W9-CTW-247

FOR REFERENCE

Do Not Take From This Room

Contemporary
Literary Criticism

Guide to Gale Literary Criticism Series

For criticism on	Consult these Gale series
Authors now living or who died after December 31, 1959	*CONTEMPORARY LITERARY CRITICISM (CLC)*
Authors who died between 1900 and 1959	*TWENTIETH-CENTURY LITERARY CRITICISM (TCLC)*
Authors who died between 1800 and 1899	*NINETEENTH-CENTURY LITERATURE CRITICISM (NCLC)*
Authors who died between 1400 and 1799	*LITERATURE CRITICISM FROM 1400 TO 1800 (LC)* *SHAKESPEAREAN CRITICISM (SC)*
Authors who died before 1400	*CLASSICAL AND MEDIEVAL LITERATURE CRITICISM (CMLC)*
Black writers of the past two hundred years	*BLACK LITERATURE CRITICISM (BLC) AND BLACK LITERATURE CRITICISM SUPPLEMENT (BLCS)*
Authors of books for children and young adults	*CHILDREN'S LITERATURE REVIEW (CLR)*
Dramatists	*DRAMA CRITICISM (DC)*
Hispanic writers of the late nineteenth and twentieth centuries	*HISPANIC LITERATURE CRITICISM (HLC)*
Native North American writers and orators of the eighteenth, nineteenth, and twentieth centuries	*NATIVE NORTH AMERICAN LITERATURE (NNAL)*
Poets	*POETRY CRITICISM (PC)*
Short story writers	*SHORT STORY CRITICISM (SSC)*
Major authors from the Renaissance to the present	*WORLD LITERATURE CRITICISM, 1500 TO THE PRESENT (WLC)*
Major authors and works from the Bible to the present	*WORLD LITERATURE CRITICISM SUPPLEMENT (WLCS)*

ISSN 0091-3421

Volume 114

Contemporary Literary Criticism

Excerpts from Criticism of the Works
of Today's Novelists, Poets, Playwrights,
Short Story Writers, Scriptwriters, and
Other Creative Writers

**Jeffrey W. Hunter
Deborah A. Schmitt
Timothy J. White**
EDITORS

**Tim Akers
Pamela S. Dear
Catherine V. Donaldson
Daniel Jones
John D. Jorgenson
Jerry Moore
Polly Vedder
Thomas Wiloch
Kathleen Wilson**
ASSOCIATE EDITORS

GALE

DETROIT • LONDON

Riverside Community College
Library
4800 Magnolia Avenue
Riverside, CA 92506

REFERENCE
PN771 .C59
Contemporary literary
criticism.

STAFF

Hunter, Deborah A. Schmitt, Timothy J. White, *Editors*

Tim Akers, Pamela S. Dear, Catherine V. Donaldson, Daniel Jones, John D. Jorgenson, Jerry Moore, Polly Vedder, Thomas Wiloch, and Kathleen Wilson, *Associate Editors*

Tracy Arnold-Chapman, Jay Daniel, Nancy Dziedzic, Linda Quigley, Paul Serralheiro, Lynn Spampinato, and Marc Standish, *Contributing Editors*

Susan Trosky, *Permissions Manager*
Kimberly F. Smilay, *Permissions Specialist*
Steve Cusack, and Kelly Quin, *Permissions Associates*
Sandy Gore, *Permissions Assistant*

Victoria B. Cariappa, *Research Manager*
Julia C. Daniel, Tamara C. Nott, Michele P. Pica, Tracie A. Richardson, Norma Sawaya, and Cheryl L. Warnock, *Research Associates*
Laura C. Bissey, Alfred A. Gardner I, and Sean R. Smith, *Research Assistants*

Mary Beth Trimper, *Production Director*
Deborah L. Milliken, and Cindy Range, *Production Assistants*

Barbara J. Yarrow, *Graphic Services Manager*
Sherrell Hobbs, *Macintosh Artist*
Randy Bassett, *Image Database Supervisor*
Robert Duncan and Mikal Ansari, *Scanner Operators*
Pamela Reed, *Imaging Coordinator*

Since this page cannot legibly accommodate all copyright notices, the acknowledgments constitute an extension of the copyright notice.

While every effort has been made to ensure the reliability of the information presented in this publication, Gale Reasearch neither guarantees the accuracy of the data contained herein nor assumes any responsibility for errors, omissions or discrepancies. Gale accepts no payment for listing, and inclusion in the publication of any organization, agency, instituion, publication, service, or individual does not imply endorsement of the editors or publisher. Errors brought to the attention of the publisher and verified to the satisfaction of the publisher will be corrected in future editions.

The paper used in this publication meets the minimum requirements of American National Standard for Information Sciences—Permanence Paper for Printed Library Materials, ANSI Z39.48-1984.

This publication is a creative work fully protected by all applicable copyright laws, as well as by misappropriation, trade secret, unfair competition, and other applicable laws. The authors and editors of this work have added value to the underlying factual material herein through one or more of the following: unique and original selection, coordination, expression, arrangement, and classification of the information.

All rights to this publication will be vigorously defended.

Copyright © 1999
The Gale Group
27500 Drake Rd.
Farmington Hills, MI 48331-3535

All rights reserved including the right of reproduction in whole or in part in any form.

Library of Congress Catalog Card Number 76-46132
ISBN 0-7876-2211-7
ISSN 0091-3421

Printed in the United States of America
10 9 8 7 6 5 4 3 2 1

Contents

Preface vii

Acknowledgments xi

Preface

A Comprehensive Information Source
on Contemporary Literature

Named "one of the twenty-five most distinguished reference titles published during the past twenty-five years" by *Reference Quarterly*, the *Contemporary Literary Criticism (CLC)* series provides readers with critical commentary and general information on more than 2,000 authors now living or who died after December 31, 1959. Previous to the publication of the first volume of *CLC* in 1973, there was no ongoing digest monitoring scholarly and popular sources of critical opinion and explication of modern literature. *CLC,* therefore, has fulfilled an essential need, particularly since the complexity and variety of contemporary literature makes the function of criticism especially important to today's reader.

Scope of the Series

CLC presents significant passages from published criticism of works by creative writers. Since many of the authors covered by *CLC* inspire continual critical commentary, writers are often represented in more than one volume. There is, of course, no duplication of reprinted criticism.

Authors are selected for inclusion for a variety of reasons, among them the publication or dramatic production of a critically acclaimed new work, the reception of a major literary award, revival of interest in past writings, or the adaptation of a literary work to film or television.

Attention is also given to several other groups of writers-authors of considerable public interest--about whose work criticism is often difficult to locate. These include mystery and science fiction writers, literary and social critics, foreign writers, and authors who represent particular ethnic groups within the United States.

Format of the Book

Each *CLC* volume contains about 500 individual excerpts taken from hundreds of book review periodicals, general magazines, scholarly journals, monographs, and books. Entries include critical evaluations spanning from the beginning of an author's career to the most current commentary. Interviews, feature articles, and other published writings that offer insight into the author's works are also presented. Students, teachers, librarians, and researchers will find that the generous excerpts and supplementary material in *CLC* provide them with vital information required to write a term paper, analyze a poem, or lead a book discussion group. In addition, complete bibliographical citations note the original source and all of the information necessary for a term paper footnote or bibliography.

Features

A *CLC* author entry consists of the following elements:

- The **Author Heading** cites the author's name in the form under which the author has most commonly published, followed by birth date, and death date when applicable. Uncertainty as to a birth or death date is indicated by a question mark.

- A **Portrait** of the author is included when available.

- A brief **Biographical and Critical Introduction** to the author and his or her work precedes the excerpted criticism. The first line of the introduction provides the author's full name, pseudonyms (if applicable), nationality, and a listing of genres in which the author has written. To provide users with easier access to information, the biographical and critical essay included in each author entry is divided into four categories: "Introduction," "Biographical Information," "Major Works," and "Critical Reception." The introductions to single-work entries--entries that focus on well known and frequently studied books, short stories, and poems--are similarly organized to quickly provide readers with information on the plot and major characters of the work being discussed, its major themes, and its critical reception. Previous volumes of *CLC* in which the author has been featured are also listed in the introduction.

- A list of **Principal Works** notes the most important writings by the author. When foreign-language works have been translated into English, the English-language version of the title follows in brackets.

- The **Excerpted Criticism** represents various kinds of critical writing, ranging in form from the brief review to the scholarly exegesis. Essays are selected by the editors to reflect the spectrum of opinion about a specific work or about an author's literary career in general. The excerpts are presented chronologically, adding a useful perspective to the entry. All titles by the author featured in the entry are printed in boldface type, which enables the reader to easily identify the works being discussed. Publication information (such as publisher names and book prices) and parenthetical numerical references (such as footnotes or page and line references to specific editions of a work) have been deleted at the editor's discretion to provide smoother reading of the text.

- Critical essays are prefaced by **Explanatory Notes** as an additional aid to readers. These notes may provide several types of valuable information, including: the reputation of the critic, the importance of the work of criticism, the commentator's approach to the author's work, the purpose of the criticism, and changes in critical trends regarding the author.

- A complete **Bibliographical Citation** designed to help the user find the original essay or book precedes each excerpt.

- Whenever possible, a recent, previously unpublished **Author Interview** accompanies each entry.

- A concise **Further Reading** section appears at the end of entries on authors for whom a significant amount of criticism exists in addition to the pieces reprinted in *CLC*. Each citation in this section is accompanied by a descriptive annotation describing the content of that article. Materials included in this section are grouped under various headings (e.g., Biography, Bibliography, Criticism, and Interviews) to aid users in their search for additional information. Cross-references to other useful sources published by Gale Research in which the author has appeared are also included: *Authors in the News, Black Writers, Children's Literature Review, Contemporary Authors, Dictionary of Literary Biography, DISCovering Authors, Drama Criticism, Hispanic Literature Criticism, Hispanic Writers, Native North American Literature, Poetry Criticism, Something about the Author, Short Story Criticism, Contemporary Authors Autobiography Series,* and *Something about the Author Autobiography Series.*

Other Features

CLC also includes the following features:

- An **Acknowledgments** section lists the copyright holders who have granted permission to reprint material in this volume of *CLC*. It does not, however, list every book or periodical reprinted or consulted during the preparation of the volume.

- Each new volume of *CLC* includes a **Cumulative Topic Index,** which lists all literary topics treated in *CLC, NCLC, TCLC,* and *LC 1400-1800.*

- A **Cumulative Author Index** lists all the authors who have appeared in the various literary criticism series published by Gale Research, with cross-references to Gale's biographical and autobiographical series. A full listing of the series referenced there appears on the first page of the indexes of this volume. Readers will welcome this cumulated author index as a useful tool for locating an author within the various series. The index, which lists birth and death dates when available, will be particularly valuable for those authors who are identified with a certain period but whose death dates cause them to be placed in another, or for those authors whose careers span two periods. For example, Ernest Hemingway is found in *CLC,* yet F. Scott Fitzgerald, a writer often associated with him, is found in *Twentieth-Century Literary Criticism.*

- A **Cumulative Nationality Index** alphabetically lists all authors featured in *CLC* by nationality, followed by numbers corresponding to the volumes in which the authors appear.

- An alphabetical **Title Index** accompanies each volume of *CLC*. Listings are followed by the author's name and the corresponding page numbers where the titles are discussed. English translations of foreign titles and variations of titles are cross-referenced to the title under which a work was originally published. Titles of novels, novellas, dramas, films, record albums, and poetry, short story, and essay collections are printed in italics, while all individual poems, short stories, essays, and songs are printed in roman type within quotation marks; when published separately (e.g., T. S. Eliot's poem *The Waste Land)*, the titles of long poems are printed in italics.

- In response to numerous suggestions from librarians, Gale has also produced a **Special Paperbound Edition** of the *CLC* title index. This annual cumulation, which alphabetically lists all titles reviewed in the series, is available to all customers and is typically published with every fifth volume of *CLC*. Additional copies of the index are available upon request. Librarians and patrons will welcome this separate index: it saves shelf space, is easy to use, and is recyclable upon receipt of the next edition.

Citing *Contemporary Literary Criticism*

When writing papers, students who quote directly from any volume in the Literary Criticism Series may use the following general forms to footnote reprinted criticism. The first example pertains to material drawn from periodicals, the second to material reprinted in books:

[1]Alfred Cismaru, "Making the Best of It," *The New Republic,* 207, No. 24, (December 7, 1992), 30, 32; excerpted and reprinted in *Contemporary Literary Criticism,* Vol. 85, ed. Christopher Giroux (Detroit: Gale Research, 1995), pp. 73-4.

[2]Yvor Winters, *The Post-Symbolist Methods* (Allen Swallow, 1967); excerpted and reprinted in *Contemporary Literary Criticism,* Vol. 85, ed. Christopher Giroux (Detroit: Gale Research, 1995), pp. 223-26.

Suggestions Are Welcome

The editors hope that readers will find *CLC* a useful reference tool and welcome comments about the work. Send comments and suggestions to: Editors, *Contemporary Literary Criticism,* Gale Research, 27500 Drake Rd., Farmington Hills, MI 48333-3535.

Acknowledgments

The editors wish to thank the copyright holders of the excerpted criticism included in this volume and the permissions managers of many book and magazine publishing companies for assisting us in securing reproduction rights. We are also grateful to the staffs of the Detroit Public Library, the Library of Congress, the University of Detroit Mercy Library, Wayne State University Purdy/Kresge Library Complex, and the University of Michigan Libraries for making their resources available to us. Following is a list of the copyright holders who have granted us permission to reproduce material in this volume of CLC. Every effort has been made to trace copyright, but if omissions have been made, please let us know.

COPYRIGHTED EXCERPTS IN *CLC*, VOLUME 114, WERE REPRODUCED FROM THE FOLLOWING PERIODICALS:

The American Book Review, v. 16, March-May, 1995. © 1995 by The American Book Review. Reproduced by permission.—*American Indian Culture and Research Journal*, v. 20, 1996. Copyright © 1996 The Regents of the University of California. Reproduced by permission.—*American Indian Quarterly*, v. XIV, Fall, 1990. Copyright © Society for American Indian Studies & Research 1990. Reproduced by permission of the publisher.—*The Antioch Review*, v. 34, Fall, 1975. Copyright © 1975 by the Antioch Review Inc. Reproduced by permission of the Editors.—*Ariel: A Review of International English Literature*, v. 25, January, 1994 for "To Understand this World Differently': Reading and Subversion in Leslie Marmon Silko's 'Storyteller'" by Linda J. Krumholz. Copyright © 1994 The Board of Governors, The University of Calgary. Reproduced by permission of the publisher and the author.—*Artforum*, v. XXVIII, March, 1990 for "Onwards & Sideways: The Films of Almodóvar" by Jeanne Silverthorne. Reproduced by permission of the publisher and the author.—*Belles Lettres*, v 10, Spring, 1995. Reproduced by permission.—*Book World- The Washington Post*, January 13, 1980 for "Walks on the Southwest Side" by Bruce Cook/ August 6, 1989 for "At Play in the Funhouse of Fiction" by Madison Smartt Bell/ v. XXVI, February 4, 1996 for "Vamps, Riffs and Breaks" by David Nicholson. © 1980, 1989, 1996 Washington Post Book World Service/Washington Post Writers Group. All reproduced by permission of the respective authors.—*Books Abroad*, v. 37, Autumn, 1963. Copyright © 1963 by the University of Oklahoma Press. Reproduced by permission.—*Bulletin of Hispanic Studies*, v. LXX, July, 1993. Reproduced by permission.—*Chicago Review*, v. 43, Winter, 1997. Copyright © 1997 by Chicago Review. Reproduced by permission.—*Chicago Tribune*, January 21, 1990 for "'Maximalist' Short Fiction from a Talented Young Writer" by Douglas Seibold. Reproduced by permission of the author.—*Chicago Tribune-Books*, April 8, 1990 for "A Storied Renaissance: The Golden Age of the American Short Story May Be Right Now" by Joseph Coates. All rights reserved. Reproduced by permission.—*The Chowder Review*, n. 14, Spring-Summer, 1980 for "Vital Assurances" by David Clewell. Reproduced by permission of the author.—*Christian Science Monitor*, February 10, 1997. © 1997 The Christian Science Publishing Society. All rights reserved. Reproduced by permission from The Christian Science Monitor.—*CLA Journal*, v. XXXVIII, December, 1984; v. XXXVII, June, 1994; v. XXXIX, June, 1996. Copyright © 1984, 1994, 1996 by The College Language Association. All used by permission of The College Language Association.—*Critique: Studies in Contemporary Fiction*, v. 38, Fall, 1996. Copyright © 1996 Helen Dwight Reid Educational Foundation. Reproduced with permission of the Helen Dwight Reid Educational Foundation, published by Heldref Publications, 119 18th Street, N. W., Washington, DC 20036-1802.—*English Language Notes*, v. XXIX, September, 1991. Reproduced by permission.—*Film Quarterly*, v. XLI, Fall, 1987 for "Pleasure and the New Spanish Mentality: A Conversation with Pedro Almodóvar" by Marsha Kinder./v. 46, Spring, 1993 for "Melodrama Against Itself: Pedro Almodóvar's 'What Have I Done to Deserve This'" by Kathleen M. Vernon. © 1987, 1993 by the Regents of the University of California. Both Reproduced by permission of the publisher and the resective authors.—*Frontiers*, v. XV, 1994. Copyright © 1994 by Frontiers Editorial Collective. Reproduced by permission.—*Harper's Magazine*, v. 292, June, 1996. Copyright © 1996 by Harper's Magazine. All rights reserved. Reproduced by permission.—*The Hollins Critic*, v. XIII, April, 1976. Copyright © 1976 by Hollins College. Reproduced by permission of the publisher.—*The Hudson Review*, v. XXXIII, Autumn, 1980. Copyright © 1980 by The Hudson Review, Inc. Reproduced by permission.—*Journal of Croatian Studies*, v. XIV-XV, 1973-74. Reproduced by permission.—*Journal of Evolutionary Psychology*, v. 15, March, 1994. Reproduced by permission.—*The Kenyon*

Review, v. XIV, Winter, 1992 for "Probable Reason, Possible Joy" by David Baker./v. XVII, Spring, 1995 for "Among Lovers, Among Friends" by Sue Russell. Copyright © 1992, 1995 by Kenyon College. All rights reserved. Both reproduced by permission of the respective authors.— *Kirkus Reviews*, v. LIV, November 15, 1986. Copyright © 1986 The Kirkus Service, Inc. All rights reserved. Reproduced by permission of the publisher, "Kirkus Reviews" and Kirkus Associates, L.P.—*London Review of Books*, v. 8, July 3, 1986 for "Afro-Fictions" by Graham Hough; v. 18, April 4, 1996 for "Pipe-Dreams" by Rob Nixon. Both appear here by permission of the London Review of Books and the respective authors.—*Los Angeles Times Book Review*, February 11, 1996. Copyright © 1996, Los Angeles Times. Reproduced by permission.—*MELUS*: Society for the Study of the Multi-Ethnic Literature of the United States, v. 12, Fall, 1985; v. 1, Spring, 1988; v. 17, Spring, 1991-1992; v. 20, Summer, 1995; v. 21, Summer, 1996. Copyright, MELUS, The Society for the Study of Multi-Ethnic Literature of the United States, 1985, 1988, 1992, 1995, 1996. All reproduced by permission.—*Midwestern Miscellany*, v. X, 1982; v. XXI, 1993. Copyright© 1982, 1990 by The Society for the Study of Midwestern Literature. All rights reserved. Both reproduced by permission.—*The Nation*, New York, April 10, 1972; v. 250, January 29, 1990; v. 262, March 4, 1996. © 1972, 1990, 1996 The Nation magazine/ The Nation Company, Inc. All reproduced by permission.— *New Statesman & Society*, v. 1, July 22, 1988. © 1988 Statesman & Nation Publishing Company Limited. Reproduced by permission.—*The New Republic*, v. 179, July 29, 1978; v. 216, June 16/30, 1997. © 1978, 1997 The New Republic, Inc. Both reproduced by permission of The New Republic.—*The New York Review of Books*, May 15, 1997. Copyright © 1997 Nyrev, Inc. Reproduced with permission from The New York Review of Books.—*The New York Times*, March 1, 1982. Copyright © 1982 by The New York Times Company. Reproduced by permission.— *The New York Times Book Review*, November 16, 1969; February 15, 1970; February 24, 1980; November 5, 1989; April 20, 1990; May 20, 1990; March 3, 1996; January 19, 1997; March 16, 1997. Copyright © 1969, 1970, 1980, 1989, 1990, 1996, 1997 by The New York Times Company. All reproduced by permission.—*The New Yorker*, v. LXXI, November 27, 1995 for "Death of a Writer" by William Boyd. © 1995 by The New Yorker Magazine, Inc. All rights reserved. Reproduced by permission of Georges Borchardt, Inc. on behalf of the Author.— *Northwest Review*, v. XVIII, 1980. Copyright © 1980 by Northwest Review. Reproduced by permission.—*Obsidian: Black Literature in Review*, Vol. 7, Summer & Winter, 1981 for "The Whitman Awakening in June Jordan's Poetry" by Melba Joyce Boyd. Reproduced by permission of the author.—*The Ohio Review*, n. 25, 1980. Copyright © 1980 by the Editors of The Ohio Review. Reproduced by permission.—*PMLA*, v. 94, January, 1979. Reproduced by permission of the Modern Language Association of America.—*The Progressive*, v. 57, January, 1993. Copyright 1993. Reproduced by permission of The Progressive, 409 East Main Street, Madison, WI 53703.—*Quarterly Review of Film and Video*, v. 13, 1991. Copyright © 1991 by OPA (Overseas Publishers Association) N.V. All rights reserved. Reproduced by permission.—*Research in African Literatures*, v. 23, Spring, 1992. Copyright © 1992 Indiana University Press. Reproduced by permission.—*The Review of Contemporary Fiction*, v. 13, Summer, 1993; v. 16, Spring, 1996. Copyright, (c)1993, 1996 by John O'Brien. Both reproduced by permission.— *The Saturday Review*, v. 52, November 15, 1969. © 1969 Saturday Review Magazine, © 1979 General Media Communications, Inc. Reproduced by permission of Saturday Review Publications, Ltd.— *Sight and Sound*, v. 4, January, 1994;v. 6, February, 1996. Copyright © 1994, 1996 by The British Film Institute. Both reproduced by permission.—*The Slavonic and East European Review*, v. XLV, January, 1967. Reproduced by permission.—*Studies in American Fiction*, v. 12, Spring, 1984; v. 16, Autumn, 1988. Copyright © 1984, 1988 Northeastern University. Reproduced by permission.—*Studies in American Jewish Literature*, no. 5, 1986 for "Tillie Olson: The Writer as a Jewish Woman" by Bonnie Lyons. Reproduced by permission.—*Studies in Short Fiction*, v. I, Fall, 1963. Copyright (c) 1963 by Newberry College. Reproduced by permission.—*The Times Literary Supplement*, July 26, 1991; July 25, 1997. © The Times Supplements Limited 1991, 1997. Both reproduced from The Times Literary Supplement by permission.—*Time*, New York, v. 147, February, 1996. Copyright © 1996 Time Warner Inc. All rights reserved. Reproduced by permission from Time.—*Tulsa Studies in Women's Literature*, v. 11, Fall, 1992. © 1992, The University of Tulsa. Reproduced by permission.—*The Wallace Stevens Journal*, v. 19, Fall, 1995. Copyright © 1995 The Wallace Stevens Society, Inc. Reproduced by permission.—*Women's Review of Books*, v. 7, April, 1993 for "Stirring the Melting-Pot" by Adele Logan Alexander. Copyright (c) 1993. All rights reserved. Reproduced by permission of the author.—*World Literature Written in English*, v. 27, Autumn, 1987. © copyright 1987 WLWE-World Literature Written in English. Reproduced by permission.

COPYRIGHTED EXCERPTS IN *CLC*, VOLUME 114, WERE REPRODUCED FROM THE FOLLOWING BOOKS:

Bauer, Helen Pike. From "'A Child of Anxious, Not Proud, Love': Tillie Olsen's 'I Stand Here Ironing'" in *Mother Puzzles: Daughters and Mothers in Contemporary American Literature*. Edited by Mickey Pearlman. Greenwood Press, 1989. Copyright © 1989 by Mickey Pearlman. All rights reserved. Reproduced by permission of Greenwood Publishing Group, Inc., Westport, CT.— Bigsby, C.W.E. From "Improvising America: Ralph Ellison and the Paradox of Form" in *Speaking for You: The Vision of Ralph Ellison*. Edited by Kimberly W. Benston. Howard University Press, 1987. Copyright © 1987 by Kimberly W. Benston. All rights reserved. Reproduced by permission of the author.—Birkerts, Sven. From *American Energies: Essays on Fiction*. William Morrow and Company, Inc., 1992. Copyright © 1992 by Sven Birkerts. All rights reserved. Reproduced by permission of William Morrow and Company, Inc., and the Helen Pratt Agency on behalf of the author.—Epps, Brad. From "Figuring Hysteria: Disorder and Desire in Three Films of Pedro Almodóvar" in *Post-Franco, Postmodern: The Films of Pedro Almodóvar*. Edited by Kathleen M. Vernon and Barbara Morris. Greenwood Press, 1995. © 1995 by Kathleen M. Vernon and Barbara Harris. Reproduced by permission of Greenwood Publishing Group, Inc., Westport, CT.—Evans, Charlene Taylor. From "Mother-Daughter Relationships as Epistemological Structures: Leslie Marmon Silko's 'Almanac of the Dead' and 'Storyteller'," in *Women of Color: Mother-Daughter Relationships in 20th-Century Literature*. Edited by Elizabeth Brown-Guillory. University of Texas Press, 1996. Copyright © 1996 by the University of Texas Press. All rights reserved. Reproduced by permission.—Flaker, Aleksandar. From "Krleza's Culinary Flemishness" in *Text and Context: Essays to Honor Nils Ake Nilsson*. Edited by Peter Alberg Jensen, Barbara Lonnqvist, Fiona Bjorling, Lars Kleberg and Anders Sjoberg. Almqvist & Wiksell International, 1987. © Stockholm Studies in Russian Literature 1987. Reproduced by permission.—Jessup, Florence Redding. From *Look Who's Laughing: Studies in Gender and Comedy*. Edited by Gail Finney. Gordon and Breach, 1994. Copyright © 1994 by OPA (Overseas Publishers Association) Amsterdam B.V. All rights reserved. Reproduced by permission.

PHOTOGRAPHS AND ILLUSTRATIONS APPEARING IN *CLC*, VOLUME 114, WERE RECEIVED FROM THE FOLLOWING SOURCES:

Almodóvar, Pedro (seated, surrounded by film equipment, in jeans and beaded jacket), 1988, photograph. The Kobal Collection. Reproduced by permission.—Ellison, Ralph (wearing suit and glasses), photograph. Archive Photos. Reproduced by permission.—Jordan, June, photograph. AP/Wide World Photos. Reproduced by permission.—Olsen, Tillie, photograph by Miriam Berkley. Photo © Miriam Berkley. All rights reserved. Reproduced by permission.—Saro-Wiwa, Ken, November 10, 1995, photograph. Rueters/Archive Photos, Inc. Reproduced by permission.—Silko, Leslie Marmon (wearing black shirt, parrot pin), photograph by Robyn McDaniels. © Robyn McDaniels.—Wallace, David Foster, photograph by Dianne Nilsen. Reproduced by permission.

Pedro Almodóvar
1949(?)-

Spanish filmmaker.

The following entry provides an overview of Almodóvar's career through 1995.

INTRODUCTION

Pedro Almodóvar's work flourished in the post-Franco culture of Spain in the late 1970s and 1980s. His films celebrate the era of individuality and acceptance that infused the Spanish cultural arts after the end of Franco's repressive totalitarian regime. In addition, Almodóvar's work is understood by some critics as a revision of the history of Spain under Franco. The characters in Almodóvars films, commonly homosexuals, transsexuals, or bisexuals, are not relegated to the subculture. Instead, Almodóvar uses these characters to represent the postmodern revolt against the repressive boundaries of Spain's history. Almodóvar's work has garnered him a reputation as an international auteur.

Biographical Information

Almodóvar was born in 1949 (some sources say 1951) in a small village, Calzada de Calatrava, and spent most of his youth attending parochial schools. Almodóvar always felt out of place in the small town and at the age of seventeen he moved to Madrid. He worked for the next ten years as a typist for the telephone company. During this time he also acted with an independent theater troupe, sang in a rock band, wrote articles and X-rated comics for an avant-garde newspaper, and composed the memoirs of the fictitious pornography queen, Pati Difusa. Almodóvar never attended film school, but by the mid-1970s he was shooting experimental 8- and 16-millimeter shorts. He completed his first full-length feature, *Pepi, Lucy, Bom y otros chicas del montón* (*Pepi, Lucy, Bom and a Whole Lot of Other Girls,* 1980) for only thirty thousand dollars. Two years later he followed with *Laberinto de passiónes* (*Labyrinth of Passion,* 1982) which attained cult status in Spain. Almodóvar's fourth feature, *¿Qué he hecho yo para merecer ésto?* (*What Have I Done to Deserve This?,* 1984) brought him popularity in the United States. His reputation has grown steadily throughout his career in both Spain and internationally. His films are played at film festivals throughout the world and have won several international awards.

Major Works

Almodóvar's films primarily focus on the lives and feelings

of women. They are usually told from the woman's perspective, but include a host of well-developed ensemble characters. His cinematic world is filled with intense imagery and outrageous situations that are made to seem ordinary. His films embrace life and individual freedom, and his main theme is the celebration, exploration, and sometimes frustration of human desires. *What Have I Done to Deserve This?* focuses on life in the housing projects of Madrid. The film's protagonist is Gloria, an overworked mother who takes amphetamines to help her face her responsibilities as a housewife and her job as a cleaning woman. Her family includes her taxi driver husband who neglects her, two sons—one a drug dealer, the other a homosexual—and a mother-in-law who longs to return to her village. Gloria is frustrated and unsatisfied in her life and takes action to change her circumstances by bludgeoning her husband with a ham bone and selling her youngest son to a homosexual dentist. *Matador* (1986) is a study in psychosexual brutality which follows the story of an ex-matador and a lady lawyer who can only experience sexual fulfillment in conjunction with killing. *Mujeres al borde de un ataque de nervios* (*Women on the Verge of a Nervous Breakdown,* 1988) is about overcoming machismo. Pepa is a Spanish television and radio actress who attempts to contact her ex-lover Ivan to tell him she is pregnant. Ivan is a cad who uses women and abandons them, but Pepa sees reconciliation, murder, or suicide as her only options. She attempts to win him back, but in the final confrontation Pepa decides to give up on Ivan and become a single mother. *Kika* (1993) tells the story of an independent heroine who is raped and then further abused by the broadcast of her victimization on television.

Critical Reception

Reviewers often point out the autobiographical nature of Almodóvar's films, including his focus on sexuality, family relationships, and life in Madrid versus life in a small town. Critics discuss Almodóvar's complicated relationship with Francoism. Marvin D'Lugo asserts, "While Almodóvar has long insisted that his cinema is without any connection to Franco and Francoism, textual evidence suggests the contrary. An essential axis of meaning in much of his filmic work lies precisely in the ways the ideas and icons of Francoist cinema—those related to religion, the family, and sexual repression—are set up as foils to stimulate the audience to embrace a new post-Francoist cultural aesthetic." Other reviewers assert that in his attempt to ignore Francoist Spain, Almodóvar turned to Hollywood melodrama for a reference point in his films. Kathleen M. Vernon states, "American film has provided him with a vehicle for articulating his distance from the themes and style of a recent Spanish film tradition obsessed with the country's tragic past." Critics assert that Almodóvar pays homage to the Hollywood melodramas of the 1930s and 40s both through his use of clips from several films and his use of melodramatic techniques. Critics also discuss Almodóvar's unconventional use of humor in his films, comparing his work to such directors as John Waters, Russ Meyer, and Luis Buñuel. Some reviewers are disturbed by the erotic themes and images in Almodóvar's films, but many critics look beyond the sensational aspects of the director's work. Peter Evans says, "Almodóvar's devotion to scandal and outrage never detracts from a serious project to explore the after-effects of repression through the combined strategies of pop and high art."

---

*PRINCIPAL WORKS

†*Pepi, Lucy, Bom y otros chicas del montón* [*Pepi, Lucy, Bom and a Whole Lot of Other Girls*] (screenplay) 1980
‡*Laberinto de pasión* [*Labyrinth of Passion*] (screenplay) 1982
**Entre tinieblas* [*Dark Habits*] (screenplay) 1983
††*¿Qué he hecho yo para merecer ésto?* [*What Have I Done to Deserve This?*] (screenplay) 1984

Matador (screenplay) 1986
La ley del deseo [*The Law of Desire*] (screenplay) 1986
Mujeres al borde de un ataque de nervios [*Women on the Verge of a Nervous Breakdown*] (screenplay) 1988
Atame! [*Tie Me Up! Tie Me Down!*] (screenplay) 1990
Tacones lejanos [*High Heels*] (screenplay) 1991
Kika (screenplay) (1993)
Almodóvar on Almodóvar (nonfiction) 1995
La flor de mi secreto [The Flower of My Secret] (screenplay) (1995)
Carne tremula [*Live Flesh*; based on the novel by Ruth Rendell] (screenplay) 1997

*Almodóvar directed all the films listed here.

†The English translation of this title varies. It is also referred to as *Pepi, Lucy, Bom and Other Girls on the Heap*, *Pepi, Lucy, Bom and Other Ordinary Girls*, *Pepi, Lucy, Bom and Other Girls Like That*, and *Pepi, Lucy, Bom and Other Girls All Like Mom.*

‡This film is also known as *Laberinto de pasiones* [*Labyrinth of Passions*].

**This film is sometimes referred to as *Sisters of Darkness.*

††Punctuation of this title varies.

CRITICISM

Pedro Almodóvar with Marsha Kinder (interview date Fall 1987)

SOURCE: "Pleasure and the New Spanish Mentality: A Conversation with Pedro Almodóvar," in *Film Quarterly*, Vol. XLI, No. 1, Fall, 1987, pp. 33-44.

[*In the following interview, which was conducted on May 25, 1987, Almodóvar discusses his approach to filmmaking, the major themes of his films, and the place of his work in the context of Spanish film.*]

Following the enthusiastic critical reception of Pedro Almodóvar's **La Ley del Deseo** (**The Law of Desire**) at this year's Berlin Film Festival, Spain's oldest and largest-circulation film journal, *Fotogramas & Video*, ran an editorial saying:

> The recent Berlin Festival has demonstrated an important fact for Spanish cinema: the interest that our cinema can arouse abroad, not only at the level of interchange or cultural curiosity, but as an exportable and commercially valid product. . . . Spanish

cinema is trying to leave the national "ghetto" and join a movement that proclaims the necessity and urgency of a "European cinema" which transcends nationalities without renouncing their specificity.

Although this editorial mentions several films at the festival to support its point, it focuses most specifically on "the enormous and overwhelming success of *La Ley del Deseo*. . . , a film that is eminently 'Spanish' but comprehensible to any person," and which confirms that "when one makes a cinema that has something to say, these things can have appeal everywhere."

Fotogramas fails to acknowledge the irony that this film being singled out as a model of "universal" appeal is an outrageous melodrama featuring homosexual and transsexual protagonists in a sado-masochistic triangle involving incest, murder, and suicide and including several sexually explicit homoerotic love scenes. It's a film that in most national contexts would be marginal, to say the least. And yet in March, when it was screened in New York, concurrent with but not as part of the Ministry of Culture's Third Annual Spanish Film Week (which included an equally extreme Almodóvar melodrama called *Matador*), *La Ley del Deseo* again received critical raves in the *Village Voice* and in the *New Yorker* where Pauline Kael devoted a full page to the film—an achievement that was duly reported as "news" in Spain's most prestigious daily, *El País.*

At the very moment when Spanish cinema may be facing its most serious economic crisis, Almodóvar's films are achieving modest success both at home and abroad. Since the death of Franco in 1975 and despite the earnest efforts of the Socialist government which came to power in 1982, Spanish films have not only failed to find adequate distribution in foreign markets, but they have steadily been losing their home audience. Spanish spectators are either staying home in droves with their VCRs or flocking to see the latest imports which increasingly dominate Spanish movie houses with their block booking. The number of total spectators who attended movies in Spain decreased from 331 million in 1970 to 101 million in 1985, and by 1985 Spanish films held only 17.5% of that diminishing home market, as opposed to 30% in 1970. Within this discouraging context, Almodóvar's early features did surprisingly well in Spain and *Matador* was an outstanding success—the third-largest-grossing Spanish film in 1986. The final figures are not yet in on *La Ley del Deseo,* but they promise to be even better. It's the first Almodóvar film to be immediately sold worldwide—virtually everywhere but in Japan.

Almodóvar's films have a curious way of resisting marginalization. Never limiting himself to a single protagonist, he chooses an ensemble of homosexual, bisexual, transsexual, doper, punk, terrorist characters who refuse to be ghettoized into divisive subcultures because they are figured as part of the "new Spanish mentality"—a fast-paced revolt that relentlessly pursues pleasure rather than power, and a post-modern erasure of all repressive boundaries and taboos associated with Spain's medieval, fascist, and modernist heritage. Almodóvar claims:

> I always try to choose prototypes and characters from modern-day Madrid, who are somehow representative of a certain mentality existing today. . . . I think that since Franco died new generations have been coming to the fore, generations that are unrelated to former ones, that are even unrelated to the "progressive" generations that appeared during the last years of the dictatorship. How do people 20 years old live in Madrid? It's quite complex. . . . The characters in my films utterly break with the past, which is to say that most of them, for example, are apolitical. Pleasure must be grasped immediately, hedonistically; that is almost the main leitmotif of their lives.

This new mentality was already present in Almodóvar's first low-budget, underground feature (made in 16mm and blown up to 35), *Pepi, Lucy, Bom y Otros Chicas del Montón* (re-titled in English *Pepi, Lucy, Bom and Other Girls All Like Mom*), where a policeman, who's married to middle-aged Lucy, rapes their young neighbor Pepi and tries to cover up his crime by planting marijuana on her balcony. Lucy responds by becoming sexually involved with a girl even younger than Pepi, a 16-year-old pleasure lover named Bom, and Pepi writes their love story. The rape is further avenged by Pepi's friends from a punk rock group who, in order to attract the rapist, disguise themselves as traditional Spanish zarzuela singers.

The new mentality of 20-year-olds was seen even more clearly in Almodóvar's second splashy feature *Laberinto de Pasiones (Labyrinth of Passions)*, which positively bristles with vibrant color and a wildly comic sexual energy. The tortuously complex plot follows the tangled passions of an ensemble of young Madrileños trying to escape the crippling influences of repressive fathers in order to pursue their own pleasure. Riza Niro (Imanol Arias) is the bisexual son of the deposed "emperor of Tehran." More interested in sex and cosmetics than in family or politics, he flees his corrupt, cancerous father and lecherous, infertile stepmother, becomes a punk singer in Madrid, and ultimately flies away with the Felliniesque Sexilia (Celia Roth), a nymphomaniac member of a feminist punk band called "Las Ex" and daughter of a world-class sex-loathing gynecologist, whose scientific detachment drives his daughter to promiscuity. Queti, a young laundress who is chronically raped by her dry-cleaning daddy on alternate days, undergoes plastic surgery to become Sexilia's surrogate on stage and at home where she enters a budding incestuous relationship with her new doctor daddy. This two-faced incestuous daughter feeds both daddies powerful potions that render one impotent, the other horny. The fleeing lovers Riza and Sexy are hotly pursued by an assortment of jealous punks and Islamic fundamentalists, but none so dogged as the superkeen-scented Sadec, a handsome Tehranian terrorist (played by Antonio Banderas) who also loves Riza in spite of politics. This "musical comedy" (for which Almodóvar himself wrote and performed some of the wildest songs) is still running on weekends as a midnight cult movie in Madrid.

Though I haven't seen Almodóvar's third feature, *Entre Tinieblas* (retitled in English *Sisters of Darkness*), it's reported to be about a community of nuns known as the "Humble Redeemers" who run a home for delinquent girls, where, among other pleasurable pastimes, the sisters keep a pet tiger, write steamy best-sellers, smoke pot, and shoot dope.

¿Qué He Hecho Yo para Merecer Ésto? (*What Have I Done to Deserve This?*), Almodóvar's first international hit, follows the travails of Gloria (Carmen Maura), a high-rise suburban housewife who toils as a maid to help support her family, which includes: a taxi-driver husband who's obsessed with a suicidal German singer and who gets involved in a plot to forge Hitler's memoirs; two sons—a teenage heroin dealer and a 12-year-old homosexual; and a dotty mother-in-law who yearns for her pet lizard and her home village. Despite these pressures, both the soapish heroine and her narrative still have time for needy neighbors—a cheerful hooker who longs to go to Las Vegas and a haughty mother who abuses her telekinetic child. Ultimately, downtrodden Gloria kills her troublesome husband, her doper son goes to live with his granny in her home village, and her homosexual prodigal son returns home from the lecherous dentist who "adopted" him just in time to save his despondent mother from suicide.

Matador is an exercise in excess, a stylish psychological thriller with extravagant costumes, lush visuals, and the narrative logic of erotic fantasy. It opens with a montage of violence against women, movie images being watched on a VCR by an ex-matador as he masturbates. Having been gored in the ring, Diego Montes (Nacho Martinez) now only *teaches* bullfighting, but to recapture the ecstasy of the kill, he murders young girls. Angered by the insinuation that he might be a repressed homosexual, Angel (Antonio Banderas), one of Diego's virginal students, tries to rape his next door neighbor Eva, who conveniently (for the Oedipal subtext) just happens to be Diego's young fashion-model mistress. Angel is sexually disturbed, not only by an evil repressive mother who belongs to Opus Dei (an extreme rightwing lay religious organization), but also by a supernatural ability to see the violent and erotic acts of others and

to imagine they are his own. Not only does he see the serial murders of his mentor Diego, but also those of his famous female defense lawyer María Cardenal, a beautiful man-killer, with a secret obsession with matadors, which she picked up while watching Diego being gored. Once Diego and María meet in a movie house during the lust-in-the-dust climax of *Duel in the Sun,* these erotic killers see their destiny and give up all other pursuits. Guiding a group of interested parties—Diego's discarded mistress Eva, the maternal psychiatrist (Carmen Maura) who gives Angel loving support, and the police inspector (Eusebio Poncela) who has eyes for Angel and other young men in tight matador pants—Angel and company try to forestall the final fatal orgasm of Diego and María, but they arrive in time only to witness with envy the blissful smiles of the dead lovers.

La Ley del Deseo is another psychological thriller of excess, but this time about two brothers, Pablo and Tina. Pablo (Eusebio Poncela) is a homosexual screenwriter/director who is in love with a young bisexual named Juan (Miguel Molina) and who rewrites Juan's love letters to make them suit his own standard of absolute passion. One of his soft-core films deeply arouses a young spectator named Antonio (Antonio Banderas), who subsequently has his first homosexual experience with Pablo and immediately is transformed into a possessive lover. When Antonio reads the love letter from Juan that was actually written by Pablo, he becomes insanely jealous and murders his rival. Stunned by grief over Juan's murder, Pablo has a car accident and suffers amnesia. Pablo's brother Tina, formerly Tino (brilliantly played by Carmen Maura), is a transsexual actress who loved and was abandoned by her father and who now hates men. The lesbian model she lives with (ironically played by real-life transsexual Bibi Andersen) has deserted both Tina and her own 10-year-old daughter Ada, who now adopts Tina as her mother and falls in love with Pablo. In order to force Pablo to see him after the murder, Antonio seduces Tina and then holds her hostage, so that he will be granted a final hour of love. Although Pablo goes to the assignation with hatred and dread, his feelings are miraculously transformed into love by the purity of Antonio's passion.

Born in 1949 in the small village of Calzada de Calatrava near Ciudad Real, Almodóvar claims he always felt "like an astronaut in the court of King Arthur" and "knew he was born to take on the big cities." By the time he was eight, this quixotic child was living in La Mancha and then in Cáceres, where he studied with the Salesianos and Franciscans and finished his baccalaureate. In 1967, at 17, he finally made it to Madrid where he immediately became a hippy and then a white-collar worker at the National Telephone Company. After hours, he became a versatile member of Madrid's artistic underground—doing comic strips for underground magazines; acting in the avant-garde theater group *Los Golliardos;* recording and performing live in a rock band called Almodóvar and McNamara; publishing journalistic articles, parodic memoirs (under the pen name Patty Diphusa), a porno photo-story, and a novella; and making experimental short films, first in 8mm and then in 16. Even after making his first feature in 1980, he still continued writing and singing. But by the time he made *Entre Tinieblas* in 1983, his first film to be sent to a foreign festival and sold outside of Spain, he was launched as an international auteur.

[*Kinder:*] *What do you think is the primary appeal of your films, especially of* **La Ley del Deseo** *which has had such international success, whereas most Spanish films have had such difficulty in getting international distribution?*

[Almodóvar:] Well, I've been striving for this over the last three years, and I think this is the fruit of my previous work. People know me more now, and it's easier for me to sell a film. On the other hand, I think my films are very contemporary. They represent more than others, I suppose, the new Spain, this kind of new mentality that appears in Spain after Franco dies. Above all, after 1977 till now. Stories about the new Spain have appeared in the mass media of every country. Everybody has heard that now everything is different in Spain, that it has changed a lot, but it is not so easy to find this change in the Spanish cinema. I think in my films they see how Spain has changed, above all, because now it is possible to do this kind of film here. Not that a film like *The Law of Desire* would be impossible to make in places like Germany, London or the United States.

I believe that the new Spanish mentality is less dramatic—although I demonstrate the contrary in my films. We have consciously left behind many prejudices, and we have humanized our problems. We have lost the fear of earthly power (the police) and of celestial power (the church), and we have also lost our provincial certainty that we are superior to the rest of the world—that typical Latin prepotency . . . . We have become more skeptical, without losing the joy of living. We don't have confidence in the future, but we are constructing a past for ourselves because we don't like the one we had.

—Pedro Almodóvar

Yes, but it would be impossible to have such a film get half of its financing from the ministry of culture in any of those countries! How would you define "the new Spanish mentality"?

I believe that the new Spanish mentality is less dramatic—although I demonstrate the contrary in my films. We have consciously left behind many prejudices, and we have humanized our problems. We have lost the fear of earthly power (the police) and of celestial power (the church), and we have also lost our provincial certainty that we are superior to the rest of the world—that typical Latin prepotency. And we have recuperated the inclination toward sensuality, something typically Mediterranean. We have become more skeptical, without losing the joy of living. We don't have confidence in the future, but we are constructing a past for ourselves because we don't like the one we had.

Do you think that the appeal of your films also has something to do with their unique tone? I know that Pauline Kael in her very enthusiastic review of **La Ley del Deseo** *stressed the uniqueness of the tone without really describing what it is.*

Well, I would like to think this is one of the reasons because this is the main difference of my films. Whether they are good or bad, my films are absolutely different from other Spanish films and even from the other foreign cinema. I mean you can talk about a lot of influences, everybody has them. But if you see all of my films, I'm sure you can differentiate them from the others, you can recognize them. I would like to think this is the main reason for their international appeal.

How would you define that tone?

It's hard for me to talk about it because I never try to verbalize about my films, but it's true there is a different tone, even in general. This is something I'm obsessed with when I'm working with the actors. They have to say my lines in a different way. Even for me this is something that's very difficult to explain to them because you have to catch it and you have to feel it. When I'm shooting, I'm obsessed with creating an atmosphere that explains exactly what is my tone. The atmosphere that I create when I'm shooting, this is the tone of my films. To take one example, I used to mix all the genres. You can say my films are melodramas, tragicomedies, comedies or whatever because I used to put everything together and even change genre within the same sequence and very quickly. But the main difference is the private morality. I think one auteur is different from another because he has his own morality. When I say morality, I don't mean ethics, it's just a private point of view. I mean you can see a film by Luis Buñuel and you know exactly that it belongs to Buñuel because it's just the way of thinking.

It seems to me that what lies at the center of your unique tone is what you were describing before, that fluidity with which you move so quickly from one genre to another, or from one feeling or tone to another, so that when a line is delivered, it's very funny and borders on parody and we spectators are just ready to laugh, but at the same time it's erotic and moves us emotionally. In this way, you always demonstrate that you're in control, that you're manipulating the spectator response.

Yes, it takes more care than other styles of acting and shooting. You have to be very careful to control the tone because it can easily run away with you and go too far. Just as you say, in my films everything is just at the border of parody. It's not only parody. It's also the borderline of the ridiculous and of the grotesque. But it's easy to fall over the line.

Other film-makers who come to mind as doing something similar with tone are David Lynch . . .

Absolutely, I recognize myself a lot in *Blue Velvet.* I love it.

I love that film, too. It allows you to be both terrified and turned on and at the same time it's also hysterically funny. And then there's Fassbinder.

But the difference is that Fassbinder, as a German, doesn't have much of a sense of humor. In *Blue Velvet* you can find a great sense of humor, but *Blue Velvet* is more morbid than my films because there is always an element of naiveté in what I'm doing. It's strangely antithetical because I'm not so naive. But this kind of purity of actions, feelings and spontaneity, that's not in *Blue Velvet. Blue Velvet* is darker, sicker, sick in every way. But, with a lot of humor. Do you think there is humor in Fassbinder's films?

Oh yes, although it's always combined with pain.

German culture is so different from Spanish culture. In our culture there is a great sense of humor but not in the German culture. Also, I believe that our culture is more visceral. Intuition and imagination influence us more than reason. There is more adventure and spontaneity. We don't fear disorder or chaos.

Your use of Hollywood melodrama—especially in ¿Qué He Hecho? where two characters go to see Splendor in the Grass *and in* **Matador** *where there's a long excerpt from* Duel in the Sun—*it seems similar to the ways in which Fassbinder used Sirk and even Billy Wilder's* Sunset Boulevard *in* Veronika Voss, *where he picked something already very extreme—and then pushed it even further to that borderline of parody. How do you see the relationship between your work and Hollywood melodrama?*

All of the influences on me and all of the film references in my films are very spontaneous and visual. I don't make any tributes. I'm a very naive spectator. I can't learn from the movies that I love. But if I had to choose one master or model, I would choose Billy Wilder. He represents exactly what I want to do.

Which Billy Wilder? His films are so varied!

Both Billy Wilders. The *Sunset Boulevard* Billy Wilder and *The Apartment* Billy Wilder, the *1-2-3* and *The Lost Weekend. The Lost Weekend,* for example, is a big, big drama but you can find a lot of humor in it and a lot of imagination in the way it develops a unique situation. It's a great challenge for a screenwriter. But to return to the question about Hollywood, I just love that big period of the classic American melodrama. I'm not just talking about Sirk but about the kinds of films Bette Davis made. I like these extreme genres where you can talk naturally about strong sentiments without a sense of the ridiculous. This is something that melodrama has. But, of course, all these films like *Splendor in the Grass* and *Duel in the Sun,* which is so outrageous, I mean you have to be very very brave to dare to go to this kind of extreme, you can really be grotesque if you don't know how to do it. This is something that I like. But I use the genre in a different way. My films are not so conventional as that kind of melodrama. Because I don't respect the boundaries of the genre, I mix it with other things. So my films appear to be influenced by Hollywood melodrama, but I put in other elements that belong more to my culture. For example, ***What Have I Done to Deserve This?*** is more like a neorealist film than melodrama. I think it's more like the films of Rossellini, Zavattini, and DeSica—more like Italian neorealism which is also a melodramatic genre. But I put in a lot of humor. That makes the reality even more awful in a way, more extreme. And I also put in a lot of surrealistic elements that completely change the genre. I think that the presence of the nonrational in my films is strong, but I never try to explain it. For example, in *¿Qué He Hecho?* I don't try to explain the girl with the telekinetic powers, the girl like Carrie. I just put her in as part of the life or plot, and this kind of element changes the genre.

There's a moment in ¿Qué He Hecho? that helps me understand what you might mean by calling it a neorealist film. In one scene the older son asks for help with his homework in assigning the labels "realist" and "romantic" to famous authors, and his granny reverses the traditional answers, calling Byron a realist and Balzac a romantic. Isn't this joke a comment on your own style? Isn't this exactly what you're doing in this movie—reversing the traditional meanings of realist and romantic?

That could be, but I had no consciousness of it.

In one of your interviews, you say you admired very much the Spanish neorealism of Marco Ferreri and Fernando Fernán Gómez, films like El Pisito, El Cochecito *and* La

Vida por Delante—*films that combined neorealism with a Spanish absurdist black humor called* esperpento. *In his new book* Out of the Past, *John Hopewell says that* ¿Qué He Hecho? *continues in this tradition. Is this connection valid?*

Yes, very much so. If you have to find some source or relation to Spanish movies for my films, I think they are related to that kind of film. And also to an early film by Francisco Regueiro, *Duerme, Duerme, Mi Amor* (*Sleep, Sleep, My Love*). It's wonderful. Have you seen that film?

Yes, it's desperately funny, and I can definitely see the connections with the absurdist black humor and the high-rise living theme in ¿Qué He Hecho?

Yes, this is one line I admire very much, and also early Belanga. For me Berlanga's *Plácido* is a model.

Is it the film's rapid pacing and its ensemble of comic characters that appeal to you?

Yes, and also this kind of tragic situation, very dark and very sad, but with great naturalness, and this kind of comedy that talks about a lot of things in life very seriously, and this kind of confusion of a lot of people all talking and doing different things at the same time.

Yes, I can see those qualities in your films, especially in ¿Qué He Hecho? . . . *I think one of the most amazing things about* ¿Qué He Hecho? *is that whereas it starts out with distanced reflexivity (with Carmen Maura walking past a film crew as she goes to work as a maid in a martial arts gym) and with burlesque (when she mimics their sword-moves with her broom and has a torrid sexual encounter with a man in a shower who proves to be impotent), still amidst all of the satiric absurdities Maura's performance miraculously remains so realistic that she still manages to generate emotional identification in the spectator. And this has a big pay-off in the final sequence when she is saved from suicide by the homecoming of her homosexual son who has just walked out on the lecherous dentist his mother left him with in order to cover the dental bill. We still get a big emotional rush from their reunion, and we're marveling, how did Almodóvar manage to pull this off!*

Yes, I tried to do that. This is always the challenge that I face whenever I make a film. . . . I try to solve the problem of how to get the big emotion from the audience, how to get emotional identification with the problem (in this case, high-rise apartment living) which lies behind the facade of absurdity, because everything just under the facade is absolutely real. And I think the audience can always recognize very clearly what I'm trying to say about life in the high-rise. And the jokes have many reasons for being there. For example, the opening titles sequence is very much like an abstract or experimental film with all the crew there making a film while the female protagonist goes to work in that place. That was the square where we were shooting; it was very direct. And in the gym where they're doing kendo, it looks like parody, but it also shows a very aggressive sport—one that releases aggression. And from the beginning you see that she's going to be in a male world and that males are the violent, strong ones who do this kind of thing. And she is just cleaning up. And then she tries to imitate them, just to be more quiet.

It also prepares her for killing her husband with an oxbone.

It's just the surface that's surrealistic, but I think you can understand very well what's just behind that surface. But I always try to work with all of these elements and to make it so that the people can feel it. Another example is the big confession scene in ***The Law of Desire*** when Carmen Maura, as Tina the transsexual, is trying to tell her brother Pablo about her relationship with their father. You know this is really hard. It's very strange, it's not easy to find a girl like that. Well, but I hope, and I felt that during this speech the audience really identifies with Tina as if she were the girl next door, someone with whom they can readily identify. I mean this is really *heavy*. She committed incest and she changed her sex to be with her father. She's one in a million. In this case, the acting is very important. It's Carmen Maura. If she hadn't been so perfect, then you never could have believed it. To do this kind of thing, you have to be very very careful. But if you succeed with that, then the audience can believe and understand everything.

Even within that scene, you seem to purposely make it even harder for yourself, I mean in the way you set it up with her brother's amnesia, which is a highly contrived and corny way of motivating why Tina has to tell him and the audience about her past at this particular moment. And then that comical touch when she mentions Madrid, and then points out the window, saying, Oh yes, this is Madrid! reminding herself and us of the amnesia. And even with these absurdities, we are still swept away by Maura's performance.

Yes, in that scene even Carmen was very surprised because she told me that when I was directing her, I asked her for exactly the opposite of what she thought was right for this scene. She was sure that everyone else would have asked her to do exactly the contrary of what I said. Because the confession was very quiet, not very dramatic. So perhaps that's why you can believe it better. I don't know.

There seems to be a movement in **La Ley del Deseo** *that is parallel to the one in* ¿Qué He Hecho?, *where you start with reflexivity, in this case a film within a film, in which someone dictates from a script how a young man is to masturbate, and a voyeuristic spectator who—*

Imitates what he sees, yes. . . .

In a way, you start out by demystifying how movies work, but then by the end of the film those same dynamics still work on the audience very powerfully. A film-maker like Buñuel, in showing you how it happens, prevents you from experiencing that kind of pleasure—he offers you a differ-ent kind of pleasure. But you demonstrate how the pleasure works and then make the spectator experience it despite the demonstration.

Yes, that's true.

My favorite moment in **La Ley** *is when all the people at the end—Tina, the little girl Ada, and the police—look up with wonder at the window of the apartment where Pablo and his murderous lover Antonio are having their final hour of passionate love.*

Yes, this is one of the moments I'm proudest of—it's like a ritual with the music. I told the cinematographer (Angel Luis Fernández), make it surprising and magical—not exactly like real magic, but like that moment when everyone looks up at the UFOs in *Close Encounters of the Third Kind.* I like it very much.

It's wonderful. Their faces are full of awe and envy. Even the police are softened and eroticized by the passion they imagine is going on inside that room. They become the quintessential Almodóvar spectators! Isn't this the third time such a spectatorial moment occurs in the film? The first is the opening where Antonio is watching and is turned on by the erotic scene from Pablo's movie. And the second occurs in the middle of the film where Tina asks a man in the street to hose her down while her brother Pablo and the child Ada watch in wonder. Isn't the film's structure controlled by these three spectatorial moments?

Yes, all three moments you have mentioned are the key to the film. The beginning is the key to understanding every-thing. I try to put the spectator into the field that I'm going to explore—the field of desire. Everyone understands that you can pay someone to make love to you. But it's very dif-ficult to recognize that you can pay someone just to *listen* to his desire, which is something very different. This sen-sual desire is more abstract. It's just the necessity of feeling desire in an absolute way. This is the problem in the film. And also, as you said, I explain how the movie is made. You see just the interior of the movie. But also I explain the director's behavior—the relationship between director and actor. The director, on the one hand, is a voyeur, but he also is pushing, dictating exactly what he wants to be enacted, he wants to be represented, and this is very important to the relationship of power and voyeurism between the director and the actor.

And yet aren't both being controlled by the script, which is probably why the script and the typewriter become so es-sential in the film—with all those huge close-ups and ex-pressionistic angles of the keyboard? I read in one interview where you say the force of Pablo's imagination is stronger than his feelings and that's why he takes the vengeance on the typewriter—why he refuses to write another script and why he throws the typewriter out the window at the end. But couldn't you also say that the script links Pablo to patriar-chal discourse?

I don't understand.

Isn't Pablo like his father—a seducer who prefers young boys and who's never totally committed? Doesn't he reen-act his father's seduction of his brother and also inspire his lovers to make a sacrifice? Pablo may want to be in con-trol, but isn't he as shaped by his father as Tina was? Aren't his scripts and movies vehicles for patriarchal ideology?

Well, I didn't think of that. Those are new ideas to me, but I agree with them and find them interesting. I like to dis-cover new explanations in my films. It makes them richer. The opening is the main sequence of desire, of abstract de-sire rather than of sensual pleasure. Sensuality and physical pleasure are far better represented in the central sequence where Tina says, "Hose me!" than in the opening where the boy says, "Fuck me!" That's an important distinction in the film.

But isn't there submission in both? Aren't they both part of the same masochistic aesthetic that also leads you to put the lust-in-the-dust ending of Duel in the Sun *in the middle of* **Matador?**

I don't see it as masochism. Masochism requires pain, and I don't find it in my films . . . I don't see masochism even in the Carmen Maura figure Tina, who is so obsessed with her past. She doesn't want to forget anything, even her worst memories. She's very engaged with her worst memories, they even feed her. This can be masochism too . . . a kind of quo-tidian masochism. In life in general you have to accept pain. It's a kind of adventure and sometimes pain is the price you have to pay; the things you get are more important than the pain. But masochism requires that you *like* to feel pain. . . . No, my films are more about pleasure, sensuality, and liv-ing—about the celebration of living. Don't forget you have to be conscious that for this celebration of absolute pleasure, often you have to pay a very high price. But the price is par-allel with the pleasure. This is the theory of *Matador.* If you can find an absolute pleasure, you also have to pay an ab-solute price. And in the reference to *Duel in the Sun,* there is, of course, what you said, but what was more important for me in this scene is just that when the ex-matador and lawyer come to the cinema, they look at the screen and see their future. It's like when you look into a magic crystal ball. When you go to the cinema, the cinema reflects not your life but your end. And it was exactly the ending of *Duel in the Sun* that is the ending of **Matador.**

But then both in **Matador** *and* **La Ley,** *watching movies seems to be a very dangerous activity.*

No, the problem is that *your* mentality is far more rational than ours, than of the Spanish people. And perhaps all of these terrible things are here inside my films. But I don't see these elements so clearly. I'm unconscious of them. I don't want to be so conscious of all these things. You explain everything. I prefer just to inspire, to suggest, not to explain.

I'm not really saying there are "terrible things" in your films, I'm just considering the implications of your choices— like the implications of having your last three films all end the same way—with an orgasmic climax in which two people are brought together in a passionate union that is somehow related to suicide and murder. In making this choice, aren't you romanticizing the price one has to pay for this absolute value? Isn't this a kind of romantic idealism that has connections with fascism since fascism also glamorizes death and sacrifice in the name of the ideal?

That sounds terrible! (laughs) . . . No, the moral of all my films is to get to a stage of greater freedom. *¿Qué He Hecho?* Is about the liberation of women, even if it takes killing. It's very dangerous to see my films with conventional morality. I have my own morality. And so do my films. If you see *Matador* through a perspective of traditional morality, it's a dangerous film because it's just a celebration of killing. *Matador* is like a legend. I don't try to be realistic, it's very abstract, so you don't feel identification with the things that are happening, but with the sensibility of this kind of romanticism. I hope that there is not this kind of fascist element in the celebration of murder. You know, murder happens. I'm not as, what should I say, as "naughty" as Patricia Highsmith. The kind of murder that horrifies me is the kind that happens in her novels—among regular people, where you agree with that murder. This is really immoral.

I think it's your tone that prevents the spectator from taking these murders seriously or from seeing them in terms of traditional morality. I know you've been widely quoted as saying you want to make films as if Franco had never existed, and I think that desire may be related to your refusal to see this potential connection between romantic love and fascism.

Perhaps I didn't fully understand what you said before about my glorification of violence.

It's not just violence, it's violence in the name of a noble

sacrifice, which one can also find in Christianity. For example, Tina has an altar in which she puts the image of the Virgin next to that of Marilyn Monroe and Liz Taylor. . . .

The Spanish people are known to be very religious. But it's not true. What we do in general is to adapt religion for our own needs, as Tina does. She needs to lean on something because she feels very much alone. Religion is there to make her feel better, to keep her company. And the altar contains, not only things of beauty, but all of her memories that accompany her, that prevent her from feeling so lonely. This is the kind of religion she needs. For her, there's a Virgin and a Dictator, and even the toys of the young girl.

Yes, but doesn't the altar serve as the backdrop for the final reunion between Pablo and Antonio, for their Passion?

Yes, in the end they form part of the altar, they become religious figures.

That's precisely what I mean. You glorify their kind of romantic love by turning it into a religion, by mystifying it with the same ideological trappings that helped to glorify fascism. But with lots of humor. . . . Maybe it's time to turn to another crucial institution that was glorified by Franco, the family. In one interview you noted that Wim Wenders chose a melodrama about the family (Paris, Texas) *to win the hearts of American spectators.*

That was just a joke. I like using the family very much.

In Spanish films, the family is typically made up of cruel mothers, absent, mythified fathers, and stunted, precocious children. And there seems to be a special Spanish version of the Oedipal narrative with a series of displacements of desire and hostility between the mother and the father. Sometimes the object of desire for the son is transferred from mother to father, as in **La Ley del Deseo,** *but mostly there's a displacement of the hostility, usually directed at the father, onto the mother. I don't find this dynamic in any other national cinema. And this is particularly odd since patriarchal power is so strong, or at least was so strong in Spain under Franco. Is it that the father is so threatening, the son has to displace his hostility onto the mother? Why do you think there's so much hostility directed toward the mother?*

I don't know. I defended the mother in *¿Qué He Hecho?* Of course, there was also a bad mother next door, but you actually find this kind of mother in Spain—the one who is so repressive to her children.

Yes, but in **Matador** *the only evil character is not the serial murderers, but Angel's repressive mother from Opus Dei.*

Yes, I find this kind of mother very hateful, but there are several other mothers in that film. . . . I feel very close to the mother. The idea of motherhood is very important in Spain. The father was frequently absent in Spain. It's as if the mother represents the law, the police. It's very curious because in my next film project, I have two young girls kill their mother. When you kill the mother, you kill precisely everything you hate, all of those burdens that hang over you. In this film, I'm killing all of my education and all of the intolerance that is sick in Spain.

Is this matricide an act of liberation or is it suicidal?

I don't want to psychoanalyze it. It's like killing the power. In my film, this is a very typical mother from the South, like Bernarda Alba. In order to frighten her two daughters, she tells them that the world is going to be destroyed and that they will be guilty. And the two girls run away. Then the two parents, both the father and the mother, supposedly die, but the mother doesn't really die. When the two girls become women, the mother suddenly appears like a ghost in order to drive them crazy, really crazy, because she behaves like a ghost. It's very surrealistic. At the end, the two girls have a duel with their mother and then, after they kill her, they discover that she was not a ghost, that she was alive. But she was very crazy. The mother's behavior is actually more murderous than that of the girls.

*It sounds fascinating. I can't think of any other national cinema that has so many matricides as the Spanish cinema. For example, in 1975, the year that Franco died, there were two major films in which matricide occurs—*Furtivos *and* Pascual Duarte. *And later in Saura's* Mamá Cumple Cien Años, *it's attempted again. And now your project! And, what's also strange, in Spanish films the killing of the father is only done by daughters, not by sons.*

It's true. . . . Fathers are not very present in my films. I don't know why. They are not in my films. This is something I just feel. When I'm writing about relatives, I just put in mothers, but I try not to put in fathers. I avoid it. I don't know why. I guess I'm very Spanish.

I guess you treat fathers like Franco, as if they never existed. . . . What is the name of your new project?

I don't know whether I'm going to change it later, but now it's called *Distant Heels.* I remember when I was a child, it was a symbol of freedom for young girls to wear high heels, to smoke and to wear trousers. And these two girls are wearing heels all the time. After running away, the two sisters live together, and the older remembers that she couldn't sleep until the moment that she heard the sound of distant heels coming from the corridor. I also like the title because it

sounds like a Western. All this happens in a desert in the South and the look is like that.

What qualities do you strive for in your mise en scène? *Can you make any generalizations about that? The visual look seems quite different from film to film.*

Yes, they *are* different. I'm learning at the same time that I'm shooting. I didn't go to any film school. So everything I learned, was learned while shooting. Also, I like so many different genres and want to go for very different qualities in each film. I have many different sides and want to develop them all. I'm not obsessed with style. I'd like each film to be absolutely different from the others in every possible way. This is a way of learning everything. And I don't want to get bored.

What impact has your success in Berlin and New York with **La Ley** *had on your new projects? Has it led to any concrete proposals for the future? Any international co-productions?*

For me the success merely means I can sell my films outside of Spain, and that's good for everybody. Right now I don't feel the temptation to make films outside of Spain because here I can work easier and faster and because it's the culture I know better than any other. I'm sure I'll make a film outside of Spain one day, but not now, not for the moment. Someday I would like to make a film in English, but later. Perhaps I'm lazy. But I want to keep working in this way. I want to feel very independent, and now I have to defend my independence even more than before.

Jeanne Silverthorne (essay date March 1990)

SOURCE: "Onwards and Sideways: The Films of Pedro Almodóvar," in *Artforum,* Vol. XXVIII, No. 7, March, 1990, pp. 146-50.

[*In the following excerpt, Silverthorne states that, "Almodóvar's world is a soup of tenses. His films simultaneously lock us in the past; celebrate our having come through, and wait for us to be born."*]

. . . Almodóvar is very conscious of his cultural surround: a new Spain, only recently released from fascism. He has observed in interviews that the generations now taking over in the country are "unrelated" to earlier ones; however, although he is clearly presenting his vision of a polymorphously perverse post-Franco generation, it is not exactly the case that his characters "utterly break with the past," as he has claimed. Where precisely in time do Almodóvar's films take us? Back to the future? Forward to the past? His approach to history is adaptive, a kind of use-it-up-and-wear-it-out attitude that is improvisation at its best. But there's a contradiction: despite all the joyfulness of his zany films, for Almodóvar, it often seems as if the past is literally the *mort-gage* (death pledge) on our future.

History grates in Almodóvar's films—literally. Baroque grilles and grillwork trace the nostalgic pull of the old Spain while geometric bars and grids map its repressiveness. In **Women on the Verge of a Nervous Breakdown,** 1987, we see the romance of the balcony in exterior shots of lovely filigreed old buildings, but the romance in the movie is one of seduction and separation, and almost every woman character struggles against it. Meanwhile Pepa (Carmen Maura), the heroine, has transformed her own balcony, a concrete shelf in a contemporary high rise, into a mini ark, installing two of every species of animal in what begins to resemble a peasant village. What to save of the past, what reject? When Gloria (Maura), the put-upon housewife of **What Have I Done to Deserve This?,** 1984, starts to commit suicide by climbing over the railing of her box of a balcony, the appearance of her son saves her—that is, it allows her to stay behind the grillwork of tradition by giving back to her a remnant (merely) of the role of loving mother, which she has persistently cast off throughout the film by, for instance, selling the son to a dentist and murdering her husband with a ham bone.

There's leakage backward and forward through the grate of the past. **Dark Habits,** 1983, concerns the adventures of a convent of nuns who write popular romance novels, keep a pet tiger, make costumes for the Virgin with an eye on Audrey Hepburn in *My Fair Lady,* sell and take drugs, and have love affairs—all in a matrix of black, tortuous religious/sexual passion in which the DNA of Saint Theresa of Avila, Billy Idol, Madonna, and Julio Iglesias seems to have recombined. If the metaphoric grille between modernity and the old-Spain world of the convent has failed completely to cloister this particular community, gothic mystery is nevertheless honored. In **Law of Desire,** 1986, a film about the homoerotic loves of a successful film director and the tribulations of his transsexual sister, it seems at first that a lighter, more pop-ish approach to religious tradition is being proposed, despite the film's tragic bent. The transsexual heroine, Tina (Maura), uses the forms of religion like an old teddy bear or bathrobe—they are something to cuddle up with or wrap herself in when she's feeling low. On her home-made altar, a figurine of Marilyn Monroe sits easily next to those of the Holy Mother. But after this makeshift altar bursts into flame at the end of the film, a long shot shows police climbing scaffolding into the burning apartment building, looking like licking flames themselves (and echoing the iconographic tradition of the Deposition, the men removing Christ's body from the Cross.) In that moment, the grid of

authoritarian law overlays a comforting sentimental mysticism.

So that in **Matador,** 1986, the story about "a retired torero and a beautiful lawyer," we are not surprised by the reciprocity of law and tradition, of prison bars and the brutal geometry of the bullring. Grids collide in checks and plaids as the tartan-suited attorney Maria Cardenal (Assumpta Serra) figures against black-and-white tiles, or stands in front of a barred window. Glimpses of gates and fences remind us of the advice of the maestro matador Diego Montes (Nacho Martinez) to a novice: "Chicks are like bulls. You need to hem them in—then it's easy." This is the only Almodóvar film to feature required heterosexual "love." But the traditional dance of courtship has become a mutual "hemming in," the gridlock of the immovable and the irresistible: accomplished serial murderers both, Maria and Diego kill each other off at the instant of their sexual climax. At one point, the matador's ex-girlfriend, angry and forsaken, eyes the lovers through the old-fashioned wrought-iron screen of an elevator shaft; she is appropriately anachronized, then, as she is also by dressing in red to attract the bull, her matador. (Colors are significant and heightened in Almodóvar's films, red being especially emphasized.) She does not recognize that where the lovers are, on the other side of some temporal mesh that separates past from present (or present from future), mutual machismo replaces the victim/aggressor pact. It's as though Almodóvar were suggesting that if heterosexuality follows its historical blueprint, it can only survive as a perversity. The joke in this film of rigid right angles is that the "straightest" of Almodóvar's erotic pairs is really the most "bent."

> The image of an overbearing, cruel, and powerful mother dissolves and reforms behind a wall of glass blocks in *Matador;* she is a recurring figure in the background of virtually every Almodóvar film, the never-quite-exorcised ancestor of the "new," postbiological mother, who is caring, adoptive, and not necessarily born female.
> —*Jeanne Silverthorne*

At times, in keeping with its osmotic quality, the grille becomes a palimpsest—that perfect symbol, in the post-Modern allegory, for bleeding time, for the shifting uncertainty of the contemporary moment. In **Women on the Verge,** Pepa, a pregnant woman on the verge of shucking off her outmoded Don Juan, is twice shown through glass panes covered with the texts of advertisements. The image of an overbearing, cruel, and powerful mother dissolves and reforms behind a wall of glass blocks in **Matador;** she is a recurring figure in the background of virtually every Almodóvar film, the never-quite-exorcised ancestor of the "new," postbiological mother, who is caring, adoptive, and not necessarily born female. And on the verge of a flight that will change her life. Yolanda (Christina S. Pascual), the nightclub singer in *Dark Habits,* is addressed by a piano player silhouetted behind a scrim. He prompts her to sing the last line of her act: "You'll come back" (a refrain).

Things always do come back, especially words. On the one hand, there is the script that imprisons. In *Dark Habits,* Yolanda is caught in her dead boyfriend's diary, which becomes the text for her conversations with her new admirer, the mother superior of the convent where she takes refuge from the police. Pablo (Eusebio Poncela), the film director in *Law of Desire,* ends up throwing out of the window the typewriter on which he has composed the various fictions that the people around him are compulsively acting out. Although it lands in a dumpster and bursts into flames, it continues to exert its influence in the form of the narrative we are watching, just as in *Women on the Verge,* suitcases and answering machines thrown away out the window remain in the plot by landing on other characters' heads. In several of Almodóvar's movies, people see films that predict or dictate their destinies. And various forgeries suggest that we slavishly imitate a script, often—like the illiterate forger of Hitler's letters in *What Have I Done to Deserve This?*—without being able to decipher it. That film alone displays not only fake letters but fake liquors, fake orgasms, fake girlfriends, fake checks, fake drugs, fake commercials, fake sadism.

On the other hand, impersonation is liberating. Yolanda may stick to the script of the diary, but she reverses the roles to put herself in control. Actually, it is by doubling her identity that she has escaped the police in the first place: seeking her in connection with the drug-induced death of her lover, they find her in the dressing room of another of the nightclub's performers, whom she impersonates, telling them that Yolanda is elsewhere. And once safe in the sanctuary of the convent, she takes over the completion of a painting begun by another, mysteriously vanished nun, somehow making available the resolution to that nun's story. (What happened to her was in part a sexual liberation.) By likewise following a script, the script for femininity, the transsexual Tina of *Law of Desire* also liberates herself, to a large extent. Lip-synching to romantic songs, characters in both films may seem to show that if no one had ever heard the word *love* (or the lyrics of a love song), no one would ever fall in love.

This lip-synching corresponds with the repeated references to dubbing. In *Women on the Verge,* Pepa is an actress who dubs in Spanish dialogue for old American films. And *Law of Desire* opens with a scene in which an off-screen male

presence directs a young man to masturbate; the words and sighs of both men, we eventually see, are provided by two distinctly unglamorous studio workers, and the whole episode, including the dubbing, turns out to be part of Pablo's latest film. While clearly about the manipulation of desire, this recurring device also shows desire cut off from its originator. Unmoored, erotic words float freely (if anxiously), belonging to everyone and to no one in particular, neither here nor there. Such ventriloquism allows characters to be in two places at once—in a café, say, and, thanks to vocal sound effects, at Le Mans. This is an increase rather than a diminution of power. Similarly, Almodóvar has produced counterfeit publicity shots and published the ongoing memoirs of an alter ego of his, Patty Diphusa, supposedly an international porn star—giving the director the gift of authorial bilocation.

Regurgitation in the films both is and exemplifies tautology. From film to film, characters vomit, an echo amplifying all of Almodóvar's recyclings: not only does he continually use the same actors, but lines of dialogue resurface, even trivial, throwaway lines like "Talking about me behind my back again?" (But then the entire contemporary world is unsuccessfully engaged in jettisoning its so-called disposable goods, right up to its typewriters and answering machines.) Prayers of thanksgiving are offered for the return of items never lost, the resurrection of people not dead. In *Dark Habits,* a mother asks about "the child," referring not to her missing daughter but to a pet tiger kept by the nuns. Still, her daughter turns out to have been a tiger, sexually, and in telescoping the daughter and this carnivorous coddled beast, Almodóvar collapses William Blake's two-faced god—the terrifying tyger and the childlike lamb. "This is the lamb of God who taketh away the sins of the lamb," improvises a priest, in a direct segue from the mother's inquiry; he is describing a sacrifice of innocence for no purpose, since the lamb has no sins. This oxymoron of innocence punished might be the definition of masochism. (Another ghost of the past: is masochism the essential ingredient of a "woman's" film like *Dark Habits?*) The frustration level is accordingly high—highest in this film, but impotence alternates with rejection throughout the oeuvre, and the rare consummated love annihilates.

The reflexiveness of the films, their placement of themselves as fictions, should deconstruct their illusion, but serves only to reinforce it. This reflexiveness is heaviest in the consistently narcissistic or voyeuristic opening sequences: that is, it is couched in terms of deferral, of waiting. Perhaps the most obvious example of this is the "fake" masturbation scene that both precedes and constitutes the beginning of *Law of Desire.* Later in the film, we watch fascinated policemen gaze up through a window at the kidnapped Pablo and his voracious lover/captor Antonio (Antonio Banderas). The scene rivets us even as we realize that we are watching a reflection of ourselves watching this film, entranced. Cinema takes us hostage and seduces us, as Antonio does Pablo. A gesture such as Tina's highly theatrical wiping away of a tear as she watches with the police makes us aware of the artifice, but no one is consequently disengaged. The way time is suspended during this hiatus—the syncopation of the police cars' keys and flashing lights makes an audible ticking—is virtually an objective correlative for the suspension of disbelief. Willing? That's beside the point.

Yet there are moments of breaking through the spell of redundancy, repetition, and regurgitation. The most stunning of these lies, once again, in the pseudofilm screened at the beginning of *Law of Desire.* For the conclusion of this sequence "gives birth" to Tina, who bursts radiantly upon us, throwing open the double doors of the theater. For a brief pause, we see her framed in the red circle on screen marking the "movie's" end, and containing the Spanish word *fin.* Thus you might say that Tina is the post-Modern pastiche (in Fredric Jameson's sense of that without norm) born after "the end" of Modernist self-reflexiveness. Moreover, she seems to have been born out of Antonio's orgasm; the close-up of his red, parted lips murmuring "fuck me" mirrors the red circle of *fin.* (For a director who sees the script as the originator of action, and words as genetic templates for lives, it's fitting that the mouth function as the birth canal. In *Dark Habits,* the mother of the vanished nun, kissing her daughter's photo, imprints the circle of her red lips around her image.) Tina, a transsexual, is conceived from the sperm of a masturbating bisexual male and delivered from the womb of film.

Like Yolanda in *Dark Habits,* with her surprising academic training in botany, Almodóvar specializes in hybrids, new possibilities. His new nuclear family takes root where it can. Children are left behind (Tina mothers one such child of a transsexual) or appropriated from inappropriate mothers. In *Dark Habits,* a whole community of "sisters" is bereft when their reverend "mother" dies; left to their own devices, they begin to mutate into a new communal shape. Crossbred genres are likewise a commonplace of Almodóvar's films. *What Have I Done to Deserve This?,* the tale of an overworked wife, mother, and domestic char, is part soap opera, part surreal fantasy, and part psychic thriller (there's a telekinetic little girl, who has no effect on the plot), all embedded in a Marxist matrix in which a pet lizard—sought for, bled upon, and witness to murder—is named Money. The movie ends with a long shot, that cinematic device for returning us to the "real" world, which juxtaposes a *free*way with the incarceral concrete apartment block in which the protagonist lives her constricted life.

In *Women on the Verge of a Nervous Breakdown* Almodóvar posits a new breed of woman. The film plays with the notion of "model," opening with a collage of photos of fashion mannequins and a shot of a scale model of the modern apartment house in which Pepa lives. Candela (Maria Barranco), a young friend of Pepa's, makes a living as a model; Pepa's ex-lover has a model ex-wife; and Pepa provides a role model to her young companions. Having established identity as artifice, Almodóvar locates it in time. Pepa sleeps with four clocks, as if with one for each of the four female characters. The fashion illustrations featured with the opening credits are from the '60s—when Franco maintained his supremacy—and they are the fashions to which Lucia (Julieta Serrano), the ex-wife of Pepa's ex-lover, clings even in the '80s. Lucia is first seen in profile against a butterfly collection; she too has been pinned and preserved. Maddened and made dangerous by her husband's infidelities and his abandonment of her, she has been intermittently institutionalized. For Pepa, who is younger but no ingenue, Lucia becomes a kind of icon, almost a Medusa into whose face a younger generation of women must look in order to "come through" into a new time. The fourth woman, the young Marisa (Rosy de Palma), who is being groomed for the old position of wife and mother (she's engaged to Lucia's son), is (accidentally) put to sleep by Pepa, and remains unconscious through much of the film. Here Almodóvar slyly rehabilitates Medea: it is the "good mother," Pepa, who makes the drugged food (gazpacho) that her protégés eat. An intermediary generation works out conflict with an older generation and then gives the result as a gift to the younger generation: at the end of the narrative, sleeping beauty wakes up, refreshed and mysteriously no longer a virgin, and Pepa, free from her obsession with her philandering boyfriend, reveals that she is going to have a child. They sit gazing at the view from the balcony and discuss the future.

True to its screwball-comedy format, *Women on the Verge* is the most optimistic of Almodóvar's works, and the only one that does not revolve around murder and suicide. Indeed, Almodóvar often seems to conflate the future with death. "When you go to the cinema," he has said, "the cinema reflects not your life but your end." And *end* means *future,* as when he talks about the lovers in *Matador* using *Duel in the Sun,* another agon resulting in a couple's simultaneous death, as a crystal ball. In personal terms, clearly the future *is* eventually an end, a death, even if it is also, and in an intimately related way, potential, change, rebirth—as with Tina's naissance out of *fin* in *Law of Desire.* In one scene in that film, Antonio shoots targets in a video arcade, waiting to see if he can pick up Pablo, director of the film that has just premiered; the numbers on the machine light up in sequence—one, two, three—as Pablo talks to a fan about his first, second, and third films. (Antonio is a "straight shooter" all right—out of the purity of his passion he will shoot and kill himself.) Numbers also appear in *Matador,* painted on pillars and abutments for the purposes of bullfighting instruction, but this time they form a countdown: spread out in time are glimpsed first a seven, then six, five, four. We are on our way to the explosive climax (there are lots of targetlike rings on the floor of the school), but the counting goes backward. The action is subliminally regressive. This may seem to reinforce the feeling that the sexual politics of *Law of Desire* are more progressive than those of *Matador.* Both films, however, conclude in fatalities. On the other hand, perhaps *Matador's* countdown of circled numbers is intended to suggest the numbers on a film strip that mark the seconds before a production starts. In a way, as the lovers march toward death, a film advances to a beginning.

So for Almodóvar, the two terms become interchangeable, subsiding back into tautology, which is his version of fate. Except for *Women on the Verge* (and the early, less resolved film *Labyrinth of Passion*), all of the films discussed end in some form of pietà, a configuration whose air of irrevocable loss seems eternal and therefore inevitable. Yet what succeeds this scene in Christian mythology? A resurrection. Still, while it is surely an innovation to replace the embracing Mary with a man (*Law of Desire*) and the prostrate Jesus with a woman (*Dark Habits*), with Almodóvar we are not fully in a brave new world. Tina may have been born after "the end" of history, Pepa may have resolved her conflicts, but both are shadowed by bulwarks of the past. Almodóvar's world is a soup of tenses. His films simultaneously lock us in the past, celebrate our having come through, and wait for us to be born.

Marvin D'Lugo (essay date 1991)

SOURCE: "Almodóvar's City of Desire," in *Quarterly Review of Film and Literature,* Vol. 13, No. 4, 1991, pp. 47-65.

[*In the following essay, D'Lugo discusses the image of Madrid and Spain's past and present in Almodóvar's films.*]

History and Desire

Madrid has figured prominently in Pedro Almodóvar's cinema, gradually coming into focus as the implicit protagonist of nearly every work. In these films, the city is regularly imaged as a cultural force, producing forms of expression and action that challenge traditional values by tearing down and rebuilding the moral institutions of Spanish life: the family, the Church, and the law.

Inspired by the conventions of cinematic representation of the city in film and, most pointedly, American filmic depictions of urban space, Almodóvar's city-scapes succeed in imitating the American cinema's unself-conscious universalization of particular milieus as the natural *mise-en-scène* of action. In the context of a cinema such as Spain's, which has

for so long been marginalized, such a project needs to be recognized as a self-affirmation of a culture that no longer sees itself as marginal and intuitively reframes and recenters its characters within a broader cultural field.

This foregrounding of the city as an assertion of a vibrant Spanish cultural identity is built around a rejection of the traditions that ordered Spanish social life for four decades. While Almodóvar has long insisted that his cinema is without any connection to Franco or Francoism, textual evidence suggests the contrary. An essential axis of meaning in much of his filmic work lies precisely in the ways the ideas and icons of Francoist cinema—those related to religion, the family, and sexual repression—are set up as foils to stimulate the audience to embrace a new post-Francoist cultural esthetic.

> **While Almodóvar has long insisted that his cinema is without any connection to Franco or Francoism, textual evidence suggests the contrary. An essential axis of meaning in much of his filmic work lies precisely in the ways the ideas and icons of Francoist cinema—those related to religion, the family, and sexual repression—are set up as foils to stimulate the audience to embrace a new post-Francoist cultural esthetic.**
>
> **—Marvin D'Lugo**

Historically, the Francoist animosity toward urban culture revealed an important conflation of politics and sexuality that would inform cultural development and particularly cinematic development decades after the end of the Civil War. Francoism constructed its own ideal of the Spanish nation against the models of social and political deviance embodied as much by the urban life styles of Madrid and Barcelona as by the external otherness of foreign political ideologies and social customs. During the 1930s and 1940s, a strongly folkloric cinema emerged that imaged a sanitized, provincial world of pure spiritual and moral values, implicitly opposing the milieu of moral corruption, sexual promiscuity, and heretical foreign ideas that was synonymous for the regime with urban culture.

One of the most striking cinematic examples of this negative conception of the city is José Antonio Nieves Conde's 1950 film, *Surcos* (*Furrows*), which chronicles the dissipation of the members of a provincial peasant family as they struggle to survive in an economically depressed Madrid. The root of the family's difficulties in the big city, as that film insists, lay in the emerging dominance of female characters who have usurped the traditional authority and power of the male in Spanish society. The film's mother and daughter expose the degree to which female sexuality had become a dangerous counter-discourse to the dominant ideology of Francoism.

The technocrats who occupied key government ministries beginning in the late 1950s helped modernize Spain's antiquated economic and social institutions. Their policies effectively discarded the doctrinaire anti-urban bias of earlier government officials. Yet, while the notion of urban culture as enemy receded as an official view, the opposing notion of the city as a haven from the ideological repression of the provinces seemed not only to persist, but even to intensify. In Juan Antonio Bardem's 1956 film, *Calle Mayor (Main Street)*, the critique of repressive provincial life is pointedly contrasted with the lure of Madrid where characters are not plagued by the close-mindedness and intolerance of the community. Hints of a similar repudiation of the provinces and of the intense appeal of the city are central to Fernando Fernán Gómez's *El extraño viaje* (1964: *The Strange Journey*).

Francoist antipathy to urban culture clearly shapes the critical opposition cinema of the 1960s and 1970s which, in turn, establishes the bridge to Almodóvar's films of the eighties. Drawing, for instance, on the commonplace of the city as refuge from the oppression of provincial life, seventies' films such as Jaime Armiñán and José Luis Borau's *Mi querida señorita* (1971: *My Dear Young Lady*), Vincente Aranda's *Cambio de sexo* (1976: *A Change of Sex*), and Ventura Pons's *Ocaña* (1979) repeatedly figure the city—Madrid and Barcelona—as the haven for characters whose sexual identity had been deformed by the repressive social environment of provincial life.

By the early eighties, Madrid became cinematically as well as socially the site of a generational schism chronicled in films as diverse as Gutiérrez Aragón's *Maravillas* (1980: *Marvels*), Carlos Saura's *Deprisa, deprisa* (1980: *Hurry, Hurry!*), and Fernando Trueba's *Opera prima* (1980). In this subgenre, urban milieus were increasingly identified as the locus of a defiant youth culture that rejected the mores and morality of its parents.

To a certain extent, this emphasis on Madrid locales is the result of the centralization of much of the film industry in and around the capital, which made it financially expedient to locate certain narratives in and near the city. Whether coincidental or intentional, however, this narrative centering has led to the rise in opposition cinema in the seventies of implicit "scenarios of the Spanish nation." In films such as Pedro Olea's *Pim, Pam, pum . . . fuego* (1975: *Bang, Bang, You're Dead*), Gutiérrez Aragón's *Sonámbulos* (1978: *Sleepwalkers*), or José Luis Garci's *Asignatura pendiente* (1977: *Pending Exam*), to name only three conspicuous examples,

the narrative is situated on the symbolic national stage, the capital city, thus transforming presumably local action into broader meditations of national historical issues.

Though Almodóvar's cinema represents in most ways an unequivocal stylistic rupture with nearly every Spanish filmic tradition that precedes it, the figuration of the city in his films enables us to recognize a similar pattern of reflection on Spanish cultural identity that the flashy surfaces of particular films may tend to belie. In Almodóvar's cinema, Madrid comes to be seen as the place where the oppression of the old Spain depicted by earlier filmmakers is deciphered, challenged, and, in quite surprising ways, displaced.

The final sequence of **Law of Desire** (1987: **La ley del deseo**) dramatizes these tendencies by foregrounding the urban *mise-en-scène* of Madrid as the medium through which this radical reformulation of Spanish cultural values is expressed. This is a cardinal moment in Almodóvar's cinema in that this cluster of narrative motifs is joined to a strategy of subject address that foregrounds the crucial thematics inscribed in the urban milieu. In that scene, Antonio, the murderous lover of Pablo Quintero, the film director, has been cornered by the police in the apartment of Pablo's transsexual sister, Tina, played by Carmen Maura. Antonio agrees to release Tina and a captured police detective in exchange for one hour with Pablo. Finally alone with his lover, Antonio puts on a phonograph record ("*Lo dudo*") that expresses the sentiments of pure, unfailing love, then proceeds to undress Pablo for their last sexual union. The camera discreetly cuts away to a shot of the street below as the assembled police and relatives look up to the window of Tina's apartment where the homosexual love scene is taking place. As Marsha Kinder describes the scene: "Their faces are full of awe and envy. Even the police are softened and eroticized by the passion that they imagine is going on in the room. They become the quintessential Almodóvar spectators!"

After the love-making scene, Antonio, understanding that he is trapped, commits suicide, shooting himself in the head and falling dead before Tina's altar of kitsch artifacts—Barbie dolls and statues of Marilyn Monroe and the Virgin Mary. Pablo rushes to his side and, in a mock recreation of Michelangelo's *Pietà*, holds his fallen lover in his arms. The film thus ends with an image that daringly transposes the scene of gay love, and perhaps the entire film, into what for some audiences must appear as a surprising religious context.

The scene is constructed around an essential historical irony. Not only is a religious discourse mobilized to valorize those sexual activities that the Church had traditionally suppressed within Francoist society, but the dramatized audience and presumably the authenticators of that new demarginalization are the police, the enforcers of those repressive social and moral codes. In short, the apparatus of Francoist social and sexual repression is reinscribed into the scene to affirm the very values that historically it had blocked and suppressed.

In highlighting the traditional institutions that articulated and enforced the social discourse of the past, the scene enunciates a basic linkage between two forms of desire: Antonio's individualized passion for Pablo and the "collective" scopic desire of the assembled audience on the street below. Madrid, as the narrative attests, constitutes a privileged space in which individual desires freely circulate, inevitably transforming the urban milieu into the site of a continual spectacle. Part of that transformation is the positioning of other madrileños to "bear witness" to the scenario of sexual liberation of the protagonists, triggering in them in turn a recognition of their own desires long repressed by the social institutions of the Francoist regime.

This subversive reinscription of the dominant discursive register of Francoist ideology in *Law of Desire* dramatizes what Michel Foucault called "effective history," that is, ". . . not [history as] a decision, a treaty, a reign, or a battle, but the reversal of a relationship of forces, the usurpation of power, the appropriation of a vocabulary turned against those who had once used it, a feeble domination that poisons itself as it grows lax, the entry of a masked 'other.'" The result of this effective history, as Foucault asserts is to open up a range of discursive discontinuities, of ruptures that will, in fact, place into question the very genealogy of received cultural knowledge. Foucault thus sees effective history as a "curative science," affirming knowledge, not as an absolute, but rather a perspective, " . . . [creating] its own genealogy in the act of cognition."

The notion of "effective history" as a strategy of subject address coincides with Linda Hutcheon's view of postmodern parody as a means through which "an artist [can] . . . speak to a discourse from within it, without being recuperated by it." "Parody," Hutcheon says, "appears to have become, for this reason, the mode of . . . 'the ex-centric,' of those who are marginalized by the dominant ideology." It is, as well, a means through which "to investigate the relation of ideology and power to all our present discursive structure." As the dramatization of an appropriation of a dominant discourse now turned against those who had once imposed it, the final scene of *Law of Desire* addresses its audience through a series of ironic reversals in the social authentication of sexual identity. These reversals of traditional Spanish ideology foreground a historicized spectatorship to Almodóvar's film. A broader cultural discourse, in other words, has been displaced onto a sexual discourse, and one comes to view the film not only in terms of the specific sexual alignments it recounts, but also as the affirmation of a new social logic of toleration and openness.

Detailing the generational cleavage that lies at the center of his films as it mirrors the larger social picture of Spain after Franco, Almodóvar observes:

> We have lost the fear of earthly power (the police), and of celestial power (the Church) . . . And we have recuperated the inclination toward sensuality, something typically Mediterranean. We have become more skeptical, without losing the joy of living. We don't have confidence in the future, but we are constructing a past for ourselves because we don't like the one we have.

The construction of a "new past" as dramatized in each of Almodóvar's films involves, as Foucault's effective history suggests, the appropriation of the language of the old order now turned against itself to constitute a new Spanishness. A close look at the function of the city within the narrative and visual structures that define these films reveals a coherent textual order that actively appropriates the social constructions of Francoist culture—the family, the Church, the police—and mobilizes them into the emerging expression of new cultural "desires."

City of Desire

Almodóvar's first two feature-length films, *Pepi, Luci, Bom, and Other Girls Like That* (1980: *Pepi, Luci, Bom, y otras chicas del montón*) and *Labyrinth of Passion* (1982: *Laberinto de pasión*) are, by the director's admission, products of the *Movida,* that effervescence of youthful energy in music, art, and popular culture that occurred at the end of the seventies. Inspired by the movement's punk style, both films express the brash self-confidence of a newly emerging youth culture that suddenly discovers Madrid as "the center of the universe." In *Labyrinth of Passion,* for instance, Toraya, the dethroned Empress of Tehran is in search of her gay step-son, Riza. She comes to Madrid because she knows he has heard it is "the most entertaining city in the world, and so modern." The ironic displacement of the traditional centers of Western culture, New York and Paris, and the improbable centering of the culture of the periphery are a source both of humor and of cultural self-affirmation.

Cityscapes in these early films tend to emphasize the concept of physical movement and social mobility underscored in the very word, *Movida,* "movement." Characters like Pepi, the heroine of Almodóvar's first film, and Riza, the hero of the second, have come to Madrid looking for a freedom obviously denied them elsewhere. They are able to seek out kindred spirits in an atmosphere that, as both films assert, is socially liberating and the impetus for new artistic creativity.

Though, as Almodóvar insists, Franco doesn't exist for these characters, the foils for his liberated protagonists turn out to be fathers and husbands who serve as transparent embodiments of traditionalist, patriarchal order. In *Pepi, Luci, Bom,* for instance, Pepi, the heroine, has been raped by a police detective who continually voices the tenets of old-guard Francoist ideology: law and order, misogyny, and homophobia. In seeking her revenge against the detective, Pepi befriends the latter's wife, Luci, who soon abandons her husband for a lesbian relationship with Pepi's girlfriend, Bom. The formerly laconic Luci is introduced to the emancipated atmosphere of a post-Franco Madrid populated by gays, lesbians, and transvestites, all of whom implicitly reject the phallocentric political and social order embodied by Luci's estranged husband.

In *Labyrinth of Passion* Almodóvar distances himself from the overt marks of the old Spain but continues the assault on conventional categories of sexuality. In the opening sequence of the film we see both Riza and Sexilia, the nymphomaniac daughter of a woman-hating gynecologist, cruising the Sunday morning flea market, the Rastro, in search not of touristic bargains, but of sexual partners. From the establishing shot that identifies the Rastro, the camera swiftly cuts to a chain of medium close-ups of crotches and buttocks as the protagonists vie for sexual mates. The point of the erotic spectacle is that both male and female characters are going after the same sexual partners. By casting the spectator in the role of voyeur of this sexual spectacle, the scene deploys the scopic register of cinema as a form of discursive resistance to patriarchal constructions of sexual identity; from the very first moment, the spectator is positioned to occupy a cinematic gaze that transcends the repressive categories of sexual identity and to enter into the film's "labyrinth of passion," which is synonymous with Madrid.

In this way, the credit sequence highlights the essential breaking down of the boundaries between public and private spaces that is one of the basic features of the cinematic characterization of Madrid in the early films. In that newly-created space of interaction between personal and social behavior, new relations are shaped; new identities are forged. That very same message is affirmed in the opening sequence of *Pepi, Luci, Bom.* The camera poses what at first appears to be an exterior shot of apartment building facades in Madrid, only to reveal the source of that view to be inside the window of Pepi's tiny apartment. The camera then pulls back and begins a brief tracking of the heroine's apartment. When the doorbell rings, Pepi answers it and we meet the detective who has been eyeing Pepi's marijuana plants from his apartment window in one of the nearby buildings we have just viewed. Confusing personal desire with social desire, the detective winds up raping the girl he had come to arrest, thus setting in motion the film's intricate narrative of revenge and friendship.

The visual and narrative blurrings of interior and exterior space as the impetus for the mobilization of desires is repeated in an elaborate scene of sexual spectacle later in the film. A contest called "General Erections" is staged among the male guests at a party held in the courtyard of an apartment building. The scene is viewed by a bisexual male, situated at the window of an apartment overlooking the orgy, who observes these actions through a pair of binoculars as he makes love with his transsexual wife.

Though seemingly motivated as affirmations of a hedonistic youth culture, these scenes also operate to secure the notion common to both films of an urban *mise-en-scène* in which the tearing down of scopic and sexual barriers leads to a series of social and sexual realignments. The individual desires that surface in this environment work, in turn, to break down the mythologies of sexuality identified within the broader cultural politics of traditionalist Spain, especially those of *machismo* and subservient females. As a city of pure, hedonistic desire, Almodóvar's Madrid thus becomes the site of a radical new series of social desires as well.

Though, from the start, female characters assume centrality in Almodóvar's cinema, it is not until *Dark Habits* (1983: *Entre tinieblas*) that the city is self-consciously figured as the site of female empowerment. The plot of Almodóvar's third film is set in motion by two female antagonists who represent the spiritual and material interests of Spain after Franco. Sister Julieta, a mother superior who leads a religious order of nuns, "*Las redentoras humilladas*" ("The Humbled Redeemers"), in a Madrid convent, confronts a crisis for her order when the convent's benefactor, the Marquis, dies and his widow refuses to continue her fascist husband's support of the convent. This situation forces the order to face the harsh economic realities of the real world. Thus the Madrid of the post-Franco era is defined implicitly as a space in contention by two opposing forces, one moral, the other materialistic, and both, importantly, embodied in strong female characters. Tellingly, all views of contemporary society in the film are mediated through female characters.

The "Humbled Redeemers" have come from the provinces to perform charitable work by providing haven from the police for youthful drug addicts, prostitutes, and murderers. It soon becomes apparent, however, that the nuns' "good deeds" are as much a liberation for them from the oppressive cloistered atmosphere of the provinces as they are a demonstration of good samaritanism. As a critique of traditional Catholicism's lack of connection with the problems of contemporary society, *Dark Habits* also weaves the historical tension between the city and Francoism's idealized provinces. Under the impetus of the urban milieu, the nuns have been led to discover the force of their own desire. Their religious faith, at best a convenient sublimation of those desires, becomes the catalyst for each woman's self-realization.

The arrival of Yolanda Bell, the fugitive torch singer who takes haven in the convent, pointedly dramatizes that linkage of individual desire and the urban *mise-en-scène.* The scene begins as the nuns are in the convent chapel preparing to take communion. They sing a religious chant of devotion to God that expresses the confusion between sacred and erotic passion that will shortly be enacted. As they sing, the nuns form a line in the aisle and approach the altar where a priest awaits them. The scene is shot from the altar so that when the rear door of the chapel suddenly opens and reveals Yolanda standing in the doorway, it is as if one sees a "divine apparition." Sister Julieta turns around and approaches Yolanda, inviting her to participate in the mass. Rear lighting from the street pours into the darkened chapel and thereby gives Yolanda the appearance of a saintly figure with a halo surrounding her head and body. The voices of the female chorus block out the noises of passing traffic on the street; yet the blending of the visual and auditory tracks of the convent and the city streets suggests a continuity between the religious fervor that appears to possess the nuns and the city that seems magically to have delivered Yolanda to the waiting arms of Sister Julieta. By foregrounding the *mise-en-scène* in this fashion, Julieta's lesbian desire for Yolanda Bell, which is the dramatic heart of the film, is defined within the play of cloistered and urban spaces that situates that melodrama within a larger context of Spanish culture in transition. Indeed, *Dark Habits* is the first of his films where Almodóvar takes aggressive control of the development of narrative space in order to develop the dramatic identity of his characters.

It is also this film where Almodóvar makes his first explicit connection between the urban milieu and moral categories, supplying us with a framework for understanding the rewriting of "celestial power" by his "Humbled Redeemers." "Jesus didn't die on the Cross to save saints," Sister Julieta tells Yolanda, "but to redeem sinners. . . . Soon, this house will be filled with murderers, drug-addicts and prostitutes, just like in earlier times."

The principles of the religion Julieta preaches are both egalitarian and sexually liberating. On one hand, the "Humbled Redeemers" appear to be recuperating Catholicism's tradition of ministering to the humble and weak, while on the other, their contacts with urban life inevitably lead each of the women to realize her own inner desires. The patron saints of this religion, according to Almodóvar, are as much Jean Genet as St. John Bosco, the founder of hospices for abandoned youths. Speaking of the portrayal of religion in the film, the director says; "In *Dark Habits* the important thing is the absence of religion, or rather religion understood from another point of view, with another subject and another object. That is to say, religious sentiments are provoked by something other than God. Religion is the language that human beings have invented for themselves to connect with something superior and that language contains a series of religious rituals that pass for piety. The paradox of the film is that these nuns have a religion, but not a religion inspired in God."

In Almodóvar's next work, **What Have I Done to Deserve This?** (1985: *¿Qué he hecho yo para merecer esto?*), the identification of Madrid with the liberation of the female and the attendant revision of the moral order become even more pronounced. Inspired in some measure by the melodramatic formulae of Italian neorealism, particularly the films of Rossellini, Zavattini, and De Sica, **What Have I Done?** is set in the recognizable working-class *barrio de la Concepción,* a neighborhood of high-rise cheap housing built in the sixties as a demonstration of Franco's modernization of living conditions in Spain. The film's setting foregrounds its neorealist intertext, suggesting to some critics an update of the opposition cinema of Bardem, Berlanga, and Ferreri, which also drew heavily on Italian neorealism.

That historical intertext is continually paired, however, with the obvious evidence of a dystopian present tense. Almodóvar says of his development of the film's exteriors: "The few times that we moved outside for exteriors it had to be like *Blade Runner,* with that atmosphere of an uncomfortable future that novels always tell us about, that continuous, disagreeable spitting of bad weather. But also that gothic enormity of *Blade Runner . . .*" Indeed, the frequent shots of the urban expressway vividly establish the image of modern-day Madrid as a European cognate of Los Angeles and therefore the anti-image of Francoist Spain.

Through the destinies of its two central female characters, **What Have I Done?** textualizes that cultural duality of a city hovering between a wretched past and an even more depressing future. Gloria (Carmen Maura) and her mother-in-law (Chus Lampreave) have both come from the same provincial village, but the older woman cannot tolerate the city and longs to return to the provinces, while, as Gloria's family dissolves around her, she comes to understand that the city is precisely her destiny. In a certain respect, Madrid shapes and directs this duality for it is both the place that symbolizes the schism between the old and the new, and also the cultural agency of the changes that will eventually liberate Gloria.

Visually debunking the Francoist dream of high-rise modernity, the narrative also attacks the Francoist myth of the ideal Spanish family. The key to Gloria's eventual deliverance from social, sexual, and emotional imprisonment lies precisely in her extricating herself from the family, which she does by accidentally killing her brutish husband in an argument. Near the end of the film, in a moment of defiance, she admits her guilt to the detective investigating the murder, but he takes her confession to be an emotional outburst occasioned by the shock of the murder. In this way, *What Have I Done?* constructs a parable around the liberating force of the city: The family, the cultural institution that traditionally has replicated Francoist ideology on the individual level, has been shattered by the city, and the father has conveniently been eliminated. With the valorizing glance of the law, however, Gloria, the embodiment of a different kind of Spanish mother, is able to free herself from the tyranny of the old patriarchy and reconstitute the Spanish family anew with her homosexual son, Miguel, while her older son, Toni, returns with his grandmother to the provinces. The film's final reconciliation between Gloria and her gay son underscores the persistent bonding of female and gay characters throughout Almodóvar's cinema as they each recognize the city as the place of their liberation from the tyrannical sexual and social codes of the patriarchy.

The identification of individual destiny with locale is foregrounded in a number of scenes in the film. One of the most pointed of these is a cinematic self-reference. Gloria's mother-in-law takes Toni to the movies to see Elia Kazan's *Splendor in the Grass.* We see the two sitting in the darkened theater as they watch the key moment when Warren Beatty tells his father that he doesn't want to go to college, but, instead, prefers to run the family farm. The film-within-the-film is obviously used to prefigure part of the denouement of *What Have I Done?* as Toni and his grandmother return to their village. But on a broader self-referential level, the use of the film-within-the-film device suggests the power of the cinematic medium, including the Almodóvar film we are viewing, to enunciate individual and collective desires.

What Have I Done to Deserve This? crystallizes the multiplicity of opposing individual and collective desires that Madrid activates for Almodóvar's characters. The film uses urban space to establish a basic historical tension that, as John Hopewell observes of a later Almodóvar film, is ". . . not a distance from the past but a sensitivity to the legacy of the past."

New Mythologies for a New Spain

While Almodóvar's early films defined the city as the embodiment of generational self-affirmation and female liberation, his next three films, *Matador* (1986), *Law of Desire* (1987), and *Women on the Verge of a Nervous Breakdown* (1988), mythify their protagonists in order to rewrite cultural identity within the matrix of a liberated and liberating Madrid.

This rewriting of the mythologies of Spain coincides with the cinematic reimaging of the city in progressively more sensuous and evocative colors. Before *Matador,* Almodóvar's films foregrounded the unattractiveness of Madrid. In fact, in *What Have I Done to Deserve This?,* his intention was precisely to capture that external ugliness that coincided with the internal tawdriness and claustrophobia of the heroine's world. Visually, *Matador* reverses that *feoísta* tendency by giving pictorial prominence to a more cosmopolitan urban imageability.

Matador situates its action in a recognizable Madrid while again playing out the ideological scenarios of otherness through the development of two mother figures: Angel's mother, Berta (Julieta Serrano), a member of the conservative Catholic lay group, *Opus Dei,* and Pilar (Chus Lampreave), the understanding and modern-thinking mother of Eva, a popular fashion model. As Almodóvar says, these women represent two notions of Spain. Yet, rather than contenting himself with what by now is the cultural platitude of the "two Spains," he stands that hoary cliché on its head when, appearing in a brief cameo as a fashion designer, he is interviewed by a reporter who asks him why he has called his fashion show 'Spain Divided.' He answers, "Because this country has always been divided in two." When she pushes him for a clarification, he responds, "On one side, there are the envious; on the other, the intolerant . . . I'm on both sides."

Reducing ideological conflict to a fashion show, Almodóvar seems to have resolved the age-old conflicts of national identity by suggesting simply that it's all a matter of changing fashion. But tellingly, the only model we ever see actually parade in this fashion show is Pilar, who walks from the dressing area to her seat simulating the movements of a model. Indeed, she is the ideal maternal model of the new Spain, liberated from the deforming values of its intolerant past.

As the film's title suggests, *Matador* is centered on the popular images of the bullfighter. Instead of repeating trite stereotypes, however, the film reformulates the bullfighter clichés into a new Spanish myth, one in which passion and death are given a contemporary meaning. The plot focuses on a curious triangle. Diego Montes, a retired torero, relives the thrill of the bullring by committing a number of murders. One of the students in Diego's bullfighting class, Angel, wracked by a sense of personal guilt instilled in him by his religious mother, confesses to the crimes. Angel, in turn, is defended by a female lawyer, María Cardenal, who also happens to be a murderous nymphomaniac and ardent admirer of Angel's teacher, Diego. Diego and María eventually form the perfect couple and achieve their long-sought erotic pleasure by attempting joint suicide at the moment of orgasm.

Our initial view of Madrid is tellingly a highly mediated one. In the first narrative sequence after the credits, we see Antonio sitting in Diego's bullfighting class and fantasizing a scene obviously triggered by Diego's description of the proper manner for killing a bull. Antonio's reverie is visualized as the scene cuts to a plaza in the city where María is seen seducing a young man for what will be her own ritual of death in the afternoon. In this way, the stereotypical bullring image of Spanish cultural space is transformed into a space of seduction in which the female, not the male, is predator. This view subsequently gives way to the image of the new Spain as a chic fashion show, and finally ends with the reworking of the matador motif into the film's final image of the two murderous lovers, draped by a bullfighter's cape in deadly embrace before the admiring eyes of the police inspector. This final pairing of Diego and María as the ideal erotic-murderous couple along with their shared identity as *matadores* suggests once again an intentional blurring of the traditional, rigid lines that defined male and female identities in the old Spain.

Even more reflective of the cultural logic of the new order, particularly its reframing of traditional ethics and morality, are the secondary characters Angel and Inspector del Valle, the police detective investigating the rash of murders committed by Diego and María. Angel is the critical link between the moral order of the past and the ethical identity of Post-Francoism. Having so deeply absorbed conservative Catholic dogma, he believes himself guilty of the murders committed by others. In a cinematic quotation of the mushroom-picking scene from Victor Erice's *Spirit of the Beehive* (1973: *El espíritu de la colmena*), Almodóvar has Angel caution the gardener at Diego's house not to pick "bad," poisonous mushrooms. As in Erice's film, the act of distinguishing between "good" and "bad" mushrooms is a metaphoric expression of the political and social judgments that were the foundation of the Francoist ethic. Angel's mouthing of the Manichean distinction works to reinforce his identity as a child of Francoism who is struggling to shake loose from the grips of the old order. His dubious confession leads Inspector del Valle to witness the new cultural ideal represented by Diego and María's ritual of passionate love and death.

This notion of transforming the old into the new is given an additional moral dimension in one key scene near the beginning of the film in which Angel's mother forces him to go to confession. After mass, Angel approaches the priest who tells him to wait a moment while he changes his vestments. In a perfectly matched cut to maintain continuity, we see Angel walk through the church with its excessive Catholic iconography, then open a door and enter what turns out to be a police station. He walks to the reception area and says to a receptionist: "I've come to confess." The radical juxtaposition of scenes constructed by this *faux raccord* crystallizes the equally radical transformation of morality and religion that have occurred in post-Franco Spain, where a new secular morality has displaced the old tyranny of the Church.

Ironically, Angel's confession is delivered to the most improbable representative of the law, Inspector del Valle. As Almodóvar describes the del Valle character: "The detective is secretly in love with Angel. . . . This is a surprising kind of police detective, subtle, sensitive, ingenious, and well-dressed, qualities which one doesn't usually attribute to a Spanish police officer. But Spain has changed a lot, and I want to believe that so have its police officials." Adding other crucial details to the conception of the detective, the director says, "He is more of a criminologist than a policeman. Justice doesn't interest him and he lacks any sense of morality." Out of such a character, who outwardly embodies the forms of continuity with the past, but inwardly disavows its stern judgmental posturings, *Matador* seeks to rewrite the mythologies of Spanish cultural identity.

In Almodóvar's next film, *Law of Desire,* Madrid once again shapes a tale about characters who, like Del Valle, embody the shifting value system that has transformed the cultural fabric of Spanish society. Almodóvar's vision of the city by night in *Law of Desire* imparts an implicit libidinous connotation to much of the action. Urban space pointedly serves as a frame for a continuous erotic spectacle that the filmic narrative persistently chronicles. Speaking of the film's *mise-en-scène,* which reveals a number of buildings and plazas in the city that are under renovation (including Tina's apartment building, the site of the film's final image) the director further notes: "Madrid is an old and an experienced city, but full of life. . . . Its restoration, which seems interminable, represents this city's desire to live. Like my characters, Madrid is a spent space for which it isn't enough just to have a past because the future keeps on exciting it."

Perhaps the most explicit marker of this erotic textualizing of the city comes in the scene on a street at night near Tina's apartment when she asks a sanitation worker to hose her down, with all the erotic visual symbolism that action implies. The on-screen audience of the transsexual's erotic spectacle are Tina's gay brother, Pablo, a popular filmmaker, and her young ward, Ada, the daughter of her former lesbian lover. In other words, the performer and audience of this erotic spectacle foreground the identification of the city as the place of a persistent breakdown of the traditional categories of sexual identity in Spanish society. That meaning is overdetermined by the centering of the scene on the transsexual's body as it signifies the dramatic collapse of sexual difference: male/female; gay/lesbian; heterosexual/homosexual. As we watch Tina's ecstatic response to the thrust of water on her body, we unconsciously bear witness to the power of the city as the agency of the individual's release from the constraints of the social suppression of body and mind.

Marsha Kinder notes the similarity between the hosing scene and the precredit sequence of *Law of Desire* in which a young man is auditioning for Pablo's gay porno film, *The Mussel's Paradigm.* The actor's delivery of the script line, *fóllame, fóllame!* ("Fuck me, Fuck Me!") will later be echoed in Tina's words to the sanitation worker, *"riégueme, riégueme* ("Hose me, hose me!"). That textual similarity retrospectively establishes the film's underlying equation between the urban *mise-en-scène* and the cinematic institution, that is to say, between social praxis and cinematic praxis. In both, scopic energies, previously institutionalized by social conventions, are now rechanneled through erotic rituals of the body that effectively undermine the viewer's socially constructed responses. The two prompters who serve as the onscreen audience of the audition momentarily lose themselves and discover, as Almodóvar says, "their relation to their own erotic desire." In the same way, the scene of Tina's sensuous release and abandon before her staged audience suggests that the spectacle triggers in those who view it a liberating sense of abandon from socially controlled responses in the city.

Almodóvar recognizes the implicit "sexual danger" in the film's opening scene. That danger is rooted in the historically repressive notions of sexuality as defined by authoritarian society. The underlying textual desire that appears to inform *Law of Desire* is one which seduces the viewing subject, as in both of those scenes of erotic spectacle, and engages that subject in the process of breaking down the differences related to sexuality as part of a more expansive revision of their identity within a social community.

This effort to subvert the power of traditional categories of sexual difference is part of the larger project of *Law of Desire,* the rewriting of the mythology of the city around the liberation of desires. The film's action centers on the intricate sexual complications in the life of a successful screen writer and director, Pablo Quintero. Pablo tries literally to "write" the desires of his lover, Juan, by sending him a letter that he wants Juan to mail back to him. The letter is eventually read and misinterpreted by Antonio, the third member of the film's love triangle. For his part, Antonio wants Pablo to write him letters signed with a woman's name to cover up the true nature of their gay love affair. These intricate narrative twists all serve to de-emphasize the fact of gay love as a social issue in the fictional world and to define the film's center of gravity as the struggle of individuals to achieve their own desires. The final sequence of *Law of Desire* connects these questions of personal desire with the shaping of the larger community's desire by staging the realization of Pablo and Antonio's final union as a "public" event that self-consciously constructs as its audience a community that did not exist previously. Individual desire as it operates in that final scene works as a magnet, bringing together members of the community and thereby setting in motion a series of collective desires that function as resistances to the traditional patterns of Spanish societal order, such as those conventionally represented by the police and the Church.

The focus on religious iconography in the final sequence of *Law of Desire* is linked to earlier actions by Tina and her young ward, Ada. When Tina reencounters Father Constantino, the priest who had seduced her as a child, he shuns her, telling her to find God in another house. "God is everywhere," he says. So Tina builds a chapel in her apartment, a pagan altar with the kitsch paraphernalia of contemporary pop culture, mixing popular religion with the adoration of movie stars. "The altar is the symbol of a pagan religion," one critic has noted: "It serves to ask for things. The Virgin Ada adopts is like the fairy godmother of a children's story who grants the protagonist three wishes. Ada asks this Virgin to help Tina land the job in Pablo's new play; to have Pablo return after he and Tina have had an argument; finally, to have Pablo resuscitate after Tina has announced that he has died."

Tina describes Father Constantino as one of the only two men she ever loved, the other being her father. In her chance meeting with the priest, she introduces Ada as her daughter. As the film progresses, it becomes increasingly apparent that Tina associates the concepts of religion and family with the episodes from her youth related to seduction and abandonment by her two "fathers." Her actions in the present are efforts to reconstitute both family and religion in terms that will construct for her a Utopian world. Indeed, the trajectory of *Law of Desire* appears centered precisely around the figure of Tina as the embodiment of Almodóvar's thesis of the contemporary Spaniard being dissatisfied with the past and therefore constructing a new one. The key to Tina's identity is inextricably tied to the destiny of the city as the site of transformation of traditional patriarchal values into a new cultural order as emblemized in the film's final scene of "adoration."

In *Women on the Verge of a Nervous Breakdown* (1988: *Mujeres al borde de un ataque de nervios*), the spectacle of the city is once more identified with the project of a rewriting cultural mythology for the Spaniard. The film focuses intensely again on the status of women, this time, however, in the context of a society that, from all perspectives, has already undergone radical transformation, yet in which the female is still emotionally tied to the archaic phallocentric order.

Religion and history are figured in a prominent discursive move that addresses the spectator at the film's beginning. Pepa speaks the film's opening lines in a voice-over as the screen reveals a close-up of an improvised farmyard showing chickens in a caged area on what will soon be identified as the terrace of her Madrid apartment; "It had been months since I moved into this penthouse with Iván. The world was drowning around me. I felt like Noah; I wanted to save myself and the world." The explicit biblical intertext invites us to read the ensuing action as the narrative of a new social and moral order authored by the female and constituting a rewriting of the relations of domination between men and women in Spanish society.

Pepa's struggle to locate the womanizing Iván to inform him of her pregnancy serves as the starting point of an intricate chain of narrative moves that organizes the film's plot. Significantly, Pepa is continually identified with places in the city (her penthouse apartment, the various locales she goes to in search of the elusive Iván), and is further characterized as an outwardly mobile woman. As the action progresses, it becomes increasingly apparent that her mobility is merely the illusion of freedom as long as she is emotionally tied to Iván. The symbol of the female's false liberation is embodied in the person of Paulina Morales, the feminist lawyer who is indifferent to the plight of women and, as it turns out, is Iván's latest conquest. Like the city with whose destiny she is intimately identified, Pepa needs to achieve more than the outward trappings of liberation; she needs an inner spiritual emancipation.

After the use of urban settings as the *mise-en-scène* of a more expansive scenario of the nation in **Matador** and **Law of Desire, Women on the Verge** appears at first to be caught up in a very localist vision of Madrid, marked by the continuing narrative device of situating actions at specific street addresses in the city (Almagro 38; Montalbán 7; Castellana 34). But such details only reinforce the notion that the character, despite her outward liberation, is still confined within the recognizable spaces of the old city. As the film suggests, Pepa's full liberation will come only from a self-distanciation from patriarchal traps. That distanciation is ironically embodied in the space of Pepa's penthouse, a space that situates her far above the city and provides her with an idealized view of the Madrid skyline.

In reality, such a view does not exist. Almodóvar has simply constructed a studio set that invents a fantasized Madrid skyline to prefigure the eventual fulfillment of Pepa's desires. From its initial appearance as a view from Pepa's terrace, this idealized Madrid flaunts its own artifice, recalling the cinematic constructions of highly legible New York and Paris cityscapes as the backdrops to fantasized cultural scenarios in American films. Indeed, the strategy of **Women on the Verge** is to use such artifices to lead Pepa to her own self-distanced lucidity.

In that context, the use of cinematic self-reference becomes a critical move. When Pepa sits on a bench across the street from Iván's apartment, she sees a female dancer rehearsing in an apartment on the first floor. She then notices a young man, pining on a terrace on one of the upper floors. The scene recalls details of Hitchcock's urban thriller *Rear Window* and pointedly places Pepa in the androgynous role that merges the functions of the James Stewart and Grace Kelly characters. That is to say, she is able to view the problems of romantic coupling at a distance as the Stewart character does, and, by virtue of a mobility identified with the Kelly character, Pepa can effect the changes that are denied the Stewart character throughout Hitchcock's film.

A more ostentatious cinematic self-reference is presented in the narrative device of having Pepa and Iván working as dubbers involved in voicing the lines from the famous "Tell me lies" dialogue of Nicholas Ray's *Johnny Guitar*. Once again cinema self-consciously writes the heroine's destiny as it did in **Matador.** Foregrounding the cynical identity of Joan Crawford's forceful character, Vienna, Pepa speaks the lines that perfectly prefigure her own eventual disengagement from her sentimental entrapment in a masochistic relationship with the egotistical and deceitful Iván.

The narrative follows the heroine's emotional itinerary from a dependency upon the male, expressed in the opening scenes in her apartment, through the various locations in the city, back to that apartment where, after definitively breaking with Iván, she is able to announce her pregnancy without concern for the father. With the "Annunciation" of a new generation, presumably one that is unfettered by the archaic patriarchy, Pepa will effectively assume the position of matriarch for the new city and the new cultural order. In one of the last lines of the film, she claims she is not going to sublet her apartment because she "loves the view."

As the denouement of the **Women on the Verge** suggests, the city in Almodóvar's films is increasingly aligned with the imaging of a new moral order. The surface impression of the hedonistic world of immediate sensual gratification that was at the heart of the early films has gradually ceded to a fairly constant framing of actions within a more tolerant moral system. This new moral matrix serves to center a group of characters who, within the culture of the dictatorship and in the immediate post Franco period, were viewed as marginal types.

The increasing focus on characters who represent "earthly power" as Almodóvar calls the law and the police, becomes a parallel to what we have already noted as the reordering of celestial power (the Church) implied by this new matrix. In **Pepi, Luci, Bom,** for instance, the narrative is set in motion by the heroine's desire for elaborate revenge against the police detective who had raped her. In **Dark Habits** Sor Estiércol (Sister Manure) declares, "the police are the natural enemies of nuns," suggesting that the progressive, liberating activities of the Humbled Redeemers are in direct opposition to the repressive tactics of the law.

The characterization of the police begins to undergo a transformation in *What Have I Done?* where Polo, an impotent police detective who keeps crossing Gloria's path, turns out to be the on-screen witness and authenticator of the heroine's actions. Near the film's end, when Polo dismisses Gloria's confession of murder as merely an emotional outburst, the law seems to valorize her spiritual and social rebirth in the city, and to help reconstitute the family around a new matriarchy.

A somewhat similar dramatization of the valorizing glance of the law occurs at the end of *Matador.* After a prolonged car chase, the police finally arrive at María's country home and view the bodies of the two murderous lovers lying naked on the floor in rapturous embrace. Inspector Del Valle speaks the last line of the film as if expressing the community's approval of sexual excess: "I've never seen anyone so happy!"

Law and Desire contains two distinct expressions of this valorizing process by representatives of the law. When Pablo arrives at the village where his lover, Juan, has been murdered, a young member of the *Guardia Civil* identifies himself as a childhood friend of Juan's. He tells the director he knows that Juan really loved him. This gentle characterization of what has been traditionally one of the most repressive and feared of Spanish institutions of authority suggests the changing spirit of the time. A more sustained narrative focus on the law as an agency of toleration comes toward the end of the film with the appearance of the father and son investigators who pester Pablo and Tina in an effort to solve Juan's murder. No longer menacing, they appear to be parodies of the hard boiled urban detective of American genre films, particularly when the father advises his son: "In order to be successful in this profession, you need to be more than unscrupulous; you need to have a sense of humor." That "sense of humor" also prescribes a distance for the spectator, a way of seeing without the authoritarian impulse to judge and condemn that for so long ordered Francoist society.

That is the logic of the constant appearance of the guardians of social morality in Almodóvar's films. Like the detectives and police congregating on the street below Tina's apartment where Pablo and Antonio experience their final hour of love, these officials become the audience that authorizes the new moral order of post-Francoist Spain. In positioning the law to witness and valorize murder, gay love, or any of the other countless acts that defy the "earthly" and "celestial" powers of the old Spain, Almodóvar's cinema continues to engage its audience in the project of imaging Spain's present by rewriting the social and moral logic of its past.

Kathleen M. Vernon (essay date Spring 1993)

SOURCE: "Melodrama Against Itself: Pedro Almodóvar's *What Have I Done to Deserve This?*" in *Film Quarterly,* Vol. 46, No. 3, Spring, 1993, pp. 28-40.

[*In the following essay, Vernon analyzes the influence of American film melodrama on Almodóvar's work.*]

Central to what might be called the purposeful eclecticism of Pedro Almodóvar's cinematic universe is the model of American film melodrama, a source which the Spanish director has appropriated to notably effective and often unexpected ends. Indeed, the presence of American film culture is palpable throughout his work, from the photographs of Ava Gardner and Elizabeth Taylor among the "greatest sinners of the world" in *Entre tinieblas* (*Dark Habits*) to the inclusion of clips from three well-known Hollywood films, Elia Kazan's *Splendor in the Grass* in *¿Qué he hecho yo para merecer esto?* (*What Have I Done to Deserve This?*), King Vidor's *Duel in the Sun* in *Matador,* and Nicholas Ray's *Johnny Guitar* in *Mujeres al borde de un ataque de nervios* (*Women on the Verge of a Nervous Breakdown*).

American melodrama holds multiple attractions for Almodóvar. On the one hand, American film has provided him with a vehicle for articulating his distance from the themes and style of a recent Spanish film tradition obsessed with the country's tragic past. Frequently quoted to the effect that he wished to make films as if Franco never existed—"I never speak of Franco; I hardly acknowledge his existence. I start *after* Franco.... The stories unfold as if he had never existed"—Almodóvar can be said to have turned to Hollywood, the quintessential storyteller for a nation characterized by historical amnesia, for an alternate source of cultural and personal references (in that respect not unlike the function of Hollywood films in the novels of Manuel Puig). However, Almodóvar's borrowings from American film do not represent an unquestioning endorsement of the ideological underpinnings of Hollywood cinema. Instead, his intertextual and international network of references serves to question the role of film itself, not only in reflecting the ideologies and values of the society in which and for which it is created, but also in implicitly perpetuating those societal structures. Specifically, his importation of *American* melodrama into *Spanish* film casts the light of suspicion onto the way both film industries have mythified the representation of historically contingent categories (such as gender and socioeconomic class) as natural, essential "identities" in their implicit construction of a larger, national self-identity.

Similarly, melodrama has allowed Almodóvar to articulate a moment of rupture in Spanish history, not merely imagining a Spain in which Franco never existed but constructing a repertoire of stories and images for a post-Franco Spain that is perhaps yet to be. Peter Brooks, in his influential study *The Melodramatic Imagination,* goes beyond thematic definitions of the genre to identify melodrama as "a mode of conception and expression, . . . a certain fictional system for making sense of experience," whose historical roots he traces to late eighteenth-century France:

> The origins of melodrama can be accurately located within the context of the French Revolution and its aftermath. This is the epistemological moment which it illustrates and to which it contributes: The moment that symbolically, and really, marks the final liquidation of the traditional Sacred and its representative institutions (Church and Monarch), the shattering of the myth of Christendom, the dissolution of an organic and hierarchically cohesive society, and the invalidation of the literary forms—tragedy, comedy of manners—that depend on such a society.

In melodrama, then, Almodóvar also finds a "new" fictional system for conceiving and representing Spanish society in the aftermath of its own "ancien régime." The death of Franco, the politically and psychically repressive patriarch, "Caudillo por la Gracia de Dios," also marks the final passing of Spain's hierarchically conceived "organic democracy" and the institutional identification of church and state. Melodrama provides the mode for exploring the breakdown of old hierarchies and the resulting dissolution of barriers and boundaries in a post-patriarchal, post-religious Spain.

It is nevertheless ironic that melodrama should play this role in Almodóvar's films. Grounded in a moral and thematic Manichaeanism, melodrama has often been read as constructing a fictional world of unambiguous absolutes, of villains vs. victims, shadow vs. light. Robert Lang has observed that the universe of melodrama depends on "clearly legible differences on all levels. It is a world of binary structures: men and women, masculine and feminine, the 'right' side and the 'wrong' side of the tracks, . . . brother and sister, work and love, material wealth and poverty." Indeed, much of the appeal of melodrama for students of film lies in this symptomatic overdetermination of societal and gender roles.

In the 1970s, feminist film critics turned to the domestic melodrama as a privileged area of investigation, a "woman's genre," where the representation of women on the screen and the (primarily female) audience's response are foregrounded and hence more accessible to and demanding of analysis. What they found there for the most part was a series of paradigmatic examples of the way "classic narrative cinema" works, and works on the spectator. They identified narrative structures and thematics which are not merely reflective of the hierarchical, patriarchal society in which they are pro-

duced; their very functioning as signifying practices and sources of pleasure and entertainment depends on the perpetuation and indeed polarization of differences and boundaries.

More recent studies have moved beyond this somewhat monolithic and generally ahistorical view to acknowledge the continuing attraction and fascination of film melodrama as a source of visual and affective pleasure and even to examine its function in creating a space for resistance against the very societal structures and values it would seem to represent. It is this provocative ambivalence in the melodramatic imagination, understood here as a mode of spectatorial response, that Almodóvar has exploited so skillfully in his films, using melodrama in some sense against itself. My aim in this essay, then, will be to show how the director has appropriated the language of Hollywood melodrama as a mediating structure that would allow him to have it both ways, to opt out of the binarism apparently inherent in classic narrative film as well as in many contemporary analyses of such cinema. What I contend in my discussion of *What Have I Done to Deserve This?* is that while the film lays bare the material reality of filmic practice, the technological, economic, and institutional apparatus behind the illusion, while it acknowledges the complicity of narrative cinema in constructing images of femininity (in Laura Mulvey's words, "cut to the measure of [masculine] desire") its aim is not exclusively deconstructive. Rather, the film holds out the possibility of rescuing an alternative, subversive visual pleasure that does not depend on an enunciatory structure grounded in sexual difference, and more particularly, in the repression of the feminine in favor of the masculine.

The initial sequences of *What Have I Done to Deserve This?,* the director's fourth feature film and his first international success, situate it as a cinematically mediated tale of frustrated feminine desire. The opening shot surveys a film crew on location in a Madrid square, closing in on the image of a woman crossing the plaza, followed by a man holding a sound boom. The music on the sound track evokes the movie scores written by Nino Rota for numerous Italian neorealist films. Our awareness of the filmic frame is further reinforced by the juxtaposition of the film's title and credits intercut with the images. The camera follows the woman (Carmen Maura) into a karate studio, cutting to rows of men dressed in monk-like robes who practice the martial art of kendo by delivering grunting blows in the air with five-foot-long sticks. As Maura goes about her chores as a cleaning woman, the class ends and the studio empties out. But while she finishes up in a mirrored dressing room in the foreground of the shot, a naked man steps into a shower stall just beyond her on the right side of the frame. Maura's character's unabashed gaze at the spectacle of the male body is reflected and framed for the spectator by the mirror on the wall. Sensing her presence, the man turns and beckons her into the shower. However, any erotic promise in the encounter for either characters or film audience is soon undercut. The sexual clinch beneath the streaming shower head responds neither to the horrific connotations of the Hitchcockesque shower scene—explicitly evoked in one shot—nor to the fantasy of instant sexual gratification in spontaneous, anonymous sex. The act itself is unsatisfyingly brief, especially for the woman, who then acts out her frustration by taking up a stick left by one of the kendo students. The sequence ends with her striking furiously at the air as the man slinks guiltily out of the building.

Through its privileging of feminine desire, coupled with the assumption of the look by the female protagonist, Almodóvar's film from the outset issues an implicit challenge to the patriarchal structures of both power and pleasure inherent in the dominant cinema tradition as theorized by Laura Mulvey and subsequent feminist critics. According to Mulvey, narrative cinema is complicit with a scopophilic regime of pleasure whereby the male spectator "possesses" (with its dual connotations of sexual and physical control or power) the female through the look—or rather the relay of looks—created by the camera, the male actor's gaze, and the male spectator who identifies with both. In *What Have I Done?*, Almodóvar seeks to opt out of the societal and filmic system that would exclude the feminine except as a projection of male desire.

Even before his fourth film, Almodóvar had earned a reputation as a man at home cinematically in a feminine universe. Both his first and third films, *Pepi, Luci, Bom y otras chicas del montón* (*Pepi, Luci, Bom and Other Ordinary Girls*) and *Dark Habits,* are set in the diverse womanly worlds of unhappy housewives, punk rock singers, and unconventional convents. While such a focus has been notably rare among Spanish film-makers, American studios cultivated women audiences for decades through the popular sub-genre known as "woman's pictures." Starring well-known actresses and concentrating on women's problems and specifically domestic issues, such films have been a staple of commercial melodrama. But as Anglo-American feminist film critics have demonstrated, while "woman's pictures" provide a privileged locus for the analysis of representations of women on the film screen, these films have tended to offer only further variations on the Hollywood repertoire of repression which reduces women to images reassuring to the male viewer. In contrast to the image of the glamorous star as fetishistic projection of phallic sexuality, the "weepie," in its address to a primarily female audience who would identify with the trials of the heroine, serves up a de-eroticized image of the women as victim, often as mother or mental patient. Such portrayals literally deflate the threat of feminine sexuality even as they channel the female viewer toward a masochistic over-identification—hence the tears—with the female protagonist.

Almodóvar would seem, at least initially, to have pursued that latter path in his characterization of the desperate housewife Gloria. Trapped in a cramped apartment with her thoughtless taxi-driver husband Antonio, her dotty diabetic mother-in-law addicted to sweet *magdalena* cakes and Catalán mineral water, and her two semi-delinquent sons (one sells drugs and the other sells his body to his friends' fathers), Gloria lives through a series of never-ending days propped up by the pills she acquires illegally from her neighborhood pharmacy. The look of the film and its heroine is unrelentingly miserable, and the actress herself speaks of the effects of playing such a decidedly unglamorous role:

> During the shooting . . . I felt terribly depressed, as I'd imagined all women with a life like hers must feel. With hair like that, all messy, with those housecoats . . . I gradually became more and more miserable and then I also got very weepy.

Maura's reactions are particularly revealing with regard to the affective axis of the film, established through the requisite identification between protagonist and audience. Nevertheless, the feelings the actress describes are not reflected in her portrayal of the hapless Gloria, whose emotional register is characterized more by lack of affect (due perhaps to drugs or lack of sleep) than by emotional excess. Instead, they testify to a process of interiorization of the spectator's role that surfaces at key moments of the film.

While the "woman's picture" can be said to function as the dominant model of spectatorial response for the film, the cultural meaning of the film as a whole accrues through a process of "semiotic layering," which operates by means of the juxtaposition of nationally and historically diverse film sources. I have already alluded, for example, to the references to Italian neorealism in the musical score. But the plot and mise-en-scène owe much more to a specifically Spanish tradition of black comedies from the fifties and early sixties. Grounded in the socioeconomic conditions of the period, these films focused on the plight of urban dwellers struggling to survive in a city unable to provide jobs and housing to a population swollen by recent arrivees from the economically even more desperate provinces. Films like Marco Ferreri's *El pisito* (*The Little Apartment,* 1958), José Antonio Nieves Conde's *El inquilino* (*The Tenant,* 1958), and particularly Luis García Berlanga's *El verdugo* (*The Executioner,* 1961) anticipate the plight of Gloria and her family in their modern cement-block urban high-rise overlooking Madrid's M-30 superhighway. Seen in this context, Almodóvar's social criticism appears all the more devastating in that it reveals the lack of fundamental change despite the intervening years—years of the so-called economic miracle and the end of Francoism. Contrary to the director's declarations about making films as if Franco never existed, *What Have I Done?* depicts a world created by the urban non-planning of the Franco years, growing out of a policy that actively sought by passive neglect of urban social services to discourage immigration to the "corrupt" cities. Like the characters from those earlier films, both Gloria and her husband have come from the *pueblo,* the *pueblo* to which her mother-in-law and older son Toni will return at the end of the film. The post-Franco city has failed them, as it fails Gloria, despite their apparently greater material well-being in a world of time-saving home appliances, the "consumer paradise" of contemporary Spain.

Still, that criticism is tempered, or at least rendered deeply ambivalent, through the persons and story of Toni and his grandmother, with their nostalgic longing for a return to the countryside. In their flight from the city they reenact the ending of the founding film of Spanish neorealism, José Antonio Nieves Conde's 1950 *Surcos* (*Furrows*). Hailed as "the first glance at reality in a cinema of papier-mâché" for its serious treatment of the problem of the rural exodus to the cities, the film—in the hands of Falangist Nieves Conde— also served as a cautionary tale about the moral corruption and destruction of family structures that awaited new immigrants to the city. The film's conclusion, rewritten by the Spanish censors, projects the family's chastened return to the fields they never should have left. Almodóvar's film can in fact be read as an ironic rewriting of Nieves Conde's.

As in the earlier film, in *What Have I Done?* paternal authority is reduced or absent, and a harried mother overly preoccupied with material survival neglects her children's moral education. But Almodóvar's treatment of the subject takes the moral absolutes of *Surcos* and uses them against the values system they purport to represent. American film culture, decried well into the fifties as the devilish tool of a foreign, materialist ideology by the regime's guardians of Spanish moral and ethnic purity, paradoxically provides the instrument whereby Toni and his grandmother are able to articulate their discontent with contemporary urban Spanish reality. Sitting with his grandmother in a darkened movie theater watching Elia Kazan's double-edged pastoral, *Splendor in the Grass,* Toni voices his identification with Bud Stamper's (Warren Beatty) rejection of his oil-baron father's ambitions and his desire to be a cattle farmer. "Maybe I'll set up a ranch in the *pueblo,*" he exclaims, as his grandmother signals her enthusiastic assent. The historical irony for the (second-degree) spectator in Stamper's desire to return to a simpler age of American existence in a small Kansas town on the eve of the Stock Market crash underscores the untimeliness, and "unplacefulness," of Toni's dream as well. The small town is portrayed as a stifling, socially and sexually repressive place in the Kazan story, just as it is in numerous Spanish films of the same period, such as Juan Antonio Bardem's *Calle Mayor.* Furthermore, as the *Surcos/ Splendor* juxtaposition reminds us, the simpler past grandmother and grandson would return to is the past of

Francoism, a past Almodóvar's films rewrite even as they seek to disavow it.

Another crucial distinction between both the Berlanga and Nieves Conde films and Almodóvar's lies in their treatment of the female protagonists, in each case a wife and mother. In the view of the earlier directors, the woman, Eve-like, draws the man into a Girardian triangle of desire with her eyes set firmly on financial gain and the acquisition of material goods. Thus the protagonist of *El verdugo,* for example, is trapped into becoming an executioner in order to provide an apartment for his wife and child-to-be. For Almodóvar, in contrast, it is the housewife who becomes a pawn in a patriarchal and capitalistic system of exchange. Obsessed by the pressures of meeting payments on the apartment, the television, washing machine, and refrigerator, Gloria's other desires are displaced onto those consumer goods. But those longings are also turned back against her. A number of critics have examined the historical links between commercial cinema as entertainment and as advertisement, a complicity which situates the female addressee of the woman's picture as potential consumer of images of herself and her surroundings. In *What Have I Done?,* once again, the character mirrors the spectator's role, for she too is being sold a bill of goods. As the director expresses it in his summary of the film: "[Gloria] would like to become a member of the consumer society, but only manages to consume herself, day by day." Thus, even as she struggles to survive, Gloria is aware of the distance that separates her life from the idealized images of women she sees in magazines in the doctor's office or in beauty shop windows. While it is the men in her life who fail to satisfy her, she interiorizes her discontent as a form of self-hatred. In a scene whose comic extremes may blind us to its incisiveness, she sells her son to a pederast dentist in order to buy a curling iron she has seen in a shop window and about which she fantasizes as the instrument of her transformation.

Almodóvar's films constantly foreground the topic of narrative cinema's collusion with the language and address of advertising. From *Pepi, Luci, Bom* to *Atame* (*Tie Me Up, Tie Me Down*) the director has delighted including mock commercials within his films. *What Have I Done?* is no exception in that regard, but here the codes of television advertising spill over into the diegesis itself. In a telling sequence early in the film, Gloria has returned from her cleaning woman's job at the karate school to her kitchen, where she takes up her other full-time job. Placing her amid a conventional kitchen setting, the camera portrays the protagonist in a series of reverse-angle shots, a classic editing figure in a two-character scene. But Gloria is alone in the room, bending first to fill her washing machine with clothes and then to remove a pan from the oven. In both instances the camera is positioned so as to show the appliances, in effect, looking back at her. While this non-naturalistic use of the reverse-angle shot is startling to the spectator, it is not entirely unfamiliar, since TV commercials for clothes washers and fried-chicken recipes long ago appropriated this particular editing figure. Framed in this way, the image of the desiring female subject of consumer society collapses into her own objectification. While foregrounding the role of the cinematic apparatus, as Charles Eckert has noted, in "fetishizing products and putting the libido in libidinally invested advertising," **What Have I Done?** once again recalls the specifically Spanish context in which it functions and consequently evokes the history of the explicit political manipulation of consumer desire under the Franco regime. Indeed, the creation of a prosperous consumer society, as theorized and promoted by arch-technocrat Gonzalo Fernández de la Mora in his 1961 book, *The Twilight of Ideologies,* was conceived as a strategy to guarantee political apathy among Spaniards. As historians of the period Raymond Carr and Juan Pablo Fusi observe: "There is nothing like the installment system to weaken the striker's resolution, nothing like relative well-being after struggle to weaken 'solidarity' as a working-class value.

Thus the two initial circuits of desire remain uncompleted; they end in apparently irreversible frustration, blocked, at least in part, by history and the persistent legacy of the Franco years. Gloria will find no satisfaction, nor even relief, in sexual or material fulfillment. Instead, the film is carried to thematic and affective closure by a third circuit, the still more exclusively feminine realm of the maternal melodrama, with its rich filmic intertext. The director himself has signaled this dimension of the film, stating that:

> It's a film about motherhood. . . . In it are reflected different embodiments of the maternal. Carmen Maura's character is that of the mother pure and simple, the mother who keeps the home together, who carries it all on her back. There are frustrated mothers like Cristal, who's a wonderful mother. And there's a very typically Spanish mother that appalls me, the kind who's always hitting her kids, that tense sort of mother I see in the streets of Madrid, the kind that, if the child falls down, on top of it all she beats him for it, very violent. And within all those mothers is my own. For me it's very significant: I was making a film about my own social class, about my origins and my family, a type of family I recognize, and I wanted my own mother to be there.

The cultural specificity of Almodóvar's cast of mothers in the film—including, as he notes, his own, Francisca Caballero, who plays the role of the white-haired lady from the old *pueblo* whom Gloria meets in the dentist's office—distinguishes his film from the ideological traditions of the maternal melodrama as described by Linda Williams in her study of that quintessential film of maternal self-sacrifice, King Vidor's *Stella Dallas.* Identifying an ethic of maternal self-abnegation as the hallmark of the genre, Williams signals the paradox in that "frequently the self-sacrificing mother must make her sacrifice that of the connection to her children—either for their or her own good." This self-canceling structure, she notes, serves as "[a] device [for] devaluing and debasing the actual figure of the mother while sanctifying the institution of motherhood in general."

In many ways, then, Almodóvar's film could not seem farther from the Hollywood ethic of glorified feminine masochism. First of all, in contrast to the traditional film mother, Gloria does not sublimate her sexual desires entirely into her maternal role. As we have seen, the film begins with an emphatic, if frustrated, expression of her sexuality. Second, until the very end of the film, Gloria gives little evidence of traditional motherly behavior. Her demonstrations of maternal affection are limited to her contacts with Vanessa, the telekinetic daughter of her neighbor Juani, the "bad mother" characterized in the Almodóvar quotation. Her ties to her own two sons, in contrast, are strained by the family's dire economic circumstances. But if we focus more closely on her relationship with her younger son, Miguel, the profile of the melodramatic movie mother may be seen to offer a more appropriate point of comparison.

In the early scenes of the film, Gloria is shown as being unable to fulfill the most archetypal of maternal functions toward Miguel: that of providing physical nourishment. When he comes home to a bare refrigerator, she is forced to send him off to her neighbor Cristal, the prostitute next door, for dinner and a sandwich for tomorrow's lunch. This ceding of maternal rights and responsibilities prefigures her later surrender of Miguel to the dentist. The defining gesture in the portrayal of Gloria within the circuit of maternal desire, this surrender bears striking similarities to Stella Dallas's sacrifice of her daughter to a "better" mother, the upper-class wife of her former husband. In Gloria's case as well, the mother seeks to provide her child with the material advantages she cannot herself give her offspring. "You know how bad it is at home. I can barely feed you," she tells her son, who then bargains with the dentist for a stereo system, a VCR, and painting lessons. In the Almodóvar version, it is true, there is an ironic slippage between the altruistic act of maternal self-sacrifice in its most characteristic movie form and Gloria's more venal desire for a hair curler, but this subversion works against the sentimentalizing tendencies of the traditional maternal melodrama and its destructive idealization of motherhood. Unlike Stella's smiling apotheosis at the end of *Stella Dallas* as a woman who has denied her very identity as mother for the daughter she loves, Gloria's act passes virtually unnoticed, even by the boy's father, who, we are later told, was never aware of his son's absence.

The conclusion to Almodóvar's film also runs a rather different course from the King Vidor classic, as ensuing events apparently intervene to liberate Gloria from her role as both wife and mother. Driven to the edge by too many demands for ironed shirts and dinner on the table, Gloria accidentally kills her husband with a ham bone. In a sense Antonio's largely comic and narratively convenient demise only serves to confirm his estrangement, throughout the film, from the rest of the household and from the film's both real-world and cinematic referents. The would-be champion of moral *decencia,* he chastises Gloria for her work outside the home and her friendship with neighbor Cristal, and as such represents the voice of an archaic values system ill-suited to current economic and social realities. Antonio's emotional distance from his family is conveyed through his obsessive playing of the Zarah Leander song "Nicht nur aus Liebe weinen," for him a nostalgic token of his love affair with his former employer, Ingrid Müller, the aging *chanteuse* for whom he forged a series of Hitler letters during a stint as a "guest worker" in Germany. Indeed, a number of viewers and critics have complained of the tangential character of this complicated Teutonic subplot. I would argue rather that this element of the film is significant, in its conception if not in its execution. Drawing this time not upon Hollywood melodrama but on one of its European cousins, as it were, the director plots the husband's story, the real historical drama of economic exile, against the suspect nostalgia of the so-called retro film. With its foregrounding of the Ingrid Müller/Zarah Leander figure, however, Almodóvar's version evokes Fassbinder's critical variation on the genre, *Veronika Voss,* or especially *Lili Marleen,* with its basis in the life story of another Nazi star, Lale Anderson.

Whatever his role in life, Antonio's death is key to the film's denouement. For with him literally out of the picture, the other members of the family leave to pursue their separate destinies, as if acknowledging their own liberation from the yoke of paternal authority. While Miguel is apparently happily ensconced with his dentist, the grandmother and Toni achieve their desired departure for the *pueblo,* thanks to bus tickets purchased with the proceeds from Toni's drug dealing. But as the director moves with characteristic verve to wrap up the remaining plot lines, a sudden change in the tone of the film provides a final twist. Gloria's good-byes to her son and mother-in-law, cued by the scene's bluesy saxophone score, evoke a surprising pathos, an emotional response blocked until this point in the film. Upon her return to her empty house, Gloria encounters a sense of overwhelming solitude rather than relief. Looking over the balcony to the pavement below, she is drawn toward the void, until she catches sight of Miguel running up the steps. Parody converges with genuine melodrama as the film's finale stages an emotional reunion between mother and younger son. Home once again, Miguel announces his decision to stay because, although the dentist was fun for a while, "I'm too young to be tied down to anyone, and besides," as he tells his mother, "this house needs a man."

The affective punch of these final scenes is heightened by the autobiographical subtext to the film. In addition to his own mother, Almodóvar has included in the character of Miguel a portrait of himself as a young film-maker-to-be. The boy's painting lessons, the Zoetrope he spins in his bedroom at night before shutting off his light, even his precocious homosexuality mark the character as a projection of the director. Thus the ending represents not simply a self-conscious restatement of classic melodramatic closure but a more broadly self-reflexive gesture which Almodóvar uses to offer a slyly open conclusion. By completing the thematic and affective circuit of the film in the realm of the maternal, the film rewrites the traditional Oedipal scenario. The playful asymmetry of the mother/son couple denies the restrictive narrative logic of the patriarchal family, both on and off the film screen. In the absence of the paternal Law, it is suggested, mother and son are free to explore—and create—forms of sexuality and sexual identity impossible under traditional societal and familial structures.

In fact, the possibilities held out by this post-patriarchal society have already been hinted at quite tellingly in the concluding sequences of the film. In a touch of canny Almodóvarian logic, the police detective investigating the death of Gloria's husband turns out to be the same impotent man with whom she shared the opening shower scene. When the distraught widow confesses her role in her husband's death, the detective refuses to believe her and the case is closed. In a world where the Law has lost its potency and the power to enforce its strictures, crimes have no consequences. Attacking the foundations of linear causality, the film affirms its power, not, as one might have thought, to forget history, the past of Francoism, but to challenge the hold of that history over future stories. Thus the ending to ***What Have I Done to Deserve This?*** ought really to be read not as a resolution but rather as a beginning to the film-maker's, and his audience's, ongoing task of rewriting post-Franco, post-patriarchal society.

Peter Evans (essay date July 1993)

SOURCE: "Almodóvar's *Matador:* Genre, Subjectivity and Desire," in *Bulletin of Hispanic Studies,* Vol. LXX, No. 3, July, 1993, pp. 325-35.

[*In the following essay, Evans analyzes how Almodóvar reworks the genre of the Hollywood melodrama and explores the issues of identity and desire in post-Franco Spain in* Matador.]

1 Introduction: The Lawless Breed

Souvent, nous parlons du monde, de l'humanité, comme s'il avait quelque unité: en fait, l'humanité compose des *mondes,* voisins selon l'apparence mais en vérité étrangers l'un á l'autre . . . Le plus frappant est qu'en chacun des mondes auxquels je fais allusion, l'ignorance, du moins la méconnaissance des autres est de règle. Même en quelque sort le père de famille oublie, jouant avec sa fille, les mauvais lieux où il entre en porc invetéré . . .

These remarks by George Bataille—recognized by Almodóvar himself as a writer to whom *Matador* is to some extent indebted—aptly describe the mechanisms of Almodóvar's films in opening up the heterogeneity of a country for almost three decades straitjacketed into the triumphalist perceptions of a powerful and reactionary ideology. Though these are by no means the only Spanish films of recent years to celebrate release from the nightmare of Francoism and its legacy, they are almost unique in doing so with an irresistible sensibility for the reinstated multifariousness of Spanish society—from the *movida* to the middle classes—a sensibility, moreover, uniquely characterized in the Spanish cinema (ignoring the proliferation of copy-cat failures), by a style mixing sublime elegance with vulgarity and kitsch. Even so, Almodóvar's devotion to scandal and outrage never detracts from a serious project to explore the after-effects of repression through the combined strategies of pop and high art.

His films are a blend of Bataille and bathos, Leiris and lewdness, Hollywood and heaviness. Even *Matador,* a film remaining more consistently within Thriller/Film Noir and Melodrama parameters, cannot always keep a straight face as it periodically lapses, even at its most intensely dramatic moments, into comic fantasy inspired as much by the work of directors, like John Waters and Russ Meyer, working outside mainstream Hollywood, as by Buñuel and other revered figures from the European Art cinema traditions. Here, while the traces of indigenous popular culture and performers are as clear as ever (the *sainete, zarzuela, foto novelas,* comics like *El víbora,* stars like Marisol, and so on), forming a patchwork quilt of cross-references to give a formal context to the films' underlying principle of cultural heterogeneity, Hollywood's contribution to the film's creative, 'intertextual' processes is even more than usually significant. In Nuria Vidal's useful book of interviews, Almodóvar has himself acknowledged the crucial references in *Matador* to *Vertigo, Strangers on a Train* (1953), *Cat People* (the 1982 version) and *Pandora and the Flying Dutchman* (1951). But the film's most direct allusion to Hollywood, one that pervades the whole film, occurs when, hotly pursued by Diego Montes (Nacho Martínez) the retired *torero,* María Cardenal

(Assumpta Serna) shelters in a cinema showing *Duel in the Sun* (1946), the last scenes of which—the shoot-out between Pearl Chavez (Jennifer Jones) and Lewt McCanles (Gregory Peck)—become through their own force but also through their evocation of a whole range of 1940s and 1950s Hollywood Melodramas a complex *mise-en-abîme* for **Matador.** Though obviously in important respects a Western, *Duel in the Sun* is also, as Laura Mulvey has already convincingly argued, a crucial Melodrama, a film exploring the vicissitudes, legacies and betrayals, laws and desires of American family life in the 1940s. By referring specifically to *Duel in the Sun,* **Matador** seems determined not only to honour the glamorous icons of the Hollywood cinema—something not restricted in the Spanish cinema to Almodóvar, as may be judged especially by the films of José Luis Borau and Pilar Miró, whose *Gary Cooper que estás en los cielos* is an elegant act of homage to its classical period—but also, by stressing the film's Melodrama-motivated complexes of subjectivity and desire, to highlight Hollywood's idiosyncratic formulations of questions less easily accommodated by other genres.

2 Genre: The Call of the Wild

While discussing complex problems of genre, point of view, audience reception theory, commodity and conditions of production, writing about Hollywood Melodrama in recent years has also, among other things, drawn attention to ways in which in the 1940s and 1950s the genre opened up possibilities for American audiences not wholly ideologized, not wholly condemned to responding to the text as *histoire* (as distinct from *discours*), to engage productively with matters of form and ideology and, in Robert Lang's words, above all to have 'special access to a *jouissance* of the body as feminine and/or maternal', as an alternative to involvement in the strategies of more consistently patriarchal texts. These issues, too complex to raise more than hurriedly here, though with as much relevance to Almodóvar as to the Hollywood Melodrama, in turn lead to questions about gender and other differences in audience response.

If Lang, Mulvey and others are right in seeing a radical potential in the genre's marginal, somewhat despised status for audiences (in the 1940s and 1950s, mainly women?), not irredeemably colonized by the consensus values of the period, one can understand why a director like Almodóvar (also appealing to, among others, hitherto marginalized audiences), reclaiming the popular, resolved to exploit the extremes of sexual difference, inflexible standards of taste and decorum, claustrophobic definitions of sexual and family life, should have found the genre in general and a film like *Duel in the Sun* in particular so appealing. The film's transgressions of genre—mixing Western with Melodrama—attracts a director himself consistently aligning comic and tragic, high and low.

Duel in the Sun confuses the boundaries of conventional Westerns. Less preoccupied with saloon-bar bravado, threadbare interiors and rugged outdoor objective correlatives for the all-American patriarchal virtues, it plunges its audiences into the cloying, suffocating, but also code-breaking *ambientes* of Melodrama and the Woman's Picture, into elaborate, 'hysterical' (a favourite word of his) *mise-en-scène,* garish, clashing colours and, above all perhaps, the labyrinths of passion, self-conscious stereotyping of women, the fetishes and castration fears of characters on the verge of nervous breakdown. Sometimes consciously, sometimes not, the genre commits itself through extremes of form and content to exposure of the contradictions and repressions of what Lacan (gestured to indirectly throughout the films, but also with comic explicitness in *Laberinto de pasiones* through the figure of the Lacanian psychoanalyst), has called the Symbolic order. Like many Melodramas, *Duel in the Sun* hyperbolizes the patriarchal text, and this is the terrain with which a director in flight from Iberian versions of patriarchy feels a natural identification.

Despite working in the far freer climate of democracy, Almodóvar (and, although he does not always appreciate the comparison, like Fassbinder before him), is obviously attracted as much by the constraints as by the creative potential of Hollywood Melodrama. Various types of constraint, or Law, to use the Almodóvarian-cum-Lacanianidiom, originating in the pre-democratic society, continue to tyrannize the majority of the main characters despite the collapse of the dictatorship. But beyond the narrowly political and sociological implications of the narratives' interest in constraints of various types, the psychological complexities of enduring obsessions with inhibiting and ultimately death-dealing laws of desire never flag. In Lacanian language, the film presents four characters struggling for release from the constraints of the Symbolic and its various laws (here represented by the police, legal, bullfighting and family worlds), seeking the liberations of the Imaginary and its promise of desire. But as the Symbolic order cannot completely be shaken off, so the film acknowledges the equation of desire with death, and takes to extremes Bataille's Freud-inspired conviction that 'il n'y aurait pas d'érotisme s'il n'y avait d'autre part un respect des valeurs interdits'. As a result, most dramatically perhaps in *Pepi, Luci, Bom, y otras chicas del montón* and *Matador,* characters like Pepi, Pablo Quintero, María Cardenal and Diego Montes are drawn to relationships predicated more on the possibility of loss than of fulfilment, with the last couple actually celebrating their reciprocal desire through a ritual act of suicide and murder, reminiscent of Mishima, *Pandora and the Flying Dutchman, Prizzi's Honour,* and other texts, but directly compared in the film to *Duel in the Sun.* Constraint as the price of limited kinds of freedom, an underlying principle of the Hollywood Melodrama, forms an apt image for *Matador's* formal/thematic obsessions with matters of life and death where, as

with its American precursor, social determinants as much as genetics are assumed to be the causes of the sometimes monstrous shapes of desire.

3 The mise-en-scene of the Family

While the term 'Melodrama' has sometimes loosely been used as a way of describing a wide variety of Hollywood genre films, recent writing has tended to restrict its application as a description of a series of films either concentrating on family narratives organized around tensions between outdated laws and freedom-seeking desires, or in what is really an offshoot of the genre, the so-called 'Woman's Picture', characterized by narratives specializing in the predicaments of women caught in the parent trap. The Hollywood Melodrama's expression of these tensions both in the operations of its narratives and, crucially, in the expressive potential of its music, colour, lighting, setting, *mise-en-scène,* provides a creative model for Almodóvar's own practice. While also reformulating some of the distinctive modes of other Hollywood genres, especially Film Noir (borrowing many of its most distinctive features, especially, of course, the *femme fatale*), *Matador* recreates the classic Hollywood Melodrama's formulae both in its dependence on traditional family narratives and in the resonant hyperboles of its baroque form.

Yet whereas a Hollywood film from the classical period would have usually had to raise its difficult questions indirectly or ambiguously, often, as it has been argued, precisely through the highly-wrought patterns of its elaborately aestheticized form, a 1980s Spanish film can ultimately be far more openly critical, making its statements far more straightforwardly. Moreover, although *Matador* reworks the patterns of the war between the generations, never failing to capture and to adapt the soaring emotions of the Hollywood prototype to its own distinctive strategies, it also moves beyond it in adding the characteristically Almodóvarian features of the almost obligatory counter-family (e.g. the school of tauromachy here, but also, for instance the *movida* worlds of *Pepi* and *Laberinto de pasiones,* or the gay/transvestite family of *La ley del deseo*), and humour (carried especially in this film by Chus Lampreave's playing of the tolerant, unshockable, positive antidote of a mother to Julieta Serrano's Berta, the monstrous, self-mortifying, predemocratic fascist ideal), neither tendency normally associated with the more doom-laden ambience of the Hollywood Melodrama. The conventional family, as oppressive here as in Hollywood classics like *Now Voyager* or *All that Heaven Allows,* is represented through the relationship between Berta and her guilt-ridden son Ángel (Antonio Banderas). Additionally, the *mise-en-scène* of the conformist household, with its symbolic mirrors, religious and other traditional icons, heavy furniture, has all the excess of its Hollywood counterpart, while the scene of Ángel's unsuccessful attempt to rape Eva (Eva Cobos), his neighbour, and mistress of his *ex-torero* idol, on whom he has been spying like some half-hearted Peeping Tom, takes place against the background of thunder and lightning in an ironic reminder of the overblown scene where, caught up in a violent storm, Pearl Chavez capitulates to her desire for Lewt McCanles. Traumatized by a mother whose slavery to the old attitudes extends to the masochistic practice of tightly securing her thighs with formidable straps, Ángel only attempts to rape the unfortunate Eva because he is attempting to live up to macho expectations, men, not women, arousing in him authentic libidinal responses, feelings allowed only limited expression through enrolment at the alternative family of Diego's school of tauromachy.

While Angel is the film's image of the hazardous odyssey towards liberation from the tyrannies of the past, Chus Lampreave's Pilar functions as one of the film's reminders of the country's alternative non-conformist traditions, all but extinguished under Franco, now revived in the less neurotic climate of democracy. Pilar has no inhibitions about sex, feels only contempt for good form and sobriety, and all too happily betrays her addiction to kitsch and the enchanting superficialities of glamour (fashion, *haute couture,* modelling, at one point herself taking the model's place on the catwalk). At its deepest levels the film sees through the ultimate shallowness and banalities of these worlds, their *apariencias* ('no te fíes de las apariencias', María warns Diego in the men's lavatory), as deceptive as any created by the masters of *desengaño* of Spain's 'Golden Age'. But, at another level, where surface pleasures provide their own justification, the film's indulgence in various John Waters or Russ Meyer inspired forms of kitsch represents for a country until 1975 so starved of colour and frivolity a necessary first stage of transgression against the austere moral and religious sobrieties of an ideology which if not by any means yet extinct, is at least neither any longer exempt from unambiguous modes of satire. As María Antonia García de León and Teresa Maldonado put it, one of the film's projects focuses precisely on the need to 'lavarle la cara a España, arrumbar su tradicional imagen negra y vetusta'. So, for instance, in *Ley,* the garish Church décor, in *Pepi,* the outrageous parody of the *zarzuela,* the erotic pop-Picasso interiors of *Laberinto,* and in *Matador,* to take just one example, the whole fashion sequence, are all moments of unapologetic self-indulgence, as gaudy as anything in, say, *Beyond the Valley of the Dolls* or *Desperate Living.* But *Matador's* kitsch, for one audience level at least, must ultimately be ironic. If kitsch is not only, as Almodóvar himself puts it, 'something that should really be awful, but instead of being awful [is] delightful', but also, in Milan Kundera's evocative definition, 'a folding screen set up to curtain off death', the film's obsession with death undermines the mode's essential force.

4 Masculinity: The Bad and the Beautiful

Almodóvar's films, as María Antonia García de León and Teresa Maldonado have argued, are conspicuously autobiographical, using the term here rather more widely than as a means of merely referring to the ordinary, documented incidents of daily life. Like other directors before him—e.g. Hitchcock, Fassbinder, Buñuel, Woody Allen—Almodóvar makes (brief) appearances in his films. Although he dismisses these as intrusions motivated either by narcissistic whim or necessity, they nevertheless have the force of stressing, in the traditions of auteurist cinema, the direct autobiographical relevance of the films' preoccupations, however indebted they might be to the modes and operations of popular genres. In this respect, in their dependence on a select group of actors and other creative personnel, their usually urban Madrid settings, their comic perspectives, these films are very much in certain restricted ways the somewhat less sceptical Spanish equivalents of Woody Allen's Manhattan films. Above all, though, in their complex confessional exploration both of the relations between the sexes and of sexual identity itself, they recall the struggles of the Allenesque hero groping for meaning in the postmodern world. The major differences are that, first, while Allen is more or less certain of his heterosexual orientation (with significant anxieties about it in *Love and Death* and elsewhere), and, second, while his characters live in a world—largely white, Jewish, liberal—paying lip-service to freedoms won and institutionalized for a considerably longer period than Spain's fledgling democracy, Almodóvar surveys both gayness and sexual/political repression far less gingerly, in a riotous, inhibition-free celebration, at all levels, of the polymorphous perverse, even if on occasions characters like Ángel in *Matador* find release from the cocoons of guilt and prejudice more awkward than the more liberated Sexilias and Pepis of other films.

Matador, like all Almodóvar's films, is double-focused: while it looks backwards for historical and ideological rationales of its sexual and political traumas, it looks forward—with relief, openness and an adolescent vivaciousness born of long-suffering patience—to a society unafraid to speak the names of its multifarious desires. In this context, traditional popular art forms are relied on both as a means of signposting their potential under difficult circumstances for bearing coded messages, and for defining their own alternative truths in societies officially attuned to the sounds of anodyne versions of the so-called higher culture. In releasing and celebrating the popular—both indigenous and foreign (mainly American)—Almodóvar achieves through Hollywood Melodrama here, but elsewhere, too, through Spanish comics, pop songs and so on, the reinstatement of traditions ignored, condemned or silenced during the Franco years.

Challenges to heterosexual norms were, of course, especially anathematized by the regime. In a society so obsessed by polarities of sexual difference, deviation from stereotype, however trivial, verged on blasphemy. The yardstick for ideal behaviour, which the regime's apologists never seem to have abandoned, was *Raza,* the Generalísimo-scriptedtriumphalist saga of the early days of the dictatorship. As someone whose sexuality has struggled for survival against the current of official standards, Almodóvar has found the Hollywood Melodrama's own problematic expression of stereotypes of gender and sexuality particularly appealing. But whereas *Matador's* interest in male homosexuality is far more muted than in *Ley* or *Laberinto,* its scrutiny of the inhibitions and limits of masculine stereotype owes a good deal to Melodramas like *Duel in the Sun,* with their emphasis on the Oedipal dramas of sons straining to live up to or rebelling against the Law of the Father.

The three principal male characters, Ángel, Diego and the Police Inspector, take up three different positions along the spectrum of masculinity: at one extreme, Diego, the arch-*macho, ex-torero* misogynist, his murder of women the appallingly conclusive sign of his wholesale socialization; at the other extreme, Ángel, desperate to assert an unnatural heterosexuality by not only attempting, unsuccessfully, to rape his idol's mistress, but also by pretending to have committed the *maestro's* crimes against women, both projects designed to appropriate some of his mentor's power; and, in the middle, with ambivalent sexual impulses (in a scene at the bullfighting school his gaze is at one point transfixed by the bulging genitalia and tight buttocks of the tyro *toreros*), epitomizing Almodóvar's suspicions about fixed categories of sexual orientation, the police inspector, simultaneously the upholder of more than just the social law, and the budding rebel, fascinated as much by Ángel's sexual aura as by his alleged criminal involvements. These are characters who, like their Hollywood counterparts, but in rather different circumstances, play out the dilemma of masculinity. While the males in *Duel in the Sun* are not even codedly racked by doubts over their sexual identities (*cf.* on the contrary *Cat on a Hot Tin Roof, Strangers on a Train,* or *Suddenly Last Summer,* among many other Melodramas, for characters who are), they nevertheless characterize the genre's meditation on socialized notions of gender. In *Duel,* the clashes between Jess (Joseph Cotten) McCanles' softened, civilized lawyer (another!), contemptuous of the tyrannical, wife-subjugating patriarch, and Gregory Peck's Lewt McCanles, the rakish, law-violating hyperbole of sexual potency, inheritor of his father's scorn for women and effeminate men, create a complex rhetoric of irony prompting audiences to re-think their concepts of masculinity, especially when, as here, Jess epitomizes well-meaning dullness, while Lewt has all the satanic allure of the eternal rebel. The latent Oedipality of these stereotypes—especially the implications of castration complexes leading to voyeurism, fetishism and punishment of the mythologized 'other' (lower case, and not to be confused with Lacan's higher

cased shorthand for the Symbolic order) of patriarchal society, here personified by the dangerously libidinal half-breed Pearl Chavez—is developed in *Matador* as all three men play out their own Oedipal dramas.

From the mother-fixated, voyeuristic, *machista* images, with all their terrible implications, *Matador* moves beyond the anxious soul-searching of *Duel in the Sun* towards the validation of alternative, redemptive possibilities for the male, in the process rescuing the hidden potential beneath transparent meanings in the substructure of this and all other great Hollywood Melodramas of the period, turning their implicit truths into the characteristically outspoken, irreverent Almodóvarian verbal and visual rhetoric. So, Almodóvarian men, capable of all the sins of their fathers, are also epitomized by extremes of emotion, sexual desire for one another, unmanly intuition, gentleness, weakness and resistance to conformist stereotype. The men may not overnight become the Utopian ideal (and they are still somewhat short of it even in *Atame,* as the outraged reviewers at the Berlin film festival predictably complained), but they do become part of a movement towards definitions of maleness where ideological repression and extremes of sexual difference, the undercurrents of much of the best Hollywood Melodramas, are exposed as the primary agents in formulations of ultimately unacceptable modes of behaviour. When Ángel's reflection merges with the Inspector's in the police station glass partition, when he attempts to sacrifice his own freedom for Diego's, when he begins through ESP, his own brand of 'angelic knowledge', to predict the future (*cf.* Sadec's—also played by Antonio Banderas—heightened sense of smell in *Laberinto*), when he has an attack of vertigo, in a deliberate reference to Hitchcock's dramatization of a man traumatized, like Ángel, by severely patriarchal expectations, the film at once celebrates, with varying degrees of confidence, the possibility of male liberation from the prisons of ideology, and the necessary destruction of the myth of the 'other', that complex sign-system through which women are relegated to a domain of marginalized but simultaneously enjoyed and dreaded mystery. While Almodóvar's films take the view that the Bad and the Beautiful need not be irredeemably linked axioms of desirable masculinity (as they are in the character of Lewt McCanles), they are, nevertheless, sufficiently realistic to accept, with ambivalent feeling, that the terrible allure of the Bad, for women as well as men, is an all too often unfortunate aspect of the Beautiful, a force probably too powerful always effectively to be resisted.

5 Femininity: First a Girl

In Hollywood Melodrama women frequently move towards the centre of the narrative and are allowed in a genre focusing more on private than on public vicissitudes greater diegetic space, even if in the majority of cases their lives are still circumscribed by the narrative closures of the genre's conscious or unconscious obedience to the demands of a pre-dominantly patriarchal culture. This holds true of *Duel,* where Pearl Chavez provides the central area of interest. *Duel* is primarily her story, her struggle for liberation from stereotype, entrapment and destiny. As Laura Mulvey has compellingly argued, the film's interest in questions of female sexuality and socialization can helpfully be discussed through appeal to Freud's notion of the 'residual phenomena of the early masculine period' in the development of female psychology. On this reading, the two principal male characters become 'different sides of her desire and aspiration'. Recuperation of the early masculine phase of a woman's life is also very much at the heart of *Matador,* a view seemingly endorsed by Almodóvar himself when he accepts that 'there are times when people show masculine or feminine behaviour, depending on the situation, even if the essence of each one is clear', going in this film to the extreme—though the point is made humorously—of making his heroine assert her pre-Oedipal masculinity in the men's lavatory at the cinema (in a place of fictions, what validity do such assertions have?).

As in all of his films, there are women characters in abundance in *Matador:* the Good Mother, the Bad Mother, the psychiatrist, the slave of desire, the transsexual. More complex than these, because still trapped in the Symbolic order, still traumatized by the legacy of social and cultural norms, because for all the advances towards sexual equality, still driven to self-destruction, is María Cardenal, the Symbolic Law's advocate and its avenger. The equivalent in her life of Jess and Lewt McCanles, the projections of Pearl's masculinity, are Ángel and Diego. While Ángel projects the guilt-tortured, mainly law-abiding and dispensing conformist side of her psyche (during their first meeting, at the prison, there are alternating shots framing each of them with prison bars), Diego is her minatory, id-prompted, sadistic side, full of style, narcissism, amorality, anti-social self-assertion, the affirmations of a liberated self that has, nevertheless, fatally confused freedom with revenge, imposing on men what she takes to be the higher law of an extremely radical form of feminist justice in the name of women's history of victimization.

Why is María a killer? As the male *matador* kills motivated by a vicious, socially-bred misogynistic desire for revenge against the female, so the female *matador* kills as an avenger (and the film's first image shows Diego masturbating in front of a pornographic video) of male degradation of women. While the wholly socialized Eva—the irony of her name compounded by the female *matador*'s unlikely symbolic association by name with the Virgin Mary (and cardinals: ironic spirituality, but also redness and maleness as well as 'cardinal', the wound of female sexuality)—bears the scar of her victimization on her face, the law- and ball-breaking advocate marks the bodies of her male victims with her deadly, pre-feminized phallic pin. In contrast to Eva (the name also recalls 'Ava' Gardner, whose photo graces Diego's dressing table), who remains quite still, pinned under her pornography-sustained lover's naked body, alone, gyrating in the act of copulation, María remains physically and symbolically on top, in control of the men she devours in the name not only of her own libidinal gratification but of all the Evas who have ever been mythologized, victimized and made to pay for Adam's expulsion from paradise. As Almodóvar himself comments, Eva is as lifeless as a slab of marble. She has internalized the mythology of female subservience to the male, ready to act out any stereotyped fantasy—to the point of accepting her role as the symbol of death, when she not only obeys his command to 'hacerte la muerta', but also uses cosmetics that give her a phantom look—as a way of appeasing and appealing to her lover: at one point, dressed up in the *femme fatale*'s diabolically scarlet costume, a forlorn last-ditch effort to rouse the dying embers of Diego's passion, her framing through the wrought-iron structures by the lift at María Cardenal's office makes her look like the goat-horned great Beelzebub himself. By contrast, María dresses, as has already been noted, alternately like *torero* and yuppie, both styles projecting independence, control and power, impressions not destroyed even when, naked, she passionately and frenziedly takes her fill of erotic pleasure, like a *torero* enjoying the foreplay of the *faena* before the kill. As the false virgin accomplishes her awesome mission, moving ever closer through each sex murder to fusion with Diego, symbol at once of her own phallic power and darker self, so the film again recalls through its excess of colour, *mise-en-scène,* music and thematics, the patterns and drives of Hollywood Melodrama, especially as they appear in the complex generic patterns of *Duel in the Sun.*

Pearl Chavez's strikingly gaudy costume colours (greens, yellows), setting up contrasts with patterns of black and white for what John Hopewell aptly describes as symbols of irrationality, become the dramatic 'cardinal' reds and blues of her own dresses and of the ex-*torero*'s *faena* cape she covets and eventually possesses. Just as the Hollywood Melodrama, invoking a long tradition (with some exceptions to the rule), usually ensures that passion is All about Eve (all those thriller dames), associated with Indians (as in *Duel*), or foreigners (*Cat People*), so in *Matador* María Cardenal, as Almodóvar himself indicates, is darkened (compare her fairer colouring in, say, Carlos Saura's *Dulces horas*), made less Iberian, more Moorish, Gypsyish (*cf.* English Gainsborough's equations of gypsies and sexuality), in keeping with Spain's own traditions of dark women, sentimental Moors (Lope, Calderón, *El Abencerraje,* etc.), passionate Gypsies (Cervantes, Lorca, Falla), and self-conscious sexuality (Buñuel's dark ladies), all given a mock-serious, positive-negative framework in the verbal and visual imagery of eclipse towards the end of the film. The *torero*'s shrine, with all its heightened phallic symbolism, evokes the erotic force of the *mise-en-scène* of corrals, horses and ranches associated with the film's Western ambience. The diegetic relevance of Dimitri Tiomkin's music is paralleled by the counter-point of the popular song, sung by Mina, with a bitter-sweet, lilting, orgasmic, almost necrophiliac lyric and melody, 'Espérame en el cielo, corazón' (*cf.* other examples of this, especially, 'Guarda che luna' and 'Lo dudo' in *Ley*). Excess lies upon excess, as Almodóvar eulogizes the time and place of hyperbole, Spain in the 1980s, a country alive again after decades of solemnity, authoritarianism and sanctimoniousness. The voice of the Hollywood Melodrama plays a major role in the project both of exposing the cradle of violence, subjugation and victimization from which the 'children of Franco' (to use Marsha Kinder's vibrant phrase), have escaped, and of looking still forward to a future of enduring permissiveness based on a principle of cultural heterogeneity that, against all the odds, the country has on the whole warmly accepted. If Bataille is *Matador's* inspiration for this credo of heterogeneity, he is also its crucial reference point for María's courtship, through her desire for Diego, of death:

> Ce qui nous marque si durement est la connaissance de la mort, que les animaux craignent et ne connaissent pas. Je montrerai plus loin qu'à cette connaissance de la sexualité, à laquelle contribuent, d'une part l'horreur ou le sentiment de la saleté de l'acte sexuel, et d'autre part, la pratique de l'érotisme, qui en est le contre-coup.

Superficially, María's desire for Diego has a Bataille (and also, of course, Freud) inspired conviction that sexual passion is inextricably linked with frissons and premonitions of death. But when she kills Diego, as Pearl kills Lewt, she neither simply intensifies the quality of her pleasure nor simply unites herself eternally, like earlier doomed other-worldly couples (Cathy and Heathcliff in *Wuthering Heights,* Jennie and Eben in *The Portrait of Jennie,* for instance), with a kindred spirit, a being so compellingly different from all other mortals (like the fatally attracted brother and sister in another of Almodóvar's allusions in this film, the 1982 version of *Cat People*), that no one else will do. In the process she also destroys tendencies she recognizes as having been created within her by a monstrous, death-dealing society. Like the butcher of Chabrol's great film, too, this butcher/*Matador* has been transformed by a macho-crazed ideology into a killing machine, as ruthlessly efficient and addicted to killing as, on his own admission, Diego has long ago become. If the *Matador,* in Michel Leiris' view, is an apt image of the autobiographer, since both are at once narcissistic, guilt-ridden and exposed to personal danger, her pricking to death of Diego creates a mirror image of her own self-destruction. The deaths of María and Diego, like Pearl's and Lewt's, are also, since the film is additionally the larger con-

fession of its creator, the desired death or exorcism of what Almodóvar may fear remains the not wholly absent spectre of his pre-1975, socialized, straighter, and far from *cañí* self.

Paul Julian Smith (essay date January 1994)

SOURCE: "Future Chic," in *Sight and Sound,* Vol. 4, No. 1, January, 1994, pp. 6-10.

[*In the following essay, Smith argues that although* Kika *is "Gloriously shot, beautifully dressed and skillfully acted," the film "is poorly plotted and characterized, its rogues' gallery of grotesques provoking little of the audience identification that Almodóvar was clearly hoping for."*]

It promises to be a cold winter in Madrid. As the long hangover from the Olympic *annus mirabilis* of 1992 drags on, Spain is facing up to record unemployment, continuing political scandal, and mounting concern over the intrusions of the newly deregulated media. In a mirror image of the UK, a long-serving government, incapable of managing either the budget deficit or the rising tide of crime, is confronted by an ineffectual opposition and an alienated electorate. The only difference is that in Spain the government is socialist and the opposition back-to-basics conservatives.

In the week that Pedro Almodóvar's *Kika* was released, 17,000 people applied for 200 clerical jobs in Madrid city council. They sat competitive examinations in the former municipal abattoir. When Almodóvar shot a bizarre fashion show in the same location for *Matador,* it was a campy joke; but as unemployment heads for a ten-year high, no one is laughing. Ever sensitive to the mood of the moment, Almodóvar's latest feature offers evidence of a new pessimism clouding a famously sunny outlook; the erstwhile muse of Madrid now proclaims the city to be "unliveable", swamped by drug-related crime.

The winter would also seem to mark a new low for the once promising Spanish film industry. Now the high hopes inspired by the generous state subsidies of the 80s have gone unfulfilled, policy has shifted to protectionism. The government has passed panic measures to reduce the dubbing licenses granted to US-hungry distributors, and is vigorously campaigning for film and television to be excluded from the GATT agreement.

At this inauspicious moment comes *Kika,* the longest-awaited and biggest-budget film of the year and the tenth feature from Almodóvar, the most profitable Spanish director in both domestic and foreign markets. Three questions arise. First, how will Almodóvar adjust to the end of the wonder years of the 80s, the decade of conspicuous pleasures and quick profits with which he is so closely identified? Second, what is his relationship to a Spanish film industry whose perpetual crisis now seems in danger of becoming terminal? And finally, why has his undisputed commercial success attracted such critical derision, both abroad, where he is often dismissed as "crazy" or "camp", and at home, where the attacks are more personal, and increasingly bitter? The answers are not what we might expect; and they derive ultimately from a suspicion of identity politics which is typically Spanish and somewhat mystifying to foreigners.

Kika still offers fans the frantic farce and gloriously saturated colours and costumes we have come to expect from its director, and in the title character we find the incorrigible optimist typical of Almodóvar's heroines. As played by Verónica Forqué (previously cast as the perky prostitute in *What Have I Done to Deserve This?*), Kika confronts the vicissitudes of urban rape and multiple murder with disturbing equanimity. By turns naive, sexy and vigorously independent, Forqué, known to Spanish audiences for her appearance in domestic farces with titles like *Salsa Rosa* (*Pink Sauce*, Manuel Gómez Pereira, 1991), suggests a curious combination of Judy Holliday and Barbara Windsor.

The benevolent Kika is matched by Victoria Abril's malevolent Andrea Caracortada (Cutface), the presenter of an exploitative real-life crime show entitled *The Worst of the Day*. This is sponsored, with conspicuous incongruity, by a milk manufacturer. Abril clearly relishes the role, sporting much-publicised black rubber outfits by Gaultier and revealing what must be the bushiest female armpits ever shown on screen. In the central scene of the film, Kika is raped by an escaped convict who has grown tired of screwing "queers" (*maricones*) in prison. The crime is presented as a comic *tour de force;* certainly it provoked much hilarity from the young, mainly female audience on the night I saw the film in the massive Palace of Music theatre in Madrid. However, Kika's humiliation comes not so much from the act itself (which she vigorously resists), as from its television screening by the wicked dominatrix Andrea, who has procured graphic video footage from a mysterious voyeur.

While such sequences will surely try the patience of UK audiences, they hint at a new social concern in Almodóvar—albeit one that is typically ironised and distanced. Once again, in the very week of *Kika*'s release, a Spanish family who were victims of a kidnapping complained of the "disgusting" exploitation of their case by a private television channel. And the newly hostile press coverage of Almodóvar himself has revealed hitherto unplumbed depths of that combination of unhealthy curiosity and ghoulish delight known in Spanish as *morbo.* Thus the film prompted reports of

Almodóvar's supposed marriage to long-time collaborator Bibi Andersen, now celebrated as a chat-show hostess and once billed as the tallest transsexual in Europe. Denying he was the source of the wedding rumours, Almodóvar compared the press coverage he has nurtured so carefully throughout his career to a "bomb", liable to explode in his face at the worst possible moment. *Morbo* is, however, a two-way street. And by including gleefully gratuitous frontal nude shots of Andersen in *Kika,* Almodóvar himself might not be seen to be upholding the highest standards of cinematic propriety.

The typically stylish credit sequence of *Kika* features a spotlight, a keyhole, and a camera shutter. This can be read socially as a reference to the increasingly intrusive voyeurism of the Spanish media; it also points quite clearly to that reflexive and ironic attention to the cinematic apparatus that has run through Almodóvar's work since his first feature *Pepi, Luci, Bom y otras chicas del montón* had its three eponymous heroines make a video version of their lives. An unlikely Spanish Godard, Almodóvar uses *Kika* to rub our faces in the self-conscious (hi)stories of cinema held to be typical of a post-modern culture. Indeed, all *Kika*'s characters are shown to fictionalise their experience: Kika herself is a make-up artist, shown at one point adding 'natural colour' to a corpse; Andrea circles Madrid with a camera on her futuristic helmet and arc lights in place of breasts; the two male leads, Kika's boyfriend Ramón (Alex Casanovas, in the Antonio Banderas role of the attractive and sensitive young man) and his stepfather Nicholas (Peter Coyote, dubbed unconvincingly into Spanish) play a voyeuristic photographer and an autobiographical novelist respectively. Most gratuitously and intrusively, Almodóvar casts his own octogenarian mother as a television presenter and has her drop knowing references to her son's profession. The viewer can only agree with her when she tells Nicholas, an expatriate American, "Nothing compares to Spain."

The commercial background of *Kika* is, however, perhaps more important than these emphatically self-conscious elements. The second co-production between Almodóvar's own company El Deseo, S. A. (Desire Ltd) and mainstream French producer CiBy 2000, *Kika*'s generous budget enables glossy production values which few films outside Hollywood could aspire to. If European cinema is in Stuart Hall's words "on the verge of a nervous breakdown", the continuing success of the Almodóvar trademark, most spectacularly in France, might provide a model elsewhere for a film practice which is both grounded in domestic concerns and attractive to foreign audiences. In the Spanish capital, where *Kika* is currently the most conspicuous local film playing the vast picture palaces of the Gran Vía (Madrid's Shaftesbury Avenue) and the only domestic product to figure in the top ten grosses (bringing in a healthy $300,000 in the first three weeks), El Deseo's dominance is such that it is claimed that industry insiders are unwilling even to criticise King Pedro the Cruel.

It seems likely, however, that Almodóvar has been a victim of his own success. Foreign audiences now expect stylish eroticism and furious farce from Spanish films, and they now have other directors such as Bigas Luna (*Jamón, jamón*) to provide it for them. In Spain itself, the newly cautious mood has made Fernando Trueba's bland period comedy *Belle Epoque* (soon to open in London) the most critically and commercially popular film of the year preceding *Kika*'s release. And an ill-timed announcement has just awarded the earnestly highbrow Victor Erice (*The Spirit of the Beehive; The Quince Tree Sun*) the National Prize for Cinematography. *Kika*'s gorgeous art design and consistently inventive cinematography (by Alfredo Mayo, an Almodóvar regular) produce pleasure, but no longer surprise. It seems only fair to ask: has Almodóvar painted himself into a corner?

Almodóvar once claimed, facetiously, that he could not wait to go out of fashion so that he could become a classic. It would seem that only the first part of his wish has been granted. *Kika* was greeted in Spain by a crescendo of critical abuse, in which Almodóvar served as an unwilling and perhaps unwitting litmus test for the problems of misogyny and homophobia which continue to dog Spain more than a decade after the socially progressive Socialists took power. The responses relate both to the film itself and to Almodóvar's typically idiosyncratic promotion of it. Based, as ever, on a cavalcade of strong women (from 'good' Kika to 'bad' Andrea by way of Rossy de Palma's gloriously 'ugly' turn as a lesbian maid in love with her mistress), *Kika* shamelessly proclaims itself a woman's film and one whose female characters are granted both the 'ultra-feminine' visual pleasure characteristic of mainstream film and the central narrative position generally occupied by men. This implicit threat to masculinity is confirmed by the male leads who, as so often in Almodóvar, are comparatively dull: the cataleptic Casanovas is muted: the saturnine Coyote merely bemused.

Moreover, as a consummate female impersonator, Almodóvar has clearly placed himself on that side of the cinematic gender division which is coded as feminine. Thus he posed cheekily for Spain's best-selling daily *El Pais* peeking out from behind a pair of curtains, an oversized polka-dotted bow in his bushy hair. The same paper carried pictures of the director in costume for all the principal roles of the film, male and female. Even *Cahiers du cinéma* ran a spread of parallel shots of director and actors acting out scenes on the set, with Almodóvar vigorously ironing the laundry or firmly bound to a chair like Rossy de Palma's maid during the rape sequence. Such antics seem to have provoked the latent homophobia of the Spanish press, usually liberal by UK standards. Indeed one paper accused Almodóvar of promoting "a homosexual fashion", an accusation he proved over-eager to refute.

At a deeper level, the threat of Almodóvar's performances is in their hints of subjective merger and fluidity. Just as his films are full of characters unable to separate from their parents or lovers (in this case the mother-obsessed Ramón), so Almodóvar's over-identification with his creations, his compulsion to repeat and act out their dilemmas both on and off the set, put fixed individual boundaries into crisis and throw the rigid divisions of gender binaries into confusion. Wilfully frivolous and superficial, Almodóvar's films can be read as identity parades, an acting-out of roles with no depth or essence. This cult of the surface is nowhere more evident than in *Kika.* Gloriously shot, beautifully dressed and skillfully acted, it is poorly plotted and characterized, its rogues' gallery of grotesques provoking little of the audience identification that Almodóvar was clearly hoping for.

> **Wilfully frivolous and superficial, Almodóvar's films can be read as identity parades, an acting-out of roles with no depth or essence. This cult of the surface is nowhere more evident than in *Kika.***
> **—*Paul Julian Smith***

But if *Kika* may well be seen as a mid-point in Almodóvar's career, in which the maestro treads water between the unselfconscious pleasures of the 80s and the more critical climate of the 90s, there can be no doubt as to the importance of that career as a whole. For as Almodóvar's films clearly reveal, far from being belated, the Spain that offers a mocking reflection of the UK's political and economic decline reveals no sign of the regressions signalled by Major's cynical appeal to "traditional values", or indeed Clinton's disingenuous call for "security". In spite of domestic horror stories, still less do we find in Spain the turn to neo-fascism exemplified by Italy. Indeed, Madrid may well be ahead of London or New York in the sexual arena.

In his love of sex and gender fluidity, his hostility to fixed positions of all kinds, Almodóvar anticipated by a full decade the critique of identity politics now commonplace in Anglo-American feminist and queer theory. Once we are weaned from the reassuring comforts of the dichotomies of gay/straight, female/male, his cinema offers us English-speakers the promise of a nightmare and a dream for the 90s. The nightmare is a future of powerlessness in which (as in Spain) feminists and gays prove unable to organise and unwilling to found a sense of community on the experiences they have in common. The dream is a future of fluidity in which (as in Spain, perhaps, once more) sexual practices are not constrained by fixed allegiances and each of us negotiates our own price in the libidinal economy. The financial metaphor is apt. For as Almodóvar's constant concern for the bottom line has shown, economic clout is essential if any dissonant voice wishes to make itself heard in an increasingly globalised entertainment industry.

Kika ends with its plucky heroine, having sped in her car from the scene of multiple murders, picking up a handsome young stranger at random from the side of the road. The scene is shot against a glorious blaze of sunflowers. Relentlessly optimistic even in extremis, Almodóvar may also, like his heroine in this sequence, have lost his sense of direction for the time being. It seems very likely, however, that the future journey will be well worth making, the cinematic and sexual adventure characteristically unpredictable. In the meantime, *Kika* remains gloriously flashy fun and Almodóvar's combination of uncompromising modernity and unabashed visual pleasure could teach the more timid and tasteful UK film industry a thing or two.

Florence Redding Jessup (essay date 1994)

SOURCE: "Women on the Verge of a Nervous Breakdown: Sexism or Emancipation from Machismo?" in *Look Who's Laughing: Gender and Comedy,* edited by Gail Finney, Gordon and Breach, 1994, pp. 299-314.

[*In the following essay, Redding Jessup asserts that "If the ending convincingly sums up Pedro Almodóvar's gender messages in this film,* Women on the Verge of a Nervous Breakdown *is a story about emancipation from machismo."*]

Introduction: May We Laugh?

Is Pedro Almodóvar's *Women on the Verge of a Nervous Breakdown* a sexist comedy about hysterical women or a story of liberation from machismo? Should our nerves jangle with Almodóvar's stereotypical treatment of women? Or, may we celebrate the happy ending and laugh with this comic film from Spain?

Even before we see *Women on the Verge of a Nervous Breakdown,* the title conjures up images of edgy, emotional, out-of-control women. Then, from the beginning until the final scenes we watch the female characters in a frenzy over men. Pepa (played by Carmen Maura) frantically searches for her lover Iván (Fernando Guillén), who has left her for another woman, to tell him she is pregnant and to get him back. Crazed Lucía (Julieta Serrano) hijacks a motorcycle in pursuit of the same Iván, to shoot him. Pepa's friend Candela (María Barranco) is in a panic fearing she will go to jail as an accomplice to her lover's plot to hijack the plane which Iván plans to take to Stockholm with his new paramour, Paulina (Kiti Manver). Before the end of the film, Candela and Iván's son Carlos (Antonio Banderas) flirt and kiss, while Carlos' fiancee, Marisa (Rossy de Palma), sleeps nearby. As Elvira Siruana notes, the women in this comedy behave as "neurotics" who chase after men, "competing" with each other as if they had "no other objective in their lives."

The conclusion of the film, however, is not in the interest of the patriarchal power which such stereotypical images of women seem to justify. After all, irrational women need rational men to tell them what to do. But in the final scenes, Pepa is an independent career woman who says "*adiós*" to Iván. She also decides, as Murphy Brown will do four years later, to become a single parent. Clearly Pepa and her baby will be better off without Iván, a macho cad. As the comedy closes, phallocentric dualisms are upset. Pepa regains control of her life, and Iván remains irrationally subjugated to the macho role he plays. If the ending convincingly sums up Pedro Almodóvar's gender messages in this film, *Women on the Verge of a Nervous Breakdown* is a story about emancipation from machismo.

In Caryn James' opinion, however, the endings of Almodóvar's films simply do not work. In "Almodóvar Adrift in Sexism," a New York Times article about *Women on the Verge of a Nervous Breakdown, Tie Me Up! Tie Me Down!,* and *High Heels,* she sees the endings as "contrived, declared by authorial fiat." She finds "a definite trace of misogyny lurking beneath his apparently fond creations of women" because the conclusions are ineffective. "The undercurrent of sexism is directly tied to the bludgeoning control that wrecks the endings of Mr. Almodóvar's films," she explains. Women in *Women on the Verge of a Nervous Breakdown,* for example, "are suddenly made self-sufficient at the end; this is a neat feminist twist but not a convincing one." Hence viewers are left with the impression that women are "frenetic and silly."

In contrast, Marvin D'Lugo believes that Almodóvar's female protagonists such as Pepa are "agents of radical cultural change" in films that reflect and further a "newly emerging social order." In his article "Heterogeneity and Spanish Cinema of the Eighties," he sums up the plot of *Women on the Verge of a Nervous Breakdown* in this way: "We trace the inner emancipation of the female who, having already achieved the outward marks of freedom and independence that have come with the social transformation of Spain, now struggles to achieve the inner liberation from a phallocentric past by means of her disengagement from the womanizing Iván." By the final scenes, in D'Lugo's opinion, Pepa represents a "cultural and social system in which the female has finally shed the ideological chains of her imprisonment in traditional Spanish patriarchy."

Rather than a deus ex machina at the end of Almodóvar's films, D'Lugo writes that viewers participate in "the emancipating function of the specular ritual," which he defines as "the audience's bearing witness and tacitly legitimizing the cultural reordering that each filmic narrative chronicles." In an analysis of the final scenes of *Law of Desire,* the predecessor of *Women on the Verge of a Nervous Breakdown,* D'Lugo notes the crowd of police and passersby who "look up to the window" where "the homosexual love scene is taking place." The audience joins spectators in the film in a "secular adoration scene." As viewers affirm liberation from past intolerances, according to D'Lugo, they "rewrite the phallocentric and repressive scenarios of Franquismo."

Pedro Almodóvar says that "his films are meant to deny even the memory of Franco," reports Vito Russo. Marvin D'Lugo identifies ironic images that negate the power over gender roles of institutions—the Church, the patriarchal family, and the police—used by Generalissimo Franco during his long dictatorship (1939-1975) to enforce conformity to gender hierarchy. Again in *Law of Desire,* D'Lugo notes the likeness to Michelangelo's *Pietà* of the final embrace of the homosexual lovers, Pablo and Antonio, in front of an "altar of pop-cultural artifacts." Tina, Pablo's transsexual brother who turned woman to become the lover of her father—although the patriarch abandons her—stands by the police in the "adoration" scene. Undermining the patriarchal order of course reaches beyond dramatic changes in Spain. Almodóvar's humorous untying of old gender strictures has international appeal.

In 1988 *Women on the Verge of a Nervous Breakdown* topped box office records and received five Goya prizes in Spain and won awards in Toronto, in Venice, in Berlin and in New York. The next year it was a nominee for an Oscar. Its images of women chasing machos have entered many brains. Elvira Siurana's and Caryn James' important concerns about the female characters' stereotypical behavior prompt a closer look at the film. As Alice Sheppard notes, "typical humor against women relies on stereotypes." But in this analysis of gender in *Women on the Verge of a Nervous Breakdown,* I will try to show that Pedro Almodóvar uses stereotypes subversively, that he directs his humor against machismo, and that the ending confirms this humorous critique.

Because this essay views Almodóvar's gender messages from the vantage point of the end of the film, I will first focus on the final scene. Inspired by Marvin D'Lugo's baptism of the ending as the "annunciation," a beginning, I will share evidence that this finale is also a nativity scene that opens the ending with hope for better gender arrangements in the future. An epilogue to the plot, the final scene follows the closure of two parodic themes, Don Juan and stereotypical women in Hollywood comedies of the 1950s and 1960s. After analyzing these parodies, which involve the central characters and the main plot of the film, I will note contributions to gender themes by other scenes and characters. My conclusion will be that *Women on the Verge of a Nervous Breakdown* is about liberation from machismo.

Almodóvar's humor in this funny film renders machismo absurd. Yet our laughter has undertones of frustration as well as optimism. Pepa overcomes her subordination to the macho; the macho continues with someone else. Machismo roves around society throughout this film; the final scenes indicate that mañana it will go away.

Ending: "Annunciation" and Nativity Scene

The final scene of *Women on the Verge of a Nervous Breakdown* follows the conclusion to the plot. In the penultimate scene, after two days and one sleepless night of frenetic searching, Pepa catches up with Iván at Madrid's Barajas Airport. By then she has nothing to say to him except *"adiós."* This leave-taking is a statement of emancipation from the macho, but there is one more scene. The last set is the terrace of Pepa's penthouse. Back from the airport, Pepa walks through her living room, past the police and others sleeping off drugged gazpacho, to reach the terrace just when Marisa wakes up. Then we watch the happy epilogue, called the "annunciation" by D'Lugo. Pepa announces her pregnancy to Marisa.

Marisa is one of seven people melodramatically entangled in Pepa's story who join Pepa in her penthouse during the second day in the fictional reality of the film. *"Sea precisamente al que tiene menos relación con ella al que le comunique su secreto"* ["it is exactly to the one with whom she has the least relationship that she communicates her secret"], points out Pedro Almodóvar. But Marisa is part of the mesh. Carlos, Iván's son and Marisa's sweetheart when they enter the apartment, leaves Marisa for Candela, as his father discards Pepa for Paulina. Marisa is abandoned while she sleeps, dreaming sweet orgasmic dreams after consuming the gazpacho that Pepa concocted for Iván. Pepa has laced this nourishing cold soup with sleeping pills to keep Iván, even if asleep, with her. Iván does not come by, and almost everyone, including Marisa, relishes this delicious culinary symbol of Spanish summers. Thus Pepa announces her pregnancy to Marisa, who is there by a series of coincidences.

The names of the characters in this final scene are not accidental; they suggest the Holy Family. Pepa is a nickname for Josefina, the feminine form of José or Joseph; Marisa is derived from María. Pepa (Joseph) will be both father and mother to her child. Marisa (Mary), blessed with immaculate intercourse while sleeping on the terrace, is no longer a virgin. Pepa is pleased and calls virgins *antipáticas* [unpleasant]. This brief discourse, reversing the veneration of sweet innocent female virgins, does not appear in the original script. By adding it, Almodóvar debunks with a few phrases the age-old cult of women's purity and undoes an obsolete myth that helps sustain macho power. If female chastity is not fiercely defended, Don Juan's valiant conquests, the macho's "scores," are mere deceptions. If a female person is not an otherworldly virgin mother, does she need a worldly patriarch to rule her and the family? Happily the Mary at the ending of *Women on the Verge of a Nervous Breakdown* is not a virgin, and the family announced will not be patriarchal.

In the final scene on the terrace, a calm conversation between two women, Pepa is free from her submission to Iván, and the baby she plans to have will not grow up under the macho's influence. She has no worries about becoming a single mother, no concerns about social or political stigma, and no financial problems. (No Spanish politician, to my knowledge, nervously pointed to Pepa as a threat to "family values," that is, to "the importance of the father.") Well-to-do Pepa can afford a penthouse on Montalbán Street, in the beautiful *Los Jerónimos* neighborhood in Madrid, a few steps from the Prado museum and from the Retiro Park. Her economic advantage glows, if we contrast her with Gloria (also Carmen Maura) from Almodóvar's 1984 film *What Have I Done to Deserve This?* After Gloria frees herself from her macho husband by whacking him over the head with a ham and baking the fatal weapon, she is still financially stuck in an awful apartment overlooking traffic on Madrid's M30 beltway. For Gloria the "outward marks of freedom and independence," noted by D'Lugo in Pepa's case, are not so brilliant. Besides, Gloria's homosexual son who returns home to be the man of the house is already tainted by his father's machismo. But the carefree ending of *Women on the Verge of a Nervous Breakdown* predicts that machismo will not spoil Pepa's baby.

Venturing beyond the hopeful finale into the future—an epilogue invites us to do so—Pepa will continue her career, as Spanish women who work outside the home now commonly do when they have children. When she gives birth she will enjoy the Spanish sixteen-week parental leave with seventy-five percent of her salary. All Spaniards have both a paternal and a maternal surname, and Pepa's baby will carry on Pepa's maternal as well as her paternal family names. Spain's low birthrate, 1.3 children per woman in 1992, indicates that Pepa probably will choose to have one child. Perhaps, like Murphy Brown, she will hire a man to care for her baby until she or he goes to nursery school. The maid Pepa mentioned as she stepped over the spilled gazpacho in the last scene will help her clean the apartment, freeing her from the *la doble jornada* [double day's work] of many career women with children, not only in Spain.

Also, the maps and planes in her apartment symbolize her freedom and imply she will travel. The film's ending encourages optimistic thoughts.

The hopeful finale suggests a nativity scene. The conversation between Pepa (Joseph) and Marisa (Mary) on the terrace with a view of Madrid's nighttime skies takes place close to a manger, or hints of one, and a light, like a star, winks above the Telephone Company building before the scene ends. Ducks and chickens are in the closing and opening sets. D'Lugo mentioned "the biblical intertext" of the "annunciation" and of the prologue. In the voice-over in the opening scene, Pepa said she, as a Noah, would have liked to have a pair of every animal but could not save the couple that mattered most to her. Happily, saving this couple, Iván and Pepa, is no longer a goal at the end of the film. Nor is this nativity scene, with Mary and Joseph and talk of a future baby, a "celebration of fertility," an element of comedy in traditional (androcentric) theory, noted by Regina Barreca. The glad tidings here are that Pepa is free from her submission to a Don Juan and that the baby will be a member of what D'Lugo calls the "presumably 'liberated' generation."

"On the Verge of Parody": Don Juan

"En mis películas todo está al borde de la parodia" ["In my films everything is on the verge of parody"], Almodóvar tells us. Throughout *Women on the Verge of a Nervous Breakdown* he parodies the legendary Don Juan. Although he does not mimic its style, Almodóvar implies actions, characters, and even the author of José Zorrilla's nineteenth-century *Don Juan Tenorio,* the drama that revitalizes the Don Juan myth with performances each year on All Saint's Day in Spain and in other Spanish-speaking countries.

The final scenes of *Women on the Verge of a Nervous Breakdown* suggest the ending of *Don Juan Tenorio.* At the end of the romantic drama, Doña Inés, willing to sacrifice her eternal life, saves Don Juan from hell. After Don Juan's last-minute repentance, the souls of Doña Inés and of Don Juan ascend into heaven in a whirl of flowers, angels, perfume and music. When Pepa saves Iván's life at the end of *Women on the Verge of a Nervous Breakdown,* Iván says *"estoy avergonzado"* ["I am ashamed"] and *"lo siento"* ["I am sorry"] and offers to talk with Pepa in the cafeteria. *"Ya es tarde"* ["It is too late"], Pepa responds. So, they go up into the sky on their separate ways. Iván prepares to board the plane to Stockholm to fly with his new lover Paulina to Beirut if the Shiite terrorists slip by the police. Pepa returns to her penthouse, to the terrace with a view of Madrid's heavenly skies.

The uplifting ending of *Women on the Verge of a Nervous Breakdown* brings the parody of the Don Juan legend to its ironic close. Pepa rejects Iván, but no woman leaves Don

Juan Tenorio. He makes the decisions. Women, numbers to win a bet, matter only as helpmates to his ego. In contrast, Almodóvar's film is the story of a woman discarded by Iván who overcomes her subordination to him. In the end, Pepa completes the task stated in an early scene when the receptionist Cristina (Loles León) advises her, *"olvídale"* ["forget him"], and Pepa responds, *"dame más tiempo"* ["give me more time"]. Two days and one sleepless night later, she says good-bye to Iván.

Almodóvar signals Pepa's progress toward this *"adiós"* throughout the film. When she burns the bed, with Manuel de Falla's "Ritual Fire Dance" from "Love the Magician" playing in the background, she begins to purge the power memories of their lovemaking have over her. Then she packs up his clothes and gifts. After lugging the suitcase up and down the steps of her apartment, she finally heaves it into the trash, ridding herself of her subordination to him. She will no longer wait for him to come by for it. After flinging the telephone through the window in two moments of frustration and frantically running to answer it with each ring, she walks calmly to answer the call from Lucía. Almodóvar's stage instructions for this scene, the fifty-ninth of the eighty-four scenes in this eighty-eight minute film, are: *"Por primera vez Pepa se dirige al auricular como una persona normal, sin necesidad de batir un record de velocidad"* ["For the first time Pepa goes to the phone as a normal person, without the need to beat a speed record"]. When she slings the record *"Soy infeliz"* ["I am unhappy"] through the window, with its slapstick landing on the neck of Paulina, she is freeing herself from the unhappiness Iván caused her. When she tosses the answering machine loaded with his lies through the window onto the hood of the car, just as Iván and Paulina are leaving, she throws his falsehoods back to him. This is a "ligera" [light] comedy, in Almodóvar's words. We have little access to Pepa's deliberations, but scenes of visual and situational humor indicate her steps toward her liberation from Iván.

Names in *Women on the Verge of a Nervous Breakdown* bring to mind *Don Juan Tenorio.* As I have suggested, Iván is a Don Juan. Ana, Pepa's neighbor—the one who asks the panic-stricken driver of the mambo taxi if he sells guns—is an ironic namesake of Doña Ana who was seduced by Don Juan Tenorio in a case of mistaken identity. Ana in the film erroneously worries that Lucía is after her sweetheart Ambite instead of Iván. Pepa's paternal surname, Marcos, is the first name of Don Juan Tenorio's servant. We hear it only in her call to Lucía, early in the film when she is servile to her feelings for Iván. Pepa's first name implies the author of *Don Juan Tenorio,* José Zorrilla, as well as the biblical Joseph. D'Lugo notes how Almodóvar in the introductory voice-over "gives the voice of the creative author to Pepa." Through Pepa, he creates a Don Juan from the perspective of a woman abandoned by the macho.

Point of view works ironies on the Don Juan myth. We see Iván through the problems he causes Pepa and Lucía. Invulnerable Don Juan Tenorio does not notice the suffering he brings about. With the exception of Doña Inés, with whom he falls in love and whose father he then kills, women are objects for seduction. Self-absorbed, after a conquest, he goes on to his next adventure. Similarly, Iván is not upset by Lucía's insanity. At the airport, even though she tries to shoot him, he pays little attention to her—only a glance and a mention of her name, as if reprimanding a little girl. If surprised by Pepa's *"adios,"* in the next moment he turns to his new lover and prepares to board the flight to Stockholm. But we see Iván through Pepa's feelings, not through his pride. He is a culprit.

Iván's machismo is to blame for Pepa's irrational actions; yet she is of sounder mind than he. He first appears in Pepa's nightmare as he passes from one woman to the next, pleased with the uninvited seductive phrases—piropos, he playfully tells them. This introduction to Iván resembles Don Juan bragging about his list of conquests, from one woman to the next, in the opening scenes of *Don Juan Tenorio.* A one-dimensional macho from this beginning of the film, Iván does not change or think. But Pepa, even when "on the verge of a nervous breakdown," figures out, for example, where Lucía lives and where Iván is going and with whom. Later, with pistols pointed at her face, she is able to try to persuade Lucía not to kill Iván. In the end, Pepa's rejection of Iván is a reasonable decision; Iván's machismo is unreasonable.

The mythic Don Juan, a fearless young hero, is reduced in *Women on the Verge of a Nervous Breakdown* to a ridiculous liar in the figure of the cowardly and middle-aged Iván. The most revealing scene of Iván's prevarications occurs when he leaves this message on Pepa's answering machine: *"No me voy de viaje, ni me voy con ninguna mujer"* ["I am not going on a trip, nor am I going away with another woman"]. While he makes the call from a phone booth because he is afraid to face Pepa, Paulina waits in the car ready to go with him to Stockholm. Pepa walks by the phone booth to put his suitcase in the trash, and Lucía passes by on her way to Pepa's apartment. Pepa and Lucía move with determination, as does Paulina when she yanks the suitcase from the dumpster and takes it to the car. Meanwhile, Iván hides cowering behind the advertisement in the phone booth, afraid to use his voice to tell the truth.

Pedro Almodóvar tells us that the inspiration for *Women on the Verge of a Nervous Breakdown* was Jean Cocteau's *The Human Voice.* When Almodóvar wrote the script, the only things remaining from Cocteau's monologue were *"una mujer sola, el teléfono y una maleta"* ["a woman alone, the telephone, and a suitcase"]. Then he added the voice of the lover and *"sus mentiras"* ["his lies"]. Almodóvar also notes that Iván talks to machines—telephones and an answering machine—that allow him to send lies without looking at Pepa. John Hopewell's comment about Antonio in Carlos Saura's *Carmen* sums up Almodóvar's condemnation of machismo in *Women on the Verge of a Nervous Breakdown:* "Machismo impedes communication. It is also quite simply a lie."

In addition to telling lies, Iván uses his voice to dub words into films, which evokes ideas about illusions of reality in the film within the film, in cinema, and in life. This early dubbing scene also hints at role-playing in machismo. Iván speaks, while the actors move their mouths, to delude future audiences who will think his voice pertains to someone else, which it does. It belongs to a beguiler. Iván is an impostor to himself.

The sad song *"Soy infeliz"* ["I am unhappy"] tells Iván, *"vive feliz en tu mundo de ilusiones"* ["live happily in your world of illusions"]. This song about hurtful delusion begins the film and later, on a record, flies through the window of Pepa's apartment. A sad bolero echoes the same message at the end of the film. Almodóvar's final commentary on machismo as represented by Iván is the song *"Teatro"* with its lyrics, *"lo tuyo es puro teatro"* ["yours is nothing but acting"].

"On the Verge of Parody": Hollywood Comedies

Another parodic theme, visible throughout *Women on the Verge of a Nervous Breakdown* and brought to its ironic closure in the final scenes, is women's behavior in Hollywood comedies of the 1950s and 1960s. Generalissimo Franco's censors welcomed these films about happy subjugation, and Almodóvar saw many of them in Spain. Speaking of *Women on the Verge of a Nervous Breakdown,* he tells us:

> *He querido hacer una especie de alta comedia al estilo de las americanas de finales de los años 50, donde un grupo de mujeres están a punto de tirarse por el balcón o de ahorcarse con el cable del teléfono porque su novio no las llama. La película está basada en esos primeros momentos del abandono, en que pierden un poco el control de los nervios.* [I wanted to make a kind of high comedy in the style of the American ones at the end of the 1950s where a group of women are ready to throw themselves from the balcony or hang themselves with the telephone cord because their sweethearts do not call them. The film is based on those first moments of abandonment, when they lose some control of their nerves.]

Pedro Almodóvar also makes clear, *"no quiero que sea una mirada complacienta sobre los sesenta, sino todo lo*

contrario." ["I do not want this to be a complaisant look at the sixties, but rather the opposite"].

In *Women on the Verge of a Nervous Breakdown* Pedro Almodóvar mimics and mocks women's stereotypical behavior in Hollywood comedies of decades past. But his message is not that women can act like funny little girls because in the end they will submit to their man who will take care of them. To the contrary, Pepa passes comically through the trauma of ending her relationship with Iván, who has discarded her. In the happy conclusion she is free to invent her own life. Significantly, the character in *Women on the Verge of a Nervous Breakdown* who remains completely dependent on her macho man is insane. Lucía, in her zany outfits from the 1960s, refuses to leave behind gender roles often prescribed by comedies of that decade and returns to the hospital. Pepa's denial of subordination, her declaration of independence, does not sanction stereotypical behavior of women as did many Hollywood happy endings of the fifties and sixties.

Almodóvar calls *Women on the Verge of a Nervous Breakdown "una comedia realista al estilo americano, o sea, muy falseada"* ["a realistic comedy in the American style, or, that is, very falsified"]. Pauline Kael mentions the tone of the fifties of the plastic-like "cosmetic layouts" of the introduction. The main set, Pepa's apartment, resembles unreal Hollywood decor of decades past. The apartment building in the prologue is a bad painting, and its interior is impeccable. The kitchen, as María Asunción Balonga notes, is like one from "Homes and Gardens." The tomatoes for gazpacho are lustrous red; the colors inside and on the terrace are brilliant. Almodóvar explains that *"Lo que pretendo es que lo único auténtico y lo único verosímil sean los sentimientos de ella"* ["What I intend is that the only authentic thing and the only credible thing will be her feelings"]. Against a backdrop of artificiality, Pepa's emotions are genuine from the beginning to the end.

We see Pepa's sincerity in an opening scene, the dialogue from Nicholas Ray's 1954 film *Johnny Guitar.* Iván first dubs Sterling Hayden's part into Spanish; later Pepa dubs Joan Crawford's words into Spanish. Iván, through Johnny Guitar's lines, asks for lies: *"Dime que siempre me has esperado."* ["Tell me that you have always waited for me."] *"Dime que hubieras muerto si yo no hubiera vuelto."* ["Tell me that you would have died if I had not returned."] *"Dime que todaavía me quieres, como yo a ti."* ["Tell me that you still love me as I love you."] Pepa says the lines with deep emotion, too heartfelt for the role Joan Crawford plays. Then she faints, which blends into the melodramatic pitch of the film. This clip shows that Iván, as a Don Juan, wants self-delusion; Pepa, authenticity.

As in *Johnny Guitar* and other Hollywood films of those

decades, *Women on the Verge of a Nervous Breakdown* takes place with sudden shifts from the stage set to the streets. One of these switches from the set is to Almagro street in Madrid, and Almodóvar's choice is significant. This is the street where Pepa looks through an apartment window and watches a woman dance, an allusion to Alfred Hitchcock's 1954 film *Rear Window,* as noted by Patricia Hart. The name of this street lined with elegant buildings suggests the wonderful seventeenth-century theater, *Corral de Comedias,* in the town Almagro, where classical drama is still performed. It brings to mind Tirso de Molina's *El Burlador de Sevilla,* the seventeenth-century model for *Don Juan Tenorio.* But Pedro Almodóvar chose this street for an additional purpose, one that states the underlying gender theme of the comedy.

The central office of the *Instituto de la Mujer* [The Women's Institute] is located at Almagro 36, and its telephone number is 410-51-12. Pepa reads its address when matching Lucía's phone number, 410-41-30, with street numbers in the Madrid directory arranged by addresses. She rushes through the numbers, "Almagro 30, 31, 32, 33, 34, 36," before arriving at Almagro 38, Lucía's address. The Center for Information on the Rights of Women, where women can receive advice on legal matters, is located at Almagro 30. Very close by on Almagro Street is the *Casa de la Mujer,* which houses various associations where women and men work for the cause of gender fairness. Lucía, ensnared in the past, lives on a street that symbolizes Spain's advances toward the goal of equality of opportunities. Her apartment is next door to the Women's Institute, a government agency dedicated to turning Spain's progressive constitutional rights for women into realities.

The Spanish government in 1983 created The Women's Institute "for the purpose of promoting the conditions necessary for equality between the sexes and for the participation of women in political, cultural, economic and social life." The Institute's work is inspired by the Spanish Constitution of 1978, which prohibits discrimination based on sex (article 14), specifically forbids discrimination based on sex at work (article 35), and declares marriage an institution based on equality (article 32). Moreover, the Constitution, in an aboutface from Generalissimo Franco's regime, promises that "the public powers" will remove obstacles in the path toward equality (art. 9.2). In the decade following its ratification, ending the year *Women on the Verge of a Nervous Breakdown* appeared, legislative and social reforms were dynamic. But, the Women's Institute notes "the difficulties in changing attitudes at the same speed as legislation" and says that "a profound change in social customs and individual behavior" is necessary.

Almodóvar turns this need into comedy in *Women on the Verge of a Nervous Breakdown.* The ludicrous juxtaposi-

tion of Lucía's apartment next to the Women's Institute on Almagro Street is a serious social commentary. Moreover Iván has walked along this same street. There too is Iván's son Carlos, who according to Lucía *"ha salido como su padre"* ["has turned out like his father"]. During the first night of the film, Pepa stalks Almagro Street looking for Iván. She sits down across the street from Lucía's apartment and from the Women's Institute, waiting for her Don Juan. Women in 1988 engaged in behavior reminiscent of Hollywood comedies of decades past and Don Juans on a street that represents progress are absurd incongruities. But the optimistic ending justifies our smiles.

The protagonist Pepa conveys Almodóvar's messages of hope for women's progress. At the end of the film, Lucía, a foil to Pepa, trapped in the past, is put away. The macho Iván, also a crazy anachronism, roams free. Naive Candela, whose name implies *cándida,* ingenuous, still has much to learn. Her sexual desires blind her again—the scene with rabbits who like turnips and with a can of Seat car oil in the background has innuendoes. She cuddles up to Carlos on the sofa, while his fiancée Marisa sleeps nearby. Where is female solidarity against machismo? By the final scenes, it is Pepa who advances from reactions reminiscent of Hollywood comedies of the fifties and sixties to actions suitable to the end of the eighties.

Gender and Other Funny Scenes and Characters

Other scenes and characters corroborate Almodóvar's messages about gender in *Women on the Verge of a Nervous Breakdown.* They also add to the ludicrous situations and juxtapositions, the wild coincidences, the exaggerations, the caricatures, and the comic tone that make this film seem frivolous. But as Pedro Almodóvar asks, *"¿Qué es frívolo y qué es trascendente?"* ["What is frivolous and what is transcendental?"]. Funny minor characters and scenes underline Almodóvar's portrayal of machismo as a lie.

Two television commercials are woven into this comedy. In the first spot, a priest puts a condom in the bride's bouquet during the wedding ceremony and warns her never to trust any man. María Barranco, the bride, later appears as Candela, deceived by a Shiite terrorist. Carmen Maura, Pepa, abandoned by Iván, dubs the words of the bride. We view the second commercial with Pepa who watches herself in the main role. "The mother of the murderer" combines detergent, murder, words of Pontius Pilate, a hint of Christ on the cross, police, and a housewife pleased with her clean wash. The advertisement for Ecce Homo laundry soap mocks housewives' delight in a clean shirt, as if it were a life or death issue, which in this case it is. Omo, by the way, was a "popular" detergent in Spain during the sixties. The police, no longer in a police state, are helpless before the stain-removing power of Ecce Homo. All blood and guts have vanished from the shirt. The mother has saved her son, the murderer. Television gives the word in the world of consumerism; detergent works miracles. The final sentence about the incredible detergent, *"Ecce Homo parece mentira"* ["Ecce Homo, it (or he) seems a lie"], suggests commercials deceive. These words can also mean, "behold, this man seems to be a lie."

Almodóvar plays with lies in this film. Chus, the Jehovah's Witness and concierge who cannot tell a falsehood, is a comic contrast to Iván and his prevarications. Lucía lies to herself about time not passing. Significantly, her mother wants to sell the outdated outfits to cure her daughter's self deception, but Lucía's affectionate father tells her she looks wonderful, *"estupenda,"* in an ugly wig. Lucía replies, *"Qué bien mientes, papá. Por eso te quiero."* ["How well you lie, father. That is why I love you."] Pepa lies to protect Candela. The police do not believe her when she tells the truth.

We do not hear the kind and funny mambo taxi driver lie, but he repeats sexist clichés. This sensitive taxi driver with his clown-like hair cries because Pepa cries and because he does not have eye drops for her. On the next trip he has the drops. Each time Pepa needs a cab, along comes the mambo taxi that offers magazines, newspapers, drinks, snacks, cigarettes, a sign *"Gracias por fumar"* ["Thank You for Smoking"], leopard seat covers, and mambo music. The taxi driver's sweetheart's sugary name, Azucena, reminds us of Don Quixote's illusory love for his sweet Dulcinea and hints at Pepa's love for Iván. Later, this Don Quixote in his Rocinante mambo cab says to Pepa that Azucena *"va a pensar que . . . ja, ja"* ["will think we are . . . ha ha"] because they meet so often. He also claims categorically that there are no dangerous women, *"si las sabe tratar"* ["if you know how to treat them"]. In the next moment he finds himself in the line of fire as perilous Lucia shoots at his mambo taxi.

In a reversal of a long-standing gender situation, women force men to partake in a wild taxi and motorcycle chase. They do not sit as companions to their crazed men who pursue each other until one car crashes—or the wheels fall off the stage coach. The mambo taxi driver, not a macho, wisely panics and gives up. He takes Pepa and Ana to the airport by a safer route. There Iván and Paulina are checking in for their flight.

Paulina, the supposedly feminist lawyer, is an ironic reversal of a feminist. She does not help women, is jealous of Pepa, and runs off with a Don Juan. Paulina Morales—her surname is also ironic—had represented Lucía in a suit against this Don Juan, Iván. Moreover, she is very "unlaughing," a term described by Regina Barreca in her introduction to *Last Laughs: Perspectives on Women and Comedy.* Barreca explains that this adjective can be "a

weapon against both the 'pretty little girls' and the 'furious females' in order to negate whatever powers of humor they seem to possess." But, Almodóvar, a feminist, does not label feminists humorless here. Rather, an implication is that feminists, not only in Spain, need humor as they further equality in masculine societies where machos still lurk.

Sexism or Emancipation from Machismo?

Almodóvar would like to be thought of as "authentically feminist" and as "one of the least macho men in the world."

> *Quizá eso de que a mí me gusta la intimidad de las mujeres no deje de ser un reflejo machista. Pero espero que no, porque a mí me interesa la mujer y su mundo en todos sus aspectos . . . Yo creo que soy uno de los hombres menos machistas del mundo, más auténticamente feminista. Lo que no quiere decir que no vea la realidad. Defiendo a las mujeres, pero no creo que sean unos arcangeles. Pero mi corazón suele estar siempre con ellas. Aunque te salgan cosas de la educación.* [Perhaps the fact that I like the private lives of women is no more than a reflection of chauvinism. But I hope not, because I am interested in women and their world in all its aspects . . . I believe that I am one of the least macho men in the world, the most authentically feminist. That does not mean that I do not see reality. I defend women, but I do not think they are archangels. But my heart is almost always with them. Although some things come out from one's upbringing.]

Pedro Almodóvar's messages about gender in **Women on the Verge of a Nervous Breakdown** are feminist. Machismo is senseless and hurtful, they say. Iván mindlessly plays the Don Juan role. Lucía's dependency on Iván to give her life meaning is an anachronism and a complicity with the macho charade. In contrast to Lucía and to Iván, Pepa, the hero, frees herself from her subjugation to machismo. When Nancy Walker, in *A Very Serious Thing: Women's Humor and American Culture,* identifies "the impulse of all feminist humor" as "the fundamental absurdity of one gender oppressing the other," she expresses an underlying theme of this film.

Some of the aspects of women's humor described by Regina Barreca, Zita Dresner, and Nancy Walker also fit Pedro Almodóvar's comic strategies. In *A Very Serious Thing,* when discussing the subversion of stereotypes in literature written by women, Walker notes "the purpose of mocking those stereotypes and showing their absurdity." In the same work she speaks of the intent to "point to the origins of these stereotypes in a culture that defines women in terms of relationships with men" and mentions portrayals of "lovelorn women" as "victims of male indifference and the double standard." These comments describe Almodóvar's subversive use of stereotypical behavior in *Women on the Verge of a Nervous Breakdown.* Also, Almodóvar's meaningful scenes of Don Juans and dependent women on Almagro Street, symbol of women's progress, come to mind when Nancy Walker and Zita Dresner note women writers "exposing the discrepancies . . . between the inequities . . . and the egalitarian ideals." Finally, the nativity scene on the terrace does "not, ultimately, reproduce the expected hierarchies," a refusal which links it to "the ending of comic works by women writers" discussed by Regina Barreca.

Yet *Women on the Verge of a Nervous Breakdown* is a film written and directed by a man. Pedro Almodóvar, as he creates his humor, does not have to deal with female social conditioning such as "standards of ladylike behavior," discussed by Walker. He, by the way, has mentioned, in speaking about his sexual orientation, "we [gay men] keep on being what they call masculine in behavior." Identification of masculine stylistic traits would be a different study. But Almodóvar is a feminist and this film reflects the hope and the need for more progress as well as dramatic changes for women in Spain. As María Antonia García de León says, Almodóvar *"no tiene una visión androcéntrica"* ["does not have androcentric vision"].

Nor do I see macho control in *Women on the Verge of a Nervous Breakdown.* Almodóvar's presence is felt in his unique humor; in the wild series of significant surprises and incongruities; and in his signatures—taxis, telephones, television, not to mention the appearance of his mother and brother in minor roles. Also, we see *la Telefónica,* the Telephone Company building with its red clock, where Almodóvar once worked, from Pepa's terrace on Montalbán Street. Rather than dominating the audience, however, as Marvin D'Lugo discusses, he invites viewers' participation. As I have noted in this essay, Pedro Almodóvar offers suggestions in *Women on the Verge of a Nervous Breakdown*—a nativity scene with a Holy Family, parodic themes of Don Juan and of Hollywood comedies, Almagro Street, Ecce Homo, Azucena—for us to ponder beyond the visual images on the screen. After a laugh of recognition of his intentions, we collaborate in the gender messages.

Women on the Verge of a Nervous Breakdown, not a realistic comedy, reflects aspects of gender in contemporary society. Although Pepa's material comfort is Hollywood-like, her situation at the end of the film—a self-sufficient career woman who decides to become a single parent—symbolizes real advances in the "outward marks of freedom and independence" for women, mentioned by D'Lugo. But the macho is still there. As Spanish women have said to me, *"queda mucho camino para andar"* ["there remains a long road to walk"], and not only in Spain. Machismo or its residues may

be around in private lives and at work until women attain more "outward marks" of equality in societies, until they hold approximately half the decision-making positions, including those on the highest levels, for example. Meanwhile, machos are absurdly irrational, says Pedro Almodóvar, and rational women overcome their submission to them, as Pepa does.

Women on the Verge of a Nervous Breakdown is a story of emancipation from the macho. Pepa's independence and the epilogue, a nativity scene that undoes the patriarchal order, end the film with the hope that future generations will be able to laugh away machismo.

Brad Epps (essay date 1995)

SOURCE: "Figuring Hysteria: Disorder and Desire in Three Films of Pedro Almodóvar," in *Post-Franco, Postmodern: The Films of Pedro Almodóvar,* edited by Kathleen M. Vernon and Barbara Morris, Greenwood Press, 1995, pp. 99-124.

[*In the following essay, Epps discusses the use of hysteria in Almodóvar's* Labyrinth of Passions, What Have I Done to Deserve This? *and* Women on the Verge of a Nervous Breakdown.]

There is something at once mad and methodical about Pedro Almodóvar's films. Frenetic, effervescent, wild, and rapturous, they are also willful, deliberate, and self-conscious. They focus on dispersion, center on marginality, and concentrate on excess. They seem designed, almost systematically, to scandalize and trouble; they seem fixed, almost obsessively, on the movement of sexual desire. They are also, of course, framed largely around figures of femininity and homosexuality: figures subject, in Almodóvar's eyes, to nervous anxiety, emotional exhaustion, and flamboyant histrionics: to hysteria. Though most visibly "characterized" as women and gay men, these figures of hysteria function on a formal level as well, pointing to problems of stillness and mobility, placement and displacement, continuity and discontinuity, framing and figuration. Hysteria is, as Michel Foucault puts it, "indiscriminately mobile or immobile, fluid or dense, given to unstable vibrations or clogged by stagnant humors." Rife with paradox, hysteria signifies, if anything, a quandary of classification, "a crisis of signification." As such, it is an oddly adequate figure for Almodóvar's films, where comedy itself is open to dramatic revision. Hysteria, then, is of critical significance for matters of gender and sexuality, form and method, genre and style, and finally, given the problem of classification, socioeconomic class. In fact, while hysteria figures in all of Almodóvar's films, I have chosen to examine three that engage diverse cultural classes: transvestites, aristocrats, and terrorists in *Labyrinth of Passions;* the working class of cleaning women, taxi drivers, seamstresses, and prostitutes in *What Have I Done to Deserve This?;* and the privileged class of professionals, psychologists, fashion models, and commercial entertainers in *Women on the Verge of a Nervous Breakdown.* Together, and separately, these films suggest through the firm but fluid figures of hysteria, a methodical madness that I entertain as critical to Almodóvar's work.

Part of what makes hysteria so cinematically suggestive is the fact that it entails a gender- and class-coded method of acting and directing, a method virtually made for the camera. Though undeniably ancient, hysteria entered the age of modern technological control in Jean-Marie Charcot's union of (largely working-class) women and photography in late-nineteenth-century France. Photographing hysterical attacks in hypnotic, "alienated" women before an audience of doctors, students, and fashionable onlookers, Charcot transformed the lecture hall of the Salpêtrière into a showplace where entertainment at times overtook medical knowledge. All the while invoking documentary objectivity and scientific neutrality, Charcot set the stage where, as Elaine Showalter remarks, "female hysteria was perpetually presented, represented, and reproduced." Representation, of course, assumes many guises; and if the first "subjects" are preserved for posterity as silent and still, Dora, under the study of Freud, is subsequently scripted as hysteria's most (in)articulate actress, oscillating between the contrasting yet connected roles of victim and heroine, object and subject, even woman and man. An individual of economic privilege, Dora upstages, as it were, the poorer women of the Salpêtrière, just as Freud, the listener, prompter, and scriptor, overshadows his teacher Charcot, "the *visuel,* the seer." Thus plotted, hysteria itself seems to move from the clinician's amphitheater to the analyst's study; remaining something of a spectacle, it becomes less public and more private, more intimate, more perilously seductive. The psychotheatrical metaphors I have been employing are neither entirely ornamental nor accidental: Charcot's use of performative and iconographic devices; Freud's description of the unconscious as *ein anderer Schauplatz,* "another showplace"; and Joseph Breuer's patient Anna O's representation of daydreaming and desire as a "private theater" all indicate the profoundly histrionic dimension of hysteria itself. Hysteria may indeed be, as so many critics assert, a spectacular construction, an invention, and a "malady through representation"; but it is one in which Charcot's camera and Freud's script, the image and the word, play a crucial role. Only a principle of motion is lacking.

Motion is, after all, fundamental to hysteria. As a condition first characterized as "a pathological wandering of a restless womb," hysteria connotes instability and errancy, "unnatural" bodily movement. Its incredibly diverse symptoms include enervation and hyperactivity, mutism and babbling (often in other tongues), depression, hypochondria, convulsions, fainting spells, amnesia, and an array of acts and attitudes like bisexuality, masturbation, promiscuity, abstinence, and anxious sexual morality. For Freud, not surprisingly, "[t]he symptoms of the disease are nothing else than *the patient's sexual activity.*" That these patients are primarily female has important ramifications for the representation of gender and sexuality in Almodóvar's films, but it is the principle of motion that I want to stress here. For if photographs and words capture a sense of hysteria, it is the art of *motion* pictures that most fully represents it. Tracking its convulsions and ramblings, its starts and stops, film captures the kinetic quality of hysteria. Film holds, however ironically, the subtle slips, the furtive quirks, the flashes and lulls of the body. It not only shows the malady but exposes it to potentially endless speculation and study. While Freud may not employ cinematic devices in his work, there is nonetheless something telling about the affinity between the (dis)continuities of hysteria and film. Stanley Cavell, among others, notes the historical coincidence of psychoanalysis, born out of hysteria, and cinema, born out of photography, and further notes how both construe woman as a principal "problem" of knowledge and representation. Lynne Kirby, shifting the focus from female to male disorder, also acknowledges the connections between hysteria and film. For her, the moves of the hysterical and the filmic body are symptoms of broad social change and commotion. According to Kirby, "cultural displacement as massive as nineteenth-century mechanization and urbanization . . . made of its traumatized victims something like female hysterics."

This brief overview of the history of hysteria may seem beyond and beside Almodóvar. After all, from one fin de siècle to another, from modernity to postmodernity, much has changed: film has become smoother, psychoanalysis more cautious, sexuality more out in the open. Hysteria itself is now seen more as a metaphor than as a malady, more as a figure than as a fact. And yet, in Almodóvar's production of nervous, rattled women; in his depiction of passion, obsession, and repression; and in his self-reflective play with voice, body, image, and movement there lies, I believe, the historical residue of hysteria, its discourses, and its spectacles. Catherine Clément has declared that hysterics are outmoded figures, that they no longer exist, but it is just this that allows them, and their condition, to be restyled and reinvested, to be revamped as postmodern cinematic camp. Fundamental to hysteria and film, motion is fundamental to the *Movida* as well.

From his first full-length feature film, *Pepi, Luci, Bom and Other Ordinary Girls,* Almodóvar appears to have his hand on the pulse, and later the purse, of Spanish society. Making the best of his modest beginnings as a telephone worker, he exploits the humor implicit in the exaggeration, pastiche, and collapse of boundaries known as postmodernism. He markets, with increasing success, the giddiness of Spain's fledgling democracy, its heady entry into the European community, and the artfully commercial madness of the *Movida:* in short, what he himself has called the new Spanish mentality. As he puts it in a 1989 "self-interview" in the significantly titled *El Europeo:* "I am utterly ignorant of everything pertaining to geography and history." Though Almodóvar undoubtedly exaggerates his ignorance, he does so to get beyond the somber fixation on the Spanish Civil War that colored much cultural production under Franco. He asserts that he actively forgets the past in order to create in the present. Where Franco's order enforced propriety and obedience, Almodóvar's (dis)order, at least on the screen, appears to enforce nothing so much as its own dissolution.

Still, while Francoist censorship, conformity, and control seem to dissolve into something radically new and different, older constraints remain. I am referring not simply to the Catholic Church, the Opus Dei, or the police force, all restyled in Almodóvar's films, but to the system of capitalist exchange that frames, and fragments, the cinema as a whole. Constraining as it is, capitalism is also the condition of possibility of the style-conscious, fashion-oriented, trend-setting vision of Almodóvar: even, if not especially, when what is in style is grungy and disgusting (*cutre, guarro, y borde*), shocking and schlocky. The *Movida,* that boisterous movement of cultural and sexual experimentation in the late seventies and early eighties, is a marvel of marketing. Sex sells, particularly when repackaged according to, possibly as, the latest fad. This is not to deny the critical power of Almodóvar's work but to acknowledge the commercial power of cultural critique itself. More important, the tense movement between critique and commercialism may well be a peculiarly compelling mode of hysteria. In fact, if hysteria itself has been seen as a symptom of "the bourgeois value system of patriarchal authority and sexual asceticism," perhaps it is here, in the wake of father Franco, a symptom of the commodification of desire, its ceaseless conversion to capital. Perhaps, that is, hysteria signals not merely the law of desire but the law of the market.

FABULOUS FRAMES IN *LABYRINTH OF PASSIONS*

> In these hysterical, convulsive gestures . . . it would be difficult, not to say impossible, to guess that virility lay hid.
>
> —Baudelaire

Labyrinth of Passions opens with a stroll through the market: Cecilia Roth as Sexilia and Imanol Arias as Riza Niro wander through the Madrid flea market, the Rastro, shopping for the fullest and most appealing crotch. Sporting sunglasses, they cross paths but do not see each other until later, in a nightclub. Lovestruck, the two renounce their erratic,

erotic romps in the market of desire for heterosexual monogamy. This is "funny," that is to say, curious, because the very promiscuity and homosexuality that make this film "positively bristle with vibrant color and a wildly comic sexual energy" are plotted as pathological, as problems to be overcome. Passion may be labyrinthine, but it apparently needs to be set straight. This rectified coming-together of a man and a woman suggests a classical, all too classical, story; but so many comings and goings elsewhere suggest a story that is unabashedly modern. Almodóvar has called *Labyrinth of Passions* a "catalogue of modernities," a sort of initiation, or "baptism," into modern being. The film is a cult classic, its modernity not limited to an amalgamation of rock music, drugs, and sexual diversity; it derives as well from what John Hopewell describes as an artful and incongruent reelaboration of tradition. This is especially apparent in *What Have I Done to Deserve This?*, where the grandmother's insistent references to her village play off the equally insistent references to the urban sprawl of contemporary Madrid. In *Labyrinth of Passions,* however, the most elaborate reelaboration targets the clinic instead of the countryside. Medicine and, more important, psychoanalysis comprise the codes and traditions that Almodóvar reworks and, in many respects, ridicules. Homosexuality, nymphomania, incest, delusion, impotence, obsession, and sublimation figure prominently in the film and are related to psychic disorder, to hysterical trauma. Both Sexilia and Riza are explicitly designated as traumatized and as suffering from their passions, though Sexilia alone is highlighted as the patient to be analyzed and cured. Those presumably responsible for analysis and cure—be it the self-designated Lacanian psychoanalyst, Susana Díaz, or the eminent gynecologist, father of artificial insemination and of Sexilia—are themselves plagued with problems. Everyone, it seems, has either too much or too little sexual desire; everyone participates in the bedlam.

Volatile as they are, these roles are tethered to an extensive tradition of Freudian narration and interpretation, but a tradition become hackneyed and exhausted by popularization and overuse. The resulting tension between meaningful content and its exhaustion or evacuation, between the classical and the modern, is of course the perilously hackneyed mark of postmodernism, itself forever on the verge of breaking down. According to Jean Baudrillard, "the characteristic hysteria of our time" is a collapse of scandal and spectacle, a loss of distance between the viewer and the viewed, and an overproduction of difference that issues in total indifference. But hysteria is also a historical staging of scandal and spectacle, a reiteration of distance, and a classical production of difference in and against the feminine, or feminized, body. Almodóvar, professing to be ignorant of history, flirts with a rhetoric that is similar to Baudrillard's, but his dogged insistence on the sights and scenes of gender and sexual orientation keeps him from succumbing completely to it. If there is a hysteria characteristic of our time, Almodóvar sees it in fairly determinate characters and characterizations; and he does so despite—or rather because of—the crisis of representation that hysteria entails. As *Labyrinth of Passions* rushes to its close, Sexilia exclaims at least three times that she is hysterical (*histérica*). The fact that this word has become so widespread in present-day Spain as to designate virtually any feeling of exasperation, confusion, or impatience does not so much empty it of content as point to a curious success. Hysteria spills over into popular discourse, becomes trivial, banal, and common, so common that it can characterize anyone and everyone. Still, in Almodóvar's world it retains a special echo for women. In no way does this mean that men are not also hysterical, or that they do not also (dis)articulate themselves in such terms. But the male hysteric, acknowledged even by Charcot and Freud, raises some peculiarly prickly problems: he shifts, among other things, the matrix of speculation to include the body of the speculator himself.

The most spectacular male hysteric is not Riza but Fabio, played by Almodóvar's one-time punk rock partner, Fanny McNamara. Shortly after Riza and Sexilia stroll through the Rastro, Fabio, vampishly posed in the La Bobia café, takes a long, luxurious whiff of fingernail polish, surveys the potential pickings of desire, and exclaims to his companion: "No money, baby. No car, no 'girl,' no drugs, no vice, no rimmel. I'm hysterical" (*¡Estoy histérica!*). Referring to himself in the feminine, Fabio takes a popular expression—*estar histérico*—and utters it in a way that renders its uterine origins risible, that is to say, humorous. A female malady of "humoral imbalance," hysteria is, as we have seen, a principle of motion with serious restrictions. Fabio's mad humor, his hysteria, is thus not simply the ecstatic sign of tolerance and openness but also the exasperating sign of the persistence, albeit in different dress, of scarcity, need, and desire. He seems to intimate this, for he declares that he is *histérica* only after enumerating the things he lacks: money, a car, sex, drugs, vice, cosmetics. While the first two objects remain more elusive, the others are all around (on and in) him. Spotting Riza at a nearby table, Fabio writes him a note in lipstick, seals it with a kiss, and has the waiter deliver it. The note is a lispy, idiosyncratic piece of writing where s is x, f is ph, and that darling of gays, Elizabeth Taylor, is tacked onto the word for happiness: "Sí me guxtaría hacerte pheliz (taylor) exta tarde" (Yes, I'd like to make you happy this afternoon). The note is untranslatable because the style is as important as the message. In that respect it resembles Fabio's speech, an effusive, polyglot babble of Spanish, English, and French: "¡Qué overdose!," "lipstick," "moving on," "un shocking," "el libro des coiffeurs, de nuit et de jour, pour les femmes," and so on. As he walks up to Fabio's table, he addresses, again in the feminine, the audience of his seduction: "Hi, hi, everyone. I'm here again, but not for you." Someone in the crowd calls him *histérica,* thereby echoing what Fabio has already announced. Coming on the heels of his declaration of lack, need, desire, and hysteria, Fabio's seduction of Riza is flamboyant, public, and to the point.

There are, however, more subtle factors at work here. Fabio makes a spectacle of himself, but he does so in a space where consumerism remains intact (in Almodóvar's Rastro, barter is consumer kitsch). Accordingly, Fabio writes a note with borrowed lipstick, but the waiter requires that someone pay for its delivery. Fabio does not hesitate to say that Riza, the addressee, will pay; and, sure enough, he does. This is a telling moment of exchange, telling for the very reason that it seems so minor. To take a note from one table to another, the waiter charges 200 pesetas (around 2 dollars), an amount at once insignificant and exorbitant. It is exorbitant not only because the waiter could deliver the note free of charge but also because Fabio, seated only two tables away, could deliver it himself, could even forgo writing anything at all; and it is insignificant because Riza Niro is the heir to the throne of Tirán, a man accustomed to a life of "sex, luxury, and paranoia." Fabio's seduction of Riza is thus realized amid insignificance and exorbitance, scarcity and excess. Epistolary in form, it is economic in function: mediated by money, it promises a release of sexual energy, a satisfactory expenditure and exchange. It *promises* a release, but it never delivers it to the audience; we see Fabio cruise Riza, proposition him, and pick him up, but nothing more.

Something more specific than sexual discretion is involved in this refusal to show and deliver. Paul Julian Smith writes of the nagging disavowal of homosexual specificity in Almodóvar's work. Poses, propositions, and promises of gay encounters abound in this film, but nowhere does homosexual pleasure succeed in showing itself. The sex between Fabio and Riza, Sadec (Antonio Banderas) and Riza, can only be imagined, for it is not to be seen. The sex between Santi (Javier Grueso) and Riza is, in contrast, a visible failure: when we get a glimpse of homosexual pleasure, when we come close to seeing it, we must imagine instead that Riza is dreaming of Sexilia, that he cannot see himself with anyone but her. On screen, homosexuality reveals itself as desiring heterosexuality. Riza is thus not really gay, not are his flirtations and caresses with Fabio and Sadec sufficient signs to the contrary. And although the sex between Riza and Sexi also remains offscreen, it comes through loud and clear: in the final shot, over the image of an airplane in ascent, we hear, amid sighs and moans, their orgasmic voices. In fact, the most explicit sexual scene is the rape of Queti by her father. The most explicit sexual scene is, in other words, a scene of violence. In the visual economy of *Labyrinth of Passions,* incest, rape, and violence are shown to succeed while homosexuality and promiscuity are shown to fail. Thus, while Fabio coquettishly responds to Riza's description of the size of his room by saying, "better too much than too little," it appears that when it comes to showing certain things, and only certain things, less is indeed better than more.

The visual economy is based on the transactions between the seen and unseen, the scene and the ob-scene. For Jean-François Lyotard, this economy is violent not only in what it succeeds in showing but also in what it fails to show: "just as the libido must renounce its perverse overflow to propagate the species through a normal genital sexuality allowing the constitution of a 'sexual body' having that sole end, so the film produced by an artist working in a capitalist industry . . . springs from the effort to eliminate aberrant movements, useless expenditures, differences of pure consumption." Tying sexual renunciation to economic restriction, repression to oppression, Lyotard questions what is at stake in such basic cinematic techniques as framing, decoupage, montage, and mise-en-scène. Exclusions, effacements, and forced unifications underwrite, as Lyotard observes, cinematic production. The result is a type of enclosure, where the norms of representation dovetail the norms of social reality. Subversion and disorder may be represented, that is, but they are represented as part of a tenacious, perhaps inevitable, order of control, authorship, and direction. This is especially important in the case of a director, or *auteur,* like Almodóvar, whose films have been seen, with good reason, as "anarchic and irreverent," as part of "a fast-paced revolt that relentlessly pursues pleasure rather than power, and a postmodern erasure of all repressive boundaries and taboos." Without disputing the spirit of such views, I want to focus on how the sexual exuberance of the labyrinth of passions is at the same time the effect of restriction, how pleasure is bound to power. It is here, again, that hysteria proves to be cinematically productive. Fabio's erratic movements and fitful speech designate him as a singularly hysterical subject, one who resists the established order even as he is an effect of that order. This tension between resistance and restriction is crucial to hysteria and leads to a number of violent figurations. Such is the hysteria that Lyotard figures as a quasi-lethal *jouissance* and Lacan figures as a fragmented body, as an aggressive, Bosch-like disjunction of form and fantasy. Such is the hysteria that Almodóvar figures, and frames, as an instance of power.

Of all the characters who populate Almodóvar's film, Fabio is the most intemperate and intractable, the campy cock of the walk, the queen of artifice and bad taste: spectacular, scandalous, hysterical. He signifies, in Susan Sontag's terms, "the sensibility of failed seriousness," "the theatricalization of experience," and "the convertibility of 'man' and 'woman,'" and in Lyotard's terms, disorder, flippancy, and flashy, nonreproductive pleasure. Enacting femininity as an aggressively masculine (im)posture and (dis)possession, Fabio signifies the persistence of a desire that does not recognize itself in the mirror of reproduction, a love that dare

not see its image. And yet, it is just this image of daring that makes Fabio so special, so much a challenge for Almodóvar. Fabio first appears in the Rastro, negotiating sex with Riza. He next appears not writhing in bed with Riza but writhing under a power drill and a camera, posing for a sado-masochistic photonovel or, as he calls it, a "foto porno sexi killer." In the move from the Rastro to the photography studio, from a scene of seduction to a scene of violence, the sexual act is lost: offscreen, ob-scene. Or rather, the sexual act is lost as anything but a violent simulacrum. To underscore this, Almodóvar himself enters the picture. As he tells the photographer what to do, he shouts to Fabio, "Enjoy it, enjoy it more, you desire this drill so much. Yeah, yeah, try to like it. You like the way it tastes, say more: 'I deserve it.'" What Fabio has done to deserve this is perhaps the subject of the photonovel, but the subject of this scene is filmmaking itself. Almodóvar directs Fabio to enact a violent ecstasy, to desire his own destruction before the camera. He exposes the theater of hysteria as a theater of model violence.

According to Almodóvar, "in every film there is always a moment when something must be done and there is no one to do it. That's where I come in. Specifically, in *Labyrinth of Passions* the scene was with Fabio." The critical moment for Almodóvar, the moment when the problem of direction caroms into the problem of representation, occurs with Fabio in the role of victim, not seducer. Fabio, Almodóvar declares, is marvelous, but he lacks control: he (mis)places himself; he threatens to slide off-frame and to slip offscreen; he says things that are funny and witty, yet inessential and imprecise; he acts and forgets everything, even, or especially, that he is acting. Against Fabio, then, comes Almodóvar, the director, placing himself directly in the scene to ensure the proper place, the essential speech, the precise movement, of Fabio. In-frame, onscreen, the director controls and commands: in a word, he authorizes. And central to his authority is the centralizing pull of the camera, the force of the frame. Faced with the possibility of an oblivious, babbling, errant actor, and hence with the possibility of a scandalously inchoate (non)spectacle, Almodóvar intervenes to reinforce, in his own terms, the frame or limit that allows the show to go on.

Almodóvar's onscreen appearances recall those of Alfred Hitchcock, although, according to Almodóvar, his interventions are performative, whereas Hitchcock's are merely figurative. And yet, Almodóvar's role entails nothing less than the authoritative figuration of Fabio, himself in danger of disfiguration and disappearance, a hyperperformance that dislocates the scene, disregards the audience, and disrupts basic cinematic standards. What is so ironic about this authoritative figuration of Fabio is that it is focused on disfiguration: Almodóvar intervenes not merely to guarantee that Fabio does not disfigure the scene, script, and film by sliding offcamera, but also to guarantee that Fabio is himself disfigured. The trouble with this is that the authoritative (dis)figuration of Fabio, appealing as it does to hysterical trauma, is at one and the same time the (dis)figuration of an image of femininity and of male homosexuality. Almodóvar makes trouble, is in trouble, directs and performs it, by exposing the violent power of limits and frames. His relationship with Fabio—Fanny is in this sense critical. For insofar as Fabio plays across the boundaries of gender and sets hysteria wandering in masculinity, he evokes the dream of an unframed imagination. He evokes, that is, the explosion of the limits of representation, the ecstasy of the cinema. Of course, to evoke such ecstasy he must, paradoxically, be contained.

Just as the persistence of lack or scarcity enables desire, so the persistence of constraints enables "anarchic and irreverent" representations. Transvestism, camp, and drag, all the signs of Fabio's wildness, are as much the effects of a constraining system of gender as they are its *mise-en-critique*. "Paradoxically," writes Marjorie Garber, "the male transvestite represents the extreme limit case of 'male subjectivity,' 'proving' that he is male against extraordinary odds." Camp and drag are likewise compromised, sadly relying on sexual identities even as they seem to undo them. Fabio's own undoing is "sad" in part because it is played for fun: as if the only figure who could be so violently disfigured and still remain "comical" had to be hysterical, gay, and a transvestite. While this may be read as a sign of Almodóvar's complicity in a system of established representation, it may also be read as a sly exposure of the pain underlying representation itself, particularly when it comes to so-called minor and marginal subjects. In this film of happy heterosexuality, it is after all with Fabio, not with Sexi and Riza, that Almodóvar comes out as a performer, not just as a singer in a nightclub but as a director. Staging hysteria in a sexually charged theater, showing it to be a spectacle under direction, and framing and cutting it as violence, Almodóvar keeps it, and his film, on the move.

DOMESTIC DUELS: *WHAT HAVE I DONE?* AND *WOMEN ON THE VERGE*

The hysterical fit is an equivalent of coitus.

—Freud

Keeping women hysterically on the move is what *What Have I Done to Deserve This?* and *Women on the Verge of a Nervous Breakdown* are all about. More centered than *Labyrinth of Passions* on heroines, homes, and work, these two films are in many respects just as hectic. Although they limit transvestites and rock musicians to advertisements on television, and banish royalty altogether, *What Have I Done?* and *Women on the Verge* buzz with everything from murder and suicide to telekinesis, burning beds, and shoot-outs. Amid all this activity, they make a compelling pair: united

and separated, as dark to light, down to up, misery to luxury. What pairs these two films is not merely the figure of Carmen Maura in contemporary Madrid but a sense of frustration, entrapment, and imminent collapse. Both Gloria and Pepa, both the working-class woman from the overcrowded Barrio de la Concepción and the professional woman from the elegant Barrio de Chamberí, rush madly across the screen, working out and against the memory of men. Popping pills and brandishing everything from ham bones to telephones, Gloria, Pepa, (and Carmen) illustrate the emotional versatility of hysteria, at once funny and sad. And yet, if their nervous condition seems to make them sisters in emotional arms, they belong to different socioeconomic contexts. In other words, the signs of cinematic hysteria do not signal a feminine uniformity, or universality, beyond class difference. Even the body of Carmen Maura, functioning as an essentialist lure, as the real beneath the role, is contextually sensitive and continually othered as acted. Pepa, as commercial celebrity, glamorizes Maura and markets hysteria as post-modern slapstick, while Gloria, as domestic servant, works Maura into a market where hysteria is melodramatic and glamour is always for someone else. Keeping in mind the interplay between these two films, between Pepa and Gloria, I want to examine some of the ties between economic class, the psychosexual body, and hysteria.

What Have I Done to Deserve This? is torn between confusion and exasperation. Its title in Spanish, *¿Qué he hecho yo para merecer esto!*, begins with an inverted question mark and ends with an exclamation mark. This detail is frequently overlooked in reviews and critiques of the film, particularly in English. I follow the tendency to pose the title as a question rather than as an emphatic declaration, but it is nonetheless significant that something, from the very outset, is either missed or eliminated. The difficulty of processing so many details engenders a sense of conflict, exhaustion, and loss. In *What Have I Done?* much is indeed missing and lost, much unnoticed. Antonio (Angel de Andrés López), Gloria's husband, does not notice that his son Miguel has left home; the exhibitionist does not notice that Cristal (Verónica Forqué), Gloria's prostitute friend and neighbor, has remained unmoved by his self-proclaimed sexual prowess; and the police do not notice that Gloria, her face visibly bruised, has murdered her husband. Men, in this film, seem especially—though by no means exclusively—oblivious to what is, and is not, before them. And yet, for all that, it is Gloria who is repeatedly designated as oblivious to her surroundings. When Gloria cannot find her watch or her "minilips" (pep pills), her mother-in-law (Chus Lampreave) shakes her head and says, "I don't know where you've got your head"; when she burns the chicken, her husband snaps, "Fuck, you're never where you should be" ("Joder, nunca estás en lo que estás"). Almodóvar has said that no one notices her, but that is not quite the case. Others do notice her. But what they notice about Gloria, when they notice her, is that she is forgetful, unmindful, scattered, and distracted; what they find, when they find her, is a woman lost. Among the missing signs of *What Have I Done to Deserve This?* is its central character.

To the eyes of those around her, Gloria is like a blank screen. To the spectator's eyes, however, she is the figure who most visibly fills the screen, its center. This figure that fills the screen as a blank screen for other figures presents a perceptual problem. Gloria is seen, by the spectator, as a woman not seen. She therefore remains the object of the spectator's gaze, but an object that is largely missed by other objects of the gaze (i.e., the other characters). This "missing" is, furthermore, closer to pure failure than to feeling. For example, if Antonio misses Gloria, it is not because he feels her to be missing from his life. The missing that is felt, and that undergirds and motivates desire, Antonio reserves for Frau Müller (Katia Loritz), his former employer in Germany. Antonio misses Frau Müller, feels her absence, and longs for her presence; but he misses Gloria, fails to acknowledge her, let alone long for her, even when he is having sex with her. Almodóvar underscores this failure of feeling in a most economical way. As Gloria asks Antonio for money to pay the bills, he grabs her, kisses her neck, and throws her onto the bed. She continues to tell him that she needs money, and the scene cuts abruptly to a program on television: a sort of Andalusian burlesque show in which Almodóvar sings to Fanny McNamara in drag. The song he sings, or rather mouths, is Miguel Molina's "La bien pagá" ("The Well-Paid Woman"), a song whose lyrics provide an ironic commentary to the goings-on in the bedroom: "I don't owe you anything, I don't ask anything from you, forget me already . . . I don't love you, don't love me." With the song winding down, the scene cuts back to Gloria, still clothed on the bed. She is smiling, but her smile soon fades because Antonio, utterly inattentive to her pleasure, has evidently climaxed. There is yet another cut, this time to the grandmother, singing along with the television: "Well-paid, well-paid, well-paid, woman, you were." Gloria, needless to say, is not well-paid, on any account; not only does Antonio not give her the money she requests, he does not give her anything (pleasure, attention, respect) at all. Put simply, Antonio sets Gloria at naught, having sex not with her but through her. When he seems to desire her most, he misses her.

Gloria is in many respects missing from the desire of others. While the encounter with Antonio in the bedroom is quietly brutal, the most poignant instance of Gloria's disjunction from desire occurs in Cristal's apartment. There, as Cristal has sex with a man, Gloria sits by, the voyeuristic presence that Cristal's client requires for his stimulation. She is an imperfect voyeur, however, for just as she is scarcely noticed by others, here she, in turn, scarcely notices what is going on beside her. Far from being excited or disgusted, Gloria is merely exhausted. Her body slouched, her face fallen, her eyes empty, her thoughts presumably elsewhere, she appears utterly estranged from the sexual activity in which Cristal is engaged. Then again, Cristal herself appears estranged. Distant from desire, she looks at her fingernails as the man on top of her asks if she is coming. She says yes, but her tone suggests boredom, even exasperation. Cristal, of course, is acting out a routine that earns her money, not pleasure. So seen, she is as much a working woman as Gloria, but with a number of important differences. She is single; she has no children; she sets her own conditions; and she is relatively solvent, feeding Gloria's children when Gloria cannot. The putatively well-paid woman, she extends and alters the earlier bedroom scene with Gloria and Antonio. Cristal is to Gloria as prostitution is to matrimony: similar yet different. Almodóvar is indebted to such well-established topics as the whore with a heart of gold and the frustrated housewife, but he invests them with a blend of humor and sadness that keeps them from being either flip or maudlin. This is a difficult blend, to be sure, for as Gloria sits drained and distracted, more attentive to her husband's arrival than to the commotion beside her, she fiddles with a newly purchased curling iron. The phallic charge of this instrument of feminine beauty is evident, vulgarly so, and indicates that Gloria's place in the order of desire may be one of displacement but not of exemption or exteriority. With Cristal and client next to her, and a curling iron in her hands, Gloria remains in a phallic economy even as she is beside it.

The curling iron functions as a Freudian joke, undercutting Gloria's somberly detached mood. It is yet another nod to a store of psychoanalytic images and instruments whose hermeneutic force has been popularized, like hysteria itself, to the point of banality. But it also has a function that is formal. Gloria's curling iron does not merely bind together the two scenes in which it figures directly; through the play of similitude, it indirectly binds together an array of scenes. Similar objects include kendo poles, mops and brooms, a rough wooden stick (the grandmother's staff), a ham bone, and a boom microphone. The film opens with a shot of Almodóvar's camera crew in a city square. Gloria traverses this space, and as she does so a sound man follows her with a microphone on a long black boom. She turns once, twice, as if menaced by the microphone, and enters a karate studio. The titles begin to roll and are intercut with shots of men practicing kendo. They wear black gowns and masks of metal mesh, hop forcefully around a room, and lunge first at the camera and then at each other with long bamboo poles. As they lunge, they emit a series of guttural shouts, ending in a lone bloodcurdling scream. The scene then cuts to Gloria cleaning the dressing rooms. A naked man enters a shower stall, and motions to her to come. She obeys, and once she is inside the shower with him, he embraces her. As the water drenches them, they have, or seem to have, sex: seem to, because it is later revealed that the man is impotent. Straightening her hair and her dress, Gloria exits the shower. To the mounting strains of a German song, Gloria grabs a kendo pole and lashes out at the air. A cut follows, visual not auditory, to Antonio singing along to the same song that has punctuated Gloria's rendition of kendo. The song expresses Antonio's nostalgic attachment to Frau Müller as well as Gloria's sexual and emotional frustration. It is replayed several times in the course of the film, and although it is most closely connected with Antonio, it is also, as the opening scene indicates, connected with Gloria, or more precisely with Gloria in the act of striking out. Later, of course, Gloria will wield not a kendo pole but a ham bone, and she will strike not the air but Antonio. But here, already, Almodóvar has made effective use of the interplay of sound and image. Having established a link between sound and a menacing phallic object (the boom microphone dogs her here as the song does later), he underscores the link by replaying it in a growing chain of sounds and visual objects. This complex audiovisual chain is no joking matter, for when Gloria holds the curling iron, she holds not just something sexual but something violent.

The links between sex and violence in *What Have I Done?* are subtly, even elegantly, cinematic. This is ironic because the story is itself rather sordid. The failed writer Lucas (Gonzalo Suárez) articulates the links between elegant form and sordid content when he tells Cristal that what he wants from her is "an elegant, sophisticated, and well-worn sadism like one sees in French movies." Cristal is unable to comply, not through any failing of her body but through a failing of her accessories. In an attempt to satisfy her client's sadomasochistic request for a thrashing with a leather whip that she does not possess, Cristal goes to Gloria. What Gloria offers her is not a whip but the grandmother's wooden stick. Taking it firmly in her hands and giving yet another powerful lunge, Gloria remarks, "you could even kill him with this." Her actions are underscored with the sound of sirens, with the insistent urban music of ambulances or police cars. The stick is in fact later examined by the police as a possible murder weapon; but here, in this prelude to sophisticated sadomasochism, Cristal takes it, rubs it, and notes with a wink how big it is. Cristal's thoughts are sexual while Gloria's are violent, and together they implicitly invest the object with the image of sexual violence.

The ramifications of such a combination are unsettling, so much so that Lucas promptly rejects the stick as too rough and rustic. Lucas's own combination of sex and violence relies on a principle of delicacy that is more in line with Roland Barthes than the Marquis de Sade. Lucas is not, as Cristal points out, a true sadist but a mime or simulator. The form of elegance he desires does not admit breaches between model (French porno films) and copy, at least when the copy is visibly modified by scarcity, when ideal whips are replaced by rough sticks. Lucas desires, that is, an elegance whose form is one of explicit correspondence, blatant mimesis: an

elegance where artifice replicates artifice. That is why Lucas is a failure as an artist and, I might add, why he serves as a counterpart to Almodóvar. For unlike Lucas, Almodóvar does not make artistic subtlety depend on the occultation of scarcity, sordidness, and need; he does not make formal elegance depend on the representation of elegant objects. In fact, Almodóvar's success may well lie in his ability to communicate what others, like Lucas, find comfortably contradictory: the elegance of sordidness and the sordidness of elegance.

Sordid objects and elegant optics: *What Have I Done?* is carefully crafted neorealism. Almodóvar acknowledges the similarities between his film and the neorealist films of Roberto Rossellini, Fernando Fernán Gómez, and Marco Ferreri, but he is careful to note that the similarities are more on the level of intention than of production and mise-en-scène. While he maintains that *What Have I Done?* has a clear political position typical of neorealist cinema, he stresses the film's dark humor and artificiality. Eighty percent of the film is shot in a studio, not on location or in the street, as is customary with "true" neorealism. For Almodóvar, true neorealism is false insofar as it denies its technical bases and naturalizes its artifice. In contrast to the neorealists, when Almodóvar takes to the street, it is to display his artistry, not to hide it. I am referring to the window-shopping scene where the curling iron first appears. It is an eminently commercial scene in which objects assume a striking ascendancy. Gloria and Juani walk along the street, passing a flower shop, a cosmetics shop, and an appliance shop. The camera follows them, but from inside the shops, not outside. Sutured so that it flows quite effortlessly, this sequence of traveling, or tracking, shots turns the tables on consumerism, showing the two shoppers to be the objects behind the glass, the consumers to be consumed.

It is in this exchange of objects and sights that Gloria and Juani consider the curling iron. "What a luxury," sighs Gloria, her eyes filled with desire for the curling iron, for the image of a more beautiful self. Gloria, as the spectator-buyer of the curling iron, sees and buys an image of herself. For John Berger, this specular, speculative dynamic is characteristic of the self in capitalism: "the publicity image steals her love of herself as she is, and offers it back to her for the price of the product." For Gloria, the price of the product is her son Miguel, whom she "sells" to a dentist in order to have the money for such a necessary luxury (as well as for rent, gas, electricity, and food). The iron is thus ridiculously rich with meaning: an instrument of beauty, a symbol of the phallus, a sign of displaced violence, a replacement for her son, a lure for her "self," a reservoir of desire, and a not so simple commodity. But more than the curling iron is at stake here; it is the way Almodóvar plays with the objects of vision that makes this scene so valuable. Reversing a naturalized order, he has us see Gloria from inside the space of commerce, an object among objects. Objects are, as Almodóvar says, "the only witnesses of her life." If Gloria is not noticed, it is in part because objectification no longer issues from other subjects but from other objects.

Watching Gloria through shop windows, ovens, washing machines, and refrigerators, we see her in a consumerist relation that is markedly different from that of Pepa in *Women on the Verge*. For while Pepa is a consummate consumer, impetuously disposing of material possessions, continuously changing her clothes, renting and retaining her penthouse, promoting household products on television, marketing her voice and her image, Gloria is consumed by her inability to consume. According to Almodóvar, she desires not the overturn of capitalism but its opening and expansion, its accommodating embrace. Frustrated in her consumerism, she is given to a kind of nervous consumption, an exasperating depletion of energy. Pepa pops downers to help her relax; Fabio sniffs nail polish to help him cruise; Gloria pops uppers (when she can get them) and sniffs dishwashing liquid to get her through her household chores. Rushing from one unsatisfying job to another and then home, she is both overworked and underemployed. She is not, at any rate, "unemployed" or "unoccupied" in the discreetly bourgeois sense that Breuer and Freud discuss as conducive to hysteria. She may suffer from "[t]he monotonous family existence without a corresponding psychic labor for the unused excess of psychic activity and energy," but neither her monotony nor her labor is that of Breuer's and Freud's typically well-heeled patients. Gloria does not "disburden" herself "through the continuous work of her phantasy" any more than she exacerbates her nervous condition through "habitual day-dreaming." In fact, far from exercising her fantasy, Gloria continuously works her body to the bone. This does not mean that she has neither the time nor the energy to be hysterical, but that hysteria itself has become, under the influence of Freud, a construction in which working-class women (and men) are in large measure missed or left unnoticed. Reversing this trend, Jan Goldstein reminds us that "the hysterics of the Salpêtrière were not bourgeois women, living within the framework of a bourgeois value system, but urban working-class women—seamstresses, laundresses, domestic servants, flower sellers." Gloria, an urban working-class woman at the end of a different century, is similarly engaged, similarly seen and missed. She may go routinely unnoticed by the people around her, yet when they do notice her, she seems flighty, volatile, and flustered: in a word, hysterical.

When, if, and how Gloria is noticed, or not, is not just a function of time and energy (repetition, routine, endurance, exhaustion) but also of space. Gloria occupies a space that is neither wildly orgasmic like Fabio's nor comfortably fashionable like Pepa's. Instead, for most of the film she inhabits a darkly domestic space whose closure the camera, largely stationary, emphasizes. Within such dim, claustrophobic surroundings, without payment or recognition, Gloria cooks, cleans, washes, and serves. A maid or charwoman outside her house, she is the same inside, except that she is also a wife and mother. The film deliberately shuffles these roles—mother and maid, housewife and charwoman—and in the process places work inside and outside of the house on the same footing. This is the context for Gloria's "nervous condition," a context and condition that Cristal articulates as follows: "She's a little hysterical, but the poor woman has two kids and spends her life working all day as a maid." Cristal's assessment is echoed by Gloria's mother-in-law and son, among others. When Gloria snaps at the grandmother, the latter responds: "Gloria, calm down, or you're going to have a breakdown." And when she offers her son a diet pill to stave off his hunger, he responds, "no, it makes me nervous; look how you are." In this close, dark, cold house where money is the name of a pet lizard (Dinero), Gloria moves, murders, and contemplates suicide. The murder itself is dramatically filmed, though quickly dedramatized in the "murder" of Money (the pet lizard), the bumblings of the police (the chief inspector is the impotent seducer of the early shower scene), the telekinetic remodeling of the kitchen, and the departure of Toni and the grandmother for the ironically idealized village. The most dramatic, or rather melodramatic, moment occurs at the very end, when Gloria returns to an empty, only partially remodeled house. Drained and despondent, she finds no calm liberation in solitude. Instead, approaching a state of emotional vacancy, beyond hysteria, Gloria goes out onto the balcony of her apartment, leans forward into a brighter, more open space, and signals a suicide that the return of her son Miguel prevents. In what may well be the film's most troubling line, Miguel announces: "This house needs a man." Gloria, after all she has so richly not deserved, after all she has so somberly resisted, after the violent elimination of "her" man, seems to agree. *What Have I Done?* ends where *Women on the Verge* begins.

Carmen Maura as Pepa utters her first lines in *Women on the Verge of a Nervous Breakdown* over a close-up shot of a scale-model building (a maquette), a cardboard sun, and the sound of quacking ducks. As is so often the case in this film, the voice does not accompany the image. It thereby announces, on the level of form, a split or separation that it affirms on the level of content. Pepa speaks, in the past tense and from someplace out of frame, of separation and splitting, absence and abandonment. She had been abandoned by her partner Iván (Fernando Guillén), an aging Don Juan with a golden voice. With his departure, she says, the world seemed to collapse around her. She struggled to save herself and her world, bound up as they were in her relationship, but to no avail. Feeling like a modern-day Noah, she set up a coop for ducks and chickens on the terrace of her penthouse, preparing herself, symbolically, for the loneliness of the flood. These past events are then depicted on screen—

unfolded, as it were, from a point of view after the flood. The film suggests a subtle circularity, then, with the final scene of Pepa and Marisa on the terrace—talking about sex, love, virginity, maternity, and feminine independence—providing a clue as to the possible site of the film's opening enunciation. Ending with a sort of bedraggled feminist triumph (women do not need men), *Women on the Verge* nonetheless opens with a house, and a woman, in need of a man. This need and its overcoming structure the body of the filmic narrative. Centered in Pepa, it is played out in a number of other women: in Candela (María Barranco), an Andalusian model suffering from betrayal by a man who turns out to be a Shiite terrorist; in Marisa (Rossy de Palma), the brusque, domineering, virginal fiancée of a man who falls for Candela; in Lucía (Julieta Serrano), the pistol-wielding, clinically insane first wife of Iván; in Paulina (Kiti Manver), the so-called feminist lawyer who insults Pepa and is going to run off with Iván to Sweden; and finally, in Vienna (Joan Crawford), the strong-willed entrepreneur who is saved by Johnny (Sterling Hayden) in Nicholas Ray's *Johnny Guitar*. These women vary significantly: they are of different ages and professions; they are even of different realities (the *mise-en-abîme* of a film within a film). But they all have one thing in common: they are all, to varying degrees of nervousness, in need of men.

The need for a man has long been posited as crucial to hysteria. As Beret Strong styles it, "[t]he hysteric is a woman in search of a man." The womb wanders, or so the story goes, but it does so in part out of unfulfilled desire, improperly channeled erotic energy, prolonged abstinence, and "amorous ardor." With respect to men, hysteria is frequently associated with emasculation and symbolic castration, with the lack of, and need for, what ostensibly makes a man a man. For better and for worse, Sexilia, Riza, and Fabio in the market of desire, no less than Gloria in the market of self-image, gravitate around things phallic. While what is at stake may ultimately be more a question of need—and of course of desire—in general than of object choice in particular, heterosexual women and homosexual men do seem to be particularly susceptible to the plays of hysteria. And yet, as the reference in *What Have I Done?* to Elia Kazan's 1960's psychomelodrama, *Splendor in the Grass,* suggests, even nice straight boys like Warren Beatty can become faint and silly when they do not have what they want, what they supposedly need. Sexual repression and renunciation, those mainstays of morality, are hence deeply implicated in the nosology of hysteria. In the words of Charles Bernheimer, "the psychological understanding of hysteria was born in complicity with moral condemnation of its victims"; or in the words of Beret Strong, "[t]he weak body appears to spread the contagion of its faulty integrity to the hysteric's morality." This moral specter, mobilizing problems of agency, responsibility, guilt, and choice, haunts *What Have I Done?* in its very title. In *Women on the Verge,* moral dilemmas are unquestionably less pressing (murder, forgery, prostitution, and the "education" of children are absent), but they continue in the guise of problems such as fidelity, honesty, and solidarity. In other words, the hysterical fixation on, and need for, a man in *Women on the Verge* runs up against the need for friendship and self-respect. Pepa comes back from the border of a nervous breakdown when she realizes, through a classically heroic act (she saves Iván from murder), that her needs need not be mediated through a man.

At the very end of the film, Pepa returns home to a house in shambles, steps over broken glass and a slew of sleeping bodies, goes out onto the terrace, and has a quiet conversation with Marisa. Unlike Gloria, Pepa contemplates not suicide but the beauty of the city under a starry sky. Never mind that both city and sky are a painted backdrop, that they are, as the film's final song indicates, "pure theater," Pepa is able to appreciate them anyway. Marisa is drowsy but luminous, and tells Pepa that she has had an intensely erotic dream in which she has lost her virginity by herself, without any real need for a man. Pepa, in turn, tells Marisa that she is pregnant, but that she will have the baby alone. Envisioning a house without a man and a child without a father, Pepa appears fatigued but content and calm. This exchange of confidences among women is indeed the calmest communication in the film. So much else is only partly communicated, or miscommunicated, or not communicated at all. Pepa and Iván play phone tag for two days, always just missing or, in Iván's case, just avoiding, the other. The telephone itself, indelibly associated with Almodóvar's job at the phone company, assumes an irksome preeminence, simultaneously denying and affirming separation. A voice in a machine is at times all that remains of human contact. In *Women on the Verge,* telephones, microphones, loudspeakers, answering machines, tape recorders, and sound tracks, far from helping people to connect, bring them apart. One of the most acutely cinematic disconnections is that of body and voice, a fact that Almodóvar exploits without marring the film's smooth Hollywood mood. Acknowledging a blend of formal experimentation and commercialism, Almodóvar has said that the film owes much to the comedies of Billy Wilder but that its origins are to be found in Jean Cocteau's *La voix humaine (The Human Voice)*. Cocteau's piece is an experimental monologue that is performed in part by Carmen Maura, as the transsexual Tina, in *The Law of Desire.* As Pepa in *Women on the Verge,* Maura acts considerably less tortured, but here, too, she waits anxiously for the phone to ring: rushing to it, screaming at it, and at one point throwing it out the window, breaking it as she herself is breaking down. The telephone is for Pepa a curious object of desire, frustration, and anger. As such, it recalls Iván, promising communication but not delivering it. When it is repaired, it hardly matters: Pepa's conversation with Marisa is not only without a man, it is without a machine.

Communication can have hysterical consequences. Along with the convulsions, fainting spells, and swings of emotion classically tied to hysteria are problems of communication: aphasia, mutism, babble, uncontrolled polyglotism, and so on. These problems are not confined to the hysterical body, however, but to the plays and replays of desire, knowledge, and language between bodies: doctor and patient, analyst and analysand, and man and woman. Almodóvar makes effective use of these problems from early on in the film. We hear Pepa before we see her, and we hear Iván before we see him. His voice is joined not to a body but to a script. And as he says, "Pepa, darling, I don't ever want to hear you say 'I'm unhappy,'" the image on the screen is a close-up of the handwritten, multicolored gloss to the preprinted list of songs that includes the song, circled for good effect, "Soy infeliz." Writing is spoken, speech is written, but what is signified is a telling desire for silence or deafness: "I never want to *hear* you say 'I'm unhappy.'" Iván spends the greater part of the film not hearing, not wanting to hear, Pepa say that she is unhappy. When he does finally offer to listen, after Pepa has saved his life, again, as with the repaired telephone, it hardly matters: Pepa no longer cares to tell him. But before, she had cared too much, so much that Iván is the stuff of her dreams.

What follows Iván's statement of deaf desire is the only dream sequence in Almodóvar's work. The dream is entered by way of three close-ups: an alarm clock ringing, a black-and-white photograph of Pepa and Iván (their first visual appearance, colorless and static), and Pepa asleep in bed (the brightly colored fabric of her pajamas contrasting sharply with the black-and-white frame of photograph and dream). The dream itself is filmed in misty black and white, and consists of a leisurely stroll by Iván, microphone in hand, past a dazzling gallery of women: Spanish, Nordic, Arabic, African, American, Asian. Iván does not speak so much to the women as into the microphone, narcissistically absorbed in the mellowness of his own voice. His remarks are trite and trivial declarations of insincere love, as airy as the wind heard in the background. The scene ends with a woman scoffing at his claim to "accept her just the way she is." The dream lays bare a number of communicative problems, but it is when the film becomes self-referential that these problems really come to the fore.

As black and white dissolves into bright red—first a light, then something like the sun—Iván makes his first true-color appearance. He appears, significantly fragmented: an extreme close-up of his lips against a microphone. He slowly licks his lips and begins to speak. "How many men have you forgotten?" he asks, then, after a pause, "tell me something nice." He speaks in Spanish, of course, but the words are not his. For as soon as he asks to hear something nice (not something unhappy), there is a cut, not to the figure of Carmen Maura but of Joan Crawford. Iván is dubbing Ster-

ling Hayden's part in *Johnny Guitar,* a film that enjoys almost a cult following in Spain. *Johnny Guitar* is, among other things, a campy melodrama, a western with a female lead. At its center is the story of a failed love affair and a woman's attempt at achieving success on her own. Crawford, as Vienna, plays a strong, swaggering character who nonetheless needs the real strength of a real man. Hayden, as Johnny, is that man, and he saves Vienna's life. The scene that Iván is dubbing is certainly the most successful in Ray's film, but it is also crucial to Almodóvar's. In it, in the original, a man feeds a woman lines, scripts her words to suit his pleasure. "Lie to me, tell me all these years you've waited, tell me," and then, "tell me you'd have died if I hadn't come back," and finally, "tell me you still love me like I love you." Truth, it seems, is engendered in lies and repetition, in one saying what the other wants to hear and then hearing it as one's own. Vienna reacts to Johnny's request first with violent derision, then with true confession: "Once I would have crawled at your feet to be near you. I searched for you in every man I met. I have waited for you, Johnny. What took you so long?" In *Johnny Guitar* this communicative exchange and emotional change lead to a happy Hollywood ending, to Johnny and Vienna walking off arm in arm. But in **Women on the Verge,** it is significantly altered. Iván dubs Johnny, doubles his artificiality, and exposes himself as a cinematic product. What is more, he dubs him without hearing anyone but himself. He experiences, in a sense, a troubling powerful male fantasy: Joan Crawford flashes across the screen, moves her lips, and keeps silent— a woman beautiful, desirable, mute. Pepa is not there to dub Vienna, but asleep in bed. The image of her sleeping, dreaming body cuts the dubbing scene, but Iván does not miss a beat. He does not need Pepa to do the scene; he needs only himself.

Pepa also plays the scene alone, but she is not as independent and distanced as her former partner. For when she speaks Vienna's lines (back) to Johnny, she is unhappily hearing Iván. Unlike Iván, Pepa is pictured wearing a hefty set of headphones. His voice surrounds her, separating her from everything else. As a guitar softly begins to play, the camera focuses on the red light of a movie projector and gradually moves back to show the black celluloid strip running through. The frontal shot changes into an aerial shot, and the camera follows the light that streams out of the projector, over the seated figure of Germán, the director of the dubbing, and toward Pepa, standing before the screen. She begins to dub, first with her voice in off, then in synchronization with Crawford's image. She tells Johnny (Iván) what he wants to hear, Vienna's truth as well as her own. She tells him that she is waiting and dying for his love. No sooner does she finish her lines and fill in the silences in the scene, than she faints. As she faints, her glasses fall beside her and before the camera, blurring her to our view. With regard to her emotional state, she remains blurred and muddled for most of the film, pausing and reflecting only to pursue Iván all the better. She does, of course, finally free herself from him, but only after much havoc (including Candela's suicide attempt, Lucía's murder attempt, and the Shiites' terrorist attempt). Continually on edge, she repeats the lines of the woman in *Johnny Guitar,* but to different effect. Here, the happy ending comes in the form of a woman without a man, a woman whose independence is communicative (witness Marisa) instead of spurious and self-absorbed (witness Iván). *Women on the Verge* is thus a revision or redoubling of *The Human Voice* and, more directly, *Johnny Guitar.* Within a deceptively conventional framework, it pushes at disjunction and desire and ends up with a woman who no longer waits for or leans on a man. But it dubs and redoubles another film as well. *Women on the Verge* takes the dark domestic needs and desires of *What Have I Done to Deserve This?* and replays them as happy, sunny, stylish slapstick, as a sort of upscale, toned-down *Labyrinth of Passions.*

This interfilmic relation need not be resolved in favor of either of the two films. It is no doubt tempting to criticize *Women on the Verge* as a falling from critical truth, as a selling out, and to celebrate *What Have I Done?* as politically committed and socially aware or, obversely, to celebrate the former as showing a woman's success (despite the figure of Paulina Morales) and to criticize the latter as showing a woman's failure. But to do so is to overlook the critical significance of tension itself. This tension is, as I have been arguing, figured here as hysteria, or at least as some postmodern simulacrum of hysteria: mad, methodical, and ever so metaphorical. Hysteria, after all, is a site of considerable tension—psychosexual, to be sure, but ethical, political, epistemological, and aesthetic as well. It involves a crisis of categories and classes, an errant diffusion of bodily signs, and a troubling generation of images that critics have denounced in terms of victimization and championed in terms of resistance. It entails the disjunctions, framings, movements, spectacles, and speculations that Almodóvar's films find as their form; and it entails the problems of language, desire, body, image, gender, and class that they find as their content. Hysteria figures the women and, at times, the men of Almodóvar's films; it does so with often uneasy humor, slipping, especially in later works, between sadness and laughter. On the whole, Almodóvar's films have been remarkably successful, commercially as well as critically, perhaps because humor is always more uneasy than we may think; perhaps because the art of histrionics is always, after a fashion, hysterical.

Pedro Almodóvar with Paul Julian Smith (interview date February 1996)

SOURCE: "Almodóvar and the Tin Can," in *Sight and Sound,* Vol. 6, No. 2, February, 1996, pp. 24-7.

[In the following interview, Almodóvar discusses his latest film The Flower of My Secret, *his cinematic process, and Spanish politics.]*

[Smith:] You've told the Spanish press that **The Flower of My Secret** *is your most La Manchan and most traditional film. But it strikes me that, with its references to NATO and Bosnia, to the newspaper* El País *and to Prime Minister Felipe González, this is your most European and most contemporary film.*

[Almodóvar:] When I say the film's La Manchan I mean it's my most realistic film yet. Of course I'm not interested in naturalism: even if I made a documentary it would turn out to be a fictional work on that subject. Between what inspires me and what I actually make, there is always an element of distance, of representation. Even when you decide where to place the camera, you're manipulating reality. So this is my most realist film, with the proviso that my realism is very personal and that there is always a touch of artifice there. It's also my most contemporary film, with references to political demonstrations and to the tension that people now feel on the street. It's based on the place where I was born, La Mancha, and the place where I now live, Madrid at this particular historical moment.

And you've also described it as the most personal of all your films.

Normally I'm very embarrassed to speak about my roots and my mother, and of myself in the first person. This time the film turned out like that in spite of myself. However, all of my films are absolutely personal; it's just that normally the things that affect me personally are hidden behind the characters. For example people often say to me: "Your films are so full of mothers, it's as if you didn't have a father." But it's not true. In **High Heels,** for example, my father is the model for elements of the mother played by Marisa Paredes: my father had cancer and returned to die in the room in which he had been born, just like the mother in the film. I haven't spoken about this before.

This is the first time in your films that the village from which the characters originate actually appears. In **What Have I Done to Deserve This?,** *the grandmother and grandson are shown leaving for the village; and in* **Tie Me Up!** *Antonio Banderas returns to his village, but it's in ruins. But in* **The Flower of My Secret** *there is an idealised view of the village, to which it's in fact impossible to return.*

In reality I myself don't go back to my village. I don't know what to do with myself there. But the mere fact of placing the camera in front of the earth, the red earth of La Mancha, is moving for me: there's something atavistic and primitive in that earth of my childhood. In the end I didn't shoot in my own village, which has changed, but in Almagro, some 20 kilometres away. Almagro now looks more like my village than my village does. This is the question of representation again.

Can we talk about this shoot? This is the first time you've worked with director of photography Alfonso Beato.

I liked his work with Glauber Rocha and Jim McBride, but I chose him because, although we have a terrible film-making crisis in Spain, 15 films were being shot in January 1995 and the cinematographers I like were already fully booked. So I had to bring in someone from abroad. Although this film has a less vivid palette than the others, it still has a colour scheme that's recognisably mine.

The image remains as stylised as in your previous work. And yet there's a very raw emotionalism also.

The look of the film is stripped down, austere. I had originally imagined the film as being more extravagant, but I gradually discovered that the more sober and austere it was, the more expressive it would be. It's the austerity that gives meaning to this film: I've made films before about women abandoned, but never such an economical film, one which speaks such a simple cinematic language.

Is it relevant that this is the first time for many years you've shot entirely on location and not in a studio?

The fact of working in a real place imposes a certain shooting style. At first it's disconcerting because, of course, you can't knock down walls to get a shot. But it gives a kind of tension and naturalism to the camerawork because you need new solutions all the time.

You make great use of mirror shots in these interiors.

Mirrors serve a number of functions. First, on a practical level, they make the space seem bigger: a real house is always too small, because you have to fit the crew in too. On the other hand they give an effect of duplication. This links up with the duplicity of the characters (Leo is a writer with several pseudonyms) and the reproductive functions of literature and the mass media: when Leo visits the newspaper *El Pais'* print works, her image is repeated in multiple windows, just as the written word is subject to reproduction. Another key scene in the film is when Leo's husband arrives home. The space was very small and we put a mirror to expand it. But instead of a single mirror I chose one made up of multiple mirrors, so that when the two characters kiss you can't see their lips. This is to show that this couple is already split apart or fragmented, from the very first moment.

There are also shots through lace, which seem to have a distancing function. And lace-making is a symbol of village life.

Lace-making is a kind of work traditionally carried out by women. I use lace to speak of the solitude of both mother and daughter, and in the key scene between them I begin by shooting through lace to show that we are in a wholly female world. La Mancha is perhaps the only place in the world where women still make lace by hand, sitting in the street enjoying the last rays of sunlight. It's an image of the woman alone and of the woman accompanied by other women, a matriarchal society. The whole film is shot from the woman's point of view: even when she's mistaken or unfair to her husband, it's her perspective.

"Leo" means "I read" in Spanish and this is a very literary film, with the main character changing literary genres just as you change cinematic genres in your films.

All my films are literary in the sense that there is a lot of dialogue. But Rohmer's cinema is literary and colloquial at the same time. For me a literary cinema is one in which language is centre stage, and is the motive force for the action.

When you start to write a film you begin with the dialogue.

That's right: dialogue is action for me. I've often said this, and it seems like a joke but it's not: in Europe we make films about people because it's cheaper to put two people in a living room talking than to make a film full of special effects. For me two girls and some good dialogue are as effective as all the FX in *The Terminator.*

Godard said that all you need for a film is a girl and a gun. But you'd rather have two girls?

Maybe they're carrying a gun in their handbag, and you can't see it. Or maybe they use their tongues as guns.

You normally try to shoot in sequence. Did you do this here?

I tried, but you can never really do that because it's too expensive. You have to shoot according to the locations and we managed to shoot blocks of action in sequence because they were all set in Leo's flat. This time I began by shooting a scene from the middle of the film: the visit of Leo's husband. I don't mind starting with a tough sequence. It gets the actors into their character and I like to be confronted by difficulties from the very beginning.

Does shooting more or less in sequence enable you to improvise on set?

There are no changes affecting the production schedule. Once I have the sets ready I rehearse for a week before shooting. That's when I adapt the script. Where the film became much richer was in the role of the mother, played by Chus Lampreave. Chus is my cinematic mother and she understands me perfectly. I gave her a lot more lines five minutes before shooting. She had to learn it quickly. But it's never she who improvises. I'm the one who improvises. Nothing happens for the first time in front of the camera. We've always rehearsed it before.

In the visually arresting first sequence you crosscut between two unrelated scenes: the grieving mother in the seminar and Leo desperate in her flat. Was this decided in the script or in the editing?

It was written that way.

The technique is reminiscent of the opening of some of your previous films, especially **Women on the Verge** *and* **Matador.**

This is a metaphor which is initially hermetic and disconcerting because the audience doesn't yet know what's happening. It involves a sequence that occurs on another level and serves as a premonition of what will happen later: in **Women on the Verge** it's the character's dream; in *Matador* it's the slasher footage. I like to begin like this.

It's cinematic, not literary at all.

Yes, it's peculiar to cinema. I'm proposing from the start that this is a representation or performance.

Marisa Paredes is extraordinary in the main role. She is famous for her work in the theatre as well as on film. How did you collaborate with her here?

Yes, she's worked more in the theatre than in films. Her performance is splendid, but it's one of the easiest jobs I've ever had. The only thing I tried to do was to lead her in a certain direction. This is almost an epic of grief and an actor might tend towards exaggeration. I kept cutting and cutting and led her in the opposite direction. To such an extent that at one point I said: "Don't move a single muscle in your face." And yet this empty mask is enormously expressive. Marisa understood at once that an economy of gesture was essential to this part.

The scenes with Chus and Rossy are marvellously comic; but they're played with a double edge of emotion also.

It's terrible to see two people who love each other at loggerheads like this. My mother treats my sister just like this and it's destroying my sister. It looks funny but it terrifies me.

If comedy is serious, is seriousness comic also? Even when Leo attempts suicide, audiences aren't quite sure how to react.

When she comes back to life in the bathtub, she looks like one of the living dead. Of course there's a lot of humour in this. It's a very risky technique, but one I've become a specialist in.

Can we talk about your first experience of film? You've compared it to the opening of Victor Erice's The Spirit of the Beehive, *when the travelling cinema comes to the village.*

My relationship with cinema started as a child in the village when I'd go with a tin can full of glowing pieces of cheap charcoal: it was right in the middle of the postwar period and to keep warm in the cold you took a tin can with you. I seem to remember that in *The Spirit of the Beehive* the characters went to just this kind of improvised cinema. My conception of cinema is still that it's something that gives me warmth, that comforts me, like that tin can.

If this is an image of the past of Spanish cinema, what of its future? You've now made three successful features in coproduction with French company CiBy 2000. Is this a model for European film-making?

My relation with CiBy is absolutely free. It's not just that they don't bother me when I'm shooting; they don't even see the film until it's subtitled in French. The film is still Spanish, although the funding is French. Moreover, my films are cheap and CiBy knows they sell all over the world. So it's good business for them. That's why I have so much freedom. If I got involved with a film like *Little Buddha* that cost $40 million I'd have more problems.

But your films are expensive by Spanish standards.

A normal Spanish film costs less than mine, that's true. I spend a lot of money on set design. I won't settle for things you can buy in the shops. I have things brought in from all over. This stylisation is expensive. I also rehearse the actors a lot, which is costly. These things are essential for my films.

What about postproduction? You've made all 11 features with editor José Salcedo.

I'm very fast with editing. I cut every day after shooting and I continue refining the rough cut as I go. It makes things cheaper, because the day after we finish shooting we have a cut of the whole film and ten days later we always have the final version. I can't shoot and wait until the end to edit. The film is alive and if you cut as you shoot you know what rhythm it's taking on and how the characters are really turning out. You can also sort out problems as you see them coming up in the editing process.

Leo has a line: "The country is on the point of exploding." Do You have any views on the political situation in Spain now?

The country is very tense. It can't stand the Socialist government and it blames Felipe González for not resigning. But when the Socialists go the [extreme right] People's Party will get in. Young people have no memory of political activism; they don't even know what it means to have a political position. They may say they're on the right but they don't realise the right will stop them living the way they live now.

Will a future rightwing government provoke a reaction against it?

Exactly. We'll all react and become more radical. We will protest once more.

Critics in the UK and US have often asked you to take up a clearer political position in your films.

My political position is perfectly clear. I've never been a member of a political party because I need to keep my independence. But I'm very much on the left. In films it's not necessary for characters to talk about politics. The politics is implicit in the film.

To finish, then. This may strike you as crazy, but there seems to be a connection between two characters called Angel: the one who comes to the aid of Leo in **The Flower of My Secret** *and the Angel (played by Antonio Banderas) who plays a similar role in* **Matador.** *They are both creatures without sex.*

This is something that hadn't occurred to me. But it's true that this Angel undergoes a process of feminisation throughout the film. By the end he and Leo have become two female writers toasting each other by the fireside, like Candice Bergen and Jacqueline Bisset in *Rich and Famous.* So the man ends up as the woman's best girlfriend. It's a very positive process.

FURTHER READING

Criticism

Cardullo, Bert. "Lovers and Other Strangers." *The Hudson Review* XLIII, No. 4 (Winter 1991): 645-46.
    Asserts that Almodóvar's *Tie Me Up! Tie Me Down!* is "as facile and tedious as his other films to reach these shores."

Dyson, Jonathan. "Hypocrite Lecteur." *The Times Literary Supplement,* No. 4764 (22 July 1994): 18.
    Complains that "despite several stunning set-pieces such as the rape, the basics of plot and characterization [of *Kika*] simply don't gel: storylines go unresolved or are unconvincingly resolved, *longueurs* abound."

Forbes, Jill. "Ivan the Terrible: *Women on the Verge of a Nervous Breakdown.*" *Sight and Sound* 58, No. 2 (Spring 1989): 135.
    Observes the comedy and ambiguities present in Almodóvar's *Women on the Verge of a Nervous Breakdown.*

Fuentes, Victor. "Almodóvar's Postmodern Cinema: A Work in Progress . . ." In *Post-Franco, Postmodern: The Films of Pedro Almodóvar,* edited by Kathleen M. Vernon and Barbara Morris, pp. 155-70. Westport, CT: Greenwood Press, 1995.
    Discusses Almodóvar's contributions and limitations as a postmodern filmmaker.

Hart, Patricia. Review of *Patty Diphusa y otros textos,* by Pedro Almodóvar. *World Literature Today* 66, No. 3 (Summer 1992): 485.
    Praises Almodóvar's *Patty Diphusa y otros textos.*

Morris, Barbara. "Almodóvar's Laws of Subjectivity and Desire." In *Post-Franco, Postmodern: The Films of Pedro Almodóvar,* edited by Kathleen M. Vernon and Barbara Morris, pp. 87-97. Westport, CT: Greenwood Press, 1995.
    Analyzes how "Almodóvar de/reconstructs heavily codified myths and institutions of Spanish culture—the nunnery, the working-class family and motherhood, the tragic love triangle, and the bullfight—revered in Francoism's exalted iconography."

Romney, Jonathan. "The Pain in Spain." *The Observer* (21 January 1996): 15.
    Questions Almodóvar's sincerity in his *Almodóvar on Almodóvar.*

Smith, Paul Julian. "*Pepi, Luci, Bom* and *Dark Habits:* Lesbian Comedy, Lesbian Tragedy." In *Post-Franco, Postmodern: The Films of Pedro Almodóvar,* edited by Kathleen M. Vernon and Barbara Morris, pp. 25-39. Westport, CT: Greenwood Press, 1995.
    Contrasts Almodóvar's *Pepi, Luci, Bom,* calling it a lesbian comedy, with his *Dark Habits,* calling it a lesbian tragedy.

Vernon, Kathleen M. "Melodrama Against Itself: Pedro

Almodóvar's *What Have I Done to Deserve This?*" In *Post-Franco, Postmodern: The Films of Pedro Almodóvar,* edited by Kathleen M. Vernon and Barbara Morris, pp. 59-71. Westport, CT: Greenwood Press, 1995.

> Discusses Almodóvar's *What Have I Done to Deserve This?* in terms of its relationship to American melodrama.

Vernon, Kathleen M. and Barbara Morris. "Introduction: Pedro Almodóvar, Postmodern *Auteur.*" In *Post-Franco, Postmodern: The Films of Pedro Almodóvar,* edited by Kathleen M. Vernon and Barbara Morris, pp. 1-23. Westport, CT: Greenwood Press, 1995.

> Traces Almodóvar's films from a cultural and historical perspective.

Additional coverage of Almodóvar's life and career is contained in the following sources published by Gale: *Contemporary Authors,* Vol. 133; and *Contemporary Authors New Revision Series,* Vol. 72.

Stuart Dybek

1942-

American short story writer, poet, and playwright.

The following entry presents an overview of Dybek's career through 1997.

INTRODUCTION

Much of Stuart Dybek's fictional world addresses adolescent life in Chicago's immigrant neighborhoods. Though often considered a member of a long tradition of Chicago writers such as Gwendolyn Brooks and Saul Bellow, Dybek is known for blurring the lines between the real and the magical, which sets his work apart from the realism of other Chicago writers.

Biographical Information

Dybek was born on April 10, 1942, in an immigrant neighborhood on the southwest side of Chicago. His father, Stanley, was a foreman in an International Harvester Plant, and his mother, Adeline, was a truck dispatcher. Dybek developed an interest in music at a young age and has said that jazz music has been an important influence on his development as a writer. He attended a Catholic high school, but soon rejected the strictures of the Catholic church. Upon graduation, Dybek entered Loyola University of Chicago as a pre-med student. He dropped out to devote himself to the peace and civil rights movements, but returned later to receive both his bachelor's (1964) and master's (1968) degrees. Dybek worked as a case worker for the Cook County Department of Public Aid, and a teacher in an elementary school in a Chicago suburb. He also worked in advertising, and then, from 1968 to 1970, he taught at a high school on the island of Saint Thomas. In 1970 Dybek turned his focus to writing; he entered the Master of Fine Arts program at the University of Iowa where he received an M.F.A. in 1973. He has taught English at Western Michigan University since 1974. Dybek has won several awards, including an Ernest Hemingway Citation from the P.E.N. American Center for *Childhood and Other Neighborhoods* (1980) in 1981; the Whiting Writers Award in 1985; and three O. Henry Memorial Prize Story Awards in 1985, 1986, and 1987.

Major Works

Dybek's collection *Brass Knuckles* (1979) combines verse and prose poems. The verse poems are clearly set in inner city neighborhoods, whereas the prose poems are not so definitive in their sense of place. Many of the poems focus on childhood, but the images are stark and often violent. "The

Rape of Persephone" is the center of the collection, describing the molestation of a child, her subsequent revenge, and her falling in love with Death at the conclusion of the poem. Other poems also rework traditional myths, including "Lazarus" and "Orpheus." Dybek's *Childhood and Other Stories* is a collection of stories about childhood in the Chicago of the 1940s, 50s, and 60s. The collection espouses Dybek's assertion that childhood is a visionary state of perception. Ethnicity is very important to the collection, and several stories have themes concerning immigrant life in the city. In "Blood Soup," two boys search the city for a jar of duck blood for an old-country remedy to help cure their grandmother. In other stories Dybek's use of ethnicity is more subtle; his protagonists are often third-generation Polish immigrants and ethnic references are more vague. Some stories in the collection have a surreal quality. "Visions of Budhardin" is about a man who returns to his old neighborhood to make amends for luring his friends into mortal sin when he was a youth. He roams his former neighborhood behind the controls of a mechanical elephant. In the process, he wrecks a church only to escape on a garbage scow with an altar boy. *The Coast of Chicago* (1990) is a combination of one- and two-page vignettes and longer short stories. "Chopin in Winter" deals with the theme of loneliness. The main character, Marcy, is pregnant by an unnamed man and living with her mother. She plays Chopin on her piano, and for a brief moment in time, the music links her to an old man, Dzia-Dzia, and his young grandson who listen to her from a downstairs apartment. To Marcy, the music represents a lament for her lost youth. To Dzia-Dzia, who spent his life moving around, the music reminds him of his life in Poland. To the grandson, who has a crush on Marcy, the music represents the grown-up world which he is on the brink of entering. Metamorphosis is also an important theme in this collection, as represented in "Hot Ice." The story focuses on an urban legend of a young virgin who drowns while fending off a sexual assault, and who is then entombed in an abandoned ice house by her distraught father. Big Antek, a former butcher, claims to have seen the virgin and her coffin of ice. He claims that while locked in the ice house one night, her presence warmed him and helped him avoid freezing. The three main characters are changed through their connection to the legend. The virgin herself, or at least her story, is metamorphosized when the protagonists free her from her icy coffin.

Critical Reception

Critics classify Dybek as a "Chicago writer" and compare

his work to that of Nelson Algren and James T. Farrell, among others. Bruce Cook calls Dybek "a true inheritor, one who stands tall in a direct line of succession with Chicago's best." Reviewers often note the black humor present in Dybek's work. They also comment that there is a blurring of fantasy and reality in Dybek's fictional world, and that there is a "transcendental, magical quality" to many of his stories, in the words of Cook. Certain reviewers have asserted that Dybek occasionally loses control of his fantastical elements and that his stories are weakened in the process. David Kubal complains that Dybek suffers from "the modern writer's urge to mythologize reality. . . ." Some reviewers discuss the difficulty of avoiding sentimentalism when writing about childhood and immigrant neighborhoods, but critics assert that Dybek avoids this fault. David Clewell states that "whether writing about adolescent sex, hoodlums, shopkeepers, or his beautifully-drawn ragmen, Dybek neatly skirts the obvious pitfalls of sentimentality." Despite his shortcomings, critics have found Dybek to be a strong and imaginative writer.

PRINCIPAL WORKS

Brass Knuckles (poetry) 1979
Childhood and Other Neighborhoods (short stories) 1980
Orchids (play) 1990
The Coast of Chicago (short stories) 1990; also published
    with six selections from *Childhood and Other Neigh-
    borhoods,* 1991

CRITICISM

Reg Saner (review date 1980)

SOURCE: A review of *Brass Knuckles,* in *The Ohio Review,* No. 25, 1980, pp. 113-19.

[*In the following excerpt, Saner reviews Dybek's* Brass Knuckles *asserting that despite unsettling subject matter, he found himself "involved."*]

One gathers that Stuart Dybek is younger by a good deal than either [John] Allman or [William] Dickey. Certainly his *Brass Knuckles* offers a collection less consistently sustained, though with plenty of compensatory energy. Since the book mixes verse and prose poems about equally it may be fair to infer that Dybek is uncertain what sort of piece he wants to write. The verse tends to focus on inner-cityscapes, while the prose poems cultivate more surreal experience not circumstantially "placed." If the latter half of *Brass Knuckles* goes deeper into the psyche, the fact that it is mainly

prose poems may be less significant than Dybek's growing experience in his art.

Since the book's dominant polarities are Eros and Thanatos, **"The Rape of Persephone"** centers the collection. In this long verse poem myth and journalism palimpsest. The scene of child molestation in an "abandoned garage" with its burnt, cat-pissed mattress might have been a neighborhood crime or newspaper item. But since no actual child would be *vagina dentata* enough to *really* seize a fallen razor and lop off the molester's penis while sucking it—like a gaucho eating beef—and since the blood on her chin is "dark as a pomegranate" we understand the scene as myth-made-new. Four pages and other contemporized existences later, a grown-up Persephone induces the cock-shorn rapist, Death, to masturbate her, drawn by his "torment, the mutilation borne / with grace and majesty. / He alone among the gods still undiminished."

But does it work? Anyone owning a penis will find one of his fears confronted in the poem, undeniably memorably. And memorability ranks high in art. My own reaction remains queazy about the poem's obvious sensationalism in relation to insights the myth ought to generate. Weeks after, I visualize the mutilation, the concluding encounter; all other significances recede. My misgivings prove that Dybek has involved me despite my uneasiness.

Certainly the Eros/Thanatos interest has been amply announced. At once, in **"Maroon,"** we find omens of child-murder by crowbar; in **"Clothespin,"** a manic ballbat; in **"The Knife-Sharpener's Daughter,"** the impending menace of his cry, "scissors! knives! axes!"; in **"Cat's Pyre,"** a combusted pet; a boy-Raskolnikov in **"Crime & Punishment"**; a father carried away by TV boxing in **"My Father's Fights"**; a hit kid slaughtered by the promo-midget driving a "wiener mobile" in **"Little Oscar"**; an insane riot of liberation in **"Bastille Day on 25th Street"**; a severed body in **"Svengali"**; a waxy cadaver coming upstairs to resume his marriage in **"Lazarus"**—not to mention spatters of blood flung aside in **"Brass Knuckles."**

> **Dybek's perhaps unconscious aim in *Brass Knuckles*—and the title supports the guess—is to acknowledge through neighborhood characters the terror he dare not admit.**
>
> **—*Reg Saner***

Dybek's perhaps unconscious aim in *Brass Knuckles*—and the title supports the guess—is to acknowledge through neighborhood characters the terror he dare not admit. The sort of childhood the book implies is one no child can wholly survive. The more sensitive the child or adolescent, the more disastrous. And the ultimate scar, "toughness."

The latter portion of the book shows Dybek emerging somewhat, giving his *anima* scope. Earlier accuracies of city detritus, dreck fallen down airshafts, excavation sites fenced by old doors, dead pennies under third rails, arm-wrestlers and VFW red-necks adding vulgar color to a working-class wedding—these give way to more dream-worldly experience, as in **"Traveling Salesman"**:

> He finds himself stepping off the bus in some burg he's already bored with. Picking his teeth for 200 miles—here's where he spits the toothpick out. Past Holiday Inn the neighborhoods get dark. All-night laundromats where women with circles under their eyes press laundered underwear, warm as bread, against their sinuses. Finally, he's signing the register at a funeral home where he knows no one, but is mistaken for a long-lost friend of the deceased, for someone who has dislocated his life to make the hazardous journey on a night when the dead man's own children have avoided him. Once again instinct has taken him where he's needed; where the unexpected transforms routine into celebration. He kneels before the corpse, striking his forehead against the casket.

This and pieces like **"The Need for Sleep,"** **"To Acquire a Beautiful Body,"** **"Night for Voyeurs"** and **"Sleepwalking Solo"** represent progress from unidimensional verse-snapshots like **"Penance"** and **"Lynn"** earlier in the book.

"My Neighborhood," the concluding poem, has better title to speak for the collection than **"Brass Knuckles,"** since Dybek's compassionate nostalgia and revulsion relax into each other. Though the poem's elements seem mere squibs of reportage, they accrue interest and emotion through their very insignificance: the daily, the nakedly ugly eye-trash and blight of cities, gritty, dingy, desolate and human. Not a line of this excellent summary poem seems contrived. In it the world of *Brass Knuckles* achieves a lucid, life-like epitome, and the poem's closing image is at once completely believable and moving.

Robert Ward (review date 1980)

SOURCE: A review of *Childhood and Other Neighborhoods,* in *Northwest Review,* Vol. XVIII, No. 3, 1980, pp. 149-57.

[*In the following excerpt, Ward discusses the inner city lives Dybek portrays in his* Childhood and Other Neighborhoods.]

If this tone of apocalypse and condemnation is where Otto's work leaves off, it is where Stuart Dybek's *Childhood and Other Neighborhoods* begins. Where Otto's stories depend for their effect on his characters' complacency, Dybek's are stories of the inner city, a panorama of ruined lives overcome by the refuse of civilization. In these longer, carefully crafted stories set in the Chicago of the 40's, 50's and 60's, Dybek's technique is a no-holds-barred assault on everything we may have smugly assumed was reality. Though his characters appear to have vitality in a world they are forced to scrape a living from, in truth they are cripples who manage only to fend off the total impotence that bellies in on them. From the ragmen of **"The Palatski Man"** who each Sunday in their impoverished warren outside the city perform a strange communion composed of liquid blood red candy, generally used for the candy apples they sell, to "crazy Swantek," of **"The Cat Woman,"** whose grandmother managed a meager living through drowning unwanted kittens in her basement washing machine, until Swantek took to hanging them out on the line to dry, it is Dybek's artistry to capture the fantasies of hope, the horrible black humor, and the details of ritual that carry these people through to their end.

This bizarre world creates for the reader an atmosphere where reality and imagination become indistinguishable; it is a confusion which Dybek takes full advantage of. In **"Visions Of Budhardin"** a homosexual outcast returns inside a huge mechanical elephant, and vents his wrath on the local Catholic church whose years of moral lies have made his inner landscape a ruin. Certainly, if we can accept the degree of the character's compulsion, the grotesque metaphor of a mammoth and mechanized nature does not seem so far fetched.

Yet in the profoundly achieved story **"The Apprentice,"** the exigencies of life make the surreal even more difficult to separate from the real. Ostensibly, an immigrant ex-taxidermist and nephew ride the highways at night to support themselves by supplying a rather exotic inner city restaurant, named "Spanish Blades," with its gruesome fare. The uncle, who bristles with imagination and black humor fantasy, a vitality charged by paranoia of Nazis and other fascists he imagines are pursuing him, describes this unusual place:

> ". . . An exclusive restaurant, a private club, for all those who'd been excluded and had finally made their way here, to this city of displaced persons. Displaced persons, DP's, who'd come from the corners of the earth evading politics and poverty; draft dodgers, deportees, drifters, illegal aliens, missing persons, personae non grata, refugees, revolutionaries, and emigré royalty, all orphans, mingling beneath the same ensign in a dining room where chandeliers rotated a crystalline light and blue poofs

of flame erupted as waiters, tuxedoed like magicians, ignited food."

And what is on the menu of such a restaurant?:

"And the road littered with the driftwood of night. Animals whose eyes have turned to quartz in the hypnosis of headlights, streamlike souls still hovering around their bodies. Rabbits, possums, coons, squirrels, pheasants—like a single species of highway animal. Some crushed beyond recognition, even their pelts useless and so left behind. But most still limp, waiting to be collected with the other highway scrap—blown tires like lizard skins, dropped mufflers, thrown hubcaps, lumber, hay bales, deposit bottles, anything that could fall off a tailgate or blow out of a car window.

The reader scarcely notices that this restaurant, in which the nephew is promised he will someday be a waiter, is only some graffiti spattered on an alley wall, that at the heart of their existence is a fantasy born from intense reality. In their comic backyard rituals these two characters bury, then revive old dolls, "mufflers and transmissions, . . . broken radios, crates of magazines, animal bones. . . . Makeshift tombstones stuck up everywhere." Near the apocalyptic ending, where the uncle, nagged by a terminal lung disease, becomes increasingly frenetic and paranoid, we begin to comprehend the great gift being passed on to the boy—the ability to stay alive in a deadly world.

Indeed, this kind of immediacy becomes even more abbreviated and accessible in Dybek's recent book of poems, *Brass Knuckles.* As the title implies, these poems are meant to shock and hurt us, swelling from volcanic sources of anger. Through such images as a twelve-year-old friend murdered with a crowbar, and the incineration of a pet cat's corpse in a garbage can, the horrible texture of the inner city rubs against us. Interspersed between this *cinéma vérité* are prose poems and redefinitions of myths whose surreal social satire is wrenchingly accurate. For example, these excerpts from **"Traveling Salesman":**

He finds himself stepping off the bus in some burg he's already bored with. Picking his teeth for 200 miles—here's where he spits the toothpick out. . . .

. . . Finally, he's signing the register at a funeral home where he knows no one, but is mistaken for a long-lost friend of the deceased, for someone who has dislocated his life to make the hazardous journey on a night when the dead man's own children have avoided him. Once again instinct has taken him where he's needed: where the unexpected transforms routine into celebration. He kneels before the corpse, striking his forehead against the casket.

But of all the techniques which Dybek uses to expose the sophisticated depth of necrophilia surrounding us, none is more successful than the contemporized refocusing of myths which for millenia have been the psyche's projection of the flux of life and death. In the tongue in cheek **"Lazarus,"** no mention of God is made, unless it is the media which has transformed the resurrected man into a celebrity. In **"Orpheus,"** the satire weaves threads of accusation, anger, confession and a lyric communion with all victims, as this latter day Orpheus leads us through the underworld of our own streets. In **"The Rape Of Persephone,"** the longest and most complex poem of the volume, the explosiveness of revitalized archetypes reaches a crescendo. Death, who is initially described as "Death in the alley, prehistory, / drooling and slobbering, guzzling wine, / and mumbling his name over and over . . ." forces the young girl into a lurid rape whose climax is her lopping off of his penis with his own razor, "Persephone / running down an alley like a canyon / his scream has cracked through skyscrapers." It is not the cycle of the seasons that is emphasized here, rather it is the return of important Death transformed, "Sleek, in silks and velvets . . . his opera cape swirls . . . he drives the alleys in a black limousine . . . He hires an angel." "And Persephone, a woman now, / keeps meeting him . . ." because he is

the one who makes her other lovers
seem adolescent, who *listens* to her,
who's interested in her soul, not just her body,
who understands the dark scars of childhood.

He reappears alternately as "Her professor of French romantics, / including seminars in de Sade," as "the dentist who calms her terror of pain / through hypnosis; the psychiatrist / she chooses at random . . . in the phone book. . . ."

If, in other writers, critics might brand this kind of vision as excessive over-statement, it is the highly crafted imagination, conscience and commitment of both Lon Otto and Stuart Dybek that will insure that their work must and will be read. As technology rockets us toward a future promising longer and better life, we see before us the possibility of an environment that may not be fit to live in. Our defense must be in the deepening resolve to comprehend ourselves. In the exploration of the human psyche, equal attention must be given to the biophilia and necrophilia that twist their complex patterns in each of us. As in the work of William Van Wert . . . we must observe all the action that takes place on the killing floor, where nothing has been decided yet. The blood that is put inescapably before us is our own blood.

Bruce Cook (review date 13 January 1980)

SOURCE: "Walks on the Southwest Side," in *Washington Post Book World,* January 13, 1980, pp. 1-2.

[*In the following review, Cook praises Dybek's* Childhood and Other Neighborhoods *and discusses how Dybek fits into the tradition of Chicago writers.*]

Along a diagonal line southwest from Chicago's Loop lies a vast terra incognita once populated almost completely by Slavic groups which has been changing over to black and Latin during the past couple of decades. Chicago has had neighborhood laureates in the past—James T. Farrell, who wrote of the south-side Irish; Gwendolyn Brooks, the fine poet who sings of the black south side; Nelson Algren, whose people are the Poles of the near-northwest side; and Saul Bellow, who has written so well about the west-side Jews. But nobody has come forward to speak for that mixed patch surrounding Douglas Park on the southwest side. That is, nobody until now. For here is Stuart Dybek to tell you what it is like to grow up there—the sights, the sounds, the smells, all of it—and this volume of his stories constitutes as impressive a debut as has been made by any of the many good writers who have come out of that "dark city," Chicago.

Of them all Dybek seems most like Nelson Algren. Although it may simply be a similarity of subject matter, I was reminded again and again while reading *Childhood and Other Neighborhoods* of the tough, beautiful stories in Algren's *The Neon Wilderness.* **"Blood Soup,"** Dybek's tale of an odyssey through decayed, changing blocks and alleys by Stefush and his brother Dove to find a jar of duck blood for the old-country remedy which they are sure will restore their dying grandmother, brought back to me Algren's frequently anthologized classic, "The Night the Devil Came Down Division Street." Sterndorf, the title character of the **"Neighborhood Drunk,"** could well be a first cousin to Drunkie John in *The Man with the Golden Arm.* And the high-schoolers yearning after culture in **"The Long Thoughts"** and **"Sauerkraut Soup"** might be Bruno Bicek's kids had Bruno only gone straight at the end of *Never Come Morning.*

Yet there are also elements here that would probably seem altogether alien to any reader of Algren. There is a kind of transcendental, magical quality to certain of the stories— **"The Palatski Man," "Visions of Budhardin,"** and **"The Apprentice"**—that is quite new to Chicago writing. It is distinctly Eastern European in flavor. The closest I can come by way of comparison would be the early stories of Isaac Bashevis Singer with all their dybbuks and devils. Yet after all, why not? Singer is a *Polish* Jew, after all. There was probably a good deal more interchange between the ghetto culture and that which surrounded it in Singer's day than is remembered now or perhaps was realized at the time.

None of this, however, is to deny the distinctive nature of Stuart Dybek's own writing. He has his own voice. It

emerges more and more clearly the deeper one reads in this collection. If he writes, for the most part, about children and adolescents here, it is always with an adult's understanding and sympathy. He speaks for the losers and victims, telling of a teen-age girl's wasted life in **"The Wake,"** and of the terror that is the daily bread of one boy's existence in **"Horror Movie."** There is anger, too—anger at the ignorance and brutality that has trapped those he writes about in their separate miseries, and anger at the system that keeps them there. This last is especially evident in **"Charity,"** in which the unnamed narrator, a social worker for the state, takes us on a tour through his case files and gives reality and some dignity to the squalid lives of his "clients." It is a harrowing story, absolutely true, I'm sure, to the author's experience, and it is the best of its kind I have read since Saul Bellow's "Looking for Mr. Green."

But there I go again, comparing and categorizing. There is a great urge for anyone who knows the literature of Chicago to see it as a whole, to try to tie it all together. The place has given so little encouragement to its writers and yet has produced so many fine ones that it is almost tempting to conclude that it is by denial and frustration, rather than generosity and help, that real writers are made. They have had to struggle similarly, and as a result there are certain similarities to their work—qualities of anger, cynicism, and sometimes a strident tone. Theirs is a tradition of deprivation and resentment.

And how does Stuart Dybek fit into this tradition? Perfectly, as a true inheritor, one who stands tall in a direct line of succession with Chicago's best. He is the real article, this guy, the McCoy, and if he is not ruined by neglect, drink, academic ennui, or the thousand other nagging miseries that sap a writer's talent, then he can be as good as any of the rest. It says here he is working on a novel. I am ready with my ten bucks to buy it the day it appears.

Ivan Gold (review date 24 February 1980)

SOURCE: A review of *Childhood and Other Neighborhoods,* in *The New York Times Book Review,* February 24, 1980, pp. 14-15.

[*In the following review, Gold praises the stories in Dybek's* Childhood and Other Neighborhoods.]

This is a collection of stories about coming of age in Chicago. Stuart Dybek's title struck me as a trifle coy, until I had finished the book. By then *Childhood and Other Neighborhoods* had come to seem as apt as any of the startling observations and sharp images that distinguish these 11 tales of growing up poor and American and urban in the middle decades of the 20th century. Mr. Dybek grounds his stories in the city's streets and alleys, in the feel his young children and adolescents have for the neighborhood landscapes of their early years, and then bends his flair for naturalism on an anvil of fantasy, with bizarre results that yet seem utterly consistent with the logic of childhood.

In **"Blood Soup,"** 13-year-old Steve sets out to find duck's blood, the primary ingredient in a soup his ailing grandmother believes will keep her alive. Equipped with the jar that had contained her holy water, Steve picks up his younger brother, Dove, and together they begin an odyssey that takes them to rooftops, to a lagoon in the black section of the city, to an abandoned tenement listing over the elevated railway. There they locate Pan Gowumpe, a raucous old man surrounded by fowl, who finally, after some frightening, funny exchanges with the pair, appears to give them what they came for. They flee, evading the addled black man who had led them there (while sure he is in hot pursuit), and when Steve discovers that they are not carrying duck's blood at all, the story ends.

In the ultra-strange **"Visions of Budhardin,"** a man who in his youth had been in the habit of luring his friends into acts of mortal sin and has now returned to the old neighborhood to make amends, sits at the controls of a mechanical elephant in an overgrown lot. Roaming the neighborhood inside his elephant, he ends up wrecking a church with a nun astride his back trying to bring him down, and escapes on a garbage scow with one of the new generation of altar boys.

The young man in **"The Apprentice"** is not sure how he has come to be gathering roadside detritus for a living, in the company of paranoid old "Uncle" ("Who are our enemies, Uncle?" "*Who?* The same as those of all peoples. The *secret* police. The KGB of the soul, CIA of the brain, SS who think they are only harmless dogcatchers. . . . KKK, FBI, ICBM, DDT, initials! Initials are our enemies, Tadeusz"), nor just why it is that he winds up clinging to the top of an opening drawbridge, gathering pigeon eggs.

The old neighborhood changes, and so do we. The more straightforward stories—**"Charity," "The Long Thoughts," "Sauerkraut Soup"**—painfully document these changes and are full of riches. This is an impressive debut in short fiction.

David Clewell (review date Spring-Summer 1980)

SOURCE: "Vital Assurances," in *The Chowder Review*, No. 14, Spring-Summer, 1980, pp. 64-7.

[*In the following excerpt, Clewell favorably reviews Dybek's* Brass Knuckles *and calls Dybek a "multi-talented, generous imagination."*]

There is a certain presence in the world of contemporary poetry that I like to think of as the "hermetic poem." This type of poem is almost always "well-crafted," riveted and tempered in all the right places so there can be no mistaking this object as *poem.* These poems would have us know that their makers are conscious, careful technicians well-versed in poesy. But the poem itself, for all practical purposes, is insulated and sealed; it is effectively impervious to any and all forces from the outside. Sometimes we are given certain clues to follow: the sky may be "cracked porcelain," a "someone" may be in a room "somewhere," as if a deliberate fuzzing of time and space inherently enhances a poem. By the time we finish with one of these poems we feel—if we feel anything at all—that we're *supposed* to feel a certain way, *supposed* to appreciate the special integration of everything we have been given. But too often we are hard-pressed for the where's and why's, as though we have been taken through a dance without ever having seen our partner. The hermetic poem, proud of its word-prowess, is self-satisfied. Partners are optional, expendable and, often, apparently unnecessary or even undesired.

Happily, there are poems being written that don't feel obliged to assure us of their validity through a rabid self-assertion of technical virtuosity. Happily, there are poems assuring us that poetry—*real* poetry, the stuff providing us with renewed ways of thinking, feeling, knowing—is still possible. It is this assurance that may provide some comfort amid the psychic wreckage the 80's seem doomed to promise us. The collections by Stuart Dybek and David Bottoms are strong and vital assurances of this kind.

Brass Knuckles, Dybek's first book, is divided fairly evenly between lined poems and prose poems. One of Dybek's fervent obsessions is with the urban neighborhood, complete with the sounds and sights of human lives scratching out room for themselves in a place where little is handed to them. This is from **"My Neighborhood"**:

> across the street Mr. Patek
> unscrewing the awning with a rusty crank,
> dropping the green shadow
> across the storefront window
> where morning donuts harden in the sun;
> a brewery truck curbs up to Andy's Tap,
> aluminum kegs thud down a wooden ramp
> into a cellar, releasing a must
> of cobwebs, ice, and yeast
> that Mrs. Kosh pauses to inhale
> as she feels her way
> along the buildings to church,
> refusing to admit she's blind.

Whether writing about adolescent sex, hoodlums, shopkeepers, or his beautifully-drawn ragmen, Dybek neatly skirts the obvious pitfalls of sentimentality. Nor is he content to make merely crafted poems of "atmosphere" where the poem never quite gets beyond its own setting of scene. We are given a sense of where we are through appropriate details, not so we can simply be there to take it all in, but so we can proceed through the process of discovery aware of the context for what we find out. Dybek takes us to a place we think of as "familiar" and shows a way of seeing perhaps never considered by us before. That "place," that way of perceiving, is Dybek's unique world—his own imagination acting on the given world.

Whether writing about adolescent sex, hoodlums, shopkeepers, or his beautifully-drawn ragmen, Dybek neatly skirts the obvious pitfalls of sentimentality. Nor is he content to make merely crafted poems of "atmosphere" where the poem never quite gets beyond its own setting of scene.
—David Clewell

The danger in poems that make extensive use of descriptive details is the lack of opportunities afforded to a reader to exercise imagination. Overstatement, too, presents problems. Although Dybek draws his details through the colors of his imagination, he still leaves us plenty of room for intimate involvement in the goings-on. When Dybek's speakers capture the magic of neighborhoods, shops, and childhood, they never close us off from the sources of that magic. Through diction and selective imagery the poet does more than allow us to participate; he pleads with us to fall into his sensibility as a necessary part of the poetry being sung. In such circumstances we are a long way from the workings of the hermetic poem. The book's opening poem, **"Vivaldi,"** begins:

> When I met Vivaldi it was dark,
> a ragman lashed his horse's bells,
> streets tilted into slow wind tunnels,
>
> no, it was another night, in winter,
> snow as soft as opium, two winoes wassailed
> down an alley through a mail truck's ruts

The poem continues, a strangely beautiful evocation of a city's musics. At the poem's conclusion, we too have met the speaker's Vivaldi, not because the speaker tells us so, but because he has let us walk *with* him, seeing and discovering as the speaker sees and discovers.

The poet's sense of humor (and God knows there are too

many poets so concerned with "being serious" that there is rarely a smile cracked in their work) is genuine, displayed at appropriate moments. It strikes a fine balance with much of the sadness and mustered toughness that fills Dybek's neighborhoods. **"Little Oscar"** epitomizes that struck balance as we encounter the midget driver of the Oscar Meyer Weiner Mobile on the day he runs over and kills a child. Or take **"Bastille Day on 25th St.,"** a prose poem chronicling strange happenings among "the mysterious stragglers we feared and envied as kids." The poem begins:

> I heard them kick the door through the next room,
> the TV explode,
> sounds and shouts of a struggle and knew I had to
> exit fast. The goddam
> window was painted stuck. I grabbed a roll of
> toilet paper and bashed it
> out with a muffled tinkle. Someone was already
> rattling the doorknob
> with diarrheic abandon, yelling 'Com'on outa der,'
> as I squeezed onto
> the fire escape.

As the poem continues we learn, in a less frantic fashion, more about these people. It ends with a wild scene as the speaker finds himself and his new allies "buckshot into History." The final stage is set:

> O Brothers! The secret bombs, fake beards, and
> dark glasses! Razor
> blades in the edges of placards, black flags nailed
> to baseball bats, songs
> and slogans flinting from teeth used to flinging out
> curses!

"In The Basement" gives us a man who for years has been throwing all manner of worldly goods into his cellar, "Having to tell potential buyers: Basement? No, there's / no basement here. This house never had a basement. The furnace? / Oh, we keep that in the attic." And finally, there is **"The Rape of Persephone"**—maybe the most remarkable poem in the book. This is Dybek's own retelling of the myth featuring a uniquely American goddess; she likes where she's being held and falls in love with Death:

> He always gives her the most exquisite gifts:
> the jeweled case of sleeping pills,
> gold plated razor, *Ariel*
> signed by the author, a long scarf of Isadora's,
> Billie Holiday's last recordings,
> an ivory handled .32.

The poem, although rollicking good fun, is never totally played strictly for yuks, and therein lies Dybek's special gift:

Death tars his stump.
For years no one sees him.
There's time to invent agriculture, the wheel,
to steal fire.
Till finally life's too good; full of gods.
Eating and drinking and fucking.
By the time he reappears men have grown bored,
crazy with immortality.

The few weaknesses in this book occur in some of the prose poems. Dybek is capable of creating spare, surrealistic descriptions and situations, tight entities full of poetry. **"Groom,"** a story of a wax figure atop a wedding cake, is wonderfully bizarre and human. **"Sunday at the Zoo"** and **"A Friend of the Family"** are quirky, surreal. But others in this mode are less self-contained. The speaker in **"Convalescence"** changes his eyes into fly's eyes. The piece is imaginative but reads like the beginning of a longer story. Similarly, **"Fascist Honeymoon," "Mr. and Mrs. Van Winkle"** and **"Grand Entrance"** are flat pieces with strained effects, too whipped into shape. Dybek's best pieces of this kind deal with people in real-world situations. **"Maroon,"** a hauntingly spare prose poem, is concerned with the death of a friend. **"Traveling Salesman"** and **"How Much"** are imaginative and exact.

The speaker in **"My Neighborhood"** says, at one point, "I have forgotten their names, / the names of the streets we passed, / weather, daydreams, legends, / the precision of fear." But Dybek has not forgotten. He gives names to new ways of knowing. The poet has also written *Childhood and Other Neighborhoods,* a collection of stories recently published by Viking. He is currently writing a novel. I look forward to more ways of knowing from this multi-talented, generous imagination. . . .

David Kubal (review date Autumn 1980)

SOURCE: A review of *Childhood and Other Neighborhoods,* in *The Hudson Review,* Vol. XXXIII, No. 3, Autumn, 1980, pp. 445-47.

[*In the following excerpt, Kubal states that Dybek's* Childhood and Other Stories *contains "stories of vigorous and brilliant unconventionality.*]

In Stuart Dybek's first book, a group of eleven uncanny stories about childhood and adolescence, we encounter a world radically different from Miss Beattie's or Mr. Vivante's. It is the Southwest side of Chicago during the 1940s, fifties, and sixties, a Slavic neighborhood gradually being overtaken by Blacks and Spanish. It is also a harsh and repulsive section of the city, which the author's singular imagination none-theless enchants, transforming it into a world of magical grotesques. With its antecedents in Russian, and, perhaps, in Yiddish literature (one is sometimes reminded of I. B. Singer's stories), as much as in Sherwood Anderson and James T. Farrell, his fiction treats Ragmen, who hold strange rituals on the outskirts of town on Sunday after Mass; an old *buzka,* the Cat Woman, and her crazy grandson, Swantek, who drowns kittens and hangs them on the clothesline to dry; Budhardin, who returns to the neighborhood inside a mechanical elephant to revenge himself on the parish church; and, the oddest of all, "Uncle" and his apprentice, who scour the highways of Cook County for dead animals to stuff and sell to restaurants. But it is not only the trolls and ogres of the city that haunt one. It is also the gruesome sights, such as the one of the fat Puerto Rican woman tied to a telephone pole by drunks on a Saturday night: "'Help,' she said in English. She didn't yell, she hardly said it, just kind of formed the word with her lips, looking straight at him with terrified made-up eyes. One of the men kicked her when she said it. It wasn't a violent kick—he brought his foot up like a punter into her breast, which lopped up and hit her in the chin." The smells of the Chicago neighborhoods linger too—of "cat sexuality" on hot summer nights, of whiskey vomit, and of blood and sauerkraut soup.

Moments of beauty are rare. In the first story, **"The Palatski Man,"** Mr. Dybek does describe the marvel of a girl coming into puberty: "She ran from the window to the mirror and looked at herself in the dark, feeling her teeth growing and hair pushing through her skin in the tender parts of her body that had been bare and her breasts swelling like apples from her flat chest and her blood burning, and then in a lapse of wind, when the leaves fell back to earth, she heard his gold bell jangle again as if silver and knew that it was time to go." Still, growth, for the most part, is agonizing, surrounded as the children are by ugliness and putrefaction. And so, predictably enough, in the last story, the Uncle's apprentice, a figure of the young artist, stands on top of a railroad bridge gathering pigeon eggs, and as the bridge opens to let barges pass, "Warning bells clanged. Finally the boy raised his arm. Through swirling birds he waved good-bye."

The artist's flight from his city on waxen wings has become, of course, a mere conceit in modern fiction, especially in first books. It is a tired convention, too easily fallen into, and should be abandoned. Besides, in Mr. Dybek's stories of vigorous and brilliant unconventionality such a scene pales. It is all part of the modern writer's urge to mythologize reality, discontented as he is with the weightiness of the familiar. To be always trying to see through the world and to elevate it to spiritual significance is to chance missing what is so splendidly there. This may account for the fact that Mr. Dybek's characters experience so little joy or sensuous pleasure and that family life is almost totally absent from the book. The impressive exception is the story **"Sauerkraut**

Soup," in which the narrator lovingly and straightforwardly tells about working in an ice cream factory, about the old immigrant workingmen, and about eating the soup, a magical ritual. If Mr. Dybek's first novel, which his publisher informs us is underway, deals with this kind of experience, it will also be well worth reading. . . .

Joseph Coates (review date 8 April 1990)

SOURCE: "A Storied Renaissance," in *The Chicago Tribune,* April 8, 1990, pp. 1, 4.

[*In the following excerpt, Coates asserts that Dybek's* The Coast of Chicago *is further proof of the renaissance of the short story.*]

The market is minuscule and shrinking further under the heat of bottom-line publishing forces—just one weekly magazine, the New Yorker, now regularly publishes short stories, as opposed to more than 50 in the days before TV. Yet the form is booming in both quantity and especially quality, as editor Shannon Ravenel confirms in her introduction to *The Best American Short Stories of the Eighties.*

> I believe the 1980s will be known as another golden age [of the short story], though for reasons very different from those which led to the story's great popularity in the teens and twenties, when writers could live off their work in a way that today's practitioners could not.

Though I not only agree with this but also will soon offer more proof of it, Ravenel's excellent collection, to which we will return, is misleadingly titled, to the extent that anyone might infer that the book includes all the best stories or writers of the '80s. To start with the most glaring omission, it hasn't one story by Stuart Dybek, whose second collection of stories establishes him as not merely a talent but a magician comparable to Eudora Welty and Joy Williams.

Not since Cyrus Colter's *The Beach Umbrella,* 20 years ago, has a book of Chicago stories hit me as hard as Dybek's *The Coast of Chicago.* Its excellence again suggests that the "renaissance" of the short story discussed by Ravenel may involve a return to regionalism among our best writers (E. Annie Proulx and Howard Frank Mosher in New England, Richard Ford, Tom McGuane and Rick Bass in the Far West and South, to name just a few), and Dybek's tone of eloquent, rueful valedictory to a childhood place gives his book specific links (probably intentional, in the spirit of homage) to the early story collections of two other Midwestern elegists, Sherwood Anderson and Ernest Hemingway.

Like Hemingway's *In Our Time,* **The Coast of Chicago** interleaves sketchy one or two-page vignettes, which are sometimes intact stories themselves, between stories of more or less standard length—though, unlike Hemingway, Dybek often links the two, the sketch serving as a prologue to the story. For example, the one-and-a-half pages of **"Bottle Caps"** describe how the child narrator's collection of beer-bottle caps, carefully harvested from the alleys behind taverns, is stolen by his kid brother: "'I've been using them as tombstones,' he said, 'in my insect graveyard.'"

This introduces an absolute marvel of a story, both macabre and funny and itself only three pages long, called **"The Death of the Right Fielder"** that could have been written by Donald Barthelme or Kafka—or, more accurately, it was written by a homegrown Kafka who knows the terminal boredom and alienation of playing right field in sandlot games. "After too many balls went out and never came back we went out to check," it begins. "It was a long walk—he always played deep. Finally we saw him, from the distance resembling the towel we sometimes threw down for second base."

This unlikely tone of hilarious, anti-sentimental eulogy is maintained even in the presence of the deceased, as his teammates try to figure out what killed him: "Nor could it have been leukemia. He wasn't a talented enough player for that. He'd have been playing center, not right, if leukemia was going to get him."

These stories are not only set in Chicago, they also breathe it. The brilliantly compressed, 27-page **"Nighthawks"** (named after the Edward Hopper painting) is an impressionistic novel-in-miniature that floats the reader on a river of rain past a kaleidoscopic view of the city at night—a Hopperesque diner, an ethnic neighborhood on the Near South Side, lovers waking at dawn in a Gold Coast apartment—complete with subtitled chapters and recurring characters.

Like George Willard at the end of *Winesburg, Ohio,* the unnamed narrator who has guided us through many of these stories is on a train and bidding farewell not only to his childhood but also its locale at the end of *The Coast of Chicago.* Both think of "little things," but George, who lived in a different time, merely visualizes the "tall woman, beautifully gowned, who had once stayed overnight at his father's hotel," while Dybek's young narrator, in the empty conductor's booth of a CTA train hurtling toward Evanston, is urgently making love to a woman he'll soon part from, as he glimpses "the landscape of the El I'd memorized from subway windows over a lifetime of rides: the podiatrist's foot sign past Fullerton. . . ."

A high school kid on a platform waves and grins as he

catches sight of the couple, and "[i]t was as if I were standing on that platform . . . on one of those endlessly accumulated afternoons after school when I stood almost outside of time simply waiting for a train, and I thought how much I'd have loved seeing someone like us streaming by."

What's interesting here is the reversal of direction. Dybek's narrator is leaving Chicago, while Willard was heading toward it. Anderson, Hemingway and Edgar Lee Masters used their early books of small-town life as weapons in a "revolt from the village" that would take them to Chicago and beyond; Dybek's lyric nostalgia looks back with almost unqualified fondness on urban neighborhoods that were like small towns in their sense of community.

It's almost as if the writers of the '80s had skipped back several literary generations to have their heroes light out for the territory with Huck Finn—the same territory as before, essentially, but settled now with clusters of academics, scientists, writers-in-residence and corporate types, all co-existing uneasily with Bobbie Ann Mason's or Russell Banks' embittered and culturally uprooted small-town natives. . . .

Michiko Kakutani (review date 20 April 1990)

SOURCE: "Lyrical Loss and Desolation of Misfits in Chicago," in *The New York Times Book Review,* April 20, 1990, p. C31.

[*In the following review, Kakutani compares Dybek's* The Coast of Chicago *with Sherwood Anderson's* Winsburg, Ohio, *stating that while it lacks a central hero and "authorial perspective to put the characters' dilemmas in context with the larger world," the collection does possess an "emotional forcefulness."*]

The narrator of one of Stuart Dybek's elegiac new stories goes to the Art Institute of Chicago and stands before Edward Hopper's "Nighthawks," that famous painting of a corner diner, done in somber tones of black and blue and brown. He stands there, closes his eyes, and thinks to himself: "It was night in Hopper's painting; the diner illuminated the dark city corner with a stark light it didn't seem capable of throwing on its own. Three customers sat at the counter as if waiting, not for something to begin, but rather to end, and I knew how effortless it would be to open my eyes and find myself waiting there, too."

Hopper's painting captures perfectly the mood of Mr. Dybek's stories—the solitary lives of his characters, the lyrical desolation of their city neighborhood, the feeling of longing and regret that encircles their hopes and dreams. As in

Sherwood Anderson's *Winesburg, Ohio,* most of the stories take place at night or twilight, that hour when the cheerful routines of day give way to more subterranean emotions, when the mundane facts of life take on a hallucinatory magic. The reader is introduced to a group of insomniacs who haunt the local diner, a pair of speed freaks who ride the deserted subways after midnight, a gang of teen-age boys who tour the darkened city of Chicago in a red convertible.

Like the characters in *Winesburg,* these people tend to be outsiders—loners, eccentrics, misfits, visionaries, who are tied to one another only by a shared sense of yearning and loss. An alcoholic butcher named Antek, who's so drunk that he has chopped off bits of his own fingers, gets himself locked in a freezer and nearly dies. A young girl, known as the local saint, drowns in the nearby park's lagoon; her father freezes her body in a chunk of ice. A fanatical altar boy named Pancho, who believes in saints and miracles and ghosts, goes crazy and winds up in jail; rumors later circulate that he has disappeared—he's hung himself in his jail cell, he's been packed off to the psycho ward in Kankakee, he's made a deal and gotten out.

In one of the most affecting stories in this volume, a beautiful, musically patterned tale called **"Chopin in Winter,"** Mr. Dybek creates a lovely portrait of three lonely people who are briefly brought together by Chopin's music; their lives intersect for a moment, then shift and move away forever.

There is a lyricism to Mr. Dybek's writing, an eagerness to read metaphors and hidden meanings in the stuff of ordinary life.
—*Michiko Kakutani*

A young woman named Marcy, who plays the waltzes and nocturnes on her piano, is living at home with her mother; she's pregnant with the baby of a man she won't name, and her impassioned playing becomes a kind of lament for her own lost youth. An old man, Dzia-Dzia, who listens to her music from a downstairs apartment, is a visitor in town; he's spent his life on the road, moving from country to country, city to city, and he hears in the music some distant reminder of the life he abandoned in Poland so many years ago. His young nephew, who narrates the story, also listens to the music; he's developed a schoolboy crush on Marcy, and he hears strange melodies in the music she plays, faint intimations of the grown-up mysteries that lie waiting in the world beyond.

By the end of the story, Marcy has left home to have her baby alone; Dzia-Dzia has also disappeared—he's set off for yet another unknown destination; and the young narrator stands poised on the brink of adolescence, ready for new adventures of his own. "It took time for the music to fade," he recalls, "I kept catching wisps of it in the air shaft, behind walls and ceilings, under bathwater." When it finally does disappear, it leaves behind a silence. "Not an ordinary silence of absence and emptiness, but a pure silence beyond daydream and memory, as intense as the music it replaced, which, like music, had the power to change whoever listened."

There is a lyricism to Mr. Dybek's writing, an eagerness to read metaphors and hidden meanings in the stuff of ordinary life. Although some of the slighter sketches in this volume take this impulse to an extreme—resulting in abstract and willfully poetic passages that read like self-conscious creative-writing class exercises—the more expansive stories ground this lyricism and the author's surrealistic flights of fancy in gritty, finely observed descriptions of character and place. Mr. Dybek lets us hear the hip, knowing dialogue of teen-agers who have grown up on Chicago's South Side; and he shows us the rhythms of life here, in the lower-middle-class neighborhoods populated by immigrants from Mexico and Poland.

It's a grimy, dilapidated neighborhood that has just been designated as an Official Blight Area by the city government. Old buildings are being torn down for an urban renewal program; old streets are being torn up for an expressway. "Blight was just something that happened, like acne or old age," says one character. "Maybe declaring it official mattered in that mystical world of property values, but it wasn't a radical step, like condemning buildings or labeling a place a slum. Slums were on the other side of the viaduct."

"Blight, in fact, could be considered a kind of official recognition, a grudging admission that among blocks of factories, railroad tracks, truck docks, industrial dumps, scrapyards, expressways, and the drainage canal, people had managed to wedge in their everyday lives."

In the end, *The Coast of Chicago* doesn't have the cumulative, mythic power of *Winesburg, Ohio:* there is no central hero like Anderson's George Willard to tie the stories together, no authorial perspective to put the characters' dilemmas in context with the larger world. Individual stories like **"Blight," "Hot Ice"** and **"Chopin in Winter,"** however, possess an emotional forcefulness: they introduce us to characters who want to take up permanent residence in our minds, and in doing so, they persuasively conjure up a fictional world that is both ordinary and amazing.

Katharine Weber (review date 20 May 1990)

SOURCE: "Windy City Dreaming," in *The New York Times Book Review,* May 20, 1990, p. 30.

[*In the following review, Weber praises Dybek's* The Coast of Chicago.]

Stuart Dybek could flip a coin and win a bet that it would land on its edge. In his second collection of stories, he gambles (usually successfully) that the paradoxical borders and margins of life are the most interesting places to locate his fiction. Some of these 14 stories are big and rich, long enough for a leisurely pace and pleasant reiterations of themes and motifs without running the least risk of seeming overstuffed or repetitious. The other stories, interleaved, are extremely short, ranging from a few paragraphs to a few pages. But these brief illuminations are no less effective, and they stand alone with a deft elegance that makes them far more than amusing little palate cleansers between courses. Crossing over to the lost territories of childhood is a recurring theme in *The Coast of Chicago.* Memories that are intensely dreamlike, as opposed to nostalgic, seem to drive many of Mr. Dybek's characters, whose thoughts circle and hover over old Chicago neighborhoods. One of the longest and most moving stories, **"Nighthawks,"** has clearly been inspired by the eponymous Edward Hopper painting of a cafe and its middle-of-the-night denizens. Mr. Dybek names the night counterman Ray and imagines him trying to sleep during the day: "Perhaps it's something other than insomnia, to lie listening to children yelling as if they've recreated light; to try to dream, but succeed only in remembering." Laden but not burdened with significant imagery, this story exemplifies Mr. Dybek's persistence in examining the edge between wakefulness and dreaming, where memories lie coiled.

David Montrose (review date 26 July 1991)

SOURCE: "Into the Underworlds," in *Times Literary Supplement,* July 26, 1991, p. 19.

[*In the following review, Montrose discusses the problems of combining two volumes of Dybek's stories into the British version of* The Coast of Chicago.]

Eight of the stories in *The Coast of Chicago,* Stuart Dybek's fine British début, have been selected from a larger volume of the same name published in America last year; the remaining six are from his previous collection, *Childhood and Other Neighbourhoods.* The titles are apposite. Dybek's fictive territory is his native patch, the Slav and Hispanic districts of Chicago's South Side (frequently during the 1950s, "those years between Korea and Vietnam"); his protagonists are often children and adolescents.

All the earlier stories are third-person narratives, the majority with children serving as the centres of consciousness. Particularly impressive are two in which pairs of children stray into alarming social netherworlds. **"The Palatski Man"** sees John and his kid sister follow a sweet-vendor back to the encampment of a gypsy-like clan of peddlers, where they witness a strange quasi-Mass. In **"Blood Soup"**, two brothers brave dangerous neighbourhoods in quest of fresh duck blood (no longer obtainable legally), an essential ingredient of a restorative potion for their ailing grandmother.

A variation on this device is employed in **"The Wake"**, in which misadventures befall a young woman returning at night to the area where she grew up, an area that has since "gone down". By contrast, the hero of **"The Apprentice"** is part of criminal society, working for his uncle, an unlicensed taxidermist and supplier of out-of-season game to restaurants. The underworld in **"Horror Movie"** is that of the imagination: a boy is unable to overcome his addiction to monster flicks even though they give him nightmares and cause him to start at shadows.

Dybek spices his naturalism with dashes of the grotesque and the surreal, to good effect. When, however, he increases the measures, in **"Visions of Budharin"**, the result is much less successful: inexplicably concealed inside a ramshackle mechanical elephant, a tycoon revisits his childhood haunts, undergoes indignities, broods on bygone injustices, wrecks a church interior, and finally floats away down a drainage canal. The plot may sound promisingly bizarre; the story is disappointingly half-baked.

The best of the later stories, **"Hot Ice"** and **"Blight"**, are rather more accomplished than their earlier counterparts, but ultimately slightly less striking. The extended (thirty-two page) **"Hot Ice"**, an O. Henry Award-winner, recounts episodically the low-lives of Eddie Kapusta and his pals. Their scenes are interwoven with a local legend concerning a drowned woman preserved in her father's ice-plant.

Dybek's style in his third-person narratives is somewhat reminiscent of Bellow's, though without the range and exuberance. The first-person **"Blight"** is plainer, closer to the standard voice of the contemporary American short story. Superficially akin to **"Hot Ice"**—dealing with four high-school buddies whose neighbourhood is "an Official Blight Area"—it is altogether jauntier: the kids have wider horizons; they read (Kerouac, Thomas Merton), write songs, start an R&R band. **"Nighthawks"** is the most satisfying of the other longer stories: a little anthology of tangentially connected *récits* whose focus is a twenty-four-hour diner modelled on the one in the famous painting by Edward Hopper. **"Bijou"** constitutes something of a departure: a tense and angry piece about turning human suffering into a commodity and the way cinematic depictions of violence desensitize our responses to the real thing.

In carving this single collection from two, the best stories have been chosen, but both volumes are rather misrepresented as a result. The variety of style and length in the later stories is deceptive: ***Childhood and Other Neighbourhoods*** contains several first-person shorter narratives, none of which has been chosen. The later "rejects" are shorter pieces, none outstanding but which achieved a cumulative impact and gave the parent volume a unity now lacking.

Thomas S. Gladsky (essay date Summer 1995)

SOURCE: "From Ethnicity to Multiculturalism: The Fiction of Stuart Dybek," in *MELUS*, Vol. 20, No. 2, Summer, 1995, pp. 105-118.

[*In the following essay, Gladsky analyzes the significance of ethnicity in the work of Stuart Dybek.*]

The new world culture and old country heritage of approximately fifteen million Americans of Polish descent are among multicultural America's best kept secrets. Historically a quiet minority, they have been eager to acculturate, assimilate, and melt into the mainstream. One of the consequences of this has been a failure to acquaint other Americans with Polish culture—its history and literature—or to establish a recognized ethnic literary tradition. This is not to say that there is not a Polish presence in American letters. From the 1830s and the arrival of the first significant body of Polish émigrés, primarily officers exiled after the 1831 uprising against the tzar, American writers have created Polish literary selves in plays, fiction, poems, and in prose works numbering perhaps as many as two hundred. Many of these contain abbreviated characterizations, predictably simplistic portraits, or, in some cases, merely composite Slavic cultural representations. At the same time, a few writers of classic ethnic and immigrant fiction, such as Karl Harriman (*The Homebuilders* 1903), Edith Miniter (*Our Natupski Neighbors* 1916), and Joseph Vogel (*Man's Courage* 1938), have sensitively explored the culture of Americans of Polish descent. Despite their efforts, what has emerged, as Thomas Napierkowski, Caroline Golab, and others have argued, is a set of stereotypes that have in certain ways attempted to transform a culture into a caricature.

Beginning in the 1930s, descent writers themselves began to examine the Polish self in a multiplicity of ways when Monica Krawczyk, Victoria Janda, and Helen Bristol turned to the immigrant generation as the subject of their poetry and fiction. Two decades later Richard Bankowsky produced a remarkable tetralogy about the arrival and dispersal of a turn of the century immigrant family. Bankowsky's *A Glass Rose* is perhaps the best novel about Slavic immigration in all of American literature. Wanda Kubiak (*Polonaise Nevermore*) and Matt Babinski (*By Raz,* 1937) have described Poles in Wisconsin and Connecticut. In a series of novels in the 1970s, Darryl Poniscan followed the fortunes of the Buddusky clan in eastern Pennsylvania and elsewhere. In fiction for children, Anne Pellowski lovingly describes growing up ethnic in the Latsch Valley of Wisconsin. In numerous poems, *The Warsaw Sparks,* and his soon to be published memoir, *Szostak,* Gary Gildner explores both old and new world selves in sensitive ways. Most recently, Anthony Bukoski looks back to a rapidly vanishing Duluth community in *Children of Strangers.* In short, when one also considers the "Solidarity generation" of Czeslaw Milosz, Eva Hoffman, Stanislaus Baranczak, Janusz Glowacki, W. S. Kuniczak, and others, the Polish experience in American literature becomes demonstrable if not exceptional.

Even so, contemporary writers of Polish descent face complex problems, some of which are, of course, shared to some degree by all those who write about ethnicity. An ever-narrowing definition of multiculturalism that virtually excludes Eastern Europeans is one. Competing waves of Polish immigrants, dividing the ethnic community into descendants of the largely peasant immigration of 1880-1914, a post-war influx of "displaced persons," and a newer, more highly educated, urban Solidarity generation, is another. Added to these are America's general unfamiliarity with Polish culture, originating during the period of great immigration when nativists tended to lump all Slavic peoples together and to promote caricatures and stereotypes of Poles in particular.

Stuart Dybek is a case in point. The author of numerous poems and short stories, including a collection of verse (***Brass Knuckles,*** 1976) and two collections of fiction (***Childhood and Other Neighborhoods,*** 1986, and ***The Coast of Chicago,*** 1990), Dybek is among the first writers of Polish descent (who write about the ethnic self) to receive national recognition. Reviewers have praised him as a regional writer (Chicago) and as a social critic who sides with those on the margin. They have compared him with Bellow and Dreiser and pointed to his city landscapes and spare, terse dialogue while, unfortunately, ignoring the ethnic dimension in his work. To be sure, Dybek does indeed write about the human condition. He gives us primarily initiation stories of urban adolescent males stretching into adulthood, expressing their sexuality, bravado and intellectual independence and realigning their social identity. Chicago with its particularized ethnic neighborhoods is a marked presence in their lives.

For Dybek, who grew up in southside Chicago, ethnicity is itself a natural and integral part of the human condition. The population in his neighborhood was mainly Eastern European and Hispanic. As he describes it: "The Eastern Europeans—Poles and Czechs—were migrating out; the Hispanics were migrating in. Each group had its own bars;

they shared the same churches." Ethnicity, moreover, is also a condition of the contemporary literary experience. If not itself the central thrust of Dybek's work, it is one of those doorways, as he prefers to describe it, that leads to "some other dimension of experience and perception that forever changes the way one sees life." It is no surprise therefore that ethnicity is everywhere in his works. In **"The River,"** a Ukrainian Kid fiddles a nocturne. The girl in **"Laughter"** is Greek. The upstairs neighbors in **"Chopin in Winter"** speak Czech. The eccentric teacher in **"Farewell"** comes from Odessa. Hispanics appear in a number of stories; but Polish ethnicity is the tie that binds Dybek's protagonists together and supplies the cultural temperament in his fiction. Young men are named Swantek, Marzek, Vukovich, Kozak, and Gowumpe. Grandmothers called *Busha* worship in churches named St. Stanislaus. Relatives refer to soup as *zupa;* the neighbors listen to the Frankie Yankovitch Polka Hour; passersby speak Polish. Here and there we hear about *mazurkas,* Paderewski, Our Lady of Czestochowa, *babushkas,* and DPs, a recurring reference to non-native born Americans of Polish descent.

But what kind of ethnicity is Dybek portraying and how does he, a third generation American at some distance from his cultural roots, choose to represent his own cultural heritage? What, in effect, is Polish about these stories and what is the relationship between old and new expressions of ethnicity inside and outside Polonia? To some, Dybek's fiction may appear to be anachronistic, in that his frame of reference excludes the post-war and more recent Solidarity immigration that has transformed the Polish community in the United States, especially in Chicago, the setting for much of his work. Dybek, it could be argued, understands ethnicity almost exclusively from the point of view of the peasant generation and its descendants. In truth, the period of immigration and old world ties has long ago ended for his ethnic Poles. Consequently, he does not focus on assimilation and acculturation; nor are his characters busily collecting and preserving bits and pieces of their old world heritage. To the contrary, his protagonists are young, streetsmart, third generation Americans who know little, if anything, about Poland's past or present or the cultural nuances of the immigrant generation from which they are descended.

> **For Dybek, who grew up in southside Chicago, ethnicity is itself a natural and integral part of the human condition.**
> —*Thomas S. Gladsky*

If anything, Dybek shows this generation resisting its ethnic impulses even as it rushes toward them. His young protagonists are updated modernists who, like Stephen Daedalus or Alfred Prufrock, wander city streets content with their own alienation and superior to the urban blight and social chaos that surround them. They are loners, eccentrics, budding intellectuals. They have no conscious sense of themselves as Polish-American or as ethnic in the usual sense of descending from a common history, religion, geography, and set of traditions. They are consumed instead with adolescence, environment, friends—with life in deteriorating and changing southside Chicago. They prefer Kerouac, the White Sox, Edward Hopper and rock music. Dybek's young Chicagoans thrive on melancholy, feast on loneliness, inhabit the "hourless times of night." They are refugees from Edward Hopper's "Nighthawks," which Dybek features prominently in his work. At the same time, they are acutely aware that they ache for something they cannot name "but knew was missing," as the narrator of **"The River"** phrases it; and that "things are gone they couldn't remember, but missed; and things were gone they weren't sure ever were there." Primarily, their narratives are remembrances of youthful things past.

For them, ethnicity and memory are interwoven naturally and succinctly. Consequently ethnicity in these stories is everywhere and yet almost beyond reach. Polish culture, for example, often enters through the back door. Dybek never identifies his characters as Poles, nor do they refer to themselves as Polish or as Polish-American. Polishness is rather cumulative, dependent partly on recurring signifiers and partly on the interconnectedness of the stories themselves. In "typical" fashion, he draws attention to the presence of cultural differences in the first few lines and then proceeds to develop a generic ethnic cultural landscape which seems to have few particular Polish markers. This approach is evident even in the first story in *Childhood and Other Neighborhoods.* The title, **"The Palatski Man,"** itself calls attention to otherness, although only midway in the story does Dybek explain that *palatski,* apparently a regional American corruption of *plocki,* the Polish word for potato pancake, was a food once sold by vendors in southside Chicago. In the first page the reader also encounters the Slavic-sounding name Leon *Sisca* and the Catholic mysteries of Palm Sunday. The children attend St. Roman's grammar school, have friends named *Zmiga* and another named Raymond *Cruz,* "part Mexican" and perhaps part Polish. In addition, the children define their surroundings in terms of their parish church, which distinguishes their neighborhood from the adjoining one where "more Mexicans lived." Apart from the fact that the *palatski* man stammers in "foreign English," no other overt references to ethnicity in general or to Polishness in particular occur.

This approach is repeated elsewhere. In **"The Wake,"** Dybek looks at one evening in the life of Jill, a southside Chicago teenager whose surname and particular cultural heritage remain anonymous. Dybek, however, establishes Jill's parameters, physical and psychological, within an ethnic landscape. On her way to the wake, she hears the bells of St. Kasimir's church and walks along the street that serves as a boundary between her neighborhood and St. Anne's, "an old Slavic neighborhood that had become Spanish." She heads toward Zeijek's Funeral home, "a three-story building domed with its fake Russian onion." Reminiscent of Joyce Carol Oates's "Where Are You Going, Where Have You Been?" Jill eventually drives off with an intrusive Hispanic whose ethnicity poses no threat to her. We learn that the culture of Jill's neighborhood is Slavic-Hispanic. She drives by the hot tamale man with his striped umbrella; she hears radios turned to Latin stations; and she refers to the young man's car as "Pancho." There is no dominant ethnic "theme" in **"The Wake,"** no social or generational problems, no hint of cultural oppression or collision. Ethnicity is muted, understood, and natural—an integral part of the contemporary urban experience and cultural context—but not exclusively tied to national boundaries, even though one suspects that Jill might be of Polish descent.

In other stories in *Childhood and Other Neighborhoods, The Coast of Chicago,* and elsewhere, Dybek constructs a more specifically Polish ethnic identity for his characters, their neighborhood, and their frame of mind. In **"The Cat Woman"** and **"Blood Soup,"** the two stories that immediately succeed **"The Palatski Man,"** Dybek repeats the pattern of the opening story, relying primarily on names, words, and surface features to establish an ethnic landscape. At the outset, the reader learns that *buzka* and *busha* are what some people call their grandmothers. The reader also meets characters with Slavic-sounding names such as Swantek and Stefush (a Polish diminutive for Stephen). The cat woman, Swantek's grandmother, fingers her rosary and tunes her radio to the polka station. She also shares cabbage soup with her neighbor, Mrs. Panova. In stories like **"The Cat Woman,"** the ethnic markers suggest a composite Slavic cultural landscape although discerning readers might interpret the markers as the outlines of Polish-American culture.

A distinctly Polish frame of reference becomes evident only in **"Blood Soup,"** the third story in *Childhood,* where, in addition to Busha "clutching the crucifix" and references to such old world Catholic practices as the kissing of holy pictures, Dybek includes more compelling evidence of Polish ethnicity. On occasion, he uses Polish words (*usiadz, dziekuje, dupa, czarnina, rozumiesz*) without translation. His young hero remembers the traditional Polish custom of blessing the Easter breakfast food: colored eggs, ham, bread, kraut, horseradish, and kielbasa. More importantly, in this story Dybek moves beyond ceremonies and the surface features of ethnicity when he tries to capture something of the old world temperament that differentiates Eastern Europeans from Americans and first generation ethnics from their descendants. At one point, Stefush recognizes that his grandmother is different in more substantive ways that merely her taste for *czarnina,* a peasant soup made from duck's blood. He senses in her "a kind of love he thought must have come from the old country—instinctive, unquestioning like her strength, something foreign that he couldn't find in himself, that hadn't even been transmitted to his mother."

Ethnicity, particularly the culture of Americans of Polish descent, is cumulative in Dybek's writing. Often one story clarifies and extends an ethnic dimension introduced in another. For example, in order to understand fully what Dybek means in **"Blood Soup"** by "a kind of love" that "must have come from the old country," we must turn to **"A Minor Mood,"** published some seven years later. This is a familiar tale of immigrants and their descendants. Joey, a young third generation American, remembers attacks of bronchitis and his granny swooping down upon him, bathing his neck with a glob of Vicks and wrapping it in her *babushka,* applying camphor to his chest, filling the rooms with steam, mixing honey, lemon, Jim Beam, and boiling water for him to drink (and for herself too). These were mornings, he concludes, "to be tucked away at the heart of life, so that later, whenever one needed to draw upon the recollection of joy in order to get through troubled times it would be there." All of **"A Minor Mood,"** in effect, develops and expands the ethnic temperament alluded to in **"Blood Soup,"** although a few ethnic signifiers can be noticed.

Only once does Dybek turn to what might be called a paradigmatic ethnic tale in order to define the contemporary Polish-American self. In **"Chopin in Winter,"** a story about the conflicting claims of descent and consent, the aging Dzia Dzia tells his own story to his grandson—his trek from Krakow to Gdansk to avoid being drafted into the tzarist army, his immigration to the coal mines of Pennsylvania and the barges of the Great Lakes. At one point, Dzia Dzia's story melts into that of another Polish immigrant and national icon, Frederick Chopin. "Chopin," he'd whisper hoarsely to Michael, pointing to the ceiling with the reverence of nuns pointing to heaven." More than telling his story, the old man provides a cultural frame for the third generation, creating an image of what it means to be ethnic.

Dybek does not mean to stop here, however, with romantic and sentimental notions of heritage; he is more interested in cultural fusion, in that uniquely American acculturating process described by Werner Sollors in *Beyond Ethnicity* as the tension between "our hereditary qualities" and our position as "architects of our fate." Grandfather, for instance, mentions in **"Chopin in Winter"** that Paderewski dearly loved Chopin; but Michael does not know Paderewski, a sign of his distance from his cultural heritage. Instinctively, Grandfather connects their American and Polish heritages in a comic but revealing and shrewd fashion, by asking, "Do you know who's George Washington, who's Joe Dimaggio, who's Walt Disney? . . . Paderewski was like them, except he

played Chopin. . . . See, deep down inside, Lefty, you know more than you think." Even in this, one of Dybek's most "Polish" stories, cultural transmission gives way to a new cultural pattern of consent and descent. For Americans of Polish descent, ethnicity means knowing about Joe Dimaggio *and* Paderewski, Washington *and* Chopin, Disneyland *and* Krakow.

Ethnicity also means Catholicism; in fact, Catholicism in the form of childhood experiences with the church, the parochial school, or the religious practices and attitudes of the immigrant generation permeates these stories and poems and often is the singular definer of Polish culture. Even here Dybek concentrates not on Polish but on *ethnic* expressions of and responses to Catholicism. In a recently published chapbook, *The Story of Mist,* Dybek begins by wondering what it is "about the belly button that connected it to the Old Country?" To explain, he immediately turns to religious metaphors, noting that "outside, night billowed like the habits of nuns through vigil lights of snow," while Busha's "rosary-pinched fingers" promised to lead inward. But it is the tolling of the bells from the steeple of St. Kasimir's that serves as the umbilical cord between old and new world culture. When he hears them, he knows that "Krakow is only blocks away, just past Goldblatt's darkened sign."

The parish church is thus the center of vision in a significant number of stories. In **"The Wake,"** Jill uses the church steeple to locate her whereabouts in the neighborhood. Ladies murmur the rosary in front of the icon of Our Lady of Czestochowa in **"Neighborhood Drunk."** In a fit of madness Budhardin destroys the inside of the parish church in **"Visions of Budhardin."** Old women walk "on their knees up the marble aisle to kiss the relics" and Eddy and Manny try to visit all the neighborhood churches in **"Hot Ice." "The Woman Who Fainted"** does so at the 11:15 mass. Stanley's girlfriend lives across from the Assumption Church, leading him to call her "the Unadulterated one." To the young protagonists in these stories, the church represents the mystery of old world culture—of Polishness itself.

Consequently, Dybek frequently turns to childhood experiences with the clergy, the parochial school, and the rituals and mysteries of Eastern European Catholicism in order to develop plot and theme. There is little that is peaceful, consoling, or even attractive in these memories and experiences, however. We read about the cruelty of Father O'Donnel. We meet Sister Monica who loses her teaching assignment because she becomes hysterical in front of her fifth grade class. We listen to the narrator of **"The Dead in Korea,"** remembering how he was made to kneel on three-cornered drafting rulers in parochial school. At the same time, Dybek writes about the mystical attractions of Catholicism that draw his young people toward familiar ritual and ceremony despite their growing skepticism. This is perhaps best expressed in **"Hot Ice,"** where Manny and Eddie reenact a childhood ritual of visiting seven churches on Good Friday afternoon. They walk from St. Roman's to St. Michael's, from St. Kasimir's to St. Anne's, from St. Pius's to St. Adalbert's, then finally to the church of St. Procopius. At first, they merely peek in and leave, "as if touching base." But soon their "familiarity with small rituals quickly returned: dipping their fingers in the holy water font by the door, making the automatic sign of the cross as they passed the life-sized crucified Christs that hung in the vestibules where old women and school kids clustered to kiss the spikes in the bronze or bloody plaster feet."

Dybek makes it clear that the pull of Catholicism is both spiritual and cultural and that it is rooted in the immigrant experience itself. He makes this connection through the recurring presence of old people, the last of the immigrant generation. Usually these characters are grandparents engaged in helping third generation youngsters understand their cultural identity. Dzia Dzia in **"Chopin in Winter,"** Busha in **"Blood Soup,"** the old man in **"The Apprentice,"** and Gran in **"A Minor Mood"** all help to introduce their grandchildren to Polish history, tradition, and temperament.

At other times Dybek integrates the immigrant generation into the mystique of Polish Catholicism. He does this primarily through repeated references to older women involved in one form of worship or another. The narrator of **"The Woman Who Fainted,"** intrigued by the ritualistic fainting that often occurs at the 11:15 mass, observes the hand of an "old woman in a babushka" that darts out to correct the dress hem of the fainting lady. In **"Chopin in Winter,"** Mrs. Kubiak joins the regulars at morning mass, "wearing babushkas and dressed in black like a sodality of widows droning endless mournful litanies." And in **"Good Friday,"** a two-page story published in *Gulf Coast,* the young narrator, entranced with the church organ, the statues, Sister Monica, the incense and the holy water, focuses ultimately on the "old women, babushkaed in black, weeping as they walk on their knees up the marble aisle to the altar in order to kiss the relic." These people, Dybek implies, are nothing less than old world culture transfigured into the new world. In this sense Dybek captures both the attraction and rejection of whatever it is that Polish culture has come to mean in post-war America.

In fact, rejection and denial and the subsequent reshaping of cultural identity are essential ingredients of the ethnicization that occurs in these stories. In a very real sense all of Dybek's fiction is about social disorganization and reorganization in the classic sense of these principles outlined by Thomas and Znaniecki in *The Polish Peasant in Europe and America.* The alienation that exists in Dybek's younger characters results as much from cultural tensions, however, as it does from socio-economics and shifting philosophical perspectives. Typically, Dybek contrasts the immigrant generation with its third generation descendants with an eye toward showing cultural transformation, or he describes the simultaneous act of acquiring and rejecting a cultural past. While "ethnicity" is still the norm by which his protagonists view the world, Dybek insists that contemporary urban ethnicity must be defined differently from that of preceding time periods. Thus he attempts to differentiate between old and new ethnicity even in his ethnically Polish characters.

For example, while Dybek on the one hand offers sympathetic portraits of grandparents and other first generation Americans of Polish descent and sensitively explores the essentials of Polish culture, he on the other hand frequently presents these cultural representatives as eccentric grotesques out of touch with the times and their adopted culture. Typically he portrays the immigrant generation as the cultural "other" rather than as the cultural norm. In fact, the more Polish the characters are, the more eccentric and grotesque they and their cultural practices tend to look to the reader. The **"Palatski Man,"** the opening story in *Childhood and Other Neighborhoods,* sets this tone and outlines this direction. The *palatski* man, not dignified with any other name, is a rather frightening and threatening figure (at least to the two youngsters in the story). He is an exotic street vendor who appears to live with the peddlers, ragpickers, and other cultural outsiders in makeshift housing near an urban dumping ground. The food he sells is culturally unrecognizable although Slavic sounding. His white clothing and white cart, while ordinary enough, are undercut by his foreign-sounding English (although we never hear him talk) and his involvement in Palm Sunday Eucharistic rituals with other ragmen. Although we do not learn the *palatski* man's cultural heritage, his characterization, his ragged associates, and their surreal surroundings create an atmosphere of strangeness and alienation toward the culture represented by the word *palatski.*

This point of view permeates those stories involving Americans of Polish descent. In **"The Cat Woman,"** Dybek almost rushes to associate ethnicity with strangeness when he calls the woman *buzka,* introduces her "crazy grandson as Swantek," and then proceeds to explain that Buzka drowned the excess neighborhood kittens in her washing machine. With this introduction, the ethnicity of the immigrant generation (*buzka*) and those (Swantek) who remain most closely associated with their old world habits is enough to divorce it from the cultural norm. "No one," Dybek succinctly comments, "brought laundry anymore to the old woman." The story ends with grotesque images of despair and degeneration. Swantek sleeps on old drapes beside the furnace, "vomiting up cabbage in the corners and covering it with newspapers," and Buzka and her old friend Mrs. Panova blow on their spoonfuls of soup "with nothing more to say," their radio turned to the polka hour. In other stories, we meet Big Antek, the local drunk; the uncle of Tadeusz, who spends his nights picking up the debris of a culture on the move; and Slavic workers missing parts of hands and arms that have been "chewed off while trying to clean machines." Such is the price of the old ethnicity, which in this case is represented as servile labor, alcoholism, a meanness toward animals, a taste for cabbage soup, and, most importantly, as descent from an inferior national culture.

In these rather traditional interpretations of second and third generation behavior, the usual signifiers of ethnicity—language, religion, history, customs and other conventional cultural markers—lose their privileged position even though they remain as a frame of reference. Nowhere is this better illustrated than in his adolescent protagonists' ambivalent relationship with Catholicism, which in Polish terms is inextricably and historically tied to nationalism. In other words a rejection of Catholicism is tantamount in these cases to a rejection of national, that is to say Polish, identity. **"Visions of Budhardin," "The Long Thoughts," "The Woman Who Fainted,"** and **"Sauerkraut Soup"** all dramatize the act of coming to terms with the religion of descent. One narrator, remembering his parochial education, explains what he regarded as the fear underlying religion, and reveals that the summer "after my sophomore year in high school was the last summer I went to church." Those who continue to attend do so from habit and custom. In **"Hot Ice,"** Eddie admits that "he had given up, and the ache left behind couldn't be called grief." In **"Visions of Budhardin,"** the protagonist, in a rage of pent up resentment, ravages the church which so callously ignored his childhood needs. But Marzek in **"Sauerkraut Soup"** speaks for all Dybek's disillusioned Polish Catholics when he says: "I had already developed my basic principle of Catholic education—the Double Reverse: (1) *suspect what they teach you;* (2) *study what they condemn.*" The words and deeds of these characters document their hostility to the culture of their ancestors and their inability to any longer understand or sympathize with this kind of ethnicity.

In effect, Dybek shows the transformation from immigrant to ethnic and beyond. Throughout, a sense of loss is coupled with an acceptance of change as his spokespersons lament the disappearance of the Polish southside. The narrator in **"Blight"** returns to his old neighborhood after a few years and confesses that he "was back in my neighborhood, but lost, everything at once familiar and strange, and I knew if I tried to run, my feet would be like lead, and if I stepped off a curb, I'd drop through space." Dybek thus points to a condition of ethnicity that characterizes the American Polish community as the recently published stories of Anthony Bukoski (*Children of Strangers*) also makes clear. In Dybek's stories, as in Bukoski's, the core of old world Pol-

ish culture is almost lost. Neighborhood demographics and Parish churches have changed, and only a few Polish-born Americans are left to transmit and interpret Polish traditions and customs. In **"Blood Soup,"** Uncle Joe's meat market is full of Mexican kids and Big Antek explains to Stefush that, in regard to his efforts to help his grandma make her beloved old world soup, "we don't sell fresh blood no more." Mrs. Gowumpe (pigeon, in Polish) tells Stefush how things were: "I used to work in the yards," he explains. "All those DPs working there . . . Polacks, Lugans, Bohunks. People who knew how to be happy." Now Mr. Gowumpe, grandma Busha, the *palatski* man, and the other first generation Poles are poor, isolated, lonely, and few in number. Nonetheless, they are the voice of cultural memory.

Dybek's fiction is not elegiac, however. Ethnicity is positive, pervasive, and dynamic in these stories; and the movement is toward a new understanding of ethnicity that is based not on national origins but on a shared sense of ethnicity as a condition of Americanness. Dybek's protagonists aren't Poles; they're not even Polish-American by traditional definition. They have, paradoxically, reinvented and reinterpreted themselves. For this generation ethnicity is a socio-political reality, a sensitivity to pluralism, and, as James Clifford phrases it, "a conjunctural not essential" state of mind. More than that, ethnicity is not even a necessary condition of descent because for Stuart Dybek cultural pluralism has supplanted nationality and a new level of multicultural awareness has replaced ethnocentricity. Dybek himself calls attention to this in an essay entitled **"You Can't Step Into the Same Street Twice"**: "Besides the ethnic tribes of Slavs and Hispanics whose language and music and food smells permeated the streets, there was another tribe, one that in a way transcended nationality, a tribe of youth, of kinds born to replenish the species recently depleted by WW II."

In his stories, Dybek replicates the tribal and cultural landscape of Chicago. Those who live in the older ethnic neighborhoods have experienced a change from a basically Eastern European population to a mixed neighborhood of Americans of Hispanic and Slavic descent, primarily Mexican and Polish. More importantly, Dybek's third generation fellow Polish ethnics are just as frequently paired with Hispanic friends as with fellow "Poles": Ziggy Zilinski and Pepper Rosado in **"Blight,"** Eddy Kapusta and Manny and Pancho Santoro in **"Hot Ice,"** Ray Cruz and John in **"The Palatski Man."** There are few instances of ethnic rivalry in this landscape. Quite the contrary, the commingling of Latino and Slav is economic, sociological, and cultural—a product of shifting demographics and resulting neighborhood changes, the result of shared environment and social class. They both identify with and like "the other." From this a new sense of ethnicity—an emblem of contemporary America—arises.

On the surface, the new ethnicity appears to be nothing more than the camaraderie of friends thrown together by demographics. In reality, the union of Pole and Chicano represents the changing face of America and of Polish Americanness. Stanley Rosado is Pepper to some and Stashu to others, reflecting his Mexican father and Polish mother. When David, the descendent of Poles, goes to a bar with a friend, he drinks a Coca-Nana rather than *vodka* or *piwo.* The Mexican music on the jukebox sounds "suspiciously like polkas." David now listens to "CuCuRuCuCu Paloma" on the radio, and Eddie Kapusta sings in Spanish. Tellingly, Eddie identifies more with Spanish than he does with the Polish language. He is struck with the word *juilota* (pigeon). It seems the perfect word because in it "he could hear both their cooing and the whistling rush of their wings." Equally telling, Eddie cannot remember "any words like that in Polish, which his grandma had spoken to him when he was little." Eddie's relatives may likely turn out to be Hispanic in the sense that Richard Rodriguez, in *Hunger of Memory,* believes that he may become Asian. In the words of Rosalie Murphy Baum, "multicultural contact has defeated the ethnic norm."

When all is said and done, Dybek's ethnic characters seem to say that "what they are" doesn't really matter in terms of history, language, geography. The new urban ethnic accepts ethnicity while rejecting nationality. Traditional ethnic borders give way to a heightened social and moral sense that replaces geographic maps and national origins. In **"Hot Ice,"** Eddie Kapusta arrives at this insight: "Most everything from that world had changed or disappeared, but the old women had endured. Polish, Bohemian, Spanish, he knew it didn't matter; they were the same . . . a common pain of loss seemed to burn at the core of their lives." Grandma in **"Pet Milk"** is illustrative. She knows about the old country and the new, where "all the incompatible states of Europe were pressed together down at the staticky right end" of the radio dial. Grandma also seems to know that ethnicity in America means something more than national origin. Consequently she is happy to listen to the Greek station or the Ukrainian or the Spanish although, of course, she would prefer listening to polkas. And in **"Hot Ice,"** Eddie elaborates on the changing face of ethnicity when he admits to himself, "Manny could be talking Spanish; I could be talking Polish. . . . It didn't matter. What meant something was sitting at the table together."

What also matters is that in Dybek's hands the Polish ethnic self assumes what some may regard as a new identity. And Dybek emerges as a writer who offers examples of the way experience, history, and ethnicity crossbreed. To be sure, Dybek does indeed try to present the preciousness of America's Polish heritage and the exceptionalism of the ethnically Polish American. He is, at the same time, eager to resist parochialism and exclusivity. His characterization of his young heroes and heroines as romantic rebels and urban-

ized American versions of Keats, Proust, Dostoevsky and others whom they have read, leads him beyond mere ethnicity even though his fiction is rooted in the cultural neighborhoods of southside Chicago. While attempting to capture the unique flavor of a particular ethnic group, Dybek has created a multi-layered and multi-dimensional ethnic self. This self reflects the image of a trans-ethnic urban America, a diorama of a diverse cultural landscape where ethnicity transcends national origins but remains vital and where the ethnic and the modern self are not only compatible but are the essence of postmodernism and, as Andrew Greeley puts it, "a way of being American."

Stuart Dybek with Mike Nickel and Adrian Smith (interview date Winter 1997)

SOURCE: "An Interview with Stuart Dybek," in *Chicago Review,* Vol. 43, No. 1, Winter, 1997, pp. 87-101.

[*In the following interview, Dybek discusses what he thinks of the label "Chicago writer," his approach to writing, and the importance of form.*]

The following interview was conducted as part of the University of Memphis's ongoing River City Writers Series; the conversation took place March 7, 1995, in Memphis. Stuart Dybek's books include two collections of short stories, **Childhood and Other Neighborhoods,** *and* **Coast of Chicago,** *as well as a work of poetry,* **Brass Knuckles.** *A recipient of a lifetime achievement award from the Academy of Arts and Letters, Dybek's writing may be found in* The New Yorker, *and* The Best American Short Stories of 1995.

[*Nickel:*] *I thought we'd start by talking about the Chicago style with which you're often identified. Let's begin with the term "Chicago Writer." I'm curious how you feel about it?*

[Dybek:] Well, at this point it might seem a little disingenuous of me to say that it was a surprise because the reviews have mentioned it so often, but it really was. When my first book of stories came out, I was living in the Keys, a long way from Chicago. And the way I had written those stories was as individual pieces until I realized that there was an organizational principle in the fact that a lot of them have to do with childhood, and a lot of them were set in Chicago. And so, I organized them around that principle, but it never occurred to me that the Chicago element was what would be picked up. As soon as it was pointed out to me, I saw it, but what was upper-most in my mind at the time was that they were stories about childhood, and that they had strong Eastern European influences.

[*Smith:*] *You talk about childhood as a neighborhood itself, calling your first short-story collection* **Childhood and Other Neighborhoods.** *What is it about childhood that makes it a neighborhood?*

Let me try and answer that question by putting it in a larger context and say that if somebody asked me what I thought my subject was, the answer wouldn't be Chicago, and it probably wouldn't be childhood: it would be perception. I think what I'm always looking for is some door in the story that opens on another world. A doorway like that can be a religious experience; in fact, that's probably the first such doorway I was aware of. When I grew up on the southwest side, the two biggest landmarks on most every corner were a church or a tavern. I would be walking down, let's say 25th street, which would represent ordinary reality. Ordinary reality would be made up by bread trucks delivering bread, people going to work, kids playing on the sidewalk, women hanging wash and so on. But by just stepping through either one of those doorways, the tavern or the church, it seemed to me that you entered a different world. In the tavern you entered a world that moved to a different time. The time it moved to was whatever song was on the jukebox. There was the smell of alcohol. People told stories and behaved in ways that they would never behave on the street. The church was the same thing. By just entering its doors you just seemed to enter the medieval ages. There was the smell of incense, and there were statues of saints and martyrs in grotesquely tortured positions. What I look for as a writer in stories are those doorways in which somebody leaves ordinary reality and enters some kind of extraordinary reality. So, to get back to your question, childhood for me is one of those doorways. To me, childhood seems like a state of extraordinary perception, and to inhabit that state or that neighborhood means that you're perceiving the world in a different way than is defined as ordinary. It's assuming that perception that interests me. It's a lens you can look through, in which the world becomes a different, hopefully fresher, more vivid place.

[Nickel:] You mention you have a reluctance to accept the term "Chicago" writer. You feel that's a label of sorts?

No, it isn't a reluctance. It's just a surprise. In fact, I was quite flattered to be included in that kind of company, and I just had never assumed that kind of lineage, that's all. I have tremendous admiration for Saul Bellow, and Algren as well. And James Farrell doesn't get mentioned enough in that company. That Studs Lonigan trilogy was really a very important book for me. But, it just hadn't occurred to me that someone would be generous enough to mention my work in that company. I really mean that.

[Nickel:] Do you see yourself as being a part of any other literary traditions?

The writers that I was thinking about at the time when I was writing those stories in **Childhood and Other Neighborhoods** were not the writers in the so-called Chicago Tradition. The reason is that the personal departure I felt I made in order to acquire some kind of a voice I was comfortable with was, especially in that first book, one that combined elements of the fantastic and the grotesque with realism. The Chicago tradition is a stubbornly realist tradition, and I didn't really see my work in that realist tradition, and therefore, I didn't see my work in the Chicago tradition. You know, what's great about Bellow, and Algren, and Farrell is just how powerfully realistic, and naturalistic in some degree, their work is. The writers I was reading were more Eastern Europeans, and some of the Hispanic writers.

[Nickel:] Now, I'm thinking of the story **"Palatski Man,"** *one of the first stories from your collection* **Childhood and Other Neighborhoods.** *It has a certain kind of magic realist quality to it, yet you're often identified with realistic, or naturalistic, writers ranging from Eudora Welty to James Joyce. How do you account for that magic realist quality? What influences were there that brought about that style?*

I'm not sure. I can tell you the anecdote though, which is a true story, of how I came to write **"The Palatski Man,"** which was the first story that I kind of wrote. At the time, I was reading mostly realistic writers. I particularly loved that kind of realistic voice that comes out of Sherwood Anderson, which you can follow through Hemingway and Salinger. It's frequently a first person voice. A lot of those writers wrote with young narrators, so I found that very familiar, and a voice I could readily adapt. But, the problem I was having with it was that it sounded like—the way that I was using it—pretty much like it would as adapted by any number of other writers, a sort of instantly recognizable, almost generic American style. And so, on some level I was dissatisfied with it because it didn't seem to me that I had found a voice, a style that in some ways expressed what I felt were my own personal rhythms. I was listening to a ton of music, and had reached the point where mostly when I wrote I listened to some kind of music. Usually it was jazz, but I was listening more and more to classical music, especially to chamber music, and I had gotten very interested in Béla Bartók. In reading about Bartók, I read about this other composer, Zoltán Kodály. Bartók and Kodály were part of a movement which tried to infuse postmodern music, mainly French impressionist music, with folk elements from their own culture. As part of the process, they took trips into the wilds of Hungary with very primitive recording devices and recorded real gypsy music—not the kind of stuff that Brahms was using. I mean it was true primitive stuff based on bagpipe riffs, and strange model chords and so on and so forth. And then they tried to integrate it into their own music.

This sounded really interesting to me. I've always loved local color. So, I got these records out of the library by Zoltán Kodály, and I put them on the record player, and I sat down and I wrote a story to his music that I had never even thought about writing, which was the **"Palatski Man."** It was literally almost like falling into a trance. I think what happened was the same thing that happens in a fifth grade classroom when the teacher brings in Ravel's "Bolero," and says to the kids, "Now, kids, today we're going to listen to Ravel's 'Bolero', and you write whatever comes into your mind." Then it begins [whistling the beginning of "Bolero"], and everybody is writing "I see camels going across the desert. They're dancing at the oasis." That music [by Kodály] just brought up all these images, but the images it brought up happened to be these Eastern European images, which, on some levels, I guess I had grown up with, but had never been able to harness or tap into them. I had really not read very much Eastern European literature with the exception of several of the Russians. I had read no magical realism at that point. I hadn't read [Isaak] Babel. I hadn't read Czeslaw Milosz. I had read very little Kafka, but as soon as I started writing those stories, I immediately developed a kind of hunger to go and see what other kinds of stories there might be like this. And that's when I started reading a lot of Kafka, and shortly thereafter, [Gabriel Garcia] Marquez's book *One Hundred Years of Solitude* appeared. But it was really the music that had generated the story and only after that did I circle back and start finding a literary base for the direction I stumbled on.

[*Nickel.*] *Are you able to recreate that feeling now?*

To my mind, a fiction writer's first allegiance is to the imagination, and so it was probably necessary for me to leave Chicago in order to write about it.
—Stuart Dybek

No. I wore it out. But for years after that I would gather all this music—Kodály, Bartók, Shostakovich, Janácek—because as soon as I put the music on, story became a physical feeling. I mean, I could almost feel it as if it guided me to some kind of biological, electrical path in my mind that would lead to a place in my brain where all this stuff lurked. I guess I reached the point where I overdrew the account. It's not quite there anymore, but by that time I had written most of the stories in that first book. By the way, two of the writers you mentioned—Welty and Joyce—I don't really see them as realistic writers. I mean, I'm sure they can be viewed that way, but to me, they're lyrical writers. I think in the second book I'd exhausted that Eastern European account that I was drawing on, in which, to me, the primary element was the fantastic, the fantastic or the grotesque. The grotesque

that is defined in a great book by Wolfgang Kayser, where he describes it as a third genre, along with comedy and tragedy. I think the technique in *Coast of Chicago* is actually closer to Welty and Joyce, which is to try to combine the lyric mode with the realistic mode. It's that combination that fascinates me about those writers—besides their incredible sense of place.

[*Smith:*] *You have obviously been influenced by the ethnic diversity of the neighborhood you grew up in. How do you think this affected your development as a writer—particularly now that you've lived away from Chicago for some time? As you said, you were living in the Florida Keys when your first collection was actually published, and you lived in New York after that, so you've had a chance to move away from those Chicago influences.* **Coast of Chicago,** *however, is still very much influenced by those experiences.*

Well, a lot of writers leave home in order to write about it as a place. I go back to Chicago frequently to kind of charge up again, too. Sometimes I'll just rent a room and live there for a while. But certainly, it depends wholly on temperament. Faulkner absolutely needed to live in the place that he wrote about whereas, clearly, Joyce did not. For me, because a lot of what I'm writing takes huge liberties with the imagination, I actually found it difficult to be writing about a somewhat imaginatively transformed El station, say the Bryn Mawr El station, and then to actually be passing the real Bryn Mawr El station. To my mind, a fiction writer's first allegiance is to the imagination, and so it was probably necessary for me to leave Chicago in order to write about it. As far as the ethnic neighborhoods and street life, that's become so impressed on my memory and personality that I don't really have to be there for it. I'd say, along with music, the other most important influence on my writing was my Polish grandmother who could hardly speak any English, even up into her nineties when she finally died. But we were able to communicate through my pidgin Polish and her pidgin English. There was a nonverbal communication that went on through body language, and the intensity of her eyes and just some kind of powerful nonverbal emotive ability that she had that was so un-American, or maybe "not-American," I suppose is what I mean. I value that foreign-ness to such a degree because it's opposite what I would consider "All-American," depending on how it's defined, could almost be a pejorative term, at least in the way that America digests and homogenizes everything and spits it back out into these McDonald's-like portions. That is what is least interesting to me about this country. What's most interesting to me is its ethnic variety, its cultural variety and its sense of genuine place, which is one of the reasons that the South fascinates me so much. The South and huge cities like New York have managed to remain somewhat impermeable to all that homogenization. A recurring motif in a lot of my stories is nonverbal experience and sometimes a longing after languages that don't exist, and that all comes from my grandmother.

[*Smith:*] *Is the powerful emotive quality of your grandmother's nonverbal communication a part of the reason the stories in* **The Coast of Chicago** *have a more consciously lyrical quality than your earlier stories?*

Maybe. I think the kinds of stories that I usually don't like are stories that are not interested in emotion. It seems to me that a risk that a writer should take is to tell a story which leaves you feeling something deeply. One of the things that is beautiful about music is that it is an emotional teacher that teaches you about different shades of emotion. In a way, all the arts are nonverbal, you know. Obviously, painting is a nonverbal art. Dance is a nonverbal art. But the narrative arts, film, theater, and particularly fiction and poetry, paradoxically, should convey a nonverbal quality. It's a total paradox of course because they're based on language. I don't know if I can articulate this, but I think that the kind of fiction I'm after is as essentially nonverbal as music is. And by that I mean, it should take you to a shading of emotion that there aren't actual words for. That is, that what you're feeling can't be paraphrased by the words we have in the language, only evoked, or approximated.

[*Smith:*] *Is the minimalism of roughly half of those stories, the ones usually set off by the gray pages, a part of that?*

Yes.

[*Nickel:*] *Speaking of feeling, I'm reminded of something you said in 1983, if I can go back 12 years to pull something out from a roundtable discussion you had with other Chicago writers. In that discussion you mention sentiment as being a part of the Chicago style, but you were careful to point out that sentiment is feeling as you've just described, and not the sentimental.*

Right.

[*Nickel:*] *Yet, a lot of your stories have a nostalgic edge to them and also contain a lot of feeling. So, I'm curious as to how you were able to do that—balance the two without crossing the line into sentimentality, which you don't.*

I can't give you a capsule answer because each story usually possesses its own, somewhat different, problem, and you kind of solve it story by story. For example, there's clearly a risk one takes when writing any childhood story. Just by its very nature a story about children runs the risk of being a corny sentimental story. And so, on either a conscious or unconscious level the writer has to, from the very start, take that into account and continually devise strategies to both harness the sentiment and the subject but, at the same time,

undercut the sentimentality. In one story it might be understatement and irony that keep it at bay, and, in another story, it might be that the incidents are so brutal that they balance off any kind of sentimental feelings. In another story, it might still be yet something else, so there isn't really one solution to it.

[*Nickel:*] *Are you aware of that dynamic, though, when you write? Are you aware that there is that danger?*

Absolutely. Sure. Nostalgia, in particular. I mean, because that nostalgia is built into the immigrant experience you can't have one without the other. It really interested me when I began reading the Hispanic writers, how much more nostalgia was a part of their emotional palette. You've got people in [Garcia] Marquez walking around saying "Oh my nostalgia" in a way that you could never get away with as an American writer. We're still linked to a British tradition that doesn't emote that way. It's not an Anglo-American feeling. So, it's an opportunity to integrate that into the American emotional palette, but it's also an immediate danger when you do it. But to ignore such emotions is to ignore a universal aspect of the American experience. To become self-indulgent about them is obviously to undermine the very feelings you're trying to evoke a genuine representation of.

[*Smith:*] *We've talked a little bit about two of the important influences on your work, music and neighborhood, and another one that keeps appearing is the presence of Mayor [Richard J.] Daley, which seems to signify a kind of wider neighborhood. In both of your short-story collections you mention the "Sorry for the Inconvenience . . ." sign which brings Daley into the story itself, and I'm wondering what it meant to you growing up in Chicago under his various administrations?*

There's about five different ways I could answer that question. The simplest one is that Daley was everywhere as I grew up, and that meant that because he was a colorful politician, well . . . as William Price Fox, a teacher of mine at the University of Iowa, once said to me about growing up Catholic, "It's good material. Use it." The same thing is true of Daley. Anybody who writes about him owes a tremendous debt to a writer I haven't talked about, Mike Royko. His book *Boss* was a wonderful book. What Royko did better than anybody else was show how funny that material could be. So, there's that comic element. Another element that interests me is the fact that Daley represented a certain kind of paternalism, and on one level or another a lot of my stories are anti-paternal. I've always wanted to use, at some time or another, that opening Bob Dylan line in "Highway 61 Revisited":

God said to Abraham, kill me a son,
Abe say Man you must be putting me on,

God said no, Abe say what?
God say you can do what you want Abe but the
Next time you see me coming you better run.
Well Abe said, Where do you want this killing
    done?
God said, out on Highway 61.

Growing up during Vietnam, when you had an older generation seeming to want to send a reluctant younger generation to war, it was no accident Dylan wrote that verse during that time. That was the time of the so-called "Generation Gap" and, in a way, Daley was representative of that tension between different ways of perceiving the world. Daley's was an older, paternalistic order that was built on the tried and true political principle of you scratch my back I'll scratch yours.

[*Smith:*] *In a number of the stories, in the ones that deal specifically with childhood in some way or another, there's an absence of the Father figure.*

Exactly.

[*Smith:*] *In **"Chopin in Winter"** and **"Blight,"** for example.*

Well, the book I'm working on now pushes that even further, but you know, because I'm working with this material, I'm kind of disinclined to fall into an analytical discussion about it. I know what it is I'm trying to say about it, but I want it said through fiction before I start talking analytically. So, if you'll let me just duck out on that one.

[*Nickel.*] *Maybe this would be a good point to switch gears and talk about the forms you write in. The short-short story seems to have gained in popularity in the last couple of years. You're a practitioner of it, and are often anthologized in books like* Flash Fiction *and* Sudden Fiction. *Do you have any insights into the rising popularity of that form?*

I really don't. I guess I've read the same things you probably have about it. People are linking it to shorter attention spans and watching MTV, and so on and so forth. I think I come to the short-short through poetry. I remember exactly how I got interested in it. A college friend named Peter Fiori, who I knew from Chicago, and I used to just read each other's work. We'd meet at a bar called "Connally's," an Irish bar on Devon, and he came walking in to the bar one day, and he had written a bunch of these short prose things, and I thought they were terrific. And so I figured I'd start writing these, too. That was long before short-shorts, flash fiction, or anything else. The only other stuff of the kind I had seen at that point I'd also liked a lot, those little vignettes that Hemingway used to separate the stories from *In Our Time.* To me they still read as fresh today as they must have

when he wrote them back in the 1920s. Those were the only two short prose things I knew, and then I finally got around to picking up some translations of Rimbaud's work, and read his prose poems, and they're still some of the best prose poems I've ever read. So, I added those to the mix, and continued scribbling my own versions of those little pieces, but never knew what to do with them, and then, almost suddenly, there was this huge prose poem mass insanity that struck American Literature in the 1960s and 1970s—long after other cultures had prose poem traditions, one might add. But there was this second wave of Frenchifying, Francophiling American poetry—this time called the continental or international style, which brought on the prose poem. So, with poets experimenting with these little semi-prose pieces, there was a channel for them. Poetry editors were now publishing it. That was great. I didn't care what they called it, and I'd been writing all of these short things anyway, so I started having my short prose poem pieces published by poetry editors. One of things I couldn't help but notice at the time was that several poets whose work I admired were trying these things, and generally I thought they were writing better in verse than in prose. That kind of started bothering me. I waited with great anticipation for a book that I knew Michael Benedict was doing. He was editing poetry at that time for *The Paris Review,* and he was publishing a lot of prose poems in that magazine, and he himself wrote prose poems, and I was really waiting for this anthology of his with great anticipation. When it came out, there was certainly stuff in it that I really liked, but a lot of the work seemed flat to me and uninteresting and disappointing. I read his cogent introduction, and one of the things that Benedict said was that the prose poem developed as part of a postmodernist anti-poetry movement, and it was at that point that I realized what was bothering me about a lot of the so-called prose poems. For full effect it was necessary to read them in the context of traditional poetry. That is, they were anti-poetry, but in order to appreciate what they were doing one needed to be totally familiar with the history of formal and traditional poetry. Like a lot of conceptual art, the prose poem often worked best if you understood what it was putting itself in opposition to. And that's always been my problem with conceptual art; that it's sometimes more interesting to talk about the theory of it than to actually read or listen to the stuff itself. I didn't want to write "anti-work," so I rethought what I was doing and began regarding the pieces as just little stories. I wanted to distance myself from the prose poem. In the 1980s, the second wave of stuff came, the short shorts, which is now supposed to be fiction, distinct from prose poems. But there's overlap. At least no one is calling them anti-stories.

[*Nickel:*] *Right. I'm thinking of **"Laughter"** which is one of those stories from the **"Nighthawks"** sequence in **The Coast of Chicago** which appeared, years earlier, in **Brass Knuckles** as poetry, but still very similar to its later prose* *counterpart. Does the change in context change the perception of that piece?*

Well it changed the writing of the piece for me. That is, one of the things I liked about the prose poem—I mean this is strictly temperamental, so I'm not claiming that this exists as an aspect of the prose poem—but for me, the freedom from line, though not from rhythm, allowed me to open up the "prose poem" in a way that I was not able, in some ways, to open up some of my poems. Then, when I freed myself from thinking of those short pieces as prose poems, I got a second burst of that feeling. So, when I started thinking about **"Laughter"** as a short fiction, rather than as a prose poem, I actually rewrote it and expanded it still further. For me, within the compressive principle of the short-short, there's still a principle of expansion that I don't find in formal poetry or in the prose poem.

[*Smith:*] *Since we've brought up "Nighthawks," I'm wondering about the relationship between the painting and that sequence. What is it about the painting that resonates so vividly that made you want to write about it and yet write about it in that form?*

Before that piece was called **"Nighthawks"** it was called "Nocturnes." I'd been working on a story called **"Chopin in Winter,"** listening to music, as I usually do, and I found myself gravitating towards the nocturnes. They were putting me in the mood I wanted for the story. So in the story itself, nocturnes start figuring heavily. But after I finished the story, I thought, would it be possible to write a series of mood pieces, which is what nocturnes are. They're less formal than a lot of musical forms. I thought, by naming it "Nocturnes" it would give the reader some clue as to how to read it, that is, what is holding all of these things together. When you're working on something that doesn't have a good straight narrative line, you're always looking for formal clues to give the reader as to how to put the piece together, since the reader doesn't have a narrative line to follow. It was only later that I started thinking about Hopper's painting. As soon as I thought about the painting, I reluctantly dropped the title "Nocturnes" because the painting gave me a whole series of images that I could also use in the form of theme variations, and it seemed to me that the painting gave the sequence a stronger sense of narrative propulsion than "Nocturnes" did. So, I switched. But basically it was the same thing I was looking for in both. That is for some way to create individual pieces that at the same time seemed linked by something other than a straight narrative line.

[*Nickel:*] *Back to form a little bit. Are you conscious of form when you write, or do you write a piece and then later realize how the piece itself realizes the form.*

A lot of what I write starts out as poetry, probably thirty per-cent of the stories I've published are actually, on some level to me, failed poems. Including stories that you would never think would have started out as a poem, like **"Blight."** Really, for a long time **"Blight"** was written as a would-be poem. I had the nutty notion on that one to turn it into a poem that imitated a Lenny Bruce monologue. It was supposed to be a comic poem mimicking the way comedians get up there and tell monologues, and I still would like, someday, to write a poem that's just based on comedian's comic monologue. Finally, what happens in these failed poems is that characters start asserting themselves, they take it over, and for me it becomes a piece of fiction. As soon as a piece has fictional qualities, I let it go. My notion is that if it can be something other than a poem, then it probably wasn't supposed to be a poem. I let it become a piece of fiction. So, just that kind of procedure means that I'm not casting these things from the start in one kind of a form or another. But, a second answer to your question, relates particularly to the short-short. I'm always looking for a way out of form, or out of traditional form. Traditional form for a short story requires a beginning, a middle, and an end. But I'm always looking for a way to explode form, and that's one of the things that I like about the short-short—nobody knows what they are yet. And there aren't the same expectations of them there are of short stories. And I like that. I'm constantly looking to read and write pieces that confuse me. I mean, sometimes they confuse me so much that they don't work. The form of **"Nighthawks"** is something I'm not going to go back and do for a while because I ended up putting way more time into that than I had envisioned myself doing and, frequently, didn't know where in the world I was with that. I had only too well succeeded in putting myself in a state of absolute floundering around. It felt great to be writing in a more traditional form after that. Sooner or later, you know, you want to keep surprising yourself. The short-short is a no-man's land between fiction and poetry, and I like it there. It's a comfortable place to be lost, and not to have to feel like you have to deliver on certain expectations that the genre has set up. I feel the same way about closure. I'm always looking for a way to close a story that isn't the kind of traditional the-character-has-a-realization so it's time to end.

[*Smith:*] *The major genre you haven't published in so far is the novel. Do you have any ambition to explode your subject matter into that form?*

I've actually been working off and on, but they haven't quite jelled yet. It's certainly a genre I want to publish in. Chapters of a novel I've been working on have actually appeared in places like *Atlantic Monthly,* and *Chicago Magazine.* It's a family novel, unfortunately, and non-literary reservations have also been part of the reason I haven't published more of it.

[*Smith:*] *As a problem for the writer, how do you approach the novel differently from the shorter works?*

Well, I'm a little reluctant to talk about something that I really don't have out there. But, a short answer to that is, what I love about the short story is that you can jump into it where it's already geared up at a high level, start out already in third gear and then kick it into fourth and fifth. The beauty of the novel is rising and falling action and, temperamentally, what I like is rising, rising, rising action. When I hit falling action, I mean the very thing that makes the novel beautiful, which is that long narrative arch, I get tremendously nervous as a writer. When I hit that falling action part, I'm filled with panic.

[*Smith:*] *Baseball appears in your work frequently.* **"The Death of the Right Fielder,"** *in particular, seems concerned with the game's metaphorical qualities. What metaphorical qualities do you see in baseball that you want to use, that you have used?*

Well, that story is self-explanatory as far as what its metaphors are, but I would go back to that earlier statement I made about perception. For me, sports are one of those doorways. Intense physical activity is one of those doorways. When you enter a sport or enter any intensely physical activity, you have again transformed your perception. You're in a different zone, a different world. I love the current sports vernacular for being "in the zone." Because that's exactly what I'm trying to talk about; so, clearly they're in a baseball zone in that story.

[*Smith:*] *In* **"Hot Ice"** *you talk about St. Roberto Clemente and when Big Antek has his miraculous experience, in the background they're talking about Joe DiMaggio. Baseball sort of enters into the larger story as a background.*

It's a sport I love though, like everybody else, I'm disgusted by what's going on right now. I spent huge amounts of my life sitting in Wrigley Field. They were some of my happiest moments. I played on ball teams well into my thirties until I tore my knees up. The entire American mythology that goes along with it fascinates me. Wrigley Field is probably one of the sights, along with Fenway Park, in Major League Baseball that still has an almost time machine element. Part of it is that we've gotten physically bigger, and the world is smaller now than when those parks were built. I have this clear recollection as a kid of sitting in this small ballpark with one of the worst pitching staffs in the history of baseball on the mound—that is the Chicago Cubs—and one of the best hitting teams in the history of baseball in the batter's box—the Pittsburgh Pirates—with guys like Stargel and Clemente and several other players, and the power of those balls firing off the bats as the Cub pitchers lobbed them in. In that small park, it really felt like you should be yelling "Incoming, Incoming." I think you can suggest, but never really ever capture, the power of a Roberto Clemente line drive coming off a bat in Wrigley Field. So, there's always that homage to him in those references in my stories.

Additional coverage of Dybek's life and career is contained in the following sources published by Gale: *Contemporary Authors,* **Vol. 97-100;** *Contemporary Authors New Revision Series,* **Vol. 39; and** *Dictionary of Literary Biography,* **Vol. 130.**

Ralph Ellison
1914-1994

(Full name Ralph Waldo Ellison) American novelist, essayist, short story writer, critic, and editor.

The following entry presents criticism on Ellison's works through 1997. For further information on his life and works, see *CLC,* Volumes 1, 3, 11, 54, and 86.

INTRODUCTION

Ellison is considered among the most influential and accomplished contemporary American authors for his highly acclaimed novel *Invisible Man* (1952). Honored with the National Book Award for fiction, *Invisible Man* is regarded as a masterpiece of twentieth-century American fiction for its complex treatment of racial repression and betrayal. Shifting between naturalism, expressionism, and surrealism, Ellison combines concerns of European and African-American literature to chronicle the quest of an unnamed black youth to discover his identity within a deluding, hostile world. Although critics have faulted Ellison's style as occasionally excessive, *Invisible Man* has consistently garnered accolades for its poetic, ambiguous form, sustained blend of tragedy and comedy, and complex symbolism and characterizations.

Biographical Information

Born in Oklahoma City, Oklahoma, Ellison was raised in a cultural atmosphere that encouraged self-fulfillment. After studying music from 1933 to 1936 at Tuskegee Institute, a college founded by Booker T. Washington to promote black scholarship, Ellison traveled to New York City, where he met Richard Wright and became involved in the Federal Writers' Project. Encouraged to write a book review for *New Challenge,* a publication edited by Wright, Ellison began composing essays and stories that focus on the strength of the human spirit and the necessity for racial pride. Two of his most celebrated early short stories, "Flying Home" and "King of the Bingo Game," foreshadow *Invisible Man* in their portrayal of alienated young protagonists who seek social recognition. Although he originally envisioned writing a war novel, Ellison instead began work on *Invisible Man* following his honorable discharge from the United States Merchant Marines in 1945. A meticulous craftsman, Ellison was working on his long-awaited second novel at the time of his death in 1994.

Major Works

Invisible Man chronicles an unnamed black youth's quest for

self-identity in a hostile world. Narrating his story from an underground cell, the anonymous protagonist describes his experiences as a student in the South, his travels in Harlem following his undeserved expulsion from college, his work with a political organization named the Brotherhood, and his participation in the Harlem race riots of the 1940s; he explains in the prologue that he is involuntarily invisible—and has thus gone underground—because society sees him only in terms of racial stereotypes. Additionally known as an essayist and nonfiction writer, Ellison collected twenty-two years of reviews, criticism, and interviews concerning such subjects as art, music, literature, and the influence of the black experience on American culture in *Shadow and Act* (1964). This volume is often considered autobiographical in intent and is noted for its lucidity and the insights it provides into *Invisible Man. Going to the Territory* (1986), which contains speeches, reviews, and interviews written since 1957, echoes many of the concerns of *Shadow and Act.* Making use of ironic humor in the manner of *Invisible Man,* Ellison here reflected on and paid tribute to such personal influences and creative mentors as Richard Wright and Duke Ellington. Two collections of Ellison's works have been published posthumously, *The Collected Essays of Ralph Ellison* (1996) and *Flying Home and Other Stories* (1997). *The Collected Essays of Ralph Ellison* contains twenty previously unpublished essays, as well as all of the essays published in *Going to the Territory* and *Shadow and Act*. *Flying Home and Other Stories* is comprised of thirteen short stories written between 1937 and 1954, and includes such stories as "A Party Down at the Square," which relates the story of the lynching and burning of a black man from a young white boy's perspective. "Out of the Hospital and Under the Bar" (1963), a short story published in the anthology *Soon, One Morning: New Writing by American Negroes, 1940-1962*, was originally intended to be a chapter of *Invisible Man*.

Critical Reception

Although attacked by black nationalists for lacking stringent militancy toward civil rights issues, *Invisible Man* garnered laudatory reviews immediately following its publication and has continued to generate scholarly exegeses. Many critics have commented on how the book's dexterous style, dense symbolism, and narrative structure lend intricacy to its plot. The narrator, who reflects on his past experiences, is observed as both an idealistic, gullible youth and as an enlightened, responsible man who actively addresses problems that may result from social inequality. The foremost controversial issue of *Invisible Man* involves its classification as either a work particularly for blacks or a novel with universal import. Critics who insist the book strictly concerns black culture maintain that the experiences, emotions, and lifestyles described could not possibly be simulated by white authors, while supporters of the more prevalent view that *Invisible Man* transcends racial concerns contend that the protagonist's problems of illusion, betrayal, and self-awareness are experienced by every segment of society. Ellison is also highly regarded for his accomplishments as an essayist. *Shadow and Act* is often considered autobiographical in intent and has been acclaimed for its lucidity and insights into *Invisible Man*. Although Ellison's collected short stories and essays are often viewed by critics as valuable only in terms of their capacity to illuminate aspects of *Invisible Man*, these works also have been lauded by critics who have noted particularly Ellison's ability to convey the universality of his characters' concerns and experiences, irrespective of race.

PRINCIPAL WORKS

Invisible Man (novel) 1952
Shadow and Act (criticism) 1964
Going to the Territory (essays) 1986
The Collected Essays of Ralph Ellison (essays) 1995
Flying Home and Other Stories (short stories) 1997

CRITICISM

Ralph Ellison with Alfred Chester and Vilma Howard (interview date Spring 1955)

SOURCE: An interview in *Paris Review*, Spring, 1955, pp. 53-55; reprinted as "The Art of Fiction: An Interview," in *Conversations with Ralph Ellison*, edited by Maryemma Graham and Amritjit Singh, University Press of Mississippi, 1995, pp. 6-19.

[*In the following interview, Ellison discusses his life and his views on writing and literature, specifically addressing his own works, so-called "protest literature," and contemporary African-American writers and literature.*]

When *Invisible Man,* Ralph Ellison's first novel, received the National Book Award for 1952, the author in his acceptance speech noted with dismay and gratification the conferring of the award to what he called "an attempt at a major novel." His gratification was understandable, so too his dismay when one considers the amount of objectivity Mr. Ellison can display toward his own work. He felt the state of U.S. fiction to be so unhappy that it was an "attempt" rather than an achievement which received the important award.

Many of us will disagree with Mr. Ellison's evaluation of his own work. Its crackling, brilliant, sometimes wild, but always controlled prose warrants this; so does the care and logic with which its form is revealed, and not least its theme: that of a young Negro who emerges from the South and—in the tradition of James' Hyacinth Robinson and Stendhal's Julien Sorel—moves into the adventure of life at large.

In the summer of 1954, Mr. Ellison came abroad to travel and lecture. His visit ended with Paris where for a very few weeks he mingled with the American expatriate group to whom his work was known and of much interest. The day before he left he talked to us in the Café de la Mairie du VI about art and the novel.

Ralph Ellison takes both art and the novel seriously. And the Café de la Mairie has a tradition of seriousness behind it, for here was written Djuna Barnes' spectacular novel, *Nightwood*. There is a tradition, too, of speech and eloquence, for Miss Barnes' hero, Dr. O'Connor, often drew a crowd of listeners to his mighty rhetoric. So here gravity is in the air and rhetoric too. While Mr. Ellison speaks, he rarely pauses, and although the strain of organizing his thought is sometimes evident, his phraseology and the quiet steady flow and development of ideas are overwhelming. To listen to him is rather like sitting in the back of a huge hall and feeling the lecturer's faraway eyes staring directly into your own. The highly emphatic, almost professorial intonations, started with their distance, self-confidence, and warm undertones of humor.

[Ellison:] Let me say right now that my book is not an autobiographical work.

[*Chester and Howard:*] *You weren't thrown out of school like the boy in your novel?*

No. Though, like him, I went from one job to another.

Why did you give up music and begin writing?

I didn't give up music, but I became interested in writing through incessant reading. In 1935 I discovered Eliot's *The Waste Land* which moved and intrigued me but defied my powers of analysis—such as they were—and I wondered why I had never read anything of equal intensity and sensibility by an American Negro writer. Later on, in New York, I read a poem by Richard Wright, who, as luck would have it, came to town the next week. He was editing a magazine called *New Challenge* and asked me to try a book review of E. Waters Turpin's *These Low Grounds.* On the basis of this review Wright suggested that I try a short story, which I did. I tried to use my knowledge of riding freight trains. He liked the story well enough to accept it and it got as far as the galley proofs when it was bumped from the issue because there was too much material. Just after that the magazine failed.

But you went on writing—

With difficulty, because this was the Recession of 1937. I went to Dayton, Ohio, where my brother and I hunted and sold game to earn a living. At night I practiced writing and studied Joyce, Dostoevski, Stein and Hemingway. Especially Hemingway; I read him to learn his sentence structure and how to organize a story. I guess many young writers were doing this, but I also used his description of hunting when I went into the fields the next day. I had been hunting since I was eleven but no one had broken down the process of wing-shooting for me and it was from reading Hemingway that I learned to lead a bird. When he describes something in print, believe him; believe him even when he describes the process of art in terms of baseball or boxing; he's been there.

Were you affected by the Social Realism of the period?

I was seeking to learn and Social Realism was a highly regarded theory, though I didn't think too much of the so-called proletarian fiction even when I was most impressed by Marxism. I was intrigued by Malraux, who at that time was being claimed by the Communists. I noticed, however,

that whenever the heroes of *Man's Fate* regarded their condition during moments of heightened self-consciousness, their thinking was something other than Marxist. Actually they were more profoundly intellectual than their real-life counterparts. Of course, Malraux was more of a humanist than most of the Marxist writers of that period—and also much more of an artist. He was the artist-revolutionary rather than a politician when he wrote *Man's Fate,* and the book lives not because of a political position embraced at the time, but because of its larger concern with the tragic struggle of humanity. Most of the social realists of the period were concerned more with tragedy than with injustice. I wasn't, and am not, concerned with injustice, but with art.

Then you consider your novel a purely literary work as opposed to one in the tradition of social protest.

Now mind! I recognize no dichotomy between art and protest. Dostoyevsky's *Notes from the Underground* is, among other things, a protest against the limitations of 19th century rationalism; *Don Quixote, Man's Fate, Oedipus Rex, The Trial*—all these embody protest, even against the limitation of human life itself. If social protest is antithetical to art, what then shall we make of Goya, Dickens and Twain? One hears a lot of complaints about the so-called "protest novel," especially when written by Negroes; but it seems to me that the critics could more accurately complain about their lack of craftsmanship and their provincialism.

But isn't it going to be difficult for the Negro writer to escape provincialism when his literature is concerned with a minority?

All novels are about certain minorities: the individual is a minority. The universal in the novel—and isn't that what we're all clamoring for these days?—is reached only through the depiction of the specific man in a specific circumstance.

But still, how is the Negro writer, in terms of what is expected of him by critics and readers, going to escape his particular need for social protest and reach the "universal" you speak of?

If the Negro, or any other writer, is going to do what is expected of him, he's lost the battle before he takes the field. I suspect that all the agony that goes into writing is borne precisely because the writer longs for acceptance—but it must be acceptance on his own terms. Perhaps, though, this thing cuts both ways: the Negro novelist draws his blackness too tightly around him when he sits down to write—that's what the anti-protest critics believe—but perhaps the white reader draws his whiteness around himself when he sits down to read. He doesn't want to identify himself with Negro characters in terms of our immediate racial and social situation, though on the deeper human level identification can become compelling when the situation is revealed artistically. The white reader doesn't want to get too close, not even in an imaginary recreation of society. Negro writers have felt this and it has led to much of our failure.

Too many books by Negro writers are addressed to a white audience. By doing this the authors run the risk of limiting themselves to the audience's presumptions of what a Negro is or should be; the tendency is to become involved in polemics, to plead the Negro's humanity. You know, many white people question that humanity but I don't think that Negroes can afford to indulge in such a false issue. For us the question should be, what are the specific *forms* of that humanity, and what in our background is worth preserving or abandoning. The clue to this can be found in folklore which offers the first drawings of any group's character. It preserves mainly those situations which have repeated themselves again and again in the history of any given group. It describes those rites, manners, customs, and so forth, which insure the good life, or destroy it; and it describes those boundaries of feeling, thought and action which that particular group has found to be the limitation of the human condition. It projects this wisdom in symbols which express the group's will to survive; it embodies those values by which the group lives and dies. These drawings may be crude but they are nonetheless profound in that they represent the group's attempt to humanize the world. It's no accident that great literature, the products of individual artists, is erected upon this humble base. The hero of Dostoyevsky's *Notes from the Underground* and the hero of Gogol's *The Overcoat* appear in their rudimentary forms far back in Russian folklore. French literature has never ceased exploring the nature of the Frenchman . . . Or take Picasso—

How does Picasso fit into all this?

Why, he's the greatest wrestler with forms and techniques of them all. Just the same he's never abandoned the old symbolic forms of Spanish art: the guitar, the bull, daggers, women, shawls, veils, mirrors. Such symbols serve a dual function: they allow the artist to speak of complex experiences and to annihilate time with simple lines and curves; and they allow the viewer an orientation, both emotional and associative, which goes so deep that a total culture may resound in a simple rhythm, an image. It has been said that Escudero could recapitulate the history and spirit of the Spanish dance with a simple arabesque of his fingers.

But these are examples from homogeneous cultures. How representative of the American nation would you say Negro folklore is?

The history of the American Negro is a most intimate part of American history. Through the very process of slavery came the building of the United States. Negro folklore,

evolving within a larger culture which regarded it as inferior, was an especially courageous expression. It announced the Negro's willingness to trust his own experience, his own sensibilities as to the definition of reality, rather than allow his masters to define these crucial matters for him. His experience is that of America and the West, and is as rich a body of experience as one would find anywhere. We can view it narrowly as something exotic, folksy, or "low-down," or we may identify ourselves with it and recognize it as an important segment of the larger American experience—not lying at the bottom of it, but intertwined, diffused in its very texture. I can't take this lightly or be impressed by those who cannot see its importance; it is important to *me*. One ironic witness to the beauty and the universality of this art is the fact that the descendants of the very men who enslaved us can now sing the spirituals and find in the singing an exaltation of their own humanity. Just take a look at some of the slave songs, blues, folk ballads; their possibilities for the writer are infinitely suggestive. Some of them have named human situations so well that a whole corps of writers could not exhaust their universality. For instance, here's an old slave verse:

> Ole Aunt Dinah, she's just like me
> She work so hard she want to be free
> But ole Aunt Dinah's gittin' kinda ole
> She's afraid to go to Canada on account of the cold.

> Ole Uncle Jack, now he's a mighty "good nigger"
> You tell him that you want to be free for a fac'
> Next thing you know they done stripped the skin off your back.

> Now ole Uncle Ned, he want to be free
> He found his way north by the moss on the tree
> He cross that river floating in a tub
> The pataleroller give him a mighty close rub.

It's crude, but in it you have three universal attitudes toward the problem of freedom. You can refine it and sketch in the psychological subtleties and historical and philosophical allusions, action and what not, but I don't think its basic definition can be exhausted. Perhaps some genius could do as much with it as Mann has done with the Joseph story.

Can you give us an example of the use of folklore in your own novel?

Well, there are certain themes, symbols and images which are based on folk material. For example, there is the old saying amongst Negroes: If you're black, stay back; if you're brown, stick around; if you're white, you're right. And there is the joke Negroes tell on themselves about their being so black they can't be seen in the dark. In my book this sort of thing was merged with the meanings which blackness and light have long had in Western mythology: evil and goodness, ignorance and knowledge, and so on. In my novel the narrator's development is one through blackness to light; that is, from ignorance to enlightenment: invisibility to visibility. He leaves the South and goes North; this, as you will notice in reading Negro folktales, is always the road to freedom—the movement upward. You have the same thing again when he leaves his underground cave for the open.

It took me a long time to learn how to adapt such examples of myth into my work—also ritual. The use of ritual is equally a vital part of the creative process. I learned a few things from Eliot, Joyce and Hemingway, but not how to adapt them. When I started writing, I knew that in both *The Waste Land* and *Ulysses* ancient myth and ritual were used to give form and significance to the material; but it took me a few years to realize that the myths and rites which we find functioning in our everyday lives could be used in the same way. In my first attempt at a novel—which I was unable to complete—I began by trying to manipulate the simple structural unities of *beginning, middle* and *end,* but when I attempted to deal with the psychological strata—the images, symbols and emotional configurations—of the experience at hand, I discovered that the unities were simply cool points of stability on which one could suspend the narrative line—but beneath the surface of apparently rational human relationships there seethed a chaos before which I was helpless. People rationalize what they shun or are incapable of dealing with; these superstitions and their rationalizations become ritual as they govern behavior. The rituals become social forms, and it is one of the functions of the artist to recognize them and raise them to the level of art.

I don't know whether I'm getting this over or not. Let's put it this way: Take the "Battle Royal" passage in my novel, where the boys are blindfolded and forced to fight each other for the amusement of the white observers. This is a vital part of behavior patterns in the South, which both Negroes and whites thoughtlessly accept. It is a ritual in preservation of caste lines, a keeping of taboo to appease the gods and ward off bad luck. It is also the initiation ritual to which all greenhorns are subjected. This passage states what Negroes will see I did not have to invent; the patterns were already there in society so that all I had to do was present them in a broader context of meaning. In any society there are many rituals of situation which, for the most part, go unquestioned. They can be simple or elaborate, but they are the connective tissue between the work of art and the audience.

Do you think a reader unacquainted with this folklore can properly understand your work?

Yes, I think so. It's like jazz; there's no inherent problem which prohibits understanding but the assumptions brought to it. We don't all dig Shakespeare uniformly, or even *Little Red Riding Hood.* The understanding of art depends finally upon one's willingness to extend one's humanity and one's knowledge of human life. I noticed, incidentally, that the Germans, having no special caste assumptions concerning American Negroes, dealt with my work simply as a novel. I think the Americans will come to view it that way in twenty years—if it's around that long.

Don't you think it will be?

I doubt it. It's not an important novel. I failed of eloquence and many of the immediate issues are rapidly fading away. If it does last, it will be simply because there are things going on in its depth that are of more permanent interest than on its surface. I hope so, anyway.

Have the critics given you any constructive help in your writing, or changed in any way your aims in fiction?

No, except that I have a better idea of how the critics react, of what they see and fail to see, of how their sense of life differs with mine and mine with theirs. In some instances they were nice for the wrong reasons. In the U.S.—and I don't want this to sound like an apology for my own failures—some reviewers did not see what was before them because of this nonsense about protest.

Did the critics change your view of yourself as a writer?

I can't say that they did. I've been seeing by my own candle too long for that. The critics did give me a sharper sense of a larger audience, yes; and some convinced me that they were willing to judge me in terms of my writing rather than in terms of my racial identity. But there is one widely syndicated critical bankrupt who made liberal noises during the Thirties and has been frightened ever since. He attacked my book as a "literary race riot." By and large, the critics and readers gave me an affirmed sense of my identity as a writer. You might know this within yourself, but to have it affirmed by others is of utmost importance. Writing is, after all, a form of communication.

When did you begin **Invisible Man***?*

In the summer of 1945. I had returned from the sea, ill, with advice to get some rest. Part of my illness was due, no doubt, to the fact that I had not been able to write a novel for which I'd received a Rosenwald fellowship the previous winter. So on a farm in Vermont where I was reading *The Hero* by Lord Ragland and speculating on the nature of Negro leadership in the U.S., I wrote the first paragraph of *Invisible Man,* and was soon involved in the struggle of creating the novel.

How long did it take you to write it?

Five years with one year out for a short novel which was unsatisfactory, ill-conceived and never submitted for publication.

Did you have everything thought out before you began to write **Invisible Man**?

The symbols and their connections were known to me. I began it with a chart of the three-part division. It was a conceptual frame with most of the ideas and some incidents indicated. The three parts represent the narrator's movement from, using Kenneth Burke's terms, purpose to passion to perception. These three major sections are built up of smaller units of three which mark the course of the action and which depend for their development upon what I hoped was a consistent and developing motivation. However, you'll note that the maximum insight on the hero's part isn't reached until the final section. After all, it's a novel about innocence and human error, a struggle through illusion to reality. Each section begins with a sheet of paper; each piece of paper is exchanged for another and contains a definition of his identity, or the social role he is to play as defined for him by others. But all say essentially the same thing, "Keep this nigger boy running." Before he could have some voice in his own destiny he had to discard these old identities and illusions; his enlightenment couldn't come until then. Once he recognizes the hole of darkness into which these papers put him, he has to burn them. That's the plan and the intention; whether I achieved this is something else.

Would you say that the search for identity is primarily an American theme?

It is *the* American theme. The nature of our society is such that we are prevented from knowing who we are. It is still a young society, and this is an integral part of its development.

A common criticism of "first novels" is that the central incident is either omitted or weak. **Invisible Man** *seems to suffer here; shouldn't we have been present at the scenes which are the dividing lines in the book—namely, when the Brotherhood organization moves the narrator downtown, then back uptown?*

I think you missed the point. The major flaw in the hero's character is his unquestioning willingness to do what is required of him by others as a way to success, and this was the specific form of his "innocence." He goes where he is told to go; he does what he is told to do; he does not even choose his Brotherhood name. It is chosen for him and he accepts it. He has accepted party discipline and thus cannot be present at the scene since it is not the will of the Brotherhood leaders. What is important is not the scene but his failure to question their decision. There is also the fact that no single person can be everywhere at once, nor can a single

consciousness be aware of all the nuances of a large social action. What happens uptown while he is downtown is part of his darkness, both symbolic and actual. No; I don't feel that any vital scenes have been left out.

Why did you find it necessary to shift styles throughout the book; particularly in the Prologue and Epilogue?

The Prologue was written afterwards, really—in terms of a shift in the hero's point of view. I wanted to throw the reader off balance—make him accept certain non-naturalistic effects. It was really a memoir written underground, and I wanted a foreshadowing through which I hoped the reader would view the actions which took place in the main body of the book. For another thing, the styles of life presented are different. In the South where he was trying to fit into a traditional pattern and where his sense of certainty had not yet been challenged, I felt a more naturalistic treatment was adequate. The college of Trustee's speech to the students is really an echo of a certain kind of southern rhetoric and I enjoyed trying to recreate it. As the hero passes from the South to the North, from the relatively stable to the swiftly changing, his sense of certainty is lost and the style becomes expressionistic. Later on during his fall from grace in the Brotherhood it becomes somewhat surrealistic. The styles try to express both his state of consciousness and the state of society. The Epilogue was necessary to complete the action begun when he set out to write his memoirs.

> **The Prologue was written afterwards, really—in terms of a shift in the hero's point of view. I wanted to throw the reader off balance—make him accept certain non-naturalistic effects.**
> **—*Ralph Ellison***

After four hundred pages you still felt the Epilogue was necessary?

Yes. Look at it this way. The book is a series of reversals. It is the portrait of the artist as a rabble-rouser, thus the various mediums of expression. In the Epilogue the hero discovers what he had not discovered throughout the book: you have to make your own decisions; you have to think for yourself. The hero comes up from underground because the act of writing and thinking necessitated it. He could not stay down there.

You say that the book is "a series of reversals." It seemed to us that this was a weakness, that it was built on a series of provocative situations which were cancelled by the calling up of conventional emotions—.

I don't quite see what you mean.

Well, for one thing, you begin with a provocative situation of the American Negro's status in society. The responsibility for this is that of the white American citizen; that's where the guilt lies. Then you cancel it by introducing the Communist Party, or the Brotherhood, so that the reader tends to say to himself: "Ah, they're the guilty ones. They're the ones who mistreat him; not us."

I think that's a case of misreading. And I didn't identify the Brotherhood as the C.P., but since you do I'll remind you that they too are white. The hero's invisibility is not a matter of being seen, but a refusal to run the risk of his own humanity, which involves guilt. This is not an attack upon white society! It is what the hero refuses to do in each section which leads to further action. He must assert and achieve his own humanity; he cannot run with the pack and do this—this is the reason for all the reversals. The Epilogue is the most final reversal of all; therefore it is a necessary statement.

And the love affairs—or almost-love-affairs—.

(*Laughing*) I'm glad you put it that way. The point is that when thrown into a situation which he thinks he wants, the hero is sometimes thrown at a loss; he doesn't know how to act. After he had made this speech about The Place of the Woman in Our Society, for example, and was approached by one of the women in the audience, he thought she wanted to talk about the Brotherhood and found that she wanted to talk about brother-*and-sisterhood*. Look, didn't you find the book at all *funny*? I felt that such a man as this character would have been incapable of a love affair; it would have been inconsistent with his personality.

Do you have any difficulty controlling your characters? E. M. Forster says that he sometimes finds a character running away with him.

No, because I find that a sense of the ritual understructure of the fiction helps to guide the creation of characters. Action is the thing. We are what we do and do not do. The problem for me is to get from A to B to C. My anxiety about transitions greatly prolonged the writing of my book. The naturalists stick to case histories and sociology and are willing to compete with the camera and the tape recorder. I despise concreteness in writing, but when reality is deranged in fiction, one must worry about the seams.

Do you have difficulty turning real characters into fiction?

Real characters are just a limitation. It's like turning your own life into fiction: you have to be hindered by chronology and fact. A number of the characters just jumped out, like Rinehart and Ras.

Isn't Ras based on Marcus Garvey?

No. In 1950 my wife and I were staying at a vacation spot where we met some white liberals who thought the best way to be friendly was to tell us what it was like to be Negro. I got mad at hearing this from people who otherwise seemed very intelligent. I had already sketched Ras but the passion of his statement came out after I went upstairs that night feeling that we needed to have this thing out once and for all and get it done with; then we could go on living like people and individuals. No conscious reference to Garvey is intended.

What about Rinehart? Is he related to Rinehart in the blues tradition, or Django Rheinhardt, the jazz musician?

There is a peculiar set of circumstances connected with my choice of that name. My old Oklahoma friend, Jimmy Rushing, the blues singer, used to sing one with a refrain that went:

> Rinehart, Rinehart,
> It's so lonesome up here
> On Beacon Hill,

which haunted me, and as I was thinking of a character who was a master of disguise, of coincidence, this name with its suggestion of inner and outer came to my mind. Later I learned that it was a call used by Harvard students when they prepared to riot, a call to chaos. Which is very interesting because it is not long after Rinehart appears in my novel that the riot breaks out in Harlem. Rinehart is my name for the personification of chaos. He is also intended to represent America and change. He has lived so long with chaos that he knows how to manipulate it. It is the old theme of *The Confidence Man*. He is a figure in a country with no solid past or stable class lines; therefore he is able to move about easily from one to the other. (*He pauses, thoughtfully.*)

You know, I'm still thinking of your question about the use of Negro experience as material for fiction. One function of serious literature is to deal with the moral core of a given society. Well, in the United States the Negro and his status have always stood for that moral concern. He symbolizes among other things the human and social possibility of equality. This is the moral question raised in our two great 19th century novels, *Moby Dick* and *Huckleberry Finn*. The very center of Twain's book revolves finally around the boy's relations with Nigger Jim and the question of what Huck should do about getting Jim free after the two scoundrels had sold him. There is a magic here worth conjuring, and that reaches to the very nerve of the American consciousness—

so why should I abandon it? Our so-called race problem has now lined up with the world problems of colonialism and the struggle of the West to gain the allegiance of the remaining non-white people who have thus far remained outside the Communist sphere; thus its possibilities for art have increased rather than lessened. Looking at the novelist as manipulator and depictor of moral problems, I ask myself how much of the achievement of democratic ideals in the U.S. has been affected by the steady pressure of Negroes and those whites who were sensitive to the implications of our condition; and I know that without that pressure the position of our country before the world would be much more serious than it is even now. Here is part of the social dynamics of a great society. Perhaps the discomfort about protest in books by Negro authors comes because since the 19th century American literature has avoided profound moral searching. It was too painful and besides there were specific problems of language and form to which the writers could address themselves. They did wonderful things, but perhaps they left the real problems untouched. There are exceptions, of course, like Faulkner who has been working the great moral theme all along, taking it up where Mark Twain put it down.

I feel that with my decision to devote myself to the novel I took on one of the responsibilities inherited by those who practice the craft in the U.S.: that of describing for all that fragment of the huge diverse American experience which I know best, and which offers me the possibility of contributing not only to the growth of the literature but to the shaping of the culture as I should like it to be. The American novel is in this sense a conquest of the frontier; as it describes our experience, it creates it.

Susan L. Blake (essay date January 1979)

SOURCE: "Ritual and Rationalization: Black Folklore in the Works of Ralph Ellison," in *PMLA,* Vol. 94, No. 1, January, 1979, pp. 121-36.

[*In the following essay, Blake illustrates how Ellison's use of black folklore aids him in "bridg[ing] the gap between the uniqueness and the universality of black experience."*]

The predominant theme in the works of Ralph Ellison is the quest for cultural identity. Although he does not realize this himself, the protagonist of *Invisible Man* seeks identity, not as an individual, but as a black man in a white society. He encounters and combats the problem Ellison identified in an interview with three young black writers in 1965: "Our lives, since slavery, have been described mainly in terms of our political, economic, and social conditions as measured by outside norms, seldom in terms of our *own* sense of life or

our *own* sense of values gained from our *own* unique American experience" [**"A Very Stern Discipline,"** *Harper's,* March, 1967, p. 78]. The invisible man searches for self-definition in terms of the sense of life and values gained from the unique black-American experience. His quest, however—like that of almost every other Ellison protagonist—ends in the conviction that the black experience is not so unique: "Who knows but that, on the lower frequencies, I speak for you?" Cultural identity becomes indistinguishable from the human condition.

I

One way that Ellison bridges the gap between the uniqueness and the universality of black experience is by use of black folklore. *Invisible Man,* most of Ellison's short stories, and the pieces of his partially published second novel, "And Hickman Arrives," are packed full of folk-tales and tellers, trinkets, toasts, songs, sermons, jazz, jive, and jokes. In his essays and interviews, Ellison has repeatedly singled out black folklore as the source of genuine black self-definition:

> In the folklore we tell what Negro experience really is. We back away from the chaos of experience and from ourselves and we depict the humor as well as the horror of our living. We project Negro life in a metaphysical perspective and we have seen it with a complexity of vision that seldom gets into our writing. (**"A Very Stern Discipline,"** p. 80)

Negro folklore, evolving within a larger culture which regarded it as inferior, was an especially courageous expression. It announced the Negro's willingness to trust his own experience, his own sensibilities as to the definition of reality, rather than allow his masters to define these crucial matters for him.

At the same time, however, Ellison insists that "on its profoundest level American experience"—and, it is implied throughout *Shadow and Act,* human experience—"is of a whole"; that behind John Henry is Hercules, behind specific folk expression, "the long tradition of storytelling . . . of myth." So when Ellison uses black folklore in his fiction, he consciously adapts it to the myths of the "larger" American and Western cultures:

> For example, there is the old saying amongst Negroes: if you're black, stay back; if you're brown, stick around; if you're white, you're right. And there is the joke Negroes tell on themselves about their being so black they can't be seen in the dark. In my book this sort of thing was merged with the meanings which blackness and light have long had in Western mythology: evil and goodness, ignorance

and knowledge, and so on. In my novel the narrator's development is one through blackness to light; that is, from ignorance to enlightenment: invisibility. . . .

It took me a long time to learn how to adapt such examples of myth into my work—also ritual. The use of ritual is equally a vital part of the creative process. I learned a few things from Eliot, Joyce and Hemingway, but not how to adapt them.

["The Art of Fiction: An Interview," *Shadow and Act*].

Ellison's use of terms is confusing here: the saying "if you're black, stay back" is not myth but folk wisdom; ritual is not completely independent of myth, it is the form through which myth is often expressed. What Ellison learned to do, in order to adapt black folk expression in literature, was to turn it into ritual and to put it at the service of a myth "larger," or other, than itself. Folklorists, myth theorists, and literary critics—as groups and as individuals—differ widely on the definition of "myth" and its relationship to the rest of folklore. Whether they say, however, that myths involve divine characters and folktales human, that myths take place in prehistoric and folktales in historic time, or that myths are believed by teller and audience and folktales told as fiction, they are acknowledging a not necessarily sharp distinction between two levels of folk belief—one concrete, temporal, and specific to the folk group; the other abstract, "eternal," and "universal." "Eternal" and "universal" are here relative terms; they refer to times and worlds larger than those of the immediate social context—how much larger is unimportant. For the purposes of this paper, "myth" refers to the abstract level of folk belief; "folk expression," to the concrete.

Ritual is the repetition of action for symbolic purpose. It abstracts experience from history by extending it over time and emphasizing form over context. We need not get into the question of whether myth or ritual comes first in order to say that ritual, theoretically at least, turns social experience into the symbol of mythic experience. When Ellison puts elements of black-American folk experience into series with similar elements of American or Western mythology, he is ritualizing them, making each experience a repetition of the other. He is removing the black experience from its historical time and place and replacing it in the long run of time, erasing its distinctiveness, heightening its similarity to other experience. He is translating an expression of the way things work in a particular, man-made, social world to an expression of the way they work in a larger, uncontrollable, cosmic world.

The specific implications of the difference between a social and a mythic view of folk experience can be illustrated by

considering Ellison the critic's discussion of the Battle Royal scene in *Invisible Man:*

Take the "Battle Royal" passage in my novel, where the boys are blindfolded and forced to fight each other for the amusement of the white observers. This is a vital part of behavior pattern in the South, which both Negroes and whites thoughtlessly accept. It is a ritual in preservation of caste lines, a keeping of taboo to appease the gods and ward off bad luck. It is also the initiation ritual to which all greenhorns are subjected. This passage which states what Negroes will see I did not have to invent; the patterns were already there in society, so that all I had to do was present them in a broader context of meaning. In any society there are many rituals of situation which, for the most part, go unquestioned. They can be simple or elaborate, but they are the connective tissue between the work of art and the audience.

["The Art of Fiction: An Interview"]

The Battle Royal is rooted in the slave experience. It goes back to the many-versioned folk-tale "The Fight," in which Old Marster and his neighbor pit their two strongest slaves against each other and stake their plantations on the outcome. It has been used by Wright in *Black Boy,* Faulkner in *Absalom, Absalom!,* and Killens in *Youngblood* to dramatize social relations between whites and blacks. It encapsulates the physical, economic, psychological, and sexual exploitation of slavery (and dramatizes the slaves' comprehension of it). By identifying this ritual of a slave society as a "keeping of taboo to appease the gods" and an "initiation ritual to which all greenhorns are subjected," Ellison turns it into an essentially religious ritual in commemoration of implicitly immutable laws and connects it with other such rituals across cultures. By emphasizing the symbolic rather than the social components, Ellison transforms a social experience into a mythic one.

The social and mythic interpretations of a ritual of situation might coexist peacefully if the situation were not a function of so abnormal a condition as slavery. But the mythic interpretation of the Battle Royal contradicts and negates its social meaning. As a social ritual, the Battle Royal reflects the limitation of blackness in the face of white power. As an initiation ritual, it reflects the limitation of youth in the face of maturity. The youth can expect to become mature; the black cannot expect to become white. The initiation ritual symbolizes the relationship of an individual to his own community; the social ritual symbolizes the relationship of an oppressed people to an oppressive people. The initiation ritual celebrates a natural process, maturation, that has been ritualized because it cannot be circumvented: the social ritual celebrates a man-made convention that has been ritualized to prevent its circumvention. Because the social ritual and the mythic ritual reflect different relationships between people and power, they do not have compatible meanings. To equate the Battle Royal with an initiation or an appeasement of the gods is to assume that the relationship between blacks and whites that it dramatizes is divinely sanctioned and eternal. Although that relationship has often seemed permanent, black folklore is based on the premise that it is not; the folk connections between Old Master and divinity are all ironic.

In his theoretical analysis, Ellison places this ritual of situation in a context that distorts its social meaning. In *Invisible Man,* he makes it one of a series of initiations that finally demonstrate not the politics of slavery but the chaos of the universe. In his fiction in general, he fits black-American folk expression into the forms of American and Western myth. To do so, he must ignore, minimize, distort, or deny the peculiarities of the folk expression. Since the peculiarities of black folklore reflect those of the peculiar institution, the effort to transcend them results in the denial of the circumstances that distinguish black experience from all others. The end of the identity quest in Ellison's fiction betrays the beginning.

II

Some of Ellison's short stories illustrate the process of adapting black folk experience to the forms of ritual and the meanings of myth. The quest for identity is the quest for manhood (quite literally: Ellison's only significant female character, Mary Rambo, *knows* who she is). Ellison mounts the quest on rituals of situation like the Battle Royal—characteristic social situations that are repeated over and over again in black life, folklore, and literature because they so accurately express the conflict between black manhood and white power in American society. In his earliest stories, Ellison exploits only the social dimensions of the rituals of situation and the social dimensions of the protagonists' struggles for manhood. In **"Slick Gonna Learn,"** an excerpt from an unfinished first novel, Slick escapes the expected retribution for accidentally striking a policeman but gets picked up by a carful of off-duty cops for a verbal assault when he thinks he is free; he escapes again when the policemen, who are planning to "give this nigger the works," get a radio call and dump him out into the rainy night with only a few kicks and some pistol shots that miss. In **"The Birth-mark,"** Matt and Clara, who have gone to the woods with a policeman and the coroner to identify the body of their brother, are forced to accept the story that he has been hit by a car, when he has obviously been lynched with the cooperation of the police. The title refers not only to an identifying mark on the body but also to the castration wound and to blackness itself. Both stories probe the helplessness and frustration of

black characters in the face of a capricious and all-powerful white law. Both use the ritual qualities of the situation to illuminate social experience.

The Buster-and-Riley stories—**"Mister Toussan," "That I Had the Wings,"** and **"A Coupla Scalped Indians"**—use folklore more symbolically. Buster and Riley are two little boys looking for adventure and fulfillment in a world circumscribed by God, the white folks, and their elders, who interpret God and the white folks for them. In **"Mister Toussan,"** they get carried away retelling the story of Toussaint L'Ouverture that Buster has heard from his teacher. In a call-and-response collective composition with the style of a toast and the rhythmic climax of a folk sermon, they create a heroic badman who makes "those peckerwoods" beg for mercy:

> 'They said, Please, Please, *Please, Mister Toussan. . . ."*
>
> ". . . We'll be good," broke in Riley.
>
> "Thass right, man," said Buster excitedly.
>
> He clapped his hands and kicked his heels against the earth, his black face flowing in a burst of rhythmic joy.
>
> "Boy!"
>
> "And what'd ole Toussan say then?"
>
> "He said in his big deep voice: *You all peckerwoods better be good, 'cause this is sweet Papa Toussan talking and my nigguhs is crazy 'bout white meat!"*

Their story of Toussan both arises from and is applied to the social conflict between blacks and whites. Buster and Riley have just been chased out of their white neighbor's yard for asking whether they could pick up cherries from under his trees—as the birds are doing undisturbed. The irony of the birds' freedom and the sound of his mother inside singing the protest spiritual "I Got Wings" makes Riley ask Buster what he would do if he had wings. Buster replies that he would go to Chicago, Detroit, the moon, Africa, "or anyplace else colored is free." The mention of Africa brings up the school books' view that Africans are lazy, and this leads to the story of the black hero. Their story of Toussan is a flight of fancy that develops the theme of freedom introduced by Buster's answer to Riley's question; identification with Toussan gives them the courage to think about another attempt on Old Rogan's cherries.

"That I Had the Wings" continues the theme of freedom

through flying, but freedom in this story means freedom from the limitations of childhood and humanity. Riley, frustrated in his own wish to learn to fly, tries and fails to teach some chicks. He is defeated by his Aunt Kate, Ole Bill the boss rooster (the identity Riley would choose if he were to die "and come back a bird like Aunt Kate says folks do"), and gravity. The obstacles to manhood in this story are not social but universal—immaturity and earthboundedness.

In **"A Coupla Scalped Indians,"** the quest for manhood is specifically sexual. Buster and Riley, who, still sore from circumcision, have been out in the woods performing Boy Scout tests (with a view to becoming, not Boy Scouts, but Indians), have to pass the house of Aunt Mackie, a reputed conjure woman, whose very name makes Riley shiver. In the course of trying to get by Aunt Mackie's dog, Riley somehow gets himself inside her yard and ever closer to her house, where he sees her dancing naked before the window and is surprised at the youthful body beneath her wrinkled face. She discovers him, brings him in, makes him kiss her ("You passed all the tests and you was peeping in my window"), demands to see his circumcision wound, and fills him with the confusing emotions of pain, need, shame, and relief. The only conflict in the story is sexual, and the elements of folklore, Aunt Mackie's "conjure" and Buster's eulogy to the dozens (a game of competitive insult usually focusing on the sexual behavior of the opponent's female relatives), are metaphors for the power of sex. The definition of manhood in the early stories becomes more and more general, and the elements of black folklore become less and less connected with specifically black social experience.

> **"That I Had the Wings" continues the theme of freedom through flying, but freedom in this story means freedom from the limitations of childhood and humanity.**
> —*Susan L. Blake*

Both **"Mister Toussan"** and **"That I Had the Wings"** make central use of the ability to fly as a metaphor for freedom and manhood. **"Flying Home"** develops this metaphor further and, through it, shows the effect of framing black folk materials in Western myth. Flying is a predominant motif in black-American folklore as well as in Western myth; its meanings vary from one tradition to another. In Greek mythology, flying represents the superhuman power of the gods; in Freudian psychology, it symbolizes male sexual potency; in black-American folklore, it means freedom. In a folk context the aspiration to fly recalls Harriet Tubman's dream of flying over a great wall, the numerous references in the spirituals to flying to freedom in Jesus, the Sea Islands legend of the Africans who rose up from the field one day and flew back to Africa, and the humorous folktale of the Colored

Man who went to heaven and flew around with such abandon that he had to be grounded but who boasted that he was "a flying black bastard" while he had his wings. Although the mythic and sexual meanings of the metaphor are of course implicit in the aspiration to freedom, the emphasis in the folk concept of manhood is on the freedom, and the obstacles to freedom are seen to be in the social structure, not in oneself or the laws of the physical universe.

"Flying Home" presents at least four folk variations on the flying motif and as many more mythic ones. The story is based on the former military practice of withholding from blacks the opportunity to fly airplanes, a historical situation that so largely bore out the folklore of flying that it immediately became part of it. The protagonist in the story is a student at the Negro air school in Tuskegee, established during World War II in response to complaints about discrimination against blacks in pilot training. The story about the school was that it trained black men to fly but never graduated them to combat. Todd, the flier in this story, who feels he acquires dignity from his airplane and the appreciation of his white officers and shame from his relationship with ignorant black men, has run into a buzzard and crashed in a white man's filed. Jefferson, the "ignorant black man" who finds him, sends for help, and keeps him company while they wait, tells him two folktales—a brief anecdote about seeing two buzzards emerge from the insides of a dead horse and the comic story of the Colored Man who tore up heaven flying.

The buzzard is a common figure in black folklore, representing sometimes the black person scrounging for survival, sometimes his predators, and always the precariousness of life in a predatory society. In one story, told by Mrs. I. E. Richards, the buzzard is represented as a bird that flies higher than the average but has to come down to get food; this story is told to impress children that "regardless of what you might have . . . we all have to live on the same level." All these folk associations are active in the references to buzzards in **"Flying Home."** The birds are black; Jefferson says that his grandson Teddy calls them jimcrows. Representing not only the black man, Todd, but the Jim Crow society, they symbolize the destructiveness of both. Todd thinks of himself as a buzzard when he cries, "Can I help it if they won't let us actually fly? Maybe we are a bunch of buzzards feeding on a dead horse, but we can hope to be eagles, can't we?" But there is also a clear analogy between him and the horse's carcass ("Saw him just like I see you," says Jefferson of the horse): he is being devoured by both the Jim Crow society and his own shame at blackness. Todd (*Tod* 'death') is, in trying to destroy old Jefferson, also feeding on his own dead self. So the moral of Mrs. Richards' buzzard story also applies to Todd: he learns that he cannot set himself above other blacks because, as Jefferson reminds him, "You black son. . . . You have to come by the white folks, too."

The tale of the Colored Man in heaven also applies to Todd, who "had been flying too high and too fast" and "had climbed steeply away in exultation" before going into a spin and crashing. Todd recognizes this application in anguish: "Why do you laugh at me this way?" he screams while Jefferson is laughing at the punch line. The point of the folktale, which Jefferson emphasizes by adding the "new turn" that "us colored folks had to wear a special kin' a harness when we flew," is that the black man is a man despite the obstacles put in his way: even with the harness, he outflies the other angels; even grounded, he remains brash and confident. Together, the moral of this story and the implications of the buzzard associations compose the explicit message of **"Flying Home"**: manhood is inherent, neither tendered nor rescinded by white society; to try to achieve manhood by escaping blackness is only self-destructive, because "we all have to live on the same level."

As Joseph F. Trimmer has pointed out, **"Flying Home"** also recalls the myth of Icarus and alludes to the myth of the phoenix, the Christian doctrine of the fortunate fall, and the parable of the prodigal son. The stories of Icarus, the fall, and the prodigal son all involve men trying to transcend their condition, as Todd is trying to transcend blackness. The story of Icarus parallels Mrs. Richards' comments on the high-flying buzzard. The idea of the fortunate fall and the story's final image of the buzzard flying into the sun and glowing gold like the phoenix both suggest, as the folk referents in the story do, that the flier's failure is in some way a victory. But there are important differences between the meanings of the myths alluded to in the story and those of the folk sources. First, the strivers in the stories of Icarus and the fall of man are trying to improve their position with respect not to other men but to God. Even the Prodigal Son is presented in that context in this story, through the opening lines of James Weldon Johnson's "Prodigal Son" in *God's Trombones,* which Todd remembers his grandmother reciting as a warning when he was a child:

> Young man, young man,
> Yo' arms too short
> *To box with God. . . .*

But Todd's fault—and that of the high-flying buzzard—is to try to set himself above other men. Second, all these myths, including that of the phoenix, which cremates and resurrects itself, imply that the hero is the sole cause of his own fall. By thus obscuring the duality of the buzzard symbol and ignoring the social basis of the story, the mythic allusions dull the irony of the folk associations and shift the emphasis from manhood to mortality. In the end, Todd flies "home" to freedom in the sense of the Sea Islands legend, by flying "home" to his people and to himself like the prodigal son. But as the final image of the buzzard glowing gold like the phoenix seems to imply, he is also dying, flying "home" to

acceptance of the universal human condition of mortality, which is not at all the same as the perpetual precariousness of life in a predatory society. Nor is it the same as the "home" or "heaven" of the black spiritual tradition, for there, in a reversal of the conventional relationship between the concrete and abstract terms of metaphor, both "home" and "heaven" often connote the geographical North and social freedom.

The mythic context subtly changes the meaning of the themes embodied in the folk foundation of **"Flying Home."** It transforms acceptance of blackness as identity into acceptance of blackness as limitation. It substitutes the white culture's definition of blackness for the self-definition of folklore.

III

The theme of *Invisible Man* is similar to that of **"Flying Home."** The novel presents itself as an epic statement of the need for black self-definition. The protagonist of the novel, characterized as a representative black man on an identity quest, finds himself only when he gives up his white masters' definition of reality and adopts that asserted by the black folk tradition. Ironically, however, the definition of reality that Ellison attributes to the folk tradition is the very one maintained by the whites.

What functions as black folklore in the novel is everything the protagonist initially rejects as manifesting a Sambo mentality and finally learns to accept as basic to his true identity. It includes almost anything rooted in or associated with slavery, the South, the established body of southern folklore, or its northern ghetto mutations. And it comes from the traditions of both the black slave and the white plantation. Nothing could be more apparently contradictory than the images of the black man offered by these traditions, which differ simply as the perspectives of slave and master. The archetypal black man of slave folklore is John, the hero of an extensive cycle of tales, who comically but constantly says "no" to Old Marster and the slave system he represents. The stereotypical black man of the plantation tradition is Sambo, who grins, sings, fawns, and otherwise says "yes" to Old Marster, old times, and the old Kentucky home. John may appear to acquiesce, but he manages to subvert Old Master's intentions; Sambo may appear mischievous, but he is fundamentally loyal. *Invisible Man* attempts to reconcile the two images through both the plot, in which the protagonist must learn to stop fleeing from Sambo in order to find himself, and the pattern of folklore allusion, which treats Sambo and John as though they were one and the same.

The novel chronicles three stages in the protagonist's life—education, employment, and political activity—framed by his entry into the life of society (or, in the novel's terms, history) through high school graduation and his exit from it through disillusionment with political organization. Each stage in the protagonist's personal history corresponds to an era in the social history of black Americans. His sojourn in a southern black college modeled on Tuskegee Institute corresponds to Reconstruction; he has entered it on a scholarship presented in a parody of Emancipation, and he leaves it under compulsion, in the company of a disillusioned World War I veteran, in a manner representative of the Great Migration. His first few weeks in New York—job hunting, working in the paint factory, encountering unionism, and undergoing electric shock treatment—contain the elements of the hopeful twenties, when industry was god, self-reliance its gospel, and unionism an exciting heresy; when timidly rebellious young heirs like Emerson, Jr., frolicked in Harlem and psychology was the newest toy. His experience in the Brotherhood reflects the Great Depression, when dispossession was the common complaint and communism the intellectual's cure; his disillusionment with the Brotherhood parallels the general post-Depression retreat from communism. And the riot in which he drops out—of sight, of history, of the novel—suggests the Harlem riot of 1943.

The protagonist enters each stage hopefully and is ejected forcibly. His hopefulness is based on faith in the word or belief or method that each historical age has offered as the solution to the difficulties blackness has always presented. In school and college, it is accommodation—the principles of Booker T. Washington, as quoted by the protagonist in his graduation speech, eulogized by the Rev. Homer Barbee in his chapel-service account of "the Founder's" life, and practiced by Dr. Bledsoe in the administration of the college. In the business world, it is capitalism, individualism, Emersonian self-reliance. In politics, it is "brotherhood—whether of class, as maintained by the Brotherhood itself, or of race, as insisted by its chief competition, the Garveyesque Ras the Exhorter. The distinction between Ras and the Brotherhood is ultimately unimportant, for all the recommended solutions to the problem of blackness—accommodation; capitalism; its briefly introduced corrective, unionism; communism; nationalism—prove to be false. Reliance on these conventional principles leads the protagonist not to security but to the chaos that propels him from one stage to another—from the Battle Royal, to the melee at the Golden Day, to the paint factory explosion, to the Harlem riot. And the proponents of these principles—Jack, Norton, Emerson—merge in the protagonist's mind by the end of the novel "into a single white figure," with which Bledsoe, too, is elsewhere associated.

Opposed to the conventional and apparently rational doctrines of the white world are the wisdom and experience of the black folk tradition, which exposes the falseness of the white view of reality and offers an alternative vision testified to by the protagonist's grandfather, the pushcart man, the vet, and, ironically, Bledsoe and Emerson, Jr. Each of these characters has some link with the folk past. The grandfather has been a slave; the pushcart man talks rhymes and fables and sings the blues; the vet, though educated and erudite, is connected in the protagonist's mind with the pushcart man; Bledsoe is modeled on Booker T. Washington, a legend in himself and a real-life reflection of the traditional trickster; even Emerson, Jr., is a primitivist, who frequents Harlem nightclubs, collects African art, and reads *Totem and Taboo*. These characters are also linked—as Bledsoe, Emerson, Norton, and Jack are on the other side—by the advice they give the protagonist for dealing with blackness.

> **What functions as black folklore in the novel is everything the protagonist initially rejects as manifesting a Sambo mentality and finally learns to accept as basic to his true identity.**
> —*Susan L. Blake*

The protagonist regards the businessmen's smoker at which he delivers his graduation speech and receives his scholarship to the state college for Negroes as his emancipation from the degradation created by slavery, but it is also here that he is compelled to participate in the Battle Royal. Folk wisdom would show this "emancipation" and each successive one to be just variations on the fundamental condition of slavery. The protagonist's grandfather warns him in a dream that the scholarship certificate in his briefcase advises "Whomever It May Concern" to "Keep This Nigger Boy Running." The prediction recalls the trick some masters played on their illiterate slaves, writing them passes that invited the reader to administer a flogging. It is fulfilled by both Bledsoe, whose treacherous letters of introduction request the reader to help the bearer "continue in the direction of that promise which, like the horizon, recedes ever brightly and distantly beyond the hopeful traveler," and Jack, who the protagonist realizes, when he sees that the handwriting on a threatening note is the same as that which has informed him of his Brotherhood name, "named me and set me running with one and the same stroke of the pen."

The principle of emancipation through accommodation is refuted by the folk storyteller Trueblood: "I done the worse thing a man could ever do in his family and instead of chasin me out of the county, they gimme more help than they ever give any other colored man, no matter how good a nigguh he was." The principle of emancipation through capitalism is punctured by the folk rhyme the protagonist remembers when he hears of Bledsoe's treachery: "They Picked Poor Robin Clean" explains not only what Bledsoe has done to him but what Liberty Paints has done to Lucius Brockway and will do to him and what capitalistic industry generally strives to do to all its workers. The irony of Brother Jack's betrayal is sharpened by the background of the John-and-Old-Marster tales: "Brother Jack," whose name is a variant of "Brother John," reminds the protagonist of "old Master," a bulldog he "liked but didn't trust" as a child, and becomes in the end "Marse Jack." Even Brotherhood—which, as both abstract philosophy and political movement, promises the ultimate liberation—offers only the same old oppression.

What the folk perspective substitutes for the "rational" programs to order chaos is acceptance of chaos as reality. Under the stream of conventional advice on how to deal with blackness runs a current of counteradvice introduced and distilled in the protagonist's grandfather's deathbed dictum: "overcome 'em with yeses, undermine 'em with grins, agree 'em to death and destruction"—the "beginning" to which the narrator returns on the first page of Chapter i. The grandfather, the vet, the pushcart man, Bledsoe, and Emerson offer a vision of reality based on contradiction: yes is no, freedom is slavery, things are not what they seem. The pushcart man sings the characteristic contradiction of the blues,

> She's got feet like a monkey
> Legs like a frog—Lawd, Lawd!
> But when she starts to loving me
> I holler Whoooo, God-dog!
> Cause I loves my baabay,
> Better than I do myself . . .

leaving the protagonist to wonder whether the song expresses love or hate and whether he himself is hearing it with pride or disgust. "Play the game, but don't believe in it," counsels the vet. "You're black and living in the South," exclaims Bledsoe, "did you forget how to lie?" "For God's sake, learn to look beneath the surface," exhorts the vet. "Aren't you curious about what lies behind the face of things?" asks Emerson, Jr. What lies behind the face of things is, like the black dope in the white paint, contradiction.

The inclusion of Emerson, Jr., and Bledsoe as spokesmen for the "folk," as well as for the white, point of view is not self-contradictory but illustrative of the simultaneous sway of opposites that Ellison sees as the heart of the folk vision. A yam may be good and sweet and call up memories of all that is good in the past and in the South; or it may be bitter. A leg shackle may be a "symbol of our progress," as Bledsoe calls the memento on his desk; or it may be a symbol of continued slavery, as Bledsoe's seems to be in comparison with Brother Tarp's filed-open shackle. The meaning is not in the thing itself but in the way it is used.

The function of folklore in Chapter xi, in which the protagonist undergoes electric shock treatment in the paint factory hospital, applies this point to the protagonist's identity and the Sambo image. When the doctors and nurses refer to Brer Rabbit in their efforts to draw the protagonist a new personality after erasing the old one electrically, they clearly have the Sambo image in mind. They have just played with the shock treatment as the traditional cracker plays with pistol shots:

> "Look, he's dancing," someone called.
> "No, really?"
>
> An oily face looked in. "They really do have rhythm, don't they? Get hot, boy! Get hot!" it said with a laugh.

When they ask in sequence "What is your name?" "Who was your mother?" "Who was Buckeye the Rabbit?" and "Who was Brer Rabbit?" they are regarding folklore as the expression of a childish personality, safe and hence "normal" in a black subject. The protagonist identifies with the folklore—"Somehow I was Buckeye the Rabbit"—but while the doctors mention the Rabbit with the expectations of the nursery, the protagonist replies in the idiom of the dozens:

> BOY, WHO WAS BRER RABBIT?
> He was your mother's back-door man. I thought. Anyone knew they were one and the same: "Buckeye" when you were very young and hid yourself behind wide innocent eyes; "Brer" when you were older.

Even Sambo, the image of subjugation, has simultaneous, opposite meanings. He is not only the embodiment of degradation but also, as Dr. Bledsoe, Trueblood, Lucius Brockway, and Tod Clifton all demonstrate in one way or another, a source of power. "I's big and black and I say 'yes, suh' as loudly as any burrhead when it's convenient," Dr. Bledsoe concedes, "but I'm still the king down here." Sambo represents not only powerlessness but the knowledge of powerlessness, not only the absence of identity but knowledge of the absence—and knowledge is a kind of power in itself. Tod Clifton, selling Sambo dolls, even being shot by the police, is in greater control of his own destiny than the protagonist, who is still being manipulated, like one of Clifton's dolls, by the Brotherhood. Clifton has acknowledged and rejected the Brotherhood's manipulation; the protagonist is still dancing on a string unawares.

Sambo is, in effect, the lesson the protagonist has rejected all along; that, in the terms of the white world he has been relying on for guidance and identity, he is nobody, invisible, Sambo—something his advisers have been telling him from the beginning. Whether invisibility is identity or nonidentity depends on your point of view: "You're nobody, son," barks Bledsoe, speaking for the white point of view. "You're hidden right out in the open," says the vet, from the black. "Identity! My God! Who has any identity any more anyway?" laments Emerson, Jr., from the nihilistic. The protagonist's challenge is to look at things from the black point of view, the underside, from which the contradiction, the chaos, is apparent.

The folk influences in *Invisible Man* define not an action but an attitude of ironic withdrawal from the white world, an attitude represented metaphorically by the lives of all those characters—Bledsoe, Trueblood, Brockway, and Rinehart—who deal with it successfully and finally by the protagonist's withdrawal into his well-lighted cellar. All the characters who function well in the white world inhabit some sort of underworld: Bledsoe's is calculated humility; Trueblood's, the subconscious; Brockway's, the cellar of Liberty Paints; Rinehart's, organized crime. And they all accept the chaos apparent from down below. "You have looked upon chaos and are not destroyed?" Mr. Norton asks Trueblood. "No suh, I feels all right." "This here's the up-roar department and I'm in charge," boasts Lucius Brockway (Lucifer Breakaway) from his cellar. Rinehart does not simply live with chaos; as Rine the runner, Rine the gambler, Rine the briber, Rine the lover, and Rine the Reverend, he *is* chaos:

> Could he be all of them? . . . Could he himself be both rind and heart? . . . It was true as I was true. . . . The world in which we lived was without boundaries. A vast seething, hot world of fluidity, and Rine the rascal was at home. Perhaps only Rine the rascal was at home in it. It was unbelievable, but perhaps only the truth was always a lie.

When the protagonist comes to this insight, realizes that he has "no longer to run for or from the Jacks and the Emersons and the Bledsoes and Nortons, but only from their confusion, impatience, and refusal to recognize the beautiful absurdity of their American identity and mine," and goes underground, he is following the model of these folk characters and the wisdom of his folk advisers and is acting out the lesson that folk allusions have helped to develop: that meaning is all in your mind.

This ironic withdrawal is presented as negation of the white world and its absurdity. The protagonist looks on his retreat as a relief from the "ill[ness] of affirmation, of saying 'yes' against the nay-saying of my stomach—not to mention my brain." The characters he is imitating are all, from the conventional point of view, a bit diabolical, and those whose advice he is following—the crazy grandfather, the insane vet, the neurotic young Emerson—are all a bit mad. It is against this perceived negation that Ellison sets the contrived reinterpretation of the grandfather's advice ("Could he have meant—hell, he *must* have meant that we were to affirm the principle on which the country was built and not the men . . .") and the unsupported retraction of the book's dramatic statement: "Perhaps that's my greatest social crime, I've overstayed my hibernation, since there's a possibility that even an invisible man has a socially responsible role to play."

But withdrawal into a hole is not negation. To say that the world is absurd, that the only reality is in the mind, is a way of saying that the world and the falsehoods that make it absurd are unimportant. And that is, if not affirmation, at least acquiescence. The goal in *Invisible Man* is to know, not to change; knowledge is presented as the equivalent of change. But knowledge does not necessarily produce change. Whether or not Sambo knows is something Old Marster never knows; it is only when Sambo shows he knows that the relationship changes—and then Sambo is not Sambo at all, but John, Old Marster's natural equal and moral and intellectual superior. When John says "yes" to Old Marster, he is either covering up his crimes against slavery or setting up new ones. The result is, at least, a couple of chickens in his pot; at most, some erosion of the power of slavery that Old Marster is forced to acknowledge: Old Marster gets whipped, Old Miss gets slapped, or Old John gets freedom. The affirmation of *Invisible Man* is neither the survival technique of John the chicken thief nor the political weapon of John the social saboteur, for the negation behind it is all in the mind. The ultimate effect of *Invisible Man*'s reinterpretation of the black folk image is not to elevate Sambo, the cellar rebel, to the status of John but to reduce the archetypal black folk hero to Sambo. Thus the result of the protagonist's identity quest is not self-definition at all but reaffirmation of the identity provided by the white culture.

There are two folk characters in the novel who have the potential for representing a positive interpretation of the black folk perspective: Mary Rambo and Brother Tarp. Both are explicitly characterized as anchors against chaos. The protagonist thinks of Mary as "a force, a stable familiar force like something out of my past which kept me from whirling off into some unknown which I dared not face." He regards Brother Tarp's gift of the sawed-open chain link as a "paternal gesture which at once joined him with his ancestors, marked a high point of his present, and promised a concreteness to his nebulous and chaotic future." Both offer the protagonist advice in direct opposition to the counsel to go underground:

> "It's you young folks what's going to make the changes," [Mary says]. "Y'all's the ones. You got to lead and you got to fight and move us all on up a little higher. And I tell you something else, it's the ones from the South that's got to do it, them what knows the fire and ain't forgot how it burns. Up here too many forgits."

Brother Tarp echoes her with the gift of the legchain link:

> "Even when times were best for me I remembered.

Because I didn't want to forgit those nineteen years I just kind of held on to this as a keepsake and a reminder.... I'd like to pass it on to you, son.... Funny thing to give somebody, but I think it's got a heap of signifying wrapped up in it and it might help you remember what we're really fighting against. I don't think of it in terms of but two words, *yes* and *no*; but it signifies a heap more...."

These passages root both the activist perspective and the stabilizing effect of Mary and Tarp in slavery, the South, the past—the black folk experience. The anchor against chaos that each provides is a clear perception of the source of the chaos, not as general absurdity, but as the specific legacy of slavery, something to be confronted in the world, not just the mind. But the perspective of Mary and Brother Tarp is not the perspective of the novel. Ellison does not follow up the implications of their characterization. Their advice is never confirmed, never refuted, never even dramatized. Though they are introduced as admirable and illuminating characters, they are soon dropped and forgotten. Mary Rambo is further developed in an unused chapter entitled **"Out of the Hospital and under the Bar,"** but even it it were included, she would still have no sustained effect on the novel. The final perspective remains that of the grandfather, who has said "no" so secretly that even his family is shocked to hear him call himself a traitor.

IV

The long-projected novel **"And Hickman Arrives"** follows up on the final, universalizing sentence of *Invisible Man:* "Who knows but that on the lower frequencies, I speak for you?"

Judging by the published fragments, **"Hickman"** explores the relationship between a representative white American and a group of blacks who are, in two ways, his. Senator Sunraider is a representative American in that he is a legislative representative, and he is a representative white man in that his views, though racist in the extreme, represent the quintessence of white consciousness of whiteness. The black characters are "his" not only in the sense that he acts as though he owns them but also, paradoxically, in the sense that he belongs to them. Senator Sunraider, like Faulkner's Joe Christmas, is a man of ambiguous ancestry. We see him in **"Juneteenth," "The Roof, the Steeple, and the People,"** and the flashback in the title story as a light-skinned foundling in a black community in the South, a child-prodigy preacher named Bliss, foster son and pupil of Rev. A. Z. Hickman, "God's Trombone." He has grown up to be, inexplicably, a white racist senator from a New England state. As Hickman and his congregation watch the Senator from the Senate visitors' gallery, they recognize in the very rhetoric with which he humiliates black people the gestures and cadences of the southern black preacher: "'why, Reveren', that's *you*! He's still doing you! O, my Lord . . . still doing you after all these years and yet he can say all those mean things he says . . . .'" The Senator is *of* what he is *against*; his roots are in what he so strenuously denies: and he denies it so strenuously *because* he is rooted in it. The implication is that the Senator's apparently bizarre relationship with Hickman is actually the archetypal relationship of white America to black: something more than brotherhood—identity, perhaps—denied.

The relationship is developed by stitching together elements of the black experience and elements of American popular culture into a patchwork myth of American identity. Like a quilter making two-color patterns, Ellison matches black folk characters to white racist stereotypes, the folklore of race relations to the conventions of southwest humor, and ultimately the emancipation of black folks from slavery to the emancipation of whites from racism. The patterns are set against a background of allusions to stories—historical and literary—that have already become myths of American identity.

Daddy Hickman, the folk preacher, and Senator Sunraider, the southern politician (though northern: North and South are one and the same) relate to each other as Uncle Remus and the Little Boy. Hickman treats the child Bliss, the grown-up Senator, and all whites with the patronizing patience characteristic of the stereotypical plantation storyteller. Bliss and Sunraider portray the two sides of the white child, who is both the child and the master, both the "son" and the "son-raider," kidnapper, castrater. The relationship between Senator Sunraider and his living past culminates when he is shot from the Senate visitors' gallery in a gesture that, ironically, recalls the assassination of Lincoln the Emancipator (and seems to divine, in 1960, an element of the American experience revealed in the ensuing decade with the assassinations of John and Robert Kennedy, Malcolm X, and Martin Luther King).

In a further twist to the irony, the assassination does emancipate Senator Sunraider by making him acknowledge his sonship and hence himself. In his delirium he calls for Daddy Hickman and reenacts sermons he has helped Hickman preach. The role of Bliss in these sermons has been to dramatize the theme of life-out-of-death. In the sermon in **"And Hickman Arrives,"** he rises on cue from a little white satin coffin clutching his teddy bear and an Easter bunny. As the Senator relives the experience of the sermon, falling again under the influence of Hickman's rhetoric as he remembers it, he undergoes the rebirth that the sermon is about. The **"Juneteenth"** sermon, preached on the annual celebration of Emancipation among blacks in the Southwest, applies the resurrection theme to the history of a people and the awakening of Senator Sunraider to the redemption of American society. In this sermon, Hickman calls the enslavement and emancipation of his people "a cruel calamity laced up with a blessing—or maybe a blessing laced up with a calamity .... because out of all the pain and the suffering, out of the night of storm, we found the Word of God." As Hickman develops this theme, Bliss acts it out. "WE WERE LIKE THE VALLEY OF DRY BONES!" he shouts. When the bones begin to stir, Bliss begins to strut. When Bliss, the child of his memory, is moved, the dry bones of the Senator begin to stir. When Senator Sunraider comes to himself, he emancipates both the blacks he has assumed power over and the blackness, the humanity, in himself.

The relationship between black and white outlined in the main plot is repeated with variations in a comic subplot in which the assassination of Senator Sunraider is parodied by the sacrifice of a gleaming white Cadillac. This episode, contained in **"Cadillac Flambé"** and **"It Always Breaks Out,"** is a chain of reactions to the Senator's half-facetious but characteristic public statement that the Cadillac has become so popular with blacks that it ought to be renamed the "Coon Cage Eight." Each of the characters in this subplot is both a racial and a literary stereotype, characterized by both the content and the form of a speech on race relations.

LeeWillie Minifees, who immolates his Cadillac on the Senator's front lawn, is the Black Militant and literary Badman. He acts in the tradition of a decade of ghetto rioters, draft-card burners, and self-immolating Buddhist monks; he speaks with the style and defiance of a Shine or a Stackolee:

"YOU HAVE TAKEN THE BEST," he boomed, "so, DAMMIT, TAKE ALL THE REST! Take ALL the rest!

"In fact, now I don't want anything you think is too good for me and my people. Because, just as the old man and the mule said, if a man in your position is against our having them, then there must be something WRONG in our wanting them. So to keep you happy, I, me, LeeWillie Minifees, am prepared to WALK. I'm ordering me some clubfooted, pigeon-toed SPACE SHOES. I'd rather crawl or fly. I'd rather save my money and wait until the A-RABS make a car. The Zulus even. Even the ES-KIMOS! Oh, I'll walk and wait. I'll grab me a GREYHOUND or a FREIGHT! So you can have my coon cage, fare thee well!

... And thank you KINDLY for freeing me from the Coon Cage. Because before I'd be in a CAGE, I'll be buried in my GRAVE—Oh! Oh!"

[**"Cadillac Flambé"**]

McGowan, a journalist who comments on the conflagration from the leather-upholstered luxury of his club, while the "inscrutable but familiar Negro waiter" Sam unobtrusively serves drinks, is both the Unreconstructed Rebel and the Big Braggart of southwestern humor. The main body of **"It Always Breaks Out"** is McGowan's long, hyperbolic dissertation on the thesis "everything the Nigra does is political." If he buys a washing machine or more than one TV, wears a dashiki or a homburg, joins the Book-of-the-Month Club or likes Bill Faulkner, drives a Volkswagen or a Cadillac or an Imperial when he can afford a Cadillac (and so on for nine pages), he is being political. "But gentlemen," McGowan concludes, with the inconsistency of wishful thinking, "to my considerable knowledge no Nigra has ever even *thought* about assassinating anybody."

The journalist who narrates both LeeWillie's action and McGowan's reaction is, in his own words, "a liberal, ex-radical, northerner"—in folk-literary tradition, the Gullible Greenhorn. He reports the conflagration on the Senator's front lawn with meticulous attention to detail, and with all the insight of the narrator of "The Big Bear of Arkansas" or "The Celebrated Jumping Frog of Calaveras County."

For now, having finished unpacking, the driver ... picked up one of the cases—now suddenly transformed into the type of can which during the war was sometimes used to transport high-octane gasoline in Liberty ships (a highly dangerous cargo for those round bottoms and the men who shipped in them)—and leaning carefully forward, began emptying its contents upon the shining chariot.

And thus, I thought, *is gilded an eight-valved, three-hundred and fifty-horsepowered air-conditioned lily!*

For so accustomed have we Americans become to the tricks, the shenanigans, and frauds of advertising, so adjusted to the contrived fantasies of commerce—indeed, to pseudo-events of all kinds—that I though that the car was being drenched with a special liquid which would make it more alluring for a series of commercial photographs.

[**"Cadillac Flambé"**]

The reporter's careful, conscientious, and convoluted report is his "speech"; he comments by his very attempt to report without commenting.

For all their difference in style, the narrator and McGowan speak from equal ignorance, obtuseness, and presumption. Neither can see the implications of his own speech; neither can conceive of a black person's destroying a symbol or representative of American society. The narrator does not see Lee Willie any more than McGowan notices Sam. The northern and southern journalists are both like the northern-southern Senator, and he is like both of them. All three deny black humanity. All three, in doing so, make themselves ridiculous. The narrator has a glimpse of this connection when he observes Sam, the one character of the four who comments by silence:

> Was he, Sam, prevented by some piety from confronting me in a humorous manner, as my habit of mind, formed during the radical Thirties, prevented me from confronting him; or did he, as some of my friends suspected, regard all whites through the streaming eyes and aching muscles of one continuous, though imperceptible and inaudible, belly laugh? *What the hell,* I though, *is Sam's last name?*

In among the jibes at journalists, liberals, and advertising stunts, the episode of the burning Cadillac makes the point that the humanity of such paper-doll characters as McGowan and the narrator is tied up in that of the Sams and the LeeWillies, that it is their refusal to acknowledge the humanity of the Sams and the LeeWillies that stereotypes them and robs them of their own humanity. If the message of *Invisible Man* and Ellison's early short stories is that blackness is humanity, the message of **"And Hickman Arrives"** is that humanity—and particularly American humanity—is blackness.

Given Ellison's acute consciousness of literary tradition and national myth, it is probably more than coincidence that Hickman bears the same name as the focal character in Eugene O'Neill's *Iceman Cometh,* another mythic rendition of the American experience. Each of them, Theodore Hickman ("Hickey") the salesman and A. Z. Hickman the preacher, is both preacher and salesman. Each comes to his potential converts—Hickey, as Iceman, "cometh" to Harry Hope's saloon, Hickman "arrives" in Washington—with a gospel of self-recognition. Each preaches birth into a new life through death to a false one. Each establishes a sense of identity between himself and his subject. Though Hickey's gospel is ultimately ironic and Daddy Hickman's straight, Ellison uses the mythic character of the consummate salesman to touch the themes of illusion and identity and to tie his conception of the American experience to what American society already accepts as an American myth. The distinction between black and white, Daddy Hickman is saying, is one of those illusions we think we need in order to live, but we do not really live until we see it as an illusion and give it up. "And Hickman Arrives" is a mythic and metaphorical amplification of the theme of an essay Ellison wrote for *Time* entitled **"What America Would Be without Blacks"** (6 April 1970, pp. 54-55). In this essay Ellison identifies two fundamental contributions of blacks to American culture: a cultural style

and a moral center—"for not only is the black man a co-creator of the language that Mark Twain raised to the level of literary eloquence, but Jim's condition as American and Huck's commitment to freedom are the moral center of the novel." A patchwork of American archetypes and stereotypes, "Hickman" attempts to give a moral center to the myth of American democracy. In the *Time* essay Ellison says that the presence of an incompletely free group of people represents both the performance and the possibilities of American democracy, and in the novel he suggests that the function of black suffering is to emancipate white humanity. As Hickman, looking back on the night in which he now realizes his foster son "began to wander," confesses to Sunraider, "all that time I should have been praying for you" ("Hickman"). Ellison's manipulation of folklore in "Hickman" subordinates black experience to American redemption.

V

Ellison's ability to adapt, rather than simply to include, black folklore in his fiction is regarded as his special contribution to the literary interpretation of both folklore and black culture. A few commentators have criticized this adaptation of black folklore for its dependence on Western mythology. Larry Neal, who singles Ellison out for his broad and profound understanding of Afro-American culture, considers the fact that Ellison "overlays his knowledge of Black culture with concepts that exist outside of it" a sign of confusion. George E. Kent regards Ellison's use of the folk and cultural tradition in *Invisible Man* with "a certain unease," "inspired by the elaborate system of interconnection with Western symbols and mythology, and our awareness that Blackness is more in need of definition than Western tradition, which has had the attention of innumerable literary masters." Both these comments treat the elements of blackness and Western tradition in Ellison's fiction as separable. But Ellison's adaptation of black folklore produces an alloy rather than a plate. The process of ritualization itself changes the meaning of the folklore.

Ellison's ability to adapt, rather than simply to include, black folklore in his fiction is regarded as his special contribution to the literary interpretation of both folklore and black culture.
—Susan L. Blake

Although rituals do undergo change, they do so much more slowly than other aspects of life, and fixity remains the principle of ritual as a form. People use ritual to deal with "those sectors of experience which do not seem amenable to rational control," or as Ellison himself puts it,

People rationalize what they shun or are incapable of dealing with; these superstitions and their rationalizations become ritual as they govern behavior. The rituals become social forms, and it is one of the functions of the artist to recognize them and raise them to the level of art.

("The Art of Fiction: An Interview")

Thus ritual, by its very nature, formalizes the relationship of individuals to an order they do not understand and think they cannot change. By formalizing, it perpetuates; by perpetuating, it celebrates. As a form, ritual tends to affirm the powerlessness of human beings and the permanence of a fixed order.

Emulation of ritual in literature applies the implications of the form to the conflict between characters and the social, natural, or metaphysical forces controlling their lives. It diminishes the role and responsibility of individuals for shaping their own world, personifies impersonal forces and dehumanizes social institutions, homogenizes human experience by emphasizing continuity rather than development, and reduces any particular human action to an insignificant gesture among many in the long run of time. Ultimately, it reduces the significance of the very conflict it expresses by setting it in the context of innumerable others, past and future, by foreordaining the outcome, and by approving the outcome as a contribution to maintaining the order.

Ritualization of black folklore applies the implications of ritual to the specific social conflict between black people and the institution of slavery or Jim Crow. It implies that this conflict is part of a general, eternal, and inescapable conflict between human beings and their limitations. It transforms the social conflict at the heart of the folk expression into the metaphysical conflict of the framing myth, thus denying the social conflict any importance of its own. But the relationship between an oppressed people and an oppressive society *is* social; it is the result of human action and can be changed by human agency. To imply otherwise is, in Ellison's own words, to rationalize.

Rationalization is in fact just what Ellison's ritualization of black folklore accomplishes. It implicitly justifies the relationship between black people and American society by effectually denying it. Putting the experience of the flier in "Flying Home" into a context that includes the stories of Icarus, the prodigal son, and the fall of man changes it from an experience with racism to an example of hubris. It changes the image of the buzzard, a folk symbol of the destructiveness of racism, to that of the phoenix, a mythic symbol of the redemptiveness of destruction. The folk advisers in *Invisible Man* offer the protagonist a way of looking at society that allows him to live with it as it is. They teach him to consider invisibility a personal asset, rather than a

social liability, to embrace chaos as the natural order, to regard Sambo as John, yes as no. But invisibility in the novel *is* a social liability; chaos is racism; Sambo is an attitude of acquiescence; and yes means no only in the mind of the speaker. In both *Invisible Man* and "Flying Home," Ellison offers folk expression as a definition of blackness, then uses folk characters and allusions to deny the social reality that has created the folk identity.

In "Hickman," Ellison uses the materials of black folklore and American popular and literary culture to broaden the context of black experience and reduce the significance of its social dimension. "Oh God hasn't been easy with us because He always plans for the loooong haul," Hickman preaches. "He's looking far ahead and this time He wants a well-tested people to work his will" ("Juneteenth"). As Hickman, in folk-preacher tradition, puts the experience of slavery into the context of Christian myth, Ellison puts it into the context of American myth. "And Hickman Arrives" characterizes the black experience as a test of American humanity and takes the same patient and paternal attitude toward its failure that Hickman takes toward the prodigal Senator Sunraider.

By enlarging the context of the relationship between black people and American society, all these works come to a positive conclusion. They suggest that the nature of the relationship can be changed by changing the perspective from which it is viewed and thus, implicitly, that the relationship exists only in the minds of the victims, as the invisible man's exists in his mind. This shift in perspective shifts the burden of change from the racist society to the oppressed race. Even in "Hickman," where Senator Sunraider, who represents American society, does apparently change, it is Hickman's uniquely paternal and pastoral attitude that effects the change. By denying the need for real change, broadening the context of black folklore perpetuates the oppressive relationship on which it is based. Thus the definition of black experience achieved by Ellison's ritualization of black folklore is ultimately not black but white—white not only because the "larger" contexts into which ritual fits the folklore are those of predominantly white American and Western societies but also because the very idea that a change in mental context can change social reality supports the interests of white society by implicitly denying those of the black. Ellison's adaptation of black folklore, however involuntarily, exchanges the self-definition of the folk for the definition of the masters—an effect it would not have if it did not undertake to define black identity.

Herbert Mitgang (essay date 1 March 1982)

SOURCE: "*Invisible Man,* As Vivid Today as in 1952," in

Conversations with Ralph Ellison, University Press of Mississippi, 1995, pp. 378-82.

[*In the following essay, which originally appeared in* The New York Times, *March 1, 1982, Mitgang uses the occasion of the thirtieth anniversary of the publication of* Invisible Man *to reflect on Ellison's life and career.*]

Ralph Ellison is 68 years old today. Relaxing in his art-and-book lined apartment on Riverside Drive above the Hudson the other day, he took a little time away from his electric typewriter to talk about his working life.

"My approach is that I'm an American writer," he said. "I write out of the larger literary tradition—which, by the way, is part Negro—from Twain to Melville to Faulkner. Another element I'm aware of is American folklore. And then all of this is part of the great stream of literature.

"Americans didn't invent the novel. Negroes didn't invent poetry. Too much has been written about racial identity instead of what kind of literature is produced. Literature is color-blind, and it should be read and judged in a larger framework."

In March 1952, Mr. Ellison's first novel, ***Invisible Man,*** was published, and Random House is marking the occasion this month by bringing out a 30th-anniversary edition, which is also being distributed by the Book-of-the-Month Club. Since 1952, *Invisible Man* has gone through 20 hardcover and 17 Vintage Books paperback printings, and there has been a Modern Library edition.

The novel can also be read in Czech, Danish, Dutch, Finnish, French, German, Hebrew, Hungarian, Italian, Japanese, Norwegian, Portuguese, Slovak, Spanish and Swedish. The author's wife, Fanny, who magically finds just about everything he has written in their home files, says that a request came in for a Polish edition just before martial law was declared in Poland. He says that the Russians are aware of his writings, but that if a translation exists in Russian, he hasn't seen any edition.

What provides the greatest continuity for ***Invisible Man*** is that it is recognized as an essential 20th-century American literary work in just about every high school and college in the country. Anne Freedgood, a Random House editor, enjoys telling the story of the 17-year-old student she knows who recently learned that Mr. Ellison had not written a second novel. "How could he?" the young woman said. "This novel has *everything* in it."

It won the National Book Award in 1953 and, in 1965, some 200 authors, editors and critics, polled by *The New York Herald Tribune,* picked ***Invisible Man*** as the most distinguished novel written by an American during the previous 20 years.

The novel, which defies easy summary because of its subtleties (a thumbnail description: It is about one nameless black man's dilemma about his position in the white world), builds from one of the most memorable opening paragraphs in modern American fiction:

> I am an invisible man. No, I am not a spook like those who haunted Edgar Allan Poe; nor am I one of your Hollywood-movie ectoplasms. I am a man of substance, of flesh and bone, fiber and liquids— and I might even be said to possess a mind. I am invisible, understand, simply because people refuse to see me.

Mr. Ellison revealed that he had meant to write a different novel—a war story rooted in some of his own experiences at sea and observations ashore as a merchant seaman in Europe in the 1940's—when he was seized by the notion of invisibility.

"I had come back on sick leave from my service in the Merchant Marine and, after a hospital stay, in the summer of 1945, my wife and I went to a friend's farm in Waltsfield, Vt. Sitting in a lumberman's cabin, looking at the hills, I wrote the first line of the book: 'I am an invisible man.'"

The original interest in his book came from Frank Taylor, who had read his short stories, and Albert Erskine, who were with the publishing house of Reynal & Hitchcock after the war. When those respected editors moved to Random House in 1947, the contract for Mr. Ellison's book went with them. Mr. Taylor went to Hollywood, and Mr. Erskine remained as his editor.

Mr. Ellison said, "Once the book was gone, it was suggested that the title would be confused with H. G. Wells's old novel, *The Invisible Man,* but I fought to keep my title because that's what the book was about." Mr. Erskine recalled. "His novel doesn't have the article in its title, although the mistake keeps cropping up, and I've been telling people to drop the word 'the' ever since the book came out."

The author was born in Oklahoma City, educated at Tuskegee Institute, worked as a researcher on the New York Federal Writers' Project before World War II and hoped to enlist as a trumpeter (he still has a trumpet, but he says, no lip anymore) in the Navy—"but they were not taking any more musicians. So, instead, I became a second cook on a Liberty ship. I was in charge of making breakfast, and I also turned out cornbread, biscuits and fried pies."

The war background—his own experiences in Europe and

his father's as a soldier during the Spanish-American War—led to planning a novel that would show how Negroes (the word he usually uses rather than "blacks" in conversation, explaining that it has historical roots) fought not only for their country but for their own recognition and rights.

He had the unwritten novel's theme worked out. It was focused on the experience of a captured black American pilot who found himself in a Nazi prisoner-of-war camp. As the officer of highest rank, the pilot became the spokesman for his white fellow prisoners. The resulting racial tension was exploited by the German camp commander for his own amusement. "My pilot was forced to find support for his morale in his sense of individual dignity and in his newly awakened awareness of human loneliness," Mr. Ellison notes in an introduction to the 30th anniversary edition of *Invisible Man.*

But then, creatively, "the spokesman for invisibility intruded," and he was captured by a richer theme that grew more out of himself—"the voice of invisibility issued from deep within our complex American underground." Today, he says, he doesn't know where the manuscript about the captured black pilot is—"I probably tore it up."

Inevitably, a talk with Mr. Ellison turns to his long-awaited work-in-progress. It will be his third book. *Shadow and Act,* a book of essays, came out in 1964. It can be reported that his second novel is progressing, and apparently it is working—certainly, the author is, steadily, every day. He has given the novel his full attention since he retired in 1980 from his teaching duties as a Schweitzer Professor of Humanities at New York University.

Author and novel suffered a setback in the summer of 1967, when 300 pages of manuscript were lost in a fire in Mr. Ellison's home in the Berkshires. "It was quite a traumatic experience watching the house burn and losing typewriters, cameras and other personal property," he said. "The only thing we saved was our Labrador retriever. After that, I tried to put together as much as I could, and I began to reconceive some of the characters; Now, we have a photocopier at home and I keep at least two copies of what I write."

Some Ellison fans, waiting so many years for his next novel, have wondered if he had writer's block.

"If so, it's a strange kind of thing, since I write all the time," Mr. Ellison replied. "The blockage is that I'm very careful about what I submit for publication. I learned long ago that it's better not to have something in print that you feel isn't ready. It's not a difficult thing to turn out more books. I had a hell of a lot more material that didn't get into *Invisible Man.* It may be a wasteful way of writing but I'm careful about what is published. There is a lot of formula writing

today. I can't do certain things as a writer, but I enjoy the act of writing even if it isn't published immediately."

There is a strong metal file cabinet containing much of the manuscript of the untitled novel. He unlocked it for a visitor, pulled out the drawer and measured the sections of manuscript with a tape measure: it came to 19 inches.

"It looks long enough to be a trilogy," he said, smiling. "It all takes place in the 20th century. I'm convinced that I'm working with abiding patterns. The style is somewhat different from *Invisible Man.* There are different riffs in it. Sections of it are publishable and some parts have already appeared, in *American Review, Noble Savage, Partisan Review, Iowa Review,* the *Quarterly Review of Literature.*

"I'm dealing with a broader range of characters, playing with various linguistic styles. Quite a bit of the book is comic. The background is New York, the South, an imaginary Washington—not quite the world I used to encounter on the board of the Kennedy Center for the Performing Arts there."

He has seen Washington from on high, in public service positions, such as membership on the Carnegie Commission on Educational Television. He was given the highest civilian honor, the Medal of Freedom, from President Lyndon B. Johnson, and he is a member of the American Academy-Institute of Arts and Letters, the ranking cultural body in the country.

"The novel has to be more than segments, it has to be a whole before it's ready for publication." He didn't say, nor was he asked, when. "But if I'm going to be remembered as a novelist, I'd better produce it soon," he said cheerfully.

Mary Ellen Williams Walsh (essay date December 1984)

SOURCE: "*Invisible Man:* Ralph Ellison's Wasteland," in *CLA Journal,* Vol. XXVIII, No. 2, December, 1984, pp. 150-58.

[*In the following essay, Walsh delineates the relationship between* Invisible Man *and T. S. Eliot's* The Waste Land.]

In *Shadow and Act,* Ralph Ellison credits an early reading of *The Waste Land* as the impetus for his "real transition to writing." *Invisible Man* reveals the profundity of this experience. Important scenes, characters, and events in *Invisible Man* recreate prototypes from *The Waste Land.* Identifying his avatars by strong patterns of allusion, Ellison creates a dry, devastated land of the human spirit which reaches into the mythic past. The protagonist of *Invisible Man* reenacts the journey of the quester in *The Waste Land.* His search for the truths which will bring spiritual renewal ends with his perception of his invisibility and his corresponding acceptance of the ideal precepts of American democracy.

Ellison establishes the connection between **Invisible Man** and *The Waste Land* early in the novel in the protagonist's description of the agricultural college he attends:

> For how could it have been real if now I am invisible? If real, why is it that I can recall in all that island of greenness no fountain but one that was broken, corroded and dry? And why does no rain fall through my recollections, sound through my memories, soak through the hard dry crust of the still so recent past? Why do I recall, instead of the odor of seed bursting in spring-time, only the yellow contents of the cistern spread over the lawn's dead grass? . . . . I'm convinced it was the product of a subtle magic, the alchemy of moonlight; the school a flower-studded wasteland, the rocks sunken, the dry winds hidden, the lost crickets chirping to yellow butterflies.

By describing the lush and fruitful agricultural college with the images of aridity and decay used by Eliot to portray the dying land of the impotent Fisher King, Ellison implies that the source of the isolation and dislocation felt by the protagonist is a spiritual sterility like that which devastates the Fisher King's kingdom. He further implies that the protagonist, like the quester in *The Waste Land,* must seek the truths which will restore spiritual vitality to black intellectual, cultural, and social life as it is symbolized by the college.

Ellison underscores the larger purpose of the protagonist's journey by unmistakably identifying the Founder of the college with the Fisher King. The Founder was impotent; his "seed" was "shriveled" in infancy. Referred to at all times by his regal title, rather than by name, the Founder has "the power of a king, or in a sense, of a god." The imagery Homer A. Barbee uses in describing the Founder's death strengthens his identification with the fertility myths: "[T]hink of it not as a death, but as a birth. A great seed has been planted. A seed which has continued to put forth its fruit in its season as surely as if the great creator had been resurrected." Fertility does invest the physical landscape of the Founder's kingdom. The spiritually deformed people who inhabit the immediate environs—the venal Bledsoe, the incestuous Trueblood, the maimed veterans—remain as evidence, however, that a spiritual rebirth has not accompanied the transformation of the "barren clay to fertile soil."

As Ellison shapes the powerful myth to include the experience of black Americans, he transforms Eliot's brittle, European characters and scenes into appropriate counterparts

in the life of the protagonist. The Trueblood episode is clearly an adaptation of "A Game of Chess." Ellison parodies Eliot's "O O O O that Shakespeherian Rag—" with the following line which announces the episode: "And Oh, oh, oh, those multimillionaires!" The petulant woman of "A Game of Chess" is the source of the woman in Trueblood's dream. The room in the mansion in which the dream woman appears is "full of lighted candles and shiny furniture and pictures on the walls, and soft stuff on the floor"; Eliot's woman sits in a similar room. Eliot's lines, "In vials of ivory and coloured glass / Unstoppered, lurked her strange synthetic perfumes, / Unguent, powdered, or liquid—troubled, confused / And drowned the sense in odours . . .," undoubtedly are the source of Ellison's description of the smell of the dream woman which gets "stronger all the time." When the woman attempts to hold Trueblood with her, she acts out the line which Eliot's woman speaks: "My nerves are bad to-night. Yes, bad. Stay with me." The bartender's call in the second scene of "A Game of Chess" perhaps suggested the clock through which the woman appears and Trueblood escapes. The account of the incestuous rape and its aftermath conjoins allusions to both scenes in "A Game of Chess." Trueblood's act parallels the rape of Philomel. His wife's attempt to obtain abortions for herself and their daughter reflects the talk of abortion by Eliot's women in the bar. The response of the white community to Trueblood's act suggests Eliot's line, "'Jug Jug' to dirty ears."

The Trueblood episode, like "A Game of Chess," demonstrates the perversions of love and potency which are symptomatic of spiritual aridity. The impotence of the king makes potency monstrous. Lust, not love, prevails. Rape and incest result. At the end of the episode, when Trueblood's young children play "London Bridge's Fallin' Down," Ellison alludes to Eliot's line in "What the Thunder Said": "London Bridge is falling down falling down falling down." In the novel, as in the poem, the words of the children's game comment on the decay and disintegration of a spiritually bereft land in which such perversions occur. The episode at the Golden Day Tavern—peopled with whores and mad veterans—further exhibits distorted and perverse sexuality. Like Eliot's bar in "A Game of Chess," the tavern is filled with "demobbed" men. In the course of the episode, the "multimillionaire" Norton inadvertently reveals an incestuous lust for his own daughter, the source of his great interest in Trueblood's story.

The chapel scene in which Homer A. Barbee delivers his eulogy to the Founder further establishes the need for spiritual regeneration in the Founder's kingdom. In this scene, Ellison alludes to "The Fire Sermon" and to "What the Thunder Said." The Founder's chapel is dedicated to his "'vast' and formal ritual." What his people celebrate, however, is "the black rite of Horatio Alger," an economic, not a spiritual, success story. Like Eliot's ruined Chapel Perilous, the

Founder's chapel extends no hope for the renewal of his land. The "thunder and lightning" in this chapel is uttered by white men. Their message to the young blacks parodies that of the sacred Thunder in *The Waste Land*; the young people must "accept and love" the limited universe proscribed for them "and accept even if [they do] not love."

In this setting, Homer Barbee narrates the life and death of the Founder, drawing parallels between the Founder and Jesus Christ, as Eliot associates Christ with the Hanged Man/Hanged God in "What the Thunder Said." Barbee, the black Buddha, describes the Founder's being saved from his enemies by a "fire that burned without consuming," a parody of the fire in the sermon of Buddha to which Eliot alludes. Ultimately, the restorative promise of the birth, death, and resurrection imagery which pervades the chapel scene collapses under the rites practiced there. The rites are devoted to economic success, not to spiritual regeneration.

Although the protagonist leaves the college, he remains in a ritual landscape when he travels north. Ellison develops one of the protagonist's first encounters in New York through allusions to the closing section of "The Burial of the Dead." Just as Stetson is hailed in the poem, a man who alludes to the life of Christ ("Why you trying to deny me?") hails the protagonist and asks, "[I]s you got the *dog*?" Furthermore, when the protagonist goes to work at Liberty Paints, Ellison identifies the action as the beginning of his descent into a hell by a brief narration of the protagonist's trip to the plant: "The plant was in Long Island, and I crossed a bridge in the fog to get there and came down in a stream of workers." The narration is an adaptation of Eliot's lines which allude to the *Inferno:* "Unreal City, / Under the brown fog of a winter dawn, / A crowd flowed over London Bridge, so many."

When the protagonist becomes involved with the Brotherhood, Ellison establishes the mythic importance of the organization by characterizing its leader in the terms of *The Waste Land.* The head of the organization, one-eyed Jack, who lapses in a moment of fury into a "foreign language," parodies the one-eyed Smyrna merchant, who speaks in "demotic French." Ellison's naming the one-eyed leader Jack identifies him with the figure found in a deck of common playing cards and provides thereby a particularly complex allusion to the Tarot card figure with which Eliot associated Mr. Eugenides. The Smyrna merchant's proposal in "The Fire Sermon" debases the messages of the fertility cult mysteries carried throughout the Mediterranean area by early Phoenician and Syrian merchants. Jack's promise to the protagonist similarly perverts the already perverse message of the rites celebrated in the Founder's chapel. The Brotherhood, nonetheless, does offer the narrator a kind of ritual rebirth, giving him a new name, new clothes, and a new address.

Ellison's continued allusions to *The Waste Land* throughout the Brotherhood section maintain the parallel between the journey of the protagonist and that of the quester in the poem. The protagonist stages a massive funeral procession—the burial of Tod—thereby literally rendering Eliot's "The Burial of the Dead." The line from de Nerval which Eliot uses in "What the Thunder Said" doubtless suggested the bell tower setting for the funeral oration, Tod Clifton having earlier been called a "natural prince" by Ras the Destroyer. When the Brotherhood denounces the protagonist for planning and executing the funeral ceremony, he seeks an answer to some of the mysteries of the cult from Sybil, the wife of one of its leaders. Ellison thus transforms the Sibyl at Cumae, the subject of the quotation from Petronius's *Satyricon* which forms the epigraph to *The Waste Land,* into a chubby, middle-aged woman who knows nothing of the mysteries but desires to be raped by a black Apollo in order to give herself an illusion of youth and desirability.

The chaos of the Harlem riot recalls Eliot's description of the chaos in Europe in "What the Thunder Said." The protagonist encounters the riot first as a "sound high in the air," then finds himself in a city which "Cracks and reforms and bursts in the violet air/Falling towers." As Harlem—a symbol of social and cultural freedom for the protagonist's black contemporaries—explodes, Ras the Destroyer singles out the protagonist for sacrifice in a death by hanging, because "only hanging would settle things, even the score." Eliot associates the Hanged Man of the Tarot with the Hanged God, who restores fertility to the land following his resurrection. While the protagonist refuses to accept the role of the Hanged Man, and death at the hands of Ras, he nonetheless thinks as he escapes down the manhole, "It's a kind of death without hanging . . . a death alive."

The underground death in life that the protagonist does accept has been foreshadowed by a series of figurative deaths by water. The first follows the explosion at Liberty Paints when he "seemed to sink to the center of a lake of heavy water" . . . . That experience leaves him feeling engulfed by an emotional ice which begins "melting to form a flood in which [he] threatened to drown . . . ." When he rides down Riverside Drive toward the riot, he feels "as if drowned in the river." During the riot, the shattered glass in the streets appears to him "like the water of a flooded river" in which he suddenly "seemed to sink, sucked under . . . ." After being pummeled by water from a broken main, he "lay like a man rescued from drowning . . . ."

Underground, alive but dead, the protagonist assumes the role that the Founder had been unable to fulfill. His dream of castration, beside a "river of black water" that suggests Eliot's Thames which "sweats/Oil and tar," profoundly identifies his assumption of the role. As Ellen Horowitz observes, "The castration acts as the ultimate dispelling of illusions whereby the hero gains the right to see. Like the Fisher King his impotence seems a prerequisite for his life-giving role." That role is the role of seer. Eliot noted that "What Tiresias sees . . . is the substance of [*The Waste Land*]." What the protagonist sees is the substance of **Invisible Man.** He sees that his individual plight—his invisibility to white Americans—must be viewed in the larger context of a spiritual failure in American society. By withholding from black Americans the rights and privileges of humanity, American society has dehumanized itself.

> **Just as The Waste Land closes with the ancient answers for the restoration of the Fisher King's domain, the Epilogue to Invisible Man contains the answers the protagonist finds for the revitalization of America and the restoration of humanity to black people.**
> **—Mary Ellen Williams Walsh**

Just as The Waste Land closes with the ancient answers for the restoration of the Fisher King's domain, the Epilogue to **Invisible Man** contains the answers the protagonist finds for the revitalization of America and the restoration of humanity to black people. The answers rest in the affirmation of "the principle on which the country was built and not the men, or at least not the men who did the violence," and in a recognition of both the diversity and the unity of the nation: "America is woven of many strands; I would recognize them and let it so remain. . . . Our fate is to become one, and yet many—." Despite the hope thus proffered, the protagonist recognizes that the sickness remains. In a passage which alludes to the opening lines of "The Burial of the Dead," he cautions: "There's a stench in the air, which, from this distance underground, might be the smell either of death or of spring—I hope of spring. But don't let me trick you, there *is* a death in the smell of spring . . . ."

For Ellison and for his protagonist the identity of black Americans depends upon the renewal of the spirit which formed the country of which they are citizens. In his National Book Award acceptance speech, Ellison remarked that he considered his attempt "to return to the mood of personal moral responsibility for democracy" to be one of the major strengths of **Invisible Man.** Ellison made this attempt because he saw his characters and their situations from a broadly human perspective. His allusions to *The Waste Land* demonstrate the perspective. The mythic tradition—the urge for spiritual renewal, the necessity for sacrifice, the desire for rebirth—speaks as strongly to the condition of black people in America as it does to the isolated and alienated condition of any people. To emphasize this concept, the closing question of the novel contains a final significant allu-

sion to *The Waste Land.* When the protagonist asks, "Who knows but that, on the lower frequencies, I speak for you?" he echoes Eliot's use of Baudelaire's line, "You! hypocrite lecteur!—mon semblable—mon frére!" Both the question and the exclamation demand the reader's identification with their speakers. The protagonist thereby insists on the universality of his experience, an experience which Ellison has nonetheless firmly tied to a failure in American values.

C. W. E. Bigsby (essay date 1987)

SOURCE: "Improvising America: Ralph Ellison and the Paradox of Form," in *Speaking for You: The Vision of Ralph Ellison,* edited by Kimberly W. Benston, Howard University Press, 1987, pp. 173-83.

[*In the following essay, Bigsby examines Ellison's paradoxical treatment of chaos and form.*]

Writing in 1937, Richard Wright insisted that "black writers are being called upon to do no less than create values by which the race is to struggle, live and die" ["Blueprint for Negro Literature," *Amistad,* Vol. 2, 1971]. In 1941 Ellison echoed this sentiment. His responsibility, he felt, was "to create the consciousness of his oppressed nation" [**"Recent Negro Fiction,"** *New Masses,* August 5, 1941]. It was a stance he was later to be accused of abandoning by those who, in the 1960s and 1970s, proposed their own prescriptions for cultural and political responsibility and who found his determined pluralism unacceptable. For although he undeniably concentrated on the black experience in America, he tended to see this experience in relation to the problem of identity, the anxieties associated with the struggle for cultural autonomy, and the need to define the contours of experience. His central concern was with the relationship between raw experience and the shaping power of the imagination. And, for him, the "imagination itself is *integrative,*" in that it is essentially involved in the process of "making symbolic wholes out of parts" ["Study and Experience: An Interview with Ralph Ellison," *Massachusetts Review,* Autumn, 1977]. Such a stance plainly has implications on a moral and social level no less than on an artistic one.

He has, indeed, always been fascinated, politically, ethically, and aesthetically, with the struggle to discover form in diversity. To his mind this was equally the problem of the Negro in America, of the individual in a democracy, and of the artist confronted with the sheer contingency and flux of events. The imaginative linking of these experiences, indeed the metaphoric yoking of the processes of invention in life and art, is a characteristic of Ellison's artistic strategy and of his moral assumptions. But it is a process which, from the beginning, he acknowledged to be fraught with ambiguity, for he was not unaware that form could imply entrapment as well as release. Thus, he argued that "for the novelist, of any cultural or racial identity, his form is his greatest freedom and his insights are where he finds them" [*Shadow and Act*], while acknowledging that that form potentially defines the limits of his freedom. To use story or myth to control experience is also, potentially, to imprison oneself in the prison house of myth. Archetype too easily becomes stereotype. To deploy language as a means of inducing coherencies is to subordinate oneself to the constraints of that language, which is, at the very least, historically stained. Thus for the writer, as for the American pioneer, "the English language and traditional cultural forms served both as guides and as restraints, anchoring Americans in the wisdom and processes of the past, while making it difficult for them to perceive with any clarity the nuances of their new identity" ["Study and Experience: An Interview with Ralph Ellison"]. It is a paradox that lies at the heart of all of his work. For Ellison, the act of writing is an act of shaping inchoate experience into moral meaning no less than aesthetic form. But it is an act that implies its own coercions. It implicates the imagination in the process of control.

This tension between chaos and form, this recognition of a profound ambivalence, is a fundamental trope of Ellison's work. He seems captivated by paradox, fascinated by apparent contradictions, drawn to the polarities of American experience, simultaneously attracted and repelled by the nervous energy of the unformed and the compelling grace of coalescence. Even his prose style seems often to turn around sets of dualities that are fused together by the writer, contained by the imagination, and exemplified in the linguistic structure, as he believes they can be so fused in the world beyond the page.

Thus, while he readily identified the metonymic reductivism implied in white attempts to mythologize Negro life, insisting that "the Negro stereotype is really an image of the unorganized, irrational forces of American life, forces through which, by projecting them in forms of images of an easily dominated minority, the white individual seeks to be at home in the vast unknown world of America," he nonetheless asserted that without myths, "chaos descends, faith vanishes and superstitions prowl in the mind" [*Shadow and Act*]. The same process contains a generative and a destructive potential.

So, too, with language. We are, Ellison insists, "language using, language misusing animals—beings who are by nature vulnerable to both the negative *and* the positive promptings of language as symbolic action" [**"The Little Man at Chehaw Station,"** *American Scholar,* Winter, 1977-78]. He addresses this ambivalence directly in an essay called, **"Twentieth-Century Fiction and the Black Mask of Humanity,"** where he suggests, "Perhaps the most insidi-

ous and least understood form of segregation is that of the word. And by this I mean the word in all its complex formulations, from the proverb to the novel and stage play, the word with all its subtle power to suggest and foreshadow overt action while magically disguising the moral consequences of that action and providing it with symbolic and psychological justification. For if the word has the potency to revive and make us free, it also has the power to blind, imprison and destroy." Indeed, to him "the essence of the word is its ambivalence" [*Shadow and Act*], more especially in a society in which the nature of the real is problematic for reasons of racial ideology. This suspicion marks all of his work, from the nonfunctional articulateness of his protagonist in the early short story **"Flying Home,"** through the deceptive speeches and documents of *Invisible Man,* to the uncontrolled rhetoric of the narrator of his later short story, **"A Song of Innocence,"** who observes, "They say that folks misuse words but I see it the other way around, words misuse people. Usually when you think you're saying what you mean you're really saying what the words want you to say.... Words are tricky.... No matter what you try to do, words can never mean meaning."

Melville had made much the same point and addressed the same ambivalence with respect to the urge to subordinate chaos to form. He, too, was aware that language itself constitutes the primary mechanism of the shaping imagination and it was not for nothing that Ellison chose to quote from *Benito Cereno* as an epigraph to his own novel. For Captain Delano, in that story, uses language as an agent of power and control, albeit a language rendered ironic by his moral and intellectual blindness; while Benito Cereno, imprisoned by a cunning and dominant black crew, who for the most part remain potently silent, deploys a language which is willfully opaque, hinting at truths that language cannot be entrusted to reveal. And yet language is the only medium through which the novelist can attempt to communicate his own truths. It was a familiar conundrum of nineteenth-century American writing and one to which Ellison was compulsively drawn.

The strict discipline and carefully sustained order of Delano's ship is an expression of his fear of an anarchy that he dare not imagine and cannot confront. And the image of that anarchy, for Delano and Cereno alike, is the Negro, whose shadow they see as falling across American history. But Melville suggests that just as their own ordered world contains its virus of moral anarchy, so what Delano takes for anarchy is perhaps a coherence he is afraid to acknowledge; the hieroglyphs of action that he chooses to translate as pure chaos can be decoded in a wholly different way. Indeed, Melville's story turns precisely on this ambiguity. So does much of Ellison's work.

Chaos and order constitute the twin poles of experience,

promising, simultaneously, vital energy and destructive flux, necessary from but threatening stasis. Indeed, he is quite capable, in a single paragraph, of presenting both order and chaos as promise and threat. Speaking of the process whereby national identity coalesces from its constituent elements, he asserted, in 1953, "Our task then is always to challenge the apparent forms of reality—that is, the fixed manners and values of the few, and to struggle with it until it reveals its insights, its truth. . . . We are fortunate as American writers in that with our variety of racial and national traditions, idioms and manners we are yet one. On its profoundest level, American experience is of a whole. Its truth lies in its diversity and swiftness of change" [*Shadow and Act*]. The task for the writer would seem to be to inhabit these ambiguities and thereby to cast light not merely on processes endemic to art but also on the struggle that the individual and the race wage with contingency. Irresistibly drawn to the primal energy of flux, the writer, nonetheless, is inevitably committed to the creation of coherent form, thereby offering hintself as a paradigm of the processes of self-invention and the distillation of cultural identity.

It is a theme that echoes throughout Ellison's work. Thus, he quotes approvingly André Malraux's observation that "the organized significance of art . . . is stronger than all the multiplicity of the world . . . that significance alone enables many to conquer chaos and to master destiny" [*Shadow and Act*], while in an introduction to Stephen Crane's *Red Badge of Courage* he chose to stress "the shaping grace of Crane's imagination," whereby "the actual event is reduced to significant form . . . each wave and gust of wind, each intonation of voice and gesture of limb combining to a single effect of meaning . . . the raging sea of life" [*Shadow and Act*] thereby being contained by an act of imaginative economy. He even insists that "in the very act of trying to create something there is implicit a protest against the way things are—a protest against man's vulnerability before the larger forces of society and the universe . . . a protest against that which is, against the raw and unformed way that we come into the world . . . to provide some sense of transcendence over the given" ["**On Initiation Rites and Power: Ralph Ellison Speaks at West Point,**" *Commentary,* Spring, 1974]. And yet he equally acknowledges that it is precisely the fear of anarchy that leads to the creation of coercive models that express nothing more than a fear of the uncontrolled and the unknown. Thus, when Leslie Fiedler identifies a homoeroticism in the relationship between Twain's Huck Finn and the Negro slave Jim, he is, according to Ellison, in reality simply shouting out "his most terrifying name for chaos. Other things being equal he might have called it 'rape,' 'incest,' 'patricide' or 'miscegenation'" [*Shadow and Act*]. Order has no preemptive rights. It requires a moral as well as an aesthetic elegance.

The history of Ellison's creative life, from his early days as

a putative musician throughout his career as a novelist and essayist, has in effect been concerned with exploring this paradox and identifying a way, at least on a metaphoric level, in which it could be resolved. To some degree he found it in music. He began his career as a would-be composer, and music has always provided a central source of imagery for him. Thus, in describing the reaction of the reader of fiction, he suggests that "his sensibilities are made responsive to artistic structuring of symbolic form" through "the rhetorical 'stops'" of his own "pieties—filial, sacred, racial" ["**The Little Man at Chehaw Station**"]. The writer, meanwhile, is described as playing upon these sensibilities "as a pianist upon a piano" ["**The Little Man at Chehaw Station**"]. But, what is more significant, he found in jazz and the blues a powerful image of the struggle to imprint meaning on experience, to reconcile the apparently contradictory demands of order and freedom. Like Richard Wright, he saw the blues as an attempt to "possess the meaning of his life" [*Shadow and Act*], while jazz offered a model for the act of improvisation that lies at the heart of personal experience. Indeed the key word becomes "improvisation," which is made to stand for the act of self-invention that is the essence of a private and a public drive for meaning and identity. It is an integrative metaphor that links his sense of racial distinctiveness to what is essentially a pluralist position: "The delicate balance struck between strong individual personality and the group during those early jam sessions was a marvel of social organization. I had learned too that the end of all this discipline and technical mastery was the desire to express an affirmative way of life through its musical tradition and that this tradition insisted that each artist achieve his creativity within its frame . . . and when they expressed their attitude toward the world it was with a fluid style that reduced the chaos of living to form" [*Shadow and Act*].

Thus, it is characteristic that in his account of growing up in the Southwest he chose to stress what he calls "the chaos of Oklahoma," as he elsewhere spoke of "the chaos of American society" ["**On Becoming a Writer,**" *Commentary,* October, 1964], but set this against his own growing fascination with the ordered world of music and literature. It is characteristic, too, that through an extension of this logic he should identify that same tension first with the nature of the American frontier experience (still recent history for the Oklahoma of his birth), then with the jazz which emerged from that same region, and then with the nature of artistic creativity itself. The move is one from the real to the metaphoric, from the pure tone to its significant resonances. Thus, he insists, "ours was a chaotic community, still characterized by frontier attitudes and by that strange mixture of the naive and sophisticated, the benign and the malignant, which makes the past and present so confusing" ["**On Becoming a Writer**"], only to go on to suggest that it is possible to "hear the effects of this in the Southwestern jazz of the 30s, that joint creation of artistically free and exuberantly creative adventurers, of artists who had stumbled upon the free-dom lying within the restrictions of their musical tradition as within the limitations of their social background, and who in their own unconscious way set an example for any Ameri-cans, Negro or white, who would find themselves in the arts" [**"On Becoming a Writer"**].

And this was a key to Ellison's attempts to square the circle, to resolve the paradox. The problem for the jazz musician, as for any artist, was how to celebrate versatility and possi-bility in a form that seemingly denied both. The key is seen by Ellison as lying precisely in improvisation, the exercise of a personal freedom within the framework of the group, an act of invention that builds on but is not limited by in-herited forms. This becomes both his metaphor for the pro-cess of artistic invention and the means whereby individual and group identity coalesce. In terms of writing this tended to be translated into an instinctive existentialism, at the level of theme, a picaresque narrative drive, and a prose style that could prove as fluid and flexible, and yet as controlled and subject to the harmonies of character and story, as the jazz musician is free and yet responsive to the necessities of rhythm and mood. In terms of social process it became a de-scription of the means whereby diverse elements are harmo-nized. Thus, speaking of the origins of American national identity, Ellison remarked, "Out of the democratic principles set down on paper in the Constitution and the Bill of Rights they were improvising themselves into a nation, scraping to-gether a conscious culture out of the various dialects, idi-oms, lingos, and mythologies of America's diverse peoples and regions." Similarly, in describing the relationship be-tween black and white cultural forms, he observed that "the slaves . . . having no past in the art of Europe . . . could use its elements and their inherited sense of style to impro-vise forms through which they could express their own unique sense of African experience . . . and white artists often found the slaves' improvisations a clue to their own improvisations" ["Study and Experience: An Interview with Ralph Ellison"].

As a boy he had been taught the rudiments of orchestration, the blending, the integration, of different instruments to form an harmonic whole. It was offered to him as a lesson in the deconstruction of a score which was to enable him to "at-tack those things I desired so that I could pierce the mys-tery and possess them"; but in retrospect it becomes a lesson in civics. True jazz, he insists, "is an act of individual as-sertion within and against the group. Each true jazz moment . . . springs from a contest in which each artist challenges all the rest; each solo flight, or improvisation, represents . . . a definition of his identity; as individual, as member of the collectivity and as a link in the chain of tradition. Thus, be-cause jazz finds its very life in an endless improvisation upon traditional materials, the jazzman must lose his identity even as he finds it" [*Shadow and Act*]. And, beyond this, jazz

becomes an image of America itself, "fecund in its inven-tiveness, swift and traumatic in its resources" [*Shadow and Act*].

The parallel between jazz and his own social circum-stances, growing up in postfrontier Oklahoma, seems clear to Ellison in retrospect. "It is an important circumstance for me as a writer to remember," he wrote in 1964, "be-cause while these musicians and their fellows were busy creating out of tradition, imagination, and the sounds and emotions around them, a freer, more complex, and driv-ing form of jazz, my friends and I were exploring an idea of human versatility and possibility which went against the barbs and over the palings [pickets] of almost every fence which those who controlled social and political power had erected to restrict our roles in the life of the country" [**"On Becoming a Writer"**].

And as a boy, he and his friends had constructed their he-roes from fragments of myth and legend, from the movies ("improvising their rather tawdry and opportunistic version of a national mythology" [**"The Little Man at Chehaw Sta-tion"**]), from music and religion, from anything "which vio-lated all ideas of social hierarchy and order" and "which evolved from our wildly improvisatory projections" [**"On Becoming a Writer"**]. In a sense this can stand as a model of Ellison's fictive and moral strategy, as of his conception of cultural identity and American pluralism. A complex eclecticism is presented as a moral necessity as much as a natural product of American circumstances. And "complex-ity" is a favorite word—sometimes "a stubborn complexity." For his is a sensibility that reaches out to absorb the varie-gated realities of American life, rejecting those who see the process of self-invention as necessitating a denial of that complexity.

The problem is to discover a means of rendering that com-plexity without reducing it through the sheer process of trans-muting experience into art. Pure energy has no shape. The challenge confronting the artist, no less than that confront-ing the uncodified, free-floating sensibility of the American individual, is to sustain some kind of creative tension be-tween a liberated and liberating imagination and the aesthetic and moral demands of an art and a life which require the subordination of random energy and an anarchic imagina-tion to the constraints of order. For just as the artist oper-ates "within the historical frame of his given art" [**"The Little Man at Chehaw Station"**], so the individual is lo-cated within the triangulation of time, space, and cultural in-heritance. Thus the writer's responsibility in America is to define the diversity of American experience in such a way as to bring to bear the "unifying force of its vision and its power to give meaningful focus to apparently unrelated emo-tions and experience" [**"The Little Man at Chehaw Sta-tion"**].

The problem is that the democratic ideal of "unity-in-diversity and oneness-in-manyness" [**"The Little Man at Chehaw Station"**] creates a vertigo which he sees as sending too many plunging into the reassurance of simplified cultural models, preferring fragment to complexly formulated whole. There is a clearly positive and negative model of chaos in his mind. On the one hand, there is a fructifying interaction of differing cultural traditions, "always in cacophonic motion. Constantly changing its mode . . . a vortex of discordant ways of living and tastes, values and traditions, a whirlpool of odds and ends" [**"The Little Man at Chehaw Station"**] which inspires a profound unease but which is the source of a creative flux. On the other hand, there is a negative chaos, a fearful splintering into component elements. And this is how he saw the black aestheticians of the 1960s. "In many ways," he insisted, "the call for a new social order based upon the glorification of ancestral blood and ethnic background acts as a call to cultural and aesthetic chaos." Yet, "while this latest farcical phase in the drama of American social hierarchy unfolds, the irrepressible movement of American culture toward the integration of its diverse elements continues, confounding the circumlocutions of its staunchest opponents" [**"The Little Man at Chehaw Station"**].

For Ellison, strength lies precisely in diversity, in the sustained tension between chaos and form, the Apollonian and the Dionysian, and this is no less true of a racial identity which he refuses to grant the simple self-evident contours demanded by some of his contemporaries. To his mind, that identity can only express itself multivocally. And so in his essay **"The Little Man at Chehaw Station,"** which is a crucial statement of his artistic and social principles, he recalls seeing a black American who seemed to combine a whole kaleidoscope of cultural influences: and whatever sheerly ethnic identity was communicated by his costume depended upon the observer's ability to see order in an apparent cultural chaos. The essence of the man, his complex identity, existed less in the apparent clashing of styles than in the eclectic imagination, the unabashed assertion of will, which lay behind it—"not in the somewhat comic clashing of styles, but in the mixture, the improvised form, the willful juxtaposition of modes" [**"The Little Man at Chehaw Station"**]. But, as ever, Ellison is not content to leave it there for, he insists, "his clashing of styles . . . sounded an integrative, vernacular note—an American compulsion to improvise upon the given," and the freedom he exercised was "an American freedom" [**"The Little Man at Chehaw Station"**].

It is not hard to see what infuriated the cultural nationalists of the 1960s. Ellison seems to be appropriating supposedly unique and definitional aspects of black life to an American cultural norm. Since America was diverse, loose-limbed, disparate, self-displaying, free-wheeling and concerned with the question of identity, with delineating its own cultural boundaries, with negotiating a relationship with its own past which would give it space for its own critical act of self-invention, the black American was apparently simply an expression of this process, one component of the American diorama. But such an assumption ignored Ellison's central conviction—the basis, indeed, of his whole aesthetic and social theory—namely, that the American identity he described was as it was precisely because of the presence of the Negro. While rigidly subordinating and segregating the black American, the whites had been shaped by what they had tried so hard to exclude. Their imagination had been penetrated, their sensibility infiltrated, by those whose experience of adjusting to a strange land and whose necessary cultural improvisations were more intensely, more deeply scarring, more profoundly disturbing than their own. As the victims of violence, as the evidence of a failure of American idealism, as an extreme case of adjustment to a hostile environment, they represented not merely a constant reminder of the poles of American moral experience but a model of possibility, a paradigm of those acts of desperate self-creation that were at the heart of the American myth. The shadow of the Negro does indeed fall across American history but not merely as promise and threat. His existence defines the nature of the American experience.

Ellison was less inclined than many to abandon the notion of the "melting pot," though he saw the image less as a promise of homogeneity than as a metaphor of "the mystery of American identity (our unity-within-diversity)," and as a symbol of those who "improvised their culture as they did their politics and institutions" [**"The Little Man at Chehaw Station"**]. The potency of the image lay in its acknowledgment of the fact that, in America, cultural traditions were brought into violent contact, that past and future were made to interact, that ideals, and the evidence of the failure of those ideals, were placed in intimate and ironic counterpoint. And, as a consequence, a series of adjustments were enforced, a process of action and reaction which, to his mind, was the very essence of Americanness. It was precisely on the level of culture that such interactions operated. Cultural appropriation and misappropriation were, to Ellison, the essence of an American development that would scarcely stand still long enough for confident definition. Indeed, since America was to him more a process than an isolable set of characteristics, such definitions carry the threat of a menacing stasis. The essence of improvisation lies in the energy released by the pure act of invention in process. In *Invisible Man* the protagonist is at his most vulnerable when he allows himself to be contained and defined by simple racial or political models. He radiates the energy of pure possibility (like the light bulbs with which he illuminates his darkness) when he abandons these restrictive definitions for the sheer flux of being—a state controlled only by the imagination, and those moral commitments that lead him out of his isolation and into the dangerous interactions of the outside world and the complex symbols of the novel, with which he seeks to address that "variegated audience" for whom the little man at Chehaw Station was Ellison's image. As he himself insists, "it is the very *spirit* of art to be defiant of categories and obstacles. . . . They [the images of art or the sound of music] are, as transcendent forms of symbolic expression, agencies of human freedom" ["**The Little Man at Chehaw Station**"]. For Ellison, "the work of art" itself "is . . . an act of faith in our ability to communicate symbolically" ["**The Little Man at Chehaw Station**"].

> **Jazz exists as a constant source of reference, an ironic counterpoint to the protagonist's earnest struggles, a celebration of his growing understanding. Ellison himself has spoken of his desire to capture the "music and idiom" of American Negro speech. . . .**
> **—C. W. E. Bigsby**

Invisible Man opens and concludes with references to jazz. At the beginning the protagonist sits in his cellar and "feels" rather than listens to the music of Louis Armstrong who has "made poetry out of being invisible." High on drugs, he responds to the off-beats, seeing meaning in the unheard sounds, the resistances to simple rhythmic structure. Music becomes a clue to his past and future. The music pulls him back to his origins, conjuring up an image of his slave past; but it also offers him a clue to his future, outside the determined structures of social life. The music, like the novel the protagonist writes, emerges from "an urge to make music of invisibility," to set it down. It is a paradoxical enterprise. But, then, as we are told at the end of the novel, the music, too, is characterized by "diversity." It, too, contains an essential conflict. And that conflict mirrors the conflict of the protagonist who reminds himself that "the mind that has conceived a plan of living must never lose sight of the chaos against which that pattern was conceived." And this, he assures us, "goes for societies as for individuals" [*Invisible Man*]. It is the virtue of jazz that its improvisations remind us of precisely this. Improvisation has its risks. In the form of Rinehart, a protean figure (whose first name is actually Proteus) who refuses all content and all commitment, it becomes pure chaos; but for the protagonist, willing, finally, to chance his own dangerous act of self-creation in the public world outside his cellar, it becomes a commitment to sustaining the tension between the twin compulsions of freedom and order.

Jazz operates in Ellison's work as image and fact. The thematic uses he makes of it have been usefully traced by Robert G. O'Meally in *The Craft of Ralph Ellison.* Jazz exists as a constant source of reference, an ironic counterpoint to the protagonist's earnest struggles, a celebration of his growing understanding. Ellison himself has spoken of his desire to capture the "music and idiom" of American Negro speech, but in fact his concern with musical structures goes much further than this. In "**A Song of Innocence**" the prose owes less to idiomatic speech than to jazz rhythms, the words being of less significance than the free flow of sound. Indeed the inadequacy of language, which is in part the subject of that story, implies the need to turn to other models, other symbols as a means of explaining the conflicting demands of pattern and chaos, form and experience, tradition and innovation. And throughout his career, Ellison turned to the improvisational thrust of jazz for that symbol, finding there a clue to the commitments required of the artist, the race, and the individual concerned with developing their own identities in the face of inherited forms: "I had learned from the jazz musicians I had known as a boy in Oklahoma City something of the discipline and devotion to his art required of the artist . . . the give and take, the subtle rhythmical sharpening and blending of idea, tone and imagination demanded of group improvisations" [*Shadow and Act*]. And "after the jazzman has learned the fundamentals of his instrument and the traditional techniques of jazz—the intonations, the mute work, manipulation of timbre, the body of traditional styles—he must 'find himself,' must be reborn, must find, as it were, his soul. All this through achieving that subtle identification between his instrument and his deepest drives which will allow him to express his own unique ideas and his own unique voice. He must achieve, in short, his self-determined identity" [*Shadow and Act*]. Like Charlie Parker, he is involved in a struggle "against personal chaos" [*Shadow and Act*]. To Ellison, much the same could be said of the writer in America, as of the individual struggling to make sense of his racial and cultural inheritance while defining a self strong enough to stand against the centripetal pull of the chaos that could manifest itself equally as pure contingency or deceptive consonance.

In an essay titled "**Society, Morality, and the Novel**" [in *The Living Novel: A Symposium,* edited by Granville Hicks, Macmillan, 1957], Ellison observed that "the writer has an obsessive need to play with the fires of chaos and to rearrange reality to the patterns of his imagination," while the novel achieves its "universality" precisely through "accumulating images of reality and arranging them in patterns of universal significance." Indeed, it seemed to him possible that the novel, as a form, had evolved in order "to deal with man's growing awareness that behind the facade of social organization, manners, customs, myths, rituals, religions of the post-Christian era, lies chaos." But since we can live neither "in the contemplation of chaos" nor "without awareness of chaos," the novel simultaneously acknowledges and seeks to transcend the fact that "the treasure of possibility is always to be found in the cave of chaos, guarded by the demons of destruction." The writer's responsibility, in Ellison's eyes, is to improvise a response that denies nothing of the force and power of disorder but will "strengthen man's will to say No to chaos and affirm him in his task of humanizing himself and the world" [**"Society, Morality, and the Novel"**], without submitting to stasis. Change and diversity are, to him, the essence of the American experience. The challenge is to bring to "the turbulence of change" an "imaginative integration and moral continuity" [**"Society, Morality, and the Novel"**]—to improvise America, as the individual creates the uncreated features of his face, and as the black American had struggled to "create the consciousness of his oppressed nation."

David J. Herman (essay date September 1991)

SOURCE: "Ellison's 'King of the Bingo Game': Finding Naturalism's Trapdoor," in *English Language Notes,* Vol. XXIX, No. 1, September, 1991, pp. 71-74.

[*In the following essay, Herman explains how Ellison both follows and deviates from the conventions of literary naturalism in "King of the Bingo Game."*]

Prima facie, Ralph Ellison's **"King of the Bingo Game"** fits squarely into the tradition of literary naturalism. Ellison's extended treatment of the bingo wheel, for one thing, figures the same overriding concern with the issue of fate versus chance—the issue of determinism—manifest in, say, the famous open-safe scene in Dreiser's *Sister Carrie,* or in the closing pages of Norris's *The Octopus.* If anything, Ellison's story addresses the notion of determinism even more explicitly than is customary in naturalistic works. For Ellison's (literally) nameless protagonist attempts self-consciously to eliminate chance, to control the wheel of fortune itself, by refusing to relinquish his grasp on the button whose release determines where the bingo wheel will stop. Ellison, in orthodox naturalistic fashion, also stresses the protagonist's gnawing hunger and his craving for the alcohol he hears gurgling appealingly in the bottle of his fellow movie-goers. Indeed, in accordance with the logic of the naturalistic genre, we witness the bingo-player's last-ditch effort to beat not only the odds, but also the resistance of a hostile or at the very least indifferent environment. Against such an environment the protagonist, having been displaced from the rural South into the urban North, must struggle, much as he struggles against the now bored and impatient, now aggressive and jeering movie audience. Rhetorically speaking, furthermore, Ellison, like Flaubert and, later, Joyce and Faulkner, mimics the disjointed thought-processes of his protagonist, a hungry, tired, desperate man, his mind roving, in the space of a single paragraph, from attempts to concentrate on the movie; to thoughts about his dying wife; to re-

flection on the mechanism of movie-projection itself; to a hypothetical revision and eroticization of the movie's script; to the fleeting and repugnant memory of a bedbug crawling on an unknown woman's neck.

Yet certain elements taken from this same compendium of thought-associations point to an emphasis in Ellison's story that competes with, and to some extent undermines, the deterministic, social-Darwinistic manner in which the author portrays the protagonist's fight to survive. What I wish to isolate in this context is the protagonist's preoccupation with the modes of projection, as well as the (possible) revision, of the film being shown as the story begins. For instance, the bingo-player finds himself drawn to "the white beam filtered from the projection room above the balcony," and amazed that "the beam always landed right on the screen and didn't mess up or fall somewhere else." Here, the protagonist's momentary fascination in effect undercuts the overt naturalism of Ellison's entire account. For the bingo-player's thoughts gesture toward the contingency, the capacity to "mess up" or "fall somewhere else," in the face of which we project cultural stories—narratives in general and Ellison's own tale in particular. The limits of Ellison's deterministic fiction are thereby exposed from within; a narrative that explains accident by fate at the same time designates as accidental the success, the cogency and coherence, with which any given narrative explains a personal, projects a collective destiny.

Consider how the notion of projection, along with those of staging and theatricalization, in fact operate throughout **"King of the Bingo Game,"** assimilating what Ellison represents as fated or determined to what the author portrays as made, constructed, "art." This assimilation of nature to art tends not only to suggest how every putatively naturalistic account remains the product of certain (literary) conventions, but tends also to break down the difference between levels or orders of representation within Ellison's narrative itself. For example, in the opening paragraph we watch, through the protagonist's eyes, the movie's "hero stealthily entering a dark room and sending the beam of a flashlight along a wall of bookcases" and then finding a trapdoor. Likewise, Ellison's bingo-player, Ellison's "hero," at first sees by means of the projector flashing images on the screen, and at last finds himself in dire need of a trapdoor of sorts at the story's end. The girl that the movie's hero finds tied to a bed, moreover, brings to mind the bingo-player's own sick and presumably bed-ridden wife. The analogy Ellison thus creates between the (in principle) alterable narrative sequence of the film, and the (in principle) unalterable or deterministic account of the protagonist's battle against fate, suggests how Ellison's own naturalistic presentation counts as only one among other possible ways of constructing the bingo-player's experiences. Ellison's staging or theatricalization of the protagonist's desperate bid to win—after all, he makes that bid before footlights and in front of an audience—further approximates ostensibly fated or determined actions to the process by which narratives are in the first place fabricated, made up. Once fate is staged, destiny theatricalized, nature itself becomes a cultural production.

In short, Ellison's treatment of the bingo wheel on the one hand implies freedom only within a limited, predetermined set of possibilities; the bingo-player finally runs around in circles in attempts to elude the police. But on the other hand, Ellison simultaneously places the closed circle of destiny within a narrative frame that, by breaking down the barrier between convention and nature, representation and what is represented, makes of fate itself an open-ended process, no more and no less "fixed" than the accounts through which we project our experiences onto the stage of culture at large. Ellison's story, by inviting speculation on the contingency of any narrative that feigns to be fixed, thereby parodies the naturalistic tradition in which **"King of the Bingo Game"** is also heavily invested. It is in the resulting dissonance of conceptual schemes that we find the only space of freedom— the sole trapdoor into alternative cultural logic—on which the bingo-player might have staked a well-calculated risk.

Sandra Adell (essay date June 1994)

SOURCE: "The Big E(llison)'s Texts and Intertexts: Eliot, Burke, and the Underground Man," in *CLA Journal,* Vol. XXXVII, No. 4, June, 1994, pp. 377-401.

[*In the following essay, Adell examines* Invisible Man *according to the theory of intertextuality expressed by Roland Barthes, noting the connections between Ellison's novel and such works as T. S. Eliot's* The Waste Land *and Fyodor Dostoyevsky's* Notes from Underground.]

Mallarmé might well have been, as Michael Gresset and Noel Polk claim, the first of the moderns to point to *intertextuality* as a key operation in literary activity when he wrote that

> all books, more or less, contain the fusion of a certain number of repetitions: even if there were but one book in the world, its law would be as a bible simulated by the heathens. The difference from one work to the next would afford as many readings as would be put forth in a boundless contest for the trustworthy text among epochs that are supposedly civilized or literate.

[*Intertextuality in Faulkner*]

Of course, Mallarmé did not know that he was articulating

a theory of intertextuality; that word has only recently come into literary terminology. But he obviously had no doubt that this "fusion of a certain number of repetitions" is not only the basis, but the very essence of literature. This notion of intertextuality and its attendant concepts, the "work" and the "text" are, of course, founding principles for structuralist and post-structuralist criticism.

Prior to the late 1970s, when a few black writers and intellectuals began to reconsider and reevaluate the relationship between black writing and the critical discourses of the literary mainstream, and the space(s) occupied by Ralph Ellison and his writing in those discourses, a dominant issue in Afro-American literary criticism was what in Barthian terms would be called the "writerliness" of Ellison's *Invisible Man.* In what John Wright refers to in "Shadowing Ellison" [in *Speaking for You: The Vision of Ralph Ellison,* Howard University Press, 1987] as an intense "war of invective" waged against Ellison by his more ideologically oriented opponents, the novel has often been attacked because it subverts much of what characterizes the "work" or classic text, and because, like the "writerly" text as Roland Barthes defines it, what "traverses it from one end to the other" are references and echoes of texts from systems that lie outside of the parameters of what has been very loosely defined as the black "experience."

An essay published in 1970 by the black aesthetician Clifford Mason entitled "Ralph Ellison and the Underground Man" [*Black World,* December, 1970] is symptomatic of this "war of invective." Guided by what the one-time-but-now-much-reformed black aesthetician Houston Baker calls the "romantic Marxism" of the black aesthetic, Mason speaks of a "proper position" with regard to black literature and white American culture which he feels that Ellison, through his "literary references," has violated:

> Black literature deserved its own references, its own standards, its own rules. Not in an abberrant denial of *anything* that came from white American culture, valid or otherwise, but as conscious insistence on the creating of an African-American text that derived its *raison d'etre* from an African-American truth that exists in spite of the fact that it has never, until very recently, had a really pervasive life in the world of literature.

Without specifying what that "truth" is, Mason argues that the amplitude of Ellison's literary references and his insistence on giving structural credit for *Invisible Man* to a number of mainstream writers rather than to Richard Wright not only makes this kind of "aggressive Black literary independence" impossible; it makes Ellison's nationalism suspect as well:

[H]is insistence on giving structural credit for *Invisible Man* to William Faulkner, and Ernest Hemingway and Feodor Dostoevsky and T. S. Eliot and James Joyce and God knows who else, when it's as plain as it can be that he owes the basic design of the book to a Richard Wright short story ... called, prophetically enough, "The Man Who Lived Underground," certainly makes his nationalism suspect. I suppose a case can be made for Dostoyevsky based on his *Notes From Underground*. But *Notes* deals with the outsider who is estranged because he is the son who cannot conform, not because he is the bastard who was never allowed to conform in the first place.

Ignoring the well-known fact that both writers read and were very influenced by Dostoevsky, Mason goes on to argue that rather than basing his writings on a "white substructure," Ellison should have stood against white literary values as did Du Bois and Alain Locke. One need look no further than Du Bois and Alain Locke themselves to see the fallacy of this argument; for indeed, their aesthetics is heavily implicated in the Western philosophical tradition and therefore inextricably bound to the "white substructure." In fact, Du Bois's thesis in "Criteria of Negro Art" is that black folk will not be recognized as human until their art is equal to that of white folk. Alain Locke shared Du Bois's thesis and defined the "poise and cultural maturity" of the black artist in terms of his ability to "bring the artistic advance of the Negro sharply into stepping alignment with contemporary artistic thought, mood, and style." He called for the kind of "transfusions of racial idioms with the "modernistic styles of expression" which he felt had already occurred in music so that "Negro thoughts" would wear the "uniform" of the modern age. Like Du Bois, he practiced what Houston Baker calls an "integrationist Poetics." His critical and theoretical perspective was based on a faith in "American pluralistic ideals" that were to be effected through an art whose impetus was lodged within the "spirit" of the restless and urban-bound Negro masses.

Ellison, whose interest in music and sculpture exposed him very early to these "modernistic styles of expression," responds to Locke's imperative for black participation in the modernist movement through his appropriation of T. S. Eliot and Kenneth Burke in *Shadow and Act,* and to Locke's and Du Bois's cultural pluralism through the many intertextual instances—Dostoevsky's *Notes From Underground* is but one of those instances—that permeate *Invisible Man.*

From Eliot's critical perspective, a writer's contemporaneity is contingent upon the extent to which he perceives, simultaneously, the pastness and the presence of the past. This historical sense, which Eliot refers to as "tradition," therefore paradoxically involves an indebtedness to the past without which a work of art not only would not be new; it would not be a work of art. The new work of art must emerge out of the past, out of the "ideal order" of the "monuments" existing prior to it. It must "reorder" and readjust the ideal order so that there is conformity between the old and the new and a parallel reciprocal relation between the past and the present: "the past should be altered by the present as much as the present is directed by the past." The imperative for the artist or poet in this relationship is that he surrender his "private mind" or personality to a "continuing developing consciousness" of the "main current" which, while abandoning nothing en route, proceeds from the past through the mind of Europe and his own country. Through this process of a continuing developing consciousness, his mind must become a medium, not for expressing his personality, but for combining, in "peculiar and unexpected ways," the passions, impressions, and experiences which constitute its (the mind's) materials. What Eliot therefore proposes—and this is a founding principle for modernism in general—is a "formal" approach to art. The poet or artist must become subordinate to the work of art. Interest must be diverted from the subject to the object, from the poet to the poem, from the artist to the art work; that is, to the way everything that has come before is recombined, reconcentrated, recast, and refined to form something new.

When Ellison writes in the introduction to *Shadow and Act* that "[b]ehind each artist there stands a traditional sense of style," ... he reiterates Eliot, whose notion of tradition, as we have seen, is related to one's perception of the past as a living present. This "traditional sense of style" was the source from which Ellison drew the forms and figures that inhabited the imaginary realm which he often shared with his boyhood friends as they attempted to escape an environment—post-World War I Oklahoma—which he describes as one which "at its most normal took on some of the mixed character of nightmare and of dream" [*Shadow and Act*]. He writes that "part of our boyish activity expressed a yearning to make any and everything of quality *Negro American*; to appropriate it, possess it, recreate it in our own group and individual images" [*Shadow and Act*]. There is, therefore, in his fiction a convergence of the styles of black jazz and blues men with those of the heroes of American and African-American literature and folklore, which in turn combine with those of the "literatures of Europe."

From out of this "vortex" of cultural contexts emerged Ellison's "Invisible Man." He resembles his Russian "ancestor" in that, like *Notes From Underground,* his memoir is "one long, loud rant, howl and laugh" [*Shadow and Act*]. He resembles Wright's "underground man" in that his underground hole is a refuge from a society determined to "keep this nigger boy running." He is also very different in that his experience, i.e., his quest for self-realization and self-definition, takes him through what Ellison describes as the black American language,

> . . . . a language swirling with over three hundred years of American living, a mixture of the folk, the Biblical, the scientific and the political. Slangy in one stance, academic in another, loaded poetically with imagery at one moment, mathematically bare of imagery in the next.
>
> [*Shadow and Act*]

As a being born into this intertextual linguistic field, the black writer, like the Invisible Man, is irrevocably linked to the "white substructure" upon which it is grounded. Consequently, despite the contention of the black aestheticians and the more recent black "anti-theory theorists" that there is something called a "unique" black experience out of which should develop "unique" cultural artifacts (with the power to transform an "American Negro into an African-American or a black man"), and "unique" critical tools for evaluation, the literary work of even the most radical black writer, and Baraka is an excellent example of this, will to some extent reflect the values—cultural, political, social, aesthetic, etc.— of that "substructure." Such is the nature of art, and particularly of literature. A work of art does not develop out of a vacuum. From Ellison's (and Eliot's) perspective, every work *proceeds* from the totality of works that *preceded* it. Thus, a more practical critical approach to African-American literature in general, and to Ellison's texts in particular, would seem to be that taken up by the writers included in Kimberly Benston's *Speaking for You: The Vision of Ralph Ellison*— that is, to analyze the skill with which the black writer is able to "rewrite" or recontextualize the literary references that echo, resound, and reverberate throughout his or her texts rather than to criticize, for purely social, political, or ideological purposes, the fact that they are there.

Ellison writes that his constant concern with the craft and technique from which his literary styles emerged and his "constant plunging back into the shadow of the past" were necessary precisely in order to transcend the limitations "*apparently* imposed by [his] racial indentity" and to resist the temptation to "interpret the world and all its devices in terms of race" [*Shadow and Act*]. He therefore takes a decidedly formal approach to literature and to literary criticism.

Ellison attributes his preoccupation with form and technique to his 1935 encounter with Eliot's *The Waste Land* and to his formal training in music with its emphasis on theory. In fact, he writes that he began to make the transition from the study of music to the study of literature after having read *The Waste Land* during his second year as a music major at Tuskegee Institute. He describes the influence it had upon him in **"Hidden Name and Complex Fate"**:

> . . . *The Waste Land* seized my mind. I was intrigued by its power to move me while eluding my understanding. Somehow its rhythms were often closer to those of jazz than were those of the Negro poets, and even though I could not understand then, its range of allusion was as mixed and varied as that of Louis Armstrong. Yet there were its discontinuities, its changes of pace and its hidden system of organization which escaped me. There was nothing to do but look up the references in the footnotes to the poem, and thus began my conscious education in literature.
>
> [*Shadow and Act*]

Thus by reading *The Waste Land,* with what F.O. Mathiessen calls its "series of scholarly notes," Ellison "inscribes" himself into modernism and the entire Western literary tradition. However, as we have seen, in so doing, he situates himself in opposition to many of his more ideologically oriented contemporaries vis-a-vis the literary "text." As Ellison explains in **Shadow and Act,** what concerned him was not an ideological or sociological interpretation of the "Negro's experience" but the conversion of that experience into "symbolic action." For Ellison, the "text" is therefore not a sociological or political construct, although it does perform a social function: "[I]t brings into full vision the processes of [man's] current social forms." Following Kenneth Burke, to whom he claims to be "especially endebted," Ellison thinks of reading/writing as symbolic actions—in the introduction to **Shadow and Act** he writes that writing was an "acting out, symbolically" of a choice (between music and writing) he dared not acknowledge—and the "text" as a "symbolic act." As William Dowling puts it in his discussion of the relationship between Frederic Jameson and Kenneth Burke, the "text," accordingly, is paradoxical, for it is at once a symbolic *act* and a *symbolic* act. This means that it is *as act* genuine, for it tries to do something to reality or the world, but this something is unabashedly *symbolic,* for it leaves the world unmarked. Thus we come to a point of ambiguity or ambivalence, which is perhaps at the heart of modernism (certainly in the form of the New Criticism) and about which Ellison is keenly aware: the relationship between the text and the world or reality or the Symbolic and the Real. One choice would be to stress the *symbolic* status of the text, to view it as a kind of passive reflection of a ("politically") chaotic reality. A second would be to stress *act* whereby the language of the text would be seen as having the power both to organize and, as it were, constitute the world. This is important, for it is perhaps the case that the world or its reality cannot be independent of language: without language the world would simply disappear. Our question is, then, where does Ellison place the stress? On the *symbolic* or on the *act*? This brings us to yet another problem: Ellison's understanding of "reality" or the "real."

In pursuing this last question, let us not forget that Ellison was greatly influenced by Burke, who believes that what we call the real is in fact the symbolic. In *Language as Symbolic Action* Burke writes that as symbol-using/misusing animals, we cling to "a kind of naive verbal realism that refuses to realize the full extent of the role played by symbolicity in [our] notions of reality," which he defines as "but a construct of our symbol system." Thus reality is for Burke, and for Ellison as well, a "clutter of symbols about the past combined with our knowledge of the present" which is dispersed through writing—through books, magazines, maps, and newspapers. Indeed, Ellison's exposure as a child to a reality different from the one he inhabited was stimulated by the media: by the radio he enjoyed tinkering with and the discarded opera records, books, and magazines—he mentions specifically *Vanity Fair*—his mother would bring from the home of her white employer. Needless to say, this reality (or symbol system) often clashed with the one to which he was confined by virtue of his being black. In any event, what is implicit here but is made explicit by Ellison in the essay entitled **"Twentieth-Century Fiction"** is that what is taken for the real, particularly in literature, is in fact the symbolic. All of its constructs, including the sociological and racial, reside in linguisticality—in the *word,* which Ellison describes as an "insidious" form of segregation:

> Perhaps the most insidious and least understood form of segregation is that of the word. And by this I mean the word in all its complex formulations, from the proverb to the novel and stage play, the word with all its subtle power to suggest and foreshadow overt action while magically disguising the moral consequences of that action and providing it with symbolic and psychological justification. For if the word has the potency to revive and make us free, it has also the power to blind, imprison, and destroy.

[*Shadow and Act*]

Ellison's concern here and in **"The Shadow and the Act,"** is with what Burke calls "language as a species of action—symbolic action [whose] nature is such that it can be used as a tool." As symbolic *action,* language posits a myth—that of the stereotypical black—(Burke refers to this stereotype as a symbol of "contented indigence") and a ritual—that of keeping the black in his place. (Jim Crow is but another symbolic [juridical] system.) Hence, according to Ellison, what is represented as a "black" reality in much of twentieth-century fiction is not the Real but the Symbolic—a system of symbols governed, as in the case of Faulkner's Chick in *Intruder in the Dust,* by "an inherited view of the world with its Southern conception of Negroes" [*Shadow and Act*]. His imperative in **"Brave Words for A Startling Occasion"** is that, like Menelaus, who in the *Odyssey* must struggle with

Proteus's ever-changing forms in order to find his way home, the modern American novelist must struggle against this "inheritance of illusion" and challenge the "apparent forms of reality" in order to find *his* way home:

> The way home we seek is that condition of man's being at home in the world, which is called love, and which we term democracy. Our task then is always to challenge the apparent forms of reality—that is, the fixed manners and values of the few, and to struggle with it until it reveals its mad, vari-implicated chaos, its false faces, and on until it surrenders its insight, its truth.

[*Shadow and Act*]

In addition to his very Burkian notion of reality as the symbolic rather than the real, what Ellison reveals here is his own paradoxical relationship to modernism. On the one hand, Ellison, like most modernists, is involved in a serious reevaluation of the limits of literary form and the possibilities for a new aesthetic in the arts generally. On the other hand, through his concern with value, he *refuses* to be modern. Furthermore, by invoking the idea of homelessness, he raises a problem with which modernism tries to grapple: what does it mean to *be-in-the-world* in the twentieth century? Indeed, Ellison tells us in the introduction to *Shadow and Act* that the question of Being is what underlies his fiction: "Fiction became the agency of my efforts to answer the questions: Who am I, what am I, how did I come to be?" In other words, as we shall see, Ellison—like the Invisible Man and his Russian counterpart, Dostoevsky's Underground Man, whose narrative we will argue forms a kind of "frame" upon which *Invisible Man* is superimposed—writes out of an urgent (metaphysical) need to *act.*

As Ellison explains in *Shadow and Act*, what concerned him was not an ideological or sociological interpretation of the "Negro's experience" but the conversion of that experience into "symbolic action."
—Sandra Adell

We have called *Notes from Underground* a "frame" for *Invisible Man* because it is in the novel's Prologue and Epilogue that Ellison's close proximity to Dostoevsky is most evident. In both novels we have an "I," a speaking subject who, after having endured about twenty years of "sickness," is suddenly compelled to write a kind of confessional. "I am a sick man. . . . I am a spiteful man," declares the Underground Man, while Ellison's protagonist writes, "I am an invisible man." The first sentence of each novel is important because it raises the question, "Who is behind the 'I?'"

"Who is writing, and to whom does he address himself?" According to Barthes, the "I" has a double status, that of character and figure, which he distinguishes as follows:

> In principle, the character who says "I" has no name.... [I]n fact, however, I immediately becomes a name, his name. In the story (and in many conversations), I is no longer a pronoun, but a name, the best of names; to say I is inevitably to attribute signifieds to oneself; further, it gives one a biographical duration, it enables one to undergo, in one's imagination, an intelligible "evolution," to signify oneself as an object with a destiny, to give a meaning to time.... The figure is altogether different: it is not a combination of semes concentrated in a legal Name, nor can biography, psychology, or time encompass it: it is an illegal, impersonal, anachronistic configuration of symbolic relationships. As figure, the character can oscillate between two roles, without this oscillation having any meaning, for it occurs outside biographical time, (outside chronology . . .).

> In short, as character, the "I" is full, a complete subject; as figure, the "I" is decentered, dispersed among its "configurations of symbolic relationships."

While Ellison claims that his Invisible Man is a "character" in the "dual meaning of the term," he posits his protagonist in much the same way that Dostoevsky posits his—that is, as a "figure." In a footnote to Part One of *Notes*, Dostoevsky describes the Underground Man as a representative of a "generation that is still living out its days among us." He is the type of man that city life had begun to breed: a man of acute consciousness whose sickness comes from his increasing awareness that the system which constitutes the social has no basis—it has no ground. His audience is nothing more than an "absent presence," an "empty device" which makes it possible for him to carry on this long dialogue with himself in which he lays out his notion of pain and suffering as one of the metaphysical grounds for human existence.

Ellison's protagonist is described by what is probably the sanest character in the novel, the "crazy" vet. He describes the Invisible Man as a product of the age of technology, the kind of man that philanthropists like Mr. Norton, who believe it is their business to see to the "first-hand organizing of human life," had begun to breed. As the "crazy" vet helps Mr. Norton to recover from his Golden Day Tavern ordeal, he tells Mr. Norton that the Invisible Man is the most perfect achievement of his dreams:

> "You see," he said turning to Mr. Norton, "he has eyes and ears and a good distended African nose,

but he fails to understand the simple facts of life. *Understand.* Understand? It's worse than that. He registers with his senses but short-circuits his brain. Nothing has meaning. He takes it in but he doesn't digest it. Already he is—well, bless my soul! Behold! a walking zombie! Already he's learned to repress not only his emotions but his humanity. He's invisible, a walking personification of the Negative, the most perfect achievement of your dreams, sir! The mechanical man!"

As a mechanical man the Invisible Man is unable to see beyond the corners of his consciousness, and when he does, as in the Prologue, he retreats. Everything else, including an understanding of "the simple facts of life," is blocked off by the "they" or the "Other" to which he looks for an image of himself. And when he finally comes to see the "nightmare" of the absurdity of all life, it is to the "they" or the "Other" that the Invisible Man articulates his need to write:

> So why do I write, torturing myself to put it down? Because in spite of myself I've learned some things. Without the possibility of action, all knowledge comes to one labeled "file and forget," and I can neither file nor forget. Nor will certain ideas forget me; they keep filing away at my lethargy, my complacency. Why should I be the one to dream this nightmare? Why should I be dedicated and set aside—yes, if not to at least *tell* a few people about it? There seems to be no escape. Here I've set out to throw my anger into the world's face, but now that I've tried to put it all down the old fascination with playing a role returns, and I'm drawn up again. So that even before I finish I've failed (maybe my anger is too heavy; perhaps being a talker, I've used too many words). But I've failed. The very act of trying to put it all down has confused me and negated some of the anger and some of the bitterness. So it is that now I denounce and defend, or feel prepared to defend. I condemn and affirm, say no and say yes, say yes and say no. I denounce because though implicated and partially responsible, I have been hurt to the point of abysmal pain, hurt to the point of invisibility. And I defend because in spite of all I find that I love. In order to get some if it down I *have* to love.

We have quoted this rather long paragraph almost entirely, because it shows some important intersections and divergences between the Underground Man and the Invisible Man. The most obvious intersection is the protagonists' need to write. But they write for different reasons. The Underground Man claims that he writes in order to relieve himself of one of the hundreds of memories that oppress him, and because he is bored. As a man suffering from "excessive consciousness," and inertia, he needs something to do. The Invisible Man writes precisely because he *does not* want to forget, and because he wants his anger and frustration to be heard. He therefore aspires to be a "readerly" writer. And in contrast to the Underground Man, who contemptuously invokes his audience only to negate it, the Invisible Man always takes his readers' sensitivity into account. He is respectful, and careful not to take advantage of them. He is apologetic for even the slightest contradiction. And at the end of the Prologue, he says, "Bear with me." He asks them to be tolerant because he needs allies; the Invisible Man does not want to dream the nightmare alone.

As the Lisa episode dramatizes, the Underground Man refuses to establish an alliance with anyone. He refuses because he considers himself more intelligent than everyone else, but more importantly, because to seek allies implies a willingness to give oneself over to the quotidian, the social, the moral, the ethical; in short, it implies a willingness to give oneself over to the nightmare which the Underground Man is attempting, through a sort of metaphysical rebellion, to escape. His escape is not without its consequences, however. The anger and bitterness that abate as the Invisible Man tries to "put it all down" only becomes more intense as the Underground Man turns it inwards. Since he denounces everything that stands for the social, he is never tempted by the fascination of playing a role for the sake of the "they" as is the Invisible Man. He does not allow himself to be drawn into the everydayness of the "they"; therefore, nothing detracts from what he, too, experiences as an abysmal pain.

The pain from which the Underground Man suffers is the "sole root" of his consciousness. It constitutes the state or condition which Dostoevsky nominates the "underground." And it is only in this condition that the Underground Man feels he can experience what ordinary existence, with its "systems and abstract conclusions," denies the human subject: that most "advantageous of advantages," absolute freedom.

The freedom about which the Underground Man speaks has nothing to do with material well-being or virtue: that falls under the rubric liberation and is always contingent upon the "they." What he articulates is a notion of freedom which is another metaphysical ground for existence as he understands it. It is a kind of existential "thinking" that negates all systems of reason and logic—it is the absolute right to choose:

> One's own free, untrammeled desires, one's own whim, no matter how extravagant, one's own fancy, be it wrought up at times to the point of madness— all of this is precisely that most advantageous of advantages which is omitted, which fits into no classification, and which is constantly knocking all sys-

tems and theories to hell. And where did our sages get the idea that man must have normal, virtuous desires? What made them imagine that man must necessarily wish what is sensible and advantageous? What man needs is only his own independent wishing, whatever that independence may cost and wherever it may lead.

In order to maintain this absolute right to his own "whim," the Underground Man must stand alone, and he must struggle against that which has already been defined. He must reject anything that makes a claim to the good, the logical, and the beautiful as being nothing more than weapons, illusions with which to combat the painfulness of "authentic" existence. And since this authenticity is what he seeks, he must always be acutely, excessively conscious. This is why in "On the Occasion of Wet Snow," he allows himself to be insulted and humiliated, then insults and humiliates Lisa, and thereby perpetuates the cycle of pain through which he grows more morbidly and sensitively self-aware.

The Underground Man is morbidly and sensitively aware of what it means to say "I am." Through his dialogue with himself, he attempts to make a distinction between the "I am" of everydayness, the "I am" that gets dispersed into the "they" and exists in terms of the "they," and the authentic self, the "I am" that can uncover what everydayness shields from the "they"—that is, the finitude of existence. He is morbidly and sensitively aware that life is nothing more than a "sequence of experiences" between birth and death and that despite the multiplicity of possibilities which lie between those boundaries, he is nothing more than a being-towards death. As such, he insists on his right to exist authentically, in his corner, away from society, and to leave "living life" to those he feels are simply too cowardly to look true subjectivity in the face and say, "*I am.*"

. . . . .

"I yam what I am," exclaims the Invisible Man as he walks along the Harlem streets enjoying a yam—piping hot and sweet and seeping with butter. Although he engages in the play on words out of a sense of exhilaration over having broken a rule of etiquette by eating in the streets, the "whatness" of the slightly distorted tautology is the metaphysical problem he spends his life trying to resolve. However, he seeks the "whatness" of his *self* in the very thing that distances the *self* from itself: in language. Only when language is temporarily wiped away, when what the "crazy" vet refers to metaphorically as his "short-circuited brain" becomes a reality after the paint factory accident, does the Invisible Man succeed in experiencing his true subjectivity.

When he recovers from the paint factory explosion, the Invisible Man finds himself in the hospital, attached to a machine, "pounded between crushing electrical pressures, bumped between live electrodes, like an accordion between a player's hand." When the pounding and pumping stop, all he feels is an intense pain and a kind of primordial vacuousness. For a fleeting moment, with his memory temporarily wiped away, he says, "My mind was blank, as though I had just begun to live." But with a second onslaught of electrical shocks, conducted to the rhythms of Beethoven's *Fifth Symphony,* the Invisible Man drifts back into consciousness, into an awareness of himself as a being existing somewhere between a fluid and painful blackness and the vast whiteness of the white world. He does indeed become, at least temporarily, a walking zombie for whom nothing has meaning. Language comes to him first as the "rhythmical differences between progressions of sound that questioned and those that made a statement," then as a "jumble of alphabets" as the voices hovering over him in a cacophony of silence try to make him understand.

As his focus becomes clearer the Invisible Man is able to recognize the jumble of alphabets that one of the doctors has written on a card as a question: "What is your name?" But its meaning does not register. Only when the question is rephrased does the Invisible Man feel a "distant light" of understanding penetrating the pain and blackness of his mind:

WHO . . . ARE . . . YOU?

As he reconstructs the incident, the Invisible Man remembers that suddenly,

> Something inside me turned with a sluggish excitement. This phrasing of the question seemed to set off a series of weak and distant lights where the other had thrown a spark that failed. Who am I? I asked myself. But it was like trying to identify one particular cell that coursed through the torpid veins of my body. Maybe I was just this blackness and bewilderment and pain. . . .

The Invisible Man is brought back into contact with what the Underground Man would call his true *self*; but it does not last. All of the subsequent cards that the doctors and technicians produce force him to contemplate the question "Who are you?" within a racial and historical context. His responses, which are a kind of internal monologue, are double-edged, two-toned, as one part of him tries to grapple with the "I am," while the other engages in a game in which he either inverts the meaning of the question or invents a text for which he provides an interpretation. For example, when one "short, scholarly looking man" writes on a small chalkboard, "Who Was Your Mother?" the Invisible Man writes, "I looked at him, feeling a quick dislike and thinking, half in amusement, I don't play the dozens. And how's *your* old lady today?" By invoking the black verbal game

of the dozens, he imposes one level of language, the vernacular, upon another, the standard, and thereby subverts the specialist's attempt to communicate with him.

The satisfaction which he derives from outwitting his interrogator is somewhat short-circuited, however, by the next question, at which the Invisible Man stares in "wide-eyed amazement":

WHO WAS BUCKEYE THE RABBIT?

I was filled with turmoil. Why should he think of *that*? He pointed to the question, word by word. I laughed, deep, deep inside me, giddy with the delight of self-discovery and the desire to hide it. Somehow *I* was Buckeye the Rabbit . . . or had been, when as children, we danced and sang barefoot in the dusty streets:

Buckeye the Rabbit
Shake it, shake it
Buckeye the Rabbit
Break it, break it . . .

Yet, I could not bring myself to admit it, it was too ridiculous—and somehow too dangerous. It was annoying that he had hit upon an old identity and I shook my head, seeing him purse his lips and eye me sharply.

BOY, WHO WAS BRER RABBIT?

He was your mother's back-door man, I thought. Anyone knew they were one and the same: "Buckeye" when you were very young and hid yourself behind wide innocent eyes; "Brer," when you were older. But why was he playing around with these childish names? Did they think I was a child? Why didn't they leave me alone? I would remember soon enough when they let me out of the machine . . .

The first question fills him with turmoil because it invokes an "I" that once was, a wholesome "I," the one that existed long before his dying grandfather spoke of the necessity of wearing a mask, of breaking the "I" in half. It is the "I" prior to its encounter with the white world, an "I" completely in accord with its own reality, with a world that is still of its own making.

Brer Rabbit is the "I" that knows how to confront the white world. He is shrewd, cunning, and like the Invisible Man's grandfather, he knows how to live with his "head in the lion's mouth." He knows how to "overcome" 'em with yeses, undermine 'em with grins, agree 'em to death and destruction" without losing himself in the process, something the Invisible Man never learns. Because he takes his grandfather's dying words too literally, he fails to understand that what the old man described as his *treachery* was nothing more than a game which he did not believe in but knew how to play to his advantage. It was a game of words: Say what they want to hear, but never believe in what you say.

Although the Invisible Man insists after his Harlem eviction speech that he does not believe what he said and that he gave the speech because he was simply angry and because he likes to make speeches, he very quickly comes to believe in the game.
—*Sandra Adell*

Although the Invisible Man insists after his Harlem eviction speech that he does not believe what he said and that he gave the speech because he was simply angry and because he likes to make speeches, he very quickly comes to believe in the game. So by the time he is indoctrinated into the ideology of the Brotherhood, he believes that by relying on language, he can free himself of the racial and historical boundaries that confine him and thus acquire a new status: that of a human being. Instead, what he acquires are new identities which make even more remote any possibilities of self-definition. The electric shock machine makes of him a "new man," whose words and expressed attitudes are not his but someone else's. They belong to some "alien personality" created by high technology and Gestalt psychology. The Brotherhood, which is another kind of machine, provides him with yet another identity, that of a "leader" and "eloquent" speaker of words. The problem is that he becomes so captivated by the magic of his own words that he begins to believe that there is some truth to what he says. For example, during his first Brotherhood speech, the Invisible Man shares with his audience what he describes as a sudden and odd experience, the experience of suddenly becoming "more human" and of feeling suddenly that he had finally come "home" after a long and desperate and "uncommonly blind" journey. The audience responds enthusiastically, and despite the disapproval of some of the brothers who argue that he was emotional rather than theoretical, the Invisible Man becomes an overnight success. But he also becomes a victim of his own discourse. After the rally, as he lies awake in his room, he realizes that he meant everything he said, even though he did not know he was going to say "those things." He writes that many of the words and phrases he used in his speech seemed to form themselves independently of him; they seemed to possess him and fall into place of their own accord. But one phrase was particularly disturbing: he did not know what he meant when he said that he had become "more human." How did this unfamiliar phrase come into his con-

sciousness? He does not know whether he picked it up from a preceding speaker or from his college literature professor, or whether it was just one of the many remembered words, images, and linked verbal echoes one hears when not listening.

The question which the Invisible Man raises is one of the key issues in Barthes' theory of intertextuality: the plurality of the "I" that "reads" the text. According to Barthes, "This 'I' which approaches the text is already itself a plurality of other texts, of codes which are infinite or more precisely, lost (whose origin is lost)." Likewise, the "I" that "writes" the text is already itself a plurality of other texts. For the invisible man, that plurality reaches back through at least two traditions: the Euro-American and the black oratorical traditions. Consequently, his Brotherhood speech is a "re-writing" of all the speeches or verbal "texts" in these two traditions. It rewrites the Reverend Homer A. Barbee's speech/text which is already itself a rewriting of other texts—the narratives of Booker T. Washington and Frederick Douglass, among others—which are themselves rewritings of other narratives, and so forth. It is also a rewriting, in a Marxist discourse, of the Old Testament myth of the Jews as a chosen people. The phrase "I have become more human" is therefore both familiar and strange to the Invisible Man, because it has always already been written.

This concept of the irretrievable origin of the *always already* is what differentiates Barthes's theory of intertextuality from theories of influence or the association of ideas. Influence implies a literary indebtedness to a traceable source, be it a particular author or a particular literary tradition, etc. In other words, the origin is not lost. We can see, for instance, Eliot's, Burke's, and—despite Clifford Mason's argument to the contrary—Dostoevsky's influence on Ellison. Indeed, Ellison points to Dostoevsky himself. It would be difficult to argue, however, that Ellison, both consciously and unconsciously, bypassed Richard Wright, for although he insists that he was much less influenced by Wright than his critics assume, his novel does share certain affinities with "The Man Who Lived Underground," which preceded its publication by several years. For example, both freddaniels and the Invisible Man come upon their subterranean sanctuaries while being chased by white men; and both manage to triumph over the white world by stealing some of its power. Where the two works diverge is in terms of the metaphysical problems they raise. Whether through a direct influence or an association of ideas, Wright's treatment of those problems more closely parallels Dostoevsky's than does Ellison's. The Invisible Man's notion of freedom is materialistic, for example. He sees it as his inalienable right to pursue any number of the infinite possibilities which he believes his world has become. In other words, he sees it as his right to try and make it to the top.

In contrast, Wright's protagonist, through his devaluation of the things that are most valuable to "the men who lived in the dead world of sunshine and rain" above, discovers the kind of absolute freedom described by Dostoevsky's Underground Man. Furthermore, as he watches the boy and the watchman being wrongly accused and punished for having stolen the radio, gun, money, rings, watches and diamonds with which he decorates and illuminates the wall and floor of his cave, he is suddenly freed from any sense of guilt. He is freed, first of all, because he feels that although they are not guilty of that particular crime, they are nevertheless guilty. They had always been guilty, because for him, guilt is the very essence of existence. It is an innate, physical feeling that one had committed some dreadful offense that can neither be remembered nor understood, but which creates in one's life a state of eternal anxiety.

Secondly, like the Underground Man, freddaniels no longer shares the conscience of the "they." He no longer thinks in terms of right and wrong, because, echoing the maxim of Dostoevsky's Ivan Karamozov that "All is permitted," he realizes that "if the world as men had made it was right, then anything else was right, any act a man took to satisfy himself, murder, theft, torture." A desire to share his insights is what impels freddaniels to return to the "dark sunshine above." He wants to share his discovery with someone, because, by doing so, he would also affirm the reality of his existence as an absolutely free man.

In contrast, the Invisible Man returns to the world above because his innate sense of guilt will not let him remain underground. It forces him to attempt to absolve himself of the blame for his sickness, his invisibility, by recognizing that in spite of it all, he nevertheless has a "socially responsible role to play." Dostoevsky's Underground Man is, on the other hand, determined to carry his acute consciousness to the bitter end. He rejects any notions of personal culpability and social responsibility and remains underground because, he tells us, "I am convinced that we underground men must be kept well reined in."

In any event, with Wright's freddaniels in the *avant guard* of what Craig Werner [in "Brer Rabbit Meets the Underground Man: Simplification of Consciousness in Baraka's *Dutchman* and *Slave Ship*," *Obsidian* 5.1-2, n.d.] refers to as a "distinguished file of black underground men, all of whom march in a column led by Fyodor Dostoevsky's original," the Invisible Man occupies a prominent position because he is the first black American "hero" to come fully clothed in the "uniform" of the modern age. He brings the black American "Hero," and perhaps black American literature, to what can be called a "fixed point" of modernism; that is, a seeking, in language, of the *self,* for this "speaking subject" in fact give himself over to language so that, ultimately, what speaks is not a subject at all, but language itself. Indeed, the novel's internal structure revolves around

language, around the sphinx-like discourse of the Invisible Man's dying grandfather, whose "truth" he thinks resides in language: in Barbee's speech, in Bledsoe's letters, and, finally, in the Marxist discourse of the Brotherhood. The characters that the Invisible Man encounters as he moves through this complex linguistic field are types of discourse, whose voices or "codes" interweave to form the intertextuality of the text. For example, much of the "crazy" vet's discourse falls under the Barthian code of psychology: he talks about the Invisible Man in terms of his psychological makeup. When his voice fades, the same code is picked up by young Emerson and intersects with yet another code, the voice or code of truth: Emerson tells the Invisible Man the "Truth" of what Bledsoe has sealed in the seven letters. In the discourse of the blues-singing and fast-rapping Peter Wheatstraw, the Harlem landlady Mary, the yam peddeler, and many of the other Harlem dwellers, there is a convergence of cultural codes. Black American history, tradition, and folk culture "speak" out of these discourses and interweave their voices into those of the white "substructure" to create the "vast stereophony of cultural languages" from which the Invisible Man challenges us to consider the question—"Who knows but that, on the lower frequencies, I speak for you?"

David Nicholson (review date 4 February 1996)

SOURCE: A review of *The Collected Essays of Ralph Ellison,* in *Washington Post Book World,* Vol. XXVI, No. 5, February 4, 1996, p. 7.

[*In the following review, Nicholson examines* The Collected Essays of Ralph Ellison *and two works by Albert Murray, providing a laudatory assessment of all three works and characterizing the two authors as "giants" in terms of their talent and achievements as writers.*]

The critic Stanley Crouch, himself no mean chronicler of the American scene, has dubbed Albert Murray and Ralph Ellison "the twin towers" of our national literature. The appellation is apt, invoking as it does both basketball (a game to which black athletes have brought both style and breathtaking improvisation all the more remarkable because performed with grace under pressure), and the black monoliths that dominate the skyline of lower Manhattan. The essays collected in these three volumes [*The Blue Devils of Nada: A Contemporary American Approach to Aesthetic Statement* and *The Hero and the Blues* by Albert Murray, and *The Collected Essays of Ralph Ellison,* edited by John F. Callahan] allow us to witness Albert Murray and Ralph Ellison in the full glory of their wit and style, and to marvel at their flights of intellectual synthesis, accomplished with all the nonchalant daring of a Charlie Parker solo. Time and again, we are reminded of their centrality as American writers—for their fiction and their essays—and American thinkers.

Only one of these books, Murray's *The Blue Devils of Nada,* is new in the strictest sense of the word, although it goes without saying that all are welcome. Murray's *The Hero and the Blues,* first published in 1973 by the University of Missouri Press, has long been unavailable. ***The Collected Essays of Ralph Ellison,*** ably edited by John F. Callahan, includes the entire contents of ***Shadow and Act*** (1964) and ***Going to the Territory*** (1986), as well as 20 other pieces. All told, ***The Collected Essays*** includes about half of the 75 occasional pieces and addresses Ellison wrote between 1937 and his death in 1984.

Reading these three volumes in concert, one is struck by how much Ellison and Murray must have influenced each other. While it would take a keener intelligence than mine to determine whose influence was the more profound, certain matters are, nonetheless, well established. Ellison, born in 1914, was just two years older than Murray. Both attended Tuskegee Institute in Alabama, where they were at least nodding acquaintances, but it was not until 1942, when Murray came to New York (Ellison had arrived six years earlier, and both would make their homes in Harlem), that they began the lifelong friendship that ended with Ellison's death in 1994.

As a result of that friendship, perhaps, certain themes recur again and again in their work. Both, for example, are insistent that black American life is best examined via art, not sociology (Ellison sharply rebuked "the specialists and 'friends of the Negro' who view our Negro American life as essentially nonhuman"). Both view the black experience as inseparable—perhaps even, in its fundamentals, indistinguishable—from the American experience, and the blues as black (and white) America's tragic poetry. Further, each sees improvisation as a hallmark, not merely of jazz, but of the American character, evident even in what seem on the surface the most prosaic activities. Thus, in an essay on Louis Armstrong, Murray remarks that "the ever-resilient and elegantly improvised ballroom choreography . . . was an idiomatic representation of an American outlook on possibility and thus also was an indigenous American reenactment of affirmation in the face of the ever-impending instability inherent in the nature of things."

That last is one of Murray's favorite themes, one that he developed at length in *The Hero and the Blues,* and that can be summarized by this passage from *The Blue Devils of Nada:* "The improvisation that is the ancestral imperative of blues procedure is completely consistent with and appropriate to those of the frontiersman, the fugitive slave, and the picaresque hero, *the survival of each of whom depended largely on an ability to operate on dynamics equivalent to those of the vamp, the riff, and most certainly the break, which jazz musicians regard as the Moment of Truth, or that disjuncture that should bring out your personal best"* [emphasis added].

Time and again, then, he and Ellison return to celebrating American improvisation and innovation, shrewdness and ingenuity, our love of adventure and exploration, our adaptability and our sense of humor, ringing new changes on these themes in much the same way as the jazz musicians who are among their favorite subjects.

Ellison, born in Oklahoma just seven years after it became a state, more than once referred to himself as a frontiersman, adding, "And isn't one of the implicit functions of the American frontier to encourage the individual to a kind of dreamy wakefulness, a state in which he makes—in all ignorance of the accepted limitations of the possible—rash efforts, quixotic gestures, hopeful testings of the complexity of the known and the given?"

At bottom, I think, Murray and Ellison were both intellectual frontiersmen, seekers of the promise of America. They went into the treacherous wilderness of our history, armed only with their imaginations and their intellects, using those tools in much the same way the frontiersmen each admired tamed the wilderness with axe and Kentucky long rifle.

It is not simply that both men are thoughtful writers, precise and insightful. ("He did not think that unguarded or loose expression represented one's true, honest, and material self," Murray notes of Count Basie, whose autobiography he co-authored. It is an observation he could easily have made of himself or of Ellison, and that painstaking quality is a large part of what makes each of them worth reading.) Nor is it that, as these essays make clear, they were men of catholic tastes, possessed of an inexhaustible intellectual curiosity, believers that the examined life, the life of the mind, was well worth living.

Were that all to Albert Murray and to Ralph Ellison, it would certainly have been enough. Where they proved themselves originals, however, breaking new ground and claiming new territory, was in uncovering and analyzing the mythopoetic aspects of black life. They did it taking the ordinary, most common stuff of life and obeying what Murray called "the vernacular imperatives to process (which is to say stylize) the raw native materials, experiences, and the idiomatic particulars of everyday life into aesthetic (which is to say elegant) statements of universal relevance and appeal."

Unlike some who would follow in the Black Arts movement of the 1960s and after, they did so in thoroughly unsentimental fashion, unreservedly acknowledging the similarities between cultures as well as their debt to other writers.

Ellison, for example, cited Eliot, Joyce and Lord Raglan, author of *The Hero,* as influences or, as he would have put it, "ancestors." Murray acknowledged Thomas Mann and Andre Malraux, and both he and Ellison owed—and readily admit to—a substantial debt to Hemingway.

In the end, however, they did what only great artists do—they took from others and made it their own. And why not? It was, and continues to be, after all, the American way.

Writing about his first months in New York, a city that he found more than a little confusing, not least because it lacked the familiar, if oppressive, guideposts of the segregated South he had known, Ellison notes that he came to the realization that "if I were to grasp American freedom, I was compelled to continue my explorations." He meant explorations of Manhattan outside of Harlem, but the idea can easily serve as a statement of his (and Murray's) artistic and aesthetic intentions.

They are truly, as Stanley Crouch implies, giants. We shall not see their like again.

Gary Giddins (review date 19 January 1997)

SOURCE: A review of *Flying Home and Other Stories,* in *The New York Times Book Review,* January 19, 1997, p. 13.

[*In the following review, Giddins offers a laudatory assessment of* Flying Home and Other Stories.]

The one-novel career, while hardly unique to the United States (Europe offers Canetti, Rilke and Lampedusa, among others), has produced a peculiar frisson of suspense in this country in the postwar era. I'm thinking not of writers who died young, like James Agee, or who consummated extended literary callings with one big fictional work, like Katherine Anne Porter, but of those who made an indelible assault on the consciousness of several generations with a prodigiously incisive novel and left us loitering, season after season, in the vain hope of a second strike.

Three cases stand out. Henry Roth published *Call It Sleep* in the 1930's, but his novel belongs as much to the 60's, when it was read and celebrated. Breaking what may be the longest silence in publishing history, he persevered to write a memory novel so long we are three volumes away from the finish (the six volumes are being published individually under the collective title *Mercy of a Rude Stream*) and lingering in a zone of cautious disappointment. J. D. Salinger would undoubtedly top best-seller lists with *The Pitcher in the Chaff,* but I suspect we have given up waiting or stopped

caring. Ralph Ellison's death in 1994, however, was a blow—prayers unanswered once and for all.

A deconstruction of race and identity fixed on the most reverberant metaphor since Melville's whale, *Invisible Man* succeeded so well in addressing what Ellison called "human universals" that we recall with a sad jolt the admiring condescension with which it was greeted in 1952. At a time when not a few white intellectuals presumed that Negro novels were—or ought to be—proletarian protest fiction (and that Negro novelists were—or ought to be—limited in their reach by a kind of intellectual ebonics), countless readers were encouraged to approach *Invisible Man* as a sociological inquiry into the Negro condition: Me Tarzan, you invisible. Not the least indication of Ellison's transfigurative powers is the chagrin engendered by that memory.

Invisible Man is a reverse Bildungsroman, in which a coming of age is refracted through the prism of ripened—indeed, nearly fatal—experience. The hibernating protagonist speaks to us "on the lower frequencies," from a coal bin illuminated by 1,369 light bulbs and the grace of Louis Armstrong, all powered by stolen electricity. If Ellison's second novel, worked on for decades, never materialized, the excerpts he infrequently let fly, as well as his essays and interviews (a forum he made artful), affirmed a comic aptitude for lighting up dark places with an ungrudging lyricism that simply could not be subverted.

John F. Callahan, who assembled a volume of Ellison's nonfiction for the Modern Library in 1995, has been entrusted with collating the books Ellison shyly or modestly or stubbornly held back. The unfinished novel is said to be an immense manuscript, so perhaps an American answer to *The Man Without Qualities* is still in the offing, though which of us isn't prepared to settle for less—say, an Ellisonian clue to life after hibernation? Ellison's early reviews, written for *The New Masses,* have never been collected; likewise, stories reworked or cut from his published and unpublished novels. We are promised a more prolific posthumous career for Ellison than most of us had expected.

Flying Home and Other Stories is a slim but shining installment, collecting 13 short stories written between 1937 and 1954, six previously unpublished. Mr. Callahan, who commands significant editorial clout (he effects "silent" emendations, omits a story he admits Ellison would have included, gives titles to two stories Ellison left untitled), has shrewdly organized the material to reflect a sequential growth that with two notable exceptions fuses the central characters as one: the stories spin outward, not only from early youth to early manhood, but from the South to the North and back, from horror to horror averted. They have a befitting unity, on the order of "In Our Time" or "Dubliners," that Ellison himself could not have intended.

The least of these stories are distinctive, the best are gripping and two are genuinely terrifying. Still, it is scarcely possible to read them without noting sundry apprenticeship connections to *Invisible Man* and to Ellison's most accomplished nonfiction, especially the disarmingly cheerful memoir **"An Extravagance of Laughter."** Nor is it difficult to see why Ellison dawdled over publishing them: it would have been like Beethoven making his name with his Ninth Symphony and, after 40 years' labor, proffering his First. Some books, however treasurable, are better dispensed by estates. Ellison was a master of recounting old tales from the haven of a hard-won maturity—these tales are fresh, even raw. Many are candidly autobiographical, and even the most skillful and symbol-laden betray his search for his own voice.

Surprisingly, Ellison, an unequivocal master of the first-person narrative, appears to have been intimidated by that mode in the 1940's. Five of the six unpublished stories are in the first person (most of those persons are unnamed); six of the seven he did publish are in the third person and, excepting the three that appeared in 1944 and that conclude the book, are conspicuously flatter. All are told exclusively from the perspective of a boy or man, almost always linked through geographical and situational connections to Ellison. The exceptions are remarkable tours de force.

"A Party Down at the Square" vividly depicts a lynching and burning from the perspective of a visiting white boy whose body rejects the horrific episode ("the gutless wonder from Cincinnati," his uncle calls him), but whose mind works hard to accept it, finally coming to rest in a kind of hapless admiration: "God, but that nigger was tough. That Bacote nigger was some nigger!" Ellison puts in the boy's mouth a few didactic asides in a futile attempt to explain or understand the inexplicable, but this is an important work in its own right because it commands a forbidden ringside view of barbarians at play. The story is also fascinating because it augurs Ellison's masterpiece. The frenzied confusion that ensues when a pilot, disconcerted by the fire, crashes his plane in the square is a foretaste of the masterly episodes of disarrangement in *Invisible Man,* from the battle royale to the Harlem riot. No less predictively, the blank-slate narration suggests the Invisible Man's early and equally unformed recollections. Obtuseness is a human condition, not a racial one.

The nattering violence in **"King of the Bingo Game"** occurs almost entirely in the head of the protagonist, a Southern black man in Harlem, whom the Oklahoma-born Ellison takes pains to distinguish from his fellow Southwesterners at the center of the other stories. This one, marked by a brief memory interlude as seamlessly woven as that in a Mizoguchi film, sneaks up on the reader like a cop with a blackjack. Overwrought and hysterical in its narrow focus on a man obsessed with the machinations of a bingo wheel,

it closes with the revelation of fate affirmed, even as it borrows Hemingway's device of disguising one fixation with another.

Hemingway's influence is rife in early Ellison, and so, in the fastidious overlay of symbols, is T. S. Eliot's. Echoes of writers Ellison admired occasionally intrude with noticeable clarity: Hemingway ("the swift rush of water in the irrigation canals and the fish panting in the mud where the canals were dry and rotting in the sun where the mud had dried"), Eudora Welty ("the horns were blasting brighter now . . . like somebody flipping bright handfuls of new small change against the sky") and William Faulkner ("his whole life was determined by the bingo wheel; not only that which would happen now that he was at last before it, but all that had gone before, since his birth and his mother's birth and the birth of his father"). At times Ellison will test a technique like a pilot taking out a new plane—trying out a Faulkner-type flashback (and Hemingway-type dialogue) in "A Hard Time Keeping Up" or a "Snows of Kilimanjaro" flashback in **"Flying Home."** At other times you can track the transition from influence to assimilation, for example in a comparison of the Faulknerian repetition of "vomit" in **"King of the Bingo Game"** and the Ellisonian repetition of "humiliation" in **"Flying Home."**

Ellison's voice ultimately prevails, from the personal metaphor ("they seem to feel just the place to kick you to make your backbone feel like it's going to fold up like the old cellophane drinking cups we used when we were kids") to the ebullient non sequitur ("When we jam, sir, we're Jamocrats!") to the more specific indicators of what was to come: minute descriptions rendered with cool detachment, gently pointed satire, expressionistic waking scenes, a naked woman dancing, the surreality of a boy attempting to snatch a plane from the sky, a humanizing grandfather, the kind of emotional violence that substitutes a chimera for reality and, perhaps most distinctive of all, the combination of terror and revelation that resolves itself in uncontrollable laughter.

The memoir-essay **"An Extravagance of Laughter"** winds up with the long-delayed punch line of Ellison erupting in ill-suited and unruly laughter during a performance of "Tobacco Road," an outburst he associates with "my emotional and intellectual development." The first incident recounted by the Invisible Man shows how violence was deflected when his own outrage turned to laughter. In Ellison, laughter is rarely unforced or natural, and nowhere is its violent yet emancipating power more hard-earned than in the story **"Flying Home"** ("Blasts of hot, hysterical laughter tore from his chest, causing his eyes to pop"). A Tuskegee airman is brought to earth by a buzzard in hellish Alabama and is caught between the possibility of casual redneck murder in the person of a plantation owner, who assumes murder is his birthright, and the shame of abiding black acquiescence, in the person of a grandfather who is sharper than the airman initially wants to admit. It is a frightening story, edgily confined to the wounded pilot's vision, and Ellison's conclusion is surprising, unsentimental and moving.

Less successful are the Buster and Riley stories, a sequence of four pastoral dialogues that take place over a period of about two years; they are filled with word games and play acting, but are undermined in their banter by touches of vaudeville and authorial intrusions, hinting none too subtly at what we ought to make of what we are invited to overhear. Yet they capture the value of imagination in quelling the insecurities of childhood. One of them, **"That I Had the Wings,"** tells of an incident Ellison related from his own past, about the time he tied parachutes to chickens. In an interview with John Hersey in 1974, he was quick to point out that none of the chickens died; in the story, one bites the dust. In **"A Coupla Scalped Indians,"** a sexual initiation story published four years after *Invisible Man,* Riley is transformed into the unnamed first-person narrator, in the manner of the novel.

Two slight but sharply told anecdotes about riding the rails address the narrators' suspicion regarding kindnesses proffered by whites, a theme given full-dress treatment in **"In a Strange Country,"** the account of a serviceman in Wales, brutalized by racists in his own division but brought to communal harmony by the patriotic singing of his Welsh hosts. Music is too much the essence of life in Ellison ("a gut language") to serve a merely symbolic end, but rarely is he as ingenuous as here, bringing the dislocated American back from a reverie of forgetfulness ("I can remember no song of ours that's of love of the soil or of country") to a restored sense of identity when the Welsh band honors him by striking up "The Star-Spangled Banner." It is invariably Ellison's stubborn Americanism that his critics find so galling—they miss even the piercing anger that gives it meaning.

A note of caution: In a long introduction, which would have served the book better as an afterword, Mr. Callahan writes, "Ellison's readers must earn the right to be interpreters." You may not have that opportunity if you read Mr. Callahan's detailed summaries and exegetical comments before encountering the stories. Save the intro for last.

David Holmstrom (review date 10 February 1997)

SOURCE: "Dark Memories in the Early Voice of Novelist Ralph Ellison," in *Christian Science Monitor,* February 10, 1997, p. 14.

[*In the following review, Holmstrom provides a favorable assessment of* Flying Home and Other Stories.]

For Buster and Riley, two fictional African-American boys created by Ralph Ellison, ebonics is the only language they speak. In [*Flying Home and Other Stories*], this collection of short stories, including three about Buster and Riley, Ellison at least establishes that the speech patterns and clipped grammar of ebonics flourished in the 1930s and '40s between two boys.

Today black children in Oakland, Calif., speak ebonics and create a stir when school officials recognize it as valid.

Ellison, the author of the famed novel *Invisible Man,* published in 1952, also establishes in these stories—written before *Invisible Man*—that the racial segregation and bias that limited the lives of "colored" people decades ago linger today.

So, even though Ellison writes with power and clarity about being black in a white world some 55 years ago, the issues haven't changed much, as seen through the burning of some black churches recently or a record racial-discrimination lawsuit against Texaco that was settled out of court.

Today the inner cities of America, for the most part, remain ethnically and economically segregated.

Thus, there is an immediacy in the echo of these stories, despite the rural setting of some of them in the days before TV, megastar black athletes, and McDonald's. And the passage of time has transformed a few of the characters into stereotypes, a situation saved only by Ellison's power to put them all in a social context from story to story. And an introduction to Ellison's life and beliefs by editor John Callahan is helpful too.

The first story, **"A Party Down at the Square,"** is the most harrowing and perhaps the sharpest-drawn of all the stories, a vast and ugly reality given a fine point in only 11 pages.

The narrator is an anonymous white boy witnessing the burning of a black man in an Alabama town square. No reason is given for the horror. The boy is first enthralled, then entertained, and finally sickened as the mob rules the night.

A small airplane, caught in winds, mistakes the fire for a landing signal. The plane clips a wire which in turn electrocutes a white woman. The boy, carried along by the crowd, is only momentarily diverted by the plane and the woman before returning to the horror of the tortured black man.

Ellison makes the boy a witness without a conscience, as surely as thousands of white boys were when witnessing the lynchings of blacks that were common in the South for years. The boy has no moral reference point provided by family or community. Because the boy vomited in a physical reaction, his uncle calls him "the gutless wonder from Cincinnati."

Other stories become quick, clear fragments pulled from Ellison's experiences. He was known to have ridden the rails as a young man, and several short pieces focus on eluding the "bulls," the railroad police who beat the rail-riding blacks with clubs and chased them off.

In the three stories about Buster and Riley—told with almost a Huck Finn quality—the boys are mischievous, always daring each other, uttering rumors as truths, and always scolded by adults who warn them about the hazards of being uppity blacks in the white world.

After Riley sings a song about being president, Aunt Kate tells him he has to learn to live in the white world while he is young so he won't be "buttin' yo head 'ginst a col' white wall all yo born days."

The collection of stories as a whole is greater than its parts.

Ellison's easy style, idioms, and simple declarative sentences, are perfectly suited for measuring the world as he saw it. Despite the hassle and danger of being black in a white world, Ellison was drawn to the inherent possibilities of his country.

In the story **"The Black Ball,"** a boy asks his father, "Brown's much nicer than white, isn't it, Daddy?"

And the father replies, "Some people think so. But American is better than both, son."

Darryl Pinckney (essay date 15 May 1997)

SOURCE: "The Drama of Ralph Ellison," in *The New York Review of Books,* May 15, 1997, pp. 52-9.

[*In the following essay, Pinckney surveys Ellison's life and career.*]

1.

Invisible Man holds such an honored place in African-American literature that Ralph Ellison didn't have to write anything else to break bread with the remembered dead. But he did try to go on, because if a writer has done one great thing then the pressures to do another are intense. A few of Ellison's short stories from the 1940s and 1950s were widely anthologized over the years. After a while it became generally known that he was at work on another novel. Though he remained aware ever afterward of the authority *Invisible Man* gave to him, no second novel followed his brilliant debut in 1952.

Ellison published essays, magisterial in tone, often on how a "specifically 'Negro' idiom" has influenced and been influenced by the larger American culture, or on the enduring predicament he saw as being at the heart of the American novel, the contradiction between the country's founding ideals and its actual, though sometimes hidden, caste and racial history. He admired nineteenth-century writers such as Melville and Twain because they believed in works of fiction as repositories of the nation's social and moral history. Before the undoing of Reconstruction, American novelists took account of the presence of blacks, and this inclusiveness suggested a brave, creative country, in Ellison's view. From its legacy he derived a lofty sense of his own purpose as an artist and of the novel as a "public gesture."

Ellison was prominent on the lecture circuit even in the Black Aesthetic days of the Sixties when his defiantly pro-American and prickly-proud intellectual act met with some hostility. Black Power nearly buried his reputation as he faced impolite audiences of black students from Harvard to Iowa, and refused to join in the mood of outrage, declining to call himself black instead of Negro. Meanwhile, chapters of his second novel appeared here and there throughout the 1960s and the 1970s. Eventually the voices of the militants whom he charged with having condescended to blacks faded and became as historical as his memory of Richard Wright falling out with black Communists in Harlem.

Whatever was said about Ralph Ellison, *Invisible Man* was considered untouchable. For a long time—pre-*Song of Solomon* days—he was the sole African-American novelist to have won anything as big as the National Book Award. Ellison held distinguished university appointments, received honorary degrees, delivered commencement addresses, granted lengthy interviews, and relished the fellowship of the American Academy of Arts and Letters. His work benefited mightily from the rediscovery of folklore in Black Studies and he lived long enough to witness the elevation of *Invisible Man* to a sort of Ur-text of blackness. "That blackness is most black, brothers, most black," people like to quote.

By the time Ellison died in 1994 he was regarded as a cultural treasure, a vindicated father figure for a generation of formerly militant and post-militant black writers who wanted folklore, blues, jazz, and black literature to be brainy yet virile subjects. The man of letters in Ellison had flourished, but maybe the writer in him up there on Riverside Drive, with his voluminous black-bound manuscript pages of a "work in progress," had found it paralyzing to think of the risks in publishing a second novel that might not measure up—or might be said not to measure up—to his one celebrated accomplishment.

To have published only one novel was part of the drama of his distinction. His standing apart because of this novel also became an allegory for one of his most cherished themes: the individuality of the Negro and therefore the complexity of the Negro as an American artist. He wanted to be read on his own terms. In some of the essays originally collected in *Shadow and Act* (1964) and *Going to the Territory* (1986), Ellison used his biography to explore the pluralistic irreversibly mixed cultural tradition in which he saw himself working, and which he didn't think most other Americans, black or white, appreciated enough for its intricacies and ironies.

Perhaps in looking back on his formative years to make his case that there was more to the lives of black people than Jim Crow, Ellison slyly confused the evidence of his own singularity with the argument for "personal realization" and affirmation of self that he claimed were available to all blacks. But Joyce, he noted, was busily establishing the conventions by which he wanted to be read even while he was writing his books. For Ellison this meant challenging misconceptions about the lives of black people and asserting what made his "sense of Negro life" different from that of other black writers.

To begin with there was Oklahoma, where Ellison was born in 1914. During his childhood Oklahoma had some of the worst riots in US history, and this was at a time when a race riot meant whites on the rampage through black neighborhoods. Still, he observed, Oklahoma "had no tradition of slavery, and while it was segregated, relationships between the races were more fluid and thus more human than in the old slave states." Ellison remembered a white boy called Hoolie, whom he'd met when his mother was working as custodian for some apartments in a white middle-class neighborhood. Hoolie suffered from a rheumatic heart, was being educated at home, and, like Ellison, was lonely for company. Race, Ellison said, didn't come into their shared enthusiasm as radio buffs and seekers after tuning coils in the garbage. Because the nine-year-old Hoolie approached electronics with "such daring," knowing him led Ellison, so he claimed, to expect more of himself and the world.

The porousness of the Jim Crow fabric in Oklahoma City not only allowed for exchanges of everyday humanity, but also for an almost subversive cultural flow up and down the social scale. "Any feelings of distrust I was to develop toward white people later on were modified by those with whom I had warm relations. Oklahoma offered many opportunities for such friendships," he said in an interview in 1961. In his late teens Ellison worked as an elevator operator in the Hub Building on Main Street to earn money for his college tuition. The building's owners, the Lewinson brothers, were pleased to find him either reading or beating out rhythms on the elevator cage. Ellison had a crush on one of the Lewinson daughters and years later in Italy he told her cousin, the writer Thekla Clark, that when he thought of a father figure he recalled Milton Lewinson's white mane.

Oklahoma had only been a state seven years when Ellison was born. The black people no less than the white people there, he said, were still imbued with the pioneer spirit. Their aggressive demeanor alone challenged the intentions of segregation. They were also mindful of the Native American elements in their ancestry and environment. This atmosphere of resistance and superiority was part of Ellison's remembrance of a black community not at all cut off from information, knowledge.

Ellison's father, a construction foreman, coal and then ice salesman who died when Ellison was three, wanted his oldest son to be a poet, as Ralph Waldo Ellison learned much later. It was not unusual for blacks of his father's generation to name their children after American heroes, including literary ones. Though Ellison's mother did not have much formal education, she nevertheless encouraged her two sons by bringing home from her jobs as a domestic discarded books, magazines, opera recordings. Just as he could grow up listening to the radio, like any white kid, he said, so, too, could anybody go to the movies, even if people had by law to sit in different sections.

Ellison remembered as a joy the public library for blacks that had been hastily organized in two large rooms of what had once been a pool hall. He first read Shaw and Maupassant in the home of a friend whose parents were teachers. As adolescents he and his friends told one another that they were going to be "Renaissance men." "We discussed mastering ourselves and everything in sight as though no such thing as racial discrimination existed." The first black graduate of Brown, Inman Page, was, in the last years of his career as an educator, principal of Ellison's high school.

Apart from the editor of the local black newspaper, Oklahoma City "starkly lacked" black writers. Ellison had been a delivery boy for several black newspapers that had nationwide distribution, but "on the level of conscious culture the Negro community was biased in the direction of music." Dr. Page's daughter was a leader of the music-in-the-schools movement that swept the nation in the 1920s. She also owned the town's one black theater and was responsible for its sophisticated repertory. "We were being introduced to one of the most precious of American freedoms, which is our freedom to broaden our personal culture by absorbing the cultures of others."

Black schoolchildren danced Irish reels and Scottish flings on their segregated playground; black Spanish-American War veterans taught them drills until dusk. Ellison credited his school's rigorous music program with teaching him the lifelong lesson of "artistic discipline." The school's teachers were conventional in their musical tastes, but jazz was inescapable as part of the social life of young black people. Ellison liked to point out that the Kansas City style had its origins among the jazzmen of Oklahoma City.

Ellison's use of his past to illustrate the workings of "cultural integration" reached beyond the wish to dress up a respectable but humble background. Ellison objected to ideas about black people that depended on a limited picture of what went on in the places blacks came from. He opposed the notion of black life as a "metaphysical condition" of "irremediable agony" because that made it seem as though the lives of blacks either took place in a vacuum or had only one theme. Ellison wanted to confound sociological categories. Consequently, the Tuskegee Institute, Booker T. Washington's citadel of accommodationism, was his prime example of how misleading the general impression of "American Negro culture" was.

At Tuskegee, where Ellison enrolled in 1933 to study music, his teacher, Hazel Harrison, let him handle manuscripts that Prokofiev had given her. There he was at the institution most associated with the bowing and scraping of vocational education, Ellison seemed to say, and yet he was being initiated into the mysteries of classical music. In *The Oregon Trail,* Francis Parkman expressed surprise at the French novels he found in a prairie cottage. Ellison answered that they didn't get there by magic and that as people moved about they became transmitters of culture, practitioners of cultural synthesis.

Ellison once rounded on Irving Howe for saying that he may have read great writers at Tuskegee, but at the same time he would not have been able to attend "the white man's school or movie house." To Ellison, this underplayed his freedom of choice and will.

> I rode freight trains to Macon County, Alabama, during the Scottsboro trial because I desired to study with the Negro conductor-composer William D. Dawson, who was, and probably still is, the greatest classical musician in that part of the country. I had no need to attend a white university when the master I wished to study with was available at Tuskegee. Besides, why should I have wished to attend the white state-controlled university where the works of the great writers might not have been so easily available?

Ellison also informed Howe that even though he had never attended a white school, he had taught at Northern white universities, just as Howe had done. Apparently he didn't ask whether Dawson, himself a Tuskegee graduate, could have

taught at white-controlled state schools, or even whether he would have wanted to. Ellison gave the impression that he, a scholarship student, could have followed Dawson anywhere.

He insisted that Tuskegee was a major musical center in the South in the 1930s. "It was to Tuskegee that the Metropolitan Opera groups came; it was to Tuskegee that the great string quartets and the Philharmonic came. It was not to the University of Alabama; it was not to white schools in this area, but to Tuskegee." But while he convinced himself that Tuskegee was one of the leaders in his field of study, he neglected to say that another black for whom Tuskegee represented the only chance to get a college education might have dreamed of going someplace else. What mattered to Ellison was that he may have been poor, orphaned, and segregated, but as a Negro he refused to see himself as deprived, a cultural outsider.

Ellison's stand about the contributions blacks had made to music as an American art, including the level of musicianship which the greatest exponents of jazz had attained, was the basis from which he judged the achievements of blacks in other forms of artistic expression.
—*Darryl Pinckney*

Ellison's stand about the contributions blacks had made to music as an American art, including the level of musicianship which the greatest exponents of jazz had attained, was the basis from which he judged the achievements of blacks in other forms of artistic expression. It was also why he expected blacks as artists to find freedom within their restricted circumstances. He was critical of those who wanted to dignify jazz's rough beginnings. Blacks knew too much about the hypocrisy of respectability, and as a youth he himself had seen more nobility in socially marginal musicians than he did in the professionals and businessmen he was urged to emulate. Ellison wanted to keep jazz's outlaw sources, but at the same time he said that the musicians he most admired were those who could jam in the roadhouses as well as read scores in the orchestra pits downtown.

He talked a great deal about things like craft, skill, and technique. No amount of emotion or raw power substituted for proper training. Black artists had to earn the mastery, a favorite Ellison word, that would let them extend any tradition they encountered. Hence his admiration for those jazzmen who were the equivalent of bilingual. Ellison spoke of black musicians as being like folk heroes, and their mastery was an example of how black artists could reclaim the debased images of folk culture, which meant something opposite to blacks from what it did to whites. Ellison agreed with the poet and critic Sterling Brown in his sense of the complexity of the folk roots of black culture, though Ellison was wary of the term "black culture" because to him it had racist overtones.

Part of what led Brown to write dialect poetry when it was considered a relic of Uncle Remus days was his contention that the psychology of the black had been erased by the minstrel images white people had imposed on him. Ellison goes further and characterizes America as "a land of masking jokers." The darkie entertainer of the minstrel tradition was, Ellison said, an exorcist, but the black-faced figure could not eradicate the country's spirit of unease, which was what led to the notion that the trickster, the smart man playing dumb in order to protect himself, is "primarily Negro." "Very often, however, the Negro's masking is motivated not so much by fear as by a profound rejection of the image created to usurp his identity." Ellison is as concerned as Brown with how folklore gets into literature, but if Brown concentrated on the psychological reality lost because of stereotyping, then Ellison wanted to add that black artists were conscious of folklore as a subversive tradition and were discriminating about standards. Folk culture was a source of stability as well as of inspiration.

He didn't falter when talking about music, but in his discussions of his literary education a frustrated Ellison emerges, which raises the question of how willful his interpretation of social reality was. At Tuskegee he and Albert Murray had talked of going to Harvard to study with "Dr. Kittredge." Ellison later conceded that he wasn't sure he could have hopped a freight to Harvard or what would have happened to him had he gotten there.

Ellison remembered the name of the grade school teacher— another cultural transmitter—who taught Negro history and from whom he'd learned about the writers of the New Negro Movement of the 1920s. They inspired pride, gave him a closer identification with poetry, excited him with the glamour of Harlem, and "it was good to know that there were Negro writers." But he also never forgot

> the humiliation of being taught in class in sociology at a Negro college that Negroes represented the "ladies of the races." This contention the Negro instructor passed blandly along to us without even bothering to wash his hands, much less his teeth. Well, I had no intention of being bound by any such humiliating definition of my relationship to literature.

At Tuskegee in 1935 Ellison read *The Waste Land* on his own, and this encounter with Modernism was a turning point. "I was much more under the spell of literature than I real-

ized at the time. *Wuthering Heights* had caused me an agony of unexpressible emotion, and the same was true of *Jude the Obscure,* but *The Waste Land* seized my mind." Its rhythms, he judged, were somehow closer to jazz than were those of Negro poets. *The Waste Land* and its footnotes began, he said, his conscious study of literature. He moved on to Pound, Ford Madox Ford. Sherwood Anderson, Gertrude Stein, Hemingway, and Fitzgerald. "Perhaps it was my good luck that they were not taught at Tuskegee."

2.

In his later essays, Ellison gives his departure from college a romantic gloss: Manhattan was his Paris and Harlem his Left Bank. In the summer of 1936 he went to New York, already aware of radical movements in politics and the arts. Ellison said that he had begun to write almost in secret, but he still thought of himself as a student "symphonist," or maybe a sculptor, while he worked odd jobs, such as being a waiter at the Harlem YMCA, hoping to earn the tuition for his senior year at Tuskegee. He never went back to college. The day after he arrived in Harlem Ellison met Langston Hughes on the street. He recognized Hughes from his photographs. Hughes took him to the Broadway play of *Tobacco Road,* and also arranged his introduction to Richard Wright.

In 1937 Wright invited the yearning Ellison to write a book review and then a short story for *New Challenge,* a magazine he was editing. It folded before Ellison's story could be published. Wright was then also working in the Harlem bureau of *The Daily Worker.* There Ellison read some of the stories that would go into *Uncle Tom's Children,* the collection that made Wright's name. "He guided me to Henry James's prefaces, to Conrad, to Joseph Warren Beach and to the letters of Dostoevsky." Then again Ellison also once said in an interview that he'd already read everything by the time he met Wright and had had to suppress his annoyance at Wright's assumption that he had not.

In 1937, when his mother became ill, he went to Ohio, where she was then living. There, with the help of one of Dayton's black lawyers, he began to devote himself seriously to writing. His mother died, and after three months of "ice and snow and homelessness," he abandoned an attempt at a novel. Back in New York he found work, with Wright's help, collecting Negro folklore for the Federal Writers' Project. He be became managing editor of *The Negro Quarterly* in 1942. It ceased publication after a year, and Ellison joined the merchant marine, which did not get in the way of his literary application. By War's end he had published a number of stories in such magazines as *Direction, Common Ground, Tomorrow,* and *The New Masses.*

The work in *Flying Home and Other Stories,* respectfully

edited by John F. Callahan, who has also served Ellison well as editor of the Modern Library edition of his *Collected Essays,* dates from this period. One of the thirteen stories was written in the 1950s, but is characters belong to a series from the 1940s. The story that opens the volume, **"A Party Down at the Square,"** is a first-person account given by a white boy from Cincinnati visiting his uncle in Alabama. He witnesses a lynching and simply relates what happens, how the crowd taunts the victim until a storm blows an airplane off course, how the crowd flees when falling wires electrocute some of the whites.

Ellison had read Wright's apocalyptic poem about a lynching. "Between the World and Me." Maybe Wright's passionate lyricism about tar and flame provoked Ellison to look at lynching through an innocent and therefore more effectively condemning observer. But **"A Party Down at the Square"** probably owes more to Faulkner's courthouse loafers and soused demobilized World War I pilots. Though one might expect to find in this collection of stories signs of Wright's influence or of Ellison's struggle to overcome it, there aren't any. Wright's intense and anguished early stories of rural blacks thrown into violent confrontation with whites are completely different from Ellison's low-key investigations of how racial situations affect an individual's perceptions. In later life Ellison would say that Wright's importance to him was intellectual, not literary. At most the work of both shows that Wright and Ellison belonged to the same social era.

Callahan has arranged Ellison's stories so that they follow the stages of a man's life. They are all about men and maybe that comes from Hemingway.

Ellison was young when he wrote them and life would have presented itself then as a series of solitary discoveries. But writing about young black characters also involved the theme that some day arbitrary limitations would be placed on them as social beings. Three stories, **"Mister Toussan," "Afternoon,"** and **"That I Had the Wings,"** for instance, depict two young black boys, Buster and Riley, at boisterous play, telling themselves tall stories about Toussaint L'Ouverture, cheering each other's baseball skills, trying to fashion parachutes for baby chicks. They don't know how dangerous it is for them to grow up with dreams of heroism. Because of their own experience the grandmothers and mothers are fearful for boys who are too bold and loud and too blatant about their wanting to be something, even if it's just a game.

By the time Ellison was publishing his first stories it was well established that left-wing publications offered black writers the chance to reach an audience. What now gets called folklorist was probably back then seen as having a *New Masses* aesthetic, the reversals that give victory to the common man, or thwart the usual expectations about how a social situation will be resolved. For instance the white man who comes up to the black janitor on the street turns out to be a union organizer, not a bigot. To white radical readers and editors these twists would have been taken as the higher truths of proletarian literature. To black writers and readers the surprises may have been enjoyed as occasions of social correction or downright payback.

Several of Ellison's stories have that *New Masses* feeling, among them **"Hymie's Bull"** and **"I Did Not Learn Their Names,"** stories in which he was able to draw on his experience of hopping freights. Their descriptive ease and tone of cool menace make them the best in the collection. They deal with a temporary or tentative fraternity among the down and out. Blacks and whites are made equal by the circumstance of being displaced. Riding on top of a boxcar, Hymie, "sick from some bad grub he'd bummed," is grabbed by a railroad cop who then beats him and attempts to throw him from the streaking train. In the ensuing struggle Hymie kills him with a knife. The narrator expresses satisfaction that Hymie manages to get away, even though black bums are the ones hauled off trains and made to pay the costs whenever a railroad cop goes missing. The narrator of **"I Did Not Learn Their Names,"** a student, waits for the elderly white couple he meets on a boxcar to act like white people. Instead they share their food and bits of their sad story. He keeps his distance, but finds himself thinking of them when not long afterward he is picked up in an Alabama railroad yard and put in jail.

The airplane still figured in American fiction as a common symbol of the romantic hope of the young for adventure, especially a poor boy's. Everywhere characters used to look up from slum doorways or cornfields and vow that they too would climb high. The title story has a downed, injured black airman embarrassed by the concern of the black farmer who has come to his aid. The airman is certain that the old man's attentions will compromise him further in the eyes of his white superiors, with whom he is already in trouble for wrecking his machine and for being a pilot who is black. He thought he'd escaped what the old farmer represented. But by the story's end their mutual understanding affords the only dignity he has.

"Flying Home" and an equally ambitious story, **"King of the Bingo Game,"** also first published in 1944, hint toward the voice Ellison was to find for *Invisible Man.* In both stories, narrative emphasis shifts from external detail to the point of view in the protagonist's head, an anxious concentration on the main character's being surrounded by uncomprehending, potentially hostile spectators. But both are apprentice work. The short story from wouldn't accommodate Ellison's need to describe experience as he had "seen and felt it," because he couldn't assume his readers would understand what he meant by the diversity of experience among blacks. His own consciousness had been formed by a multiplicity of sensations, from a love of observing the weather to listening to different styles among Negro preachers.

Neither the naturalism nor the straight realism of the short story suited his temperament. He wanted to extend realism somehow to find a way to include the chaos of life as it had passed before him. Soon after Ellison had completed these exercises he made his leap. Ellison began *Invisible Man* in 1945. Two years later a segment appeared in *Horizon* in a special issue on America. It would be another five years before the work was finished.

3.

Ellison had almost as much to say about *Invisible Man* as his critics did. In his preface for the thirtieth-anniversary edition he recalled that his novel's prologue came to him as a voice that interrupted the war novel he was writing about a black American pilot imprisoned in a German camp. Ellison respected message from that empire, the unconscious, and he described himself as being suddenly in the service of "a taunting, disembodied voice." His "spokesman for invisibility" would not be one of those protagonists in African-American fiction who were "without intellectual depth." He said he was trying to avoid writing what would amount to just another novel of racial protest instead of the "dramatic study in comparative humanity" that "any worthwhile novel should be."

Ellison in his preface said that he had associated his invisible man "ever so distantly" with the narrator of Dostoevsky's *Notes from Underground,* but the connection is clear. Golyadkin remembers trying to pick a fight with a six-foot-tall blond officer, who moved him to another spot and walked on. "I could have forgiven blows, but how could I forgive just being moved like that and being so completely ignored?" Golyadkin could not treat the officer as an equal even on the street. He stepped aside, "nothing but a fly before all that fine society."

Ellison's unnamed narrator recalls the night he bumped into a tall blond man who then uttered an insult. The narrator seized him and demanded an apology. The black man kept kicking and butting him until the white man went down. He was ready to slit his throat. "when it occurred to me that the man had not seen me, actually; that he, as far as he knew, was in the midst of a walking nightmare!" He is talking about the habit of whites not to notice blacks, not to differentiate among them. While Dostoevsky's narrator, speaking "from under the floor," inspired Ellison's metaphor of invisibility, it was the marginal urban philosopher himself who may have given Ellison confidence in the fluency of his narrator's hallucinations.

Dostoevsky's clerk is socially superfluous but well read. He says that the only external sensations available to him are in reading. Apart from his reading, he has nothing to respect in his surroundings. He mocks the romantic pretensions in Russian thinking at the time by identifying with them, by knowing all the fashionable phrases. Ellison's narrator has a similar relationship to the talismanic phrases of Negro uplift and education. In his search for Negro leadership he tries a variety of styles, and his dreams of success prove as false as Golyadkin's literary postures.

Invisibility, Ellison said, also sprang from the "great formlessness of Negro life" which produced personalities of "extreme complexity." This complexity explains why Ellison was enthralled by the narrative voice he had found. The narrator's sheer articulateness is his advantage over racial prejudice. It gives him the victory of the more profound understanding. The tragic face behind the comic mask that Ellison felt was so central to black folk culture was really intelligence, the black person's conscious refusal to accept any interpretations of reality other than his own.

Dostoevsky's example of a deracinated, educated character freed Ellison from the piety of the articulate black first-person narrators of earlier black fiction, who were resolutely middle-class. The anonymous narrator of James Weldon Johnson's novel *The Autobiography of an Ex-Colored Man* (1912) is a precursor of Ellison's invisible black man. His is also a story retold in isolation. Johnson's narrator remembers a series of disillusioning experiences as a young, aristocratic mulatto. But he looks back on his life as a black from the psychological prison of having chosen to pass for white. Ellison's narrator doesn't pass, but he disappears underground, in order to start talking. Ellison wanted to comment on the theme of upward mobility by having his character go down and "rise" by expressing his inward self while down, the "transformation from ranter to writer."

Ellison's narrator has made the journey from the rural South to the urban North often related in autobiographies by blacks. He recalls the experience in black politics that he survived before he went underground, from Southern paternalism at a Tuskegee-like college to radical agitation in a volatile Harlem. Crammed with incident, dense with metaphor and symbol, the novel is full of speech makers: black educators, left-wing organizers, a West Indian black nationalist. The invisible man himself makes speeches in his helpless progress from naive class orator performing, for his hometown big shots to embittered eulogist of a fellow political organizer in Harlem. When he is not wondering where he is or how he got there, someone is talking at him or around him, usually a working-class black man or black woman. How they talk and what they talk about from the "underground of American experience" that is Ellison's main subject.

They tell stories within the story. They are the carriers of the friendly down-home customs, playful ways of speaking, and relaxed attitudes about daily life that the invisible man thinks he must repudiate in order to advance. The sharecroppers, war veterans, bartenders, landladies, street vendors, and random pedestrians he meets from a chorus of folk values. They are "too obscure for learned classification, too silent for the most sensitive recorders of sound; of natures too ambiguous for the most ambiguous words." These transitory people "write no novels, histories or other books" and have no one to applaud the glamour of their language. But the unwritten history contained in their sayings and songs contradicts the political theories and sociological prejudices from which the narrator has been trying to forge his identity.

He can only appreciate these folk truths once he has broken with the Brotherhood, an organization much like the Communist Party. Ellison not only made room for so many recognizable social types in his narrator's odyssey, he also had a talent for rendering traits that were usually laughed at into something strange and threatening, like the suspicious black men in the narrator's rooming house who hold menial jobs but nevertheless dress fastidiously and observe a strict social code. Ellison is merciless in his portrayal of the cynicism of the Brotherhood's members. His narrator makes cuckolds of the leaders. Their women pine for black brutes. To all of them he is either a tool or an entertainer. They no more want him to think than they expect Paul Robeson to be able to act on stage.

He submits to the Brotherhood's discipline. "If I couldn't help them to see the reality of our lives I would help them to ignore it until it exploded in their faces." But the Brotherhood dupes him and abandons Harlem to black nationalist forces. Harlem erupts following a cop's shooting of an idealistic black organizer who, disgusted by his misplaced faith, had resorted to selling Sambo dolls on the street. At first the invisible man exults in the destruction as an action by the people that did not come from ideology. But the smashing and burning convince him that the Brotherhood was willing to sacrifice Harlem, that its new alliances in city politics meant that it welcomed the repression of blacks. He falls down a manhole and escapes.

He tells himself to stop running from the people in authority who had always had control over him and to run instead from "their confusion, impatience, and refusal to recognize the beautiful absurdity of their American identity and mine." After his surreal descent from politician to looter to someone hibernating and speaking "on the lower frequencies," the narrator, "hurt to the point of invisibility," wonders if maybe blacks didn't have to "affirm the principle on which the country was built, and not the men, or at least not the men who did the violence," or even to take responsibility "for

the men as well as the principle in order to find transcendence.

This message of enlightened endurance is unexpected because, apart from some gorgeous nostalgic passages about Southern settings early on, *Invisible Man* is grim in its scenery and paranoid in mood. The narrator reminisces as someone who has been taught to behave from the conviction that everyone he encounters is conspiring to do something to him. He is in command of the solitude of his hiding place, a hole in a basement that he has wired with 1,369 filament light bulbs. Perhaps the paranoia is fitting for a novel about blacks as a transplanted, unwelcomed people.

But Ellison's idea of the complexity and resilience of black folk also included the possibility that they were capable of a mournful patriotism in spite of everything that had gone wrong since Reconstruction. Ellison's narrator is more likely to speak of American society than of white society, because the plurality of the term, American, would indicate that he has a share in the national life, "the whole unhappy territory and all the things loved and unlovable in it." Though Ellison in his novel has contempt for white paternalism of any kind, the anti-communism of *Invisible Man* shows the change in the Party's image since the war. Ellison had praised *Native Son* as a philosophers book when it appeared in 1940. But as a novel of political ideas *Invisible Man* shows no sympathy for the radical alliances of the Depression that informed Wright's best-known work.

McCarthyism's power was increasing when *Invisible Man* was published in 1952. The same year *Partisan Review* declared that American artists were at last discovering enough on their own shores to sustain them. Langston Hughes was soon to face committee hearings; Richard Wright was in exile in Paris, ignored, he feared, by American critics. James Baldwin had attacked protest writing in *Partisan Review* in 1949, but he, like Chester Himes, was also living in Europe. Ellison, however, after a stint at the American Academy in Rome from 1955 to 1957, returned to America and stayed American—not bohemian, not queer, not married to a white woman, not a former Marxist, not a novelist of racial victimization.

In the immediate aftermath of World War II black writers like Wright, Himes, and Anne Petry had brought out works of protest, but not until the 1960s would there again be anything comparable to their aggressiveness in exposing the country's racial violence. Realism is always a vital force. It never goes out of date, providing one has a new subject. As the cold war took hold, the cultural moment, in fiction by blacks, seemed to belong to introspective coming-of-age novels, to Baldwin's *Go Tell It on the Mountain* (1953) or Paule Marshall's *Brown Girl, Brownstones* (1959). What sets the fabulism of *Invisible Man* apart from the realism of its time is the atmosphere it conveys of Ellison's having asked as much of the novel, stylistically, as he did of his subject matter.

Invisible Man gives a sense of Ellison's having patiently saved up a great stock of observation and ideas for the release of composition. Though some of the incidents in the novel were based on actual events, it is not a transcription of experience. It is clearly an invention, and its incidents are so fantastic that it can't remotely be read as a case study. Ellison had no interest in pretending that his book was like life, an expression perhaps of his Modernist disdain for journeyman realism. To judge from some "Working Notes" on the metaphor of invisibility, written around the time he began *Invisible Man,* he had higher aspirations for his novel.

His perfectionism counted for everything—in the meticulousness of the novel's conception, the confidence of its structural devices, and especially in the lavishness of its rhetorical displays. For a story about someone remembering his own spiritual fog, the narrator is precise in his language and perceptions, in his recall of so many idioms, as though they were reproduced by an ear trained for musical memory. Ellison's governing presence is never far from the frame of the narrator's personality, and the virtuosity of his narrative voice was central to Ellison's ambition. In Philip Rahv's historical view which split American literature into the two camps of paleface and redskin, Ellison would have wanted to be counted among the patricians of sensibility.

He was a paleface with a subject long dominated in his youth by redskins. A high literary finish was therefore the quality that would most distinguish Ellison's prose style from Wright's broad stream of speech. It's no scandal that Ellison might have wanted to produce a work free of or even superior to Wright's. When Ellison was at work on *Invisible Man,* Wright was the most famous black writer in the US, the first to enjoy the financial relief of a best-seller. In 1945 Ellison wrote a thoughtful review of *Black Boy* in which he tried to reconcile Wright's bleak picture of the South with his own idea of the black community as a place where the imaginative life is encouraged.

However, the same year, 1953, that Ellison spoke at the National Book Award ceremonies about *Invisible Man*'s significance being in its "experimental attitude," its presentation of "the rich diversity" of American "unburdened by the narrow naturalism" that had led to so much "unrelieved despair" in current fiction, Wright published an "existentialist" novel, *The Outsider,* to very mixed reviews. In a *Time* magazine article dismissible of the fears of totalitarianism in the US expressed in the novel, and suspicious of Wright's residency in France, Ellison is quoted as saying, "After all, my people have been here for a long time. It is a big wonderful country, and you can't just turn away from it because some people

decide it isn't your country." The *New Masses* feeling was obsolete.

Wright himself had been trying to find an alternative to the racial situations of his earlier fictions. *The Outsider* had its origins in a long story. "The Man Who Lived Underground," published in 1944 in an anthology, *Cross Section.* In this story about the nature of guilt, Wright combines naturalism with stream-of-consciousness techniques. It opens with a man, not immediately identified as black, eluding police by slipping down a manhole into a sewer. He'd been beaten into signing a confession for a murder he didn't commit. He becomes a phantom hunter-gatherer, eventually rigging his cave with electricity.

Holes in brick walls allow him to spy on the daily life of others. He gains access to a jewelry shop, which he robs. When out of curiosity he goes back to the jeweler's he observes the night watchman accused of the robbery kill himself after a brutal police interrogation. Driven by inchoate feelings he returns to the surface. He is unable to remember his name and his story isn't believed. He sounds like just another raving black man. The murder he was almost framed for has been solved, but the police decide not to risk that he had indeed witnessed their torture of the night watchman. He leads them to his manhole. "You've got to shoot his kind. They'd wreck things." Sewer waters carry the body off.

4.

Wright died in 1960. In the years that followed Ellison had occasion to reflect on his relation to Wright, especially when critics linked him with Baldwin as a black writer whose aestheticism had betrayed the social mission of black literature as exemplified by Wright. In response Ellison on invoked "the American Negro tradition" that abhors trading on one's anguish and teaches strategies of survival instead. A tenacious hold on the ideal of ultimate freedom, he contended, was as characteristic of blacks as the "hatred, fear, and vindictiveness" that Wright chose to give emphasis to. One wonders why Ellison assumed that holding on to ideals of freedom was separate from or contradictory to the fear and anger of the lives Wright investigated.

Ellison asserted his belief that "true novels," even the most pessimistic, arose from the compulsion to celebrate human life, that they were therefore "ritualistic and ceremonial at their core." Wright on the other hand, in Ellison's summary, believed in the novel as a weapon or an instrument of public relations. Wright, he said, was more of a problem for a young black writer like Baldwin than he was for him anyway. Wright was not the "father" in his way because they were too close in age. "I simply stepped around him." By 1940, he said, Wright had begun to view him as a rival and he had ceased to show Wright his work. Had he wanted to study a protest novel in the first place, Malraux's *Man's Fate* was superior to *Native Son* in his opinion.

> To me Wright as a writer was less interesting than the enigma he personified: that he could so dissociate himself from the complexity of his background while trying so hard to improve the condition of black men everywhere; that he could be so wonderful an example of human possibility but could not for ideological reasons depict a Negro as intelligent, as creative or dedicated as himself.

Bigger Thomas was intended as "a subhuman indictment of white oppression." Wright could imagine Bigger, Ellison said, but someone like Bigger could not imagine a black man like Richard Wright. Even if Ellison recoiled from the tabloid sources of Wright's plots, one wonders why Ellison overlooked how hard it is to make a simple person convincing on the page. Wright made Bigger uncertain in speech, but he did not leave him without powers of reflection.

Ellison illustrated through his articulate narrator the black presence in the country as a king of "pure" intelligence. It's as though he thought of the memories and feelings of blacks as being like signals not detected by others by which certain people recognize one another. But what Wright made intelligible through Bigger was the inner state of someone unseen, even by himself, because of his caste. Wright broke psychological and physical taboos in his portrayal of how race affected human relations. In some ways as a popular writer he was more innovative than Ellison, a "custodian of the American language," as he called himself.

Wright had told Ellison in Paris that after his rupture with the Communists he had no place else to go. To Ellison Wright's main problem was that Marxism closed off to him the world of black folk because it had made him so negative about it. He claimed that Wright didn't understand the "catharsis of tears," the release of shouting in church, and that because Wright didn't know anything about jazz, he was not in full possession of African-American culture.

Ellison said his goal in *Invisible Man* had been "to transcend, as the blues transcend the painful conditions with which they deal." Perhaps that was why he sometimes seemed to be talking about his book as though it were a trickster tale, whose blameless narrator's voice, for all his forthrightness, was a clever means of making his "truths" palatable, of sneaking them up on readers without setting off racial radar. When he maintained that the motives behind his own writing were "by no means racial" and that he had resolved not to succumb to "the deadly and hypnotic temptation to interpret the world and all its devices in terms of race," he was looking at black life as a kind of inexhaustible, abiding reserve that would make the fictions that could

capture its essence immune to changes in social mood. "Novels are time-haunted. Novels achieve timelessness through time."

Folklore, as Ellison discussed it, was above politics; it existed in nature, like a river that never stopped flowing, but was different from the idealized ruralism white writers had invested with conservative social values, from the plantation tradition of the 1830s to Agrarianism. Yet it's not always clear what Ellison meant by folklore: a recognizable style in the arts in some cases, in others an art form in itself. Most often he seemed to classify it as the "rich oral literature" that had been a part of the cultural climate of his upbringing. Folklore provided "the first drawings of a group's experiences" but these drawings were usually "crude." The feeling found in churches, school-yards, barbershops, and cotton-picking camps was a resource that was waiting until, in his explanation. Dostoevsky and Joyce taught him that he, too, could make it the stuff of literature. To Wright, however, folklore was the back-water hell he had fled.

Regardless of their different attitudes to folk culture, Wright and Ellison were both products of their reading, as Ellison tirelessly pointed out. And they read the same things, as he noted less often. Writings by blacks from the nineteenth century were unavailable to them in their youth in a way that is inconceivable now. Perhaps very little of it would have satisfied their standards. It is very moving that they shared a passion for the weird English of the Constance Garnett translations, that circulated widely in the US beginning in the 1920s. For both, nineteenth-century Russian literature, with its drifting urban characters, tied-down serfs, and worries about Westernization, was an alternative literary past. Their own common themes had antecedents in a literature that did not require the filtering out or the explaining away of how blacks were depicted.

Still, Ellison reacted very strongly to the way blacks were portrayed in American literature. Over the years he returned to the same great writers in essay after essay, refining his judgments, redefining his relation to them. He was especially drawn to ponder the examples of Twain and Hemingway. Ellison cherished *Huckleberry Finn* because Twain had allowed the runaway slave to stand with all his ambiguity as a universal symbol of Man. But what Twain achieved in the character of Jim and his friendship with Huck signaled, for Ellison, a missed opportunity. He lamented the disappearance, beginning in the twentieth century, of "the human Negro" from American fiction. Writers of the Lost Generation were only interested in their personal freedom, which made their cries of alienation a "swindle." Hemingway was more concerned with "technical perfection" than with "moral insight." Ellison also criticized Hemingway for wanting to excise the anti-slavery theme from *Huckleberry Finn,* thus reducing it to a boy's story.

Ellison took personally the overall absence of blacks in Hemingway's American reality. It is easy to imagine the effect Hemingway had on Ellison when he first read his stories in *Esquire* in an Alabama barbershop or when he hiked through the Ohio winter to get the New York newspapers with the dispatches Hemingway sent from Republican Spain. Ellison said Hemingway's struggle with form made him "a cultural hero," but he also probably identified with the trout fishing or with Nick Adams remembering the face the undertaker had put on his father. Also, Hemingway had become famous while still in his twenties.

In time Ellison forgave Twain's heir by looking beyond Hemingway's bias, he said, in order to appreciate the truths revealed by his art. He proclaimed that Hemingway had been "the true father-as-artist" of aspiring writers of the 1930s. Ellison no longer accused Hemingway of moral diffidence. Ellison also said that he learned to lead a bird from reading Hemingway and as a result was able to feed himself and his brother by hunting in the Ohio woods.

No doubt Twain and Hemingway appealed to Ellison as writers of masculine adventures. The work of these redskins also represented to him the literary arrival of the American vernacular, just the sort of contribution he hoped to make to American literature, if in paleface terms. Ellison's sense of what literature was, like Wright's, came mostly from white European and white American writers, who seemed to set the standards because their work survived fashion. Both had grown up in the days when black literature was regarded as necessarily inferior, still in its "infancy," which was why they were determined to rescue those white writers whom they admired. Wright once worried about his fondness for Gertrude Stein's *Three Lives* after reading an article that condemned her as decadent. He gathered a group of black stockyard workers together in a Chicago Black Belt basement and read "Melanctha" to them. They laughed, stomped, and howled, he said. "They understood every word."

Poor frivolous, forgotten Harlem Renaissance. Hughes was very much around when Wright and Ellison were starting out, but they were ambivalent about his work. One would think both would have been more sympathetic to a literary movement among blacks that had as a driving force the wish to assimilate some of the developments of Modernism. But just as blacks tend to look at the political and social advances of the generation before them as being partial, incremental, so, too, the literature of a previous generation seems to require completion. As such, books by blacks from an earlier era were treated as raw material—somewhat like folklore, in Ellison's case. He had criticized William Attaway's novel about the migrating folk, *Blood on the Forge* (1941), for being too despairing, as if to say the ingredients were there but Attaway had got it wrong and the subject needed the corrective of Ellison's more forgiving optimism.

A biography of Ellison may one day tell us whether or not he read James Weldon Johnson or Claude McKay, with their bookish main characters inhibited by their education and trying to get back to their roots. Ellison's invisible man does pretty much the same, deciding to breathe the stench and sweetness of Louis Armstrong's Old Bad Air.

It would have been Jim Crow thinking. Ellison said, for him to model himself only on other black writers. He was adamant about the distinction between his literary "ancestors"—Melville, Twain, Crane, Hemingway. Faulkner—and his literary "relatives"—Hughes, Wright, Baldwin. There still is a tendency among black writers to compete with one another, as if only one of them could be left standing by the chair marked Black Writer, in the way that many women writers really compete with other women writers, not with men. What at first glance looks like snobbery on Ellison's part was perhaps an attempt to withdraw from that kind of competition, to try instead to occupy one of the chairs marked, simply, Writer, (Interestingly enough, both Wright and Ellison wrote scenes in which blacks are manipulated into boxing for the amusement of a white audience.) Nevertheless, everything Ellison did not want to be mistaken for made him fetishistic in his attitude toward tradition. Some Jim Crow thinking seeped into Ellison's resentment of Wright's shadow, as though having to define himself against a black writer were not as literary as Henry James marking his departure from another New Englander, Hawthorne.

Invisible Man came out roughly in the middle of Ellison's life, dividing his biography, and, just as a prism bends light, giving to his contemplations after 1952 a meaning altogether different from the quests of his apprenticeship. The longer he worked at his second novel, the more his identity as a writer was invested in his first novel's reputation. His later essays defend his slowness and the mastery implicit in his taking his time. Ellison wrote superbly about Mark Twain or Stephen Crane, but he was also prone to windy meditations on the novel as an abstract form. Someone unafraid of titles such as "The Novel as a Function of American Democracy" is gripping a top branch in the Tree of Seriousness.

Perhaps Ellison's fortress tone had something to do with his being largely self-educated. The cultural climate in which it was customary to wonder about black's educational or intellectual preparation may be why one can sometimes sense in Ellison's saturation in the New Criticism, in his devotion to speculations about form, symbol, and myth, a determination to show that a black writer could be terrifically thoughtful about what he was up to that he could respond to Kenneth Burke or hold his own against Trilling. It was also a way for him, as a black, to participate in American culture. Moreover, literature was the god that had not failed. Consequently, Ellison stood by the black writer's right not to be a spokesman, a leader. The only mention of Du Bois in his essays is a suggestion that one ought to ask why Du Bois failed to become as powerful a politician as Booker T. Washington and that if Du Bois was not as good a sociologist as Max Weber one ought to say so. Maybe he meant that Du Bois had tried to be too many things. Ellison said he believed that black people recognized a division of labor in the struggle, that his being the best novelist he could be was his contribution to that struggle, and that this effort required that he resist distractions and reductive thinking. He made a distinction between art and politics, as in his criticism of Robert Lowell for declining an invitation to the White House in 1965 as a protest against US involvement in Vietnam. Ellison had accepted the invitation, saying the evening had been about art, not politics.

Ellison's Americanism was like his pride in his literary pedigree: it seemed proof of his independence of mind as a black. His strict attention in public to literary matters was also a way of resisting other people's ideas about how to be "a good Negro," even though, traditionally, it was the angry black who was urged to be good. He said that he found it less painful to move to the back of a bus than to "tolerate concepts which distorted the actual reality of my situation or my reactions to it."

Modernism was the great universalizer, which was what Ellison was responding to when he read *The Waste Land* all alone down there in Tuskegee. It crossed national and linguistic boundaries. Why not the color line? As liberating as Modernism was, the cost for the doctrine of newness was the culture of forced originality that haunts us still. With Ellison the burden translated into regarding his work as a culmination, an indisputable summing up. Often a writer can't repeat the inspiration of his or her first book, but it is unusual when that work is of the order of *Invisible Man.* What came after *Ulysses*? The saying that a first novel is never finished, merely abandoned, does not apply to Ellison. Something like the opposite happened. He finished *Invisible Man* and that monument to literary longings held him hostage for the rest of his dignified life.

Karl Miller (review date 25 July 1997)

SOURCE: "Notes of a Native Son," in *Times Literary Supplement,* July 25, 1997, p. 22.

[*In the following review, Miller provides a positive assessment of* Flying Home and Other Stories.]

Ralph Ellison's celebrated novel *Invisible Man,* seven years in the making, appeared in 1952. It is an American Gothic delirium. Writing about it in such terms, a few years later, in his great book of the 1960s, *Love and Death in the Ameri-*

can Novel, Leslie Fiedler saw a method in the "madness" he took it to contain. The reason why this madness carried conviction was that "the Negro problem in the United States" was "a gothic horror of our daily lives".

The old-fashioned apartheid expression, "the Negro problem", should not prevent one from accepting that the novel's first-person narrator is an incarnation of the problem which America's Negroes have had to live with. Their very name has been a problem, and has been subject to change. What has been done to them can become the question of who they are. The narrator's identity is projected in the novel as uncertain, phantasmagoric. And his invisibility is as phantasmagoric as his identity. The vivid black people who figure in it are, in one way, far from uncertain; nor, in that way, is the narrator. But Ellison is pledged to these ideas. And if it isn't always clear, in the more discursive passages of the book, what he means by them, that can in part be construed as almost certainly part of its point.

As with other fictional accounts of the sufferings of American blacks, there is a problem here for any reader who cares about these sufferings. The historical realities that enter *Invisible Man* are likely to seem as grievous to such a reader as *Beloved*'s scarred back is to the reader of Toni Morrison's novel, and there are times when the anxiety they provoke can almost appear to distract attention from what Ellison is writing. The American magazine *Commentary* recently praised a black American's "very American sense of right and wrong". Those compatriots who tortured and exploited their black underclass for generations may be presumed to have been deficient in that sense, and they are commemorated in the reading difficulty of a kind which some parts of Ellison's novel can present. One aspect of this difficulty, of this anxiety, is a longing for the novel to succeed. In a letter of his youth, to Richard Wright, Ellison exclaimed: "Workers of the World Must Write!!!!" Ellison wrote, and wrote well, about matters which had to be treated, which must sometimes have seemed almost impossible to treat, and which can make for hard reading of the kind referred to. All honour to him.

There is death in the novel, and love. The narrator says in due course that despite his hate and bitterness he is able to affirm, to say yes as well as no. He has been "hurt to the point of abysmal pain, hurt to the point of invisibility". But "in order to get some of it down I *have* to love". Ralph Waldo Ellison affirms America, at times. "American is better than both, son", better than brown or white, advises a small boy's father in one of the stories in *Flying Home.* The narrator's enemies and manipulators in the novel, of both colours, who include a quivering, self-pitying white liberal by the name of Emerson, are said in Existentialist style to have refused to recognize "the beautiful absurdity of their American identity and mine".

Flying Home is a selection of the early stories, some of them discovered by John F. Callahan in a drawer after Ellison's death in 1994. There are thirteen of them, written between 1937 and 1954. **"Hymie's Bull",** possibly his first, describes the murder of a murderous guard by a freight-hopping hobo—Ellison rode the boxcars himself on his journey south from Oklahoma to the Tuskegee Institute for black students. During the war, service in the Merchant Marine took him to Wales, and there's a story in which the narrator receives a welcome in the valleys and joins in the singing, having been beaten up by some white fellow Americans on the way. The stories are offered as the best of Ellison's published and unpublished "free-standing" short fictions; material associated with the work-in-progress towards a second novel which was to occupy him over the years until his death is excluded. While charged with interest for its admirers, they are stylistically distinguishable from *Invisible Man.* In the novel, there is a Melville presence. In the stories, Hemingway hovers, not least in the one that starts the book. Editorially titled **"A Party Down at the Square",** this is a story about a lynching.

It has in it both Hemingway and Huckleberry Finn. "I was sick, and tired, and weak, and cold." This is not the voice of the black man who is about to be burned to death, before an enthusiastic crowd of moralists, one cyclonic Southern night. It is that of the boy from Cincinnati who witnesses the incineration. The Twain irony whereby Huck helps Jim while thinking it wrong to do so is perceptible here in the narrative of someone who has yet to learn that lynching people is wrong: in one sense, an unreliable narrator, but a narrator who gets it all down with a shocking immediacy that can make it difficult to attend to the literature, so to speak, of this well-crafted story.

Flight is a dominant concern throughout. Two country boys chat about flying away from African cannibals intent on sticking spears in their behinds, and attempt to teach a chicken to fly. Elsewhere, in a story set during the Second World War, a black man learns to fly, and flies into turbulence. The pilot is a young man for whom the thought of flight has brought a lump to the throat. But there is more to this than the "lonely impulse of delight" pursued by Yeats's poetic Irish airman. Upward mobility is found to have more than one face. When he hits a buzzard in mid-air and crashes, he is looked after by an old Negro "peasant", who angers the injured pilot, but protects him from a malicious redneck. When the old man asks the pilot why he wants to fly, he thinks to himself; "Because it's the most meaningful act in the world. . . ." Yeatsian enough, perhaps. But there's another reason which occurs to him: "because it makes me less like you". What he actually says is: "It's as good a way to fight and die as I know." But, continues the peasant, "how long you think before they gonna let you all fight?" By the end, the flyer has been brought down to earth, but is uplifted too,

by feeling that he is like the old man and his boy, after all. The story belongs to a time when black pilots talked as other people did about "the enemy", as if in their case there was only the one.

"A Coupla Scalped Indians", perhaps the most memorable item, shows the narrator and a friend, two youths recently circumcised, descending through woods towards a carnival. A *son du cor* floats up towards them in the depths of the woods (Ellison played the cornet in his youth and went to Tuskegee to study composition). The narrator then encounters a wise woman of the neighbourhood, Aunt Mackie, a talker with spirits, who is unusual among literature's wise women in being game for a cuddle. A fierce dog barks in her yard. The woman is as young as she is old. The narrator's bandaged condition joins with Aunt Mackie's strange kiss, with her "smooth body and wrinkled face", to produce the magic appropriate to a rite of passage. Summoned by its horns, he moves off, an older man, in the direction of the fairground, wondering what can have happened to his friend.

FURTHER READING

Bibliography

Nadel, Alan. *Invisible Criticism: Ralph Ellison and the American Canon.* Iowa City: University of Iowa Press, 1988, 181 p.
   Full-length bibliography.

Biography

Callahan, John F. "Frequencies of Memory: A Eulogy for Ralph Waldo Ellison (March 1, 1914—April 16, 1994)." *Callaloo* 18, No. 2 (Spring 1995): 298-309.
   An expanded version of a eulogy delivered at Ellison's funeral on April 19, 1994.

Cannon, Steve. "Reminiscin' in C: Remembering Ralph Waldo Ellison." *Callaloo* 18, No. 2 (Spring 1995): 288-91.
   Cannon reminisces about his experience with Ellison and his perceptions of the author's works.

Forrest, Leon. "Ralph Ellison Remembered." *Callaloo* 18, No. 2 (Spring 1995): 280-82.
   Writer and educator Forrest remarks on various aspects of Ellison's life.

Stern, Richard. "Ralph Ellison." *Callaloo* 18, No. 2 (Spring 1995): 284-87.
   Stern recalls his acquaintance and experience with Ellison.

Criticism

O'Meally, Robert G. "On Burke and the Vernacular: Ralph Ellison's Boomerang of History." In *History and Memory in African-American Culture,* edited by O'Meally and Geneviève Fabre, pp. 244-60. New York: Oxford University Press, 1994.

　　Explores Ellison's approach to history and links that approach to Kenneth Burke's notion that history is "the flow of experience or even 'the world.'"

Scott, Nathan A., Jr. "Ellison's Vision of *Communitas*." *Callaloo* 18, No. 2 (Spring 1995): 310-18.

　　Essay in which Scott examines Ellison's treatment of the concept of community, or *communitas,* in his novel and essays.

Additional coverage of Ellison's life and career is contained in the following sources published by Gale: *Authors and Artists for Young Adults,* **Vol. 19;** *Black Literature Criticism*; *Black Writers,* **Vol. 1;** *Concise Dictionary of American Literary Biography,* **1941-1968;** *Contemporary Authors,* **Vols. 9-12R, and 145;** *Contemporary Authors New Revision Series,* **Vols. 24, and 53;** *DISCovering Authors*; *DISCovering Authors: British*; *DISCovering Authors: Canadian*; *DISCovering Authors Modules: Most-Studied,* *Multicultural,* **and** *Novelists*; *Major Twentieth-Century Writers, Second Edition*; *Dictionary of Literary Biography,* **Vols. 2, and 76;** *Dictionary of Literary Biography Yearbook,* **1994;** *Short Story Criticism,* **Vol. 26; and** *World Literature Criticism.*

June Jordan
1936-

American poet, novelist, essayist, playwright, critic, biographer, and author of children's books.

The following entry provides an overview of Jordan's career through 1998. For further information on her life and works, see *CLC*, Volumes 5, 11, and 23.

INTRODUCTION

Although best known as a poet, June Jordan has published a substantial number of children's works, novels, essays, and plays. Jordan's works explore the African-American experience in America, focusing on a wide range of topics including conflicts in Nicaragua and Africa, and more personal issues of love and self-awareness. Critics have praised Jordan for uniting in poetic form the personal, everyday struggle and political oppression of African Americans.

Biographical Information

Jordan was born in 1936 in Harlem, the only child of immigrants from Jamaica. When she was five, the family moved to the Bedford-Stuyvesant area of Brooklyn. Jordan's father, a post-office clerk, introduced her to poetry, from the Scriptures to the writings of African-American poet Paul Laurence Dunbar, and her mother, a nurse, provided an example of community service. Jordan's parents jeopardized their daughter's developing sense of identity, however, with harsh treatment—beatings from her father, and her mother's failure to intervene—and by opposing Jordan's ambition to become a poet. Coming to terms with her parents and her childhood became a major biographical theme in Jordan's writing. For a year, Jordan was the only African-American student in the high school she attended; she then spent three years at the Northfield School for Girls in Massachusetts before entering Barnard College in 1953. At Barnard she met Michael Meyer, a white student at Columbia University, and they were married in 1955. The marriage ended in divorce in 1965, but the couple's child, Christopher David Meyer, provided another biographical theme in Jordan's writing: motherhood and, by extension, nurturing for the broader African-American community. Her first book, *Who Look at Me* (1969), was dedicated to Christopher, as was her autobiographical essay collection *Civil Wars* (1981). Jordan has also enjoyed a distinguished university teaching career, including positions at the State University of New York at Stony Brook and the University of California-Berkeley.

Major Works

Who Look at Me is a long poem that turns on the image of eye contact between the races to treat the history of African Americans in a prejudiced white America. Twenty-seven paintings of African Americans from Colonial days to the present complement the poem and reinforce the theme of looking at others as individuals rather than stereotypes. In her first poetry collection, *Some Changes* (1971), Jordan explored her efforts to find her poetic voice despite her troubled relationship with her parents. While continuing to address the African-American experience, she elucidated her artistic ideals, appealing for a revision of the literary canon that would incorporate African-American writers and writing on social consciousness. *His Own Where* (1971) is a novel for teens in which a young man and woman make themselves a place to live in the midst of urban ruin. This book is noteworthy in part for Jordan's use of Black English, which she fervently espouses and promotes through her work. Jordan's second poetry collection, *New Days* (1974), deals with the civil rights movement and returns to the poet's evolving perception of her mother, for whom she had found a kind of surrogate in Mrs. Fannie Lou Hamer during trips to Mississippi in 1969 and 1971. A poem in the collection is addressed to Hamer, who is also the subject of a 1972 biography for young readers. A major collection, *Things That I Do in the Dark* (1977), contains poems from earlier works as well as pieces never previously published. The essays collected in *Civil Wars* are a good source of information on Jordan's life, thought, and development as a writer. Jordan's books for children and young adults include, in addition to *His Own Where* and *Fannie Lou Hamer* (1972), the novels *New Life, New Room* (1975) and *Kimako's Story* (1981). In *Naming Our Destiny* (1994) Jordan achieves unity between her lyrical poetic voice and the political voice of her essays. She uses a variety of voices and personas to convey her investigation of the "we/us" versus "they/them" rhetoric which she sees as central to the divisiveness of American culture.

Critical Reception

Susan McHenry in *Nation* remarked that "Jordan's characteristic stance is combative. She is exhilarated by a good fight, by taking on her antagonists against the odds." This commitment to urgent political issues, this need to, as Matthew Rothschild put it, "make America live up to its promise," is combined with a concern for the quotidian. This is reflected in a style which is "oratorical," inviting comparisons, from critic David Baker, to Carl Sandburg and the blues, as Jordan "makes public art out of public occasion." An avoidance of the scholarly and academic veins of discourse is one of her strengths. She may deal with weighty political and social issues like race, gender, and social justice but she does so with imagery and language taken from the world readers recognize, using situations with which readers are familiar. The ideas are delivered, Dorothy Abbott believes, by a "politically grounded writer," with a "lyric precision and a beautiful sense of celebration." This praise is corroborated by several critics, like Honor Moore who commented in *Ms.* that Jordan "never sacrifices poetry for politics," and that the details of her craft are "inseparable from political statement." In terms of literary community and intellectual trends, P. Jane Splawn places Jordan in the category of "New World consciousness," an aesthetic and sensibility traceable to Walt Whitman and postcolonial thinker and activist Frantz Fanon, and which is characterized by a heterogeneous, pluralistic, and democratic spirit.

PRINCIPAL WORKS

Who Look at Me (poetry) 1969
Soulscript: Afro-American Poetry [editor] (poetry) 1970
The Voice of the Children [editor] (poetry) 1970
Some Changes (poetry) 1971
His Own Where (juvenile novel) 1971
Dry Victories (juvenile novel) 1972
Fannie Lou Hamer (biography) 1972

New Days: Poems of Exile and Return (poetry) 1974
New Life, New Room (novel) 1975
Things that I Do in the Dark (poetry) 1977
In the Spirit of the Sojourner (drama) 1979
Passion: New Poems (poetry) 1980
For the Arrow that Flies by Day (drama) 1981
Civil Wars (essays) 1981
Kimako's Story (juvenile) 1981
Naming Our Destiny: New and Selected Poems (poetry) 1989
Technical Difficulties (essays) 1992
Haruko/Love Poems (poetry) 1994

CRITICISM

James A. Emanuel (review date 16 November 1969)

SOURCE: A review of *Who Look at Me,* in *The New York Times Book Review,* November 16, 1969, p. 52.

[*In the following review, Emanuel acquaints the reader with the theme and voice in Jordan's first collection of poetry.*]

Opposite the title page of **Who Look at Me** is a painting simply entitled "Portrait of a Gentleman." The gentleman is black. June Jordan's book suggests all black Americans are as unknown as the anonymous early 19th-century artist and his subject.

"We do not see those we do not know," she writes. "Love and all varieties of happy concern depend on the discovery of one's self in another. The question of every desiring heart is, thus, 'Who Look at Me?' In a nation suffering fierce hatred, the question—race to race, man to man, and child to child—remains: 'Who Look at Me?' *We answer with our lives.* Let the human eye begin unlimited embrace of human life."

By intermixing 27 paintings of black Americans from colonial times to the present with an original, understated but intense poem that comments indirectly on the paintings and enhances their meaning, she has given children a splendid opportunity to "begin unlimited embrace of human life."

Her text begins with a question: "Who would paint a people black or white?" The implied answer is that centuries of derogatory generalizations about Negroes have done precisely that. Consequently **Who Look at Me** displays paintings of black people in all their human and historical variety: slave, revolutionary, sailor, lover, artist, civil rights marcher.

The accompanying poem reveals its unity through repeated words, and themes and records with psychological deftness the evolution of the black man's racial pride. In it Miss Jordan says pithily to whites, "To begin is no more agony than opening your hand." She cautions them "I am black alive and looking back at you." Her black man is the seed that "disturbed a continent," the truth-teller saying "NO / to a carnival run by freaks." Having survived "the crazy killing scorn" of his oppressors in "a hungerland / of great prosperity," he sees America as "the shamescape" and "that lunatic that lovely land / that graveyard," where he dies ritualistically. And this grim vision is supported by a final reminder:

> "I trust you will remember how we tried to love
> above the pocket deadly need to please
> and how so many of us died there
> on our knees."

Each picture is worth framing, and each section of poetry has lines that we must remember.

Melba Joyce Boyd (review date Summer and Winter 1981)

SOURCE: "The Whitman Awakening in June Jordan's Poetry," in *Obsidian,* Nos. 2 & 3, Summer and Winter, 1981, pp. 226-28.

[*In the following review, Boyd discusses the influence of Whitman evident in Jordan's* Passion.]

In the preface of June Jordan's latest book of poetry, *Passion,* the poet acclaims Walt Whitman as the Great White Father of American poetry. She explains she has most recently realized his significance because during her academic preparation, Whitman was overlooked and obscured by the establishment literati of eastern universities. I suppose this is possibly true of some educational experiences, but it's difficult to imagine.

At any rate, this revelation about Whitman has sharply altered Jordan's cultural acceptance of progressive White American poetry. She says, "What Whitman envisioned we, the people and the poets of the New World, embody. He has been punished for the political meaning of his vision. We are being punished for the moral questions that our very lives provoke."

June Jordan was a poet of the sixties, or the Black Arts Movement—Renaissance II. These writers were strong nationalists who were sometimes too quick to categorically dismiss English and American writers into a ruble of racist reactionaries who articulated the insensitive values and attitudes of a repressive ruling culture. This active resistance to prevent the europeanization of her art was a necessary divorce from the dominant culture, incorporating their rhythms, and their tones in the expressions of pain, joy and frustration. But many of those Black writers totally succumbed to this artistic separation, and are still beleaguering a cultural position that produces inflated images and flat, predictable language confined to the limited dimensions of the obvious and the overstated.

Jordan has taken the initiative to identify the restrictions of the reactions of the cultural separatists, and thereby re-examines the validity of those White American writers who have contributed to New World poetry and sung from the true democratic spirit that is particularly American in character and style. By resurrecting Whitman, Jordan hopes to identify him as a thematic constituency of Black American Literature and thereby justify her acceptance of him. Such a stance may not be readily approved by her peers. However, in support of her move, let me remind the Nationalists that the poetic voice of Whitman was the voice of the Abolitionists, and the New Marxists should review Whitman as a working class writer in touch with reality and humane ideals.

But, I'm not sure *Passion* is the best title for the poems. The motion and meaning of the poetry do not always swing deep enough for a passionate encounter. Rather, they are often too direct, too pointed and too typical of the propagandistic personality of Black poetry of the sixties. The lines are too familiar and they collapse on the ear. And unlike Whitman, her vision is often circumvented by anger and impatience. In **"Poem About Police Violence,"** she writes:

> Tell me something
> what you think would happen if
> everytime they kill a black boy
> then we kill a cop
> everytime they kill a black man
> then we kill a cop
>
> you think the accident rate would lower
> subsequently?

One of the interesting aspects of Jordan's poetry is that she writes in both Standard English and Black dialect. She writes in the language of the people and still takes advantage of the flexible linguistic structure of the standard. When the speed of thought and the intensity of emotion increases, she drops the "do" and the weight and emphasis of the statement fall on __. But passion is the thrust of the book, and at peak moments, the love poetry is breathtaking.

> You said, "In Morocco they make
> deliberate mistakes."

Next to you I do nothing
to perfect my safety

How should I dispel
the soul of such agile excitation?

(from **"Night Letters"**)

Her use of oblique rhyme ("mistakes" and "safety") and the interplay of fricatives, plosives, and sibilants create a soft tone that generates feeling of the poem. When Jordan sustains this rounded perspective in her political poems, it insulates and expands the themes.

I am a woman searching for her savagery
even if it's doomed
Where are the Indians?

In **"Poem for Nana,"** Jordan lifts the raw history of America and searches for some truth hidden in the unwritten. She fondles a few lines with Native American imagery and makes you feel the spirit of our ancestors who died on the Trail of Tears.

the people of the sacred trees
and rivers precious to the stars that told
old stories to the night

"Poem About My Rights" is probably the most passionate poem in the book. She leaves nothing out.

as I need to be
alone because I can't do what I want to do with my
own body and
who in the hell set things up
like this

She traces the outrage of racism and sexism by connecting rape and apartheid to legal definitions that defend these injustices perpetrated by political and economic control.

I am the history of rape
I am the history of the rejection of who I am
I am the history of the terrorized incarceration of
my self

This poem moves with incisive rhythm and intricate interplay of metaphors and absurdities that are appropriate to reality. The poem is inspired by her anger, but the energy enraptures the images and compounds the meaning. When Jordan writes like this, we can feel her tearing open wounds. Such a voice is so valuable when most White American poetry has retreated to the obscurity of confessional kvetch (insensitive suspension); and when most Black American poetry is a faint call caught in a quagmire of self adoration (victim poems). Meanwhile, the world is shrinking and so is the time and space we're living in.

When June Jordan begins from a personal base and then intertwines the complexities and despair of human frustration and dilemma, her writing carries a stronger sense of identity and purpose. This is when she is attuned to the New World voices, not just the Black ones, or the Brown ones or the inbetween ones. Unlike those words nurtured in the skull of a disembodied history, these powers echo Whitman and the earth and sky that gives art life.

Marilyn Hacker (review date 29 January 1990)

SOURCE: "Provoking Engagement," in *The Nation,* Vol. 250, No. 4, January 29, 1990, pp. 135-39.

[*In the following review, Hacker surveys the themes and techniques in Jordan's* Selected Poems *and evaluates some of the poet's positions and propositions.*]

June Jordan's new book [*Naming Our Destiny: New and Selected Poems*] is an anthology of causes won, lost, moot, private and public, forgotten and remembered. Anyone who doubts the relevance and timeliness of poetry ought to read Jordan, who has been among the front-line correspondents for almost thirty years and is still a young and vital writer. So should anyone who wants his or her curiosity and indignation aroused, or wants to read a voice that makes itself heard on the page.

There are as many kinds of poetry as there are novels and plays. But some critics, who would not fault a novel of social protest for failing to be a novel of manners or a *nouveau roman,* seem to want all poetry to fit one mold. June Jordan epitomizes a particular kind and strength of American poetry: that of the politically engaged poet whose commitment is as seamlessly joined to her work as it is to her life.

> **Jordan's poems are strongest when they deal with interior issues, when she begins with a politics of the personal, with the articulate and colloquial voice of, if you will, "a woman speaking to women" (and to men) and ranges outward to illustrate how issues, lives and themes are inextricably interconnected.**
> **—*Marilyn Hacker***

What makes politically engaged poetry unique, and primarily poetry before it is politics? Jordan's political poetry is, at its best, the opposite of polemic. It is not written with a preconceived, predigested agenda of ideas and images. Rather, the process of composition is, or reproduces, the process of discovering how events are connected, how oppressions are analogous, how lives interpenetrate. Jordan's poems are strongest when they deal with interior issues, when she begins with a politics of the personal, with the articulate and colloquial voice of, if you will, "a woman speaking to women" (and to men) and ranges outward to illustrate how issues, lives and themes are inextricably interconnected. One of the most powerful examples is **"Poem About My Rights,"** first published in 1980, which begins as an interior monologue of a woman angry because, as a woman, the threat of rape and violence keeps her from going where she pleases when she pleases:

> . . . without changing my clothes my shoes
> my body posture my gender identity my age
> my status as a woman alone in the evening/
> alone on the streets/ alone not being the point
> the point being that I can't do what I want
> to do with my own body because I am the wrong
> sex the wrong age the wrong skin

But she moves from the individual instances to the laws defining rape, and from rape to other questions of violation:

> which is exactly like South Africa
> penetrating into Namibia penetrating into
> Angola and does that mean I mean
>   how do you know if
> Pretoria ejaculates

then deftly to Nkrumah and Lumumba, also in the wrong place at the wrong time, and to her own father, who was at once "wrong" himself as a working-class black male in his daughter's Ivy League college cafeteria and an oppressor who defined his child by her deficiencies. When Jordan concludes this poem with a defiant challenge to anyone seeking to physically or ideologically circumscribe her, we believe her and have made leaps—possibly new ones—of consciousness.

She uses a similar technique of accumulating incident/fact/detail in **"Gettin Down to Get Over,"** a poem for her mother which swells to a litany of praise for black women and the African-American family. **"Free Flight,"** another late-night stream of consciousness, though it stays closer to the "personal," builds momentum and depth with Whitman-esque inclusiveness to consider the humorously identical possibilities of consolation by a female or a male lover before settling on self-respect as the best way to get through the night.

Where Jordan is unlike Whitman is in her creation of a quirky, fallible persona (apart from her creation of personae that are clearly different from that of the poet), an alter ego by which readers accustomed to identifying the poet with the speaker of a poem may sometimes be taken aback, if not shocked.

Jordan plays skillfully with this post-Whitman, post-Williams but also post-Romantic expectation in **"Poem From Taped Testimony in the Tradition of Bernhard Goetz,"** an ironically issue-oriented dramatic monologue which transcends its headline-bound issue. Jordan's speaker breathlessly appropriates to a black perspective the reasoning Goetz used to justify arming himself and firing on black youths in the New York City subway. Is a black woman who has suffered every kind of violence from ridicule and exclusion to invisibility, battery and rape at the hands of whites also justified in assuming the worst and acting accordingly? Justified if she carries a gun and fires not on a racist cop or armed rapist but on the white woman beside her at an artists' colony dinner table whose loose-cannon talk was the last straw? The poem is at once horrifying and funny, as a tall tale is meant to be, and hard to dismiss (even if, "logically," a reader who rejected Goetz's reasoning would reject that of Jordan's speaker as well).

The inevitability and passion of this poem, as well as its wit, will keep it valid and readable after the "issue" of Goetz is forgotten. The connection between being spat at on the way to third grade, seeing a neighborhood friend beaten by the police, being ignored in a New England drugstore and being raped in a college town may not necessarily be apparent to all white (or even black male) readers. It's to Jordan's credit that she concretizes the link by juxtaposition, with the accelerating energy of deceptively ordinary speech. From her opening she establishes not only her speedy and frenetic "I" but the "they" that is, more than any "I," the opposite of "thou": the "they" that, be its antecedent "blacks," "whites," "Jews," "Muslims," "women" or "men," is the essential evil agent in any prejudiced discourse. Describing an incident that was perhaps only an eye contact made or avoided, the speaker here is confused—paranoid, the reader might think—or is she?

> . . . I mean you didn't
> necessarily see some kind of a smile
> or hear them laughing but I could feel
> it like I could feel I could always
> feel this shiver thing this fear take
> me over when I would have to come
> into a room full of them and I would be by myself
> and they would just look at you know what
> I mean you can't know what I mean
> you're not Black.

Of course Jordan's proposition is farcically surreal, exaggerated to show the fallaciousness of its white equivalent, absurd (as the murder of twenty-two black children in Atlanta, the murder of fourteen women students in Montreal, the murder of one homeless man in New York's 103d Street subway station, are absurd; they all died for being "they" to someone). Nonetheless, a reader some-where will categorize Jordan as a rabble-rousing reverse racist, missing the point of her "Modest Proposal": the quantum leap from grievance to slaughter and the culturally triggered impulse to jump it.

How can a white critic say that a black poet has a spectacular sense of rhythm? Modestly, or courageously. Jordan writes (mostly) free verse. Many writers of free verse produce a kind of syntactically disjointed prose, expecting line breaks to provide a concentration and a syncopation not achieved by means of language. In Jordan's best poems there is a strong, audible, rhythmic counterpoint to the line breaks, a rhythm as apparent to the reader as it is to the auditor who hears the poet deliver them. This is true of her poems that have been set to music by Bernice Reagon of the a cappella group Sweet Honey in the Rock (**"Alla Tha's All Right, but"** and **"A Song of Sojourner Truth"**), but it's equally true of dramatic monologues like **"The Talking Back of Miss Valentine Jones"** and **"Unemployment Monologue,"** and of the interior monologues evolving into public declaration, like **"Poem About My Rights."**

The fluid speech-become-aria quality of Jordan's free verse poems also makes them difficult to quote, though never difficult to remember. They are not made of lapidary lines and epigrammatic stanzas. They gather momentum verbally, aurally. Most often, the effects of the voice and the statement are cumulative.

Why is this important? Because it fixes the poems in the reader's memory; because it makes these poems, even those on the most serious subjects, paradoxically fun to read. It is a reason for these texts to be written in verse, to be poetry. They are not fiction, journalism, essays or any other form of prose, even when they share qualities with these other genres. When Jordan's poems are unambiguous and straightforward, as well as when they are figurative, ironic or complex, her words create a music, create voices, which readers must hear the way they were written: Her poems read themselves to us.

Like many contemporary poets, Jordan sometimes ventures back into fixed forms. There are five sonnets and a loose ghazal sequence among the forty-three new poems here. Unfortunately, in the new sonnets the poet too often uses grandiose statement and inflated diction as if they came with the form:

> From Africa singing of justice and grace

> Your early verse sweetens the fame of our Race.

("**Something Like a Sonnet for
Phillis Miracle Wheatley**")

Or she seems tone-deaf to the meter, which may always be broken, but for a purpose:

> I admire the possibilities of flight and space
> without one move towards the ending of my pain.

("**A Sonnet from the Stony Brook**")

She can also come up with a gem of a line like "A top ten lyric fallen to eleven" to refer to a fading love affair. Still, it's a long way from her best work, such as **"The Reception,"** which depicts vividly imagined characters and action in iambic pentameter quatrains:

> Doretha wore the short blue lace last night
> and William watched her drinking so she fight
> with him in flying collar slim-jim orange
> tie and alligator belt below the navel pants uptight.

> ". . . I flirt. Damned right. You Look at me."
> But William watched her carefully his mustache
> shaky she could see him jealous "which is how he
>   always be

> at parties."

Some of Jordan's most successful poems are the farthest from polemic. They are vignettes, short dramatic monologues, observations of characters who may or may not be in some interaction with the narrator, like **"Newport Jazz Festival," "Patricia's Poem"** and **"If You Saw a Negro Lady":**

> sitting on a Tuesday
> near the whirl-sludge doors of
> Horn & Hardart on the main drag
> of downtown Brooklyn

> solitary and inconspicuous as plain
> and neat as walls impossible to
> fresco and you watched her self-
> conscious features shape about
> a Horn & Hardart teaspoon
> with a pucker from a cartoon
> she would not understand
>   . . .
> would you turn her treat
> into surprise
> observing
> happy birthday

"The Madison Experience" expands this quick-take technique into a fourteen-part sequence that is a tender and surprising love song to one swath of Middle Western America. Its clean primary colors and color-blind courtesy impress the poet (who nevertheless "went out / looking for traffic") as much as the juxtaposition of rain-washed fresh produce, a rally for Soweto and "fathers / for Equal Rights." As much as anything, Jordan appreciates an untroubled solitude:

> Above the backyard mulberry tree leaves a full
>   moon
> Not quite as high as the Himalaya Mountains
> not quite as high as the rents in New York City
> summons my mind into the meat and mud
> of things that sing

Jordan hints at but does not politicize an "incorrect" sexuality. There are love poems to men and love poems to women, to black and to white partners, poems in the aftermath of loving, poems on the erotic edge of friendship, love poems that (no surprise) broadcast mistrust, question the accepted definitions of relationships. There has been pressure in the past three decades on black writers and on feminist writers to put their personal lives on the line, or to make them toe one (revolutionary black heterosexual monogamy; radical feminist lesbian ditto). "The subject tonight for/public discussion is/our love," Jordan writes ironically in **"Meta-Rhetoric."** Her only manifesto on her private choices has been her refusal to let them be the subject of discussion, at once revealing and sufficiently circumspect to make either name-calling or roll-calling impossible.

Often the glancing, yearning glimpses through language are more suggestive, more erotic than a clear depiction would be. (The word "lesbian" occurs only once in Jordan's book: the poet "worried about unilateral words like Lesbian or Nationalist." The word "gay," usually but not always in reference to men, is positively stated and vindicated.)

Rape is a subject about which Jordan is unambiguous. It is not sexual in nature but violent, and it is, she illustrates, analogous to other forms of violence motivated by lust for power, by "thou" becoming "they." She is not speculating. She reveals that she has been raped twice: "the first occasion / being a whiteman and the most recent / situation being a blackman actually / head of the local NAACP" (**"Case in Point"**). Her poems re-examine these violations through description, through metaphor (**"Rape Is Not a Poem"**) and through theory (**"Poem About My Rights"**). If there is a "silence peculiar / to the female" (**"Case in Point"**), it is that of the forcibly silenced. **"Poem on the Road"** reiterates, through other women's stories, that no racial combination explains or excuses sexual violence. I think the double betrayal of black-on-black assault makes her angriest.

Another depiction which is mercilessly specific is that of one particular black nuclear family: the poet's own, beleaguered from without, reproducing the conditions of oppression within. West Indian strivers (a postal worker and a nurse), her father tried to beat his "Black devil child" into submission while making sure she was educated for rebellion, while her mother personified both submission and endurance to her daughter. We meet these people on the first pages of *Naming Our Destiny* and are back in their kitchen in the last poem, written thirty years later. The effect is much that of reading a novel in which new points of view reveal different, complementary truths about a character or situation, culminating in **"War and Memory,"** which delineates how the dynamics of what we now call a dysfunctional family woke a bright child to the power of words and the possibility of dissent.

A *Selected Poems* is a second chance for an author and for readers. Work gone out of print can be rediscovered, the development and evolution of themes and style underlined. Poems bound too closely to an outdated topicality, or ones which are simply not good enough, can be cut out, thus placing the best-realized work into sharper relief. There are deleted poems I miss in this book: from *Things That I Do in the Dark,* "Uncle Bullboy" and the second "Talking Back of Miss Valentine Jones"; from *Passion,* "For Lil' Bit" and especially the two **"Inaugural Rose"** poems; from *Living Room,* "To Sing a Song of Palestine" and "Notes Toward Home." There are also texts that upon rereading seem to be occasional pieces whose occasion has passed: **"On Moral Leadership as a Political Dilemma," "Some People," "What Would I Do White?"** (wear furs and clip coupons; this reader optimistically thinks a white June Jordan would still be more June Jordan than Ivana Trump) and **"Memo."** In the newer work, **"Poem Instead of a Columbus Day Parade," "The Torn Sky"** and **"Take Them Out!"** pose the same problem. The events are current, but the poems don't transcend the level of chants, captions or slogans:

> Swim beside the blown-up bridges
> Fish inside the bomb-sick harbors
> Farm across the contra ridges
> Dance with revolutionary ardor
> Swim/Fish/Farm/Dance
> Nicaragua Nicaragua
>
>   (**"Dance: Nicaragua"**)

Likewise, printing the word "chlorofluorocarbons" nine times down a page, with an odd simile in the middle, is less informative about the destruction of the ozone layer than was last week's exchange of letters in *The New York Times,* and less productive of thought and action on the issue.

There are, in short, too many propaganda poems, where the

activist's desire to touch every base, to stand up and be counted on every current issue, took precedence over the poet/critic's choice of what ought to be published, not in a newspaper or a flyer but in a book that will be kept, read and reread. One need only compare Jordan's elegy for Martin Luther King Jr., which is entirely, though musically, public, with her poem for Fannie Lou Hamer—also a public figure, but this time a person Jordan knew well and worked beside. There's life, a voice, no hagiography but a lively portrait in **"1977: Poem for Mrs. Fannie Lou Hamer"**:

> Humble as a woman anywhere
> I remember finding you inside the laundromat
> in Ruleville
> lion spine relaxed/hell
> what's the point to courage when you washin
> clothes?
>   . . .
> one solid gospel
>   (*sanctified*)
> one gospel
>   (*peace*)
> one full Black lily
> luminescent
> in a homemade field
>
> of love.

This could have been a poem for an aunt/sister/mother (the feeling of blood tie is so strong) as well as a poem about any brave friend. The fact that its subject was also a public (now historical) figure gives it another dimension, and the poet a status she or he has rarely held in this country: someone who writes as an intimate of the makers of history, as an actor in significant events—and who also reminds us that the face of history can be changed to a familiar, to a family face.

One public issue with which Jordan has been closely associated in recent years and which has become a recurrent subject of her poetry is the conflict in the Middle East, including Lebanon, and the struggle of the Palestinian people for self-determination in the West Bank and elsewhere. It's an issue that has at times polarized some readers' responses to her work. I too have stopped myself to examine my own responses to texts like **"Apologies to All the People in Lebanon," "Living Room" and "Intifada."** What I find is that Jordan does in these poems what she satirizes and exposes in the Bernhard Goetz monologue: She creates an undifferentiated "they" with no stated antecedent, which embodies evil or at least the evil done to the Palestinians. A reader familiar with the events will know that Jordan's "they" sometimes refers to the Lebanese Christian Phalangist militia, sometimes to the Israeli Army, sometimes to the present Israeli government. Because these names do not appear, what

the "they" represents becomes unspecified, a monolith. Once a name has been written it is more difficult to use it unilaterally: There is the Lebanese Army and the Israeli Army, and also the Israeli opposition and the Israeli peace movement. There is a poem in Jordan's previous collection, **_Living Room,_** that expresses confusion and dismay at the paradox of Lebanese-on-Lebanese violence. There is also one envisioning peace and cooperation, dedicated to an Israeli peace activist. These weren't included in the present collection. A poet, a worker with words, should use those words to clarify, not to obfuscate.

> **One public issue with which Jordan has been closely associated in recent years and which has become a recurrent subject of her poetry is the conflict in the Middle East, including Lebanon, and the struggle of the Palestinian people for self-determination in the West Bank and elsewhere.**
> **—Marilyn Hacker**

The best American writing I've read about Vietnam has been by black and white vets who were there (Yusef Komunyakaa's *Dien Cai Dau* is a moving recent example), not by antiwar activists who weren't. I think the best poetry of the *intifada* will be written by Palestinians, and by Israelis—and that a writer who is neither, who hasn't been there except by analogy, runs the risk of letting exhortation and indignation replace observation and introspection. Adrienne Rich's recent poems about the Middle East are essentially the meditations of an American Jew who finds herself implicated in the conflict whether she chooses to be or not. Therein lie the tension and interest of the poems. The source of Jordan's involvement may be equally specific, but we don't know what it is. She gives us catalogues of the atrocities "they" performed; she seems to have no questions and to know all the answers. I think it is necessary to add that I write this as a Jew who is sickened by the Likud-led government's historically overdetermined version of apartheid, who is also opposed to and frightened by the conflation of that government with "Israelis" and "Jews" too easily made by right-and left-wing lobbyists and politicians.

Jordan's Palestinians and Nicaraguans are too often one-dimensional hero/victims. Jordan's African-Americans, small-town Middle Western whites and long-distance Brooklyn lovers of any race or sex are complex, even when glimpsed quickly in a hardware store or from a cab crossing a bridge at midnight. In spite of rage and outrage, even a rapist is not "they" but "thou":

> . . . considering the history

that leads us to this dismal place where (your arm
raised
and my eyes
lowered)
there is nothing left but the drippings
of power and
a consummate wreck of tenderness/I
want to know
Is this what you call
Only Natural?

("Rape Is Not a Poem")

The desire to reread and to pass a book on to others are two strong strands of a writer-reader connection. I don't know how many times I've read Jordan's work to myself and out loud to friends and students. At a writers' conference in Grenoble last November I read **"Poem About My Rights"** to illustrate that North American feminist poetry could not be segregated from a tradition of politically engaged writing, and also to show how a poet could create a voice that would be heard as intended, no matter who was reading the poem. What is it about June Jordan's work that I like as much as I do? Its capacity to unsettle and disturb me, for one thing, to make me want to pursue the discussion, write something in response. In **"War and Memory"** she recounts that, as a child, she related the suffering of Jewish concentration camp prisoners—described factually by her father and symbolically, in terms of women's pain, by her mother—to the war and internal bleeding in her home. The two-way trajectory between reporting and metaphor, between personal and global politics, is floodlit in Jordan's writing. Engaged as she is with the issues of the day and the irreducible issues of human life, her work provokes engagement with the reader, something too few readers now expect of poetry, something June Jordan gives back to poetry generously.

David Baker (review date Winter 1992)

SOURCE: "Probable Reason, Possible Joy," in *The Kenyon Review,* Vol. 14, No. 1, Winter, 1992, pp. 152-57.

[*In the following excerpt, Baker reviews Jordan's* Naming Our Destiny: New and Selected Poems *in the context of contemporary American poetry, pointing out what he perceives as the strengths and weaknesses of Jordan's work.*]

Occasionally I feel about Diane di Prima's poems the way I do about June Jordan's—that she writes poems as if poetry were sometimes rather far down on her list of interests. That is both compliment and complaint. Jordan is obviously devoted to the poetics of politics and judgment; she's a poetry activist. Her aesthetic includes, not only the casual or demo-

cratic sensibilities of free verse, but also the bald, repetitive, encantatory powers of oratory; hers is persistently spoken poetry, whose closest contact with song is the chant and, occasionally, the heavily stressed, feigned naïveté of the blues, as in **"Winter Honey"**:

Sugar come
and sugar go
Sugar dumb
but sugar know
ain' nothin' run me for my money
nothin' sweet like winter honey

[Poet Henri] Coulette is a good representative of some of the ongoing influences of Neoclassicism in American poetry, and di Prima charts the development of at least one strain of Romanticism; June Jordan reminds us that, while these two aesthetics have comprised the dichotomy of Western philosophy and literature for thousands of years, they are incomplete in expressing the more various cultural heritages of this country. Jordan's prosody may derive primarily from the free verse liberties of Romanticism, and her decidedly nontranscendental, socially aware sympathies may align in intriguing ways with Neoclassical worldliness; still, Jordan's most immediate tradition and her most notable accomplishment correspond with her development of a distinctly African-American poetry. Much of her power stems from her antagonisms—intended or not—with the two more predominant forces in our poetry. That's why I said earlier that, though her interests do not seem to reside wholly in poetry, I find that stance to be critically valuable. For Jordan, to adopt the techniques of a Western aesthetic is to risk forgetting the history of an African past—and an importantly African present:

What kind of person would kill Black children?
What kind of person could persuade eighteen
different Black children to get into a car or
a truck or a van?
What kind of person could kill or kidnap
these particular
Black children:
        Edward Hope Smith, 14 years old, dead
        Alfred James Evans, 14 years old, dead
        Yosef Bell, 9 years old, dead. . . .

"Test of Atlanta 1979" exemplifies the sternest and most blunt qualities of Jordan's poetry. It is expressly unpoetic, ungarnished; it is virtually prose in lines. Yet the power of its testimonial rhetoric, the plain and undeniable fact-making embedded in the poem, produces a voice capable of moving beyond mere shock, blame, or stupor into an accumulating indignation leading toward action. Jordan's well-chosen title to this volume reiterates one of her most urgent tasks: to name names, in order to rehearse the details of one's past; to identify the face of one's oppressor; and actively to take part in the creation of one's future.

> **For Jordan, to adopt the techniques of a Western aesthetic is to risk forgetting the history of an African past—and an importantly African present.**
> —*David Baker*

Imagine the liberating importance of naming for a culture whose identity has, for centuries, been refigured or erased by a more dominant or controlling one. There are names abounding in *Naming Our Destiny:* in titles (**"A Richland County Lyric for Elizabeth Asleep"**), in dedications (to her son Christopher, to Jane Creighton, to Adrienne Rich, or in "commemoration of the 40,000 women and children who . . . presented themselves in bodily protest . . . at The United Nations, August 9, 1978"), and in the characterizations within virtually every poem. The nominal and spiritual transformation of Saul to Paul provides, in Jordan's important "Fragments from a Parable," a paradigm for another crucial naming: the naming or recreating of oneself. As if directly to confront the paradox of an artist—the desire to be original while employing the received technique and traditions of one's art form—Jordan opens her poem in purposefully tentative fashion:

> The worst is not knowing if I do take somebody's
> word on it means I don't know and you have to
>   believe
> if you just don't know. How do I dare to stand as
> still as I am still standing? . . .
> Always there is not knowing, not knowing
>   everything
> of myself and having to take whoever you are at
>   your
> word. About me.

Elsewhere in *Naming Our Destiny,* the trope of nomination produces a push toward responsibility and duty, as well as a sense of kinship or sympathy; in **"Fragments from a Parable,"** the drive to name participates in the fundamental process of self-identity. The speaker must invent herself, must give birth to herself, not only as artist, but as person. Ellison's terrible figure of invisibility must be surmounted through distinct verification: "She seeks to authorize her birth." To authorize is to certify as well as to transcribe. Jordan's speaker moves from the distances of third person ("And this is my story of Her. The story is properly yours to tell. You have created Her, but carelessly. . . . Your patterns deny parenthood; deny every connection suggesting a connection; a consequence") into the immediacy of first person: "I am. // My name is me." The subsequent narrative

reimagines her birth and childhood, and the speaker continues to confront the pressures which attend her race and gender: "My father loved the delusion he sired. The fundamental dream of my mother, her unnatural ignorance refreshed him . . . He said to my mother many nouns." Finally, the speaker seeks to move beyond even her own creation: "Let me be more than words: I would be more than medium or limestone. I would be more than looking more than knowing. . . ." The poem concludes in an act of personal liberation, having served as a vehicle for self-creation.

The issues of race and self-reliance (artistic and otherwise) are not the only political topics to which Jordan returns persistently. She speaks searingly in behalf of the hitherto silenced or subjugated; women, the poor and hungry, the imprisoned, the politically tyrannized in Nicaragua, the enslaved in Manhattan. I can think of very few contemporary American poets who have been so willing to take on other people's troubles; decidedly, this is not the poetry of a sheltered, introspective confessional, not the work of a tidy scholar or a timid dormouse. Jordan's variety of poetic stances enacts her drive to connect and represent, for in addition to her principal mode of delivery—the poet talking directly to an audience—she also speaks through a number of other characters in persona poems, giving sympathetic articulation to lives, idioms, and concerns beyond her own. Like Carl Sandburg, she makes public art out of public occasion and the available word, and she does so with confidence and conviction.

While I admire the task of such writing, such purposely unartistic or democratically accessible art, I do nonetheless tire of some elements of Jordan's work. It is finally hard to read page after page by somebody who is always right:

> Some people despise me be-
> cause I have a Venus mound
> and not a penis
>
> Does that *sound*
> right
> to you?

"Some People," quoted entirely, may articulate a feminist corrective, but it is certainly inadequate as a poem; it's more like a sound bite, a facile commercial for rightness. Especially when her tone steps over from witness to blame, or when her accusations don't seem grounded within the body of the work itself, Jordan's voice resounds with self-righteousness and sanctimony rather than urgency:

> They said they were victims. They said you were
> Arabs . . .
>
> Did you read the leaflets that they dropped

from their hotshot fighter jets?
They told you to go . . .

I didn't know and nobody told me and what
could I do or say, anyway?

Yes, I did know it was the money I earned as a
    poet that
paid
for the bombs and the planes and the tanks
that they used to massacre your family

But I am not an evil person
The people of my country aren't so bad

You can't expect but so much
from those of us who have to pay taxes and watch
American tv

You see my point;

I'm sorry.
I really am sorry.

Here in **"Apologies to All the People in Lebanon,"** sarcasm, obvious irony, and feigned helplessness prevent the
poem from becoming a more serious indictment of American brutishness. The result is something closer to the sentimentality of mere or obvious correctness. Jordan's more
powerful social critiques occur in poems which implicate her
speaker more personally in events. "Poem about My Rights,"
for instance, is explicitly about the relationship of personal
experience and general history-telling. Here the trope of rape
operates as a figure for both individual and social damage,
as the poem moves from the speaker's regret that "I can't
do what I want / to do with my own body because I am the
wrong / sex the wrong age the wrong skin," to France where
"they say if the guy penetrates / but does not ejaculate then
he did not rape me," to the literal and political rape of
Namibia and its citizens by South Africa. The speaker becomes both a voice of specific indignation and a voice of
more wide-ranging, accumulating rage: "I am the history of
rape / I am the history of the rejection of who I am / I am
the history of the terrorized. . . ." In a serious pun on her own
title, the speaker asserts her own "right"—her legal and
moral liberty as well as her correctness—as the poem concludes in another important act of verification and naming:

> *I am not wrong: Wrong is not my name*
> My name is my own my own my own
> and I can't tell you who the hell set things up like
>   this
> but I can tell you that from now on my resistance
> my simple and daily and nightly self-determination
> may very well cost you a life

"Apologies to All the People in Lebanon," quoted earlier,
provides an example of my second complaint with Jordan's
work: her occasionally rather wearying approach to technique. It is sometimes as if design and prosody are incidental bothers to her, things to be quickly dispensed with, rather
than integral and integrated parts of the whole poetic effect.
This is often an inevitable result of a public poetry whose
primary foundation is oral rather than visible or written. Even
while I can rationally explain the purposeful raggedness and
homeliness of her work as a visible resistance of the conventions of power implicit in Western poetry, I still wish she
were capable of applying more formal pressures to her material. In **"Ghazal at Full Moon,"** for example, she ironizes
or complicates her work by a juxtaposition of technique and
subject matter. Borrowing the Mediterranean form originally
designed to celebrate love and drinking, Jordan uses its independent couplets paradoxically, not pastorally, to represent the variety of cultures vaguely named by the term
"Indian"—from the "dead man" on the obsolete nickel to the
cultures of Guatemala, Pakistan, and elsewhere. Much of the
poem's power and tension derive from the formal progres-
sion embedded in the closed couplets, as well as from the
speaker's accumulating sense of injustice done to many cultures wrongly named and blurred. In other poems, though, I
occasionally feel that Jordan's work reads too easily, as if
she can't be worried by technique when there is so much
other "real" work to do.

Even given my complaints, Jordan's work is a reminder that
poetry might yet be a viable and persuasive form of social
corrective, that its more oratorical modes may have the ca-
pability to mobilize as well as inspire. Her project is especially whelming, given her ethnic as well as artistic fidelities:
she requires of herself, and invites us, to review some of the
most basic assumptions about myth, identity, and influence
that writers as various as Henri Coulette and Diane di Prima
more willingly inherit and more generally take for granted.
Together, these three Californians suggest the depth, difference, and significance of current American poetry. The point
for us is not to elect one of these three voices over the others; it is to learn how to listen to them all.

Matthew Rothschild (review date January 1993)

SOURCE: A review of *Technical Difficulties: African-
American Notes on the State of the Union,* in *The Progressive,* Vol. 57, No. 1, January 1993, pp. 33-4.

[In the following excerpt, Rothschild favorably reviews
Technical Difficulties: African-American Notes on the State
of the Union.*]*

For those who are June Jordan fans, as I am, *Technical Dif-*

ficulties is an exhilarating collection of some of her best essays and speeches from the last six years, many of which appeared first in these pages. Every time I read Jordan's work, I am struck and re-struck by her authentic voice, her fresh poetic style, and, above all, the intensity of her commitment to justice and equality.

Like most great American agitators, and she is proudly an agitator, Jordan holds up our country's ideals and points out the distance we are from realizing them. Hers is a patriotic quest in the best sense: to make America live up to its promise.

In **"My Perfect Soul Shall Manifest Me Rightly: An Essay on Blackfolks and the Constitution,"** Jordan documents the problems in our society. "There is a terrible trouble across the land," she writes. "As a nation we have become a beacon for tyrants, greed-driven entrepreneurs, and militaristic fantasies. As a people we have become accustomed to the homeless, the beggars, the terrorized minorities, and the terrified elderly. As an electorate, we have become the craven subjects of deceitful, lawless, and inhumane leadership. As African-Americans, we have become coast-to-coast targets for resurgent racist insolence and injuries."

But characteristically, she finds hope. After detailing other terrible troubles, she reverses field. "There is a terrible trouble across the land because We, the People, are becoming more powerful," she writes. "Despite the limited intentions of the Fathers of this republic, We, the People of America, are forcing a democracy out of Pilgrim Rock. . . . This was not always the case. This was not meant to be."

Jordan offers more than just politics, narrowly defined. She includes a warm tribute to her West Indian immigrant parents; a poignant account of how she rejected the isolated, individualistic life of a secluded poet and decided to return to a city and community; a couple of rousing commencement addresses; a funny and pointed piece—given as the keynote at an Activists' and Socialists' Conference—that begins memorably, "Two weeks ago my aunt called me a communist"; a laudatory yet critical essay on Martin Luther King Jr., entitled **"The Mountain and the Man Who Was Not God,"** and an exuberant recollection of Jesse Jackson's 1988 bid for the Presidency.

I always find June Jordan inspiring and empowering, and it is a treasure to have some of my favorite *Progressive* essays—such as **"Waiting for a Taxi," "Can I Get A Witness?",** and **"Requiem for the Champ"**—collected under one cover. But it is a particular delight to discover some earlier pieces that display her talents and her humanity in all the rich and dazzling hues that have come to characterize her distinguished work.

Adele Logan Alexander (review date April 1993)

SOURCE: "Stirring the Melting Pot," in Women's Review of Books, No. 7, April, 1993, pp. 6-7.

[*In the following review, Alexander surveys the range of concerns and discusses the style of address in Jordan's essay collection* Technical Difficulties: African-American Notes on the State of the Union.]

"I am one barbarian who will not apologize," June Jordan shouts [in ***Technical Difficulties: African-American Notes on the State of the Union***]. (Because I can hear her voice's clarion call, I'm sure that she shouts these words, although I only read them on the printed page.) "Two weeks ago my aunt called me a Communist," she confides, acknowledging the outrage that her opinions have caused her kin. "Calling someone a Communist," she continues, "is an entirely respectable, and popular, middle-class way to call somebody a low-down dirty dog." Yes, Jordan often must have outraged her relatives because she is such an unapologetic "barbarian," so piercing in her analysis, often so provocative beyond apparent reason. Yet after all, reason prevails in ***Technical Difficulties,*** this new collection of essays. Kinfolk notwithstanding, Jordan scarcely could be considered anyone's cup of tea (warm, sweet, milky—if that's what one seeks) or even their meat and potatoes; she is, rather, the very finest bitter vetch, the best champagne or straight shot of Stoly.

Technical Difficulties is a book about America—subtitled, as it is, "The State of the Union." This is America observed and found both noble and nurturing, brutal and malformed—often at the same time—by a brilliant and mature African American scholar who has looked at our country with her own unique clarity of vision and focus. Her subjects include affectionate tributes to her own Jamaican heritage (**"For My American Family"**) and that of those other immigrants, not the Poles, Russians, Irish, or Germans but the too-often invisible and darker-skinned newcomers whose journeys through New York harbor, past the Statue of Liberty and Ellis Island, have been largely overlooked in our romantic imaging of the American melting-pot.

Although these less chronicled voyagers harbored dreams much like those of America's white immigrants, they came not from the *shtetls* of Eastern Europe, but rather from places like "Clonmel, a delicate dot of a mountain village in Jamaica." They settled their families down in black communities such as Brooklyn's Bedford-Stuyvesant that sociologists in the 1950s characterized as "breeding grounds for despair," where teachers taught Jordan "all about white history and white literature." Yet there, in her parents' "culturally deprived" home, she "became an American poet." In her essays Jordan combines love and respect with scorn and mistrust for this America where her parents—her "faithful American family"—created a new life and nurtured this "barbarian" of a writer.

In another essay, **"Waking Up in the Middle of Some American Dreams,"** Jordan directs her attention to an analysis of her own deliberate self-isolation and the intrusions upon it by a lifetime of memories, a single ring of the telephone, and then, violently, by a rapist. She inserts this brutal assault into her narrative with just three words, but those words carry the potency of a drop of paint splashed into a bucket of water—spreading out to infuse the entire pail with its livid pigment. Questioning "American illusions of autonomy, American delusions of individuality," she had created her own "willful loneliness," designed to nurture her own creative process. She had sought and found an isolated spot where she could ask herself such questions as "what besides race and sex and class could block me from becoming a clearly successful American, a Great White Man," only to have her illusions of Eden-like solitude shattered by violence. Her conclusion, "I do not believe that I am living alone in America," is countered by the fearful question, "Am I?"

"Don't You Talk About My Momma" and **"No Chocolates for Breakfast"** both traverse Jordan's familiar home ground—the lives of African American women. With wit and steel, she lashes out at men such as Daniel Patrick Moynihan who would endlessly analyze and put down her "Momma," "If Black women disappeared tomorrow," she argues persuasively, "a huge retinue of self-appointed and *New York-Times*-appointed 'experts' would have to hit the street looking for new jobs." Her own 1965 **"Memo"** to Moynihan elegantly encapsulated her opinion of these self-righteous analyzers and experts:

> You done what you done
> I do what I can
>
> Don't you liberate me
> from my Black female pathology
>
> I been working off my knees
> I been drinking what I please . . .
>
> But you been screwing me so long
> I got a idea something's wrong
> with you
>
> I got a simple proposition
> You take over my position
>
> Clean your own house, babyface.

"When and Where and Whose Country is This, Any-way?" continues in this vein. Fannie Lou Hamer's declaration at the 1964 Democratic Convention that "We didn't come all the way up here for no two seats," provides the essay's keynote. As an African American woman, Jordan wants to know just what she and other intruders at the great American banquet have to do to get more than just the "two seats" they have been told they deserved. In **"No Chocolates for Breakfast"** she reiterates her conviction that Black women have been doing for others while no one has been doing for them—with the near-perfect observation that "I can't think of a single Black woman who has a wife." Combining this point with her observations about Moynihan, Jordan revises Aretha Franklin's familiar lyrics: "Don't Send Me No Experts; I Need a Man Named Dr. Feelgood—and I could also use me a wife."

Moving along from the experts to the icons, Jordan tries to develop a revised perspective on a deeply admired but nonetheless flawed Martin Luther King in **"The Mountain and the Man Who Was Not God."** "Any time you decide to take on a mountain," she observes, "you just better take good care." (Take on Dr. King? No wonder her aunt called her a Communist.) But Jordan only wants to demythify King, not dishonor him, and she urges us to remember and revere others as well. She recalls "Jo-Ann Robinson, Diana Nash, Rosa Parks, Ruby Doris Robinson, Septima Clarke, Bernice Reagon, Ella Baker, Fannie Lou Hamer, and, of course, Angela Davis"—all of them stalwarts of the civil rights movement—calling them "just a handful of the amazing components of The Invisible Woman whose invisibility has cost all of us an incalculable loss." As they struggled in the movement without the continuing domestic support enjoyed by men such as King, who knows how often Hamer and Parks might have thought "I could also use me a wife"?

> **June Jordan has a prolific intellect and a vast reservoir of extraordinary and broad-based knowledge, yet her writing maintains its solid grounding in everyday experience.**
> **—*Adele Logan Alexander***

Jordan tackles and dissects familiar themes: family, race, neighborhood ("two-and-a-half years ago," she writes, "I . . . returned to my beloved Brooklyn where, I knew, my eyes and ears would never be lonely for diversified, loud craziness and surprise"), the love of men, women and children, the mutable American Constitution, education, creativity and politics (of nations and of sexuality, the "correct" and the "incorrect"). For many years she has been a teacher and writer, with several books of essays, including *Civil Wars, Moving Towards Home* and *On Call, to* her credit, as well as collections of her poetry, including the less well-known

Who, Look at Me?—poems for children about African American artists and their work. These new essays, though they cover a variety of topics, come together into a unified and consistent whole. Adapting the Cubists' technique of viewing a subject from many different perspectives at once, Jordan sees all sides and then reassembles the fragments into a consistent, if multifaceted, whole. One should not say *Technical Difficulties* is "better" than what preceded it, but it is surely "more," and though a little of Jordan's well-muscled prose goes a long way, in this case it is also true that "more is better."

June Jordan has a prolific intellect and a vast reservoir of extraordinary and broad-based knowledge, yet her writing maintains its solid grounding in everyday experience. (The frustrating disempowerment of Black women, for example, is captured in the impossibility of getting a taxi on a rainy afternoon.) The luminous accessibility of these essays keeps them well clear of the murky pits of obfuscation that trap those scholars who write for the purpose of garnering accolades from others in the academy. Jordan's is an intricate and often jarring patchwork collage of Americans and American life. Attempting in her **"Alternative Commencement Address at Dartmouth College"** to define this "American," puzzling over how to characterize that slippery and complex essence, Jordan observes that "*He* was not supposed to be an Indian. *He* was not supposed to be a *She*. He was not supposed to be Black or the African-American descendant of slaves. And yet, here we are, at our own indomitable insistence, here we are, the peoples of America."

"Finding the Haystack in the Needle" is one of the more intriguing titles I've come across recently, but it surely fits the skewed perspectives, insolent assumptions and refreshing ambiguities of Jordan's work. "Why would you lose the needle in the first place?" she wonders. Perhaps we have worried too much about that minuscule, even insignificant, needle, while failing to notice the importance of the hay: "How come nobody's out looking for that common big messy thing: that food, that playground that children and lovers enjoy?" she asks, and now, so do I. And hungry as I sometimes find myself, I look forward to more of Jordan's intellectual "food" and more recess time spent in her "playground."

Jordan vigorously rants at our familiar "emperors," from George Washington to Ronald Reagan. She reminds us of the meaty, but non-mainstream, substance that has been deliberately omitted and obscured from our educational, cultural and political lives. I look to her not only to rail at the way things have been ("if you're not an American white man and you travel through the traditional twistings and distortions of the white Western canon, you stand an excellent chance of ending up *nuts*," she says) but to knock our white,

male-centered world cockeyed from its moorings and provide more of the revised visions that we need.

For my next feast, I would like to order from June Jordan a little less Dr. Spock and more Dr. May Chinn; less Martin and more Fannie Lou; less Jesse and more Sojourner; less Clarence ("whose accomplishments as former head of the Equal Employment Opportunity Commission do not cleanly distinguish him from David Duke") and more Anita; less Thomas Jefferson and more Sally Hemings—and more Aretha, more Marys (Magdalene, Church Terrell, McLeod Bethune and many others come to mind) and more Josephines (both Empress and Baker, perhaps) as well.

I admire what you've given us here, Ms. Jordan. It's quirky enough to make us giggle out loud, and then in turn it's heart-wrenchingly sad. It's always provocative. To employ the new jargon, you're really "pushing the envelope." It's great stuff—but please, come back soon and feed us some more.

Margaret Randall (review date March-May 1995)

SOURCE: "Dreams Deferred," in *American Book Review*, Vol. 16, No. 6, March-May, 1995, p. 26.

[*In the following review, Randall presents an appreciation of Jordan's skill and thematic range in* Haruko/Love Poems.]

June Jordan's work, at this point and for many years now, is perfect. That is, not a word too many, none too few, nothing at all other than it must be. She says exactly what she means to say, and says it so powerfully that the reader (or fortunate, listener) *hears* each phrase; isolated, made specific, an essential part of the whole. From the collected poems in *Naming Our Destiny* to the precise columns in *The Progressive* and spartan essays (*Civil Wars; On Call, South End,* and *Technical Difficulties*), hers is a voice that epitomizes wise sister, alter ego, conscience, song. She manages to tap that place where race and sexuality, class and justice, gender and memory come together. She doesn't go with the cutting-edge idea but reaches for that difficult terrain where others may fear to tread.

I have yet to teach a college class in which I haven't read out loud Jordan's essay **"Many Rivers to Cross"** at one of the early sessions. It focuses the students. And renews my sense that we have writers now—most of them women, many of them women of color—who simply know how to say what must be said, with brilliance.

Haruko/Love Poems is an ambitious collection. The poems that make up its first part speak of and to a love that fails. Or does it? This is love in its most comprehensive definition. Perhaps it would be better to say that love here does not follow the boy-meets-girl-and-both-enjoy-happy-ending formula. This is the love of one woman for another, one culture for another, one age for another; and the happy ending doesn't happen.

Jordan's narrative takes us through the heights and pits of passion: ". . . my soul adrift / the whole night sky denies me light / without you," And,

> Wind chimes murmuring into the atmosphere
> and high above this peaceful
> house
> a 90 year old willow tree
> sucks on the sunlight
> with a thousand toothless leaves . . .

Then cradles itself in lines of affirmation:

> . . . I do,
> I ride these tracks to meet you:
> moving through
> an upright register
> of shadow and of light
> moving through
> eclectic ganglia of open cities
> nervous
> nowhere immaculate nowhere a mystery
> to match this urban earthquake travelling
> stop by stop
> into reunion
> with the highway wonder
> of your eyes.

The last of the *Haruko* poems ends:

> . . . the roots
> for a connection that can keep
> Japan and San Francisco
> and Jamaica and Decorah
> Iowa and Norway
> all in one place palpable
> to any sweet belief
> move deep below
> apparent differences of turf
> I trace them in the lifeline
> of an open palm
> a hand that works
> its homemade heat
> against the jealous
> hibernating blindness
> of the night
> plum blossom plum jam
> even the tree becomes something

> more than a skeleton
> longing for the sky.

Neither is Jordan's fine humor absent: "'Haruko: / Oh! It's like stringbean in French?' / 'No; / It's like hurricane / in English!'" Or the poem **"Taiko Dojo Messages from Haruko"** with nothing more than variations on the word no. The poet wrote the poems to Haruko and put this entire collection together at a time when—in her own words—she "could not, by [herself], do many things." She was suffering from breast cancer, that plague which has taken so many women from us. Survival must have required such energy. And yet these poems, this collection, is living testimony to the fact that we often do more than we know. Facing death, the great artist pushes through to the other side.

The second part of the book gathers earlier love poems, 1970-91. Here again, the meaning of love is stretched. And in these poems it does not move through the space of a single relationship but many: the Roman poems (to men, man), the beautiful **"Poem for Joy"** (for the poet Joy Harjo, and dedicated to the entire Creek Tribe of North America), the extraordinary **"The Reception,"** and **"Poem for Mark"** in which so much of Jordan's exquisite ability to merge race, class, global and other visions comes together:

> England, I thought, will look like Africa
> or India with elephants and pale men
> pushing things about
> rifles and gloves
> handlebar mustache and tea
> pith helmets
> riding crop
> the Holy Bible
> and a rolled up map of plunder
> possibilities . . .

The word "map" in the next to last line of the preceding fragment reads "man" in the book, but I wonder (I believe it is a typo, or should be). In any case the poem continues, ending as the political becomes absolutely personal: "I knew / whoever the hell 'my people' / are / I knew that one of them / is you."

One last look at what Jordan can do with words, the way she has of saying so much more than their sum:

> OK. So she got back the baby
> but what happened to the record player?
> No shit. The authorized appropriation
> contradicts my falling out of love?
> You're wrong. It's not that I gave away my keys.
> The problem is nobody wants to steal me or my
> house.

This is **"Onesided Dialog."** Jordan's poems convince us one side is both, or all we'll ever need.

Sue Russell (review date Spring 1995)

SOURCE: "Among Lovers, Among Friends," in *The Kenyon Review,* Vol. XVII, No. 2, Spring 1995, pp. 147-53.

[*In the following excerpt, Russell illustrates her appreciation of Jordan's* Haruko/Love Poems.]

Both Ted Berrigan and June Jordan have shown an inclination to see themselves as outsiders from the literary elite, defined by such external rewards as prestigious grants and *New Yorker* publication. For Berrigan, the distinguishing criteria might be class and circle of friends, while for Jordan, they are race (black), politics (radical), and sexuality (ambiguous). According to Alice Notley, "Ted came from a working-class background and was very realistic about choices in America. You weren't poor if you had gone to college. On the other hand, you would not get certain kinds of poetic recognition in your lifetime if you had gone to Something State rather than Harvard; or if you hadn't involved yourself in one of what he called 'the serious jack-off scenes'". June Jordan displayed a similar understanding of the pernicious effect of the old-boys' network in her preface to *Passion: New Poems, 1977-1980,* which proposes a new perspective on the American literary tradition through recognition of the prototypically independent voice of Walt Whitman. She offers a potent description of the poetic energy that exists outside of the grant-giving, book-publishing, white, heterosexual male mainstream:

> I kept listening to the wonderful poetry of the multiplying numbers of my friends who were and who are New World poets until I knew, for a fact, that there was and that there is an American, a New World, poetry that is as personal, as public, as irresistible, as quick, as necessary, as unprecedented, as representative, as exalted, as speakably commonplace, and as musical, as an emergency phone call.

> (*Passion*)

Jordan's latest collection, *Haruko/Love Poems,* embodies all these divergent qualities. The individual sections in the initial sequence of **"Poems for Haruko"** are so immediate and vibrant in their effect that they seem to be happening right there on the page. The push and pull of syllabic stress and line against line mirrors the tension of the relationship in question, as in these lines from **"Poem for Haruko":**

> Now I do

> relive an evening of retreat
> a bridge I left behind
> where all the solid heat
> of lust and tender trembling
> lay as cruel and as kind
> as passion spins its infinite
> tergiversations in between the bitter
> and the sweet

We know that Jordan is not the kind of poet to use a multisyllabic word like "tergiversations" without a good reason. In addition to sounding just right, it suggests both the changing face of love and, through the root meaning of "verse" (*versari*—to turn), the movement of a poetic sequence which records these changes as they occur.

The tautness of these poems reflects a narrative stance of readiness, equating love with the martial arts, as expressed here:

> Why I became a pacifist
> and then
> How I became a warrior again:
> Because nothing I could do or say
> turned out okay
> I figured I should just sit
> still and chill
> except to maybe mumble
> 'Baby, Baby:
> Stop!'
> AND
> Because turning that other cheek
> holding my tongue
> refusing to retaliate when the deal
> got ugly . . .

After a number of further "because's," the poem comes to its strong and righteous end with these lines:

> I pick up my sword
> I lift up my shield
> And I stay ready for war
> Because now I live ready for a whole lot more
>
> than that

There is no mention here of Haruko, no sensual detail, no reminder that the speaker here is concerned about the love between two women. But it is clear from the context of the surrounding poems that the analogy between love and war helps the narrator to sustain a position of strength.

Another poem, **"Speculations on the Present through the Prism of the Past,"** continues the image pattern with the recollection of a time in which the narrator "at 29 . . . climbed on a motorcycle / for my first date / with this guy." Climbing aboard here meant giving up "my house / my life" for a benevolent dictator who kept her " . . . well fed / absolutely / clean / and (in general) well satisfied / on the sexual side / but scared to say anything / about the 25 foot leather whip / memento from his military duties." Memory of time spent in the war zone leads finally, two poems later, to a meditative stillness which makes it possible to say "Ichiban / Good bye. / I do not choose / to collaborate." The final movement in the sequence combines regret with the return of a clearer vision and the ability to see oneself as part of the larger world:

> even the tree becomes something
> more than a skeleton
> longing for the sky

A generous selection of love poems from Jordan's work from 1970-1991 fills out the collection. Included here are such personal favorites as **"Free Flight,"** which offers a memorable catalog of the array of ingredients that make up a lonely midnight snack. The clear distinction between what is desired and what is available is carried in the detail:

> I must arise
> and wandering into the refrigerator
> think about evaporated milk homemade vanilla ice
> cream
> cherry pie hot from the oven with Something Like
> Vermont
> Cheddar Cheese disintegrating luscious
> on the top while
> mildly
> I devour almonds and raisins mixed to mathemati-
> cal
> criteria or celery or my very own sweet and sour
> snack
> composed of brie peanut butter honey and
> a minuscule slice of party size salami
> on a single whole wheat cracker no salt added

The "selected" poems are well-chosen and well-paced, with short lyrics interspersed among longer explorations. In addition, the book as a whole is handsomely designed on glossy white stock with an aesthetically pleasing arrangement of text and marginal space. This careful attention may be because collections of love poems are often thought to be audience pleasers. If the word "love" attracts a broader audience to Jordan's work, those new readers will undoubtedly be grateful. I predict that this book will be taken up like that strangely various midnight snack, for Jordan's poems are as necessary and basic as food for the hungry. They will satisfy in that hour of need.

Dale Edwyna Smith (review date Spring 1995)

SOURCE: "The Mother Tongue," in *Belles Letters,* Vol. 10, No. 2, Spring, 1995, pp. 68-70.

[*In the following excerpt, Smith considers the thematic and stylistic features of Jordan's prose.*]

The twinning of politics and poetics as a literary strategy in African-American women's writing is dictated by a variety of circumstances, combined with temperament, intellect, and literary perspicacity. Even so, the tradition has become over time an almost indigenous response, like race memory, a kind of mother tongue; and these titles, with one exception, embrace it well. Among them are June Jordan and Nikki Giovanni, unquestioned exemplars of those currently practicing this art successfully.

Melding memoir to the presentation and analysis of the cultural and political evolution of an entire community is a tricky business. However, particularly in the case of a "nonpublic" person, it is critical that insight into the universal application of the individual life be clear and unambiguous, and the tale engagingly told. June Jordan, in both of her new books, shows us how this is best accomplished. Essays in her *Moving Towards Home: Political Essays* (1981) and her *Technical Difficulties* (1992) initially appeared about a decade apart, providing the reader a fortunate retrospective as well as a bird's-eye view of Jordan's own literary evolution. Her prose, like the finest poetry, perfectly distills emotion into snapshots of verse. And her work is unapologetically Afrocentrist and gynecentrist in outlook, in part because, as she states in *Moving Towards Home:*

> *Race* and *class* . . . are not the same kind of words
> as *grass* and *stars. Gender* is not the same . . . as
> *sunlight.*

But of course! We knew this; and though our failure to speak plain is at the bottom of our cultural conundrums, it comes from our consistent failure to see plain. Jordan sees, plain, and then writes it down, for us, in pristine, unadorned prose. A teacher, her hope is also in educating the next generation, as she states in *Technical Difficulties:*

> The best higher education . . . in the USA has meant
> that you could graduate *summa cum laude* . . .
> knowing about the fictive tragedy of King Lear, but
> . . . ignorant about the actual prayers . . . of Native
> Americans . . . You would never . . . split an infini-
> tive . . . but you could not understand why . . . Af-
> rican-Americans . . . seemed so stubbornly
> dependent upon . . . their own "weird" mother
> tongue . . . Why couldn't they learn to speak or
> write "plain English"?

Thus, Jordan translates the "specificity" that is "the idiosyncratic truth of [her] personal experience" into language that we can understand.

Jacqueline Vaught Brogan (essay date Fall 1995)

SOURCE: "Planets on the Table: From Wallace Stevens and Elizabeth Bishop to Adrienne Rich and June Jordan," in *The Wallace Stevens Journal,* Vol. 19, No. 2, Fall 1995, pp. 273-75.

[*In the following excerpt, Brogan situates Jordan in a philosophical context along with poets Wallace Stevens, Elizabeth Bishop and Adrienne Rich.*]

In Jordan [. . .] we find a poet, at least in her latest works, far more persuaded of the primacy of words, and possibly of the primacy of speech as a redemptive force, despite her acute awareness of the violence cultural scripts impose all over the world. When she "says" she does not want to speak of those who "describe human beings" in certain violative ways, she also says such words "are the ones from whom we must redeem / the words of our beginning"—invoking a faith in what Stevens calls "The thesis of the plentifullest John"—or that we have traditionally inherited as "In the beginning was the Word." Jordan herself admits to being drawn to this phrase as a child, suggesting that it empowered her early on as a poet: "Early on, the scriptural concept that 'in the beginning was the Word and the Word was with God and the Word was God' the idea that the word could represent and then deliver into reality what the word symbolized—this possibility of language, of writing, seemed to me magical and basic and irresistible." It may well be much to the point that Jordan, writing at the end of this century rather than at the beginning, interprets this "possibility of language" as a possibility of *writing* rather than one of *speaking* (with the implicit logocentric and largely phallocentric notions traditionally associated with this biblical passage). At least as she interprets John's thesis, the *essential* rupture of language (or words, or writing)—that it *represents* a reality—does not preclude its power to then call that reality into being. In this way, Jordan both accommodates and then challenges poststructuralist theories of language. This is to say, that for Jordan, as for [Wallace] Stevens, we are responsible for the "planets on our table." Precisely because language is a rupture, because it is secondary and arbitrary, it opens the possibility for redemptive future constructs.

In terms of both her poetry and this essay, Jordan's most important work to date is the concluding poem to the volume appropriately entitled *Naming Our Destiny* (1989)—that is, **"War and Memory,"** a poem once again set during World War II in its beginning sections, moving through the Span-ish Civil War, the Vietnamese War, and the War on Poverty to Chinese Revolutionaries and the killing streets of Washington, D. C. In the first sections of the poem, itself highly reminiscent of "In the Waiting Room," a young girl (Jordan) discovers that looking at pictures of Jewish girls in Nazi concentration camps proves the occasion of recognizing her placement within a gendered, racial, and family war of her own. Subsequently various scripts, from the TV to clichés and to slogans—"Hell no! We won't go!"—to poverty and propaganda, prove overwhelming and disillusioning to a child who thought she "was a warrior growing up," who had written "everything [she] knew how to write against apartheid." The belated and somewhat nostalgic recognition of her innocence and idealism could well, it seems to me, turn at this point to despair, giving in to the kind of nihilism I believe has been wrongly associated with deconstruction.

However, with a tone that is equally as forceful as that of [poet Adrienne] Rich's "Final Notations" but is clearly more expansive, Jordan seeks at the end of *Naming Our Destiny* to redress the patriarchal scripts that have so conscripted our world with a literal "mother tongue." I cite the last lines of the poem:

> and I
> dared myself to say The Palestinians
> and I
> worried about unilateral words like Lesbian or
> Nationalist
> and I
> tried to speak Spanish when I travelled to
> Managua
> . . . .
> and I wrote everything I knew how to write against
> apartheid
> and I
> thought I was a warrior growing up
> and I
> buried my father with all of the ceremony all of
> the music I could piece together
> and I
> lust for justice
> and I
> make that quest arthritic/pigeon-toed/however
> and I
> invent the mother of the courage I require not to
> quit

If, indeed, an event has occurred in relation to the history of the concept of structure, Jordan's poetry suggests that such an event or "rupture" may not necessarily be a bad thing, but rather may reveal the ethical space in which a new story, as it were, for the world and the words in it may be written.

Thus, even if it is true that for [poet Elizabeth Bishop] ultimately the "world seldom changes" and that for Rich it is primarily "the difficult world," Jordan, like Stevens before her, carries an ironically reinscribed faith in the capacity of language to mean and to redeem—actually to create what Stevens had called for earlier, a "world / In which *she* sang" as the "maker" of her world instead of as the victim of a world in which she is silenced (italics added). Similarly, from the urgency of his sense that "the theory of description matters most" *because* "what we say of the future must portend," to such late poems as "Two Illustrations That the World Is What You Make of It" and "Prologues to What Is Possible," Stevens evokes a powerful faith in that linguistic rupture as constituting the space in which we might redeem our actual world. However, the pass from Stevens' sense of the power of this linguistic rupture to that of Jordan's more personally charged and politically specific poetry depends upon the more sobering route taken from *Esthétique du Mal,* through Bishop, and through Rich. In fact, this poetic history or journey, which is of course highly selective, nonetheless again anticipates one of the most recent and most important moves made by Jacques Derrida, with whom I began.

In a recent article published in the *Cardozo Law Review,* Derrida has attended more specifically to the potential ethical dimensions and consequences of deconstruction. Most succinctly, the overriding thesis of "The Force of Law" is that the "law" (a highly patriarchal and domineering construct in that essay, as it is for some of the poets here) can be deconstructed precisely because it has been constructed, but that justice, if it exists, cannot be. This, it seems to me, is the "good news" of that "rupture" or "event" with which I began, and one with which our poets, from Stevens through Bishop and Rich to Jordan, would ultimately concur. It is in fact that very rupture that allows us, however variously, to realize a multitude of planets on the table, some of which we may be blessed to read. As Stevens says, perhaps with no more faith in a logocentric authority than Derrida, "Out of this same light, out of the central mind, / We make a dwelling in the evening air, / In which being there together is enough"—lines that might indeed have our world blazing, spiritually, if we were ever to take the "response-ability" to make the "actual candle" of the "artifice", which those lines describe, truly the actual poetic and political lines of the planet, of which we are a part.

P. Jane Splawn (essay date June 1996)

SOURCE: "New World Consciousness in the Poetry of Ntozake Shange and June Jordan: Two African-American Women's Response to Expansionism in the Third World," in *CLA Journal,* Vol. XXXIX, No. 4, June 1996, pp. 417-31.

[*In the following essay, Splawn examines the work of Ntozake Shange and June Jordan, in which she finds examples of "a New World aesthetic."*]

And who will join in this standing up
and the ones who stood without sweet company
will sing and sing
back into the mountains and
if necessary
even under the sea

we are the ones we have been waiting for.

—June Jordan, **"Poem for**
South African Women"

of course he's lumumba
see only the eyes/bob marley wail
in the night ralph featherstone
burning temples as pages of books
become ashen and smolder by his ankles
walter rodney's blood fresh soakin
the streets/leon damas spoke poems
with his face/cesaire cursed our
enemies/making welcome our true voice.

—Ntozake Shange, "irrepressibly
bronze, beautiful & mine"

I

Poet June Jordan asks in the first line of the epigraph to this paper, "And who will join this standing up"—this standing up for every individual, regardless of race, nationality, gender, and sexuality? The words in the epigraph invoke a call to the many African-descended peoples throughout the world and to their allies, be they black (by race or by political-class identity) or white. Jordan, activist, author, scholar, and poet, seems to suggest that those who hear and will heed this call are those who aspire to a New World vision of strength in diversity, and love in our differences. This is the message that June Jordan delivers in exemplary poems from her oeuvre, such as **"Poem about My Rights."** In **"Poem about My Rights,"** Jordan unfolds the pervasive nature of the oppression that diasporan women face in their day-to-day lives. Similarly, poet, activist, dramatist Ntozake Shange, in the preceding epigraph, links the oppression which African-descended people resist from one part of the globe to another. In this excerpt from "irrepressibly bronze, beautiful & mine," Shange shows how Patrice Lumumba's eyes, Bob Marley's wail, and Walter Rodney's blood blend, forming one unifying consciousness that I am calling the consciousness of the New World artist. Thus, New World consciousness is (1) grounded specifically in the experience of oppression diasporic women face; (2) linked to African-descended people throughout the globe; and (3) serves as a call to connect with allies who are oppressed elsewhere (i.e., in the Middle East, Central America, etc.)

This paper proposes to lay out the idea of a New World aesthetic as gleaned from the writings of June Jordan and Ntozake Shange, two African-American writers and activists, and will argue, in the words of Ntozake Shange in "Bocas: A Daughter's Geography," that though "our twins salvadore & johannesburg / do not speak the same language, . . . we fight the same old men / in the new world." These women writers see a very clear analog between their victimization as blacks and as women globally and the perpetuation of racist and expansionist regimes. June Jordan sees this connection clearly in the previously alluded to **"Poem about My Rights"** when she identifies two forms of terrorism in the brutal raping of women in the expansionist ideology of a country, in this case South Africa, which "penetrat[es] into Namibia [which then in turn] penetrat[es] into Angola."

In the New World aesthetic, women are engaged in the struggle to overcome oppression equally with men. Historical data is invoked in the poetry to reclaim the place of women in the liberation struggle. Section II of Shange's "irrepressibly bronze, beautiful & mine" reveals the solidarity in the struggle of George Jackson and Angela Davis, two African-American political activists whose stance on justice cost them time served in prison. Shange opens this section of the poem with the following portrayal of a typical day in the life of two leaders,

> he's of course george jackson
> doing push-ups and visiting with angela
> soledad soledad
> confined to his beauty alone
> fighting cement walls for air.

The final line, "fighting cement walls for air" is an allusion to "combat breathing," Fanon's term for the measured response of oppressed people to their oppression. Indeed, one might argue that it is exactly upon Fanon's conception of how oppressed people respond to their oppression that Jordan and Shange base the New World aesthetic.

II

But what is the New World aesthetic, the New World consciousness espoused in the writings of Ntozake Shange and June Jordan? The use of Fanon and Walt Whitman reflects the openness to which New World consciousness situates its literary and theoretical antecedents. June Jordan comes to a definition of New World consciousness by beginning with the vision of pluralism espoused in Walt Whitman's *Democratic Vistas* and in his representative poems, and then tracing this radical vision of democracy in the writings of activist

poets in the Americas and in the Caribbean. On Whitman's vision, she writes in the introduction to **Passion,** "New World does not mean New England. New World means non-European: it means big, it means heterogeneous, it means unknown, it means free, it means an end to feudalism, caste, privilege, and the violence of power. It means wild in the sense that a tree growing away from the earth enacts a wild event."

In that same introduction, Jordan further argues:

> In the poetry of the New World, you meet with reverence for human life, an intellectual trust in sensuality as a means of knowledge and of unity, an easily deciphered system of reverence, aspiration to a believable, collective voice and, consequently, emphatic preference for broadly accessible language and/or "spoken" use of language, structure of forward energies that interconnects apparently discrete or even confidential balancing of perception with vision: a balancing of sensory report with moral exhortation."

Indeed, one might argue that while we are acutely aware of the many variations of our "Africanisms," a New World consciousness problematizes the imposed division between blacks in the New World and blacks in other parts of the globe. In fact, it problematizes all kinds of divisions, be they gender, racial, or sexual. An example of the New World writers' response to this can be seen in Shange's "New World Coro":

> the earth hums some song of her own
> cuz
> we have a daughter/mozambique
> we have a son/angola
> our twins
> salvadore & johannesburg/cannot speak
> the same language
> but we fight the same old men/in the new world
> we are so hungry for the morning
> we are trying to feed our children the sun
> but a long time ago/we boarded ships/locked in
> depths of seas our spirits/kisst the earth
> on the atlantic side of nicaragua costa rica
> our lips traced the edges of cuba puerto rico
> charleston & savannah/in haiti
> we embraced &
> made children of the new world
> but old men spit on us/shackled our limbs
> old men spit on us/shackled our limbs
> for but a minute . . .
> you'll see us in luanda or the rest of us in chicago.

> (*A Daughter's Geography*)

The line "see us in luanda or the rest of us in chicago" signals the interconnectedness of African-descended people to suggest that African-descended people are really the same people who are merely separated by geographical location. Despite overwhelming historical odds against survival of the Middle Passage, Africans en route to the New World did survive and, generations later, women and men descendants of those African survivors seek to "feed [their] children the sun," a line reminiscent of Zora Neale Hurston's memory of her mother's prodding of herself and of her siblings to "jump at de sun," or reach for the heights of success, in her autobiography *Dust Tracks on a Road.* Also the repetition of the syntactical unit "but old men spit on us/shackled our limbs" twice powerfully underscores the theme of racially based oppression by powerful, though cowardly, elites who spat on the enshackled women and men in the New World who could not, by virtue of their being enshackled, retaliate. It should be noted as well that this refrain is repeated in the longer poem, "Bocas: A Daughter's Geography." In that poem Shange pointedly states,

> there is no edge
> no end to the new world
> cuz i have a daughter/trinidad
> i have a son/san juan
> our twins
> capetown & palestine/cannot speak the same
> language/but we fight the same old men
> the same old men who thought that the earth waz
> flat
> go on over the edge/go on over the edge old men.

> (*A Daughter's Geography*)

The first two lines in the above quote underscore Shange's view and, I might add, the view of other contemporary activists such as Audre Lorde and Jean Binta Breeze—that people of color comprise four-fifths of the globe; thereby, leaving terms like "minority" open to interrogation. And though there is "no edge to the new world," the speaker in this section invites the old men, who elsewhere in the poem "spat on us," and who deign themselves the discoverers of the New World, to "go on over the edge." This alludes to the prevailing view about the shape of the earth during the time of the most notable of those "old men," Christopher Columbus, that the earth was flat and that therefore one could fall off the edge if one attempted to sail around it. It is worth noting that as with the line "but old men spit on us/ shackled our limbs," this line is also repeated, underscoring Shange's emphasis on reclaiming African-descended peoples' right to determine their own destiny.

III

For Shange and Jordan, however, our consciousness is not simply confined to our individual struggles in particular countries in the New World; they are also entwined with our collective struggles as "global Africans," Vibert Cambridge's term for African and African-descended peoples throughout the world, as well as with those of the people of Central America and the Middle East. Solidarity lies with other oppressed groups who are struggling. As Audre Lorde puts it, "Yet there is a vital part that we play as Black people in the liberation of consciousness of every freedom-seeking people upon this globe, no matter what they say they think about us as Black Americans."

Based on a line from Bob Marley's "Heathen," Shange's "Rise Up Fallen Fighters" addresses this theme pointedly:

> david's warriors
> rise up rise up fallen fighters
> show me the promised land
> show me round the universe
> our fathers' land
> rise up
> announce the comin of the kingdom's rightful
> heirs
> i climbin to the moon on the rasta-thruway
> our father lands
> risin up
> the land even sing & jump
> the sky want to jam all thru the day
> the stars forget they weakness
> & dance
>
> rise up fallen fighters
> unfetter the stars
> dance with the universe
> & make it ours
>
> rise up fallen fighters
> unfetter the stars
> dance with the universe
> & make it ours
>
> oh, make it/make it ours
> oh, make it/make it ours.

> (*A Daughter's Geography*)

"[O]ur father lands / risin up" and references to the "fallen fighters" connote the collective struggle of African-descended people and their ancestors for freedom. These fallen fighters—like Petion, L'Ouverture, and Dessalines in Haiti, to whom Shange addresses her plea for their spiritual return during the Duvalier regime in "A Dark Night in Haiti: Palais National"—comprise the dead African and African-descended warriors, both male and female, who had been so successful in the past in breaking the tyranny of their enslavers. The line may also be a reference to more recent warriors who, while still alive, have experienced set-backs (hence, the reference to "fallen") in the struggle for freedom. Since the speaker asks the "fallen fighters" to "rise up" and "unfetter the stars," a role that only mythic figures who have been immortalized as constellations, etc., can do, the poem fuses Todorov's fantastic with magical realism and traditional African religion.

June Jordan speaks of another kind of resistance in **"A Song for Soweto,"** by opening the poem with the issue of language imposed on the colonized. Her use of phrases like "devil language" and "falls slashing" denotes a cultural moment when one's language and one's oppression are interconnected. For as the speaker states,

>   Where she would praise
>   father
>   They would teach her to pray
>   somebody please
>   do not take him
>   away
>   Where she would kiss with her mouth
>   my homeland
>   They would teach her to swallow
>   this dust.

This interconnection does exist, "[b]ut words live in the spirit of her face and that / sound will no longer yield to imperial erase." Thus,

>   Where they would draw
>   blood
>   She will drink
>   water
>   Where they would deepen
>   the grave
>   She will conjure up
>   grass
>   Where they would take
>   father and family away
>   She will stand
>   under the sun/she will stay
>   Where they would teach her to swallow
>
>   this dust
>   She will kiss with her mouth
>   my homeland
>   and stay
>   with the song of Soweto
>   stay
>   with the song of Soweto.

The Soweto girl embodies the New World consciousness in her resistance to colonization. Though she has been made to face insurmountable odds, she takes for herself the beauty of "[her] homeland."

Expanding on themes raised in **"A Song for Soweto,"** Jordan makes a powerful statement about the oppression of women and of Third World countries by the superpower countries in **"Poem about My Rights"**:

>   which is exactly like South Africa
>   penetrating into Namibia penetrating into
>   Angola and does that mean/mean how do you
>   know if
>   Pretoria ejaculates what will the evidence look
>   like the
>   proof of the monster jackboot ejaculation on
>   blackland
>   and if
>   After Namibia and if after Angola and if after
>   Zimbabwe
>   and if after all my kinsmen and women resist
>   even to
>   self-immolation of the villages and if after that
>   we lose nevertheless what will the big boys say
>   will they
>   claim my consent.

(Passion)

The implications of Pretoria's "monster jackboot ejaculation on Blackland" are particularly rich if one considers the rise of certain countries to superpower status due to military, rather than economic, power. Further, "if Pretoria ejaculates what will the evidence look like?" is a reference to the difficulty of providing legally sanctioned "proof" in the judicial system, not only of rape but also of other forms of oppression, such as racism. The more trenchant aspect of Jordan's question, however, points to the New World consciousness concerns. That is, what do the manifestations of Pretoria's "jackboot ejaculations" mean for African-descended people? Such evidence could take on a range of effects, including material, psychosocial, and spiritual manifestations of oppression. Later in the poem, Jordan makes reference to a kind of "penetration with or without the evidence of slime" (*Passion*), another example of the pervasive nature of victims having to provide the burden of proof in order to exact justice.

IV

see what the man have done
*   done*
see how the red blood run
*   run.*

—June Jordan, **"Atlantic Coast Reggae"**

Thus begin the opening lines to Jordan's **"Atlantic Coast Reggae,"** lyrics from a reggae the poet describes in an essay in *On Call: Political Essays,* in which she describes a little girl's matter-of-fact reflecting in a street song that she sings about the people of Nicaragua's attitudes about expansionism from the West in her country. The refrain to the song is sung by a five-year-old girl who, like most people living on the Atlantic side of Nicaragua, is black and English-speaking. The refrain—the New World consciousness refrain, that sees the systemic paradigms of power and, while never accepting its invasive effects, situates the responsibility for the effects of war and destruction where they belong (i.e., with the colonial powers)—reminds us how banal the realities of occupation are for African and African-descending people. It is, in the words of Ntozake Shange, "like drinking morning coffee." My point of emphasis here is that the speaker is a young girl who, like her male peers, is actively engaged in the struggle for liberation. As I have indicated in the first section of the paper, women are engaged in the New World struggle on a par with men. Women give their lives for the Revolution. Jordan makes explicit in **"Fourth Poem from Nicaragua Libre: Report from the Frontier"** the high price that women pay for their involvement in the struggle for liberation:

> gone gone gone ghost
> > gone
> > both the house of the hard dirt floor and the
> church
> > next door
> > torn apart more raggedy than skeletons
> > when the bombs hit
> leaving a patch of her scalp
> like a bird's nest
> in the dark yard still lit by flowers.

The "piece of scalp with hair attached" provides shocking evidence of the price exacted from one woman for her fight for freedom. Left "like a bird's nest" scattered in the debris of the bombed community, the visible remains of what once was a vibrant human being testify to Nicaraguan women's engagement in the struggle for liberation.

In a more personal vein than the previous poem, the woman speaker in the following poem makes clear her distaste of gender abuse:

> I AM NOT STILL As i stand here like a phony
> catatonic:
> > aggressively resisting. I am not, it is not
> > > important
> > am i an impermeable membrane. This resis-
> > > tance
> > provokes the madness of enumeration
> > I am insensible to a,b,c,d,e,f,g,—

> And the gamble of elimination:
> A*, B*, C*—
> The energy this resistance requires is itself an
> alteration of temperature, at least.
> So I surrender. I surrender and I multiply:
> Polybot:
> Sponge.

(Naming Our Destiny)

This passage invokes Stuart Hall's reminder that the body is the only cultural capital that we have. The speaker expresses her defiance via negation. Even in her impassive stance, she resists total denial of self. Her "surrender" is a negotiated one, whether her oppressors realize it or not; for as Audre Lorde tells us, one's oppressors must overcome their victims, but resistors need only survive. Thus, her position in the poem is one that she mediates for herself: echoing Langston Hughes's resisting speaker in "I, Too," she elects to "surrender" and "multiply:" [p]olybot:" "[s]ponge."

Jordan presents a further example of women's commitment to the battle for liberation in her poem **"To Free Nelson Mandela":**

> They have murdered Victoria Mxenge
> they have murdered her
> victorious now
> that the earth recoils from that crime
> of her murder now
> that the very dirt shudders from the falling blood
> the thud of bodies fallen
> into the sickening
> into the thickening
> crimes of apartheid
>
> Every night
> Every night Winnie Mandela
> Every night the waters of the world
> twin to the sofly burning
> light of the moon.

(Naming Our Destiny)

Jordan's use of assonance in the near-refrain, "into the sickening / into the thickening / crimes of apartheid" approximates the blues pattern. Images of "dirt shuddering," "falling blood," "thud[s] of bodies," however, add a morbid twist to the blues motif. Nonetheless, the speaker suggests that despite the perverse conditions, women, like Victoria Mxenge and Winnie Mandela, inspire hope through their resistance. It should be noted that though feminist issues are expressed in Shange's and Jordan's writing, they are inextricably linked to issues encompassed in the New World aesthetic.

V

I am not wrong: Wrong is not my name
My name is my own my own my own
and I can't tell you who the hell set things up like
this
But I can tell you that from now on my resistance
my simple and daily and nightly self-determina-
tion
may very well cost you your life.

—June Jordan, Conclusion to
"Poem about My Rights"

In conclusion I would like to underscore Jordan's and Shange's too often overlooked message. For these African-American women writers, the era of the Euro-American liberal, whether in academia or in various other professions, has passed. We are in an age of radical artists, thinkers, and leaders who do not seek to join the established bureaucracy. Furthermore, these writers resist essentialist postures that seek to offer definitive expressions of their expressions of their experiences as women in the African diaspora; they write, as Issac Julien puts it, "from the African diaspora," as opposed to "of the African diaspora." These women would give their lives for the establishment of a New World. In such a world men and women share equally in the full benefits of freedom. Difference is not only tolerated but celebrated. Jordan's and Shange's vision of a New World is not a philosophical retreat of perpetual ecstasy nor complacency, but rather a world of striving. Echoing Frederick Douglass'

maxim that there is "no progress without a struggle," Jordan's and Shange's vision of the New World epitomizes that foreshadowed by Fanon in *A Dying Colonialism,* in which men and women engage in "combat breathing," a measured response to oppression. But with regard to colonizers, Jordan and Shange make clear that although they and other African-descended and indigenous people "[did not] set things up like this," they will not be silenced. Indeed, one might argue that these writers feel a need to retaliate against their oppressors. As Shange goads the "old men" in "Bocas: A Daughter's Geography" to "go on over the edge," these writers write about retribution even as they speak of empowerment and equality.

FURTHER READING

Criticism

Jordan, June. "Writing and Teaching." *Partisan Review,* Vol. XXVI, No. 3 (1969): 478-82.

An essay in which Jordan explains her perception of issues of language related to the production, teaching and understanding of literature.

Moramarco, Fred. "A Gathering of Poets." *Western Humanities Review,* Vol. XXIV, No. 2 (Spring 1970): 201-07.

Considers Jordan's first book of poetry in the context of several poetry collection by other contemporary American poets.

Additional coverage of Jordan's life and career is contained in the following sources published by Gale: *Authors and Artists for Young Adults,* Vol. 2; *Black Literature Criticism Supplement; Black Writers,* Vol. 2; *Contemporary Authors,* Vols. 33-36; *Contemporary Authors New Revision Series,* Vol. 25; *Children's Literature Review,* Vol. 10; *Dictionary of Literary Biography,* Vol. 38; *Discovering Authors: Multicultural Authors Module; Discovering Authors: Poets Module; Major Authors and Illustrators for Children and Young Adults; Major 20th-Century Writers;* and *Something About the Author,* Vol. 4.

Miroslav Krleza

1893-1981

Croatian dramatist, novelist, essayist, short story writer, poet, critic, and autobiographer.

The following entry presents criticism of Krleza's career through 1987. For further information on his life and works, see *CLC,* Volume 8.

INTRODUCTION

Considered the most significant Croatian literary voice of the twentieth century, Krleza wrote more than five dozen books, but has been generally ignored by Western academics and readers. Only a small portion of his work has been published in English—two novels, a short story collection, and selected writings issued in periodicals. His commitment to radical humanism led the Yugoslav government to ban most of his work until 1940, but by the early 1950s Krleza had become a major proponent of the artistic integrity of indigenous Yugoslav cultures. A master stylist who is often compared to such Western literary luminaries as James Joyce and Marcel Proust, most of Krleza's writings concern the downfall of the Austro-Hungarian empire and its transformation into a modern socialist state, while giving expression to often ambiguous themes and politics. Ante Kadic has explained that Krleza's "materialist convictions—conveyed with strong emotional impetus, his Marxist and liberal philosophy, his socialism mingled with sincere defense of personal freedom, and his readiness to defend his point of view with his own life—made Krleza highly controversial."

Biographical Information

Born in Zagreb, Yugoslavia, Krleza was sent to Hungary after graduating from high school to attend an officers' school in Pécs and then a military academy in Budapest. Although trained as an Austro-Hungarian officer, Krleza nonetheless sympathized with the Serbian nationalist cause and volunteered his services to the Serbian army in their war against the Turks in 1913. Suspicious Serbian officials, however, expelled Krleza, who consequently was arrested by Austrians, deprived of his rank, and sent to the front lines as a private when Austro-Hungary declared war on Serbia in 1914. This was the same year that Krleza made his literary debut with the publication of the anti-religious drama *Legenda* (1914). Krleza's experience on the fronts in Galicia and Austria during World War I brought him into contact with Croatian peasants and workers, with whom he shared the horrors and hardships of war, which became a principal theme in many of his writings. Inspired by the 1917 Octo-

ber revolution in Russia, Krleza and other leftist writers founded several short-lived, underground literary journals, including *Plamen* (1919), *Knjizevna republika* (1923-27), *Danas* (1934), and *Pecat* (1939-40). Despite official restrictions on his works in the period between the World Wars, Krleza proceeded to write not only plays but also novels, poetry, short stories, and essays. He continued to write during World War II, but he refrained from publishing his writings until later. Publicly disgraced after 1945 because he did not actively support the Partisan cause during the war, Krleza was rehabilitated by Yugoslav President Josip Broz Tito during the early 1950s and went on to win numerous Yugoslavian literary prizes and several international awards, including the Heder Prize. In 1950 he was named director of the Yugoslav Lexicographic Institute—a position he held for the rest of his life—and from 1955 to 1971 he served as editor-in-chief of *Enciklopedija Jugoslavije*. In 1967 Krleza actively joined the cause of Croatians to publish in their own dialect, but when Tito issued an edict in 1971 against Croatian political leaders and intellectuals forbidding them to do so, Krleza retreated into silence. He died in Zagreb in 1981.

Major Works

Krleza's early plays, often likened to the romantic, symbolist style of Oscar Wilde, depict historical personages as legendary individuals struggling with self-doubt about their visionary goals and about validation of their ideas by the masses. *Legenda* portrays the relationship between Jesus and Lazarus's sister, Mary, who suffers unrequited love for Jesus despite the presence of his "shadow," or alter ego, which insists that Jesus betrayed his own self and his true feelings for his high ideals. *Mikelangelo Buonarti* (1925) presents the artist as the sensitive soul who rejects all earthly delights in favor of solitary pursuit of creative endeavors, while *Kristofor Kolombo* (1918) represents the explorer as a dreamer aware that his discovery of a new world will certainly succumb to the evils of the old. Themes of the horrors of war, the nullification of the past by a brighter future, and the peace obtained amid native landscapes inform Krleza's poetry collections, most notably *Lirika* (1919), *Knjiga lirike* (1932), and *Pjeseme u tmini* (1937). Written in the dialect of northern Croatia and influenced by Croatian folk poetry, *Balade Petrice Kremepuha* (1936), regarded as Krleza's formal and stylistic poetic masterpiece, traces the history of Croatian peasants from the 1570s to the 1930s, protesting the consistently intolerable conditions of peasant life under the nobility, the clergy, and the modern bureaucracy. Krleza's short stories and novels contrast the hardships of Croatian peasants with the decadence of the aristocracy and the bourgeoisie. Intended to represent the rise and fall of capitalistic society, a series of eleven stories and three plays describe the history of the Glembay family, whose rise out of peasantry to middle class prosperity is accompanied by moral degeneration. The plays in the so-called "Glembay cycle" feature the psychological method of dramatist Henrik Ibsen and include *Gospoda Glembajevi* (1928), *Leda* (1930), and *U agoniji* (1931). The novel *Povratak Filipa Latinovicza* (1932; *The Return of Philip Latinovicz*) tells the story of a once-renowned painter, who returns to his childhood home after a twenty-year absence and confronts unhappy memories. Similarly, the first-person narrative of *Na rubu pameti* (1938; *On the Edge of Reason*) recounts the story of a Zagreb lawyer's alienation from his society, which gradually resolves in his descent into madness. Krleza's other novels, *Banket u Blitvi* (1938-9) and *Zastave* (1967), focus on the relationship between the individual and his government, particularly in dictatorships reminiscent of those that came to power in the 1920s and 1930s. Krleza's numerous essays on subjects ranging from politics to literary criticism display his powers of persuasion and his vast, though sometimes inaccurate and biased, knowledge.

Critical Reception

Critics have regarded Krleza as a highly controversial writer, whether on the basis of his literary style and themes or his politics and philosophy. According to Kadic, only a few Central and Southern European critics have emphasized that "Krleza is the real initiator of Yugoslav revisionism." Although most scholars of his native land have recognized Krleza as the most significant Croatian and Yugoslavian writer to emerge during the twentieth century, some have attempted to discredit or minimize his literary and cultural achievements, particularly for his refusal to accept government interference in cultural and literary domains. Kadic has noted that "Krleza's skirmishes with the 'socialist' theoreticians were just as bitter and dangerous as were those with the bourgeois camp." In the English-speaking West, Krleza remains relatively unknown due to the paucity of his works published in translation. Some critics have maintained that this neglect stems in part from the narrow-mindedness of Western publishers and their public, while others have attributed his obscurity in the West to the ambiguous nature of Krleza's themes and politics. The link between his politics and writings has constituted the central debate among commentators, the majority of whom have remarked on the inherent duality of Krleza's vision, which simultaneously embraces socialist revolutionary ideals and the importance of moral and artistic integrity. Some have stressed the political activist perspective of Krleza's works, arguing that his Marxist leanings show the moral and political inefficacy of the middle class, but others have coun-

tered that the common thread throughout his literary corpus affirms an abiding belief in humanist ideals. Kadic has concluded that "Krleza was and shall remain a pivotal figure, and no one interested in twentieth-century Croatian and South Slavic literature can ignore him. . . . He fully deserves to be ranked among the luminaries of contemporary world literature."

PRINCIPAL WORKS*

Pan (poetry) 1917
Tri simfonije (poetry) 1917
Kraljevo (drama) 1918; published in *Hrvatska rapsodija*
Kristofor Kolombo (drama) 1918; published in *Hrvatska rapsodija* as *Christoval Colon*
Lirika (poetry) 1919
Hrvatski bog Mars (short stories) 1922
Izlet u Rusiju (travel essays) 1926
Gospoda Glembajevi (drama) 1928
Leda (drama) 1930
†*U agoniji* (drama) 1931; expanded edition, 1962
Glembajevi (drama) 1932
Knjiga lirike (poetry) 1932
Moj obracun s njima (essay) 1932
Povratak Filipa Latinovicza [*The Return of Philip Latinovicz*] (novel) 1932
‡*Legende* (dramas) 1933
Michelangelo Buonarroti (drama) 1925
Balade Petrice Kerempuha (poetry) 1936
Pjesme u tmini (poetry) 1937
§*Banket u Blitvi* (novel) 1938
Na rubu pameti [*On the Edge of Reason*] (novel) 1938
Dijalekticki antibarbarus (criticism) 1939
Djetinjstvo u Agramu 1902-1903 (autobiography) 1952
Aretej; ili, Legenda o Svetoj Ancili (drama) 1959; published in periodical *Mogucnosti*
Saloma (drama) 1963; published in periodical *Forum*
#*Zastave* (novel) 1967
The Cricket beneath the Waterfall, and Other Stories [*Cvrcak pod vodopadon*] (short stories) 1972
Selected Correspondence (letters) 1988

*Dates for dramas represent first publication, except for the drama *Leda*.
†This work was originally produced in two acts. A third act was produced in 1959.
‡This work contains the dramas *Legenda, Michelangelo Buonarotti, Kristofor Kolumbo, Maskerata, Kraljevo,* and *Adam i Eva*.
§The first volume of this work was published in 1938, the second in 1939, and the third in 1956.
#This work originally appeared in four volumes; a fifth volume was added in 1976.

CRITICISM

Ante Kadic (essay date Autumn 1963)

SOURCE: "Miroslav Krleza," in *Books Abroad,* Vol. 37, No. 4, Autumn, 1963, pp. 396-400.

[*In the following essay, Kadic provides a thematic and generic overview of Krleza's writings.*]

Miroslav Krleza should not be treated as a man of letters only: his significance lies in various fields. One can safely state that his role in the establishment of the Communist dictatorship in Yugoslavia was extremely significant. There is no one who did more than Krleza to discredit bourgeois society and to orient a great number of intellectuals toward socialism.

To understand and appreciate Krleza one must locate him in his milieu, in Zagreb, during and after the First World War, when the Austrian empire was rapidly disintegrating and royalist Yugoslavia was in the process of formation. Krleza was one of the first who revolted against the megalomania and mythomania of the military clique in Belgrade, which considered the non-Serbian lands a conquered territory.

Krleza was born in Zagreb on July 7, 1893. After completing high school, he was sent first to the officers' school in Pécs and then to the military academy in Budapest. At that time the Croatian intelligentsia hoped that Serbia would play the role of Yugoslav Piedmont in national liberation and unification. Although an Austro-Hungarian officer, Krleza espoused this ideal, crossed the border and volunteered in the Serbian war against the Turks (1913). The Serbian authorities became suspicious of him and expelled him; Krleza was thereafter arrested by the Austrians, deprived of his rank and, a year later, sent to the front as a private.

In Galicia and on other Austrian fronts, Krleza came into close contact with the Croatian peasants and workers who were being killed en masse for the "despised German Kaiser"; these simple and honest people had a deep yearning for decent family life, social justice, and the expulsion of all exploiters from their fields and villages.

Disillusioned over his "nationalistic" dreams and suffering now with the underprivileged who were slaughtered like sheep, Krleza greeted the October Revolution as a promising earthquake, as a starting point for a new and better world.

Alone or with other leftist writers Krleza edited literary journals (*Plamen,* 1919; *Knjizevna republika,* 1923-27; *Danas,* 1934; *Pecat,* 1939-40). Although most of them were short-lived, being banned by police authorities, these magazines played an important role in orienting several Yugoslav writers toward leftist goals. Already in *Plamen* Krleza expressed his conviction that the flame which was burning in the hearts of the oppressed would soon burst forth; he insisted that the working class would be able to govern itself and others.

During World War II Krleza was in constant danger; rumors were spread abroad that he was dead. He wrote much, but more of this work remains unpublished; only fragments have appeared here and there (as e.g., his exceptionally revealing *Djetinjstvo u Agramu,* 1902-03). A recently launched magazine *Forum* has published several of his essays and his long novel *Zastave* (*Banners*, first volume), dealing with World War I and its aftermath.

Krleza is the Director of the Lexicographic Institute in Zagreb; he is the editor-in-chief of *Enciklopedija Jugoslavije,* a unique enterprise of historic importance; unfortunately, it omits or slanders enemies of the regime and over-praises partisans.

Krleza's first published work was his anti-religious play *Legenda* (1914). In it he portrays Jesus and his relations with Mary, the sister of Lazarus; she is in love with him; he knows it, but he prefers to reject her advances, being afraid that they could impede him in his obstinate search for truth and eternity. His Shadow, which is his alter ego, tries to convince him he should not fly too high, because only terrestrial things have real substance and can procure worthy pleasure; the rest is smoke and purely cerebral invention. Jesus is presented as an illegitimate child, who later abandoned his weeping mother and numerous brothers. The resurrection of Lazarus was arranged; Judas's betrayal was his revenge for rejection by Mary, who preferred the misty eyes and soft skin of the Preacher. The play, full of historical allusions and premonitions, is hard to perform; its unity lies in the writer's conviction that Jesus was untrue to himself and his better feelings. In the same spirit and pattern—a mixture of history, materialist preaching and rejection of any religious belief—Krleza wrote other short plays (such as *Kristofor Kolombo,* 1917; *Michelangelo Buonarroti,* 1918).

In 1917 Krleza published his "expressionistic" poem *Pan.* Here again, through the fragmented sketches, he chants the beauty of nature and joys of life as opposed to the Christian self-abnegation; he is sure that the final triumph will be with man's natural inclinations. His boys and girls wonder why, instead of love and merriment, people are taught by clergymen to pray, and lament for uncommitted sins. Krleza's most significant "symphony" is one called **"A Street in an Autumn Morning"** (**"Ulica u jesenje jutro"**), in which he deplores the stupidity of his countrymen who boast about military success, forgetting that their dear ones are hungry and their roofs are already falling in. He sees the shining Star, but is alone, because the masses still find solace in wine and military songs.

The same or similar themes—war and its horror, the rejection of the past and belief in a bright future, peace of mind found in the midst of the native landscape—are to be found in his subsequent collections of poetry (the most important being: *Lirika,* 1919; *Knjiga lirike—A Book of Lyrics,* 1932; *Pjesme u tmini—Poems in the Darkness,* 1937). In his **"Plameni vjetar"** (**"The Burning Wind"**) he foresees the final destruction of all lies, and in his famous **"Noc u provinciji"** (**"Night in the Province"**) he compares the reactionaries to dogs barking at the moon.

Krleza's masterpiece in form and style is his *Balade Petrice Kerempuha* (*The Ballads of Petrica Kerempuh,* 1936). Kerempuh is an equivalent of the German Till Eulenspiegel, a peasant clown who enjoys playing tricks on persons of higher rank. In his ballads Krleza describes the sufferings of the Croatian peasants, from the time of Matija Gubec and his comrades (1573) to the present. The Illyrian movement and abolition of serfdom (1848) did not change their intolerable situation. Kerempuh does not hope, as the poet Gundulic did, that the ruling classes will one day serve their former servants; he realizes that peasants, like himself, were always exploited by noblemen, clergymen, and bureaucrats. In Petrica's songs, very much under the influence of folk poetry, Krleza is bitter, but effective; his protest is conveyed in such a masterly way that even those who were mercilessly attacked were shaken by the truth and depth of his analysis.

The hardships of the Croatian peasants, particularly during the First World War, and the decadence of the middle class are main themes of Krleza's short stories and plays; in these he reaches his greatest achievement.

> **In Petrica's songs, very much under the influence of folk poetry, Krleza is bitter, but effective; his protest is conveyed in such a masterly way that even those who were mercilessly attacked were shaken by the truth and depth of his analysis.**
> **—Ante Kadic**

In his deeply moving collection of short stories, *Hrvatski bog Mars* (*The Croatian God Mars,* 1922), all dealing with the Croatian *domobrani* (home guards), there are three particular stories which are considered among the best works in world literature about war and its atrocities. The first story, **"Bitka kod Bistrice Lesne,"** describes the tragic end of seven Croatian peasants in Galicia, while at home their children are starving, their wives drink out of desperation, their parents have nobody to take care of them, and their fields remain uncultivated. **"Baraka pet be"** (**"Hut Five B"**) deals also with the bloody fighting in Galicia and points to its consequences: a hospital full of patients who are divided into three catagories—those with broken and protruding bones, those with amputated legs and arms, and those whose last moment is rapidly approaching. The student Vidovic belongs to the third group. When he hears the Austro-Hungarian doctors and nurses celebrating a small victory with champagne, he decides with the last drop of his energy to throw his excrement at their rich table. *Hrvatska rapsodija* is a vision of Croatia and its centuries-long suffering under the cruel Magyar domination: a train is carrying the entire nation toward the battlefield; sick, hungry, mad, desperate, and bigoted people are sketched in the same tableau. Krleza is convinced that such a train must fall into an abyss to make room for a more logical life.

As many other great writers have done, Krleza also depicts a particular family, Glembay, in an effort to portray the ascent and decline of capitalistic society. In eleven stories and three plays Krleza narrates how this Croatian family, whose peasant ancestor became rich in the eighteenth century by killing a Styrian goldsmith, gradually moved into higher circles; its descendants were bankers, businessmen, government officials, and generals. Their moral dissoluteness grew in proportion to their wealth. They could prosper only in the anti-national and anti-social Austro-Hungarian empire of which they were most obedient servants. When in 1918 Austria was officially proclaimed dead, all these Glembays were already nervous wrecks, ready to commit crimes or suicide. Krleza shows them in the moment of their downfall as degenerates and criminals; through them he castigates the capitalistic system of which they were representatives.

Whereas in his *Legenda* Krleza was romantic and symbolist (*à la* Wilde) and in his *Hrvatska rapsodija* concentrated on the external action, in his plays about the Glembays he tried a new method: a psychological dialogue, with few characters and extremely limited action.

Gospoda Glembajevi (*The Glembays,* 1928) centers on the conflict between Ignjat Glembay and his son Leone; whereas the old Glembay is an embodiment of the negative aspects of his class, Leone (his son by his first marriage) is an educated and refined gentleman, who would be relieved if he could free himself from the stains of his ancestral blood. In a violent quarrel with his father he shouts that his second wife is a prostitute; the old man is ready to kill him, but dies from a heart attack; after his death it becomes evident that his "fabulous" fortune is nonexistent. His wife is desperate; losing control of herself, she uses bad terms about Leone and the nun Angelica who shares Leone's views; he becomes furious and kills his stepmother. Leone, though a strange character, is an honest man. Krleza believes that the Glembay circle, as a social monster, was predestined for self-destruction; when hidden passions and hatred surge to the surface, all polished appearances give way and petty characters betray their real nature. Krleza is a master of words and action: in the first act, when very little is happening, we sense the oncoming storm in the innuendoes between father and son; the intensity of the dialogue keeps the reader in suspense.

U Agoniji (*In Agony*) was written in the same year (1928). In the first act Baron Lenbach, after a humiliating quarrel with his wife Laura, commits suicide; Laura, who for three years has loved a lawyer, Ivan Krizovec, and hoped to be his wife, discovers then that she was only his transient flirt. Lenbach is degenerate and a drunkard; Krizovec wants to succeed even in this new non-Magyar environment, while Laura vibrates with intelligence, passion, and sincerity. There are few pages in South Slavic literature where psychological perception and intensity are so superb. Laura's faint suspicion suddenly becomes certitude; she is at once able to draw conclusions from certain movements, from certain expressions; she had noticed these same details before but was unable to comprehend them because she was blindly in love. Now when it is too late, she grasps everything; "I remember in the semi-darkness of the auditorium, everything happened between you and me that could possibly have happened. The light was shining on you. To your right, two rows in front of us, sat an unknown woman. You were flirting with her. All that was like a flash, and then it went out. I forgot it, but now I see that what happened in that flash was everything. Your glance in the eyes of that strange woman, my movement toward you, that was everything! I wanted a child by you that night! Yes, I so wanted to feel your hand, but you. . . ."

In the eighth edition of this play (1962) a third act has been added; Laura attempts suicide at the end of the third instead of the second act. It is true that we learn more about Krizovec, about this extremely evasive character and his capacity for presenting his selfish motives as the benevolent gestures of a gentleman, but the question nevertheless remains if this third act adds anything to our understanding of the protagonists.

There persists the same discussion about Krleza's third play *Leda* (1930) as about Chekhov's *The Cherry Orchard:* is it comedy or drama? The author calls it "a comedy of a carnival night" and certain stage-directors in presenting it put the accent on the word "comedy." *Leda* is a logical conclusion of the two previous plays from the Glembay cycle: a knight, Oliver Urban, knows well that his family's prosperous days are forever gone and now attempts to obtain from life whatever he can; as a former aristocrat he has great charm which he abundantly uses in seducing the wives of his friends; the fortune is gone, but moral depravity is in his bones. Besides Urban, there is a parvenu, a green Yugoslav capitalist and

industrialist, Klanfar, whose mentality is no better than that of the Glembays. The old and new exploiters are symbolically rejected by an old cleaning woman, who feels only disgust while sweeping up the remnants of their debauchery.

Krleza's novel *Povratak Filipa Latinovicza* (*The Return of Philip Latinovicz,* 1932) describes almost the same society as do his Glembay plays. Philip does not know who his father is, he has no respect for his mother of easy morals, he is devoid of any national feelings, and becomes involved with a nymphomaniac, Bobocka, who is later killed by her neurotic husband. Philip has neither roots nor principles; he believes that only art could sublimate him and mankind. Sick and tired of cosmopolitan life, he returns to his native Zagorje to find peace of mind. When his dreams evaporate under the brutal analysis of a vagabond, Kyriales, Philip loses his last chance for salvation. This novel, broad in perspective, unmasking the moral nakedness of selfish individuals, and full of sophisticated digressions, contains several passages hard to read; its action in general moves slowly.

In 1938 two novels by Krleza appeared: *Banket u Blitvi* (*Banquet in Blitva,* first and second volumes, the third having been published only in 1962, in the magazine *Forum*) and *Na rubu pameti* (*On the Brink of Reason*).

Although in the first novel everything is presented as happening in some northern land and Krleza uses allegorical language, it is obvious that he is depicting the regime of royal Yugoslavia; the main character is Barutanski (King Alexander): a cretin who considers himself an emanation of divine will and rules the country in a most arbitrary fashion. "Banquet in Blitva," masterfully composed, is enjoyable reading for it has not lost its actuality: it is a solid historical work presented in attractive, imaginative form.

Na rubu pameti is about an individual who revolts against the higher society to which he belongs by his education and wealth; he is proclaimed mentally deranged. He is not a mouthpiece of the author; on the contrary, Krleza often ridicules him because of his ineffectiveness. *On the Brink of Reason* is a mixture of realistic snapshots given in monologue form. Some critics (e.g., Marakovic) have viewed this novel as evidence of Krleza's decline.

Another of Krleza's fascinating books is *Izlet u Rusiju* (*A Trip to Russia,* 1926; second somewhat shortened and modified edition, 1958). Although he went to the Soviet Union favorably disposed toward the new socialist system, he did not write as a propagandist; he saw there both positive and negative sides. Krleza was glad to observe the enthusiasm of a working man in rebuilding his country, but he also saw the bureaucrats who enjoyed many privileges and were a great obstacle to the normal development of socialism. This travelogue is a lyrical and human document; the author understands the tragedy even of those who were dethroned by the new order. Krleza proved to be an artist who looks with open eyes at those whom he loves; he is convinced that final victory is with the proletariat, and therefore he was not afraid to point to its weaknesses.

Krleza has written numerous essays on foreign and Croatian artists. He wrote interesting, though often controversial pages on many prominent Croats (such as Juraj Krizanic, Frano Supilo, Stjepan Radic, Ivan Mestrovic and others). In reading these studies one should not expect absolute correctness in his statements or an objective and balanced judgment about his opponents (e.g., about Mestrovic "who believed in God"), but appreciate Krleza's intuition, persuasion, expressive power, and melodiousness; one should accept the necessity for his repetitions, his similes, and antitheses. When he writes, he quarrels with himself and other imaginary or real antagonists. Right or wrong, all his essays bear the stamp of his extraordinary talent and not one should be disregarded.

There are few writers who are so deeply esteemed but were so bitterly opposed as Krleza; while the majority of critics (Marijan Matkovic, Marko Ristic, Milan Bogdanovic, Sime Vucetic and others) consider him the most outstanding Yugoslav writer between two wars, the others (e.g., Ivo Lendic, Stanislav Simic) did everything they could to discredit him. Krleza did not remain silent; being a man of strong convictions and temperament, he defended himself and his beliefs. In his famous ***Moj obracun s njima*** (***My Squaring of Accounts with Them,*** 1932) there are precious autobiographical items (e.g., about his nationalistic enchantment and later disappointment).

From his appearance on the literary horizon until 1941, and again after 1948, Krleza was constantly in the forefront. His materialist convictions, conveyed with a tremendous emotional impetus, his sometimes hard to grasp but always powerful sentences, his Marxist and liberal philosophy, his socialism mixed with sincere defense of personal freedom and his readiness to defend his point of view with his own life—all this made Krleza highly controversial and unacceptable both to the nationalists and rigid Communists. Few critics stress the fact that Krleza is the real initiator of Yugoslav revisionism. He never accepted the political *ukase* in literature. The writer should have, according to him, progressive ideas and then write as he thinks best. Krleza's skirmishes with the "socialist" theoreticians were just as bitter and dangerous as were those with the bourgeois camp. His death sentence was pronounced both by Stalinists and by *ustashis.*

To stress the unusual power of Krleza's writing does not prevent the realization that, at times, he appears to be an author not easy to read. To appreciate his formal and thematic innovations does not hinder one from seeing the light of other stars. To recognize Krleza's importance does not imply acceptance of his ideology. To respect his courage does not mean approval of his recent silence.

Ante Kadic (essay date January 1967)

SOURCE: "Krleza's Tormented Visionaries," in *The Slavonic and East European Review,* Vol. XLV, No. 4, January, 1967, pp. 46-64.

[*In the essay below, Kadic establishes a biographical context for an examination of Krleza's early works, tracing his preoccupation with "tormented" protagonists.*]

Since Miroslav Krleza (born in 1893) is the leading Yugoslav Communist writer and as such believes in the progress of mankind and the ultimate victory of the proletariat, Yugoslav critics have been understandably reluctant to analyse his early output, especially the plays written at a time when he was a nihilist and sceptic. A thorough examination of the early work of Krleza, in which his doubts remain unsolved, is worth-while.

For an appreciation of Krleza's early plays in which, at the beginning of his literary career, he portrayed certain well-known historical figures as idealists who gradually became disillusioned both with their own visions and with their followers, some biographical details are relevant. This distinguished Croatian writer is generally considered to be at least as good as, if not superior to, Ivo Andric. Whereas Andric (born in 1892) excels in form, Krleza's strong individuality, his early revolutionary and subsequently revisionist ideas are real cornerstones of contemporary Yugoslav leftist literature.

I

Krleza's solid catholic and biblical education, and his constant attachment to catholic liturgy, empty cathedrals and even village chapels should not be overlooked; it should also be stressed that he did not become an atheist and materialist through Marx, but rather by reading Feuerbach, Schopenhauer, Darwin's evolutionary theory, and Nietzsche's *Also sprach Zarathustra.* Like another Croatian poet, Silvije Kranjcevic (1865-1908), whose influence on his early writing is obvious, Krleza shouts about the great nonsense that reigns in this world; he rejects the supernatural origin of Christ and his teaching, but he believes in his sincerity and goodness. He is never indifferent toward Christ: sometimes he writes that he is a 'bastard' and seducer of the weaker sex (in the poem **"Jeruzalemski dijalog"**) and sometimes he would like to save him from himself and his illusions, as if he were his brother or friend.

> **If it is remembered that Krleza began to write in 1914, at the beginning of World War I, it will not be found surprising that the absurdity of human life and death were his favourite themes.**
>
> —*Ante Kadic*

In 1913 Krleza attempted to enlist in the Serbian army but was expelled from Serbia as a spy and then tried by a Hungarian military court as a deserter. Though an officer by profession, he was sent in 1915 to the Galician battlefield as a private. He became ill and feared that his last moments were approaching. His countrymen were being slaughtered en masse on various fronts for the interests of the Austrian and Hungarian militarists and imperialists.

If it is remembered that Krleza began to write in 1914, at the beginning of World War I, it will not be found surprising that the absurdity of human life and death were his favourite themes. In his first published poem, characteristically entitled **"Pietà,"** there is the following refrain: 'We were slaughtering each other, my dear mother . . . Oh, why were we slaughtering each other, my dear mother?' ('Mi smo se klali, mati moja draga . . . O zasto smo se klali, mati moja draga?'). In his famous essay **"Moja ratna lirika"** (**"My War Poetry,"** 1933), he frankly states that his early poetry was predominantly funereal. There were so many freshly-dug graves—how could he see anything else but death? In an entry in his 'Diary' for 1914 he depicts an abysmal collective cataclysm, because he saw trains incessantly bringing thousands of wounded and mutilated victims who were admitted to the hospitals for a short while and then inevitably carried to the cemeteries. On the city's streets only funeral processions were seen. It is no surprise then that Jesus, the innocent victim of Golgotha, and the laments from the Good Friday services and *Dies irae* ('confutatis maledictis, flammis acribus addictis . . . ') became Krleza's frequent leitmotiv and cherished image.

Krleza saw dark forces on every side surrounding him and those whom he loved. He knew that God was dead for him, but he saw Satan and his abominable assistants taking God's place everywhere. Having rejected the Christian faith and reached a pessimistic view of the human condition, Krleza looked in vain for a solution. He was desperate, for he envisioned his beloved Croatia, with the rest of the world, as a runaway train moving rapidly toward an unavoidable abyss (*Hrvatska rapsodija,* 1917).

Then suddenly, in October 1917, he heard about the Russian Revolution and Lenin. Lenin came as Krleza's salvation. Subsequently he was to devote many hymns to him which did not portray the real Lenin but Krleza's 'fantasy'

about him. Lenin had replaced the Christian God: when Krleza utters the name of his idol, he is on his knees, his imagination runs free and the litany of eulogies becomes endless.

When the Yugoslav Communist Party was organised in 1919, Krleza became one of its most zealous and influential members. Between the wars he launched four literary periodicals (*Plamen, Knjizevna republika, Danas* and *Pecat*), all of them extremely important for students of Yugoslav political, ideological and cultural life.

In December 1939, Krleza published in *Pecat* a vitriolic diatribe against the 'orthodox' socialist realists (e.g. Ognjen Prica, Radovan Zogovic, Jovan Popovic and Milovan Djilas.) Panic, disarray and turmoil grew in leftist circles. Krleza was attacked as a renegade and revisionist; he had several faithful supporters (such as Milan Bogdanovic, Marko Ristic and Vaso Bogdanov) but the majority of the 'progressive' writers sided with those who viewed literature as a 'tendentious' instrument of propaganda. The Party hierarchy was thankful to Krleza for his undeniable contribution to the Communist cause but henceforth considered him a stubborn and incorrigible individualist and heretic.

These pre-war skirmishes perhaps explain why in 1941, when the Communists started to organise 'the war of liberation' against the foreign occupying forces, Krleza did not join the Partisan movement: his bitter enemies (such as the two Montenegrins, Djilas and Zogovic) were by then in the high command. It can thus be understood why, during the entire war period (1941-45), though in constant danger, Krleza remained in Zagreb, on the territory of the 'Independent State of Croatia'. It is almost unbelievable that 'the father of the Yugoslav leftist intellectuals' remained at home, while Vladimir Nazor (1876-1949), a leading Croatian nationalist poet, far from any leftist tendency, left his comfortable residence, though old and sick, for a precarious existence in the Bosnian mountains.

In post-war Yugoslavia Tito, after leaving Krleza for a short period in disgrace, made him one of his most intimate associates and thus placed him in a position of great power. The fanatics, such as Zogovic and Djilas, who had been courageous fighters on the battlefields, became a disturbing element during the reconstruction process: Zogovic openly supported the Cominform in 1948 and Djilas, in 1953-4, became impatient because of the slow democratisation within the new class. Krleza, on the contrary, a rationalist moderate, supported the regime; at the same time he devoted his remarkable intelligence and energy to the raising of Yugoslav cultural standards (he has various encyclopedias and precious bibliographies to his credit) and continued, with erudite and thundering eloquence, to defend creative freedom against all Party encroachments. In his numerous essays and speeches, particularly in his speech delivered during the Writers' Congress in Ljubljana, 1952, Krleza has brilliantly condemned any kind of Zhdanovism or bureaucratic intervention in the cultural domain. The present writer believes that he accepted Marxism in the economic and political fields but has remained an indomitable individualist in literature, and that he knows well—from experience—that he has created good literature when writing in accordance with his own 'sinful and fallible inspiration'.

Krleza is very popular in Yugoslavia, and enjoys the benefits of his privileged position, but he continues to live and dream in an ivory tower. The playwright Marijan Matkovic, one of the best connoisseurs of Krleza's drama, writes that Krleza is 'tragically a lonely man, lonely when he judges, when he suffers, when he doubts, when he fights'; his numerous admirers have accepted his leadership, but few have risen to the level of this giant whose 'feet are deeply immersed in the mud of Yugoslav historical reality while his head is touching the stars'.

Krleza is not different from his heroes, from his Christ, Christopher Columbus and Michelangelo, all of them surrounded by a small élite which remained passive just when their masters were sweating blood in mental agony. Regarding the masses, Krleza is firmly convinced that the head stands above and guides the movements of the lower parts of the body.

II

In his autobiographical essay *Djetinjstvo u Agramu 1902-1903* (*Childhood in Agram 1902-1903*) Krleza shows such exceptional knowledge of patristic and scholastic theology, Latin hymnology and catholic liturgy that one readily believes his statement that the main interest of his childhood was his daily attendance at divine service. He was so involved in religious mysticism that he constructed a small altar at home. Later he decided to transform it into a stage for his plays.

In whatever he has written, from his first to his latest work, and in spite of his various changes in other domains, Krleza has remained adamant in his attempts to destroy those beliefs which were dear to him in his 'teens. As if he were ashamed of how stupid he was when accepting catholic dogmas blindly, as if he were suspicious that his personal enemies would accuse him of religious relapse (as they did many times), Krleza regularly raises his voice whenever he touches upon the subject of the catholic church and its hierarchy. There is such a dose of hatred in his vocabulary that one suspects it was caused by something more than mere ideological discrepancies; it seems as if something of a personal nature happened.

Krleza insists in *Childhood in Agram* [*Djetinjstvo u Agramu*] that it was Charles Darwin who opened his eyes and freed him from religious hallucinations. Having discovered that clergymen 'hide an ape's tail under their cassocks', the young Krleza became a different person. He had previously believed in original sin. Now he was glad to discover that the former ape was able to stand erect and, thanks to his own effort and creative power, constantly move upward and finally take the place of the imaginary god. When man was still superstitious, he needed the divinities, but now he knows that they were a simple product of his imagination. God, his saints, and whatever they represent, are dead forever; even man is unable to resurrect them any more.

> **There is such a dose of hatred in his vocabulary that one suspects it was caused by something more than mere ideological discrepancies; it seems as if something of a personal nature happened.**
> **—*Ante Kadic***

Nietzsche's *Zarathustra* was translated into Croatian in 1912, and Krleza published his poem in prose **"Zaratustra i mladic"** (**"Zarathustra and the Youth"**) in 1914. In this paradoxical sketch Krleza's concluding sentence is most revealing: 'Doubt is in my thoughts' ('Sumnja je u mislima mojim'). Krleza also assiduously read his favourite Croatian poet Kranjcevic, whose best known poem *Mojsije* ('Moses', 1893), with its insistence upon the destructiveness of doubt, made a deep impact upon him.

Krleza has often written about historical figures; he is attracted by those who have played a significant role in human history; he feels an inner urge to formulate and express his own opinion about all of them; he is neither objective nor fair when he does not agree with them. But even when we disagree with Krleza's judgment we are forced to recognise that he is usually knowledgeable and never dull.

Krleza's early 'expressionistic' short plays are interesting for their consistent existentialist philosophy but are uneven in literary value and offer difficulties for theatrical presentation. In the manner of a French existentialist writer, Krleza first tests his philosophical concepts in his literary works, and then proceeds to formulate them as theses. All his books are a kind of artistic laboratory testing the anxiety, absurdity and paradox of human existence. His philosophical outlook does not fit into any definite doctrine, but is personal and original.

Krleza wrote his play *Legenda* in 1913 at the age of twenty, and published it the following year in Marjanovic's *Knjizevne novosti*. It contains the well-known triangle of

Christ, Lazarus's sister Mary and Judas. Judas is mad with jealousy; he loves Mary but she is attached to Christ. Christ is aware of Mary's love; they meet in the garden lit by the moonlight, Mary caresses his feet, timid but ready to surrender; instead, Jesus asks her lovingly to leave him alone. Judas has decided to buy a piece of property with the thirty pieces of silver he will receive for the betrayal of Jesus, and thus he hopes to convince Mary to marry him.

This plot lacks originality and often approaches cheap erotic literature. All the prerequisites for a passionate encounter are there: two young lovers are left alone, surrounded by the moonlight, singing birds and floating stars. As Krleza later recognised in his speech at Osijek in 1928, his early plays suffered from 'too much lyricism and moonlight' ('puna lirske mjesecine').

The interesting aspect of **Legenda** is the fact that Krleza has adroitly introduced into an otherwise trite framework the Tempter, whom he labels 'the Shadow' ('Sjena'). The Shadow is in fact none other than Christ himself, his alter ego, his earthly side, which would prefer Mary's charming presence and embraces to the snoring of the three rude and boastful fishermen. The Tempter has convincing arguments: he shows to Christ, in a panorama of historical events, that his church, in due time, will not differ a bit in financial undertakings from the Jewish temple. Christ is shaken, and he appears to be ready to concede that he was wrong, but he also realises that he has gone too far and consequently there can be no honourable face-saving for him. He is aware that if he should show the slightest hesitation, he would be immediately laughed at, and would soon become either a forgotten imposter or a small carpenter in provincial Nazareth. There he would constantly meet the accusing eyes of his mother and numerous brothers, whom he has previously abandoned in utter poverty. Only if he appears firm will he be respected, become a martyr and a saint. People will then build sumptuous cathedrals in his honour, and a throng of women will weep at his tomb. Rather than an abject existence, Christ chooses posthumous fame: his spiritual pride is greater than his instinct of self-preservation.

There is a basic difference between Krleza's Shadow and the Devil who tempts Christ in the desert (*Matthew* 4:I-II). The biblical Tempter offers Christ terrestrial things, for which he shows no interest. He is tempted, as any other Jew would have been, by material benefits which the Jewish people expected their Messiah to bring them. In the temptations as reported in the Bible the divinity of Christ remains intact; he comes out as an incontestable victor; his inner being remains undisturbed. As soon as doubt is put into Christ's mind, and Krleza does this persistently, he is deprived of his divine aureole and placed in the category of the captain who is ready to abandon the ship because it is apparently sinking. Furthermore, Krleza's Christ is unwilling to sacrifice his own life for the sake of those who would leave him at the first disappointment.

Krleza's Christ does not belong to the category of visionaries such as T. S. Eliot's Thomas Becket. In his magnificent play *Murder in the Cathedral,* Eliot introduces four tempters; the first three remain in line with Christ's three temptations: they are 'temporal tempters with pleasure and power at palpable price'. These tempters encourage Becket to return to his early life, when he enjoyed merriment and women, to take supreme power in England and to become the national hero by restoring Norman political independence. Such temptations were going through Becket's mind, he knows them well and therefore is able to reject them, giving preference to penitence, spiritual power and friendship for Henry. The real danger, which Becket did not expect, arises when the fourth tempter puts into his mind the suspicion that he is relinquishing all these transient pleasures for spiritual vanity, in order to become a martyr and saint, and thus to be remembered much longer than if he had held political power in England. Kings are forgotten, but saints become powerful after their death, they 'rule from the tomb'. Thomas counters by putting his confidence in the 'good angel whom God has appointed to be his guardian'. Becket is concerned only with God's glory and therefore remains calm and confident; his faith overcomes all his human imperfections.

Whereas Eliot suggests that his hero will die for his ideals, Krleza deprives his 'dreamer' even of this honourable exit: his Christ suspects that he is mistaken, but his vanity does not allow him to retreat. Eliot accepts spiritual forces, while Krleza judges everything from the materialist point of view. Krleza's visionaries all succumb, in despair or futile bravado, because there is nothing worth dying for.

Oscar Wilde's *Salomé* was performed in Zagreb in 1905 and published as a book in 1912. It had a direct impact on a number of Croatian poets and dramatists, particularly on Fran Galovic (1887-1914). It likewise influenced Krleza, who drafted three variants of the play **Saloma** between 1913 and 1918. For instance, the name of John the Baptist in Croatian is Ivan, but because Wilde called him Jokanaan, Krleza made his name Johanaan.

Krleza's idea that Salome was madly in love with John and passionately kissed his dead lips (at the end of the first scene in **Legenda**) does not come from the Bible at all (*Mark* 6:14-28; *Matthew* 14:1-12), but from Oscar Wilde. Krleza writes that there was a happy expression on John's dead face when Salome kissed him, and a blissful tear fell from his eyesocket onto a silver plate. John had realised that certain things which he had ignored or despised in life could have brought him greater pleasure than eating locusts and wild honey and wearing a garment of camel's hair. In Oscar

Wilde's *Salomé,* Salome bites John's mouth 'with her teeth as one bites a ripe fruit'; she senses 'a bitter taste of love' on John's lips. Wilde does not go further; he stops after having hinted that perhaps John would have loved Salome if only he had known her better, because 'the mystery of love is greater than the mystery of death'.

Although Wilde's play created a famous scandal in Britain, it is moderate compared to Krleza's *Saloma.* Whereas Wilde pictures Salome in her perverted pleasure, Krleza in his play describes John the Baptist as an illiterate and stupid fanatic who succumbs easily to his first real temptation. In order to deprive John of any dignity, Krleza makes Salome an intellectual, an honest person, searching for truth and ready to accept John's ideals if only he could convince her 'of the existence of immaterial values'. But John fails miserably.

In *Saloma* John is an energumen who raves against Herod, Herodias and her daughter Salome. Salome plans to accept a renewed proposal of marriage from Herod, her step-father; Herodias claims that Herod is Salome's real father, but she does not believe her mother, who killed her former husband to marry his brother. Salome fears that Herodias intends to kill her too.

Salome has saved John in the past, because he aroused her sympathy by his readiness to lose his own life, wishing to put some moral decency into the royal court. She orders that John be brought to her and then tells him how much she is impressed by him. Her flattery and intimacy, particularly her perfumed body, easily turn John's head; he instantly forgets what he has been preaching and behaves as an 'uncontrollable Jew' who cannot resist the power of female proximity. Salome spends a night with him but afterwards becomes disgusted and personally asks for his head.

Here again Krleza is closer to Wilde than to the Bible: the Evangelists say that Salome requested John's head at her mother's suggestion, while Wilde writes that John became the victim of Salome's revenge. According to Wilde, she wanted him dead because he had refused her advances. Krleza implies that John was pointing an accusing finger at the sins of his countrymen because he was afraid of recognising his own weakness: only those who have experienced and accepted their human condition can be understanding and merciful toward others.

An obvious comparison comes to mind between Krleza's *Saloma* and Somerset Maugham's *Rain* (1921): Davidson too has taught his parishioners 'to make sins out of what they thought were natural actions,' while Sadie Thompson takes pleasure where she finds it. John and Davidson are severe because they are basically weak; they have about them 'a look of suppressed fire'. Both Salome and Sadie are ready to accept truth and undergo radical changes in their lives,

but finally discover that both missionaries are 'filthy, dirty and hateful pigs'. Both women, previously looked upon with scorn, feel triumphant in the end.

There is, nevertheless, a great difference between Maugham's Davidson and Krleza's John: Davidson is so disillusioned with himself that he cuts his own throat; John is such a weakling that he is denied even the dignity of despair. John does not judge himself; he is instead repudiated by one whom he once called 'a harlot and a wanton'. Salome emerges as a heroine and he as a moral tramp.

In June 1914 Krleza submitted *Saloma* to the director of the Croatian theatre, Josip Bach, who found it impossible to produce on the stage; he remarked that it belonged to the category of such 'dramas' (!) as the *Song of Solomon,* the *Psalms of David* and Nietzsche's *Zarathustra.* Krleza needed both the stage experience and money, but Bach remained uncooperative.

In the autumn of 1915 Krleza tried his luck again by offering to Bach a new short play *U predvecerje* ('On the Eve'), but he rejected it as 'obscene' and an imitation of Stanislaw Przybyszewski. This Polish dramatist was then popular in Croatia; Krleza's introduction of Satan ('Necastivi') into his plays was probably due to the influence of this Polish 'Satanist'.

The sketch 'On the Eve' is a parody of the relationship between man and woman. Satan encourages man in his egoistic pursuit and he consequently strangles his sweetheart. Man is obsessed by high ambitions: he would like to become a famous writer and escape to Paris, but he lacks everything, particularly the intellectual and moral strength. He is typical of those good-for-nothings who spend their time playing cards and hope to achieve great things by pure wishing.

Krleza feverishly wrote further plays, which were refused either by Bach or by publishing houses. He became an 'angry young man'. Military call-up did not improve his already nihilistic attitude toward the established order. Upon his release from service in the spring of 1917 he wrote other plays which were considered equally 'unacceptable'. He then entered into bitter polemics against all authority.

Nevertheless, Krleza proved to be too powerful a writer to be neglected. As early as 1917 his poems and prose began to be published (*Tri simfonije, Hrvatska rapsodija*). He was no longer considered a megalomaniac, bohemian, and writer without taste. Josip Bach then showed a willingness to produce Krleza's most interesting plays, such as Christopher Columbus and Michelangelo; but in spite of their unusual plots, lyrical passages and undeniable originality, they were incompatible with the customary laws of stage production. Krleza is a much greater playwright than such men as Josip

Kosor, Milan Begovic or Ivo Vojnovic, particularly during the latter's deplorable 'nationalist' period; but these three knew stage technique, which for Krleza was at this time still *terra incognita.*

Although *Cristoval Colon* (the title was later changed to *Christopher Columbus*) was written in 1917 and *Michelangelo* [*Mikelandjelo*] in 1918, it will be appropriate first to examine *Michelangelo,* which is much closer in content, ideology and structure to *Legenda* than is *Columbus.*

Krleza seems to have been fascinated since his youth by Michelangelo. He identifies himself with the great sculptor and painter and uses him as a mouthpiece for his own views on art, artistic freedom and creative experience. In his 'Diary' Krleza writes (1917) that only Moses carrying the Ten Commandments can be compared with Michelangelo working on the scaffolding in the Sistine Chapel. Both were fighting, Moses with Jehovah for the sake of his people, and Michelangelo with the Unknown ('Nepoznati'), who tried to convince him how heavenly it is to lead a normal existence. Krleza confesses his attachment to those who dare to face and defy the Prince of Darkness. The golden calf and all worldly pleasures cannot procure any satisfaction comparable to that experienced by those who conceive and create their own universe.

Although *Legenda* is filled with lyrical elements (moonlight, stars, birds, and two lovers who speak in the language of the *Song of Solomon*), the present writer finds *Michelangelo* the more poetic. Krleza does not here indulge in lyrical phraseology; rather is his Michelangelo a sensitive soul who loves roses, caresses a spider within its web, feeds mice, sings to the rays of the sun, and is enchanted by the magic power of colours. Krleza's Michelangelo reminds one of Francis of Assisi, and at certain moments we are aware that the author recalls the *Cantico del Sole* and has given his hero many of the Franciscan traits.

Michelangelo was willing to renounce legitimate pleasures, such as wine and women, for the solitary path of artistic creation; he had to say goodbye to his beloved Vittoria Colonna. To paraphrase Chekhov's statement, an artist may have a legitimate wife (his daily job) but his mistress (art) is dearer to him than his wife. Michelangelo and Krleza were each happy in the exclusive company of his mistress.

Krleza insists that men who accomplish indestructible things are victorious even in death. Michelangelo lives through his work in mankind's grateful memory.

In *Legenda* Krleza had already demonstrated his pungent sarcasm against the catholic church: he had written of bloody crusades, the Inquisition, the destruction of forbidden books and the burning of free-minded individuals at the stake; depicted temples, cold and dark like wine cellars, full of statues honouring the 'madmen' who flagellated themselves and denied life; ridiculed the pope and his claim of infallibility. *Michelangelo* ends with a scene that stresses how the catholic church has enchained the great artist. In order to earn a piece of bread and pay the bills for himself and his two apprentices, Michelangelo is expected to kiss the pope's slipper and to keep silent while the 'fat and asthmatic dignitary' talks nonsense and meddles in delicate problems beyond his comprehension. The supreme pontiff departs babbling sanctimonious platitudes, his retinue eagerly and piously swallowing his passing remarks, while the artist holds in his hands thirty gold coins (like Judas) which were given to him because he had betrayed himself. He feels miserable and defeated, but he will continue to create and find meaning and satisfaction in his work.

In his novel *Na rubu pameti* (*On the Brink of Reason,* 1938), Krleza writes an inspired chapter about Michelangelo. The main character, who reminds us somewhat of the author himself, comes to Rome and visits the Sistine Chapel. In general rebellious and neurotic, he here becomes genuinely infuriated because people behave as if they were promenading on the public square; they walk in armed with guides, cameras and binoculars, look for a while at this or that painting without discrimination, exchange a few remarks, are delighted if they are found witty, and then rush out. For Krleza this place is sacred, not because it is a chapel, but because it contains Michelangelo's *Dies irae,* and therefore should be respected as a shrine. Everyone who has eyes to see and a brain to comprehend has an opportunity here to see and appreciate a unique work of art.

Krleza is often very sceptical about man's progress: civilisation goes forward, he says, the world is changing, but man is not. In his play *Aretej* he writes: 'The fact that we telephone is less important than the fact that the gorilla still speaks through us. But here, in the Sistine Chapel, Krleza points out that the theory could be accepted that human life has a deeper meaning ('nas zivot ipak ima neki dublji smisao'). Michelangelo was able to create such a masterpiece because he did not follow any formulas or dogmas, but was guided solely by his own inspiration; such a giant did not need any command—he was able to see by himself. The real artists do not accept this or that doctrine, they obey an inner voice and not external dictates; such artists create works which bear witness to man's extraordinary creative power.

The chapter 'Intermezzo in the Sistine' in the novel *On the Brink of Reason,* in large part reproduced in the polemic *Dijalekticki antibarbarus,* is of cardinal importance in Krleza's work for two reasons. First, he was fighting, at the time of writing, against those socialist realists who were trying to prescribe to the leftist writers what and how they should write in order to fulfil their duty as Party members. Krleza emphatically declares that an artist should form his own ideas and then 'create from a surplus of his energy through an inspirational process,' as he thinks fits him best. Secondly, although the leading Communist writer, Krleza never had any patience with the masses and their stupidity, and above all he is sarcastic about their lack of sensitivity to beauty. He is appalled by crowds that behave, when looking at the Last Judgment, as if they were examining a piece of cloth or a pair of shoes. Not only the candles, which damage the picture, but also all 'cloven-footed ruminants' should be removed from the Sistine Chapel, which has no parallel in the world; only those should be admitted who are able and ready to realise, in silence and contemplation, that art alone differentiates man from the rest of the animal world.

Christopher Columbus is the most consistent among Krleza's visionaries: he does not succumb to doubt like Christ and does not humiliate himself like Michelangelo; he continues to believe in the accessibility of the astral world and accepts no compromise. Christ dies so that others shall cherish his memory, while he himself is aware that his cause is forever lost; Michelangelo degrades himself in order to create beauty for which mankind would gladly forgive him his weakness; Columbus discovers the New World, but he immediately senses that his great discovery will serve purposes totally alien to his goals—in the new continent, as in the old, there will be interest and profit, banking enterprise, greediness, slaves, rulers and ruled, rich and poor. Columbus undertakes his perilous adventure in the hope that the New World will be really new in every respect, will be a striking denial of the poverty, stupidity, tyranny and bigotry prevailing in the Spanish realm.

Columbus lets 'the pygmies' enjoy the fruits of his labours. He sails on because he cannot stop for a second; he is much in advance of his contemporaries. He is one of those predestined to dream because no reality can satisfy their yearning. Even stars become muddy for them in contact with the earth and its inhabitants. Columbus is never motivated by hope of personal triumph, posthumous glory. When he is assailed by the Tempter ('Nepoznati') he does not vacillate, because he is made of an indestructible spiritual substance. He derives his strength from a faith that the stars can be reached, not for his own benefit but for that of others, so that their lives may become bearable through change and constant improvement.

Columbus dies crucified by his own crew, repudiated because he will not accept the New World as a second edition of the old one. He is another Prometheus, but his destiny is much worse than that which was suffered by Aeschylus' legendary hero; Prometheus was chained to a Caucasian mountain by the envious Zeus, but here human beings crucify and spit at their benefactor. Whereas the biblical Christ dies on his cross praying: 'Father, forgive them, for they know not what they do' (*Luke* 23:34), Krleza's Columbus expires shouting to the sailors that the approaching land is a great fraud and all their leaders are impostors.

In 1955 the Belgrade theatre finally succeeded in producing *Christopher Columbus.* Krleza then wrote an epilogue in which the dying admiral expresses his faith in the victory of man, in the possibility that man will be able to bring his life into accord with the high ideals of humanism and beauty.

Krleza indicated, first in his speech at Osijek (1928) and then in *Moj Obracun s njima (My Squaring of Accounts with Them,* 1932), that as a student and apprentice dramatist he had read many writers (such as Petöfi, Tolstoy, Wedekind, Strindberg), but he paid special tribute to Ibsen, saying that his own dramatic trilogy *Glembajevi (The Glembays)* was 'qualitative, psychological, and concrete in the Ibsen manner'. Ibsen is already present in the early plays of Krleza, in which exceptional individuals stand isolated and apart from the masses.

Two of Ibsen's dramas in particular come to mind here: *An Enemy of the People* and *The Master Builder.* Public opinion is unstable, Dr Stockman realises, for the same man one day is considered a savior, only to be rejected the following day as 'the enemy of the people'. Dr Stockman therefore despises the masses and believes solely in individual action. The master builder Solness hangs a wreath around the vane on his house-top and then falls to his death. Hilda hears a song in the air, because she alone believes in the master builder and encourages him to mount to the top. Solness is hated by his assistants because, by his extraordinary personality and achievements, he has kept them subordinate for so long; they would like to see him stay quietly below. But the old master cannot become one of them; his greatness and his tragedy consist in being different from them.

Ibsen's characters stand above the crowd; there is no contact between the two. Even physically they are not on the ground, not to be found among common people, on the market place; they stand high, close to the stars, as if the proximity of *terra ferma* were incompatible with their being. Krleza's protagonists are also unusual characters; they fight their battles and are despised by ordinary people. They too stand above the ground: Michelangelo works high on the scaffolding and Columbus, like Christ, is crucified on the mast.

In all his early plays Krleza emphasises the lack of understanding and communication between leaders and followers. In *Legenda,* during Christ's agony in Gethsemane his three favourite apostles are sleeping; not only is he betrayed by one of his disciples, but Peter, to whom he gave the keys of his kingdom, becomes frightened by a simple maidservant and swears that he does not know him. Michelangelo is equally alone: he has said goodbye to Vittoria Colonna, because he feels that she would be an impediment to his creation; he who loves all God's creatures has no friends among human beings. Churchmen do not trust Michelangelo's art, and artists are jealous of him; his two assistants, who help in his work and eat with him, do not understand their master. There is no one with whom to speak, no one to whom he can express his doubts or confide why his work is not progressing. When he attempts to mix with people, they immediately recognise that he is not one of them and chase him away. In *Columbus,* as in *Legenda,* there is a small élite around the leader: they interpret the admiral's plans to the rebellious crowd; they are intermediaries between this solitary figure and those who do not understand his language. But even this élite, 'the salt of the earth, the light of the world', abandons the admiral, turns the tired and greedy sailors against him, and crucifies him when it becomes evident that they do not share the same ideas.

Neither in these early plays nor in his later work, written when he was well indoctrinated and accepted as a foremost Communist writer and ideologist, does Krleza assign a leading role to the proletariat. It is true that he has written with great understanding and sympathy about peasants and workers—particularly in *Hrvatski bog Mars* (*Croatian God Mars,* 1922) and *Balade Petrice Kerempuha* (*The Ballads of Petrica Kerempuh,* 1936), and that he has done his best to see their miserable condition improved; but whenever he conveys his ideas on how the world should be destroyed or reformed, he chooses his mouthpieces from among the intellectuals, who are incapable of and uninterested in establishing meaningful contact with their fellow-men—for example in his novels *Povratak Filipa Latinovicza* (*The Return of Philip Latinovicz,* 1932), *Na rubu pameti,* 1938, and *Banket u Blitvi* (*Banquet in Blitvia,* 1938-9).

III

Christopher Columbus, in which the admiral is rejected and crucified not only by the rank and file but also by his intimate collaborators, Krleza dedicated in the autumn of 1917 to none other than Lenin! The author soon realised the incongruity of this dedication and a year later, when he published the play, he omitted any mention of him. Krleza's detractors (particularly Josip Bach) noticed this change and claimed that he was hiding his leftist leanings.

Five years later, in 1924, Krleza gave an interesting explanation. Thinking about Lenin, he confesses, he imagined him as a circle revolving around itself, a solipsist, a disciple of Stirner and Schopenhauer. 'Since at that time I did not look at things clearly, but through misty symbolism, I did not think of Lenin as Lenin, but as a desperado, who like Bakunin

would like to ram through the wall with his own head.' Lenin was for him another solitary Columbus who torments himself and sails toward nirvana. In this mood he wrote *Columbus* 'which with Lenin as such had no connection. The events of the spring and summer of 1918 convinced me that this dedication of mine was a random shot, and having realised this, I decided to remove it.' Lenin afterwards became for him a symbol of 'humanism, willpower, self-confidence, and sailing under a full wind'.

This passage shows not only how Krleza had conceived of Lenin during the October Revolution, but also helps us to understand the spirit in which he wrote the play about the admiral who, obsessed by doubts as to whether it is worthwhile to discover the new continent, decides to sail toward nothingness.

We have seen Krleza's predilection for depicting important historical figures as legendary heroes, visionaries, individuals tormented by anxiety over the validity of their own goals or the capacity of the masses to follow them. Lenin too, in Krleza's subsequent writing, has much in common with all those who have suffered for their ideals. Lenin is not a real man, such as we know him from history; he is a myth, an idol whom Krleza has adorned with super-natural qualities; he is the saint whose shrine is in the middle of Moscow, and Krleza is happy to worship there; very few of the faithful in Mecca or Jerusalem could compete with Krleza when he starts to enumerate the Herculean deeds of this new divinity.

Krleza's obituary of Lenin is written in his usual half-biblical, half-mythical jargon. This new Archimedes who dared to uplift the globe, this second Prometheus, is the hero of the final Palm Sunday whom thankful mankind welcomes by 'cutting branches from the trees, by spreading cloaks upon the road and shouting jubilant Hosannas'. He who was lonely, like Bakunin, and treated like a madman when he predicted events which nobody would believe, is now a gigantic lighthouse on the other side of the shore; he is the only guide to the harbour of salvation.

The May 1924 issue of the periodical *Knjizevna republika* was devoted entirely to the memory of Lenin. Therein appeared Krleza's story presenting Lenin through the eyes of the home-guards Gebes and Bencina. This story is interesting both because it reveals the home-guard Gebes' enthusiasm for Lenin on account of his anti-militarist slogans, and because it shows that Krleza had heard about Lenin from the Croatian soldiers who were prisoners in Russia. In this sketchy story Lenin is compared to the Croatian peasant leader Matija Gubec, who in 1573 led a rebellion against the feudal lords with the slogan 'for the old rights' ('za stare pravice').

A year later Krleza visited the Soviet Union and wrote *Izlet u Rusiju* (*A Trip to Russia,* 1926) which has recently enjoyed two new editions, enlarged and partly changed. Its most revealing chapter is entitled 'Leninism on the Moscow Streets' ('Lenjinizam na moskovskim ulicama'). Here again Krleza uses biblical phraseology: he calls Lenin master and rabbi, the Word at the beginning and the Light in the darkness. According to Krleza, Lenin said to his disciples: 'And I say unto you, the gates of hell shall not prevail against me!' Lenin is compared with Christ and Mohammed, who became more powerful after their deaths than they had been during their lifetime. The guard around Lenin's mausoleum reminds Krleza of the holy sepulchre on Good Friday. Lenin is already deeply rooted in the soul of the Russian people; his name sounds soft, warm, quiet and peaceful. He is slowly captivating Moscow as a strange and 'unbelievable legend'.

Krleza's Lenin is closer to Mayakovsky's portrayal in his poem on Lenin (1924) than to Gor'ky's (1924). Whereas Mayakovsky identifies Lenin with the Party (for him the two are the same), Gor'ky's warm tribute to Lenin, one of the best pieces written about the Soviet leader, shows the vast contradictions between the man and the politician. Krleza lacks Gor'ky's knowledge of the facts and Mayakovsky's emotional involvement with the goals of the deceased 'prophet' and his anguish for the future of the Russian proletariat.

Krleza has continued to write periodically about Lenin. His articles and occasional writings were collected in 1963, in the Belgrade newspaper *Borba,* under the title 'Themes on Lenin' ['Lenjinske teme']. Lenin is called the Lighthouse, Ideologue, Constructor, Hope of the Slaves, Standard-Bearer, and so on. But Krleza himself recognises that he has not yet depicted Lenin artistically.

This is perhaps understandable when Lenin's significance for Krleza is recalled. Lenin delivered him from his terrible depression in 1917, caused by personal disillusions and by war and its atrocities. Lenin came at the right moment for Krleza, who welcomed his anti-militarist slogans like manna from heaven; he captivated Krleza, gave him courage to live and made dialectical materialism his professed creed. Krleza is unable to look at such a man objectively. His heart is guided by principles which are alien to human logic; without Lenin the chaotic world would have been complete darkness for him.

Krleza has never ceased questioning, doubting, and being disappointed by almost everyone and everything. It seems that he is a successful writer when depicting protagonists who struggle with their tempters but not when placing someone on an altar in place of the Christian God. Such a posture of worship does not correspond to his nihilistic mentality. He is more convincing when destroying old temples than when erecting new.

Vasa D. Mihailovich (review date 15 November 1969)

SOURCE: A review of *The Return of Philip Latinovicz,* in *Saturday Review,* Vol. 52, No. 46, November 15, 1969, p. 48.

[*In the following review, Mihailovich discusses the themes in* The Return of Philip Latinovicz, *lamenting Krleza's lack of recognition by readers in the West.*]

Paris had its Balzac and Zola, Dublin its Joyce, and Croatia has its Miroslav Krleza. Many of his works deal with the tribulations of the Croats under the ungainly Austro-Hungarian Empire. He is one of the two leading Yugoslav writers today (the other is Ivo Andric), a distinction he won almost half a century ago with the short-story collection *Croatian God Mars* [*Hrvatski bog mars*]. His other major works include the plays *In Agony* [*U agoniji*] and *Aretheus* [*Aretej*] and the novels *On the Edge of Reason, Banquet in Blitvia* [*Banket u Blitvi*] and *The Banners* [*Zastave*].

The Return of Philip Latinovicz, Krleza's first novel, was published in 1932, during the modernistic, almost expressionistic phase in his development. The novel's main dialectic—art vs. life—is also a variation on the *Return of the Native* theme.

After spending twenty-three years in West European capitals, where he was imbued with *savoir-faire,* dilettantism, and world-weariness, Philip, a young painter, returns to his home town in a Godforsaken Croatian plain. The time is the late 1920s. Though the trappings of Austrian rule have become things of the past, life in the small town has hardly changed; on the contrary, everything seems to be as usual—the powers-that-be, the thin crust of intelligentsia alienated from the people, the squalor and hopelessness of a "stuffy backwater." Philip, "a godless, westernized, restless bird of passage, nervy and decadent," soon realizes that even here "somebody is always being hunted" and that "devouring goes on everywhere."

Yet these philosophical conclusions seem to bother Philip less than his inability to cope with two women, each in her own way diametrically opposed to his artistic nature: his primitive, sensual mother, concerned with her unbridled lust and with the perpetuation of her privileged status as a woman of pleasure for the provincial establishment; and a youngish widow, the *femme fatale* of the novel, who is just as sensual and morally loose but who wields a much greater destructive power because of the illusion of happiness she offers her men. In addition, Philip has been plagued since childhood with the question of his father's identity. All these trials make his homecoming a tortured experience and his future increasingly doubtful. He tries to find refuge in his art, only to realize that "art is a fine thing but life is a serious matter."

The love story and the dilemma of the artist in a prosaic world are only two aspects of this short but significant work. They serve Krleza as a framework for his commentaries upon life, *Kulturphilosophie,* social order, and human foibles. As a far-left revolutionary, he is bitter, blunt, and pessimistic about the future of bourgeois society. The world he presents is filled with mud, slime, rot, perfidy, bleakness:

> People move like wax dolls, scratch the napes of their necks, chew tobacco, and leave behind them a cloud of cigar smoke, the reek of their bodies and of misery. Every individual drags around with him the enormous circles of his own existence, his own warm entrails and other persons' warm entrails, from which he has issued like a worm, to crawl and twist, to bite and prick with his poisonous sting, to eat and devour; and others devour him, and have harnessed him, and beat him about the head with a whip. Everything moves in circles of resistance and starvation and horror, and amid all this painting is a largely unknown and superfluous matter.

This pessimistic stance does not derive from Krleza's obvious fondness for philosophizing but rather from his indictment of an industrialized capitalist society and its by-product—a neglected provincial town.

The author walks the tightrope of social criticism without slipping over into preaching. Moreover, due to his artistry this traditional, almost old-fashioned novel is still charming and refreshing. A certain long-windedness and seemingly endless descriptions are compensated by a wealth of detail, exquisite character sketches, fine nuances, and a sharp eye for color and shape. Krleza is a master of hint and allusion, and he knows how to keep his distance. His pessimism— even at times nihilism—and his irony, often turning to sarcasm, are tempered with humor and compassion. Though somewhat contrived and methodical, his novel still packs a terrific punch. The final scene resembles that of Dostoevsky's *Idiot,* when Rogozhin and Prince Myshkin sit numbly and disconsolately beside Nastasya's corpse.

Many Yugoslav writers are indebted to Krleza, more than they realize or admit. One of the most political of Yugoslav authors, he is at the same time one of the most accomplished, profound, and meaningful, not only in Yugoslav but in European literature. That he has been bypassed for the Nobel Prize bespeaks the sad fate of many excellent but little-known writers from "peripheral" countries. *The Return of Philip Latinovicz* is Krleza's first major work to be published here. In this excellent translation it should convince the reader of the author's power.

Ernst Pawel (review date 15 February 1970)

SOURCE: A review of *The Return of Philip Latinovicz,* in *The New York Times Book Review,* February 15, 1970, pp. 4, 26.

[*In the following review, Pawel praises Krleza's "demythification" of evil and commitment to moral and artistic integrity in* The Return of Philip Latinovicz.]

Miroslav Krleza (Kirlezha), the formidable Croat who has dominated Yugoslavia's literary landscape for nearly half a century, remains virtually unknown in the West. His is not the only such case and again reflects at least in part the parochialism of Western publishers and their public; but the ambiguities of Krleza's themes and politics have no doubt contributed to the neglect of a writer who, ironically, happens to be quintessentially Western—or more precisely Central European—in the scope and sources of his work.

Born in 1893 in the then Austrian city of Zagreb, raised in a Budapest military academy, Krleza came of age in the twilight gloom of the Hapsburg empire and shares unmistakable affinities with his German-language contemporaries of the Prague-Vienna literary renaissance, from Kafka to Kraus and from Schnitzler to Musil. What set him apart from the very beginning was an unfashionably undespairing commitment to radical humanism, that is, faith in radical politics tempered by a clear-eyed awareness of its limits in the affairs of men. Most of his lifelong troubles as a citizen and author stem from a stubborn refusal on his part to betray these principles or modify them in accordance with political expediency.

His first major work was a play born of his World War I experiences, a powerful protest in the manner of the early O'Casey whose timely relevance—a Croat officer going against his conscience and following orders by executing a peasant woman for some trivial offence—probably points up nothing more profound than the essential timelessness of inhumanity. The play was banned an hour before its scheduled opening, the rulers of newly independent Yugoslavia having quite accurately read its message as anti-murder rather than anti-Austrian and considered it subversive.

This dramatic debut in 1920 set a pattern. Krleza, with a versatility probably unique in contemporary letters, has since then created an immense body of work consisting of over fifty volumes of plays, novels, poetry, essays, political and literary journalism, all of it impressive and much of it outstanding. But up to 1948, through the successive eras of monarchy, military dictatorship, Nazi occupation, liberation and until Tito's break with Stalin, most of his output remained officially proscribed.

The ban, largely ineffectual at first, given the well-organized Communist-led underground of the twenties and thirties, served to project Krleza into the role of revolutionary idol. He accepted it gracefully enough, but when it came to the inevitable test, he proved quite unwilling to barter away his artistic integrity in the interest of party loyalty. His slashing attack on what he characterized as the nonsensical notion of Socialist realism not only cost him the adulation of the student rebels of his day but also, by depriving him of underground support, effectively condemned him to silence until Yugoslav communism itself deviated sufficiently to forgive one of its prodigal old men. By 1950 all his books were in print for the first time in his life; he himself has since than been heading the Yugoslav Lexicoggraphic Institute, but a panoramic four-volume novel published over the past five years bears witness to the fact that neither age nor a full eight-hour day in a major executive position can seriously interfere with his creative drive.

Such prolific vitality has its drawbacks, especially since none of Krleza's books represents more than a fragment of his genius. But *The Return of Philip Latinovicz,* the only one thus far available in English, is not a bad choice by way of introduction. This uncommonly sensitive translation by Zora G. Depolo, originally published in 1960 and now reissued, captures the echo of Krleza's own voice in a novel written nearly 40 years ago but vibrant with a kind of lyrical cynicism oddly contemporary and at the same time characteristic of its author.

> The indissoluble unity of moral and artistic integrity is one of Krleza's recurrent themes; so is his demythification of evil, an almost serene acceptance of decadence, decay and death as sources of life rather than of either guilt or redemption.
> —*Ernst Pawel*

The protagonist is a has-been painter come home to the small town of his childhood after a 20-year absence. Languidly he probes a past composed of bright visions and dark secrets, trying to retrieve some inspiration for his canvases. His painter's eye records the profiles of land and people; but beyond the surface features lies the desert of the soul, and Philip's quest, as he himself well knows, is doomed right

from the start. His mother, now smugly settled into near-respectability, had once been a high-class whore, the favorite of counts and bishops, and could not possibly reveal to him the true identity of his father even if she wanted to. Philip in turn proceeds to re-enact the fatal myth by drifting into a sado-masochistic *liaison-à-trois* with a nymphomaniac ex-countess fallen on bad days and the ex-lover who tripped her. The obsessive affair yields a brief burst of creative inspiration before exploding in the sterility of violence and leaving Philip face to face with his own death in life.

The indissoluble unity of moral and artistic integrity is one of Krleza's recurrent themes; so is his demythification of evil, an almost serene acceptance of decadence, decay and death as sources of life rather than of either guilt or redemption. Both are aspects of his abiding commitment to the concepts that have inspired all his work.

Alan Ferguson (essay date 1973-74)

SOURCE: "A Critical Literary Approach to Miroslav Krleza's *The Return of Filip Latinovicz,*" in *Journal of Croatian Studies,* Vol. XIV-XV, 1973-74, pp. 134-44.

[*In the essay below, Ferguson assesses the meaning of* The Return of Filip Latinovicz, *distinguishing between Krleza's viewpoint and Filip's to suggest the novel's tragic intent.*]

The most noticeable feature of criticism of Miroslav Krleza's novel *The Return of Filip Latinovicz* is the divergence of opinion as to "what the novel is about." Potential difference of opinion appears all the more remarkable when it is considered how little surrounds other Croatian novels regarding "what they are about." Should this novel be read as a treatment of man's search for identity in society or his attempt to flee from society and himself; as a political statement by Krleza about the shallowness of bourgeois society; as a dramatic presentation of a discussion upon the importance of beauty and art; as an assertion of man's fundamental need of love for life to be meaningful; as a revelation of the psychological problems created by an acute sensitivity towards life; or even as a sort of comic-fantasy? To suggest that the novel is a *mélange* of these interpretations may in fact be nearer the truth. This would imply, however, that *The Return of Filip Latinovicz* is characterised by thematic inconsistency and contradiction. Yet Filip as a character is highly consistent in his psychological make-up: no episodes strike the reader as being out of place or in any way unnatural to Filip's behaviour. Similarly, the structure of the novel exhibits a cohesion which can be broken only by artificial distinctions. A distinction might be drawn between Filip's actual return from Kaptol railway station to Kostanjevec (parts 1-8) and his residence at Kostanjevec (parts 8-end), yet this distinction does not comply with any thematic change in the novel. Furthermore, the introduction of other characters as the novel develops does not result in any thematic changes, despite the fact that several parts of the novel are used for the purpose of the narrator's extensive probing into their backgrounds. Filip remains central to the novel, for it is he who is the psychological recipient of the existence and actions of the other characters. This stems from the fact that the reader enters the novel with Filip and perceives its action from his point of view. It is from this last statement that most of the problems as to "what the novel is about" arise. Formally, it is the difficulty for the reader to distinguish between the narrator's voice and the voice of Filip. Informally, it is the difficulty to distinguish which is the author's point of view and which his character's. The problem is evident throughout the novel, but a single example will clarify the point:

1. He was dreaming of his new composition, a bare, female
2. belly, darkly illumined by a boy's sad and morbid
3. experience.
4. The only creative reality is what initially shocks
5. our senses: man really sees only what he notices for
6. the first time. Painting is and should be nothing else
7. but a visionary experience of the space before us, for,
8. if not that, it has no justification. Otherwise it is
9. only the sticking together and patching up of familiar
10. and already painted pictures, a mere multiplying of
11. what has already been seen. It is like that boring
12. children's pastime in winter of sticking transfers on
13. to paper, wetting them with their fingers. Sticking
14. together and rearranging, that is all artistic styles
15. and trends and schools are, but all this had
16. nothing to do with Filip since he refused to follow
17. any artistic trend, style or school.

How does the reader distinguish between Krleza's and Filip's "point of view" in this passage? Lines 1-3 are purely narrative, the words "he was dreaming" possibly preparing the reader for an insight into Filip's thoughts in the following lines. Yet the lines 4-13 might come from either the voice of the narrator or the thoughts of Filip. Lines 13-17 are also problematic since although the indication is that the narrator is speaking (Filip/he), there is a continuation of the train

of thought of lines 4-13, and there has been no change of paragraph. There is a further potential ambiguity in that if Filip is thinking in lines 4-13 then he may be addressing himself in lines 13-17. It is difficult to illustrate the full extent of this stylistic weakness in the novel as a whole without much broader reference. It is, however, easy to see the consequences of the reader's inability to distinguish the points of view of narrator and character in this particular context. The reader can not be sure whether the passage is introspection on the part of Filip or a statement from the narrator. Thus, there is an implicit accompanying problem as to what the relationship is between the narrator and his central character Filip. The reader may wish to sympathise with true introspection on the part of Filip, but objectively criticise any statement inserted by the narrator. According to how he "reads" this context, the reader can state that it is either about an individual searching his mind, or an intrusion by Krleza so that he can expose his views about the true nature of artistic creation.

If one conceives of this problem on a general scale throughout the novel where it is not purely descriptive, it becomes immensely difficult to find a workable answer to the overriding question—"what is the novel about?" Even if one were to suppose that Krleza and Filip have identical points of view, the difficulty is still not resolved. In sympathising with Filip, the reader must necessarily be sympathising with the author's own point of view and thus he is denied any objective view-point towards the novel and events in it. But should the reader fail to sympathise with Filip, the novel will then appear as a bias from the author and the whole purpose of writing the novel from Filip's point of view will be of an entirely negative effect.

It is, therefore, of axial importance that the reader should have an understanding of both Krleza's and Filip's point of view disassociated one from the other. It is essential also that the reader should have some knowledge of the author's attitudes independent of his novel. Only in this way can the reader explain the incongruity of an author who is inseparable from his hero. Furthermore, an understanding of the author's point of view will resolve much of the trouble confronting the reader considering the question "what is the novel about?" for it will inform the reader of the author's attitude towards Filip. The crucial question in this respect is to what extent does Krleza see art as being realistic.

In the same year as the publication of *The Return of Filip Latinovicz,* in 1932, the concept of socialist realism was developed and adopted by the Association of Soviet Writers. In essence it required the artist "to represent reality in its revolutionary course of development, in a true and historically concrete manner." Krleza's attitude towards his novel was fundamentally different from the socialist realist outlook. He supported the idea of "art for art's sake," since for him it was a protest against the reality of the time, on which the artist turned his back in disgust. Since the debate on socialist realism did not reach any profound level until after 1948 in Yugoslavia, one may safely assume that the attitude which Krleza expressed in a search in this debate in 1952 is representative of his earlier attitude:

> Artistic creation is linked to the temperament of the artist . . . to write down does not mean to describe the realities of life, for if writing in the literary sense meant simple everyday description, then every clerk would be a writer.

For Krleza, art was not obliged either to serve society or directly to reflect reality. In other words, it all depended upon "the temperament of the artist." He is thus, undoubtedly sympathetic towards Filip when he writes: "he refused to follow any artistic trend, style or school." It is interesting here to notice the main argument leveled against Filip's artistic attitude. This argument dominates at least three parts of the novel and it comes not surprisingly from the cold, intellectual philosopher Kyriales. It is not merely coincidental that the Greek is also a suicidal.

> A self-respecting cosmopolitan civilisation should have its windows open on reality, it should have parks and fountains, but real parks and real fountains: for the civilised people of tomorrow there will be no need of baroque-scene-painting! From the beginning painting has only been a sort of substitute for reality! What do I want today with your picures of people with bad teeth and debts? What is the purpose of such paintings? They are absolutely useless.

Kyriales opinion is essentially two-fold. First, that art is a substitute reality. Secondly, that as such it is devoid of any sense of purpose and is utterly useless. Krleza shows this attitude to be hopeless in that Filip has a burning desire to paint a "street scene" but the artist can not reflect the reality of that scene *in totum,* as he can not capture the smells, sounds and movements of the scene in reality, in his painting. That Kyriales should have a hopeless attitude toward art is a clear indication of his suicidal attitude towards reality. Art is useless for the Greek simply because it can not fulfil an impossible task. Whilst Kyriales is a decadent bourgeois, his argument is similar to that of the later concept of socialist realism, in which it was argued that art did not need to falsify reality.

The increasing awareness of Filip as an artist that he can not reflect reality becomes a dynamic force in the novel. It leads him into the psychological state in which he can perceive of his situation as being "comic." More profoundly it leads to the tragedy of the novel—the tragedy that Filip's condi-

tioning by one social reality can not be acted against within that same social reality, even though as an artist he may perceive something outside his conditioning by the bourgeois social reality. This point will be returned to since it is the key to the overriding question "what is the novel about?" Before it can be analysed in detail, two other aspects of the novel must be considered: one in relation to Krleza, the other in relation to Filip.

Krleza's attitude towards art tells the reader something fundamental about the attitude of the author towards *The Return of Filip Latinovicz:* that the novel is not an attempt to reflect social reality, in some way to re-create in literature bourgeois society *in totum.* "To write down does not mean to describe the realities of life." Thus, a criticism of this novel on the grounds that bourgeois society is "not like that in reality" is a misplaced criticism, although as has been shown it is to some extent pardonable due to the difficulty of distinguishing between the "points of view." But since the novel is written from Filip's point of view in the broadest sense of that term, the criticism is misplaced in that it necessitates an *objective* view of "what bourgeois society is really like" whilst the novel for the greater part presents bourgeois society as Filip *perceives* it, a *subjective* viewpoint. Filip is characterised quite deliberately by Krleza as being ultra-sensitive, so that the environment of Kostanjevec naturally appears all the more hostile in his eyes. To criticise the novel on the grounds that it is based on an inaccurate description of the "reality" is thus unjust, unless it is applied purely to the areas in which Krleza is writing objective narrative. More important, however, is the fact that a criticism which is based upon how true a picture of reality the novel presents, will miss much of the psychological depth of the work and the profound symbolism which is contained in the sub-consciousness of the artist, Filip.

Only rarely is symbolism a direct representation of objective realism. Symbolism must be associated with a particular perception, that of a character, of reality, and as such may be quite different from what is the objective reality. In *The Return of Filip Latinovicz* there are two angles from which symbolism enters the novel: Krleza's and Filip's. Most frequently their two views are intricately associated. Above, it was suggested that criticism based upon what was "reality," as the reader perceived it, was unjust unless applied to the areas in which Krleza has an "objective narrative" viewpoint. The discovery though, that Krleza uses symbolism, and that extensively, throughout the novel, undermines any assertion that there is any attempt by the author to make "objective narration." The whole novel is in a sense symbolic; it is "a return," not only to Kostanjevec but to the problems of Filip's childhood, a search for home, for a father, for the childhood *ego* of the adult being. To understand the animal symbolism of the novel, the reader must appreciate the lack of "objective narrative," and the psychological vein of

Krleza's interests must come to the forefront of the reader's attention. To suppose an "objective narrative" from Krleza makes recurrence of the characters symbolised as animals quite ridiculous, as people are not in objective terms "animals" although bestial sides to their character might exist. The direct influence of Darwin on Krleza can be detected in this symbolism. For Krleza "it is art that differentiates man from the rest of the animal world." Thus, since both the author and Filip are artists, they will both symbolise characters in the form of animal imagery. Similarly, the colour imagery of the novel comes both from the narrator's descriptions ("the grey Pannonian mists") and from the perception of Filip ("for Filip everything was grey"). Colours interact throughout the novel, just as the characters do—greys predominate, symbolising the gloom of Filip's mood; reds appear in association with blood and sexuality; greens are symbolic of degeneration frequently generating reds. Black and white, darkness and light, in both mental and physical contexts, are often quite crudely juxtaposed within descriptions of incidents and scenes. Colour symbolism is an important feature of the novel, a feature which substantiates the suggestion that Krleza's attitude towards the novel is far more complex than an attempt "merely to describe reality." When Balocanski questions Filip on the latter's relationship with Bobocka, it is the candle and the light which it creates, stunning Balocanski's eye-sight, that forces him out into the open, into the light.

> "The fact is: there are times in life when one . . ." Balocanski fell silent again. He was not looking at Filip, but at the orange halo round the candle, the light green ring which radiated red light, like some strange rocket. This circle of light had attracted his attention and he was aware that he had to talk about certain decisive matters here, but the light was something completely apart from everything else, as if placed above everything and it spluttered loudly and flickered in a drop of molten tallow as if alive. This lasted for some time and then as if awakened from sleep and stepping into a newly revealed space, he said in a very low voice, almost intimately: "I know everything that is going on between you and Boba!"

As in the above context, psychological reality and objective actuality constantly relate. Nowhere is this more pronounced than in the mood of Filip. It is the result of his situation in bourgeois society, his past, his ultra-sensitivity, his artistic perception and his febrile introspection. The decay of bourgeois society is paralleled by the decay in the mentality of Filip:

> Life began to split up in Filip into its component parts; within him the incessant, analytical disintegration of everything grew increasingly active, be-

coming an end in itself, a process which, for quite some time now, had automatically tended towards disintegration. This mental destruction of everything that came to his hand, or appeared before his eyes, was slowly giving rise to an idea which began to haunt him more and more obstinately, from one day to the next: according to his own conception of his subjective life, all meaning, even the slightest, was disappearing. His own life had somewhere broken away from its foundations and had begun to turn into a phantom that had no reason whatsoever for existence; and this had been going on for some time and was growing more and more burdensome and exhausting.

It is this mental breakdown of Filip which provides the essential link between the bourgeois society depicted in the novel and the tragedy of the novel; that one social reality, perceived as hostile by Filip's mind, can not be acted against within that same social reality. A criticism of the novel on the grounds that Filip does not break out of this society, that his awareness of its corruption does not lead to any action on his part against that society, can not appreciate the psychology of Filip. He can neither react against nor break out of his society precisely because his mind is disintegrating as a parallel to the disintegration which he sees all around him.

> Wretched and helpless in his present frame of mind, Filip looked on with the nervous impatience of someone powerless, yet desperate, ceaselessly digging in his own darkness with a lamp in his hand. . . . It was simple: he had just to take a cab and drive over to the Kaptol railway station and there get on the first train. It became ever increasingly clear to Filip that this hesitation was fatal in every sense: if any one of the persons involved in it had felt the fatality of every insignificant event from the very beginning of this passionately-dangerous game, it had been himself.

More than any other factor, it is Filip's hostile environment which determines his mental disintegration and consequent lack of action. All the characters which surround him and work upon his psyche are representations of decline, decay, corruption and superficiality. Masks, changes of name, sexual deviance and the conversation of polite society are features of each of the bourgeois characters. In such surroundings life becomes meaningless and unreal for Filip. The "gloomy morass of present-day reality" overpowers the ultra-sensitivity of Filip. He finds himself engulfed in unreal events, or rather in events which a common-sensical outlook on reality can not explain. Stomachs are slashed open, woods burn for three days, houses burn as the result of curses cast upon them, cows die mysteriously, wolves come back from extinction, princely coachmen are seen driving in the night, a man is found hanging from a tree with a wallet still in his pocket. Moreover, Filip finds himself taking risks, risking his life even to rescue Hitrec's bull, yet he can not explain to himself what made him do it.

Even the continuity of his "self" becomes somehow unreal as a result of Filip's return to Kostanjevec.

> Weary daydreams seemed to float round him— thoughts of the ephemerality of human existence in space and time, of the incomprehensible extent of life's reality compared with that flickering phenomenon called the subjective self and with the trifling, quite insignificant, unreal details—outside the subject which constituted the sphere of perception of that subject, which in itself was nothing but a detail in a series of details. . . . Strange . . . to be the thinking subject and to be conscious of the identity of one's own subjective self.

The strangeness, the unreality of life become the dynamic forces of Filip's perception, not the social acts, the rejection of the hostile environment. How is he to act against a social reality which he cannot help perceiving as unreal? The tragedy of the novel is explicit: Filip cannot react against social reality since idealisation of it brings with it a derealisation. Filip's situation is tragic since he has no choice but to suffer the infernalisation of reality. It is a condition into which he has been born.

> Intensely troubled by the uncertainty of his own origin, all beginnings were inscrutable mysteries to Filip, and for him all contacts with reality had from the first remained enigmatic . . . The dead, the unknown hypothetical dead, in Filip, were all made up of endless complexes of the most impossible hypotheses and obsessions . . . Man is nothing but a vessel full of other people's tastes and experiences! There were times in his life when he was convinced that it was not he, personally, subjectively, who was seeing the things he saw, but some distant and unknown being within him who had been looking at things of his own, in his own way . . . Thinking about himself and his own existence in time, about his beginnings and about the limits of his own personality, Filip lost himself in vague pictures and could not find his bearings.

Clearly, the awareness of social reality as Filip perceives it leads to the psychological state of madness rather than rational reaction against that reality. Filip is not a caricature in the novel, he is not created to provide the reader with a reassurance of man's ability to overcome all: he is an individual rather than a pawn of socialist realism. He is isolated "in the circle of his own emotions;" the insanity which develops as a consequence makes the idea of any action impossible.

> Filip was seized with a restlessness which grew more and more intense. He had always felt isolated in the circle of his own emotions and he knew very well from long experience how difficult it is to rouse people around one to the intensity of one's own feelings. Man lives in his closed world, has his own beauties, his own nervous excitements, intense and often rapturous and genuinely beautiful—but to inspire others with this beauty, with the genuineness of one's own rapture, is hard and very often impossible of achievement. Impossible indeed!

Despite the "trap" of Filip's psychology, the novel possesses considerable development within the limits imposed by a need for general consistency in the work. For instance, the sexual images are developed in Filip's mind until a point is reached where they saturate all other "motifs." Boba becomes the object of Filip's affections. It becomes irrelevant to him that his emotion stems from sensuous sources. So that unconsciously he falls more and more under her influence. His obsession with sexual deviance leads him into animal behaviour and jealousy of the decrepit Balocanski. "Filip was overcome by an unreasonable repugnance full of animal hatred." Filip loves Boba precisely because, like himself, "most of her life was in the past." His love is typical of the bourgeois love reality, being motivated primarily by sexuality, indifferent to an understanding of the partner, leading to destruction.

> Filip had no idea who she really was and what was going on in her and around her . . . Filip had known that nothing worthwhile or concrete could or would come of it.

Filip is incapable of having a meaningful relationship and it is precisely this that attracts Boba to him. Sexuality with Filip, as with all the other bourgeois characters, becomes a refuge from reality. It relieves his awareness and leads to his abortive return to painting.

> Just lately, he had turned everything around him into pictures and with his every breath he had a vivid feeling of how much progress he had made, of how he had broken through his inertia of the last years.

The search for a direct contact with life has eluded Filip from the very start of the novel:

> It was there (Kostanjevec) long ago, at the very beginning, that he had rejected the direct contact of

life and for thirty years he had run after that contact, but he had never caught up.

However, there is one static theme that runs the whole course of the novel: Filip's isolation, due to his psychological make-up, from society. No matter how much Filip falls into the errors of the bourgeois life style he will always remain essentially isolated. "Man lives in his closed world." His greater awareness and perception of life, the consequence of his artistic ability, lead to the person (Filip) who can best offer an understanding of the shortcomings of society in the novel, into isolation and a sense of unreality. His sense of beauty is suffocated by awareness, the tragedy becoming all the more real for the reader since those moments when Filip does have a visionary experience of life are vividly described by Krleza:

> In a glade of newly-cleared land in the forest, he sat down on a felled tree and remained for a long while absorbed in his thoughts . . . In the valley below the glade the Blatnja wound between the vineyards and the meadows in its deep-cut bed, and in the distance, in the ash-grey mist of the summer dusk, one could discern the contours of the hills increasingly clear, blue and transparent as in a Japanese drawing. In the changing shades of evening color, a line of willows stood out in the distant plain, each one distinct, plastic as if put in with charcoal, while the colors merged into a monochrome horizontal bar above the haystacks and distant dark-green cornfields. The glade was filled with the bitter evening beauty of solitude. . . . To breathe.

To suffocate the bitter evening beauty of Filip's solitude is left to the social reality in which he lives. Particularly it is left to the arguments of Kyriales. He provides the antithesis of the visionary experience of man in nature. Once again, the animal image is not merely coincidental:

> Man is an animal who, in individual isolation, is a melancholy object and, it might be said, quite out of place in nature.

His notion of man is that he is the lowest kind of animal. The tragedy of Filip's inability to answer Kyriales is implicit: how can a person explain the visionary experience of art and of life to an animal? What is artistic intuition to an animal? Filip is aware that "the Greek talked about art, but he really had no conception of it," so he is utterly unable to convey the importance of art in society.

Thus far, little mention has been made of the actual nature of the society in which Filip is the victim, other than it is bourgeois, decadent, corrupt and is superficial—for Krleza simply "animal-like." In the novel the nature of society is carefully portrayed by the author in all its morbid detail. Its participants, with the possible exception of Boba and Kyriales, are not of a particular significance. What is important is that drawn together and viewed *en masse* by the reader, they form a collage and foil against which Filip is isolated. Some of the details with which each character is described are perhaps indulgences by the author. Where the details have little importance to the psychological state of Filip and merely repeat previous details, they tend to detract from the tragedy of the novel. If Krleza's political stance, if it can be so called, is indulged in at all in the novel it is not in respect to Filip, but rather to the numerous lesser characters who constitute the social collage. Filip is isolated from it because, although it has an effect upon his psyche, there is no counter-effect. Filip then, and not the bourgeois society itself, is the central point of the novel. Society is the indispensable back-cloth to the tragedy. If the back-cloth is decadent, this does not mean that Krleza as an artist is decadent. We cannot assume that because Filip does not possess all the potentials of the positive man, Krleza is incapable of possessing an adequate sense of human possibilities. Filip's attitude to sexuality is not necessarily Krleza's—"an unpleasant memory of wretched perspiring bodies, as irrelevant as the noise of pots and pans behind a closed door."

It is thus possible to say with confidence precisely what the novel is about. Most profoundly, it is tragedy, not comic-fantasy induced by the recurrence of "animals," of character descriptions, of comic situations, for this interpretation fails to conceive of the depth of significance which all the apparently comic aspects have for both Filip and Krleza. Neither is it a novel about "love," for such a relationship is meaningless in the society depicted in the novel. The interpretations enumerated at the outset fall down similarly. The response which the novel provokes in the reader is essentially the tragic. Given a dynamic approach, the novel is frighteningly convincing. Given an inadequate approach, failing above all to distinguish between the views of Filip and Krleza, the novel is a weak example of political exposition. The mood of Filip when considering his art should be a clue to the reader's attitude towards the novel: "one should feel how underneath it a child's soul had been violated and murdered."

The Antioch Review (review date Fall 1975)

SOURCE: A review of *The Cricket beneath the Waterfall and Other Stories,* in *The Antioch Review,* Vol. 34, No. 1, Fall, 1975, pp. 234-35.

[*In the following review of* The Cricket beneath the Waterfall, *the critic comments on Krleza's narrative style.*]

The Croatian Miroslav Krleza is among the most neglected of the world's great writers. European critics have long paired him with Bosnian novelist Ivo Andríc, as deserving contenders for the Nobel Prize (Andríc won the Prize, in 1961).

Krleza's stories display the same panoramic density that enlivens Andríc's magisterial chronicles of sturdy Balkan sub-kingdoms emerging from centuries of oppression into the modern age. But Krleza is the more overtly "political" writer—and his pungent, unsparing studies of human isolation paradoxically resonate with a swooping sense of cultures struggling, strangely formed powers laboring to surface. A satirically observed complex of military-political careerists reveals "the immeasurable wretchedness of Croatian military glory." A village boy dreams, romantically, of Paris—and a harsh sardonic vision descends, to shake him from his "sick illusion." (A favorite focus of Krleza's wit is the intellectual fop who rejects his own nationality and culture.)

A desperate young man, whose stubbornly narrow imagination betrays him into drunken nihilism, writhes suspended in mutual revulsion with his stolid peasant father: the son flaunts a truth intended to kill; the old man only shrugs it off. Their worlds never touch. The title-story's hero claims communication with the dead; this continuity, once established, withers into an acknowledgement of existential despair. These stories [in *The Cricket beneath the Waterfall*] derive their universal significance from Krleza's grave Olympian perspective. Sometimes mocking, sometimes gently probing, he views vulnerable, isolated lives within a context of expansive history that is itself a speck upon a swelling cosmos of constant dissolution and mutability. The force that drives each story is Tolstoyan, but Krleza's laconic complexity seems utterly distinctive.

Krleza's novel *The Return of Philip Latinovicz* was published in 1969 by Vanguard, which has announced for future publication another Krleza novel, *On the Edge of Reason.* If these are equal to his short stories, they are important reading.

Aleksandar Flaker (essay date 1987)

SOURCE: "Krleza's Culinary Flemishness," in *Text and Context,* edited by Peter Alverg Jensen, et al., Almqvist & Wiksell International, 1987, pp. 185-92.

[*In the following essay, Flaker examines the role and various function of food in some of Krleza's works, particularly* Balade Petrice Kerempuha *and* Zastave.]

In his comparison of Krleza's *Balade Petrice Kerempuha*

(*The Ballads of Petrica Kerempuh*) to the poetry of Eduard Bagrickij, Russian poet from Odessa, Zdravko Malic calls one of the chapters of his study *I Consume, Therefore I Am,* and, consequently, dubs the "point of view from which the world starts to assume the shape of an object of culinary interest" "*pantagruelism*", after Rabelais, of course, but without reference to Bachtin's chapter *Pirsestvennye obrazy u Rable* (The Feasting Scenes of Rabelais). "Pantagruelism" is seen as a "caricature of every spiritual interpretation of the world, its materialization in the most drastic form, and thus highly characteristic of the Ulenspigelian tradition". Malic gives numerous examples of the "pantagruelism" of *Balade* on the level of style: comparisons and metaphors in which the first member is a man and his action while the second is an "object of culinary interest", but—we might add—from socially varied menus.

As for "objects of culinary interest" in the *Ballads,* the most representative is certainly the *Keglovichiana,* in which we find an entire catalogue of edibles and scenes of feasting prepared in heaven for the late Count Kegloic. It is observed from the wings like a "heavenly paradise" by "Imbro Skunkac, chicken filcher and thief" who, on earth, "pecked at corn with the turkeys and the chickens", but who is then taken from the heavenly feast and thrown into hell. The point of view in this "Ballad" is that of the people, a Kerempuh-Ulenspigel point of view, and the *popular* source of the main motif is confirmed by a Russian, somewhat earlier example. In 1923, the Soviet "proletarian" and folk poet Demjan Bednyj, relegated today to the margins of literature, published his sacrilegious text *Kak 14 divizija v raj sla* (How the 14th Division Went to Paradise), in which the "Lord's virgin" Malanja must wait at the gates to heaven while the entire 14th division, after having stumbled on a mine field (in the World War), enters—with the generals and priests at its head, of course. The *cook,* in the very rear, takes pity on God-fearing Malanja. Bednyj's "folk buffonade" was performed on the Moscow music hall stage in 1932. In both works, Krleza's as well as Bednyj's, those who ruled, and (in Krleza) gorged themselves on earth, are the ones who enter heaven, while simple people are outsiders there. In Krleza's work there is an emphasis on the "particular connection of food to death and hell", significant also in the folk rituals of "karmine" (among the Catholics) and "daca" (among the Orthodox)—in South-Slavic areas post-funeral feasts equivalent to a wake—treated by Mickiewicz as well in the beginning of his dramatic text *Dziady* (Forefathers' Eve): a "feast with many dishes, beverages and fruit, to which the spirits of the deceased are invited". In the imagination of Mickiewicz's folk "fiddler" heaven is also filled with edibles ("doughnuts, pasta, milk and fruit and strawberries") which goes together with the basic refrain of this part of the text where the chorus points out that "he who has never tasted bitterness" on earth "will never taste sweetness in heaven" (to be stressed here are the concepts of 'bitterness' and 'sweetness', belonging to the sense of taste!). In Krleza's text the reverse applies, for with a glance from "below", Krleza claims that whoever has tasted of pleasure on earth will taste of it in heaven as well; heaven becomes an extension of earthly space, undergoing a "drastic materialization".

Krleza's text (the **Balade** in general) is based on a duality in the folk picturesque, dedicated to feasts and food: the representatives of the ruling classes eat differently from ordinary people, who within the categories of their own diet dream more of food than eat: the rulers of life, in distinction from the oral tradition (Kraljevic Marko in the poetry of the Serbian or Croatian language), "are not feasting in the name of the people, but at the expense of the people and to the people's detriment", but—with Bachtin—it is important to add that "the bread stolen from the people does not cease to be bread, wine is always good, even when the Pope is drinking it. *Wine and bread* have their logic, their *truth,* their *irresistible urge for an abundance that spilleth over . . .*"

It is important to stress, when discussing the "Flemishness" of Krleza's **Balade** and in particular Bruegel as their artistic model (or more correctly one of the artistic models), that the abundance and variety of edibles enumerated by Krleza is not paralleled in Bruegel's work. In the painting *The Fight Between Carnival and Lent* (1559), a picture Krleza had seen at the Viennese *Kunsthistorisches Museum,* the prince of the carnival rides on a barrel, his weapon is a skewer with a pig's head on it, and his shield—a ham impaled on the barrel; and in another painting from the Viennese museum, *Peasant Wedding* (1568) wine is poured in the foreground and dishes are carried, but the edibles on the table are hidden by human figures, Bruegel is indeed modest in his portrayal of feasts in comparison to Krleza. Only *Schlaraffenland* (1567, *Alte Pinakothek,* Munich) has that "irresistible urge for abundance" that Bachtin speaks of, although its heaps of porridge, roasted suckling pig and fences made out of sausages are principally disputed as sinful. Sometimes Krleza is closer to Bosch than to Bruegel, as in the phantasmagorical folk grotesque *Scherzo* with its search for the "god of Bacchus" and a "Pauline friar with a tuft like 'mlinci'" (mlinci—a popular pasta dish), a friar who concludes that "of all literary chines, the most healthy are the sweet pheasant chines!", in *Sanoborska* (Samobor Ballad) with its series of grotesque "images" in which pigs lay "eggs" and little "suckling pigs" crow, or in *Komendrijasi* (The Buffoons) with its popular-grotesque parallels drawn between people and edibles (a "baron" is compared to "strukli" (cheese filled dumplings), "beans", "marinade", "goat", "ox", "tomato" and "lemon").

However, Krleza's culinary Flemishness can be seen not only in **Balade,** where it is based on the cultural models of the 16th century, it also comes forth in the novels. Although we will be dealing here with examples from the last of his novels—**Zastave** (Banners), it should not be forgotten that the opening scene of the novel *Na rubu pameti* (**On the Edge of Reason**) is the chapter *Dinner Party in Domacinski's Vineyard,* and that the act of the "domestic" capitalist who produces chamber pots for Persia, namely his murder of a peasant—an act that brings forth the indignnation of the narrator and thus furthers the plot—is committed in the "defense of his own Riesling". The novel in which Krleza attempts to generalize the question of the mechanism of power in the states of Central Europe bears the characteristic title of **Banket u Blitvi** (Banquet in Blithuania), stressing in the title itself that it is a text in which there will be *conversations* between representatives of governments and those strata that attend "banquets". Although the "banquet" here is not a chronotope of the novel, it is important to note that the title indicates a "feast as the essential framework of wise words, speeches, merry truth" for "between words and feasts there is an underlying bond" rooted in the "antique symposion". The banquet is not, of course, a symposion, but a place where statesmen and politicians on the highest level meet with representatives of (official) culture and art, and such a gathering, with its inevitable disputes and mutual setting of accounts, is the fundamental principle of the novel's organization with its dialogue and soliloquy sections. In this connection one of the basic chronotopes of *The Brothers Karamazov* deserves mention, a tavern in which Ivan and Alyosha meet to converse on God "with fish soup, tea and jam", a situation Krleza clearly used as a model in the novel *In extremis.* The "tavern", as Sklovskij established, is a locus of "geometric intersection of individual lines of the novel", it was "patented with purely literary goals" by Cervantes, and, early on, this "literary tavern" became one of the frequent chronotopes of the novel, as for instance in Stendhal's and Balzac's novels, where the characters meet in the parlor-salon; the importance of the salon is signalled by the fact that "there dialogues develop which acquire a special meaning in the novel, they disclose the characters, their 'ideas' and 'passions'". Krleza is relying on this tradition in the compositional pattern of **Zastave,** even if the novel is "dispersive" in many aspects, making plot and composition less important. Organized formally and compositionally around the basic chronotope "path", as a projection of the metaphor "path of life" that "permits (the novel) to witness everyday life [*byt*] broadly", **Zastave** underlines already in the headings of its chapters the meaning of the chronotope of "tavern", or, in Krleza's work, restaurant or "parlor"; in any case the *table,* around which the characters of the novel gather to lead dialogues, is where Krleza's Flemishness comes to the foreground. In the following chapter headings the "table" is emphasized: *Dinner in Honor of Mr. Stevan Mihailovic Gruic, Dinner at Old Kamráth's, A Silver Anniversary at the Jurjaveski Home, Dinner at the Grand Hotel.* Furthermore we encounter within the novel restaurants, inns, bodegas or (Hungarian) *esárdas* as *loci* facilitating dialogic interaction, lovers' trysts or as places of social characterization. Some of these loci can be identified. The Budapest "restaurant, reserved for the select of the presidential cream" is called "At King Matthias's" in the first editions, but even under the name "Hungarian Crown" it is recognizable as the *Mátyás Pince*; a comparison of newspapers with "Gerbaud's Profiterollen" invokes the famous Budapest Konditorei, and Kamilo meets with Kamráth at an "evening at Gundel's", a restaurant renowned even today in Budapest, where they "serve Balaton fish, bedewed with a yellow mist of butter from steaming, silver casseroles". There Kamilo looks at the "dark blue, tempestuous landscape on his platter: slender, chivalric towers, dark ominous Scottish fortresses on a misty shore", clearly an allusion to the famous Wedgewood china!

The vision of the first of the *loci* is marked iconic:

> Under age-old attics and with rustic, crudely hewn tables, with a floor of red, varnished brick, in the dim glow of orange lampshades, everything was patriarchal, everything was an imitation of a Renaissance tavern from the old days of Corvinus, with servants in tails, silver casseroles, crayfish, Balaton *fogas* in jelly, Martell, Courvoisier, "Szürkebarát" from Tokai, Transdanubian "Bikaver", rabbit, venison, game in general, pheasants, mayonnaise, English meat, grilled Danubian sturgeon, pineapple bowl, and of all these Kamilo chose the stuffed pepper.

This is certainly not Grosz's satiric vision of a scene from the opulent Berlin restaurants of the 1920s, so esteemed by Krleza, but a catalogue of edibles, situated in the framework of an architectural "imitation" of the European Renaissance, and disputed within Kamilo's opposition to his "illustrious" father by his choice of a popular dish, and thus transferred into a culture to which the main character of the novel belongs, by genealogy alone. A similar catalogue of "rich" food will appear later in Kamilo's "half-dream" in which the *locus* of a meeting will become the "store window of a delicatessen bodega" on the corner of *Váci street* "with mixed pickles, Italian mortadella and salsas, with salmon and pickled herrings, with French cheeses and Cointreau", and then the *intérieur* with "pink pastries in marzipan, the pink glaze of punch and cream, with a large, massive cake in the middle of the dining room, as massive as a mill wheel", while in *Dinner at Old Kamráth's* the iconic model of these enumerations discloses the Budapest culinary opulence, with *game, fish* and *cheeses* in the focus of attention. In fact, we learn little of the menu of this "dinner" which actually serves only as a framework motivating the dialogue. All that we know is that "black coffee with Chartreuse was served" at the end, while at the beginning of the chapter, attention is focused on the iconography of the chronotope, i.e. on

the still gloomy and funereal mood that reigned in the dark, heavy oak-panelled *Dutch* dining room, decorated with equally dark *still-lifes,* on which the *oily, pink fish* on *silver platters* stood out from *brown molasses,* and with slaughtered *corpses of furry rabbits,* on which veinal blood had clotted in the open wounds.

This classic Dutch *still-life,* familiar from the paintings of Snyder or Weenix, exhales death, as an accompaniment to food, and in this same vein of painting bloody corpses we furthermore find the "Quartered Ox" by Krleza's friend Petar Dobrovic (1936, Dobrovic Gallery, Belgrade) painted at the same Mlini, near Dubrovnik, where the *Portrait of Miroslav Krleza* (1938, same gallery) was made. "Dutch Settecento Stilleben" appears in an *intérieur* still later, but with the correction that these "still-lifes are not Dutch, but Dalmatian, probably by a provincial Venetian master—in the countryside, in our cities, there are many such things".

In the chapter *The Call of the Emperor's Trumpet* in which Kamilo becomes "an Austrian recruit" in the World War, a *locus* of farewell is the Hungarian *csárda* which appears as a popular inn on the outskirts of Budapest, on the Danube, with "sterlets on the grill and fisherman's soup, and fresh Sombor cheese, and wine thick and dark as ox blood" ("Bikaver" wine, in which the comparison with ox blood is included in the name). However, amid the "oily mass of fish meat" Kamilo recalls the "lordly" Budapest drinks of "cherries in rum of Mistress de Szemera, and cognac in a café, and Tokai and Kirsch and Armagnac". "In the maelstrom of images" which passes through his mind culinary motifs from other cultural regions appear, arosen by the memory of his already dead Serbian friend: faith in life, as faith in the "innocent joys of life, in Smederevo wine, grilled bulls' balls, good coffee. Turkish demi-tasse, Turkish coffee pot, decasyllable, gypsy violin"—and it should be pointed out that in this inner monologue the culinary motifs are placed in one and the same category as the decasyllable, the "heroic" verse meter of the oral epics mythologized in this culture.

In the chapter *Dinner in honor of Mr. Stevan Mihailovic Gruic,* dedicated to the Serbian-Croatian dispute on the eve of the World War, the "dinner" in the Zagreb "salon" is only a framework for the conversation, but this framework explains why the "retired Serbian minister" is characterized with the aid of elements of popular culinary culture. Stevca returns from his military service "with a huge Uzice smoked ham, two kilos of caviar from Kladovo, and a 5-liter jug of juniper brandy". He recalls in culinary concepts the Serbian army in the Balkan war: "heaps of amorphous masses of mutton wallow in the mud, skewers with pilfered rolls are turned here and there, juniper brandy is downed". Here contrast is also made to food from official banquets in the Kingdom of Serbia—"surprise with cognac and crêpes flambée", on the other hand, and popular dishes, "kaimak cheese from Uzice or cevapcici" on the other. The opposition between two cultural regions is designated sarcastically in culinary terms: "bloody liver" stands for the Serbian and "a silver casserole" for the Croatian side.

At the above-mentioned dinner with father and son in a Budapest restaurant, within the exposition of the novel, Emericki *senior,* representative of the traditional values, complains of the Croatian cuisine:

> We don't even know, brother, how to cook, no, not even how to cook, and all we can think about are some ideas, we've been ruined by Viennese cuisine, the devil knows why we've forgotten how to cook, a little of the old Croatian cuisine has held on in Varazdin, but that is disappearing by and by, I remember when I was there in secondary school, those turkeys, those sausages, those roast sirloins, buckwheat patties and mlinci pasta, those were dishes, and it is all disappearing, the good traditions are melting like snow, and that is our modern time. . . .

In accordance with such a description, the chapters that bring the characters of the novel to the *table* in Croatian loci do not abound in information on "Croatian cuisine". The chapter *A Silver Anniversary at the Jurjaveski Home* is a real "banquet" chapter which collects the social elite around the table, and where the exposition of the chapter is dedicated to the culinary content of the "jubilee" table—a description of a dinner that

> began with richly served caviar, on ice slabs, and progressed from turtle soup and chilled crayfish in their shells with mayonnaise to turkey with mlinci, only to continue with hunting-style venison and end with hot carnival doughnuts. . . .

However, there is later mention of "a roast bearing the famous name of Archduchess Stephanie, served at Glavacki's with a spicy mushroom sauce", "a burgundy of the Cazma prevost", comparable to (Hungarian) Tokai wine, and at the end of the chapter, there appears even a "sizeable gilthead fish" and a "suckling pig", half of which is devoured by one of the guests "with head and brains"; but this table is no longer presented as a *tableau.* The menu is composed of elements of representative European dining, but also of the "national" dishes of northern (turkey with mlinci) and maritime (gilthead fish) Croatia.

Dinner at the Grand Hotel, conveying the nervous mood of the three characters in an "agonizing, crepuscular and deadly game", gathered around the table, introduces titbits from the hotel menu ("vol-au-vent of chicken livers with a mushroom

sauce", "asparagus soup", "perch", "Odeschalchi's burgundy") in an argument with the waiter; "huge silver platters full of fish" appear on the table once more, with associations to "various tasty specialties" of the domestic cuisine, but this is only a "dinner of friends, where all *pretend* to dine, though no one feels like eating", and where the tension among the three persons grows when they are to select the "salon wine"; coffee is finally served, and Kamilo Emericki, by now Mirkovic, remains with Ana Borongay, and a "bottle of Armagnac". It is worth remarking, however, how at the culmination of this tragic situation of the two loners, Ana, a poetess of Hungarian modernism, who has already embraced fashionable Cocteau and Picasso, drinks a "mysterious mixture of pale green absinthe" only to turn, a moment later, to the "coloristic perfection of her already slightly *wilted self-portrait*" (my italics A. F.). These emphatically ironic details point to Picasso's painting *La buveuse d'absinthe* (1902. The Hermitage, Leningrad), all the more so since Ana, with the pathetic, tragic exclamation of "ah, my dear mask", intended for herself, turns to the waiter to continue the rounds of Armagnac.

And it is only at the end of the novel, in the chapter *Finale,* when Ana and Kamilo descend to the "abyss" of their love affair, in the brutal atmosphere of a tavern on the outskirts of the town, on the banks of the Sava (recall the csárda on the Danube!) where the waiter offers "gypsy-like concoctions", that a local, more plebeian menu appears— "Presswurst or fine, home-made head cheese with warm corn bread", and "for dinner: strukli, blood sausage, devenica sausage, garlic sausage, pecenica sausage", and then "à la carte: crambambuli, Glühwein, pancakes with rum, barley, chicken soup, hot brandy, Eier-Cognac, Butellenwein, as you wish, and if you would have a French liqueur as well, then 'Heidsieck' and 'Veuve Cliquot'".

This is no longer the Dutch *Settecento-Stilleben,* nor is it Picasso's melancholic woman with absinthe and a siphon; this brothel-like atmosphere is thick with the "sweetly sickening smells" of spices, and dishes are not served in "silver casseroles", but instead "clay jugs" with "peasant grog" are put on the table. This opposition of popular dishes to the predominantly high class "banquet" meals in *Zastave,* Krleza's last novel, is strictly functional and related to the pivotal events of the novel.

In *Zastave* the bearers of the textual structure are not ordinary people, and hence there is no "pantagruelism"; it has been replaced by a "Flemishness", shaped iconically only in the Budapest scenes. It appears, however, in the novel in which the grotesquely caricatured Grosz-like "noble" world is confronted with a peasant and a poacher, to whom "man is a gut with nine windows", a peasant who farts in pantagruelian style, dreaming of a mother who baked strukli (cheese pie) and cooked "tripe" that peasants "can't afford,

God bless 'em", or of "slabs of bacon", and where someone steals the officers' chocolate rations, someone who is named after the most filling Zagorje dish—Valent *Zganec* (*zganci*—corn mush), a name that reminds us of the important place that food occupies in Krleza's texts, and of its very varied functions.

FURTHER READING

Criticism

Fried, István. "Miroslav Krleza's Anti-Utopia." *Acta Litteraria Academiae Scientiarum Hungariace* 29, Nos. 1-2 (1987): 163-78.

> Discusses the relationship between Krleza's distinctly Croatian-Hungarian anti-utopian vision in his works and the development of Western European anti-utopian literature.

Miletich, John S. "Toward a Stylistic Description of Expressionist Lyric: The German Phenomenon and Its Croatian Analogs." *International Journal of Slavic Linguistics and Poetics* XXV/XXVI (1982): 281-89.

> Explores "stylistic tendencies" of German expressionism as used by Antun Branko Simic and Krleza in their lyrics, showing that "Krleza's lyrics are organized around the use of imagery involving violent movement and sound as well as the extended use of personification."

Suvin, Darko. "On Dramaturgic Agents and Krleza's Agential Structure: The Types as a Key Level." *Modern Drama* XXVII, No. 1 (March 1984): 80-97.

> Dramaturgical analysis of Krleza's use and meaning of "stock characters" primarily in his plays of his expressionistic phase, particularly the Woman, the untranslatable *Nervchik,* and the subsidiary types of the Patriarchal Tyrant, the Parasite, and the Knower.

Additional coverage of Krleza's life and career is contained in the following sources published by Gale: *Contemporary Authors,* Vols. 97-100, and 105; *Contemporary Authors New Revision Series,* Vol. 50; and *Dictionary of Literary Biography,* Vol. 147.

Tillie Olsen

1913-

American short story writer, novelist, and essayist.

The following entry presents an overview of Olsen's career through 1998. For further information on her life and works, see *CLC,* Volumes 4 and 13.

INTRODUCTION

Olsen's work—which focuses on the plight of the poor, the powerless, and women—has earned her almost universal praise. Although she has published relatively little throughout her career, her short stories and novel are of the highest quality. Her fiction and her essays have placed her in a role as a chronicler of the working class as well as a leading feminist writer.

Biographical Information

Olsen was born on January 14, 1913 (some sources say 1912) in Omaha, Nebraska. Her Jewish parents had been political activists in Russia and immigrated to the United States after the failed 1905 revolution. While a teenager, Olsen read Rebecca Harding Davis's *Life in the Iron Mills* and was so moved by the description of the working class that she vowed to become a writer. After high school, Olsen took a variety of jobs to supplement her family's income and became active in leftist politics, joining the Young People's Socialist League and the Young Communist League. While working in Kansas City, Olsen was arrested in 1931 for encouraging packinghouse workers to unionize. While in prison, Olsen developed pleurisy and incipient tuberculosis. Upon her release, she moved to Minnesota to recover. There she began her first novel *Yonnondio: From the Thirties,* working on it until 1937 when she abandoned it, not to publish it until 1974. In 1936 she married Jack Olsen, a longshoreman, and raised four daughters in a working class neighborhood of San Francisco. She published some poems, articles and short stories about the plight of the working class in socialist periodicals such as *Partisan,* the *Waterfront Worker,* and the *Daily Worker.* In 1954 she enrolled in a writing class at San Francisco State University and won a Stanford University Creative Writing Fellowship. Another grant enabled her to finish *Tell Me a Riddle,* which was published in 1961. The 1970s where the most prolific time for Olsen as she published three works and gained wider recognition. Since then she has held a number of visiting professorships, writer-in-residence, and lecturer positions across the country.

Major Works

Olsen has only published a small volume of material: a handful of short stories, a book of essays and speeches, and one unfinished novel. Writing about working class families and their search for self-fulfillment, Olsen again and again returns to the tension in characters' lives between the demands of living in poverty and the need for accomplishment and meaning. Olsen has particularly focused upon the relationship between mothers and their children, arguing that the greatest demands are place upon mothers, often to the detriment of the women's hopes and dreams. *Tell Me a Riddle,* which won the O Henry Award for best American short story in 1961, consists of four short stories. Most famous is the title story which is often compared to Leo Tolstoy's "The Death of Ivan Ilyitch." It chronicles a grandmother's efforts to make sense of her life as she is dying of cancer, surrounded by the family for whom she has sacrificed all her own ambitions. **"I Stand Here Ironing"**, also in this collection, focuses on a mother's internal conflict as she remembers all the trials and failures she has encountered as she tried to raise her daughter. She mourns that her daughter has not had more advantages and fears that her daughter will be forced to endure a life much like her mother's. In *Silences,* a collection of essays and speeches, Olsen discusses the sacrifices that women writers have had to make for their families, and refutes common held beliefs that women writers have not been as successful as men because they are not as talented. *Yonnondio,* her only full length (though unfinished) novel, takes its name from Walt Whitman's poem. The book follows the lives of a working class family in the 1930s as they struggle against the Depression. Centering on two strong women, it presents their lives in terms of failures and successes, always locating the source of their strength within themselves.

Critical Reception

Critics have been unanimously overwhelming in their praise of Olsen's fiction. As one critic states, "Olsen writes with an elegance, compassion, and directness rare in any period." Although she has published little, reviewers agree that her short stories and novel are peerless in their portrayal of the working class, of women, and of the powerless. Blanche Gelfant comments on the recurring theme of human survival, even when the characters' "lives seem broken and futile, and life itself full of pain." Stylistically, scholars praise Olsen's use of dialect, internal conflict and flashbacks, as well as her ability to evoke a scene or experience with a brevity of words. However, critics have some reservations about Olsen's role as a leading feminist writer. Ellen Cronan Rose argues, "Olsen has made the mistake, in her recent oratory, of confusing the general human situation and the particular plight of women in our society. What she emphatically knows because she is an artist she thinks she knows because she is a woman." Critics point to her convincing male characters in the short stories "Hey Sailor, What Ship?" and "Requa" as evidence of her ability to address the human condition regardless of gender. Scholars such as Mickey Pearlman point out that some of Olsen's popularity is based upon her life experiences and what she represents to women. Reviewers find that her book of feminist essays, *Silences,* is far less evocative and convincing than her fiction.

PRINCIPAL WORKS

Tell Me a Riddle: A Collection (short stories) 1961
"Requa" (short story) 1970
Yonnondio: From the Thirties (novel) 1974
Silences (essays) 1978

CRITICISM

William Van O'Connor (essay date Fall 1963)

SOURCE: "The Stories of Tillie Olson," in *Studies in Short Fiction,* Vol. 1, No. 1, Fall, 1963, pp. 21-5.

[*In the following essay, O'Connor praises Olsen's short stories, for the power of their scenes of everyday life.*]

Tillie Olsen writes about anguish. One character thinks: "It is a long baptism into the seas of humankind, my daughter. Better immersion and in pain than to live untouched. Yet how will you sustain?"

In one story a soft-hearted sailor has lived a boisterous, rowdy, hard-drinking life. His world is empty, meaningless and in an eerie flux of days and nights at sea, transient acquaintanceships at bars and brothels when he is very drunk. His only refuge is a man whose life he had once saved, and the man's family. He has given the wife and children presents and much needed money. They have all loved him, and welcomed his visits. But now that he can tolerate his anguish only by constant drinking, during which he uses foul language and is an embarrassment before their friends, they are torn between devotion to him, or to what he once was, and their own respectability. Not being able to tolerate their disapproval, he leaves. Drunken, he looks back from a hill at their house, an island of light and warmth. The image blurs, and the house becomes impersonal and anonymous. One knows the sailor will find release from his pain only in the bottle, and finally in death.

An early scene in a second story presents a white girl in her early teens at a Negro church meeting. The singing, shouting, and strange rhythmic movements terrify her, and she faints. She has been very friendly with a colored girl her own age, having shared dolls, parties, and secrets. But white girls, in white society, eventually go their own paths, and, reluctantly, the girls give each other up. The white girl discovers she is filled with shame and guilt, and wants her mother to explain why there is so much misery and unhappiness. The mother embraces her, at the same time wondering where she herself would find that "place of strength" and "the gloved and loving hands" waiting "to support and understand."

In a third story, a mother, standing over her ironing board, ponders the life of her nineteen year old daughter. Someone, presumably a principal or counselor, has asked the mother "to come in and talk with me about your daughter." As she irons, she thinks back over the girl's life. The daughter was born in the depression. The father, unable to endure their poverty, leaves them. The mother works, puts the child in a nursery, then sends her to live with her husband's family. The mother remarries. There is never enough money, and they move frequently. The girl is not good in school, even though she tries hard. She has no close friends. She is small and dark, and not at all out-going. She does have one talent—she can be a sad-eyed clown, able to hold an audience enthralled; but a lack of money prevents the mother from helping her develop the talent. Eventually, the girl gives up in despair. The bomb becomes her symbol of frustration, and she justifies her passive opposition to society on the grounds that "we'll all be atom-dead" soon and nothing will matter. The mother believes that despite poverty and suffering there is "still enough to live by." But she does not know how to convince her daughter.

The story about the sailor is **"Hey Sailor, What Ship?"** The story about the white and colored children is **"O Yes,"** and the one about the mother and daughter is **"I Stand Here Ironing."** The three stories have anguish and despair as the antagonists. The protagonists hope, but with no real confidence. There appears to be no margin on the far side of despair for the sailor to reach. The children in **"O Yes"** find that friendship dissolves under economic, racial and social pressures. And the mother merely hopes that she can communicate her own sense of the value of life, even of lives lived in desperate circumstances.

A fourth story, **"Tell Me a Riddle,"** is about a Jewish couple who have been married for forty-seven years. The husband wants to retire to his lodge's Haven. He longs to be near other people, and to be free from economic worry. His wife wants to remain in her own house and to be free from all entanglements except the basic quarrel she has with her husband. Her quarrel with him has roots in the dim past. They have had many children, and were always poor. She resented his going out at night to visit with his cronies. She also had literary interests, but the pressure of work made it impossible for her to pursue them. Instead of reading, she sewed and scrubbed. Now in their old age they fight. Sometimes he cajoles her, hoping to win a victory; but she ridicules him, and soon he is calling her unpleasant names. Each gets a perverse joy out of their struggle, although he would be agreeable to a truce. Their children find all this distressing and unavailingly introduce many rational arguments about why it is foolish for their parents to quarrel.

She becomes ill, and after repeated refusals to visit a doctor she is examined. An operation follows, and the family learns she has cancer. She has about one year to live. A round of visits with their children follows. The grandchildren are noisy, and she is constantly tired. One child says, "Tell me a riddle, Grammy"; and she replies, "I know no riddles, child." In pain, she watches the activities of her children changing diapers; grandchildren climbing trees, hiding in closets; observes people in the streets, listens to sounds, and remembers. She relives her life, as a child in Europe, the birth of her children, the quarreling with her husband, and much else. Sometimes she sweats, sometimes she retches.

In California, they sit together on benches at the beach, watching other people playing, and looking out to sea. A grandchild who is a nurse lovingly attends her. He, the husband, feels death pursuing them, and refuses to take his wife home. These are the last two paragraphs:

> That last day the agony was perpetual. Time after time it lifted her almost off the bed, so they had to fight to hold her down. He could not endure and left the room; wept as if there never would be tears enough.

> Jeannie came to comfort him. In her light voice she said: Granddaddy, Granddaddy, don't cry. She is not there, she promised me. On the last day, she said she would go back to when she first heard music, a little girl on the road of the village where she was born. She promised ·me. It is a wedding and they dance, while the flutes so joyous and vibrant tremble in the air. Leave her there, Granddaddy, it is all right. She promised me. Come back, come back and help her poor body to die.

"Tell Me a Riddle" is as full of anguish as "The Death of Ivan Ilytch." It is also as serene, with the distance and calm of tragedy. Miss Olsen shows the human being's capacity to endure his own suffering, his own irrationality, and his own despair. Only creatures capable of a great and transforming idealism could turn such suffering into peaceful acceptance. They are defeated, but they are not routed. Subjected to enormous indignities, they remain dignified. **"Tell Me a Riddle"** exhibits once again the classic tragic stance, and does it magnificently.

Miss Olsen's stories are quite skillfully put together. On occasion, San Francisco seems to be the locale of a story, but generally the setting is not specifically identified. There is a city, the ocean, or a poor neighborhood, and it could be any city, either ocean, and almost any poor neighborhood. The stories push away from the individual and the unique, toward the world of Everyman.

The sailor is any lonesome human being who hopes against hope that he can be free from his wretchedness. The white child is any child discovering ineradicable evil. The mother is any mother who has failed, or believes she has failed, in rearing her child. The Jewish couple are a man and a woman facing death.

Miss Olsen's method is reminiscent of [Thorton] Wilder's in *Our Town*, [Dylan] Thomas' in *Under Milk Wood*, and [Thomas] Hardy's in *The Dynasts*. She names characters, but usually one finds out very little about them. Sometimes they are only a voice. Conversations are universal rather than particularized. The voice of the Jewish husband—"You have important business, Mrs. Inahurry? The President wants to consult with you?"—is other Jewish voices one has heard, first generation immigrant, mocking, with ages of patience and suffering back of them. The sailor's language is any sailor's language: "She don't hafta be jealous. I got money for her." The young colored girl adopts jive talk: "Couple cats from Franklin Jr. chirp in the choir. No harm or alarm." The lonely child in the convalescent home writes an anguished letter: "I am fine. How is the baby. If I write my letter nicely I will have a star." And "There never was a star."

Characters are rendered only as much as is necessary to place them in a certain kind of environment. The homes of the children in **"Tell Me a Riddle"** are not described. One does not know much about their husbands or wives. The voices come in over one another. One is married to a doctor, whom she quotes. Another can't bear to see her mother suffer. A third needs more money. They are people. They breathe, suffer, wonder.

The chronology or sequence of events in the stories is ordered not as these occurred, but as they impinge on a character's memory. As in [William] Faulkner's *Absalom, Absalom!* or *The Sound and the Fury*, Miss Olsen's stories seem gradually to "discover" themselves for the reader. She does, however, give the reader more assistance than Faulkner does. She does not immerse him so deeply in the dark recesses where events are happening but have not as yet been explained. She sets a scene quickly, usually with a few sentences. Then the characters take over, talking, remembering, laughing or crying. Occasionally the author intrudes with a refrain, such as *"Hey Sailor, what ship?"* or a rhetorical commentary, such as *"So it is that she sits in the wind of the singing, among the thousand various faces of age."* But mostly the action belongs to the characters.

When Miss Olsen is at her best, as in **"Tell Me a Riddle,"** she is a writer of tremendous skill and power. Her productivity has been small, but she would not have to write a great deal more than she has to earn a place among the eminent writers of short stories.

Elizabeth Fisher (review date 10 April 1972)

SOURCE: "The Passion of Tillie Olsen," in *The Nation,* Vol. 715, No. 15, April 10, 1972, pp. 472-74.

[*In the following review of* Tell Me a Riddle, *Fisher praises Olsen's efforts as a feminist writer.*]

You won't find her in *Who's Who* . . . nor is her name going to be listed in the forthcoming reference book, *World Authors.* Her total published work probably runs to under 200 pages: the first story came out in 1934, the latest in 1970. In between there were the four stories in *Tell Me a Riddle,* reissued in paperback this August after being out of print for several years, stories written and published between 1953 and 1960, and—its own kind of explanation—the essay, **"Silences, When Writers Don't Write,"** published in *Harper's* magazine in 1965. "I have had special need to learn all I could of this over the years, myself so nearly remaining mute and having let writing die over and over again in me." Yet in the 116 pages of *Tell Me a Riddle*—small ones with large type and large margins, too—are contained several lives and lifetimes, as if all the writing Tillie Olsen didn't do has coalesced in intensity and packed itself into these stories.

The title story is her masterpiece. My first reading of it was one of those shattering discoveries, an experience that, at first, reminded me of coming on Henry Roth's *Call It Sleep,* because that book, too, had been "buried," had a strong emotional impact, and dealt with poor immigrant Jews. However, Olsen's work has neither the particularity nor the special faults of Roth's; it has such compression and such scope that the analogy made by a friend of mine—her first reading of "The Death of Ivan Ilyitch"—seems to me a better one. With this difference: Tillie Olsen is not only a great writer, she is a feminist artist. Till the very end, we do not even know the name of the old woman whose long dying is the framework on which **"Tell Me a Riddle"** evolves. She is the mother, the wife, the grandmother. Only in the last 3 pages do we learn that she is Eva. But in the magic weaving of past and present which goes from Olshana in prerevolutionary Russia to death in a strange impersonal Los Angeles, what comes out most strongly is the disadvantaging of woman, the denial of intellect and aspiration, the utter thanklessness of the mother's role. Seven children are brought up, through the vicissitudes of a working-class life during the past fifty years, and make the successful climb into the middle classes, but at what a cost, what a cost. The young girl steeped in 19th-century idealism gives way to the exigencies of 20th-century American materialism. Always "don't read, put your book away," and she dies shutting out her husband, babbling of the great world of books and culture, philosophy and music of which she has had only the most fleeting glimpses in her practical everyday life: "The children's needings; that grocer's face or this merchant's wife she had to beg credit from when credit was a disgrace; the scenery of the long-blocks walked around when she could not pay; school coming, and the desperate going over the old to see what yet could be remade; the soups of meat bones begged 'for the dog' one winter. . . ." About Olsen's men it might be said, as of the husband in [Samual] Beckett's "Happy Days," how can they help others when they can't even help themselves? Her women can, but it is never enough, never right, never whole.

"The love—the passion of tending—had risen with the need

like a torrent; and like a torrent drowned and immolated all else. . . . Only the thin pulsing left that could not quiet suffering over lives one felt but could no longer hold nor help." People have drawn on her, feeding, demanding more, more, so that, at last, drained without replenishment, she says, no, enough.

"Never again to be forced to move to the rhythms of others. Being at last able to live within, and not to move to the rhythms of others." This is the refrain of the tired old woman, battered by too much life, but free at last on her own limited terms. "If they would but leave her in the air now stilled of clamor, in the reconciled solitude to journey to her self." Hunched in the closet, she hides from the hurly-burly of family, from her daughter's "spilling memories," unable to touch the baby, "warm flesh like this that had claims and nuzzled away all else and with lovely mouths devoured . . . the drawing into needing and being needed." And later, "at the back of the great city" where her husband had brought her "to the dwelling places of the cast-off old," as she makes for "the far ruffle of the sea . . . though she leaned against him, it was she who led." What images and what economy, what a world is here compressed!

"I Stand Here Ironing" is the story told by a mother of how, wanting to do the best for her daughter, she was so often forced to do the worst, and it is one that every parent can recognize. In tight, economical prose she tears us with the parental experience, how we listen, wrongly, to other people, or are just imprisoned by events we could not foresee—desertion, poverty, expanding families; it is also a hopeful story of how children survive, sometimes even making strength, or talent, out of the deprivations they've endured. Tillie Olsen's is an unsparing but tender vision in which love is need that is rarely answered, a vision of communication on strange, imperfect levels, and, above all, of resilience, a belief that human beings are not passive, that there is more in them "than this dress on the ironing board, helpless before the iron."

The two other stories in this volume, strong and well worked, would be accounted great if someone else had written them; they fade only beside the raw strength of the first-named ones. **"Hey Sailor, What Ship?"** tells of an alcoholic seaman who cannot survive ashore and who yet seeks the warmth of a family; it tells also of the limitations and cruelties and affections of the family trying to hold on to an earlier time's hope and community.

In **"O Yes"** there is a marvelous evocation of the black religious experience: "The crucified Christ embroidered on the starched white curtain leaps in the wind of the sudden singing"; "You not used to hearing what people keeps inside, Carol"; and a depiction of the snob and class pressures that drive apart two 12-year-old girls, one black, one white. The

white girl doesn't want to be oppressed by life; "Why is it like this and why do I have to care?" Her mother knows, but is helpless with her own unassuaged needs, as she answers, inside to herself, "Caring asks doing. It is a long baptism into the seas of humanity."

> **What is wonderful is that, engaged, feminist, Olsen's work is also utterly transcendent—a contradiction of the art-for-art's sake purists.**
> **—*Elizabeth Fisher***

Olsen's women alternatively reject and demand the full intensity of life. They are conscious, terrifyingly frighteningly conscious, and it is this that makes their pain and ours. Mortality presses on them with an awful weight, the finiteness of the human animal as opposed to the infinitude of the human spirit, or even to the possibilities of the human, being. "*Humankind one has to believe.*" And we feel with Lennie, Eva's son, "for that in her which never lived (for that which in him might never live) . . . *good-bye Mother who taught me to mother myself.*"

What is wonderful is that, engaged, feminist, Olsen's work is also utterly transcendent—a contradiction of the art-for-art's sake purists. Though the subject matter may be autobiographical, the author is everywhere and nowhere; this is indeed writing that consumes all impediments; incandescent, it glows and it burns. Read the stories; they will not be forgotten.

Ellen Cronan Rose (essay date April 1976)

SOURCE: "Limming: or Why Tillie Writes," in *The Hollins Critic,* Vol. XIII, No. 2, April, 1976, pp. 1-13.

[*In the essay below, Rose explores Olsen's philosophy on writing and suggests that Olsen, a renowned feminist, is as powerful at depicting men as she as at depicting women.*]

Tillie Olsen was born in Nebraska 65 years ago. In 1960, when she was 50 years old, she published her first book, a slim volume of short stories called *Tell Me A Riddle.* In 1974 she finally published a novel—*Yonnondio*—she had begun in 1932 and abandoned in 1937. To women in "the movement" she is a major literary figure, not so much despite as because of the paucity of her publications.

Since 1971, when Delta reissued *Tell Me A Riddle* in paperback, Olsen has been stumping the country, speaking about women who have been prevented by their sex from utilizing their creative talents. These are her words:

> In the twenty years I bore and reared my children, usually had to work on the job as well, the simplest circumstances for creation did not exist. When the youngest of our four was in school, the beginnings struggled toward endings. . . . Bliss of movement. A full extended family life; the world of my job; and the writing, which I was somehow able to carry around with me through work, through home. Time on the bus, even when I had to stand, was enough; the stolen moments at work, enough; the deep night hours for as long as I could stay awake, after the kids were in bed, after the household tasks were done, sometimes during. It is no accident that the first work I considered publishable began: "I stand here ironing." In such snatches of time I wrote what I did in those years, but there came a time when this triple life was no longer possible. The fifteen hours of daily realities became too much distraction for the writing.
>
> As for myself, who did not publish a book until I was 50, who raised children without household help or the help of the 'technological sublime' . . . who worked outside the house on everyday jobs as well. . . . The years when I should have been writing, my hands and being were at other (inescapable) tasks. . . . The habits of a lifetime when everything else had to come before writing are not easily broken, even when circumstances now often make it possible for the writing to be first; habits of years: response to others, distractibility, responsibility for daily matters, stay with you, mark you, become you. I speak of myself to bring here the sense of those others to whom this is in the process of happening (unnecessarily happening, for it need not, must not continue to be) and to remind us of those (I so nearly was one) who never come to writing at all. We cannot speak of women writers in our century without speaking also of the invisible; the also capable; the born to the wrong circumstances, the diminished, the excluded, the lost, the silenced. We who write are survivors, 'onlys.' One—out of twelve.

I heard Olsen speak these words to a class at Dartmouth College last year, and I observed their galvanic effect on the students—mostly women—who heard them. My first exposure to Tillie Olsen was to Olsen the feminist. It was with this preparation that I first read *Tell Me A Riddle* and *Yonnondio.* I was thus unprepared for their impact on me.

For in her books, Olsen is no politician, but an artist. Her

fictions evoke, move, haunt. They did not seem, when I read them, to belong to any movement, to support any cause.

And so I returned to Olsen's words about the situation of the woman writer to see if there was something I had missed, something the women's movement had missed.

In **"Silences: When Writers Don't Write,"** originally delivered as a talk to the Radcliffe Institute for Independent Study in 1963, Olsen asks, "What are creation's needs for full functioning?" The answer *women* have heard is an echo of Virginia Woolf's "£500 a year and a room of one's own"—independence, freedom, escape from the restriction of traditional feminine roles. This is the answer Olsen herself gives on the lecture circuit. But in this early Radcliffe speech, her question seems not so much political as aesthetic.

It is no accident that the first work I considered publishable began: "I stand here ironing." In such snatches of time I wrote what I did in those years, but there came a time when this triple life was no longer possible.

—Tillie Olsen

Wondering what keeps writers from writing, Olsen turns to what writers—*men* writers—have themselves said about their unnatural silences, not periods of gestation and renewal, but of drought, "unnatural thwarting of what struggles to come into being, but cannot." She points to Hardy's sense of lost "vision," to Hopkins, "poet's eye," curbed by a priestly vow to refrain from writing, to Rimbaud who, after long silence, finally on his deathbed "spoke again like a poet-visionary." She then turns to writers who wrote continuously, in an effort to understand what preserved them from the unnatural silences that foreshortened the creativity of Hardy, Hopkins, Rimbaud, Melville, and Kafka. She cites James's assertion that creation demands "a depth and continuity of attention," and notes that Rilke cut himself off from his family to live in attentive isolation so that there would be "no limit to vision." Over and over in these opening paragraphs of "**Silences,**" Olsen identifies the act of creation with an act of the eye.

In order to create, the artist must see. Margaret Howth, in Rebecca Harding Davis's novel of that name, is the type of the artist for Olsen, "her eyes quicker to see than ours." And one of the special handicaps of the woman writer, confined traditionally to her proper sphere in the drawing room or the kitchen, is that she is restricted to what Olsen calls "trespass vision" of the world beyond that sphere. But although she echoes Charlotte Bronte's lament that women are denied "facilities for observation . . . a knowledge of the world," Olsen does not equate the reportorial with the creative eye. Vision is not photography. Olsen quotes, approvingly, Sarah Orne Jewett's advice to the young Willa Cather: "If you don't keep and mature your force . . . what might be insight is only observation. You will write about life, but never life itself."

In Rebecca Harding Davis's *Life in the Iron Mills,* to which Olsen has added an appreciative biographical afterword, the distinction between vision and mere seeing is dramatized in the reactions of two viewers to the statue Hugh Wolfe has sculpted out of slag. The mill owner's son has brought a party of gentlemen to see the mill. On their way back to the carriage, they stumble on Hugh's statue, the crouching figure of a nude woman, with outstretched arms. Moved by its crude power, the gentlemen ask Hugh, "But what did you mean by it?" "She be hungry," he answers. The Doctor condescendingly instructs the unschooled sculptor: "Oh-h! But what a mistake you have made, my fine fellow! You have given no sign of starvation to the body. It is strong,—terribly strong." To the realist, a portrait of starvation must count every rib. But Mitchell, who is portrayed as the dilettante and aesthete, a stranger to the mill town and of a different cut than the doctor, foreman, and newspaperman who round out the party, "flash[es] a look of disgust" at the doctor: "'May,' he broke out impatiently, 'are you blind? Look at that woman's face! It asks questions of God, and says, "I have a right to know." Good God, how hungry it is!'"

So Olsen's vision is, in a sense, trespass vision. It is "insight, not observation," the eye's invasion of outward detail to the meaning and shape within. It is this creative trespassing that Rebecca Davis commends in Margaret Howth, whose eyes are "quicker to see than ours, delicate or grand lines in the homeliest things." And it is precisely that quality in Rebecca Davis herself that makes her so significant to Tillie Olsen, who says of her that "the noting of reality was transformed into comprehension, Vision."

Tillie Olsen's edition of *Life In the Iron Mills,* published by the Feminist Press, is central to an understanding of what she means by the creative act. It may or may not be one of the lost masterpieces of American fiction. Olsen herself admits that it is "botched." But it fascinates her because it is a parable of creation, a portrait of the artist. And significantly, that artist is a sculptor.

One of the unsilent writers Olsen quotes in **"Silences"** is the articulate Thomas Mann, who spoke of the act of creation as "the will, the self-control to shape a sentence or follow out a hard train of thought. From the first rhythmical urge of the inward creative force towards the material, towards casting in shape and form, from that to the thought, the image, the word, the line." Vision is perceptive seeing, which sees beneath and within the outward details the essential shape of the meaning of the thing perceived. Doctor May saw only the anatomy of Hugh's statue; Mitchell saw through to the woman's soul.

Sculpting is cutting away the exterior surface to come to the shape within the block of marble. Hugh spends months "hewing and hacking with his blunt knife," compelled by "a fierce thirst for beauty,—to know it, to create it." His struggle is first to see the beauty within and then to give it form, Mann's urge towards the material and then casting it in shape and form.

Olsen writes of Davis's art in similarly sculptural words: "It may have taken her years to embody her vision. 'Hewing and hacking'" like Hugh. The first pages of *Life in the Iron Mills* are the narrator's injunction to the reader to "look deeper" into the sordid lives of the mill workers, to ask whether there is "nothing beneath" the squalor. This preamble concludes with the artless confession that "I can paint nothing of this" inner reality, "only give you the outside outlines." But the strength of the tale is in Davis's ability to sculpt that inner reality, to dissolve the outside outlines and uncover the moral shape of her simple tale. For Olsen it is "a stunning insight . . . as transcendent as any written in her century."

Vision is not photography. Sculpting is not cameo carving. Rebecca Harding Davis excoriated the Brahmins she met on her trip north from her native Wheeling, West Virginia. Emerson and Bronson Alcott, she wrote in her journal, "thought they were guiding the real world, [but] they stood quite outside of it, and never would see it as it was . . . their views gave you the same sense of unreality, of having been taken, as Hawthorne said, at too long a range." In other words, they imposed their vision of the world on the world of fact, pasted their carvings on the surface of things. Davis criticized them for ignoring the "back-bone of fact." To see the inner shape, you have at least to acknowledge the contour of the surface.

In her own tale of the down-trodden, **Yonnondio,** Olsen addresses the Brahmins of our day:

> And could you not make a cameo of this and pin it
> onto your aesthetic hearts? So sharp it is, so clear,
> so classic. The shattered dusk, the mountain of
> culm, the tipple; clean lines, bare beauty—and
> carved against them dwarfed by the vastness of
> night and the towering tipple, these black figures
> with bowed heads, waiting, waiting.

The aesthetic eye sees "at too long a range." It abstracts from surface detail a pleasing pattern. But the creative eye, the visionary eye, apprehends the surface in order to comprehend the inner shape which gives it meaning.

Thus by accreted detail, Olsen's definition of the creative act comes into focus. The artist stands, always, in relation to a world of fact. He can record it or he can transform it. In the one case, the standard by which he measures his achievement is fidelity to fact. In the other, his standards are formal. Between these extremes, Tillie Olsen places the creative act. Fidelity to fact, but essential fact. Form and pattern, but exposed, not imposed.

It is not surprising that, of all the literary people she met on her northern trip, Rebecca Davis should have been drawn to Hawthorne. This aesthetic stance in relation to reality that I have discerned in Olsen and Davis is also, as I understand it, the method of Hawthorne's romances. Coming to Hawthorne's tales early in her life, Davis was "verified" in her feeling that "the common-place folk and things which I saw every day had mystery and charm ... belong to the magic world [of books] as much as knights and pilgrims." *Ethan Brand*, that tale of another furnace tender, sees under the surface of fact a fable of the unpardonable sin; *Life in the Iron Mills*, as Olsen points out, is about "another kind of unpardonable sin," but its method of uncovering that sin is akin to Hawthorne's. It is not an abstraction from reality—that is the method of the cameo cutter, the formalist—but a reduction of facticity to its primary form.

When I began this study of Tillie Olsen, I was motivated by my sense that beneath the polemic about the predicament of the woman writer lay something like this more comprehensive aesthetic. What gave me this sense, or suspicion, was Olsen's fiction, which transcends her oratory. But before I turn to an appreciation of that fiction, I want to examine briefly the source of the disparity between Olsen's real aesthetic and her current feminist articulation of it.

Throughout her non-fiction writing, as we have seen, Olsen uses the metaphor of sculpture to define the creative act. To be a writer, one must "be able to come to, cleave to, find the form for one's own life comprehensions." But in an article published in *College English* in 1972, **"Women Who Are Writers in Our Century: One Out of Twelve,"** Olsen uses this sculptural imagery to describe, not the artist, but the situation of women, who are "estranged from their own experience and unable to perceive its shape and authenticity," prevented by social and sexual circumscription from the essential act of self-definition and affirmation. The paradox of female reality, as Olsen understands it, is that immersion in life means loss of perspective, or vision.

The artist-visionary can supply that perspective, can "find the form" which constitutes the "shape and authenticity" of what Olsen calls "common female realities."

Thus in **"One Out of Twelve"** and on the lecture circuit, Tillie Olsen exhorts women artists to take women's lives as their subject matter, finding a therapeutic link between the situation of women in our society and the peculiar kind of discovery implicit in the aesthetic creation. Accordingly she feels "it is no accident that the first work I considered publishable began: 'I stand here ironing'."

It is possible to read the first of the four stories that comprise *Tell Me A Riddle* as an exemplum of Olsen's feminist aesthetic. The mother-narrator of **"I Stand Here Ironing"** looks back over a life where there has been no "time to remember, to sift, to weigh, to estimate, to total." Caught in the mesh of paid work, unpaid work, typing, darning, ironing, she has suffered, but never had time and leisure to perceive and shape, to understand, the passionate arc of motherhood. Helplessly she looks back over her memories of her daughter's childhood and concludes, "I will never total it all."

What Olsen does, in **"I Stand Here Ironing,"** is to perceive and give form to the meaning of her narrator's motherhood, that "total" which the mother has no time to sum. As every female reader I have spoken to attests, this story movingly succeeds in articulating what Olsen calls "common female realities."

It is also possible to fit the title story of the collection into the Procrustean feminist aesthetic Olsen propounds in **"One Out of Twelve."** "Tell me a riddle, Grammy. I know no riddles, child." But the grandfather "knew how to tickle, chuck, lift, toss, do tricks, tell secrets, make jokes, match riddle for riddle." Why? Clearly because during all the years when she "had had to manage," to contend with poverty, to raise five children, to preserve domestic order, he "never scraped a carrot or knew a dish towel sops." The man is free, the woman bound. Women cannot "riddle" or form the experience they are utterly immersed in.

But **"Tell Me A Riddle"** is far more than a feminist document. In it, Olsen riddles the inscrutable by perceiving the meaning beneath and within the old woman's life and death. But this service is not rendered solely to the grandmother, but to all the characters in the story, and to the reader as well. Lennie, her son, suffered "not alone for her who was dying, but for that in her which never lived (for that which in him might never live)." And keeping his vigil by the dying woman's bedside, the grandfather achieves an epiphany, which the reader shares:

> The cards fell from his fingers. Without warning, the bereavement and betrayal he had sheltered—compounded through the years—hidden even from himself—revealed itself,
> uncoiled,

released,
sprung
and with it the monstrous shapes of what had actually happened in the century.

"Tell Me A Riddle" is a story about "common female realities," but it is also a story about "common *human* realities." We are all bound slaves, all immured in immanence, pawns of economic and political forces we cannot comprehend. Stepping from moment to moment, we do not see that we are pacing out the steps of a "dance, while the flutes so joyous and vibrant tremble in the air."

Olsen has made the mistake, in her recent oratory, of confusing the general human situation and the particular plight of women in our society. What she empathically knows because she is an artist she thinks she knows because she is a woman, that our greatest need is to "be able to come to, cleave to, find the form for [our] own life comprehensions." In her fiction, if not in her rhetoric, Olsen does not reserve that need to the female half of the race.

Like the mother in **"I Stand Here Ironing,"** the protagonist of **"Hey Sailor, What Ship?",** the second of the *Tell Me A Riddle* stories, has spent his life day by day, immersed in "the watery shifting" from one port to another, the animal rhythm of work/pay check/binge/hangover. Yet Olsen rescues this inchoate history into meaning, by showing how Whitey fits in to a larger pattern, of which he himself is unaware. To his old friends in San Francisco, to whom he continually returns no matter how wide the arc of his dereliction, he is "a chunk of our lives." When Jeannie, the ruthless teenager, says, "he's just a Howard Street wino, that's all," her mother insists, "You've got to understand."

> Understand. Once they had been young together. To Lennie he remained a tie to adventure and a world in which men had not eaten each other; and the pleasure, when the mind was clear, of chewing over with that tough mind the happenings of the times or the queernesses of people, or laughing over the mimicry. To Helen he was the compound of much help given, much support; the ear to hear, the hand that understands how much a scrubbed floor, or a washed dish, or a child taken care of for a while, can mean.

With understanding, Whitey's sordid life is illuminated and valued. For us, who view it by way of Olsen's trespass vision, his life has meaning.

If Olsen, like Rebecca Harding Davis, owes her aesthetic to Hawthorne, it is with another American writer that she shares her sympathies. In a revealing remark to a class of Dartmouth students, Tillie Olsen said that when she began writing her tale "From the Thirties" in 1932, she knew she would call it *Yonnondio*. Furthermore she has another unfinished novel she also calls *Yonnondio*. Like Walt Whitman's, from whom she borrowed the name, her fiction is one continuous poem, dedicated to the common man.

Yonnondio, as the subtitle reminds us, is a tale "From the Thirties." It records several years in the life of the Holbrook family, as they move from a mining town in Wyoming to a tenant farm in South Dakota to the slaughter-houses of Denver. But although the settings and their squalor have equivalents in other writing "from the thirties," Olsen is neither Upton Sinclair nor John Steinbeck. *Yonnondio* is not a protest, but a perception.

Olsen told the Dartmouth students she was "fortunate" to have been brought up "working class, socialist." She thus credited her strength as an artist, not to her sex, but to her roots, her heritage, her sense of belonging to a living culture. It is her sympathetic love for the common people she identifies with that leads her to perceive in their lives the luminous beauty she limns, to articulate the inarticulate, to give voice to what might otherwise be a note as fleeting as JimJim's song in *Yonnondio:*

> a fifth voice, pure, ethereal, veiled over the rest. Mazie saw it was Jimmie, crouched at the pedals of the piano. "Ma," she said after the song was done, "it's Jimmie, JimJim was singin too." Incredulous, they made him sing it over with them and over and over. His words were a blur, a shadow of the real words, but the melody came true and clear.

Olsen's ears are quick to catch that ethereal melody, and her pen is incomparable at notating it.

Olsen's fiction is full of privileged moments, instants prized from the flux of time and illumined by a vision of their essential meaning. For the characters, the moments are fleeting. At the end of a day of gathering greens and weaving dandelion chains, a day wrested from the stink and squalor of Slaughterhouse City, Mazie sees her mother's face transfigured, senses in her "remote" eyes "happiness and farness and selfness." Anna's peace suffuses the place where she sits with the children, so that "up from the grasses, from the earth, from the broad tree trunk at their back, latent life streamed and seeded. The air and self shone boundless." But the sun sinks, Ben gets hungry for supper, and "the mother look" returns to Anna's face. "Never again, but once, did Mazie see that look—the other look—on her mother's face."

For Mazie, the privileged moments are so evanescent that she sometimes wonders if they ever occurred: "Where was the belted man Caldwell had told her of, lifting his shield against a horn of stars? Where was the bright one she had run after into the sunset? A strange face, the sky grieved above her, gone suddenly strange like her mother's." Snatched from the grinding, degrading poverty of her life's daily texture, such moments of beauty as Mazie had with the old man Caldwell, who directed her näive eyes to Orion and his luminous companions, are so rare that they might never have existed, might be dreams, or promises, like the books the dying Caldwell wills her and her father sells "for half a dollar."

> **Olsen's fiction is full of privileged moments, instants prized from the flux of time and illumined by a vision of their essential meaning.**
> —*Ellen Cronan Rose*

More often, the privileged moments do not "come to writing" for Olsen characters. "Come to writing," a favorite phrase of Tillie Olsen's, expresses her vitalistic conception of the creative process. It means the inarticulate finding words, the dumbly sensed becoming sensible, the incipient meaning finding form. For the writer, it is breaking silence. For the actor in an Olsen fiction, it is a moment of perceiving, of knowing that there is shape and direction in the ceaseless flow of what must be. Mazie comes to writing occasionally; so does her mother, Anna, who "stagger[s]" in the sunlight and moves beyond the helpless "My head is balloony, balloony" to sing her love for her eldest child and her joy in motherhood: "O Shenandoah, I love thy daughter, / I'll bring her safe through stormy water."

But more often, when Mazie is immersed in a potentially luminous moment, she perceives it as "stammering light" and when "she turns her hand to hold" it, "she grasps shadows." Anna moves through the daily drudgery "not knowing an every-hued radiance floats on her hair." As for Jim, her husband, "the things in his mind so vast and formless, so terrible and bitter, cannot be spoken, will never be spoken—till the day that hands will find a way to speak this: hands."

The hands are Olsen's hands, grasping her pen to copy a fragment of Walt Whitman's poem as the epigraph to her novel "From the Thirties":

> No picture, poem, statement, passing them to the
>   future:
> Yonnondio! Yonnondio!—unlimn'd they dis-
>   appear;
> To-day gives place, and fades—the cities, farms,
>   factories fade;
> A muffled sonorous sound, a wailing word is
>   borne through the air for a moment,
> Then blank and gone and still, and utterly lost.

Yonnondio! That evocative word is the emblem of Tillie Olsen's aesthetic. It is her plea, and her pledge: that the unobserved should be perceived, that the fleeting should be fixed, that the inarticulate should come to writing.

Joyce Carol Oates (review date 29 July 1978)

SOURCE: "Silences," in *The New Republic,* Vol. 179, No. 5, July 29, 1978, pp. 32-4.

[*In the following review, Oates contends that* Silences *suffers from omissions, uneven tone, and faulty logic.*]

The highest art appears to contain an entire world in miniature: entering it, one experiences the illusion of entering into the very center of the human cosmos, penetrating immediately the depths of the human imagination. If the most perfect forms of art have the quality of being "static"—in Joyce's sense of the term—it is because they are beyond and above time. Of course they exclude a great deal, and yet they give the impression of excluding nothing. They are complete; they point to nothing outside themselves; one grasps them as esthetic wholes, moved by their authority.

There is no more powerfully moving a piece of fiction in recent years than Tillie Olsen's long story **"Tell Me a Riddle,"** which was first published in *New World Writing* in 1960, and reprinted as the title story in Tillie Olsen's first book, in 1969. Forty-seven years of marriage, hard work and impoverishment and the dizzying passage of time, an old woman's death by cancer, a frightened old man's realization of love: bitter, relentless, supremely beautiful in its nuances, its voices and small perfect details: and certainly unforgettable. All of the stories of *Tell Me a Riddle* are superb but the title story is the one that remains most vividly in the mind. It will withstand repeated readings—and the sort of close, scrupulous attention ordinarily reserved for poetry.

Tillie Olsen tells us in her new book, *Silences,* that her fiction came very close to never having been written. The mother of four children, she was forced for many years to work at low-paying jobs in addition to her ceaseless labor as a wife and mother "without the help of the technological sublime." Since women are traditionally trained to meet others' needs before their own, and even to feel (in Olsen's words) these needs as their own, she was not able to write for 20 years, and did not publish her first book until she was 50. During this time she was haunted by the work that demanded to be written, which "seethed, bubbled, clamored, peopled me."

Some stories died. Deprived of the time and energy to imagine them into being—for writing requires not simply passion and self-confidence but periods of solitude that will allow for the slow maturing of work—Tillie Olsen lost them forever. The present book, *Silences,* is partly autobiographical, and partly a wide-ranging discussion of the phenomenon of "unnatural" silences in literary history. Its main focus is a feminist concern, and anger, with the enforced silences of women, but it also deals—in an informal, conversation, and frequently scattered way—with the "silences" of such disparate writers as Hopkins, Melville, Rimbaud, Hardy, and Baudelaire. Virginia Woolf is ubiquitous: in fact her voice seems to compete with Tillie Olsen's own. And there is a consideration of the meaning of certain statistics (as gauged by appearances in 20th-century literature courses, required reading lists, anthologies, textbooks, etc., there is only one woman writer for every 12 men) in terms of our patriarchal society.

A miscellany of Olsen's speeches, essays, and notes, written over a period of approximately 15 years, *Silences* is necessarily uneven, and it is certainly not an academic or scholarly study. It was written, as Olsen states in her preface, out of passion: love for her incomparable medium, literature, and hatred for all that, societally rooted, lessens and denies it. Most of its content consists of excerpts and quotations from other writers who have experienced the agony of being, for one reason or another, unable to write; and there is a complete section on the relatively unknown American writer Rebecca Harding Davis, whose "classic" *Life in the Iron Mills* was published in 1861 (and more or less forgotten until its reissue in 1972). Olsen's sympathy with her numerous subjects is evident, though one might wish that she had concentrated more on her own experiences, which would have been of great interest, and less on a recounting of familiar situations (Melville's fate of being "damned by dollars" and his subsequent silence, for instance). Admirers of Tillie Olsen's fiction will be rather disappointed to discover in *Silences* dozens of extremely familiar passages from Virginia Woolf, a lengthy excerpt from *The Life of Thomas Hardy* (ostensibly by Florence Emily Hardy), parts of numerous poems by Emily Dickinson, and scattered quotations by artists as unlike as Van Gogh, [Joseph] Conrad, Katherine Anne Porter, Isaac Babel, Charlotte Brontë, and Henry James . . . and nothing but the most cursory and summary of remarks about Olsen's own life. (Yet the book is being advertised as "astonishingly autobiographical.")

The book's strengths lie, however, in its polemical passages. Olsen asks why so many more women are silenced than men; she asks why there is only one woman writer "of achievement" for every 12 men writers; why our culture continues to reflect a masculine point of view almost exclusively. She quotes disapprovingly Elizabeth Hardwick's remark (about Sylvia Plath's suicide), "Every artist is either a man or a woman, and the struggle is pretty much the same for both," and Cynthia Ozick's "The term 'woman writer' . . . has no

meaning, not intellectually, not morally, not historically. A writer is a writer."

She notes the distressingly low earnings of "established" writers, men and women both, and the current unhealthy publishing situation, in which more and more publishing houses are owned by large conglomerates. She speaks critically of the literary atmosphere that sets writers against one another, breeding an absurd spirit of competition. One of her chapters lists the proportion of women writers to men writers in 20th-century literature courses (six percent women, 94 percent men), in critical studies (seven percent women, 93 percent men), in interviews (10 percent women, 90 percent men), in anthologies and textbooks (nine percent women, 91 percent men), in terms of various prizes and awards (the National Book Awards, for instance, in the years 1950-73, were given to 52 people, only six of them women). The figures are often rounded off, the estimates rough, but the message is certainly clear.

Norman Mailer is quoted and allowed to make a fool of himself once again ("I have a terrible confession to make—I have nothing to say about any of the talented women who write today. . . . I do not seem able to read them."); the English critic A. Alvarez speaks condescendingly toward Sylvia Plath (". . . No longer a housewifely appendage to a powerful husband, she seemed made solid and complete. Perhaps the birth of a son had something to do with this new confident air."); Auden is quoted in one of his sillier passages ("The poet is the father who begets the poem which the language bears. . . . Poets, like husbands, are good, bad, and indifferent."). Books like *Silences* are enormously strengthening in that they polarize attitudes, freezing people into one camp or another, suggesting unlikely sisterhoods (Virginia Woolf, who wrote so many novels, and that marvelous Diary, and those essays and reviews—and those letters!—a sister to a woman writer who, thwarted by family responsibilities and lack of freedom, has never managed to publish a single word?) and bizarre bedfellows (Hopkins, Rimbaud, Scott Fitzgerald—who "sacrificed" his talent by writing *too much,* in order to live out his sophomoric notion of the Good Life).

One feels the author's passion, and cannot help but sympathize with it. Certainly women have been more generally "silenced" than men, in all the arts. But the book is marred by numerous inconsistencies and questionable statements offered as facts. Why, for instance, are Elizabeth Hardwick and Cynthia Ozick wrong? Their views differ from mainline feminist views but are not, surely, contemptible for that reason. Why are men in general the enemy, but some men—perhaps weaker men—welcomed as fellow victims, and their "unnatural silences" accorded as much dignity as that of women? Does Baudelaire's "silence" as a consequence of syphilitic paralysis have anything at all to do with Tillie

Olsen's 20 years of "silence"? I see no connection, yet the book ends with excerpts from *My Heart Laid Bare,* as if they somehow summarized Olsen's position. And why are men who exploit women criticized on the one hand, and Rilke, who kept himself aloof from responsibilities to his family, admired, on the other hand, for being shrewd enough to guard his creative energies against emotional entanglements. . . ? We are told that women are not to be trapped into the role of being *women writers*; yet it turns out to be quixotic, and halfway traitorous, to "proclaim that one's sex has nothing to do with one's writing." Feminist homiletics are always troublesome not only because they are often self-contradictory but because they never seem to apply to anyone of originality or stature.

An angry book must stir anger. Hence there is little or no mention of successful women writers of our time—among them Doris Lessing, Flannery O'Connor, Eudora Welty, Isak Dinesen, Iris Murdoch, Elizabeth Bishop, Marianne Moore, Jean Stafford, Lillian Hellman, Mary McCarthy, Muriel Rukeyser, Penelope Mortimer, Joan Didion, Edna O'Brien, Margaret Drabble, Anne Tyler, May Swenson, and innumerable others. Tillie Olsen must have felt justified in subordinating—or silencing—her own considerable artistic instincts during the composition of *Silences,* and I would not quarrel with her decision. It was a generous one: she wanted to reach out to others, to the living and the dead, who have, evidently, shared her own agony. One must respect such an impulse. But the thinking that underlies *Silences* is simply glib and superficial if set in contrast to the imagination that created *Tell Me a Riddle* and *Yonnondio,* Olsen's novel. Unexamined, unverified, and indeed unverifiable statements are offered as facts again and again. For instance, someone at a national conference on creativity in 1959 said, "Creativity was in each one of us as a small child. In children it is universal. Among adults it is nonexistent"—not only a doubtful proposition, but sheer malarkey—and Olsen quotes it with approval.

She never confronts the most troublesome question of all: What has "creativity" as such to do with "art"? Are all silences equally tragic? On what basis can a writer resent his society's indifference to his art, so long as society is free to choose its values? I was reminded of that cruel but witty passage in the chapter "Economy" in *Walden,* in which Thoreau speaks of an Indian who has woven straw baskets no one wants to buy, and who is amazed and resentful at the world's indifference. He had not discovered, Thoreau says, that it was necessary for him to make it worth the other's while to buy them, or at least make him think that it was so. And there is Flannery O'Connor's sardonic response to a question put to her at a reading, about whether universities stifled writers. O'Connor replied: "They don't stifle enough of them." (Which is one of the reasons, I suspect, that O'Connor cannot be taken up by feminist critics with much comfort.)

A final comment on the book's editing, or lack thereof. Since the various chapters were published at different times there are many, many repetitions of key phrases and quotations. And nearly every page is marred by small, inconsequential footnotes that qualify or update statements made in the text. In practically every case these footnotes should have been incorporated into the text or eliminated: their busy, gnat-like presence is injurious to the reading experience, and in most instances their nature undercuts the seriousness of the book. For instance, in the chapter "One Out of Twelve: Writers Who Are Women," Olsen quotes Hortense Calisher with disapproval, and then admits in a footnote that her remarks are unfair, because the copy of Calisher's essay she read had an important (and unnoticed) page missing. "My abashed apologies," Olsen says. Yet surely it would not have been too much trouble to type over a single page and eliminate the negative reference to Calisher . . . ? These are signs of haste, and of an editor's indifference. In a book that sets itself up as a literary manifesto of the women's movement, one which has been eagerly anticipated by a considerable number of readers, offenses such as these are saddening, and inexplicable.

Sara Culver (essay date 1982)

SOURCE: "Extending the Boundaries of the Ego: Eva in 'Tell Me a Riddle.'" in *Midwestern Miscellany X,* edited by Marilyn J. Atlas, Midwestern Press, 1982, pp. 38-48.

[*In the following essay, Culver discusses Olsen's views on self-fulfillment and motherhood.*]

And if a blight kill not a tree but it still bear fruit, let none say that the fruit was in consequence of the blight.

Fruit from a blighted tree will always be sparse. Tillie Olsen's collected works weigh lightly in one hand, yet they weigh more heavily in the mind than many more luxuriant volumes.

Her fiction, a rich trove from a gift "nursed through the night," cherished and preserved against the forces that could have killed it—motherhood in straitened circumstances—retains some of the bleakness where it had to endure. It is remarkably condensed. In **"Tell Me A Riddle"** she sketches an entire life in fifty-three pages; she writes as if she were distilling the experiences from a crucible in her own body.

This story reveals the depth of wasture which results from using as a servant and breeding machine a woman whose intellect, courage and idealism served only to make her painfully aware of the distance between her life as it was lived, and her life as it could have been lived. Gifts that rot unused in the bearer breed poisonous resentment and the bitterness that seeps up through the surface of daily life is a residue that destroys the soul.

Tillie Olsen's protagonists are frustrated in their expression of artistic or intellectual gifts, people whose lives are blighted by poverty, racism, ignorance, or all of these. What she shows in her vignettes is how all people's lives are made even poorer by this blighting of intellectual capacity in women. While in *Silences* she takes issue with those who say that women aren't well represented in the arts because there are very few talented women, in her fiction she does not deal with such luxuries as artistic creation. Her women—in *Yonnondio,* in **"I Stand Here Ironing,"** and in **"Tell Me a Riddle"**—all battle for mere survival. The question of artistic creation never arises. The struggle to maintain their children's bodies demands all the women's effort; the luxury in this bleak world is to give their children love and understanding. The only other writer who comes to mind as having portrayed the reality of grinding necessity so vividly is James Agee. It is impossible to read *Let Us Now Praise Famous Men* and come away mouthing platitudes about the possibility of choice being open to all. Olsen, in much terser vein, does the same thing for mothers.

> **Though Olsen shows us that the wastage and loss are real, that something precious has been lost to the world, she somehow manages to convey a sense, not of futility, but of transcendence.**
> —*Sara Culver*

In *Silences,* Olsen points out that the German poet, Raina Maria Rilke, would not come to his own daughter's wedding because it interfered with his writing time. History forgives him his choice, but when a woman leaves her children to the care of a father or grandparents, she become a monster. For a woman to leave her children is considered at best, extremely irresponsible and selfish, and at worst, criminal. The fact that a man can leave his family, as did the father in **"I Stand Here Ironing"** without being considered either a madman or a criminal, makes it obvious that a man has a wider range of options open to him, even after fatherhood, than does a woman after motherhood. While even poor men who have become fathers are at liberty to dispose of their lives as they wish, poor women who become mothers are not. And women, especially in the past, have been made responsible for lives whose presence has not been wholly a matter of choice on their part.

There have been a multitude of commentators about those women who neglect their children for art or intellectual pursuits or who (selfishly) fail to produce children in order to pursue their private careers. What isn't very often shown is the blight on children whose mothers fail to bring forth the intellectual and artistic harvest within themselves.

Olsen shows us this side of the coin. She shows how spiritually impoverished the children must be whose mothers have no legacy of accomplishment in the wider world to leave them, whose lives have been squeezed away in the wringer of necessity, whose words are unspoken or unheard. The mothers who have never had a chance to experience a wider world than their families can rarely bequeath to their children a kind of wisdom that will serve them beyond the narrow boundaries of self. If they have acquired such wisdom, it is often despised, for our culture designates women's knowledge as "trivial" if it is not acquired in the male-dominated world outside the home.

Another author who deals with this theme is Susan Griffin whose book, *Pornography & Silence,* has just come out. When I read it, Tillie Olsen's heroine, Eva, came to mind as an archetypal example of what Griffin means when she discusses the artificially imposed split between nature and culture which our society demands.

> A woman who is a mother is divided from culture. And because of this she must be split in her own soul. Despite the propaganda of a culture which excludes women, women have a capacity for culture which is as large as the human capacity. But culture has ordained that women has no need of culture and culture has no need of her, and so she is excluded from the life of her society. One of the means of this exclusivity is to make her a mother.

Eva—mother of all—is the protagonist in **"Tell Me a Riddle."** The original creatrix and law-giver for humankind has become a drudge whose words are unheeded, whose wisdom is despised. Yet, though Olsen shows us that the wastage and loss are real, that something precious has been lost to the world, she somehow manages to convey a sense, not of futility, but of transcendence. What prevents her portrayal of Eva from being merely a sad and pathetic story, what gives us a sense of being profoundly moved to pity and terror and " . . . of being one and indivisible with the great of the past," is Olsen's ability to convince us that her heroine is a woman of some stature. She doesn't give herself much space in which to accomplish this task.

The woman in this story is a Russian Jew. Before or during the 1905 revolution she suffers exile and imprisonment—solitary confinement, actually—in Russia—for her political activities. She is freed, emigrates with her young husband to the United States—presumably in search of a better life in "the land of peace and freedom." But Eva in the United States fares little better than Eva in Russia. She becomes a kind of serf to her husband and family. While the level of the family's poverty is not so severe as it would have been in Russia, her spiritual life is smothered in the daily struggle against the humiliations poverty imposes in the U.S. and her voice is silenced just as effectively as the voices of her mothers before her.

But when we are introduced to her, at the beginning of the story, we know nothing of Eva's past. Olsen deliberately shrouds the grandeur of this woman's spirit in the rags of her servitude. In fact, when we first meet Eva, she has become a stranger to herself. In the eyes of her daughter-in-law, Nancy, she is merely an embittered drudge, whose one way of making herself useful—cleaning house—is seen as an implied reproach. "I can't enjoy Sunday dinner, knowing that half-blind or not she's going to find every speck of dirt. . . ." Nancy prefers the company of her father-in-law.

> "When I think of your dad, who could really play
> the invalid with that arthritis of his, as active as a
> teen-ager, and twice as much fun. . . ."

The reader can see the effects of the blight in Eva's sharp tongue, in her bitterness, and in her desire for solitude, or rather, hermitude.

Neither Nancy nor the reader can see into the past for the reasons behind her mother in law's bitterness and her father-in-law's cheerfulness. She can only see the grandmother's bitterness, feel her grudging struggle with life. She does not connect her father-in-law's light-hearted attitude with her mother-in-law's dour practicality. She can't understand that when Eva was young, her few chances for happiness and pleasure were sacrificed for the convenience and preference of the young man who was her husband. When he tries to persuade her that they should sell their home and move to a retirement village, she replies,

> "Now, when it pleases you, you find a reading circle
> for me. And forty years ago when the children were
> morsels and there was a circle, did you stay home
> with them once so I could go? Even once? You
> trained me well. I do not need others to enjoy."

Her husband's main reason for wanting to sell their home is the fact that he dislikes having to do any repair work around the house. His conviction that his comfort and his desires legitimately outweigh any needs or desires his wife might have is congruent with his behavior as a young man. Since his wife had to shoulder the ultimate responsibility for the children, naturally he's cheerful. Why shouldn't he be cheerful? If things got too rough, it was up to her to bicker with the landlord and the corner grocer for credit, and up to her to see that the children had clothes decent enough for school.

. . . from those years she had had to manage, old humiliations and terrors rose up, lived again, and forced her to relive them. The children's needings; that grocer's face or this merchant's wife she had had to beg credit from when credit was a disgrace; the scenery of the long blocks walked around when she could not pay; school coming, and the desperate going over the old to see what could yet be remade; the soups of the meat bones begged "for-the-dog" one winter. . . .

He could have made life easier for her, had he chosen to do so. But it was not easy or convenient for him, and in bearing the full weight of responsibility, she has become bent out of shape. She has tried to numb her longings by work, first work that was needed by others, and later by herself.

Any dreams she had had were drowned in the need to provide for her children. The children of her soul, her visions, her passion, her ideas, her hopes for a better world were simply made flesh incarnate, and instead scattering her words on the wind, food for dreams, food which can sustain the hearer beyond the single day, she provided her family with "dog-bone" stew.

If the cruelty and wretchedness of her betrayal could have been embodied in any physical form, then perhaps she would, like her friend, have leapt for its jugular. But there was no single human being upon whom to lay that blame. The culture that had socialized her husband and herself to look upon her children and household as her primary responsibilities, and made her husband only secondarily responsible for the physical well-being of their children, made it effectively impossible for her to break the shackles of her life.

When she becomes seriously ill (apparently from her husband's relentless nagging) her husband's cruel selfishness is apparent in his reaction to her pleas for his companionship. That he could have the company of others if he chooses it, without imposing it on her who had become a stranger to the world, is apparent in the fact that he goes out for a night of socialization when she is ill and frightened and lonely. And finally, she curses him.

Eva's smoldering intelligence has been banked, but never fully extinguished . . . just as with the slowly dying young mother of *Yonnondio,* whose senses and imagination revive under the influence of spring in a blossoming meadow, Eva's thirst for meaning still persists. She has some sense, in her illness, that it is important for her to remember what brought her to where she is now, how she came to be this person. We have a sense that she is a stranger to herself as well as to those around her. She seems to be only dimly aware of how she lost herself entirely in the struggle to give her six children the love and nourishment they needed.

It seems that she has literally forgotten who she had been before her children came. She had forgotten the *feelings,* the passionate belief that she could matter, that her life would make the larger world a better place to live. Her emotional struggles to come to terms with her feelings, to go back in herself to a source of passion that was not the new body of a human being, are portrayed in terms we can believe; these feelings have their source in a woman's body and can be described in terms of bodily sensation. They are real feelings. These are not abstractions. What is it to experience "motherly love?" Why does the aged woman shudder and sweat when she is offered a baby to hold?

Eva's life has been co-opted by others for so many years that they take her sacrifice of self as their due. This refrain runs over and over through her thoughts (as her husband continually exhorts and admonishes her to give up her home), ". . . never to be forced to move to the rhythms of others." Her need for space and time for herself has always been and still is completely disregarded by her husband and family, and she finds it nearly impossible to press her own claims against theirs. As Olsen quotes Rilke in **Silences,** "Anything that makes demands, arouses in me an infinite capacity to give it its due, the consequences of which completely use me up." While Rilke could get away from his family long enough to create, there is a strong taboo on a mother closing the door on her family for even an hour. That Eva's own conscience prevented her from doing this is apparent in her reaction to her grandson. When they bring him to her to hold she shudders and sweats. Her body can no longer tolerate the voracious demands of others, and since for her to acknowledge the need of the other is to feel compelled to fill it, she must turn away. She cannot bring herself to hold him.

What Eva needs are solitude and stillness; she must have these in order to recall from oblivion a self different from, more powerful than the bewildered one which is drawing to the end of its journey, and must absolutely make some sense of its terrible past: "Still the springs were in her seeking. Somewhere an older power that beat for life. Somewhere coherence, transport, meaning."

But she is not allowed either solitude or stillness until she is quite literally on her death-bed. Even after major surgery, and while she is supposed to be convalescing, the only way she can find some peace and quiet and avoid her boisterous grandchildren is to hide in the bedroom closet. And even there they track her down.

The most remarkable aspect of her dying is her desire to make contact with humankind in a wide, far-reaching sense. She has been shut up and excluded from participation in the culture by the fact of her motherhood; this has been a kind of death for her. Her attempt to remember what she had been, what she used to share with humanity, is her attempt to extend the boundaries of her ego, an attempt to transcend the confines of her life. Her one year in the frozen wastes of Siberia, her solitary confinement, was to be the metaphor of her entire life. Her triumph is in her finally bursting through the dammed-up forces to the repressed desires and passions of her youth.

The first real indication we get that this is not an ordinary woman is the incident with the rabbi at the hospital. She has no desire to escape into what she considers superstition. She has a deeply religious attitude, but her real religion is belief in the shared consciousness of humanity. She considers religious customs—as they have been handed down—merely one more way to divide humanity. "Tell them to write: race, human, religion, none." She is cultured, in the best sense of the word. She has courage. She does not, even in her most miserable hours, turn to supernatural forces to rationalize or explain the degradation and misery of her life.

Her outlook seems rather starling to the reader in light of her having so little interest in her neighbors, in light of her apparently empty life, and in light of her approaching death. She has taken shape as a fairly conventional woman up to this point. True, she had mentioned that "she never did like queens" but we don't guess how vehemently she disliked them until we hear that she had been imprisoned for her revolutionary activities.

In Eva's delirium, the youthful orator of the 1905 revolution comes to life again and speaks so eloquently that her husband would silence her if he could. Her hopeful, joyous words, issuing from the lips of a woman already nearly a corpse, resonate through his encrusted layers of compromise and despair and he is shaken to his bones by a sudden painful shock of realization that he too, had lost what had given his life meaning. He tries to justify the sacrifice by pointing at their grandchildren—but even they cannot make up to him his loss.

The narrator gives us a little of her style:

> Heritage. How have we come from our savage past, how no longer to be savages—this to teach. To look back and learn what humanizes—this to teach. To smash all ghettos that divide us—not to go back, not to go back—this to teach. Learned books in the house, will mankind live or die, and she gives to her boys—superstition.

From the fact that she tells us she had tried to stay awake to read after the children were in bed, we know that she liked reading, but do not realize how fiercely she wanted to learn to read until she is tossing with fever, near death.

"Have I told you of Lisa who taught me to read?

Of the highborn she was, but noble in herself. I was sixteen; they beat me; my father beat me so I would not go to her. It was forbidden, she was a Tolstoyan. At night, past dogs that howled, terrible dogs, my son, in the snows of winter to the road, I to ride in her carriage like a lady, to books. To her, life was holy, knowledge was holy, and she taught me to read. They hung her. Everything that happens one must try to understand why. She killed one who betrayed many. Because of betrayal, betrayed all she lived and believed. In one minute she killed, before my eyes (there is so much blood in a human being, my son), in prison with me. All that happens, one must try to understand."

Yet Eva—as a young woman—is not clearly presented to us. It seems that she was ardently dedicated to learning, to political causes, that she took risks, and that she had courage and integrity. But beyond this she is hazy. She is an archetype of a youthful revolutionary. She was—or seemed to be—destined for an heroic fate. As a young woman, she suffered from her country's cruelty to youth and poverty; as a mother she suffers from her culture's cruelty to women. She became a spiritual hermit in order to forget how much she had dreamed of for humanity, to forget how much she had wanted to share her dreams with others.

To force a woman to live as Eva is to limit her influence to only that small circle of flesh she can call her family. She has to choose between the universal and the particular. The universal is uncertain; who knows what one's influence will be beyond the grave? And then there are needs, the need to love and be loved, to welcome and be welcomed after a battle, to be made safe. The knowledge that one has sheltered and fed and comforted another human being can be far more potent even than the need to express one's deepest beliefs. It is true that in order to produce much of artistic value, a mother has always had to divide her time between her children and her work. This is not in the nature of fate, however, but in the way in which society is structured: in accord with the values of the culture. What women need, what mothers need, is a sense of participation in all humanity. There is a wealth of learning and wisdom to be shared by all children of all mothers. Mothers are mothers of the spirit as well as mothers of the body, and for the individual child to be the sole responsibility of a particular parent, especially of a woman in a world where women have no authority, is to make a selfish and ferocious community of human beings, who learn only to snarl and bite and seize each other for what they can devour. They learn that the world is cruel, that the world is uncaring and selfish, that their own individual survival in what matters, that they have not a common substratum of being with all humanity, that their experiences will never transcend their narrow margins of birth and death, and that they must, for that reason, fear and hate and deny death above all other thing. They learn to believe that material goods are to be cherished as the only means of protection against death, that it is acceptable to watch other human beings die of poverty and neglect and despair, that it is all right to watch a mother lose all of her joy in life as a drudge for others, and that if she bears children of her own body then she has no right to bear children of the spirit.

Eva's knowledge—her long-stored dreams of humanity's fulfillment—are not valued by her culture because she is a woman. When she speaks, breaking a life-long silence, her husband's immediate response is. "Where are the pills for quieting? Where are they?" But also her knowledge of the body is denigrated, by herself as well as by others. She sees in her grandchildren only "lovely mouths" that devour.

Griffin would say that mothers' experience isn't valued because this culture does not value knowledge of the body; this culture attempts in every way to deny the finitude and mortality of the body, to reject limitations and death. Yet Eva's knowledge, of the body's vulnerability, its susceptibility to scarring, is vital knowledge; it is what she learned with her living, and it is what her children need to know.

Eva is twice betrayed. First, because she is a woman her culture confines her to motherhood and despises her thirst to participate in the larger world. Then again, after she has bitterly learned the lessons of motherhood and poverty and death and birth, the tenderness and vulnerability of human love and human flesh, her knowledge is despised, because it is finite knowledge, knowledge that acknowledges finitude and limitations, that has no pretensions to omnipotence or eternal grandeur—vulnerable knowledge, for it will vanish with its bearer. Too late her family realizes what they have lost. Eva's eldest daughter—Clara—asks,

> "... where did we lose each other, first mother, singing mother? ... I do not know you, mother. Mother, I never knew you."

And her son, "Lennie, suffering not alone for her who was dying, but for that in her which never lived (for that in him which might never live)," is aware that his mother's spiritual impoverishment has also been his own.

When Eva's children finally come together to stand by their mother's death-bed, and the riddle hangs in the silent air: "And what did you learn with your living, mother, and what do we need to know?" We hear nothing, for their mother is past coherent speech.

Blanche H. Gelfant (essay date Spring 1984)

SOURCE: "After Long Silence: Tillie Olsen's 'Requa'," in *Studies in American Fiction,* Vol. 12, No. 1, Spring, 1984, pp. 61-9.

[In the following essay, Gelfant addresses the protagonist's need to find meaning and self-renewal during the Depression in Olson's short story "Requa."]

No one has written so eloquently about silences as Tillie Olsen, or shown as poignantly that a writer can recover her voice. In her most recent fiction, a long story called **"Requa,"** she reclaims once more a power of speech that has proved at times extremely difficult to exercise. Silence followed the publication, almost fifty years ago, of sections from her early and still unfinished novel *Yonnondio.* Then came *Tell Me a Riddle,* bringing Olsen fame but not the sustained power to write she needed, and for another long period her voice was stilled. In 1970 **"Requa"** appeared, an impressive work which received immediate recognition and was reprinted as one of the year's best stories. [**"Requa"** is part of a larger work-in-progress Olsen plans to complete.] For apparently fortuitous reasons, it is now little known, though as Olsen's most innovative and complex work of fiction, it deserves critical attention it has yet to receive. Complete but unfinished, **"Requa"** is a still-to-be-continued story that develops the theme of human continuity in ways which seem almost subversive. Its form is discontinuous, as though to challenge its theme, and the text is broken visibly into fragments separated from each other by conspicuous blank spaces, gaps the eye must jump over and the mind fill with meaning. However, the story repudiates the meanings that might be inferred from its disintegrated form and from its imagery and setting, both influenced by literary traditions of the past that Olsen continues only to subvert. She draws obviously upon poetry of the twenties for her waste land motifs, and upon novels of the thirties for her realistic portrayal of America's great Depression. Waste and depression are Olsen's subjects in **"Requa,"** but Olsen's voice, resonant after long silence, is attuned to her vision of recovery.

In his poem "After Long Silence," Yeats had defined the "supreme theme" of recovered speech as "Art and Song." Patently, these are not the themes of Olsen's story. **"Requa"** is about uneducated, unsung working people struggling against depression, both the economic collapse of the thirties and the emotional depression of its protagonist, fourteen-year-old Stevie. The story begins with Stevie traumatized by his mother's death and the loss of everything familiar. Alone and estranged from the world, he is being taken by his Uncle Wes from his home in San Francisco to a small California town set by the Klamath River. Here men fish for salmon, hunt deer, and lead a life alien to a city boy. Stevie arrives at this town, named by the Urac tribe Rekwoi, or Requa, broken in body and spirit. A wreck of a child, still dizzy from the long bumpy truck ride, heaving until he "can't have'ary a shred left to bring up," he seems utterly defeated, unable "to hold up." From the beginning, his obsessive death wish leads to Stevie's withdrawal: "All he wanted was to lie down." He refuses to speak; he sees human faces dimly or not at all; he huddles in bed, hiding under his quilt and rocking. A "ghostboy" with dazed eyes and clammy green skin, he seems ready to lie down forever. But the story turns aside from death to describe a miraculous recovery, nothing less than Stevie's resurrection, for at the end the silent boy springs spectacularly to life. In the "newly tall, awkward body" he has grown into, he runs, "rassles," "frisks" about like a puppy; and when at last Stevie does lie down, he falls into a sweet sleep from which, it seems, he will awaken rested and restored.

Given the time and place, that recovery should become the pervasive action of the story seems as miraculous as a boy's resurrection. The time is 1932, and the setting a junkyard, the natural stopping-place for dispossessed people on the move during America's great Depression. "Half the grown men in the county's not working," Wes tells the boy, no jobs anywhere. Wes himself works in the junkyard; a realistic place described in encyclopedic detail and a symbolic setting suitable to the theme of loss and recovery. At the junkyard mounds of discarded and disjunct things represent tangibly a vision of disorder, disintegration, and waste. "U NAME IT—WE GOT IT," the yard sign boasts: tools, tees, machine parts, mugs, quilts, wing nuts, ropes, reamers, sewing machines, basket hats, "Indian things," baby buggies, beds, pipe fittings, five-and-dime souvenirs, stoves, victrolas. These wildly proliferating abandoned things form "Heaps piles glut accumulation," but the growing lists of material objects Olsen interjects into the story—or rather, makes its substance—undermine a common assumption that accumulation means wealth. On the contrary, things can reveal the poverty of a person's life. All the souvenirs that Stevie's mother had accumulated, now passed on to her son, are "junk." The more souvenirs the story mentions, the more it shows how little the mother had, though obviously she wished to possess something pretty even if it was only "a kewpie doll [or a] green glass vase, cracked" or a "coiled brass snake Plush candy box: sewing stuff: patches, buttons in jars, stork scissors, pincushion doll, taffeta bell skirt glistening with glass pinheads."

But things that at first seem worthless take on a strange incandescence in the story, initially perhaps because of the narrator's tone, a musing, mysterious, reverent tone that imbues isolated objects with emotional meaning. And the lives that seem wasted in the story also begin to glow. The dead mother's felt presence becomes stronger and brighter, shining through characters who help her son and through Stevie himself as he begins to recover. Even the junkyard changes. Piled with seemingly useless things, it gives promise of renewal, for the "human mastery, [the] human skill" which went into making machines, now broken and disassembled, can be applied again and the strewn parts made to function. Olsen's waste land inspires "wonder" at the technological genius that can rehabilitate as well as invent, though it has rampantly destroyed. Olsen expresses no nostalgia for a by-gone pastoral past which many American writers wish recovered. She visualizes instead a reclamation in the modern world of the waste its technology has produced. In her story everything can be recycled, and anything broken and discarded put to new use. Nothing is beyond the human imagination that can create even out of waste, the "found" objects in a junkyard, a poetic text. Placed side by side, the names of these objects begin to form a concrete poem the story will interrupt, continue, and complete as it moves along. The first stanza, a listing of ingenious devices, implicitly extols human inventiveness and skill: "Hasps switches screws plugs faucets drills Valves pistons shears planes punchers sheaves Clamps sprockets coils bits braces dies." If these disconnected nouns form also a litany of waste, it is one that introduces the hope of redemption, for Olsen describes "disorder twining with order," a combination which qualifies chaos and may signify its arrest. Moreover, Olsen's final inchoate sentence traces a search through the "discarded, the broken, the torn from the whole; [the] weathereaten weatherbeaten: mouldering" for whatever can still be used or needed, for anything that can be redeemed.

At the junkyard, Stevie sees people as depleted as himself still hoping for redemption. The faceless, nameless migrant workers who stop to pick up a used transmission or discarded tire reflect widespread social disintegration, but like the migrant workers in John Steinbeck's *The Grapes of Wrath,* they persist in trying, struggling, moving. Battered as they are, they refuse the temptation to lie down, and they trade their last possession, a mattress or gun, for whatever will keep them going. "We got a used everything," Evans the yard-owner says, seeing to it that trashed and broken things are fixed and made usable again for people on the move. Evans is tough and wants the "do-re-mi," but whatever his motives, he is crucially involved in the process of recovery. His yard attracts people whose lives have been shattered, the dispossessed migratory workers and, in time, Stevie. The junkyard also sustains Wes, who keeps his self intact as he makes broken parts useful, working capably and even happily, "singing . . . to match the motor hum as he machines a new edge, rethreads a pipe." Meanwhile Wes is trying to make a new life for his nephew: "I'll help you to catch hold, Stevie," he says, "I promise I'll help." Other characters, barely identified, also help, and the story sketches in the outlines of people variously involved in the boy's recovery. Besides Evans, who gives Stevie a chance to work, the Chinese cook at the boardinghouse keeps him company, and the sympa-thetic landlady takes him on an outing that will complete his recovery.

As **"Requa"** describes the "concern" underprivileged or struggling characters show for each other, it raises Olsen's thematic questions about human responsibility and about the relationship between love and survival. Implicitly it asks why Wes, a lone workingman, should give his skill and energy to make trash useful to others and an alienated boy valuable to himself, and why anyone should care, as everyone does, whether a "ghostboy" recovers. The story thus restates Olsen's recurrent riddle, which is, essentially, the mystery of human survival as evidenced by people who continue to live and to care even though their lives seem broken and futile, and life itself full of pain. If human existence has meaning, as Olsen's fiction asserts, then suffering, bereavement, poverty, despair, all inseparable from day-to-day survival in a waste land, must be explained. So must the secret of recovery, which prevails against depression.

This is a complicated achievement already described in Olsen's earlier stories. In **"I Stand Here Ironing,"** a pock-marked girl becomes beautiful, her talent realized, her unhappy deprived childhood, never forgotten, transcended; and a mother, recalling this childhood, straightens out confused emotions and gains a sense of her own identity. Before the Grandmother dies in **"Tell Me a Riddle,"** she too searches through the past to see what of value she can retrieve; and as she becomes reconciled to her own painful life, now coming to an end, she finds meaning and continuity in all human existence. Olsen can describe such recoveries because she has a strong sense of history as both a personal past that gives one a continuous identity and a social legacy that links generations. This legacy, however, is neither whole nor complete, for history is a dump-heap strewn with broken promises and wrecked hopes, among which lie examples of human achievement. Someone must sort through the junk of history, redeem its waste, and salvage whatever can be useful for the next generation. This is the task of reclamation Olsen has assumed as a writer and assigns to her characters, often unnoted, unlikely, inarticulate people for whom she speaks. Indeed, this is why she must recover her own speech, no matter how long her silence, so that Wes, and Stevie, and the dying Grandmother can have a voice.

In **"Requa"** Stevie continues the quest of the Grandmother in **"Tell Me a Riddle."** Different as they are, the resurrected boy and the dying woman are both searching for a transmittable human past that will give significance to their present struggle. Both need a history as reusable as Wes's rethreaded pipes. The Grandmother finds hers in the record of humanity's continuous progress toward self-realization. She appropriates this history as a shared "Heritage": "How have we come from the savages, how no longer to be savages—this to teach. To look back and learn what humanizes man—this to teach." Young as he is, Stevie also looks back to learn from his past the secret of recovery, of how he might claim his rightful place as a human being. As the story begins he seems dehumanized, so broken and apathetic that he is unable to relate to anyone else or to himself, unable to see the people in the boarding-house or the beauty of the countryside that will in time shake him with "ecstasy." Described as a "ghostboy," he appears doomed to inanition, but the story struggles against this fate and insists in hushed portentous tones that something will save him: "The known is reaching to him, stealthily, secretly, reclaiming." Both mysterious and obvious, the *known* is Stevie's personal past, experiences from which he will in time draw the strength to live. This strength comes mainly from the remembered love of his mother, the person in his past who has provided him with a "recognizable human bond" which must sustain him and matter more than the losses that life makes inevitable. Even in his withdrawal, a quest for "safety" from the shocks he has suffered, Stevie recognizes that the bond is holding, that Wes is taking the place of his mother by showing "concern." Wes is in Stevie's "corner," willing to share whatever he knows. "I got so much to learn you," he says, looking to the future; and looking back at the past, he vows not to let Stevie "[go] through what me and Sis did." Though he is an orphan, Stevie belongs to a family bound together by ties Olsen insists can remain irrefragable, even in a landscape of waste. When Wes becomes helpless, falling on his bed in a drunken stupor, Stevie tends to his uncle as once he had been cared for by his mother. He takes off Wes's muddy shoes and covers his body with blankets: "*There now you'll be warm,* he said aloud, *sleep sweet, sweet dreams* (though he did not know he had said it, nor in whose inflections)." Then he stares at the sleeping face in a crucial moment of recognition: "Face of his mother. *His* face. Family face."

The salvaging effect of work, even the work of salvaging, dramatizes the theme of "Requa" and shows Olsen's experience of the 1930s still shaping her social vision.
—*Blanche H. Gelfant*

Once Stevie can see clearly the *"human bond"* created by the human family, he begins to see objects and people that had been vague: The windows in the dining room which had been "black mirrors where apparitions swam"; the Indian decorations on the wall; the bizarre family resemblance between a bearded face and the face of his landlady. The forces of reclamation are finally reaching Stevie, forces shaped by the care and concern that have linked generations together in an endless chain of human relationships. Thus, though **"Requa"** describes the fragmentation of a life disrupted by death, it creates in the end a vision of relatedness that gives

the displaced person somewhere to belong. Wes's loyalty to his sister's child makes possible Stevie's recovery of the life he lost when his mother died; and Stevie's consciousness of recovery begins when he recognizes the face of his mother in any human being who cares for another, his uncle, his landlady, himself. In an unexpected way, Olsen speaks of the power of mother love as a basis for the continuity of one's self and of one's relationships with others. History keeps a record of these relationships, preserving and fostering the ties of one generation to another; and literature extends these ties as it creates a bond of sympathy between the reader and such unlikely characters as Stevie, whose experience of depression and death is universal.

As the story continues, work reinforces a recovery made possible by extended acts of love, and Stevie's apprenticeship period at the junkyard proves therapeutic. Understanding perhaps that he can learn from things as broken as he is, Stevie has begged to work with Wes rather than attend school. As he undertakes the task of sorting out the accumulated junk in the yard, the story begins to sort out its contents, separating order from disorder; and Stevie sorts out his life. He bungles and fails at his job in the junkyard, but he keeps trying because "*the tasks*" are there, "*coaxing.*" Describing these tasks, ordinary daily labor, Olsen dignifies the menial worker and his work. Stevie sees Wes showing "concern" for a trashed car as "he machines a new edge, rethreads a pipe." A man's labor expresses his love; and a boy's tasks pull him "to attention, consciousness"; they teach him "trustworthiness, pliancy"; they force him "to hold up." The salvaging effect of work, even the work of salvaging, dramatizes the theme of **"Requa"** and shows Olsen's experience of the 1930s still shaping her social vision. During the Depression she had seen jobless men lose their self-respect, and she learned a simple tautological truth: economic recovery, as well as the recovery of a broken individual, comes with work. Even the most menial task, as she would show in **"Requa,"** can be redemptive. Instinctively, Stevie knows this and wants a job, "a learn job, Wes. By you." Work will bond him to another and teach him the secret of survival. At the junkyard Stevie slowly acquires skill and patience, which give him a sense of self-respect. He can put things together, including himself. As he sorts through heaps of waste, he finds a rhythm to his life: The incremental repetition of tasks produces a sense of pattern and continuity, of meaning. He is becoming someone who keeps working, making order, and making himself into an integrated person, like Wes. Slowly, "coaxed" by his tasks, he too is showing "concern."

The climactic moment of Stevie's return to life occurs, oddly enough, as he commemorates the dead. On Memorial Day, Mrs. Edler, the landlady, takes Stevie to church for a requiem celebration and then to several cemeteries. At church, encountering other "families, other young" who remember their dead, he realizes that loss, like love, constitutes a human bond. Moreover, as long as the dead are remembered they are never entirely lost, for the human community includes both mourners and the mourned. At the cemetery, Stevie embraces a stone lamb that may represent the ultimate in-explicability of death, the mystery of its arbitrariness as it claims an infant's life. The quaint consoling verse on the lamb tells that the baby is safely sleeping, and it seems to lull Stevie to rest: "The lamb was sun warm. . . . He put his arm around its stone neck and rested." Calmly embracing a figure of death, Stevie at last finds peace at the Requiescat in Pace cemetery. His story, however, is not over, for the act of recovery is never entirely consummated. **"Requa"** concludes with the word "reclaiming," after which there is nei-ther the end parenthesis the text requires nor a final period—as though the process of reclamation still goes on and will continue with no sign of ending. [In effect, Olsen has recovered the site of Requa as she knew and loved it, for many aspects of her setting no longer exist. The grave-yard was vandalized; the salmon are few; and the town of Klamath has become a shopping-center with that name.]

In the last scene, Stevie's "newly tall" body suggests that time has effected recovery simply by letting the boy grow; but the natural gathering of strength that comes with the body's maturation needs the reinforcement of human rela-tionship and love. A faceless woman, merely a name in the story, Mrs. Edler or Mrs. Ed, has taken Stevie in hand and acted as catalyst for his recovery. [Tillie Olsen intends the landlady, Mrs. Edler, to play a larger part in Stevie's life in the version of **"Requa"** she hopes to complete. Wes, appar-ently, will die, and Mrs. Edler will carry on his role as "mother".] She does this, apparently, because she feels sorry for an orphan boy, though Olsen's characterization of Stevie raises questions of why she should mother him. Stevie is a silent, withdrawn, and ghostlike boy, if not sleeping then vomiting, and awake or asleep, dripping with snot. However, the characters in **"Requa"** have a clairvoyance that comes from caring, and they see beyond appearances, just as they communicate without words, or with curses and insults that express love. Throughout the story, Wes calls Stevie "dummy" and "loony" and swears the boy will end in the crazy house; but Wes's insults in no way affect his action nor show disaffection. Rather they express frustration as he waits for Stevie's recovery. Wes's happiest moment comes at the end of the story when he looks at the blissfully sleep-ing boy and says, "blowing out the biggest bubble of snot you ever saw. Just try and figger that loony kid."

Olsen's style in **"Requa"** is conspicuously varied. Lyrical passages are juxtaposed to crude dialectic speech, and stream of consciousness passages to objectively seen realistic de-tails. Numerous lists of things represent a world of objects proliferating outside the self; but a mind encompasses these objects and tries to find in their disorder a way of ordering an inner tumult expressed by the roiling fragments of the story. Like the junkyard, the story is the repository of bits and pieces: sentences broken into phrases separated into words, words isolated by blank spaces. Single words on a line or simply sounds—"aaagh/aaagh"—mark the end of nar-rative sections, some introduced by titles such as *Rifts* and *Terrible Pumps.* Even the typography is discontinuous, so that the text seems a mosaic of oddly assorted fragments. In creating a visibly discontinuous text, in effect turning **"Requa"** into a design upon the page, Olsen attracts atten-tion to her form, which always refers the reader to a social world that **"Requa"** presents as real, recognizable, and out-side the fiction. Still **"Requa"** exists as an object: its var-ied typography creates truncated patterns of print that catch the eye; words placed together as lists or as fragmentary re-frains form distinct visual units; blocks of nouns separated from the text produce concrete poems; intervening spaces turn into aesthetic entities. Mimetic of her theme, Olsen's form is enacting the story's crucial phrase: "*Broken exist-ences that yet continue.*" As a text, **"Requa"** is broken and yet continuous, its action extending beyond its open-ended ending. The story transforms a paradox into a promise as it turns the polarities of fragmentation and continuity into ob-verse aspects of each other. Merged together, the broken pieces of **"Requa"** create an integrated self as well as an aesthetic entity. The story enacts a process of composition to show broken existences continuing, order emerging from disorder, art from images of waste, and speech from the void of silence.

Among the many reasons for silence that Tillie Olsen has enumerated, another may be added. Perhaps what the writer has to say is too painful to express: mothers die, children sorrow, working families are evicted from homes and left with nothing to trade for a gallon of gasoline. Olsen speaks of knowledge ordinarily repressed, and while she dignifies her characters and their work, her story denies the cherished illusion that childhood in America is a happy time of life. But **"Requa"** preaches no social doctrine; unlike the novel *Yonnondio,* which also describes a child caught in a period of depression, it preaches nothing at all, although a preacher's fragmentary phrases of consolation help restore the boy. Rather, the story contains a secret that must be pieced together from disconnected fragments, inferred from blank spaces on the page, melded out of poetic prose and vomit, snot, and violence. This secret, that broken existences can continue, is stated explicitly. Left unsaid is another truth that both affirms and subverts the view of the poet. Yeats had described speech after long silence as an extended dis-course upon Art and Song, "we descant and yet again des-cant." In **"Requa,"** Olsen has said nothing about art. Her speech, resumed after ten years of silence, simply *is* art. This is the secret inherent in Tillie Olsen's story of recovery, in which a child's renewed will to live becomes inseparable from an artist's recovered power to write.

Rose Kamel (essay date Fall 1985)

SOURCE: "Literary Foremothers and Writers' Silences: Tillie Olsen's Autobiographical Fiction," in *Melus,* Vol. 12, No. 3, Fall, 1985, pp. 55-72.

[*In the essay below, Kamel discusses the elements which are common within Olsen's writings.*]

Ellen Moers observes the consistent and fervent penchant for women writers, themselves rendered invisible by patriarchy, to read other women's writings, even those from whom they were geographically and culturally distanced:

> Not loyalty but confidence was the resource that women writers drew from possession of their own tradition. And it was confidence that until very recently could have come from no other source. . . . The personal give-take of the literary life was closed to them. Without it, they studied with a special closeness the works written by their own sex, and developed a sense of easy, almost rude familiarity with the women who wrote them.

Moers supports this observation with extensive examples of nineteenth-century women writers reading their counterparts' lives and texts. She also notes that despite changes for the better in the lives of twentieth-century writers, women persist in reading and writing about other women:

> In the case of most women writers, women's traditions have been fringe benefits superadded upon the literary associations of period, nation, and class that they shared with their male contemporaries.

> In spite of the advent of coeducation, which by rights should have ended this phenomenon, twentieth-century women appear to benefit still from their membership in the wide-spreading family of women writers.

Tillie Olsen's well known apologia, *Silences,* a lamentation for her own sparse literary output, laments as well the waste of creative potential in working class and women's lives. Indeed, mourning others' silences so exceeds mourning her lost opportunities, that the reader of *Silences* must diligently search Olsen's self-reference. Born in 1913 to East European Jews living in Nebraska, Olsen had no formal college education, but read voraciously. She became a longshoreman's wife raising four daughters in working-class San Francisco, taking low-paying jobs, becoming active in radical politics, and organizing unions. Only when the last of her children entered school could she concentrate on writing. A Ford grant apparently allotted Olsen the solitude she needed but "time granted does not necessarily coincide with time that can be most fully used." Dishearteningly often, writer's paralysis diminished her productivity.

In 1954, when she was fifty, Olsen published the brilliant short story **"I Stand Here Ironing,"** having served a prolonged apprenticeship during which "there was a conscious storing, snatched reading, beginnings of writing" and always "the secret rootlets of reconnaissance." This reconnaissance involved not only obsessive reading but internalizing the lives of women writers, especially writers who were also mothers.

> Their emergence is evidence of changing circumstances making possible for them what (with rarest exception) was not possible in the generations of women before. I hope and I fear for what will result. I hope (and believe) that complex new richness will come into literature; I fear because almost certainly their work will be impeded, lessened, partial. For the fundamental situation remains unchanged. Unlike men writers who marry, most will not have the societal equivalent of a wife—nor (in a society hostile to growing life) anyone but themselves to mother their children.

Nowhere is Olsen's reading of another woman writer, her identification with this writer's concerns so elegiac, as in *Silences'* reprinting of Olsen's postscript to Rebecca Harding Davis' *Life in the Iron Mills,* a postscript longer than Harding's poignant novella. This postscript almost seamlessly blends critical analysis with self-scrutiny.

In particular, two patterns in Davis' life story parallel Olsen's. The first is an awareness of working class hardship. Rebecca Harding Davis, daughter of an affluent businessman, moved to the raw industrial town of Wheeling, Pennsylvania, in 1936 when she was five, and spent most of her childhood observing the human misery trudging to factory and mine; she was separated from them by more than the pane of glass through which she watched them go by:

> It was in front of the Harding house that the long train of mules dragged their masses of pig iron and the slow stream of human life crept past, night and morning, year after year, to work their fourteen hour days six days a week. The little girl who observed it grew into young womanhood, into spinsterhood, still at the window in that house, and the black industrial smoke was her daily breath.

The second was Davis' frustration as a woman. Of her father she later wrote: "We were not intimate with him as with our mother." [Olsen learned this, haveing perused all of Davis' writings "accessible to me for reading," from letters, official biographies and old issues of *The Atlantic Monthly.*]

Secluded in his study with Shakespearian volumes, he refused to confront the give and take of domestic life and was cold to his wife and children:

> The household revolved around him. Her mother ("the most accurate historian I ever knew, with enough knowledge to outfit a dozen modern college educated women") was kept busy running the large household *noiselessly.* [my italics]

Consistently Olsen links Davis' sensitivity to both social/political issues and women's private misery. Graduating from a female seminary in Washington did not assuage Davis' "hunger to know," and at seventeen she left Wheeling for Washington State College where she met Francis LeMoyne, a physician, radical reformer, and agnostic whose beliefs opposed those embodied by her family. LeMoyne's recognition of "the gulf of pain and wrong . . . the underlife of America" deepened Davis' perception of the twin injustices she would write of in *Margaret Howth* and *Life in the Iron Mills*.

First, however, the long literary apprenticeship. After graduation she returned to Wheeling, refusing the restrictions marriage would put on a Victorian wife, assuming, instead, the thankless role of eldest daughter:

> There was much help to be given her mother in the commonplace necessary tasks of caring for family needs, younger children; keeping the atmosphere pleasant especially for her father. The bonds of love were strong—she writes of the protection and peace of home—"but they were not bonds of mutuality." She had to keep her longings, questionings, insecurities secret.

Although Davis published minor works about problems of dutiful daughters, difficult fathers, and older women pariahs, articulating "the vein of unused powers, thwarted energies, starved hopes; the hunger for a life more abundant than in women's sanctioned sphere . . . ," it was thirteen years later that *The Atlantic Monthly* published *Life in the Iron Mills,* which brought her fame.

Painstakingly, Olsen follows the twists and turns of her literary fore-mother's life. Feted by the transcendentalist pundits at Concord, Massachusetts, Davis found their ideals false to reality. Unmarried until the age of thirty-one, she was the object of pity, curiosity, sometimes scorn. When she finally married Richard Harding Davis (much to her father's dismay at losing his eldest daughter's unpaid services), Davis discovered that wife-motherhood drained her of time and energy to write, even though she continued to do so. From her husband and literary critics she received little encour-agement or recognition. At the age of seventy-nine she died in relative obscurity.

Davis' voice permeates at least two recurring themes in Olsen's autobiographical fiction: The tyranny of class struggle eroding the bodies and minds of workers and the children of workers; household drudgery and child care undermining a woman writer's creativity. But another still small voice, Olsen's own, is heard in her depiction of *Jewish* mothers and daughters struggling for selfhood in the promised land and of Jewish immigrant experience shored up in secular humanism. Characteristically, Olsen justifies her autobiographical focus by citing yet another other woman writer, Ntozake Shange: "When women do begin to write . . . we write autobiography. So autobiographically in fact that it's very hard to find any sense of any other reality."

When still a young writer in the 1930s, having assimilated Davis as foremother, and long before she ever heard of Shange, Tillie Olsen wrote *Yonnondio,* a clumsy yet powerful depiction of a working class family driven from a rural village to a hog-slaughtering factory in the Midwest where all succumb to grinding poverty and spiritual attrition.

Yonnondio's title is taken from Walt Whitman's poem. It undercuts the good grey poet's celebrating an America with limitless space, endless opportunity. Not that Olsen doesn't share Whitman's vision of collective human dignity; like Davis, Whitman's *contemporary*, she is outraged at an ideal being betrayed:

> When in 1861 industry was considered at all, it was as an invasion of pastoral harmony, a threat of materialism to the *spirit.* If working people existed— and nowhere were they material for serious attention, let alone central subject—they were "clean-haired Yankee mill girls," . . . or Whitman's "workwomen and workmen of these states having your own divine and strong life."

Anna and her daughter Maisie respond as intensely as Whitman did to nature. The nature images suggest an extension of women's bodies—"the trees dipped and curtsied, the corn rippling like a girl's skirt"; the clouds are likened to Anna's belly big with child. But nature aligned with ruthless capitalism blights their lives, becomes a domesticity yoked to industrial waste: "Indeed they are in hell: indeed they are the damned, *steamed, boiled, broiled, fried, cooked, geared*, meshed."

Olsen's compiling of passive verbs links two spaces inhabited by working women. The first renders the stifling August air of a slaughter house where at a temperature of 108 degrees immigrant women swelter below in "casings," their task to dismember hog carcasses because men working on the floor above cannot endure the stench of pigs' blood and entrails. The second is Anna's kitchen, where she rhythmically stirs jam, tends a sick child while other children tap her flagging energy. Anna also is "geared and meshed"; she thinks of drowned children while softly singing a childhood song, "I saw a ship a' sailing." In this context the sea fantasy obliquely evokes the pivotal immigrant experience Olsen will return to in **"Tell Me a Riddle."**

In *Yonnondio,* the plaintive immigrant voice only faintly infuses Anna's American dream:

> School for the kids Maisie and Willie Jim her Protestant husband working near her, . . . lovely things to keep, brass lamps, bright tablecloths, vines over doors, and roses twining. A memory unasked plunged into her mind—her grandmother bending in such a twilight over lit candles chanting in an unknown tongue, white bread on the table over a shining white table-cloth and red wine—and she broke into song to tell Jim of it.

These occasional roses succumb to the struggle for bread. Linking factory and kitchen drudgery makes inevitable the reduction of iron-willed humans to scrap; in such an environment, analogous to Upton Sinclair's *The Jungle,* it is small wonder that Anna loses her baby, takes sick, and dies.

> Earth sucks you in, to spew out the coal, to make a few bellies fatter. Earth takes your dreams that a few may languidly lie on their couches and trill "How exquisite" to be paid dreamers.

Far more than her faint allusion to Jewish immigration, Anna suggests Davis' Korl Woman, the central metaphor in *Life in the Iron Mills.* Fashioned in pig iron by Hugh Wolfe, the wretched miner in Davis' story, this sculpture is "a nude woman's form, muscular, grown coarse with labor, the powerful limbs instinct with some one poignant longing. One idea: there it was in the tense muscles, the clutching hands, the wild, eager face. . . ." Hardly a Galatea, the Korl Woman symbolizes nearly all Olsen's narrator-personae, from Anna to Eva in **"Tell Me a Riddle,"** women of extraordinary potential wasted by capitalism and patriarchy. Whether pure or scrap, the iron image resonates throughout Olsen's texts.

"I Stand Here Ironing" depicts a nameless mother-narrator, who, having received a phone call from her daughter Emily's high-school guidance counselor that Emily is an underachiever, pushes an iron to and fro across the board on which Emily's dress lies shapeless and wrinkled. The narrator begins "dredging the past and all that compounds a human being." Her thoughts flow with the rhythm of the iron as she attempts to grasp the "rootlet of reconnaissance" to explain why it was that her oldest child was one "seldom

smiled at." What would appear as understandable reasons—the Depression, the nineteen-year old mother, who at her daughter's present age worked at menial jobs during the day and at household chores at night, the iron necessity that made her place Emily in a series of foster homes, the desertion of her first husband, bearing and rearing four other children of a second marriage, all clamoring for attention—should account for Emily's chronic sorrow; but somehow they do not. Necessity dominating the mother's life could have tempered Emily, but the reader soon perceives that there may be another reason why Emily and the mother-narrator are silenced counterparts. The mother has remarried, but material comforts, an emotionally secure middle-class existence, cannot assuage her loneliness. Never having experienced the celebratory rituals of working-class communality, middle-class anomie distances her from other women. Her entire adult life has been interrupted by child care described by Olsen quoting another women writer:

> My work "writing" is reduced to five or six hours a week, always subject to interruptions and cancellations . . . I don't believe there is a solution to the problem, or at least I don't believe there is one which recognizes the emotional complexities involved. A life without children is, I believe, an impoverished life for most women; yet life with children imposes demands that consume energy and imagination at the same time, cannot be delegated—even supposing there were a delegate available.

In **"I Stand Here Ironing,"** characteristic stylistic clues embedded in the occasionally inverted syntax, run-on sentences interspersed with fragments, repetitions, alliterative parallels, an incantatory rhythm evoke the narrator's longing not only for a lost child but for a lost language whereby she can order the chaotic dailiness of a working mother's experience.

> She was a beautiful baby. The first and only one of our five that was beautiful at birth. You do not guess how new and uneasy her tenancy in her now-loveliness. You did not know her all those years she was thought homely, or see her pouring over her baby pictures, making me tell her over and over how beautiful she had been—and would be, I would tell her—and was now to the seeing eye. But the seeing eyes were few or non-existent. Including mine.
>
> . . . . .
>
> Ronnie is calling. He is wet and I change him. It is rare there is such a cry now. That time of motherhood is almost behind me when the ear is not one's own but must always be racked and listening for the child to cry, the child call. We sit for awhile and I

hold him, looking out over the city spread in charcoal with its soft aisles of light. "Shoogily," he breathes and curls closer. I carry him back to bed, asleep. *Shoogily.* A funny word, a family word, inherited from Emily, invented by her to say: *comfort.*

Emily's word play appears rooted in Yiddish (*shoogily—meshugah*) and there is something archetypically talmudic in her fascination with riddles (for which a younger sibling gets recognition) "that was *my* riddle, Mother, I told it to Susan . . . ," foreshadowing the leitmotif Olsen will orchestrate in **"Tell Me a Riddle."** When language inventiveness fails to mitigate against Emily's lack of achievement at school, when she tries and fails to authenticate herself, she escapes into another's role. Desperate for attention, identity, she responds to the mother's suggestion that she try out for a high school play—"not to have an audience is a kind of death"—and becomes a comic crowd pleaser to the sound of thunderous applause. Thus, Emily finally commands some attention and affection and to a limited extent a control of life's randomness. Nonetheless, only articulation through language can free her from oppression. Silenced at home she lacks and will probably continue to lack centrality.

The story ends with the mother still ironing out the wrinkles in Emily's dress; like Emily she is "helpless before the iron," aware that this Sisyphus-like ritual cannot atone for the past, nor can she ultimately answer the riddle Emily poses within and without the family constellation. Certainly the chains of necessity should have justified the mother's past relationship with her eldest child.

> We were poor and could not afford for her the soil of easy growth. I was a young mother. I was a distracted mother. There were the other children pushing up, demanding. Her younger sister seemed all that she was not. There were many years that she did not want me to touch her. She kept too much to herself, . . . My wisdom came too late. She has much to her and probably nothing will come of it. She is a child of her age, of depression, of war, of fear.

Who speaks for the autobiographer? A nameless narrator once a poor Jewish parent, now part of a middle-class nuclear family. Emily, her silenced daughter, is in fact a disembodied dress pushed and pulled by her mother's iron. Shunted, stunted, despite her comic pandering to a mass audience at high school, Emily is a version of the narrator's atrophied self, a contemporary Korl Woman.

If not to have an audience is a kind of death, who listens to the autobiographer? Olsen has always sought a community of women readers identifying with her silences, carefully scrutinizing her self-censorship as she herself has done in the remarkable close reading of Rebecca Harding Davis' *Life in the Iron Mills.* It is this kind of imaginative scrutiny we must bring to a reading of **"O Yes,"** where once again working class communality is negated by middle-class distancing and silence defeats clamor on behalf of the poor.

Deceptively simple, this aforementioned theme emerges during a Black baptismal service for twelve year old *Pariahlee* Phillips (my italics). The only whites attending the all Black service are Pariah's closest friend Carol and Carol's mother, Helen, liberal, Jewish, middle class. The over-heated, tumultuous service, enveloping one parishioner after another, pounds against Helen and Carol's class inhibitions. Terrified, Carol faints in church:

> And when Carol opens her eyes she closes them again, quick, but still can see the new known face from school . . . , the thrashing, writhing body struggling against the ushers with the look of grave and loving support on their faces, and hear the torn, tearing cry "Don't take me away."

> And now the rhinestones in Parry's hair glitter wicked, the white hands of the ushers, fanning, foam in the air; the blue-painted waters of Jordan swell and thunder; Christ spirals on his cross in the window, and she is drowned under the sluice of the slow singing and the sway.

The timeless sermon that recapitulates Old and New Testament suffering and redemption, serves two functions. The first is a subtle reminder to Helen and Carol of their de-facto segregation from the Black community, strongly personified by Alva, Parry's vital resilient mother. The second underscores a Judaic-Christian patriarchal heritage that obscures women, but also makes them aware of how the power of the word mitigates against silence. The preacher arouses the congregation to feverish pitch:

> He was your mother's rock. Your father's mighty tower. And he gave us a little baby. A little baby to love.
>> *I am so glad*
> Yes, your friend when you are friendless. Your father when you are fatherless. Way maker. Door opener
>> *Yes*
> When it seems you can't go on any longer, he's there You can, he says you can
>> *Yes*
> And that burden you have been carrying—ohhh that burden—not for always will it be. No, not for always.
>> *Stay with me, Lord.*
> I will put my *Word* in you and it is power

I will put my *Truth* in you and it is power.
          [Italics in the last two lines, mine]

Unfortunately, the frustration inherent in middle-class women's powerlessness censors Helen's need to voice passion and shape inchoate experience into language. In the hectic event following the service Helen's silence is especially telling. Heretofore, Carol and Parry have loved each other, but Carol's fainting at church marks the beginning of their estrangement:

> "How are you doing now, you little ol' consolation prize?" It is Parry, but she does not come to the car or reach to Carol through the open window: "No need to cuss and fuss. You going to be sharp as a tack, jack." Carol answering automatically: "as cool as a fool."
>
> Quick they look at each other.
>
> "Parry, we have to go home now, don't we mother?"

Not Helen but iron-willed Alva Phillips, seasoned in adversity, who unlike the mother in **"I Stand Here Ironing,"** chooses immersion into rather than withdrawal from life.

> *When I was carrying Parry and her father left, and I was fifteen years old, one thousand miles away from home, sinsick and never believing, as still I don't believe all, scorning, for what have it done to help, waiting there in the clinic and maybe sleeping, a voice called: Alva, Alva. So mournful and so sweet: Alva. Fear not, I have loved you from the foundation of the universe. And a little small child tugged on my dress.*

This passage suggests the similarity and difference between the white and Black mother. Both women have felt isolated, skeptical of religious orthodoxy. But whereas Helen internalizes this estrangement, distancing herself from the immediacy of passion, and remains static and Korl-like, Alva allows communal celebration to temper her and thus sets her spirit free:

> *Eyes he the small child placed all around my head, and as I journeyed upward after him, it seemed I heard a mourning: "Mama, Mama, you must help carry the world." The rise and fall of nations I saw. And the voice called again Alva, Alva, and I flew into a world of light, multitudes singing, Free, free, I am so glad.*

Helen, who cannot even conceptualize this kind of force, feels divided not only from Alva but from herself. A dichotomy exists between Helen's (and by extension Carol's)

head and heart, ultimately inhibiting the words she needs to comfort Carol and convey the meaning of Black communion.

> *Emotion,* Helen thought of explaining, *a characteristic of the religion of all oppressed peoples, yes your very own great-grandparents*—thought of saying. And discarded. *Aren't you now, haven't you had feelings in yourself so strong they had to come out some way?* ("What howls restrained by decorum")—thought of saying. And discarded.

Carol lives out the consequences of her mother's ambivalence. In the months to come, Carol and Parry seem as intertwined as they were before the baptism. But Jeannie, Carol's older sister, has warned her parents that the future holds little promise for that friendship. Both girls will shortly enter Junior High where a rigid hierarchy of social cliques divides academic performance/social conformity from the pariahood of those who cannot or choose not to comply.

And what of Parry? If at the threshold of adolescence Carol seems to exemplify Helen's liberalism gone defensively rigid, Parry's uninhibited pride in her budding sexuality should affirm Alva's earthiness. But contradictions between the institutional racism of the school and the communality of the church have also damaged Parry. She must hurry home after school to look after younger siblings because Alva works the night shift. In the societal sorting process predicted by Jeannie, who has gone through it earlier, Parry falls behind the achievers, her dignity violated by a dress code incompatible with her exuberant sexuality. Carol's rejecting her eats away as Parry's breezy self-confidence. Visiting Carol, sick with the mumps, Parry brings over the assignments teachers have written down, not trusting Parry to remember what they were. Nervously Parry tries the old banter:

> Flicking the old read books on the shelf but not opening to mock declaim as once she used to. . . . Staring out the window as if the tree not there in which they had hit out and rocked so often . . . Got me a new pink top and lilac skirt. Look sharp with this purple? Cinching in the wide belt as if delighted with what newly swelled above and swelled below. Wear it Saturday night to Sweets . . . (Shake my baby, shake). Asking of Rembrandt's weary old face looking from the wall. How come (softly) you long-gone you.
>
> Touching her face to his quickly, lightly.

White culture denied her, Parry departs forever, announcing that from now on someone else would stop by with Carol's homework.

And yet Olsen never knots the complex strands of human experience. Years later, remembering the ecstasy of that church service, Helen and Carol discuss the bleak lives of Carol's Black high school mates whom, identifying with in some deep recess of her being, Carol cannot easily dislodge:

> "Mother, I want to forget about it all, and not care.... Why can't I forget? Oh why is it like it is and why do I have to care?"

> Caressing, quieting.

> Thinking: *caring asks doing. It is a long baptism into the seas of humankind, my daughter. Better immersion than to live untouched.... Yet how will you sustain?*

> *Why is it like it is?*

> Sheltering her daughter close, mourning the illusion of the embrace.

> *And why do I have to care?*

> While in her Helen, her own need leapt and plunged for the place of strength that was not-where one could scream or sorrow while all knew and accepted, and gloved and loving hands waited to support and understand.

The seas of humankind, reminiscent of Anna's sailing song in *Yonnondio,* remind us as well how landlocked, trapped are the Annas and Parrys whose youth will erode under an exploitative system offering them little bread and no roses. Anna, Emily, and Parry, daughters; all three are young. Two are victims, the third possibly a survivor, for industrial violence and the depression are over and young Black women will eventually foment change. Their author's self-referential voice, decorous in *Silences,* becomes an extended wail in **"Tell Me a Riddle."** Her incantatory prose encapsulates Rebecca Davis' lament for the laboring poor, for women's souls reduced to scrap iron. Olsen's voice is an elegiac tribute to the Jewish immigrant experience gone sour in the promised land, adding a powerful dimension to the lives of Olsen's literary foremothers dead and Jewish mothers dying.

Not knowing she is dying, Eva, the grandmother in **"Tell Me a Riddle"** recognizes that for the better part of her existence she has lived "between" and "for" but "not with people." "Your sickness was in you, how you live," her husband Max tells her, recalling a penurious and cluttered past when she weighed each morsel of food and yet felt "hungry for the life of the mind." It would be simple enough to assume that Eva's cancer, like the one consuming Tolstoy's

Ivan Ilytch becomes an extended metaphor for the unexamined life: marrying Max, bearing five children, conforming thereby to the iron tenets of Jewish patriarchy. Unlike Ivan Ilytch's marriage, however, one of chronic bad faith, Eva's relationship to Max is not loveless; he has been a union worker and has labored long for an earned retirement. And for too long Eva has surrendered, albeit uneasily, to the unspoken dictum that biology equals destiny.

After 47 years of living an unfulfilled life with Max, all the children grown and on their own, Eva's iron willpower undermines her gregarious husband's proposal that they move to a rest "Haven" he has chosen for them to live out their retirement. Accustomed to psychic privation, she intends to spend an old age on her own and private terms: "Let *him* wrack his head for how they would live. She would not exchange her solitude for anything. *Never again to be forced to move to the rhythms of others.*"

Bitterly the couple wrangle. Eva, wearing a hearing aid and turning on the vacuum cleaner in order to drown out Max's haranguing, rejects his plea that she owes them both an earned rest at the cooperative for the aged where others would do their chores and minister to their leisure needs. He enlists the aid of their adult children. Eva refuses point blank to hear these arguments.

> "Because I'm use't."

> "Because you're use't. This is a reason, *Mrs. Word Miser?* Used to can get unused!" "Enough unused I have to get used to already.... Not enough?" turning off the vacuum a moment to hear herself answer. "Because soon enough we'll need only a little closet, no windows, no furniture, nothing to make work, but for worms. Because now I want room....

> . . . . .

> Over the dishes coaxingly: "For once in your life to be free, to have everything done for you like a queen."

> "I never liked queens."

> "No dishes, no garbage, no towel to sop, no worry what to buy, what to eat."

> "And what else would I do with empty hands? Better to eat at my own table when I want and to cook how I want."

For Olsen, however, marriage signifies more than living falsely, acquiescing to the rhythms of others. Eva needs Max; they have become interdependent. Eva's ties to husband and children are a source of bonding as well as bondage. The symbiotic relationship unfolds early in the story before Eva's stomach pains and fatigue are diagnosed as symptoms of inoperable cancer. For example, during a heated quarrel on an unbearably humid evening, Max storms out, slamming the door despite his wife's uncharacteristic plea that he stay with her. The air is rent with Eva's cursing in Yiddish, a language she has not used in years:

> She was not in their bed when he came back. She lay on the cot on the sun porch. All week she did not speak or come near him; nor did he try to make peace or care for her. He slept badly, so used to her next to him.

> After all the years, old harmonies and dependencies deep in their bodies; she curled to him, or he coiled to her, each warmed, warming, turning as the other turned, the nights a long embrace.

In the first passage Olsen's punning (used to it, uses) reveals the nuances of domestic drudgery. In the second a characteristic overflow of infinitives, gerundives, incantatory parallels underscores the reciprocity of a marriage that will not be reduced to bondage alone. Bonding, in fact, has always proved seductive to Eva:

> Immediacy to embrace, and the breath of that part; warm flesh like this a new grandchild placed on her lap that had claims and nuzzled away all else and with lovely mouths devoured; hot-living like an animal—intensely and now. . . .

And troubling:

> It is distraction, not meditation that becomes habitual; interruption, not continuity . . . work interrupted, deferred, relinquished makes blockage—at best lesser accomplishment. Unused capacities atrophy, cease to be.

Her illness diagnosed, the information withheld from her, Eva is taken on a round of family visits she does not know are final. At Vivi's house, the younger daughter weeps nostalgically and when grandchildren clamor for attention, Eva withdraws in silence:

> It was not that she had not loved her babies, her children. The love—the passion of tending had risen with the need like a torrent; and like a torrent drowned and immolated all else. But when the need was done—oh the power that was lost in the painful damming back and drying up of what still surged, but had nowhere to go.

Nor is Eva's response bizarrely ungrandmotherly. It is honest, indicating a sub-rosa recalcitrance rejecting patriarchal categorizing (and Orthodox Jewish patriarchy codifying wife-mother behavior for thousands of years is unyielding, even today) of a grandmother's behavior according to Jewish custom. For the immigrant women transplanted to American soil the confluence of Jewish and Gentile patriarchy proved difficult to resist. Erika Dunkan writes:

> In Jewish literature by *women,* mothers are the "bread givers" who try to make feeding into a replenishing ecstatic act. But the mothers are themselves starved in every way, sucked dry and withered from being asked almost from birth to give a nurturance they never receive. They are starved not only for the actual food they are forced to turn over to others, but for the stuff of self and soul, for love and song.

Thus, Eva, remembering her lost youth spent borrowing, scrimping, hoarding so that her brood could survive in America is the Korl woman grown old, resistive, being shaped in another image, fearful that she might drown in nurturing a grandchild, rather than immersing herself in the sea. Instead she bends her will to concentrate on what an older precocious grandson is exploring for his science project. To persistent queries—"Tell me a riddle, Grandma," she responds "I know no riddles," defining riddles as childs' play that only Max, the fun loving grandfather can supply because his life has been freer. Alone, she holds a magnifying glass over young Richard's rock collection, laboriously repeating terminology—"trilobite fossil, 200 million years old, . . . obsidian, black glass,"—signifying Darwinian geology: "igneous, sedimentary, metamorphic."

If Eva's hearing aid drowns out the others claiming her attention, the magnifying glass represents an intense attraction for enlightenment, a rejection of ghetto irrationality she experienced at the turn of the century. She retains pre-atomic age optimism equating evolution with social progress. Lying in a hospital bed, her mind clouded in the aftermath of anesthesia, she is aroused by the chaplain:

> I think he prays. Go away please, I tell him. I am not a believer. Still he stands while my heart knocks with fright.

> You scared *him,* mother, he thought you were delirious [answers Paul, Eva's son-in-law].

> Who sent him? Why did he come to me?

> It is a custom. The men of God come to visit those of religion they might help. The hospital makes up the list for them—race—religion—and you are on

the Jewish list. Not for rabbis. At once go and make them change. Tell them to write: Race, human. Religion, none.

In the same way she rejects Max's plea that for the sake of family harmony she shares in her daughter Hannah's benediction of the Sabbath candles: "Superstition! From the savages, afraid of the dark, of themselves: mumbo words and magic lights to scare away ghosts."

Eschewing the healing effect of ritual, Eva remembers too well the time when ghetto orthodoxy was "the opiate of the people," especially of women for whom the way out of dogma was through education. Thus, Olsen's use of Eva's magnifying glass is an inspired metaphor, allowing the old woman to peer through a glass clearly and see the world "steadily and whole."

Taking leave of her children, Eva allows Max to bring her to a frayed Los Angeles boarding house by the sea where she will spend the final weeks of her life. One afternoon, on the beach, feeling an upsurge of strength, Eva runs toward the ocean that brought her to America, followed by a stumbling Max who cannot stop her. Tripping over a rock, she puts it in a bag "to look at with a strong glass." The rock held against her cheek, Eva gazes at "the shore that nurtured life as it first crawled toward consciousness millions of years ago."

Although she affirms evolution, Eva, like Olsen and her foremothers, does *not* endorse the Social Darwinism that dominated turn of the century intellectual life, probably because such a belief would validate a nature "red in tooth and claw," a determinism: predatory, male, offering no hope of the progressive humanism she really worships. Eva's nurturing impulses have always included ministering to the wretched of the earth, from saving scraps of food and clothing for the poor to reading books that espouse doing away with outmoded social orders. Like Rebecca Harding Davis, whose mind Dr. Le Moyne opened to ethical radicalism, Eva remembers a girlhood mentor in the ghetto of Olshana, Lisa, a brilliant and artistic Russian revolutionary, who taught her to read. Despite beatings at home, Eva would sneak away to meet the idealistic Tolstoyan in much the same way Davis absorbed Le Moyne's subversive ideas in Wheeling, Pennsylvania prior to the Civil War.

> At night past dogs that howled, terrible dogs, my son, in the snows of winter to the road, I to ride in her carriage like a lady, to books. To her, life was holy, knowledge was holy, and she taught me to read.

An informer having betrayed their underground cell, Lisa killed him in prison and was hanged.

Everything that happens one must try to understand why. She killed one who betrayed many—betrayed all she lived and believed. In one minute she killed, before my eyes (there is so much blood in a human being, my son) in prison with me.

Lisa's revenge on those that would stultify ideas of human liberation live on in Eva's fading memory. To sustain what minuscule life she has, Eva must desperately reach out through time and space linking her selfhood with Lisa, a dead foremother, whom she must internalize before she can allow herself to die. Heartbreakingly for the husband and children who watch the agony of her final days, Eva turns from them to ideas, words, gleaned from books, recapitulated at the ultimate moment. Delirious she hears snatches of songs, sings, quotes: "Pain I answer with tears and cries, baseness with indignation, meanness with repulsion—for life may be hated or wearied of, but never despised." Captive to her fragmented utterances, Max, himself fearful of cancer, helpless before Eva's suffering, impoverished by the cost of her medical care, wearily tries to understand:

> "It helps, Mrs. Philosopher, words from books: It helps?" And it seemed to him that for seventy years she had hidden a tape recorder, infinitely microscopic, with her and that it had coiled infinite mile on mile trapping every song, every melody, every word read, heard, and spoken, and that maliciously she was playing back only what said nothing of him, of the children, of their intimate life together.

It is with a special intensity that Clara, Eva's eldest daughter, an "Emily" hardened to bitter middle age, listens to her mother's dying words. Old wounds throb anew as Clara recalls the deprived childhood in which she stood by helplessly as Eva begged storekeepers for extended credit, hoarded bits of meat and bone for soup, mended ragged clothing, drudged for others with no time to communicate with her first born:

> *Pay me back, Mother, pay me back for all you took from me. Those others you crowded into your heart. The hands I needed to be for you . . .*
>
> *Is this she? Noises the dying make, the crab-like hands crawling over the covers.*
>
> *The ethereal singing.*
>
> *She hears that music, the singing from childhood; forgotten sound—not heard since, since . . . And the hardness breaks like a cry: Where did we lose each other, first mother, singing mother?*

In silence Clara asks this profound Olsen riddle for which the answer would only exacerbate the wound. For Eva trusts only two women. The first was Lisa, her foremother, hanged in a Russian prison. The second is her granddaughter Jeannie, who understands Eva's starved soul and is reminiscent of Lisa in her dedication to alleviating human suffering. It is Jeannie who tries to bridge the gap between Eva and Max. A nurse and a talented artist, Jeannie not only moves into Eva's room to care for the dying woman, she paints her grandparents lying side by side, hands intertwined.

> As Harold Bloom has explained, literary forefathers have always influenced their writing sons, often causing them the "anxiety of 'this' influence." For Tillie Olsen, literary foremothers help engender and empower otherwise silenced women writers.
> —*Rose Kamel*

Perhaps Jeannie represents Olsen's attempt to affirm the artistic continuity transcending generations she experienced reading Rebecca Harding Davis. If so, this attempt is flawed. Jeannie's breathless buoyancy cannot unleash the suppressed creativity that adds up to an appalling waste of Eva's (and Clara's) potential.

Yet Olsen has given the closest reading possible to silenced writers, demonstrating two basic premises underlying their writing. The first, an ongoing tension between an artist (worker, Black, woman, Jew) in need of a voice, and a silence societally imposed, psychically internalized. The second, an imperative to find an audience for that energy, that authentic voice, an audience unlike the wealthy dilettantes in *Life in the Iron Mills,* fascinated by the Korl Woman while they allow its sculptor to rot in prison. If *not* to find an audience is always a kind of death, discovering the responsive reader valorizes the obscured artists' suffering and strength, giving them the power to formulate riddles we have never addressed, let alone redressed. As Harold Bloom has explained, literary forefathers have always influenced their writing sons, often causing them the "anxiety of 'this' influence." For Tillie Olsen, literary foremothers help engender and empower otherwise silenced women writers.

Bonnie Lyons (essay date 1986)

SOURCE: "Tillie Olsen: The Writer as a Jewish Woman," in *Studies in American Jewish Literature,* No. 5, 1986, pp. 89-102.

[In the following essay, Lyons argues that while Judaism shapes Olsen's work, her writing is most influenced by her experiences as a woman.]

That Tillie Olsen's work is radically perfectibilistic in spirit and vision is obvious to most of her readers. Less obvious is that the two principal sources of that vision derive directly from her experience as a Jew and as a woman.

What is most deeply Jewish in Olsen is the secular messianic utopianism she inherited from her immigrant parents. That is, her political and social ideology directly reflects the radical Jewish background in which she grew up. But while her Jewish background provides a foundation for Olsen's basic political vision, it would be a mistake to view Jewishness itself as the living core, either in theme or imagery, of her work. Her experience as a woman is much more central, and is especially noticeable in her patterns of imagery. From the weak propagandistic early poetry to the great **"Tell Me a Riddle,"** Olsen repeatedly emphasizes the human body and the mother/child relationship, aspects of human experience strongly identified with the female.

This is not to suggest that Olsen's explicit "femaleness" makes her work restricted in scope or marginal. Her habitual focus on the body does not suggest, for example, that the human is *merely* a body. On the contrary she grounds the spiritual *in* the body in very concrete and physical terms, emphatically insisting on the wholeness of the human. For Olsen the physical body makes the spiritual condition manifest: disfigurement, mutilation, and especially starvation are body images or ideas employed repeatedly to reflect both self-estrangement and estrangement from the world. Generally, hunger, eating, and feeding (nurturing) are the pivotal experiences that directly link the mother/child relationship on the one hand to the Jewish radical political vision on the other.

Olsen's vision lies between the Realist emphasis on victimization and the puniness of the individual, and the over-optimistic emphasis on the sheer human potentiality of some of the Romantics. In Olsen, human beings experience ravening hungers of all kinds: physical, emotional, intellectual, spiritual. But when these hungers are fed, the individuals develop their potential and give to others and to the world at large: fulfilled people are productive and nurturing in turn. In Olsen's view the deepest human hunger is to be fruitful, so human beings satisfy their own needs best by giving. The negative conclusions of this Rousseauvian view are likewise drawn: those who are prevented by circumstances from developing their productive and nurturing natures will be inclined in turn to become victimizers and stultifiers of others.

The Rousseauvian dimension of Olsen's work is most obviously demonstrated by the fact that in each of her fictions there is a child at or near the center of the story. The child poetically embodies mankind's two dominant characteristics: potential and hunger. Moreover, since she sees each individual human life and all human life in general as parallel journeys toward greater consciousness, what happens to the child is emblematic of the condition and fate of humankind.

Since for Olsen the deepest human hunger is to be fruitful, mothering, in its ideal form, is an example of intense fulfillment. It is also a source of knowledge. Through the experience, the mother discovers human potential and all the forces that operate to limit it; she comes to see human beings as born with enormous possibilities for joy, growth, and productivity which are unnaturally thwarted through class, age, sex and race prejudice.

[Olsen's] habitual focus on the body does not suggest, for example, that the human is *merely* a body. On the contrary she grounds the spiritual *in* the body in very concrete and physical terms, emphatically insisting on the wholeness of the human.
—Bonnie Lyons

What is implicit about nurturing and motherhood in her fiction is made explicit in *Silences,* where she insists on the "comprehensions possible out of motherhood" and specifies that these comprehensions include "*the very nature, needs, illimitable potentiality of the human being—and the everyday means by which these are distorted, discouraged, limited, extinguished.*" Moreover, Olsen asserts that because motherhood is a neglected theme in literature (neglected because mothers are not usually able to become writers), these comprehensions have not yet "come to powerful, undeniable, useful expression." Thus there are "aspects and understandings of human life as yet largely absent in literature." Olsen's own fiction is itself an attempt to redeem that "loss in literature."

The next section of this essay will explore what is Jewish in Olsen's work, the following two will focus on what is female: first, her treatment of the body and second, the mother/child relationship both as fact and metaphor. Tillie Olsen has said "What is Yiddish in me . . . is inextricable from what is woman in me, from woman who is mother." The concluding section will suggest the accuracy of that self-analysis.

II
"Still Eva Believed and Still I Believe"

Olsen's Jewishness is a thorny subject. Because her mother was a non-Jew, for Orthodox Jews Olsen is not, in fact, Jewish. Moreover, Olsen considers herself an atheist and proudly describes her father as "incorruptibly atheist to the last day

of his life." Nonetheless, Olsen considers herself a Jewish atheist, and **"Tell Me a Riddle,"** her greatest fiction, is also one of the finest works of American Jewish literature.

Olsen hardly affirms all things Jewish. She looks at traditional Judaism as having served a useful purpose in the past by providing a sense of solidarity and strength, a refuge in a terrible world of oppression. But for all its positive effects, traditional Judaism for Olsen is inextricably linked with much that is negative or limiting: superstition, patriarchy, parochialism, and an enclosed, static life which reinforced life-stifling traditions as the price of security and continuity.

In an interview, Olsen recently remarked, "I still remain with the kind of *Yiddishkeit* I grew up with." By this she refers to her Jewish socialist background. According to her, that background fostered two essential insights. First, "knowledge and experience of injustice, of discrimination, of oppression, of genocide and of the need to act against them forever and whenever they appear." And second, an "absolute belief in the potentiality of human beings."

Olsen's vision of the world parallels Eva's in **"Tell Me a Riddle,"** and Eva is on the one hand a spiritual portrait of the artist as an old woman and, on the other a wonderfully moving evocation of a segment of the Jewish community. That is, even Eva's insistence "Race, human; religion, none," is a not atypical Jewish response.

Olsen has said that she began **"Tell Me a Riddle"** in order to "celebrate a generation of revolutionaries," and her portrait of Eva and David is indeed a celebration of fervent Jewish revolutionaries during the early years of the century and of a time of boundless hopes and richly humanist fervor. These Jewish socialists, whom Irving Howe also celebrates in *World of Our Fathers,* were dedicated to building a new society, a world-wide international community in which all human beings "would live without want in freedom and fulfillment." Theirs was a socialism that was more than political and economic; it was founded on a profound idealism, an idea of human liberation and secular utopia. Opposed to traditional Judaism, socialist Jews transferred messianism, one of the traditional elements of Jewish experience, to secular dreams.

"Tell Me a Riddle" then is a deeply Jewish story. The Yiddish-inflected speech and "old country curses" are obviously of Jewish origin. David's ideal, to retire in dignity and community to his workers' haven evokes memories of Jewish Workmen's Circles. Even the bait with which David unsuccessfully tempts Eva to the home is particularly Jewish; he tells her there is a reading circle which studies Chekhov and Peretz, a Russian and a Jewish author united by their understanding and love of the ordinary person, of basic, un-improved humanity.

For all its positive effects, traditional Judaism for Olsen is inextricably linked with much that is negative or limiting: superstition, patriarchy, parochialism, and an enclosed, static life which reinforced life-stifling traditions as the price of security and continuity.
—Bonnie Lyons

Through Eva, Olsen makes her clearest fictional statement about traditional Judaism. When one of her children tells Eva that the hospital puts patients on lists so that "men of God may visit those of their religion" and that she is on the Jewish list, Eva responds: "Not for rabbis." It is not that Eva denies being Jewish but that she refuses the religious views and consolation of the rabbis.

When asked by her daughter Hannah to light the Sabbath candles, Eva refuses and accuses Hannah of doing it for ignoble reasons: "Not for pleasure she does it. For emptiness. Because his [her husband's] family does. Because all around her do." She calls Hannah's heritage and tradition "superstition! From the savages afraid of the dark, of themselves: mumbo words and magic lights to scare away ghosts." Eva's dismissive attitude toward ritual parallels that of her "real life" contemporaries: in the early years of the century young Jewish radicals held costume balls on Yom Kippur to flaunt their separation from a "benighted" past. What infuriates Eva most is Hannah's nostalgia for the past. For the forward-looking Eva the past means "dark centuries" when religion stifled women and encouraged the poor to buy candles instead of bread. It was when the poor chosen Jew was "ground under, despised, trembling in cellars" and later a Holocaust victim—"and cremated. And cremated." When her husband David asks whether the terrible victimization of the Jews is the fault of religion, Eva does not answer. But clearly she sees Judaism as a backward religion and has no faith in a God who permits his chosen people to suffer so excruciatingly. Instead of traditional religion she believes Hannah should teach universal humanism: "to smash all ghettos that divide us—not to go back, not to go back."

Eva's undying faith in their youthful messianic hopes, "Their holiest dreams" is the story's vision of a secular utopia. Both the vision and the faith in human possibility mirror Jewish socialism of the early years of the century and Olsen's own abiding *Yiddishkeit*: "*that joyous certainty, that sense of mattering, of moving and being moved, of being one and indivisible with the great of the past, with all that freed, ennobled man.*" Although Eva's sacred text is not the Bible but the Book of Martyrs, and Socrates not Moses is her hero, her vision embodies both the messianic hope and universalist worldview of a particular kind of secular Jew.

The complete familiarity with Jewish immigrant culture revealed in **"Tell Me a Riddle"** is particularly striking because Jewishness barely touches Olsen's other work. In *Yonnondio* it appears and disappears suddenly and briefly. Enroute to a farm after finally escaping from a brutalizing coal mining town, Anna Holbrook momentarily blossoms with memories and plans: "School for the kids, Jim working near her, on the earth, lovely things to keep, brass lamps, bright table-cloths, vines over the doors, and roses twining." Suddenly a memory flashes: "her grandmother bending in such a twilight over lit candles chanting in an unknown tongue, white bread on the table over a shining white tablecloth and red wine." Elenore Lester has suggested that "the way Anna's Jewishness is injected and then withdrawn without casting some subtle coloration over her, suggests that the author was cauterizing a rich vein of associations which might have worked for her." Since the novel was never completed there is no way of knowing for sure if or how Olsen would have developed this Jewish thread. As is, the very slightness of the Jewish memory functions to keep the Holbrooks a representative American proletarian family and supports the universalizing aspects of the novel. To explore or develop Anna's Jewishness may well have seemed to the young Olsen to risk parochialism and to undermine the one world vision. The word Jewish itself is mentioned as one of many nationalities, neither first nor last: "Na-tion-al-it-ies American Armenian Chinese Croatian . . . Irish French Italian Jewish Lith. . . ."

The candle lighting ceremony links *Yonnondio* with **"Tell Me a Riddle."** That candle lighting is clearly positive in the early novel and denounced by Eva in the later story superficially suggests a change in Olsen, a deepening disaffection and disavowal of her Jewish roots. But the contexts and function of the scenes differ crucially in the two texts. In *Yonnondio* candle lighting is positive to Anna because her recent past has been so physically and spiritually crippling. Candle lighting in her mind is linked with order and beauty, with home and sweet domesticity. In **"Tell Me a Riddle"** the candle lighting occurs in the home of Eva's son-in-law, a Jewish doctor. That is, in an affluent, educated home where there is no real need to look back, no need for religion whose purposes have been, in Eva's and Olsen's eyes, outgrown.

"O Yes," the only other Olsen story mentioning Jewishness even obliquely supports this analysis of Olsen's religious attitudes. That story celebrated the Negro church as a place where oppressed Negroes release pent up emotion and "the preaching finding lodgment in their hearts." When her daughter Carol becomes hysterical because of all the intense feeling in the church, Helen thinks of explaining that emotion is "*a characteristic of the religion of all oppressed peoples, yes your very own great-grandparents.*" Traditional religion as a resource, a rock for oppressed people is affirmed, but only as a stage along the way. This is Olsen's overt message. Interestingly, however, at the end of **"O Yes"** Helen is unable to explain the cruelty and suffering of the world to Carol and feels her own emptiness: "her own need leapt and plunged for the place of strength that was not." What Helen is missing is the warmth and comfort of the church "where one could scream or sorrow while all knew and accepted, and gloved and loving hands waited to support and understand." The Negro church and the religion of her grandparents seem equally impossible solutions.

III
"We are the injured body"

A section of **Silences** ends with the words, "*We are the injured body. Let us not desert one another.*" Throughout her work Olsen expresses the ways people are psychologically as well as physically thwarted and diminished through bodily images. In her earliest, rather obvious polemical poetry, she denounces capitalist exploitation by envisioning the effects on the workers' bodies. Here the body, standing for the whole self, is destroyed in various ways; in particular, the poor workers' bodies are *consumed* by the rich.

In **"I Want You Women Up North to Know,"** [the poem appeared in *The Partisan*, (March 1934), 4, under the name I. Lerner] the seamstresses' bodies are stitched into the garments bought by the wealthy. The dainty dresses that the poor women sew are "dyed in blood," stitched in wasting flesh; "bodies shrivel" in "parching heat." Skeletons and starved children abound. Parallel examples of exploitation and bodily disfigurement and consumption are portrayed: women reduced to prostitution and venereal disease, and an injured male worker "remembering a leg, and twenty-five years cut off from his life by the railroad." Didactic and simplistic, the early poems divide the world into innocent victims whose bodies are eaten, and wicked victimizers with fat, bloated bodies.

The novel **Yonnondio**, also begun in the thirties, evokes a similar vision of the world and employs similar body imagery. In the first chapter the nameless narrator mourns the waste of a young boy's life as he enters the coal mines and contrasts the "skeletons of starved children" with the "fat bellies" of the capitalists. Later in the novel when the Holbrook family loses their farm despite their unceasing work, the politicians are seen as vultures, and the father, Jim Holbrook, says that the banks "batten on us like hogs."

Olsen also uses two body images to integrate major sections of the novel and to establish parallels and contrasts between the two sections. The opening section (part of which was first published under the title **"The Iron Throat"**) is dominated by an image of the mine as the "earth's intestines," as a place where the earth "sucks you in." The climax of the terror comes when an insane miner (a victim turned into a crazed victimizer) attempts to throw a child, Mazie Holbrook, into the mine: the miner imagines the mine as a ravenous woman "hungry for a child" to devour. The very fact that the miner sees woman as devourer rather than nurturer demonstrates the extremity of his condition, a result of the economic and social conditions in general.

The third major section of **Yonnondio**, like the opening one, is dominated by a nightmare body image: the packing house is a monstrous heart, which, rather than pumping healthy blood, pumps "the men and women who are the streets' life-blood, nourishing the taverns and brothels and rheumy-eyes stores, bulging out the soiled and exhausted houses, and multiplying into these children playing so mirthlessly in their street yards where flower only lampposts."

In the stories the human condition is not seen in such dichotomous terms—victims and victimizers—but the same body and eating imagery abounds, developed in subtler, more complex ways. In these stories Olsen often uses eating as symbolic of a character's sense of self and world, as the link between the individual and the universe. Eating is a clear indication of a character's psychic state, and healthy eating indicates a sense of total well-being, an at-homeness in the universe.

Eating is significant because to eat is to assert and fulfill the claims of the self. Eating also means taking a part of the world, making it part of the self, absorbing part of the world. In Olsen's work the eating process reflects the ultimate mystery of life and death and an awareness that humans kill other living organisms in order to survive. For Olsen the proper response to the plant or animal sacrifice necessary to human life is a kind of reverence or natural piety. Her characters express this natural piety by eating, not to become bloated, but in order to grow and produce and, in turn, nourish others: they eat so that they can feed others.

In **"I Stand Here Ironing"** the daughter Emily's thinness, her early inability to eat, and her subsequent ravenous appetite all suggests her lack of nourishment on every level. Although the narrator/mother remembers the "sleek" young society women who raise money for an institution where children like Emily wear "gigantic red bows and ravaged looks", it is not just the fat bellies who cause Emily's thinness. Sent to an institution to gain weight by a well-meaning mother and social worker, Emily returns thin and stays thin. As her mother tells it, "Food sickened her, and I think much of life too."

Here the problems are not all solvable by eliminating the

vultures of the earth. Emily's hunger and subsequent legendary appetite have many causes, including her mother's youth and anxiety, her father's cowardice and withdrawal, her own slowness and darkness in a world that prizes quickness and blondness. Her hunger also has one surprisingly positive effect: out of her despair, expressed by both her early thinness and later insatiable appetite, she develops a gift, the art of comic mimicry. And while the memory of a heartless teacher who belittled Emily for her fear has "curdled" in the mother's memory, the mother refuses to see Emily as doomed or as passive victim—a dress "helpless before the iron."

"Hey Sailor, What Ship?" also interweaves body and eating imagery into its texture in important ways. Some of the imagery reflects the social/political concerns of the earlier work. For Lennie, Whitey is a tie to "*a world in which men had not eaten each other.*" One of the memories Whitey tries to drown in liquor is the time of brotherhood when "*whoever came off the ship fat shared.*" Now part of Whitey's problem with authority on the ship stems from his complaint about "rotten feed"—symbolic of the exploitation of the workers.

Whitey's present failing condition is also given digestive terms: he hardly eats, and he drinks not to nourish himself, but to poison himself. The key to his woes also seems bodily: he cannot have sex unless he is drunk. And now he also drinks because there are "*memories to forget, dreams to be stifled, hopes to be murdered.*" His body expresses his estrangement from himself and the world; now he has a "*decaying body, the body that was betraying him.*" His desperate attempt to connect with Lennie and Helen and their children, who represent not only family but also his memories, his earlier self, and a hopeful future, is symbolized by his attempt to provide and share a meal with them, a communion through shared food.

In **"Tell Me a Riddle,"** the deepest hungers are embodied, hungers of every kind. In Russia, Eva and David experienced physical hunger as well as hunger for learning, for holy knowledge. In America they had hungry children and hungry souls—hungry for beauty, meaning, sense of purpose, and progress. As the story progresses, Eva wastes away, consumed by cancer until the final day when the "agony was perpetual." Still she refuses to give up the dream of fulfilled human life which is embodied in the old Russian revolutionary song she continues to sing. At the climax of the song, which is interrupted by a "long strangling cough," her husband suddenly awakens from his years-long sleep and self-blindness: "Without warning, the bereavement and betrayal he had sheltered . . . revealed itself,/uncoiled,/releases,/*sprung*/and with it the monstrous shapes of what he had actually happened in the century." His reaction is immediate and "Olsenian": "ravening hunger or thirst seized him."

Despite the bitterness, recriminations, rage, and disappointment, Eva and David and their love finally triumph. On her last night and in Jeannie's picture they are holding hands: "their hands, his and hers, clasped, feeding each other." The image of love as mutual nourishment, as two people *feeding* each other, is the antithesis of and the "answer" to the earlier vision of a world of eaters and eaten. And this image of mutual nourishment is linked to another: David looks at Jeannie's art, her drawing of Eva and himself "and as if he had been instructed he went to his bed, lay down, holding the sketch (as if it would shield against the monstrous shapes of loss, of betrayal, of death) and with his free hand took hers [Eva's] back into his." Their life, their love, their humanity nourish Jeannie's art, which in turn, nourishes and instructs their life: life and art feed each other.

Silences is about artists' failure to produce because of inadequate nourishment: here Olsen analyzes the multiple causes that produce silence—all the nagging hungers that thwart productivity. The hunger/feeding metaphor is pursued insistently at every level. In the very acknowledgments of the book Olsen mentions earth, air, and others as "sustenance" for her own efforts. The major theme of her long afterword to Rebecca Harding Davis's *Life in the Iron Mills* is Davis's hunger to make use of herself and her powers, her hunger to give and produce. Olsen explores the many kinds of hunger in Davis's life and the lives of her characters, whose miserable circumstances meant soul starvation. As Davis identifies with her characters, so Olsen identifies with Davis, especially her "hunger to know."

Repeatedly Olsen blames unsatisfied hunger for non-productivity. Analyzing Katherine Anne Porter's long delay in finishing *Ship of Fools,* Olsen observes that "subterranean forces" need feeding: "before they will feed the creator back they must be fed, passionately fed." Similarly, Olsen describes the destruction of her own powers as a failure in the necessary mutual feeding of art and life: "So long they feed each other—my life, the writing—;—the writing or hope of it, my life—; but now they begin to destroy;."

IV
"Mama Mama you must help carry the world"

Mothers and children are at the heart of almost every Olsen work. The child embodies man's potential greatness and his needy vulnerability. The degree to which adults can mother and nurture children is frequently a sign of their own psychic condition. Because the link between the individual family and the family of man everywhere penetrates Olsen's work, her focus on the nuclear family does not seem narrow or claustrophobic.

In *Yonnondio* Olsen repeatedly uses the word "baby" to suggest beauty and tenderness. Mazie feels a breeze as "soft, like the baby laughin." Gorgeous colors of fire seem to her "like babies' tongues reaching out to you." The healing beauty of the baby-tongued fire melts "the hard swollen lump of tears" into a "swell of wonder and awe." And when the Holbrooks escape from the coal mines, "the sun laid warm hands on their bodies" and "the air was pure and soft like a baby's skin."

Mothers and children are at the heart of almost every Olsen work. The child embodies man's potential greatness and his needy vulnerability.
—Bonnie Lyons

Erina, the epileptic, crippled child from an impoverished, brutalized, and brutalizing family, symbolizes the most humiliated, abused humanity: the child or human as innocent sufferer. The horror of Erina's life is most movingly evoked through her linguistic errors. In the author's brilliant use of children's linguistic errors and connections, *Yonnondio* resembles another Thirties novel, Henry Roth's *Call It Sleep.* But while the confusion of Roth's David Schearl about the ordinary coal and the coal which purified Isaiah's lips is central to a redemptive vision, Olsen's two most memorable uses of this technique are unequivocally pathetic. Olsen first uses the technique early in the novel when Mazie confuses the word "operator" with the idea of a surgical operation and cannot understand how the privileged coal operator "cut up a mine." In the reader's mind the error is suggestive, for the coal operator does indeed cut up the land and the miners themselves. The later use of the device is much more chilling. The monstrous distortions of her life have taught Erina, a most Dostoevskian character, to interpret the Biblical line, "suffer the children," as "the children suffer." Erina's twisting of the meaning of the word *suffer* from "allow" into "bear painfully" perfectly embodies Olsen's outraged sense of the world's derangement. It is worth noting that even Erina is not totally reduced to inhumanity. On her way home, "where she will be beaten," she sees a bird "bathing itself, fluttering its wings in delight." Erina feels in herself "the shining, the fluttering happiness" and for a few minutes walks "in the fluttering shining and the peace."

Erina is the novel's deepest and most frightening image of human suffering; Bess, the Holbrook baby, represents human possibility and power. In the midst of an oppressive heat wave, Bess, while playing with a fruit-jar lid, discovers her powers: "Lightning in her brain." the novel celebrates her coming to consciousness: "Centuries of human drive work in her; human ecstasy of achievement; satisfaction deep and fundamental as sex: *I can do, I use my powers*; I! I!" With her "eternal dream look" Bess is the promise, the possibility.

In **"I Stand Here Ironing,"** the mother speaks of Emily as a tender young plant, bemoans the fact that Emily never had "the soil of easy growth," and concludes that "all that is in her will not bloom." She also remembers Emily's miraculous capacity for learning and delight when she was a baby and trusts that "there is enough left to live by." Similarly, the uncollected story **"Requa"** suggests that early damage can be overcome, that a hurt, withdrawn child can be reclaimed, that later care can revive a wilting plant.

In **"Hey Sailor"** Whitey's sense of loss, of his lost past and empty future, is most acute when he touches his friends' children: "It is destroying, dissolving him utterly, this helpless warmth against him, this feel of a child—lost country to him and unattainable." Even more terrible to him is the general horror: "The begging children and the lost, the thieving children and the children who were sold." The relative financial and emotional security of Lennie and Helen's home coupled with their sympathy and moral sense will help to bring their children to fruition, but the reality of other children's lost and wasted lives is not forgotten, never forgiven.

In several of her stories Olsen focuses more on the mother and nurturing process than on the child. In particular, **"O Yes"** is a story of mothering, especially the moral and emotional aspects. Two women "mother" Carol. Parry's mother Alva tries to teach Carol about the meaning of their release and ecstasy in church, and Helen tries to ease Carol through the *"long baptism into the seas of humankind."* Alva's classic death and rebirth dream-memory embodies several mother/child relationships. A small boy leads Alva on her journey; in order to ascend, Alva needs her own mother's hands, and the final injunction to Alva as mother completes the journey. The child leads the mother whose journey is helped by her own mother and who is enjoined as mother to "help carry the world." Nurturing is thus the road and the rule.

In *Silences* Olsen describes motherhood as both the *"core* of woman's oppression" and her "transport as woman." This dual description of motherhood is most vividly embodied in **"Tell Me a Riddle,"** which brilliantly evokes the complexity and depth of the mother/child relationship, as well as the wisdom and richness that motherhood has brought to this aging mother and grandmother.

Eva looks back at her youthful mothering and remembers the poverty and want, the "old humiliations and terrors," and the "endless defeating battles" of housekeeping. Part of her bitterness is about the poverty, and part is directed at her husband who never thought of her needs, never helped at home, never stayed with the children so that she could have some life outside the home.

But her memory is not just of the chafing limitations but also "the love—the passion of tending" that had "risen with the need like a torrent." Eva has now lived through that period: "the need was done." Unlike more limited, traditional women suffering from the empty nest syndrome, she is sure there is more: "Somewhere an older power that beat for life."

Eva is characterized as more than just a biological mother of a large family; she is also a woman concerned since her youth about developing human potential. When she first sees the Pacific Ocean, she looks "toward the shore that nurtured life as it first crawled toward consciousness the millions of years ago." As biological and symbolic mother, Eva looks back at her own family history and at human history, especially the history of life in this century. She sees the revolutionary dreams and the monstrous facts, including millions with "no graves—save air," the holocaust victims. As the seashore reminds Eva of the developing human infant, the aged, including her pathetic friend Mrs. Mays, suggest the terrible waste, the incompletion. The unfulfilled aged suggest that the overall direction may not be higher consciousness but rather destruction and self-destruction: "Everywhere unused the life. . . . Century after century still all in us not to grow."

V
"A song, a poem of itself—the world itself a dirge"

Directly, as in the early poetry, and indirectly, as in Eva's dream in **"Tell Me a Riddle,"** Olsen celebrates human potential, mourns what has been lost, and anticipates a time when the world will be changed so that human capacities will not be wasted.

"A song, a poem of itself—the word itself a dirge," these three phrases of Whitman's introductory explanatory note to his poem "Yonnodio" are emblematic of Olsen's vision and her borrowing of this title for her one and only novel is noteworthy. In Olsen's art, the song and dirge are the poles of human life: the fruit and the blight.

The dirge is not primarily a response to any natural calamity or death. This is clearest in **"Tell Me a Riddle."** There Eva's excruciating physical decline into death is not the deepest source of pain. In fact, her decision to experience her own death—refusing the sterile, painless, numb hospital death—is a personal triumph: she has chosen a death of her own. She stays with her family and experiences everything, including her own terrible physical pain. For her and for the reader, the deepest agony is, on the contrary, the realization of what has died prematurely in her, what through unnatural causes never flowered. For her the dirge laments what has been thwarted by circumstances—primarily poverty but also rigid sex role prescriptions. Even more than the limitations of her own life, Eva and the author mourn Eva's

(and mankind's) dream of peace, freedom, education, humaneness: the fulfillment of the individual and a harmonious society. The deepest dread is the either/or that mankind faces—growth and progress or annihilation. Wasted lives, unused potential, and the threat of nuclear holocaust—this is the dirge in Olsen's work.

The song, the other pole, celebrates what mankind can experience and express. It is the possibility, the undying hope, that never totally relinquished dream. It is the part of Olsen that, in **Silences,** after listing the lost and ruined writers and analyzing the multiple causes of the blight, insists, "AND YET THE TREE DID—DOES BEAR FRUIT." It is embodied in Eva (with whom Olsen explicitly identifies in *Silences*) who continues to dream, whose continued hope keeps the dream alive and verifies its essential value and possibility: the "stained words" of her youthful dream song, stained by what the century did to kill the dream, "on her working lips came stainless."

Olsen's exploration of the dirge and song of human life reflects her experience as a Jew and as a woman. Her ideology recapitulates the radical Jewish socialist background in which she grew up; her analysis in terms of the body and the mother/child relationship reflect her deeply felt experiences as a woman. Song and dirge alike emerge from the one radical (in the sense of root, fundamental) condition: the single individual in all his vulnerability, hunger, and yearning potentialities. The uncanny bitter-sweet harmonies Olsen has created by interweaving dirge and song, by vividly depicting the sheltering of or preying upon vulnerabilities, the nurturing or starving of hungers, the fulfillment or blighting of potentials—these give her own music its intense emotional resonance, as the song and dirge merge into a luminous, all encompassing chord: "the poem of itself."

Michael Staub (essay date Autumn 1988)

SOURCE: "The Struggle for 'Selfness' through Speech in Olsen's *Yonnondio: From the Thirties,*" in *Studies in American Fiction,* Vol. 16, No. 2, Autumn, 1988, pp. 131-39.

[*In the following essay, Staub traces Olsen's focus on self-articulation and the freedom it brings.*]

Tillie Olsen's only novel, **Yonnondio: From the Thirties,** written between 1932 and 1937 but not published until 1974, concerns a migrant family's impossible dream: the search for happiness and security in a world they never made. It is an often shocking book, one that makes vivid the brutal consequences of homelessness and poverty on a married couple, Jim and Anna Holbrook, and their five children: Mazie, Will, Ben, Jimmie, and baby Bess. As it proceeds, however, it is apparent that the novel belongs primarily to Anna and to Mazie, her oldest daughter, and their efforts to speak and be heard in a hostile environment. From its opening sentence ("The whistles always woke Mazie") through to its final description ("He is too dazed to listen" [p. 154]), *Yonnondio* is a highly compressed catalogue of sounds and silences. As the family migrates eastward from a Wyoming coal-mining community to a South Dakota tenant farm to the slaughter-houses of Kansas City, a theme emerges: that women and girls of the working class will never identify their own concerns at home or in the society at large, and will never be able to change their lives for the better, until they can create forums where their individual stories are heard, shared, and debated.

In this way, *Yonnondio* is part of a much larger body of 1930s "consciousness-raising" literature (James Agee and Walker Evans' *Let Us Now Praise Famous Men* on white Southern tenant farmers, John Neihardt's *Black Elk Speaks* on Native Americans, and the Federal Writer's Project's *These Are Our Lives* on black Southern tenant farmers) that counseled middle-class Americans to *listen* to impoverished minorities before presuming what assistance they needed and then acting on their behalf. What distinguishes *Yonnondio,* and what makes it an especially valuable contribution to any examination of the Depression era, is its presentation of a working-class feminism that defends the human rights of all working women to be freed from abusive relations within their families and communities and to achieve what the novel calls "selfness" through speech. From the perspective of the book, to be denied an audience that cares to listen, or fails to listen, women—and particularly poor women—will die or descend into madness. For such women, the struggle for "selfness" was often nothing less than a struggle for survival.

A great deal of *Yonnondio* concerns the trials of working-class girlhood, and this subject is pursued by chronicling the articulations and subsequent subjugation of the visions and instincts of a female child. This child, Mazie Holbrook, represents "poverty's arithmetic": the slow, pained subtraction of dreams and wonder from the young lives of the dispossessed. Mazie is a bright girl, but one who never will get the chance to break the double bonds of being poor and female. Her initiation into social awareness is suffused with violence, hunger, and shame. Over the course of the book, her hopes become lost in a crazy quilt of oppressive relationships and banal afflictions. Mazie's voice, at first hesitant but insistently curious, seems to disappear altogether amidst the images and voices at the end of Olsen's disjointed narrative.

Speech and "selfness" are related in *Yonnondio* by the presentation of "a reverse case": Mazie's speechlessness results in her identity confusion. Life for Mazie meant the power of pushing "her mind hard against things half known, not

known," and she struggles with her limited comprehension of the world around her. Thus she becomes a near-perfect vehicle for innocent observation and vulnerability. Mazie's mental health appears to depend on an ability to speak and to know the meaning of what she sees. Consequently, when continually rebuffed and silenced, Mazie descends into a trancelike madness over the course of *Yonnondio.* "I know words and words," Mazie says in *Yonnondio's* opening pages. "Tipple. Edjication. Bug dust. Superintendent." But the words, like the world from which they arise, are disjointed pieces of a whole whose meaning eludes the young girl.

Quite unsentimentally, Olsen conveys the brutality of the cacophonous world Mazie must decipher with a memorable expressiveness from the opening paragraph:

> The whistles always woke Mazie. They pierced into her sleep like some guttural-voiced metal beast, tearing at her; breathing a terror. During the day if the whistle blew, she knew it meant death— somebody's poppa or brother, perhaps her own— in that fearsome place below the ground, the mine.

The Wyoming coal mine is a living organism for Mazie Holbrook, and the whistle that sounds the work shifts and announces deaths is this creature's vocal chord or "iron throat." This "voice" tears into Mazie's sleep each morning, waking her to a strange and dangerous reality. "Bowels of earth," Mazie says to herself. "It means the mines. Bowels is the stummy. Earth is a stummy and mebbe she eats the men that come down." The men, including Mazie's father, enter the iron throat each morning and return each evening blackened with coal. The half-knowledge of the work her father does and the feeling that the mine is a living thing fill Mazie with fear and pain. She wants to know "what makes people a-cryen" and whether or not ghosts live down in the mines . She asks this of her father, "half cringing," although "somehow the question she had meant to have answered could not be clamped into words." Thus from the very outset in *Yonnondio,* Mazie is silenced by her fears.

From the perspective of [*Yonnondio*], to be denied an audience that cares to listen, or fails to listen, women—and particularly poor women—will die or descend into madness. For such women, the struggle for "selfness" was often nothing less than a struggle for survival.
—*Michael Staub*

Soon after, Mazie once again finds herself voiceless when she encounters Sheen McEvoy, a miner who has lost his face and his mind in a mine blast. Like Mazie, McEvoy believes that the mine is alive, a hungry goddess of the earth. In McEvoy's imagination, sacrificing Mazie to the mine shaft would save the lives of countless numbers of men. "Give her a sweet baby," McEvoy says, "and she'll want no more." As he stands beside the mine shaft with Mazie in his arms, he addresses the mine directly: "I am giving you your baby." Mazie is unable to speak or to scream:

> Screams tore at Mazie's throat, caged there. Sweat poured over her. She closed her eyes. He strode toward the shaft. He kissed her with his shapeless face. In Mazie her heart fainted, and fainted, but her head stayed clear. "Make it a dream, momma, poppa, come here, make it a dream." But no words would come.

A night watchman appears just in time and saves Mazie's life. When this other man appears, Mazie finally screams and McEvoy drops her just beside the iron throat of the shaft. The two men fight, the night watchman pulls a gun, shoots three times, and McEvoy stumbles and falls in the mine shaft and is himself sacrificed to the earth mother.

The consequences of this incident are profound for the Holbrook family. They decide that they must leave the mining town as soon as their limited finances permit. But more important are the undefined scars left on Mazie; the episode leaves her in a state of shock: "In her delirium Mazie laughed—terrible laughter, mocking, derisive, not her own. Anna and Jim, hearing it mix with their words, shuddered." Although Mazie will go on with her life, she begins to experience "a voiceless dream" in which "suddenly she would see before her a monster thing with blind eyes and shaking body that gave out great guttural sobs." As the story unfolds, Olsen continues to stress Mazie's horrible silent visions and how her inability to speak both results from and causes an ill-defined sense of self.

The one hopeful interlude in this progressive deterioration is short-lived. When the family arrives on a farm in South Dakota where they become tenants, Mazie finds the first confidant she has ever had. He is an old man named Caldwell, "who had come west from college and wealth and chosen to live and build out of the wilderness." Caldwell offers Mazie a hint of the knowledge she could be learning; he teaches her about the stars and constellations. He also offers her poems, books (although her father sells them for fifty cents), and a bit of wisdom (although "the words were incomprehensible"): "Mazie. Live, don't exist. Learn from your mother, who has had everything to grind out life and yet has kept life. Alive, felt what's real, known what's real. People can live their whole life without knowing." But, as expected, Caldwell's death signals new hard times for Mazie. For example, when her family moves yet again, this time to

Kansas City, she begins to induce her visions again by pressing her fingers into her eyes. Her "wondering dazed eyes" imagine that the move to the city was "just a dream, a bad dream." Mazie fails her report card in school and is soon imagining skeleton babies in her visions, starved and grotesque. "The nightmare feeling" she has felt ever since her encounter with Sheen McEvoy becomes more common and pronounced. Further, when she wishes now to relate the awful visions to her parents, she is not able: "There was something she wanted to say, but she could not remember it."

There are further moments in *Yonnondio* that concern Mazie's confusion over her identity and how her dementia relates to an inability to speak and be heard. For example, when Mazie attends school for the first time and learns to read, "the crooked white words on the second-grade blackboard magically transforming into words known and said", her schooling brings with it unintended side-effects: "For the first time, Mazie was acutely conscious of her scuffed shoes, rag-bag clothes, quilt coat." With new knowledge came a new shame and self-consciousness at her poverty. As a consequence, Mazie retreats from the classroom lessons and "spent most of [her] time listening secretly to the upper grades recite jography and history—far countries, strange people." She is far better at listening to spoken words and stories than she is at reading aloud. For Mazie, like the rest of the Holbrook children, "had been judged poor learners, dumb dumb dumb" because of a disinterest in their studies. Even "onceuponatime and theylivedveryhappyeverafterfairy tales" can not hold Mazie's attention. Although she becomes literate over the course of the novel, she never puts this ability to use. Her intelligence lies dormant and neglected, and Mazie retreats further into a fantasy world.

Towards the end of *Yonnondio,* the confusions that have arisen in Mazie reach a new point of crisis. Her fears and terrors locate themselves in another moment of visions: "O it's us again, thinks Mazie, it's us. Then in clenching fear: Now something bad's going to have to happen. Again." It is not clear, however, what this passage signifies. Mazie faints from the extreme summer heat, she is teased by a group of children, but at the end she is asked by her younger brother, Ben, to explain bad dreams: "'Splain to me about bad dreams,' he whispers into her ear, 'tell me about boogie mans and scaredies and ghosts and hell.'" There is no doubt that Mazie is the right person in the Holbrook family to ask about such things, but Mazie never responds. Mazie's movement towards madness is left half-formulated. Whether or not she would emerge from her dreams and visions to live a saner life is left unanswered. It is implicit, however, that she will not.

Mazie's mother, Anna Holbrook, is a character whose power of speech relates directly to her "selfness." In the opening pages, Anna speaks to her husband, Jim, about a woman friend whose son will go to work for the first time that morning. The friend, whose husband was killed in a mine blast, "talks about the coal. Says it oughta be red, and let people see how they get it with blood." "Quit your woman's blabbin'," Jim Holbrook tells his wife. Jim's defeated attitude and misdirected anger deafens him to the truths Anna articulates about the pain of their lives. For the most part, Jim's dreams hurt too much; they only remind him of what he never had himself. Anna, unlike her husband, has a dream for her children and does put into words (when she can) what it is she wants them to have. For example, when Mazie asks her mother "What's an edication?" Anna responds:

> "An edjication?" Anna Holbrook arose from amidst the shifting vapors of the washtub, and with the suds dripping from her red hands, walked over and stood impressively over Mazie. "An edjication is what you kids are going to get. It means your hands stay white and you read books and work in an office. Now, get the kids and scat. But don't go too far, or I'll knock your block off."

Anna's struggle for "selfness" in *Yonnondio* is fired by her hope of saving her children. With her oldest daughter traumatized, her husband stuck in horrible working conditions, her oldest son, Will, growing up in the streets, and her youngest child possibly in need of expensive medical attention, Anna still struggles to make a better life for her family and simply will not give up. She does, however, bear the weight of her dreams, and she suffers fainting spells, a dazed illness, a miscarriage, and a disconcerting fantasy-life not unlike that of her daughter. When a neighbor suggests she try a tonic that says it is for "all female complaints," Anna responds, "all female complaints, huh? Well, I guess I got all of them."

Anna carries the unenviable burdens for maintaining a semblance of home and family life during constant crisis and dislocation. When the family moves to a tenant farm in South Dakota, it is with the aim of "a new life." But the phrase, first spoken by Jim in earnestness, becomes for Anna an ironic expression of despair that things will never get better for her and her children. Jim Holbrook, a "good" and well-intentioned man, refuses to accept full responsibility for his actions and wavers between the terrible non-choices of abandonment, alcoholism, and abusive behavior. In *Yonnondio,* Anna suffers the consequences of each of these tendencies in her husband.

There are a variety of ways in which Anna's speeches identify her struggle for "selfness." For example, it is Anna, more than anyone else in the novel, who loves to sing:

> I saw a ship a sailing
> her mother sang.

> A sailing on the sea

Mazie felt the strange happiness in her mother's body, happiness that had nought to do with them, with her; happiness and farness and selfness.

> I saw a ship a sailing
> And on that ship was me.

The fingers stroked, spun a web, cocooned Mazie into happiness and intactness and selfness. Soft wove the bliss round hurt and fear and want and shame—the old worn fragile bliss, a new frail selfness bliss, healing, transforming.

The dreaminess and peace of this moment is shortly broken when one of her children announces that he is hungry. Anna retreats from her tenuous pleasure and returns to her pressing task as a mother of five. But singing provides "selfness" for Anna *and* Mazie at several points throughout *Yonnondio.* It is a mechanism for coping with sorrows and unfulfilled dreams.

The sense of how strong Mazie's mother is, and how remarkable her daily triumphs over the privations of poverty are, emerges slowly. Much of the second half of the novel chronicles the consciousness of Anna, and what is made most explicit is the torment that her dreams for her children may be battered beyond hope. Nevertheless, while Anna's silences often reflect a day-to-day straining against exhaustion and defeat, Anna in small moments is able to speak her hopes.

For example, after her miscarriage, Anna is bed-ridden, unable to clean the house or keep track of her kids. When she is finally able to rise, Anna pulls herself weakly through the empty house:

> The kitchen stood blank and empty in glaring afternoon sun. It was a long while before she could make out the potato peels turning black on the garbage in the sink, the dirty dishes, the souring bottle of milk about which flies droned. Flies, the poster said, Spread Germs. Germs Breed Disease. Cleaving to the table for support, disregarding the flame of agony in her engorged breasts, she swatted feverishly. The flies lifted and evaded. Disease . . . Your children . . . Protect . . . The soap was gone, the water spluttered malevolently at her. She rinsed the dishes, scooped the garbage up into a pot, and went out into the yard.

Anna finds the cover off the garbage pail, and she stuffs both pot and garbage into the pail, then jams the cover on. Nausea overcomes her, but Anna "scarcely realizing that she was doing so," goes back to the pail and removes the slippery pot, despite the horrible stench of the trash. It is perhaps her only pot, and it can scarcely be thrown away so casually, and so Anna almost instinctively retrieves it. Trembling, she returns to the house: "All she could do was sit there, her head against the screen door, her eyes closed, waiting for the trembling and faintness to cease. Slowly, slowly, her fingers loosened, and the pot slipped from her hand to the ground."

This could be interpreted, as one critic has suggested, as part of "a terrible losing battle, the battle to get out from under that the poor almost never win." The pathetic effort Anna makes to save the pot seemingly confirms this interpretation that the novel chronicles "a terrible losing battle" of migrant life through the most commonplace of everyday details. However, what follows this "defeat" is especially striking:

> Softly, she began to sing. Now a train puffed by, and the long wail dissolved in distance. The wind just lifted against her cheek. Ben came from nowhere and nozzled against her. Momma, he said. She held him warm into her singing.

To interpret an intimate and private moment like this one as representative of failure is to erase and undervalue the dignity and spirit of Anna Holbrook's life. Anna is a woman of great human capabilities, operating under severe limitations, and yet managing nonetheless to express herself with sensitivity, pride, and compassion. Anna is constantly pressed-down economically, socially, and psychologically. Yet she always presses back through singing, loving her children, and affirming what she believes is right.

Not long after the incident with the pot, Jim confronts Anna; he tries to argue his sick wife back into bed. She refuses angrily. Jim insists and Anna again articulates her faded hopes for her children:

> "Dont sweet Anna me. Who's to do it if I'm not up? Answer. *Who?* Who's to . . . look out for . . ." Gasping hoarsely. "Who's to care about 'em if we dont? Who? . . . *Who?* Answer me . . . Oh Jim," giving in, collapsing into his reaching embrace, "the children." Over and over, broken: "the children. What's going to happen with them? How we going to look out for them? O Jim, the children. Seems like we cant do nothing for them in this damn world."

The intensity of Anna's speech at this point in the narrative is a crucial moment. Anna's credo becomes enacted over the course of the novel; the singing and this speech represent the core of her resistance to submission. It is her method for reaffirming her human spirit and her children's right to a life better than the one she had been born into. Anna's efforts to express her own needs and values underscore the theme

of the novel as a whole: That a person's self-articulation leads to self-knowledge which can lead to an end to oppressive familial and social relationships. Anna's few speeches that dot the landscape of *Yonnondio* become critical for an understanding of the connections made between speech and "selfness." Anna's remarkable character is not expressed through dramatic action but rather through dramatic speech. Thus one key to a fuller understanding of this novel depends upon an ability to see the speaking and silences of its two central characters as linked to their survival.

In her unpublished notes and drafts for the novel, Olsen reflects further on the near-impossibility of creating the circumstances that allow articulation for women. "How easily women give up the battle after marriage—become mothers and wives, secondary, instead of mothers and wives—*and growing human beings*—." In another passage, Olsen wrote:

> MY BABIES, MY CHILDREN—
>
> Anguished cry that breaks soundless in her throat. Outside nothing answers. There is only the smell of the earth, expectant of rain, the mysterious blue light that is on everything, the trees moving secretly against the sky, the sound of a freight starting up, hoarse, strained, labored. Heavy to take up again, the burden of being poor and a mother.

From the available notes and drafts it appears that Olsen had several different ideas on how to proceed with her unpublished novel. In one version, Jim Holbrook, the ambivalent breadwinner, runs off and abandons his family. In another, Jim leads a strike and is blacklisted. In a third, Anna attempts suicide by leaving the gas jets on and blocking all the doors in the room. In another, it is Will, the oldest boy, who runs off and becomes a vagabond waif, a common sight during the Depression years.

Despite the drama of these possibilities, the focus on the relationship between articulation and the female search for self is once again reinforced in the final pages of the novel. There is a last irrepressible celebration of life, this time by the youngest female character, baby Bess. It is summer during a terrible heat wave. Jim sits dazed from the intense heat and from working, the children are having bad dreams, and Anna sings to her baby, Bess, at the kitchen table:

> *Bang!*
>
> Bess who has been fingering a fruit-jar lid—absently, heedlessly dropped it—aimlessly groping across the table, reclaims it again. Lightning in her brain. She releases, grabs, releases, grabs. I can do. Bang! I did that. I can do. I! A look of neanderthal concentration is on her face. That noise! In trium-

phant, astounded joy she clashes the lid down. Bang, slam, whack. Release, grab, slam, bang, bang. Centuries of human drive work in her; human ecstasy of achievement; satisfaction deep and fundamental as sex: *I can do, I use my powers*; I! I!

The relationship between sound and "selfness" is once more made clear. But there the novel ends, and thus in the 1930s *Yonnondio* itself became a silenced text that could not be fully articulated. While some critics agree with Jack Salzman that *Yonnondio* is "a magnificent novel," others debate whether or not the lack of "polish" in the book is a problem. For example, Selma Burkom and Margaret Williams have commented that "*Yonnondio* flies off in many directions, not all of which are equally developed or coalesce with the others." On the other hand, Amy Godine says of *Yonnondio:* "The absence of a finished, flowing, conventional plot simply underscores [Olsen's] point that it is the incidental, commonplace, fragmentary detail that really imperils the quality of human life."

But the question of how "unfinished" *Yonnondio* is diverts attention from its extraordinary accomplishments. Unlike many of the poor in 1930s literature, Olsen's characters refuse to die, kill themselves, or submit to any higher authority. They err, hurt one another, and dream unfulfilled dreams, but they do not acknowledge their own second-class existence. "I was writing about great human beings," Olsen says, "and the circumstances in which they find themselves. I was writing about how circumstances shape people and how children are formed and deformed. My writing came out of what I knew and saw in other human beings." *Yonnondio* establishes how people make changes in their lives when things grow intolerable and further argues "that it is *all wrong* that people have to live in such circumstances [like the Holbrooks] when they are capable of so much. The Holbrooks were who I would be if I had led that life. You feel such respect when you know them and the agony of their defeats. They never realize what possibilities there could have been."

Yonnondio, after all, is a novel about possibility. The variety of possible directions Olsen considered for the conclusion of *Yonnondio* can best be seen as representative of the sense of hope and promise she held out for her novel and for her characters. And Olsen's struggle to write a novel that captured the authenticity both of the suffering of the poor and of their self-articulation is testimony to her hope that speaking out about injustice is the first step towards righting wrongs.

Helen Pike Bauer (essay date 1989)

SOURCE: "'A Child of Anxious, Not Proud, Love': Mother and Daughter in Tillie Olsen's 'I Stand Here Ironing,'" in *Mother Puzzles: Daughter and Mothers in Contemporary American Literature,* edited by Mickey Pearlman, Greenwood Press, 1989, pp. 35-9.

[*In the following essay, Bauer remarks on the themes of hope and despair within the mother-daughter relationship in* "I Stand Here Ironing."]

"I stand here ironing" begins the narrator in Tillie Olsen's short story that takes its title from that opening line. These are words that would never introduce a male narrator, and the facts of her woman's life, its emotional as well as economic exigencies and constraints, provide the context for this unnamed mother's meditation on her daughter Emily. A school counselor has asked to meet with her to discuss Emily, a child the counselor finds troubled and in need of help. The mother's unspoken response, "what good would it do?", introduces the questioning note on which the story expands. It is a tale of virtually unalleviated strain on the mother and daughter. But the conflicts in the story are not between them; they are within the mother. She weighs her own responsibility for the circumstances of Emily's life, acknowledges both her own power and powerlessness. And she looks with dread toward her daughter's future, afraid that it will be a joyless, meager existence consequent upon a childhood when there was not enough money or time for emotional nourishment. She fears that her daughter's life will be merely an extension of her own, the bitter fruit of labor and privation. Indeed, throughout most of the story Emily seems to reflect, in her complex and fragile psychological state, her mother's lifelong economic precariousness. But Emily comes to embody not only the immediate effects such a mother's life can have on a child, but also her mother's strength, the still living impulse toward life and harmony that she has maintained and protected.

Her mother's evocation of Emily's past life is an attempt to understand her daughter's character. Emily we are told repeatedly, has been an unhappy child. Although beautiful and joyous in infancy, nurtured by her mother, sensuously alive to light and music and texture, Emily was soon left with neighbors, then with relatives, and finally with day-care institutions to allow her mother, abandoned by her husband, to go out each day to work. It is this displacement and deprivation, Emily's being shunted off to indifferent, unresponsive strangers, that her mother feels have created the somberness, the passivity and repression that seem to characterize the present Emily.

Part of the mother's analysis, then, is a sorting out of responsibility for Emily's personality. Her child is troubled and this mother searches through the experiences of her own life to see if she could have done better. But the narrator does not take on a burden of excessive guilt. She is acutely aware of the brutal restrictions on her life. Economically alone and lonely, overworked, tired, she gave Emily all she could. But she could not give her the abundant time allowed to those in easier circumstances.

In this story, time is the first casualty of poverty. And Olsen emphasizes lack of time as the first and last restriction in the mother's consciousness. "I wish you would manage the time to come in," says the counselor. "When is there time?", thinks the mother. The tyranny of the timetable is felt repeatedly in the story. Though her infant cries and the mother trembles with the urge to feed her, she "waited till the clock decreed." For those authorities, medical and sociological, who set models of behavior for others, often define those models in terms of time; natural impulses must give way to a schedule. Jobs have their appointed hours too, and at the end of each day the mother rushes home on the streetcar to pick up her baby at a neighbor's and spend a few evening hours with her. Emily, too, suffers consciously under time's insistent power. It is the clock that she throws away when she lies awake waiting for her mother and stepfather to come home. "The clock talked loud," she explains; "it scared me what it talked." The clock, a symbol of our communal agreement to measure our lives inexorably, is placed against human rhythms that do not scare but create a natural medium for the mutual love between a mother and child. The luxury of that kind of time did not exist for Emily, although it does for the narrator's other children. We see the mother at leisure with her youngest child: "we sit for a while and I hold him, looking out over the city spread in charcoal with its soft aisles of light." Her quiet sitting, looking outward peacefully, holding the baby in her arms until he falls asleep, contrasts forcefully with the one scene we have of Emily's infancy. The narrator, at the end of a working day, would rush to the babysitter's to retrieve her child; "when she saw me she would break into a clogged weeping that could not be comforted, a weeping I can hear yet." Giving the claims of motherhood their due time allows those claims their proper fulfillment; a tired child falls asleep in his mother's arms. But Emily's weeping, the result of her mother's absence at work, is a sound that is never silenced; her mother hears it forever.

Lack of money and lack of time constitute the dimensions of the mother's powerlessness. She describes her decisions repeatedly in terms of having to do something. "I had to leave her daytimes"; "I had to bring her to his family"; "I had had to send her away again." The story is filled with expressions of compulsion and lack of choice: "It was the only place there was. It was the only way we could be together, the only way I could hold a job." And Emily shares these constrictions. Sent away to a convalescent home, she received "letters she could never hold or keep." Back home, "she had to help be a mother and housekeeper, and shopper. She had to set her seal." Emily, like her mother, must

accept the hard realities of life and act within its limitations. In this, they differ from Emily's father, who gives up the struggle and abandons his family. Emily and her mother do not give up.

Indeed, the mother and daughter share strengths of which the mother is not always aware. The narrator has struggled through intensely difficult times. Without money, education, skills, deserted at nineteen with an eight-month-old child, she worked to support the two of them. She reared, often while working outside the house, several other children, seemingly without much help from her second husband. And she has lived through it all. But she fears that Emily's life will be simply the grim reprise of her own impoverished existence of struggle, fear, too little time, too little money, that Emily will come to share her look of "care or tightness or worry." And, indeed, the mother sees herself in Emily; "her face is closed and sober." She sees too the ways that Emily differs from her younger brothers and sisters in both appearance and personality. Susan, the next youngest, grows into a blonde, lively, lovely child with a talent for being companionable and attractive to others. Emily, thin, dark, silent, awkward, is always aloof. For the younger children are the products of less austere times, members of a family with its attendant noise and comfort. Emily spent her young life without such easements. Like her mother, she has known long years alone and has felt their toll. Her mother understands this and fears for Emily. If much modern fiction reveals a daughter's dread of reliving her mother's life, Olsen's story dramatizes a mother's dread of that fate for her daughter.

But the reader sees the mother's strength more fully than the mother does herself. Indeed, the narrator's ability to survey her life and apportion responsibility for it shows her keen intelligence; her ability to meet life's demands without succumbing to either a paralyzing guilt or an emotional dessication shows her strength of character. And Emily shares some of her mother's power.

> **Olsen's story ["I Stand Here Ironing"] is a dialogue between circumstances and desire, constraint and love, absence and presence, silence and speech, power and helplessness.**
> **—*Helen Pike Bauer***

Emily, however, also possesses qualities all her own. She is nineteen in the story, the same age her mother was when she was deserted. But Emily's life at this moment is very different from her mother's. She is in school, and although the counselor is disturbed by her, we do not readily see why. The one glimpse we have of her is the laughing, witty young woman who teases her mother before running off to bed,

"Aren't you ever going to finish the ironing, Mother? Whistler painted his mother in a rocker. I'd have to paint mine standing over an ironing board." And, in fact, her mother is surprised by the energy and spark that Emily possesses. Emily has a comic talent, a gift for pantomime that shocks her mother. The first time she saw Emily on the stage, her mother could not believe it was her somber daughter. "Was this Emily? the control, the command, the convulsing and deadly clowning, the spell, then the roaring, stamping audience, unwilling to let this rare and precious laughter out of their lives." Emily's talent for mimicry and movement, the comic exaggeration that is pantomime, cannot be accounted for by her mother's memories. And although her mother fears that Emily's gifts will never be fully developed because the family lacks the money and resources to aid and encourage her, we see, even in the small flowering of her talent and her youthful, high spirits, a sign of hope for Emily.

In the story's powerful final paragraph, the mother utters a kind of prayer. "Let her be. So all that is in her will not bloom—but in how many does it? There is still enough left to live by. Only help her to believe—help make it so there is cause for her to believe that she is more than this dress on the ironing board, helpless before the iron." Throughout the story the mother has acknowledged how little she could do for her daughter, at first how little money and time, and, in a larger sense, how little self-confidence and joy she could provide. But Emily has withstood her privations and proved her strength. Human life contains the possibility of the inexplicable gift, the spark for which others can take neither praise nor blame. The mother, in surveying her daughter's life, sees the threads that form the pattern, but she is still surprised by the figure that emerges, and is still able to hope. And the reader, perhaps because we do not know what occasioned the counselor's fears, perhaps because the only Emily we see directly is this laughing young woman, has reason to believe that the mother's prayer may be answered. Emily's character may bear the mark of her childhood's deprivations, but she has talent and strength, an auspicious alliance.

Olsen's story resists easy optimism, however. The author makes her characters' circumstances as difficult as possible. Theirs is a world of poverty, monotonous labor, estrangement, and sickness. Children are taken away; friends are taken away; when people most need each other, the quarantine of illness separates them. The mother's life is economically and spiritually hard, and her sense of human existence reflects that. She speaks of her children as "needing, demanding, hurting, taking"; she defines motherhood as the time "when the ear is not one's own but must always be racked and listening for the child cry." Although she is only thirty-eight years old, she sees her productive life as past. Olsen's art depicts a world of physically exhausting, spiritually enervating labor and its psychic and domestic costs.

In *Yonnondio,* her unfinished novel, Olsen explores the lives of the poor on the farm and in the factory during the 1930s. But in that fragment, Olsen's characters never achieve the self-knowledge that can make meaning out of pain. Acutely but inchoately aware of their plight, they yearn for a finer reality, but never move beyond the life they know. In *Silences,* her book-length compendium of reflections on creativity and the forces that impede it, she speaks of the particular burdens attendant upon being both poor and female: the toil, responsibility, triviality, and distractions that prevent such artists from expression. These are her subjects—the forces in the lives of the poor, especially poor women, that are inimical to life and voice. In **"I Stand Here Ironing,"** however, the reader, moving through memory to vision and finally to prayer, can contemplate not just the iron, the force of fate, but the desire for fulfillment that begins to find an answer in reality.

Olsen's story is a dialogue between circumstances and desire, constraint and love, absence and presence, silence and speech, power and helplessness. Much of what the mother sees is negative. But the inner world, the domain of love and desire, are not entirely helpless before the outer world. Emily has her own personality. People respond to her and want to help her. The physical beauty that she had as a baby has returned; her early love of motion, light, color, music, and textures has found a resurrection in art. And that state which Olsen so often uses as a metaphor for repression and silence, here exemplified in the mother's reluctance to speak with the counselor, is transformed through Emily's medium, pantomime, into the creative expression of art.

Olsen portrays powerfully the economic and domestic burdens a poor woman bears, as well as the sense of both responsibility and powerlessness she feels over her children's lives. Olsen sees, however, the particular tie between a mother and daughter, explored both here and in *Yonnondio.* In **"I Stand Here Ironing,"** she develops a mother's two vantage points, reflection and projection. She can review her own experience and wish her daughter to escape it, to break the pattern, be released into a fuller intellectual and emotional life. The biological tie between mother and daughter is often extrapolated into a cultural presumption that defines girls' lives as following their mothers'. But this mother does not define Emily in traditional female terms; she does not, for example, focus on her daughter's likelihood of becoming a wife and mother. Instead she hopes for a defined selfhood for Emily, a core of self-confidence, a sense of self-worth. Even in the flinty world that this story traces, Olsen demonstrates enough faith in human resilience to hope that a daughter might find a better path than her mother trod.

Kathy Wolfe (essay date 1993)

SOURCE: "'Coming to Writing' Through the Impressionist Fiction of Tillie Olsen," in *Midwestern Miscellany XXI*, edited by David D. Anderson, Midwestern Press, 1993, pp. 57-67.

[*In the following essay, Wolfe compares "I Stand Here Ironing" with "Hey Sailor, What Ship?" as she explores Olsen's concept of universal hope.*]

Trying to define Tillie Olsen's "place" in the history of the short story is difficult, not only because of her comparatively small output, but also because she is "known and admired much more because of what she represents than because of what she has written." Olsen is best known for her insights (chronicled in *Silences*) into the difficulties—such as poverty, illness, family responsibilities, etc.—that block the way to success, especially in writing (and especially concerning women). She speaks of, and to, "the gifted among women (*and men*) [who] have remained mute, or have never attained full capacity . . . because of circumstances, inner or outer, which oppose the needs of creation."

Olsen herself experienced such circumstances, both first hand and through her family. She was born in Eastern Nebraska in either 1912 or 1913 to Ida and Samuel Lerner, Russian Jewish immigrants who came to America to escape punishment for their involvement in the failed 1905 uprising against the Czar. Her father worked several blue-collar jobs—packinghouse worker, farm laborer, painter, paperhanger—to support the family, and served for several years as the state secretary for the Nebraska Socialist Party. Tillie, who left high school to take a factory job, belonged to the Young Communist League and, later, the Communist Party; she was devoted to helping the working class, as is evidenced by her two stints in jail for involvement in the organization of labor strikes.

To illustrate the plight of workers and their families during the Depression, Olsen began in 1934 to write her novel *Yonnondio,* which has been called "well deserving to be put aside John Steinbeck's *Grapes of Wrath* as testimony to the suffering and the dreams and the disasters of the time." However, increased financial pressure on Olsen and her husband, Jack, and the heightened scrutiny of Communist Party members by the Dies Committee (which contributed to that financial pressure) forced the writer to abandon the novel in 1937 and concentrate her efforts on working various jobs and raising her children (she had four daughters in all).

Due to these responsibilities and time constraints, Olsen was kept from any productive writing until the early 1950's, when she began writing the four short stories that, in 1961, were collected as *Tell Me a Riddle.* Following this, she again had to return to work, and published almost nothing until the short story *Requa,* and an article in *College English,* in 1971-2. The *Yonnondio* manuscript was found and finally published, still unfinished, in 1974. *Silences* (a collection of essays and quotations) followed in 1978, and since then Tillie Olsen, now 80, has been in great demand as a public speaker and visiting instructor.

While Olsen is best known for portrayals of women in stifling circumstances, her themes of hope are not intended to apply solely to the female gender. . . .
—*Kathy Wolfe*

Though Olsen is no longer "silenced," she has experienced the circumstances that keep people from realizing their full potential; she had, as she says, "lost consciousness. A time of anesthesia . . . as if writing had never been." Though she still feels that she lacked the opportunity to write to the best of her creative ability, she did manage to largely overcome her difficult circumstances, and it is that kernel of hope in her own life that extends to become central to her stories, surrounded though that kernel may be by apparent despair. This is most evident in the stories which make up *Tell Me a Riddle*; in Abigail Martin's words,

> Each simply tells of lives caught in frustration and pain—caught, but not, in the end, overcome. She [Olson] shows that humanity can never be stifled. Dreams remain, and remnants of beauty—even hope.

In the refusal of Olsen's characters to be utterly determined by the seemingly insurmountable obstacles in their lives, her fiction is, I believe, lifted out of the mire of naturalism and into impressionism. To illustrate this, I've chosen to examine the first and second stories in *Tell Me a Riddle,* which I believe are the most and least familiar, respectively. **"I Stand Here Ironing"** has been anthologized over fifty times, and illustrates Olsen's particular concern with the difficulties faced by women. On the other hand, **"Hey Sailor, What Ship?"** is seldom examined, and is the one story in the collection whose focal character is not a woman. While Olsen is best known for portrayals of women in stifling circumstances, her themes of hope are not intended to apply solely to the female gender; my examination of these two stories will focus on the universal nature of that hope instead of differentiating it between the sexes. As Pearlman states,

> Tillie Olsen is interested in the silences shared by all people, and not in what she sees as the current overemphasis on . . . sub-definitions of human experience, which, in her opinion, serve only to divide us further.

In not being strictly bound by the tenets of naturalism, Olsen somewhat resembles Sherwood Anderson, who is described by Danforth Ross as "influenced by naturalism because it was in the air he breathed, but there was also a good deal of the romantic in him. . . . [he] poignantly suggest[s] the contrast between ideal and actuality." Olsen, in illustrating similar contrasts, utilizes the "typical themes" of impressionism as put forth by Ferguson—alienation, isolation, the quest for identity—and her writing style, including that in **"I Stand Here Ironing"** and **"Hey Sailor, What Ship?"** is largely representative of characteristics of that movement.

The first, and most important, of these is the emphasis put on presenting the inner experiences of the characters, while playing down physical action; the "action" in an impressionistic story is comprised chiefly of the evolving thoughts and emotions of the characters. Weaver states that

> Olsen's technique is an innovative combination of third-person narrative, dialogue, and interior monologue that reveals her characters' thoughts, memories, and perceptions . . . Olsen's [stories] move from dialogue inward, focusing on individual instants of experience.

The movement of **"I Stand Here Ironing"** is related almost wholly as interior monologue, the most immediate and, I think, dramatic way in which to focus on the inner life of a character. The mother, as she carries out the careful yet drudging chore of ironing, also carries on the story of her oldest daughter's neglected childhood, periodically asking questions of the non-existent (and unspoken) school official who wishes to "help" the girl:

> Even if I came, what good would it do? You think because I am her mother I have a key, or that in some way you could use me as a key? She has lived for nineteen years. There is all that life that has happened outside of me, beyond me.

There is brief dialogue toward the end of the story, when the daughter enters the room; the short exchange shifts the emphasis partially away from the introspective mother, and gives the reader a very fleeting firsthand glimpse of the inner life of the girl which the mother has been remembering for us: "Aren't you ever going to finish ironing, Mother? Whistler painted his mother in a rocker. I'd have to paint mine standing over an ironing board."

There is more of a combination of techniques in **"Hey Sailor, What Ship?"** As the story begins, we hear Whitey's inebriated interior thoughts, which return periodically throughout the story amid the third-person narrative and dialogue. As the degenerating seafarer sits at the bar, those thoughts are revealed with little intrusion from the narrator:

"Gotta something. Stand watch? No, din't show last night, ain't gonna show tonight, gonna sign off. Out loud: Hell with ship. You got any friends, ship? Then hell with your friends."

Even the sensory details of the setting in the story are chosen to reflect the state of mind of the character who is perceiving those details; at the outset of the story, we see Whitey's surroundings through his eyes:

> The grimy light; the congealing smell of cigarettes that had been smoked long ago and of liquor that had been drunk long ago; the boasting, cursing, wheedling, cringing voices, and the greasy feel of the bar as he gropes for his glass.

The reality in each of these stories is necessarily subjective; In **"Ironing,"** we see everything as though we are inside the mother's mind, and in **"Hey Sailor"** nearly all of the story's atmosphere is revealed thoroughly through Whitey, who trembles with alcoholism and has a fresh scar on his face but can't comprehend how awful he appears. He doesn't recognize his own deterioration, and is shocked to see the age in the face of Lennie's wife: "(Helen? so . . . grayed?)."

This illustrates a paradox which Olsen frequently discusses as an obstacle to understanding, and changing, one's own life; that "immersion in life means loss of perspective, or vision." Olsen, as the narrator, uses what she terms "trespass vision" in order to gain for her readers that perspective. This is not readily apparent in **"Ironing;"** due to the internal nature of the narrative, readers are as immersed in the mother's over-whelming exhaustion as the mother is herself. The mountains of memories she must tunnel through to try and explain her daughter are recalled by the pile of ironing she must methodically deal with, chasing the iron back and forth.

Olsen's "trespass vision" is more easily ascertained in the second story. Whitey is so mired in his drunkenness that he does not consciously articulate the choice he must make between his two lives; the knowledge manifests itself indirectly as two refrains which continually counterpoint in his mind: "Hey sailor, what ship? and "Lennie and Helen and the kids."

Olsen's emphasis on this repeating pattern in both the mother's life (her repeated dredging up of memories to try and smooth them, as she does with clothing in her continuous ironing) and in Whitey's life (his seesawing between debauchery and domesticity) represents, in part, what Ellen Cronan Rose sees as "Olsen's definition of the creative act" and the artist's relationship to her material; "Fidelity to fact, but essential fact. Form and pattern, but exposed, not imposed." I don't entirely agree. However subjective the realities of the mother's and Whitey's characters may be, no matter how immersed they are in them—Olsen, in *exposing* that, necessarily *imposes* some part of her *own* subjective reality upon those of her characters. I don't believe it's possible to expose without simultaneously imposing, either deliberately or unconsciously. For instance, the ironing the mother is doing may be linked to the flat, repressed quality of Emily's childhood. Similarly, the undulating quality of Whitey's life connects very smoothly (too smoothly for coincidence) with the water imagery and wave metaphors that Olsen plants throughout the story.

The use of metaphor (and metonymy) is another hallmark of impressionism. Reminders of ironing are found throughout the first story, such as the overwhelming, neverending pile of memories that the mother relates; just as a chore like ironing is never completely done, she can't articulate all of the things that have affected her daughter, she "will never total it all." Emily is explicitly compared to the flattened, ironed clothes themselves: "Only help her to know . . . that she is more than this dress on the ironing board." Though the mother may stand there and attempt to smooth out the wrinkles in Emily (the result of her unavoidable neglect), she knows that they will never completely or permanently disappear.

Constantly present in **"Hey Sailor"** are images of water; apropos of Whitey's occupation, water and waves permeate the story. For example, the bottles behind the bar "glisten in the depths;" the rain-wet street is "clogged" with traffic; and Helen remarks that she is "keeping [her] head above water." The very way that Whitey's life has moved back and forth between life at sea and life with Lennie's family, and up and down from a height of youth and pride to a low of age and alcoholism is suggestive of the movement of the waves on which Whitey has lived; the "watery shifting: many faces, many places." And at the end, he sees Lennie and Helen's house atop a "crest" of the waves of the city buildings, and while it remains at the top, "he goes down." Whitey rides the waves of his existence while he drowns within "the bottle" metonymically, the object is suggestive of the unspecified drink. It could be whiskey or cheap wine; it doesn't matter what's in the bottle, only that Whitey is a prisoner inside it.

Readers of these stories are also prisoners, as we've seen; chiefly of the mother's and Whitey's points of view. Even our perceptions of time are necessarily their perceptions; while the pieces of Emily's life are related in order in **"Ironing,"** the events in **"Hey Sailor"** do not always happen chronologically, but rather are related as they occur to Whitey's troubled memory. William Van O'Connor praises Olsen for "set[ting] a scene quickly and then let[ting] the characters take over," and this limitation of point of view lends economy to Olsen's style. As the narrator, she does not in-

dulge in lengthy explanations of events, but instead allows the reader to glean information from the characters.

That is, until the fourth and final section of **"Hey Sailor,"** in which Whitey returns drunk to Lennie's house after being admonished not to leave. Lennie and Helen are angry at Whitey's behavior around the children, and hurt in their imminent realization that he is beyond help, and older daughter Jeannie is embarrassed by Whitey and cannot understand the relationship between this man and her parents; "He's just a Howard Street wino now—why don't you and Daddy kick him out of the house? He doesn't belong here." The characters aren't communicating anymore; they cannot articulate the heightened tension between them, the various memories flooding their minds so Olsen steps in and articulates it for them.

It begins with a sentence, explaining Whitey's unconscious probing of his own facial features; "Tracing the scars, the pits and lines, the battered nose, seeking to find." After Jeannie's outburst to Helen, the explanation grows to two paragraphs, ending with ". . . there were memories to forget, dreams to be stifled, hopes to be murdered." A page later, three paragraphs are needed; "Understand. The death of the brotherhood . . . Remember too much, too goddam much." Finally, just as Lennie poignantly comments "Jesus, man, you're a chunk of our lives," an entire page of narrator intrusion is required to handle the rush of memory and emotion that is triggered in Whitey, ending yet again with the refrain "the memories to forget, the dreams to be stifled, the hopeless hopes to be murdered."

Although Whitey ultimately, and abruptly, leaves for good— "I'm goin' now . . . Go own steam. Send you a card"— Lennie *had* gotten to him, as evidenced by the conflated history of their friendship that crashes through his mind. Amid the tension, there is a moment of connection.

> Looked at one way, **"Hey Sailor, What Ship?"** is a cheerless story; but examined in a different light its beauty of almost perfect devotion shows forth. Lennie and Helen and Whitey rise above surface things . . . Poverty and trouble exist, but they cannot touch the core of love deep within these people.

The moments of communication in these two stories may be rare, but shared experiences permeate the relationships between Emily and her mother and between Whitey and Lennie and Helen; and this very communion, coupled with the perseverence each main character musters at the end of each story, is central to Olsen's writing. Though her characters are so often stifled by circumstance, something of their lives is eventually illuminated in them, and gives them some kind of hope; that illumination is part of what Olsen terms "Come to writing:"

"Come to writing" . . . expresses [Olsen's] vitalistic conception of the creative process. It means the inarticulate finding words, the dumbly sensed becoming sensible, the incipient meaning finding form. For the writer, it is breaking silence. For the actor in an Olsen fiction, it is a moment of perceiving, of knowing that there is shape and direction in the ceaseless flow of what must be.

In **"I Stand Here Ironing,"** the mother's cumulative remembrance of the encouragement that was lacking in Emily's upbringing culminates in the arrival of Emily herself, who "runs up the stairs two at a time with her light graceful step." It is "one of her communicative nights," and she converses lightly with her mother. Though the mother's melancholy reminiscing has exhausted her enough that even this banter seems oppressive ("because I have been dredging the past, and all that compounds a human being is so heavy and meaningful in me, I cannot endure it tonight"), the fact that her daughter is capable of it at all gives her hope to hang on to. She realizes that the circumstances of her early parenting have made it difficult for Emily to ever reach her full potential; but what is most important is her further realization that Emily may rise above that, at least a little, despite being "a child of her age, of depression, of war, of fear." While this perception is anything but jubilant, "There is still enough left to live by."

This story is almost certainly autobiographical, in the mother we see Tillie Olsen, who had herself been stifled between *Yonnondio* and this writing, and whose first daughter endured many of the same hardships that Emily has endured. We can assume that the mother here, due to her responsibilities in the home, will never find out what creative capacity she possesses, so she hopes for this in her daughter instead, who has shown a talent for performing. Olsen may have felt that way herself, but refused to give up; as the mother in **"Ironing"** (and, potentially, the daughter) discovers hope, Olsen illustrates the moment of "coming [back] to writing" in her own life.

The events in **"Hey Sailor"** build toward Whitey's own pinnacle of perception. He is confused when he first arrives at Lennie and Helen's house; he has "imaged and entered it over and over again, in a thousand various places a thousand various times," and the memory has sustained him during his long jaunts at sea. But this time he isn't bursting in with gifts, feeling on top of the world. He's sick, has trouble climbing the front steps, and is too weakened to gracefully endure the children's enthusiastic greetings; "Whitey's just gonna sit here. . . .

Later in the night, when Allie climbs onto his lap after a bad dream (she was "losted"), Whitey welcomes her, but his protection is bittersweet because he knows deep inside him that he will never get to play this father role; "He starts as if he has been burned . . . It is destroying, dissolving him utterly, this helpless warmth against him, this feel of a child-lost country to him and unattainable." Finally the unaccustomed distraction and attention of the family overwhelms Whitey— he needs solitude, much as Olsen's silenced writers need uninterrupted solitude in which to devote their efforts to their creativity. So he "endures" their good-night affections and is left alone.

When he wakes, however, the complete silence of the empty house troubles Whitey; he is used to hearing the sounds of people, the ship, the sea. Being apart from his usual life does offer Whitey some perspective on that life—he realizes that he misses the accustomed sounds of shared mornings. He wanders through the house, noting the work that needs to be done, and remembers how useful he formerly was to the family. While that makes him proud, he knows that he's no longer up to it, and that knowledge "hurts in his stomach."

It is when Whitey returns again, drunk, and the atmosphere in the house is so raucous and tense, that he—and, perhaps, Lennie and Helen—finally realize at a conscious level that he has chosen to devote whatever time remains to him to his seafaring life, that he is returning for good to this room where he can yell or sing or pound and Deeck will look on without reproach or pity or anguish." This recognition of Whitey's direction arrives at the moment he answers Lennie roughly, "Shove it . . . So you're a chunk of my life. So?"

This is not a happy ending, by any means; Whitey is beyond help and headed for death, and will never experience the family life that Lennie has found. But he is not without a certain dignity; as he recites "Crown 'n' Deep" for the children, its words connect him with the hero of the poem; "I shall be speech in thy ears, fragrance and color/Light and shout and loved song . . . /O crown and deep of my sorrows, I am leaving all with thee, my friends." Whitey asserts his independence, and while his approaching end may be a sad one, he has displayed a kind of strength in taking a measure of control over his life and that instant of perception, and the taking of control, represents a "coming to writing" for his character.

Tillie Olsen believes that the potential to "come to writing" exists in every person:

> Unlike many of her modern and contemporary peers who espouse individualism and the cult of self, Olsen believes in Matthew Arnold's communal "human struggle bursting the thick wall of self."

Her fiction reveals a deep understanding of stifling circumstances, but offers a glimmer of hope. If, as a colleague has asserted to me, Joyce Carol Oates is a "postmodern romantic, then perhaps Tillie Olsen is her immediate precursor—a modern romantic whose work is ultimately a "celebration of human beings," containing a belief that "there is so much more to people than their lives permit them to be."

Jean Pfaelzer (essay date 1994)

SOURCE: "Tillie Olsen's *Tell Me a Riddle:* The Dialectics of Silence," in *Frontiers,* Vol. XV, No. 2, 1994, pp. 1-22.

[*In the following essay, Pfaelzer discusses the ways in which Olsen uses language and silence in* Tell Me a Riddle *to represent Eva's journey from alienation to engagement.*]

Logos, the expressed word, empowers. "God *said,* 'Let there be light,' And there was light" (Gen. 1:3). By the act of speech, God ascribed reality and assigned meaning to the object of his desire. Inevitably, man arrogated this divine power to himself: "Out of the ground the Lord God formed every beast in the field and every bird in the air, and brought them to the man to see what he would call them: whatever the man called every living creature, that was his name" (Gen. 2:19). And the word reified.

But by what word shall woman call every living creature? For the past decade, feminist critics have debated the phallocentric nature of language—the relationship between patriarchy and language, the relationship between patriarchy and silence. Feminist theorists Helene Cixous and Monique Wittig argue that phallocentrism is logocentrism; they find that a woman's speech, even rebellious or dissenting speech, is made up of the signs and signifiers of patriarchy. Hence, they call for a retreat from language, directly through silence or obliquely, through the discontinuities and disruptions of avant-garde rhetorical practices. Many feminist novelists, however, particularly ones who write from the "margins" of the American literary canon, such as Rebecca Harding Davis, Zora Neale Hurston, Alice Walker, and Tillie Olsen, appear to reject the notion that language is inevitably repressive and that silence is inevitably resistant. In narratives about reclaiming women's power and/or ethnicity, these authors thematize female language. And they do not conclude that language is his. Tillie Olsen's *Tell Me a Riddle* (1956), is a powerful study of the politics of voice and suggests to us that there is a way to represent silence, not normatively, but historically and dialectically. This reading of *Tell Me a Riddle* explores the ways in which speech is marked by gender, ethnicity, class, and the tensions of bilingualism. Inevitably, it thereby considers differences between empiricist, Lacanian, Marxist-feminist, and post-structuralist theories of female speech.

Set in the 1950s, **"Tell Me a Riddle"** is the story of the death of Eva, an old Russian Jewish woman who emigrated to the United States as a young bride and surrendered her political voice and identity while she raised seven children in poverty. As Eva (Eve—the first woman, the first mother) faces cancer and death, we watch her negotiate the silence that represents first her alienation and then her freedom. Unaware of the true nature of her illness, Eva allows her husband to take her on a long voyage to visit the families of her grown children. Initially, her passage from involuntary to voluntary silence, from repression to quietude, forces her to relinquish her mothering role with its speech of comfort and self-abnegation. This verbal isolation precedes the recovery of her youthful political voice—the hopeful words she spoke and the songs she sang as a leader in the 1905 Russian revolution. Thus, silence marks Eva's passage from alienation to engagement and reconnection as Olsen rescripts the romance quest; **"Tell Me a Riddle"** begins where a domestic novel used to end, in marriage, and questions whether husband, love, motherhood, and family compensate for the atrophy of a woman's voice. Eventually, through the rediscovery of her political voice, Eva rediscovers her capacity to love.

> **Many feminist novelists, however, particularly ones who write from the "margins" of the American literary canon, such as Rebecca Harding Davis, Zora Neale Hurston, Alice Walker, and Tillie Olsen, appear to reject the notion that language is inevitably repressive and that silence is inevitably resistant.**
>
> **—Jean Pfaelzer**

Marguerite Duras, French novelist and deconstructionist, suggests that a woman who writes within the existing symbolic order is either a plagiarist or a mere translator of male discourse. Men, she observes,

> have established the principle of virile force. And everything that emerged from this virile force—including words, unilateral words—reinforced the silence of women. In my opinion, women have never expressed themselves. It is as if you asked me: "Why aren't there writers in the proletariat? Why aren't there musicians among workers?" That's exactly the same thing. There are no musicians among the workers just as there are no musicians among women ... To be a composer you must have total possession of your liberty.

In **"Tell Me a Riddle"**, Tillie Olsen suggests that neither workers, immigrants, nor women, groups that of course are not necessarily distinct, have waited for the "total possession of their liberty" to sing or write. Rejecting repression as the sole explanation of female identity, Olsen inscribes silence, not just as a repudiation of male discourse, but as a way to represent radical subjectivity in the process of coming into being. In this regard, **"Tell Me a Riddle"** confirms critic Chris Weedon's observation that language is how we represent to ourselves our "lived relation" to our material circumstances. For Helene Cixous, the possibility of self-expressive language—for woman, man, or "ungendered individual"—assumes that a preexisting subjectivity awaits expression. By contrast, Eva's rediscovery of a radical subjectivity through the recovery of her speaking identity challenges the view that a woman's speech fixes her in either a "womanly" or an "alienated" position. In **"Tell Me a Riddle",** language itself is the site of struggle; verbal contact with other expressive and rebellious people who celebrate their historical and ethnic heritage transforms Eva's identity. Her language and consciousness evolve collectively, through the simultaneous processes of differentiation from and identification with her family and old radical Jewish friends. Which is to say, Eva's language and consciousness evolve dialectically, through the negation of silence as negation as she recuperates her political voice. Thus, **"Tell Me a Riddle"** offers an alternative to silence on the one hand or the recovery of an essentialist, ahistorical identity on the other. For Olsen, language is social, rebellious, and portends the possibility of change.

Eva, in a sense, like any woman, resides in what Elaine Showalter has termed the "wild zone," an abstract space that exists outside of ideology. Pictured by Showalter as a circle that overlaps that of the dominant culture, the "wild zone" survives and, indeed, thrives outside of patriarchy, its hegemonic but not enslaving neighbor. In this precarious geography, I believe women can speak of constriction, exclusion, dispossession, and resistance. And not in *his* tongue. While **"Tell Me a Riddle"** predates the contemporary debate over female utterance, Olsen defines the radical and feminist potential of language; in effect, she implicitly rejects the post-structuralist conclusion that language is a male activity, and she repudiates the romanticization of silence.

Xavière Gauthier has aptly described the trap of yielding language to men, nothing that throughout the course of history women "have been mute, and it is doubtless by virtue of this mutism that men have been able to speak and write. As long as women remain silent, they will be outside the historical process. But if they begin to speak and write AS MEN DO, they will enter history subdued and alienated; it is a history that logically speaking their speech should disrupt." Olsen invokes a disruptive voice when Eva, on her deathbed, remembers and sings the revolutionary lyrics of Victor Hugo, while her husband longs for loving words of comfort and recognition. Olsen reproduces but subverts Hugo's lyrics through the pain of Eva's misdiagnosed disease and the rage

of her repressed female life. Through Olsen, we find that we need not force feminist discourse completely outside the symbolic order, a sociolinguistic system reserved by Lacanians for patriarchy.

Issues of silence and repression have pervaded Tillie Olsen's life. She was born to Ida and Sam Lerner "somewhere" in Nebraska, in 1912 or 1913; "No birth certificate seems to exist," she has said. She recalls that in an articulate and lively family of Russian-Jewish emigrés who were active in socialist politics, she was a child who stuttered. Olsen found her voice, however, in writing politically engaged fiction, although this voice was frequently repressed by economic and political pressures. Deborah Rosenfelt has observed that few of Olsen's contemporary admirers realize the extent to which her "consciousness, vision and choice of subject" are rooted in the communist "Old Left" of the 1930s and 1940s; Olsen's early skits for the Young People's Socialist League, her membership, at age 17, in the Young Communist League (the youth organization of the Communist party), and her organizing projects for the congress of Industrial Organizations (CIO). During these years of imprisonment, work in a ties factory, community organizing, and mother hood, she published some poems in the *Daily Worker* and, for a time, a column in the *People's World.* After her first story, **"The Iron Thread,"** appeared in *Partisan Review* in 1934, two prominent editors failed to locate her because she was in jail, officially charged with vagrancy but in fact imprisoned for refusing to answer questions about her communist activities. The implications of this arrest frame her first study of silence and repression, "The Thousand Dollar Vagrant," published in 1934. Soon thereafter Bennett Cerf and Donald Klepfer of Random House heard an early version of her first novel, ***Yonondlo,*** and offered her a stipend to write a chapter a month to complete the text. Even though she sent her daughter off to relatives in order to have time to write, Olsen never finished ***Yonondio,*** which was eventually published in its incomplete form in 1974.

Material pressures persisted during the forties and fifties. After her marriage to Jack Olsen, a union printer, and the birth of three more daughters, Olsen continued to write— on busses or after the children were in bed. In 1959, when she finally received a Ford grant that would give her the time that only money can buy, she observed, "I am a partially destroyed human who pays the cost of all those years of not writing, of deferring, postponing, of doing others work—its in my body too (deafened ear from transcribing) etc." In *Silences* (1962), her eloquent study of the circumstances that frustrate voice, Olsen wrote, "Literary history and the present are dark with silences: some the silences for years by our acknowledged great; some silences hidden; some the ceasing to publish after one work appears; some the never coming to book form at all. . . . The silences I speak of here are unnatural."

In **"Tell Me a Riddle"**, Eva's silence is "unnatural" because it results from and is conceived within the repressions of immigration, poverty, housework, Post-holocaust fear, and the Cold War. When the story opens, Eva has refused her husband David's plea to sell their old house and move into his union's retirement home, "The Haven":

> "What do we need all this for?" he would ask loudly for her hearing aid was turned down and the vacuum was shrilling. "Five rooms" (pushing the sofa so she could get into the corner) "furniture" (smoothing down the rug) "floors and surfaces to make work. Tell me, why do we need it?" And he was glad he could ask in a scream.
>
> "Because I'm use't."
>
> "Because you're use't. This is a reason, Mrs. Word Miser? Used to can get unused!"
>
> "Enough unused I have to get used to already . . . Not enough words?" turning off the vacuum a moment to hear herself answer. "Because soon enough we'll need only a little closet, no windows, no furniture, nothing to make work, but for worms. Because now I want room. . . . Screech and blow like you're doing, you'll need that closet even sooner. . . . Ha, again!" for the vacuum bag wailed, puffed half up, hung stubbornly limp.

The couple's only shared activity is housework, but for Eva, without work, now there is only death. To sell the house would deprive her of her only power, if only the illusion of power. Overworked, she finds herself paradoxically "unused," a woman's pun on unfulfilled and unfamiliar. Olsen marks this couple's conflict as a struggle between sound and silence. As Eva attacks David for his postured speech, "screech and blow," he attacks her for her silences, "Mrs. Word Miser," with the masculine assault at verbal female withholding. Yet both Eva and David are empty; if Eva is "unused," David is associated with the limp, half-puffed-up vacuum bag, here a pitiable loss of male power. At this point Eva's only act of resistance is to "turn off her ear button so she would not have to hear." In this gesture that fails to stop David from selling their home, Eva mistakes silence for control.

One reading of this text might situate the repressions of Eva's language, and thereby her desire, in representation itself. The post-structuralist proscription against representation derives, in part, from the Lacanian view that the phallus is the enscriber and enactor of patriarchy. Helene Cixous, for example, argues that women, historically, have been "matter subjected to the desire he wishes to imprint." Eva's social condition would thus emerge as an analogy of her biology—

a space, a gap, empty, waiting to be filled or defined. Along similar lines, Xavière Gauthier suggests that "women find their place within the linear, grammatical, linguistic system that orders the symbolic, the superego, the law. It is a system based entirely upon one fundamental signifier: the phallus."

One of the few ways out of this colony of silence is through the ruptures of the avant-garde. Julia Kristeva observes that because women are "estranged from language" they have no access to the phallocentric order, which adheres in symbolic discourses. If women do want to "have a role to play in this on-going (historical) process, it is only in assuming a negative function: reject everything finite, definite, structured, loaded with meaning." Otherwise, as in most novels written by women, language will seem "to be seen from a foreign land."

Likewise, Helene Cixous endorses "only the poets—not the novelists, allies of representation. Because poetry involves gaining strength through the unconscious, and because the unconscious is the place where the repressed manage to survive." Hence, only "a Kleist" or "a Rimbaud" can speak the feminine. For Kristeva and Cixous, according to Gayatri Spivak, evocative literature alone has "the power of indeterminate suggestion rather than determinate reference" and only indeterminacy can "overwhelm and sabotage the signifying conventions." (It is interesting that both Cixous and Kristeva focus on the white male avant-garde.)

Mary Jacobus, however, suggests that such a plea for a feminine language of indeterminacy returns us to "the pre-Oedipal phase of rhythmic, onomatopoetic babble which precedes the symbolic but remains inscribed in those pleasurable and rupturing aspects of language identified particularly with avant-garde literary practice." She concludes that this definition of women's language marks either a rejection of language itself or a return to a specifically feminine linguistic domain of oppression and confinement.

To avoid the masculine hegemony of connotation and denotation, should feminists talk baby talk? Another problem: this alternative female discourse, like male discourse, is hegemonic and appears to eradicate difference, dialect, and interpretation. Moreover, it does not account for languages of resistance. If phallogocentrism determines all our "signifying conventions," from whence comes the language that names and defines agents of repression? From whence come the linguistic constructions of a rebellious subjectivity?

It seems to me that earlier in the century, while understanding full well what Cixous would later term the "solidarity of phallocentrism and logocentrism," Virginia Woolf recognized defiant possibilities in referential language. In *A Room of One's Own,* she describes how a man uses a woman's word to inflate his power: "Women have served all these centuries as looking glasses possessing the magic and delicious power of reflecting the figure of man at twice its natural size. Without that power, probably the earth would still be swamp and jungle. The glories of all our wars would be unknown." The female speaker, essentially an author, has participated in the creation of a fictitious hero/listener who is convinced by her speech of his omniscience. But here Woolf is identifying only the traditional activity of speech (*la parole*), not the very tools of speech (*la langue*). She adds, if woman "begins to tell the truth, the figure in the looking glass shrinks; his fitness for life is diminished. How is he to go on giving judgement, civilizing natives, making laws, writing books, dressing up and speechifying at banquets unless he can see himself at breakfast and dinner at least twice the size he really is?" For Woolf, oppression derives from the content and function of language rather than from words and symbols themselves. While she often played with language herself, she also saw that women can use words to "tell the truth." Therein lies the liberating potential of language: referential discourse can rupture the mystifications upon which patriarchy survives.

Clearly, as Sheila Rowbotham notes, "Language conveys a certain power. It is one of the instruments of domination." How to usurp this power? Donna Stanton, while accepting the concept of phallogocentrism, suggests that a woman can "deconstruct the myths of objectivity and truth, and challenge the authority of the Word only by using fragments, both *materia* and methods, from the phallocentric heritage she questions. And these relics from the past must ultimately be reinscribed within the bounds of the discourse she seeks to subvert, since no other exists which can transmit her visions." And this, I suggest, is what Olsen would have us do.

What then do Eva's gestures toward silence and her ultimate recovery of language signify? Eva's subjectivity is not solely an effect of language, nor is it solely constituted by language.

Likewise, Eva's silence hardly comes from the inward folds and tunnels of her anatomy. She has been silenced by religion, history, class, and gender—shamed by her children for her accent, isolated from community by long hours of hand washing and repairing used clothes for seven children. Thus, when David tries to tempt her to move from their house by announcing that there is a reading circle in the "Haven," she responds: "'Enjoy!' She tasted the word. 'Now, when it pleases you, you find a reading circle for me. And forty years ago when the children were morsels and there was a Circle, did you stay home with them once so I could go? Even once? You trained me well. I do not need others to enjoy."

Images of eating inscribe Eva's anger as she "spews forth" words and accuses David of "diarrhea of the mouth." Food, in Olsen's story, is a layered metaphor for oppression and

expression, suggesting a mixture of love and hate, dependence and autonomy, nurture and aggression, poverty and abundance, and significant domestic labor. To evocative oral associations, Olsen adds women's literal work of providing, buying, and cooking food; for example, Eva shamefully recalls asking the butcher for "dog bones" with which she would feed her family.

Thus images of silence and food mark this story of female deprivation and resistance. Soon after David announces his plan to sell their house, Eva becomes quite ill, with "a ravening inside," again the metaphor of hunger unfulfilled. Ironically, the doctor first suggests that Eva "get a new hearing aid," in essence, listen, internalize, respond. Eventually, he discovers that Eva has cancer of the stomach, a cruel irony for a woman who saw her life as one of feeding others. Again, the two images fuse: "More and more she lay silent in bed . . . a bellyful of bitterness," a mute surrender that precedes her quest for identity and social integration. In contrast, David uses words to placate, to be obsequious to other men and to lie to her. To Eva, who still sees language as betrayal, David is "a babbler," a "yesman, entertainer, whatever they want of you."

David has betrayed Eva by secretly selling their house, forcing her on a death-bound and homeless journey to their various grown children—a symbolic diaspora. For Eva the long cross-country trip becomes a journey into memory and silence, prompted and contextualized by the social choices her children and grandchildren have made, choices that she will reject. Her eldest daughter has returned to Judaism, which signifies gender betrayal and genocide to Eva: "Swindler! does she look back on the dark centuries? Candles bought instead of bread and stuck into a potato for a candlestick? Religion that stifled and said: in Paradise, woman, you will be the footstool of your husband, and in life—poor chosen Jew—ground under, despised, trembling in cellars. And cremated. And cremated." Her second daughter, consumed by mother-love, is raising four children with the "drowning into needing and being needed." At this daughter's house Eva refuses to hold the "warm, seductive babies," seeking, instead, to be "stilled of clamor, in the reconciled solitude, to journey to her self." Only in a grandson's rock collection does she find temptation, in a piece of obsidian, "frozen to black glass, never to transform the fossil memory." The silent and invulnerable stone resists imprint and rejects entanglement.

Motherhood, for Eva, represents a powerful symbiotic relationship that she must relinquish on this "journey to her self." In *Silences,* written at the same time as *Tell Me a Riddle,* Olsen observed:

> "In motherhood, as it is structured, circumstances
> for sustained creation are almost impossible . . . the

need cannot be first . . . Motherhood means being instantly interruptible, responsive, responsible. Children need one *now* (and remember, in our society, the family must often try to be the center for love and health the outside world is not). The very fact that these are needs of love, not duty, . . . *that there is no one else responsible for these needs,* gives them primacy. It is distraction, not meditation, that becomes habitual. . . . Work interrupted, deferred, postponed makes blockage. . . . Unused capacities atrophy, cease to be.

Olsen also portrays the contradictions of maternal subjectivity through the children's reactions to Eva's "journey to her self." Her daughters, in particular, bitterly resent her retreat. One, for example, calls Eva an "unnatural grandmother, not able to make herself embrace a baby."

As Nancy Chodorow has observed, many daughters learn from their mothers to repress their own dependency needs while mimicking the mother's nurturing skills. Often daughters (as well as sons) first construct autonomous subjectivity through conflicts with their mothers: "Differentiation, separation and disruption of the narcissistic relation to reality are developed through learning that the mother is a separate being with separate interests and activities that do not always coincide with just what the infant wants at the time." Although a child generally accepts her father's independence early on, she comes to understand her mother's autonomy more gradually. Over time, she may view her mother in particular, and women in general, with fear and dependency, anger and desire.

Perhaps a daughter's awareness of maternal mortality finally establishes her mother's autonomy. Despite the children's resentment of Eva's cancer, the dying woman comes to understand that she must repudiate mother-love en route to her recovery of an integrated self: "It was not that she had not loved her babies, her children. The love—the passion of tending—had risen with the need like a torrent; and like a torrent drowned and immolated all else. . . . Only the thin pulsing left that could not quiet, suffering over lives one felt, but could no longer hold nor help." The passion of motherhood, posed as a metaphor for language itself, is the hardest to "quiet." As Eva withdraws from motherhood she begins to put forth a radical alternative, "To look back and learn what humanizes—this to teach. To smash all ghettos that divide us—not to go back, not to go back—this to teach." Her utopian moment resides in historical memory and anticipates the recovery of her political identity and voice.

Silence for Eva, then, is a historicized muzzle that reinscribes rather than resists marginality. At first Eva finds that just as language secures authority, silence provides shelter. Initially, silence loosens the power of David's language of assertion and the children's language of need. As her journey progresses, she begins to identify the violence of their familial language. During one of the enforced visits to her grown children, Eva escapes from the family gathering of "blows and screams." Hiding on a shelf in a closet she discovers the silence found behind frilly dresses. This significant moment ends in empathetic reengagement with a granddaughter:

It was the afternoons that saved.

While they thought she napped, she would leave the mosaic on the wall (of children's drawings, maps, calendars, pictures, Ann's cardboard dolls with their great ringed questioning eyes) and hunch in the girls' closet on the low shelf where the shoes stood, and the girls' dresses covered.

Blows, screams, a call: "Grandma!" For her? Oh please not for her. Hide, hunch behind the dresses deeper. But a trembling little body hurls itself beside her—surprised, smoothered [sic] laughter, arms around her neck, tears rub dry on her cheek, and words too soft to understand whisper into her ear (Is this where you hide too, Grammy? It's my secret place, we have a secret now).

And the sweat beads, and the long shudder seizes.

Neither the enclosed domestic space of the closet, the frills of girlhood dresses, nor the possibly metaphoric dark and wombic retreat in fact protects her from the assaults of expectations. This passage recalls Eva's earlier experiences of defenseless enclosure in a Russian prison, thereafter on a steerage deck on an immigrant ship, and finally in her house; it also suggests Olsen's scattered references to shelves of stacked bodies in concentration camps and slave ships. The private is historical.

Both the structure and style of **"Tell Me a Riddle"** provide us with tools to consider alternative explanations of female speech and silence. Olsen was well aware of the problematics of gendered language. In 1981 she said, "I'm tormented by things having to do with the language we use, and whether it is indeed poisoned language, male language." However, as Eva reclaims her political identity, her language suggests radical possibilities of disjuncture. Unlike those who privilege the avant-garde for its attack on representation *per se,* Olsen accounts for the fissures in Eva's language and memory through her political, religious, economic, and sexual oppression. Indeed, **"Tell Me a Riddle"** is a modernist text. The narrative is discontinuous, with movements back and forth across time, in and out of omniscience and internal dialogue, the perspective deliberately disjointed. Olsen scripts Eva's voyage to identity through gaps, fractured discourse, written intervals, and disassembled point of view.

At the last stage of her enforced journey (paradoxically westward), David takes her to Venice, California, which, in the 1950s, was an impoverished beach community of retired Jewish immigrants, the "cast off old," who spend their days sitting on peeling park benches and looking out to sea. There, Eva and David encounter an old friend, Ellen Mays, who lives in one stench-filled attic room: "Thirty years are compressed into a dozen sentences; and the present, not even in three." Again, the metaphor of language fuses with images of poverty and repression. Similarly, the houses and the old Jews alike are "abandoned . . . all boarded up and still." Stunned by Ellen's poverty, Eva observes:

> Shrinking the life of her   into one room   like a coffin   Rooms and rooms like this   I lie   on the quilt and hear them talk
>
> Please, Mrs. Orator-without-Breath
>
> Once you went for coffee   I walked   I saw   A Balzac   a Chekhov to write it   Rummage Alone On scraps.

"Scraps" becomes a metonym for hunger, aging, speech, and the politics of Chekhovian realism, which might enscribe female poverty.

On the one hand, Luce Irigary, a disciple of Lacan, might interpret this kind of disjointed speech as an analogue of female anatomy wherein a woman "at least when she dares to speak out . . . retouches herself constantly. She just barely separates from herself some chatter, an exclamation, a half-secret, a sentence left in suspense—When she returns to it, it is only to set out again from another point of pleasure or pain." Irigary finds that the distinguishing feature of a woman's statement is one of "contiguity. They touch (upon). And when they wander too far from this nearness, she stops and begins again from 'zero'; her body-sex organ." The implication of this view, as Chris Weedon has observed, is that there is no space for resistance within the terms of symbolic language, and hence, women who do not wish to repress their femaleness have no access to representation. They abdicate any claim to the symbolic order and must retreat into separateness.

In contrast to Irigary, Rachel Blau DuPlessis' view of ruptures in the conventional sentence and sequence in women's narratives comes closer to Olsen's historicized and politicized intentions: "Breaking the sentence severs dominant authority and ideology. Breaking the sequence is a critique of narrative, restructuring its orders and priorities precisely by attention to specific issues of female identity and its char-

acteristic oscillations." Establishing her critique through an analysis of ideology rather than biology, DuPlessis refuses to define a universal or normative female form and also refuses to reduce female subjectivity to female sexuality. Following Woolf, she observes that a woman's sentence is a "psychological sentence," first, because it "deepens external realism with a picture of consciousness at work," and second, because it involves a critique of "her own consciousness, saturated as it is with images of dominance." DuPlessis finds nothing exclusively female about this sentence because writers of both sexes have used this "elastic" and "enveloping" form. Nevertheless she suggests that it is a woman's sentence "because of its cultural and situational function, a dissension stating that women's minds and concerns have been neither completely or accurately produced in literature as we know it. Breaking the sentence is a way of rupturing language and tradition sufficiently to invite a female slant, emphasis or approach."

Olsen's sentences in **"Tell Me a Riddle"**—fractured, evocative, representational, self-critical, and self-conscious—suggest a decentered and bicultural subjectivity rooted in the material as well as the psychological ruptures of lived history and daily life. Consider, for example, Olsen's description of Ellen May's rented room:

> Singing.   Unused   the life in them.   She   in this poor room   with her   pictures   Max   You The children   Everywhere unused the life   And who has meaning?   Century after century   still all in us not to grow?

Absent punctuation marks, there is no indication regarding the status of this comment as dialogue, internal dialogue, or narration. Through Olsen's careful use of Russian-Jewish dialect, abbreviated phrases indicate the inversions and ellipses of Eva's partial bilingualism. The incomplete sentences also articulate the choppy phrases and pauses of a dying woman who is trying to catch her breath. Additionally, they articulate the choppy phrases and pauses of unutterable anger. Thus the prose inscribes Eva's "unused" gender and her psychological and historical "unused" particularities, while at the same time it subverts the authority of the omniscient narrator. Eva's final two questions, "And who has meaning?" and "still all in us not to grow?" betoken uncertainty and possibility. This decentered utterance is neither pre-conscious, pre-Oedipal, nor irrational. The social relations of the Jewish-American, the elderly, the Cold War victim, and the homeless are constituted within Eva's language. Olsen never presumes that Eva is the sole author of her thoughts. In the final weeks of her life, Eva's language has become both the site and the subject of her struggle about identity and about speech itself. In **"Tell Me a Riddle"** Olsen has also ruptured the traditional narrative sequence. The narration is a discourse of gaps, discontinuities, flashbacks, and written intervals. The non-linear sequence and the unexplained interruptions inscribe the development of Eva's memories and associations; the narrative form reproduces her repression. Each textual interruption contributes to the representation of Eva's frustrations: housework interrupted by the needs of family, comprehension interrupted by misunderstood English, her tired bedtime reading interrupted by David's sexual expectations or by her babies' needs to nurse. The gaps also represent Eva's minimal assertion of control, as she turns off her hearing aid to shut out the demands of others. Olsen's modernism has little to do with the shape of women's bodies but much to do with Eva's experience of exile, motherhood, and poverty.

Finally, in Venice, California, Eva comes to understand that rebirth involves an awareness of connections, both social and historical. Lying by the Pacific Ocean, she cradles herself in the sand and looks toward the "shore that nurtured life as it first crawled toward consciousness the millions of years ago." Through the relationships Eva forms in California, with the timeless creatures of the sea, with Ellen Mays, with her granddaughter Jeannie, and eventually with David, it becomes clear how Olsen's view of female subjectivity differs from that of either Sigmund Freud or Nancy Chodorow, both of whom argue that selfhood is largely achieved by separation. Olsen's notion of identity is closer to developmental theorist Jessica Benjamin's theory of "intersubjectivity"— identity that evolves through reciprocity and rapprochement. Eva's journey culminates in a "sing-along" at a community center with other impoverished Jewish exiles, where the lyrics penetrate her self-imposed deafness in an epiphany of sounds of an insurgent past and a hopeful future: "children-chants, mother-croons, singing of the chained love serenades, Beethoven storms, mad Lucia's scream, drunken joy-songs, keens for the dead, work-singing." As the faces become sound and the sounds become faces, they press from her the essential and real question: "On scraps Yet they sang like Wondrous! Humankind one has to believe So strong for what? To rot not grow?" Earlier in the story Eva rejected her children's medical, psychological, and political answers and also refused to pose the riddle: "Tell me a riddle, Grandma. (*I know no riddles.*)" The riddle: the manipulated question, the false question with the trick answer, the pun, which controls, frustrates, and undermines meaning. But here, in Venice, the answer emerges as the capacity for change and affirmation: "one has to believe."

In **"Tell Me a Riddle"** Olsen demystifies the Western notion of the self as separate, bounded, and autonomous and puts forward, in its place, a view of female identity that reflects a balance of separation and intimacy. For Olsen, independence need not exclude connection; hence, it need not exclude language. Eva's story appears to support Jessica Benjamin's analysis that the self does not proceed from oneness to separateness, but evolves by simultaneously differentiating and recognizing the other, by alternating between "being with" and being distinct—a materialist view of development. Eva's subjectivity, realized through her speech, evolves dialectically through relationships. Dependence, marked by communication, defines Eva's sense of political identity. Hence, her subjectivity has little in common with the solipsistic self of postmodern feminism (the refusal of identity) or the liberal humanist discovery of a buried essential or true self (the romanticized sovereign subject).

> **Olsen's notion of identity is closer to developmental theorist Jessica Benjamin's theory of "intersubjectivity"—identity that evolves through reciprocity and rapprochement.**
>
> **—Jean Pfaelzer**

In **"Tell Me a Riddle"** Tillie Olsen, like Eva, is again articulating history after a long silence. Eva's relationships designate a return to speech and consciousness within the context of contemporary history: the recovered memory of her son buried in an unknown grave in Germany, the "heavy air" of Los Angeles smog, the challenge of a grandchild insisting, "Mother, I told you the teacher said we had to bring it all filled out this morning. Didn't you even ask Daddy? Then tell me which plan and I'll check it: evacuate or stay in the city or wait for you to come and take me away?" The imperatives of Cold War ideology frame his patriarchal question, "Didn't you even ask Daddy?" Olsen's antinuclear stance also appears in the school's naive plans for evacuation. **"Tell Me a Riddle"** was written at a time when Olsen was seriously concerned about the threat of nuclear war, what she calls the "technological sublime." In *Silences* she observed that the atom bomb was in manufacture before the first washing machine. The final re-emergence of Eva's articulate and radical subjectivity develops through her granddaughter Jeannie, a public health nurse who, Eva sees, offers respectful and caring attention to Mexican patients. One day Jeannie brings Eva a Mexican cookie, modeled after a little girl who had died the day before. The cookie, "*pan del muerto*" (bread of death), is an image in food that suggests to Eva a culture's refusal to bury guilt, loss, and memory. Another day, Jeannie invites a Samoan friend to perform a native dance for the dying woman who weakly tries to imitate his beckoning hands and his low plaintive calls. Through Jeannie's visits, Eva discovers an aesthetic diversity of self-representations and she contrasts these experiences to her grandchildren's play, which mirrors televised identities. Finally, Eva realizes that Jeannie reminds her of Lisa, the "Tolstoyan" woman who taught her to read when they were imprisoned together over fifty years ago. She is then able to tell her son, who has come to her deathbed, the story of Lisa:

Like Lisa she is, your Jeannie. . . . I was sixteen, they beat me; my father beat me so I would not go to her. . . . To her, life was holy, knowledge was holy, and she taught me to read. They hung her. Everything that happens one must try to understand why. She killed one who betrayed many. . . . In one minute she killed, before my eyes (there is so much blood in a human being, my son), in prison with me. All that happens, one must try to understand.

Jeannie, like Lisa, represents the difference between speech and betrayal, reading and repression, intimacy and compromise.

For Olsen, history resides in memory, in economics, and in a social text that establishes a connection between Eva, her listener/son, and the reader. The recovery of history is the means of the recovery of both Olsen's voice and Eva's voice; it is also, I would argue, the subject of **"Tell Me a Riddle."** Eva's integration of her history is set against her grandchildren's ignorance of the Russian revolutions, the Holocaust, and the Cold War. Rather than deconstructing the subject, therefore, Olsen offers a model of consciousness mediated through relationships with other subjects who are also positioned historically. It is an aesthetics that accounts for alienation and communication.

Language is a mediation. It has the capacity to arise from and interact with history, to reflect, reproduce, and create change and to alter consciousness. Silence is repression. Silence is rebellion. But it is not freedom.

—*Jean Pfaelzer*

In dying, Eva begins to speak again, answering David's insistent question of life, "For what?" At first she speaks incessantly, and to David it seems "that for seventy years she had hidden a tape recorder, infinitely microscopic, within her, that it had coiled infinite mile on mile, trapping every song, every melody, every word read, heard, and spoken— and that maliciously she was playing back only what said nothing of him, of the children, of their intimate life together." Like Virginia Woolf's narcissistic speechifier, David initially rejects the words that do not glorify him, or even pertain to him, and he calls Eva "Mrs. Philosopher," "Mrs. Miserable," and "Mrs. Babbler," insults that hide his grief and dependence, insults that connote Eva's new ability to articulate her sense of political loss and challenge his passivity.

Eva's death is neither the price exacted for her resistance nor the emblem of her defeat, as it might have been in ear-

lier narratives. Rather, as David finally comes to understand, it represents the merging of past and future, and the continuity of collectivity, idealism, and meaning itself. In the end Eva, no longer "Mrs. Word Miser," becomes "First mother, singing mother," hoarsely chanting passages from radical speeches, books, and songs, from memories of a year imprisoned in solitary confinement, from earlier fragmented memories of a sore-covered child dancing her ecstasy alone at a crossroads village wedding. The story ends in a contest of sounds as Eva, in dying, hoarsely chants Victor Hugo's songs of revolutionary possibility while David noisily slaps playing cards on the table, ironically loud and cynical in a game of solitaire:

> Deuce, ten, five. Dauntlessly she began a song on their youth of belief:
> > *These things shall be, a loftier race*
> > *than e'er the world has known shall rise*
> > *with flame of freedom in their souls*
> > *and light of knowledge in their eyes*
> King, four, jack "In the twentieth century, hah!"
> > *They shall be gentle, brave and strong*
> > *to spill no drop of blood, but dare*
> > *all . . .*
> > > *on earth and fire and sea and air*

Finally we do not know whether David or Eva is speaking; the boundaries between them, indeed, the boundaries between male and female, dissolve through dialogic voices. Her songs of freedom release David's disjointed memories of the "monstrous shapes of what had actually happened in the century," of his American grandchildren who never hunger, who go to school, who live unravaged by disease, and of Eva, the "mother treading at the sewing machine singing with the children," the "girl in her wrinkled prison dress, hiding her hair with scarred hands, lifting to him her awkward, shamed imploring eyes of love," and his wifely lover, "in all the heavy passion he had loved to rouse from her." Through Eva's deathbed songs he understands that the political and private endure as one in her, and he asks her his final question: "Still you believe? You lived by it? These things shall be?" Once articulated, her polemic becomes communal. And David loses both the freedom of noncomprehension and despair of the future.

Olsen here has avoided several dangers of representing the decentered self: superficiality, flatness, attention to form per se, and a waning of human affect. Indeed, Olsen recovers human affect by representing alienation. Discontinuities, fluctuations between voices and between past and present, signify the possibility of inscribing understanding and change. For Olsen, meaning endures through words. David decides to let Eva die and "with her their youth of belief out of which her bright, betrayed words foamed; stained words, that on her working lips came stainless." Eva's "working lips" have subverted, reclaimed, and purified the "stained words."

What is really at stake in this debate over language, which Elaine Showalter calls one of the most exciting debates in gynocriticism? Postmodernists, following Lacan, have predicted radical social and political consequences from the discovery of the "solidarity of logocentrism and phallocentrism." By bringing this solidarity to light Helene Cixous, for example, announces that she has "threatened the stability of the masculine edifice which passed itself off as eternal-natural." She wonders, as did Woolf, what "if it were to come out in a new day that the logocentric project had always been understandable to '*fonder*' (to found and to fund) phallocentrism, to insure for masculine order a rationale equal to history itself? Then all the stories would have to be told differently, the future would be incalculable, the historical forces would, will change hands, bodies." But unlike Woolf, Cixous goes on to propose that "another thinking as yet not thinkable will transform the functioning of all society." What we need to do, she concludes, is "invent another history." But history, as our studies of utopia have shown, cannot be "invented." And "thinking," in and of itself, does not create change.

An alternative to inventing history is not to invent at all. Gauthier observes, "Perhaps if we had left these pages blank, we would have had a better understanding of what feminine writing is all about." Similarly, in *Les guerilleres,* Monique Wittig observes,

> The women say the language you speak poisons your glottis tongue palate lips. They say the language you speak is made up of words that are killing you. They say the language you speak is made up of signs that rightly speaking designate what men have appropriated. Whatever they have not laid hands on whatever they have not pounced on like many-eyed birds of prey does not appear in the language you speak.

But where does it appear? Wittig finds it only "in the intervals that your masters have not been able to fill with their words of proprietors and possessors; this can be found in the gaps, in all that which is not a continuation of their discourse, in the zero, the o, the perfect circle that you invent to imprison them and to overthrow them." And so, women fall into the gap—the quiet enclosed space of their own anatomy.

Fredric Jameson calls this silent telos the "cultural logic" of postmodernism:

> Insofar as the theorist wins, therefore, by constructing an increasingly closed and terrifying machine,

to that very degree he loses, since the critical capacity of his work is thereby paralyzed, and the impulses of negation and revolt, not to speak of those social transformations, are increasingly perceived as vain and trivial in the face of the model itself.

There are, nonetheless, interesting, and perhaps ironic, similarities between the postmodernist's and Marx's view of language. Language, for Marx, is a distorted instance of false consciousness, a type of communication that is unauthentic and alienated. Often it disguises the realities of exploitation and struggle. As Jean Bethke Elshtain observes, when Marx "drops Hegel's dialectic of self-conscious awareness as a linguistically grounded activity . . . the speaking subject goes too. . . . If the only voice in which man speaks is one of rationalization or 'false consciousness' . . . woman's relegation to public silence seems a less important deprivation, a less total denial of her subjectivity."

According to Julia Kristeva, "it seems that certain feminist demands revive a kind of naive romanticism—a belief in identity" unlike her own perspective of "la femme ce n'est jamais ca." But if woman's meanings lie beyond language, how do we even talk about her? **"Tell Me a Riddle,"** I suggest, (re)presents this ineffable woman. Luce Irigary, Julia Kristeva, and Helene Cixous propose a feminine semiotic language that has its roots in pre-symbolic and pre-Oedipal expressions. These nonrational discourses arise in the unconscious, which is the site of resistance to the masculine symbolic order. Only the semiotic discourses can enscribe a radical subjectivity. Further, they alone have the capacity to challenge the social and economic orders of patriarchy. Thus the postmodern concept of social change merges with the concept of subjectivity in a view that is tied to a model of psychosocial development that is particularly resistant to change. It appears to preclude the impact of historical activities and the power of rhetorics to shape consciousness. Implicitly, it puts forth a universalist view of personal development that crosses cultures and epochs. [It is not surprising, then, that postmodernism is not primarily concerned with the project of canon reform.]

Tillie Olsen, by contrast, proposes that politics, work, and love can purge language, which is itself purgation. Language is a mediation. It has the capacity to arise from and interact with history, to reflect, reproduce, and create change and to alter consciousness. Silence is repression. Silence is rebellion. But it is not freedom.

Robert J. Kloss (essay date March 1994)

SOURCE: "Balancing the Hurts and the Needs: Olsen's 'I Stand Here Here Ironing,'" in *Journal of Evolutionary Psychology,* Vol. 15, Nos. 1-2, March, 1994, pp. 78-86.

[In the following essay, Kloss examines the daughter's emotional deprivation in "I Stand Here Ironing."]

Few modern short stories move readers to feel as much compassion toward the inherent vulnerability of the human child as does Tillie Olson's **"I Stand Here Ironing."** In the mother's wrenching narration of simple fact in response to a school psychologist's inquiry about her troubled nineteen-year-old daughter, she reveals all her anguish, past and present. At the same time, she tries not to ". . . become engulfed with all I did not do, with what should have been and what cannot be helped."

Indeed, this tale does raise significant questions about what can and cannot be helped in the upbringing of a child, and discussions of the story usually center on emotional deprivation, personal responsibility, and the question of guilt. Linda Kirschner, in her brief consideration, phrases her inquiry this way: "Yet, how much guilt must the mother bear for Emily's sense of alienations? For how much is she truly responsible?"

Though the question is certainly paramount, at least three separate and separable definitions of *responsible* become conflated and confused in examinations of this tale. Two of them (the third will be cited shortly) raise the issue of guilt and, for many naive readers, blame: To be responsible can mean to be ethically accountable for the care or welfare of another, as are all parents of minors. It can also mean, on the other hand, to be the source or cause of something—in this instance, Emily's difficulties.

It is virtually impossible, however, to tease out once and for all the complexities of the emotional relationships in this story. Nor is it useful. Fixing blame on any one of the characters or events as the source of Emily's problems does not help. As Alexander Portnoy discovers while lying on his analyst's couch, "it alleviates nothing fixing the blame—blaming is still ailing."

What may be useful, though, is to understand why—specifically—Emily suffers as she does and, as well, observe how Olsen, with consummate artistry, creates an integral pattern of maternal-filial interaction that is more than a clinical case study to be filed by the psychologist whose question precipitates the narrative.

In the story, as Joanne Frye has observed, we get motherhood "stripped of romantic distortion." Frye would make of motherhood a metaphor of developing a responsible selfhood, concluding that "We must trust the power of each to 'find her way' even in the face of powerful external constraints on individual control." From the mother's point of view, this may indeed be true, as she attempts in extreme adversity to balance her own hurts and needs. But common

sense tells us that this simply cannot be true for the child. Given her helplessness, what infant or toddler can possibly have it within her power or control to "find her own way," or, as Frye phrases it elsewhere, "can act only from the context of immediate personal limitations but must nevertheless act through a sense of individual responsibility?"

To maintain this is to project adult sensibilities and capabilities into an infant. While the mother can find reasonable and mature ways to satisfy her own needs and allay her hurts (e.g., a job, a new husband), Emily must somehow, first as infant, then child, cope with and defend against persistent, overwhelming fears and fantasies as best she can. As Nancy Chodorow, in her pioneering feminist re-examination of mothering, states it, "At first, the infant is absolutely dependent and, because it does not experience itself as separate, has no way of knowing about maternal care and can do nothing about it. It 'is only in a position to gain profit or to suffer disturbance.'"

To understand the story, then, from the inside out—that is, from Emily's point of view—the third definition of *responsible* can help: to be responsible is to be able to be trusted or depended upon. It is in this respect that the nurture of the child is significantly deficient, for whatever reason, and there are many; and it is this deficiency that so scars the child, making her a source of anguish to the mother and an object of concern to the psychologist. From Emily's vantage point, the world itself is simply not to be trusted ever: nothing, no one is reliable, can be counted on to be there, consistently through time.

Olson demonstrates this lack of basic trust but has so skillfully structured the narrative with flashbacks, for instance, that she obscures the fact that by actual count, Emily suffers at least one dozen traumatic separations from significant people and objects before she is even seven years old.

From Emily's vantage point [in "I Stand Here Ironing"], the world itself is simply not to be trusted—ever: nothing, no one is reliable, can be counted on to be there, consistently through time.
—Robert J. Kloss

A brief summary of these may be in order. The first comes when her mother nurses her not on demand but by book, separating the infant from her and her nurturance, both nutritional and emotional. The father has already abandoned them both—another separation—and when Emily is eight months old, she is placed with the woman downstairs so the mother can work to support them. When she finally gets a night job so she can be with the child days, she is then forced to leave her with her grandparents, a stay lengthened by chicken pox until the child is two years old. At that point, Emily is separated from her mother once more by being sent to nursery school. When a new father enters the picture, the parents leave the child alone nights (she is now five) when they go out.

Shortly afterward, Susan is born, and Emily, separated from the mother who goes to the hospital to give birth, contracts measles and is prevented from going near mother and baby when she returns, prolonging the separation. Emily never fully recovers and is sent to a convalescent home for eight months, an institution that separates her from close friends and from personal belongings like letters from home. When she returns, she pursues a potential boy friend who rejects her blandishments. We learn here that Emily has no friends at all because the family has "moved so much", and we discover as well that she has lost another significant object: World War II is being fought, and the new father is now in the service.

Caring figures thus come and go—the woman downstairs, the grandparents, the mother, the nurses. As the child is moved from house to house to institution to yet another house, even the environment itself does not remain stable. From the child's vantage point then, it seems clear that nothing or no one can be depended on. That these separations are traumatic to Emily can readily be inferred from the fact that they eventuate in significant symptoms. At one time or another throughout her childhood Emily suffers from nightmares, eating disorders (either overeating or undereating), failure to thrive, and at the end of the tale, depression. She exhibits, in fact, the classic symptoms of the syndrome known as separation anxiety disorder.

In his discussion of this problem, Richard Gardner notes that DSM-III [*Diagnostic and Statistical Manual: Mental Diseases*] enumerates its manifestations as follow unrealistic fears that the mother will be harmed or that she will leave and not return, unrealistic fears that a calamitous event will separate the child and the mother, persistent reluctance or refusal to go to school in order to remain home with the mother, persistent reluctance or refusal to go to sleep without the mother, complaints of physical symptoms on school days, signs of excessive distress upon separation or in anticipation of separation, social withdrawal, apathy, and sadness.

A glance at these reveals that they appear to virtually catalog Emily's conflicted behavior throughout the story, especially in infancy and early childhood. Emily's problems indeed begin when the mother, in the ignorance and innocence of youth herself—she is but nineteen—chooses to nurse the newborn Emily as she does " . . . With the fierce rigidity of first motherhood. I did like the books then said

Though her cries battered me to trembling and my breasts ached with swollenness. I waited till the clock decreed. Why do I put that first? I do not even know if it matters or if it explains anything." Intuitively, however, she appears vaguely aware of the enduring significance of her not supplying food to the infant when she needed it and that it does provide a partial explanation for Emily's conflicts. We hear, as well, in her choice of "battered" and "ached" the emotional pain she suffered, and the infant as well, in abiding by the authorities instead of her own maternal sense.

More frequent breast feeding, for instance, would have offered to both mother and infant the opportunity to gaze into each other's even, smiling in mutual satisfaction. Emily's mother, however, dissuaded by experts, does otherwise, and the old man in back reminds her one day. "You should smile at Emily more when you look at her" By the end of her tale the mother, while attempting to deny it, finally does admit that "She was a child seldom smiled at." She wonders that Emily did see in her face and tries to smile more often at her successive children, but admits that Emily herself, as a consequence, "does not smile easily." her face being "closed and sober."

Saunder has observed that any infant needs its mother's attempt to induce a smiling response as an appropriate social stimulus to interaction with others. "The degree to which mutuality will be established," he says, "seems to depend, in part at least, on the balance the mother can maintain between her empathy with what she feels are the child's needs and her objectivity in viewing [her] as an individual apart from her own projections and displacements." We see, then, the initial instance of the mother's difficulty in balancing hurts and needs, of moving beyond the "fierce rigidity," her own anger at being abandoned, toward concern for her newborn. Yet, given her poverty and arduous struggle, can we really blame the mother for not smiling enough, however much that might have been?

The mother's own needs to escape, to enjoy the outside world again with her husband, prompt her to leave the five-year-old Emily alone nights, a fearful time for any child that age. Emily's separation anxiety manifests itself here in several ways. She remains awake, "rigid," until the parents return, and she defends against her fears by denial: "I didn't cry. Three times I called you, just three times. . . ." As well, she engages in typical magical behavior in order to constrain the mother to return sooner: "I ran downstairs to open the door so you could come faster. The clock talked loud. I threw it away, it scared me what it talked." Had mother been psychologically sophisticated, she would have known that the clock's message (actually, of course, Emily's internal fear projected) was "Your mother is never coming back!"

It is this fear, never allayed, that manifests itself as the school phobia from which the child suffers. At the age of two, again because authorities say it is appropriate for the child and because she desperately needs to hold a job, the mother places Emily in a nursery school which she eventually realizes is just a "parking place for children." From the start, though, she admits that "Even without knowing, I knew. I knew that the teacher was evil" because of the way she treated the other children. The mother acknowledges that Emily hates leaving her, yet "she did not clutch and implore 'don't go Mommy' like the other children, mornings." She wonders why there was "never a direct protest, never rebellion. . . . What in me demanded that goodness in her? And what was the cost, the cost to her of such goodness?"

The cost to Emily, of course, is depression, and we see here its evidence in submissiveness masking and defending against powerful emotions. Mackinnon and Michels explain the relationship between the intense separation anxiety and such passive posture by noting that "perhaps the simplest psychodynamic basis for this is the patient's anger at the lost love object for abandoning him." But " . . . Any outward expression of hostility is dangerous—he might destroy what he most needs. He therefore turns it against himself in the form of self-accusation and condemnation, a cardinal feature of depression." This self-accusation will appear later, in Emily's adolescence.

As Emily grows older, she does indeed refuse to go to school. This behavior is consistent with Gardner's finding that "Generally, the younger the child the greater is the fear element. And the older the child, the greater is the refusal element." We learn, too, that the mother is frequently complicitous in Emily's manipulations, rationalizing that "We had a new baby, I was home anyhow." Indeed, she eventually allows the younger child, Susan, to stay home as well, "to have them all together." She claims she is trying hard to establish a warm environment and create rapprochement between the sisters, where now only "poisonous feeling" and "corroding resentment" reign. Her attempts she labels "that terrible balancing of hurts and needs", for Emily's emotional conflicts have become significantly worse since the birth of her younger sister.

Part of the mother's explanation for allowing Emily to absent herself from school is that the child was sick, "though sometimes the illness was imaginary." We should not be surprised that Emily's affliction is asthma, a condition clinically linked to the dependent character which expresses an "exaggerated need for a bond with the mother . . . accompanied by an acute fear of loss of the mother's love. . . ." The asthmatic seizure itself, as Fenichel points out, is first and foremost "an anxiety equivalent. It is a cry for help, directed toward the mother, whom the patient tries to introject by respiration in order to be permanently protected." It accomplishes its purpose in Emily's case by constraining the

mother to attend to her every need, and the latter seems half aware that the attack resolves a conflict, for she notices that Emily's "breathing, harsh and labored, would fill the house with a curious tranquil sound."

Susan's birth has contributed to Emily's distress by precipitating this asthma and other symptoms. Still recovering from measles upon her sister's arrival, Emily "stayed skelton thin, not wanting to eat, and night after night she had nightmares." Olsen's use of "skelton thin," prefigures the deadened affect of Emily's depression and speaks as well to the deadliness of emotional deprivation. Emily's not eating in this instance most probably serves multiple functions, expressing both her insatiable desire for attention from the mother and her own extreme defensive denial that she needs food, which has understandably become equated with both love and mother.

Emily engages in a similar hunger strike, for example, when she is sent to the convalescent home to recover from the measles and loses seven pounds during her stay. These oral conflicts continue, interfering seriously with the child's growth. The mother observes of Susan, for instance, that "for all the five years difference in age [she] was just a year behind Emily in developing physically." We thus obliquely discover that Emily's emotional deprivation has resulted in an actual lack of physical growth, a not uncommon phenomenon.

The child's psychic dwarfism may also have other, defensive functions, serving, for example, to reject adulthood. To not grow up is to not become an adult with all attendant responsibilities. The mother herself has informed us that responsibility was thrust on Emily, now with four younger siblings, much too soon. "She had to help be a mother, and housekeeper, and shopper. She had to set her seal." Regression under these conditions is common, especially when those whose own emotional needs haven't been adequately met are constrained to nurture others. As Gardner has noted, " . . . Adolescents may regress and entrench the dependent tie with the mother to provide protection from venturing forth into a demanding and less benevolent world."

And Emily has already discovered that the outside world is less than benevolent. She had "painfully" loved a little boy for a year and stole money from her mother's purse to buy him candy daily, "but he still liked Jennifer better'n me. Why, Mommy? The kind of question for which there is no answer." Though we too cannot answer the child's poignant question, we can understand why Olsen chooses this particular enactment to express symbolically Emily's disappointment in love. Raiding mother's purse is typical behavior among children who are excessively dependent. "Some children steal as a way of acting out hostility, and anything that can reduce their anger may be helpful. Others do it because of feelings of deprivation of affection, the stolen object symbolizing love or a prized possession or present." Both of these motives are consistent with what we already know of Emily, and it is additionally interesting that she chooses to bribe the little boy with food to obtain love, that is to do actively to someone else what she most fervently would like done to her.

The sleep disorders typical of separation anxiety disorder also begin with Susan's birth when Emily begins having nightmares, crying out for the mother. The mother, however, refuses to tend her in her anguish and gets up only twice when she has to get up for Susan anyway. The mother's indifference may be due to her exhaustion and distraction, but it is also possible to see it as stemming from hostility, perhaps unconscious.

Olsen herself has provided us with a clue to this aspect of the mother's troubled relationship with Emily during the child's chicken pox. Having been sent to the in-laws so that the mother could hold a job down, Emily returns home, and says the mother, " . . . I hardly knew her, walking *quick and nervous like her father, looking like her father,* . . . all the baby loveliness gone" (italics added). It is a reasonable inference to discern in the child's resemblance to the abandoning father the source of mother's hostility toward her, displaced from him. This helps us better understand why the mother finds it so difficult to balance her own hurts and needs and why despite her continual best intentions, aside from external reality factors (her job, etc.), she seems unable to act beneficially in the child's best interests, giving her enough food, enough love of herself.

Emily, however, eventually ceases her hunger strikes and develops "her enormous appetite that is legendary in our family", probably using food as a substitute for love. The mother refers to this change as taking place only as "in those years," but it appears to be during high school and World War II since the mother occasionally writes "V-Mail to Bill." This, of course, tells us that as a consequence of the war, Emily's second father has, from her point of view, in a sense, "abandoned" her and his family.

As important as mother is to Emily, we should not underestimate the significance of these various fathers and their presences and absences on the psychic development of the child. Chodorow points out that "The child uses its father not only in its differentiation of self. The father also enables more firm differentiation of objects. The infant, as it struggles out of primary identification, is less able to compare itself and its mother, than to compare mother and father, or mother and other important people she relates to This comparison indicates the mother's boundedness and existence as a separate person. The comparison also reveals the mother's special qualities—finding out that the whole world does not provide care increases her uniqueness in the child's eyes." How much more poignant, then, that from Emily's point of view neither mother nor the world—represented here by father—provides adequate care.

In her adolescence, of course, the separation anxiety symptoms persevere and others develop. She "tomented herself about not looking like the others", like a typical teen, and it is probable that this self-accusation is fed by the hostility felt against the mother but deflected toward the self in order not to endanger the relationship. Frye, though, sees in it "the limitations of a parent's capacity to foster a child's growth in selfhood . . . ," noting that "a human being cannot rely on the perpetual presence of external seeing eyes to validate her own authenticity as a separate self."

While this is to some extent true, what Frye overlooks is the reason Emily still seeks that validation: she has never had her own existence and separateness from her mother fully confirmed by adequate *mirroring,* the reciprocal gazing into the eyes of the mother that establishes the basic trust of consistency, continuity, and sameness of care provided by that mother. Through this process, intimately linked to breast feeding and stimulation of the smile response, the infant makes mother, once an outer predictability, into an inner certainty, a sense that the world is a good place where one's needs are provided for. "Hopefully," as Robert Coles has put it, "the infant is held and feels held, craves food and finds his appetites satisfied, looks and sees in return his mother's eyes." In these eyes, the infant finds confirmation of his own existence, the initial sense not of *who* I am but *that* I am.

The infant, literally mirrored in his mother's eyes, apparently constructs a series of connected notions: "(1) the infant-child in the mother's eyes (that is, the actually observed reflection); (2) the infant-child in the mother's eyes (that is, as she sees him); (3) the primitive self observation, the earliest mirror of self; and (4) the gradually developing sense of reality—what I really am, as compared with what the mirror tells or seems to tell of what is my identity." Optimal mirroring therefore aids the child in consolidating his own identity because it enables him as a separate entity and to realize the existence of a separate object out there, an "I" vs. a "not-I." On the other hand, poor mirroring—insufficient holding, smiling, gazing, nurturing—leads to deeply rooted conflicts such as those Emily exhibits.

Olsen, however, strikes a single optimistic note when she provides the child with, if not an ostensible path to salvation at least a means of obtaining attention and adulation and alleviating her anguish. This is, of course, of Emily's talent for producing laughter in others. "Sometimes," the mother says, "to make me laugh or out of despair, she would imitate happenings or types at school." A chance remark of the mother's encourages her to enter a school talent show which she wins, starting her amateur career as a comedian. As the mother phrases it, "Now suddenly she was Somebody, and as imprisoned in her difference as she had been in her anonymity", the statement revealing the confirmation of separateness in the eyes of others that she had not been able to find in the eyes of the mother.

We should remember, too, that earlier Olsen has stated that Emily would relate jokes and riddles to Susan with which the latter would then amuse the mother and company, while Emily sat silent and resentful, complaining later that they were *hers* originally. In her public career, then, she appears to be imitating her younger sister's method of finding favor with the mother. The latter harbors her own suspicions that Emily's levity has its origins in the darker recesses of the girl's conflicted mind, as revealed by her speculation that it is done "out of her despair" and by her own anguished remark that her daughter's talent is "deadly clowning."

This deadliness appears in Emily's final words in the story when she reveals her fantasy about the future. Asked by her mother about her midterms as she kisses her goodnight, Emily blithely responds, " . . . In a couple of years when we'll all be atom-dead they won't matter a bit." Frye believes that this does not indicate Emily "succumbing to that despairing view; rather she is asserting her own right to choice as she lightly claims her wish to sleep late in the morning." This unwarranted optimism, however, conveniently overlooks virtually all the evidence of the girl's depression and despair. Given this, it is impossible not to see in Emily's remark both her projected rage and a fantasy of her ever undependable world violently disappearing. It symbolizes that long-feared calamitous event that would separate her absolutely and forever from the mother she has longed for since birth.

Indeed, the mother herself finds the remark unbearable: "She has said it before. She *believes* it." Returning then to her symbolic ironing, she tries to remove the wrinkles of life and stress, hoping that Emily will recognize that she is "more than this dress on the ironing board, helpless before the iron." The probability is low. Kirschner, like the mother, retains hope for Emily, yet is forced to admit that "a childhood of poverty and emotional deprivation have obviously taken their toll . . . ," and that there are "lasting psychological implications that Emily may never overcome."

These psychological implications are enormous, for the findings in regard to children like Emily are consistent: significant personality disturbances almost inevitably result from "repetitive separations associated with other traumatic and depriving experiences," and that "reversibility becomes improbable with increased age." It is no wonder then that, from Emily's point of view, the future seems hopeless, and the world she could never trust or depend upon may vanish shortly in a tremendous roar, a blast of light, and a mushroom cloud.

Martin, in her biographical sketch of the author, has observed that "Though Olsen disclaims the 'autobiographical' label for her work, she does admit that this story is 'somewhat close to my own life.'" This is a courageous statement on the author's part, and yet that "somewhat" spans the often vast distance between reality and artistic creation. Whatever the former, the latter is a faithful depiction, compassionate to both, of a mother and daughter trapped in circumstances frequently not of their own making and struggling as best they can to win out over those circumstances. The portrait is clear, the harrowing anguish of both evident.

Abandonment by an irresponsible father, the innocence and ignorance of youth on the mother's part, an unstable home situation, chronic illness, birth order, poverty and deprivation—all these combine to affect Emily deeply, and perhaps irrevocably. The mother, trying to balance her own hurts and needs, does her best trying to help Emily balance hers, hoping out of desperation that the child may prove more than the inert dress from which she attempts to press the symbolic wrinkles and creases.

It is testimony to her heroism that she irons throughout her narration and continues to do so at story's end, her Sisyphean labor depicting her maternal love for her daughter and her desperate hopes for her well-being. A chance remark about a talent show, after all, once saved Emily, moved her from anonymity to being Somebody; some other event just might again change her life for the better. In a world as bleak as theirs, one must hope for the best and, like a Beckett character who can't go on, simply go on.

FURTHER READING

Criticism

Coiner, Constance. "Literature of Resistance: The Intersection of Feminism and the Communist Left in Meridel Le Sueur and Tillie Olsen." In *Radical Revisions: Rereading the 1930s Culture,* edited by Bill Mullen and Sherry Lee Linkon, pp. 144-66. Urbana: University of Illinois Press, 1996.

> Places Le Sueur's and Olsen's work against the backdrop of Leftist culture in the 1930s.

Connelly, Julia E. "The Whole Story." *Literature and Medicine* 9 (1990): 150-61.

> Explores the roles of patient and physician in Olsen's "Tell Me a Riddle" and Leo Tolstoy's "The Death of Ivan Ilyitch."

Neihus, Edward L. "Polar Stars, Pyramids, and 'Tell Me A Riddle.'" *American Notes and Querries* XXIV, Nos. 5-6 (January-February 1986): 77-83.

> Explains the significance of the reference to pyramids and pole stars in "Tell Me a Riddle."

Additional coverage of Olsen's life and career is contained in the following sources published by Gale: *Contemporary Authors,* **Vols. 1-4R;** *Contemporary Authors New Revision Series,* **Vols. 1, and 43;** *Dictionary of Literary Biography,* **Vol. 28;** *Dictionary of Literary Biography Yearbook: 1980;* *DISCovering Authors; DISCovering Authors: Canadian; DISCovering Authors: Most-studied Authors Module; Major 20th-Century Writers;* **and** *Short Story Criticism,* **Vol. 11.**

Ken Saro-Wiwa
1941-1995

(Full name Kenule Beeson Saro-Wiwa) Nigerian novelist, essayist, diarist, poet, short story writer, playwright, television writer and producer.

The following entry provides an overview of Saro-Wiwa's career through 1997.

INTRODUCTION

Saro-Wiwa achieved popularity in Nigeria as a satirist of Nigeria's notoriously corrupt government, but gained worldwide fame as a political activist executed for his vocal protest of multinational exploitation of local culture. His nonfiction works detailing Nigerian corruption and his own imprisonment have been widely praised as provocative and compassionate.

Biographical Information

Born in Bori, in southeastern Nigeria, in 1941, Saro-Wiwa was a member of the Ogoni tribe, one of Nigeria's many ethnic minorities. His father was Chief J. B. Wiwa, a civil servant, and his mother was Widu Wiwa, a trader and farmer. Recognized early as a gifted student, Saro-Wiwa attended the Native Authority School from 1947 to 1954 and went on to the distinguished Government College Omaha until 1961. There he took advantage of the school's extensive library to study literature and explore his proclivity for writing and publishing. After graduating, Saro-Wiwa taught at the school for a year before his acceptance into the University of Ibadan, where he furthered his study of English as well as French and German literature and began working in drama. He graduated in 1965 and taught at Stella Maris College in Port Harcourt, Nigeria, and then at Government College Omaha before returning to the University of Ibadan for further study of drama. His work there was cut short by the political violence that escalated into civil war in 1967. Saro-Wiwa held two more teaching positions before entering the political sphere as an administrator for Bonny, Rivers State, after its liberation from Biafran forces and as a member of the Interim Advisory Council of Rivers State. Shortly thereafter, Saro-Wiwa began his literary career with his radio play *The Transistor Radio* (1972), which tied for fourth place in the British Broadcasting Service competition in drama. He published books for young people and plays in the next year, and then his career in government ended when he was forced to resign his post as commissioner in the Ministry of Works, Land, and Transport, the Ministry of Education, and the Ministry of Information and Home Affairs when the governor

of the state objected to Saro-Wiwa's play *Eneka*. Over the next twelve years Saro-Wiwa became a successful businessman and eventually founded Saros International Publishers to publish his own works. He also wrote and produced a highly successful situation comedy on Nigerian television, *Basi and Company,* a satire that lampooned widespread Nigerian corruption. In 1985 his first self-published works appeared—a collection of poems entitled *Songs in a Time of War* and his most acclaimed novel, *Sozaboy*. At this point, Saro-Wiwa began focusing more, in both his writing and his personal life, on Nigeria's devastating civil war and on the oppression of the Ogoni people by government forces and multinational oil companies whose efforts to profit from the oil fields beneath the Ogoni region had left the land blighted. Saro-Wiwa launched a campaign against Shell Oil—which had been drilling in the region since the 1930s and had left the land severely polluted and infertile—with a group called Movement for the Survival of the Ogoni People (MOSOP). Dedicated to seeking redress from Shell and in calling government complicity with Shell genocide, the group incurred the suspicion of the militaristic regime. Saro-Wiwa was arrested in 1993 and charged with treason. He was released after several months, but was again arrested when a MOSOP rally, not attended by Saro-Wiwa, erupted in violence and four Ogoni elders were killed. Saro-Wiwa and eight others were charged with murder and imprisoned for over a year. The affair prompted international outrage from political and environmental organizations, who unsuccessfully tried to pressure the Nigerian government into dropping charges. After the trial—largely considered to be merely a staged publicity stunt to appease the opposition—Saro-Wiwa and the others were executed.

Major Works

Saro-Wiwa's literary career is generally considered to fall into two distinct periods: the early 1970s, and the 1980s until his death. His first two published works, *Tambari* (1973) and *Tambari in Dukana* (1973) are adventure stories for young readers in which Saro-Wiwa employs qualities of traditional African folktales and oral story-telling set against colorful descriptions of village life. Embarking on a business career, Saro-Wiwa gave up writing until 1985, when he began publishing his own works. In *Songs in a Time of War* (1985), his first collection of poetry, Saro-Wiwa depicts the tragedy of Nigeria's civil war largely in pidgin (or "rotten") English. His next published work, *Sozaboy* (1985), is written entirely in pidgin to offer a rhythmic, lyrical sense of authenticity. His most acclaimed work of fiction, the novel concerns a young man who dreams of becoming a "sozaboy," or soldier boy, in the civil war. He is instead captured and forced to fight for the enemy's side, and upon his return home, he learns of his wife's and mother's death in the war and is shunned by his family. *A Forest of Flowers* (1986), Saro-Wiwa's first short story collection, evokes village life in Nigeria both before and after the civil war. In the 1980s Saro-Wiwa wrote and produced a highly successful television series called *Basi and Company*. A farcical situation comedy, the show spoofed the widespread corruption in Nigerian government and society. Saro-Wiwa also published a series of books based on the television series. He again satirized the Nigerian government in *Prisoners of Jebs* (1988), his third novel. The prison portrayed in the novel represents the African continent in microcosm, and this allows Saro-Wiwa the ability to comment on the social and political atmosphere in post-colonial Africa. Saro-Wiwa gained great respect as a critic of Nigeria's—and Africa's—political system beginning with his autobiographical novel *On a Darkling Plain* (1989), in which he focused on the devastating effects of the war on the Ogoni people of his homeland. After two more volumes of short stories—*Adaku and Other Stories* (1989) and *The Singing Anthill* (1991)—Saro-Wiwa turned to nonfiction in *Nigeria* (1991) and *Similia* (1991), both of which address the oppression of the Ogoni people. In 1992 Saro-Wiwa published *Genocide in Nigeria*. In this book, he openly accuses the Nigerian government of genocide because of its compliance with multinational oil companies. Saro-Wiwa's final publication was the posthumous *A Month and a Day* (1995), the diary he secretly kept during his imprisonment prior to his execution.

Critical Reception

While Saro-Wiwa has been praised for his experimentation with pidgin English and his sensitive evocation of village life in his fiction, as well as the biting satire on his television series, *Basi and Company,* he received the highest praise for his nonfiction works critical of Nigeria's corrupt government. His passionate pleas to end the exploitation of the Ogoni people earned him high regard from environmental and human rights activists around the world.

PRINCIPAL WORKS

The Transistor Radio (radio play) 1972
Bride by Return (radio play) 1973
Tabari (children's fiction) 1973
Tambari in Dukana (children's fiction) 1973
Songs in a Time of War (poetry) 1985
Sozaboy: A Novel in Rotten English (novel) 1985
A Forest of Flowers (short stories) 1986
Basi and Company: A Modern African Folktale (novel) 1987
Prisoners of Jebs (novel) 1988
Adaku and Other Stories (short stories) 1989
Four Farcical Plays (plays) 1989
On a Darkling Plain: An Account of the Nigerian Civil War (novel) 1989
Nigeria: The Brink of Disaster (essays) 1991
Pita Dumbrok's Prison (novel) 1991
Similia: Essays on Anomic Nigeria (essays) 1991
The Singing Anthill: Ogoni Folk Tales (short stories) 1991
Genocide in Nigeria: The Ogoni Tragedy (nonfiction) 1992
A Month and a Day: A Detention Diary (diary) 1995

CRITICISM

Graham Hough (review date 3 July 1986)

SOURCE: "Afro-Fictions," in *London Review of Books,* Vol. 8, No. 12, July 3, 1986, pp. 22-3.

[*Hough is an English author and educator. In the following review, he praises Saro-Wiwa's ability to capture the peculiarities of Nigerian life in* A Forest of Flowers.]

Ken Saro-Wiwa's extremely accomplished collection of short stories [*A Forest of Flowers*] stands to Nigeria in something of the same relation as Joyce's *Dubliners* to Ireland. They are brief epiphanies, each crystallising a moment, a way of living, the whole course of a life. When as a youngster I first read *Dubliners* I remember being baffled by the way eerie characters and their bizarre motivations were calmly accepted as part of the ordinary nature of things. Saro-Wiwa's tales bring back something of this feeling. There is great variety in these glimpses. The book is divided into two parts—innocence and experience, you might call them. The first part deals with Dukana, a village community, the second with the more sophisticated life of the towns. Not that there is anything idyllic about the village; it is sunk in dirt, apathy and superstition. An educated girl comes back there, thinking of it as home, and eager to see an old friend from school-days. But she finds the friend has disappeared, been driven out, no one knows where. She has committed the misdemeanour of having twins. A solitary man who talks to nobody but gets on with his farming by himself is suspected of witchcraft, simply because he is a loner, and is burnt alive in his hut. Yet all the families are close and affectionate; and an element of placid bargain-keeping does something to mitigate the harshest arrangements. A beautiful girl is married, and married well, since it is to a lorry-driver; but she turns out to be barren and so is repudiated—with the agreement of all, including the girl herself. She simply pays back her bride-price, goes back to her mother, and resumes her life as before, without resentment or disgrace. Less sombre are the vagaries of the Holy Spiritual Church of Mount Zion in Israel, and the complex arrangements to defeat the Sanitary Inspector—involving, of course, the defeat of all attempts at sanitation.

This brings us on to Part Two, where the towns, repositories of government and business, are exposed in all the depths of their squalor, incompetence, chicanery and corruption. Some of this is the stuff of comedy: in the negotiations about the Acapulco Motel muddle and cheating seem to be tolerantly expected on all sides. But in the two stories **'The Stars Below'** and **'Night Ride'** we get a steady look at the heartbreaking hopelessness of this society. In each case an idealistic young official surveys the ruin of his life, the wreck of the world around him in the aftermath of a ghastly civil war, and the doubt whether the old apathetic stagnation or the new conscienceless greed is worse.

But I have made these stories seem more sombre than they are. An unlovely world, but much of it is rendered with affection; and there is immense satisfaction for the reader in the adroitness and variety of the presentation. A few of the tales are in pidgin, which I can hardly judge. Others use interior monologue and make a wonderfully happy accommodation between the idiosyncrasy of the characters and the decorum of the English language; while the parts where the narrator speaks in his own person have a straightforward elegance that is extremely attractive.

Though the colonial past of Nigeria is not very far away, it plays little or no part in the awareness of Saro-Wiwa's characters. The new regime is self-determined, and the new official class has so successfully appropriated the privileges of its colonial predecessors that there is no room for *ci-devant* resentments. Whatever the social results of this, the literary effects are benign. It means that the writer can get on with his own job without taking on the burdens of others. . .

Ken Goodwin (review date Autumn 1987)

SOURCE: Review of *Songs in a Time of War* by Ken Saro-Wiwa, in *World Literature Written in English,* Vol. 27, No. 2, Autumn 1987, pp. 232-33.

[*Goodwin is an Australian author and educator. In the following review, he praises Saro-Wiwa's evocation of war-time Nigeria in* Songs in a Time of War.]

In this modest contribution to Nigerian poetry in English [*Songs in a Time of War*], Ken Saro-Wiwa writes chiefly about the political manipulation and human waste of warfare. The war references are to the Biafran war, during which Saro-Wiwa served as a Federal administrator. Though these poems lack the immediacy and vivid particularity of J. P. Clark's war poems, they do convey a constant longing for silence and for the soft-breathing life of peaceful nighttime, as well as a sense of open landscape with a slightly menacing quality.

"The Escape" is a poem detailing the author's flight from the Delta region to Lagos as the Biafran troops advanced westward in September 1967. Among its images of fear and apprehension are one of the day hung out in front like a curtain, "A drawn-out horizon taut with uncertainty." During the river voyage he comes upon a scene in which

> White birds stood on stumps in mid-stream
> Silent and watchful . . .

In the same poem, the slightly archaic (Edwardian or First-World-War) diction that Saro-Wiwa uses can be sensed in "Naval guns boom as of yore." His point here is that, though his repetition of colonial experience might encourage a sense of *déjà vu,* in a civil war within an independent country "the issues are far greater."

Despite Saro-Wiwa's abhorrence of war and his concentration on the sorrow and pity of it all, he cannot resist some condemnation of Biafra's leaders, particularly in **"Epitaph for Biafra"**:

Didn't they test the hardness of the egg
On the skin of their teeth
Before dashing it against the rocks?

It is in such images that he manages to rise above the prosaic and declaratory quality of much of the verse. His best poems have a sensory quality that vivifies them, whether it is the "white balls of fire" that "Ascend the sky at dusk" in a war poem or the witty image of the "Tired and breathless spaceman" who, remembering an encounter with a courtesan, is able to "Toil on for the pleasures / Of the final splashdown."

The last poem in this small volume is a long satire in pidgin. In it the words "Nigeria" and "confusion" appear as a refrain, as Saro-Wiwa expresses both lament for and condemnation of Nigeria's openness to exploitation, corruption, and the temptation to borrow (both fiscally and culturally). Addressing the country, he says

Nigeria, you too like borrow borrow
You borrow money, cloth you dey borrow
You borrow motor, you borrow aeroplane
You dey borrow chop, you borrow drink
Sotey you borrow anoder man language. . . .

It is a poem written in sorrow, not in resignation or hopelessness, for he has faith in the natural resources of the country and he does not despair of all the people, for

Oh yes, som Nigerian pickin get sense
And better go follow dem all.

Adewale Maja-Pearce (review date 22 July 1988)

SOURCE: "Nigeria Laughs at Itself," in *New Statesman and Society,* Vol. 1, No. 7, July 22, 1988, pp. 44.

[*Maja-Pearce is a Nigerian-born author, editor, and educator. In the following review, she finds that while its subject matter is worthy of satire,* Prisoners of Jebs *is not entirely successful.*]

Prisoners of Jebs is a collection of 53 sketches, first published as a weekly column between January 1986 and January 1987 in the Nigerian *Vanguard* newspaper. In the **"Author's Note"**, Ken Saro-Wiwa tells us that he wanted his column to "examine weekly events in Nigeria", and to the extent that a knowledge of Nigerian politics of this period is helpful for an appreciation of many of the references, it is unlikely that the book will have much appeal to non-Nigerians.

The scene is set in the first sketch, **"The Building of the Prison"**, in which we are told that the Organisation of African Unity, celebrating its 25th anniversary, decide that "prisoners drawn from member-nations, locked up in a pollution-free environment and forced to think day and night about the problems of the continent . . . would certainly usher in progress". Nigeria is unanimously chosen as the site, and an off-shore prison, courtesy of the Dutch and the Bulgarians, is duly constructed.

This leaves the way for the kind of satire of Nigerian life that has now become the stock-in-trade of a number of inventive Nigerian journalists. Nigerians have never been slow to criticise their society; on the other hand, Nigerian society affords plenty of material: "The Nigerians had voted millions for the running of Jebs. The Nigerians always vote millions for the running of their institutions. And as is usual in Nigeria, Jebs' millions disappeared in no time. It was quite astounding, the ability of Nigeria's millions to perform the disappearing trick."

Or again: "In keeping with its reputation as Africa's most populous state, Nigeria had the most prisoners. And they were the loudest inmates. They showed off, broke all queues, played loud music, shouted at the top of their voices, refused to do manual labour, and ate and drank most."

Almost every Nigerian newspaper, of which there are an estimated 23 dailies and 29 weeklies, delights in this kind of social comment. This probably represents the nation's greatest hope: nobody can accuse Nigerians of being unable to laugh at themselves, a pre-requisite for fundamental social change.

Social satire of this kind also serves a useful function if you happen to be stuck in a car in Lagos during one of the legendary "go-slows"—the experience of anybody who has to go to work every day. Unfortunately, journalism rarely survives longer than the date on the newspaper. After the first half-dozen sketches in *Prisoners of Jebs* I found myself growing just a little weary, partly because the joke had worn a little thin, partly because the form itself precludes any development of character.

Ken Saro-Wiwa (essay date Spring 1992)

SOURCE: "The Language of African Literature: A Writer's Testimony," in *Research in African Studies,* Vol. 23, No. 1, Spring 1992, pp. 153-57.

[*In the following essay, Saro-Wiwa justifies his choice of writing in English rather than any of the various Nigerian languages.*]

I was born to Ogoni parents at Bori on the northern fringes of the delta of the Niger during the Second World War. I grew up speaking one of the three Ogoni languages—Khana, my mother-tongue—and listening to and telling folk tales in that language.

> **If Europeans speak of French literature, Spanish literature, and English literature, why do we insist on having an "African literature" and debating what language it should be written in?**
> —*Ken Saro-wiwa*

When I went to primary school in 1947, I was taught in my mother-tongue during the first two years. During the other six years of the primary school course, the teaching was done in English, which soon imprinted itself on my mind as the language of learning. Khana was the language of play, and it appeared on the class time-table once or twice a week as "vernacular"—wonderful, story-telling sessions in Khana. We spoke Khana at home, and we read the Bible at church in Khana. It was enough to make me literate in Khana to this day.

The Ogoni lived a simple, circumscribed life at that time; farming and fishing were their sole occupations. There were a number of primary schools in the area, but no secondary school. All those who wished or were able to go to secondary school had to move to other parts of the country.

Accordingly, in 1954, at about 13, I proceeded to Government College, Omaha, which was the best school in the area. I was the only Ogoni boy in the entire school. Others were mostly Igbo, Ibibio, Ijaw, and representatives of other ethnic groups in what was then Eastern Nigeria. A few came from the Cameroons, which was at that time administered as a part of Nigeria. The English language was a unifying factor at the school; in fact, there was a regulation forbidding the use of any of our mother-tongues at work or during recreation. This rule ensured that boys like myself did not feel lost in the school because we could not communicate with any other boy in our mother-tongues. There were no books in any other language, apart from English, in the school's excellent library. We worked and played in English. One result of this regime was that in a single generation, the school produced Chinua Achebe, Gabriel Okara, the late Christopher Okigbo, Elechi Amadi Vincent Ike, and I. N. C. Aniebo, who was my contemporary.

There, at Government College, I began to write poems, short stories, and plays in English, the language which, as I have said, bound us all together. There was no question of my writing in Khana because no one else would have understood it.

From Government College, I proceeded in 1962 to the University of Ibadan, where I met young men and women from different parts of a vast country. By then, Nigeria had become independent. The language of instruction at Ibadan was English of course. There was no restriction as to what language we could use outside the lecture halls. So, those who were there in sufficient numbers invariably spoke their mother-tongues among themselves. However, English was what enabled students from different ethnic backgrounds to communicate with each other. English was also the official language of the country, by necessity. I wrote poems, short stories, and plays in English. Once again, there was no question of my using my Khana mother-tongue, which no one else at the university would have understood. I was studying English and, at that time, had come across the argument of Obi Wali (whom I was later to meet and know intimately). According to him, English was the dead-end of African literature.

In those days, African literature was a fashionable course of study, although I did not find it so. I had read most of the novels published by Africans in English and did not feel that they added up to much as a course of study. I was also preparing to be a writer, and I was not impressed by Dr Wali's arguments for the simple reason that I did not consider myself as a writer of African literature. I wanted to be a good storyteller, no more, no less. Putting me in a category would be the business of the critics. In any case, I was yet to publish anything. That was 1963 or thereabouts.

Nigeria had become independent three years earlier, and the country was gradually gravitating towards war. As a boy, I knew that I was an Ogoni. Of that, there was never any doubt. I also knew that Khana was my mother-tongue. Most Ogonis spoke Khana. It was a secure world.

Growing up at Government College in Omaha, I interacted with boys my age from different parts of the Eastern Region of Nigeria. And because the school taught us to be good citizens, I had learned the necessity of being a good Nigerian. By independence in 1960, I had taken the fact for granted. I had travelled to different parts of the country and knew something of the great mixture of peoples that is Nigeria. Somehow, as long as I could speak and read English, it was easy to relate to the rest of the country—away from my Ogoni home. So, English was important. Not only as the language which opened new areas to me, but as a link to the other peoples with whom I came into contact during my day-to-day life.

I had barely graduated from the University of Ibadan when I was contented with the true nature of Nigerian society as an agglomeration of peoples and cultures, much like the rest of Africa. By the way, school taught me about Africa. As a boy in my Ogoni home, the idea of Africa never arose. It is not an Ogoni concept. Nor was Nigeria. But to get back to 1965. The great argument that later tore Nigeria apart and led us to a murderous civil war was already raging. By 1967, the war had broken out. I was then a Graduate Assistant at the University of Nigeria, Nsukka.

During that war, I played a role which I had not bargained for. Forced to choose between Nigeria and Biafra, I clung to the former because the arguments for Biafra were the same as the arguments for Nigeria. Simply put, Biafra was a mish-mash of peoples and cultures, where the Igbo predominated oppressively just as Nigeria was a mish-mash of peoples and cultures where the Hausa-Fulani, the Igbo, and the Yoruba predominated oppressively.

Yes, colonialism is not a matter only of British, French, or European dominance over Africans. In African society, there is and has always been colonial oppression. In my case, the Ogoni had never been conquered by their Igbo neighbors. But the fact of British colonialism brought both peoples together under a single administration for the first time. And when the British colonialists left, the numerically inferior Ogoni were consigned to the rule of the more numerous Igbos, who always won elections in the Region since ethnic loyalties and cultural habits were and continue to be strong throughout Nigeria. Biafran propaganda invariably claimed that the Biafrans were one. But this was a lie, a hoax. I saw it as my responsibility to fight that lie. I did.

Since the end of that war in 1970, I have been engaged, as a writer and as a man of public affairs, in fighting the oppression and bad faith of the majority ethnic groups—the Igbo, the Hausa-Fulani, and the Yoruba—in Nigeria. The end of that struggle is not in sight. The facts of it are so sordid that even well-known Nigerian writers would gladly keep them away from the rest of the world. For that reason, not much has been heard about it outside Nigeria.

All the foregoing might seem irrelevant to the question of the language of African literature. Yet what I have tried to show is that, using Nigeria as an example, different languages and cultures exist in Africa. The fact that we share a common color or certain common beliefs or a common history of slavery and exploitation are not enough to just lump all Africa into a single pigeon-hole.

If Europeans speak of French literature, Spanish literature, and English literature, why do we insist on having an "African literature" and debating what language it should be written in? Africa is the second largest continent in the world. It has a multiplicity of languages and each language has its own literature. So, there is an Ogoni literature, a Yoruba lit-

erature, a Wolof literature. Most of this literature is oral because these societies are, in most cases, preliterate. That is a fact.

However, the need to communicate with one another and the rest of the world, and the fact of colonialism (which is also real) have forced us to write in the languages of our erstwhile colonial masters. I, for one, do not feel guilty about this. Were I writing in Khana, I would be speaking to about 200,000 people, most of whom do not read and write. Writing in English as I do, I can reach, hypothetically speaking, 400 million people. That cannot be bad. So, for me, English is a worthy tool, much like the biro pen or the banking system or the computer, which were not invented by the Ogoni people but which I can master and use for my own purposes. Writing in English has not prevented me from writing in my Khana mother-tongue. I am, indeed, working on a Khana novel at the moment, but that is not because I want to prove a point. I am writing this novel so I can offer it to my seventy-year old mother. She is always reading the Bible—the only book which exists in the Khana language—and I would like to give her some other literature to read.

But I am also writing this novel because I can self-publish it. I am lucky to be in a position to do so; none of the established publishers in Nigeria or anywhere else in the world would have accepted to publish it for the simple reason that it would not be profitable to do so. I have also self-published most of the twenty books I have written in English because publishers of fiction by African writers are few and far between. But that is another story.

> **I have examined myself very closely to see how writing or reading in English has colonized my mind. I am, I find, as Ogoni as ever.**
>
> *—Ken Saro-wiwa*

I am aware of Ngugi Thiongo's argument about decolonizing the mind and his determination to write in his native Gikuyu. He is of course welcome to do so. In Nigeria, many writers have been writing in their mother-tongues for a long time. There are newspapers in Hausa and in Yoruba. There is no need to blow this matter out of proportion. Besides, I detect some posturing in Ngugi's stance. Because he had already made his mark as a writer in English, his works have become instant subjects of translation into English, enabling him to live by his writing. If this were not the case, he might not be so sure of his decision. I also wonder if he has thought or cares about the implications of his decision for the minority ethnic groups in Kenya and for the future of Kenya as a multiethnic nation or, indeed, as a nation at all.

Furthermore, I have examined myself very closely to see how writing or reading in English has colonized my mind. I am, I find, as Ogoni as ever. I am enmeshed in Ogoni culture. I eat Ogoni food. I sing Ogoni songs. I dance to Ogoni music. And I find the best in the Ogoni world-view as engaging as anything else. I am anxious to see the Ogoni establish themselves in Nigeria and make their contribution to world civilization. I myself am contributing to Ogoni life as fully, and possibly even more effectively than those Ogoni who do not speak and write English. The fact that I appreciate Shakespeare, Dickens, Chaucer, Hemingway, *et al.,* the fact that I know something of European civilization, its history and philosophy, the fact that I enjoy Mozart and Beethoven—this a colonization of my mind? I cannot exactly complain about it.

I am also aware of the proposition that Africa should adopt one language—a continental language. Wole Soyinka once suggested the adoption of Swahili. Quite apart from the fact that the idea is totally impracticable, it seems to me to lack intellectual or political merit. Once a language is not one's mother-tongue, it is an alien language. Its being an African language is a moot point. As I said earlier, Africans have practiced colonialism as much as Europeans. In most cases, this colonialism has been harsh and crude; it is as detestable as European colonialism. The position in today's Nigeria is a case in point. The Sausa-Fulani, Yoruba, and Igbo have inflicted on three hundred other ethnic groups a rule that is most onerous. Were I, as an Ogoni, forced to speak or write any of these languages (as is presently proposed), I would rebel against the idea and encourage everyone else to do the same. Moreover, people of the same tongue are not always of the same mind.

African literature is written in several languages, including the extra-African languages of English, French, and Portuguese. As more and more writers emerge, as criticism responds to their works, as African languages increasingly acquire written form, and as communities become more politically aware of the need to develop their languages and cultures, African literature will break down into its natural components, and we will speak of Ogoni literature, Igbo literature, Fanti literature, Swahili literature, etc. But there will continue to be an African literature written in English and French and Portuguese. The fact that these languages have been on the continent for over a hundred years and are spoken by many African peoples entitles them to a proper place among the languages that are native to the continent.

With regard to English, I have heard it said that those who write in it should adopt a domesticated "African" variety of it. I myself have experimented with the three varieties of English spoken and written in Nigeria: pidgin, "rotten," and standard. I have used them in poetry, short stories, essays, drama, and the novel. I have tried them out in print, on stage, on the radio, and with television comedy. That which carries best and which is most popular is standard English, expressed simply and lucidly. It communicates and expresses thoughts and ideas perfectly.

And so I remain a convinced practitioner and consumer of African literature in English. I am content that this language has made me a better African in the sense that it enables me to know more about Somalia, Kenya, Malawi, and South Africa than I would otherwise have known.

William Boyd (essay date 27 November 1995)

SOURCE: "Death of a Writer," in *The New Yorker,* Vol. LXXI, No. 38, November 27, 1995, pp. 51-5.

[*Boyd is an acclaimed English novelist. In the following essay, he eulogizes his friend Saro-Wiwa and describes events that led up to his execution.*]

Ken Saro-Wiwa was a friend of mine. At eleven-thirty in the morning on November 10th, he was hanged in a prison in Port Harcourt, in eastern Nigeria, on the orders of General Sani Abacha, the military leader of Nigeria. Ken Saro-Wiwa was fifty-four years old, and an innocent man.

I first met Ken in the summer of 1986 at a British Council seminar at Cambridge University. He had come to England from Nigeria in his capacity as a publisher and had asked the British Council to arrange a meeting with me. He had read my first novel, *A Good Man in Africa,* and had recognized, despite fictional names and thin disguises, that it was set in Nigeria, the country that had been my home when I was in my teens and early twenties.

Ken had been a student at the University of Ibadan, in western Nigeria, in the mid-sixties. My late father, Dr. Alexander Boyd, had run the university health services there, and had treated Ken and come to know him. Ken recognized that the Dr. Murray in my novel was a portrait of Dr. Boyd and was curious to meet his son.

I remember that it was a sunny summer day, one of those days that are really too hot for England. In shirtsleeves, we strolled about the immaculate quadrangle of a Cambridge college, talking about Nigeria. Ken was a small man, probably no more than five feet two or three. He was stocky and energetic—in fact, brimful of energy—and had a big, wide smile. He smoked a pipe with a curved stem. I learned later that the pipe was virtually a logo: in Nigeria, people recognized him by it. In newsreel pictures that the Nigerian military released of the final days of Ken's show trial, there's a shot of him walking toward the courthouse, leaning on a stick, thinner and aged as a result of eighteen months' incarceration, the familiar pipe still clenched between his teeth.

Ken was not only a publisher but a businessman (in the grocery trade); a celebrated political journalist, with a particularly trenchant and swingeing style; and, I discovered, a prolific writer of novels, plays, poems, and children's books (mostly published by him). He was, in addition, the highly successful writer and producer of Nigeria's most popular TV soap opera, *Basi & Co. Basi & Co.,* which ran for a hundred and fifty-odd episodes in the mid-eighties, was reputedly Africa's most watched soap opera, with an audience of up to thirty million. Basi and his cronies were a bunch of feckless Lagos wide boys who, indigent and lazy, did nothing but hatch inept schemes for becoming rich. Although funny and wincingly accurate, the show was also unashamedly pedagogic. What was wrong with Basi and his chums was wrong with Nigeria: none of them wanted to work, and they all acted as though the world owed them a living; if that couldn't be acquired by fair means foul ones would do just as well. This was soap opera as a form of civic education.

What was wrong with Basi and his chums was wrong with Nigeria: none of them wanted to work, and they all acted as though the world owed them a living; if that couldn't be acquired by fair means foul ones would do just as well.
—William Boyd

Whenever Ken passed through London, we'd meet for lunch, usually in the Chelsea Arts Club. His wife and four children lived in England—the children attended school there—so he was a regular visitor. And, though I wrote a profile of him for the London *Times* (Ken was trying to get his books distributed in Britain), our encounters were mainly those of two writers with something in common, hanging out for a highly agreeable, bibulous hour or three.

Ken's writing was remarkably various, covering almost all genres. *Sozaboy,* in my opinion his greatest work, is subtitled "A Novel in Rotten English" and is written in a unique combination of pidgin English, the lingua franca of the former West African British colonies, and an English that is, in its phrases and sentences, altogether more classical and lyrical. The language is a form of literary demotic, a benign hijacking of English, and a perfect vehicle for the story it tells, of a simple village boy recruited into the Biafran Army during the Nigerian civil war. The boy has dreamed of being a soldier (a "soza"), but the harsh realities of this brutal conflict send him into a dizzying spiral of cruel disillusion. *Sozaboy*

is not simply a great African novel but also a great antiwar novel—among the very best of the twentieth century.

Sozaboy was born of Ken's personal experience of the conflict—the Biafran War, as it came to be known—and, indeed, so were many of his other writings. Biafra was the name given to a loose ethnic grouping in eastern Nigeria dominated by the Ibo tribe. The Ibo leader, Colonel Chukwuemeka Odumegwu Ojukwu, decided to secede from Nigeria, taking most of the country's oil reserves with him. In the war that was then waged against the secessionist state, perhaps a million people died, mainly of starvation in the shrinking heartland.

Not all the ethnic groups caught up in Ojukwu's secessionist dream were willing participants. Ken's tribe, the Ogoni, for one. When the war broke out, in 1967, Ken was on vacation and found himself trapped within the new borders of Biafra. He saw at once the absurdity of being forced to fight in another man's war, and he escaped through the front lines to the federal side. He was appointed civilian administrator of the crucial oil port of Bonny on the Niger River delta, and he served there until the final collapse of the Biafran forces in 1970. Ken wrote about his experiences of the civil war in his fine memoir, *On a Darkling Plain.*

Ken's later fight against the Nigerian military, as it turned out, was oddly pre-figured in those years of the Biafran War: the helplessness of an ethnic minority in the face of an overpowering military dictatorship; oil and oil wealth as a destructive and corrupting catalyst in society; the need to be true to one's conscience.

This moral rigor was especially apparent in Ken's satirical political journalism (he was, over the years, a columnist on the Lagos daily newspapers *Punch, Vanguard,* and *Daily Times*), much of which was charged with a Swiftian *saeva indignatio* at what he saw as the persistent ills of Nigerian life: tribalism, ignorance of the rights of minorities, rampant materialism, inefficiency, and general graft. Apart from *Basi & Co.,* his journalism was what brought him his greatest renown among the population at large.

In the late eighties, I remember, Ken's conversations turned more and more frequently to the topic of his tribal homeland. The Ogoni are a small tribe (there are two hundred and fifty tribes in Nigeria) of about half a million people living in a small area of the fertile Niger River delta. The Ogoni's great misfortune is that their homeland happens to lie above a significant portion of Nigeria's oil reserves. Since the mid-nineteen-fifties, Ogoniland has been devastated by the industrial pollution caused by the extraction of oil. What was once a placid rural community of prosperous farmers and fishermen is now an ecological wasteland reeking of sulfur, its creeks and water holes poisoned by indiscriminate oil spillage and ghoulishly lit at night by the orange flames of gas flares.

As Ken's concern for his homeland grew, he effectively abandoned his vocation and devoted himself to lobbying for the Ogoni cause at home and abroad. He was instrumental in setting up the Movement for the Survival of the Ogoni People (MOSOP) and soon became its figurehead. That struggle for survival was an ecological more than a political one: Ken protested the despoliation of his homeland and demanded compensation from the Nigerian government and from the international oil companies—Shell in particular. (He resented Shell profoundly and, with good reason, held the company responsible for the ecological calamity in Ogoniland.) His people, he said, were being subjected to a "slow genocide." But from the outset Ken made sure that the movement's protest was peaceful and nonviolent. Nigeria today is a corrupt and dangerously violent nation: it was enormously to the credit of the Ogoni movement that it stayed true to its principles. Mass demonstrations were organized and passed off without incident. Abroad, Greenpeace and other environmental groups allied themselves with the Ogoni cause, but, ironically, the real measure of the success of Ken's agitation came when, in 1992, he was arrested by the Nigerian military and held in prison for some months without a trial. The next year, Shell Oil ceased its operations in the Ogoni region.

At that time, the Nigerian military was led by General Ibrahim Babangida. Ken was eventually released (after a campaign in the British media), and Babangida voluntarily yielded power to General Abacha, a crony, who was meant to supervise the transition of power to a civilian government after a general election, which was duly held in 1993. The nation went to the polls and democratically elected Chief Moshood Abiola as President. General Abacha then declared the election null and void and later imprisoned the victor. Nigeria entered a new era of near-anarchy and despotism. Things looked bad for Nigeria, but they looked worse for the Ogoni and their leaders.

Over these years, Ken and I continued to meet for our Chelsea Arts Club lunches whenever he was in London. In 1992, he suffered a personal tragedy, when his youngest son, aged fourteen, who was at Eton, died suddenly of heart failure during a rugby game. Strangely, Ken's awful grief gave a new force to his fight for his people's rights.

We met just before he returned to Nigeria. From my own experience of Nigeria, I knew of the uncompromising ruthlessness of political life there. Ken was not young, nor was he in the best of health (he, too, had a heart condition). As we said goodbye, I shook his hand and said, "Be careful, Ken, O.K.?" And he laughed—his dry, delighted laugh—and replied, "Oh, I'll be very careful, don't worry." But I knew he wouldn't.

A succession of Nigerian military governments have survived as a result of the huge revenues generated by oil, and the military leaders themselves have routinely benefitted from the oil revenues, making millions and millions of dollars. Any movement that threatened this flow of money was bound to be silenced—extinguished. With the ascendance of Abacha and his brazenly greedy junta, Ken was now squarely in harm's way. Even so, he returned to Nigeria to continue his protests. These protests were now conducted in a more sinister country than the one I had known—a country where rapes, murders, and the burning of villages were being carried out as a deliberate policy of state terrorism. There have been two thousand Ogoni deaths thus far.

In May of last year, Ken was on his way to address a rally in an Ogoni town but was turned back at a military roadblock and headed, reluctantly, for home. The rally took place, a riot ensued, and in the general mayhem four Ogoni elders—believed to be sympathetic to the military—were killed.

Ken was arrested and, with several others, was accused of incitement to murder. The fact that he was in a car some miles away and going in the opposite direction made no difference. He was imprisoned for more than a year and then was tried before a specially convened tribunal. There was no right of appeal. This "judicial process" has been internationally condemned as a sham. It was a show trial in a kangaroo court designed to procure the verdict required by the government.

On Thursday, November 2nd, Ken and his co-defendants were found guilty and sentenced to death. Suddenly the world acknowledged the nature of Nigeria's degeneracy.

Things did not augur well. But, instinctively wanting to make the best of a bad situation, I hoped that the publicity surrounding Ken's case, along with the timely coincidence of the Commonwealth conference in New Zealand (a biennial gathering of the former members of the British Empire), would prevent the very worst from happening. Surely, I reasoned, the heads of state congregating in Auckland would not allow one of their members to flout their own human-rights principles so callously and blatantly? General Abacha, however, did not dare leave his benighted country, which was represented by his Foreign Minister instead.

The presence of Nelson Mandela at the conference was especially encouraging, not only for me but also for all the people who had spent the last months fighting to free Ken. (We were a loose-knit organization, including International PEN, the Ogoni Foundation, Amnesty International,

Greenpeace, and others.) We felt that if anything could persuade the Nigerians to think again it would be Mandela's moral authority. We were baffled and confused, though, when Mandela did little more than persistently advocate that we should all be patient, that the problem would be resolved through an easy, low-key diplomacy.

Despite Mandela's advice, there was a clamorous condemnation in the media of the Nigerian military. In response, Abacha's junta released newsreel pictures of Ken's trial to establish the legality of the "judicial process." One saw a row of prisoners, still, faces drawn, heads bowed, confronting three stout officers, swagged with gold braid, ostentatiously passing pieces of paper to each other. In the background, a soldier strolled back and forth. Then Ken addressed the court. His voice was strong: he was redoubtably defiant; he seemed without fear, utterly convinced.

These images both defied belief and profoundly disturbed. If Abacha thought that this would make his tribunals look acceptable, then the level of naïveté, or blind ignorance, implied was astonishing. But a keening note of worry was also sounded: someone who could do something this damaging, I thought, was beyond the reach of reason. World opinion, international outrage, appeals for clemency seemed to me now to be nugatory. Abacha had painted himself into a corner. For him it had become a question of saving face, of loud bluster, of maintaining some sort of martial pride. I slept very badly that night.

The next day, November 10th, just after lunch, I received a call from the Writers in Prison Committee of International PEN. I was told that a source in Port Harcourt had seen the prisoners arrive at the jail at dawn that day, in leg irons. Then the executioners had presented themselves, only to be turned away, because—it was a moment of grimmest, darkest farce—their papers were not in order. This source, however, was "a hundred and ten per cent certain" that the executions had eventually occurred. Some hours later, this certainty was confirmed by the Nigerian military.

So now Ken was dead, along with eight co-defendants: hanged in a mass execution just as the Commonwealth Conference got under way.

I am bitter and I am dreadfully sad. Ken Saro-Wiwa, the bravest man I have known, is no more. From time to time, Ken managed to smuggle a letter out of prison. One of the last letters I received ended this way: "I'm in good spirits . . . There's no doubt that my idea will succeed in time, but I'll have to bear the pain of the moment . . . The most important thing for me is that I've used my talents as a writer to enable the Ogoni people to confront their tormentors. I was not able to do it as a politician or a businessman. My writing did it. And it sure makes me feel good! I'm men-

tally prepared for the worst, but hopeful for the best. I think I have the moral victory." You have, Ken. Rest in peace.

Rob Nixon (review date 4 April 1996)

SOURCE: "Pipe Dreams," in *London Review of Books,* Vol. 18, No. 7, April 4, 1996, pp. 18-19.

[*Nixon is an English author and educator. In the following review of Saro-Wiwa's detention diary,* A Month and a Day, *he describes conditions in Nigeria after the encroachment of transnational companies—such as Shell Oil—into developing countries.*]

Ken Saro-Wiwa squints at us from the cover of his detention diary, the posthumous *A Month and a Day.* His moustache looks precise and trim; his eyes are alight; the distinctive gash scrawls across his temple. But the picture is governed by his pipe. It's an intellectual's accessory, a good pipe to suck and clench, to spew from and lecture with. He had hoped tobacco would kill him: 'I know that I am a mortuary candidate, but I intend to head for the mortuary with my pipe smoking.' In the end, it was another kind of pipe that got him, spilling toxins indiscriminately into the land, rivers and lungs of his Ogoni people.

Saro-Wiwa believed that his writing would return to haunt his tormentors. Shortly before his execution in the Nigerian city of Port Harcourt last year on trumped up charges of murder, he declared: 'The men who ordained and supervised this show of shame, this tragic charade, are frightened by the word, the power of ideas, the power of the pen . . . They are so scared of the word that they do not read. And that will be their funeral.' Saro-Wiwa's conviction that the pen is mightier than the goon squad may sound, to European and North American ears, like an echo from another age. In the era of the World Wide Web, books and newspapers are often dismissed as waning powers. But across much of Africa the certainty persists that writing can make things happen.

Saro-Wiwa was a voluminous, protean writer who pitched his ambitions high. In one of his final letters from detention, he assured his friend, the novelist William Boyd:

> There's no doubt that my idea will succeed in time, but I'll have to bear the pain of the moment . . . the most important thing for me is that I've used my talents as a writer to enable the Ogoni people to confront their tormentors. I was not able to do it as a politician or a businessman. My writing did it . . . I think I have the moral victory.

Elsewhere, he prayed that his work would have as visceral

an impact as André Gide's 1927 journal, *Voyage au Congo,* which prompted an outcry against Belgian atrocities. Saro-Wiwa saw himself as part of that testimonial tradition, a witness to what he called the 'recolonisation' of Ogoniland by the joint forces of the oil companies and the Abacha regime, which together have turned the Niger delta into a Bermuda triangle for human rights.

Shell has ducked behind the Nigerian military regime and ignored appeals by the Ogonis and neighbouring minorities for a share of oil revenues, some measure of environmental self-determination, and economic redress for their oil-drenched environment. By the time Saro-Wiwa was executed, the Nigerian military and the Mobile Police Force had killed two thousand Ogonis—either they straightforwardly murdered them or they burnt their villages. Ogoni air had been fouled by the flaring of natural gas, croplands scarred by oil spills, drinking and fishing water poisoned. Although Shell was driven out of Ogoniland in 1993, it has since moved to other parts of Nigeria's once lush 'delta of death', and its legacy continues to seep into Ogoni waterways, Ogoni earth, and the bodies of the local farming community which, unlike the corporation, has nowhere else to go. The Ogonis, roughly half a million of them, retain nominal ownership of most of their densely populated territory. What they have suffered in the four decades since oil extraction began is subterranean dispossession. Shell, Chevron and successive Nigerian regimes have siphoned thirty billion dollars of oil from beneath Ogoni earth. Yet the locals still find themselves lacking a hospital, electricity, piped water and basic roads, housing and schools. The community has found itself, in the fullest sense of the word, utterly undermined.

Faced with the neo-colonial politics of mineral rights in the Niger delta, Saro-Wiwa was confident that written testimony, backed by activism, could make a difference. Like many African authors before him, he recognised that, in a society with frail democratic institutions and a small intellectual élite, interventionist writing required versatility and cunning. His life as a public intellectual was distinguished by a profound strategic intelligence and a keen sensitivity to local and international changes in audience and occasion. He produced over twenty books including novels, plays, stories, histories, political tracts and children's tales. But across Anglophone West Africa Saro-Wiwa achieved his greatest renown as the creator of the popular TV comedy **Basi and Company:** 150 primetime episodes were watched on Wednesdays by thirty million Nigerians. Saro-Wiwa was, by turns, a humorist, a moralist and a robust satirist. After the death of his son in 1992, however, he devoted himself single-mindedly to the Ogoni cause, becoming the chronicler of his people's persecution and, finally, a death-row diarist.

Saro-Wiwa's versatility, his belief in an instrumental aesthet-

ics, and his obsession with land rights place him in an established tradition of African writing. But in East and Southern Africa, such tendencies have been routinely associated with writers whose anti-colonialism—or anti-neo-colonialism—has been inseparable from their socialism. One thinks, for instance, of Ngugi wa Thiong'o's *Barrel of the Pen* and Mafika Gwala's essay, 'Writing as a Cultural Weapon' (the credo for a generation of South African writers). Saro-Wiwa was unusual in cultivating an international sensibility and stood aside from the lineages of African socialism.

> **Faced with the neo-colonial politics of mineral rights in the Niger delta, Saro-Wiwa was confident that written testimony, backed by activism, could make a difference.**
> —*Rob Nixon*

He was the first African writer to articulate the literature of commitment in environmental terms. And as a successful small businessman—successful enough to send a son to Eton—he was never anti-capitalist as such. But he did find himself perfectly (and painfully) placed to chronicle one of the most notable developments of the Nineties: the resurgent power and mobility of transnational corporations—five hundred of which control 70 per cent of global trade—in the face of weakening nation-states, above all in the underdeveloped South.

It is a testament to Saro-Wiwa's strategic imagination that his political prose documents far more than the devastation of Ogoniland. While his work is passionately devoted to that cause, he came increasingly to situate it in a global framework. He began to discern certain patterns: most important, he understood how in countries weakened by structural adjustment, transnational firms and the national soldiery consider themselves at liberty to vandalise minority communities. He also saw that the justice of a cause—an African cause especially—was insufficient reason for it to attract international attention. So he strove to analogise, to turn what he called the 'deadly ecological war against the Ogoni' into a struggle emblematic of our times. His writing thus lays the ground for a broader estimation of the human cost of the romance between unanswerable corporations and unspeakable regimes.

Saro-Wiwa's political realism was tempered by a determined optimism, however. Writing in the Preface to his **Genocide in Nigeria** (1992), he took heart from three developments in the Nineties: 'the end of the Cold War, the increasing attention being paid to the global environment, and the insistence of the European Community that minority rights be respected, albeit in the successor states to the Soviet Union and in Yugoslavia'. But, he worried, 'it remains to be seen whether Europe and America will apply to Nigeria the same standards which they have applied to Eastern Europe.' His doubts have proved well-founded.

A Month and a Day includes a record of his efforts to capitalise on these new forms of international concern. Initially, human-rights and ecological groups proved equally unreceptive to the Ogoni cause. An African intellectual claiming ethnocide by environmental means? Saro-Wiwa seemed, at first, eccentric and unplaceable. At Boyd's prompting, he decided to contact Greenpeace. They replied that they did not work in Africa. Amnesty International said they could only take up the Ogoni cause if the military was killing people or detaining them without trial, a process that had yet to begin. Saro-Wiwa responded with frustration: 'The Ogoni people were being killed all right, but in an unconventional way.' Later he elaborated:

> The Ogoni country has been completely destroyed by the search for oil ... Oil blow-outs, spillages, oil slicks and general pollution accompany the search for oil ... Oil companies have flared gas in Nigeria for the past 33 years causing acid rain ... What used to be the bread basket of the delta has now become totally infertile. All one sees and feels around is death. Environmental degradation has been a lethal weapon in the war against the indigenous Ogoni people.

Despite the unresponsiveness of Greenpeace, Amnesty, Friends of the Earth and Survival International, Saro-Wiwa persisted in arguing that the Ogoni were victims of an 'unconventional war', prosecuted by ecological means. Undeterred, he sought to educate himself further through travel. An odyssey through the rupturing Soviet Union confirmed his sense of a growing international context for the articulation of minority claims. A visit to Colorado gave him access to an environmental group that had successfully salvaged a wilderness from corporate and governmental assaults. Through Michael van Walt van der Praag, a Dutch lawyer long active in the Tibetan cause, he made contact with the Unrepresented Nations and Peoples Organisation. This gave him access to the United Nations Working Group on Indigenous Populations, which he addressed in Geneva in 1992. (That same year, another Ogoni leader addressed the Earth Summit in Rio on behalf of the delta peoples.) Saro-Wiwa discovered that 'in virtually every nation-state there are several "Ogonis"—despairing and disappearing peoples suffering the yoke of political marginalisation, economic strangulation or environmental degradation, or a combination of these.'

From 1992 onwards, the combined invocation of minority and environmental rights became fundamental to the campaign waged by his Movement for the Survival of the Ogoni People (Mosop). The human-rights and ecological organisations that had earlier found the Ogoni issue enigmatic now became its staunchest international supporters, and other groups, like Abroad, Friends of the Earth and the Body Shop, also rallied to the Ogoni cause.

These developments gave Saro-Wiwa's campaign a resonance it had previously lacked, and challenged stereotypes about environmental activists: that they are inevitably white, young, middle-class Europeans or Americans who can afford to hug trees. Saro-Wiwa's campaign for environmental self-determination will prove critical to the development of a broader image of ecological activism. We have seen how the concerns of privileged white feminists in the Seventies gave way to a more internationally diverse array of feminisms, locally led and locally defined. So, too, we are now seeing indigenous environmentalisms proliferate under the pressure of local necessity. As ideas of what qualifies as environmental activism expand, it becomes harder to dismiss it as a sentimental or imperialist discourse tied to European or North American interests. Nor does the case for this diversification any longer rest solely on Amazonian experience.

Saro-Wiwa understood that environmentalism needs to be re-imagined through the lives of the minorities who are barely visible on the global economic periphery, where transnationals in the extraction business—whether oil, minerals or timber—operate with maximum impunity. Environmental justice became for him an invaluable concept through which to focus the battle between subnational macroethnicities and transnational macro-economic powers. As an Ogoni, suffering what he called Nigeria's 'monstrous domestic colonialism', Saro-Wiwa had no reason to trust the nation-state as the unit of collective economic good. Instead, he advocated a measure of ethnic federalism in which environmental self-determination would be acknowledged as indispensable to cultural survival.

After the execution of Saro-Wiwa and his eight co-accused, public outrage divided between those who primarily condemned the Abacha regime and those who went for Shell. For Saro-Wiwa, however, the blame was indivisible: the Ogonis were the casualties of joint occupying powers. Shell has sought to put a positive gloss on this relationship, with PR primers like 'Nigeria and Shell: Partners in Progress'. But the real character of the relationship is more accurately portrayed by a leaked Nigerian government memo addressing protests in Ogoniland. Dated 5 December 1994, it reads: 'Shell operations still impossible unless ruthless military operations are undertaken for smooth economic activities to commence.'

In Africa Shell waives on shore drilling standards that it routinely upholds elsewhere. Indeed, 40 percent of all Shell oil-spills world wide have occurred in Nigeria. When operating in the Northern hemisphere—in the Shetlands, for instance—Shell pays lucrative rents to local councils; in the Niger delta, village authorities receive little compensation.

The company's double standard would, however, be inoperable without backing from a Nigerian regime whose record on minority rights is appalling. Saro-Wiwa has likened the fate of the Ogoni during the oil-rush to their fate in the Biafran War, when the conflict among Nigeria's three dominant ethnicities left them flattened 'like grass in the fight of the elephants'. In a military kleptocracy with two hundred minority groups, all constitutionally unprotected, the Ogonis suffered the extra misfortune of living over oil.

The fact that the Ogonis have been casualties of both racism and ethnic hatred may help explain the low-key American response to the executions. The outcry in Britain, South Africa and France was far more vocal and sustained. In the British case, this is understandable: Shell is an Anglo-Dutch company and thanks to colonial links with Africa the British media always cover Africa more carefully than the Americans do. (The reverse is true in the case of Latin America.) But there is more to the American media's indifference than that. In US political discourse, racial oppression and minority discrimination typically function as identical terms, which makes it difficult for liberal Americans to condemn in a single breath a European corporation for racism against Africans and an African regime for oppressing its minorities. Saro-Wiwa never hesitated to make such controversial connections. As he wrote in his prison diary,

> skin colour is not strong enough to stop the oppression of one group by another. Sometimes it reinforces oppression because it makes it less obvious. White people oppressing blacks in South Africa draws instant condemnation because it is seen to be racism. But black upon black oppression merely makes people shrug and say: 'Well, it's their business, isn't it?'

Some years back, the Philippine Government placed an ad in *Fortune* magazine that read: 'To attract companies like yours, we have felled mountains, razed jungles, filled swamps, moved rivers, relocated towns . . . all to make it easier for you and your business to do business here.' The Philippines is just one of a succession of poor nations to have wooed transnationals in a manner indissociably catastrophic for the environment and local minorities. This process has been most acutely damaging in the world's equatorial belt, from Ecuador, Bolivia and Brazil, to Surinam and Guyana, on through Nigeria, Cameroon, the Central African Republic, Gabon and Zaire, to the Philippines, Sarawak and New

Guinea. Rich equatorial ecosystems could sustain a higher concentration of discrete language groups than was possible in less fertile regions. Today most of these minorities find themselves in undemocratic, destitute nation-states that register in the global economy principally as sites for the unregulated extraction of oil, minerals and timber. It is thus no coincidence that indigenous environmentalism has burgeoned most dramatically in this zone, as minorities battle for the survival of their land-dependent subsistence cultures.

West Papua has an even higher concentration of minorities than the Niger delta. And, like the delta peoples, West Papuans have the curse of wealth—some of the world's richest deposits of copper and gold—seaming beneath their land. They face a similar alliance between an occupying military power and a transnational corporation. The same Indonesian regime that was responsible for the second-worst genocide of our century, in East Timor, has colonised West Papua with a brutality that has seen 43,000 indigenous people killed. Their accomplice in this endeavour is the Louisiana-based mining transnational Freeport McMoran. Since the arrival of Freeport in 1967, the indigenous people have had inflicted on them detention without trial, torture, forced resettlement, disappearances, the plunder of their mineral wealth and the uncompensated degradation of their environment. Freeport's private security officers and the Indonesian military have, on occasion, combined to shoot and kill unarmed local protesters. In an alliance even more devastating than that between the Abacha règime and Shell, the Indonesians and Freeport have pursued ethnocide as a condition of mandatory development. In this deadly battle, the locals have fought back in a language that combines new modes of environmental defiance with a more traditional reverence for the land. As one Amungme leader put it, 'Freeport is digging out our mother's brain. That is why we are resisting.'

Some of these indigenous actions have begun to take effect—in the oil-rich Oriente region of Ecuador, for example, where Texaco had devastated Indian territory in a manner similar to Shell's despoliation of Ogoniland. Drinking water, fishing grounds, soil and crops have all been polluted. According to the Rainforest Action Network, Texaco spilled 17 million gallons of crude oil in the Oriente, leaving the residents with a legacy of chronic health problems. Here again, the seepage of oil-contaminated waste was the result of a general jettisoning of procedures for onshore drilling that are standard in the Northern hemisphere.

Ecuador's Acción Ecológica has led a successful national boycott of Texaco and has helped drive the corporation from the region. In addition, a coalition of indigenous federations, mestizos, grass-roots environmentalists and human-rights groups has pursued an innovative avenue of redress, filing a $1.5 billion class action suit in New York against Texaco.

The suit has earned the support of Ecuador's Confederation of Indigenous Nationalities, the country's largest Indian organisation. Following the Ecuadorian example, Ogoni villagers are suing Shell for $4 million for spillages that have robbed them of their livelihood.

One result—one more result—of the growing power and freedom of the transnationals and of the willingness of Third World governments to collude with them has been a reversion to concessionary economics in which forested or mineral-rich areas are sold for a song. It is in this context that Saro-Wiwa's talk of recolonisation and his invocation of André Gide sounds eerily apposite. When Shell can pump out 30 billion dollars' worth of oil and the trade-off for the locals is a crumbling infrastructure, absent services, violence, disease, military occupation and an end to self-sustaining agriculture, the process seems more redolent of turn-of-the-century colonial buccaneering than it does of fin-de-millennium international trade.

At the national level, the kleptocrats and the soldiery demand their palm-greasing; at the local level, the chiefs request their cruder versions of the same. Late last year, for example, near the delta village of Sangama, a group of foreign explorers arrived by ship at the head of a marshy river. They sought to establish a station there. After lengthy bartering with a local chief, they settled on a local cut: £1000, 12 bottles of cognac and 12 of gin. But as the foreigners pushed deeper into the hinterland, they found villagers blocking their river-route with a barricade of palm fronds and canoes. The explorers' leader felt bewildered and betrayed. He reported that 'there were about a hundred people ahead of us. If we'd pressed ahead we would have risked killing them. So we took a boat and went back to get Chief Jumbo.' More bargaining, more demands. Another £300 changed hands, an extra bottle of gin, an agreement to repair a building. The chief sacrificed a goat to the water gods; the barricade was lifted; the foreigners passed through. If they hadn't had an oil rig in tow, this could have been an entry from Gide's journal or the opening scene of a lost Conrad novel.

Joshua Hammer (essay date June 1996)

SOURCE: "Nigeria Crude: A Hanged Man and an Oil-Fouled Landscape," in *Harper's Magazine,* Vol. 292, No. 1753, pp. 58-68.

[*Hammer is a journalist working in Africa. In the following essay, he covers the trial and execution of Saro-Wiwa and examines conditions in the Nigerian government and Shell Oil.*]

The Commissioner went away, taking three or four

of the soldiers with him. In the many years in which he had toiled to bring civilization to different parts of Africa he had learned a number of things. One of them was that a District Commissioner must never attend to such undignified details as cutting a hanged man from the tree. Such attention would give the natives a poor opinion of him. In the book which he planned to write he would stress that point. . . . He had already chosen the title of the book, after much thought: *The Pacification of the Primitive Tribes of the Lower Niger.*

—Chinua Achebe, *Things Fall Apart*

To fly into the Niger Delta is to fall from grace. From the air, the silvery waters seem peaceful. Dubbed "The Venice of West Africa" in 1867 by British explorer Winwood Reade, the Delta stretches 290 miles along the Atlantic coast from the Benin River in the west to the Cross River in the east. In between, the powerful Niger feeds an intricate network of tributaries and creeks that partition sandbars and mangrove islands into cookie-cutter shapes as they meander toward the Gulf of Guinea.

Yet far beneath the belly of the airplane, oil fields mottle the landscape, their rigs ceaselessly pumping crude and natural gas from deep underground. The gas burns incessantly in giant geysers of flame and smoke, and at night the flares that ring the city of Port Harcourt and fishing villages deep within the mangrove swamps cast a hellish glow. As the smoke from the flares rises above the palm trees, methane and carbon dioxide separate from the greasy soot. The gases rise but the grime descends, coating the trees, the laundry hanging on lines, the mud-daubed huts, and the people within. There is nothing pure left in Nigeria.

In May of 1995, I traveled to Nigeria to scout the front lines of the struggle for the country's soul that pits the indigenous peoples of the Delta against Royal Dutch/Shell, other petroleum producers, and the military government. It is a conflict that threatens the fabric of Nigerian society, and by that I don't mean the political fabric—which, like most African nations, was never much more than a crazy quilt of hundreds of tribal groups haphazardly stitched together by colonial governments—but the character of the people. Easy oil money has created a culture of corruption that, even for Third World military dictatorships, is breathtakingly epic. It wasn't just that on a short drive out of Port Harcourt my taxi driver was stopped twelve times by police demanding bribes, or that the military was exporting its methods of intimidation, graft, and outright thievery to Liberia as part of its U.N. "peacekeeping" duties there, or that foreign businesses have to anticipate extra expenditures to cover kickbacks and payoffs. It was that in Nigeria, even the innocent are sullied, their expectations lowered, their complicity expected, perhaps even inevitable. Crude oil, once viewed as the means of Nigeria's ascent to greatness, had instead greased the skids into chaos.

The latest manifestation of Nigeria's descent was the trial of Ken Saro-Wiwa, a member of a Delta tribe called the Ogoni, who six years ago began organizing his people against the petroleum producers and the military regime. His efforts earned him a Nobel Peace Prize nomination and landed him—along with fourteen other members of the Movement for the Survival of the Ogoni People, or MOSOP—in prison on trumped-up charges that he ordered the murder of four Ogoni chiefs who had disagreed with his increasingly militant actions. I was to attend the trial later in my visit, and although the government had preordained his guilt, the question was larger than whether Saro-Wiwa would be executed or merely imprisoned indefinitely. The question was whether one man, dead or alive, had started an indigenous revolt against the tenth-largest, and the most profitable, corporation in the world, or, in the long view, had failed to prevent that company from poisoning his country.

I hired a small skiff at the Port Harcourt waterfront. Five minutes down the Bonny River the sounds of the city were lost to the whine of the outboard and the syncopated percussion of a tropical downpour. For three hours, as I crouched beneath a thick tarpaulin, the boat threaded through a network of creeks, overtaking fishermen in canoes—their paddles rhythmically dipping into the coffee-colored water—river taxis, oil barges, and ghost ships scuttled among the mangroves. Herons and egrets flapped by, and occasionally telltale plumes of smoke from gas flares wafted above the trees. At last I arrived in Okoroba: a cluster of weather-beaten, rain-sodden wooden huts and dugout canoes huddled around a splintered pier. Six years ago, Shell had dredged a canal through Okoroba to reach a new well. Since then, the company had yet to produce oil—but it had tapped deep reserves of frustration and rage.

Paramount chief Steven Joel Engobila, a near-toothless man in a black bowler hat, sat on a battered cushioned sofa in his dim hut. Its walls were bare except for a faded 1991 Shell Oil calendar. He led me outside for a tour of Okoroba. Heavy rain had turned the dirt alleys into quagmires; filthy, naked children ran out of huts, excitedly screaming "Oibo!" (white man). The village had no electricity, no paved roads, no shops, and a primary school with broken wooden chairs and a leaking roof. A trip to the nearest doctor took four hours by canoe. As we walked across a swamped soccer field, sinking to our ankles in the muck, Engobila ran through a list of Shell's misdeeds. The canal builders had knocked down the village health center, he said, flattened most of the village's coconut palms, and damaged the local fishing industry by flooding freshwater creeks with salt water.

"We tried to grow new coconuts, but they died. We don't know why," he said. Shell had paid a few dollars' compensation for the destroyed trees, built a water tank, and contracted with a local firm to construct a new health center, but the workers had abandoned the structure after a few months. "This is empty public relations," Engobila said, waving his hand at the roofless concrete-block building. "Shell brought us nothing but anguish." The chief felt powerless. "We are ignorant people. What can we do?" Most people in the region were so destitute, Engobila admitted, that they lived in constant hope that an oil spill would bring them even a small settlement from the company.

It is nearly impossible to overstate Shell's role in Nigeria. Today, under the terms of its OPEC quota, Nigeria produces about 2 million barrels of crude a day, bringing about $10 billion a year to the military junta and accounting for about 97 percent of export revenues. Half of that total is pumped by Shell, making the company by far the dominant economic force in Nigeria. The relationship between the company and the country is not exactly colonial. Colonialism is unwieldy, expensive, and risky. Shell, like the multinationals in Mexico and Indonesia, merely recognizes a good business climate when it sees one, and that is all it chooses to see. That much, Nnaemeka Achebe, Shell's polished and articulate general manager and the highest-ranking Nigerian in the company, cheerfully admitted when I visited him in his plush Lagos office with sweeping views of the Gulf of Guinea. "For a commercial company trying to make investments, you need a stable environment," Achebe said. "Dictatorships can give you that. Right now in Nigeria there is acceptance, peace, and continuity."

In truth, Nigeria has never really known peace. This country of 100 million people, whose boundaries were established by the British in 1914, is a pastiche of more than 250 ethnic groups, and between many of them are ancient, even violent divisions of language, religion, and culture. Violence escalated with the arrival of the Dutch and British, who used the Delta waterways to build the largest slave trade in West Africa. But these revenues paled in comparison with what followed. In 1937, the British government gave Shell D'Arcy, as the Anglo-Dutch company was then called, the exclusive right to prospect for oil. For more than two decades, exploration parties traveled by raft, canoe, barge, and on foot through the malarial swamps of the Delta, conducting seismographic surveys and core drilling. Wild-catters struck their first commercial deposits in 1956. During the following decade, as Nigeria gained independence from Great Britain, Shell laid pipelines through the Delta and opened the Bonny Island oil terminal downriver from Port Harcourt.

At that time, Nigeria was poised to become the undisputed leader of Africa. In addition to huge deposits of crude, the country had rich farmland, an educated population, and a democratic government. Its three dominant tribes—the Hausa-Fulanis in the Muslim north, the Yorubas in the west, and the Ibos in the east—were proud, artistic people with histories dating back a thousand years. Wole Soyinka and Chinua Achebe stood at the vanguard of an African literary renaissance.

Over the past generation, however, the promises of Nigeria have given way to disappointment and failure. In 1966, a military dictatorship from the northern Hausa-Fulani tribe seized power, and northern-dominated juntas have ruled the country for twenty-six of the thirty years since. They have profited enormously from the country's vast oil resources while deepening the misery of just about everyone else.

Immediately after the Hausa-Fulanis seized power, the Ibos led the Biafran region—which included the Delta, home of the Ogoni, Ogbia, Ijaw, and Andoni minority tribes—into a bloody revolt that lasted three years. After the Ibos were routed in 1970, Shell and the government were free to enter into a joint venture known as the Shell Petroleum Development Company of Nigeria, or SPDC. Shell put up the bulk of exploration and equipment costs, and in return it got to export 30 percent of the crude oil pumped, with 55 percent going to the government and the rest to two European companies, Elf and Agip. (American oil companies also have operations in Nigeria.) Collective gross oil revenues mushroomed from $600 million in 1973 to $26 billion in 1981.

While Shell and the other companies did all the work, the government sat back and collected its share of the profit. Between 1970 and 1974, the portion of government revenue derived from oil production jumped from 26 percent to 82 percent, about where it remains today. This surge in oil profits transformed Nigerian politics. Controlling the country now meant access to an ever-filling jackpot, and the "Kaduna Mafia," the Muslim-dominated military-industrial cabal named after a city in Nigeria's north, rose to unchallenged power. Officials awarded themselves billions of dollars' worth of inflated government construction contracts, lined their pockets with lucrative kickbacks, and transformed the British system of indirect rule through local chiefs into ethnic rivalry, nepotism, and institutionalized graft. Today the country is far better known for its heroin traffickers and financial scam artists than for its novelists.

The new wealth also created new poverty. While the average Nigerian scrapes by on less than $300 a year—down from about $1,200 in 1978—the country's oil elite dwell in lavish compounds with fleets of Mercedes, imported food and wine, and fat overseas bank accounts. According to Western diplomats, when oil prices soared during the Gulf War, former leader General Ibrahim Babangida reported no corresponding rise in the federal income; the equally

kleptocratic current dictator, General Sani Abacha, has also siphoned off billions of dollars in oil profits. Meanwhile, the junta dropped any pretense of accountability to the people. In June 1993, Babangida annulled Nigeria's democratic presidential election. Five months later, Abacha, a participant in three previous coups who is known by his ritual scars and fondness for epaulets, seized power, abolished all democratic institutions and regional governments, shut down newspapers, and jailed most of the opposition, including the winner of the 1993 presidential election, Moshood Abiola. Such corruption, and the resultant neglect of infrastructure and development, has only furthered Nigeria's dependence on petroleum. Agriculture, which once accounted for 90 percent of export income, is in ruins. Nigeria's cities, swollen by the mass migration from rural areas during the 1970s oil boom, are smog-choked zones of anarchy.

Such as Port Harcourt. The city, home of Shell's Eastern Division headquarters, has swelled in population in the last twenty-five years from 80,000 to over a million. Lured by the promise of money, nearby tribespeople walked away from their fields and fisheries only to find themselves living here in concrete hovels in the shadow of glass office buildings and billboards advertising cellular phones and direct TV. A miasma of pollution hangs over potholed streets teeming with oil tankers, fertilizer trucks, overcrowded buses, and secondhand foreign imports known as tokumbos. Barefoot teenage vendors weave through the seemingly endless traffic jams, known as "go slows," hawking welcome mats, cap guns, hangers, Q-tips. They compete with polio victims who thrust their twisted limbs through car windows, pleading, "Mastah. Please, Mastah, just give me five naira only."

Known in imperial times as the Garden City, Port Harcourt today is dirty and denuded; virtually the only oasis is Shell Camp, a heavily guarded compound where 180 expatriate (and some high-ranking Nigerian) Shell executives live in air-conditioned luxury amidst manicured lawns, tennis courts, and a golf course, as if in some far-flung fragment of Sacramento. Contact with ordinary Nigerians is intentionally limited: on workdays, executives travel by company car to the division headquarters, and from there by helicopter to oil facilities throughout the Delta.

Except for the gates, visitor badges, and security checks, Shell Camp could have been a location for a 1950s family sitcom, but outside the compound's fences was a very different story. By May of 1995, Ken Saro-Wiwa was in prison, the government had closed Ogoniland to outsiders, and troops had beaten foreign reporters attempting to get in. MOSOP members who were not already in jail were living semi-clandestinely in a kind of anxious limbo; no one was eager to act as my guide into their homeland.

Eventually Batom Mitee, a bearded, bespectacled man in his late thirties whose brother Ledum was on trial with Saro-Wiwa, agreed to escort me the next morning to the epicenter of the resistance, though he dared not cross the border in my company. I set out in a truck conspicuously marked "Liverpool School of Tropical Medicine," sitting next to bona fide medical personnel and clutching a set of fake credentials; Mitee followed in another vehicle. At 8:00 A.M. it was already pushing 90 degrees; the air was thick with swamp decay and diesel exhaust.

When we reached the border an hour later, the soldiers demanded a small payoff and waved us through. In Ogoniland's Gokana district, I met up with Mitee in his home village of Kegbara Dere. Here was a place and a people utterly subservient to the production of oil. High-pressure oil pipes snaked amid plots of yam and cassavas, past mud-brick huts, even through people's yards; I watched as one woman climbed over a tangle of pipes to get to her front door.

Ogoniland has a population of 500,000 crammed into 400 square miles. It contains ninety-six oil wells, four oil fields, one petrochemical plant, one fertilizer plant, and two refineries. By some estimates, the region has produced about 600 million barrels of crude during the past forty years. But despite the billions of dollars it has provided to Shell and various military regimes, Ogoniland has no hospitals, few jobs, one of the highest infant-mortality rates in Nigeria, and a 20 percent literacy rate. Moreover, frequent blowouts and leaking pipes have damaged crops and streams, sometimes irreparably; Ogoniland suffered 111 oil spills between 1985 and 1994. (Shell claims that 77 of those spills were the result of sabotage.)

"In the old days in Gokana you could fish, farm, and survive without money," said Mitee. We were sitting beside an abandoned natural-gas flare; until increasingly violent protests caused Shell to cease operations in Ogoniland in 1993, it had spewed a toxic cloud of smoke and flame 100 feet into the air above Kegbara Dere twenty-four hours a day. "But oil exploration spoiled the creeks and the seas, and you can't fish like you did before. We used to have a lot of land, but Shell made much of that unusable. Also, there's never been any family planning here, so there's growing pressure for land. My father has five sons—we can't all have his land. So we have to look for jobs. But there aren't any jobs. Everybody is suffering."

It was in this landscape that I began to apprehend what had compelled Ken Saro-Wiwa to confront the perversion of Nigeria. Born in the Khana district of Ogoniland in 1941 to a tribal chief, Saro-Wiwa attended mission schools, eventually winning a scholarship to the University of Ibadan, near Lagos. He served as administrator of the Bonny Island oil depot during the Biafran war, and between 1968 and 1973

he was a regional commissioner for education. When his militant views on Ogoni rights got him sacked, he launched successful real estate and grocery businesses, a publishing company, and a writing career that made him famous throughout Nigeria. His first novel, *Sozaboy: A Novel in Rotten English,* was an antiwar tale about a village youth recruited into the rebel army during the Biafran conflict. Later came *On a Darkling Plain,* an autobiographical account of the Biafran war, and *Basi and Company,* a TV sitcom watched by 30 million Nigerians that lampooned the country's get-rich-quick attitude. But a political role beckoned. "Ken had this idea from the time he was fifteen," says Batom Mitee. "He wanted to create a campaign modeled after the American civil-rights movement, with mass protests, sit-ins, boycotts, vigils. He started mobilizing in 1990."

For decades, Shell had pumped oil in the Delta virtually free of burdensome environmental regulations. There were few or no requirements to conduct environmental impact studies, recycle oil waste, or lay subterranean oil pipes instead of cheap aboveground pipes. According to Greenpeace, between 1982 and 1992, 37 percent of Shell's spills worldwide—amounting to 1.6 million gallons—took place in the Delta. And according to data compiled for Shell by the World Wide Fund for Nature and leaked to the British newspaper the *Independent,* 76 percent of the natural gas pumped up with crude in Nigeria is burned off—compared with 20 percent in Libya, Saudi Arabia, or Iran; 4.3 percent in the United Kingdom; and 0.6 percent in the United States. Each year, gas flares in Nigeria emit 34 million tons of carbon dioxide and 12 million tons of methane, making petroleum operations in Nigeria the biggest single cause of global warming, according to the *Independent.*

The Ogonis claim that the gas flares cause acid rain that kills crops and fouls drinking water. But they have no legal recourse to fight the destruction of their environment. In 1978, the military declared all land in Nigeria the property of the federal government, freeing the petroleum companies from troublesome negotiations with locals sitting on top of oil. Four years later, the government agreed to allocate 1.5 percent of federal revenues to the 12 million people living in oil-producing areas. In 1990, after the paramilitary police—known as the Kill and Go Mob—massacred more than fifty residents of Umuechem who were demanding that Shell provide them with potable water and scholarships, the figure was raised to 3 percent. But most of the money has been siphoned off by corrupt officials, and Shell has shown little initiative to make reparations itself. In the nearly forty years that it has pumped oil in Ogoniland, Shell has by its own calculation put in only $2 million worth of improvements, including a smattering of schools and some medical equipment.

About the same time as the Umuechem massacre, Saro-Wiwa

launched the Movement for the Survival of the Ogoni People with a handful of other members of Ogoniland's educated elite. They drafted an Ogoni Bill of Rights and demanded $10 billion in reparations from Shell and a measure of political autonomy for Ogoniland. Matching incendiary rhetoric with organizational skill, Saro-Wiwa became MOSOP's spokesperson. He was by all accounts a magnetic speaker, calling Shell's operations "genocide" and "systematic extermination," and urging the Ogonis to fight for their rights. On January 4, 1993, Saro-Wiwa drew international attention to their cause by leading a peaceful protest march of 300,000 people through Ogoniland.

Yet like so much in Nigeria, how dedicated Saro-Wiwa was to pacifism is a matter of great dispute.
—Joshua Hammer

Yet like so much in Nigeria, how dedicated Saro-Wiwa was to pacifism is a matter of great dispute. Against the wishes of other MOSOP leaders, Saro-Wiwa formed a more radical youth wing of the movement. Sabotage and threats to Shell workers increased; in January 1993, Shell ceased manned operations in Ogoniland, a move that cost the company and the government 28,000 barrels of crude oil a day. Although that amount was just 3 percent of oil production in Nigeria, MOSOP's actions signified unprecedented defiance of the junta, which feared that another secessionist movement was brewing in the Delta. The general manager of SPDC asked the government to protect Shell's installations across the Delta. During the summer of 1993, the government began replacing Ogoni police officers with officers from different ethnic groups, who prompted neighboring tribes into a series of attacks that left thousands of Ogonis dead or homeless.

In response, Saro-Wiwa called for the Ogonis to boycott the upcoming democratic presidential election, a tactic that widened schisms between the elite and the younger, poorer activists. Four MOSOP officers resigned, leaving Saro-Wiwa in charge of the organization. Ogoniland was quickly polarized, with many Ogoni activists becoming increasingly angry at the region's "traditional chiefs," hereditary leaders who oversaw the local distribution of government jobs and oil-cleanup, road, and construction contracts. When the chiefs warned Ogoni youths to desist from violence, posters appeared throughout the region branding the chiefs "vultures" and calling for their punishment. "MOSOP was changing the traditional structure," said Dr. David Owens Wiwa, Ken's younger brother. "Those who benefited from the old establishment, from government contracts, were seen as depriving the people of their due."

Revenge against the "vultures" could be harsh. Priscilla Vikue, the director-general of the Ministry of Education in Port Harcourt, was one of those branded a collaborator by Ogoni militants. "The youths requested that I resign my government appointment," she told me. "I refused. That's when they burned my house to the ground, along with those of six traditional chiefs."

Saro-Wiwa always publicly maintained that he sought to restrain the troublemakers, even asking the Nigerian military to arrest certain "hoodlums," but Vikue and other members of the elite who testified against him maintain that his anti-establishment rhetoric fueled the youths' actions. "I complained to Saro-Wiwa," said Vikue. "I said, 'Have you heard what they did to me? To my house?' He said, 'Look, Priscilla, there is a revolution in Ogoniland. You'd better go with it because heads will roll.' I was shocked," Vikue said. "He told the people they were qualified to live like kings and queens, that they would all be millionaires. And the people were unemployed. They believed him. I told him, 'You're misleading them. Not everyone can drive a Mercedes.'"

By 1994, the government had decided to escalate its efforts against MOSOP. A May 5 internal memo authored by Major Paul Okuntimo, head of the regional arm of the military, the Rivers State Internal Security Force, warned of what was to come: "Shell operations still impossible unless ruthless military operations are undertaken for smooth economic activities to commence.... Recommendations: Wasting operations during MOSOP and other gatherings making constant military presence justifiable. Wasting targets cutting across communities and leadership cadres especially vocal individuals of various groups." Four hundred more troops were sent to Ogoniland, and the memo notes that the government was pressuring the oil companies to underwrite the operation. "This is it," Saro-Wiwa told Greenpeace after the memo was leaked to MOSOP. "They are going to arrest us all and execute us. All for Shell."

Saro-Wiwa's prediction may have been melodramatic, but it was also prescient. Shortly before noon on May 21, 1994, the traditional chief of the village of Giokoo hosted at his palace a meeting of about 100 other Ogoni chiefs and supporters. The event had been well publicized, and many young Ogonis were suspicious that the chiefs were planning to collaborate with the military to quell MOSOP. Suddenly, recalled eyewitness Al-Haji Kobani, "there was the sound of a loud motorcycle outside. A guy came in and said, 'Ken has been arrested on the way to a political rally.' Three minutes later the place was surrounded by over 2,000 people. There was no escape route. They removed our wristwatches, shoes, belts, and everything that was in our pockets. They escorted about 50 people to safety. Then the rest were left in the hall for killing. They attacked us with bottles, stones, iron bars, and machetes. I tried to talk sense to them. But they said, 'Ken Saro-Wiwa is going to bring us a kingdom.'"

Al-Haji's brother Edward Kobani, a Gokana chief, former Rivers State government official, and one of MOSOP's founders, was killed on the spot by a rake driven into his skull. The other victims, all erstwhile friends of Saro-Wiwa's who broke with him in 1993, were Albert Badey, a former secretary to the Rivers State government; Chief Samuel Orage, a former Rivers State commissioner, an Ogoni chief, and the brother-in-law of Saro-Wiwa's wife, Maria; and his brother, Chief Theophilous Orage, also a traditional leader. All three were chased down and murdered at a nearby market. According to witnesses, the killers stuffed the corpses inside a Volkswagen, doused them with gasoline, and set them on fire.

The chief's palace in Giokoo remains a monument to the violence unleashed by MOSOP. All of its louvered windows were smashed, and shards of glass covered the veranda. I could still make out faint bloodstains on the eggshell-blue walls of the large living room—the spot where Edward Kobani died. Overturned easy chairs, broken glass, cooking pots, leaves, and empty bottles of schnapps—a traditional gift to village chiefs—littered the bare cement floor. A narrow hallway led to the juju shrine behind the house to which Al-Haji Kobani crawled during the mayhem, managing to save himself. Inside the shrine, chameleons scurried over sacks of cement, more empty schnapps bottles, and a pile of rodent skulls. As I looked over the palace, the intoxicating mixture of euphoria and rage that drove the killers seemed almost palpable. Rousing the Ogoni masses from passivity and despair, Saro-Wiwa had filled them with a sense of entitlement and rancor toward the old order. He may have been miles from the scene of the killings in Giokoo, but he was, in some way, responsible.

One day after the killings at Giokoo, a brigade from the Rivers State Internal Security Force stormed into Ogoniland, arrested MOSOP activists, and allegedly murdered and raped hundreds of civilians. Major Paul Okuntimo, the author of the secret "wasting" memo, led the troops. He was later implicated by one of his own soldiers in the rape of at least two women.

After I left Giokoo, I went to visit Okuntimo at his family's bungalow at the Bori military camp in Port Harcourt. He had a disarmingly charismatic presence—muscular, handsome, and well-spoken. Wearing a white jogging suit and smiling, he invited me into his house. Faded Christmas ornaments, wedding photos, and a plaque proclaiming MY FAMILY IS COVERED WITH THE BLOOD OF JESUS decorated the dusty, dark living room. Promoted to lieutenant colonel as a reward for his achievements in Ogoniland, Okuntimo is said to be planning a career in the evangelical Christian ministry when he retires from the army.

He disappeared into a back room and emerged five minutes later dressed in crisp fatigues. Then we climbed into his Toyota Land Cruiser and roared down a rutted dirt road to the headquarters of the military's Second Amphibious Brigade. Soldiers snapped to attention as he strode into his office, which was dominated by portraits of General Abacha and the army chief of staff. Okuntimo sat down behind an empty desk and leaned forward. "Look," he began, assuming a tone of restraint. "The Ogoni organization was established in good faith. But their nonviolent campaign metamorphosed. These young vigilantes took over the leadership, they set up roadblocks, they seized weapons from police stations, they began executing anyone they viewed as the enemy. At a certain point, Saro-Wiwa simply lost control.

"There was no relationship between the army and Shell. There were no discussions before the operation," he insisted. I asked Okuntimo about the admissions of some of his troops, cited in a Human Rights Watch/Africa report, that they had gunned down dozens of civilians on his orders. He laughed dismissively, and if he was lying—and I believe that he was—then it was accomplished with ease. "Where did I throw the corpses? In the creeks? They would float. Did I bury them? They could dig them up. These are all lies spread by Ogoni sympathists."

On May 17, 1995, I took a seat in the upstairs gallery of a small, high-ceilinged courtroom in a secure government compound in downtown Port Harcourt where Saro-Wiwa and fourteen other Ogoni activists, including top officials and members of the youth wing, were facing capital murder charges for having incited the killings at Giokoo. Frayed red carpets, peeling plaster walls, and forty whirring ceiling fans gave the courtroom a sad, neglected feeling. Two dozen soldiers armed with automatic weapons lined the walls, guarded the entrance, and peered in the windows from the garden outside. On the dais sat the three judges—two civilians in gray suits and a uniformed lieutenant colonel with a doctorate in criminology. Their verdict was unappealable, pending confirmation by General Abacha.

At one o'clock, the shuttered prison van carrying Saro-Wiwa and his codefendants arrived from the military barracks where they'd been detained for one year. Saro-Wiwa's appearance hushed the murmur of journalists and the families of the defendants and victims. He was a tiny, compactly built man, no more than five foot three, and wore goldrimmed glasses, a brightly dyed green, blue, and white caftan, and leather sandals. Obviously in deteriorating physical condition, he leaned on a carved wooden cane as he slowly wobbled toward the dock. The day's first prosecution witness, a former MOSOP official, recounted a meeting in late 1993 during which Saro-Wiwa had allegedly ordered the murder of the four chiefs at Giokoo. The story sounded rehearsed and implausible. Saro-Wiwa pointedly ignored him, keeping his face buried in a United Nations report on military abuses in Ogoniland. One by one, prosecution witnesses took the stand. None would make eye contact with the defendants; each intoned the same rote account.

Midway through the proceedings the judges called a brief recess, and two of Saro-Wiwa's defense attorneys ushered me out of the courtroom. In a dimly lit lounge down the corridor, Saro-Wiwa sat on a couch smoking a pipe, surrounded by a dozen soldiers and policemen. He looked at the policemen nervously, then stood up, balanced himself on his cane, and shook my hand. "Did you get my letter?" he whispered. I nodded. The day before, he had had a ten-page handwritten reply to a dozen questions of mine smuggled out of jail. In it, he denied instigating the murders, claimed his movement was entirely nonviolent, and accused the government of framing him. "These people are criminals," he told me with a dismissive wave. "They're going to find me guilty. So I don't even bother to listen to the testimony. I'm not going to let these goons have any advantage over me." Moments later, the soldiers cut him off and escorted me from the lounge. I returned to the courtroom, but my hope that the proceedings would clarify Saro-Wiwa's complicity in the escalating violence in Ogoniland had evaporated. Whatever transgressions he had committed—and I don't believe that ordering the murder of the four chiefs was among them—Saro-Wiwa would get no fair hearing in this court. Of the nineteen prosecution witnesses called, two of the most damaging would later admit to having been bribed by the junta. In June, the defense team, led by pro-democracy activist Gani Fawehinmi, resigned en masse, claiming that the trial was rigged. Fawehinmi was almost immediately arrested and was held for two weeks.

The pit into which Saro-Wiwa fell was only thirteen feet deep, and the fall failed to break his neck. It took him twenty minutes to die.
—*Joshua Hammer*

Six months later, on November 10, Saro-Wiwa and the eight other prisoners who had been duly found guilty were awakened at dawn, chained at their ankles, and driven from Bori military camp to the central prison of Port Harcourt. There they were herded into a bare cell. A few minutes later, Saro-Wiwa was called into the records room. As a sobbing priest performed last rites, he was made to sign a register and surrender his remaining property: a purse in which he kept his pipe and tobacco. Wearing a loose-fitting gown and bath-

room slippers, he was handcuffed and shuffled off to the gallows. A few minutes before noon, a black cloth sack was placed over his head and he mounted the gallows. The pit into which Saro-Wiwa fell was only thirteen feet deep, and the fall failed to break his neck. It took him twenty minutes to die. The execution was videotaped, the cassette sent by courier to General Abacha, as proof that the Ogoni leader was really dead.

When the BBC broadcast the news of Saro-Wiwa's hanging, thousands of Ogonis wandered into the streets, disoriented and distraught. Within hours, the Nigerian military deployed 4,000 troops throughout Ogoniland, beating anyone caught mourning in public. In the week following the executions, the United States, Canada, South Africa, and several European countries withdrew their ambassadors. At the behest of British prime minister John Major and South African president Nelson Mandela, the Commonwealth of former British colonies suspended Nigeria. Even the Organization of African Unity, which once had greeted Idi Amin with standing ovations, expressed dismay.

That same week Shell announced it would put up the bulk of $3.8 billion to build a natural-gas plant on Bonny Island. The announcement suggested that, in ordering the executions, Abacha had taken a calculated gamble. Even from the seclusion of his presidential mansion at Aso Rock, the dictator surely knew the killings would disgust the world and possibly provoke sanctions. Yet, for Abacha, international opprobrium was a fair exchange for internal stability. Abacha probably could have predicted too that despite calls for an oil embargo from civil-rights leaders around the world, neither the United States, which imports almost half of the oil produced by Nigeria, nor any other country found the resolve to do it.

One month after the executions, I returned to Shell's Nigerian headquarters on Lagos Island. Shell was running full-page ads in the *New York Times* saying: "Some campaigning groups say we should intervene in the political process in Nigeria. But even if we could, we must never do so. Politics is the business of governments and politicians. The world where companies use their economic influence to prop up or bring down governments would be a frightening and bleak one indeed. Shell. We'll keep you in touch with the truth." But despite this bit of corporate agitprop, the company was under siege; the public relations desk was blanketed with faxes from around the world deploring the company's environmental record in the Niger Delta and its failure to prevent Saro-Wiwa's hanging.

General manager Nnaemeka Achebe again welcomed me into his office, though his demeanor was far less chipper than when we had met the previous spring. He pointed out that after the death sentences were announced on October 31,

Shell's chairman, Cor Herkstroter, had sent a personal letter to Abacha requesting mercy. Going further than that, Achebe explained, would have compromised Shell's "business principles." "Obviously we have significant economic power in the country," Achebe said. "Yet we must be mindful not to interfere with local politics and be a government of some sort. . . . We're helping the cake grow bigger, and how that the cake is divided is up to the people to decide."

Achebe ticked off a list of development projects Shell was undertaking in the Delta. (In 1995, the company spent $9 million on improvements to the region, three times what it spent in 1990.) At the top of Achebe's list was the new gas plant, which would liquefy the natural gas, thus reducing pollution. "It's in the best interest of Nigeria for the project not to collapse," Achebe said. "The whole local economy around Bonny will benefit—small contractors, welders, electricians."

Shell's newfound interest in the environment and economy of the Delta is not surprising. During the past three years MOSOP has spawned at least half a dozen imitators, including the Ijaw National Congress and the Movement for Reparation to the Ogbia, and protests have paralyzed Shell's and other oil companies' operations in dozens of Delta locations. In one recent month alone, 5,000 people in Izere besieged Shell oil wells to protest the state of the roads and to demand a water project; hundreds of protesters in neighboring Olomoro seized a Shell flow station and hijacked eighteen vehicles belonging to Seismograph Services Ltd., a Shell contractor; and a convoy of villagers in canoes from Opuama took control of a Chevron drilling platform, demanding compensation for pollution. Protests were costing Shell and the other oil producers millions of lost barrels a year. "Shell is the victim in this," insisted Achebe. "We are caught in a situation where the communities can't get at the real target—the government—to express their grievances, so they attack us."

And so Shell was making amends to these little villages because, for now, it was in its best interest to do so. It was a payoff, a way of buying a measure of peace, of silencing the fax machines and the college kids camping out in front of the company's London headquarters. A few clinics and some asphalt was a small price to pay for continuing to operate without accountability.

In Port Harcourt and Ogoniland, meanwhile, the regime was trying to mute the local press and obliterate any trace of Saro-Wiwa's influence. In the absence of reliable information, rumors flourished. The executioners were said to have poured acid on the corpses of the Ogoni nine to speed their decomposition and discourage Ogoni activists from attempting to take possession of the bodies. When I tried to visit Saro-Wiwa's grave in a weed-chocked cemetery in central

Port Harcourt, I was escorted away by a phalanx of soldiers and brought before Colonel Dauda Musa Komo, who had supervised the executions.

Komo denied me permission to see the grave but said that the military should be commended for having treated the bodies with respect. "We buried each one in a coffin in his own grave. We could have just thrown them all in a pit," he said. "We have no regrets. We don't owe anybody an explanation."

To counter reports of military repression in Saro-Wiwa's home region, the regime had launched a propaganda campaign and insisted on providing me with a government escort, Fidelis Agbiki, the glib young press secretary to the Rivers State military administrator. "Everything is completely normal in Ogoniland," Agbiki cheerfully assured me as we passed one of the roadblocks set up at intersections throughout the region. "Most Ogonis stopped supporting Saro-Wiwa a long time ago."

But at a primary school in the Ogoni village of Bera, I met Principal M. A. Vite, a dapper, middle-aged man. He fidgeted behind a battered wooden desk in the stifling heat, nervously peering toward the front gate, where Agbiki waited in the government Peugeot. Around Vite sat a dozen Ogoni teachers: shabbily dressed men with solemn faces. "If you have a brother and your brother is killed—that's how we feel," Vite said, as his colleagues nodded and murmured in agreement. "But the moment we express anger they may say, 'Kill all of them.' It's futile to face machine guns with empty hands."

"If the military sees two or three people gathering, they may imprison you. If you wear black, they may beat you," said a science teacher who refused to give his name. "If you carry newspapers, they will seize them. Our headmaster was arrested last week as a warning to us not to discuss Ken in the classroom. Pastors were arrested because they prayed for Ken Saro-Wiwa. They take away people every day."

In the five months since I left Nigeria, the government has jailed hundreds of minority and pro-democracy activists, union and human-rights leaders, journalists, teachers, and lawyers. The State Department has warned that Nigeria's human-rights record is deteriorating, noting that "police and security services commonly engaged in extrajudicial killings and excessive use of force to quell antimilitary and prodemocracy protests." Shell set up a commission to investigate environmental destruction, but the head of the commission quickly resigned, citing his doubts about its impartiality. On March 12, the Clinton Administration announced that it had been trying to persuade U.S. businesses and foreign governments to stop all investment and freeze Nigerian assets. Resistance to this proposal was so strong that the harshest sanction that seemed possible was a ban on Nigerian participation in the Olympics. On that same day, incidentally, Shell announced that one of its joint ventures with the Nigerian government had made a major offshore oil discovery. The discovery was no coincidence. If "Bongo 1" and other deep-water reserves prove commercially viable, Shell and the government could abandon mainland production in turbulent areas. Lacking an effective venue for protest, the plight of the Nigerian people could easily be ignored. In the Delta, the hospitals would crumble, the ramshackle schools would rot and fall, and the half-built roads would slowly be swallowed up by the swamps.

David Rieff (review date 16 June 1997)

SOURCE: "The Ruin of Nigeria, the Ruin of Africa. The Threat of Death," in *The New Republic,* Vol. 216, No. 24, June 16, 1997, pp. 33-41.

[*Rieff is an American political writer. In the following review of* A Month and a Day: A Detention Diary *and Wole Soyinka's* The Open Sore of a Continent: A Personal Narrative of the Nigerian Crisis, *he examines the current political, social, and economic state of Nigeria in particular and Africa overall.*]

I.

The hangmen who, on November 10, 1995, carried out the execution of the Nigerian writer Ken Saro-Wiwa and eight of his colleagues from MOSOP, or the Movement for the Salvation of the Ogoni People, the militant tribal advocacy group that he had helped to found five years earlier, were flown into the southeastern Nigerian city of Port Harcourt, where the doomed men were being held, from the far north of the country. Since hangmen are not in short supply in any region of Nigeria, it can be taken as read that the decision to use outsiders was based on the assumption that as northerners, and as Muslims, they could be relied upon to have not a flicker of sympathy for the Christian southerners whose judicial murder they were to carry out. And they passed this test of loyalty to the dictatorship of General Sani Abacha, himself a northerner. It was only the killings themselves that they bungled.

Saro-Wiwa and his colleagues were arrested in May 1994 on charges of having murdered four Ogoni tribal chiefs who had opposed MOSOP's activities. They were tried by a special tribunal and condemned to death. It was generally assumed, abroad and in Nigeria, that the Abacha regime was divided about what to do with Saro-Wiwa even after the death sentence, and so it would move slowly. Since the Nigerian army again took control of the country at the end of

1983 (the only respite was a three-month-long return to civilian rule at the end of 1993), each of the generals ruling over Nigeria has been more brutal. Babangida turned out to be worse than Buhari, and Abacha has been the worst of all. Yet even Abacha does not rule on his own.

For the elite whose consent Abacha needs to govern, the execution of Saro-Wiwa posed risks. It was one thing to send forces into Ogoni territory, as the Nigerian state had done in 1993 and 1994; but it was quite another to kill a man who had many friends and supporters abroad. In other cases that had drawn criticism from abroad, the regime had compromised. The other miscarriage of justice that excited interest in the West, the life sentence handed down against General Olusegun Obasanjo, another military leader who had been Nigeria's president, was eventually commuted to a prison term of fifteen years.

To the end, there were rumors in Nigeria that Abacha was trying to cut a deal with Saro-Wiwa, as he had done with many other opponents from within the Nigerian elite. Others believed that the Shell Oil Company, whose despoliation of Ogoniland in the Nigerian southeast had been the focal point of MOSOP's protests, would persuade Abacha to spare Saro-Wiwa's life, if only to spare itself the certain prospect of the renewal of protests and the surprisingly effective boycott that Greenpeace had mounted in 1993. Shell had been coping with other public relations problems, and it did not need more bad publicity.

It turned out that these relatively sanguine assumptions did not take into account what Wole Soyinka rightly identifies in *The Open Sore of a Continent,* his remarkable book on the collapse of Nigeria, as the Abacha regime's determination "to make it impossible for the victims of oil exploration to present a united front in their demands for reparations for their polluted land, a fair share in the resources of their land, and a voice in the control of their own development." Having tried, and failed, to stifle the movement through terror, and having imposed direct military rule on Ogoniland, with a similar lack of success, the regime opted to kill its leader. It hoped that, with Saro-Wiwa dead, MOSOP would wither, and Shell, which had withdrawn under pressure from Ogoniland in 1993, would resume its operations.

For the Abacha regime, the stakes could not have been higher. Oil has always been the lifeblood of the Nigerian state. Nigeria is the world's ninth largest petroleum producer, and Shell is by far the most important petroleum company operating in the country. A typical leaflet issued by Shell, at the height of MOSOP's campaign, was titled *Nigeria and Shell: Partners in Progress.* In reality, as even Shell officials conceded, the tensions in Ogoniland had hardly been invented by MOSOP. As a Shell "Briefing Note" put it in 1993, people throughout the oil-producing areas believe that they "are not getting a fair share of the oil revenues." The company insisted, though, that this was none of its concern. Saro-Wiwa, it argued, was trying to "internationalize the problem." Shell was simply trying to do its work in what it referred to as "a difficult operating environment, much of it swamps." As for the Ogoni's complaints, they were "Nigerian problems."

Saro-Wiwa claimed repeatedly that the Anglo-Dutch multinational had behaved with particular callousness in the Niger River Delta. He was right. Unfortunately, and this excuses nothing, Shell's conduct was not very different from the conduct of other oil companies in places where they were free to operate more or less as they pleased. Oil companies have earned a particularly bad reputation in this regard, as the recent attempt of Unocal to expand its operations in Myanmar demonstrated once again. Indeed, almost all multinationals involved mainly in the extraction of natural resources in Third World countries exhibit abysmal standards on political and environmental issues. The reason is simple: their only need is for a secure environment in which to mine or to drill. They are not trying to create markets in the countries in which they are operating, and so they do not trouble themselves about the social requirements of a market. All they need is a crude political stability. A terrorist kleptocracy will do nicely.

The notion that these swamps were the Ogoni's homeland, and that Shell's operations were gradually making great areas of it uninhabitable, is never mentioned in the company's brochures and press releases. Saro-Wiwa, a Shell official once wrote, is either "a mild nuisance or a great threat." Although they have never admitted as much publicly, there seems to have been some division within Shell over whether Saro-Wiwa represented a threat or a nuisance. Shell officials monitored Saro-Wiwa's activities with increasing alarm and mounted a campaign in Europe and North America against MOSOP's claims; but how seriously they took MOSOP is unclear.

The Nigerian authorities seemed to have had no such doubts. Shell's drilling operations might have despoiled Ogoniland, but the revenues that the Nigerian federal authorities received from oil-related activities, one-half of which came from Shell's operations (they also generated 90 percent of the country's foreign exchange), were all that stood between the regime and economic collapse. At a time when, as the saying went in Lagos, "this country dey as if e no dey" (this country was as good as dead), the Abacha regime needed desperately to increase oil revenues. It could not tolerate the prospect of seeing the cash impeded by the civic activism of small delta tribes such as the Ogoni.

Even many opponents of the regime found the Ogoni question somewhat distant and mystifying. As Soyinka observes,

for the majority of Nigerians, Ogoni is only some localized problem, remote from the immediate, overall mission of rooting out the military from Nigerian politics, rescuing the nation's wealth from its incontinent hands, and terminating, once and for all, its routine murders of innocent citizens on the streets of Lagos and other visible centers of opposition. The massacres in Ogoni are hidden, ill-reported. Those that obtain the just publicity of horror, mostly in government-controlled media, are those that are attributed to the Ogoni leadership movements, such as MOSOP.

The news, in 1994, that Ogoniland had been declared a military zone under the direct rule of a federally appointed "Task Force on Internal Security" was greeted indifferently in most parts of Nigeria. And when reports began filtering back to Lagos that in Ogoniland whole villages were uprooted, there was little public outcry. Soyinka saw clearly that, as he puts it, "Ogoniland is the first Nigerian experimentation with 'ethnic cleansing'"; but ordinary Nigerians in Lagos often read about violent incidents whose perpetrators cannot be identified. In 1994, a number of apparently unprovoked attacks on Ogoni villages in which hundreds of people were slaughtered was described by the Nigerian government as the result of "disputes" with other villages. How the attackers got their hands on sophisticated weapons, and why the local Ogoni police were ordered out of the area before the attacks, was never discussed.

What happened in Ogoniland in the early 1990s, once the Nigerian authorities realized that local opposition to the despoliation of the region was growing stronger, was a massive campaign of state terror in which the state-run media would insist that nothing at all was happening, or, if reports of bloodshed could not be suppressed, that government forces were responding to "terrorist" attacks. The Russians tried the same tactic in Chechnya. In Ogoniland, unlike in the Caucasus, the tactic largely worked.

In all likelihood, the attackers were members of the Nigerian armed forces. Still, whatever the army's exactions, nothing that the authorities undertook in the Niger River Delta was effective in suppressing the campaign that Saro-Wiwa had initiated. MOSOP's tactic of singling out Shell and demanding reparations for the environmental damage that the company's operations had done to Ogoniland were gathering strength at the time that Saro-Wiwa was arrested. Shell had declared that its decision to stay out of Ogoniland would remain in force until the civil disturbances ceased. But the trouble showed no sign of diminishing.

The Abacha regime was furious about this development, and it was under no illusion about the threat that an expansion of this kind of tribal activism to other Niger delta tribes posed. MOSOP had to be isolated. Otherwise there loomed the danger that many of the peoples of the delta would revolt against the oil companies. In that sense, Shell's shiny patter about the partnership between the company and the federal state was all too accurate. To Abacha and his cronies, an assault on one was an assault on the other. Small wonder, then, that Lieutenant Colonel Dauda Komo, a protégé of Abacha who was then the military governor of Rivers State, the region that encompasses Ogoniland, reportedly had made up his mind that Saro-Wiwa had to die.

The trial was a farce from the start, with witnesses testifying and then recanting their testimony, and the judges doing everything they could to prevent MOSOP's lawyers from mounting a proper defense. The condemned men doubtless knew of the regime's desire to destroy them. In the aftermath of the tribunal, protests against the sentences began to gather in intensity. Before the trial, the Ogoni cause had interested mainly environmental activists, a few committed journalists, and the governments of Denmark, Sweden, Norway and the Netherlands; but now even allies of the Nigerian government such as John Major and Boutros Boutros-Ghali, and notably unsentimental leaders such as the head of the European Union, the Secretary-General of the British Commonwealth, and President Nelson Mandela of South Africa, joined in the appeals to spare Saro-Wiwa's life. The condemned men had at least some reason to hope (though some prescient outsiders such as Soyinka had concluded that their fates were sealed). It seems that none of them realized, on that morning when they were taken from the military camp where they had been held for eighteen months to the Port Harcourt prison, that they were going to their deaths.

They had all faced death before. To be an antigovernment activist in Nigeria in the Abacha era has been an increasingly perilous business. But to stand up, as Saro-Wiwa and his colleagues had done, not only to the Abacha regime, but also to the interests of the Shell Oil Company, was to court extinction. And yet Saro-Wiwa had already had the experience of being jailed and released before. In 1993, he was imprisoned in the same prison in Port Harcourt. In his memoir of that time, *A Month and a Day: A Detention Diary,* he wrote of the "great number of people in Nigeria and abroad [who] had taken steps to save me." So there was at least some reason for Saro-Wiwa and his fellow prisoners to assume that the attention that their cases were receiving in Europe and North America would once again stay the regime's hand. Rumors persist in Lagos to this day that Saro-Wiwa could have made a deal and saved his life. But he laughed when Abacha tried to buy him off, and this slight cost him his life.

Saro-Wiwa was taken out first, and led into a room in which a makeshift scaffold had been erected. A black hood was pulled over his head; a noose was cinched around his neck. But when the chief hangman sprang the lever to drop the trapdoor beneath the prisoner's feet, nothing happened. For minutes, as the bound Saro-Wiwa stood there, the executioners tried to get the lever to operate properly. Then it was decided that Saro-Wiwa would not be killed first. One of the other prisoners would enable the hangmen to assure themselves that the scaffold was working properly.

Saro-Wiwa was led back to the holding cell where his eight comrades—John Kpunien, Barinem Kiobel, Baribo Bera, Saturday Dobue, Daniel Grakao, Monday Eawo, Felix Nwanie and Paul Levura—waited their turn to be murdered. Kpunien was chosen and led into the execution chamber. This time the trapdoor worked. Kpunien's body was removed, and Saro-Wiwa was brought in. But the trapdoor failed. Saro-Wiwa was led to one side, and waited as the henchmen tried to get the thing to do its job, as it had done a few minutes earlier when Kpunien died. At this point, Saro-Wiwa is reported to have screamed: "Why are you people doing this to me? What kind of a nation is this?"

On the fifth try, the Nigerian government's judicial murder of Ken Saro-Wiwa was accomplished.

II.

It is not inaccurate to describe Ken Saro-Wiwa as a Nigerian writer who became the leading advocate of the rights of his people; but he was more than that. From the beginning of his career, he wore many hats. As a writer, he was prolific. He wrote novels, polemics, memoirs, political journalism, plays, poems and children's books. He was born in Bori, on the southern coast of Nigeria, in 1941, the son of an Ogoni chief, J. B. Wiwa, and at different times in his life he did energetic service as a publisher, a businessman, a government official and a television producer. The fame that he enjoyed within Nigeria to the end of his life was due to his having conceived and written *Basi & Co.,* Nigeria's most popular television soap opera. As the English writer William Boyd remarks in his affecting preface to *A Month and a Day,* the show "was unashamedly pedagogic. What was wrong with Basi and his chums was wrong with Nigeria: none of them wanted to work, and they all acted as though the world owed them a living. . . . This was soap opera as a form of civic education."

Compared to Wole Soyinka or Chinua Achebe, the major writers of contemporary Nigeria, Saro-Wiwa's writing falls short. He had great energy, and a fertile, impatient imagination, but his literary gifts were more appropriate to the writing of film and television scripts than novels and short stories. Boyd's claim that he was a major writer does his heart credit, but not his head. Saro-Wiwa had only a modest talent. For the most part, his non-fiction is far more powerful than his fiction. Readers with no great knowledge of Nigeria would be most likely to admire, and to profit from, and to be moved by, *A Month and a Day: A Detention Diary,* an account of a period of imprisonment in 1993. It is a cry from the heart of someone who is beginning to realize that he will not prevail. "I had been detained for a month and a day," Saro-Wiwa wrote in the book's conclusion, "during which I had witnessed the efficiency of evil. . . . The genocide of the Ogoni had taken on a new dimension. The manner of it I will narrate in my next book, if I live to tell the tale."

Compared to Wole Soyinka or Chinua Achebe, the major writers of contemporary Nigeria, Saro-Wiwa's writing falls short. He had great energy, and a fertile, impatient imagination, but his literary gifts were more appropriate to the writing of film and television scripts than novels and short stories.
—David Rieff

In his lifetime, Saro-Wiwa did write one important novel, *Sozaboy,* whose subtitle is *A Novel in Rotten English.* It appeared in 1985. Told in West African pidgin, *Sozaboy,* or "Soldier Boy," is the story of a young boy conscripted into the Biafran army during the civil war of 1967-70. It chronicles what Saro-Wiwa saw as the pointless horrors of that conflict with bitter verve and originality. At the end of the book, the young recruit simply flees. His message is clear and unflinching: "And I was thinking how I was prouding myself before to go to soza and call myself Sozaboy. But now if anybody say anything about war or even fight, I will just run and run and run. Believe me yours sincerely." It was advice that Saro-Wiwa was not to take himself.

The plaudits of ordinary Nigerians, especially for *Basi & Co.,* were not the main reason that Saro-Wiwa was able to get away with his thinly disguised criticism of his society. His story is a complicated one. Despite his long history of activism on behalf of the Ogoni people—he was agitating for them since his school days—Saro-Wiwa was anything but an anti-establishment figure in Nigeria. Indeed, during the Biafran War of 1967-70, he won favor with an earlier generation of Nigerian military rulers by fiercely opposing the Ibo secessionists. He did so not out of a great belief in Nigerian federalism. As he would later explain in *On a Darkling Plain* (1989), his memoir of his role in the war, the Biafran conflict was not, in his view, about the right to self-determination of the Ibo people and the other southeastern tribes that sided with them, as the secessionists had claimed at the time. The war was, rather, "mostly about the control of the oil resources of the Ogoni and other ethnic groups in the Niger River Delta." Saro-Wiwa was utterly convinced that the choice was between "the Ogoni existing as one of 200 or so ethnic groups in Nigeria or as one of 30 or so ethnic groups in secessionist Biafra." And so "I identified with the federal government."

Most Ogonis had in fact sided with Biafran secession, and viewed the federal troops re-entering the Niger River Delta as occupiers, and so the value of Saro-Wiwa to the Nigerian authorities was substantial. And the rewards that he reaped personally for his anti-Ibo stance were immediate and considerable. Since his murder, this part of Saro-Wiwa's story has tended to be swept under the rug by his allies, as has the fact that, unlike Soyinka, he had not always been a steadfast critic of Nigeria's various despots. Yet to insist upon it does not in any way call into question the authenticity of his ever braver resistance to the authorities in the 1980s. By the early '90s, certainly, all his other activities had receded in importance for him, and he was devoting almost all of his energies to the cause of his own Ogoni people, inside Nigeria through the Movement for the Salvation of the Ogoni People, and in any foreign capital where he could get a hearing.

In the beginning, though, the swift rise of a 27-year-old academic, whose only published work was a pamphlet called *The Ogoni Nationality Today and Tomorrow,* owed more to preferments offered by the authorities during, and in the immediate aftermath of, the Biafran war than to anything else. Saro-Wiwa became a member of the government of the newly created Rivers State, which the Nigerian government had created as part of its decision, taken while the area was still controlled by Biafran forces, to transform southeastern Nigeria administratively, so that there would never again be an Ibo secession. As federal forces pushed their way into Ogoniland, Saro-Wiwa was appointed the civilian administrator of Bonny, an oil port on the Niger River Delta that adjoins Ogoniland. In 1968, after federal troops had regained control of all of Rivers State, he became a minister in the government there. He would remain in the post until 1973, three years after the final crushing of Biafra.

To the end of his life, Saro-Wiwa was unrepentant about his role in the Biafran conflict. The rebel Biafran government of Colonel Odumegwu Ojukwu, as he wrote in *On a Darkling Plain,* and repeated in *A Month and a Day,* was "hostile to the Ogoni . . . people." For this reason, while Saro-Wiwa is now a hero to almost every decent Nigerian in Lagos, Kano, or Abuja, as well as to his many supporters abroad, he was a controversial figure among non-Ogonis in his own region of southeastern Nigeria during his lifetime, and he has remained one after his death. Saro-Wiwa was, in truth, a paradoxical figure, a cosmopolitan ethnic, an ethnic cosmopolitan, a tireless campaigner for human rights who was also a tireless tribalist.

That he had wanted no part of Biafra did not mean that Saro-Wiwa had all that much faith in a unitary Nigeria. It was, in his opinion, simply the least bad alternative. He was, to be sure, a member in good standing of the Nigerian elite, who claimed senior Nigerian employees of Shell among his schoolmates, and who had sent his children to be educated in Britain. (His youngest son died in 1992 while at Eton.) But he always saw himself first and foremost as an Ogoni. The more dangerous he saw the situation of the tribe becoming, the more he threw in his lot with it. "My worry about the Ogoni," he wrote in *A Month and a Day,* "has been an article of faith, conceived of in primary school, nurtured through secondary school, actualized in the Nigerian civil war in 1967-70 and during my tenure as a member of the Rivers State Executive Council, 1968-73."

It is understandable, I guess, that his Ogoni identity impelled him to side with the federal authorities in 1968-71, though it must also be noted that many other Ogonis, probably the majority of them, opted for Biafra. The Biafran secession was itself fought largely over oil. The Ibos, who dominated the Nigerian southeast, felt that its oil should be theirs to control; and when the military coup in 1966 put an end to the first Nigerian republic, which had been a fairly equal federation of regions with three regional governments, and most of the power that the Ibos had exercised in the eastern region was assumed by the federal authorities (the southeast was to be divided into three states), the Ibos opted for independence. In a sense, Saro-Wiwa's view of the Ogoni relationship to the Ibos was the Ibo view of their own relationship to the rest of Nigeria.

Would Biafra have been better or worse for the Ogoni? It is impossible to know what a Biafran state would have looked like. Where Saro-Wiwa was almost certainly right, though, was in perceiving that Ojukwu was no friend of the Ogoni people. Under the circumstances, it was perfectly plausible that he would welcome the new three-state arrangement, since it offered the possibility that in the future the Ogonis rather than the Ibos would play a dominant role in what had become Rivers State.

Saro-Wiwa hoped that the constitutional arrangements that would be created after the war would "take strong cognizance of our desires with regard to the companies prospecting or operating on our soil." Still, long before his arrest in 1994, he was writing that "I realize how pious my hopes were [in the after-math of the Biafran war], and how much they failed." Having crushed the Biafran secession, the government of General Yakubu Gowon turned out to be no more interested in looking after the cultural or the material interests of numerically insignificant tribes such as the Ogoni than their predecessors had been. There are only half a million Ogonis in a country of more than 100 million. The central authorities, Saro-Wiwa observed bitterly, might pay lip service to the idea of Nigerian federalism, and to the protection of the rights of ethnic minorities, but their assurances were lies.

Unfortunately for the Ogoni, the aftermath of the Biafran war coincided with the oil boom of the 1970s, with the era of OPEC. The Nigerian authorities were obsessed with exploiting the resource. Within a few years of the end of the civil war, there had occurred a huge increase in exploration and extraction activities in Ogoniland, and it was becoming clear to Saro-Wiwa that the same officials who had found non-Ibo southeasterners such as himself useful during the conflict were now bent on developing the natural resources of Ogoniland, no matter what the human or environmental damage. The tribe's interests no longer mattered in a state besotted by fantasies of wealth and global importance. This was a time when there was much talk within the Nigerian elite of the country acquiring an "African" nuclear bomb and a seat on the Security Council, when the government believed that Nigeria was destined not only to lead Africa, but also to be a beacon for the African diaspora in Europe and North America.

Things looked very different in Ogoniland. As Saro-Wiwa put it in *A Month and a Day,* "the Rivers State itself did not prove to be any better than the Eastern Region in reconciling the interests of its component ethnic groups." All the peoples of the Niger delta had suffered tremendously during the Biafran war. Now the oil that lay beneath their soil was putting their physical survival at risk as surely as the fighting had done. And yet the determination of the federal authorities to exploit the delta was unshakable. As Saro-Wiwa pointed out, by the end of the 1970s oil had become "the be-all and end-all of Nigerian politics and the economy, as well as the central focus of all budgetary ambitions." The new federalist ethos provided a useful cover. Who were the Ogoni to stand in the way of Nigeria's progress? What this post-Biafran "unitarism" really meant, Saro-Wiwa wrote bitterly, was that "the resources of the Ogoni and other ethnic minorities in the Niger River Delta could be more easily purloined while paying lip service to Nigerian federalism and unity."

Oil revenues began to play an important role after the first large strikes were made in the mid-1950s by Shell Oil's corporate predecessor, Shell D'Arcy, which had been given exclusive rights to look for oil in 1937. It was in the 1960s, however, that the real profits began to materialize, once Shell finished a pipeline running from its fields in the Niger River Delta to the Bonny Island terminal near Port Harcourt. When Nigeria became independent, it was widely assumed that it would be one of the great success stories of the continent. Oil would provoke economic development, and the processes of modernization begun under colonialism would accelerate, this time to the benefit of Nigerians rather than foreign companies and Western consumers.

In the aftermath of the Biafran war, royalties from the oil companies became more and more critical to the country's survival. Nigeria was ruled by a succession of military regimes—beginning with General Gowon and including the regime led by General Obasanjo, who, since he has been imprisoned unjustly by General Abacha, is now wrongly regarded as having behaved a great deal better than other Nigerian military leaders—and these regimes had not the faintest idea of how to manage the Nigerian economy. It was a period in Africa when everyone was paying lip service to development. The reality was that neither the Gowon regime in the early 1970s, nor the Murtala-Obasanjo administration that succeeded it, was able to improve the real situation of the Nigerian economy. The only question is whether these rulers were venal or incompetent.

As a result of vastly increased revenues, Nigeria's rulers vastly increased state expenditures. The World Bank's Structural Adjustment Program in Africa is notoriously controversial—as Helmut Schmidt once said, "what is good for the World Bank must not necessarily be good for Africa"—but the Bank's report of 1994, *Adjustment in Africa,* is utterly convincing when it describes "Nigeria's missed opportunity" during the oil boom of 1973-83. As the report points out, the post-1973 increases in the price of oil meant that, for the subsequent decade, Nigeria and Indonesia received extra revenues amounting to about 20 percent of their Gross Domestic Products. The Indonesians used the windfalls ably. Nigeria's rulers squandered it. They directed spending to prestige projects in the cities (where government officials and their cronies lived), grotesquely increasing government consumption, and in many cases stealing outright.

When oil prices buckled in the mid-1980s, the Nigerian economy was totally unprepared. The country's rulers had come to view the oil monies as little more than what Tom Forest, an economic historian of modern Nigeria, has described as "the opportunity for the large-scale personal acquisition of wealth by those with access to state power." Put more starkly, long before the collapse of the Nigerian economy in the 1980s, the elite was already robbing the state blind. All the while, foreign governments kept insisting that all was well, and putting Nigeria forward as a force for stability in Africa—an ideal regional hegemon, to use the conception favored by the Nixon and Ford administrations. Chinua Achebe's intuition that "Nigeria will die if we keep pretending that she is only slightly indisposed" went unheeded. The corruption, the mismanagement, the repression, the clientelism, and the incompetence of the Nigerian state increased. And the bust was even more dangerous than the boom: the more the economic situation

deteriorated, the more the desperation of the satraps to hold on the their power grew.

Saro-Wiwa saw all this clearly. As the crisis deepened, and the situation of the Ogoni became more and more embattled, he came to recognize that his hopes had been in vain. He saw that, from the Biafran War to Abacha's seizure of power, oil on their land had been a catastrophe for Ogoniland. In the immediate aftermath of Nigerian independence, things had been somewhat different. Until the civil war, the practice had been for the authorities to share the oil revenues that they received from foreign companies such as Shell with local administrations on oil-bearing areas. Usually, the federal-local split was fifty-fifty. By 1980, however, only 1.5 percent of the proceeds were going to the people in the areas from which the oil was being extracted. And exploration and drilling were proceeding at a breakneck pace, with not the slightest regard for environmental or safety standards.

Ogoniland was being turned into a disaster area. And Nigerians outside the southeast were not especially perturbed. The previous arrangement, after all, had not favored the majority of Nigerians living in non-oil-producing parts of the country. For them, the despoliation of the Niger River Delta was a matter of passing concern. Economic times were hard, and the oil revenues were almost all that Nigeria could count on. To go back to the old system, in which the small tribes who lived in the oil production areas got a disproportionate share of the revenues, was a very unpopular idea. It was inevitable that, when Saro-Wiwa and his colleagues in MOSOP began to expose what was taking place in Ogoniland, when they carried their case to the National Minorities Council of the United Nations, the Nigerian authorities would respond with fury; but neither Saro-Wiwa nor his foreign supporters seem to have foreseen that there would be little sympathy for the Ogoni there among other Nigerians.

> **There has been a tendency since Saro-Wiwa's death to overstate the support that he received in Nigeria during his lifetime, and also the commitment that existed outside the country to the Ogoni struggle.**
> **—David Rieff**

There has been a tendency since Saro-Wiwa's death to overstate the support that he received in Nigeria during his lifetime, and also the commitment that existed outside the country to the Ogoni struggle. Until Saro-Wiwa's arrest, detention, and death, the Ogoni cause stirred little interest, except among a few environmental activists and Anita Roddick, the owner of the Body Shop stores. Saro-Wiwa's trial, the image of the plucky writer with his pipe in his mouth standing up to a corrupt regime bent on murdering him, changed all that. Suddenly there was international outrage. It was fortunate for the Ogoni that they had a leader with Saro-Wiwa's charisma. Many other small tribal peoples, from the Amazon basin to southern Sudan, are uprooted and massacred without ever striking a resonant chord in the small number of rich countries whose public opinion can alter their fate. The real surprise is that the Saro-Wiwa case managed to compel as much attention as it did in our tragedy-saturated world.

III.

In *The Open Sore of a Continent,* Wole Soyinka observes that Nigeria has become a state without sense or purpose, except for the enrichment of the murderous kleptocracy that surrounds General Abacha. He ends his book with the suggestion that Saro-Wiwa's murder may have sounded the death-knell for Nigeria, that there is nothing left for decent Nigerians to defend any more, that, with the Abacha regime, "we may be witnessing, alas, the end of Nigerian history." It is hard to disagree. A nation that is now being underwritten largely by oil revenues that are put to no constructive purpose, and also now serves as the transit point for 50 percent of the heroin that arrives in the United States, may indeed be irredeemable. Indeed, the Nigerian disaster is so deep and so pervasive that it may well lead, in the very near future, to the breakup of Africa's most populous and (potentially) most rich and most important country.

What is most striking about Soyinka's book is that he no longer finds it possible to lament the end of Nigeria. He ends his book wrathfully. If Saro-Wiwa's death does lead to the end of the Nigerian nation, he writes, it "would be an act of divine justice richly deserved." It is by no means clear, however, that this collapse—Soyinka seems simultaneously to fear it and to look forward to it—will take place. Indeed, there is some evidence, despite intercommunal violence, continued unrest in some parts of the country, and a recent spate of mysterious bombings in Lagos, that in the past year the Abacha regime has solidified its grip on power and broadened its base of support.

Indeed, the most ominous sign that Soyinka may be wrong, that the rulers in Lagos may dodge their just deserts, may be the fate of Soyinka himself. In March 1997, he was condemned to death in absentia by another of General Abacha's tribunals on charges of "levying war" against Nigeria. Unlike Salman Rushdie, of course, Soyinka has all along insisted that the Abacha regime had to be toppled at all costs. Soyinka has not involved himself with antigovernment violence, but he has refused to condemn it. The death of Saro-Wiwa was, for Soyinka, the last straw; and, like Saro-Wiwa, Soyinka demands to know, in his book, "what sort of a nation is this?"

In Lagos, meanwhile, it is business as usual. And business as usual means, well, business. Businessmen who work in Nigeria say that they are finding it easier to conduct their affairs these days. And the political opposition is fragmented. Abacha continues to promise elections and a return to civilian rule, and many Nigerian politicians have chosen to participate in this charade, even though Moshood Abiola, the man who was legally elected president of Nigeria in 1993, continues to rot in jail. Anyway, the chances that a civilian government, of the sort that will stand up to the Nigerian military, might get elected are almost nil.

Nor can Nigeria rely upon what we complacently and inaccurately call "the international community." The aftermath of Saro-Wiwa's execution illustrated this perfectly. There was much talk of imposing serious sanctions against Nigeria, of expelling it from the British Commonwealth, of other steps against it. President Mandela was particularly outspoken. But the South African volte-face has been particularly startling. South African officials account for it privately by insisting that Mandela yielded to pressure from other African leaders who insisted that he tone down his criticisms of the Abacha regime. The administration in Pretoria has its hands full at home. Judging by its behavior during the crises in Liberia, Zaire, Rwanda, Burundi and Nigeria, and by its response to the American proposal to establish an African crisis intervention force, the Mandela government will not take the lead.

The important Western governments have been equally inconstant. As Aryeh Neier pointed out recently, we have a double standard about human rights. In countries of little or no economic or strategic importance, we stand on our principles. But Nigeria is not negligible. Its oil is important, as is the role that it plays in West African security, notably in the Nigerian-led ECOMOG peacekeeping force in Liberia. The Assistant Secretary of State for Human Rights can issue all the reports on abuses in Nigeria that he likes, but when the American ambassador to Abuja has to negotiate a renewal of the Nigerian commitment to ECOMOG, he needs the co-operation of the same regime that his colleagues in Washington have so strenuously condemned.

The dissociation between the rhetoric and the reality of the Clinton administration's policy toward some of the very worst regimes in the world has distorted also its African diplomacy. It is true that American policymakers sometimes have the decency to be troubled by their own inconsistencies; they have not quite attained the cynicism of the Europeans. Still, these scruples did not prevent the United States from cultivating its ties to Mobutu Sese Seko's regime, when Zairean support for Savimbi's forces during the Angolan civil war was important, or, in the aftermath of the cold war, when Western governments needed Zaire to continue allowing the Hutu refugees from Rwanda to remain on Zairean soil. Washington withdrew its support for Mobutu at the last minute, to avoid the embarrassment of backing a loser. (It is not Washington that is to be blamed, though, for the discouraging fact that the alternative to Mobutu Sese Seko is Laurent Kabila.)

The United States could never deal firmly with Nigeria because of the Nigerian government's willingness to lead the African force trying to stabilize the situation in Liberia. Any pressure on the Abacha regime from Washington would have led to the withdrawal of Nigerian troops—a development that Washington, supremely unwilling to commit American troops, has been desperate to avoid. It is impossible to ask Abacha for favors one day and threaten him the next. There is no reason to think that the Clinton administration will behave any differently when the next group of dissidents are murdered by the Nigerian state. And that day may not be far off. Nineteen other MOSOP members are in jail in Port Harcourt. And now there is a government contract out on Soyinka.

IV.

For Wole Soyinka, the most important lesson of Ken Saro-Wiwa's life and death is the extent to which the last twenty years of Nigerian history has been simply the story of Ogoniland writ large. The really crucial question, though, is whether Nigeria is not Africa writ large. Are the pathologies that Soyinka lays bare in his own country not to be found also in almost all of sub-Saharan Africa? The *Open Sore of a Continent* is an important achievement not least because, without always making the case explicitly (although his brief remarks about the Rwandan genocide are very moving), the fate of Nigeria is, for Soyinka, the fate of Africa. The continent is itself beginning to seem like an open sore.

It must have cost Soyinka a great deal to come to this terrible conclusion. For a man with his anti-colonialist, nationalist, pan-Africanist sympathies to have witnessed the death of so many of his dreams, and to have admitted to his disenchantment so candidly, is remarkable. But if Soyinka is prepared to give up on so much, it is owing not only to his despair over the situation in Nigeria, but also to his commitment to the truth. All writers who turn their attention to politics say that they are committed to the truth. This writer really is. He does not seem to be worried that what he has to say will give aid and comfort to the "wrong" people.

If only the friends of Africa in the West could be as candid. Given the magnitude of the continent's crisis, treating Africa to the same unsentimental analysis that Soyinka has applied to his own country seems long overdue. At the political level, despite the efforts of Randall Robinson at the TransAfrica Institute to rouse support for protests against the Nigerian dictatorship, little of the fervor that accompanied

anti-apartheid activism in the United States has proved transferable to abuses in Nigeria, or, for that matter, to what has taken place under Mobutu in Zaire or Arap Moi in Kenya.

Consider only the case of Carol Moseley-Braun. The only African American in the U.S. Senate, she has shown herself to be anything but an opponent of the Abacha regime. She has strenuously opposed the Nigeria Democracy Act, which would have imposed American sanctions, and she met in Abuja with General Abacha and his wife (whom she commended for her support and promotion of family values), and she even traveled to Ogoniland in 1996, where she praised Lieutenant Colonel Daud Komo, the regional governor and the Nigerian official most responsible for Saro-Wiwa's murder. Moseley-Braun made at least one of these trips, in the company of her erstwhile fiancé and former campaign manager, Kgosie Matthews, who was at one time a lobbyist for the Nigerian government. And so Abacha, Mobutu and Arap Moi all continue to have their defenders in Washington, including a number of important African American political leaders. (And the odd Reaganite, too, such as Steve Symms, the former senator from Idaho, whose firm lobbies for Nigeria, thereby losing one for the Gipper.)

Too many people in Washington wish to ignore the truth about Africa, for reasons of business, solidarity, or—this seems to be the case with the Clinton administration's pronouncements on African affairs—because they fear that thinking gloomy thoughts makes them true. But the truth about Africa is almost unrelievedly awful. As even the most cursory look at the economic indicators reveals, an African revival is not what lies ahead. The urgent task in Africa, all the rosy predictions of the World Bank notwithstanding, is not to engineer recovery, it is to mitigate catastrophe. Officials at the Bank sometimes argue that countries such as South Korea were just as badly off in the 1950s as many African states are today, but with good economic management they became prosperous. Such an argument elides the difference between the economic conditions that obtained half a century ago, when labor was in high demand and the technological skills required for average workers fairly primitive, and the economic conditions today, when there is worldwide overproduction of low-end goods, a vast surplus of labor, and the need for a much more technologically proficient workforce. As in the colonial period, commodities such as oil are almost the only thing Africa has to offer, and many of these are available more cheaply elsewhere.

Africa has almost nothing to offer advanced global capitalism. There are better educated and better disciplined workers willing to work for very low wages all over the world. A collapsing infrastructure makes investment in much of Africa more expensive than in many other regions, no matter how low wage-scales can be forced. Political corruption and political instability further raise the costs for most corporations. And the enormous population increase in Africa means that it is inconceivable that enough jobs can be created for all the people being born. The population of Rwanda was 1.5 million in 1940. Today, even after the genocide, it is over 7 million. The current estimate of the Nigerian population puts it at about 120 million (though census figures are notoriously unreliable). It will double in the next thirty years.

The end of the cold war, moreover, robbed the continent of its strategic urgency, and it is too far away from the borders of the rich countries to pose a threat of mass migration, as Mexico and the Caribbean do for the United States, and the Maghreb does for Western Europe. Africa, in sum, offers many reasons for indifference about Africa. From human rights to the environment, from demography to infrastructure, the news from Africa could hardly be worse. It is no longer a question of the independent African states not having lived up to the expectations of their citizens. (Thirty years ago, General Obasanjo could still insist with a straight face that he fully expected Nigeria to be "among the greatest nations in the world by the year 2000.") It is now a question of survival. Will large parts of sub-Saharan Africa ever exist at more than subsistence level? Will its people ever come to know anything better than Hobbesian horror?

In this dark setting, there is something especially exemplary about Soyinka's analysis. He does not harp upon the incontrovertible fact that the crippling legacy of imperialism, however much it has been used by African politicians and soldiers to cover up their crimes and blunders, remains pervasive. When people in the West consider, say, Zaire, bemoaning its savagery and its corruption, they link these failings to the fact that the Belgians all but cut off higher education to the Zaireans, and to the fact that, at the time of independence, that vast country could boast only a few thousand university graduates with advanced degrees. But Soyinka will brook no excuses for what has happened. He will not allow history to be made into an alibi.

"We have lost thirty years to the sergeants," President Yoweri Museveni of Uganda, one of the few promising political leaders on the continent, has said. He is right. In an era in which the process of economic development by means of free (or freer) market activity is going well in most of the world, does anyone really care to do something for Africa? This is not a matter of aid. Sub-Saharan Africa has received more development aid per capita than any other region of the world over the past quarter of a century. Aid programs—most recently Boutros Boutros-Ghali's proposal for a $25 billion fund for African development—continue to be devised. Will the new assistance be more effective in fostering prosperity than the old assistance?

There will always be bankers and consultants willing to do one more survey, arrange one more loan, organize one more

exercise in "capacity building"; but with no economic remedy and political reform in sight, the international response to the African crisis is likely to be damage control. To a large degree, the expansion of humanitarian aid is a concession to three notions: that Africa does not matter, and so development aid can be decreased; that Africa will be in a shambles, and so monies for disaster relief need to be increased; that Africans cannot look after themselves, and so foreign nongovernmental organizations need to take over certain basic services, whether these involve security, as the South African mercenary organization Executive Outcomes is providing in Sierra Leone, or medical care, as the American evangelical humanitarian group World Vision is providing in Mozambique.

But disaster relief is, by definition, an admission of defeat. It is in no sense a solution, as its best practitioners are the first to admit. But this, I fear, is the point: nobody has any realistic ideas about what to do. There is little in the present climate that the United Nations, which the late Anthony Parsons once described as a "decolonization machine," can do for Africa. The religion of development has not worked, as even most officials now reluctantly concede. Proposals still regularly issue from the United Nations, of course, ranging from U.N. trusteeships for failed states—a solution increasingly in vogue among international relief groups—to the massive payment of reparations by the European Union countries and the United States, an idea floated most recently by the historian Ali Mazrui. So here we are, reduced to the serious discussion of recolonization and reparation.

As Julius Nyerere has pointed out, without the anchors of the most important African states, above all Nigeria, Zaire, Kenya and South Africa, there can be no progress on the continent. It is all very well to linger over promising developments in the Ivory Coast, or Uganda, or Ghana, but those are small places. Even if they do better than expected economically, and are rewarded by international institutions such as the World Bank and the International Monetary Fund, the collapse of their huge neighbors will swamp them. If Zaire (or as it is now called, Congo) collapses, its neighbors will not be unscathed. The refugees alone will undo whatever progress they have made; and the skewing of resource allocation will see to the rest. And what holds true for Zaire holds true for Nigeria.

Similarly, if the most important countries on the continent remain dictatorships, any prospect of smaller, neighboring countries remaining or becoming democratic seems farfetched. This is one of the reasons why, to the extent that foreign governments care at all about the fate of Africa, the questions of democracy and human rights will be critical in the coming period. A few years ago Amartya Sen showed in these pages that there has never been a famine in a free society. It seems equally safe to say that without democracy there will never be any recovery in Africa, hard as a democratic Africa is to imagine in present circumstances.

The moral reason is the best reason for caring about the ruin of Africa, and it may be the only reason. If help comes to Africa, it will be offered on grounds of decency, not on grounds of strategy. This, of course, is tantamount to saying that help will not come. The world does not work that way.

FURTHER READING

Criticism

George, Karibi T. "Myth and History in Ken Saro-Wiwa's *Basi and Company: A Modern African Folktale.*" In *African Literature and African Historical Experiences,* edited by Chidi Ikonne, Emelia Oko, and Peter Onwudinjo, pp. 107-15. Ibadan, Nigeria: Heinemann Educational Books Nigeria PLC, 1991.

> Uses an African traditionalist aesthetic criticism to explore Saro-Wiwa's use of the oral story-telling tradition in *Basi and Company.*

Maja-Pearce, Adewale. "Do It Yourself." *New Statesman* 112, No. 2885 (11 July 1986): 32-33.

> Brief review of *A Forest of Flowers* that praises Saro-Wiwa's use of pidgin English as well as his commitment to self-publishing under difficult conditions.

Additional coverage of Saro-Wiwa's life and career is contained in the following sources published by Gale: *Black Writers,* **Vol. 2;** *Contemporary Authors,* **Vols. 142, and 150;** *Contemporary Authors New Revision Series,* **Vol. 60; and** *Dictionary of Literary Biography,* **Vol. 157.**

Leslie Marmon Silko
1948-

American novelist, poet, essayist, and short story writer.

The following entry presents an overview of Silko's career through 1996. For further information on her life and works, see *CLC,* Volumes 23 and 74.

INTRODUCTION

Silko is considered among the foremost authors to emerge from the Native American literary renaissance of the 1970s. In her works she blends such western literary forms as the novel and the short story with the oral traditions of her Laguna Pueblo heritage to communicate Native American concepts concerning time, nature, and spirituality and their relevance in the contemporary world. Her protagonists, often of mixed Laguna and Anglo heritage, must draw upon the moral strength of their native community and its traditions in order to overcome the often repressive, alienating effects of white society.

Biographical Information

Of Laguna Pueblo, Plains Indian, Mexican, and Anglo-American descent, Silko was born in Albuquerque, New Mexico, on March 5, 1948, and raised on the Laguna Pueblo Reservation in northern New Mexico. As a child she attended schools administered by the Bureau of Indian Affairs and learned about Laguna legends and traditions from her great-grandmother and other members of her extended family. She graduated magna cum laude from the University of New Mexico in 1969 and briefly attended law school before deciding to pursue a writing career. Silko taught at Navajo Community College in Tsaile, Arizona, for two years, and then spent two years in Ketchikan, Alaska, where she wrote her first novel, *Ceremony* (1977). Silko taught at the University of New Mexico and then at the University of Arizona before receiving a five-year MacArthur Foundation grant in 1981 which enabled her to work on *Almanac of the Dead* (1991). She has also received a National Endowment for the Humanities Grant to make films based on Laguna oral traditions.

Major Works

Silko's work is concerned with the common representation of Native Americans in literature and her attempt to overcome what she sees as misrepresentation. *Ceremony* is a novel about healing and discovering one's identity. The main character, Tayo, is a mixed-blood Native American strug-

gling to come to terms with his ancestry, his wartime experiences, and the changing culture of the Laguna. It is through traditional rituals and his relationships with Betonie, an old man who is also a mixed breed, and T'seh, a medicine woman who represents the feminine principal, that Tayo will achieve healing, regain his identity, and grow into manhood. *Storyteller* (1981) is a collection of traditional Pueblo stories, Silko's own family stories, poems, and conventional short stories. The collection expresses the importance of storytelling to cultures and individuals alike. By making Native American stories relevant to contemporary society and by celebrating oral tradition, Silko overcomes the common misperception of Native Americans as a dying and primitive people. *Almanac of the Dead* is an apocalyptic tale which lacks the harmonizing effects of *Ceremony.* The novel tells the story of the Americas since the conquest by the Spanish, who arrived in the Yucatan and burned the entire written record of the Mayan people. The premise of the book is that one of the Mayan almanacs was smuggled to safety and is now passed down from generation to generation in a family charged with its protection. Citing a world filled with violence, cruelty, and crime, the book argues that 500 years of European civilization has failed in the Americas, and that all land should be returned to Indians, who have always been its true caretakers. Rampant individualism has torn people from the community and spirituality on which survival depends. Despite the repressive brutality of the novel, Silko leaves the room to hope that in throwing off Euroamerican individualism and embracing community, the Americas will survive. *Sacred Water* (1993) contains forty-one short tales with water as their guiding principal. The stories tell of Silko's own experience, her family's experience, Laguna society's experience, and Native Americans' experience with water in the arid region of the Southwest. Water is a life-giving force, and the book focuses on the integral nature of water to the spiritual life of the Pueblos.

Critical Reception

Critics consistently note Silko's use of subtle, Native American humor, and assert that white audiences may miss the many instances in her work. Reviewers note the positive nature of Silko's *Ceremony* and her attempt to show the value of both Anglo and Native American traditions. In her discussion of Silko's *Ceremony,* Elizabeth N. Evasdaughter states, "Ultimately, she demonstrates that combining our cultures, as her narrative does, has the power to civilize both." Reviewers had a mixed response to *Almanac of the Dead* and were often put off by the harsh judgement made against Anglo society. Some reviewers, however, found Silko's conclusions warranted. Linda Neimann states that "she does succeed in creating a world, eerily like the world we read about in the newspapers, that one would be only too glad to help overthrow." Another common complaint about *Almanac of the Dead* was that its sprawling nature and huge cast of characters were out of control and lacked focus. Silko's ability to render the feeling of oral tradition in a written form has been noted by many critics. In her discussion of *Storyteller,* Linda J. Krumholz states that "by eliding distinctions between genres and between old and new stories, Silko creates a dynamic juxtaposition that duplicates the way in which meaning is created in the oral tradition through a constant interaction between the stories and the material circumstances of the community, between the old stories and the on-going creation of meaning." Critics praise the fluidity of Silko's writing and assert that she does not see books as finished, unchanging products. Many reviewers discuss the importance of myth and ritual in Silko's fiction, and her ability to draw those outside of the Native American community into her narratives. *Ceremony* is Silko's most recognized and praised book, but Silko's entire body of work expresses a consistency and continuity that makes her an important figure in the continuing tradition of Native American literature.

PRINCIPAL WORKS

Laguna Woman: Poems (poetry) 1974
Ceremony (novel) 1977
Storyteller (poetry and short stories) 1981
With the Delicacy and Strength of Lace: Letters Between Leslie Marmon Silko and James Wright [with James A. Wright] (letters) 1985
Almanac of the Dead (novel) 1991
Sacred Water (short stories) 1993
Yellow Women and a Beauty of the Spirit: Essays on Native American Life Today (essays) 1996

CRITICISM

Elizabeth N. Evasdaughter (essay date Spring 1988)

SOURCE: "Leslie Marmon Silko's *Ceremony:* Healing Ethnic Hatred by Mixed-Breed Laughter," in *MELUS,* Vol. 15, No. 1, Spring, 1988, pp. 83-94.

[*In the following essay, Evasdaughter asserts that, "the celestial laughter" Silko evokes in* Ceremony *"shows that Indian civilization is living and has the potential to transform anglo culture."*]

In *Ceremony,* Leslie Silko brilliantly crosses racial styles of humor in order to cure the foolish delusions readers may have, if we think we are superior to Indians or inferior to whites, or perhaps superior to whites or inferior to Indians. Silko plays off affectionate Pueblo humor against the black humor so prominent in 20th-century white culture. This comic strategy has the end-result of opening our eyes to our general foolishness, and also to the possibility of combining the merits of all races. Joseph Campbell wrote in *The Inner Reaches of Outer Space* of the change in mythologies away from the local and tribal toward a mythology that will arise from "this unified earth as of one harmonious being." *Ceremony* is a work that changes local mythologies in that more inclusive spirit.

Silko is the right person to have written this book. She herself is a mixed-blood, and her experience has evidently given her access not only to a variety of problems, but also to a variety of styles of clowning and joking. Although Elaine Jahner has mentioned the presence of jokes in the novel, I have known whites to read *Ceremony* as not comical at any point. Probably their power of recognition had been switched off by "the picture of the humorless Indian . . . so common in so much of the literature, in so many of the film and television depictions of Native Americans." Although *Ceremony* is serious, offering a number of valuable propositions for our consideration, the narrative also spins a web of jokes in the morning sun. If readers' cultural background has not prepared them for Pueblo reverence for the maternal spider, they could think of Silko's writing as resembling the turning and darting of a brown-and-white bird hunting insects in the air, at one moment flashing white sunlight, the next nearly invisible against the browns of this beautiful Earth.

> **Although *Ceremony* is serious, offering a number of valuable propositions for our consideration, the narrative also spins a web of jokes in the morning sun.**
> **—*Elizabeth N. Evasdaughter***

The ceremony Silko narrates is that of a Navajo sing, but one not sung exactly as it would have been done before whites arrived in New Mexico, nor sung by a pure-blood Indian, nor sung on behalf of a pure-blood Indian. As is traditional, the ceremony is to be completed after the sing by the sick man, a Laguna named Tayo. His efforts to finish the ceremony by correct action form the last half of the novel, just as the first half was composed of the events which made him sick. These two series of events, taken together, make it clear that what the Veterans' Administration doctors have labeled *battle fatigue* is, in Tayo's case at least, really a struggle to make a decision about death. He tries two ways of responding to its invasion of his life that do not work—self-erasure and killing an agent of death. Finally he is able to find a way of opposing destruction which will not lead to his erasure as a force on the reservation, not allow anyone to kill him, and most important, not change him too into an agent of death.

Tayo's difficulty is grave, yet Silko jokes about it frequently. The belief among whites that Indians never laugh is contradicted continually by the sounds of Indians responding to subtle in-jokes or to a corrective kind of teasing crystallized in the work of ritual clowns. Black Elk speaks of clowns appearing when people needed a good laugh. At that time, he says, the clowns based their performance on the minor frustrations of life or on our minor flaws as human beings, such as our tendency to exaggerate our plight. Anne Cameron, too, in *The Daughters of Copper Woman,* has written of the dedication of a sacred clown, in this case a female Salish or Cowichan clown, to the eradication of foolish behavior and injustice, whether it originated with Indians or whites. I believe that Leslie Marmon Silko is in effect a sacred clown, turning the light of laughter against evils which might otherwise weaken us all.

Most of the clowning in *Ceremony* is not a deliberate performance by the characters. Tayo, passive, weeping and vomiting, does not apparently experience any amusing dimension of his depression, nor does his audience within the novel seem to think of him as funny, yet the Penguin edition cover painting, "Unfinished Crow," by Fritz Scholder,

which can be seen as a portrayal of the sad clown type, applies perfectly well to Tayo's condition as the story unfolds.

Animals also clown in this exhilarating book. The cross-breed cattle who take flight at every opportunity are eventually the death of Uncle Josiah, but this sad outcome eventually turns comic, in the symbolic sense that although half-breeds are the solution to our problems as a nation, they are not an easy solution, or again, that although Tayo correctly grieves over Josiah's death, he is wrong to freeze the moment of that death. By way of ethical comment, animal clowns point up the ridiculous flight of Tayo and his long-time friend Harley toward the nearest bar. While Harley rides a black burro that always veers to the left, Tayo rides a blind gray mule, which although it usually walks in blind circles, now follows the black burro in equally blind confidence. As with the ornery cross-breed cattle, Silko uses or allows story to bring out the light contained in these emblems. Readers soon forget Harley's comical burro, as Harley himself veers more and more toward leaving the road; Tayo's blind mule too, has been only a comical way of introducing Tayo's apparent preference of the gray area between good and evil, his determination to plod along as if he could not see that his fellow veterans are heading down a far worse path than the path to the bar.

Human clowning of a farcical type, exposing our human flaws in a manifestly physical way, builds up Silko's philosophy. The drunk Indian veterans who had attempted to fight over Helen Jean "started pushing at each other, in a staggering circle on the dance floor. The other guys were cheering for a fight. They forgot about her." Their lack of real love for women goes with their general ineffectuality. The whole scene parodies the war, all its supposedly ardent love for motherland, all its proclaimed desire to protect wife and home forgotten in the blundering, futile rituals of fighting.

These clowning scenes become more elaborate as the novel continues. An example of this is the size and complexity of the expedition organized to capture Tayo at his most harmless. He is carefully surrounded at night by V.A. doctors in dark green government cars, Bureau of Indian Affairs police, and some of the old men of the pueblo, just as if he were insane, hostile, and armed, when we as readers know he has spent the summer outdoors looking after his skinny cattle and rediscovering the old religion, or if you like, dreaming of a beautiful Indian woman. The absurdity of this great stake-out does not cancel, but accompanies and points up the danger to Tayo. As readers, we both fear for him and half-expect the ambush will be 100% ineffectual.

If the stake-out nearly loses its humor altogether, the cause is its origin in the evil mind of Emo. His humor is like the glimmerings and grim streaks of a distorting mirror which reflects and mocks the sacred clown. Emo's love of loud laughter at the expense of others is not a part of traditional Pueblo life, to say the least. His amusement at downfall and death is only a parody of the witticism of the Hopi clown who arranged ahead of time for his own corpse to be dressed in his clown costume, swung to and fro on the roof, and thrown into the plaza by his nephews and sons. Again, Emo devoted himself to ritual sacrifice though it hurt others and left him unscathed; a diametric contradiction of the risks and death undergone by the great Salish or Cowichan female clown in order to oppose the exploitation and warping of Indians.

Clearly Silko does not practice Emo's type of humor, for she teases her readers in a gentle manner that can enlighten. When Tayo is ordered to shoot a Japanese soldier and suddenly sees him as his Uncle Josiah, everyone around him tells him that Josiah couldn't be in two places at the same time or that hallucinations are natural with malaria or battle fatigue. This thinking, even though Tayo's cousin Rocky practices it, is anglicized, afraid to contradict Aristotle, afraid to hear about hallucinations because of their association with psychosis, anxious not to reflect on their content. The joke is on readers who believe that Tayo has had a symptomatic hallucination, for if we have allowed this smoke screen to be raised between us and the import of the hallucination or vision, we have to wait many many pages for another chance to understand Tayo's great love for his people. Actually the vision, which I would call a projection of Tayo's or Josiah's mind, illustrates for Tayo the universality of human goodness and the evil of killing. When, reading along, we finally realize this, it's natural to smile at our earlier foolish Europeanized faith in our ideas of mental illness.

Silko teases white readers in a similar way by letting us know the head of an Indian family may say to a grown daughter, "Church . . . Ah Thelma, do you have to go there again?" or by noting that the Indians in the area credited a certain medicine man, the mixed-blood Betonie, with the ability to aid "victims tainted by Christianity or liquor." Perhaps too, Silko is teasing us a little by getting us to read a book about a group of men whom many whites would refer to as "drunk Indians." She understands white Americans well enough to know that we need to be led to a vantage point where we have to admit that the great spiritual war between good and evil may take place among those our country rejects as being automatically morally inferior. She seems to enjoy arousing our stereotypical interpretations of events so that she can present a different and better interpretation. In this way she can tease us and enlighten us, not only about the issue under discussion, but also about our customary presumption of certitude.

Her Indian readers get a similar gentle ribbing, on occasion. The Laguna medicine man attempts to convince Tayo that he would have received more complete religious training had he had an Indian father, but in reality Tayo's maternal grandmother and his maternal uncle have formed the little boy perfectly. They are the people ancient custom would have preferred as his teachers. While they told him stories and explained their beliefs, Tayo always listened with love and a desire to learn more. Some of the old ways, he rediscovered before the war; after it, he continues to discover the accessibility and power of the old religion. Being a half-breed never kept him from listening to his elders of both sexes, from living with his mind open to the natural world, or from wondering about the sacred manner of life.

Silko lets her special mixed-blood medicine man Betonie answer those Indians who oppose any change in traditional rituals, while she herself modifies those traditional tales she includes in the novel. A happy example is her retelling of the Battle of the Seasons over Yellow Woman, a summer fertility spirit, leader of the Corn Maidens. In Silko's version, Yellow Woman, now called Ts'eh Montano or Water Mountain Woman, still prefers Summer, now represented by Tayo. In Silko's tale, however, the bad spirit of Winter is represented by the hostile cowboy who wants to put Tayo in jail, and a second, good spirit of Winter is introduced in the form of the Mountain Lion, who also appears as an old Indian hunter. As the mountain lion, Winter tricks the cowboy into hunting it so that Tayo can escape. In the form of the Hunter, the good spirit of Winter gives the early snowstorm, not now interpreted as a battle, but as a friendly help in Tayo's recovery of the rustled family cattle. The Hunter, who is most knowledgeable in the old ways, accompanies the younger man down the trail to safety and offers him hospitality. When this old man discovers Tayo's love for Ts'eh, he is not at all distressed. He smiles and makes no objection to her going off with Tayo. When Ts'eh comes to join Tayo where he has pastured the spotted cross-breed cattle, the novel makes it more and more evident that she is a mountain spirit helpful to all forms of life. Perhaps the once wild cattle can be read as Summer's equivalent of the mountain lion, and the once crippled yellow bull as Tayo now in his full health. This affectionate revision is the very opposite of the deterioration or distortion feared by those Indians, perhaps older, who say the old ways must not be changed. To change and expand the story to such an extent while making it an expression of Indian values better suited to this time, when we must get rid of battles and bombs, is a way of teasing while reassuring the traditional minded.

Silko turns her teasing also toward younger Indians like Helen Jean, who evaluates Tayo as the least friendly male at the Y Bar, when in fact he is the only one who cares, even briefly, what is going to happen to her. As for half-breeds like Tayo, Silko repeatedly exposes his gullibility toward erroneous white beliefs. His difficulty in believing that someone other than an Indian will steal, much less that a white man will steal, is typical of Indian jokes about oppression.

Silko does not exclude herself from being teased either. At the end of her innovative portrayal of evil, she allows Tayo's grandmother, the archetypal storyteller, to indicate her boredom at the story of Emo's downfall:

> Old Grandma shook her head slowly, and closed her cloudy eyes again. 'I guess I must be getting old', she said, 'because these goings-on around Laguna don't get me excited any more.' She sighed, and laid her head back on the chair. 'It seems like I already heard these stories before . . . only thing is, the names sound different.'

This narrative irony is a little joke at all of us—Silko for feeling she had written an original work about evil, any Indians who might have been worrying about her modernization of the stories, any whites who might have believed the test of art is originality, or maybe entertainment, rather than spiritual power. The serious effectiveness of Silko's tale is indicated by the passage which follows: "Whirling darkness / has come back on itself . . . It is dead for now."

All the instances of Indian humor in *Ceremony* have been overlooked by some of the white readers I have talked with, possibly because of lack of contact with non-European communities or culture. Indian irony can be "either so subtle or so keyed to an understanding from within of what is funny to a people that an outsider would fail to recognize it." Such outsiders tend to take many light passages in *Ceremony* as solemn or tense, and wear themselves out before the real crisis comes. Yet Silko has given non-Indian readers enough clues to enjoy her inside jokes. Although she grew up on the Laguna Pueblo reservation, she is familiar with our European culture, as she has correctly called it. She went to white schools, and she has read Steinbeck, Faulkner, Poe, Borges, and Flannery O'Connor, some with great interest, others with fascination. She understands this culture so well that she has been able to play with European black humor, which responds, not to the beautiful blackness of the black people, of nighttime outdoors, or of the forest shadows; the blackness involved in black humor is the darkness of opposition to light. Silko splits black humor as she did the spirit of Winter. She delineates one type of black humor, characterized by Emo, which bases its world view on black or unrelieved hatred and acts as the agent of hatred. She deploys a second type of black humor related to the irony of Indian ritual clowns, characterized by Tayo and Betonie, which includes hatred and white oppression in its world view without allowing them to monopolize the world. The former blackness enjoys the degradation of others; the second jokes about degrading things as they are, but shouldn't be. The first is death-dealing; the second, death-paralyzing.

Tayo at times carries irony as far as black humor. When other barflies buzz about their equality with whites, Tayo tells a more truthful, and by contrast, more ironic narrative about their status. When Emo repeatedly brings up how whites have taken everything the Indians had, Tayo wisecracks to himself, "Maybe Emo was wrong; maybe white people didn't have everything. Only Indians had droughts." This private shot of wry acknowledges both white injustice and Emo's dishonesty, thus mentally challenging blackness, not just learning to endure it. By blaming Indian deprivation on whites, however truly, Emo thinks he can deny Indian responsibility to take care of the arid land the Indians do have. Harley laughs over the decimation of a flock of sheep he had left unguarded, but this laughter warns Tayo of the presence of evil. Tayo sometimes goes drinking with these defiant veterans, but what he defies is the blackness in their hearts, what he regrets is their spiritual death.

> **All the instances of Indian humor in *Ceremony* have been overlooked by some of the white readers I have talked with, possibly because of lack of contact with non-European communities or culture.**
> **—*Elizabeth N. Evasdaughter***

Readers with sensitivity to the Red Power movement may object to Emo's apparent sympathy with the cause of justice to Indians, but his habit of objecting to Anglo domination is in time exposed as a synthetic wolf-hide masking his hatred for Indian culture and for his Indian brothers. As Joseph Bruchac points out in his article, "Striking the Pole: American Indian Humor," Indian humor gives lessons which "include the importance of humility and the affirmation that laughter leads to learning and survival."

Emo's humor, in contrast, has the blackness of an abandoned house in winter, for his amusement comes from his arrogance and negation, his apathy and love of stasis. His pride is in thinking he can equal whites in their black malice. He cherishes what he thinks was the message of the U.S. Army to him:

> He was the best, they told him; some men didn't like to feel the quiver of the man they were killing. Some men got sick when they smelled the blood. But he was the best; he was one of them. The best U.S. Army.

Emo mocks traditional Indian values, despises everything living, and spends his time spreading contempt, resentment, idleness, pleasure in the humiliation and suffering of other people—in short, hatred. His first diatribe in *Ceremony* is against reservation ranchlands: "Look what is here for us. Look. Here's the Indians' mother earth! Old dried-up thing!" By breaking the law of reverence, his sarcasms raise loud laughter. By speaking only of white women, he gets his fellow veterans, except Tayo, to laugh and cheer at stories about bringing women down. By referring to Japanese soldiers always and only as Japs, as officers, as enemies, he tricks the others into rejoicing at the smashing of fellow people of color. They are fooled because Emo's jokes resemble jokes made "not to take our minds off our troubles, but to point out ways to survive and even laugh." Unfortunately, Emo's references to troubles do not carry hints about survival or corrections of faults. Not noticing the difference, Emo's bar buddies, most of them, commit themselves by every laugh to discard a little more of Indian tradition, their only possible road to a satisfying life.

Emo's gags are those of revulsion; he is a script writer of black comedy. He uses his full artistry when he organizes the complicated stake-out against Tayo. The stake-out puts Tayo in a triple bind, for the outcome must be, Emo thinks, that Tayo will be shot, locked up, or something worse. If captured, Tayo's punishment will be witty by Emo's standards, for Emo has reported him to the authorities for bestiality, for thinking he is a Jap, for living in caves as if he had reverted to the primitive. These slanders invert Tayo's best qualities as an Indian, for he loves caves and pictographs which are connected to the traditional religion, he recognizes his bond with the Japanese people, he works hard to secure and care for the family cattle, and he loves women in a fully sacred, sexual way that Emo has no notion of. Similarly, Emo's reason for including the old men in the stake-out is apparently not only to cut the pueblo off from the help Tayo can give with ideas like that of the hybrid cattle, but also to hurt Tayo for wanting so much to be accepted by the elders. Readers who don't want to believe anyone would think such a downfall funny have only to note Emo's laughter at the novel's climax.

Emo's aim in all his activity is not just to get a laugh. Betonie describes his aim and that of other evil-wishers as:

> The trickery of the witchcraft ... they want us to believe all evil resides with white people. Then we will look no further to see what is really happening. They want us to separate ourselves from white people, to be ignorant and helpless as we watch our own destruction.

Betonie would rather see a separation between good and evil, starlight and blackness, than between Indian and white. Ts'eh Montano gives the novel's second description of Emo's aim when she calls him and others like him

> the destroyers: they work to see how much can be lost, how much can be forgotten. They destroy the feeling people have for each other ... Their highest ambition is to gut human beings while they are

still breathing, to hold the heart still beating so the victim will never feel anything again ... Only destruction is capable of arousing a sensation, the remains of something alive in them.

This lust to end the interior life of others is why Emo's joking around eventually leads to cruelty. When his own laughter finally surfaces, he is openly laughing at the flaws and vulnerability of his loyal friends—at their falling over and insulting each other, at their fighting and mutual contempt, and at the same time at the moral degradation, mutilation, desexing, loss of individuality, death and dehumanization of the only one of his friends who had attempted to befriend Tayo. Emo's perverse comic ecstasy seems to derive from his having proved to his satisfaction that Indians are as worthless as greedy whites have always claimed they are. The validation of his black interpretation of the world makes him laugh, but, having carried laughter at the expense of others to its logical conclusion, he laughs alone.

Some time before this scene at the abandoned uranium mine, Betonie had told Tayo about a witches' contest in which the evilest action award is won by a witch who invents white people with nuclear capabilities. Betonie tells the story to inject laughter into Tayo's overwhelming preoccupation with white dominance. But Betonie does not—and Silko does not—mean to discount destructiveness. In *Ceremony* Silko calls attention, as she has explained in an interview, to the irony of Los Alamos being so close to the Pueblo people, who "have always concentrated upon making things grow, and appreciating things that are alive and natural, because life is so precious in the desert." Her ironies about uranium mines have thus a good chance to overcome any habits Anglo readers may have of ignoring not only Los Alamos, but also the Pueblo Indians. If the character of the Pueblos is allowed an influence on American life equal to that of other ethnic groups, we will find ourselves not only acknowledging the danger of nuclear and other forms of destruction, but "making things grow and appreciating things that are alive and natural."

Silko sees through Emo's descriptions and can see where his black philosophy must end. To acknowledge evil and study it, has not made a convert of her, however. She plays a worse trick on Emo than he wanted to play on Tayo; as a true comic novelist always does, she thwarts evil and establishes the good in a new and more complete harmony. Hers is the laughter that rises in the spirit, when the preachers of inferiority and inevitable doom have been disproved and defeated. What is finest in her, I believe, is the wisdom of her method of bringing the good out of its trials safely. Her wisdom is that of choosing love. Silko weaves traditional tales, as I mentioned earlier, into her narrative. These tales reveal the only principles by which Tayo can escape Emo and even stop Emo's work against a revitalization of the pueblo. Tayo comes to his most difficult task, to *not* kill Emo, in the context of two Pueblo tales, those of the Gambler and of Arrowboy. These tales also deal with the worst realities honestly, but in a victorious or comic manner. Tayo, and equally the novel, needs the tales in order to find some way to prevent Emo's triumph without bringing Tayo down. As LaVonne Ruoff has argued,

> Silko emphasizes the need to return to the rituals and oral traditions of the past in order to rediscover the basis for one's cultural identity. Only when this is done is one prepared to deal with the problems of the present . . . Silko demonstrates that the Keres rituals and traditions have survived all attempts to eradicate them and that the seeds for the resurgence of their power lie in the memories and creativeness of her people.

When Tayo resists all the forces that have been turned against Pueblo holiness, he acts much as the legendary Arrowboy and the Gambler act when they oppose the witchery and its sadistic works. Although Tayo had been taught in school to scorn the old stories, he believes them and understands their modernity, their applicability to his situation. This reversal is the ultimate joke about the delusion of the whites who married into Silko's family, who like many other Protestants thought Protestant Christianity should replace Laguna paganism. Not because of Christianity, but because the Gambler attempted to trick the Sun into killing him, Tayo realizes that he must not kill Emo, and even that he must refuse the more adamantly, the more cleverly Emo tempts him to attack. Instead, Tayo has to watch and know, to avoid being seen or known, to resist every pressure, even appeals to his goodness. If he will simply stay out of range, Emo's most powerful attack will whirl back on its point of origin. Tayo has realized before the final show-down that: "He had to bring it back on them. There was no other way." Though Kenneth Lincoln takes the series of deaths that follows as pointless and hasty, he forgets that the young men whose death he regrets have just committed a pointless murder for the fun of it. Silko would be distorting life if she pretended that the natural consequences of their choices could be awarded off or denied.

Although the last scenes of *Ceremony* have a number of surprises, they have been prepared for. Tayo's refusal to be caught up in the dynamics of mutual destruction is comical because it seems cowardly, as whites judge bravery, even disloyal, by Army standards. In truth, his hiding behind the rock is his least white, least hateful action, even, perhaps, a sort of yellow humor, to go with his Asian connection.

Not only does Silko as novelist arrange for the defeat of Emo's plan either to sacrifice or to corrupt Tayo. She also plots a punishment for the villain which is more appropri-

ate and funnier than the one he has planned for Tayo. In the outcome, Silko, and readers who side with her, laugh, perhaps silently, but also happily at Emo's final defeat, hearts lifting because "he got his". In this way, as a comic novelist, Silko has brought in a third type of black humorist, the one who steals the tricks of the blackest jokers and uses them against their owners. I have found that Anglo or anglicized readers easily miss Silko's punishment of Emo, thinking he has gotten away scot-free. That's because she outfoxes him as Tayo did, aikido style, without violence. He might have died, but the old men of the pueblo only exile him, and he chooses to go to California, the epitome of all that he admires. The joke of it is seen by the now gentle Tayo: "'California,' Tayo repeated softly, 'that's a good place for him.'" This brief and quiet comment scores off evil more aptly than Emo ever scored off good. Emo will be in harmony with California; the apex of his desires is as bad as he is. This joke mocks the White Lie, the delusion that whites are superior, for in it Silko is using the most prosperous part of her region, a proud achievement of white culture in this country, as the most severe punishment she can assign, far worse than mutilation, an early death, or life in Gallup. Emo's exile is a joke, too, about the self-proclaimed superiority of white institutions. If the old men were to bring charges against Emo, government courts would probably either discredit Tayo's testimony or execute Emo. None of their methods would stop Emo's impact on the pueblo. The Laguna answer to capital punishment is more intelligent, avoids imitating murderers, and punishes them less mercifully.

Whites with some appreciation for Indian culture sometimes express a surprising certitude that "this once great culture is being lost or replaced by an Anglo culture that does not have the same respect for nature . . . and is in some ways morally inferior to it." The celestial laughter Silko calls forth by her *Ceremony* shows that Indian civilization is living and has the potential to transform anglo culture. As she said in a 1978 interview, "These things will only die if we neglect to tell the stories. So I am telling the stories." Moreover she has turned the quietest laugh against the loudest. With the help of Indian humor, even if we do not entirely get her jokes, she purifies us of our illusions about white culture, and those about Indian culture as well. Ultimately she demonstrates that combining our cultures, as her narrative does, has the power to civilize both.

Susan Blumenthal (essay date Fall 1990)

SOURCE: "Spotted Cattle and Deer: Spirit Guides and Symbols of Endurance and Healing in *Ceremony*," in *American Indian Quarterly*, Vol. XIV, No. 4, Fall, 1990, pp. 367-77.

[In the following essay, Blumenthal analyzes the symbolism of the spotted cattle and their importance to Tayo's journey for healing in Silko's Ceremony.*]*

Spotted cattle. Running with the grace and delicacy of deer, but tough, rugged, enduring, lost in a landscape of desert and mountains. Deer. Silent, spiritual sentinels whose being nourishes the soul as well as the body of its slayer when properly honored in Pueblo ceremonial traditions.

Spotted cattle and deer are strong but subtle thematic strands in the complex web of symbols, stories and images Leslie M. Silko weaves through *Ceremony;* they are the messengers of ancient wisdoms vital to Tayo's quest for healing and identity.

> **Spotted cattle and deer are strong but subtle thematic strands in the complex web of symbols, stories and images Leslie M. Silko weaves through *Ceremony;* they are the messengers of ancient wisdoms vital to Tayo's quest for healing and identity.**
> **—*Susan Blumenthal***

Critics have posited interpretations of spotted cattle but this thematic element has never been explored in sufficient depth because, as Kathleen M. Sands suggested . . . : "certain aspects of the novel reasserted themselves over and over . . ." And indeed most critical analysis of *Ceremony* has focused on several primary areas, which Sands identifies as: "the natural world, the use of myth and ritual in the novel, and the formal design of the work."

While the spotted cattle could be considered an aspect of the first category, "the natural world," there is perhaps a more appropriate designation—animal spirit guides.

Spotted cattle as spirit guides? Charles Larson in a collection of essays, *American Indian Fiction,* interpreted the cattle much differently, in the context of what Sands called "the natural world" theme:

> The cattle are a part of his [Tayo's] people's future. When they disappear after Josiah's death, Tayo feels he has not only neglected his responsibility to his people, but severed his relationship with the land.

In contrast, Peter G. Beidler in a critical study "Animals and Human Development in the Contemporary American Indian Novel," offered a more psychological analysis, describing the cattle as a type of role model for Tayo. He states: "The animals Tayo comes most dramatically to imitate are the hardy Mexican cattle, those cattle which are closer to nature than are stupid white-man herefords."

Both conclusions are valid representative interpretations. Further study however, reveals the concentric nature of the symbol of spotted cattle; ordinary animals/quest object and spirit guides.

Animal spirit guides or helpers are a fundamental part of Native American spirituality and are a common element in the literature. If Tayo seeks wisdom, healing and self-identity, because of emotional traumas suffered during the war, then Paula Gunn Allen's discussion of the importance of spirit guides and self-empowerment in *The Sacred Hoop* seems particularly appropriate to his situation:

> The seeker hopes to gain a vision because through doing so he will also gain a secure adult identity and some "medicine", that is, some personally owned item will empower him in certain ways. He might get a song or a ritual. He might get a powerful crystal, a particularly charged stone, or a spirit guide who is some creature like an eagle, a wolf, a coyote, an ant, but who in any case counsels the seeker in certain crucial situations that have a bearing on the seeker's "path".

James Welsh explores the notion of animal spirit guides in both a contemporary context in *The Death of Jim Loney* and a historical context in *Fools Crow.* The protagonist in *The Death of Jim Loney* is a deracinated alcoholic who has a reoccurring vision of a bird. Loney admits: "This must have some meaning. Sometimes I think it is a vision from my mother's people I must interpret it, but I don't know how."

Fools Crow, set in the nineteenth century, contrasts the confusion of twentieth century Jim Loney. A young Pikuni Blackfeet, White Man's Dog, has no trouble identifying his animal spirit guide. Without hesitation he follows a raven who speaks to him, asking for assistance in freeing a wolverine caught in a trap. After White Man's Dog frees the wolverine [Skunk Bear], the raven tells him: "Dream of all that has happened here today. Of all the two-leggeds [humans], you alone will possess the magic of Skunk Bear."

Jim Loney and White Man's Dog are at opposite ends of the spiritual spectrum. Loney has no understanding of the mystical wisdom of his people; White Man's Dog has not experienced the spiritual brain-washing of the dominant culture which insists it is impossible for ravens and other animals to communicate with humans. Tayo of *Ceremony* is a character whose innate spiritual insights are somewhere between these two extremes. Silko explains: "He [Tayo] never lost the feeling he had in his chest . . . he still felt it was true, despite all they had taught him in school—that long, long ago things *had* been different, and human beings could understand what the animals said. . . ."

Through the course of the novel, Tayo discovers the ancient path of wisdom in his own way, one which reflects the technological and cultural aspects of the twentieth century.

Consider the spotted cattle. These are not animals from traditional Pueblo mythology or storytelling tradition. However, by emulating Native American syncretic traditions, Silko created them to represent the hybridization of Indian culture. Indians in the southwest are not a dying race. They select certain desirable elements from the dominant white culture and incorporate these into their own culture to keep it alive and vigorous. Even though the Native American culture in the Southwest often appears in the midst of cultural crisis, it endures and survives. Betonie describes this attitude when he tells Tayo: "She taught me this above all else: things which don't shift and grow are dead things."

As part of their dual symbolic role the spotted cattle are one of the metaphors for this syncretism. Silko describes how they "run like antelope," how they "were tall and had long legs like deer. . . ."

In essence the spotted cattle are a cross between domesticated cattle and wild animals. The Indian people survived on wild game for thousands of years but contemporary white society restricted use of that food source. Native people turned to livestock as a means of maintaining self-sufficiency. Unfortunately ranch-bred livestock are poorly suited to the harsh environment of the reservation. Survivors, such as Tayo's uncle Josiah, must constantly seek ways to overcome even the seemingly insurmountable obstacle of cattle that die during drought. As a leitmotif for survival, the spotted cattle enter to echoes of Spider Woman's Story: "I'm thinking about those cattle Tayo. See things work out funny sometimes."

In the poem which opens the book Silko tells us that stories are origins, beginnings; thoughts are the creative fountain of reality:

> Ts'its'tsi'nako, Thought Woman
> is sitting in her room
> and whatever she thinks about appears.

Josiah and Tayo think about the ideal breed of cattle and they appear:

> They would breed these cattle, special cattle, not the weak, soft herefords that grew thin and died from eating thistle and burned-off cactus during the drought. The cattle Ulibarri sold them were exactly what they were thinking about.

The metaphor of the spotted cattle, as related to Native American people who have not abandoned their traditional ways and knowledge, is quite pointed; "These cattle were descendants of generations of desert cattle, born in dry sand and scrubby mesquite, where they hunted water the way desert antelope did."

In the same passage Josiah reinforces this image with one of the more profound insights in the book when he tells Tayo:

> Cattle are like any living thing. If you separate them from the land too long, keep them in barns and corrals, they lose something. The stomachs get to where they can only eat rolled oats and dry alfalfa. When you turn them loose again they go running all over. They are scared because the land is unfamiliar and they are lost. They don't stop being scared either, even when they look quiet and they quit running. Scared animals die off easily.

Beidler comes to a similar conclusion regarding the metaphor of the spotted cattle as Indians who survive, and offers this reflective analysis:

> And like the wild animals of nature, they are able to forage for themselves in the desert. Unlike the fat, white-faced Hereford (acculturated Indians?) they do not stand stupidly around artificial water tanks (bars?). Instead they find their own water in desert springs, their own food in desert grasslands. They trust their own instincts, drift to the south where they came from, and survive by their own native and natural abilities.

While the symbol of the spotted cattle as a hybrid survivor representative of Native Americans who have retained tradition and adapted to white culture is easily identified as a thematic element, there is also a more subtle symbolism involved. The spotted cattle are not only physical hybrids they are also spiritual hybrids. They have the bodies of livestock but their spiritual essence is deer/antelope, the primary large game animal(s) of the Pueblo people for thousands of years.

Nearly all of the Silko's descriptions of the spotted cattle contain a deer/antelope simile. The cattle run "like antelope." They hunt for water like "the desert antelope." They "had little regard for fences." "They were tall and had long, thin legs like deer. . . ." And, most specifically, they were "more like deer than cattle. . . ."

This emphasis on cattle as a spiritual hybrid of deer or antelope is particularly significant in terms of Pueblo philosophies concerning these animals. The reverence bestowed on deer by the Laguna people is illustrated in the novel when

Silko describes the ceremony that will be performed on the deer slain by Rocky and Tayo:

> He knew when they took the deer home, it would be laid out on a Navajo blanket, and Old Grandma would put a string of turquoise around its neck and put silver and turquoise rings around the tips of the antler. Josiah would prepare a little bowl of corn-meal and place it by the deer's head so that anyone who went near could leave some on the nose.

The deer are honored, not exploited by the Laguna people. It is important that all the proper ceremonies be performed so the spirit of the deer will not be offended. In this way a balance is maintained: The deer spirits are honored and the deer return to give their lives as sustenance to the people. Silko portrays this relationship when Josiah and Tayo kneel beside the deer's body:

> They sprinkled cornmeal on the nose and fed the deer's spirit. They had to show their love and respect, their appreciation; otherwise the deer would be offended, and they would not come and die for them the following year.

Not only does the ceremonial feeding from the deer's spirit insure future hunting successes, it is a reaffirmation of the circular and interconnected life patterns fundamental to Native American spirituality. As Paula Gunn Allen states:

> At base, every story, every song, every ceremony tells the Indian that each creature is part of a living whole and that all parts of that whole are related to one another by virtue of their participation in the whole being.

This point of view is not embraced by the majority of the white culture, and for a young man like Tayo who must straddle two cultures it renders the task of self-acceptance and self-understanding particularly difficult. It also challenges the reader's perceptions—Silko wants them to accept realities they may not understand or believe. Critics have remarked on this aspect of *Ceremony* before. Writing in the *South Dakota Review* about the concentric story aspects of *Ceremony* Dennis Hoilman notes: "An acceptance of the Laguna world view (as presented in *Ceremony*) involves a radically different perspective from the empirically derived perspective of the white culture."

It is this "radically different" perspective that tints the analysis of many images. If viewed from the white perspective, elements such as the spotted cattle and deer are metaphors; from the traditional Indian point of view they are the magical aspects of reality. Or, as Robert Bell notes about this aspect of the novel: "she [Silko] intends for us to perceive in

the duality of natural and super natural a fundamental equivalence."

This philosophy of dual realities, visible and invisible is expressed with deer, not only in the ceremonial traditions accorded the slain deer, but also with Tayo himself.

Tayo appears to have a special relationship with deer. In the opening pages of the novel, he tries to hold the image of a deer in his mind in an effort to anchor himself in reality and find comfort in a familiar spiritual image rather than drugs: "And if he could hold that image of the deer in his mind long enough, his stomach might shiver less and let him sleep for awhile."

The symbol of this special relationship seems to be reinforced when Tayo remembers tenderly examining the deer he and Rocky have killed:

> When he was a little child he always wanted to pet a deer, and he daydreamed that a deer would let him come close and touch its nose. He knelt and touched the nose; it was softer than pussy willows, and cattails, and still warm as a breath . . . he knew what they said about deer was true.

This type of spiritual understanding of animals or a particular animal is not regarded as imaginary in Native American culture, and those who do have such a relationship with a particular species of animal are often regarded as healers or holy people. It is interesting to compare the preceding quoted passage describing Tayo's feeling toward deer with the recollections of Don Talayesva in *Sun Chief: Autobiography of a Hopi Indian* published in 1942 when Talayesva was in his fifties. *Sun Chief* recounts the experience of a young man raised with traditional native customs who is not influenced by the dominant white culture and is therefore encouraged to explore and understand the other realities he perceives:

> As soon as I was old enough to wander about the village my grandfather suggested that I go out to the Antelope Shrine and look for my deer people who were invisible to ordinary human beings. Sometimes I thought I would see antelopes who changed into people. Whenever I dreamed of antelopes in the village my parents would say, "That is to be expected, for you are an antelope child."

While there may be philosophical differences between Hopis and Lagunas regarding very specific spiritual matters and traditions unique to each pueblo, all Pueblo people share this reverence for the spirit world of animals, plants and nature, which they believe coexists, unseen, with the physical world. Therefore, Talayesva's visions could be compared to Tayo's instincts about deer. But where Talayesva's spiritual gifts were recognized and encouraged, Tayo's were ignored and even his traditional respect for the spirit of the deer is questioned by his cousin Rocky when Tayo covers the slain deer's head with his jacket: "Why did you do that?" But Tayo loves deer and knows they deserve respect even if it means derision from Rocky.

The subtle theme of Tayo as "antelope child", as Talayesva calls it, takes on special significance in the theme of healing. Tayo suffers emotional wounds from the war and feels guilt for the drought which has desiccated the land around Laguna. He feels responsible for the drought because he prayed away the jungle rain when he was in the war: "He damned the rain until the words were a chant . . . He wanted the words to make a cloudless blue sky. . . ."

From the perspective of modern psychologists Tayo's concerns about damning the rain would be considered an abnormal guilt response. Silko illustrates that Tayo's awareness of the unity and connectedness of all things has not been diminished by his exposure to white culture. What has been diminished is his sense of personal power and knowledge that he can reverse the situation. This is what he must discover through his pursuit of the spotted cattle and his interaction with supernatural beings.

All of these experiences may appear purely metaphorical to the non-Indian reader. However, Silko is actually illustrating other realities of which most people have little or no understanding. Allen explains this dichotomy of perceptions in *The Sacred Hoop:*

> In English, one can divide the universe into two parts; the natural and supernatural. Humanity has no real part in either, being neither animal nor spirit— that is, the supernatural is discussed as though it were apart from people, and the natural as though people were apart from it. This necessarily forces English-speaking people into a position of alienation from the world they live in. Such isolation is entirely foreign to American Indian thought.

The self-discovery Tayo comes to realize in the course of the novel/ceremony is that, because he is an 'antelope child,' he is closely associated with rain-bearer spirits and therefore has the ability to affect the drought. As Hamilton A. Tyler writes in *Pueblo Animals and Myths:* "In Pueblo thinking there is a very close relationship between Kachina dancers and deer since both of them are rainmakers."

This belief that deer spirits are rainmakers provides the basis for another interpretation of Tayo's quest for the spotted cattle which disappear after Josiah's death. When Tayo sets off to find the spotted cattle he in essence embarks on a vision quest to bring back the rain and heal his emotional wounds. The quest begins with old Betonie's prophecy at the end of the healing ceremony: ". . . the ceremony isn't finished yet . . . Remember these stars," he said. "I've seen them and I've seen the spotted cattle; I've seen a mountain and I've seen a woman."

Tayo realizes that he must find the spotted cattle, both to honor the commitment to his dead uncle and to continue the ceremony of healing. In this respect he becomes the hunter and the healer, and the spotted cattle become his guide. They bound through his dreams and in essence lead him to his meetings with the mountain spirits Ts'eh and mountain lion man.

> He dreamed about the spotted cattle. They had seen him and were scattering between juniper trees through tall yellow grass, below the mesas near the dripping spring . . . He tried to run after them, but it was no use without a horse. They were gone . . . He wanted to leave that night to find the cattle; there would be no peace until he did."

In contemporary terms Tayo's quest for the spotted cattle can be juxtaposed to a traditional quest by Don Talayesva for the deer spirit people. When Talayesva returns to his village with yellow stains around his mouth, his family remarks that they know he had been eating sunflowers, which according to Hopi tradition are the food of deer spirits: "They knew I had been feasting with my relations [deer spirit people] and I would probably use my special power soon to heal some person who was sick and unable to urinate.

Yellow represents spiritual food to the Hopis and the Lagunas (cornmeal and pollen) and, as Tayo begins his spiritual quest for the spotted cattle, Silko emphasizes this color in her imagery. As Tayo travels north in the early spring (yellow is the color for north in Laguna mythology), he encounters Ts'eh Montano, a mountain spirit woman who wears yellow and has "ochre eyes . . . slanted upward from her cheekbones like the face of an antelope dancer's mask."

It is likely Silko meant to represent "the Keresan game goddess Kochinako, or yellow woman," in the character of Ts'eh. She initiates the completion of the healing for Tayo and the return of the rain. There are numerous references to water when Tayo and Ts'eh are together. Ts'eh's moccasin buttons have "rainbirds carved on them." Her blanket has "patterns of storm clouds." Tayo could "feel the damp wide leaf pattern that had soaked into the blanket where she lay." "He squatted down by the pool and watched dawn spreading across the sky like yellow wings."

Tayo makes love to Ts'eh, an act which balances his male power with female power and increases his luck as a hunter:

"Other powers such as sex may be especially directed into channels which will aid the hunt."

Tayo dreams of the spotted cattle again and even in that vision there are images of water: "he saw them scatter over the crest of the round base hill, running away from him, scattering out around him like ripples in still water."

After encountering a huge mountain lion, an omen of good fortune and power, Tayo fills the lion's tracks with "yellow pollen." He then discovers the cattle "grazing in a dry lake flat. . . ."

When Tayo returns to Ts'eh he encounters Mountain Lion man, another mountain spirit portrayed as the brother or husband of Yellow Woman, carrying a recently killed deer. All of these visions combine to reinforce the spiritual nature of Tayo's quest and confirm that he is a special person, an 'antelope child'.

Tayo returns again in the summer to find Ts'eh and first sees her "walking through the sunflowers. . . ," the food of the deer spirit people. It is during this second liaison with Yellow Woman that Tayo truly begins to heal as he realizes that love always endures, even if the object of that love (in his case Rocky and Josiah) dies:

> The damage that had been done had never reached this feeling. This feeling was their life, vitality locked deep in blood memory, and the people were strong, and the fifth world endured, and nothing was even lost as long as the love remained.

In reality Tayo's soul, as a reflection of the spirit of the pueblo people, can be compared to the desert Spadefoot Toad. This remarkable animal can remain buried in a state of suspended animation, waiting. Waiting, buried in the sand up to ten feet deep; enduring for as long as a decade for the rain necessary for its mating and reproduction. Silko describes these "children of the rain" as Tayo watches them at the edge of the seeping spring.

> They were the rain's children. He had seen it happen many times after a rainstorm. In dried up ponds and in the dry arroyo sands, even as the rain was still falling they came popping up through the ground, with wet sand still on their backs. Josiah said they could stay buried in the dry sand for many years waiting for the rain to come again.

Tayo has learned to endure, with love, dignity and no bitterness. Spiraling ever inward in the ceremony of his spiritual journey, Tayo resists the vortex of evil when he watches the murder of his friends Harley and Leroy. He knows his involvement would only lead to his own destruction too. Indeed, Tayo has recognized the futility of war and violence and how these forces upset the delicate balance of the cosmos. This too is a fundamental Pueblo philosophy which is associated with rain. Allen explains this concept: "The rains come only to peaceful people, or so the Keres say. As a result of this belief, the Keres abhor violence or hostility."

His spiritual odyssey complete, Tayo goes to the Kiva where he tells the elders he has seen Yellow Woman. They do not dispute or deny his encounter with a sacred mountain spirit, rather they want to know all the details: "It took a long time to tell them the story; they stopped him frequently with questions about the location and time of day; they asked questions about the direction she had come from and the color of her eyes." Tayo is then accorded the respect due a spiritually gifted person when the elders chant:

> You have seen her
> We will be blessed
> again.

As spirit guides, the spotted cattle led Tayo, the deer/antelope child on a journey of remembrance and healing. He learned to forgive himself and release the guilt burdens from the war. He chased the spotted cattle, with their infinity-symbol brand, through dreams and into the desert and mountains and learned that love is eternal. As a deer/antelope child he instinctively knew of the deer's love: "They said the deer gave itself to them because it loved them, and he could feel the love as the fading heat of the deer's body warmed his hands." But in the course of the novel/ceremony he learned of the eternal love of people as well. Perhaps it is Yellow Woman, perhaps his mother he thinks about when the healing is complete: "He thought of her then; she had always loved him, she had never left him; she had always been there. He crossed the river at sunrise."

Edith Swan (essay date Spring 1991-1992)

SOURCE: "Laguna Prototypes of Manhood in *Ceremony*," in *MELUS,* Vol. 17, No. 1, Spring, 1991-1992, pp. 39-61.

[*In the following essay, Swan discusses the male relationships in Silko's* Ceremony *and how they relate to the customs and practices of the Pueblo of Laguna.*]

Leslie Marmon Silko's novel **Ceremony** unfolds a halfbreed's search for identity amidst fragmented shards of his own tribalism, a way of life torn asunder by centuries of oppression. His story is written by a Laguna woman of mixed ancestry who does not speak the old language. Neither does her hero whose name is Tayo. Both however, make their homes at the Keres Pueblo of Laguna, New Mexico, and both must forge bridges spanning their biogenetic footing in diverse cultural systems.

Tayo is lost, and his quest is to find his place so that he may attain his identity as a mixed-breed person within the world fabricated by Thought Woman, the Spider. Paula Gunn Allen characterizes this source in *The Sacred Hoop,* stating, "In the beginning was thought, and her name was Woman" or as Silko puts it in her article, **"Language and Literature from a Pueblo Perspective,"** "In the beginning . . . Thought Woman thought of all these things, and all these things are held together as one holds many things together in a single thought." Spider Woman's tightly woven universe is woman-centered, spun with the warp and weft of matrilineal structure. Edward Dozier isolates three salient criteria of Pueblo social order: first, descent is reckoned along the female line so children belong to the clan of their mother; second, men move to the home of their wife upon marriage so the couple continues to live with or near the bride's mother, forming a residential system congregating women related by blood; and third, women own most property. On the subject of gynecentric groups, Allen remarks that "male relationships are ordered in accordance with the maternal principle; a man's spiritual and economic placement and attendant responsibilities are determined by his membership in the community of the sisterhood."

At the heart of Silko's literary enterprise is the study of relationships: "the perspective I have involves very definitely Laguna and Laguna people and Laguna culture . . . what I write about and what I'm concerned about are relationships." Therefore, in the ensuing discussion, we shall consider various patterns for masculine relationships not only as they emerge from Silko's pen, but also in terms of how they compare with norms in the milieu of custom and practice at Laguna.

We will chart Tayo's maturation process, noting key prototypes of manhood which frame and influence his behavior. From the "Social Models" established by the men of his immediate family (Uncle Josiah, Robert and Rocky), we will turn to the breed's identification with a traditional figure in folklore in "Tayo as Culture Hero." Next, we will analyze his induction into the travails of manhood in "Lessons for a Warrior" and "Becoming a Hunter," examining the fit between tradition and the literary model. We will conclude by broadening our scope to "Tayo and the Land (Yellow Woman)," showing the articulation between manhood and the feminine principle.

Social Models

For a young Laguna boy, the most important adult male model within his social domain is his mother's brother (Uncle Josiah). Adrift between the Indian world she has come to scorn, and the white world which attracts but won't accept her, Tayo's mother (Laura or Sis) abandons her four-year-old son; she "pushed him gently into Josiah's arms." Tayo's childhood is spent in his matrilineal family trying to reach an equilibrium between his pride about being Indian (through his mother) and his shame about being White (through his father). He attends grade school near home, subsequently going with his cousin/brother Rocky to board at the Indian School in Albuquerque. Both complete their secondary education at the local high school, and throughout mainly have teachers who are Anglo (white), not Native American. As their formal schooling progresses, Rocky increasingly affiliates himself with white values; concomitantly, Tayo grows more skeptical and fearful of Indian beliefs.

Within matrilineal cultures, the extended family forms a household based on the corporate kinline through women; it consists of a mother (Grandma), her spouse and her daughters (Auntie and Sis), their inmarrying husbands (Robert) who move to the wife's place of residence, their unwed brothers (Josiah), children (Rocky and Tayo) and grandchildren. In such families, the father is expected to come and go, but in Tayo's case his biological pater is completely absent. By contrast, mother's brother is fixed, stable and reliable, and the maternal uncle possesses the male jural role for the matriline. Prior to marriage, a man stays with his sister(s) and mother; afterwards, he would leave his wife's house periodically and return to his natal family in order to execute obligations due his maternal kinfolk. He has authority over the children of his sister rather than his own biological offspring, who in turn belong to the clan of his wife. There they would fall under the jurisdiction of her brother, his brother-in-law. To his sister's children, mother's brother is their primary teacher, guardian and disciplinarian; he is the source of their inheritance, makes arrangements for their marriages, and has responsibility for collecting the brideprice for his nephews' marriages. According to Fred Eggan, an anthropologist, the closeness of this relationship is marked at Laguna, and indicated in kinship nomenclature with the reciprocal term *"anawe"*—the form of address exchanged between mother's brother (Josiah) and sister's son (Tayo, son of Sis, and Rocky, son of Auntie).

Silko's portrait of Uncle Josiah in the novel conforms closely to social standards held for his status as mother's brother. He is warm and affectionate with his nephews; he jokes with them, teaches about life with its hardships and temptations, and guides their behavior. From him, Tayo and Rocky learn masculine tasks pertaining to livestock, horsemanship and hunting. Josiah cooperates with his mother and sister in the management of family affairs and solving problems, although "the sheep, the horses, the fields and everything belonged to them including the good family name." Josiah introduces Tayo to his Mexican girl friend, Night Swan, who bestows sexual favors on both uncle and nephew. Furthermore, she urges Josiah to purchase cattle from her cousin in Sonora; as Swan illustrated in "Symbolic Geography," it is likely that the Mexican herd constitutes Tayo's bridewealth for his union with Ts'eh. Although Josiah dies while Tayo is stationed in the Philippines during World War II, he persists through Tayo's thoughts about him, memories of what Josiah said or did while the boys were growing up. Their interaction is wrought with "all the love there was," and even after Josiah's and Rocky's deaths, Tayo knows that

> Josiah and Rocky were not far away . . . And he loved them as he had always loved them, the feeling pulsing over him as strong as it had ever been . . . The damage that had been done had never reached this feeling. This feeling was their life, vitality locked deep in blood memory, and the people were strong, and the fifth world endured, and nothing was ever lost as long as the love remained.

In Tayo's legacy from Josiah, his uncle's words prevail. Speech and thought are fundamental human faculties in Laguna precepts. Since words embody thoughts, they create reality. The cosmos sprang from Spider Woman's process of ideation in *Ceremony* as well as in Laguna origin legends where her intrinsic power is the ability to name. She is regarded, as we have seen, as being the supreme "mastermind" who is the "creator of all" or she is said to have "finished everything." Words mark the inception of reality, so reality becomes a projection of thought made concrete through speech in the verbal art of stories, and storytelling.

Josiah is a consummate storyteller. Silko offers the opinion that "language *is* story. At Laguna," she continues in **"Language and Literature from a Pueblo Perspective,"** "many words have stories which make them. So when one is telling a story, and one is using words to tell the story, each word that one is speaking has a story of its own too." With all the richness of stories wrapped in stories, Josiah's teachings explain the way the world works. In addition, stories reveal appropriate sanctions indicating what will happen if one breaks normative prescriptions. Behavior and belief among the pueblos unify human with the divine, culture with nature, and thought with reality—they become a single, comprehensive, complex and closely interlocked network. For a people without writing, history is stories. Stories encode the knowledge of generations about how the world and human beings came to be as they are. Stories teach what one must know in order to belong, to have health and prosperity, to survive crisis and rear one's children. Stories are knowledge and knowledge is power over the word. Silko beautifully summarizes this perspective in *Ceremony:*

> They are all we have, you see, / all we have to fight off / illness and death. / You don't have anything /

if you don't have the stories . . . / So they try to destroy the stories / let the stories be confused or forgotten. / They would like that / They would be happy / Because we would be defenseless then.

> Everywhere he looked, *he saw a world made of stories,* the long ago, time immemorial stories, as old Grandma called them. It was a world alive, always changing and moving; and if you know where to look, you could see it, sometimes almost imperceptible, like the motion of the stars across the sky. (emphasis added)

As Josiah's stories recur, they continually refresh and inform his cherished place in Tayo's mind. "Memory insures the preservation of tribal heritage . . . Thus memories heal Tayo as they make the whole Laguna experience cohere." Tayo comes to understand his terror, realizing that "nothing was lost; all was retained between sky and earth, and within himself. He had lost nothing." One might say, perhaps, the story is there within him all the time but it needs to be drawn out, remembered so to speak from the vantage point of a retrospective view. Ts'eh, his lover, pinpoints memory as the device used to maintain and protect reality. She tells Tayo, "As long as you remember, it is part of this story we have together." Likewise, memory enables the continuance of Tayo's and Josiah's story. In Tayo's recollections, Josiah's words bespeak the reality of tradition, respect for his people's sayings, responsibility for nature, and adherence to conventional practice. Tayo's wrongdoings are firmly but kindly corrected through stories, reminders affirming the "time immemorial stories" weaving Tayo's behavior into the fabric of the Laguna world view, thereby spinning him into the material of "blood memory."

Josiah's death triggers a series of major changes for Tayo. When his American comrades are ordered to execute the Japanese soldiers, Tayo sees them killing the Laguna. He witnesses Uncle Josiah among the victims despite Rocky's patient explanations that this could not be true: "it was impossible for the dead man to be Josiah, because Josiah was an old Laguna man, thousands of miles from the Philippine jungles and Japanese armies." Yet Tayo is convinced Josiah was there, and further that his own inaction was instrumental in Josiah's death. He tells the healer Betonie, "He loved me. He loved me, and I didn't do anything to save him."

Robert, Auntie's husband, substitutes for Josiah. He assumes his brother-in-law's *"anawe"* role when nephew Tayo returns from the Veteran's Hospital after the war suffering from the illness the white doctors called "battle fatigue." Robert works with Tayo, has warm words of support, brings him supplies at the sheep camp, helps in caring for the livestock and gathering firewood, and assists Tayo in his search for Josiah's spotted cattle.

After Grandma's decision that Tayo needs treatment by the native methods, she turns first to an elder Laguna priest, Ku'oosh. In "Symbolic Geography" Swan suggests that Ku'oosh serves as a "father" in the absence of Tayo's unknown white father through the ritual sponsorship of Tayo into the Kurena medicine society. At Laguna, religious identity and access to ideology pass through men, so a child belongs to the ceremonial Kiva and dance group of their father. Therefore, it is Robert, now Tayo's surrogate mother's brother, who takes Tayo westward to the hills above Gallup for ministrations at the hands of a Navajo shaman, Betonie, whom Ku'oosh recommends to Grandma.

Consequently, we are left with an impression of the temporary and mobile nature of social designs for manhood within the family circle. In terms of the structural dictates of matrilineality, this logic makes sense, for it is women who represent constancy—they ground the system, own property, and confer identity in the clan name. Men move into and out of the corporate web of relationships keyed to their mothers, sisters and wives. The message is clear—men are transitory. Upon each construct of masculinity in the novel is imprinted the metaphor of substitution: Josiah is replaced by Robert, Ku'oosh acts in lieu of Tayo's biological father, Betonie takes up where Ku'oosh left off, Rocky dies, and Tayo exists in his stead:

> It didn't take long to see the accident of time and space: Rocky was the one who was alive, buying Grandma her heater with the round dial on the front; Rocky was there in the college game scores on the sports page of the *Albuquerque Journal.* It was him, Tayo, who had died, but somewhere there had been a mistake with the corpses, and somehow his was still unburied.

To all intents and purposes, Tayo appears as the converse of Rocky, hence he may serve as a counter for his brother. [A table follows in Blumental's essay, which lists the following traits of each character. Rocky is: object of pride, full-blood, wanted, given advantages, can leave, cleancut, all-American, oriented toward white culture, dead; Tayo is: object of shame, half-breed, unwanted, deprived of advantages, must stay, drinking, irresponsible Indian, avoids white ancestry, alive.] Significant oppositions arise in their upbringing; Auntie treats the boys differentially, even though both stand in a relationship where each would call her *"naiya"* or mother.

The narrative sets forth Rocky as Auntie's "pride" whom she always favors over the unwanted child of her dead sister. When others are around she "pretended" to handle the boys the same, "but they both knew it was only temporary." Kinship protocol would have Tayo and Rocky address each other as *"tiume"* or brother, but in **Ceremony** Auntie explicitly

prohibits this term of reference, insisting on the Anglicized concept of "cousin." Tayo knows he is expected to remain behind and help so that "Rocky would be the one to leave home." Rocky "withdraws" from his mother (Auntie), and similarly moves away from "what village people thought" without plans for remaining on the reservation. Rocky pursues Anglo definitions of success: "he was an A-student and all-state in football and track. He had to win . . . (he) understood what he had to do to win in the white outside world" and he accepts the premise of deferred gratification for that success because he "believes in the word 'someday' the way white people do."

The common perception that Rocky is a hero is inscribed by the insults heaped upon Tayo by his war buddies, especially Emo who compares Tayo to Rocky: "You think you're hot shit, like your cousin. Big football star. Big hero . . . One thing you can do is drink like an Indian, can't you? Maybe you aren't no better than the rest of us, huh?" What Emo "hates" is the fact "that Tayo is part white." Tayo deeply loves his brother—"he was proud that Emo was so envious." When Rocky is badly wounded, Tayo struggles desperately to carry the stretcher, save his brother, and fulfill his parting promise to Auntie, "I'll bring him back safe." The jungle rains are endless and to Tayo they quicken Rocky's passing. He curses the drenching downpours, praying away the rain in a chant that "flooded out of the last warm core in his chest."

Tayo's universe is founded on a "world made of stories." Consequently, he construes his words as causing the drought afflicting his people and their environment. His illness is cultural. It reflects the deprivation brought on by voicing his destructive thoughts, making him in part responsible for his state of alienation. Also, it echoes his disorientation from tribal modes of thought coded in Spider Woman's universal geometry.

These events initiate Tayo's metaphysical quest when he finally returns home, a sick battle-weary veteran. He moves from the social sphere to that of the sacred where he must, according to indigenous tenets, encounter the mentors requisite for his process of recovery.

In turn Tayo, like Rocky, must become a hero.

Tayo as Culture Hero

Another model of the male individuation process appears in stories providing a behavioral code embedded in the lore of a society nourished by an oral tradition. This mythic description of masculinity is crucial as a prototype because Tayo, hero of the novel, is congruent with a traditional folklore hero.

Among the mythologies of many American Indian societies, tales reporting ceremonies, myths and ritual dwell on the character of a "Culture Hero." Spencer presents a cogent synthesis of the series of events in which the hero commonly engages, a sequence which I have annotated with reference to the personnel and plot of *Ceremony:*

> Typically, the hero experiences a series of misfortunes in which he needs supernatural assistance if he is to survive. Sometimes he precipitates the misadventure himself by actively courting danger or intentionally disregarding prohibitions; . . . *behind the hero's seeming passivity in suffering catastrophe the stories show a deep preoccupation with his active responsibility* for provoking the mishaps that plague him [cursing the rain]. *Rejection by his family* [Auntie and his Mother] or *ridicule* and *scorn* on the part of associates [Emo] may set the stage for the hero's reckless behavior. His misadventures usually occur during *sexual or hunting exploits* [The War might be counted here as well as his relationship with Night Swan, Ts'eh, the Hunter and Mountain Lion] . . . The hero's misadventures are usually bodily attack or capture by animals, natural phenomenon, supernaturals, or aliens. They may *leave him ill, destroyed bodily, transformed* [Coyote Witchery], or stranded in an inaccessible place. In this predicament the supernaturals come to his rescue or protect him from further harm. *They restore him by ritual treatment* [Ku'oosh and Betonie] *and from contact with them he acquires ceremonial knowledge and power. Usually it is the restoration ceremony performed over him as the patient that he learns in all its details* [Betonie and Shush] . . . With each misadventure and restoration he gains in . . . ritual knowledge and power of his own *to be able to protect himself* [Star map on war shield] with little or no help from supernaturals. In the final events of the story the *hero returns to his own people* [story in Kiva and family], without resentment for whatever part they may have played in his misadventures. (emphasis added)

In the novel, Tayo displays the attributes normally assigned to the Culture Hero as a mythic archetype. Without question, Silko has crafted her hero in this time-honored persona so popular to native storytelling traditions, showing Tayo's metamorphosis from being a wastrel to his status as a full-fledged hero.

Moreover, to a Laguna youngster, the name "Tayo" would be as familiar as Superman or Batman is to a white child. *He is a traditional folklore hero.* His story tells of being taken to the sky by his pet eagle, and in flight he sings and the people see him. They go to the mountain at the zenith in the upper world where he goes "northward down" to the home of Spider Woman, then hunts with her grandsons snaring robins to procure a gift for her. He stays for a while.

In Boas' collection entitled *Keresan Texts,* he comments that Tayo's words are Hopi; furthermore, he notes that originally this was a Hopi tale brought to Laguna presumably along with many other elements derived from Hopi and Zuni. If so, Silko named her hero after a borrowed Laguna mythic hero who at a minimum flies on wings of eagles, sings in Hopi and lives with Spider Woman. In addition, the status of the folklore Tayo may have been enhanced by belonging to a Hopi story, a people reputed to be sophisticated and spiritually prominent among the Western Pueblos, exemplifying how cultural admixture is recognized and incorporated into Laguna mythology.

Lessons for a Warrior

This prototypic scenario of the mythic individuation process buttressed by Tayo's correlation with a relatively minor cultural hero sets the core parameters for Tayo's development into adulthood. Tayo's coming of age as a man rests on gaining prowess first as a warrior and then as a hunter. During Tayo's lessons on becoming a warrior, his fundamental battle is within himself, and he must combat witchcraft. His learning is mediated through symbolic themes stressing incarceration, war trophies (scalps and teeth), and connections to the Japanese through evolution, transformation and uranium. Comparable to his analog in folklore, Tayo's journey starts with the outstretched wings of an eagle. When Rocky and Tayo join up, the Army recruiter gives them a glossy pamphlet featuring "a man in a khaki uniform with gold braid . . . in the background, behind the figure in the uniform, was a gold eagle with its wings spread across an American flag."

In *Ceremony,* the theater of Indian/white conflict moves from the arid southwestern desert to the rain forest jungles of the Philippines where Indians and whites are pitted against a common enemy, the Japanese. As Tayo learns, the real antagonist is not the Japanese but witchery, and his relationship to the Japanese acts as a foil for identifying this enemy both within and without. The war in the Pacific islands is a pale shadow, a prelude for the witches' plan of nuclear holocaust. Tayo must come to understand that it is all a matter of transitions and transformations—mistaken identities and knowing the clan to which you belong—mixtures requiring that he unfuse and sort out confusing combinations.

Tayo's white sergeant orders his unit to kill the Japanese prisoners in front of the cave and Tayo sees Uncle Josiah among them: "it wasn't a Jap, it was Josiah, eyes shrinking back into the skull and all their shining black light glazed over by death." Thereafter, Tayo, Rocky and the others are captured, but are not executed outright—instead they are marched to a prison camp. On the way there carrying the blanket holding Rocky, Tayo curses the incessant rain, praying for it to stop. And the wounded Rocky dies. Tayo confuses the tall Japanese soldier, who butts Rocky's skull with a rifle, with an Indian from his school days and "the tall soldier pushed Tayo away, not hard but *the way a small child would be pushed away by an older brother*" (emphasis added).

Prison camps are jails like internment camps. Internment camps are like reservations and asylums, places to fence in those a given society deems undesirable. Liberated from the Japanese prison camp, Tayo is shipped back to the mental ward of the white Los Angeles Veterans' Hospital. He is discharged. In the L.A. train station on the way home to the Laguna reservation, Tayo faints and receives help from Japanese women and children recently released from the internment camps where Japanese-Americans were captives during the war: "he could still see the face of the little boy, looking back at him, smiling, and he tried to vomit the image from his head because *it was Rocky's smiling face* from a long time before, when they were little kids together" (emphasis added).

Variations on themes of capture and imprisonment are further enhanced by Laguna notions about war trophies. While Tayo was in the Philippines barely surviving the Bataan Death March, Emo, Harley and Leroy Valdez were on Wake Island; "they were MacArthur's boys," "they had all come back with Purple Hearts." White medals for bravery in combat stirred warrior hearts. It brought pride and a sense of belonging; camaraderie spawned carousing, sharing "good times", and swapping stories. Emo had other war souvenirs—the Bull Durham sack containing "teeth knocked out of the corpse of a Japanese soldier . . . a Jap colonel." He kept rattling the bag; Tayo fought against the rising tide of nausea caused by the sound associated with death and killing. In the bar, Tayo watches Emo play with the teeth; "he pretended to put them in his mouth at funny angles. Everyone was laughing":

> the little Japanese boy *[whom Tayo identifies with Rocky]* was smiling in the L.A. depot; darkness came like night fog and someone was bending over a small body . . . "Killer!" he screamed. "Killer!" . . . Emo started laughing . . ." You drink like an Indian and you're crazy like one too—but you aren't shit, white trash. You love Japs the way your mother loved to screw white men."

Tayo attacks the real slayer of his brother—*Emo the witch, one of the destroyers.*

It is kinship bonds which disclose the actual enemy, his Laguna buddies who have joined other practitioners on the evil side. Following the courtesy of giving an "inside" place to outsiders, kin status is extended to the Japanese by Tayo, a process of filiation sanctioned by Betonie's reference to shared heritage, "Thirty thousand years ago they were not strangers." So the Laguna men closest to Tayo "become" Japanese in his eyes. Uncle Josiah becomes a Japanese soldier, brother Rocky becomes a Japanese child wearing an army hat, and a Japanese soldier acts towards Tayo as an "older brother" to a child—they are family, kinfolk, members of the same clan:

> From the jungles of his dreaming he recognized why the Japanese voices had merged with Laguna voices, with Josiah's voice and Rocky's voice; the lines of cultures and worlds were drawn in flat dark lines on fine light sand, converging in the middle of witchery's final ceremonial sand painting. *From that time on, human beings were one clan again . . .* united by a circle of death that devoured people in cities twelve thousand miles away. (emphasis added)

Thinking about this casual reference to Hiroshima and Nagasaki as he watches Emo extract bloody chunks from Harley's quivering body during the witches' rites, Tayo freely associates the atomic destruction of the Japanese with his own abandonment by his drunken mother. Tayo sees himself and the Japanese as mutual victims of American aggression. Thoughts about bombs echo once more as he is talking with both medicine men about his war sickness. To Betonie: "I wonder what good Indian ceremonies can do against the sickness which comes from their wars, their bombs, their lies?" With reference to Ku'oosh: "Ku'oosh would have looked at the dismembered corpses and the atomic heat-flash outlines, where human bodies had evaporated, and the old man would have said something close and terrible had killed these people. *Not even oldtime witches killed like that*" (emphasis added).

Oldtime witchery and newtime witchery commingle around the traditional prize of war, the scalp. Laguna warriors joined the scalp society, or *opi'*, after they had slain or touched the enemy and taken the scalp—the same Scalp society Silko poetically represents in *Ceremony.* This group performs in the Scalp Ceremony or War Dance which was held after battle to welcome, cleanse and celebrate the return of the courageous victors. During the course of this ritual "the warriors eat the flesh of the scalp." Honoring the practice of counting coup, they ingested the enemy, assumed aspects of prowess belonging to the dead, and grew in status in the eyes of their community. It's just that Emo was empowered by teeth instead of scalps: "Tayo could hear it in his voice when he talked about killing—how Emo grew from each killing. Emo fed off each man he killed, and the higher the rank of the dead man, the higher it made Emo."

Another figure said to feed on the exploits of warriors is K'oo'ko—a Katcina giantess:

> They had things / they must do / otherwise / K'oo'ko would haunt their dreams / with *her great fangs* and / everything would be endangered . . . *The flute and dancing* / blue cornmeal and / *hair washing.* / All these things / they had to do. (emphasis added)

These precautionary "things" comprise the Scalp Ceremony in which K'oo'ko, the Katcina, dances exhibiting her giant teeth like Emo did in jest. Returning to the text, it is the Scalp Ceremony which Ku'oosh conducts for the returning Laguna war veterans—it "lay to rest the Japanese souls in the green humid jungles, and it satisfied the female giant who fed on the dreams of warriors." But it isn't enough according to Ku'oosh, "There are some things we can't cure like we used to," he said, "not since the white people came. The others who had the Scalp Ceremony, some of them are not better either." However, Betonie states "there was something else"; "it was everything they had seen—the cities, the tall buildings, the noise, and the lights, the power of their weapons and machines. They were never the same after that: they had seen what the white people had made from the stolen land."

Uranium was among the stolen resources. Theft provided the nuclear reaction for the atomic bomb foreshadowing the witches' holocaust. The A-Bomb. Grandma saw the test explosion at White Sands from her kitchen window while Tayo was gone. The bomb that evaporated the Japanese in Hiroshima and Nagasaki, but not to the extent that Emo wanted. The bomb made from uranium taken from Mother Earth beneath Laguna feet, mined from their own Cebolleta land grant. The bomb alluded to in Betonie's origin story of witchery as he outlines the destructive and monstrous outcomes of the witches' use for these "beautiful rocks."

The *Opi'* society for warriors was said to be a "shamanistic society." That is, members assisted in the making, care and feeding of the Katcina masks, called "our mothers," and they were "allowed to impersonate Katcinas." Shamans were thought to possess the same kind of magical powers as deities. Thus, "warriors are believed to know all songs and understand the language of animals and plants"; after they perform the war dance "four seeds of every kind, melon, squash, piñon nuts, and corn are put away to be planted the next spring in order to obtain success in planting." Just as Tayo must learn the lessons of warfare with witchery and whites, so too must he understand the spiritual teachings and discipline requisite for ensuring respect and positive interactions (language) with the network of forces animating his environment. Like *Bushido,* the way of the warrior in Japan.

Becoming a Hunter

Tayo's mastery of Laguna ideology rests on the balance between giving/taking or providing/killing found in the masculine endeavors of warfare, raising livestock and hunting. This focus is foretold in Betonie's prophecy visioning the elements guiding Tayo's odyssey: *"Remember these stars,"* he said, *"I've seen them and I've seen the spotted cattle; I've seen a mountain and I've seen a woman"* (emphasis added). These four signs provide critical symbolic markers for various fields of events composing "the Ceremony" Betonie initiates for Tayo's cure. Briefly, the ceremonial structure is this: Tayo travels, spending a sequence of four specific nights on different mountain peaks undergoing treatment and teaching, a plan conforming to the ritual model of many Navajo chantways. On the one hand, his journeys enact the legend of the hero. On the other, his physical movement itself traces the sacred sunwise circuit ordained by Spider Woman, an action intrinsic to his recovery. This was because "his sickness was only part of something larger, and his cure would be found only in something great and inclusive of everything."

Tayo's pursuit of his prophetic signs is related in the second half of the novel. He searches for the spotted cattle, metaphorically portrayed as "desert antelope" on Mount Taylor, Betonie's mountain. The mountain, San Mateo/Mount Taylor, is the mountain where Tayo finds Ts'eh (the Woman), the spotted cattle and himself. It is the Laguna home of Our Mother, Spider Woman with her Emergence Place, and *Cakak,* the *Shiwana* rainmaker of snow personified as Winter. (The reader is referred to Swan, "Symbolic Geography," for a more detailed analysis of the underlying structure of this symbolism). Also, it is the stage for scenes of confrontation on the Floyd Lee Ranch. Laguna conceptions include the idea that mountains provide a skeletal framework for the earth; in addition, they become an integral structure within the human being for "It is in their bones." Mountains and bones are coterminous clarifying why Betonie says "It is the people who belong to the mountain" and in ***Storyteller*** Silko writes that Mount Taylor is "our mother" where the deceased go to be reborn.

Mount Taylor is the place where aspects of thought so dear to Spider Woman abound—understanding, seeing, prophecy, divination, knowledge, learning and naming—because "Thought Woman, the Spider / named things and / as she named them / they appeared." Powers of this sacred peak are best told in separate Laguna myths presented as Appendix B. These legends endow the Emergence Place (*Shipap*) and/or Place of Divination with symbolic attributes essential to Tayo's development as a warrior and hunter. The first story is the account of *Ts'i'motc'inyi*-man (a katcina) entering into a cave or hole on the northern peak of Mount Taylor. His gift to humankind is *teeth*—teeth that chew; that frame sound into words; that K'oo'ko displays to warriors in dreams and the Scalp Ceremony; that frighten children during initiations when they are whipped by the Katcina, *Ts'its'initsi'*, called "big teeth"; that Emo took in battle as a war trophy. A primary attribute of Thought Woman is her teeth, spider teeth that slant backward to hold her prey. In addition, the identical site is visited by those who wish to see the future as revealed in the story of *Ho'tc'ani-tse*. This is the spot where you see "anything you think about," surely the epitome of Thought Woman's powerful ability to name.

For Tayo, this awesome power of Mount Taylor is condensed into a deathlike experience where he contacts "the center"— either Spider Woman's Emergence Place where the dead return or the Place of Divination, both of which are situated on Mount Taylor: "He was aware of the center beneath him . . . he knew how it would be: a returning rather than a separation . . . he would seep into the earth and rest with the center, where the voice of silence was familiar and the density of the dark earth loved him." He goes to be reborn. There he falls under the aegis of Mountain Lion.

On the flanks of this sacred mountain of the North, Tayo encounters the sacredness of the yellow mountain lion. In Laguna beliefs, yellow is the color of the north, and Mountain Lion authors hunting techniques for the North: he is the sacred animal of the North and the helpmate of hunters. While riding up the North Top of Mount Taylor, Josiah's story about the mountain-lion cub occurs to Tayo, for it describes this locale as traditional Laguna hunting grounds—a fitting background for Tayo's emergence as a hunter. Then, Tayo greets Mountain Lion in person:

> He waited for the mare to shy away from the yellow form that moved towards them . . . The eyes caught twin reflections of the moon; *the glittering yellow light penetrated his chest and he inhaled suddenly* . . . Tayo held out his hand. "Mountain Lion," he whispered, "mountain lion, becoming what you are with each breath, your substance changing with the earth and sky." The mountain lion blinked his eyes; there was no fear . . . and disappeared into the trees, his outline lingering like yellow smoke, then suddenly gone. (emphasis added)

Having gained the hunter's power, Tayo rides in the direction from whence the cougar had come and finds the spotted cattle. He herds them through the hole he cut in the fence on the perimeter of the Floyd Lee Ranch only to lose them. Here Tayo is captured, this time by the Ranch border patrol. Later, the Mountain Lion helps "the hunter" once more, for when the cowboys spot the lion's tracks they decide to let Tayo free so they can pursue new "game," Tayo's mentor of the hunt.

Tayo's offering of pollen in the "four footprints" of the sacred animal stands in stark relief to this wasteful killing by the hunters, which angers Tayo: "he wanted to follow them as they hunted the mountain lion, to shoot them and their howling dogs with their own guns," a reaction expressing his desire to be a trustee of the natural environment, to protect the animals and the earth from the willful, ongoing exploitation of the destroyers.

Imagery of approved hunting techniques continues as Tayo descends Mount Taylor looking for evidence of the cattle's movement. He hears the deer song chanted in Laguna by a hunter who appears carrying a dead deer on his shoulders; Tayo sees blue life feathers adorning the tips of its antlers. The man wears turquoise, silver and traditional garb, "but the cap he wore over his ears was made from tawny thick fur which shone when the wind ruffled through it; *it looked like mountain-lion skin*" (emphasis added). It seems this is the human personification of mountain lion—"you say you have seen her / Last winter / up north / with Mountain Lion / the hunter." Mountain Lion Man is a katcina who controls game in the North; legends depict him carrying a deer on his back.

From interviews and stories, Boas ascertained that hunters and warriors wear hats made from animal skins. Presumably, then, Ts'eh's companion is the katcina, Mountain Lion Man, since humankind always hunt in pairs rather than alone. They may also possess war shields fabricated from animal skins like the one the Hunter leaves for Tayo to see:

> It was made from a hide, elk or maybe buffalo, heavy and stiff enough to stop stones and arrows; long dry years had shrunk and split the edges, and it had lost the round shape. At first he thought the hide had turned black: from age, but he touched it and realized it had been painted black. There were small white spots of paint all over the shield. He stepped back: it was a star map of the overhead sky in late September. It was the Big Star Constellation Old Betonie had drawn in the sand.

Betonie's astronomy elucidates Tayo's sign in the stars. It starts with the story of *Kau pa'ta*, the evil magician or witch known as the Gambler. He takes the storm clouds—the *Shiwana* of the cardinal directions—and hangs them on the walls of his house. Capturing the clouds makes the rain cease as effectively as Tayo's curse when he prays away the rain. In both cases, the land and animals dry up. We are told that after receiving a gift, Spider Woman gives the hero (Sun Man) medicine, warnings and instruction; she reveals the secret knowledge he needs to win the guessing game where the stakes are his life and death. She tells him the names of the stars—Pleiades and Orion. So "it happened / just the way Spider Woman said"; he cut out the Gambler's eyes and "threw them into the South sky / and they became the horizon stars of autumn." That is, Pleiades and Orion.

Spider Woman's gift of knowledge to Sun Man permits him to free the clouds so the rains resume. The folklore Tayo visits her, too, and Tayo, hero of the novel, gains her protection (in the form of the stars) ultimately winning back the rain himself like Sun Man does.

Pleiades and Orion, these are Tayo's stars, manifest in the stars Old Betonie drew in the sand; the stars Tayo beholds his first evening with Ts'eh; the stars forming the constellations depicted in the star map painted on the war shield hung on the North wall of Ts'eh's house; the stars heralding the start of autumn—the transition between Summer and Winter when the sun moves "from its Summer place in the sky"; and the stars announcing the fragility of the world at the autumnal equinox. He observes these stars above on his night of nights—his shield:

> . . . but he saw the constellation in the North sky, and the fourth star was directly above him; the pattern of the ceremony was in the stars . . . *His protection was there in the sky, in the position of the sun, in the pattern of the stars.* (emphasis added)

> Accordingly, the story goes on with these stars of the old war shield; they go on, lasting until the fifth world ends, then maybe beyond. The only thing is: it has never been easy.

During this night of his trial by witchcraft, Tayo consciously refrains from acting out his desire to kill Emo. This decision determines his victory over the witchery practiced by his war buddies. Thereby, Tayo negates the "death" imagery and symbolism associated with his roles as warrior and hunter, destructive aspects of his manhood which might be subject to control by the manipulators of witchcraft. His first action, in consequence, is to collect the plant "of light" which Ts'eh asked him to gather. So he plants the seeds "with great care in places near sandy hills . . . The plants would grow there like the story, strong and translucent as the stars." Finally, Tayo assumes the shape of the culture hero he was destined to be. He displays the divine knowledge of the Katcina, possesses the "magic of supernaturals," and "understands the language of animals and plants." Tayo's development as "the taker of life" and "shedder of blood" essential for establishing his identity as warrior/hunter is paralleled by another cycle, growing into the opposite side of this duality. To wit: becoming a provider, the planter of seeds, and a caretaker, the keeper of animals. In short, a man connected to life, nurturance and stewardship of the land.

Our review of Laguna prototypes of manhood remains incomplete until we examine a central notion in *Ceremony*—

"we came out of this land and we are hers" (emphasis added). For the Laguna the fundamental feminine entity is the earth—it is a holy place. Tayo must, therefore, be reunited with the land. Harmony must be re-newed, integrating nature and culture, the delicate balance shattered by his heedless words praying away the rain.

That humanity and nature are intertwined, a single community in fact, may be seen in Uncle Josiah's sayings. "You see," Josiah said, . . . "This is where we come from, see. This sand, this stone, these trees, the vines, all the wildflowers. This earth keeps us going . . . It's people, see. They're the ones. The old people used to say that droughts happen when people forget, when people misbehave."

Tayo's words impacted the wider environment and his illness symptomatically reflects the land's barrenness, brought on by the desiccating consequences of his praying. This can be seen in the dehydration of his tongue and his inability to speak and think of names, especially his own. Without words, Tayo lacks reality; anonymity has dislocated him from Spider Woman's dialect. Literally and figuratively, he has lost the definition granted by a name; he is dried up, "slipping away with the wind," an ephemeral being like "invisible white smoke." His thoughts articulated in words effect him just as they effect the earth to which he is inextricably bound. As the land is waterless and eroding, he is speechless, thoughtless and nameless. His disease is mirrored in his environment.

Tayo regains density of form as well as the capacity for voicing "names" in a healing process activating Josiah's words— to be and become one with the earth. Laguna metaphysics engendered by Spider Woman's thought process make the land just as much a product of her conceptualization as Tayo is since it is Silko's words (her story) which confirm the substance of Spider Woman's ideology. In essence, Tayo must become re-aligned with the mechanisms employed by the Laguna to structure meaning in their society, it might be said that he must assume the tongue and cosmography of Spider Woman.

Like real Laguna youth, Tayo learns the social and ceremonial nature of gender within this matrilineal society through his mentors of both sexes: social identity is mediated through women and access to religious knowledge passes through men. In considering characteristics of the cast of personnel from the sacred precincts of *Ceremony,* I have noted that Silko's attribution of their powers to the respective cardinal directions accords with a master paradigm of space and time. Moreover, Tayo must also be "turned sunwise" so he is consonant with the cycle of movement ordained by Spider Woman as she places the sun: "His protection was there in the sky, *in the position of the sun . . .*" (emphasis added). This sunwise circuit determines the basic path of order. It controls good, by re-establishing wholeness, well being, purity and harmony after evil and disorder are re-moved. As Tayo re-traces the footsteps of the hero portrayed in the legend of Ghostway, he experiences ritual re-instatement. He is re-created through the curative power of words rooted in chants and rites performed upon cardinally-oriented mountain tops. Re-cognition is essential to Tayo's cure through remembrance; he realizes that the placement of the peaks is mapped "in the pattern of the stars" sketched earlier by Betonie in the sand, a position re-inforced and re-presented in the picture adorning the Hunter's old war shield. Tayo's re-turn to the mountain(s) in a sunwise fashion brings re-birth at the home of the Mother, Mount Taylor.

Tayo's re-connection to the enduring feminine principle inherent to Laguna cosmogony is rendered in a gradual process of identification depicted by Silko through imagery of immersion with light, water, the land and women which I analyze in "Feminine Perspectives." This unification takes place in the joining of Tayo with Spider Woman. We have seen the parallel structure between Tayo in folklore as he flies on the wings of an eagle and resides with Spider Woman, while Tayo of the novel goes to war under the insignia of the Army's golden eagle before he lives with Ts'eh, who is a personification of Spider Woman. Allen elaborates this association in her article entitled "The Feminine Landscape of *Ceremony*":

> Our Mothers, Uretsete and Naotsete, are aspects of Grandmother Spider. They are certain kinds of thought forces if you will. The same can be said of Ts'eh.

> Ts'eh is the matrix, the creative and life-restoring power, and those who cooperate with her design serve her and, through her, serve life. They make manifest what she thinks.

Ts'eh signifies Yellow Woman, the heroine of many a tale at Laguna and Acoma. ". . . Yellow Woman," contends Allen, "is in a sense a name that means Woman-Woman because among the Keres, yellow is the color for women . . . and it is ascribed to the Northwest." Continuing, Allen adds this figure is a "role model" for contemporary Laguna women, "she is . . . the spirit of Woman." Embodying the feminine principle of the spider matrix, Ts'eh is the source—she becomes Tayo's lover and teacher, his maker and salvation.

But yellow is also the color of personhood at Laguna, a quality invoked in the naming ceremony held for each child. Tayo converts into the color yellow symbolizing the fulfillment of his native identity, a catalytic change fostered by his relationships with both Mountain Lion, who is "yellow smoke," and the Yellow Woman, Ts'eh. Consequently, Tayo's transmutation from one color (white) to another (yellow) in the mythic level may be regarded as a logical transformation of the biological factors enmeshed in his racial identity—he is a half-breed vacillating between the conflicting demands of his paternal "white" blood versus his maternal "yellow" Laguna blood.

This intricate allegory about Tayo's "yellow" nature, then, conveys his re-covery of an Indian name after losing "the thick white skin" that had enclosed him silencing the sensations of living, the love as well as the grief. Following his re-vitalization and re-storation into a sacred manner, Tayo is re-worded with a named position in the linguistic fabric of Spider Woman's theology.

In sum, Tayo emerges as an androgynous being with the content of prototypic models of manhood bonded to the maternal principle which originates and organizes planes of meaning in the Laguna world view. Ultimately, Tayo is defined in terms of Her, the Creatrix, knowing "she had always loved him, she had never left him; she had always been there." Tayo and his people are loved; there is a new sense of belonging as Tayo returns home on the autumnal equinox. He comes as the Katcinas do—at sunrise. Balance is restored as He and She become as one, blending time and space with gender, nature and culture, a union built according to the terms governing the sacred and mundane orders of Laguna experience. Tayo achieves his half-breed stature via the masculine and feminine aspects of his manhood which delimit his place in Spider Woman's cosmic tapestry, and in the end normalcy returns to Laguna. The Culture Hero has safely returned home, and the rainclouds are freed to gather once more. As Grandma says, "It seems like I heard these stories before . . . only thing is, the *names* sound different" (emphasis added). Now Tayo is a person with a name, a story that brings people together, a story that is inseparable from the land and the one who made it all possible in the first place, Thought Woman.

Edith Swan (essay date Fall 1992)

SOURCE: "Feminine Perspectives at Laguna Pueblo: Silko's *Ceremony*," in *Tulsa Studies in Women's Literature,* Vol. 11, No. 2, Fall, 1992, pp. 309-28.

[*In the following essay, Swan analyzes the influence of matriliny typical of the Laguna Pueblo on Silko's* Ceremony.]

If we are to grasp the social and symbolic significance of *the feminine* in Native American writing, then western presumptions must be set aside so that they do not adversely bias or manipulate tribal structures of meaning. Native premises must be allowed to stand on their own terms. Therefore, in the following study of ethnology evident in Leslie Marmon Silko's novel *Ceremony,* feminine perspectives are discerned within Keresan theory, the tenets of which Laguna/ Sioux critic Paula Gunn Allen reports derive from a society "reputed to be the last extreme mother-right people on earth." My aim is to portray an archetypical configuration of feminocentric values distilled from literary and cultural dimensions at Laguna Pueblo where these are rooted in solid feminine bedrock. My intent is to encourage others to apply this synopsis more widely, to illuminate critical factors shaping contemporary literature penned by American Indians, especially when either author or text is affiliated with matriliny.

Keres is the language spoken by Silko's and Allen's kinfolk, the Laguna. Their pueblo is located in northwestern New Mexico at the foot of a towering volcanic peak called Mount Taylor, a mountain sacred in traditional theology. Mixed blood predominates due to Laguna's founding, and this community is unique in this respect among the other matrilineal pueblos of the Southwest. Instead of exhibiting the common denominators of genetic and cultural homogeneity, Laguna is a proverbial melting pot, uniting diverse groups and their varying cultures. In an autobiographical interview entitled "I Climb Mesas in My Dreams," Allen remarks, "they were a polyglot people." The resulting social matrix emphasizes the female line inscribed by a hybrid past: in every sense of the term "Laguna is a breed Pueblo."

Scholars employ useful devices for unraveling the organizational fabric of kinship and cognitive systems, and these will help us appreciate the inherent models operational behind the literary form, enhancing our comprehension not only of the novel but also of its internal dynamics. Silko's words energize by granting form, substance, and worth in a way consistent with basic Laguna ideology: the spoken word (a name) brings existence into being, and thought as knowledge informs the conception of words. The font of thought combined with sacredness of the word defines concepts requisite for understanding the inception and continuity of an oral tradition. Because words create, they unify the quintessence of things, on the one hand, and fuse object to referent, on the other; the telling remains undifferentiated from what is told.

At Laguna, thought and the word emanate from a woman. Knowledge and belief are equated; thus both origin legends and *Ceremony* posit the cosmos as Spider Woman's creation:

> She is sitting in her room
> thinking of a story now
>
> I'm telling you the story
> she is thinking.

"She" is spoken of as "Ts'its'tsi'nako, Thought-Woman." In Silko's article **"Language and Literature from a Pueblo Indian Perspective"** we learn that Spider Woman's script incorporates "the whole of creation and the whole of history and time," and it serves as the basis for "the structure of Pueblo expression [which] resembles something like a spider's web—with many little threads radiating from a center, criss-crossing each other." As author, Silko taps Spider Woman's vivifying principles of articulation: Silko becomes Her voice, Her storyteller, following Her techniques. So Silko attributes her story as well as her literary conventions to the authority of ontological genesis, to the feminine universe maker who is a spinner of names.

Woman/word: My unfolding of the picture of the feminine at Laguna Pueblo will take place through consideration of complementary layers of the novel. The first section of this essay, "Women in the Social Sphere," presents the characters typifying everyday life in the form of Auntie, Grandma, and the hero's mother, Laura or Sis. These figures are also secular representatives of "Women in the Sacred Order" discussed primarily in the third section, which gives attention also to Night Swan and Ts'eh. Each signifies aspects of female power, and like the facets of a diamond refracting the prismatic interplay of light, the faces of "Woman" at Laguna are individual personifications condensing into a central being, the "The Mater-creatrix" discussed in the second section, variously known as Spider Woman/Yellow Woman/ Thought Woman.

> Everything belonged to them, including the good family name.

Examination of relationships is central to Silko's assessment of her writing: "What I write about and what I'm concerned about are relationships." At Laguna, the hub of kinship relations is located in the women, who form the web of belonging that integrates her people. According to Tewa scholar Edward Dozier, major features of social structure in the western pueblos (Hopi, Hano, Zuni, Acoma, and Laguna) "emphasize matrilineal exogamous clans, the importance of women in the ownership of houses and garden plots, [and] matrilocal residence." Unpacking this terminology one finds that descent is reckoned through females so that children belong to the clan of their mother (matrilineality). Exogamy means that a person must marry outside of her clan, yet at marriage a bride continues to live with or near her mother (matrilocality), requiring that her husband move to her household (uxorilocality, stressing residence with the wife), thus spatially concentrating women of the same bloodline. Living patterns arranged by this skein of lineation are briefly alluded to in the novel, as when the hero, Tayo, learns that the woman Ts'eh is eligible:

> The tone of her voice said that of course he knew

what the people said about her family, but Tayo couldn't remember hearing of that family.

"Up here, we don't have to worry about those things." She was right. They would leave the questions of lineage, clan, and family name to the people in the village, to someone like Auntie who had to know everything about anyone.

Tayo is reared in a matrilineal extended family composed of Auntie and her husband Robert who live with her mother, Grandma, and her unmarried brother, Josiah. Sis is Auntie's dead sister, Laura, who is Tayo's mother. Her waywardness begot Tayo, and subsequently she left her son, relinquishing his care to her sister and mother. This situation nonetheless exemplifies Allen's definition of a unified household: "one in which the relationships among women and their descendants and sisters are ordered."

Auntie's acceptance of Tayo, however, is at best grudging, cloaked with suffering as she emulates the saints and martyrs. Auntie is a "Christian woman," characterized as entrusting propriety to white authorities; she is swayed by opinions of teachers and by those published in books and newspapers. The written word distinguishing Anglo outsiders brings "importance and power" for anyone who writes and reads; such skills she takes pride in for Rocky (Auntie's son), Josiah, and to some extent, Tayo. She dotes on practices of Anglo doctors and the solace or guidance of Catholic priests. Influenced particularly by the power of the word in gossip, a controlling guide in societies without writing, what others think and what Auntie concludes they are saying about her— their stories—hold her firmly to Christian ethics and styles of conduct. In *The Sacred Hoop,* Allen notes that "among many American Indians, family is a matter of clan membership . . . membership in a certain clan related one to many people in very close ways, though the biological connection might be so distant as to be practically nonexistent." This notion of the clan's spiritual kindred appears in *Ceremony* at the heart of the conflict surrounding Auntie, who is waging a fight that only Tayo sees and apprehends, and it ties the two despite the barriers she enforces between them. As Anglo values mingle and confound Laguna assumptions, her war becomes a cultural one revolving around "her terror at being trapped in one of the oldest ways"—her own Indian mindset.

Rules of lineal descent give Auntie no choice about her obligation to raise the half-breed child of her dead sister since that child is viewed as hers—her son. An illustration of this taxonomic merging is, perhaps, most obvious in the fact that Tayo would call his mother (Laura or Little Sister), his mother's sister (Auntie), and the mate of his mother's brother Josiah (Night Swan) all by the same name, *naiya* or mother. The narrative treats Night Swan as Josiah's lover or Mexi-

can girl friend rather than his wife, but the commitment between the two is deep, and practice of Laguna social mores would have sanctioned their intimacy by marriage if Josiah had lived. In her discussion of *Laguna Genealogies,* anthropologist Elsie Clews Parsons documents matings as "casual," and "couples may live together before the ceremony" in the Catholic Church. By the standard nomenclature of Keresan ontology, then, Night Swan stands in the position of "mother" to Tayo. She is also to him a lover (like Ts'eh) and sexually initiates him. Western sensibilities would dwell on apparent incest here and generational difference of oedipal proportions, but the logic of matrilineal categories permits this possibility without the negative overlay of western interpretation. Simply, clans where intermarriage takes place have the ongoing potential of supplying further spouses to men of the same lineage as to Josiah or Tayo. In addition, male descent-group members are called by the same word. For example, a self-reciprocal term occurs with *anawe,* mutually identifying "mother's brother" (Josiah) and "sister's son" (Rocky and Tayo). Likewise, Tayo and Rocky should address each other as *tiume* or "brother," although Auntie continually tries to prevent this association from happening.

Indulgent and nurturing relationships between grandparents and grandchildren tend to characterize matrilineal societies. Alternate generations at Laguna are classified together using the self-reciprocal of *papa:* to each other, Grandma and Tayo are *papa.* Anthropologists regard this dyad as being unusually close at Laguna. Grandparents bear responsibility for childcare when the parents are busy, but execute their charge with gentleness, patience, and goodwill; they are also prominent in naming ceremonies. Tayo's warm, positively toned relationship with Grandma is often repeated in the novel, mirroring Silko's strong affection for her own Grandma A'mooh, which she amplified in *Storyteller.* In *Ceremony* Grandma is traditional, bearing her Laguna heritage with pride. She exemplifies a generation that adheres to native teachings, respects the wisdom and status of the elders, and honors the way it has always been. She is convinced of the dignity and efficacious nature of tribal methods for curing and sanity—precepts undergirding her insistence that medicine men (Ku'oosh and Betonie) treat her grandson Tayo. As maternal figurehead, Grandma is the living reference point for the "good family name." She is as stubbornly persistent in her survival strategies as she is a powerful force in determining family affairs. Grandma embodies the traditional Laguna ethos in counterpoint to the bicultural entrapment in which Auntie struggles.

Like Silko's great grandmother, Grandma is a storyteller— she wields language with a quick and practiced tongue. Thriving amidst the "goings on" at Laguna, she brokers in gossip: "She liked to sit by her stove and gossip about the people who were talking about their family. . . . She pounded her cane on the floor in triumph. The story was all that counted. If she had a better one about them, then it didn't matter what they said." Moreover, Grandma relates the "long ago, time immemorial stories" to her grandsons, Rocky and Tayo, sees to it that they receive Indian names from her sister, and overall represents caring, nourishment, and "home."

As indigenous lore would have it, Grandma makes the ritual offering for the deer's spirit, asks Tayo to gather Indian Tea, and in the end feeds members of the medicine society led by Ku'oosh when Tayo speaks in the kiva. Grandma is sensitive to the divisive currents eroding her family, her people, but she does not impose adherence to her viewpoint. However, in keeping with the influential role of maternal grandmothers in matriliny, Silko grants Grandma the last narrative comment in the novel: "It seems like I already heard these stories before . . . only thing is, the *names* sound different" (my emphasis).

Ease, humor, and affection mark relationships with grandparents, and this contrasts with the authority and respect vested in the parental generation. In *Matrilineal Kinship* David Schneider and Kathleen Gough contend that the empirical disposition of group placement runs through women, giving men access to lines of authority through the female line. It is of minor concern in *Ceremony,* then, that Tayo's father is missing, for it is the mother's brother (Josiah) who acts as the authority figure for the children (Tayo and Rocky) of his sisters, reinforcing the strong bonds of interdependence between a woman (Auntie) and her brother (Josiah). He is the children's teacher, disciplinarian, and source of inheritance; he plans their marriages and provides the brideprice in the wedding of his nephews. So it is not coincidental that *anawe,* Josiah, sends Tayo to Night Swan carrying a note on blue-lined paper. Further, one may speculate that Josiah's cattle, purchased at Night Swan's urging, serve as Ts'eh's marriage "gift" (bridewealth), thus illustrating how old practices may resurface in new forms. Following norms of ownership, the Mexican longhorns would become Ts'eh's property (or her family's), which she might dispose of as she pleased. Ts'eh indeed tends the cattle and then returns them to Tayo's care after he comes to be with her again in accordance with custom.

Matrilineal principles underscore the "good family name" of Auntie and Grandma. Auntie claims that in the past it commanded esteem: "Our family, old Grandma's family, was so highly regarded at one time. She is used to being respected by people." Several lineages tracing descent from a common ancestor are aggregated, forming the clan, a social unit above the level of the extended family. Parsons's *Genealogies* discloses 19 clans among the 124 houses scattered through the 8 village settlements comprising the pueblo of Laguna. The name of the maternal line (the matriline) bestows social identity shared with those in the tribe possessing the same name—it makes "relatives." This all-important clan name endows status, ensures etiquette, and gives knowledge of where one belongs. Social place is prescribed as is collective responsibility and life force, expressed in the novel as the "vitality locked deep in blood memory."

Clans have their own stories. Such stories become integral components of *Ceremony,* blending different personae into the oldtime beliefs and fusing them to the architecture of Spider Woman's cosmic blueprint. Legends record clan origins entwining ancestors with certain plants or animals either during the time of Emergence from the underworlds or in the Migration thereafter. Fundamentally, "the Origin story functions basically as a maker of our identity—with the story we know who we are," Silko says in **"Language and Literature from a Pueblo Indian Perspective,"** then continues with an example: when "Antelope people think of themselves, it is as people who are of *this* story [how Antelope and Badger widened the Emergence Place], and this is *our* place, and we fit into the very beginning when the people first came, before we began our journey south." In *Ceremony,* Ts'eh is connected to Antelope and Descheeny to Badger. Clan stories furnish a rich inventory of symbolism as well as the familiar mythic backbone of historical precedent, augmenting the poetic scope and sweep of Silko's literary repertoire.

There are also family stories, which "keep track" of the events, "both positive and not so positive—about one's own family." Family stories, like clan stories, mold Laguna character because the idiosyncratic details making a family history unique are related countless times in the communal process of remembering and retelling. In *Ceremony,* Auntie fears and Grandma relishes these stories. Each generation hears and tells the stories anew—time and again family members learn their family's account of itself, of themselves:

> the people shared a single clan name and they told each other who they were; they recounted the actions and words each of their clan had taken, and would take; from before they were born and long after they died, the people shared the same consciousness.

Silko states in **"Landscape, History and the Pueblo Imagination"** that "human identity is linked with all the elements of Creation through the clan." Clan names stem from the natural environment. At Laguna, Parsons found them divided into a dual entity: among the western clans one finds Bear, Parrot, Coyote, Roadrunner, and Oak—the winter people— under the aegis of the Kurena medicine society, while the Koshare have jurisdiction over the eastern, summer cluster of Sun, Turkey, Corn, Water, and Turquoise. Laguna myth assigns most clan names to one of the four cardinal directions, thus linking the clan to a discrete set of symbols and harnessing the power grounded in that direction. For instance, Ts'eh's "antelope" qualities draw on the South. In turn, this prompts a series of associated symbols, including those of Summer, Thunder and Lightning, Eagle, Red, Red Corn, Wildcat, and Badger. Principles of classification produce a symbolic dictionary or cluster of synonymous symbols, if you will, and a careful reading of the text shows Ts'eh in relationship to these images.

Composing a systematic framework of symbolic representations, the matri-clans thus weave social customs to land, nature, and gender, while knitting the individual into ontology by acknowledging a common source for all existence. Everything germinates from Spider Woman's ideational process, an image beautifully sketched by Silko in **"Language and Literature from a Pueblo Indian Perspective":** "In the beginning, Tséitsínako, Thought Woman, thought of all these things, and all of these things are held together as one holds many things together in a single thought." All in one, all is one.

> Their theory is that reason (personified) is the supreme power, a master mind that has always existed, which they call Sitch-tche-na-ko [Spider Woman]. This is the feminine form for thought or reason.

Paula Gunn Allen in "The Psychological Landscape of *Ceremony*" argues that

> it is clear that the land is female . . . the nature of Woman associated with the creative power of thought. Nor is ordinary thinking referred to in connection with Her. The Thought for which She is known is that kind that results in physical manifestations of such as mountains, lakes, creatures and philosophical/sociological systems.

All systems of order are writ larger than life where the cognitive schema bond culture with nature and arise from a powerful gynocratic foundation cementing the Laguna conception of womanhood.

The Mother loves and cares for the Laguna as her children or her family. She lives at Spider Woman's Emergence Place, *shipap,* in the North, where she ascended with the Kurena shamans from the underworlds. Specific accounts of the Laguna origin myth render several beings as "Our Mother(s)." Her profile is drawn in the following sentiments:

> She is the deepest in heart and, through her, religious feeling is most fully expressed. When a baby smiles, the old women say that [Iyatiku] is talking to it, when it cries, [she] is scolding. [She] is mentioned first in prayer, ritualistic origins are dictated by her and . . . her symbol is too sacred to be exposed commonly to view. . . . In the ritual, Iyatiku

is the cotton-wrapped ear of corn which is possessed by the *cheani* and set out on altars. . . . In myth . . . Iyatiku lived with the earth at shipap . . . and with her sisters remained within.

Thought Woman is immortal; She is origin and summary, and, to the Laguna, Her presence is all-encompassing, as Fred Eggan explains:

> One important pattern at Acoma, which is characteristic of Keresan villages generally, and which contrasts with the Hopi and Zuni to a considerable extent, is the emphasis on the concept of "mother." In the Origin Myth we have seen that the central figure is Iyatiku, who is the "mother" of the people whom she created and whom she receives at death. The corn-ear fetishes represent her and have her power.

Women making themselves women constitutes an act that discloses the pivotal symbolism of matriliny. In *Ceremony,* Silko puts it this way:

> . . . Thought-Woman,
>   is sitting in her room
> and whatever she thinks about
>   appears.
> She thought of her sisters. . . .

As Silko further elaborates in **"Landscape, History and the Pueblo Imagination,"** "they helped her think of the rest of the universe . . . including the Fifth World and the four worlds below."

Thought Woman is the source of names, language, and knowledge. She is termed the "creator of all," or she is said to have "finished everything." Some versions call her "mother" or, in Kenneth Lincoln's gloss, "Thought Woman, the matrix, deifies an old integrated regard for ideas, actions, being, plots, and things." Anthony Purley, a Keres scholar, writes, "Tse che nako is the all-fertile being, able to produce human beings and all other creatures: 'She is the mother of us all, after Her, mother earth follows in fertility, in holding, and taking us back to her breast. . . .'" Yet another tale sets Thought Woman as being identical to Iyatiku, who is the mother of colored corn women.

If not synonymous with the Mother, female creator of women and people, then Thought Woman figures as her sister in a society that conjoins sisters. Variously, She is Mother, Sister, Grandmother—the syncretic woman who is the "naming" and "knowledgeable" creatrix birthing the universe of stories spun from her abdomen; She is the "mastermind" teaching, nourishing, determining how things will be, and deciding what must be done. A Laguna spokeswoman explains:

My tribe, the Keres Pueblo Indians of the Southwest, put women at the center of their society long
ago. . . . Where I come from, the people believe traditionally that nothing can happen that She does not
think into being, and because they believe this they
say that the Woman is the Supreme Being, the Great
Spirit, the Great Mystery, the All-Being. This
WomanGod, Thought/Thinking Woman they call
Spider Grandmother, acknowledging her potency as
creator, as Dream/Vision Being, as She Who
Weaves existence on all material and supernatural
planes into being.

Women in the Sacred Order

Our Mothers, *Uresete* and *Naotsete,* are aspects of Grandmother Spider, are *She* at lower voltage, so to speak. The
same may be said of Ts'eh, who is Tse-pi'na, the Western
Woman Mountain.

Let us expand Allen's statements in the above epigraph and
suggest that the entire cast of female characters in **Ceremony**
are individual permutations of Spider Woman—each is "*She*
at lower voltage." Allen goes on to contend that the cure for
Silko's hero rests in living in harmony with nature and being "*initiated into motherhood.* . . . For Tayo it is planting
Her plants and nurturing them, it is caring for the spotted
cattle, and it is knowing that he is home," for "he has loved
the Woman who brings all things into being, and because
he is at last conscious that She has always loved them, his
people and him."

Tayo's *"initiation into Motherhood"*—his rite of passage—
develops throughout the novel, encoded in his interactions
with and indoctrination by women situated in the social and
sacred domains. But his biological mother deserts him: "the
birth had betrayed his mother and brought shame to the family and to the people." She is sister to Auntie, and in kinship nomenclature sisters are grouped together, depicting
Allen's assertion that "male relationships are ordered in accordance with the maternal principle; a male's spiritual and
economic placement and attendant responsibilities are determined by his membership in the community of sisterhood." The sisters called *naiya* (mother) by Tayo both reject
him. He is alienated from his "mothers," literally and figuratively abandoned: as Allen points out, "Failure to know
your mother . . . is the same as being lost."

Tayo's sexual instruction starts with Night Swan who is
Mother/Lover: "Mother," by virtue of kinship terminology
in her relationship with Josiah, and "Lover," by virtue of initiating Tayo into the restorative pathway of feeling, preview-
ing the love borne to him by Ts'eh. "You will recognize it
later. You are part of it now," she says. Night Swan is timeless, likened to "the rain and the wind"; analytically, she is

associated with spring, the color of blue, and cardinal West.
She is Grandmother with "no age," emblematic of the
matriliny, since all her descendants are female. "She moved
under him, her rhythm merging into the sound of the rain,"
and Tayo is immersed, "swimming" in the water that Night
Swan represents. Then Night Swan vanishes abruptly after
Josiah's death rather like the spring rains seeping into the
thirsty earth to become clay.

Analogous to Night Swan, Ts'eh personifies elemental forces
of nature, and she too is a Lover/Mother. Her color is yellow. Yellow denotes North, invoking the phenomenology of
a symbolic category whose members may stand in lieu of
one another or for whom the mention of one implies a reference to the rest: this class of the North includes Mountain
Lion as the sacred animal, Mount Taylor the sacred peak,
Yellow, Yellow Corn, Snow, and Winter. Yellow pervades
scenes involving either Ts'eh or her residence, located on
an upper plateau of the sacred northern mountain. Eventide
in the late autumn sunset is the temporal stage for Tayo's
first glimpse of Ts'eh. She stands beneath an apricot tree
wearing a yellow skirt. After acknowledging his presence,
she invites him into her house and feeds him chili containing dried corn. To the Laguna, corn is not only a fundamental food staple with its welcome harvest in the fall, but
socially it is the name of a clan that is segmented into groups
of different colors. Esoterically, corn is the staff of life—
the visible form (corn ear fetish) of "Our Mother" fashioned
by the Kurena priests and cared for by the *cheani,* the shamanistic leadership. Corn codifies the origin, maintenance,
and blessings of life; it represents sustenance and becomes
a critical attribute connoting the essence of matriliny and the
matrix—it symbolizes above all the feminine. Allen summarizes: "As the power of woman is the center of the universe
and is both heart (womb) and thought (creativity), the power
of the Keres people is the corn that holds the thought of the
All Power (deity) and connects the people to that power
through the heart of Earth Woman, Iyatiku."

It is significant, then, that after enjoying Ts'eh's food and
hospitality, Tayo rises to greet "the dawn spreading across
the sky like yellow wings"; he remembers the bells and
rattles of a late November dawn when the Katcina appear
at the moment of "sunrise" after the "pale yellow light," and
he haltingly says the prayer welcoming the Sun. Katcinas are
supernaturals impersonated by men inducted into certain
medicine societies; the initiated don elaborate masks and
costumes portraying parts taken by these spiritual beings
during performances of the sacred dances. Arrival of the
Katcina heralds the start of the winter ceremonial season.
Tayo has the impression that Ts'eh is a Katcina, an Antelope Katcina, when he sees that Ts'eh's "eyes slanted up with
her cheekbones like the face of an antelope dancer's mask."
In the creation myth, Antelope uses her hooves to butt
against *shipap,* helping Badger enlarge the Emergence Place

so the holy people can arrive on the surface of the present world. Stories tell it clearly: the Antelope Clan is one of the oldest to have been formed; it is a founding clan at Laguna and associated with the South; it is preeminent among all clans, the hearth of leadership for both Laguna and Acoma Pueblos; unquestionably, Ts'eh's clan is the most venerable of all.

The symbolism of Ts'eh's "antelope" features converges with that of the spotted cattle, which Tayo, Rocky, and Josiah call "desert antelope," cows obtained from the southern climes of Sonora. Uncle Josiah purchased the Mexican herd at Night Swan's behest, and, as I noted earlier, they served as Tayo's bridewealth. If Ts'eh and her cattle are symbolically equivalent, Tayo's "husbandry" illustrates the sophisticated metaphors used by Silko in knotting the social with the natural strata in Spider Woman's thought. The mystical and supernatural are involved as well. Tayo quietly observes Ts'eh preparing her herbs and medicines, paraphernalia signaling her role as a medicine woman and rainmaker. She brings lifegiving moisture—the snow and rain—using her stormcloud blanket and crooked willow staff, and her potency is encoded in the eagle rainbirds imprinted on the silver buttons of her moccasins.

This set of symbols reappears interestingly in connection with a woman in a prophecy made by the Navajo healer, Betonie, midway through the novel: "Remember these stars," he said. "I've seen them and I've seen the spotted cattle; I've seen a mountain and I've seen a woman." This woman is Yellow Woman, who is all women. Heroines and holy women in Laguna myth often live in the North and are named "Yellow Woman." Among these, one Yellow Woman is the wife of Winter. Yellow Woman is the maternal source of the Antelope Clan. Yellow Woman is in fact the generic name—the core integrative symbol—for all female Katcinas. There can be little doubt that Ts'eh is Yellow Woman, the personage Allen considers to be an ultimate "role model . . . She is, one might say, the Spirit of Woman."

Conforming to the paradigm set by Ts'eh, the hero follows suit: Tayo becomes yellow himself. This metamorphosis occurs when both Tayo and his urine change color. His color symbolism switches from white (father) to yellow (mother) as he takes on qualities of his maternal blood in the process of assuming his tribal identity; in Allen's idiom, Tayo is no longer "lost" and is learning "to know" his Mother once more.

During the illness, which the white doctors called "battle fatigue," Tayo projects himself as being "white smoke" fading into and out of the white world:

> For a long time he had been white smoke. . . . He inhabited a gray winter fog on a distant elk moun-

tain where hunters are lost indefinitely and their own bones mark boundaries. . . . It was not possible to cry on the remote and foggy mountain. If they had not dressed him and led him to the car, he would still be there, drifting along the north wall, invisible in the gray twilight.

Tayo gets drunk at the Dixie Tavern and fights his war buddy, Emo. That night his urine has no color, but yellow surrounds his body: "The yellow stained walls were at the far end of the long tunnel between him and the world. . . . He looked down at the stream of urine; it wasn't yellow but clear like water." Responding to Emo's insults, Tayo attacks him: "He moved suddenly, with speed which was effortless and floating like a mountain lion." But he is not the archetypical hunter, not yet. It is highly probable that the distant elk mountain, covered with gray winter fog located "along the north wall," is in Tayo's projection none other than Mount Taylor, sacred mountain of the North, which the Laguna call "Tse-pi'na, the woman veiled in clouds": "The mountain had been named for the swirling veils of clouds, the membranes of foggy mist clinging to the peaks, then leaving them covered with snow." The mountain lion that Tayo encountered near the summit of this sacred peak is "yellow smoke," Tayo's Indian alter ego. Furthermore, Ts'eh's companion there is the Hunter. The Hunter is the human manifestation of Mountain Lion Man, the Katcina charged with the welfare of all game: he is deity of the hunt and serves as a mentor to Tayo. The Hunter's animal counterpart is the cougar, sacred animal of the North, the animal that Tayo speaks to and is identified with: "mountain lion, becoming what you are with each breath."

Now the change occurs: Tayo is yellow, as he "pissed a yellow steaming slash through the snow," while the whiteness of the blizzard's cocoon remains outside his skin. He expresses the quality of personhood—yellowness—spoken in prayer when he receives his sacred "Indian name." Shortly after birth, each child is presented to the sun by the maternal grandmother or her sister, the naming ceremony is held, and the child's sacred name is spoken; thereby she becomes known, the gods recognize her. The child is said to be "yellow"—either a "yellow woman" or "a yellow youth"—the colored essence of Laguna identity. It is not certain whether "Tayo" is a sacred name or a nickname, but it is clear that "Tayo" is a twinned name since the novel's hero shares it with a folklore hero. "Tayo" is the name of a traditional folklore hero at Laguna whose pet eagle takes him to visit and hunt at the home of Spider Woman. Secret names are carefully guarded and rarely mentioned, which leads to the use of "nicknames" such as those of "Ts'eh" or "Rocky."

Both Tayo's environment and Tayo himself have become saturated with the color yellow. He has become a "yellow" person through his love for Ts'eh, the Yellow Woman, a mutation that was catalyzed by inhaling the penetrating yellow moonlight reflected in mountain lion's eyes. This transformation culminates in the slanting rays announcing early morn when "he crossed the river at sunrise." Just as the Katcina reach this river at dawn, Tayo's "safe return" occurs at sunrise at a critical moment of the seasonal cycle: the autumnal equinox when winter commences and summer ends. These diurnal and seasonal periods of time governed by the Kurena shamans prompt the suggestion that Ku'oosh, the Laguna medicine man who treats Tayo, is the *cheani* heading the Kurena medicine society, and Tayo may also be meeting with its membership in the kiva. Kurena songs are performed early each morning during the calendar of ceremonial dances. "The Kurena lead the people back from the harvest," explains Boas, an event placing their songs in the seasonal cycle between the corn harvest and the winter solstice; they are custodians of the Sun's "turning back," leaders of the winter moiety.

The connection between Ku'oosh and Ts'eh dramatizes the story of the Kurena and Our Mother in Laguna philosophy. Mythology recounts that the Kurena came up with Our Mother from the underworlds, an event ranking the Kurena foremost among the medicine societies. They make and tend the sacred corn fetishes named "Our Mother." "The Shamanistic groups prepare the masks in the houses of Antelope [Ts'eh] and Badger [Descheeny] clans"—masks that Tayo discovers stored in the southwest corner of the kiva, hidden from the eyes of the "uninitiated." The entire "Katcina cult remained under the control" of these two clans, who were the guardians of all spirits. The Kurena go to live in the Northeast—the same direction taken by Ts'eh when she parts from Tayo at the end of *Ceremony*. But their provenance is in the West, as in Ts'eh's in her guise as *Tse-pi'na*, whom Allen terms "Western Mountain Woman." The Kurena (Ku'oosh) are the male caretakers of the visible aspect (corn fetishes) of the key female personae in Laguna belief, so it is logically consistent that Ts'eh would share a common destination with them.

Going home, Tayo is bathed in pale light, like the "sunrise" in Silko's verses that open and close the novel; the word "sunrise" also ends the Kurena's dawn songs. This reiterates an earlier baptism by the sun when Tayo was in utero. Auntie reports watching his mother: "Right as the sun came up, she walked under that big cottonwood tree, and I could see her clearly: she had no clothes on. Nothing. She was completely naked except for her high-heel shoes." Silko notes it was customary for Laguna lovers to meet down among the willows and tamarisk beside the San Jose River, so it is a place for conception.

Life is made by Our Mother just as it is taken away, so it is not a surprise that abortions occur in a similar setting. One day near Gallup, a child finds where his mother disposed of bloody rags; the place was "near the side of the arroyo where she had buried the rags in the yellow sand." Instead of being bathed in sunrise's yellow light, he is covered and filled with pale yellow sand like the rags discarded by this mother. Just as the fetus is buried, Tayo is cast off by his social mothers. He is lost. In dreams his loss masquerades as a burial in yellow sand, like that of Old Betonie, the breed medicine man, who was also buried just after birth before he was rescued from the trash pile by his mother. Abandoning unwanted life, mothers leave the fetus or newborn to die in the arroyos, the cutting edge of the landscape.

Comparable imagery recurs in connection with Ts'eh as both mother and lover, though for lovers some of this imagery is revised. To achieve conception of his own life, Tayo penetrates the sand beyond his body and thus preempts the action of burial that signifies death. The first time the two make love, he "felt the warmth close around him like river sand," and later, "he dreamed he made love with her there. He felt the warm sand on his toes and knees; he felt her body, and it was warm as the sand, and he couldn't feel where her body ended and the sand began." Traversing the "sandy ridge" with Ts'eh, crossing the ruins left by the ancient ones, he is struck with the immensity of the grand scheme, "the way the arroyo sand swallowed time" and intuits that Ts'eh is the land, the Mother, and that she is eternal: "He could feel where she had come from, and he understood where she would always be." Ts'eh walks toward the Northeast where the Kurena reside; she admonishes Tayo to "remember everything" and tells him, "I'll see you." Her departure provokes another dream like the one caused by a mother's leaving.

Mother and lover, birth and sex, yellow light and yellow sand. Tayo achieves his identity in union with the land through women. Yellow Woman, the infinite, is the Laguna composite model of Woman—a facet of the Spider mater and creatrix, Thought Woman.

Various ideological principles at Laguna reflect core feminocentric values within a matrilineal system of descent. This model has been detailed as a guide to characteristic structures underlying the powerful feminine in Laguna culture. By summarizing its salient points, I hope to encourage scholars to apply this exemplar more broadly for understanding non-Keresan texts authored by other Native Americans.

In numerous ways, Tayo starts out as being "lost"; his ultimate achievement, therefore, is "belonging." Rites for his "initiation into Motherhood" are eventually completed, and the half-breed finds himself continuously striving for equilibrium within Spider Woman's teleological doctrines. On the human level, the culture hero returns to his natal home, reentering the bosom of his family. Tayo's social position is determined by the maternal line within family, clan, and cosmos—a view confirmed by Tayo's waking dream that "Josiah was driving the wagon, old Grandma was holding him, and Rocky whispered, 'my brother.' They were taking him home." On the supernatural level, Tayo reaches unity with Yellow Woman; he knows at last his Indian identity, his name.

Tayo is mobile and mortal. Ts'eh is grounded and enduring; through her Tayo comprehends the sacred reality that the tribe embodies. She is the source, the female fulcrum of this gynocratic system.
                                                          —Edith Swan

---

Tayo is mobile and mortal. Ts'eh is grounded and enduring; through her Tayo comprehends the sacred reality that the tribe embodies. She is the source, the female fulcrum of this gynocratic system. As she thinks, reality is named: cosmogony is woven into her linguistic universe. Fashioning celestial and earthly bodies with their finely wrought spatial/temporal designs, the mater-creatrix fabricates women, deities, animals, and humankind, all of which participate in the dialect of creation and are related to everything else material and spiritual; and She designs systems of order according to the cardinal directions, the cycle of the sun, and matriliny. Myth sanctifies the primacy of matrilineal symbolism on the one hand and decrees the sacred vital force of the clan on the other, and this vitality becomes manifest in yellowness, color of the stuff of corn, personhood, women, and Our Mother.

Utilizing methods predicated on the art of telling stories at Laguna, Silko gives shape poetically to Spider Woman's thought world. Her focal point is Tayo as he undergoes a ceremony reuniting him with the land, the place from which he originates, because, as Silko declares, "we came out of this land and we are hers." He can only be healed by enacting Josiah's teachings about being and becoming one with the earth. Silko depicts this transformation through metaphors of Tayo's immersion in women, light, water, and the land: congruent symbols formulating the generative, conceptual power of Spider Woman, who symbolizes the ultimate feminine principle, the template for Yellow Woman/All Women.

Tayo portrays the culture hero, the lyric figure of a yellow man returning to Laguna beneath the shelter of the golden leaves of the old cottonwood where his Mother-Lover stood in another dawn pregnant with his seed. Coming full circle, he arrives in the end at sunrise: whole, loved, and home at last, like the Katcina. His homecoming transpires near the autumnal equinox under the dominion of the Kurena medicine society. In the kiva, thought to replicate Spider Woman's

home within the earth at *shipap,* he is confirmed ceremonially after relating his journey to the world of Spider Woman—a journey that parallels the visit of his analogue in folklore. This is Silko's portrait of the questing half-breed, who overcomes his alienation and untangles the twisted cords of his ancestry.

Out of forgetfulness, Tayo cursed away the rain and became lost. Now he wins back the rain by native rules through his relationship with Yellow Woman when he remembers, realizing that "she had always loved him, she had never left him; she had always been there." Standing on the bridge outside of Gallup, on the way to visit Betonie, Tayo makes a prophetic wish for a "safe return." His self-fulfilling thought is transformed into a named reality, for his ritual process is one of being "called back." Through utterance, Tayo is transported "back home" where "belonging," "long life," and "happiness" prevail, becoming, in other words, a person "our Mother would remember." He has found interconnectedness through Her, the one who makes the unmade into all things: he has a name, he has a place, he has a story, he has returned to his people and the land, he is one with Thought Woman and Her metaphysics—he is laced paradoxically into Her "verbal" legacy of "blood memory."

Linda J. Krumholz (essay date January 1994)

SOURCE: "'To Understand This World Differently': Reading and Subversion in Leslie Marmon Silko's *Storyteller,*" in *Ariel,* Vol. 25, No. 1, January, 1994, pp. 89-113.

[*In the following essay, Krumholz discusses Silko's collection,* Storyteller, *asserting that the author "appropriates the terms of the colonizer in order to change forms of representation, to change readers, and to change the world."*]

Leslie Marmon Silko's **Storyteller** is a book of stories and a book about stories: it contains traditional Pueblo Indian stories, Silko's family stories, poems, conventional European style short stories, gossip stories, and photographs, all woven together to create a self-reflexive text that examines the cyclical role of stories in recounting and generating meaning for individuals, communities, and nations. **Storyteller** has been described as an uniquely Native American form of autobiography and as a simulation of the oral tradition in written form. The book simulates the oral tradition both in the compilation of many stories that create their own interpretive context (functioning like an oral community) and in the lack of discrimination made between the many kinds of stories. By eliding distinctions between genres and between old and new stories, Silko creates a dynamic juxtaposition that duplicates the way in which meaning is created in the oral tradition through a constant interaction between the stories and the material circumstances of the community, between the old stories and the on-going creation of meaning. Her image for the oral tradition is a web: strong, flexible, resilient, everchanging, interconnected, and in dynamic relationship with the rest of the world.

Silko's book functions in the "contact zone," a phrase coined by Mary Louise Pratt to describe "social spaces where cultures meet, clash, and grapple with each other, often in contexts of highly asymmetrical relations of power, such as colonialism, slavery, or their aftermaths as they are lived out in many parts of the world today." Pratt describes a certain kind of text created by the colonized or conquered, by those made "other" by the dominating social group, as an "autoethnographic text," "a text in which people undertake to describe themselves in ways that engage with representations others have made of them." Pratt argues that

> [autoethnographic texts] involve a selective collaboration with and appropriation of idioms of the metropolis or the conqueror. These are merged or infiltrated to varying degrees with indigenous idioms to create self-representations intended to intervene in metropolitan modes of understanding. Autoethnographic works are often addressed to both metropolitan audiences and the speaker's own community. Their reception is thus highly indeterminate.

Silko's *Storyteller* is an autoethnographic text, a book that engages with the dominant representations of Native Americans in order to appropriate and transform those representations. The book contains many of the forms of expression and faces many of the perils that, according to Pratt, distinguish writing in the contact zone:

> Autoethnography, transculturation, critique, collaboration, bilingualism, mediation, parody, denunciation, imaginary dialogue, vernacular expression—these are some of the literate arts of the contact zone. Miscomprehension, incomprehension, dead letters, unread masterpieces, absolute heterogeneity of meaning—these are some of the perils of writing in the contact zone.

Pratt emphasizes the perilous and indeterminate nature of the reception of texts in the contact zone. In this essay I focus on the role of the reader in Silko's book in an attempt to negotiate the charged terrain of the contact zone. I read *Storyteller* as a ritual of initiation for the reader into a Laguna Pueblo representation and understanding of the world, a reading that emphasizes the potential for the text to transform consciousness and social structures. Finally, I consider the position of literary criticism and my own work in this paper within this contact zone.

Silko explains in a talk entitled **"Language and Literature from a Pueblo Indian Perspective"** that "a great deal of the story is believed to be inside the listener, and the storyteller's role is to draw the story out of the listeners. This kind of shared experience grows out of a strong community base." But how does the storyteller address both those inside the community base and those outside it as well? In describing *Storyteller* as an autoethnography and as an initiation for the reader, I will focus on the reader as outsider, the non-Laguna and non-Indian reader. What serves as an act of transformation for a non-Indian reader may serve as an affirmation for the Indian reader. But insofar as Silko engages with and challenges the dominant representations of Native Americans, she confronts the ideologies that all "Americans" are subject to in varying degrees—many Native Americans have also been educated in Euroamerican schools, for example. Silko begins *Storyteller* with stories that correlate with, and repudiate, the Euroamerican representation in which American Indians are tragic figures, scattered remnants of a dying culture. As the reader moves through the book, she or he gains greater familiarity with Native American stories and perspectives, until the final stories of the book use the humour and subversion of Coyote stories, stories of the quintessential Native American trickster, to show the vitality and humour of Indian culture, while also laughing at the dominant representations of power, of history, and of American Indians. Silko engages with the terms of the dominant culture and then moves them progressively into a Laguna context, shifting the reader's perspective from one interpretive position to another. Thus Silko creates "resistance literature"; she appropriates the terms of the colonizer in order to change forms of representation, to change readers, and to change the world.

One of the central ways that Silko challenges dominant representations of Native Americans is by contesting the relegation of Native Americans to the past, and by breaking down the oral/written distinction that is used to support the past/present (them/us) dichotomy. Native American arts and storytelling were for a long time in the academic purview of anthropology, and European anthropologist Johannes Fabian argues that anthropological temporal categories served to construct the colonized "other" as part of the past, excluded from contemporaneity, in order to justify the colonial mission. He writes:

> Anthropology contributed above all to the intellectual justification of the colonial enterprise. It gave to politics and economics—both concerned with human Time—a firm belief in "natural," ie., evolutionary Time. It promoted a scheme in terms of which not only past cultures, but all living societies were irrevocably placed on a temporal slope, a stream of Time—some upstream, others downstream. Civilization, evolution, development, acculturation, mod-

ernization (and their cousins industrialization, urbanization) are all terms whose conceptual content derives from whatever ethical, or unethical, intentions they may express. A discourse employing terms such as primitive, savage (but also tribal, traditional, Third World, or whatever euphemism is current) does not think, or observe, or critically study, the "primitive"; it thinks, observes, studies *in terms* of the primitive. *Primitive* being essentially a temporal concept, is a category, not an object, of Western thought.

Clearly Fabian's analysis of Western temporal categories applies to the colonization of the United States, a colonization justified by a narrative in which Europeans discovered a New World that was empty except for a few nomadic savages who could only profit from contact with a more advanced society, primitives who needed to be brought from the past to the present (even if it killed them). There are also other contemporary manifestations of this evolutionary time concept, as in romantic ideas of Native Americans—new versions of the "noble savage"—that relegate them to some idyllic past to which other Americans wish they could return. Jimmie Durham, a Cherokee artist and writer, states that in "the United States, people phrase their questions about Indians in the past tense."

The distinction between oral and written cultures has been used in anthropology to define the preliterate, prehistorical, and primitive (that is, static and dead) cultures in opposition to the literate, historical, and, by implication, contemporary (European) people. These reified divisions between oral and literate cultures have been criticized by contemporary Euroamerican anthropologists, such as Joel Sherzer and Anthony Woodbury, who argue that

> [some statements describing an oral/written distinction] do not come to terms with the nature of oral discourse, but tend rather to take written discourse as a model and then view oral discourse as less complicated, less advanced, and seemingly deficient in relation to the written texts of literate, technological societies. . . . there is no simple dichotomy between oral and written discourse, between nonliterate and literate societies. Rather there is considerable and quite interesting continuity between the oral and the written, showing diversity within each: There are oral genres in Native America that have such "written" properties as fixed text, "planning," and abstraction form context, and written genres in European-based societies have such "oral" properties as spontaneity and "repair," scansion into pause phrases, and context-dependent interpretability.

In *Storyteller,* Silko challenges the distinctions between oral

and written by constructing the written as a secondary and diminished version not simply of verbal presence but of the entire dynamic situation of place, people, and stories in the oral community.

Silko also works against the representations of traditional Native American stories as simplistic and static, without any contemporary applicability or pleasure, ideas perpetuated by anthropologists' stylistic choices in transcription and translation. Silko disdains the work of ethnologists Franz Boas and Elsie Clews Parsons, who "collected" stories of the Laguna Pueblo in their book *Keresan Texts* in order to preserve what they considered a dying culture. Dennis Tedlock, a Euroamerican anthropologist, has also criticized Boas's and Parsons's methods of transcription and translation as another way of rendering Native American people as primitive precursors. He writes:

> [When translating from oral to written] the direction of movement is opposite to that of translation as practiced between two written traditions: whereas the professional translator brings what was said in another language across into the saying of his own, the professional linguist takes his own language partway across to the other, artificially creating a new variety of broken English. Not only that, but as Dell Hymes has pointed out, those who wish to keep what was said in the other language at a great distance, whether giving it the status of an early link in their own evolutionary past or filling out the spaces in a literary bestiary, will even take this broken English as a sign of authenticity.

Tedlock proposes that Native American oral narratives should be written on the page like dramatic poetry to emphasize oral and performative stylistics as they shape the meaning and aesthetics of oral narratives, thereby stressing the continuity of forms between the oral and the written. Silko uses some of the typographical devices that Tedlock suggests (not necessarily at his urging). She uses the ends of lines to indicate verbal pauses, she indents to indicate visually the structural importance of repetition, and she uses italics to indicate verbal asides to the audience. These textual indicators control the pacing and reception of the stories, increasing the accessibility and emphasizing the poetic and narrative effects for readers. Silko also blurs the distinction between oral Pueblo stories and written short stories as *Storyteller* progresses, in part by rendering them all in writing, but also by obscuring the formal differences on the page until in the final stories the forms of poetry, traditional stories, and European style short stories are virtually indistinguishable.

While blurring the distinctions between oral and written arts and asserting the contemporaneity of Native American verbal arts, Silko also carries Native American concepts of language into her written text. In Native American oral traditions, language is neither a lens offering a mimetic representation nor a problematic social structure—language has the power to create and transform reality. Numerous students of Native American culture have noted the efficacious power of the word. Kenneth Lincoln offers a description of "tribal poetics": "Ideally generative, words make things happen in Native America; language is the source of the world in itself." Elsewhere, Brian Swann writes, "The Word, in fact, is a sacrament, a vital force, so that, for instance, a hunting song is not just a pleasant aesthetic experience, but possesses an active relationship with the hunting act." He elaborates: "A truly sacramental sense of language means that object and word are so fused that their creation, the 'event,' is itself creative, bringing into this time and place the enduring powers which truly effect that which the event claims, and such action cannot be undone." The term "sacramental," with its religious echoes, conveys spiritual concept in which a symbol becomes what it symbolizes—there is no gap between signifier and signified. The spoken word is thus a powerful creative or destructive force.

The creative and transformative power of language connects linguistic acts to the transformative processes of ritual. Storytelling is a central element in Native American rituals, and Silko refers to the creative and destructive powers of language throughout *Storyteller.* Anthropological theories of ritual and liminality may be applicable to all acts of reading. But I wish to connect Silko's *Storyteller* to ritual in order to propose the transformative potential of this book in its particular position in the contact zone and to read the structure of the work as a tool in the transformative process.

Storytelling is a central element in Native American rituals, and Silko refers to the creative and destructive powers of language throughout *Storyteller.*
—*Linda J. Krumholz*

Rituals are formal events in which symbolic representations, such as dance, song, story, and other activities are spiritually and communally endowed with the power to shape real relations in the world. The anthropologist Victor Turner divides the ritual process into three stages: rites of separation, rites of limen or margin, and rites of reaggregation or integration. Turner theorizes "marginality" or "liminality" as a space and time within ritual in which social classifications break down and social relations are transformed. The rites of separation and reaggregation frame and mediate between the social structure and the status-free experience of liminality. Within the limen, a time and space outside of categories is created, a place where dangers have free play

within the limits set by the ritual. This is the arena of the "other" where the power of mystery supersedes the power of the social structure. Within the limen all participants, having temporarily put off their status, will see the world differently. Ritual thus creates a time and space in which the non-differentiation of *communitas* and the powers of otherness can break into, while being contained within, the pre-existing power structures in the society.

Turner's three phases of ritual can also describe the process of reading, in which ritual processes of separation and re-aggregation are compared to the (less formalized) actions of sitting alone with a book and then putting the book down. In this analogy, the act of reading correlates to the liminal phase of ritual. Liminality, according to Turner, is the central phase of ritual, a pedagogical phase in which neophytes about to be initiated are all of equal status outside of structures of social order while a ritual leader has absolute powers. Turner's description of the liminal phase as a time and space of possibility could well describe the ideal reading process:

> . . . the liminal phase [is] in the "subjunctive mood" of culture, the mood of maybe, might-be, as-if, hypothesis, fantasy, conjecture, desire . . . Liminality can perhaps be described as a fructile chaos, a fertile nothingness, a storehouse of possibilities, not by any means a random assemblage but a striving after new forms and structure, a gestation process, a fetation of modes appropriate to and anticipating postliminal existence.

The narrative is a liminal space, both within and outside daily life, a place and time in which a reader may take imaginative risks that may transform his or her perception of the world.

But the conjunction of reading and ritual also has a particular strategic value for Silko writing in the contact zone. Ritual is an indigenous idiom for many Native Americans, and it is a formal element in many contemporary Native American narratives. Paula Gunn Allen asserts that many contemporary novels by Indian authors "derive many of their structural and symbolic elements from certain rituals and the myths that are allied with those rituals." This use of ritual can be read as autoethnography, a way of carrying Indian forms of representation into the European-derived form of the novel, which has the consequence of altering the novel. The convergence of ritual and written narrative brings into the novel—by implication, structure, or artistic effect—more of the physical, spiritual, and communal aspects of ritual that tend to be deemphasized in the individual, intellectual, and often secular experience of reading novels. Beyond this, the assertion of ritual properties in written narratives creates a potent model for change, similar perhaps to narratives aimed at religious conversion, in which the narrative seeks to provide a visionary experience. Silko gives *Storyteller* ritual properties: the sense of a community of voices, a spiritual vision, a visual, physical relationship to the text, and a structure that moves both progressively towards a vision and in a circle, suggesting cyclical and balanced relations rather than a sense of closure. But the complexity of *Storyteller* as a text correlates with the danger of the heterogeneity of meaning and the indeterminacy of reception that Pratt noted. As I trace some of the structures I find in the text, I hope my attention to reception can help me to avoid a homogenized reduction of the web of reading and meaning that Silko has constructed while making its powerful vision more accessible to the reader.

In order to describe the structural movements of *Storyteller* and the way it functions as a ritual of initiation for the reader, I designate six thematic divisions in the text. The first two sections are drawn from Bernard A. Hirsch's discussion of *Storyteller,* the four remaining sections correspond to those designated by Linda Danielson in her work on the book. Hirsch designates the first section as the survival section and describes this section and *Storyteller* as a whole as "a self-renewing act of imagination/memory designed to keep storytellers as well as stories from so tragic a fate" as to be lost to memory. In this section, Silko establishes the familial and collective transmission of stories as vital cultural forces. The stories depict the determination of Native Americans to resist the forces that are dismantling Indian families, traditions, and interpretations. Most of the stories in this section are also tinged with a sense of loss and displacement caused by "European intrusion" and the tensions between Native American and Euroamerican cultures. In the two short stories **"Storyteller"** and **"Lullaby,"** the characters reaffirm the power and continuity of the stories, but the situation of the storytellers is perilous. At the end of **"Storyteller,"** the Yupik protagonist is imprisoned literally by the Euroamerican authorities and figuratively by their interpretations of her story, for which they brand her as criminal or crazy. In **"Lullaby,"** the old Navajo woman sings her song of continuity as she sits outside with her husband, preparing to freeze to death after a lifetime of losing everything including all of their children, to white social workers and doctors and white wars. In both **"Storyteller"** and **"Lullaby"** stories and songs provide consolation for Native American people besieged by white culture and authority, but the survival of the people and the stories is threatened by Euroamerican legal and interpretive structures within which these stories are meaningless or unheard. This threatens not only Native Americans; the apocalyptic imagery of **"Storyteller"** suggests that the survival of the earth depends upon the perpetuation of these stories.

Some of the stories in the Survival section also tell of the matrilineage of storytelling, its power and its tensions. Silko tells two traditional stories that her Aunt Susie told her as a young girl. Both stories—the story of the young girl who killed herself because her mother would not make her *yashtoah* (her favourite food) and the story of the two little girls who lost their mother in a flood and turned to stone—portray severed relationships between mothers and daughters, and may well have served as solace for Silko in her relationship with her mother. Silko also shows her writing to be a continuation of a female lineage of storytellers, such as Aunt Susie, in her family photographs and reminiscences. When Silko recollects her Aunt Susie's stories she writes:

> I remember only a small part.
> But this is what I remember.

In the balance of these two lines, Silko embodies both the loss of so much of the oral tradition, as well as the perpetuation of the oral tradition in her own memory and her own retellings. In the Survival section the reader is made to feel the depth of loss both of the stories and of the people who attempted to tell the stories and live by them. But Silko does not simply present the tragedy of the loss; she creates in her readers the need, the desire, and the ability to hear and understand those stories from a Native American interpretive perspective.

The second section, dubbed "Yellow Woman" by Hirsch, contains a number of stories about Yellow Woman, or "Kochininako" in Keres, a generic female character in Laguna Pueblo stories. Yellow Woman encompasses a great diversity of traits: in some stories she is loyal, beautiful, or powerful; in other stories she is selfish, thoughtless, or, worst of all, a witch. Here, Silko focuses especially on the so-called abduction stories, in which Yellow Woman is taken from her husband and children by a powerful male figure—Whirlwind Man, Buffalo Man, or the Sun—but in Silko's stories the woman is drawn into the adulterous relationships as much by her own desire as by the man's. Hirsch argues that this focus on women's sexuality shows that "individual fulfillment can be equally important to a tribal community" as individual sacrifice, since in this section, and especially in the poem/story **"Cottonwood Parts One and Two,"** Silko's retelling of two traditional stories, Yellow Woman's desire and agency bring benefits to the people.

In the Yellow Woman section, Silko tells stories of women's roles developing within the dynamic exchange of old and new stories. In the short story **"Yellow Woman,"** for example, the first person narrator tries to figure out if, in her experience of abduction, she is Yellow Woman: "I was wondering if Yellow Woman had known who she was—if she knew that she would become part of the stories." The narrator's relationship to the old stories is ambiguously resolved both in the title to Silko's story and in the last line of the story, when the narrator thinks "I was sorry that old

Grandpa wasn't alive to hear my story because it was the Yellow Woman stories he liked to tell best." The narrator's proximity with the old stories gives her experience a significance and a place in the life and stories of the people. As Silko writes in her poem **"Storytelling,"** a humorous juxtaposition of traditional and gossip stories, "You should understand / the way it was / back then, / because it is the same / even now."

It is especially pertinent to consider the relations of old and new in the treatment of women's roles. Silko's description of her hunting experiences in this section, connected by a story she was told as a child about a great young girl hunter, point out some of the ways in which "traditional" roles for women mean something quite different for Native American and Euroamerican women. Rayna Green makes these differences explicit:

> The ironies multiply when, contrary to standard feminist calls for revolution and change, Indian women insist on taking their traditional places as healers, legal specialists, and tribal governors. Their call is for a return to Native American forms which, they insist, involve men and women in complementary, mutual roles. I underscore these differences because they may teach us more than analyses of Indian female "oppression." I am not suggesting that a return to tradition in all its forms is "correct" but that attention to the debate about the implications of such retraditionalization would mean healthier, culturally more appropriate scholarship on Indian women.

Silko's focus on women's roles in this section of *Storyteller* compels the (white?) reader to reevaluate ideas of tradition, often considered by Euroamericans as something static, repressive, and unyielding. The way women construct and imagine their roles and their relation to tradition in Silko's stories parallels the give and take between old and new stories that gives the oral tradition its continuing vitality and relevance.

The next two sections, coming in the centre of the book, comprise a cycle from drought to rain. The Pueblo Indians, as well as the other Indians living in the arid southwest, focus many of their stories and rituals on the need for rain. Drought results from disruptions of harmony, from witchcraft, from bad thoughts or deeds, or from forgetting the old stories and the old ways. Rain results from an establishment of the right order and balance and sometimes from a ritual of healing to counter witchcraft. In Pueblo and Navajo religions, witchcraft is a reversal of the right order and balance of things—it is a destructive rather than a creative use of power.

In the Drought section, Silko recasts the terms of power, so that white power, which is often represented as overpowering and absolute, is treated as a misunderstanding and a misuse of power—the sort of power to bring drought rather than rain. In two stories, the short story **"Tony's Story"** and the poem/story of the creation of white people by witches, the association between white power and witchery is explicit. In the creation story, in which a witch tells a story of white people that creates them as it is spoken, white people are described as people who objectify their surroundings and who bring death and destruction to people, animals, and land (with clearly historical allusions). The witch's evocation concludes with the white people's use of the rocks "in these hills": "They will lay the final pattern with these rocks / they will lay it across the world / and explode everything." In **"Tony's Story,"** Silko recounts a true story about a traditional Indian who killed a white state patrol officer. Since the story is told from Tony's (the Indian's) perspective, the reader is left to ponder both the delusions of Tony's vision and the logic of his assumption that the cop is a witch because his manifestation of power seems lifeless, arbitrary, and destructive.

The story of the Ck'o'yo magician connects white "power" to the illusions of "magic" by inference rather than by explicit reference. In the poem/story the magician disturbs the balanced relationships between the people and the land, the animals, and the spiritual powers, and thus he brings drought. The Ck'o'yo magician fools the people with tricks, "magic," that look like power but prove to be a false power. Like the power of technology, the Ck'o'yo magician can create magical and impressive visions while ignoring and even trampling on the cycles of worship, balance, and reciprocity required for fruitful relationships and necessary to bring the rain.

Following a group of photographs, the Rain section begins with a rain chant, "The Go-wa-peu-zi Song," written first in phonetic anglicized Laguna and then in English: "Of the clouds / and rain clouds / and growth of corn / I sing." This section continues from the previous one, but the emphasis has shifted from the disruptions that cause drought to the positive and creative forces the rain represents. The stories in the Rain section are lighter and more humorous, written in a lighthearted tone that celebrates the creativity, growth, and balanced relationships that bring the rain and that the rain signifies.

This section, halfway through the book, signals a shift into a Laguna Pueblo "language" and understanding. As Pratt has described it, autoethnography collaborates with and appropriates the representations the dominant group has of the dominated. In *Storyteller,* Silko uses the process of initiation to transform the reader and to shift the interpretive vantage point and the definition of terms from the Euroamerican to Native American. At this point in the book Silko moves toward affirmation and representation of Native American philosophical and spiritual beliefs from a more Native American centred world view. For example, both **"Tony's Story"** in the Drought section and **"The Man to Send Rain Clouds"** in the Rain section end with the promise of rain, but in the former story Tony's beliefs seem disturbing and out of touch with his surroundings, while in the latter story it is the Anglo priest whose beliefs seem disturbing and out of touch within the Laguna community. Although the perspective throughout the book is clearly Native American, the weight of Euroamerican representations lifts in this section, and the storyteller exhibits a greater confidence in the reader's ability to engage with Native American concepts and representations.

This shift in the emphasis of the collaborative enterprise is depicted most clearly in **"The Man to Send Rain Clouds."** In the story an old Laguna man is found dead by his relatives who prepare for his burial ritual and who ask him to send them rain clouds. It is believed that when the dead leave the fifth world (the world we are most familiar with) and travel to the other worlds below (which have no resemblance to Hades or Hell) they can carry an appeal to the rain clouds to bring rain to the fifth world. When the Anglo priest in the story is asked to bring his holy water to the burial ceremony, the Euroamerican character and belief system are put into the Native American context; the priest is the outsider who cannot comprehend the religious and cultural forms that surround him. The readers are put in the Laguna position, finding humour and pathos in his misunderstanding. In the end of the story, as the priest watches in bafflement as his holy water soaks into the sand, we see the sacred powers of the priest and the symbolism of his water get engulfed by the ceremony and beliefs of the Laguna and their (and our) understanding of the symbolism of the water.

The other stories in this section describe productive relationships and growth as part of the cyclical processes of the world. To illustrate the vastness of the natural and spiritual cycles, Silko depicts the dissolution of illusory boundaries of time and space. Four lyric poems in this section best exemplify this concept, especially **"Prayer to the Pacific"** in which the cycles of rain become a continual process that links the very origins of life and time to the present and the future, and every part of the globe to every other. Thus Silko presents a world of temporal and spatial coexistence, a world without boundaries, in which all things are interrelated.

The story **"The Man to Send Rain Clouds"** provides a link between the Rain section and the Spirits section, since the earth's cycles are connected with the processes of life and death and the presence of the spirits of the dead. The concept of temporal coexistence in the Rain section has direct bearing on concepts of ancestral presences, as Johannes Fabian observes:

> . . . all temporal relations, and therefore also contemporaneity, are embedded in culturally organized praxis. . . . To cite but two examples, relationships between the living and the dead, or relationships between the agent and object of magic operations, presuppose cultural conceptions of contemporaneity. To a large extent, Western rational disbelief in the presence of ancestors and the efficacy of magic rest on the rejection of ideas of temporal coexistence implied in these ideas and practices.

The dissolution of temporal boundaries in the Rain section prepares the reader for an understanding of spiritual presences and our relationship to them.

In the Spirits section, Silko tells a number of stories about family members who have died, especially about her Grandpa Hank; the section is framed by photographs of her Grandpa Hank and her Grandma A'mooh. The Deer Dance becomes a model for the reciprocal relations between the living and the dead. Silko describes the Deer Dance which "is performed to honor and pay thanks to the deer spirits who've come home with the hunters that year. Only when this has been properly done will the spirits be able to return to the mountain and be reborn into more deer who will, remembering the reverence and appreciation of the people, once more come home with the hunters." This cyclical relationship is also used in poems in the section to describe the pain and homage in love relations, in **"A Hunting Story," "Deer Dance / For Your Return,"** and **"Deer Song";** and to describe the relations between the old stories and the new with a deeper spiritual dimension than in the Yellow Woman section. **"Where Mountain Lion Lay Down with Deer"** is a beautiful poetic evocation of the processes by which stories bring the spirits of the past back into existence. And in Silko's description of the anthropologists' explorations on the Enchanted Mesa, she describes a different kind of death that has threatened Indians, when pieces of the past are buried in museum basements, and the spirits and stories of the past are taken out of circulation.

In the last two stories of the section, which are two versions of a story, Silko describes spiritual transformations that affect the living. In one version a young boy taken by the bear people is brought back gradually to his humanity by a medicine man, but he will always be different after his connection to the bears. In the other version, **"Story from Bear Country,"** the reader, referred to as "you," is in the position of the young boy, and we are being lured back from the beauty of the bears' world by the narrator—the poem is the song by which the storyteller, in the role of the medicine man, calls the reader back. In these stories Silko conveys the power of stories to create spiritual transformations, thus offering stories that help to understand the reader's initiation and transformation in the ritual process of the book.

In the last section of the book, Silko tells stories of Coyote, the Native American trickster figure and ultimate survivor, to complete the shift to a Native American perspective and tradition. Coyote stories, common in the western and southwestern parts of North and Central America, differ among various people and regions, but the central feature of Coyote is his or her propensity for trickery, immorality, and deception. Exemplifying reprehensible, anti-social behaviours, Coyote is depicted as a lecher, a glutton, a thief, and a clown, whose uncontrolled appetites lead him to death again and again, though his death is never permanent. Jarold Ramsey describes Coyote's outlawry as a focus of social censure and of group humour that provides moral examples and psychological release, education and entertainment. But Coyote's foolish errors, his appetite, and his laziness are not just amusing character flaws, they are characteristics that have shaped the world—thus he is also a very human character. William Bright argues that Coyote stories, while teaching morality through Coyote's negative examples, also depict the foolishness and the power of humanity. In this last section of *Storyteller,* Silko introduces a character who represents human foibles and human creativity, as well as the power of Native American, and human, survival.

At this point, two structures can be seen in Silko's *Storyteller:* there is a progressive initiation into the Laguna Pueblo "language" and systems of belief and representation, and there is a mirror or circular structure. The Rain section responds to the Drought section, the Spirits section deepens the dynamics of change treated in the Yellow Woman section, and the Coyote stories reconsider the Survival section, and now the Indian perspective, traditions, and values pass judgment on the white world. The structure of the book can be envisioned as a butterfly: the two halves of the book provide two sides to a Native American perspective—on one side the sadness and struggle, on the other the humour and subversion—and both parts are necessary for a full understanding of power relations. At the same time, through the progressive movement of the book, Silko deflates the "dominant" vision of a "dominating" system of power.

The reader's experience of the text may be compared to the experience of Silko's great-grandfather Robert G. Marmon, a white man who married a Laguna woman and lived the rest of his life in Laguna. Near the end of *Storyteller* Silko looks at a photograph of Marmon as an old man, and she writes, "I see in his eyes / he had come to understand this world / differently." Her observation, rendered in poetry to control the pace and emphasis, conveys the depth and importance of this difference in her great-grandfather's altered vision. Silko's book works to transform the reader's vision as a lifetime at Laguna did for her great-grandfather—to convey and reinforce the power and beauty of the Laguna vision.

This final section of my essay focuses on a story in the Coyote section, **"A Geronimo Story,"** that exemplifies the process of initiation that *Storyteller* as a whole enacts. In **"A Geronimo Story,"** the reader learns, along with the narrator's younger incarnation, how to "read" Laguna meanings through an understanding of the strategies of humour and subversion. The narrator, Andy, tells the story of a trip he made as a naive young man, when he accompanied the Laguna Regulars, led by his uncle Siteye and a white man, Captain Pratt, on an assignment to track and capture Geronimo. The United States Army, at war with Geronimo and the Apaches in the early 1880s, took advantage of inter-Indian hostilities and employed Laguna men to help them against their Apache enemies.

The narrative voice of the mature Andy follows the young Andy as he learns, through the subtlety of his uncle Siteye's humour and wisdom, about the ability of the trickster to turn white authority back on itself. The reader is put in the same position as the young Andy; the narrator provides the reader with the knowledge Andy already had when he went on the trip, but he does not explain the lessons he learns as the trip proceeds. To understand the story and how it affects Andy, the reader must, like Andy, learn to understand the humour of Siteye.

The story begins by establishing Andy's "horse sense"; he describes his uncle's larger Mexican horse and his own smaller Navajo horse as he ropes and saddles them for the trip. But Andy does not understand why the group heads for Pie Town when Siteye and Captain Pratt know Geronimo is not in that direction. Captain Pratt, a "squaw man" (as was Silko's great-grandfather Robert Marmon), has married a Laguna wife, adopted many of the Laguna ways, and is respected by the Laguna. Captain Pratt, in his respect for Siteye's opinions and for the Laguna people, is contrasted to other white men. Major Littlecock is the other kind of white man, whose authoritative stance, repeated errors of judgment, and racist underestimation of the Laguna are a source for the Laguna of amused contempt, a contempt also signified by his name.

The camaraderie, stories, and lessons of the trail end when the Laguna Regulars reach the white people's town, Pie Town, and encounter the white people's distrust and hostility, at which the full power of the Laguna sense of humour is released. The more fiercely and foolishly Major Littlecock acts out his authority and prejudice, the faster the jokes fly, until a joking session ends with Siteye's words and Andy's comprehension:

> Siteye cleared his throat. "I am only sorry that the Apaches aren't around here," he said. "I can't think of a better place to wipe out. If we see them tomorrow we'll tell them to come here first."

We were all laughing now, and we felt good saying things like this. "Anybody can act violently—there is nothing to it; but not every person is able to destroy his enemy with words." That's what Siteye always told me, and I respect him.

The Laguna strategies of humour and collaboration become clearer to Andy by the end, when he puts them fully into the context of survival. First there is the following exchange with Siteye:

> Before I went to sleep I said to Siteye, "You've been hunting Geronimo for a long time, haven't you? And he always gets away."
>
> "Yes," Siteye said, staring up at the stars, "but I always like to think that it's us who get away."

Siteye's sentence can be read two ways—to mean that it is "us" who escape from Geronimo, or that he *is* "us." Anything enigmatic in the statement is made clearer when, the following day, they prove to Littlecock that he was wrong about the Apaches' proximity. Andy thinks Littlecock was wishing he were still in Sioux country, which was more familiar to him. Silko writes, "Siteye felt the same. If he hadn't killed them all, he could still be up there chasing Sioux; he might have been pretty good at it." The sarcasm and subtle humour of Silko's story suggest that the Laguna "collaboration" is both a strategy for survival and a deception of the white military authorities—a pretense of collaboration.

The journey becomes an initiation ritual for Andy, as he learns new places and the unspoken relations between Laguna and white men. Siteye teaches Andy tracking, explaining the process of memory based on an awareness of details and an ability to etch them into one's mind. The process of tracking Geronimo becomes a metaphor for Andy's initiation process, as he learns not only how to find him, but why they *do not* seek him. In Siteye's stories of the Apaches and the white soldiers, the soldiers' stupidity is a more prominent element than the murderousness of the Apaches; although there is no love lost between the Laguna and the Apache, the Laguna have even less respect for the white people with whom they ostensibly collaborate. The process of tracking and the idea of the hunt also become metaphors for the reader's initiation, as we trace through the subtlety of Silko's humour to figure out what Andy has figured out. Geronimo is, in a sense, the ultimate trickster figure of the story, the absent focus around whom the Laguna play with the whites and Silko plays with the reader. The hunt for Geronimo comes to mean much different things to the white authorities and to the Laguna. By the end of the story, Andy and the reader understand, without having heard it directly, that a successful hunt for Geronimo means *not* to find him, and that Siteye's final words in the story—"'You know,' he said, 'that was a long way to go for deer hunting'"—are a great joke on the white men.

Immediately following this story in *Storyteller* there is a photograph of "The Laguna Regulars in 1928, forty-three years after they rode in the Apache wars." The photograph of a group of older men, some in jeans and workshirts, others in suits and ties, gives Silko's story historical authenticity, while also attesting to the survival of the Laguna Regulars. By bringing together the photograph with the story, Silko demonstrates how history can be rewritten as a Coyote story, which should subsequently enable the reader to reread history. In Silko's version, the power relation generally assumed is reversed. Her story suggests that the Laguna did not act in complicity with white people against other Indians, but instead that they had found better ways to survive white domination than direct retaliation.

In **"A Geronimo Story,"** Silko uses humour to establish a relationship with the reader and thus to insinuate the reader into another way of understanding Native American history and people; the humour becomes a means of reinterpreting history, power relations, and strategies for survival. Humour, the predominant feature of Coyote tales, is an essential ingredient in Silko's construction of a Native American perspective in the last section of *Storyteller.* In *Custer Died For Your Sins,* Vine Deloria, Jr. writes:

> One of the best ways to understand a people is to know what makes them laugh. . . . Irony and satire provide much keener insights into a group's collective psyche and values than do years of research.
>
> It has always been a great disappointment to Indian people that the humorous side of Indian life has not been mentioned by professed experts on Indian Affairs. Rather the image of the granite-faced grunting redskin has been perpetuated by American mythology.

In humour, more than in other kinds of stories, the teller depends on common viewpoints and sensibilities. In the Coyote section, Silko uses humour as a final stage in an initiation process, showing Indian humour, resilience, and self-awareness along with her trust in the reader's ability to laugh with and at Coyote.

Throughout *Storyteller,* Silko reflects on the role of storytellers; in the final section, she connects the storyteller's art and her own role as storyteller to the strategies of Coyote. The storyteller is, like Coyote, a culture creator and transformer. But the analogy also connects to the subversive role of Coyote, in which Coyote's reversal of power relations and subversion of rules serve to expose the deceptions of white people or to represent Indians undermining white power. In an interview, Silko says:

> Certainly for me the most effective political statement I could make is in my art work. I believe in subversion rather than straight-out confrontation. I believe in the sands of time, so to speak. Especially in America, when you confront the so-called mainstream, it's very inefficient, and in every way destroys you and disarms you. I'm still a believer in subversion. I don't think we're numerous enough, whoever "we" are, to take them by storm.

By the end of *Storyteller,* Silko appears to be a Coyote figure herself, as she subverts the dominant representations of history, power, and knowledge.

Finally, I want to raise a question: is it possible for white or non-Indian literary critics, or any critics in white academic institutions, to resist a reading practice that appropriates and diffuses Native American literature and its potentially subversive differences? As Fabian argues, objectification through distancing in time is not just a part of anthropology; it is part of Western epistemology. So although moving the study of Native American literature from the domain of anthropology to departments of English may be an improvement—a recognition that Native American art exists as art—the study still remains in the domain of the colonizer (and here I mean institutions more than individuals). Wendy Rose, a Hopi poet and anthropologist, refers to the current "literary-colonial canon" as another form of "cultural imperialism." To revise Fabian's subtitle, how does literary criticism make its object, and is it possible to avoid objectification in our practice?

I have tried to suggest in this paper that one way to treat these stories may be to ask how they might change us as subjects, as readers—to rephrase Silko's description of the storyteller's role: what story does this book draw out of us? The concept of double consciousness could give those of us who are part of the white institutional structure a means of reconsidering our own subject positions, of viewing ourselves differently. The African American theorist W. E. B. Du Bois identifies "double consciousness" as both a gift of second sight and as an unwelcome psychological repercussion of racism; he describes "this sense of always looking at one's self through the eyes of others, of measuring one's soul by the tape of a world that looks on in amused contempt and pity." Autoethnography is, in some sense, an act of double consciousness, a means of addressing the disparity between the two perceptions. The autoethnography, if it does capture the attention of the subjects in the "dominant" social position or institutions, can impose on those readers a "second sight" that reveals their own misunderstandings and misrepresentations of others and of themselves. In the process of initiating the reader in *Storyteller,* Silko puts the reader (and especially the Euroamerican reader) into this self-critical situation. The Native American perspective and interpretive context that Silko creates puts white readers in the position of feeling the humour *and* the discomfort of our historical roles and responsibilities. For the subject in the so-called "dominant" social position or institution to take on the responsibility of double consciousness may make possible a less authoritative and a more self-conscious approach to our own reading practice.

Perhaps it will also lead us to rethink our conception of the United States, replacing the vision of an inviolable, "indivisible" political, economic, and ideological entity with a vision of fragmented nation, a contact zone, in which colonized nations are demanding their land and their sovereignty, demanding that international laws and treaties be upheld. And maybe our ideas of contemporaneity as well as of the future will change. In this regard, I conclude with Silko's ideas about the future:

> The Pueblo people, of course, have seen intruders come and intruders go. The first they watched come were the Spaniards . . . But as the old stories say, if you wait long enough, they'll go. And sure enough, they went. Then another bunch came in. And old stories say, well, if you wait around long enough, not so much that they'll go, but at least their ways will go. One wonders now, when you see what's happening to technocratic-industrial culture, now that we've used up most of the sources of energy, you think perhaps the old people were right.

Perhaps we need to learn a Pueblo vision for the future, for the survival of all of us.

Karen L. Wallace (essay date 1996)

SOURCE: "Liminality and Myth in Native American Fiction: *Ceremony* and *The Ancient Child,*" in *American Indian Culture and Research Journal,* Vol. 20, No. 4, 1996, pp. 91-119.

[*In the following essay, Wallace discusses Silko's* Ceremony *and N. Scott Momaday's* The Ancient Child *and states that the novels "are attempts to articulate the survival of those people who are known as indians."*]

An indian [Wallace explains in a footnote that "For the purposes of this paper, I will use *indian* rather than *Indian* to defamiliarize the term and to refocus attention on the history on which its significance depends"] identity is a tricky thing to define. It is perhaps debatable whether it should be defined at all. As a construct imposed on the indigenous peoples of the Americas, the conceptualization of the indian is fraught with problems. How does one determine who exactly is indian and, perhaps more importantly, who is responsible for that designation? Further, what is the distinction between, for example, a Sioux indian and a Cherokee indian? How can they both be indian yet not the same? The list of questions is infinite. Nevertheless, there are college courses on American indian studies and sections in bookstores on Native Americans that exist ostensibly to study this vague character. "In spite of its wide acceptance, even appropriation, by Native Americans," writes Louis Owens, "it should be borne in mind that the word *Indian* came into being on this continent simply as an utterance designed to impose a distinct 'otherness' upon indigenous peoples. To be 'Indian' was to be 'not European.'" Indigenous peoples, now Indians, are all the same by virtue of this "othering." Pantribalism is based on this very concept of "sameness": In relation to the U.S. and its history of expansion, non-indians perceive native peoples as an undifferentiated whole, a view sometimes shared, though for different reasons, by indians themselves.

Thus there has been a tendency in American scholarship to cling to either the myth of the Noble Savage or the idea that indians are, in a social darwinistic kind of way, a dying race. These presumptions deny the diverse and continuing experiences of those natives who have survived, often thriving in our contemporary society. "Early novels by American Indian novelists," comments Paula Gunn Allen, "leaned heavily on the same theme of the dying savage partly because it was most acceptable to potential publishers. In addition, popular and scholarly images of Indians as conquered, dying people had deeply affected American Indian self-perception, leading even Indian novelists to focus their works on that stereotype." This tendency is perhaps easiest to explain by virtue of the fact that it is difficult to talk intelligently about specific native groups, given pervasive ignorance and cultural myths. The indian—who is this simple and apparently doomed creature?

Stereotypes of Native Americans are, like other misconceptions, often based on some bit of truth. There were and are indians who drink just as there are indians who are noble or perhaps even savage. They are Cherokee and Navajo and Winnebago. They live in San Francisco or in Detroit, in Navajoland or at Jemez. They are full-bloods and mixed-bloods, "apple" indians and fancy dancers. Which of them is the most, or most authentically, Indian?

Many authors, including the most frequently taught writers such as Leslie Marmon Silko, N. Scott Momaday, or James Welch, write of an indian who is invariably male and of mixed racial descent, apparently ill-equipped to function in either Native America or Anglo America. "[I]t is through iso-lated alienated men," writes Judy Antell, "that the authors are able to demonstrate the negative severity of the twentieth century on the lives of Indian people. Indian men are more suited than Indian women to the notion of the 'vanishing savage.'" These novels are attempts to articulate the survival of those people who are known as indians. In challenging the myths of the Noble Savage or the drunken indian by contextualizing and historicizing them, these works are able to create a space within the margin that redetermines liminality and its potential for the reconstruction of self. In discussion of her own writing on marginality, bell hooks writes, "I was not speaking of a marginality one wishes to lose, to give up, or surrender as part of moving into the center, but rather as a site one stays in, clings to even, because it nourishes one's capacity to resist. It offers the possibility of radical perspectives from which to see and create. . . ." *Ceremony* by Leslie Marmon Silko and *The Ancient Child* by N. Scott Momaday are novels written according to this line of reasoning: By gaining competence in their tribal communities, the protagonists also acquire a renewed and secure sense of self that allows them to participate successfully in the dominant culture as well.

The interstices of culture that these figures inhabit do not represent the exile that Edward Said describes as "the unhealable rift forced between a human being and a native place, between the self and its true home," but rather the site of resistance that bell hooks advocates. Some of these characters are conspicuous within their tribal communities by phenotype, distinguishable by traits such as light-colored eyes, like Tayo in Silko's *Ceremony* or Grey in Momaday's *The Ancient Child,* but all are marginalized by virtue of their acculturation, by immersion in non-Indian culture and its institutions. As such, they are, at first glance, modern versions of the Noble Savage who can attain mental and physical health only by returning to their traditions—ceremonies and lifeways that require a return to the reservation and an almost total rejection of modern cultural adaptations. The indian is relegated to the past, to Said's exile. As Gunn Allen comments,

> Indians used the colonization theme coupled with the western plot structure of conflict-crisis-resolution to tell their own stories largely because these structures appeared to explain tribal life and its chaotic disorganization since invasion and colonization. In such westernized Indian novels the Indians are portrayed as tragic heroes, beset by an unjust but inexorable fate. . . . In all of the novels that use the story of conquest, devastation, and genocide as their major theme, white civilization plays the antagonist and becomes imbued with demonic power reserved in classic literature to fate and the gods.

While it is important, necessary, to reclaim and celebrate

one's traditions and heritage, there is a significant danger if the cost is the refusal or even the inability to participate in the modern world. Thus the communities to which these protagonists return are vulnerable to the technological and political incursions of a twentieth-century United States, but they are not destroyed. They remain viable options as places of origin and of future for indians.

These authors also demonstrate the capacity indians have to process what is useful from both worlds to create a functional social system that incorporates both tradition and innovation. As Vine Deloria, Jr., comments, "[W]e have seen the appearance of young people who have found a way to blend the requirements of modern industrial consumer life with traditional beliefs and practices." This, I would argue, is not a new phenomenon but rather a newly appreciated one. It is because of the success of indians writing about themselves that both indian and non-indian have had a basis from which to critique and also appreciate what it means to be indian. From D'Arcy McNickle to Wendy Rose, indians represent themselves in a variety of scenes that illustrate their achievements and concomitant survival.

"We are what we imagine," says N. Scott Momaday, "Our very existence consists in our imagination of ourselves. . . . The greatest tragedy that can befall us is to go unimagined." Silko and Momaday, who are themselves acculturated and of mixed racial descent, write of indians who perhaps define themselves or allow themselves to be defined in this way. For those indians who are not, at first glance, recognizable as such, there is a need and at times a demand to assert their ethnic identification. Consequently, in the frequent controversy over who is "really" indian, these novels are, in both content and structure, representative of a unique and evolving genre of writing particular to Native Americans in the U.S. that is in large part a response to this challenge to identity and cultural accommodation. They are in many ways a reclamation of the term *indian* and an attempt to imbue the construct with positive and inclusive characteristics.

The characters presented in these texts occupy fluid positions within and between the cultural spheres they inhabit. They remain in the interstices of cultures yet are still able to function as liaison or at least mediator between more than one system of living in which they feel competent, in the manner of Malcolm McFee's "150% Man":

> [I]ndividuals may learn new ways without abandoning the old. . . . Frequently they occupy important roles as mediators between white and Indian societies; they live with Indians and maintain Indian identity, yet are well educated and capable of competing successfully in the white community. . . . In the perspective of this article, the traditional prob-

lems of the "marginal man" can be seen as advantages rather than liabilities. Rather than being "lost between two cultures," those persons with bicultural capabilities can be seen as having unique combinations of skills which may serve the advantage of both Indian and white society.

This perspective allows for a position within tribal society from which indians who are acculturated or who define themselves as mixed-bloods can function without denying any aspect of their experience. These characters transform the margins from a space in which they are powerless to sites from which to resist. In turn, their liminality and the process of transformation force those in the center to acknowledge the margins as sites of action.

Victor Turner writes in his discussion of ritual,

> Liminality, marginality, and structural inferiority are conditions in which are frequently generated myths, symbols, rituals, philosophical systems, and works of art. These cultural forms provide men with a set of templates or models which are, at one level, periodical reclassifications of reality and man's relationship to society, nature and culture. But they are more than classifications, since they incite men to action as well as to thought.

For the American indian of mixed descent, the novel is a means by which to articulate and reconceptualize the social pressures affecting marginalized peoples. Due to the radical changes native peoples have undergone and continue to experience, the mixed-blood often survives in this liminal position as a nonparticipant. Consequently, mixed-bloods in particular (again, often read as acculturated indians) are central to contemporary indian fiction as a new space in which to "act and to incite action." They are able to reconcile the tensions between the dominant culture and native traditions by using a tribal perspective from which to view that which is alien to it and to themselves.

In each of these novels, traditional paradigms of ritual and myth mediate the dominant tropes of cultural incompatibility and psychological trauma. It is this synthesis that allows Silko and Momaday to recontextualize the interstices of culture as liminal space. The "indian novel" is a work by an indian writer that explores or reflects the difficulty of making the margins a site of resistance. Although it adapts various techniques of the *bildungsroman,* it is unique in that it retains much in the way of non-Western form and content (most generally referred to as the oral tradition). "Literature," as Gunn Allen stresses," must, of necessity, express and articulate the deepest perceptions, relationships, and attitudes of a culture, whether it does so deliberately or accidentally. . . . What are held to be the most meaningful experiences of human life, from levels which completely transcend ordinary experience to those which are commonplace, are those experiences celebrated in the songs and cycles of the people." Authors such as Silko and Momaday are successful in incorporating these aspects of their tribal heritages to redefine and affirm who indians are without qualification.

In the novels *Ceremony* and *The Ancient Child,* the mixed-blood protagonists are psychically split between cultures and, consequently, are unable to maintain any enduring sense of self. The ultimate solution in each comes to be an acknowledgment of tradition and of his own power in that context following a rupture or violent upheaval. Each character's process depends on the conscious assimilation of those elements in himself that are modern and/or "American" through a native framework. This resolution is most explicit in Leslie Silko's novel *Ceremony.*

As she constructs her story of Tayo, a Pueblo mixed-blood, Silko weaves a Laguna creation story into her narrative to illustrate Tayo's affliction. The stories are inseparable, yet remain distinct and parallel until the end, when Tayo's story enters the mythic framework, the very process reflecting Tayo's recovery. For example, Silko begins the novel by writing,

> Ts'its'tsi'nako, Thought-Woman,
>   is sitting in her room
>   and whatever she thinks about
>   appears.
>
>   . . .
>
>   She is sitting in her room
>   thinking of a story now
>
>   I'm telling you the story
>   she is thinking.
>   . . .
>
>   *What She Said:*
>   The only cure
>   I know
>   is a good ceremony,
>   that's what she said.

The structure of the narrative is thus self-referential and conspicuous, pointing to ritual; Silko reconstructs the protagonist's story in her vision of a native framework, as part of the Laguna worldview and experience. The two stories, so different in form, refer one to the other in content and emphasize the fact that Tayo's life depends on his mastering certain responsibilities within the Laguna community and reconciling them with his experiences off-reservation.

Modern indian texts tend to incorporate the oral tradition through a traditional paradigm: Silko's novel *Ceremony* is ostensibly Tayo's story expressed through a Western narra-

tive form, yet because Tayo cannot establish a sense of balance or belonging, Silko integrates clan stories of Reed Woman and Corn Woman. As Silko's narrative progresses, we can see how Tayo is living the stories and that his recovery depends on the completion of the proper ceremony. As Susan Perez Castillo writes, "[T]he text emerges, not as a passive mirror of reality, but as a space in which two or more distinct and often mutually exclusive worlds battle for supremacy." Thus, in terms of the novel as a space for action, the story is Tayo's as well as Silko's own.

Silko introduces Tayo as he returns to the pueblo from a veteran's hospital in Los Angeles. A veteran of World War II, he comes home to find the community devastated by drought. Tayo is sure that he is responsible, but he does not know how to repair the damage. He believes that his prayers, made so far from home, have caused the drought in much the same way that Corn Woman causes the water to disappear:

> Corn Woman got tired of that
>   she got angry
>   she scolded
>   for bathing all day long.
>   Iktoa'ak'o'ya-Reed Woman
>   went away then
>   she went back
> to the original place down below.
> And there was no more rain then. . . .

Tayo is significantly aware of his place as a Pueblo indian but is totally unable to express that identity because he is estranged from his family and their community.

Raised by his aunt, Tayo feels guilty, too, for having returned alive from the war in which his cousin Rocky, her son, was killed. The terms in which Silko defines his guilt are indicative of the trouble Tayo has reconciling vastly divergent cultural values and, therein, understanding his sickness:

> It didn't take Tayo long to see the accident of time and space: Rocky was the one who was alive, buying Grandma her heater. . . . Rocky was there in the college game scores on the sportspage. . . . It was him, Tayo, who had died, but somehow there had been a mistake with the corpses, and somehow his was still unburied.

Tayo had never been perceived as a contributing member of either the household or the community, having inherited the alienation his mother had both suffered and caused. Presented as a consequence of his mixed blood, Tayo's alienation is compounded by his inability to master either American or Laguna codes of behavior. Therefore, when Tayo returns, Rocky's death only aggravates his situation.

It is Tayo, not Rocky, his aunt seems firmly to believe, who should have been sacrificed. Because of her anger and despair at having lost her only son, Tayo is left on the edges of both his aunt's and the community's life. He is denied because his presence only provokes the sorrow of their loss.

Following his return from the hospital, and in reaction to his liminal status, Tayo is emotionally paralyzed. He has no tools with which to ameliorate his situation, and he realizes the extent to which Rocky's success in school had neutralized his own perceived failure. Finally it is Tayo's grandmother who addresses his alienation and isolation and proposes a solution. She sends him to a medicine man, Betonie, a mixed-blood who successfully negotiates the margins of cultures, maintaining a position in each through his liminal status. Betonie initiates the ceremony revealed at the start of the narrative; through his intervention and care, Tayo regains substance and power and ultimately becomes a significant and active force in his community.

Marked as "other" by his light eyes, Tayo is the legacy of an absent Mexican father. It is via this trait that he "sees" his marginality at Laguna:

> "I always wished I had dark eyes like other people. When they look at me they remember things that happened. . . ." His throat felt tight. He had not talked about this before with anyone. . . . "They are afraid, Tayo. They feel something happening, they can see something happening around them, and it scares them. Indians or Mexicans or whites—most people are afraid of change. They think that if their children have the same color of skin, the same color of eyes, that nothing is changing. . . . They are fools. They blame us, the ones who look different."

Tayo's identification with Betonie, a mixed-blood Navajo, intensifies his discomfort. An outsider because he is mixed and because he is Navajo, Betonie is able to utilize resources that Tayo does not know how to access. Cognizant as he is of his liminal position as well as its concomitant power, Betonie can articulate the need to synthesize seemingly disparate and, at times, contradictory modes of both thought and behavior; he is an outsider, but he is still indian. His seemingly irrelevant collection of junk symbolizes his facility with the material information of Anglo culture:

> (Tayo) could see bundles of newspapers, their edges curled and stiff and brown, barricading piles of telephone books with the years scattered among cities. . . . He wanted to dismiss all of it as an old man's rubbish, debris that had fallen out of the years, but the boxes and trunks, the bundles and stacks were plainly part of the pattern.

At first Tayo is reluctant to trust the man, but Betonie is reassuring:

> All along there had been something familiar about the old man. Tayo turned around then to figure out what it was. . . .
>
> He looked at his face. . . . Then Tayo looked at his eyes. They were hazel like his own.

Tayo manages to describe his stay at the hospital in Los Angeles for Betonie, to explain the difficulty he is experiencing:

> "They sent me to this place after the war. It was white. Everything in that place was white. Except for me. I was invisible. . . . Maybe I belong back in that place." Betonie answers, "Die that way and get it over with. . . . In that hospital they don't bury the dead, they keep them in rooms and talk to them."

Betonie confronts Tayo's insecurities and passivity in the face of his supposed worthlessness. He shows Tayo that he must reconnect with the memory of his mother as an indian woman and with the landscape of his people. Only then can Tayo accept his liminality and transform it into a productive space: His is "a transformation from the 'undead' to marginal/powerful."

As Victor Turner states,

> The attributes of liminality or of liminal personae ("threshold people") are necessarily ambiguous, since this condition and these persons elude or slip through the network of classifications that normally locate states and positions in cultural space. Liminal entities are neither here nor there; they are betwixt and between the positions assigned and arrayed by law, custom, convention and ceremonial. As such, their ambiguous and indeterminate attributes are expressed by a rich variety of symbols in the many societies that ritualize social and cultural transitions.

Accordingly, Betonie is literally between worlds, yet still participates in each. He lives alone in the hills above Gallup, New Mexico, a troubled community in the midst of Navajoland:

> "People ask me why I live here," he said, in good English, "I tell them I want to keep track of the people." "Why over here?" they ask me. "Because this is where Gallup keeps Indians until Ceremonial time. Then they want to show us off to the tourists."

He is on the edges of Gallup, but also of his own community, not because he is mixed, although this is the most convenient reason, but because of his stable identity as a "breed." In a ritualized context, as Turner indicates, difference takes on connotations of power as well as danger.

The mythic structure that Silko juxtaposes with Tayo's story supersedes a world in which most indians are poor and trapped in circumstances not of their own making. "[In the] fusion of the universal and the personal, the spiritual and the secular," writes Kristin Herzog, "identity is established and rootedness revealed. But it is seldom an individualistic identity, and Tayo, after being reintegrated into his tribe, in no way resembles the isolated, individualistic male protagonist of many American novels." As he regains his health, Tayo becomes aware of himself as being responsible to and part of his community. Thought Woman's words then envelop a history with which Tayo must come to terms and in which it is crucial that he participate.

In *Ceremony,* the consequences of European/Anglo expansion are never far from the consciousness of the author and do much to inform the text. When Tayo searches for his uncle's stolen cattle, for example, he finally understands his position in the superficial hierarchy that he had never before thought to question:

> (Tayo) was thinking about the cattle and how they had ended up on Floyd Lee's land. If he had seen the cattle on land-grant land or in some Acoma's corral, he wouldn't have hesitated to say "stolen." But something inside him made him hesitate to say it now that the cattle were on a white man's ranch.... Why did he hesitate to accuse a white man of stealing but not a Mexican or an Indian?

As he becomes aware of his increasing power, Tayo is able to articulate for himself the circumstances against which the pueblo is struggling and, through this articulation, make it a part of the story over which he is beginning to exert influence.

The factors that necessitate acculturation—for example, leaving the reservation to seek work, or accepting severalty and attempting to master non-Indian systems of land management—put into question tribal affiliation and, concomitantly, rights or access to federal aid. Therefore, due to the legal definitions of *indianness* that recognize native peoples by their relationship to the federal government, of which Silko is as aware as she is of Laguna constructs regulating social/cultural mores, mixed-bloods were and are in a necessarily awkward position. It is by establishing the legacy of U.S.-indian relations within the context of a Laguna narrative structure that Silko redefines what it is to be indian and the extent to which the boundaries of definition can be pushed: Tayo is indian not because of the color of his eyes or skin, but because of his inherent connection to the story Silko presents and therein to his people and their land.

Tayo's experience is analogous to the experience of the Laguna people as a whole, as tribal nations are forced to enter—often unsuccessfully and certainly with difficulty—into the mainstream of American culture. As Tayo relearns his own heritage and traditions, he adapts them to current circumstances without ignoring the purposes for which they were initially created. Tayo's experience with the ceremony represents his transition from a passive, disenfranchised position to an active and powerful, liminal one in which he is aware of his own agency. Thus, as Tayo re-engages with Laguna society through the bear cure, Silko mirrors the process of his healing with her story of the emergence of evil into the world and the pueblo's subsequent efforts to protect against it, if not to control it. We see the history of interaction between the U.S. and Laguna Pueblo through Silko's vision of Laguna cosmology. She writes, for example,

> Long time ago
> in the beginning
> there were no white people in this world
> there was nothing European.
> And this world might have gone on like that
> except for one thing:
> witchery.
> This world was already complete
> even without white people.
> There was everything
> including witchery.

The myths she creates, told as a related series of events that shape the Laguna worldview, confirm each time the self-referential and thus ritual nature of the book as well as Tayo's experience as a Laguna. As Betonie comments in response to the horrific circumstances in Gallup,

> "It strikes me funny, ... people wondering why I live so close to this filthy town. But see, this hogan was here first. Built long before the white people ever came. It is that town down there which is out of place. Not this old medicine man."

Tayo overcomes his suspicions by accepting what seem to him at first to be serious contradictions. Yet Betonie remarks to him,

> "That is the trickery of witchcraft.... They want us to believe all evil resides with white people. Then we will look no further to see what is really happening. They want us to separate ourselves from white people, to be ignorant and helpless as we

watch our own destruction. But white people are only tools that the witchery manipulates."

It is Tayo's responsibility to learn enough about Laguna tradition to challenge the witchery. Silko impresses upon the reader that, because Tayo embraces Laguna culture as a means by which to understand the world as a whole, his experience both on and off the reservation is conflated into one and thus is intelligible. In the end, as a liminal being and a ritual transgressor, Tayo must survive a crisis that foments the moment of his ascension to power: "He knew why he felt weak and sick; he knew why he had lost the feeling Ts'eh had given him, and why he had doubted the ceremony: this was their place, and he was vulnerable." To be healthy, Tayo must reconcile the fragments of his past. Thus he recalls the history of the pueblo, of uranium mining, and of the detonation of the atomic bomb:

> [Tayo] cried with the relief he felt at finally seeing the pattern, the way all the stories fit together—the old stories, the war stories, their stories—to become the story that was still being told. He was not crazy; he had never been crazy. He had only seen and heard the world as it always was: no boundaries, only transitions through all distances and time.

From this realization comes the decision to accept his place in the story and guard against the witchery and the destroyers. Unfortunately, it is not the U.S. government or even the Navajo who are the enemy, but Laguna people themselves. Tayo must resist his supposed friends to overcome the drought:

> He smelled a fire and saw three figures bending over a small fire . . . Leroy, Pinkie, and Emo . . . The destroyers. They would be there all night, he knew it, working for drought to sear the land . . . leaving the people more and more vulnerable to the lies.

Tayo, who is sick and afraid, watches as his three friends kill Harley, the man who failed to secure Tayo as the sacrificial victim and must therefore take his place. It is finally clear to Tayo that the ritual of the Laguna Pueblo and adherence to tradition are his cure. The problem, Silko demonstrates, is not white people but rather those Laguna who refuse to trust in their community and the history that binds them. Tayo's failure, in other words, would not have made the dominant culture, but rather the pueblo itself, culpable:

> At home the people would blame liquor, the Army, and the war, but the blame on the whites would never match the vehemence the people would keep in their own bellies, reserving the greatest bitterness and blame for themselves, for one of themselves they could not save.

Thus Tayo can reclaim power and agency for himself and for his people.

In light of the implicit refusal or even inability of many indian people to participate off-reservation, Tayo and Betonie, "threshold people," are powerful and essential to their communities as they mediate between cultures. They transform the margins into powerful space, allowing for a self-awareness from which indians may assert themselves. Thus Silko writes, "The witchery would be at work all night so that the people would see only the losses . . . since the whites came. . . . [T]he old priests would be afraid too, and cling to ritual without making new ceremonies as they always had before." "He had seen them now and he was certain; he could go back to tell the people." Tayo, in completing his cure, sees the position he may occupy within the tribe as a liminal and active one. After this crisis of identity, Tayo returns home, literally and figuratively:

> His body was lost in exhaustion; he kept moving, his bones and skin staggering behind him. He dreamed with his eyes open that he was wrapped in a blanket in the back of Josiah's wagon. . . . Josiah was driving the wagon, old Grandma was holding him, and Rocky whispered "my brother." They were taking him home.

Ku'oosh invites Tayo to tell his story to the "old men" and, as his grandmother comments later, "It seems like I already heard these stories before. . . . [O]nly thing is, the names sound different." Much of Tayo's anguish stems from the fact that he is a mixed-blood; his aunt took him in because of his mother's alcoholism, but she never lets him forget what he owes her or the shame he keeps in the family. Mixed-bloods, a real consequence of colonization, are in a position to bridge the chasm between cultures. However, before Tayo can act in this capacity, he must come to terms with the fact that he equates his indianness with loss. Therefore, he makes the whole of his experience, including the time spent in the Pacific Islands, part of a liminal context: Tayo can never change the color of his eyes or the circumstances of his birth, or even his exposure to the dominant culture, but he possesses and acts upon the ability to make his marginality a part of his identity as a Laguna. His aunt, too, despite herself, accepts Tayo as family and they are able to move forward together:

> Auntie talked to him now the way she had talked to Robert and old Grandma all those years, with an edge of accusation about to surface between her words. But after old man Ku'oosh had come around, her eyes dropped from his face as if there were nothing left to watch for.

The invitation to enter the kiva and participate in the ceremony signifies acceptance and integration. Tayo reestablishes kinship and community ties, emphasizing the significant relationship between the two, and secures himself as an integral member of the pueblo.

In his novel *The Ancient Child,* N. Scott Momaday also attempts to resolve the conflicts of the mixed-blood by melding the traditions of native and Anglo America. Like Silko, Momaday structures his novel to incorporate myth and weave the past with the present. For example, book 1 of *The Ancient Child,* entitled "Planes," exposes the multiple levels of consciousness that inform the story. The narrative traverses time and space to allow for the mythic framework that determines the fate of Momaday's protagonists. He begins, following a list of the characters, with the "Kiowa story of Tsoai," the story of the genesis of the Big Dipper: The transformation of the boy into the bear, whose metamorphosis is the catalyst for the formation of the Pleiades, is the focal point of Momaday's narrative. He therefore presents the bear, "the mythic embodiment of wilderness," from the worldview of the Kiowa, establishing a native cosmology as normative before beginning his own narrative.

Set, like Tayo, is estranged, yet the integration of past with present, and Anglo with indian lore, creates a liminal space for Set to occupy within Momaday's story: "The main protagonist and the major turning points of his life," writes M. M. Bakhtin, "are to be found *outside everyday life.* He merely observes this life, meddles in it now and then as an alien force, he occasionally even dons a common and everyday mask—but in essence he does not participate in this life and is not determined by it." As in Silko's text, there is a larger sacred narrative of which these characters are a part and with which they must be reconciled, which in turn determines their mundane, daily experience. Set's fate depends on his acting within Kiowa narrative space, not within "everyday life." "As in traditional storytelling," comments Louis Owens,

> we know the outcome of the story at the beginning, a fact that should shift our attention to the performance itself, to the way the story is told. An audience schooled in Native American storytelling will recognize in the prologue the typical pattern of the questing culture hero and realize that the well-known outline of a traditional story is being adapted to comprehend contemporary circumstances.

Momaday's manipulation of a variety of perspectives is consequently an interesting example of Bakhtin's chronotope as the defining feature of the novel: Set's ultimate transformation into the bear depends on the fluidity and confluence of space and time within the narrative.

Momaday reinforces the centrality of ritual by framing his narrative with both historical and mythic stories. From the mythic time during which the world was first created, Momaday jumps to the more recent past of Billy the Kid, circa 1881, and on again to the present. In this novel, Set and Grey occupy the margins and make them into a productive space, their combined experience effecting a change similar to that in *Ceremony.* They are both outside everyday life, yet they are able to participate and they are expected to do so.

Locke Setman—Set—a middle-aged painter of Kiowa descent, was raised in California by his Anglo guardian, Bent Sandridge, "a retired man, humane and wise." His father's death estranged Set from his heritage and prevented his connecting with or integrating the past. The theme of the indigenous man estranged from his tribal roots through acculturation is emphasized in this work far beyond Silko's novel. Set, raised in an urban center, is aware of his indianness through a somewhat haphazard recollection of his parents and the stories his father told, decontextualized and thereby stripped of significance. He has no idea how to implement the ideals or cultural information the stories impart. Significantly, Set's mother, who was not indian, represents his despair. It is in terms of her absence that Set perceives his sickness. Momaday introduces Set in the throes of some psychic illness brought on by this estrangement from his traditions:

> In Loki [Set] there was a certain empty space, a longing for something beyond memory. He thought often of his mother, dead almost the whole of his life. He knew she was not the pale, lewd ghost of his dreams; she was the touchstone of his belief in the past. Without knowing her, he knew of her having been. . . . Her reality was that of everything on the bygone side of his existence.

A singular awareness of his power as it is manifested in his art supplants the success by which Set has learned to measure his life: "Art—drawing, painting—is an intelligence of some kind, the hand and eye bringing the imagination down upon the picture plane; and in this a nearly perfect understanding of the act of understanding." Yet, as the first signs of his transformation begin to show, Set becomes afraid and disoriented, bereft of any source of self-definition. His Anglo upbringing and concomitant alienation cause his transformation to be something foreign and frightening: Locke Setman had not thought of himself as indian before and must become Kiowa, using his artistic talents to process that identity. Although he has a vague awareness of the Bear through the myth his father told him about the boy/bear and his sisters, Set, in San Francisco, is surrounded by people for whom his "illness" means little more than a loss of revenue. It is next to impossible, then, for his metamorphosis to be completed in the city:

[T]here was insinuated upon his consciousness and subconsciousness the power of the bear. It was *his* bear power, but he did not yet have real knowledge of it, only a vague, instinctive awareness, a sense he could neither own nor dispel. He was afflicted. He was losing his physical strength . . . or he was losing control over the strength within him . . . He could not tell anyone what was wrong, for he did not know.

Before his role is revealed to him, Set necessarily withdraws. Never having known his native community, he becomes less and less sure of himself without understanding why:

[T]here was a conviction in him, and a commitment to be his own man. And therefore he struggled. Now, at forty-four, he found himself in a difficult position. He had compromised more than he knew . . . [H]e had become sick and tired. . . . Yes, he had become sick and tired. And he did the only thing he could think to do under the circumstances; he withdrew—not completely, not all at once, but deliberately. . . . He would endeavor to save his soul.

Unlike Tayo, who is socialized in a system with which he is familiar and to which he returns, Set resists "becoming" indian because it seems so thoroughly foreign. Ultimately, however, he has no choice. Despite himself, and very much like Tayo, he is overcome by the process:

I did not let the unknown define my existence, intrude upon my purpose, if I could help it. But now there was an intrusion that I could not identify and could not resist. Something seemed to be taking possession of me. It was a subtle and pernicious thing; I wasn't myself. . . . I began to feel helpless now.

Set's identity is broken down almost completely and reconstituted under Grey's influence. Ritualizing his experience is the way to reconceptualize and then reintegrate his past in terms of an unfamiliar cultural framework. Once he "returns" home to Oklahoma, it is his identity as a painter and the skills he perfected as an artist that allow him to make a successful change. From the crisis he survives, Set emerges as a person of power.

With more complex concerns about her European heritage than either Set or Tayo, Grey is an indian woman, a powerful seer, who has embraced and takes pride in her difference. A mixed-blood of Navajo, Kiowa, and Scottish descent, she remains outside the core existence of her family, despite her power and the apparent ease with which she traverses boundaries. "In Grey," suggests Owens, "Momaday illustrates the act of appropriation essential to the marginalized culture that

would wrest authenticity away from the authoritative center. Within the rich heteroglossia of her Kiowa-Navajo-Euramerican life, Grey rejects the world's deadly narrative of epic 'Indianness' with its tragic implications." As a seer, she is of course susceptible to visions, and it is significant that they include Billy the Kid. Throughout the novel, there is an ongoing, supplementary story in which Grey is Billy the Kid's lover and sometime accomplice. Momaday has said that Grey "finds great satisfaction in assuming the dimensions of the stereotype. So she goes around affecting western dialect. She fantasizes about Billy the Kid and talks about him a lot." Thus, while Momaday never explicitly states the purpose of this counternarrative in his plot, it seems indicative of a struggle over which Grey has little control, although it is not necessarily disruptive.

The counternarrative becomes most significant when, early in the novel, Grey is raped by a white man, her lover's father. She is jolted from a vision of Billy the Kid into the realization of being brutalized:

In this unspeakable happening she was forced for the first time to a hatred of the world, of herself, of life itself. . . . In some feeble resistance she thought of Dog, of how Dog would trample into dust the flesh and bones of this despicable, vicious man. In her delirium, because she so needed, she saw Dwight Dicks looking up into the muzzles of the gun in Billy's hands, seeing beyond them the expressionless, nearly colorless, steady, steady eyes. . . .

The catalyst for Grey's maturation as a medicine person is this assault, precipitating a moment in which her various identities merge. Mirroring Tayo's confrontation with the destroyers in *Ceremony* and Set's total disintegration of self, Grey's rape is a moment of transgression, the blurring or even obliteration of boundaries. Her vision of love-making with Billy the Kid merges with the brutality of Dwight's attack. Thus, in the same way that Set is no longer able to compartmentalize disparate aspects of his life and is thereby incapacitated, Grey's dream life is shattered by the violence of her waking life. Just as Set must confront his identity as the Bear, Dwight's assault on Grey provokes the fusion of the discrete fragments of her perception. It is from this crisis that she perceives clearly, and accepts, her power as a liminal being.

Grey, in imposing order on her world, is able to exact revenge on the man, but it is thoughts of Billy the Kid, not any traditional native culture hero, that sustain her. Once she has freed herself from this devastating scene, it is a feminine image from her heritage that reconfirms her power: "Then, still naked, she rode the horse Dog hard to the river and bathed herself for a long time. There was an orange moon. There was the voice of the grandmother on the water."

In his treatise on eroticism, Georges Bataille writes that the violence inherent in the sex act foments an instance of the continuity that he claims is the dissolution of the self: "[T]he individual splits up and his [sic] unity is shattered from the first instance of the sexual crisis." "The urge," Bataille goes on to say, "is first of all a natural one but it cannot be given free rein without barriers being torn down, so much so that the natural urge and the demolished obstacles are confused in the mind. . . . Demolished barriers are not the same as death, but just as the violence of death overturns—irrevocably—the structure of life so temporarily does sexual violence." He writes of transgression—therefore, that "[c]ontinuity is reached when boundaries are crossed. But the most constant characteristic of the impulse I have called transgression is to make order out of what is essentially chaos. By introducing transcendence into an organized world, transgression becomes a principle of an organized disorder. The work of the liminal being is to make sense of chaos, to control (or at least to interpret) what is otherwise inaccessible to the community.

Bataille's discussion, in many ways a critique of Catholicism, sheds light on *The Ancient Child*'s ritualized violence. Momaday, like Silko, foreshadows the ultimate syncretism that is Set's and Grey's solution by incorporating traditional elements alongside images of American culture, including representations of the church. In this novel, Set's recollections of his father and the stories he told are juxtaposed with memories of Sister Stella, the nun at the orphanage where he lived until his adoption. As Momaday writes, "And then Cate [his father] was gone. Set could not clearly remember the sequence of things. There was Sister Stella Francesca, who appeared to him in his dreams. . . . It had been difficult for him to leave the Peter and Paul home. Curious. . . . But he loved [Sister Stella], for he was a child, and there was no one else to love. And Set remembered. It is an important story, I think, Cate said, all those years ago." Momaday is able to illustrate that, despite the problems besieging indian communities, there remains a constant tie to the past that serves to support the people as they create new ways that blend traditional culture and adaptations of Western culture. The centrality of ritualized violence—a significant aspect of Catholicism—as a means of transformation is crucial to an interpretation of *The Ancient Child.*

Momaday prefaces his novel with a quote from Luis Borges: "For myth is at the beginning of literature, and also at its end." Then comes the story of the origin of the Big Dipper (Ursa Major), the transformation of the boy into a bear and the escape of his seven sisters into the sky to form the constellation. Accordingly, Set is equated with the bear and is literally transformed. "Most people cannot recover nature,"

says Momaday during an interview, "But this boy is an exception. He turns into a bear; that means that he reconstructs that link with nature. Significantly, we must interpret these characters with both tribal and Western mythology and folklore, the second viewed through the framework of the first. This ensnares Set and Grey and their story in the complicated experience of the author: "*Set,* my work in progress, is about the boy who turns into a bear, and in a sense I am writing about myself. I'm not writing an autobiography, but I am imagining a story that proceeds out of my own experience of the bear power." Even on his first trip to Oklahoma, for example, Set begins to feel the power of his Kiowa heritage:

> He had a strange feeling there, as if some ancestral
> intelligence had been awakened in him for the first
> time. There in the wild growth and the soft glow-
> ing of the earth, in the muddy water at his feet, was
> something profoundly original. It was itself genesis
> . . . not the genesis in the public domain, not an Old
> Testament tale, but *his* genesis."

Momaday describes Set's experience in terms of myriad traditions. Section 12, entitled "They sit so, like mother and child," evocative perhaps of the Pietà, ends with the calling forth, resurrection almost, of the bear: "The grandmother Kope'mah had begun to speak names: Set-page, Set-tainte, Set-angya, Set-mante. Setman. Set." As a complement to this image, Set's introduction in the following section begins with his disassociation from the persona he has constructed. Reflecting on his endeavors as a painter leads him to ponder the nature of God: "What sustains Him is the satisfaction, far deeper than we can know, of having created a few incomparables. . . . He used both hands when he made the bear. Imagine a bear proceeding from the hands of God!"

Correspondingly, Grey is reminiscent of the Lady Godiva, a figure steeped in the traditions of the West, when she rides past Dwight's barn, asking after his health following his "circumcision," the revenge she has taken on the man. She, naked and wearing a mask in the form of an "unearthly turtle," rides past on a horse named Dog. According to Barbara Walker, the original purpose of Lady Godiva's ride was to "renew her virginity," comparable to Grey's successful attempt to restore her sense of self following Dwight's assault. Thus Grey's ride on the horse called Dog is significant in several ways. Momaday comments,

> Dogs and horses are closely related in my mind. The
> horse . . . was called "Big Dog" by certain Indians
> in early times. And dogs were horses for the Kiowas
> before the horse came along. . . . So the dog is an
> ancient animal and a fascinating creature.

Walker also writes that dogs were most often considered

companions to goddesses and to powerful mortal women or witches and that they are associated with funerary customs: "In myth, dogs accompanied only the Goddess, guarding the gates of her afterworld, helping her to receive the dead."

In their association with death, horses allow for the possibility of rebirth and restoration. Walker states that they represent ritual sacrifice and the phallus or castration. For example, "Death was the significance of Father Odin's eight-legged gray horse Sleipnir, symbol of the gallows tree, where human sacrifices were hung in Odin's sacred groves. Skalds called the gallows 'high-chested rope-Sleipnir', the horse on which men rode to the land of death. . . ." Western narrative thus reconfirms the ritual nature of the violence Grey suffers and in turn inflicts. Additionally, the horse is related to Set, who is alternately known as the "Ass-headed Egyptian deity, once ruler of the pantheon" and the "Good Shepherd Osiris." These stories complete the underlying paradigm for their story. As Walker writes, "Set and Horus were remnants of a primitive sacred-king cult. . . . The story of the rival gods appeared in the Bible as Seth's supplanting of the sacrificed shepherd Abel." Grey, remarkable in part for her eyes, is linked to Horus, who became known as a female judge: "I am the all-seeing Eye of Horus." Set, when he comes to Oklahoma, usurps the place of Grey's boyfriend Murphy who, being Dwight's son, assumes guilt by association, and both father and son are expelled from her life. Balance is regained through adherence to tradition, the acceptance of "folk-mythological time."

In discussing the temporal-spatial dimension of the traditional Greek romance, of which *The Ancient Child* is reminiscent, Bakhtin writes,

> The novel as a whole is conceived precisely as a test of the heroes. Greek adventure-time . . . leaves no traces—neither in the world nor in human beings. No changes of any consequence occur, internal or external, as a result of the events recounted in the novel. At the end of the novel that initial equilibrium that had been destroyed by chance is restored once again. Everything returns to its own source. The result of this whole lengthy novel is that—the hero marries his sweetheart. And yet people and things have gone through something, something that did not, indeed, change them but that did . . . affirm what they, and precisely they, were as individuals, something that did verify and establish their identity, their durability and continuity. The hammer of events shatters nothing and forges nothing—it merely tries the durability of an already finished product.

The separation of real time from mythic time, the mundane from the sacred, becomes less definite and requires media-

tion. These threshold figures or liminal personae reside on the boundaries between; they belong to both and, as such, are inviolate within the larger story.

Ultimately, though, each character is inseparable from his or her tribal history and from the others: Set is the ancient child, and he needs Grey to help him come into the power of this position. Despite the other influences undoubtedly interspersed throughout Momaday's narrative, it is the story of the bear that provides the frame for the novel. Grey's power and vision allow Set to give up the ambiguity of the periphery, with its concomitant lack of responsibility, and enter into a tribal social structure. Grey has always been aware of her own agency and liminal status; as she admonishes Set while driving to their new home in Navajoland,

> "Don't imagine that you have a choice in the matter, in what is going on, and don't imagine that *I* have one either. You are *Set;* you are the bear; you will be the bear, no matter what. You will act accordingly, in the proper way, because there is no other way to act."

She, like Tayo, becomes part of a whole that is in itself marginal, deriving strength and power.

Momaday writes of Grey,

> She had not decided to become a medicine woman. Such things are not decided after all. She was becoming a medicine woman because it was in her to do so; it was her purpose, her reason for being; she *dreamed* it. . . . In her dreams she knew of things that had long since been lost to others. She knew of things that lay in remote distances of time and space. . . . And she knew of the ancient child, the boy who turned into a bear.

Set embraces his liminal role, his indianness, and leaves San Francisco and his career there to marry Grey and live at Lukachukai. Regardless of Grey's power and guidance, however, it is not until Set feels he has lost control of himself that he is willing to commit to being indian, to being the bear. Upon the death of his adopted father, he returns to San Francisco from Oklahoma and becomes more and more disoriented:

> In his desperation he became steadily more self-destructive. There was no longer a design to his existence. His life was coming apart, dis-integrating. He drank heavily, and he did not eat or sleep for long periods. . . . He began to shake, and a terrible cold came upon his extremities. His whole being suffered a numbness, a kind of paralysis. . . . Even on the verge of madness there were times of pro-

found lucidity. The dissolution of his life seemed an illusion. . . . Yes he believed, there is only one story, after all, and it is about the pursuit of man by God, and it is about man who ventures out to the edge of the world, and it is about his holy quest . . . and it is about the hunting of a great beast. . . . He must be true to the story.

By accepting Grey's articulation of his marginality, if not his obligations, and by purposefully entering the story of the bear, he accomplishes what Tayo does in entering the story told by Thought Woman. The stories that underlie both *Ceremony* and *The Ancient Child* are therefore essential to the theme of identity in each.

The characters that Silko and Momaday introduce must, as liminal personae, come to terms with conflicting aspects of their personalities and somehow make their "otherness" a source of power. Consequently, the stories of which they become a part are pushed to the foreground, making these archetypal roles central and structuring the transgression within the narrative. Set and Grey use the whole of their experience, rather than discrete fragments, to determine what it is to be indian, but the ritual demands a crisis by which this may occur. The story of the bear and the story of Billy the Kid, for example, are both crucial elements of Grey's experience, and both serve to define who she is. In this way, the ritualizing of transgression, not necessarily the specificity of Momaday's story, confirms who these characters are as liminal people and the space they occupy.

Hence Tayo and Betonie, Set and Grey are able to establish a new normative space. Betonie and Grey are holy people, revered and feared by their communities because they transgress boundaries. By entering into relationships with them, Tayo and Set are made aware of and participate in their power. Thus the structure of the traditional society is maintained while, along its edges, things change. The narrative focus shifts to the threshold figures who negotiate this reinvigoration. "Prophets and artists," offers Victor Turner, "tend to be liminal and marginal people, 'edgemen', who strive with a passionate sincerity to rid themselves of the clichés associated with status incumbency and role-playing and to enter into vital relations with other men in fact or imagination." Liminal people may acceptably defy the rules that define the rest of community. As Silko and Momaday illustrate, it is along the edges of tribal cultures that indians reconsider survival. It is from these spaces that one may generate and control the kind of power to effect change through rituals adapted to uncertain circumstances.

As Paula Gunn Allen writes,

> For all its complexity, Native American literature possesses a unity and harmony of symbol, structure,

and articulation which is peculiar to itself. This harmony is based on the essential harmony of the universe and on thousands of years of refinement.

Ceremony and *The Ancient Child* affirm indianness by allowing their protagonists to extract from their experiences a perspective informed by both native and Western associations. Like these characters, indians who find themselves participating in often conflicting circumstances must turn what are first perceived as obstacles into sources of regeneration. These characters and their dilemmas illustrate the potential of the liminal positions that many indians occupy and the ways in which it is possible to integrate these roles into the larger context of their traditional cultures without a fragmentation of self. The narrative structures of *Ceremony* and *The Ancient Child* reflect and supplement the experiences of these marginalized indians, adapting the conventional Western narrative style of the *bildungsroman* to incorporate a style of presentation derived from traditional modes of storytelling.

By articulating the liminal experience, Silko and Momaday show the integration of their own experiences in the larger context of native cosmology. The oral tradition, which recalls the history of each group and provides guidance and boundaries for behavior, is now being enhanced by a different but certainly compatible form in the "indian novel." These texts are valuable in shedding some light on the problems and possible solutions that are affecting the lives of people in indian country, but they are also the voices of modern Native America. Theirs are attempts to recoup and reconstruct the indian as a viable means of identification. The margins in which indians live, be they Kiowa, Laguna, or Cherokee, are sites of power and, in revisualizing their potential, of resistance.

Janet St. Clair (essay date Summer 1996)

SOURCE: "Death of Love/Love of Death: Leslie Marmon Silko's *Almanac of the Dead*," in *MELUS,* Vol. 21, No. 2, Summer, 1996, pp. 141-56.

[*In the following essay, St. Clair discusses the wasteland of contemporary America as portrayed by Silko's* Almanac of the Dead, *yet acknowledges the expression of hope contained in the conclusion of the novel.*]

Leslie Marmon Silko's second novel, *Almanac of the Dead,* portrays a nightmarish wasteland of violence, bestiality, cruelty, and crime. Deformed by grotesque familial relationships and debauched by sexual perversion, its characters are incapable of love. Even more chillingly, they seem—except for a few enraged revolutionaries—incapable even of hatred.

Almanac reveals an utterly amoral and atomized society in which each isolated member is indifferent to everything but the gratifications of his own enervated passions. He is connected to nothing: all existence outside himself is reduced to a stock of commodities for which he must compete. There is cause to use the masculine pronoun here: Silko's focus of attack is explicitly the misogynistic, arrogantly hierarchical, and egocentric traditions of Western liberal individualism. The rejection and subsequent disintegration of communal tradition and ethical discipline have left a rutting ground for witchery. Silko's monstrous characters demonstrate that the philosophy of the primacy of the individual has in fact stripped individuals of the social and spiritual structures that define their humanity. Redemption depends upon reclamation of what seems irretrievably lost: a credible *telos* for ordered conduct and the essential interconnections that lend substance and coherence to such conduct.

The sink of depravity and effete self-absorption the novel records stuns both intellect and imagination: the pages are crammed with atrocities almost too heinous to imagine. Its characters induce nightmares; its plot, paranoia. And the villains (the word is too feeble) are Euro-American males. Vicious, manipulative homosexuality and injurious—even murderous—sexual perversions become relentless metaphors of the insane solipsism and phallocentric avarice that characterize the dominant culture. Gone is even a vestigial sense of those virtues which undergird community: there are no personal values because the triumph of individualism has eroded every rationale for moral discipline; there are no institutional ethics because social systems are inevitably infected by the corruption of their constituents. There is no accountability because there is no one to whom one accounts; each man is his own arbiter. Contemporary Euro-American culture is spiritually and ethically rotted by an ideology that rewards egotism. It is characterized by blind obsessions with infantile self-gratification made terrifying by the vicious, power-mad adult's capacity to seize that with which it is obsessed. Control, sex, and wealth are the prizes of unscrupulous aggression; ruthlessness becomes the fundamental pragmatic. The collation of savage white men, each with his own horrific aberrations, staggers the reader almost into numbness, as if to prove how easily, how willingly, we are desensitized to, and individually dissociated from, the horror of moral vacuity and anomie.

The unrestrained greed and brutality of these hollow men is continually emblematized in dissipated sexual perversions that provide entropic substitutes for anything remotely resembling love. Men's equation of carnal gratification with the infliction of pain and their gynophobic attraction to male partners reveal an endemic phallocentric, misogynistic, and egocentric savagery. The ability to feel even the ecstasy of orgasm is so vitiated that the men typically vacillate blandly between drug-induced stupors that deaden their *in*ability to

feel and sexual acts bizarre or sadistic or dangerous enough to titillate them into imagining that they *can* feel. Beaufrey, who knew even as a small child that "He had always loved himself, only himself," recognizes that his indifference to other people affords him enormous power to manipulate them. As an international broker in torture pornography and snuff films, he has amassed fortunes in proving his theory that men can be divided into "those who admitted" that they "enjoyed watching torture and killing" and "those who lied." Films and videos do not sexually arouse him, however. Because "others did not fully exist—they were only ideas that flitted across his consciousness then disappeared"—Beaufrey requires the warm corpses of young male lovers he has driven to suicide.

The violent, phallocentric self-absorption that characterizes Beaufrey informs the incapacity to love that typifies every so-called "successful" man in Silko's novel. The pseudo-intellectual Mexican General J. confirms Beaufrey's theory on men's appetite for savagery: his favorite scholarly topics with his powerful lunch buddies are bloodshed and rape. He theorizes that the sight and smell of blood is a natural aphrodisiac because "bloodshed dominated the natural world, and those inhibited by blood would in time have been greatly outnumbered by those who were excited by blood"; rape, for the General, is the happy conjunction of bloody violence and sexual subjugation. The corrupt Judge Arne, who presides over the Federal District Court in Phoenix, shares Beaufrey's indifference toward other people. But whereas for Beaufrey women figure only as temporary annoyances to be dispassionately erased, the Judge manifests his gynophobia by physically injuring women during the sex act. Although he claims that he "did not think gender really mattered; sex after all was only a bodily function, a kind of expulsion of the sex fluids into some receptacle or another," he is clearly hostile to women. He becomes aroused in a brothel only by imagining his male companion ramming himself bestially into a shuddering woman, and he maintains his erection by pinching the nipples and clitoris of the gasping, protesting woman he is with until he draws blood. Far more than with prostitutes of either gender, however, who require the exchange of a few words, the judge enjoys sex with his four mute basset hound bitches and his accommodating accomplice, the basset stud.

The gynophobic, phallocentric self-involvement implicit in loveless, degenerate individualism perhaps culminates in the character of Serlo. Disgusted by the touch of men and horrified by even the thought of contact with women, he tries to mate with himself, by himself. Arrogant of his *sangre pura,* he jealously saves and freezes each opalescent drop of his precious semen in stainless steel vials. Cringing at the filth and corruption of the genetically flawed human female, he invests part of his exploited wealth in his own research center to develop perfect human specimens from his own sperm in artificial uteri, and part of his wealth to develop "Alternative Earth modules . . . designed to be self-sufficient, closed systems," where he and his hybrid progeny might live in hermetic protection from the defilements of earthly existence.

The absolute self-absorption and consequent utter lovelessness that characterize these men lead them predictably enough to obsessions with personal power. Empty of the sentiments that define humanity, each tries to give himself a sense of substance by amassing more sex, money, and control than anyone else. The social hierarchies that form, accordingly, are determined by the degree to which each can wrest the instruments and emblems of power from the others. Max Blue, suave and despotic mastermind of an international ring of flawlessly disciplined contract killers, spends his time in apparent indolence at the Tucson Country Club, playing golf with his affluent and influential clients. His services are much in demand because Max has elevated cold-blooded murder to an art form. Each job is a custom-designed set piece suspended, isolated and inviolable, in time and space; each death becomes a tangible badge of someone else's supremacy. Max, meanwhile, protected by a network of implicated officials and entrepreneurs, maintains a significantly regal bearing, receiving or refusing to receive supplicants and treating each other with whatever graciousness his station merits.

Beaufrey and Serlo accord themselves the highest position in the social hierarchy by virtue of their aristocratic lineage. Beaufrey sees everything as already belonging to him by birthright. As a child, his "favorite book had been about the Long Island cannibal, Albert Fish . . . because they shared not only social rank, but complete indifference about the life or death of other human beings." As a college student, "Beaufrey had read European history" and "realized there had always been a connection between human cannibals and the aristocracy": the rest of humanity, by his calculation, is his to devour. His proprietary conviction is at one point briefly ruffled by an apprehension that he may lose total control over David, one of his sex and cocaine slaves, if David comes to love the child he has mindlessly sired on the woman Seese. He needn't have worried about being confounded by love: David's fascination with his child's features is entirely narcissistic. In his ingenuous arrogance, David has long since fallen prey to Beaufrey's "game"—one that begins with Beaufrey's encouraging "gorgeous young men such as David to misunderstand their importance in the world." David fancies himself an artist, a type Beaufrey finds "the most fascinating. . . . Because they participated so freely" in their own destruction. And David does participate, helping to drive their lover Eric to suicide, then shooting pornographically lurid photos of the naked mangled corpse. But in Beaufrey's theater, "one act followed another": he kidnaps the baby from its mother to watch David's egocentric

absorption with his replicated image, then kidnaps the child from David when he recognizes that "David is ripe" for the "final moves of the game." After David is driven to death upon seeing the 35mm color proof sheets of his baby's dismembered cadaver, Beaufrey calmly takes commercial photos of David's broken corpse and turns, in dispassionate gladness, to his next source of cannibalistic satisfaction.

Serlo elevates the importance of his aristocratic blood even more highly. Investing his entire identity in his conviction of hereditary genetic superiority, he perhaps prefigures the end result of misogynistic, earth-gutting, Eurocentric individualism. Fearing the day when the world would be "overrun with swarms of brown and yellow human larvae called natives," he coolly plans their mass extermination and stocks the underground vaults of his huge Colombian estate with food, water, and currency. Acknowledging a certain *noblesse oblige* to rape underling women and so infuse their tawdry strains with *sangre pura,* he nevertheless recoils in horror at the thought of so basely defiling his own purity. Casting himself in a godlike image, Serlo disdains the very planet he and his kind have despoiled. He plans his own ascension within space stations that "could be loaded with the last of the earth's uncontaminated soil, water, and oxygen and would be launched in high orbits" where "the select few would continue as they always had, gliding in luxury and ease across polished decks of steel and glass islands looking down on earth . . . still sipping cocktails" while the rabble killed each other for a share of the dwindling resources of a dying planet.

In a hegemony where status is determined by how much one is capable of taking and keeping, everything—land, money, materials, human bodies and lives—are commodified, priced, and labeled for consumption. Max Blue's anonymous victims, Beaufrey's torture videos that "progressed conveniently into the 'autopsy' of the victim," Serlo's acres of stockpiles that he will surely never use—each characterizes the fundamental mindset of what Silko calls "vampire capitalists." Their motto: buy low, sell high. Beaufrey's raw material includes kidnapped children and street punks lured by cocaine. Trigg, broker in human organs, processes hitchhikers and the homeless. When it occurs to him that men who agree to sell their blood are men who would seldom be missed, Trigg identifies an entrepreneurial opportunity. Those he determines to be alone in Tucson are "slowly bled to death, pint by pint" while Trigg gives them blow jobs to distract them from their own murder. Even at that price, Trigg feels "they got a favor from him": after all, "They were human debris. Human refuse. Only a few had organs of sufficient quality for transplant use." In another case, a police chief capitalizes upon his own resources at hand. As his investment in a lucrative pornography ring, he allows a cameraman to film official interrogations where women are sexually tortured and mutilated. An apt businessman, he recognizes a competitive threat: when he senses that the security of his position may be compromised by the cameraman's excesses, he arranges and videotapes the castration of his potential rival.

The sadistic greed of the police chief reveals the pervasive venom of individual morality. In a commodified and atomized society where malevolence and depravity are prerequisites to power and status, the highest and noblest social institutions are inevitably as corrupt as the men who control them. The novel portrays American justice and judicial systems in which justice and law are never even remote issues. Those characters who wield power within governmental agencies regard their positions quite purely as avenues of access to unbounded power and profit. No one feels anything—except mistrust—for anybody. Senators do business with contract killers over salad at the country club. CIA directors deal with sleazy arms brokers to protect the flow of mind-deadening cocaine across national borders. Drug kingpins arrogantly demand apologies and reparation when they are inconvenienced by inept policemen. Cops are either stupid and depraved, or smart and depraved. The smart ones manipulate the stupid ones, and grow stupendously wealthy through cordial and intimate business relationships with top-level criminals. Jamie, one of the stupid ones, is sexually obsessed with and chemically dependent upon the drug-smuggling Ferro until he is assassinated by his fellow officers at a theatrically staged drug raid. His boss, one of the smart ones, wisely appreciates the prudence (and the profit) in accommodating such manipulators and swindlers as Max Blue, Judge Arne, the senator, the CIA, and the border patrol. The men charged with enforcing the law and upholding the principles of the justice are among the most viciously criminal and egomaniacal characters in a novel full of egomaniacally lawless villains.

The church, that institution which most directly assumes responsibility for teaching and modeling the virtues of human community, is revealed more as the source of moral degeneracy than as an energized force against it. Silko's Indian characters perceive the Judeo-Christian tradition as irrational, bloody, cannibalistic, and cruel. Menardo's full-blood grandfather, explaining Europeans' chronic rootless alienation, compassionately calls them "the orphan people," wounded and eternally broken "because the insane God who had sired them had abandoned them . . . throwing them out of their birthplace, driving them away." Menardo's driver Tacho (who together with his brother El Feo emblematizes the mythically redemptive Sacred Twins) sees white people's blind violence as culturally systemic: "The European invaders had brought their Jesus hanging bloody and dead from the cross; later they ate his flesh and blood again and again" yet, "typical of sorcerers or Destroyers, the Christians had denied they were cannibals and sacrificers." The old Yaqui grandmother Yoeme notes that "even idiots can understand

a church that tortures and kills is a church that can no longer heal": it does not surprise her that the spiritually lacerated whites who came to the Americas sought "to dress their wounds in the fat of slain Indians." The church's culpability in failing to stop the extermination of Indians in the Americas is noted on several occasions by various characters. In a chapter entitled **"A Series of Popes Had Been Devils,"** the paranoid Mosca, whose clarity of thought is revealed in drug-induced visions, damns the clergy for lechery, theft, and duplicity. He sees the good deeds of the church as the work of a few "potential troublemakers" who are deviously coopted to give the Church "good publicity." There is some small ambivalence in Silko's attitude toward Christianity: its efforts—however feeble and spotty—to alleviate poverty and injustice are grudgingly acknowledged. And Menardo, who is both irritated and threatened by educated Indians, blames the priests for having "treated them like human beings." Generally, though, Silko seems to endorse the anti-Christian attitudes expressed by her Indian (and several of her white) characters, who interpret the brutal perversions of Christianity as "the betrayal of Jesus" and of "Jesus' creed of forgiveness and brotherly love." Like the justice and judicial system of the government, the Church is another example of an ideologically compassionate and communally protective institution that has been raped and butchered by the combative avarice of androcentric Euro-American individualism.

Even the civil institution of marriage, which might have served as a refuge against the isolation of individualism, is doomed to fail within a social context that values only self-gratification. Despite an enormous cast of characters, there are few marriages in this novel, and neither love nor contractual fidelity between partners. Trust, respect, and compassion again succumb to the inevitable betrayals of egocentric self-interest. Menardo, the Mexican mixed-blood, thinks he has won a valuable prize when he marries the fair-skinned Iliana with the stainless European lineage. Her prize is incredible wealth. Menardo thinks the polished and cosmopolitan Alegria is an even rarer prize and marries her immediately after Iliana's untimely death. Alegria wants Menardo's money and protection, but joylessly sleeps with the abusive and insensitive Marxist Bartolomeo and yearns after the promiscuous Sonny Blue, who so despises women that he prefers to take them in the dark. The old smuggler Calabazas is married to Sarita, but wants her sister Liria; while he's in bed with his sister-in-law, his wife is in bed with the Monsignor. When Leah Blue learns of her husband Max's death, "she had to fight an impulse to laugh . . . she felt relief, not loss."

The women characters, while they are typically less vicious and offensive than the men, are nevertheless incapable of love as well. Survival among misogynists has given them few choices. They can adopt the male value system of aggression, greed, and callousness; resist subjugation through a defiant and dehumanizing scorn; or fall in speechless defeat. The cruelest and the most ineffectual women are white: real estate tycoon Leah Blue takes by force what she cannot buy and gives no thought to the consequences that others must inevitably suffer. Hoping—significantly—to impress her father and brothers, she manipulates a corrupt legal system into awarding her the underground water rights to a vast area of drought-choked Arizona in order to fill the network of streams, fountains, and canals in her luxury development, Venice. Training and experience has rendered her incapable of human affection and insensitive to any conception of selfless reciprocity: Leah only takes. Indifferent to her husband and sons, she alleviates her ennui with meaningless exploitative sexual affairs. The most fully developed of her loveless dalliances is with the wheelchair-bound but eternally erect Trigg, whom she callously nicknames "steak-in-a-basket." When she hears he has been brutally murdered and interred in his own organ deep-freeze, she is only marginally interested to note that she "didn't feel anything." Instead of grieving, she immediately begins to hope she'll be questioned about his death "because that young police chief was really quite sexy."

The character Seese is ostensibly the opposite of Leah. Beaten into chronic silence by ruthless misogynists, Seese looks for protection in the invisibility of listless acquiescence and the insensibility of drug-induced torpor. Formerly a topless dancer in a sleazy nightclub where the girls are required to perform "bizarre sex acts for paying customers," she becomes David's lover, unaware that he is merely using her to make Beaufrey jealous, as Beaufrey had used Eric to make David jealous. She accedes under pressure to one abortion, but insists, uncharacteristically, upon carrying her second pregnancy to term. After the baby is kidnapped by Beaufrey's thugs, Seese vacuously dedicates herself to finding her child, putting her entire vague confidence in the psychic powers of Lecha, the mixed-blood, drug-addicted T.V. psychic who can locate only dead people.

The Indian women, likewise victimized and perverted by male aggression and oppression, are equally incapable of love. Zeta and Lecha, twin sisters and putative protagonists of *Almanac,* are sexually molested by their Uncle Federico throughout their childhoods; Lecha is tricked into surrendering her virginity to him with the apparent complicity of the local priest. Neither woman ever loves a man. Zeta has one sexual experience as an adult—her compensation to the fat and stinking Mr. Coco for a job promotion—then chooses a life of celibacy. Lecha, conversely, amuses herself with strings of casual and indiscriminate sexual affairs but evades even the most tenuous of emotional ties. The strident vituperation of their Yaqui grandmother, Yoeme, is the result of a lifetime of oppression at the hands of white men. Forced to marry a man she typically refers to as "that fucker Guzman"—whose name is clearly meant to recall the monstrous image of "pig-anus [Nino] de Guzman," whose infamous administration exterminated and enslaved Indians by the thousands in the sixteenth century—she spends her lifetime resisting powerful men whose greed and cruelty threaten the earth and the lives and welfare of the Indians who respect it. The revolutionary activist Angelita La Escapia, who names herself "The Meathook," has sex with men who are weaker than she, but cares only for the overthrow of the globally destructive and evilly avaricious institutions that characterize Euro-American males.

Predictably, natural physical and emotional bonds are eroded by the same obsessive self-absorption that debases individuals and institutions. Those men who engage in sex with women see them as commodities to be acquired, consumed, and discarded; those who do not see women as vile, contemptible earth-crawlers who exist beneath their antiseptic intellectual concern. Everyone except Zeta is having sex with multiple partners, but no one loves anyone, and the sex is fruitless. The only children in the novel are the mythical nomadic guardians of the Almanac and Seese's memory of her baby Monte, who is dead before the action in the novel begins.

But even maternity is incapable of engendering love. Although Seese's child is both conceived and kidnapped while Seese is in her usual cocaine-and-alcohol fog, she is the best mother in the novel: she at least feels keenly the loss of her baby. None of the other women seem to care particularly for their children, and the characters almost invariably despise their mothers. Zeta and Lecha, keepers of the sacred pages of the Almanac, are something like co-mothers to the hopelessly maladjusted Ferro. Lecha bore him "one Friday morning"—there is no mention of his father's identity—but "by Sunday noon Lecha had been on a plane to Los Angeles, leaving Zeta with her new baby." Zeta names and rears him, but makes it plain to him from the outset that she is motivated by duty, not affection.

Lecha and Zeta are taught by their Indian grandmother to reject their own mother; Yoeme sees Amalia, the twins' mother, and her other children as sickly, weak-willed, and worthless progeny of Guzman. Lecha's friend Root, understanding that his mother is ashamed of his speech impediment, hates her with a murderous fury. Trigg, who also feels that his mother rejects him out of shame, dreams of somehow making enough money to win even faint favor. Sonny and Bingo, adult sons of Max and Leah Blue, call their mother by her given name, unable to think of her as mother to anyone, much less to them; Bingo fantasizes that she is killed, just to see if he would be able to feel anything if it really happened. Beaufrey, born because his mother was more afraid of abortion than of childbirth, is the unwelcome product of his mother's final middle-aged Parisian fling.

Serlo's parents abandoned him to his pederastic grandfather, and Mosca was taken from his incompetent mother and thrust into a series of foster homes. Traditionally regarded as nurturers and instinctual protectors of their children, women are portrayed as emotionally eviscerated victims of misogynistic, egocentric European traditions. Listening to another of gunrunner Greenlee's crass sexist jokes just before she blasts him with her .44 magnum, Zeta "still had to marvel at the hatred white men harbored for all women, even their own." Raped and degraded by centuries of male oppression, women's survival has come to depend upon their ability *not* to feel.

This malevolence against mothers in particular and women in general is figurative as well as literal: women in the novel are invariably victims of male fear and hostility, but their treatment also metaphorically reflects the culturally male contempt for the female earth. The earth is repeatedly referred to as the Mother by various characters—not all of them Indian. Throughout the novel the word "rape" is applied uniformly to land and women, and to the land as woman. Yoeme argues that the white man's "gaping emptiness" results from his having "violated the mother earth"; Korean computer wizard Awa Gee plots the destruction of the empires so that the "earth that has been seized and torn open, would be allowed to heal and rest in the darkness"; and Sterling, the banished Laguna Indian, recalls the old folks' warning of the terrible consequences of the brutal wounding and scarring of "Mother Earth."

The metaphor is underscored by the correlation between men's relationships with women and their connection to the land and, analogously, their degree of sterile, narcissistic self-absorption. Again, Serlo emblematizes the final result of misogynistic disdain for the earth. He owns and retains sole authority over vast tracts of land, yet he has no emotional or moral connection with it whatsoever, just as he is incapable of the most elemental relationship with any woman, including his mother. He speaks distastefully of raping women not because of even the vaguest sense of human affinity but because rape would necessitate the squalor of physical contact. Just as he has dissociated himself completely from the company of women, he dreams of dissociating himself from the earth, living in a sterile, androgynous womb of steel and glass within sealed orbiting space units.

The women, conversely, must protect both themselves and the earth from such male psychoses. The mission of the strong Indian women—Lecha, Zeta, Yoeme, and the warrior Angelita—is to reclaim the ravished and impoverished land and restore it to its place of respect. Yoeme at first marries the hated Guzman to prevent him and other whites from breaking their land-use agreements with the Yaquis. When that fails, she adopts guerrilla tactics to subvert the silver miners' wanton rape of the earth and barely escapes death

for treason and sedition. Angelita, champion of tribal rights to the earth, laments the Euro-American failure to understand that "the earth was mother to all beings." She sees the aliens' exploitative intellectual separation from the earth as artificial and ultimately doomed, because "No human, no individuals or corporations, no cartel of nations, could 'own' the earth; it was the earth who possessed the humans and it was the earth who disposed of them."

Setting and imagery further emphasize the plaited themes of egocentric violence, loveless sterility, and dissociation from the land. The story takes place primarily in Tucson, a "city of thieves" that "had always depended on some sort of war to keep cash flowing," and the surrounding deserts of Arizona and Mexico. The relentless sun is murderous to those who will not learn the land, and the dearth of water threatens all life. Dead lawns of Tucson—*tucson,* as Calabazas ironically notes, means "plentiful fresh water" in Papago—can scarcely be distinguished from gray pavement, and the spindly landscaping reflects the moral and spiritual drought suffered by its inhabitants. Existing water is so polluted it stinks. "Pools" are typically of blood; "waves," of nausea or hatred. Clear ponds of water are the surfaces upon which float the severed heads of diplomats or the tiny bloated corpses of unwanted newborns. The only remaining pure water belongs to Leah, who is literally sucking the earth dry to create her model desert city for the incredibly wealthy white elite.

There is little vegetation, and when flowers are mentioned, it is almost invariably in connection with grisly death. When Beaufrey's boytoy Eric blows his head apart with a .44 revolver, the critics rave about David's glossy photographs of the suicide that evoke "a field of red shapes which might be peonies—cherry, ruby, deep purple, black—and the nude human figure nearly buried in these 'blossoms' of bright red." When Menardo sees a wall of vining purple flowers he can think only of the "twists of human intestines." The assassinated motorcyclist hanging upside down in the blossoming paloverde tree is reported as a "strange fruit" by the woman who sights the corpse as she drives to work. Water, the source of all life; flowers, the harbingers of renewed harvest; and fruit, the fulfillment of the flowers' promise; are all distorted into sinister images of detached, meaningless death, inevitable legacy of a tradition of isolate, amoral self-absorption.

And yet, the novel is by no means without hope. Rather, it addresses from another perspective the potentials of witchery and the creative value of stories so gracefully expressed in Silko's profoundly hopeful first novel, *Ceremony. Almanac* is an apparent miscellany of isolated stories that gradually assumes design in the reader's consciousness. This growing awareness of interconnection is, according to the author, the function of stories, which "are always bringing us together, keeping this whole together," combating people's natural tendency "to run off and hide or separate themselves from others" in times of "violent emotional experience."

The Almanac, an ancient collation of sacred story abstracts, serves as metaphor for the importance of memory—one of the central themes of Silko's first novel. As Susan Scarberry-Garcia observed in her early and seminal essay on *Ceremony,* memory "becomes the bedrock of our humanity" in helping us to define ourselves and to "forestall the witchery which is advanced, if not generated, through forgetfulness." Both novels evoke mythic images to instruct readers, as Paula Gunn Allen has so frequently observed, that "We are the land"; that self-respect is impossible when respect for our sources and sustenance is neglected and forgotten. *Ceremony* attacks specifically the threat of those who

> grow away from the earth
> then they grow away from the sun
> then they grow away from the plants and animals.
> They see no life
> when they look
> they see only objects.

Almanac of the Dead garishly illustrates the realization of that threat. Yet this story, like Tayo's, becomes dynamically charged within the consciousness of the hearer, and so promises the possibility of a different course.

Bonnie TuSmith sees *Ceremony* "as an American writer's challenge to the cult of individualism in contemporary society"—as Silko's reminder "that we are all in this together." *Almanac of the Dead* states both the challenge and the reminder more brutally, but with a similar undercurrent of tenacious faith. As the novel's Euro-American power structure sinks into the morass of depravity borne of its own misguided ideologies of individualism, a resurgence of communality is occurring. Ironically (perhaps), the redeemers of social organization and spiritual values are found among those who are most disenfranchised by the dominant white male "community." Saved from total corruption by the marginalization that has been thrust upon them, various individuals and groups are rising up and converging, nourished by the very injustice that was designed to starve them. Roy, the deeply disillusioned Vietnam veteran, is organizing his Army of the Homeless to fight the "fat cats" who own the government and police. He "had seen for himself women and children hungry, and sleeping on the streets. . . . Police beating homeless old men," and he had concluded that "This was not democracy. . . . Something had to be done." Clinton, another veteran, sees the oppression of women and minorities as a carefully planned conspiracy by white men to retain power and wealth. To him, "the entire war in Southeast Asia had been fabricated as a location and occasion for the

slaughter of the strongest and most promising young men of black and brown and poor-white communities"; his solution is to declare war upon the deathmongers and "to reclaim democracy from corruption at all levels." Telecommunications genius Awa Gee specializes in network break-ins and the creation of fake identities. Indifferent to personal power, "Awa Gee did not plan to create or build anything at all. Awa Gee was interested in the purity of destruction . . . in the perfection of complete disorder and disintegration" within a system founded on waste, oppression, and greed. Ecoterrorists are "recruiting the terminal and dying . . . who saw the approach of the end of nature and who wanted to do some good on their way out" by martyring themselves in kamikaze missions to blow up the restrictive economic infrastructures.

All subversive action will eventually culminate in the overthrow of the destructive Eurocentric and androcentric governments of the Americas, which will make way for a sacred reclamation of land and social solidarity. Divisive distinctions between colors and genders will be transcended as people identify their common oppressor. In Tucson, the white man Roy and the black Indian Clinton come together to lead a burgeoning army of women and men who "all said they'd rather fight. They'd rather burn down the city, take a police bullet, and die quick, because that way they died fighting, they died warriors, not slaves." Roy, Clinton, The Barefoot Hopi, Weasel Tail, and others—each invokes anxious and concerned people of all colors to come together because "this was the last chance the people had, and they would never prevail if they did not work together as a common force."

Community is being built even within the collective unconscious. Tribal healers and spirits are visiting the dreams of prisoners, preparing them to rise up fraternally against the enemies of land and humanity. People everywhere, sensing danger, are beginning to react "without being conscious of what they [are] preparing for," as yet unaware that "their plans would complement and serve one another in the chaos to come." Meanwhile, hundreds of miles away, Angelita La Escapia and the young twins Tacho and El Feo are organizing the masses for the march northward to reclaim the sacred earth and all the interconnections that reclamation implies. It might require generations, but the prophecies are clear: "all traces of Europeans in America would disappear and, at last, the people would retake the land."

Hope, though, rests chiefly on faith and patience: Silko extends little reason for immediate triumphant optimism. Schisms continue among those who are committed to revolution. Men versus women, the humble versus the power-hungry, black versus brown versus white, those who believe in the possibility of peaceful transitions versus those who strain toward a purgative bloodletting—the same mistrustful divisiveness they are challenging threatens the unity upon which their success depends. And so far, only a tiny minority of "scattered crazies" with "feverish plots and crazed schemes" are involved at all.

> **The hope that undergirds *Almanac of the Dead* is more implicit, then, than evident . . . . The contemporary America of the novel is on the surface a wasteland of dead possibilities, a treacherous desert where the promise and refreshment implicit in love have been blasted by the rapacious brutality of white male egoism.**
> **—Janet St. Clair**

Most find passivity their best defense. The novel's most likable (and least threatening) character is Sterling, a dispossessed Laguna Indian who stands ineffectually at the peripheries, watching the violence and betrayal in mute, bewildered horror. Driven from his homeland by tribal injustice, he wanders aimlessly to Tucson where he accidentally lands a job on Lecha and Zeta's ranch. He stays because it is easier than leaving, and he finally leaves because there is no place to stay. The novel closes with Sterling's return to the reservation from which he has been banished, where he takes up solitary and unobtrusive residence in the remote sandstone hut of the family sheep camp.

Sterling's apparent passivity notwithstanding, he serves as something of a repository of the atrophied but reawakening virtues of communal heritage. Like Tayo, he had been advised by white counselors to beat his depression by forgetting his past. Devoted to white notions of "self-improvement," he tries to forget, but finds in the end that wholeness comes through acts of remembrance. In his youth he had been scolded by his elders "because he wasn't interested in what they had to say," but upon his return "home" he tries "to remember more of the stories the old people used to tell" so that he can better understand the connections they revealed. The ancient myths, whose neglect had resulted in "all the violence and death" he had witnessed, assume profound significance as he begins to piece together his shadowy recollections "of the old folks' beliefs." He sees the resurrection of the south-facing stone snake from the tailings of the Destroyers' uranium mines as a promise of eventual redemption, and looks with the mythic snake "in the direction from which the twin brothers and the people would come" to liberate individuals from alienation. But Sterling's recovery is only beginning. Even as he attempts to remember, he attempts to forget: he blocks from his consciousness an acknowledgment of what he knows exists, gently—but falsely—reassuring himself instead that "the world was not like that. Tucson had only been a bad dream."

The hope that undergirds *Almanac of the Dead* is more implicit, then, than evident. As Silko once said of Pueblo storytelling, "a great deal of the story is believed to be inside the listener, and the storyteller's role is to draw the story out of the listeners." The contemporary America of the novel is on the surface a wasteland of dead possibilities, a treacherous desert where the promise and refreshment implicit in love have been blasted by the rapacious brutality of white male egoism. Among the empowered, all human emotion, sentiment, and compassion have atrophied in the withering aridity of European individualism. Avarice is the only remaining motivation for action; suspicion is the only remaining human connection. Even the sexual urge, the most primal guarantee of regeneration, has turned inward upon itself to produce a mutant brood of scrofulous monstrosities. And yet, although scourged and blighted, hope remains alive. The reclamation and restoration of loving relationships among people and with the land will come, according to Silko's optimistic Indians. The healing will take time, and it will require vigilant attention to history if we are to identify and resist the present sources and manifestations of witchery. But the prophecies of the Almanac are explicit: the blood-maddened male Death-Eye Dog will die; a renewed era of active spiritual and social community in the Americas will ultimately prevail.

Charlene Taylor Evans (essay date 1996)

SOURCE: "Mother-Daughter Relationships as Epistemological Structures: Leslie Marmon Silko's *Almanac of the Dead* and *Storyteller*," in *Women of Color: Mother-Daughter Relationships in 20th-Century Literature,* edited by Elizabeth Brown-Guillory, 1996, pp. 172-87.

[*In the following essay, Taylor Evans asserts that, "One of the basic unspoken feminist assumptions—that women are essentially powerless—is debunked within Silko's texts, for the mothers and daughters are bastions of the American Indian society in times of great crisis."*]

For the past twelve thousand years, most cultures have practiced the tradition of passing on the explanation of "being" and "becoming" to their offspring. While this function is not gender specific, the recipient of this information must have full faith and confidence in the one who is teaching. In many cultures, women carry the ontologies to their offspring. According to Leslie Marmon Silko, the Native American woman has been "the tie that binds her people together, transmitting her culture through song and story from generation to generation."

In Silko's *Storyteller* and *Almanac of the Dead,* grandmothers serve as mother-surrogates for Native American daughters. This grandmother-granddaughter pairing forms an intergenerational unit, sometimes supplanting the mother-daughter dyad. Native American women often bear the title "aunt" or "auntie" whether the familial relationship is grandmother, mother, aunt, sister, or neighbor. The grandmother or "auntie"-daughter relationship is taken quite seriously in American Indian culture; one of its major functions is to become the "histor" or repository of knowledge for Native Americans. The mother-daughter pair becomes an epistemology or "way of knowing." Mothers and daughters serve as the bridge of continuity for Native American posterity; thus they help preserve the embodiment of cultural values, of the past, and of the individual and collective identities of Native American people. The knowledge they transmit is essential to redemption or survival for a threatened or endangered society and helps maintain their true identity by providing the cultural underpinnings that counter the invasive and corrosive influences of Western culture.

Weaving ancestral/supernatural spirits into her narrative, Silko combines the oral tradition or literal "storytelling" (the past) into writing (the present), which are reconciled by a process of artistic development in her works. An offspring of this union is the highly intricate and almost protean relationship which exists between Native American mothers and daughters formulating myriad epistemological structures. The grandmother-granddaughter storytellers and their stories communicate, as accurately as the medium allows, the reality of the Native American existence.

Storytelling had always fascinated Silko as a child in the Laguna Pueblo district of Arizona. In a matrilineal community, especially the society in *Storyteller,* the female/mother is a powerful person who is oftentimes the storyteller. In her anthology, Silko establishes the significance of the "story" and discusses the transformation of the oral text to a written one.

In a matrilineal community, especially the society in *Storyteller,* the female/mother is a powerful person who is oftentimes the storyteller. In her anthology, Silko establishes the significance of the "story" and discusses the transformation of the oral text to a written one.
—*Charlene Taylor Evans*

Silko reminisces about her Aunt Susie, actually her great grandmother, Marie Anaya Marmon, and contends that at a certain point in the history of the American Indian "the atmosphere and conditions that had maintained the oral tradition had been irrevocably altered by the European intrusion." The onus lay on mothers/grandmothers to protect and to

transmit to their daughters an accurate explanation or accounting of the Native American past. These stories were sometimes communicated through pictures, song, and dance. Silko heard her great-grandmother, Aunt Susie, saying "a'moo'ooh," a Laguna expression of endearment for a young child, and she and her sisters began calling her Grandma A'mooh. Grandma A'mooh spent much time with Silko and Wendy and Gigi, her sisters. The girls stayed with her while their mother worked; it was quite convenient since they lived next door to each other. Silko slept with her "in case she fell getting up in the night" (Grandma A'mooh was eighty years old at this time) and was immensely influenced and nurtured in this relationship with her great-grandmother. Silko reveals in the *Storyteller* volume that Grandma A'mooh used "to tell me and my sisters about the good old days when they didn't have toothpaste and cleaned their teeth with juniper ash." She also notes that when she was only seven or eight years old Aunt Susie (Grandma A'mooh) was in her mid-sixties and listened to all of her questions and speculations. A seasoned practitioner of the oral tradition, Aunt Susie was the last of a generation at Laguna that passed an entire culture and history by word of mouth:

> . . . an entire vision of the world
> which depended upon memory
> and retelling by subsequent generations

In moving from orality to literacy or "technologizing the word," to use Walter Ong's phrase, Silko suggests that she attempts to use in her writing "certain phrases, certain distinctive words" that her Aunt Susie "used in her telling." Her writing emerges from the auditory and is a retelling:

> . . . I write when I still hear
> her voice as she tells the story
> . . . I remember only a small part.
> But this is what I remember
> . . . This is the way I remember.

The role of the grandmother is to "tell" and "re-tell," and the mother-daughter pair serves as a custodian of culture. In *Storyteller,* Silko accepts the challenge of being a storyteller as a part of the continuum. She is a "new age" storyteller in that she utilizes another medium—the written page. She also broadens her audience by switching from orality to literacy. Noting the loss in meaning when an oral culture is reduced to writing, Silko, along with numerous scholars and linguists, perceives the inadequacy and inaccuracy of the written word and uses individual portraits, landscape pictures, and other media to facilitate and enhance her story: "'Yes, that's the trouble with writing,' I said. 'You can't go on and on the way we do when we tell stories around here.'"

It is the responsibility of the storyteller or grandmother/mother figure to preserve the integrity of the written text.

In a 1986 interview with Kim Barnes, Silko discusses other techniques she has used to minimize the loss of meaning in the written text: "I play around with the page by using different kinds of spacing or indentations or even italics so that the reader can sense, say, that the tone of the voice has changed. If you were hearing a story, the speed would increase at certain points."

Silko's mothers and daughters occupy a symbiotic relationship as daughters thrive and flourish because of the knowledge passed on to them by their mothers/grandmothers, and mothers/grandmothers likewise thrive because of the knowledge they have transferred to their female offspring. In Grandma A'mooh's last years, she was sent to Albuquerque to live with her daughter, Aunt Bessie. Because Aunt Bessie worked, Grandma A'mooh "did not have anyone to talk to all day." "She might have lived without watering morning glories and without kids running through her kitchen but she did not last long without someone to talk to." The dyadic structure of mother-daughter relationships is essential to the "being"/survival of the Pueblo female. Silko describes the storytelling as a "whole way of being." "I mean a whole way of seeing yourself, the people around you, your life in the bigger context . . . in terms of what has gone on before, what's happened to other people."

Personal ontologies and epistemologies are tied to the stories and the storytellers. The mothers and daughters are the fountains and reservoirs of knowledge as they interact and exchange on numerous levels. More importantly, the mothers and daughters transfer information for understanding who Native Americans are as a people. The highly revered position of the female as creator of life and preserver of culture is maintained from generation to generation:

> In the beginning was thought, and her name was Woman. The Mother, the Grandmother, . . . is celebrated in social structures . . . and the oral tradition. To her we owe our lives, and from her comes our ability to endure. . . . She is the Old Woman who tends the fires of life. She is the Old Woman Spider who weaves us together in a fabric of interconnection. She is the Eldest God, the one who Remembers and Re-members.

The matrix of life and being in the American Indian society is the female. Her role is paramount to God, as the first lines in the excerpt from *The Sacred Hoop* are reminiscent of John 1:1: "In the beginning was the Word, and the Word was with God, and the Word was God."

The initial dedication of the **Storyteller** evokes an aspect of timelessness and circularity which also relates to a sense of being for the American Indian, especially the female. An understanding of this infinite relationship between the storyteller and the story, the present and the past, lays the foundation for individual ontologies. The reader can experience the fluidity of time; the past is omnipresent: "This book is dedicated to the storytellers as far back as memory goes and to the telling which continues and through which they all live and we with them."

The role of the grandmother is to "tell" and "re-tell," and the mother-daughter pair serves as a custodian of culture. In *Storyteller*, Silko accepts the challenge of being a storyteller as a part of the continuum. She is a "new age" storyteller in that she utilizes another medium—the written page.
—*Charlene Taylor Evans*

Memory is an important variable on this historical continuum. Likewise, the storyteller and the story are inextricably linked. The focused and deliberate narratives in *Storyteller* depict the storyteller or "histor" as a highly revered member of society. Because the "telling" establishes a permanence and maintains the culture, the storytellers (grandmothers and daughters who will become mothers/grandmothers) have a unique relationship with the past. Silko's sense of the role of mother/daughter is very much like Rayna Green's expression of matrilineage in *That's What She Said*:

> The clay shapers, fiber twisters, picture makers, and storytellers—the ones who said what was and what will be—they've always been important in Indian Country. Whether it comes directly from the storyteller's mouth and She writes it down or someone writes it for her, the story has to be told. . . . Before European writing, there were voices to sing and speak, dances to make real the stories that the people told or to honor the retelling anew. There were hands that talked and drew and shaped. . . . They kept them [the stories] even when no one asked to hear them—even when the whiteeyes came and asked only the men what they knew. Thus the women have always kept the stories. . . .

Having a spirit-centered culture, Native Americans search for alternative yet appropriate avenues of expression for their ontologies. Not being familiar with the Native American culture, Euro-Americans thought that men were the keepers of the information.

Preserving and maintaining the accuracy of the stories is an enormously difficult task. Silko's mothers and daughters extract from portraits or graphic "rememories" from the past to ensure accuracy. Sethe, the female protagonist in Toni Morrison's *Beloved,* remembers significant events from her past in colorful flurries of visual slides of meaning called "rememories." Although in an interview Silko denies any similarity to Morrison, Silko's "rememories" bear a striking resemblance to Sethe's visions in *Beloved.* They also place emphasis on recall and the vivid snapshots of life that tell all and remain eternally etched in one's mind. Silko associates these graphic visual memories with storytelling. Sensitivity to memory and remembering, an important attribute for the mothers and daughters, is illustrated in **"Lullaby."** Ayah, the protagonist, defines old age as a time of memories: "She [Ayah] felt peaceful remembering . . . and she could remember the morning her baby was born. She could remember whispering to her mother, who was sleeping on the other side of the hogan." This emphasis on the past and remembering, its relevance and relationship to the present (birth), illuminates the timelessness of the contexts that the mother-daughter dyads draw from as sources for the stories.

Native American literature is significantly different from Western literature, for the underlying assumptions about the cosmos and their experiential bases are different. According to Paula Gunn Allen and Roxanne Ortiz, Native Americans seek—through song, ceremony, legend, myths, and tales—to articulate and share reality, to bring the private self into harmony and balance with their Native American reality, to verbalize the sense of the majesty and reverent mystery of all things, and to actualize, in language, those truths that give humanity its greatest significance and dignity. As innocuous as the stories may sometimes appear to be, they are powerful weapons against assimilation. The emphasis is of course on the "telling," and remembering is a vital element of the telling and of survival, individually and collectively. Silko hallows the stories in *Almanac of the Dead* by characterizing the narratives as analogues for the actual experiences, which no longer exist, an embodiment or mosaic of memory and imagination. The past is embodied within the rememory: "An experience termed past may actually return if the influences have the same balances or proportions as before. Details may vary, but the essence does not change. The day would have the same feeling, the same character, as that day has been described having had before. The image of a memory exists in the present moment."

Frederic Jameson, a Marxist theorist and philosopher, suggests further that literary form (the story) is deeply engaged with a concrete reality: "narrative is not just a literary form or mode but an essential 'epistemological category'; reality presents itself to the human mind only in the form of stories." This again reinforces the idea of the omnipresence of the past (the story) and suggests that the story vivifies and objectifies experience. Just as females are lifegivers in the physical biological sense, they likewise generate, maintain, and sustain the lives of the Native American people through the narratives. Daughters inherit the stories and must tell and retell them to maintain and sustain their culture.

One of the major themes communicated by the mothers and daughters in **Storyteller** is the resilient and remarkable relationship between Native Americans and their natural physical environment. Individuals are an expression of the cosmos. Natural phenomena and objects in geophysical space are their kin. Complementing the idea of the past and its omnipresence is the idea of the natural environment being an integral part of the Native American ideology. In **"Lullaby"** Ayah, an old woman now, remembers the song she sang to her babies. "She could not remember if she had ever sung it to her children, but she knew that her grandmother had sung it and her mother had sung it." The song metaphorically asserts familial relationships between nature and Native Americans:

> The earth is your mother,
> she holds you.
>
> . . . .
>
> Sleep, sleep.
> We are together always
> There never was a time
> when this was not so.

The belief that American Indian children do not belong to their biological parents but to the land and to the heavens is also implied in the lyric. The last two lines of the song Ayah sings, "There never was a time / when this was not so," suggest an ancient and infinite relationship between the earth (Mother) and the Native American. The people are the earth and the earth is "being," as all creatures are "being." The life-sustaining forces are female in gender. The land (Mother) and the people (mothers) are the same.

Within the web of other familial relationships, mothers and daughters deliver the blueprint for the survival of their culture to the Native Americans. Exactly ten years after the publication of **Storyteller, Almanac of the Dead** addresses the desecration and violation of the land (the Americas) and the Native American people by Euro-Americans and depicts the mother-daughter unit as the interpreter and purveyor of the American Indian past. American Indians' overriding concern to regain tribal lands is expressed in Silko's assertion of the Indian connection to the resistance movement against Euro-American oppression of people of color in **Almanac of the Dead:** "Sixty million Native Americans died between 1500 and 1600. The defiance and resistance to things European continue unabated. The Indian Wars have never ended in the Americas. Native Americans acknowledge no borders; they seek nothing less than the return of all tribal lands" (epigraph). The climate of turmoil is exacerbated by the Native

Americans' unwillingness to assimilate into the Euro-American culture. *Almanac of the Dead* chronicles the moral deterioration of the Native Americans brought on by the onslaught of alien aggressors. There is a nostalgia for the past and the restoration of their former lifestyles. Mother-daughter units (combinations of Old Yoeme, the grandmother, and Zeta and Lecha, her twin granddaughters) quietly brace themselves for war and make attempts to protect and preserve their epistemologies.

An example of the protean or shape-shifting nature of the American Indian mothers and daughters is their becoming literal caretakers of Native American history. A chapter entitled **"Stone Idols"** in *Almanac of the Dead* affirms the significance and reverence the Native American females, in particular, have for their past (represented by stone figures). The narrator notes that the care and protection of stone figures passed from generation to generation to an elder clanswoman. Readily accepting their responsibility, women are the recipients and conscientious caretakers of these figures; many precious objects belonging to the Indian culture were destroyed by Europeans or sold by weak-hearted Native Americans. These stones are valued for their intrinsic spiritual life force and are extensions of the supernatural beings they represent. Feeding these objects a mixture of cornmeal and pollen sprinkled with rainwater, the women lift the stone figures as tenderly as they had lifted their own babies and call them "esteemed and beloved ancestors." The use of cornmeal is an important part of the birth ritual in the Laguna Pueblo culture. Clearly, reverence and dedication are illustrated in these mother/offspring or characteristically feminine actions.

In *Almanac of the Dead,* Silko's mother-daughter units delve into the supernatural. Old Yoeme (the grandmother-figure) and Lecha and Zeta, her twin granddaughters, defy categorization and illustrate the supernatural influences of the surrogate mother-daughter unit.
—*Charlene Taylor Evans*

George Lakoff and Mark Johnson support the idea of the investment of meaning in objects into their essay "Ontological Metaphors": "Understanding our experiences in terms of objects and substances allows us to pick out parts of our experience and treat them as discrete entities or substances of a uniform kind. . . . We can refer to them, categorize them, group them, and quantify them—and, by this means, reason about them." Certain objects in the Native American culture are spiritual embodiments which take on "life" or "being." These objects also serve as epistemologies and may be referred to, grouped, and quantified as Lakoff and Johnson

suggest. Because many of these figures/objects are extensions of supernatural beings, the mother-daughter dyad takes on, of necessity, a supernatural aspect.

In *Almanac of the Dead,* Silko's mother-daughter units delve into the supernatural. Old Yoeme (the grandmother-figure) and Lecha and Zeta, her twin granddaughters, defy categorization and illustrate the supernatural influences of the surrogate mother-daughter unit. Yoeme is an important influence in the self-definition and moral development of both of her granddaughters, and she preoccupies herself with the guardianship of the epistemology or the ancient, arduously preserved journals that contain the history of her own people—a Native American Almanac of the Dead. The ancient prophecies maintain that all things European will disappear from the Americas and that a decipherment of the ancient tribal texts of the Americas foretells the future of all Americans. The future is encoded in arcane symbols and old narratives. It is Zeta's duty to seek, interpret, and tell Lecha, her sister, what to add to the growing epistemology. This spiritually powerful female triumvirate is more than capable of the tedious and painful task of transmitting and preserving the sacred history and future plans for the American Indian culture.

The powerful and supernatural influence of Yoeme over her granddaughters cannot shield them from the hypocrisy and dangers presented by the contemporary American society in which they live. Silko's panoramic view of the Native American diaspora highlights an insidious yet forceful and highly programmed assault by Euro-Americans on the American Indian way of life. Shackled by restrictions and demands for mandatory assimilation, the Native American woman does not respond to this oppression in the weak and reactionary manner in which the Euro-American society has stereotyped her male counterpart. She does not resort to alcoholism or silence. Instead the mother-daughter unit is about the business of fortifying its ranks by enlightening the Indian masses. Old Yoeme speaks to Zeta and charges her with the responsibility of interpreting and keeping the notebooks containing information about the past which is integral to their future. She warns Zeta that nothing must be added to the manuscript that was not already there. Because of the assault of the American Indian culture, the need for secrecy is clearly transmitted from mother to daughter. Again there is the implication of the inaccuracy and distrust of the written word. The window of opportunity to embellish and distort the text is present, yet it must not be considered. Consequently, to assure that they are guarding and transmitting truth, Yoeme and Zeta must be in direct communication with ancestral spirits and the dead.

Yoeme teaches Zeta to communicate and to rely on the big bull snake. The notebook of the snakes is the key to understanding the rest of the old almanac. Yoeme had always consulted "the big bull snake out behind the adobe woodshed." The mystical and ritualistic conferences with the snake conjure elemental truths of being for the Native American:

> [Yoeme] had her own picture of things. Snakes crawled under the ground. They heard the voices of the dead; actual conversations, and lone voices calling out to loved ones still living. . . . Snakes moved through the branches of trees. They saw and heard a good deal. . . . It [talking to the bull snake] was something Zeta did alone with her grandmother.

Zeta learns from her grandmother Yoeme that death is not final or the end of life; it is a part of the universal cycle. This circular orientation encompasses reincarnation. People do not die unless descendants lose memory of them. In the fall Zeta had watched her grandmother Yoeme pick up the big bull snake while it sunned itself behind the woodshed. Cradling the snake against her chest, Zeta understood that the big snake recognized Yoeme "because he lay quietly, only his tongue moving slowly in and out at Zeta." Zeta never discusses this with Lecha because words cannot explain how one talks to snakes. Because the snake does not actually speak, the information is transmitted in a higher, more spiritual form. The telepathy between the woman and the serpent contributes to the epistemology. Much of the information is already in the notebooks in code; the snake validates and provides information for the void. Communicating with the serpent empowers the mother-daughter pair supplying information for the survival of Native American culture. This operates counter to the Judeo-Christian myth of the serpent corrupting Eve in the Garden; rather than bringing sin and death into the world, this snake supplies positive knowledge for the Indian peoples through the women—mothers and daughters.

The powerful and supernatural influence of Yoeme over her granddaughters cannot shield them from the hypocrisy and dangers presented by the contemporary American society in which they live.
—*Charlene Taylor Evans*

Once the notebooks are transcribed, Lecha feels that she will figure out how to use the old almanac. Then she will be able to foresee months and years to come. Interestingly, when Yoeme tells Lecha a story on the beach, Lecha writes the story on the blank pages of the notebook in English. Afterward, Yoeme demands to see it, for she is uncertain about Zeta's competence and intentions. Zeta waits for Yoeme to break into a fury, but instead she sighs with pleasure: this is the sign the keepers of the notebooks had long awaited. Tran-

scribing this information into English marks the fusion of the present with the past.

Lecha recognizes that the almanac is a great legacy, and Yoeme and others believe the almanac has living power within it to unite all the tribal people of the Americas to retake the land. Finally, Lecha feels the life, energy, and power of the words; she recognizes her power and authority as female interpreter and purveyor of life. In "Discourse in the Novel," Mikhail Bakhtin discusses the world of "authoritative discourse," which is represented in *Almanac of the Dead* as the old almanac:

> The authoritative word demands that we acknowledge it, that we make it our own; it binds us, quite independently of any power it might have to persuade us internally; we encounter it with its authority already fused into it. The authoritative word is located in a distanced zone, organically connected with a past that is felt to be hierarchically higher. . . . It is a *prior* discourse. . . . It is akin to taboo. . . . It demands our unconditional allegiance.

Because Yoeme believes that power resides within certain stories, the power ensures the retelling of the story, and with "each retelling a slight but permanent shift [takes] place." The story is given to the daughter so that she can know and actualize her role of histor; the importance of the story and its relationship to life is succinctly stated in the final entry of Old Yoeme's notebook addressed to Native American posterity: "One day a story will arrive in your town. There will always be disagreement over direction; whether the story came from the southwest or the southeast. The story may arrive with a stranger . . . or brought by an old friend. . . . But after you hear the story, you and others prepare by the new moon to rise up against the slave masters."

Convinced of the authenticity of the notebooks and the prophecy, Lecha becomes a conscientious guardian of that history. She is now acutely aware of her function in the mother-daughter dyad. After receiving much notoriety and money from her psychic predictions, the old and now cancerous Lecha hires the blond mixed blood Seese to help type the notebook. The fragments from the sacred notebooks address the importance of the narrative which facilitates the perpetuation of the American Indian culture. The mother-daughter pairing symbolizes the merging of past and present and undermines or minimizes the assault of the Western culture of the Native American people.

In *Almanac of the Dead,* Silko makes continual reference to the African American/Native American relationship. The Native American and African American cultures share striking similarities in many areas. Historically, the griot figure (histor) in the African society was male, and he transmitted knowledge of the past orally to subsequent generations. Like the Native American, the African followed a pattern of oppression and dispossession in America. The African male histor was replaced by an African American female. Understanding one's past is an essential element of empowerment, and both cultures understand the significance of the past and work to eradicate myths, distortions, and omissions in their respective histories. Most importantly, the common mission and agenda of the African American and Indian American peoples coalesce as a part of the final prophecy in Leslie Silko's *Almanac of the Dead.* In a section of the text called "Africa," Clinton, the central character, identifies the histor or African griot-figures in his life. Interestingly, they are also women speaking to other women/daughters. Clinton recalls the elderly women talking about the branches of their family, including intermarriages with whites and American Indians. One whole branch in Tennessee had married "Native Americans."

Throughout this section of the novel, Clinton validates the link between the African American and Native American female histor:

> Clinton remembered those old granny women sitting with their pipes or chew, talking in low, steady voices about in-laws and all the branches of the family. . . . [He] remembered the old grannies arguing among themselves to pass time. The older they got, the more they talked about the past; and they had sung songs in languages Clinton didn't recognize. . . .

It is important to note this similarity because Silko notes the interconnectedness of missions for the Native American and African American peoples. *Almanac of the Dead* with its heavily symbolic and highly allusive style presents five discrete narrative lines. Both African American and Native American cultures are represented by Damballah and Quetzalcoatl, two giant snakes. Quetzalcoatl is the winged serpent and god of amalgamation or expansion. The following is the sacred prophecy guarded by the Native American mothers and daughters:

> In Africa and in the Americas too, the giant snakes, Damballah and Quetzalcoatl, have returned to the people. I have seen the snakes . . . they speak to the people of Africa, and they speak to the people of the Americas; they speak through dreams. The snakes say this: From out of the south the people are coming, like a great river flowing restless with the spirits of the dead who have been reborn again and again all over Africa and the Americas, reborn each generation more fierce and more numerous.

> Millions will move instinctively; unarmed and unguarded, they begin walking steadily north, following the twin brothers.

Silko refers to Native Americans and African Americans symbolically as snakes and "twin brothers." Native Americans and the earth (Mother) are also kin and have been ravaged by the Europeans. The parallels between both cultures and the earth are obvious, and the conclusion of the novel states the final prophecy and a call to action for a united effort by American Indians and African Americans.

To borrow Zora Neale Hurston's "mules of the world" metaphor, the tremendous burden on women gives rise to and necessitates a mother-daughter relationship of incomprehensible proportions. Using the appropriate media for maintaining and transmitting their sacred and important history, the designated female units in the Native American society labor to provide a pipeline for the people. One of the basic unspoken feminist assumptions—that women are essentially powerless—is debunked within Silko's texts, for the mothers and daughters are bastions of the American Indian society in times of great crisis. They hold the fortress after the male power has failed. In *The Sacred Hoop,* Allen and Ortiz present a society controlled by women: "In a system where all persons in power are called Mother Chief and where the supreme deity is female, and social organization is matrilocal, matrifocal, and matrilineal, gyarchy is happening. However, it does not imply domination of men by women as patriarchy implies domination by ruling class males of all aspects of a society."

Unlike Western society, a struggle for dominance between the sexes does not exist in Native American culture. The various ontologies and epistemologies depicted in Silko's *Storyteller* and *Almanac of the Dead* exhibit a strong sense of the reality of the Native American experience. Unfortunately, Native American culture has not been kept completely intact by the stories transmitted by and in the care of these tenacious mothers and daughters. The acculturation of the Native American into Western society has been a rather slow and painful process. Native Americans have courageously resisted total assimilation into Western culture and struggled to survive near extinction. For millennia the social system of the Native Americans has been based on ritual, spirit-centered, woman-focused world views. Consequently, Western culture has difficulty making sense of "who" these people are. The mother-daughter units constitute the complex and fluid Native American relationships which provide representative visions and voices "invoking the inestimable power of the earth and all the forces of the universe" to resolve and complete the Indian American mission of survival.

FURTHER READING

Criticism

Beidler, Peter, ed. "Silko's Originality in 'Yellow Woman.'" *Sail* 8, No. 2 (Summer 1996): 61-84.

> Series of essays comparing Silko's short story "Yellow Woman" with the traditional Keresan versions of the Yellow Woman story.

Copeland, Marion W. "*Black Elk Speaks* and Leslie Silko's *Ceremony:* Two Visions of Horses." *Critique* 24, No. 3 (Spring 1983): 158-72.

> Discusses the vision of horses in *Black Elk Speaks* and Silko's *Ceremony.*

Evers, Larry. "A Response: Going Along with The Story." *American Indian Quarterly* 5, No. 1 (February 1979): 71-5.

> Evers asserts that "the special burden of the contemporary American Indian writer is that if he is to survive as an American Indian and as a writer, he must not only get his community but all of us to go along with his story," and holds that Silko has this ability.

Perez Castillo, Susan. "Postmodernism, Native American Literature and the Real: The Silko-Erdrich Controversy." *The Massachusetts Review* XXXII, No. 1 (Summer 1991): 285-94.

> Discusses the issues that divide Silko and fellow Native American writer Louise Erdrich.

Sale, Roger. "Hostages." *The New York Review of Books* XXIV, No. 9 (26 May 1977): 39-42.

> Reviews Anne Tyler's *Earthly Possessions,* Thomas Berger's *Who Is Teddy Villanova?* and Silko's *Ceremony.* Praises Silko's promise, but asserts that the novel wavers in the second half.

Shaddock, Jennifer. "Mixed Blood Women: The Dynamic of Women's Relations in the Novels of Louise Erdrich and Leslie Silko." *Feminist Nightmares: Women at Odds,* edited by Susan Ostrov Weisser and Jennifer Fleischner, pp. 106-21. New York: New York University Press, 1992.

> Argues that the work of Silko and Louise Erdrich "is significant for feminist theories of oppression in that it posits strategies of resistance through language, specifically through story, and, in the process, retheorizes oppression itself."

Additional coverage of Silko's life and career is contained in the following sources published by Gale: *Authors and Artists for Young Adults,* **Vol. 14;** *Contemporary Authors,* **Vol. 115, and 122;** *Contemporary Authors New Revision Series,* **Vol. 45, and 65;** *Dictionary of Literary Biography,* **Vol. 143, and 175;** *DISCovering Authors; DISCovering Authors: Canadian Edition; DISCovering Authors Modules: Most Studied, Multicultural,* **and** *Popular Fiction and Genre Authors;* **and** *Native North American Literature;* **and** *World Literature Criticism Supplement.*

David Foster Wallace
1962-

American novelist, essayist, and short story writer.

The following entry presents an overview of Wallace's career through 1997. For further information on his life and works, see *CLC*, Volume 50.

INTRODUCTION

Wallace received considerable attention for his first novel, *The Broom of the System* (1986). Wallace presented an ambitious, eccentric, and lengthy book of stories within stories that featured elaborate wordplay, a large cast of characters, and philosophical speculation that recalled the previous generation of American writers. Wallace's book contrasted sharply with much of the American fiction of the 1980s, which featured minimalist stories, thinly developed characters, plots with little action, and cynical, nihilistic themes. Wallace followed his initial novel with a collection of short stories and novellas, *Girl with Curious Hair* (1989), critical articles and essays, and the nonfiction study *Signifying Rappers* (1990). In 1996, Wallace released a complex and extravagant novel, *Infinite Jest*. At 1,079 pages, the voluminous work has cemented Wallace's critical reputation as the "Generation-X" version of "metafictionists" such as Thomas Pynchon, John Barth, William Gass, and Don DeLillo.

Biographical Information

Born in Ithaca, New York, in 1962, Wallace has described his childhood as relatively ordinary and uneventful. Both of his parents were teachers and he was encouraged to read, which he did avidly and widely. As an undergraduate at Amherst College, Wallace showed great facility in mathematical logic, enjoying what he calls a "click" as steps in mathematical structure fit into place. Many of his philosophy professors considered him a strong candidate to achieve success in their field. Increasingly, though, he felt the "click" from his own philosophical speculations in fictional forms. After receiving his A.B. from Amherst in 1985, he went on to earn an M.F.A. degree from the University of Arizona in 1987. By the time he completed his coursework at Arizona, he had published *The Broom of the System,* and his literary career was under way.

Major Works

Taking its title from Ludwig Wittgenstein's *Tractatus, The Broom of the System* presents Wallace's exploration of the philosopher's theories of language and meaning. Set in and around Cleveland in 1990, the novel follows Lenore Beadsman's quest to find her great-grandmother. Beadsman's namesake and self-appointed intellectual mentor, the elder Lenore, herself a former student of Wittgenstein, has disappeared from her nursing home and is believed to be hiding in the Great Ohio Desert (G.O.D.). The story is told from multiple perspectives and features alternating journal entries, conversations, stream-of-consciousness reflections, and third-person narratives. Lenore's efforts to sort out the confusion that surrounds her are complicated for her, and for the reader, by an array of sub-plots, frequent interruptions of the story, a large cast of characters, and Wallace's extravagant and suggestive wordplay. The same techniques are employed in a variety of contexts in the short story collection *Girl with Curious Hair*. Again Wallace explores themes of communication, identity, and meaning in an age dominated by popular culture. "Little Expressionless Animals" tells of the "Jeopardy!" game show producers' plot to unseat the longest running champion of their show because they fear the consequences of the public learning of her lesbian relationship. In "My Appearance" an actress tranquilizes herself into a stupor attempting to relieve her anxiety over appearing on the "David Letterman Show." The novella "Westward the Course of Empire Takes Its Way" follows a group of former child actors on their way to a reunion. *Infinite Jest* is in some respects a summary statement of the first decade of Wallace's career. Set in a not-too-distant future in which numeric years have been replaced by corporate sponsor designations like the "Year of Glad" and the "Year of the Depend Adult Undergarment," *Infinite Jest* is the story of the creation, loss, and attempted recovery of the perfect entertainment, a film entitled *Infinite Jest,* which is so funny that anyone who sees it must see it again to the exclusion of any other films. At more than a thousand pages with over one hundred pages of pseudo-scholarly footnotes, *Infinite Jest* physically recreates the themes it examines.

Critical Reception

Response to Wallace's work has been mostly enthusiastic. His many awards include the Whiting Writers' Award (1987), a nomination for the Pulitzer Prize in Nonfiction (1990), and a MacArthur Foundation Fellowship (1997). *The Broom of the System* received a great deal of attention, in part because of its dual-edition release. Wallace was immediately compared with Thomas Pynchon, both favorably and unfavorably. Nearly all early reviews heralded Wallace as a major talent. But many critics faulted him for excessive and self-indulgent wordplay, derivative style, and sophomoric humor. A critic for *Kirkus Reviews* wrote that *The Broom of the System* "suffers from a severe case of manic impressiveness" and goes on to characterize Wallace as a "puerile Pynchon, a discount DeLillo." Wallace's work has continued to receive such sharply divided responses, sometimes within the same review.

PRINCIPAL WORKS

The Broom of the System (novel) 1986
Girl with Curious Hair (short stories and novellas) 1989
Signifying Rappers [with Mark Costello] (nonfiction) 1990
Infinite Jest (novel) 1996
A Supposedly Fun Thing I'll Never Do Again: Essays and Arguments (essays) 1997

CRITICISM

Kirkus Reviews (review date 15 November 1986)

SOURCE: A review of *The Broom of the System,* in *Kirkus Reviews,* Vol. LIV, No. 22, November 15, 1986, p. 1686.

[*In the following review, the critic finds that Wallace's first novel displays flashes of genius but also suffers from an immature and derivative style.*]

This unusual debut, the first novel to be published simultaneously in hard-cover and as a paperback in Penguin's "Contemporary American Fiction" series, suffers from a severe case of manic impressiveness. Wallace, a recent Amherst grad, is something of a puerile Pynchon, a discount Don DeLillo, and even a bit of an original.

> **Brimming with subplots, stories within stories, countless one-liners, and a cast of characters worthy of some sort of postmodern Dickens, this bulky fiction, when it isn't plain tedious, seems to be a big inside-joke.**
> **—*Kirkus Reviews***

Brimming with subplots, stories within stories, countless one-liners, and a cast of characters worthy of some sort of postmodern Dickens, this bulky fiction, when it isn't plain tedious, seems to be a big inside-joke. Almost every male in the book went to Amherst, from Rich Vigorous (class of '69), the head of Frequent and Vigorous Publishers, to Andrew Sealander "Wang-Dang" Lang (class of '82), a former frat boy and campus swell, now married to Mindy Metalman, a "Playboy-Playmatish JAP from Scarsdale," whom Wanger met one night on a roll to Holyoke. But that doesn't begin to explain how Vigorous, with his abnormally small penis, and the strapping preppy meet in Amherst in 1990, the year in which most of this self-consciously strange book takes place. The connection between them, and between just about everyone else here, from sexy Candy Mandible to cruel Stonecipher Beadsman III, is the former's roommate and the latter's daughter, Leonore Beadsman, an overeducated switchboard operator at the Bombardini Building in Cleveland, Ohio. That's not far from the corporate headquarters of Stonecipheco, the family-owned baby-food company in fierce competition with Gerber's. Also nearby is the nursing home from which Leonore's great-grandmother, a former student of Wittgenstein (that "mad crackpot genius"), has strangely disappeared, thus setting into motion the hyperactive narrative. Jokes about fiction by "a nastily troubled little collegiate mind" should give readers further reason to pause.

Wallace dabbles in big ideas, with too many pseudo-Wittgensteinian pauses ("". . . .") and much callow satire on consumer/evangelical America. Despite flashes of real genius, it's a heady *Animal House* vision.

Madison Smartt Bell (review date 6 August 1989)

SOURCE: "At Play in the Funhouse of Fiction," in *Washington Post Book World,* Vol. 19, No. 32, August 6, 1989, p. 4.

[*In the following review of* Girl with Curious Hair, *novelist Bell places Wallace in the context of "metafictionists" like John Barth and Thomas Pynchon in order to discuss how Wallace seeks to differentiate himself from that label.*]

The appearance of his immensely long first novel, ***The Broom of the System,*** caused David Foster Wallace to be lumped in with "metafictionists" such as Barth, Coover, Pynchon & Co. Evidently Wallace is not altogether pleased with this categorization, and in his new and also sizeable first collection of stories he takes some pains to correct it. The volume ends with what by virtue of its length might be called a novella, **"Westward the Course of Empire Takes Its Way,"** which is simultaneously a parody of, homage to, and rebellion against John Barth's story, "Lost in the Funhouse." The Barth story, which constantly interrupts its progress to comment explicitly on its own techniques, is regarded by Wallace as a sort of metafictional manifesto, and here he uses somewhat similar devices to write a rather different manifesto of his own.

"Westward" is crammed with a lot of rather superfluous plot material—superfluous since the plot doesn't actually lead anywhere much and isn't supposed to. Appropriately enough, the story begins inside "The East Chesapeake Tradeschool Writing Program," directed by a Professor Ambrose (Barth himself in thin disguise). Here D. L. Eberhardt, a self-declared "postmodernist" who writes, for instance, a 20-page-long poem consisting of nothing but punctuation and whose "pheromones are attractive only to bacteria," has through the stratagem of a false pregnancy contrived to get married to Mark Nechtr ("one of those late-adolescent chosen who radiate the kind of careless health so complete it's sickening"), another grad-student fiction writer of a more realist persuasion, who is, however, completely blocked. This mismatch provides occasion for a certain amount of sniping about fictional technique, but the elaboration does not stop there.

One of the great many peculiarities of D. L.'s background is that she is a former child actor in McDonald's commercials produced by adman and franchise potentate J. D. Steelritter. Steelritter is now on the point of launching, in partnership with Ambrose, a new chain of homogenized discotheques to be called "Funhouses," after the ur-Funhouse of the Barth story (here supposed to have been written by Ambrose). Steelritter is opening the first Funhouse in his "hometown," a crossroads amid the cornfields called Collision, Illinois, and to add to the fanfare he is bringing all the former child actors back there for a humongous reunion. Thus Mark and D. L. find themselves (very eventually) passengers en route from the airport to Collision along with Steelritter and two other McDonald's "alumni," Tom Sternberg and Magda Ambrose-Gatz, in a homemade car built and driven by Steelritter's son DeHaven, who is decked out in the full regalia of his official role as Ronald McDonald.

At this point, with all the ingredients for a typical metafictional circus in place, the plot thickens to a sort of jelly, and begins to be constantly broken up by "Blatant and Intrusive Interruptions," labeled as such. Like the interruptions in the original "Lost in the Funhouse," though much longer, wilder and hairier, these are commentaries on fictional technique. Their content is thematically interlaced with the story's action, which has now been reduced to conversation amongst the people stuck in the car, which with increasing obstinance refuses to reach its destination. The story has much to say about various relationships between art, life, and advertising, but what it finally says about metafiction (through the head of Mark Nechtr) is that "itself is its only object. It's the act of a lonely solipsist's self-love . . ." Nechtr, however, "desires, some distant hard-earned day, to write something that stabs you to the heart . . . The stuff would probably use metafiction as a bright smiling disguise . . ."

> **If Wallace has assumed the mission of seizing the methods of metafiction while rejecting its self-reflexive ends, the question becomes, can he do it? And the answer is, not always.**
> —*Madison Smartt Bell*

If Wallace has assumed the mission of seizing the methods of metafiction while rejecting its self-reflexive ends, the question becomes, can he do it? And the answer is, not always. **"Westward"** itself does not quite manage to escape the toils of its own cleverness, but there are nine more stories in the book. In several of them (**"John Billy," "Here and There," "Say Never," "Everything Is Green"**), Wallace overindulges in the merely ingenious. In several others, however, he meets his own standards in a quite impressive way.

Of the successes the simplest is **"Luckily the Account Representative Knew CPR,"** a close-up account of one man attempting to manage another's heart attack in the depths of an empty parking garage. The most moving may be **"Little Expressionless Animals,"** a sort of psychodrama mostly set on the stage of "Jeopardy." The most frightening is the title story, which depicts the perverse mesalliance between a gang of unusually violent punk rockers and a psychotic Young

Republican. The most improbable is an affectionate portrait of Lyndon Johnson, seen through the eyes of a fictional aide.

Promiscuous mingling of real-life celebrities with fictional characters, fantastically absurd situations, puns and other self-referential gestures—the standard metafictional maneuvers are present everywhere. Even when he's just fooling around, Wallace is a good deal funnier than the average metafictionist, so some of the stories are worth reading for laughs alone. But the best of them do what he promises for them: they go beyond talking about only themselves to say something serious and sincere about the world that the rest of us have to live in.

Jenifer Levin (review date 5 November 1989)

SOURCE: "Love Is a Federal Highway." in *New York Times,* November 5, 1989, Sec. 7, p. 31.

[*In the following review, Levin finds Wallace's collection of short stories evidence of both an impressive talent and a tendency toward excess.*]

With this collection of stories [*Girl with Curious Hair*], David Foster Wallace, the author of the novel ***The Broom of the System,*** proves himself a dynamic writer of extraordinary talent, one unafraid to tackle subjects large and small. Ever willing to experiment, he lays his artistic self on the line with his incendiary use of language, at times seeming to rip both the mundane and the unusual from their moorings, then setting them down anew, freshly described.

Mr. Wallace is particularly interested in flux as a partial definition of human nature, in distance as a component of love and —most important to him, perhaps—in the obvious as well as the subtle linking of seeing and vision, masks and the truth behind them.

Mr. Wallace is nothing if not audacious. Real-life heroes, villains, historical figures, sports legends, television personalities—even dinosaurs—appear in these stories alongside his fictitious characters, who themselves run the gamut from banal to psychotic. In "**Little Expressionless Animals,**" for example, a young woman with an incredible winning streak on the television game show "Jeopardy!" is finally defeated by her psychologically disturbed brother—the whole encounter engineered when the producers become too touchy about her ongoing lesbian love affair. In "**Lyndon,**" David Boyd, a fictitious mail clerk who joins Lyndon Johnson's Senate staff, tells the story of his companionship with Lady Bird and describes his own arranged marriage to a wealthy alcoholic and his long homosexual union with a Haitian "with diplomatic immunity." More than mere storytelling, his is an attempt to probe the meaning of love and responsibility to individual people and to his country against a background of multiple declines: Johnson's from heart disease, Boyd's and his lover's from AIDS, America's from Vietnam.

"Love is simply a word," says Mr. Wallace's fictional incarnation of Lady Bird Johnson. "It joins separate things. Lyndon and I, though you would disagree, agree that we do not properly love one another anymore. Because we ceased long ago to be enough apart for a 'love' to span any distance. Lyndon says he shall cherish the day when love and right and wrong and responsibility, when these words, he says, are understood by you youths of America to be nothing but arrangements of distance." She goes on to explain that her husband's "hatred of being alone is a consequence of what his memoir will call his great intellectual concept: the distance at which we see each other, arrange each other, love. That love, he will say, is a federal highway, lines putting communities, that move and exist at great distance, in touch. My husband has stated publicly that America, too, his own America, that he loves enough to conceal deaths for, is to be understood in terms of distance."

In another story, the witty "**My Appearance,**" a successful television actress agonizes over her upcoming spot on the David Letterman show, pops one tranquilizer after another and muses (with emotionally disastrous results) over the differences between the way things appear to be and the way they really are. And in the title story, "**Girl with Curious Hair,**" the narrator—a successful young corporate lawyer, the graduate of a military academy and several Ivy League universities, the second son of an honored military family who also happens to be a psychotic sociopath—reveals the childhood source of his sadistic sexual compulsions while reminiscing about a Keith Jarrett concert that he attended with a group of savagely lost punk-rocker companions.

If Mr. Wallace's characters include the transcendent as well as the maimed, his style is similarly varied, running from prosaic to lyrical. "I've just never liked it," one of his characters says of poetry. "It beats around bushes. Even when I like it, it's nothing more than a really oblique way of saying the obvious." To which her friend replies, "But consider how very, very few of us have the equipment to deal with the obvious."

Mr. Wallace might as well be commenting on modern fiction in general here. He himself is more than capable of dealing with the obvious. However, he is obsessed not only with the appearance of things but with their true nature, with objects and relationships as they really are, beneath the veils that hide them. Interestingly enough, his ability simply to describe is superb. And it is when he allows his observations to speak for themselves, when he does not permit himself to become pedantic by overstating the obvious, that he is at his most effective. When showing rather than telling, Mr. Wallace allows his characters to function in both a symbolic and a living context. When showing rather than telling, he is tender enough and strong enough not to shy away from love—whether he's attempting to define it or (better yet) simply daring to expose it.

> **Mr. Wallace is such a bold writer that his failures can be almost as interesting as his successes. Unfortunately, he sometimes slides into a kind of showboating, a smug display of sheer knowledge and cleverness.**
> **—*Jenifer Levin***

Mr. Wallace is such a bold writer that his failures can be almost as interesting as his successes. Unfortunately, he sometimes slides into a kind of showboating, a smug display of sheer knowledge and cleverness. And so the pieces that don't work (**"Luckily the Account Representative Knew CPR"** and a ponderous novella, **"Westward the Course of Empire Takes Its Way"**) come off as the sort of inside jokes that might play best in a creative writing seminar; they're meaningful and witty, perhaps, to those who are willing to sacrifice substance to stylistic or symbolic experimentation, but tiresome to the rest of us.

And yet, when Mr. Wallace is at his best he is undoubtedly among the very best. The most successful fiction in *Girl with Curious Hair* has the quality of a dream: powerful, fixating, explosive and mysterious. Mr. Wallace brings us, time and again, to hidden, mythic places that are strange yet oddly familiar, larger than life yet inexplicably known—and knowable. He is definitely interested in what a television executive in one of the stories calls "the capacity of facts to transcend their internal factual limitations and become, in and of themselves, meaning, feeling."

This is especially true of the extraordinary story **"John Billy,"** a luminous explosion into the realm of myth in which a bandy-legged Oklahoman is transformed by a near-fatal brush with death (and evil) into a creature of both darkness and light, one whose damaged eyes extend like the waving ends of antennae from his head, capable of finally seeing things. Those eyes are his undoing, for they show him the wasted and bleeding countryside, linking him (like the Fisher King of myth) to the death of the land.

In this daring exploration of the mythological and metaphysical context of fiction—and thus of life itself—Mr. Wallace demonstrates his remarkable talent. He succeeds in restoring grandeur to modern fiction, reminding us of the ecstasy, terror, horror and beauty of which it is capable when it is released from the television-screen-sized confines of minimalism.

Douglas Siebold (review date 21 January 1990)

SOURCE: "'Maximalist' Short Fiction from a Talented Young Writer," in *Chicago Tribune,* January 21, 1990, Sec. 14, p. 7.

[*The following review highlights Wallace's distinctiveness from his predecessors, "the metafictionists," and his contemporaries, "the minimalists."*]

David Foster Wallace is probably the most talented of the writers under 30 who have been forced on the reading public over the past five or so years by publishers excited by the commercial success of such books as Jay McInerney's *Bright Lights, Big City* and Bret Easton Ellis' *Less Than Zero.*

Most of the work of these writers has been forgettable, in some cases even regrettable. But if the work of Wallace's contemporaries mostly consists of thin, under-nourished volumes that together form the body of the so-called "minimalist" school of American fiction, his work is resoundingly maximalist.

A 1985 graduate of Amherst, he developed his senior thesis into *The Broom of the System* (1987), a novel distinguished by the sprawling vigor of its prose as well as by its author's obvious ability, ambition and disdain for literary fashion.

Broom suggested that Wallace was an heir to such "metafictional" writers as John Barth, Donald Barthelme, Robert Coover and Thomas Pynchon. But in *Girl with Curious Hair,* his new collection of stories, Wallace makes irrelevant any distinction between schools. With his irrepressible narrative energy and invention, he is unafraid to extend his talents and take risks.

The Broom of the System (the title is from Wittgenstein) revealed that Wallace already had achieved a precocious mastery of metafictional techniques and conceits. In the nine stories and the concluding novella of *Girl with Curious Hair,* he demonstrates that his impressive facility with language and philosophical concepts (the son of a University of Illinois philosophy professor, Wallace himself is now doing graduate study in philosophy at Harvard) extends as well to literary styles.

One story, **"Everything Is Green,"** fulfills every cliche associated with minimalist writing; it almost reads as though Wallace were attempting to define the stereotype by example. But the story, a gem of a thousand words at most, is one of the best and most affecting in the collection. In writing it, Wallace demonstrates that those minimalist conventions have become cliches only through their repeated abuse at the hands of less imaginative and less passionate writers. Many of the stories here deal with television, a subject Wallace handles with intelligence, understanding and respect. He recognizes the way television both informs and deforms our lives—particularly those of younger Americans who have grown up with television occupying as much as a quarter of their time.

In **"Little Expressionless Animals"** Wallace creates the greatest champion in the history of the game show "Jeopardy." **"My Appearance"** treats the fear and trembling faced by a middle-aged actress preparing for a guest shot on David Letterman's talk show. Wallace neither condescends to television nor underestimates its significance in the lives of his characters and readers. It also provides the context for some of his funniest stuff.

In the climactic novella, **"Westward the Course of Empire Takes Its Way,"** the TV show "Hawaii Five-O" and its star, Jack Lord, figure tangentially, as the story's characters (including its maddening narrator) address such larger issues as the possession of stories, the frying of roses, their greatest fears, the Vietnam War, archery, advertising and much, much more—mostly while packed into a car bouncing over the back roads of central Illinois.

The Broom of the System **(the title is from Wittgenstein) revealed that Wallace already had achieved a precocious mastery of metafictional techniques and conceits. In the nine stories and the concluding novella of** *Girl with Curious Hair,* **he demonstrates that his impressive facility with language and philosophical concepts. . . . extends as well to literary styles.**
                          —Douglas Siebold

"Westward" takes up somewhere near where *The Broom of the System* left off in terms of Wallace's involvement with "the apocalyptically cryptic Literature of Last Things, in exhaustion in general, and metafiction," in the words of the story's heroine. As Wallace has it, parts of the story "are written in the margins of John Barth's *Lost in the Funhouse* and Cynthia Ozick's *Usurpation (Other People's Stories)*." The piece is erudite, extremely funny, and infuriating in its open-endedness, a Zeno's arrow that never quite reaches its target. The effect is impressive but unsatisfying—it's a work of virtuoso throat-clearing.

Wallace concluded a recent essay on his fledgling literary generation with an acknowledgment that many of his writing contemporaries—and perhaps those who may become the best of them—are as yet unpublished, learning and refining their craft. But among the young writers who are developing in public view, Wallace appears to be doing just fine. And though it may not amount to much more than apprentice work, *Girl with Curious Hair* is evidence that, as good a writer as he is now, he is getting better.

Sven Birkerts (essay date 1992)

SOURCE: "David Foster Wallace," in *American Energies,* William Morrow and Co., Inc, 1992, pp. 386-92.

[*In the essay below, critic and educator Birkerts sets Tom Wolfe's call for a return to fiction of social realism on the nineteenth-century model against contemporary techniques of story-telling to present Wallace as the exemplar of a viable alternative for a new approach to serious literature in our age.*]

Tom Wolfe, as we all know, has a positive genius for wetting his index finger and getting it up there into the weather. In his recent essay in *Harper's,* "Stalking the Billion-Footed Beast: A Literary Manifesto for the New Social Novel," he raised a call for a return to subject matter in fiction. Wolfe holds that in our postmodern and minimalist era the art has all but withered away. Novelists and storytellers are busy with academic exercises; they are ceding the job of transcribing reality to journalists.

Wolfe, whose own grand social novel, *The Bonfire of the Vanities,* has achieved spectacular popular success, professes himself dumbfounded. Never in history has there been so much material. The big, gritty world is all but posing for the writer; our newspapers brim with outlandish and revelatory narratives. "American society today," Wolfe asserts, "is no more or less chaotic, random, discontinuous, or absurd than Russian society or French society or British society a hundred years ago, no matter how convenient it might be for a writer to think so."

Wolfe has proved himself often prescient—and always provocative—and at first his call appears to be just what we need. The serious novel is in crisis; bony tales of domestic trauma are the order of the day. But a more thoughtful reading of Wolfe's manifesto brings pause. His premise, that our society, while different in its particulars, is in its essentials unchanged, no more "chaotic" or "random" than the societies of Tolstoy's, Zola's, or Thackeray's day, is astonishing. It short-circuits modernity altogether, ignoring the catastrophic and all-transforming impacts of nuclear fission, the microchip, telecommunications, the multinational corporation, the all but total decimation of the farm economy. Wolfe is making a brash end run around modernism, attempting for fiction what he once attempted for architecture. His summons to a new social novel is, on closer inspection, a kind of retreat.

The success of *Bonfire* seems to have blinkered Wolfe's vision. Perhaps he interprets his sales figures as an endorsement of his literary principles. But he is confusing popularity with artistic attainment. *Bonfire* is a delightfully engaging popular novel—it is not great literature. It stands on a par with works by John O'Hara and Sinclair Lewis (whom Wolfe extols in his essay), and when its cultural moment has passed, it, too, will pass. Accurate as *Bonfire* is in capturing the social mores and commodity fetishism of late-twentieth-century urban America, its penetration of culture and human character is superficial. The novel, and Wolfe's proclamation, have little bearing on the deeper purposes of literature.

In the arts, as in human life, there is no going back to the past except in memory. We may deplore the triviality or aridity of current productions and long for the vigorous amplitude of an earlier day, but we cannot snap our fingers and will its recurrence. So-called "serious" literature is bound to both reflect and reflect *upon* the continuing evolution of the human; it must interrogate our meaning—individual and social—in the light of the history we keep making. Writers find their forms for this presentation not by reaching blindly into a grab bag of former modes but by extending or refuting the forms that their predecessors have used.

Let me try to illustrate the current dilemma. Picture two travelers. One is a man sitting at a table at a roadside inn in England in the late nineteenth century. The other is a man sitting under the crackling fluorescents of a mall cafeteria in late 1980s America. The first man, positioned naturally and comprehensibly in his environment, is a ready subject for the kind of novel Wolfe espouses; we recognize both man and inn from Hardy, Dickens, and Thackeray. Reading about him, we make a set of assumptions about the solidity and coherence of the world around him.

The man in the mall, however, presents a problem. The table in front of him is plastic; the food he eats is generic pulp. He sits not in silence or amid the low murmurs of others like him, but is enfolded in the ambient distraction of Muzak. He studies the napkin holder. Nearby a kid with an orange Mohawk bashes a video game. The swirl of energies around our subject all but erases him. The writer cannot simply plunk him down and get on with the business of narration. A thousand changed circumstances have combined to vaporize his human solidity—or its illusion.

Wolfe is on target in identifying subject matter as the great-est challenge facing the contemporary writer. But in proposing the panoramic approach, he has bypassed the underlying problem entirely. To work on the scale that Wolfe demands, to get at the big ironies and moral collisions of modern urban life, characters have to be flattened and typed until they are nearly cartoons; situations have to be heightened to tabloid contrast. Which is all very interesting but has little to do with the truth about how life is experienced by the individual in our time.

Yes, there is a crisis in the arts. The crisis is that the greater part of contemporary experience has fallen out of the reach of language—or very nearly so. We no longer till fields; most of us don't even make things—our attention is increasingly dispersed among inchoate signals. So much of our time is passed in talking on phones, driving on freeways, staring at terminals or TV screens, and waiting in lobbies. Larger and larger portions of what our lives are made up of cannot be encompassed in coherent narrative form. The writer must either distort or else work around the expanding blank spots.

The minimalists, pilloried by Wolfe, have at least recognized the nature of the problem. But their response (I'm thinking here of writers such as Ann Beattie, Amy Hempel, Frederick Barthelme, and Mary Robison) is to retreat from the internal. These authors give us the descriptions of the places, the name brands, the clips of conversation, and we must infer what the innerscape is like.

Minimalism is ultimately a cul-de-sac, leaving the larger part of modern life untouched. The new social novel that Wolfe would sponsor is, by contrast, open to *stuff,* to big events and dramatic conflicts. It can incorporate in documentary fashion large masses of familiar material, including the brands and places beloved of the minimalists. But its scale and its hothouse sensationalism—its Dickensian ambition—forbid closer inspection of the conditions of our changed sensibilities.

What is the fiction writer—the writer who would try to catch us undistorted in our moment—to do? What prose will raise a mirror to our dispersed condition? One sort of answer is now offered in a collection of stories entitled ***Girl with Curious Hair,*** by David Foster Wallace. He is Wolfe's compass needle turned 180 degrees.

Wallace's stories are as startling and barometrically accurate as anything in recent decades. The author, still in his twenties (his novel, ***The Broom of the System,*** was published in 1987), writes what his adoring flap copy calls "*post*-postmodernism." Much as I revile flap copy, I have to say that the tag is right. We sense immediately that Wallace is beyond the calculated fiddle of the postmodernists. He is not announcing as news the irreparable fragmentation of our cultural life; he is not fastening upon TV and punk culture and airport lounges as if for the first time ever. Wallace comes toward us as a citizen of that new place, the place that the minimalists have only been able to point toward. The rhythms, disjunctions, and surreally beautiful—if terrifying—meldings of our present-day surround are fully his. Wallace is, for better or worse, the savvy and watchful voice of the *now*—and he is unburdened by any nostalgia for the old order.

> **Wallace comes toward us as a citizen of that new place, the place that the minimalists have only been able to point toward. The rhythms, disjunctions, and surreally beautiful—if terrifying—meldings of our present-day surround are fully his. Wallace is, for better or worse, the savvy and watchful voice of the *now*—and he is unburdened by any nostalgia for the old order.**
> —*Sven Birkerts*

Girl with Curious Hair collects ten of Wallace's stories, four or five of which are strong enough to inflict the scorpion's sting on the workshop verbiage that passes for fiction these days. The first piece, **"Little Expressionless Animals,"** is one of these. In swift, artfully elided passages, Wallace tells the story of Julie Smith, for three years undefeated queen of the television quiz show *Jeopardy*! (She is, of course, an invention.) But the customary descriptions, I realize, will not work here. Wallace does not, in fact, *tell the story.* Instead, he inhabits for extended moments the airspace around Julie, her lover Faye (a researcher for the show), Faye's mother, Dee (the producer), and Alex Trebek (the host); or else he slips, as omniscient narrator, back into essential episodes from Julie's past. What emerges is a legend of real-life damage and media vampirism that dots the reader's flesh with goose bumps.

Here, as elsewhere, Wallace sets nearly all his scenes in the drab and untenanted places that writers avoid—in hallways, empty conference rooms, on the flashing plastic set of the show. And, episode by episode, there is little or no action. The reviewer butts against impossibility, for the whole effect of these fictions derives from the cumulation and cross echo of these elided moments. Citation would distort more than it would reveal.

I can, however, try to describe the effect. As readers, we feel we have made contact with a new dimension. We touch not the old illusion of reality that fiction has always traded in but the irreality that every day further obscures the recognizable. We enter a zone where signals flash across circuits; where faces balloon across monitors and voices slip in and

out of clear sense; where media personnel work night and day to mask and stylize the merely personal; where Alex Trebek, master of poise, confesses to his psychiatrist that he's worried about his smile: "That it's starting to maybe be a tired smile. Which is *not* an inviting smile, which is professionally worrying."

"Girl with Curious Hair," the title story, reconnoiters adjacent terrain, but in a very different manner. A businessman by day, punk by night named Sick Puppy tells about an evening spent with friends at a Keith Jarrett concert. He sits with Big and Mr. Wonderful, and with his girlfriend, Gimlet, who wears her hair styled up to resemble an erect penis. The shock is less in the premise or the rude antics of the friends; it is in the idiom that Wallace has given his narrator. Tuning in on Sick Puppy at random, we hear:

> Her friend and confidante Tit sculptures Gimlet's hair and provides her with special haircare products from her career as a hair stylist which makes Gimlet's hair sculpture rigid and realistic at all times. I have my hair maintained at Julio's Unisex Fashion Cut Center in West Hollywood, with an attractive part on the right side of my hair.

By story's end precious little has happened, but we are reeling. The calculated pastiche of the prose, its phrasings drawn from TV, ad brochures, and commercial newspeak, forces the larger question: if we are as we speak, then where is Sick Puppy? He has put his expression together from everywhere; he is frighteningly, *awesomely,* nowhere.

Wallace's other stories, the best of them, set us straight into the heart of this newly seen present. In **"My Appearance,"** a young woman worries for thirty pages about her guest spot on the David Letterman show. **"Westward the Course of Empire Takes Its Way"** recounts the journey through the Midwest of a group of former actors from McDonald's commercials; they are on their way to a grand reunion of all former players from McDonald's commercials. (Wallace's scenarios are as funny as they are uncanny or suggestive.) Again and again, nothing—or nearly nothing—happens. But the way that nothing happens, the eerie space it opens for stray turns and encounters, captures a feeling that often threatens to engulf us in our lives: the feeling that we are not fully hooked in, that the tide of distraction laps ever more forcefully at our boundaries and threatens to spill over one day soon.

To achieve this peculiar verisimilitude, Wallace is forced to steer away from the staple binding ingredient of most fiction: narrative drama. His stories go untensed by any overt conflicts or movements toward gratifying resolution. They are, like Pynchon's fictions, difficult to read over long stretches, and for many of the same reasons. Yet time and again we shake our heads to say, "It's true. That's what it's like out there."

Between Wolfe and Wallace, we find ourselves in a strange bind. If fiction is to win and hold a readership, it will probably have to move Wolfe's way. But the new social novel does not hold much of the truth about the changed conditions of our subjective lives, our feel for the contemporary, except in caricature. The other compass direction, which leads us closer to the man—or woman—hunched over coffee in the mall, cannot easily render that life and remain gratifying as narrative. Where shall we get the picture of who we are? It seems that the present keeps moving, with ever greater acceleration, out of the reach of language. It may take new geniuses and new genres to bring it back.

Larry McCaffery (interview date Summer 1993)

SOURCE: "An Interview with David Foster Wallace," in *Review of Contemporary Fiction*, Vol, 13, No. 2, Summer, 1993, pp. 127-50.

[*In the following interview, McCaffery questions Wallace on matters of style, technique, and substance in his writing, as well as his relationship to the popular culture that figures so prominently in his work.*]

[*Larry McCaffery:*] *Your essay following this interview is going to be seen by some people as being basically an apology for television. What's your response to the familiar criticism that television fosters relationships with illusions or simulations of real people (Reagan being a kind of quintessential example)?*

[*David Foster Wallace:*] It's a try at a comprehensive diagnosis, not an apology. U.S. viewers' relationship with TV is essentially puerile and dependent, as are all relationships based on seduction. This is hardly news. But what's seldom acknowledged is how complex and ingenious TV's seductions are. It's seldom acknowledged that viewers' relationship with TV is, albeit debased, intricate and profound. It's easy for older writers just to bitch about TV's hegemony over the U.S. art market, to say the world's gone to hell in a basket and shrug and have done with it. But I think younger writers owe themselves a richer account of just why TV's become such a dominating force on people's consciousness, if only because we under like forty have spent our whole conscious lives being *part* of TV's audience.

Television may be more complex than what most people realize, but it seems rarely to attempt to challenge or disturb its audience, as you've written me you wish to. Is it that

sense of challenge and pain that makes your work more "serious" than most television shows?

I had a teacher I liked who used to say good fiction's job was to comfort the disturbed and disturb the comfortable. I guess a big part of serious fiction's purpose is to give the reader, who like all of us is sort of marooned in her own skull, to give her imaginative access to other selves. Since an ineluctable part of being a human self is suffering, part of what we humans come to art for is an experience of suffering, necessarily a vicarious experience, more like a sort of *generalization* of suffering. Does this make sense? We all suffer alone in the real world; true empathy's impossible. But if a piece of fiction can allow us imaginatively to identify with characters' pain, we might then also more easily conceive of others identifying with our own. This is nourishing, redemptive; we become less alone inside. It might be just that simple. But now realize that TV and popular film and most kinds of "low" art—which just means art whose primary aim is to make money—is lucrative precisely because it recognizes that audiences prefer 100 percent pleasure to the reality that tends to be 49 percent pleasure and 51 percent pain. Whereas "serious" art, which is not primarily about getting money out of you, is more apt to make you uncomfortable, or to force you to work hard to access its pleasures, the same way that in real life true pleasure is usually a by-product of hard work and discomfort. So it's hard for an art audience, especially a young one that's been raised to expect art to be 100 percent pleasurable and to make that pleasure effortless, to read and appreciate serious fiction. That's not good. The problem isn't that today's readership is *dumb*, I don't think. Just that TV and the commercial-art culture's trained it to be sort of lazy and childish in its expectations. But it makes trying to engage today's readers both imaginatively and intellectually unprecedentedly hard.

> We all suffer alone in the real world; true empathy's impossible. But if a piece of fiction can allow us imaginatively to identify with characters' pain, we might then also more easily conceive of others identifying with our own. This is nourishing, redemptive; we become less alone inside. It might be just that simple.
> —*David Foster Wallace*

Who do you imagine your readership to be?

I suppose it's people more or less like me, in their twenties and thirties, maybe, with enough experience or good education to have realized that the hard work serious fiction requires of a reader sometimes has a payoff. People who've been raised with U.S. commercial culture and engaged with it and informed by it and fascinated with it but still hungry for something commercial art can't provide. Yuppies, I guess, and younger intellectuals, whatever. These are the people pretty much all the younger writers I admire—Leyner and Vollmann and Daitch, Amy Homes, Jon Franzen, Lorrie Moore, Rick Powers, even McInerney and Leavitt and those guys—are writing for, I think. But, again, the last twenty years have seen big changes in how writers engage their readers, what readers need to expect from any kind of art.

The media seems to me to be one thing that has drastically changed this relationship. It's provided people with this tele-vision-processed culture for so long that audiences have forgotten what a relationship to serious art is all about.

Well, it's too simple to just wring your hands and claim TV's ruined readers. Because the U.S.'s television culture didn't come out of a vacuum. What TV is extremely good at—and realize that this is *all it does*—is discerning what large numbers of people think they want, and supplying it. And since there's always been a strong and distinctive American distaste for frustration and suffering, TV's going to avoid these like the plague in favor of something anesthetic and easy.

You really think this distaste is distinctly American?

It seems distinctly Western-industrial, anyway. In most other cultures, if you hurt, if you have a symptom that's causing you to suffer, they view this as basically healthy and natural, a sign that your nervous system knows something's wrong. For these cultures, getting rid of the pain without addressing the deeper cause would be like shutting off a fire alarm while the fire's still going. But if you just look at the number of ways that we try like hell to alleviate mere symptoms in this country—from fast-fast-fast-reliefantacids to the popularity of lighthearted musicals during the Depression—you can see an almost compulsive tendency to regard pain itself as the problem. And so pleasure becomes a value, a teleological end in itself. It's probably more Western than U.S. per se. Look at utilitarianism—thatmost English of contributions to ethics—and you see a whole teleology predicated on the idea that the best human life is one that maximizes the pleasure-to-pain ratio. God, I know this sounds priggish of me. All I'm saying is that it's shortsighted to blame TV. It's simply another symptom. TV didn't invent our aesthetic childishness here any more than the Manhattan Project invented aggression. Nuclear weapons and TV have simply intensified the consequences of our tendencies, upped the stakes.

Near the end of "Westward the Course of Empire Takes Its Way," there's a line about Mark that "It would take an architect who could hate enough to feel enough to love enough to perpetrate the kind of special cruelty only real lovers can

inflict." Is that the kind of cruelty you feel is missing in the work of somebody like Mark Leyner?

I guess I'd need to ask you what kind of cruelty you thought the narrator meant there.

It seems to involve the idea that if writers care enough about their audience—if they love them enough and love their art enough—they've got to be cruel in their writing practices. "Cruel" the way an army drill sergeant is when he decides to put a bunch of raw recruits through hell, knowing that the trauma you're inflicting on these guys, emotionally, physically, psychically, is just part of a process that's going to strengthen them in the end, prepare them for things they can't even imagine yet.

Well, besides the question of where the fuck do "artists" get off deciding for readers what stuff the readers need to be prepared for, your idea sounds pretty Aristotelian, doesn't it? I mean, what's the purpose of creating fiction, for you? Is it essentially mimetic, to capture and order a protean reality? Or is it really supposed to be therapeutic in an Aristotelian sense?

I agree with what you said in "Westward" about serious art having to engage a range of experiences; it can't be merely "metafictional," for example, it has to deal with the world outside the page and variously so. How would you contrast your efforts in this regard versus those involved in most television or most popular fiction?

This might be one way to start talking about differences between the early postmodern writers of the fifties and sixties and their contemporary descendants. When you read that quotation from "Westward" just now, it sounded to me like a covert digest of my biggest weaknesses as a writer. One is that I have a grossly sentimental affection for gags, for stuff that's nothing but funny, and which I sometimes stick in for no other reason than funniness. Another's that I have a problem sometimes with concision, communicating only what needs to be said in a brisk efficient way that doesn't call attention to itself. It'd be pathetic for me to blame the exterior for my own deficiencies, but it still seems to me that both of these problems are traceable to this schizogenic experience I had growing up, being bookish and reading a lot, on the one hand, watching grotesque amounts of TV, on the other. Because I liked to read, I probably didn't watch quite as much TV as my friends, but I still got my daily megadose, believe me. And I think it's impossible to spend that many slack-jawed, spittle-chinned, formative hours in front of commercial art without internalizing the idea that one of the main goals of art is simply to *entertain*, give people sheer pleasure. Except to what end, this pleasure-giving? Because, of course, TV's *real* agenda is to be *liked*, because if you like what you're seeing, you'll stay tuned. TV is completely unabashed about this; it's its sole *raison.* And sometimes when I look at my own stuff I feel like I absorbed too much of this *raison.* I'll catch myself thinking up gags or trying formal stunt-pilotry and see that none of this stuff is really in the service of the story itself; it's serving the rather darker purpose of communicating to the reader "Hey! Look at me! Have a look at what a good writer I am! *Like* me!"

Now, to an extent there's no way to escape this altogether, because an author needs to demonstrate some sort of skill or merit so that the reader will trust her. There's some weird, delicate, I-trust-you-not-to-fuck-up-on-me relationship between the reader and writer, and both have to sustain it. But there's an unignorable line between demonstrating skill and charm to gain trust for the story vs. simple showing off. It can become an exercise in trying to get the reader to like and admire you instead of an exercise in creative art. I think TV promulgates the idea that good art is just that art which makes people like and depend on the vehicle that brings them the art. This seems like a poisonous lesson for a would-be artist to grow up with. And one consequence is that if the artist is excessively dependent on simply being *liked,* so that her true end isn't in the work but in a certain audience's good opinion, she is going to develop a terrific hostility to that audience, simply because she has given all her power away to them. It's the familiar love-hate syndrome of seduction: "I don't really care what it is I say, I care only that you like it. But since your good opinion is the sole arbiter of my success and worth, you have tremendous power over me, and I fear you and hate you for it." This dynamic isn't exclusive to art. But I often think I can see it in myself and in other young writers, this desperate desire to please coupled with a kind of hostility to the reader.

In your own case, how does this hostility manifest itself?

Oh, not always, but sometimes in the form of sentences that are syntactically not incorrect but still a real bitch to read. Or bludgeoning the reader with data. Or devoting a lot of energy to creating expectations and then taking pleasure in disappointing them. You can see this clearly in something like Ellis's *American Psycho:* it panders shamelessly to the audience's sadism for a while, but by the end it's clear that the sadism's real object is the reader herself.

But at least in the case of American Psycho *I felt there was something more than just this desire to inflict pain—or that Ellis was being cruel the way you said serious artists need to be willing to be.*

You're just displaying the sort of cynicism that lets readers be manipulated by bad writing. I think it's a kind of black cynicism about today's world that Ellis and certain others depend on for their readership. Look, if the contemporary condition is hopelessly shitty, insipid, materialistic, emotion-

ally retarded, sadomasochistic and stupid, then I (or any writer) can get away with slapping together stories with characters who are stupid, vapid, emotionally retarded, which is easy, because these sorts of characters require no development. With descriptions that are simply lists of brand-name consumer products. Where stupid people say insipid stuff to each other. If what's always distinguished bad writing—flat characters, a narrative world that's clichéd and not recognizably human, etc.—is also a description of today's world, then bad writing becomes an ingenious mimesis of a bad world. If readers simply believe the world is stupid and shallow and mean, then Ellis can write a mean shallow stupid novel that becomes a mordant deadpan commentary on the badness of everything. Look man, we'd probably most of us agree that these are dark times, and stupid ones, but do we need fiction that does nothing but dramatize how dark and stupid everything is? In dark times, the definition of good art would seem to be art that locates and applies CPR to those elements of what's human and magical that still live and glow despite the times' darkness. Really good fiction could have as dark a worldview as it wished, but it'd find a way both to depict this dark world *and* to illuminate the possibilities for being alive and human in it. You can defend *Psycho* as being a sort of performative digest of late-eighties social problems, but it's no more than that.

Are you saying that writers of your generation have an obligation not only to depict our condition but also to provide the solutions to these things?

I don't think I'm talking about conventionally political or social-action-type solutions. That's not what fiction's about. Fiction's about what it is to be a fucking *human being.* If you operate, which most of us do, from the premise that there are things about the contemporary U.S. that make it distinctively hard to be a real human being, then maybe half of fiction's job is to dramatize what it is that makes it tough. The other half is to dramatize the fact that we still *are* human beings, now. Or can be. This isn't that it's fiction's duty to edify or teach, or to make us good little Christians or Republicans; I'm not trying to line up behind Tolstoy or Gardner. I just think that fiction that isn't exploring what it means to be human today isn't good art. We've got all this "literary" fiction that simply monotones that we're all becoming less and less human, that presents characters without souls or love, characters who really are exhaustively describable in terms of what brands of stuff they wear, and we all buy the books and go like "Golly, what a mordantly effective commentary on contemporary materialism!" But we already all *know* U.S. culture is materialistic. This diagnosis can be done in about two lines. It doesn't engage anybody. What's engaging and artistically real is, taking it as axiomatic that the present is grotesquely materialistic, how is it that we as human beings still have the capacity for joy, charity, genuine connections, for stuff that doesn't have a price? And can these capacities be made to thrive? And if so, how, and if not why not?

Not everyone in your generation is taking the Ellis route. Both the other writers in this issue of RCF *seem to be doing exactly what you're talking about. So, for example, even though Vollmann's* Rainbow Stories *is a book that is in its own way as sensationalized as* American Psycho, *the effort there is to depict those people not as flattened, dehumanized stereotypes but as human beings. I'd agree, though, that a lot of contemporary writers today adopt this sort of flat, neutral transformation of people and events into fiction without bothering to make the effort of refocusing their imaginations on the people who still exist underneath these transformations. But Vollmann seems to be someone fighting that tendency in interesting ways.*

This brings us back to the issue of whether this isn't a dilemma serious writers have always faced. Other than lowered (or changed) audience expectations, what's changed to make the task of the serious writer today more difficult than it was thirty or sixty or a hundred or a thousand years ago? You might argue that the task of the serious writer is easier today because what took place in the sixties had the effect of finally demolishing the authority that mimesis had assumed. Since you guys don't have to fight that battle anymore, you're liberated to move on to other areas.

This is a double-edged sword, our bequest from the early post-modernists and the post-structuralist critics. On the one hand, there's sort of an embarrassment of riches for young writers now. Most of the old cinctures and constraints that used to exist—censorship of content is a blatant example—have been driven off the field. Writers today can do more or less whatever we want. But on the other hand, since everybody can do pretty much whatever they want, without boundaries to define them or constraints to struggle against, you get this continual avant-garde rush forward without anyone bothering to speculate on the destination, the *goal* of the forward rush. The modernists and early postmodernists—all the way from Mallarmé to Coover, I guess—broke most of the rules for us, but we tend to forget what they were forced to remember: the rule-breaking has got to be for the *sake* of something. When rulebreaking, the mere *form* of renegade avant-gardism, becomes an end in itself, you end up with bad language poetry and *American Psycho*'s nipple-shocks and Alice Cooper eating shit on stage. Shock stops being a by-product of progress and becomes an end in itself. And it's bullshit. Here's an analogy. The invention of calculus was shocking because for a long time it had simply been presumed that you couldn't divide by zero. The integrity of math itself seemed to depend on the presumption. Then some genuine titans came along and said, "Yeah, maybe you can't divide by zero, but what would happen if

you *could*? We're going to come as close to doing it as we can, to see what happens."

So you get the infinitesimal calculus—the "philosophy of as if."

And this purely theoretical construct wound up yielding incredible practical results. Suddenly you could plot the area under curves and do rate-change calculations. Just about every material convenience we now enjoy is a consequence of this "as if." But what if Leibniz and Newton had wanted to divide by zero only to show jaded audiences how cool and rebellious they were? It'd never have happened, because that kind of motivation doesn't yield results. It's hollow. Dividing-as-if-by-zero was titanic and ingenious because it was in the service of something. The math world's shock was a price they had to pay, not a payoff in itself.

Of course, you also have examples like Lobochevsky and Riemann, who are breaking rules with no practical application at the time—but then later on somebody like Einstein comes along and decides that this worthless mathematical mind game that Riemann developed actually described the universe more effectively than the Euclidean game. Not that those guys were breaking the rules just to break the rules, but part of that was just that: what happens if everybody has to move counter-clockwise in Monopoly. And at first it just seemed like this game, without applications.

Well, the analogy breaks down because math and hard science are pyramidical. They're like building a cathedral: each generation works off the last one, both its advances and its errors. Ideally, each piece of art's its own unique object, and its evaluation's always present-tense. You could justify the worst piece of experimental horseshit by saying "The fools may hate my stuff, but generations later I will be appreciated for my ground-breaking rebellion." All the beret-wearing *artistes* I went to school with who believed that line are now writing ad copy someplace.

The European avant-garde believed in the transforming ability of innovative art to directly affect people's consciousness and break them out of their cocoon of habituation, etc. You'd put a urinal in a Paris museum, call it a "fountain," and wait for the riots next day. That's an area I'd say has changed things for writers (or any artist)—you can have very aesthetically radical works today using the same features of formal innovation that you'd find in the Russian Futurists or Duchamp and so forth, only now these things are on MTV *or TV ads. Formal innovation as trendy image. So it loses its ability to shock or transform.*

These are exploitations. They're not trying to break us free of anything. They're trying to lock us tighter into certain conventions, in this case habits of consumption. So the *form* of artistic rebellion now becomes . . .

. . . yeah, another commodity. I agree with Fredric Jameson and others who argue that modernism and postmodernism can be seen as expressing the cultural logic of late capitalism. Lots of features of contemporary art are directly influenced by this massive acceleration of capitalist expansion into all these new realms that were previously just not accessible. You sell people a memory, reify their nostalgia and use this as a book to sell deodorant. Hasn't this recent huge expansion of the technologies of reproduction, the integration of commodity reproduction and aesthetic reproduction, and the rise of media culture lessened the impact that aesthetic innovation can have on people's sensibilities? What's your response to this as an artist?

You've got a gift for the lit-speak, LM. Who wouldn't love this jargon we dress common sense in: "formal innovation is no longer transformative, having been co-opted by the forces of stabilization and post-industrial inertia," blah blah. But this co-optation might actually be a good thing if it helps keep younger writers from being able to treat mere formal ingenuity as an end in itself. MTV-type co-optation could end up a great prophylactic against cleveritis—you know, the dreaded grad-school syndrome of like "Watch me use seventeen different points of view in this scene of a guy eating a Saltine." The only real point of that shift is "Like me because I'm clever" which of course is itself derived from commercial art's axiom about audience-affection determining art's value.

What's precious about somebody like Bill Vollmann is that, even though there's a great deal of formal innovation in his fictions, it rarely seems to exist for just its own sake. It's almost always deployed to make some point (Vollmann's the most editorial young novelist going right now, and he's great at using formal ingenuity to make the editorializing a component of his narrative instead of an interruption) or to create an effect that's internal to the text. His narrator's always weirdly effaced, the writing unself-conscious, despite all the "By-the-way-Dear-Reader" intrusions. In a way it's sad that Vollmann's integrity is so remarkable. Its remarkability means it's rare. I guess I don't know what to think about these explosions in the sixties you're so crazy about. It's almost like postmodernism is fiction's fall from biblical grace. Fiction became *conscious* of itself in a way it never had been. Here's a really pretentious bit of pop analysis for you: I think you can see Cameron's *Terminator* movies as a metaphor for all literary art after Roland Barthes, viz., the movies' premise that the Cyberdyne NORAD computer becomes conscious of itself as *conscious,* as having interests and an agenda; the Cyberdyne becomes literally self-referential, and it's no accident that the result of this is nuclear war, Armageddon.

Isn't Armageddon the course you set sail for in "Westward"?

Metafiction's real end has always been Armageddon. Art's reflection on itself is terminal, is one big reason why the art world saw Duchamp as an Antichrist. But I still believe the move to involution had value: it helped writers break free of some long-standing flat-earth-type taboos. It was standing in line to happen. And for a little while, stuff like *Pale Fire* and *The Universal Baseball Association* was valuable as a meta-aesthetic breakthrough the same way Duchamp's urinal had been valuable.

I've always felt that the best of the metafictionists—Coover, for example, Nabokov, Borges, even Barth—were criticized too much for being only interested in narcissistic, self-reflexive games, whereas these devices had very real political and historical applications.

> **. . . when you talk about Nabokov and Coover, you're talking about real geniuses, the writers who weathered real shock and invented this stuff in contemporary fiction. But after the pioneers always come the crank-turners, the little gray people who take the machines others have built and just turn the crank, and little pellets of metafiction come out the other end. The crank-turners capitalize for a while on sheer fashion, and they get their plaudits and grants and buy their IRAs and retire to the Hamptons well out of range of the eventual blast radius.**
> **—David Foster Wallace**

But when you talk about Nabokov and Coover, you're talking about real geniuses, the writers who weathered real shock and invented this stuff in contemporary fiction. But after the pioneers always come the crank-turners, the little gray people who take the machines others have built and just turn the crank, and little pellets of metafiction come out the other end. The crank-turners capitalize for a while on sheer fashion, and they get their plaudits and grants and buy their IRAs and retire to the Hamptons well out of range of the eventual blast radius. There are some interesting parallels between postmodern crank-turners and what's happened since post-structural theory took off here in the U.S., why there's such a big backlash against post-structuralism going on now. It's the crank-turners' fault. I think the crank-turner's replaced the critic as the real angel of death as far as literary movements are concerned, now. You get some bona fide artists who come along and really divide by zero and weather some serious shit-storms of shock and ridicule in order to promulgate some really important ideas. Once they triumph, though, and their ideas become legitimate and accepted, the crank-turners and wannabes come running to the machine, and out pour the gray pellets, and now the whole thing's become a hollow form, just another institution of fashion. Take a look at some of the critical-theory Ph.D. dissertations being written now. They're like de Man and Foucault in the mouth of a dull child. Academia and commercial culture have somehow become these gigantic mechanisms of commodification that drain the weight and color out of even the most radical new advances. It's a surreal inversion of the death-by-neglect that used to kill off prescient art. Now prescient art suffers death-by-acceptance. We love things to death, now. Then we retire to the Hamptons.

This is also tied to that expansion of capitalism blah blah blah into realms previously thought to be uncommodifiable. Hyper-consumption. I mean, whoever thought rebellion could be tamed so easily? You just record it, turn the crank, and out comes another pellet of "dangerous" art.

And this accelerates the metastasis from genuine envelope-puncturing to just another fifteen-minute form that gets cranked out and cranked out and cranked out. Which creates a bitch of a problem for any artist who views her task as continual envelope-puncturing, because then she falls into this insatiable hunger for the appearance of novelty: "What can I do that hasn't been done yet?" Once the first-person pronoun creeps into your agenda you're dead, art-wise. That's why fiction-writing's lonely in a way most people misunderstand. It's yourself you have to be estranged from, really, to work.

A phrase in one of your recent letters really struck me: "The magic of fiction is that it addresses and antagonizes the loneliness that dominates people." It's that suggestion of antagonizing the reader that seems to link your goals up with the avant-garde program—whose goals were never completely hermetic. And **"Westward the Course of Empire Takes Its Way"** *seems to be your own meta-metafictional attempt to deal with these large areas in ways that are not merely metafiction.*

"Aggravate" might be better than "antagonize," in the sense of aggravation as intensification. But the truth is it's hard for me to know what I really think about any of the stuff I've written. It's always tempting to sit back and make finger-steeples and invent impressive-sounding theoretical justifications for what one does, but in my case most of it'd be horseshit. As time passes I get less and less nuts about anything I've published, and it gets harder to know for sure when its antagonistic elements are in there because they serve a useful purpose and when they're just covert manifestations of this "look-at-me-please-love-me-I-hate-you" syndrome I still sometimes catch myself falling into. Anyway, but what I think I meant by "antagonize" or "aggra-

vate" has to do with the stuff in the TV essay about the younger writer trying to struggle against the cultural hegemony of TV. One thing TV does is help us deny that we're lonely. With televised images, we can have the facsimile of a relationship without the work of a real relationship. It's an anesthesia of *form.* The interesting thing is why we're so desperate for this anesthetic against loneliness. You don't have to think very hard to realize that our dread of both relationships and loneliness, both of which are like sub-dreads of our dread of being trapped inside a self (a psychic self, not just a physical self), has to do with angst about death, the recognition that I'm going to die, and die very much alone, and the rest of the world is going to go merrily on without me. I'm not sure I could give you a steeple-fingered theoretical justification, but I strongly suspect a big part of real art-fiction's job is to aggravate this sense of entrapment and loneliness and death in people, to move people to countenance it, since any possible human redemption requires us first to face what's dreadful, what we want to deny.

It's this inside/outside motif you developed throughout **The Broom of the System.**

I guess maybe, though there it's developed in an awful clunky way. The popularity of **Broom** mystifies me. I can't say it's not nice to have people like it, but there's a lot of stuff in that novel I'd like to reel back in and do better. I was like twenty-two when I wrote the first draft of that thing. And I mean a *young* twenty-two. I still thought in terms of distinct problems and univocal solutions. But if you're going to try not just to depict the way a culture's bound and defined by mediated gratification and image, but somehow to redeem it, or at least fight a rearguard against it, then what you're going to be doing is paradoxical. You're at once allowing the reader to sort of escape self by achieving some sort of identification with another human psyche—the writer's, or some character's, etc—and you're *also* trying to antagonize the reader's intuition that she is a self, that she is alone and going to die alone. You're trying somehow both to deny and affirm that the writer is over here with his agenda while the reader's over there with her agenda, distinct. This paradox is what makes good fiction sort of magical, I think. The paradox can't be resolved, but it can somehow be mediated—"re-mediated," since this is probably where post-structuralism rears its head for me—by the fact that language and linguistic intercourse is, in and of itself, redeeming, remedy-ing.

This makes serious fiction a rough and bumpy affair for everyone involved. Commercial entertainment, on the other hand, smooths everything over. Even the *Terminator* movies (which I revere), or something really nasty and sicko like the film version of *A Clockwork Orange,* is basically an anesthetic (and think for a second about the etymology of "anesthetic"; break the word up and think about it). Sure, *A*

Clockwork Orange is a self-consciously sick, nasty film about the sickness and nastiness of the post-industrial condition, but if you look at it structurally, slo-mo and fast-mo and arty cinematography aside, it does what all commercial entertainment does: it proceeds more or less chronologically, and if its transitions are less cause-and-effect-based than most movies', it still kind of eases you from scene to scene in a way that drops you into certain kinds of easy cerebral rhythms. It admits of passive spectation. Encourages it. TV-type art's biggest hook is that it's figured out ways to *reward* passive spectation. A certain amount of the form-conscious stuff I write is trying—with whatever success—to do the opposite. It's supposed to be uneasy. For instance, using a lot of flash-cuts between scenes so that some of the narrative arrangement has got to be done by the reader, or interrupting flow with digressions and interpolations that the reader has to do the work of connecting to each other and to the narrative. It's nothing terribly sophisticated, and there has to be an accessible payoff for the reader if I don't want the reader to throw the book at the wall. But if it works right, the reader has to fight *through* the mediated voice presenting the material to you. The complete suppression of a narrative consciousness, with its own agenda, is why TV is such a powerful selling tool. This is McLuhan, right? "The medium is the message" and all that? But notice that TV's mediated message is *never* that the medium's the message.

How is this insistence on mediation different from the kind of meta strategies you yourself have attacked as preventing authors from being anything other than narcissistic or overly abstract or intellectual?

I guess I'd judge what I do by the same criterion I apply to the self-conscious elements you find in Vollmann's fiction: do they serve a purpose beyond themselves? Whether I can provide a payoff and communicate a function rather than just seem jumbled and prolix is the issue that'll decide whether the thing I'm working on now succeeds or not. But I think right now it's important for art-fiction to antagonize the reader's sense that what she's experiencing as she reads is mediated through a human consciousness, one with an agenda not necessarily coincident with her own. For some reason I probably couldn't even explain, I've been convinced of this for years, that one distinctive thing about truly "low" or commercial art is this apparent suppression of a mediating consciousness and agenda. The example I think of first is the novella **"Little Expressionless Animals"** in *Girl with Curious Hair.* Readers I know sometimes remark on all the flash-cuts and the distortion of linearity in it and usually want to see it as mimicking TV's own pace and phosphenic flutter. But what it's really trying to do is just the *opposite* of TV—it's trying to prohibit the reader from forgetting that she's receiving heavily mediated data, that this process is a relationship between the writer's consciousness and her own, and that in order for it to be anything like a real full human

relationship, she's going to have to put in her share of the linguistic work.

This might be my best response to your claim that my stuff's not "realistic." I'm not much interested in trying for classical, big-R Realism, not because there hasn't been great U.S. Realist fiction that'll be read and enjoyed forever, but because the big R's form has now been absorbed and suborned by commercial entertainment. The classical Realist form is soothing, familiar and anesthetic; it drops us right into spectation. It doesn't set up the sort of expectations serious 1990s fiction ought to be setting up in readers.

The Broom of the System *already displays some of the formal tendencies found in the stories in* **Girl with Curious Hair** *and in your new work—that play with temporal structure and flash-cuts, for instance, for heightened rhetorical effects of various sorts, for defamiliarizing things. Would you say your approach to form/content issues has undergone any radical changes since you were a "young twenty-two"?*

Assuming I understand what you mean by "form/content," the only way I can answer you is to talk about my own background. Oh boy, I get to make myself sound all fascinating and artistic and you'll have no way to check up. Return with us now to Deare Olde Amherst. For most of my college career I was a hard-core syntax wienie, a philosophy major with a specialization in math and logic. I was, to put it modestly, quite good at the stuff, mostly because I spent all my free time doing it. Wienieish or not, I was actually chasing a special sort of buzz, a special moment that comes sometimes. One teacher called these moments "mathematical experiences." What I didn't know then was that a mathematical experience was aesthetic in nature, an epiphany in Joyce's original sense. These moments appeared in proof-completions, or maybe algorithms. Or like a gorgeously simple solution to a problem you suddenly see after filling half a notebook with gnarly attempted solutions. It was really an experience of what I think Yeats called "the click of a well-made box." Something like that. The word I always think of it as is "click."

Anyway, I was just awfully good at technical philosophy, and it was the first thing I'd ever been really good at, and so everybody, including me, anticipated I'd make it a career. But it sort of emptied out for me somewhere around age twenty. I just got tired of it, and panicked because I was suddenly not getting joy from the one thing I was clearly supposed to do because I was good at it and people liked me for being good at it. Not a fun time. I think I had kind of a mid-life crisis at twenty, which probably doesn't augur real well for my longevity.

So what I did, I went back home for a term, planning to play solitaire and stare out the window, whatever you do in a crisis. And all of a sudden I found myself writing fiction. My only real experience with fun writing had been on a campus magazine with Mark Costello, the guy I later wrote **Signifying Rappers** with. But I had experience with chasing the click, from all the time spent with proofs. At some point in my reading and writing that fall I discovered the click existed in literature, too. It was real lucky that just when I stopped being able to get the click from math logic I started to be able to get it from fiction. The first fictional clicks I encountered were in Donald Barthelme's "The Balloon" and in parts of the first story I ever wrote, which has been in my trunk since I finished it. I don't know whether I have much natural talent going for me fiction-wise, but I know I can hear the click, when there's a click. In Don DeLillo's stuff, for example, almost line by line I can hear the click. It's maybe the only way to describe writers I love. I hear the click in most Nabokov. In Donne, Hopkins, Larkin. In Puig and Cortázar. Puig clicks like a fucking Geiger counter. And none of these people write prose as pretty as Updike, and yet I don't much hear the click in Updike.

But so here I am at like twenty-one and I don't know what to do. Do I go into math logic, which I'm good at and pretty much guaranteed an approved career in? Or do I try to keep on with this writing thing, this *artiste* thing? The idea of trying to be a "writer" repelled me, mostly because of all the foppish aesthetes I knew at school who went around in berets stroking their chins calling themselves writers. I have a terror of seeming like those guys, still. Even today, when people I don't know ask me what I do for a living, I usually tell them I'm "in English" or I "work free-lance." I don't seem to be able to call myself a writer. And terms like "postmodernist" or "surrealist" send me straight to the bathroom, I've got to tell you.

I spend time in toilet stalls myself. But I noticed you didn't take off down the hall when I said earlier that your work didn't seem "realistic." Do you really agree with that?

Well, it depends whether you're talking little-r realistic or big-R. If you mean is my stuff in the Howells/Wharton/Updike school of U.S. Realism, clearly not. But to me the whole binary of realistic vs. unrealistic fiction is a canonical distinction set up by people with a vested interest in the big-R tradition. A way to marginalize stuff that isn't soothing and conservative. Even the goofiest avant-garde agenda, if it's got integrity, is never, "Let's eschew all realism," but more, "Let's try to countenance and render real aspects of real experiences that have previously been excluded from art." The result often seems "unrealistic" to the big-R devotees because it's not a recognizable part of the "ordinary experience" they're used to countenancing. I guess my point is that "realistic" doesn't have a univocal definition. By the way, what did you mean a minute ago when you were talking about a writer "defamiliarizing" something?

Placing something familiar in an unfamiliar context—say, setting it in the past or within some other structure that will re-expose it, allow readers to see the real essence of the thing that's usually taken for granted because it's buried underneath all the usual sludge that accompanies it.

I guess that's supposed to be deconstruction's original program, right? People have been under some sort of metaphysical anesthesia, so you dismantle the metaphysics' axioms and prejudices, show it in cross section and reveal the advantages of its abandonment. It's literally aggravating: you awaken them to the fact that they've been unconsciously imbibing some narcotic pharmakon since they were old enough to say Momma. There's many different ways to think about what I'm doing, but if I follow what you mean by "defamiliarization," I guess it's part of what getting the click right is for me. It might also be part of why I end up doing anywhere from five to eight total rewrites to finish something, which is why I'm never going to be a Vollmann or an Oates.

You've mentioned the recent change about what writers can assume about their readers in terms of expectations and so on. Are there other ways the postmodern world has influenced or changed the role of serious writing today?

If you mean a post-industrial, mediated world, it's inverted one of fiction's big historical functions, that of providing data on distant cultures and persons. The first real generalization of human experience that novels tried to accomplish. If you lived in Bumfuck, Iowa, a hundred years ago and had no idea what life was like in India, good old Kipling goes over and presents it to you. And of course the post-structural critics now have a field day on all the colonialist and phallocratic prejudices inherent in the idea that writers were *presenting* alien cultures instead of *"representing"* them—jabbering natives and randy concubines and white man's burden, etc. Well, but fiction's presenting function for today's reader has been reversed: since the whole global village is now presented as familiar, electronically immediate—satellites, microwaves, intrepid PBS anthropologists, Paul Simon's Zulu back-ups—it's almost like we need fiction writers to restore strange things' ineluctable *strangeness,* to defamiliarize stuff, I guess you'd say.

David Lynch's take on suburbia. Or Mark Leyner's take on his own daily life—

And Leyner's real good at it. For our generation, the entire world seems to present itself as "familiar," but since that's of course an illusion in terms of anything really important about people, maybe any "realistic" fiction's job is opposite what it used to be—no longer making the strange familiar but making the familiar *strange* again. It seems important to find ways of reminding ourselves that most "familiarity" is mediated and delusive.

"Postmodernism" usually implies "an integration of pop and 'serious' culture." But a lot of the pop culture in the works of the younger writers I most admire these days—you, Leyner, Gibson, Vollmann, Eurudice, Daitch, et al.—seems to be introduced less to integrate high and low culture, or to valorize pop culture, than to place this stuff in a new context so we can be liberated from it. Wasn't that, for example, one of the things you were doing with Jeopardy *in* **"Little Expressionless Animals"**?

One new context is to take something almost narcotizingly banal—it's hard to think of anything more banal than a U.S. game show; in fact the banality's one of TV's great hooks, as the TV essay discusses—and try to reconfigure it in a way that reveals what a tense, strange, convoluted set of human interactions the final banal product is. The scrambled, flash-cut form I ended up using for the novella was probably unsubtle and clumsy, but the form clicked for me in a way it just hadn't when I'd done it straight.

A lot of your works (including **Broom***) have to do with this breakdown of the boundaries between the real and "games," or the characters playing the game begin to confuse the game structure with reality's structure. Again, I suppose you can see this in* **"Little Expressionless Animals,"** *where the real world outside* Jeopardy *is interacting with what's going on inside the game show—the boundaries between inner and outer are blurred.*

And, too, in the novella what's going on on the show has repercussions for everybody's lives outside it. The valence is always distributive. It's interesting that most serious art, even avant-garde stuff that's in collusion with literary theory, still refuses to acknowledge this, while serious *science* butters its bread with the fact that the separation of subject/observer and object/experiment is impossible. Observing a quantum phenomenon's been proven to alter the phenomenon. Fiction likes to ignore this fact's implications. We still think in terms of a story "changing" the reader's emotions, cerebrations, maybe even her life. We're not keen on the idea of the story sharing its valence with the reader. But the reader's own life "outside" the story changes the story. You could argue that it affects only "her reaction to the story" or "her take on the story." But these things *are* the story. This is the way Barthian and Derridean post-structuralism's helped me the most as a fiction writer: once I'm done with the thing, I'm basically dead, and probably the text's dead; it becomes simply language, and language lives not just in but *through* the reader. The reader becomes God, for all textual purposes. I see your eyes glazing over, so I'll hush.

Let's go back for just a moment to your sense of the limits

of metafiction: in both your current RCF *essay and in the novella* **"Westward"** *in* **Girl with Curious Hair,** *you imply that metafiction is a game that only reveals itself, or that can't share its valence with anything outside itself—like the daily world.*

Well, but metafiction is more valuable than that. It helps reveal fiction as a mediated experience. Plus it reminds us that there's always a recursive component to utterance. This was important, because language's self-consciousness had always been there, but neither writers nor critics nor readers wanted to be reminded of it. But we ended up seeing why recursion's dangerous, and maybe why everybody wanted to keep linguistic self-consciousness out of the show. It gets empty and solipsistic real fast. It spirals in on itself. By the mid-seventies, I think, everything useful about the mode had been exhausted, and the crank-turners had descended. By the eighties it'd become a godawful trap. In **"Westward"** I got trapped one time just trying to expose the illusions of metafiction the same way metafiction had tried to expose the illusions of the pseudo-unmediated realist fiction that came before it. It was a horror show. The stuff's a permanent migraine.

Why is meta-metafiction a trap? Isn't that what you were doing in **"Westward"**?

That's a Rog. And maybe "Westward"'s only real value'll be showing the kind of pretentious loops you fall into now if you fuck around with recursion. My idea in **"Westward"** was to do with metafiction what Moore's poetry or like DeLillo's *Libra* had done with other mediated myths. I wanted to get the Armageddon-explosion, the goal metafiction's always been about, I wanted to get it over with, and then out of the rubble reaffirm the idea of art being a living transaction between humans, whether the transaction was erotic or altruistic or sadistic. God, even talking about it makes me want to puke. The *pretension.* Twenty-five-year-olds should be locked away and denied ink and paper. Everything I wanted to do came out in the story, but it came out as just what it was: crude and naive and pretentious.

Of course, even **The Broom of the System** *can be seen as a metafiction, as a book about language and about the relationship between words and reality.*

Think of *The Broom of the System* as the sensitive tale of a sensitive young WASP who's just had this mid-life crisis that's moved him from coldly cerebral analytic math to a coldly cerebral take on fiction and Austin-Wittgenstein-Derridean literary theory, which also shifted his existential dread from a fear that he was just a 98.6-degree calculating machine to a fear that he was nothing but a linguistic construct. This WASP's written a lot of straight humor, and loves gags, so he decides to write a coded autobio that's also a funny little post-structural gag: so you get Lenore, a character in a story who's terribly afraid that she's really nothing more than a character in a story. And, sufficiently hidden under the sex-change and the gags and theoretical allusions, I got to write my sensitive little self-obsessed bildungsroman. The biggest cackle I got when the book came out was the way all the reviews, whether they stomped up and down on the overall book or not, all praised the fact that at least here was a first novel that wasn't yet another sensitive little self-obsessed bildungsroman.

Wittgenstein's work, especially the Tractatus, *permeates* **The Broom of the System** *in all sorts of ways, both as content and in terms of the metaphors you employ. But in the later stages of his career, Wittgenstein concluded that language was unable to refer in the direct, referential way he'd argued it could in the* Tractatus. *Doesn't that mean language is a closed loop—there's no permeable membrane to allow the inside from getting through to the outside? And if that's the case, then isn't a book only a game? Or does the fact that it's a language game make it somehow different?*

There's a kind of tragic fall Wittgenstein's obsessed with all the way from the *Tractatus Logico-Philosophicus* in 1922 to the *Philosophical Investigations* in his last years. I mean a real Book-of-Genesis-type tragic fall. The loss of the whole external world. The *Tractatus's* picture theory of meaning presumes that the only possible relation between language and the world is denotative, referential. In order for language both to be meaningful and to have some connection to reality, words like *tree* and *house* have to be like little pictures, representations of real trees and houses. Mimesis. But nothing more. Which means we can know and speak of nothing more than little mimetic pictures. Which divides us, metaphysically and forever, from the external world. If you buy such a metaphysical schism, you're left with only two options. One is that the individual person with her language is trapped in here, with the world out there, and never the twain shall meet. Which, even if you think language's pictures really are mimetic, is an awful lonely proposition. And there's no iron guarantee the pictures truly *are* mimetic, which means you're looking at solipsism. One of the things that makes Wittgenstein a real artist to me is that he realized that no conclusion could be more horrible than solipsism. And so he trashed everything he'd been lauded for in the *Tractatus* and wrote the *Investigations,* which is the single most comprehensive and beautiful argument against solipsism that's ever been made. Wittgenstein argues that for language even to be possible, it must always be a function of relationships between persons (that's why he spends so much time arguing against the possibility of a "private language"). So he makes language dependent on human community, but unfortunately we're still stuck with the idea that there is this world of referents out there that we can never really join or know because we're stuck in here, in language, even if we're

at least all in here together. Oh yeah, the other original option. The other option is to expand the linguistic subject. Expand the self.

Like Norman Bombardini in **Broom of the System.**

Yeah, Norman's gag is that he literalizes the option. He's going to forget the diet and keep eating until he grows to "infinite size" and eliminates loneliness that way. This was Wittgenstein's double bind: you can either treat language as an infinitely small dense dot, or you let it become the word— the exterior and everything in it. The former banishes you from the Garden. The latter seems more promising. If the world is itself a linguistic construct, there's nothing "outside" language for language to have to picture or refer to. This lets you avoid solipsism, but it leads right to the postmodern, post-structural dilemma of having to deny yourself an existence independent of language. Heidegger's the guy most people think got us into this bind, but when I was working on **Broom of the System** I saw Wittgenstein as the real architect of the postmodern trap. He died right on the edge of explicitly treating reality as linguistic instead of ontological. This eliminated solipsism, but not the horror. Because we're still stuck. The *Investigation's* line is that the fundamental problem of language is, quote, "I don't know my way about." If I were separate from language, if I could somehow detach from it and climb up and look down on it, get the lay of the land so to speak, I could study it "objectively," take it apart, deconstruct it, know its operations and boundaries and deficiencies. But that's not how things are. I'm *in* it. We're *in* language. Wittgenstein's not Heidegger, it's not that language is us, but we're still *in* it, inescapably, the same way we're in like Kant's space-time. Wittgenstein's conclusions seem completely sound to me, always have. And if there's one thing that consistently bugs me writing-wise, it's that I don't feel I really *do* know my way around inside language—I never seem to get the kind of clarity and concision I want.

Ray Carver comes immediately to mind in terms of compression and clarity, and he's obviously someone who wound up having a huge influence on your generation.

Minimalism's just the other side of metafictional recursion. The basic problem's still the one of the mediating narrative consciousness. Both minimalism and metafiction try to resolve the problem in radical ways. Opposed, but both so extreme they end up empty. Recursive metafiction worships the narrative consciousness, makes *it* the subject of the text. Minimalism's even worse, emptier, because it's a fraud: it eschews not only self-reference but any narrative personality at all, tries to pretend there *is* no narrative consciousness in its text. This is so fucking American, man: either make something your God and cosmos and then worship it, or else kill it.

But did Carver really do that? I'd say his narrative voice is nearly always insistently there, *like Hemingway's was. You're never allowed to forget.*

I was talking about minimalists, not Carver. Carver was an artist, not a minimalist. Even though he's supposedly the inventor of modern U.S. minimalism. "Schools" of fiction are for crank-turners. The founder of a movement is never part of the movement. Carver uses all the techniques and anti-styles that critics call "minimalist," but his case is like Joyce, or Nabokov, or early Barth and Coover—he's using formal innovation in the service of an original vision. Carver invented—or resurrected, if you want to cite Hemingway—the techniques of minimalism in the service of rendering a world he saw that nobody'd seen before. It's a grim world, exhausted and empty and full of mute, beaten people, but the minimalist techniques Carver employed were perfect for it; he created it. And minimalism for Carver wasn't some rigid aesthetic program he adhered to for its own sake. Carver's commitment was to his stories, each of them. And when minimalism didn't serve them, he blew it off. If he realized a story would be best served by expansion, not ablation, he'd expand, like he did to "The Bath," which he later turned into a vastly superior story. He just chased the click. But at some point his "minimalist" style caught on. A movement was born, proclaimed, promulgated by the critics. Now here come the crankturners. What's especially dangerous about Carver's techniques is that they seem so easy to imitate. It doesn't seem like each word and line and draft has been bled over. That's part of his genius. It looks like you can write a minimalist piece without much bleeding. And you can. But not a good one.

For various reasons, the sixties postmodernists were heavily influenced by other art forms—television, for instance, or the cinema or painting—but in particular their notions of form and structure were often influenced by jazz. Do you think that your generation of writers has been similarly influenced by rock music? For instance, you and Mark Costello collaborated on the first book-length study of rap (**Signifying Rappers**); *would you say that your interest in rap has anything to do with your writerly concerns? There's a way in which I can relate your writing with rap's "postmodern" features, its approach to structure and social issues. Sampling. Recontextualizing.*

About the only way music informs my work is in terms of rhythm; sometimes I associate certain narrators' and characters' voices with certain pieces of music. Rock music itself bores me, usually. The phenomenon of rock interests me, though, because its birth was part of the rise of mass popular media, which completely changed the ways the U.S. was unified and split. The mass media unified the country geographically for pretty much the first time. Rock helped change the fundamental splits in the U.S. from geographi-

cal splits to generational ones. Very few people I talk to understand what "generation gap"'s implications really were. Kids loved rock partly because their parents didn't, and obversely. In a mass mediated nation, it's no longer North vs. South. It's under-thirty vs. over-thirty. I don't think you can understand the sixties and Vietnam and love-ins and LSD and the whole era of patricidal rebellion that helped inspire early postmodern fiction's whole "We're-going-to-trash-your-Beaver-Cleaver-plasticized-G.O.P.-image-of-life-in-America" attitude without understanding rock 'n' roll. Because rock was and is all about busting loose, exceeding limits, and limits are usually set by parents, ancestors, older authorities.

But so far there aren't many others who have written anything interesting about rock—Richard Meltzer, Peter Guralnik . . .

There's some others. Lester Bangs. Todd Gitlin, who also does great TV essays. The thing that especially interested Mark and me about rap was the nasty spin it puts on the whole historical us-vs.-them aspect of postmodern pop. Anyway, what rock 'n' roll did for the multicolored young back in the fifties and sixties, rap seems to be doing for the young black urban community. It's another attempt to break free of precedent and constraint. But there are contradictions in rap that seem perversely to show how, in an era where rebellion itself is a commodity used to sell other commodities, the whole idea of rebelling against white corporate culture is not only impossible but incoherent. Today you've got black rapper who make their reputation rapping about Kill the White Corporate Tools, and are then promptly signed by white-owned record corporations, and not only feel no shame about "selling out" but then release platinum albums about not only Killing White Tools but also about how wealthy the rappers now are after signing their record deal! You've got music here that both hates the white GOP values of the Reaganoid eighties and extols a gold-and-BMW materialism that makes Reagan look like a fucking Puritan. Violently racist and anti-Semitic black artists being co-opted by white-owned, often Jewish-owned record labels, and celebrating that fact in their art. The tensions are delicious. I can feel the spittle starting again just thinking about it.

This is another example of the dilemma facing avant-garde wannabes today—the appropriation (and ensuing "taming") of rebellion by the system people like Jameson are talking about.

I don't know much about Jameson. To me rap's the ultimate distillate of the U.S. eighties, but if you really step back and think not just about rap's politics but about white enthusiasm for it, things get grim. Rap's conscious response to the poverty and oppression of U.S. blacks is like some hideous parody of sixties black pride. We seem to be in an era when oppression and exploitation no longer bring a people together and solidify loyalties and help everyone rise above his individual concerns. Now the rap response is more like "You've always exploited us to get rich, so now goddamn it we're going to exploit ourselves and get rich." The irony, self-pity, self-hatred are now conscious, celebrated. This has to do with what we were talking about regarding **"Westward"** and postmodern recursion. If I have a real enemy, a patriarch for my patricide, it's probably Barth and Coover and Burroughs, even Nabokov and Pynchon. Because, even though their self-consciousness and irony and anarchism served valuable purposes, were indispensable for their times, their aesthetic's absorption by U.S. commercial culture has had appalling consequences for writers and everyone else. The TV essay's really about how poisonous postmodern irony's become. You see it in David Letterman and Gary Shandling and rap. But you also see it in fucking Rush Limbaugh, who may well be the Antichrist. You see it in T. C. Boyle and Bill Vollmann and Lorrie Moore. It's pretty much all there is to see in your pal Mark Leyner. Leyner and Limbaugh are the nineties' twin towers of postmodern irony, hip cynicism, a hatred that winks and nudges you and pretends it's just kidding.

Irony and cynicism were just what the U.S. hypocrisy of the fifties and sixties called for. That's what made the early postmodernists great artists. The great thing about irony is that it splits things apart, gets us up above them so we can see the flaws and hypocrisies and duplicities. The virtuous always triumph? Ward Cleaver is the prototypical fifties father? Sure. Sarcasm, parody, absurdism and irony are great ways to strip off stuff's mask and show the unpleasant reality behind it. The problem is that once the rules for art are debunked, and once the unpleasant realities the irony diagnoses are revealed and diagnosed, *then* what do we do? Irony's useful for debunking illusions, but most of the illusion-debunking in the U.S. has now been done and redone. Once everybody knows that equality of opportunity is bunk and Mike Brady's bunk and Just Say No is bunk, now what do we do? All we seem to want to do is keep ridiculing the stuff. Postmodern irony and cynicism's become an end in itself, a measure of hip sophistication and literary savvy. Few artists dare to try to talk about ways of working toward redeeming what's wrong, because they'll look sentimental and naive to all the weary ironists. Irony's gone from liberating to enslaving. There's some great essay somewhere that has a line about irony being the song of the prisoner who's come to love his cage.

Humbert Humbert, the rutting gorilla, painting the bars of his own cage with such elegance. In fact. Nabokov's example raises the issue of whether cynicism and irony are really a given. In Pale Fire *and* Lolita, *there's an irony about these structures and inventions and so forth, but this reaction is*

deeply humanistic rather than being merely ironic. This seems true in Barthelme, for instance, or Stanley Elkin, Barth. Or Robert Coover. The other aspect has to do with the presentation of themselves or their consciousness. The beauty and the magnificence of human artistry isn't merely ironic.

But you're talking about the click, which is something that can't just be bequeathed from our postmodern ancestors to their descendants. No question that some of the early postmodernists and ironists and anarchists and absurdists did magnificent work, but you can't pass the click from one generation to another like a baton. The click's idiosyncratic, personal. The only stuff a writer can get from an artistic ancestor is a certain set of aesthetic values and beliefs, and maybe a set of formal techniques that might—just might—help the writer to chase his own click. The problem is that, however misprised it's been, what's been passed down from the postmodern heyday is sarcasm, cynicism, a manic ennui, suspicion of all authority, suspicion of all constraints on conduct, and a terrible penchant for ironic diagnosis of unpleasantness instead of an ambition not just to diagnose and ridicule but to redeem. You've got to understand that this stuff has permeated the culture. It's become our language; we're so in it we don't even see that it's one perspective, one among many possible ways of seeing. Postmodern irony's become our environment.

Mass culture is another very "real" part of that environment—rock music or television or sports, talk shows, game shows, whatever; that's the milieu you and I live in, I mean that's the world . . .

I'm always stumped when critics regard references to popular culture in serious fiction as some sort of avant-garde stratagem. In terms of the world I live in and try to write about, it's inescapable. Avoiding any reference to the pop would mean either being retrograde about what's "permissible" in serious art or else writing about some other world.

You mentioned earlier that writing parts of **Broom of the System** *felt like recreation for you—a relief from doing technical philosophy. Are you ever able to shift into that "recreational mode" of writing today? Is it still "play" for you?*

It's not play anymore in the sense of laughs and yucks and nonstop thrills. The stuff in **Broom** that's informed by that sense of play ended up pretty forgettable, I think. And it doesn't sustain the enterprise for very long. And I've found the really tricky discipline to writing is trying to play without getting overcome by insecurity or vanity or ego. Showing the reader that you're smart or funny or talented or whatever, trying to be liked, integrity issues aside, this stuff just doesn't have enough motivational calories in it to carry you over the long haul. You've got to discipline yourself to talk out of the part of you that loves the thing, loves what you're working on. Maybe that just plain loves. (I think we might need woodwinds for this part, LM.) But sappy or no, it's true. The last couple years have been pretty arid for me good-work-wise, but the one way I've progressed I think is I've gotten convinced that there's something kind of timelessly vital and sacred about good writing. This thing doesn't have that much to do with talent, even glittering talent like Leyner's or serious talent like Daitch's. Talent's just an instrument. It's like having a pen that works instead of one that doesn't. I'm not saying I'm able to work consistently out of the premise, but it seems like the big distinction between good art and so-so art lies somewhere in the art's heart's purpose, the agenda of the consciousness behind the text. It's got something to do with love. With having the discipline to talk out of the part of yourself that can love instead of the part that just wants to be loved. I know this doesn't sound hip at all. I don't know. But it seems like one of the things really great fiction-writers do—from Carver to Chekhov to Flannery O'Connor, or like the Tolstoy of "The Death of Ivan Ilych" or the Pynchon of *Gravity's Rainbow*—is *give* the reader something. The reader walks away from real art heavier than she came to it. Fuller. All the attention and engagement and work you need to get from the reader can't be for your benefit; it's got to be for hers. What's poisonous about the cultural environment today is that it makes this so scary to try to carry out. Really good work probably comes out of a willingness to disclose yourself, open yourself up in spiritual and emotional ways that risk making you look banal or melodramatic or naive or unhip or sappy, and to ask the reader really to feel something. To be willing to sort of die in order to move the reader, somehow. Even now I'm scared about how sappy this'll look in print, saying this. And the effort actually to do it, not just talk about it, requires a kind of courage I don't seem to have yet. I don't see that kind of courage in Mark Leyner or Emily Prager or Brett Ellis. I sometimes see flickers of it in Vollmann and Daitch and Nicholson Baker and Amy Homes and Jon Franzen. It's weird—it has to do with quality but not that much with sheer writing talent. It has to do with the click. I used to think the click came from, "Holy shit, have I ever just done something good." Now it seems more like the real click's more like, "Here's something good, and on one side I don't much matter, and on the other side the individual reader maybe doesn't much matter, but the thing's good because there's extractable value here for both me and the reader." Maybe it's as simple as trying to make the writing more generous and less ego-driven.

Music genres like the blues or jazz or even rock seem to have their ebb and flow in terms of experimentalism, but in the end they all have to come back to the basic elements that comprise the genre, even if these are very simple (like the blues). The trajectory of Bruce Springsteen's career comes to mind. What interests fans of any genre is that they really

know the formulas and the elements, so they also can respond to the constant, built-in meta-games and intertextualities going on in all genre forms. In a way the responses are aesthetically sophisticated in the sense that it's the infinite variations-on-a-theme that interests them. I mean, how else can they read a million of these things (real genre fans are not stupid people necessarily)? My point is that people who really care about the forms—the serious writers and readers in fiction—don't want all the forms broken, they want variation that allows the essence to emerge in new ways. Blues fans could love Hendrix because he was still playing the blues. I think you're seeing a greater appreciation for fiction's rules and limits among postmodern writers of all generations. It's almost a relief to realize that all babies were not tossed out with the bathwater back in the sixties.

You're probably right about appreciating limits. The sixties' movement in poetry to radical free verse, in fiction to radically experimental recursive forms—their legacy to my generation of would-be artists is at least an incentive to ask very seriously where literary art's true relation to limits should be. We've seen that you can break any or all of the rules without getting laughed out of town, but we've also seen the toxicity that anarchy for its own sake can yield. It's often useful to dispense with standard formulas, of course, but it's just as often valuable and brave to see what can be done within a set of rules—which is why formal poetry's so much more interesting to me than free verse. Maybe our touchstone now should be G. M. Hopkins, who made up his *own* set of formal constraints and then blew everyone's footwear off from inside them. There's something about free play within an ordered and disciplined structure that resonates for readers. And there's something about complete caprice and flux that's deadening.

I suspect this is why so many of the older generation of postmodernists–Federman, Sukenick, Steve Katz and others (maybe even Pynchon fits in here)–have recently written books that rely on more traditional forms. That's why it seems important right now for your generation to go back to traditional forms and re-examine and work those structures and formulas. This is already happening with some of the best younger writers in Japan. You recognize that if you just say, "Fuck it, let's throw everything out!" there's nothing in the bathtub to make the effort worthwhile.

For me, the last few years of the postmodern era have seemed a bit like the way you feel when you're in high school and your parents go on a trip, and you throw a party. You get all your friends over and throw this wild disgusting fabulous party. For a while it's great, free and freeing, parental authority gone and overthrown, a cat's-away-let's-play Dionysian revel. But then time passes, and the party gets louder and louder, and you run out of drugs, and nobody's got any money for more drugs, and things get broken and spilled, and there's a cigarette burn on the couch, and you're the host and it's your house too, and you gradually start wishing your parents would come back and restore some fucking order in your house. It's not a perfect analogy, but the sense I get of my generation of writers and intellectuals or whatever is that it's 3:00 A.M. and the couch has several burnholes and somebody's thrown up in the umbrella stand and we're wishing the revel would end. The postmodern founders' patricidal work was great, but patricide produces orphans, and no amount of revelry can make up for the fact that writers my age have been literary orphans throughout our formative years. We're kind of wishing some parents would come back. And of course we're uneasy about the fact that we wish they'd come back—I mean, what's wrong with us? Are we total pussies? Is there something about authority and limits we actually *need*? And then the uneasiest feeling of all, as we start gradually to realize that parents in fact aren't ever coming back—which means *we're* going to have to be the parents.

David Kipen (review date 11 February 1996)

SOURCE: "Terminal Entertainment," in *Los Angeles Times Book Review,* February 11, 1996, pp. 1, 9.

[*In the following review of Wallace's second novel,* Infinite Jest, *Kipen invokes the legacy of Thomas Pynchon to note Wallace's similarity and superiority to that legendary figure.*]

It takes a special kind of nerve to write a book with roughly the mass of a medicine ball and then end it so abruptly and unsatisfactorily that the poor reader perversely finds himself wishing it longer. But David Foster Wallace's coda disappoints only because the preceding 3 1/2 inches of *Infinite Jest* have succeeded so well at projecting a world of brainscalding complexity.

Wallace has given us a meditation on addiction—the addiction of a tennis prodigy to organic narcotics, of a paroled second-story man to inorganic ones, of the terrorist to his cause, of the couch potato to mindless pleasures and, ultimately, the unkickable addiction of readers to all those old storytelling conventions Wallace gleefully blows up like a rotten kid cherry-bombing an electric train.

The biggest addiction may be Wallace's own to writing, a habit so consuming that the only way for him to shake it is with an abrupt, cold-turkey ending. Luckily, savingly, *Infinite Jest* has a second serve to fall back on—its authentically hysterical, drink-milk-at-your peril humor.

Here's Wallace doing a high school tennis announcer whose quest for synonyms for *beat* and *got beat by* is never-ending and serious and a continual source of irritation to his friends: "Lamont Chu disemboweled Charles Pospisilova 6-3, 6-2; Peter Beak spread Ville Dillard on a cracker like some sort of hors d'oeuvre and bit down 6-4, 7-6. . . . Diane Bridget Boone drove a hot thin spike into the right eye of Aimee Middleton-Law 6-3, 6-3. . . . Felicity Zweig went absolutely SACPOP on P.W.'s Kiki Pfefferblit 7-6, 6-1, while Gretchen Holt made PW's Tammi Taylor-Bing sorry her parents were ever in the same room together 6-0, 6-3. . . ."

This is comic overkill of the foremost possible water, the sort of stuff good for reading aloud to one's more indulgent friends ("Wait, just one more!"), taking care to leave out expressions like "SACPOP," which Wallace doesn't see fit to explain until 100 pages later in a slapstick set-piece so funny you forgive him immediately. The tennis passage is also symptomatic of another of Wallace's bad habits, namely, too many characters too quickly introduced and never adequately differentiated—nota bad metaphor for the whole high school experience, but also a hallmark of the fat book.

Infinite Jest should find a kind posterity in just about any near future except the one where it takes place, sometime early in the next century. Books don't count for much in Wallace's dystopia, the only one mentioned being a copy of William James' *Varieties of Religious Experience* long since hollowed out as a stash box.

Just how early in the next century this all is can't be pinned down, as the Gregorian calendar has long since made way for Subsidized Time, which takes the concept of commercial sponsorship to its logical terminus by rechristening AD 2001 or 2020 or whatever year it is as the Year of the Perdue Wonderchicken, the Year of the Depend Adult Undergarment, etc. This tactic is mysterious at first, a scream when Wallace lets you in on the joke and kind of a pain after a while. Mercifully, he starts abbreviating them . . . then changes his mind and goes right back to spelling them out.

The novel begins with Hal Incandenza, tennis prodigy antihero, suffering a mysterious seizure during an Arizona college interview early in the Year of Glad, as in trash bags. We then flash back to the rigorously regimented Enfield Tennis Academy near Boston, Hal's and our home off and on for the bulk of the book. E.T.A. is the brainchild of Hal's late father, J.O., a man of high and wide attainments, last but not least of them committing suicide by artfully cutting a large hole into the door of a microwave oven, inserting his head and letting it rip.

J.O.'s place on campus and in Hal's mother's bed has fallen to a shady relation, giving rise to the suspicion, reinforced by the book's title, that what we've really signed on for is some hyper-modern pastiche of "Hamlet." This holds water as far as it goes, which is until Wallace starts cross-cutting between the academy and its Enfield neighbor, a dilapidated halfway house for dipso- and other maniacs. At this point, a fresh scenario pokes its head out of the verbal thicket. "Hamlet is just a red herring and Wallace is really concocting a sort of elephantine variation on "Entropy," Thomas Pynchon's classic short story of contrasted chaos and regimentation.

Wallace's earlier novel, *The Broom of the System,* has already elicited cries of "Pynchonesque!" from diverse quarters; some of them, to be sure, using the adjective in its usual sense, i.e., as reviewer's code for "I didn't finish it," others so besotted with Pynchon that they see his scat everywhere, a few finding genuine similarities. Both men do share a head for science, a stomach for gross-out humor, a great ear and a soft spot for the word "maffick," but of the two, Wallace definitely has the lower opinion of sloth.

> **The Broom of the System, has already elicited cries of "Pynchonesque!" from diverse quarters; some of them, to be sure, using the adjective in its usual sense, i.e., as reviewer's code for "I didn't finish it," others so besotted with Pynchon that they see his scat everywhere, a few finding genuine similarities. Both men do share a head for science, a stomach for gross-out humor, a great ear and a soft spot for the word "maffick," but of the two, Wallace definitely has the lower opinion of sloth.**
> **—David Kipen**

This emerges from a third thread in *Infinite Jest* one that puts it beyond the realm of homage to either Shakespeare or Pynchon. Hal's father, during his avant-garde filmmaker phase, has somehow made a movie so enjoyable as to be 100% lethal. All viewers unfortunate enough to catch even a snippet of this mortally popular production (it's called "Infinite Jest") at once live only to see it again and again, lapsing into a persistent vegetative state from which only drool-drowning will ever deliver them. All copies have now gone missing, and the post-NAFTA Organization of North American Nations (O.N.A.N.) is ineptly racing to find them before they can fall into the Wrong Hands, namely those of a splinter group of legless Quebecois separatists in wheelchairs.

If this starts to sound a mite daffy, it's also deadly serious. Like *1984* and *A Clockwork Orange,* both of which he unmistakably invokes, Wallace's critique of a future society whose only Grail has become the hangoverless bender, the

infinite jest—the never-ending Year of Glad—rings so true and contemporary that it's almost passé.

In a way, of course, it is. Lots of people have tilled this ground before, from Neil Postman in "Amusing Ourselves to Death" to 10,000 Maniacs in "Candy Everybody Wants." What keeps it fresh is Wallace's prose style, a compulsively footnoted amalgam of stupendously high-toned vocabulary and gleeful low-comedy diction, coupled with a sense of syntax so elongated that he can seem to go for days without surfacing. At times, he appears determined to end each sentence with a preposition or not at all with perhaps a slight edge going to not at all. A Wallace sentence finally draws to a close amid reluctance and relief, like a hitting streak. Half the time you'll want to pitch the damn book clear into the next room, with or without benefit of doorway, but the other half you can actually feel your attention span stretching back out to where it belongs.

Then contrary to the reader's occasional renegade suspicion, it ends. Little gets resolved, least of all a reason for Hal's first-chapter seizure, although at least three good guesses come to mind. Several well developed characters and one improbably touching romance all come to naught. Pynchonesque, some will say, but with Pynchon, he's playing with the whole idea of narrative closure, not thumbing his nose at you for giving a damn.

Finishing *Infinite Jest,* one feels less played with than toyed with. Still, better to be toyed with by a genius than pandered to by some second rater who'd write a few hundred pages and then give up. And Wallace has a toy box to do Pandora proud.

R. Z. Sheppard (review date 19 February 1996)

SOURCE: "Mad Maximalism," in *Time,* Vol. 14, No. 8, February 19, 1996, pp. 70, 72.

[*In the following review, Sheppard demonstrates his approval of* Infinite Jest *by emulating its humor and irony.*]

A 1,079-page novel that concludes with 100 pages of annotation and calls itself *Infinite Jest* is doubly intimidating. First, there is its length, which promises an ordeal like driving across Texas without cruise control. Second, the title itself hints that the joke may be on the reader. By definition, infinite means no punch line.

Yet David Foster Wallace's marathon send-up of humanism at the end of its tether is worth the effort. There is generous intelligence and authentic passion on every page, even the overwritten ones in which the author seems to have had a fit of graphomania. Wallace is definitely out to show his stuff, a virtuoso display of styles and themes reminiscent of William Burroughs, Thomas Pynchon and William Gaddis. Like those writers, Wallace can play it high or low, a sort of Beavis-and-Egghead approach that should spell cult following at the nation's brainier colleges.

Set in the year 2014, *Infinite Jest* projects the U.S. as a grotesquely extrapolated present. Entertainment and commercialism have reached a climax. Everything is product. Numbered years have been replaced by sponsors' names. There is the Year of Glad, the Year of Dairy Products from the American Heartland, the Year of the Depend Adult Undergarment. The technology of pleasure has driven people deeper into themselves. There is a new political structure known as the Organization of North American Nations whose acronym is ONAN. Get it?

Much of Wallace's humor is cute the first time around, less so the second, third, fourth and fifth. One gag that holds up is the Great Concavity. This is a chunk of New England turned over to Canada and used as a dump site by the U.S. The method of garbage disposal suggests that environmentalism has ended up in the dustbin of history: monster catapults situated near Boston hurl their toxic loads northward.

But wit is only a part of the story or, more accurately, stories. In a culture—ours—in which the national sport is channel surfing, Wallace dares out-of-shape readers to keep up with dozens of oddballs and intermingling plots. One is the tale of the upscale Incandenza clan, a family of high achievers. Mother Avril is a professor of language structure, and father James made a fortune inventing optical instruments, retiring to produce avant-garde films with cheeky titles such as *The American Century as Seen through a Brick, Dial C. for Concupiscence* and *Infinite Jest,* a feature described as "lethally entertaining."

Counterpointing the Incandenza chronicle is the sorry saga of Don Gately, a former burglar and reformed drug addict who would rather suffer the agony of a gunshot wound than risk getting rehooked by pain killers. Ghosting through both densely detailed narratives is a group of legless Quebec separatists tasked with stealing *Infinite Jest.* They want to use its deadly amusing powers as a weapon. Filmmaker James Incandenza, was so entertained that he committed suicide by sticking his head in a hot-wired microwave oven.

Annihilating diversions in an age of addictive entertainment is one of Wallace's big themes. His variations sometimes come from stock dystopian fiction. But his drug scenes at a detox center have the bumpy rhythms and details that suggests reality rather than fantasy: "Tiny Ewell, in a blue suit and laser chronometer and tiny shoes whose shine you could read by, is sharing a dirty aluminum ashtray with Nell

Gunther, who has a glass eye which she amuses herself by usually wearing so the pupil and iris face in and the dead white and tiny manufacturer's specifications on the back of the eye face out."

An artificial eye turned inward is not a bad metaphor for the world according to Wallace. So is tennis, as represented here by the Incandenzas' son Hal, a teen court prodigy with a gift for lexicography and a taste for recreational drugs. The game as Wallace portrays it is a good illustration of the paradox that there is no freedom without rules and limits. But where mindless circuitry and drugs prevail, human connections break and emotional blindness ensues. Gone too is that key imperative of Western civilization, "Know thyself." Hal, ever the global-village explainer, logs his own symptoms: a feeling of emptiness and an inability to feel pleasure. He also notes another mark of this equal-opportunity disorder: the sort of icy sophistication that often hides fears of social and intellectual embarrassment.

Wallace juggles all this and more with dizzying complexity. You can sign on for the long haul or wait for some post-Pynchon academic to parse it out. Or you can just wade in, enjoy Wallace's maximalist style and hope that unlike the fatal film, *Infinite Jest* the novel won't . . . ARRRRRRGH!

Jay McInerney (review date 3 March 1996)

SOURCE: "The Year of the Whopper," in *New York Times,* March 3, 1996, p. 8.

[*In the following review of* Infinite Jest, *novelist McInerney praises Wallace's talent while lamenting his self-indulgent prolixity.*]

Reading David Foster Wallace's latest novel, *Infinite Jest,* I couldn't help thinking at times about 7-year-old Seymour Glass's book-length "letter" home from camp, published in *The New Yorker* in 1965 as "Hapworth 16, 1924." I felt a similar feeling of admiration alloyed with impatience veering toward strained credulity. (Do you suppose Seymour's parents actually read the whole thing?) I had previously been a great admirer of Mr. Wallace's collection of stories, *Girl with Curious Hair,* and, to a lesser extent, of the loose, baggy monster that was his debut novel, *The Broom of the System,* which I confess to not finishing. If Mr. Wallace were less talented, you would be inclined to shoot him—or possibly yourself—somewhere right around page 480 of *Infinite Jest.* In fact, you might anyway.

Alternately tedious and effulgent, *Infinite Jest* is set in the near future, specifically in the Year of the Depend Adult Undergarment, which would seem to be about 18 years from now. The United States has become part of the Organization of North American Nations (ONAN), federated with Canada and Mexico; most of northern New England has been transformed into a huge toxic waste dump and palmed off on the Canadians. Quebecois separatists, many of them in wheelchairs (les Assassins des Fauteuils Rollents), prowl the lower, nontoxic states, performing terrorist acts, understandably more bilious than ever now that giant fans along the border blow Northeastern American waste products in their direction. President Limbaugh has been fairly recently assassinated, and the calendar has been sold to the highest corporate bidder, giving us the Year of the Whopper, the Year of the Tucks Medicated Pad and so on.

If Mr. Wallace were less talented, you would be inclined to shoot him—or possibly yourself—somewhere right around page 480 of *Infinite Jest*. In fact, you might anyway.
        —*Jay McInerney*

All of this might—and sometimes does—feel cartoonish in the extreme. But this skeleton of satire is fleshed out with several domestically scaled narratives and masses of hyperrealistic quotidian detail. The overall effect is something like a sleek Vonnegut chassis wrapped in layers of post-millennial Zola. Mr. Wallace's earlier fiction revealed him as a student of literary post-modernists like John Barth and Robert Coover, flirting with metafictional tropes and self-referential narratives. Here, despite the *Gravity's Rainbow*-plus length and haute science flourishes, Mr. Wallace plays it straight—that is, almost realistically—and seems to want to convince us of the authenticity of his vision by sheer weight of accumulated detail. The weight almost crushes the narrative at times—as when, for example, we are treated to 10 dense pages about the disassembly of a bed, complete with diagrams.

The two overlapping microcosms of this nonlinear narrative are the Enfield Tennis Academy, a Boston-area institution founded by the mad genius James O. Incandenza, whose clan of athletic and academic prodigies still resides there, and Ennet House, a residence for recovering drug addicts and alcoholics just down the hill. James O., a former tennis prodigy, physicist specializing in optics and avant-garde film maker, has by the time the story opens killed himself by sticking his head in a microwave oven. Surviving him are his sons: Orin, a pro football kicker; Hal, a 17-year-old student at the academy who is as gifted mentally as he is physically and Mario, who is severely deformed and mildly retarded.

The details of day-to-day life at the academy are rendered in something very close to real time, as are several matches between the junior athletes; Mr. Wallace knows his serve and volley from his baseline game: readers may feel qualified toward the end to march down to the court and challenge the club pro to a match.

The mechanics and rituals of the recovering addicts are also represented with mind-numbing fidelity. Central to this narrative is one Don Gately, a recovering burglar and Demerol man, the slogging Leopold Bloom to Hal Incandenza's Stephen Dedalus. Mr. Wallace's knowledge of pharmaceuticals and the psychology of addiction is encyclopedic; if not for the copious footnotes, which among other functions annotate the dozens of narcotics and psychedelics mentioned in the book, all but the most hard-core drug enthusiasts would need a copy of the *Physician's Desk Reference* just to keep track of who was up or down at any given moment.

Recovering at Ennet House from a serious freebase habit is one Joelle van Dyne, who was supposedly featured in a cartridge (i.e., film) made by James Incandenza before he died. This film is said to be so mesmerizing that anyone viewing it—like the famous lab rat with the cocaine dispenser—is rendered helpless and insensible to everything except the desire to keep watching it.

These plot lines eventually converge, although as a narrator Mr. Wallace reminds me of his character Lateral Alice: his momentum tends to be sideways rather than forward, with chapters often seeming interchangeable with the almost 400 footnotes, some a dozen pages long. As the title—a nod to Hamlet's Yorick—indicates, the emergent theme is that we as a nation are amusing ourselves to death. A legless Canadian terrorist tells his American counterpart: "You all stumble about in the dark, this confusion of permissions. The without-end pursuit of a happiness of which someone let you forget the old things which made happiness possible." The terrorist is trying to find Joelle van Dyne in the hope of locating the master copy of the cartridge, code-named "the Entertainment." This would constitute the ultimate terrorist weapon, a device to facilitate the American penchant for entertaining ourselves senseless.

What makes all this almost plausible, and often pleasurable, is Mr. Wallace's talent—as a stylist, a satirist and a mimic—as well as his erudition, which ranges from the world of street crime to higher mathematics. While there are many uninteresting pages in this novel, there are not many uninteresting sentences. And there are dozens of set pieces that double as dazzling mini-entertainments—like an essay on the etiquette of videophones and a street brawl between drunken Canadian separatists and a houseful of recovering addicts. Equally lively is Mr. Wallace's rendition of a New Age 12-step men's group in which bearded hulks sit in a circle clutching teddy bears that represent their inner infants. "Can you share what you're feeling, Kevin?" asks the group leader. "I'm feeling my Inner Infant's abandonment and deep-deprivation issues, Harv," answers a weeping, bearded bear-clutcher.

In this ONAN-ite world, everybody's in a 12-step group of some kind, like Phob-Comp-Anon, a "12-step splinter from Al-Anon, for co-dependency issues surrounding loved ones who were cripplingly phobic or compulsive, or both." The satirical narrative distance evident in both these passages collapses, however, in the long sections about Ennet House and Boston A.A. (the only institution treated with a certain earnestness and even reverence), which seem somewhat out of tune with the book's overall omniscient-hipster narrative stance.

These two strains are never quite synthesized. It's as if Mr. Wallace started with the Glass family whiz-kid plot and then got more interested in the gritty church-basement world of A.A. But, in the end, it is the dogged attempt of the recovering addict Don Gately to reclaim the simple pleasures of everyday life that overshadows the athletic, intellectual and onanistic pyrotechnics of the Incandenzas—and makes this novel something more than an interminable joke.

Rick Perlstein (review date 4 March 1996)

SOURCE: A review of *Infinite Jest,* in *Nation,* Vol. 262, No. 9, March 4, 1996, pp. 27-9.

[*In the review below, Perlstein calls* Infinite Jest *"a daring and brilliant exercise" but one that ultimately fails because the novelist's compulsion overwhelms his art.*]

Jazz apocrypha has it that Miles Davis once asked his sideman John Coltrane to play shorter solos. Coltrane, who could never reach a satisfying conclusion, asked how, and Miles, ever laconic, replied: "Take the horn out of your mouth." Coltrane never did take Miles's advice. Until he explored every harmonic implication of every chord, or couldn't physically play anymore, Coltrane's horn stayed in his mouth. For a while, this made for a gorgeous noise indeed. But soon enough Coltrane was stretching his fantasies into half-hour, then hourlong clots of solipsistic caterwauling. His longtime sidemen left him; his last albums became unlistenable. Although he aimed at transcendence, his compulsion overwhelmed his art.

Call it the Reefer Madness Effect. Satisfaction is always fugitive: It ups its own stakes as the effects of each pleasure achieved wear off and compel you to new heights of risk for ever grander pleasure, until you can't enjoy yourself at all for your very compulsion. In his new cinder block of a book, ***Infinite Jest,*** David Foster Wallace spies this menace ev-

erywhere. We are doubly fallen creatures because our every move toward redemption takes us farther from our goal.

Staggering and audacious, ***Infinite Jest*** covers 1,079 pages and features 388 footnotes, some themselves featuring footnotes. Like Coltrane at his bleary worst, the book ends in sheer exhaustion. Characters struggle for peace of mind and career ever farther from it, until their story lines are simply broken off. Art, love, altruism, entertainment, politics, family: All possible roads to transcending the self become gateway drugs to a junkie-like abyss. The harder you try to pull yourself out, the deeper you dig yourself in. Wallace calls the concept "annularity"—which means ringlike, the infinite downward spiral toward shame, alienation and abjection— and it's the novel's skeleton key.

Not that knowing this will make the book any more manageable. Wallace has set himself the daunting task of conjuring up a fabulist, sci-fi America a decade hence, in a worm's-eye concatenation of details—while allowing himself none of the perspectival tricks authors use to make imaginary worlds act real. It opens *in medias res:* Hal Incandenza, an 18-year-old tennis star who has memorized the entire Oxford English Dictionary, is being interviewed for an athletic scholarship to the University of Arizona after graduating from his parents' tennis academy—or more accurately his mother and half-uncle's tennis academy, his father, James, having committed suicide by hacking open a hole in a microwave door, sealing it around his head with duct tape and making like a bag of Orville Redenbacher. The Enfield Tennis Academy is a Nick Bollettieri-like gulag where adolescents slave at Zen and the Art of Groundstrokes under the tutelage of a sadistic old German and an Indian guru who takes his spiritual sustenance from licking the sweat off the lads' foreheads. Hal writes papers like "Tertiary Symbolism in Justinian Erotica" and "The Emergence of Heroic Stasis in Broadcast Entertainment." He is, in other words, a Prodigy, that annular species that lives to please parents who never will be; an affectless wreck, he also smokes a lot of pot.

Across the road from the E.T.A. is Ennet House, a halfway facility for recovering drug addicts. One of them, Joelle van Dyne, is the former lover of Hal's brother Orin, late a junior tennis star, now a professional football punter (lobs were always his specialty). But what really links drug addicts to success addicts—and to avant-garde artists, and overbearing mothers, and everyone else in this desk reference of self-loathing—is their overwhelming victimization at the hand of their own desires.

Ambition is especially self-destructive. During his meeting with the Arizona officials, Hal Incandenza loses his mind. In a scene reminiscent of "The Metamorphosis," everyone who sees him recoils in horror, to his uncomprehending consternation. Hal, like Gregor Samsa, flushed with the stress of paying off his father's debts—in junior tennis, Hal says, "reaching at least the round you're supposed to is known at tournaments as 'justifying your seed'"—is rendered anti-human. It happens in the midst of showing off his skill at reeling off the O.E.D. There will be no redemption in precociousness, which is just another compulsion that overwhelms healing.

Fatal ambition runs in the family. Before his unseemly run-in with the microwave, the distant, brooding father, James Orin Incandenza, a former junior tennis star and a retired physicist who pioneered cold fusion by harnessing the dark power of—you guessed it—annularity, founded the Enfield Tennis Academy, and then took up a career as an "apres-garde" filmmaker. He is much loved by academic film theorists for projects like installing a hidden camera in the front of an art-house theater audience and projecting the crowd of espresso-sippers to themselves in real time, until the last gullible trendies figure out the ruse. "The *New Yorker* guy, the film guy who replaced the guy who replaced Rafferty," said that Incandenza's "anti-confluential" films "were like the planet's most psychotic psyche working out its shit right there on the screen and asking you to pay to watch him." Joelle begins to act in these films not long before she and Orin break up. Orin goes annular, seducing as many women as possible in annular downward spiral of vindictive shame.

Here is where the wheelchair-bound Quebecois separatist terrorists come in and things get a little nutty. Due to a nuclear chain reaction whose provenance is left obscure, several Northeastern states have been rendered uninhabitable. What's more, the countries in the Northern Hemisphere have united into the Organization of North American Nations (the acronym is one of this rather masturbatory novel's self-deprecating winks). America rids itself of the tainted land by giving it outright to Canada.

A gang of French Canadian thugs called les Assassins des Fauteuils Rollents—assassins in wheelchairs, naturally—decide to exploit the situation. A harebrained scheme is launched to force ONAN to surrender Quebec by attaining a master copy of Infinite Jest, an unreleased Incandenza production starring Joelle van Dyne. Soon wheelchair-bound people with funny accents and suspicious alibis start poking around both the tennis academy and Ennet House looking for *Infinite Jest*. Why? Because it is an entertainment so perfectly realized that to watch it is to never want to stop watching it until you die. He who controls Infinite Jest controls the world. It is the pleasure that, finally, has the power to satisfy. Which means that it is death.

The A.F.R. terrorists want to set into motion the mother of all annularizations, but it's really the same game as everyone else's: They just want to be happy, but they always end

up sad. Pleasure is fugitive; it ups its own stakes, infinitely. Maybe conquering the world will break the spell.

Readers who stay with the novel until the pages thin will come to realize that Wallace has no intention of revealing whether les Assassins des Fauteuils Rollents succeed or fail in their quest. Nor whether Don Gately of Ennet House stays sober; whether Orin will master his awful desires; whether Madame Psychosis will ever return to the airwaves; or whether Hal Incandenza will sacrifice himself to the Oedipal grail. Readers will turn the last page, in other words, without learning anything they need to know to secure narrative succor. Like the characters, the farther they press on, the less they will be satisfied. They will say to themselves: I Have Just Read an Avant-Garde Novel.

> **Readers will turn the last page, in other words, without learning anything they need to know to secure narrative succor. Like the characters, the farther they press on, the less they will be satisfied. They will say to themselves: I Have Just Read an Avant-Garde Novel.**
> **—*Rick Perlstein***

I wonder if it was intentional on Wallace's part that the criticisms in the book that people make of Incandenza's avant-garde film apply so aptly to Wallace's avant-garde novel:

> Technically gorgeous . . . [but] oddly hollow, empty, no sense of dramatic towardness—no narrative movement towards a real story; no emotional movement towards an audience. Like conversing with a prisoner through that plastic screen using phones . . . . cold, allusive, inbent, hostile; the only feeling for the audience one of contempt.

These comments raise the right questions about whether this long-awaited and much-hyped novel ultimately matters or not. Wallace takes drug addiction—the sine qua non of annularity—as his model for the lives he renders, the world he renders them in and the narrative form in which these are simultaneously explained and obscured. He suggests it is the model for our own benumbed, repressively tolerant world as well. His is a familiar pursuit in art and social criticism: to anatomize, then point out a way to transcend, the various opiates of the people—a sort of annular quest in itself. Dreamers plot redemptive schemes like class struggle and psychoanalysis, but redemption remains fugitive (we are fallen creatures); and so Wallace joins the likes of Marcuse and Foucault in a race to the bottom to find ever more intractable sops to our redemption—humanism itself is the problem!—until compulsion overwhelms criticism (or art), and criticism (or art) becomes solipsistic caterwauling.

Wallace is painfully aware of this dilemma, musing about "why so much aesthetically ambitious film was so boring and why so much shitty reductive commercial entertainment was so much fun." He is both the author and the enemy of this jeremiad, because *Infinite Jest* is ambitious, boring and too clinical besides to carry through its own ethical insights. The jokes fall flat, though some may take pleasure in Wallace's language. He writes sentences like the one I'm writing right now pretty much, with these endless, oozing can-you-remember-where-this-started switchback clauses, and if you like this, the sentence you're reading right now, and can imagine more or less 1,000 pages of them, then you'll like this novel, prose-wise.

His precious style abuts his airless nihilism uncomfortably. At least the nihilism, though, is not unremitting. Wallace intimates the possibility of redemption across the street from the Enfield Tennis Academy, in the 12-step recovery culture at Ennet House. There, addicts have their substances taken away from them, lose their minds and find them again through radical withdrawal from enslaving ambition of any sort: a guerrilla assault on annularity, life by homily. "One day at a time." "Grass grows by inches but it dies by feet." People care for one another in this utopia of the anti-utopian. It is, Wallace seems to suggest, a way out, for all of us who feel, who are all addicted.

But Wallace doesn't make it feel like a way out. Amid all his formal experimentation, he wants to render the genuine human pain of addiction and the miracle of its transcendence. But turn again to the criticism of Incandenza's avant-garde film: "Where he dropped the technical fireworks and tried to make the characters move," one "began to see little flashes of something . . . but he wanted to get them by as quickly and unstudyably as possible, as if they compromised him somehow."

In a telling scene near the novel's end, one character dares another to dress up as a bum to see if anyone will touch him. The guy dutifully avoids bathing for a few weeks, then hits the streets. "Touch me, just touch me, please," he says. Confused passers-by drop change into his hand, thinking this is some new beggar slang. But the more he begs to be touched, the more money people give him. Other beggars on the street catch on: They, too, start saying, "Touch me, just touch me, please."

Infinite jest: Each new beggar who takes up the cry makes it harder for the first guy to convince people that, in fact, he wants to be touched. Exhausted, he loses his bet, no satisfying resolution achieved—until he becomes a bum himself. That failure is also Wallace's. He tries to touch us by showing us how hard it is to touch, and how each failure to touch redoubles our alienation and ill resolve. It's a daring and brilliant exercise. But its compulsion overwhelms its art.

Steven Moore (review date Spring 1996)

SOURCE: A review of *Infinite Jest,* in *Review of Contemporary Fiction,* Vol. 16, No. 1, Spring 1996, pp. 141-42.

[*In the following positive review, Moore places Wallace firmly in the tradition of encyclopedic American novelists like William Gaddis, Thomas Pynchon, and William Gass.*]

While reading William Gass's *The Tunnel* last year at this time, I feared I was witnessing the last of a dying breed, the encyclopedic American novel that began with Gaddis's *Recognitions* in 1955, hit its stride in the sixties and seventies (*Giles Goat-Boy, Gravity's Rainbow,* Gaddis again with *J R, The Public Burning, LETTERS*), went baroque in the eighties (*Darconville's Cat, Take Five, Women and Men, You Bright and Risen Angels*), then raged against the dying of the light in the nineties with Powers's *Gold-Bug Variations* and Gass's massive masterpiece. Who was left to write such novels, or to read them at a time when some scorn such books as elitist, testosterone-fueled acts of male imperialism? For those of us who regard these works as our cultural milestones, not as tombstones in patriarchy's graveyard, David Foster Wallace demonstrates that the encyclopedic novel is still alive and kickin' it.

As with *The Tunnel,* sheer style is the first attraction of *Infinite Jest.* Even in his precocious first novel, *The Broom of the System* (1987), Wallace was unfurling long, complex sentences, by turns sonorous and satirical, that were a joy to behold. *Infinite Jest* displays a wider range of styles—from the subliterate monologue of a poverty-stricken abused woman to technical explications of the properties of various pharmaceuticals—but the main narrative style is both casual and complex, slangy and erudite, a kind of slacker mandarin with comically manic specificity of detail. Even if you have trouble following the multiplex narrative at the macro level Wallace offers huge entertainment value at the micro level, flaunting (u in a good way) an amazing command of late- twentieth-century English, with its proliferating technical terms, street slang, and babble of late capitalism. Only Gaddis and Pynchon have this range, and Wallace takes the language places even those two don't go.

At the macro level, *Infinite Jest* consists of numerous "anticonfluential" (Wallace's word) episodes set a dozen years or so in the future (as was *The Broom*), at a time when numerical designations for years have been sold to corporate sponsors: hence we have the Year of the Depend Adult

Undergarment (in which most of the novel takes place), the Year of Glad, the Year of Dairy Products from the American Heartland, and so on. The narrative focuses on two suffering individuals: Hal Incandenza, a brilliant student and gifted tennis player attending the Enfield Tennis Academy and smoking way too much pot; and Don Gately, a petty criminal and recovering narcotics addict on staff at the nearby Ennet House Drug and Alcohol Recovery House ("Redundancy *sic*"), and the narrative shuttles between these two locations (both in the metro Boston area) with occasional side-trips to Arizona, where Hal grew up and where other members of the Incandenza family live. (There is a subplot concerning Québecois separatists and a lethally entertaining video cartridge.) Thematically, the narrative shuttles between addiction and recovery.

Addiction struck William S. Burroughs at midcentury as an encompassing metaphor for many facets of American life, and at century's end Wallace finds a similar metaphor in the recovery from addiction. While Burroughs dwelled with sadistic glee on the horrors of addiction, Wallace takes on the horrors of withdrawal; addiction in Burroughs was largely a response to the need to conform in the Eisenhower fifties, while in Wallace addiction is a response to stress, to the need to excel in the Reagan eighties (the novel's "ethical" setting, if not its historical one). Again like Burroughs—who is named in the text and seems a pretty clear influence—Wallace uses insect imagery to heighten the repugnance of addiction and detoxification. *Infinite Jest* is a *Naked Lunch* for the nineties.

But there's more: tennis as a metaphysical activity; a hundred pages of endnotes, some with their own footnotes; a parody of an annotated filmography; mindbending excursions into game theory; a Workers' Comp claim worthy of a Roadrunner cartoon; an essay-length explanation of why video-phones are doomed to fail; and some incredibly sad stories of damaged human beings with more problems than you'll ever have. The novel is so brilliant you need sunglasses to read it, but it has a heart as well as a brain. *Infinite Jest* is both a tragicomic epic and a profound study of the postmodern condition.

Tom LeClair (essay date Fall 1996)

SOURCE: "The Prodigious Fiction of Richard Powers, William Vollmann, and David Foster Wallace," in *Critique*, Vol. 38, No. 1, Fall, 1996, pp. 12-37.

[*In the following essay, LeClair contrasts three roughly contemporaneous younger novelists against their innovative forbears, especially Thomas Pynchon, and makes his case for a new and scientifically more astute voice in American literature that broadens and deepens the commentary and critique begun by the so-called metafictionists.*]

Since the publication of *V.* in 1963, when Thomas Pynchon was twenty-six, he has been the reigning, if now aging, prodigy of contemporary American fiction, the gifted author of two prodigious novels, the 492-page *V.* and the encyclopedic *Gravity's Rainbow.* Reviewing the more modest *Vineland* in 1990, Richard Powers addressed Pynchon as a composer of bed-time stories: "So tell us another one, Pop, before it gets too dark". Powers, William Vollmann, and David Foster Wallace all admit within their novels their filial debt to "Pop" Pynchon. A major character in Powers's *The Gold Bug Variations* has Pynchon as his "favorite living novelist", several references to *Gravity's Rainbow* appear in Vollmann's *You Bright and Risen Angels,* and a major character in Wallace's *Infinite Jest* is constructed from the obsessions of Pynchon's biggest book. Of the three younger writers, Wallace is the most ambivalent toward Pynchon: Wallace praises *Gravity's Rainbow* as generous in its gift-giving but also calls Pynchon, along with Nabokov, "a patriarch for my patricide". Though still alive, Pynchon seems to have retired from novelistic mastery to become the grandfatherly proprietor of an amusement park called *Vineland.* As we head toward the millennium, Powers, born in 1957; Vollmann, born in 1959; and Wallace, born in 1962, are our new prodigies.

By age thirty-three, Powers had published three novels—the *V.*-like *Three Farmers on Their Way to a Dance, Prisoner's Dilemma,* and the 639-page *The Gold Bug Variations,* which reviewers frequently compared to *Gravity's Rainbow.* At the same age, Vollmann had published a travel book, a collection called *The Rainbow Stories,* and four novels, two of which exceed 600 Pynchon-dense pages. At the age of thirty-four, Wallace had coauthored a book on rap music and had published a collection of stories, a long first novel, and the 1,089-page *Infinite Jest.* Although Powers's first book appeared in 1985, Vollmann's and Wallace's in 1987, and although all have been well-reviewed and have received prestigious awards—Powers a MacArthur Grant, Vollmann and Wallace the Whiting Award—none has attracted the academic attention one would expect for their learned, experimental, and political work. Recent surveys of younger American writers—Jon Aldridge's *Talents and Technicians* and Jerome Klinkowitz's *Structuring the Void*—do not even mention Powers, Vollmann, or Wallace. They are also missing from Patti White's *Gatsby's Party,* a study of contemporary fiction influenced by science, a natural sub-category for the three writers. At a parallel stage in Pynchon's career, numerous essays and one book had been written about his fiction.

Powers, Vollmann, and Wallace deserve essays of their own. I have chosen to treat them and their most remarkable novels—*The Gold Bug Variations* (1991), *You Bright and Risen Angels* (1987), and **Infinite Jest** (1996)—together because fundamental similarities among the authors and these three works illustrate their relation to and differences from Pynchon, as well as other large-minded novelists of Pynchon's generation. Although the Pynchon of *V.* displayed a precocious familiarity with history, geography, and multiple literary forms, what set him apart was his scientific knowledge, which became more central in *The Crying of Lot 49.* Despite his scientific training at Cornell, Pynchon has said in *Slow Learner* that his early knowledge of a concept as crucial as entropy was "second-hand". Still, his use of technical terms and references to scientists such as James Clerk Maxwell made Pynchon a prodigy for most literary readers still living in an era of "Two Cultures." *Gravity's Rainbow* with its detailed development of cybernetics, physics, and other sciences confirmed Pynchon's reputation. Not long after *Gravity's Rainbow* was published other prodigious novels influenced by information theory and scientific systems began to appear: DeLillo's *Ratner's Star,* Heller's *Something Happened,* Gaddis's *JR,* Coover's *The Public Burning,* McElroy's *Women and Men,* Barth's *LETTERS,* and Le Guin's *Always Coming Home.* I do not mean to suggest that *Gravity's Rainbow* led these writers to what I have called "the systems novel," but that from early on in his career Pynchon exemplified a new kind of learning in fiction. Unlike Pynchon, these writers did not receive academic training in science, and their early works, though sometimes concerned with technology, do not exhibit the influence of theoretical science present in *V.* and *Lot 49.* DeLillo and the others came later in their careers to cybernetics and to the sciences—such as economics, ecology, meteorology, and mathematics—that saturate their prodigious texts.

Unlike the literary elders I have mentioned, Powers, Vollmann, and Wallace were educated in the Age of Information; and they acquired an expertise nowhere evident in the work of the previous generation, Pynchon's fiction included. Although not much is known about the specific educational backgrounds of Powers, Vollmann, and Wallace, biographical sources do indicate that in their twenties, the age at which Pynchon was reading Norbert Weiner, Powers and Vollmann both worked as computer programmers. Their professional experience with information systems is manifested directly in their first novels, which are at least partially set in the computer industry. In *Three Farmers On Their Way to a Dance,* the protagonist-narrator is educated in computer science, works for a magazine aimed at the "microcomputer design readership", discusses the differences between digital and analogue technology, and brings a cybernetic awareness to his commentaries on mathematics, physics, and other sciences. The two narrators of *You Bright and Risen Angels* are computer programmers working in Silicon Valley; the characters they write about are both persons from their past and electronic alphanumerics these program-

mers call up from the graveyard of memory files. Like Powers's narrator, Vollmann's keyboarders are protagonists and antagonists whose lives mingle with figures from the historical past. In Vollmann's succeeding novels about early North America, information storage and retrieval are no longer explicit subjects but everywhere implicit in the detailed research necessary to write those books. In *The Gold Bug Variations,* after writing a novel based on game theory, Powers returns to the information industry: two of his three main characters are programmers and caretakers of a large bank of Manhattan computers. Wallace, although not a programmer, studied in college the mathematics and logic that underlie the programming Powers and Vollmann have done. One of Wallace's stories is dedicated to Kurt Goedel, and references to mathematics and theoretical physics abound in **Infinite Jest.**

> **I am not suggesting only that Powers, Vollmann, and Wallace write more explicitly about information than the earlier systems novelists or that their fluency with technical or mathematical languages distinguishes their work. Rather I believe these younger writers more thoroughly conceive their fictions as information systems, as long-running programs of data with a collaborative genesis.**
>
> **—*Tom LeClair***

I am not suggesting only that Powers, Vollmann, and Wallace write more explicitly about information than the earlier systems novelists or that their fluency with technical or mathematical languages distinguishes their work. Rather I believe these younger writers more thoroughly conceive their fictions as information systems, as long-running programs of data with a collaborative genesis. In the information industry, prodigies age quickly and generations change rapidly. In the novel industry, the cyberpunk strain of science fiction in some of its formal experiments has already exceeded the programming or systems influence found in Powers, Vollmann, and Wallace. However, among writers who set their fiction on this planet, those three novelists are, I think, most advanced in their knowledge of and most sophisticated in their use of information.

Compared with most of the older novelists mentioned above, Powers, Vollmann, and Wallace know more about the life sciences and ecology. Pynchon, Gaddis, McElroy, and Le Guin are all concerned with biology in their encyclopedic books, but only Barth in *LETTERS* registers as a central influence the most revolutionary experimental science of the Information Age: genetics, the discipline that was probably most aided by and that has the most conceptual overlaps with cybernetics. The Watson-Crick paper that propelled contemporary genetics was published in 1953, four years before Powers's birth in 1957. That is, symbolically I assume, the year in which Powers sets the genetics research group called Cyfer that introduces the dense scientific discourse of *The Gold Bug Variations.* Post Watson-Crick biology is also the intellectual substratum of *You Bright and Risen Angels*; "insect genetics" supports Vollmann's encyclopedic analogues between the human and insect kingdoms. In those two works about literary, literal, and figurative bugs, a detailed knowledge of contemporary biology underwrites, like the genetic code itself, a depiction of nature as vast and intricate collaborations of information and energy, a model for fiction even more prodigious than the mainframe computer. For Barth, genetics was a trope supporting a sequel, a backward look at and synthesis of his previous six books. Powers and Vollmann find in genetics and entomology information and symbols for urgent meditation on the future of all life. For Wallace, theoretical biology and zoology are not as central as they are for Powers and Vollmann, and yet, like them, Wallace is particularly interested in the effects of physical mutations, how waste turns two-legged and four-legged animals into monsters.

These young, obviously gifted authors' combined experience with information and knowledge of life science generates new meanings of prodigy and prodigious. Both words have as their root the Latin "prodigium," which meant "omen, portent, monster." In archaic English, a prodigy was "something out of the usual course of nature (as an eclipse or meteor) that is a portent." More recently, the word has come to mean "an extraordinary accomplishment" or "a highly gifted or academically talented child." Beginning as a natural event, the meaning of prodigy changed to a human accomplishment. Now the word is most generally applied to an individual person with a precocious skill or high intelligence. Although Powers, Vollmann, and Wallace may be such persons (Powers graduated with an "A" average from Illinois; Vollmann and Wallace graduated summa cumlaude from, respectively, Cornell and Amherst) and young, precocious characters populate *The Gold Bug Variations, You Bright and Risen Angels,* and **Infinite Jest,** the novels as wholes suggest that prodigies need not be only those hard-wired and solitary geniuses of tradition. In the world of Powers and Vollmann, collaboration with computers and other technology-assisted persons can create a contemporary prodigy, one less dependent on genetically inherited synapses, more free to direct the development of his or her own consciousness, more defined by the information he or she possesses. For Wallace, the notion of prodigy spreads even wider, incorporating physical talents and emotional capabilities, both trained in communities of the naturally gifted and culturally afflicted.

These new fiction-writing prodigies both find and create a world of information that is prodigious: "extraordinary in bulk, extent, quantity, or degree (enormous, immense, vast)." These synonyms for "extraordinary" have connotations of cosmic width and breadth, physicists' extra-planetary exploration or sub-molecular investigation. The "Infinite" of Wallace's title, which alludes to Cantor's mathematics as well as to Shakespeare's jesting Yorick, best represents the scale of prodigious fiction. The discoveries of contemporary genetics brought near-infinity to biology, exploding beyond what Powers calls "the complexity barrier" (514) information about all life all over the globe for all of history. The Human Genome project alluded to in *The Gold Bug Variations* has been called the most ambitious scientific project ever undertaken. Trying to keep up with genetics research in 1985, a Powers character says information in the field doubles every two years. For Vollmann, insects are the symbol of prolific life and proliferant information about life, millions of species breeding, multiplying, and changing, forever exceeding scientists' ability to catalogue them. The irony of both proliferations is that the four-letter genetic code generating life and information is itself not so much a prodigy as a hyperactive idiot savant. "Prodigious diversity of *macroscopic* structures of living beings," Powers quotes Jacques Monod, "rests in fact on a profound and no less remarkable unity of *microscopic* make-up". It is knowledge of this new law of the very many and the one, the large and the small, that in Powers's work modifies the behavior of old-fashioned prodigies and offers a model for the work of new collaborative prodigies. Vollmann's novel implies a similar conclusion, but only through a reversal of its characters' attempt to reduce and then destroy the many, "equality's brood", that threaten entrenched power in America, power personified by the novel's pioneering prodigy, robber baron, and multinational CEO, Mr. White.

The effect of both the prodigy and the prodigious—exciting amazement and wonder—is also, I believe, the purpose Powers, Vollmann, and Wallace pursue with their gifted massiveness: amazement at the natural world they depict circulating through us and buzzing around us, wonder at the intricate and dense fictions they offer as imitative forms of that world. Like Pynchon and the other systems novelists of the 1970s and 1980s who were influenced by cybernetics, Powers, Vollmann, and Wallace insist on transforming the synecdochic scale of traditional realism, "overloading" their stories to reflect the accessibility and relevance of technical information in the lives of contemporary characters. The new prodigies also supplement the digital mode of print with iconic or analogue representation such as diagrams and drawings, the mapping of quantitative information in visual displays that has characterized recent developments in computer design.

The artistic pressures exerted by the magnitude of their subjects and by their desires to elicit powerful responses to revolutionary information about life push Powers, Vollmann, and Wallace toward literary means that sometimes seem "prodigal": "profuse and wasteful expenditure of capital," "given to reckless extravagance," and "giving or yielding abundantly." Like the older novelists who practice an "art of excess," Powers and, even more, Vollmann and Wallace exceed expectations, deform genre, and write extravagantly, but they are not, as some reviewers complain, self-indulgent. If their works exceed the social politeness of most realism and the political correctness of their decade, they do so from, if anything, a too-earnest concern for readers and other living things. It is that concern for the future that propels the second halves of *The Gold Bug Variations* and *You Bright and Risen Angels*—and all of **Infinite Jest**—toward the original root of prodigy (omen, portent, monster) and the archaic English meaning (out of the usual course of nature) as the authors warn against mankind's leaving the course of nature and becoming a monster in the world web of life, destroying itself in the process. In these three massive novels, creators, created, and audience are all braided together under the sign of the Latin "prodigy-."

Although *The Gold Bug Variations* was published five years after *You Bright and Risen Angels* and although Powers mentions Vollmann as one of two contemporary American authors he admires, I treat Powers's novel first because it is more explicitly about prodigies and new scientific paradigms. The central character of *The Gold Bug Variations,* Stuart Ressler, genetics researcher become caretaker of computers, "was the prodigy once". In the first grade, he took over his teacher's "abortive lesson on the language of bee dancing". Given an adult encyclopedia at the age of seven, Stuart proved that his "precocity exceeded even his parents' guess" by breaking its spines with rereading in two years. A little later he "lavished this precocious life [of learning] on the home nature museum—a walk-in catalog of the planetary pageant" that he spread around his house. "A boy completely, passionately in love with links," Stuart as a sixth-grader derived "a perfect copy of Gauss's great work" on mathematical summation, a significant discovery in this novel about responding to large numbers. "By junior high, he had proved to disbelieving high schoolers that almost all possible numbers have an eight in them, or a seven, or nine, but an infinity of numbers contain none of these. In late teens, he announced to an uncomprehending English teacher that the word 'couch,' repeated a thousand times at high speed, deteriorated into semantic nothingness". Pursuing "not what a thing *is,* but how it connects to others", young Stuart Ressler moved from observation of nature to mathematical formalism, metamathematics, and to an experimental knowledge of noise, breakdown of the meanings he had recognized or constructed.

Ressler's rapid youthful progress is replicated at a slower rate during the rest of his life, which Powers dramatizes in two primary time periods: 1957-58, when Ressler is a postdoctoral researcher, and 1983-84, when his life has new vitality under the sentence of an early death from cancer. After studying physiology as an undergraduate, Ressler reads the Watson-Crick paper in 1953 and changes his graduate area to genetics in order to "rush the frontier," believing "all significant breakthroughs were made by novices free from preconceptions or vested interests. In six months of ferocious precocity, he'd made believers of everyone". Accepting at twenty-five a postdoctoral fellowship at Illinois, Ressler feels "under the gun. Miescher was twenty-five when he discovered DNA ninety years before. Watson was twenty-four. If the symptoms of breakthrough don't show by thirty, forget it. . . . Research—America in '57—is no country for old men". In chapters alternating with chapters about the early 1980s, Powers describes Ressler's joining the Cyfer group of six scientists from different disciplines, their stumbling advance on explaining how genetic processes work, Ressler's falling in love with his married colleague Jeannette Koss, their stumbling advance on consummating their relation, Ressler's conceptual breakthrough, and a double renunciation: Jeannette of Ressler, he of his research.

Trying to uncover Ressler's achievements and then understand his renunciation and years of obscurity are Franklin Todd, Ressler's twenty-five-year-old coworker, an all-but-dissertation in art history at Columbia, and Jan O'Deigh, a thirty-year-old reference librarian who becomes Todd's lover as she helps him delve into Ressler's past and interest him in the present. In this novel with numerous character doublings, collaborative triplings, and coded quadruplings, Jan, the primary narrator of the book, is closest to Ressler in childhood interests and background. "From birth," she says, "I was addicted to questions. When the delivering nurse slapped my rump, instead of howling, I blinked inquisitively". Her early "why" questions were for a time answered by her mother's gift of "a multi-volume children's encyclopedia," but this strategy backfired because Jan could "ask about things that hadn't even existed before". The first time Jan touched her cello it made a wonderful sound she never duplicated; she soon turned to the piano and became a rather mechanical player. Like Ressler, Jan lost her father when she was twelve. Although she had scientific curiosity and artistic training that Ressler did not receive until he was twenty-five, Jan was no prodigy. As an adult, her skillful information searches are primarily directed by library patrons, though she does initiate "The Quote Board" and "This Day in History," small ways of extracting and communicating some significant bits of "the disjointed stockpile". Researching questions from a patron with a Down's syndrome child, Jan makes what John Paulos calls an "Innumerate" interpretation of the data she finds on the causes of retardation. Her miscalculation of her own risk is partly responsible for her renunciation: a tubal ligation. Her four-year relationship with the adrenal ad-writer Keith Tuckwell also illustrates her defensive passivity, for she uses his nonstop commentary on competitive life in the city as a substitute for a more active life and as a source of entertainment. Like Oedipa Maas at the beginning of *The Crying of Lot 49,* Jan is susceptible to a search that will take her out of her library of trivia and trivialized personal relationship.

Todd challenges her to find out why Ressler was once famous. A student of physics in college, Todd switched to art history and is working the night shift with Ressler instead of finishing his dissertation on the life and work of a minor sixteenth-century Dutch painter. While Jan's searches in the information had are primarily seeded by others, Todd actively lavishes his attention on other people and their eccentricities. He treats New York as his "home nature museum," with the emphasis on museum. His apartment is an archive of art objects and musical recordings. Todd's formalist training gives him a Resslerian awareness of links, but Jan repeatedly thinks of Todd as childish, his curiosity unfocused, his "unfortunately high intelligence" spent in passionate dilettantism. During spare hours at work, Todd cuts up *The New York Times,* pastes its information into his notebook, and surrounds the facts with elaborate sketches, turning information into a private aesthetic object. He treats the information in his computers like a video game.

The Ressler that Todd knows in 1983 appears to have both technical and personal control of the information glut. He teaches Todd programming skills, and Ressler's almost monastic manner and obsession with Bach's *Goldberg Variations* appeal to the widely scattered younger man. As Todd and Jan get closer to Ressler, he moves out of his self-imposed isolation, becomes a father figure to them, and tries to direct their attention away from his personal life to the biosphere he has spent his life studying, if not researching, since leaving Cyfer for cybernetic caretaking. After Ressler's death, Jan quits her job, uses her life savings to support herself while investigating the state of genetics in 1957, and keeps a journal of her research and her life during the research. After spending time with Ressler just before his death, Todd writes an account of Ressler's early life rather than his dissertation. What the reader does not know until the last page is that the book just finished has been the product of combining Jan's journal and Todd's biography, a recognition that requires rereading with this new knowledge. This readerly recursion of a book about recursions—and dense with them—finds that the text has not been, as Todd suggests at the end, a product of "splicing" but has been, to use a programming term from the novel, a product of "backstopping", recursive revision. Information, language, and sensibilities developed separately cross over the textual borders and get translated differently in their new context. Clues to this interpenetration or cross-fertilizing occur in chapter 17, when Todd's programming language appears in

Jan's narration, and in chapter 22, when information about Ressler in Illinois breaks into a section presumably told by Jan. Locally cooperative, the text is globally collaborative. Its chapters and subsections simultaneously obey two formal codes—genetic and musical—that neither "author" could have managed to follow or impose alone. Although neither Jan nor Todd is, like Ressler, a prodigy capable of an imaginative "breakthrough" to the reductive secret of all life, they do combine his top-down power of abstraction and his bottom-up power of observation to understand the secrets of his life and learning, using this knowledge to form an artistically patterned text. Like Ressler's breakthrough, Jan and Todd's collaboration would have been impossible without love: their love of Ressler and his altruistic example, their learned love of each other. *The Gold Bug Variations* is, therefore, their "baby", a creation with some of the chromosomal complexity present in every child, the being Ressler called nature's "model of miraculous miniaturization".

At 692 pages, *The Gold Bug Variations* is a miniature simulation of the natural world described in it. The collaboration that produces the text is learned at the center of it, a chapter called "The Natural Kingdom II." In a book very concerned with formal symmetry, as well as the asymmetry that creates mutations, "The Natural Kingdom II" is the fifteenth of thirty chapters. Unlike most chapters, it is wholly composed by Jan, a four-part summary of the principles ruling the world populated by the four-letter genetic code, principles she had begun to understand in one of four parts of chapter 12, the subsection entitled "The Natural Kingdom." In chapter 12 she quotes Melville's Ishmael on natural classification ("the draft of a draft") and meditates upon difference and similarity. She learns how huge the genetic "gap between individuals is" and how the human genome "represents only the slightest of divergence from . . . chimp and gorilla". With her developing knowledge of genetics, Jan corrects her misconceptions about evolution: it is "not about competition or squeezing out, not a master plan of increasing efficiency." Evolution is "a deluge, a cascade of mistaken, tentative, branching, brocaded experiment . . .". She ends this subsection by quoting Monod on "prodigious diversity," the theme with which chapter 15 begins by returning to Ishmael's comparison of nature to texts: "Books may be a substantial world, but the world of substance, the blue, species-mad world at year's end outstrips every card catalog I can make for it". In "A. Classification" Jan learns that "Living things perpetuate only through glut" that resists and embarrasses all human classification schemes: "Nothing exceeds like success. Excess of issue. Surplus of offspring". In "B. Ecology" Jan replaces "competition" with a new set of more appropriate, historically denigrate terms—"parasitism, helotism, commensalism, mutualism, dulosis, symbiosis"—and extends her book metaphor: the planet as "lending library—huge, conglomerate, multinational, underfunded, overinvested . . . No competition, no success, no survival of the fittest. The world I am looking for, the language of life, is circulation". The next subsection, "C. Evolution," is "an explosive deflation" of her library metaphor, for it is only through error, genetic chance that evolution proceeds: "Mutations cause cancer, stillbirth, blindness, deafness, heart disease, mongolism—everything that can go wrong. Yet faulty copying is the only agency for change". For metaphor to represent the Darwinian revolution's effect—"tailspin anxiety . . . soul's distress"—she turns to *The Goldberg Variations,* its midpoint fifteenth, "terminal descent" from which the succeeding variations rise. "D. Heredity" is "the last, delicious twist . . . Evolution is the exception, stability the rule", a recognition that returns her to the chapter's beginning: "proliferation results from one universal and apostolic genetic code" produced by "the prodigal gene".

This twenty-page chapter enunciates a new naturalism, one that revises and reverses early twentieth-century naturalism's determinism and struggle for power, preserving the metaphor of hierarchy in the word "Kingdom" but undermining this vertical notion and the concept of Creation Jan first learned in her catechism. Born out of chance, affected by ecological constraints beyond its control, spreading and perpetuating itself by improbable variation, life is not designed. Once the notion of design disappears, Jan remembers Ressler theorizing, so will the destructive notion of improving life. Although spiritual distress has been the widespread response to the world as a "'Monte Carlo game'", the prodigious odds against life ever appearing on the planet and the prodigal diversity of its forms stimulate in Ressler "wonder and reverence", reactions he believes are the appropriate purposes of science. "'The proper response'" to the observed world, Jan quotes Ressler, "'ought not to be distress at all. We should feel dumb amazement. Incredulous, gasping gratitude that we've landed the chance at all, the outside chance to be able to comprehend, to save any fraction of it'". The natural science that Jan, Todd, and the reader learn from Ressler teaches a series of analogous lessons: that life is a prodigy, a highly unlikely phenomenon on a planet dead for millions of years; that humankind is a recent prodigy on the timeline of life; that every normal child with its brain of a "hundred trillion synaptic bits" is a prodigy within the realm of biology; and that humans had better employ their natural curiosity, the information stockpile, and pattern-recognition to become new kinds of prodigies—emerging, collaborating, maturing rather than declining with age, creating an "ecology of knowledge". For Ressler, humankind is the "caretaker" of the earth who must learn the most fundamental lesson of genetics: "small initial changes ripple into large differences".

The wisdom of "The Natural Kingdom II" can be fed backward in time to evaluate the Cyfer group in 1957-58 and fed forward in the text to judge the actions of Jan, Todd, and

Ressler in 1983. The seven scientists in Cyfer are brought together in a Cold War intellectual environment with reminders of the Manhattan Project, the possibility of nuclear apocalypse, and the launch of Sputnik. Despite these examples of theoretical physics turned into practical threat, the Cyfer scientists look to a local achievement—the invention of the transistor by two Illinois professors—to reinforce their collective belief that they are producing knowledge that will improve life. Supposedly pure scientists, their research is pressured by review boards and funding mechanisms. Initially collaborating, the group breaks up into two camps with Ressler as liaison and eventually the camps break down because of the difficulty of the project or the interference of the scientists' personal lives. Tooney Blake, locked for a night in the library, experiences information overload and leaves the group for a life of hopeless generalism. Joe Lovering, who has an imaginary girlfriend and an impossible computer task, kills all the lab's animals and, on a sudden impulse, himself. Woytowich, unwilling to admit in his personal life the long odds he investigates in the lab, breaks up his marriage and gives his intellectual energies to rating TV programs. Jeannette Koss sacrifices her role in the breakthrough and her love for Ressler to a 1950s version of womanly nobility. Ulrich, the administrator, and Botkin, the European scientist comfortable in two cultures and a reminder of Nabokov, who used the name as a pseudonym, are the only members of the group by the year's end. The novel's sections about Cyfer suggest that scientific discovery is almost as lucky—as dependent upon variables scientists of the 1950s tried to ignore—as life itself.

Ressler's passionate love of Jeannette affects his own refusal of the breakthrough, but equally important is his vision of the future, the next generation of prodigies and science. While working backward to the genesis of life, Ressler observes two children of his colleagues in Cyfer. Margaret Blake, at age seven, has been trained to recite long passages of romantic poetry that she does not understand. The Woytowichs' infant child Ivy is also being conditioned to be a prodigy, picking out alphabet blocks when her father names them. Both children are directed to second-order experience—language they do not understand, letters they cannot, know, ciphers—rather than being placed in proximity to first-order nature that language names. They see arbitrary links before experiencing things. They may well grow up to be facile cross-referencers and glib conversationalists like Jan and Todd, but these "prodigies" will lack the curiosity about and wonder at nature that Ressler and, I believe, Powers maintain are the source of science and its grand understandings. Poised at the edge of such a break-through, Ressler sees what biotech will and has become. Koss's husband—engineer turned food technologist, master of cheese in a can—is the parody version of useful knowledge. More dangerous is engineering life, creating genetic combinations that, like cheese in a can, cannot be put back in once sprayed out. For Ressler, the benefits of medical science are not worth the risks to the million-year-old genetic library, which can be snipped and cut a million times faster by human intervention than by evolutionary mutation. When he loses Jeanette and the possibility of the two of them standing as symbols of scientific renunciation, Ressler gives up the gold associated with the Nobel Prize and patented life forms. He spends the next twenty-five years recovering from what Powers suggests is the "gold bug," the financial flu, of mid-century science.

Poe's "The Gold Bug" is first referred to in the Illinois sections and serves best as a commentary on the period and the searches of the book's first half. Bach's *Goldberg Variations* are also introduced in the Cyfer group, but they are more important in the second half of the book and in the 1980s sections. The fact that "Variations" is capitalized on the title page implies that this word is more important than either of its predecessors. The characters who comment on story, Ressler included, are interested in the intellectual power and knowledge that the self-aggrandizing Legrand uses to break the code and dig up the treasure. For Powers, I think, other features of the story are equally important. Legrand is a naturalist whose curiosity about life on the seashore is responsible for first turning up the unusual golden bug. After that a series of accidents involving his servant, the weather, his friend the narrator, his dog, and a small error with huge consequences help lead him to the prodigious riches in Captain Kidd's chest, natural stones worked into human treasure immorally amassed and then covered by skeletons of men Kidd presumably killed. This wealth Legrand shares with his servant and the narrator who spends little time meditating on the sources of the wealth.

Whether it is the possible wealth that produces feats of analysis or whether code-breaking is a natural proclivity of the brain that accidentally produces financial rewards, intellectual prowess is a metaphoric piracy. The "breakthrough" that Ressler achieves is a kind of break-in: "Putting One's Hands Through the Pane" that separates life from our understanding of it.

The plot of the last third of the novel provides a contemporary analogue of piracy and the dangers of interfering in the prodigious web of interconnected information inside or outside the gene. In December 1983, Ressler, Todd, and Jan take a weekend holiday in New England. When they are snowed in, their supervisor, a boy-man named Jimmy without computer skills, futilely attempts to keep the information processing working. Feeling guilty and sorry for the overworked Jimmy, Todd uses the programming skills he has picked up from Ressler to break into the company records and give Jimmy a raise. This altruistic hacking inadvertently cancels Jimmy's insurance. When the raise is investigated, the innocent Jimmy has a stroke and requires long-term care

and therapy no longer covered. To right this wrong, Ressler, Todd, and Jan create an elaborate computer violation that breaks no laws but embarrasses the company into reinstating Jimmy's insurance before firing Ressler and Todd. Their clever manipulation of programming knowledge and literary quotation can close the gap in coverage, but nothing can repair the broken blood vessel in Jimmy's head. Like the genetic code and the life it produces, the brain is prodigiously dense and complex. But as Jimmy's accident implies, the brain that makes us prodigies is also exceedingly delicate, small changes producing huge unanticipated effects, a single event turning the rest of Jimmy's life and speech into noise.

Personal collaboration, man-machine cooperation, financial conglomeration, and overpopulation create massive scales of information, organization, and environment in *The Gold Bug Variations*. Magnitude and number pose a question that Powers asks in his other novels: how can the single person believe she or he matters? In collaborating to help Jimmy, Ressler, Todd, and Jan renounce the selfish desires percolating up into behavior from the selfish gene and act, according to Jan, by the morality dictated by "a new complex mathematics, one dependent on the tiniest initial tweaks". Her "notion that the entire community was accountable to the infinitesimal principle of a single life" has as its basis the nonlinear science of chaos and fractals, a paradigm that has emerged since the explosion of genetics and a paradigm that finds in both life and inanimate matter the kind of delicate patterning and noisy order of genetics. I have discussed in some detail in *The Art of Excess* the influence of nonlinear science on Joseph McElroy's *Women and Men*. The terms of that analysis can be easily mapped onto *The Gold Bug Variations*. Particularly relevant to Power's novel are the sources of this new paradigm: fractal theory arose from Benoit Mandelbrot's mathematical formalism and chaos theory came out of early large-scale sorting of phenomena made possible by the computer. Both theories rely on computer graphics, reducing their prodigious digital information into analogue forms, to communicate their beauty and validity. Key to both theories is the recognition that initial changes in a dynamic system create huge and unanticipatable results. This unpredictability—from the processes of genetics to an individual's brain to ecosystemic processes—is the fundamental basis of Powers's critique of scientific mastery and human intervention in the biosphere.

If old-fashioned and new prodigies turn their energies away from engineering nature and tinkering with biological information, they can learn how to imitate the new paradigm of nature in their lives and works. Jan and Todd create the collaborative biography of Ressler, who spends his last years investigating music's relationship to the brain and composing his own music. In this work about science and art, Gold Bug and Goldberg, Bach's music dominates the second half, culminating in chapter 27 where Powers uses both digital and analogue means to explain the multiple levels, overlapping orders, and recursive structures of the *Goldberg Variations*. I will leave a detailed analysis of the Bach influence to someone more knowledgeable about music than I, but it is clear from Power's use of the Goldbergs and his comments on them that the central feature uniting this music and the new science, whether genetic or nonlinear, is correspondence. For Powers, self-similarity and variation replace Newtonian cause and effect as the fundamental principles of nature. And correspondence is a pervasive principle in the novel from its molecular structure—puns, puzzles, riddles, translations—to its metaform—doublings, splittings, triplings, recursions, and expansions.

The correspondence between Bach's *Goldberg Variations* and Powers's *The Gold Bug Variations* also represents the novel's deceptive prodigality. Opening with an "Aria" that insists upon its simplicity, Powers takes the reader into a fairly conventional realistic novel about failed love and gradually overloads the reader with functional information about genetics that shows prodigality is life's rule. Then through parallels with the "Goldbergs" and through commentary on them Powers reveals the prodigality—the superabundant connections—of his novel. The result is what one of Powers's characters in *Prisoner's Dilemma* calls "Crackpot Realism", a fusion of traditional representational methods with contemporary paradigms that will seem like crackpot ideas to readers clinging to the common-sense empiricism of traditional realism. This fusion creates a mutation, the "'hopeful monster'" known in biology as "the Goldschmidt variation". With his collaborative artistic method, Powers elicits the emotional effect of realistic representation—the reader's sympathetic engagement with characters—while building toward the final response of wonder, the reader's amazement at the world created in and through this book made by an author "giving or yielding abundantly."

William Vollmann employs as artistic methods the more negative meanings of prodigal—"profuse and wasteful expenditure," "reckless extravagance"—from the very beginning of *You Bright and Risen Angels*: a vicious epigraph from Hitler; a subtitle that announces the book as a "Cartoon"; another epigraph defending exaggeration; a dedication to "bigots everywhere"; the author's autograph accompanied by hermetic signs not explained until an "Author's Note" on page 636; a four-page "Social Gazette of the Personalities Interviewed for this Book" too dense with information to be of use; a four-page "Transcendental Contents" that includes chapters of a second volume that does not exist; and a prologue entitled "Shape-shifting" in which the narrator says "I may disguise myself as any other animate or inanimate object in what follows". The profuse frames and extravagant ironies of the first few pages are followed by Shandy-like chapters, often eccentrically titled and decorated with multiple, esoteric epigraphs; a plethora of

human and insect characters in several wandering plots; an amorphous time and space, historical and imagined; a style as digressive and metaphorically diffuse as Tom Robbins's; and a humor as parodically broad as that of Robert Coover and William Burroughs, both of whom are alluded to in the novel. Unlike Powers, who suggests the prodigal quality of his novel arises from its protagonist-narrators, Vollmann calls attention to himself as the prodigy source of his book's more than crackpot hyperreality. But the author who signs his name in the text at the beginning and signs again in hermetic symbols at the end is only one manifestation of the actual author whose printed name in capital letters in the paperback edition) precedes the text. How the lower-case author becomes the capitalized Author is a central story of the novel: the development from personal hermeticism to a role as public Hermes, the prodigal god of science and art, orators and thieves celebrated as a parasite by Michel Serres. The prodigy who wrote *You Bright and Risen Angels* between 1981-85, when he was in his early twenties, *became* that prodigy: the author learned to become the Author by collecting and using prodigious information as a computer programmer, what he calls a "glorious profession" in the only partly ironic "Social Gazette."

Reconstructing this development requires assembling into chronological order details about the self-referring "author" that occur piecemeal throughout the novel. This author lived in San Francisco with a girl named Clara Bee, who called him "Beetle" and kept snakes in a glass case warmed by electric lights. Tiring of him and his parasitical dependence, Clara ended their relationship, the author attempted suicide, and began what he terms his "bug blazoomises" to forget his personal unhappiness. The hero of these cartoons (and of *You Bright and Risen Angels*) is the nameless "Bug," a bookish and vulnerable outsider like the author. Although Bug remembers everything he reads, neither he nor the author seems inherently gifted with creative abilities. Bug's "great sensitivity" to insects is largely the product of some wax earplugs that a bug-eyed boy gives Bug at summer camp. From childhood Bug's nemesis is a snake-like character named Parker Fellows, who continues to plague Bug like some Poe double even after college and after Bug joins with "The Great Beetle" to wage war against humankind and electricity. In addition to the parallels between the author and Bug, bits of information about them and what the author's note reveals about Vollmann—that he went to Cornell, visited Afghanistan, and that he lives in San Francisco—also overlap. What Vollmann suggests with these seeming or partial self-references is that the cartoon, a form for children, arose from the author's child-like vulnerability and took its imagery and names from his rather juvenile romantic relation. "As children," Vollmann has his author say, "when we pulled the covers over our heads to protect us from monsters at night, we knew that if the monsters ever came they could rip the blankets silently with their claws and then eat us . . . but with an *exoskeleton* we'd be as invulnerable as Superman".

Much of the mid-section of the book—about Bug's years at summer camp, on a high school swim team, at college, in a protest group, and finally as leader of a violent revolutionary cell that includes Milly, Clara Bee's best friend—parodies with its exhaustive, frequently excessive detail the sentimental, Holden Caulfield *bildungsroman* and the political revenge fantasy, mocking the obsessive personalizing that characterizes both forms. Although as a boy Bug, like Stuart Ressler, was a student of trees and interested in insects, his later ecoterrorism develops more from his emotional alienation than from an informed ideology. He decides to be a revolutionary when he sees the powerful effect the wind has on women's skirts. The most ideological member of his little band is the "meta-feminist" Milly, whose alliance with Bug is a symbolic defeat of Clara Bee. The group retreats in Alaska to the "Caves of Ice" that Bug read about in a Tom Swift book. Bug's attraction to guns and violence is equally juvenile and again bookish, reality developing out of the gun catalogues that he once collected. In the revolutionary cartoon, the alienated author reverses Superman's alliance with the law and order of dominant culture. Bug is a Spiderman gone native, back to his insect roots.

What metamorphoses *You Bright and Risen Angels* from a parodic cartoon about adolescent monsters to a serious attack on a larger enemy is the author's job as a computer programmer working for a "math nerd" supervisor named Big George. Incorporated as a character in the cartoon, Big George meddles with the author's favored creations. Then Big George rises above his status as character, interferes with the author's use of his word processor, and takes over long stretches of narration as alternative author. The reader experiences this conflict between authors early in the text, but understands their competition and the fact that Big George has been the speaker of "Shape-shifting" only later in the novel and in the epilogue, also called "Shape-shifting." Initially Big George appears to be a cruel manipulator of the author, substituting a long "History of Electricity" where the author would like to tell the personal lives of his characters, but the reader eventually welcomes Big George as a source of public information. Although Big George's history is ideologically distorted by his alliance with the Blue Globes, the personifications of electricity whose initials he shares, his tall-tale celebration of American pioneering imperialism and rampant industrialism are a welcome relief from the exaggerated sentimentality of the author. He attempts to depict Big George as a traitor to electricity, but he is "the eternal winner". By the end of the book the parasitical, shape-shifting, and monstrous Big George appears to be in almost complete command: as night shift supervisor, he keeps the author locked in the "Training Room" of the computer center, where he sleeps next to snaking extension cords and finds it diffi-

cult to "believe in the outdoors". Big George also controls the "tape drives" where the characters' lives exist, the "disk drives where the action of this novel takes place", and the "end of-file mark" that shortens the book from its "Transcendental" length to its real one-volume existence.

During Big George's final "justification subroutine", he becomes more than a commercial editor cutting the young author's text, more than a personification of technological power unsympathetic to sensitive art. At the end, the reader understands a much-earlier comment by the author—that Big George is "pure electrical consciousness itself, insinuating itself everywhere, drifting in and out of all stories and machines". Ultimately the relation between Big George and the author is a cartoon projection of several recent ideas coming out of neurobiology and the cognitive revolution. In *The Gold Bug Variations* the brain is described as an evolutionary "kludge," a "walkie-talkie wrapped around a shrew-screech encasing a lizard's intuition". In these terms (what Carl Sagan called "the triune brain"), Big George is the big brain, the evolutionary top of the head, a "walkie-talkie" become a calculating machine consciousness. Daniel Dennett in *Consciousness Explained,* which summarizes cognitive research of the last decade, posits a "Multiple Drafts model of consciousness" in which "information entering the nervous system is under continuous 'editorial revision' . . . accomplished in the brain by parallel, multitrack processes of interpretation and elaboration". For Dennett, consciousness is competitive and collaborative, selecting, editing, and revising the information we call personal (as well as "objective") truth. The conflicting voices of the author and Big George are two methods of cognitive interpretation and elaboration. What Vollmann calls "pure electrical consciousness" does not, according to J. Allan Hobson, turn off during sleep. In *The Dreaming Brain,* Hobson offers a physiological explanation of dreaming as an "endogenous process with its own genetically determined dynamics" (15), the work of a brain processing information without "external space-time data" and "the internal chemical controls necessary for logical thought". By the end of *You Bright and Risen Angels,* the author is sleeping at the computer center and Big George is speaking, his electrical voice "insinuating itself everywhere." Like Stuart Ressler's attempt to map the effects of music in the brain, the theories of Hobson and Dennett have a reductive effect. Hobson does away with the autonomy of the Freudian or Jungian unconscious, often cited as the source of artistic imagination. Dennett attempts to destroy the vestiges of Cartesian identity, replacing the central processor with the connectionist model of consciousness. They make humans more electrical, more like machines, even more like fireflies. But in destroying several bases for mankind's lordly separation from and authority over nature, his inherent, reified powers, Hobson and Dennett also increase human responsibility. If we are electrical information processors, if we are the summation of our information as well as our evolution, we must attend more carefully to the data about the world and ourselves that we take in.

Former programmer, Author Vollmann knows "garbage in, garbage out." This external Author programs his novel's programmers, controls the internal authorial conflict, and creates from its forcible collaboration—not a spliced or matched text like *The Gold Bug Variations*—but a prodigious garbage heap. Its prodigality represents the uncompromising extremities of its internal authors and satirizes the wasteful failures and reckless, also wasteful successes of their political positions. This satire has its dramatic climax near the end of the book when the author's hero Bug attacks the computer complex where the author and Big George work. The Luddite Bug and his companions smash terminals, murder programmers, capture two Blue Globes, and torture them. The author is helpless. Big George escapes and the conflict between reactionaries and revolutionaries, machines and bugs escalates into further violence and repression. In *Gold Bug* Powers reports the origin of the expression "bug in the machine": a "moth that crashed a complex program on one of the first sequential logic machines". Powers's cyberpunks get inside the computer and use its capabilities against the powerful people who buy control over and through it. Vollmann's author's revolutionaries are like the moth: they destroy a few machines and programmers and are then destroyed. Vollmann as Author is a parasite: he learns the computer's language and procedures, shows how it helps perpetuate an economic and political system, illustrates how it can be a model of consciousness, and then imitates its prodigious storage and instantaneous revision to create *You Bright and Risen Angels,* a giant bug in the system of literature. Eating away from inside the decayed or useless forms it parodies, enlarging itself like "The Great Beetle" and Big George, the book does not molt, does not become a winged creature, whether angel or butterfly. It remains, like the winged Hermes, an instructive monstrosity, something "out of the course of nature," a "portent" of American life and politics.

In his biographical sketch for *Contemporary Authors,* Vollmann calls himself an "Environmentalist egalitarian". Where Powers described the genetic code uniting all living things, Vollmann spreads his environmental net even further, linking all things animate and inanimate with their shared electricity. Even a rock and a computer have this in common. The primary symbols of his egalitarianism, however, are insects and, more particularly, beetles, which include fireflies and cockroaches. Vollmann enlarges human sympathies for insects by showing how humans treat other humans like bugs (how must bugs feel when the scale of victimization is even larger?) and by incorporating objective entomological information into the book. The latter method, present primarily in "The Great Beetle" chapter, parallels Powers's introduction of the "Natural Kingdom." After emphasizing, like Powers, the similarities between mankind and the "lower orders"—their common need for space, the desires to eat and mate, the survival tricks they learn—Vollmann focuses on ecological interdependencies, particularly the beetles' parasitical relation with ants, wasps, and bees. After man enters the scene in a crop-dusting plane that kills prodigious numbers of harmless insects, the encyclopedic account metamorphoses into cartoon imagination and Vollmann describes "The Great Beetle," an individual bug "capable of many feats of mentation". The Great Beetle organizes the insects' defense against man, a mission almost completely devoted to gathering information, "bugging" man's conversations for his future plans. A prodigy among the bugs, "The Great Beetle" preaches collaboration among orders as an alternative to mankind's aggression.

Bugs and mankind coexisted for millions of years. In ancient Egypt, Vollmann reminds us in his tale of "The Great Beetle," beetles were worshipped as symbols of cyclic process and immortality. In Vollmann's history of the world, the nineteenth-century taming of electricity, what an early experimenter called "blue globes," was the achievement that made man a dangerous prodigy in the ecosystem, a threat to all nature's continuance. Using quotes from Thomas Edison's writings, Vollmann metamorphoses the father of electricity into Jack White, pioneer of Big Power. With the help of his student Newton Payne, a prodigy of "superior mentation" who is credited with 950 inventions, and marketing genius William S. Dodger, White turns America into an electric monopoly in the first decades of this century. In the cartoon time of the novel, Mr. White is still living in the late twentieth century and now controls the computer industry. The "Blue Globes" of industrial electricity have become electronics, miniaturized into microchips that are, in a turn of the book's metaphor, alarmingly "like bugs": "tiny ubiquitous pellets inside the NMOSFET chips and other silicon wafer wonders . . . turning away from human concerns, the young ones, and playing diffusion gate games which we will never understand and they frolic as the snakes used to do in the great jungles of the Americas". The prodigy of this silicon age is the snake-man Parker Fellows, who has a Midas-like gift of developing pictures with a touch of his finger. This master of the image is also working on an invention called "The Great Enlarger," a technology obviously inimical to little bugs or other beings attempting to avoid the scrutiny of Mr. White's information empire. The author attempts to diminish Parker's power by making him suffer the puppy love of the author's own life. Originally interested in electricity because of the male body's ability to "conduct electrolysis of a concentrated sodium chloride solution" in a woman's body, the author contrives as a fantasy solution to electrical and electronic monopoly a Martian takeover of White's empire.

Vollmann the Author's solution is to offer a frightening metaphor of the future, a planet-wide final solution that emerges through Big George's "Shape-shifting" epilogue and gathers together the book's numerous references to Hitler's extermination of the Jews. For the "Environmentalist egalitarian," the political terms of the novel—reactionaries and revolutionaries—shift shapes twice. Meant to sympathize with the insect revolutionaries' battle against reactionary, White power, readers ultimately have to recognize that humans are the true revolutionaries on the planet, manipulating time and space that other life forms could only react to over long periods of adaptation. In his final words, Big George indicates his future work, "electrifying" all that is left of the Amazon, an "almost dried-up canal" that "stretches all across the east-west axis of our Great Republic, the two ends forming it into a fine palindrome". When this waste sink and breeding ground for insects is brought *inside* the empire of electric civilization, America and the planet it stands for will become an ecologically closed system, what Vollmann calls, in a section just preceding "Shape-Shifting," the "World in a Jar." Newt Payne, White's prodigy, studies life in a glass case. The author brings home an insect, puts it in a jar, and finally finds it has destroyed itself after it has molted. In "World in a Jar," Vollmann recalls these two experimenters and creates a compact, economic metaphor for the future of man. Bugs placed in a closed jar eat h food there, multiply, cover the glass with waste, and cover the food with their own bodies. The bugs have been trapped in glass. Supposedly more intelligent, information processing humans trap themselves in the glass of the Greenhouse Effect: "the cars snorted and farted in the blue-grey air, the yellow taxicabs especially idling and idling and double-parking, pouring out gases, while the flies buzzed and swarmed inside the darkening vial . . . but they went on buzzing and swarming until the vial dried up completely and then they were still. The vial went into the trash" This gassing of life is a final solution, however, that destroys both the controllers and victims of industrial civilization. We turn ourselves into trash, garbage, prodigal waste.

Bugs rise to blue globes above the swimming pools in suburban backyards. Inside the homes children are glued to the blue globe of the television screen. At the office, parents are affixed to the blue globes of their monitors increasing human efficiency everywhere. To break the magnetic power, Vollmann creates a book that, like electricity itself, attracts and repels, a black and white cartoon for readers reared on television, and a prodigious store of information that has what Michel Serres calls abuse, rather than use, value. Though Vollmann and Powers share numerous ideas and concerns, Vollmann's alienation effects, pop culture parodies, and surrealistic imagination are more like Pynchon's methods. Where Powers provides charts and tables to represent the intricacy of genetics, Vollmann includes childish line drawings and grotesque wood-block prints analogous to the

Tarot-card future Pynchon lays out at the end of *Gravity's Rainbow*. Perhaps that is why Vollmann's two allusions to Pynchon are to children: "the Counterforce Kid" and "The Kamikaze Kidz". To be a counterforce in post-Pynchon fiction and in postindustrial culture, Vollmann implies, an Author may have to be like a Kamikaze, attacking like a swarm of gadflies, crashing like the moth that crashed the computer, risking that artistic prodigality in a time of blue globes will be recognized as functional. Treated as an organized profusion, *You Bright and Risen Angels* is neither wasteful nor reckless but generous, a prodigious text that uses its "monster masks and giant glow-in-the-dark Spiderman cut-outs to frighten" readers away from a glassed-in future.

Vollmann and Powers are among the seven young novelists David Foster Wallace has said he admires. These three and Jonathan Franzen also compose what Wallace has called, in a short *Harper's Bazaar* profile, the school of "white male novelists over six feet", which suggests big authors write big books. *Infinite Jest,* though not quite as prodigious as its title proclaims, is only 150 pages shorter than *The Gold Bug Variations* and *You Bright and Risen Angels* combined! I do not want to suggest that Wallace, who wrote his book between 1992 and 1995, was substantially influenced by the earlier novels, but *Infinite Jest* can be most economically described as synthesizing and extending characteristics of its predecessors. The setting of *Infinite Jest* extrapolates from much of the history, politics, and technology in the imagined worlds of Powers and Vollmann. In Wallace's post-millennial future (about 2015), he is identified by its sponsors: "Year of the Depend Adult Undergarment," "Year of Glad." "Annular physics," something like cold fusion, supplies energy, and "teleputers" (tele-computers) provide nearly infinite in-home entertainment. Giant fans and catapults send U.S. waste into northern New England, which has been ceded to Quebec by President Johnny Gentle, former Vegas crooner now president of the United States and leader of the Organization of North American Nations (ONAN). Into this onanistically ominous age, Wallace inserts a monster more deadly than Pynchon's rocket or the gigantic corporations of Powers and Vollmann: a movie (or "cartridge," with its explosive connotations) so powerfully seductive that it fixates its viewers and destroys their brains. The movie, possibly entitled "Infinite Jest," extends the cyberthreat of *Gold Bug* and *Angels* to mass entertainment and gives *Infinite Jest* an international political dimension not present in those novels. As Quebecois terrorists and ONAN agents attempt to locate the master tape and identify the Master who made it, Wallace plays off the small, more traditional culture of Quebec with the gigantic, post-postmodern world of ONAN.

Within this imaginary setting and Pynchonian quest plot, Wallace creates two more contemporaneous worlds populated by Powers-like prodigies and Vollmann's victims of childhood. Living at the Enfield Tennis Academy, founded by physicist and then filmmaker James O. Incandenza and his Canadian wife, Avril, are two of the Incandenzas' sons: nineteen-year-old Mario, a physically stunted but precocious cameraman, "the family's real prodigy"; and seventeen-year-old Hal, a "lexical prodigy" who quotes from the *OED*. Hal's best friend, Michael Pemulis, is a math-science genius as well as a drug dealer. Other mostly white and rich residents at the Academy—ages ten to eighteen—have specialized intellectual abilities, and all are tennis prodigies sent away from home to prepare for "The Show," the worldwide pro tour.

Just down the hill from the Academy in its Boston suburb is the Ennett House Drug and Alcohol Recovery facility populated by mostly impoverished white and black street people like those who enter the last pages of *Angels*. The focal character at Ennett House is Don Gately, a twenty-seven-year-old former narcotics addict of enormous size who is "a prodigy of vitriolic spine". As a live-in staffer, Gately attends Alcoholics Anonymous meetings and listens to the stories of his residents. Among them is Joelle van Dyne, a former coke addict, a member of UHID (Union of the Hideously and Improbably Deformed), and a former actress in James Incandenza's underground films.

> **In a novel where waste is propelled into a border area, Ennett House first seems a disposal site for the underclass. But as Wallace reveals the tennis prodigies' individual lives and probes the histories of Ennett's adults, the two social worlds begin to overlap and the radically disjunctional novel starts to cohere as a profound cross-class study of parental abandonment and familial dysfunction.**
>
> **—Tom LeClair**

In a novel where waste is propelled into a border area, Ennett House first seems a disposal site for the underclass. But as Wallace reveals the tennis prodigies' individual lives and probes the histories of Ennett's adults, the two social worlds begin to overlap and the radically disjunctional novel starts to cohere as a profound cross-class study of parental abandonment and familial dysfunction. Sent away to the Academy to become top-flight entertainers (or pre-teen failures), the tennis kids play self-destructive games and take recreational drugs to relieve the pressure. The founding family is itself sick. After finding his father dead, having committed suicide by sticking his head in a microwave oven, Hal—a boy of "prodigious talent"—loses interest in tennis, becomes dependent on marijuana, and moves toward mute-

ness. At the novel's end he visits Ennett and attempts to recover from his dependence.

"Conditioning" is a central concept Wallace uses to connect Enfield and Ennett. The kids are physically conditioned and scientifically coached, like circus animals, for performative success. In their childhood, many of the Ennett residents have been trained by their parents or conditioned by the media to be providers of sexual pleasure or consumers of reductive entertainment. Gately's mother, for example, spent much of his youth in an alcoholic haze while his stepfather became an obsessive watcher of *M*A*S*H*. The underclass's adult escapes from parental and cultural abuse are alcohol and drugs. The killer movie, perhaps made by James Incandenza, is the logical extension of other addictions and suggests that the higher world of Enfield has corrupted with mass-produced pleasure the lower world of Ennett.

What distinguishes *Infinite Jest* is Wallace's passion for the particularities and histories of characters, both intellectual prodigies such as Power's characters and figures even more psychologically deformed than Vollmann's. In case readers of *Infinite Jest* do not understand why it provides more detail than Power's novel and proceeds more slowly than Vollmann's, Wallace enters his narrative as a tall, lexically gifted, and etymology conscious "wraith." To a semi-conscious Gately, the wraith explains his desire to give voices to "figurants", the mute, background characters of most literary fiction. The wraith calls his project "radical realism", which accurately names Wallace's method, for no matter how story lines wander both major and minor characters dig down and articulate the childhood roots ("radicalis") of their personalities. "Radical realism" also corresponds to the kind of fiction Wallace calls for in his interview with Larry McCaffery: "'Let's try to countenance and render real aspects of real experiences that have previously been excluded from art'". The number of Wallace's characters, the intelligence or sensitivity of some of them, Wallace's dedication to imagining the etiologies of muffled geniuses or fast-talking idiots, and the instructive value of placing these characters in contrasting cultures are some of the factors that necessarily press *Infinite Jest* to its prodigious size.

In the McCaffery interview and an accompanying essay on television, Wallace describes the contemporary fiction to which "radical realism" is an alternative. He criticizes younger writers for becoming purveyors of "image-fiction", surface realism that resembles TV, and "crank-turners" of postmodern irony, both of whom respond in limited ways to an earlier generation of great experimenters such as Nabokov and pynchon: "The postmodern founders' patricidal work was great, but patricide produces orphans, and no amount of revelry can make up for the fact that writers my age have been literary orphans throughout our formative years". Although the serious business of *Infinite Jest* is diagnosing how figurants" are produced in families, social systems, and national cultures, the novel can also be read as a meta-fictional allegory of this aesthetic orphanhood. James O. Incandenza brought a "scientific-prodigy's mind" to several fields—first optics, then physics—before turning to experimental films that often resemble—in their themes and parodic methods—outtakes from *Gravity's Rainbow* and Pynchon's other work. In his last movie before committing suicide, "Infinite Jest," Incandenza creates a parental apology—a long series of variations on "I'm sorry. I'm so sorry."—that he hopes will bring his prodigy son Hal out of his inward-turning "hiddenness," but Hal never sees the film. After the Pynchon figure dies, the Academy is run by Avril, an obsessive-compulsive primarily concerned with organized housekeeping and sexual relations, possibly a representation of domestic realism. The Incandenzas' oldest son, Orin, a punter for the Arizona Cardinals, enjoys the love of the crowd but fumbles at his attempts to give love. Perhaps he represents the Brat Pack, to which Wallace condescends in his interview. Mario, the physically and intellectually challenged boy who walks around with a Bolex camera on his head, is "image-fiction." Lexical game player Hal, who becomes increasingly withdrawn and ironic after his father's suicide, is postmodern talent without passion or position. Although Wallace's personal background most resembles Hal's, and although the "wraith" sounds like a combination of Hal and his father, the Wallace who wrote *Infinite Jest* is a prodigious collaboration of the three sons' qualities—and of Don Gately's sympathy for the victims whose stories he hears. Even in the realm of aesthetic allegory, Wallace is true to the history-mining of his "radical realism," for he imagines the alcoholic James O. Incandenza's childhood with an overbearing father from whom a dominated mother could not rescue the unhappy boy.

In neither the aesthetic allegory nor in the realistic family relations Wallace depicts is he satisfied with the Abuse Excuse. When the wraith attempts to explain his past to Gately, this veteran of Boston A. A. critiques the wraith's self pity and victimhood, which recalls A. A.'s policy on "causal attribution": "if you start trying to blame your addiction on some cause or other . . . everybody with any kind of sober time will pale and writhe in their chair". A.A.'s suspicion of causality and "Analysis Paralysis" is in turn critiqued by a college instructor at Ennett who argues with Gately's defense of the "Program":

> "You can analyze it till you're breaking tables with your forehead and find a cause to walk away, back Out There, where the Disease is. Or you can stay and hang in and do the best you can."

> "AA's response to a question about its axioms, then, is to invoke an axiom about the inadvisability of all such questions."

Instead of choosing between mechanistic causality and A.A.'s "Miracle" pragmatism, Wallace allows them to alternate with and supplement each other. "Infinite Jest" the movie is repetitive and single-voiced, seductive and possibly destroying because it depicts a parent blaming herself for causing the viewer's unhappiness. *Infinite Jest* the novel, though, is more like an A.A. meeting: multifarious and multivocal, engaging in its verisimilitude, and possibly rescuing because it depicts mysterious, even miraculous recoveries for addiction and anhedonia.

Like Powers and Vollmann, Wallace refers to the sciences of both chaos and cognition as contexts for the sometimes unpredictable actions of his characters and, I think, for the militantly "anti-confluential" character of his narrative. Describing the imagined heir of nonlinear science, "Extra-Linear Dynamics," Wallace says it deals with "systems and phenomena whose chaos is beyond even Mandelbrosian math's Strange Equations and Random Attractants". An M. I.T. building within which Joelle van Dyne does her "Madame Psychosis" radio show is described in great details as a huge brain. The inherent disorder of dynamical systems and the neurological noise of mental illness may well be conceptual bases for Wallace's critique of mechanistic causality, yet his central scientific interest is as old as Western medicine: orthopedics. The three Incandenza boys are all deformed: Mario's whole body at birth, Orin's left leg by repetitive punting, Hal's left arm by tennis strokes. The bodies of other kids at the Academy break down under the constant stress of training and competition. The bodies of people at Ennett House, including its stroke-afflicted director, are deformed by their addictions or behavior. Don Gately, who "grew to monstrous childhood size" watching TV, has covered his huge body with ugly tattoos. Joelle van Dyne's face was, in the novel's argot, "demapped" by an accident with acid. During one of her radio shows, she recites hundreds of deforming diseases. Minor Ennett characters are in various stages of physical decay. Out in the larger world, Quebecois terrorists have had their legs cut off or crippled by trains in an initiation rite. In the waste disposal zone, it is rumored, feral animals grow huge and an occasional gigantic child wanders out of the zone to terrorize normal people. While some of these deformities are the results of accidents or political policy, many of the monstrosities are self-inflicted, the results of addiction that has its culminating symbol in the film "Infinite Jest," described as a lethal "angelic monster".

Infinite Jest is a "hopeful monster," more extreme in both those terms than *Gold Bug* and *Angels* because Wallace extends Powers's sense of possibility to people without huge intellectual gifts or first-rate educations and because Wallace makes Vollmann's warning more plausible with "radical realism." To defamilarize the ordinary and to familiarize the exotic require even more prodigal means than Powers's "crackpot realism" and Vollmann's "cartoon," so Wallace combines and modifies the methods that the other prodigies use to deform the "classical Realist form" that Wallace calls "soothing, familiar and anesthetic". The rigorously controlled dual collaboration of *Gold Bug* is opened up by Wallace's multiple points of view, both first- and third-person; stylistic tours de force in several dialects; a swirling associative structure; and alternations in synecdochic scale. These methods produce, not just length, but a prodigious density because parts do not disappear into conventional and easily processed wholes. Wallace seems to allude to this effect with his references to mosaics and to an "*in*foliating . . . Cantorian continuum of infinities". This infolding density frequently manifests itself in Wallace's references to the historical, often physical roots of the words he uses. The wraith lists some of Wallace's key words in caps when he talks to Gately. Although Vollmann's relatively small number of cartoon characters are replaced in *Infinite Jest* by a host of physical or emotional grotesques, Wallace, like Vollmann, does employ numerous facsimile documents—such as formulae, transcripts, letters, and other documents—to deface the novel's textual surface and constantly remind readers that they are experiencing "mediated consciousness," a quality Wallace insists upon in his interview.

The novels of Powers and Vollmann imitate coded abstractions: the genetic chain and the cartoon. Wallace's special achievement is to make his book recall and resemble a prodigious human body. In a note that begins with a discussion of "Volkmann's contracture," a "severe serpentine deformation of the arms following a fracture," Wallace discusses "bradyauxesis": "some part(s) of the body not growing as fast as the other parts of the body". He then explains the "medical root 'brady,' from the Greek 'bradys' meaning slow" and applies the word to reading. Two notes later, Wallace mentions "hyperauxetic" in connection with Mario Incandenza's head, which is "two to three times the size of your more average elf-to-jockey-sized head and facies". *Infinite Jest* is self-consciously and intentionally both "brady-" and "hyperauxetic." In addition, relations between the novel's "big-headed" title, the body of the text, and Wallace's "Notes and Errata," which make up about one-tenth of the whole book, are both misleading and disproportionate. Although often humorous and satiric, *Infinite Jest* is more like the root of "jest"—"gest": story or exploit—than an extended joke. The notes (which might have appeared at the *foot* of the page) often function less as supplemental or clarifying material than as crucial information of the kind that would appear in an epigraph or *headnote*. The eight-page "Filmography" note is a prime example, for the brief descriptions of Incandenza's movies are seeds for larger narratives in the main text. In this book about addicts' bodies and athletes' extremities, the head and its abstractions are not as crucial as in books by writers of a more militantly intellectual cast. Wallace has not, like Incandenza, put his own head in

a microwave, but much of the learning in *Infinite Jest* is physical, sensory, rather than bookish or filmic. The text and the notes have, like torso and extremities, a collaborative and reciprocal relation. The only "errata" in the final section are those of readers who do not switch back and forth between the two sections and who, therefore, do not appreciate how Wallace has deformed his novel to be a gigantic analogue of the monsters—hateful and hopeful—within it. In its microscopic materials and macroscopic art, *Infinite Jest* makes 1996 the "Year of the Whopper," for Wallace's novel is a larger lie than *The Gold Bug Variations* or *You Bright and Risen Angels*. *Infinite Jest* is also a grand omen—frightening warning against the feral future it depicts, invigorating evidence that a Pynchon protege can both collaborate with his fellow prodigies and create prodigious original work.

Richard Stern (review date 9 March 1997)

SOURCE: "Verbal Pyrotechnics," in *Chicago Tribune Books,* March 9, 1997, pp. 1, 11.

[*In the following review, Stern examines Wallace's collection of essays,* A Supposedly Fun Thing I'll Never Do Again, *and equates Wallace's accomplishment with that of the classic essayist Montaigne.*]

'I go out of my way," wrote Essayist Number One, "but by license not carelessness. . . . I want the material to make its own divisions . . . without my interlacing them with words, with links and seams put in for the benefit of . . . inattentive readers." As to style, "I love a simple, natural speech, the same on paper as in the mouth . . . succulent and sinewy, brief but compressed . . . better difficult than boring . . . irregular, disconnected and bold."

Montaigne's 400-year-old prescription works to describe these wonderful essays by David Foster Wallace. The best essays—blends of fact, scene, observation, analysis, portraiture and commentary—Wallace says, are often written by fiction writers, "oglers" who "watch over other humans sort of the way gapers slow down for car wrecks: they covet a vision of themselves as *witnesses.*"

It's this ogler's greatest charm—as it was Montaigne's—that he supplies a piecemeal but consistent self-portrait that runs through the book. The portrait is of a precocious, physically timid, endlessly self-conscious, endlessly curious, naive sophitcate, a great shower and explainer, a loved and loving son, neurotic, brilliant, good-hearted and self-deprecating ("extremely sensitive: carsick, airsick, heightsick; my sister likes to say I'm 'lifesick.'").

In the best of these essays, he shows up as a fledgling journalist, one who forgets to bring a notebook, is astonished at his press perks and is puzzled by journalistic requirements ("how many examples [do] I need to list in order to communicate the atmosphere?").

It may be this self-portrait, as much as the constraints of Wallace's journalistic assignments, that saves these essays from what old-fashioned novel-readers like me thought was the narrative-killing excess of his 1,000-plus-page novel, *Infinite Jest*. Some of that mastodon meat is in the essays—tennis, teens, television—and some of its manner, too—footnotery, abbreviations, acronymania. But only here and there, say in the tribute to director David Lynch ("Eraserhead," "Twin Peaks," the new "Lost Highways"), does the "IJ"-shy reader want to call for halter, bit, reins and whip.

Perhaps the gem of the book's four gems is a 54-page essay on the 1993 Illinois State Fair. There is more about the look, sounds, smell (Wallace is a great smeller), feel and meaning of rural Illinois here than I've seen in such small space since, say, Bellow's 1957 10-pager for *Holiday* magazine. . . .
—*Richard Stern*

The title—and longest—essay is a blow-by-blow account of an expenses-paid, week-long luxury cruise in the Caribbean, a counter to a "polished, powerful, impressive . . . best that money can buy . . ." essaymercial by a writer Wallace admires, Frank Conroy (who tells Wallace that he's ashamed of having written it). No one will mistake Wallace's uproarious demolition of the "sybaritic and nearly insanity-producing indulgence and pampering" on board the Nadir (his rechristening of the cruise ship Zenith) for an essaymercial. It has more interesting characters than most novels, as much solid information as a technical brochure, and its genial depiction of the commerce of "Managed Fun" is as devastating as Henry James' analysis of the economic significance of the skyscraper in "The American Scene" (1907). Fifty times more amusing—and 500 times cheaper—than the cruise itself, Wallace's account of it may lose him a thousand perks for every hundred new readers.

There are two essays on tennis, one about becoming a teen-age tennis whiz by learning to play the winds and cracked surfaces of central Illinois courts, the second the best essay I've read on professional tennis. Its focus is the world's 79th-ranked player, Michael Joyce, competing in a recent Canadian Open, but it's prodigally full of tennis lore, wisdom and thumbnail portraiture: Michael Chang, with his "expression of deep and intractable unhappiness," and his mother, who "may have something to do with the staggering woe of

Chang's mien"; Jim Courier, who "can hit winners only at obtuse angles, from the center out"; Petr Korda, who "has the body of an upright greyhound . . . plus soulless eyes that reflect no light and seem to 'see' only in the way that fish's and birds' eyes 'see'." (There is even a lethally seductive sentence about Du Maurier cigarettes. If Wallace loses his journalistic assignments, he can moonlight as a copywriter.)

Perhaps the gem of the book's four gems is a 54-page essay on the 1993 Illinois State Fair. There is more about the look, sounds, smell (Wallace is a great smeller), feel and meaning of rural Illinois here than I've seen in such small space since, say, Bellow's 1957 10-pager for *Holiday* magazine: "Miles and miles of prairie slowly rising and falling . . . a sense that something is in the process of becoming or that the liberation of a great force is imminent, some power like Michelangelo's slave only half-released from the block of stone." Wallace's lyrics are more staccato and his assessments swifter and less powerful than Bellow's, but he has lots more space and covers much more: not just the fair but its visitors, officials, reporters, the governor ("impressive") and his wife (whose tragic flaw is her voice), the prize horses, cattle and swine, the auto races (though, "What I know about auto racing could be inscribed with a dry Magic Marker on the lip of a Coke bottle"), baton-twirling, clogging, ag people, Kmart people, message-bearing T-shirts, the flatness, the space, the loneliness of the Midwest where he grew up and from which, years ago, he fled.

Perhaps the highlight of the state fair essay is this great scene:

Wallace has invited Native Companion, his old Philo High prom date, to go around the fairgrounds with him. N.C., who "teaches water-aerobics to the obese and infirm," is now married, has three children, and bungee jumps. She accepts a carny's offer to try out The Zipper, the wildest of the near-death-experience rides. Our "airsick, heightsick" author manages, with "an act of enormous personal courage," to watch as she's strapped into a cage and spun, hurled and tumbled "like stuff in a dryer" in a horrifying ellipse. A long scream, "wobbled by Doppler," comes from the cage. "Then the operator stops the ride abruptly with Native C.'s car at the top, so she's hanging upside down inside the cage," with her dress hanging down over her head. The operator and a colleague ogle her. After another scream from the cage, "as if Native C.'s getting slow-roasted," Wallace, outraged, almost summons enough saliva to "say something stern." But at this point the two carnies, "laughing and slapping their knee," start bringing her down. Finally, N.C. bounds out of the cage and, in a burst of expletives, tells them" 'that was . . . great.'" Wallace is furious. "'They were looking up your *dress*. . . . I saw the whole thing,'" N.C. looks at him. Her color is high. "'You're so . . . *innocent,* Slug,'" she says.

Four hundred years ago, dear old Montaigne described falling off his horse and "dying." For 400 years, readers have loved him for his account of it. Perhaps 400 years from now readers will love Not So Intrepid and Not So Innocent Slug Wallace.

Laura Miller (review date 16 March 1997)

SOURCE: "The Road to Babbittville," in *New York Times,* March 16, 1997, p. 71.

[*In the following review of Wallace's* A Supposedly Fun Thing I'll Never Do Again, *Miller sees the writer fulfilling the promise and allaying the suspicions generated by his much-discussed novel* Infinite Jest.]

Many readers young and old (but especially the young and media-saturated) regarded David Foster Wallace's mammoth novel, *Infinite Jest,* with suspicion. Jaded by too many middling writers heralded as the Next Big Thing, they wondered if, as its title intimated, this daunting tome wasn't just a big joke. *Infinite Jest* itself didn't quite clear things up. Messy, demanding and stubbornly unresolved, it was also frequently brilliant. Yet Mr. Wallace's penchant for pointed satire and flashy tricks often obscured the book's passion. Ultimately, *Infinite Jest* felt noncommittal, leaving some readers unconvinced that Mr. Wallace offered anything more than a lot of energy and a dazzling but heartless cleverness.

A Supposedly Fun Thing I'll Never Do Again should settle the matter at last. This collection of "essays and arguments"—originally published in *Harper's, Esquire and Premiere,* among other magazines—reveals Mr. Wallace in ways that this fiction has of yet managed to dodge: as a writer struggling mightily to understand and capture his times, as a critic who cares deeply about "serious" art, and as a mensch.

The most outright amusing pieces here are Mr. Wallace's two journalistic forays into Middle American culture: "**Getting Away from Already Being Pretty Much Away From It All**," about a visit to the Illinois State Fair, and the title essay, in which Mr. Wallace takes a seven-day luxury cruise to the Caribbean. These vivid, hilarious essays attracted much attention when they were originally published, but they also made Mr. Wallace vulnerable to accusations, as a friend of mine put it, of "sneering at ordinary people." Rereading them lays such reservations to rest. The primary butt of Mr. Wallace's humor is himself, and if he seizes upon his experiences to reveal ugly aspects of the American character, he always does it through the lens of his own worst impulses. Compulsively analytical, he no sooner notices something— the at first irritating "bovine and herdlike" movement of Mid-

western fairgoers, for example—than he's formulated a grand and quite credible theory about it: "the vacation-impulse in rural IL is manifested as a flight-toward. Thus the urge physically to commune, melt, become part of a crowd."

With Mr. Wallace on assignment, readers will learn how everything smells (the aroma of cow manure is "wonderful— warm and herbal and blameless—but cows themselves stink in a special sort of rich biotic way, rather like a wet boot") and receive a detailed report on all forms of junk food. This manic observational faculty never seems to shut off; even while cooling his heels in a dreary waiting room with several hundred other cruise passengers, he's noting "driven-looking corporate guys . . . talking into cellular phones while their wives look stoic" and counting the different makes of camera.

This inclination to record his every impression doesn't bog down Mr. Wallace's writing as often as you might think, but he is open to accusations that he lacks discipline. "**David Lynch Keeps His Head**" is a baggy monster of a profile that suffers from too much rumination on Mr. Lynch's significance to the budding artistic sensibility of the young Mr. Wallace. Nevertheless, this essay and others show a side of him that's refreshingly ardent and sincere. When it comes to the people he admires, Mr. Wallace wears his heart on his sleeve. And it turns out that he harbors high ideals for art in general and fiction in particular, despite the "irony, poker-faced silence and fear of ridicule" that enervate the work of many of his contemporaries. "The new rebels," he speculates, "might be artists willing to risk the yawn, the rolled eyes, the cool smile, the nudged ribs, the parody of gifted ironists, the 'Oh, how banal.' To risk accusations of sentimentality, melodrama. Of overcredulity. Of softness."

That daring has begun to blossom in Mr. Wallace's own fiction, as it does in this collection's most ambitious critical essay, "**E Unibus Pluram: Television and U.S. Fiction.**" Of course, as Mr. Wallace himself observes, it's easier to draft manifestoes than it is to fulfill them. As a novelist, he hasn't entirely jettisoned the crutch of irony, but in this essay he thoroughly demolishes it as an option. "Television," he argues, "has been ingeniously absorbing, homogenizing and re-presenting the very same cynical post-modern esthetic that was once the best alternative to the appeal

> of Low, over-easy, mass-marketed narrative." In other words, the illusion of transcendence by mockery is just another kind of trap.

Finally, Mr. Wallace's distinctive and infectious style, an acrobatic cartwheeling between high intellectual discourse and vernacular insouciance, makes him tremendously entertaining to read, whatever his subject. *A Supposedly Fun Thing*

I'll Never Do Again proves that his accomplishment is far more than just a stunt.

Alexander Star (review date 30 June 1997)

SOURCE: A review of *A Supposedly Fun Thing I'll Never Do Again,* in *New Republic,* Vol. 216, No. 26, June 30, 1997, pp. 27-34.

[*In the following review, Star discusses the often contradictory nature of Wallace's writing.*]

Most novelists strive to extinguish the traces of juvenile self-consciousness from their work. Selfconsciousness is an adolescent twitch, a mannered style, a way of holding back from the potency of one's materials. It's an obstacle to communication, and a low form of candor, David Foster Wallace is not such a writer. He can't escape from self-consciousness; or he doesn't want to. Instead, he makes the sheer awkwardness of carrying a self through the world the central theme of his madly exfoliating compositions. The unpleasant sensation of being looked at and the corresponding urge to hide are the torments that drive his work into labyrinths of ever greater complexity. At any moment, his prose seems about to collapse under the mere strain of being visible.

Since the publication of his novel *Infinite Jest* last year, Wallace has become rather visible himself, lauded and mocked as a recklessly verbose chronicler of drug addiction, daytime television, and the unsettling distractions of high technology and halogen-lit trauma. To his detractors, he is the monstrous progeny of Thomas Pynchon and Don DeLillo, a fidgety, immature observer of his generation's media-saturated anomie, the perpetrator of "the grunge novel." To his admirers, he is a verbal magician, conjuring up a grimly hilarious landscape of TV-induced hallucinations and congenitally stunted characters.

In fact, Wallace's accomplishments are more considerable—and more volatile—than either of these estimations proposes. With implacable resolve, he tries to write intimate, heartfelt fiction about a nation overrun with information and images, and inhabited by an "atomized mass of self-conscious watchers and appearers." The urge to withdraw from this unhappy state of affairs and the compulsion to know about it are kept in a state of permanent revolution. With a weird kind of energy, he reaches out toward the very surfaces from which he shrinks.

The result is a very peculiar body of work. Often enough, it appears Wallace is simply trying to sabotage himself. He wants to explode the literature of "trendy, sardonic exhaustion" and "reflexive irony," but to do so he weaves a thick sardonic skein of irony into his work. He wants to take off the "empty, jaded mask" of the media-saturated citizen, but he keeps putting it back on again. His warmest episodes are scattered with cruel digressions. Yet Wallace's self-demolitions are not as pointless as they may seem. He hopes to satirize "everything that is cliched and hyped and empty and banal," and to show the presence of actual human beings in this sad landscape, and to do this he extends himself widely and deeply. The results can be overinflated, glibly superior, just plain irritating. But in his best work—in his big novel, especially—Wallace is a far more empathetic, tangible and vivid writer than his self-undermining methods may suggest.

Infinite Jest is a massive assemblage that creeps forward at an awkward gait, typically at cross-purposes with itself. It is an earnest and compassionate novel about the mutual incomprehension between fathers and sons; a painstaking study of addicts' stumbling efforts at recovery; and a solemn protest against the necessity of being seen in a culture that is obsessed with appearances. It is also a deliberately frustrating and sometimes malevolent compilation of satire, which often reads more like a madcap encyclopedia of grotesque violence, shaggy-dog sages and self-reflexive pranks than a story that might ever near its end. Wallace piles up vast banks of information and takes them down again. He generates a wave of emotion and then puts it behind a pane of shatterproof glass.

Inevitably, a novel such as *Infinite Jest* gets compared to *Gravity's Rainbow,* but in this case the comparison is reasonably apt. Like Pynchon, Wallace wants to make the esoteric vocabularies of science and technology touch the pulpy languages of pop culture; and like Pynchon, he situates his characters in the midst of inscrutable conspiracies and counterconspiracies, a world in which everyone looks like they are "at least a double agent." Both books take the form of a meandering, endlessly interrupted quest: in *Gravity's Rainbow,* for the rocket that heralds a new order of "money and death"; in *Infinite Jest,* for a lethally addictive entertainment cartridge whose circulation precipitates a "continental emergency." Finally, each novel contains its own half-buried democratic philosophy: in *Gravity's Rainbow,* the Puritan heresy which insists that the "Preterite" are saved; in *Infinite Jest,* the belief that every side-character must have a speaking part, and become "the rational and articulate protagonist of his own drama." Where Wallace most departs from Pynchon is in his approach to characterization. His major characters are not as brittle and as schematized as the worlds they live in. Instead, Wallace tries to give them an accumulating emotional resonance.

Like many experimental novels, *Infinite Jest* doesn't suffer from an absence of plots so much as from an excess of them, mostly set in the near future, inside a vaguely dystopian America where datic political and environmental rearrangements have taken place while the surface of everyday life remains roughly intact. The novel's setting is the low-rent districts of metropolitan Boston, which Wallace portrays in precise and affecting detail: the seedy streets and storefronts of Inman Square and Allston, the trash compactors behind the Boston Public Library, the "Depressed Residential" three-deckers, the imaginary and dismal "gray line" subway that runs from Watertown to Cambridge.

On the edges of this world sit two institutions, each inhabited by refugees from a nation given over to a debilitating fascination with "watching and being watched." The Enfield Tennis Academy is a school for precocious children with the "aluminum sheen" of the privileged, and the Ennet House Drug and Alcohol Recovery House is a gathering place for a motley array of recovering addicts: a verbose college professor, a sleazy coke dealer, a suicidal data-entry clerk. Most of the novel's characters swarm around these settings, where they subject their battered psyches to elaborate forms of discipline.

In the background, however, a different kind of novel develops: a kind of slow-motion send-up of a techno-political thriller. With Vonnegut-like weirdness, Wallace reveals that the United States and Canada have merged into the Organization of North American Nations, a.k.a. onan; large areas of Quebec and northern New England have become a vast toxic waste dump; and the United States is ruled by a former nightclub crooner named Johnny Gentle, whose "Clean U.S." Party unites xenophobes and environmentalists in the pursuit of a "tighter, tidier nation." Into this surreal geopolitical situation arrive rumors of a mysterious videotape that paralyzes its viewers with pleasure, leaving them in a subverbal, near catatonic state. A wheelchair-bound Quebecois terrorist and a drag-wearing onanite agent launch parallel campaigns to find the tape, which becomes known to them as "the samizdat" or "the entertainment"—as well as by its true name, *Infinite Jest*. Wallace's most significant gift is the comic dexterity of his prose, a bizarre organism that manages to feed on its own many contradictions. His sentences are elaborate constructions, packed with jokes, information, all manner of narrative twists and turns, and occasional stabs at beauty. But not too many. With a kind of systematic cunning, Wallace resists conventional eloquence, or even its echo. Instead, he endeavors to employ virtually all the silliest and ugliest colloquialisms in the American tongue. Again and again he forces dead technical language to yield unexpectedly vivid meanings ("Ruth vanCleve's chatter is as listener-interest-independent as anything Kate Gompert's heard") or ridiculous euphemisms (a woman explains that her drug dealer boyfriend is in prison for "operating a pharmaceutical company without a license"). When participants in a tennis tournament are told to "justify your seed," no implication of the phrase is left unnoticed.

Wallace writes with particular relish of the vague notational ways in which information is transmitted in a culture that's sick with the stuff. Midway through the novel, the teenage tennis player Hal Incandenza reflects that "recreational drugs are more or less traditional at any U.S. secondary school, maybe because of the unprecedented tensions: post-latency and puberty and angst and impending adulthood, etc. To help manage the intra-psychic storms, etc." Later, when Hal arrives at the door of a deserted institutional building, he finds that "there is no obvious bell, but the doors are unlocked. They open in that sort of pressurized way of institutional doors. The savanna-colored lobby is broad and still and has a vague medical-dental smell. Its carpet's a dense low tan Dacronyl weave that evacuates sound. There's a circular high-countered nurse's station or reception desk, but nobody's there."

Wallace specializes in this particular blend of offhandedness and precision. He mimics the fatigued, indifferent mannerisms of everyday speech, even as he describes a predicament or a place with almost forensic accuracy. And he applies the same methods to thought itself. He likes to show how a long line of argument can twist or turn, plummeting in midair and then righting itself again. Wallace's characters think compulsively; but they can't think straight.

> **Wallace specializes in this particular blend of offhandedness and precision. He mimics the fatigued, indifferent mannerisms of everyday speech, even as he describes a predicament or a place with almost forensic accuracy. And he applies the same methods to thought itself. He likes to show how a long line of argument can twist or turn, plummeting in midair and then righting itself again. Wallace's characters think compulsively; but they can't think straight.**
>
> —*Alexander Star*

Much of Wallace's novel tries to coax humor and pathos out of its own convolutions. Important events happen as if by accident, and no one notices them. Emotions are hidden in mounds of information. Pitiless, recursive loops are everywhere: a hospital patient who has been struck dumb finds that "without a pencil and notebook he couldn't even seem to get across a request for a notebook and pencil"; a self-help group urges its members to don veils in order to be "open" about the need to hide; a potent street drug is said to be like "acid that has itself dropped acid"; two people who recognize each other in a revolving door swirl around and around forever, trying to meet.

But can Wallace have his human beings and his anti-humanism at once? The premise of his fiction is that nothing takes place on purpose, that the world is composed of grotesque and comic coincidences, that all of his characters are in the grip of overwhelming infantile needs that rob them of their will and, ultimately, of their consciousness. At the same time, his characters speak frequently of the difficult struggle to make choices and to accept the responsibility for making them. Even under the worst of circumstances, they look for "guides" to follow and "values" to affirm. In this way, Wallace practices both the art of black comedy and the art of moral realism. Those are very different aesthetics; but, even if they don't fuse into a single tone or style, he does pursue each of them with great faithfulness.

Wallace assembles a large cast for his complex "entertainment." Dr. James Incandenza, the late founder of the Enfield Tennis Academy, is the ghost who hovers over the banquet. After developing the physics of "cold annular fusion," he had invested his considerable earnings in the creation of a sports academy, before turning to a new career as a director of opaque experimental films. Wallace devotes a long, and meticulously detailed, footnote to Incandenza's filmography: There's *Death in Scarsdale, The American Century as Seen Through a Brick,* and *The Joke,* in which audience members are unwittingly invited to watch themselves on a screen until they get fed up and walk out. When the last moviegoer leaves, the film is over. Even as Wallace has a lot of fun parodying the "antiempathetic" obscurities of avant-garde cinema, he incorporates Incandenza's aesthetics into his own: an unmistakably "anti-confluential" approach to narrative, or the tenet of "radical realism" that even the most peripheral character must enjoy a moment in the footlights.

Several years before the novel's action begins, the director acquires the delusion that his son Hal—a "lexical prodigy" and talented tennis player—cannot speak. Distraught by his son's apparent silence, he smothers his sorrow with Wild Turkey before killing himself by intruding his head into a microwave. The unhappy Hal is left without a father and with a daily habit of "getting high in secret." Much of the novel charts the growing sadness that gradually removes him from the world. "Why is Hal sad?" is the simple, plainly put question that reverberates through the book.

Hal's surviving family members certainly give him little relief. His mother is an icy linguist who once organized the "militant grammarians of America"; his oldest brother, Orin, is a relentless womanizer who betrayed the family tradition of tennis playing to become a star punter in the NFL. Hal's closest confidante is his brother Mario, a badly deformed midget who is not retarded but "ever so slightly epistemologically bent," and whose kindness wins him affection as a "(semi)-walking miracle."

The school itself is a place of recreational drugs and unrecreational sports, its medieval curriculum designed to create professional athletes who can make a living on the commercial circuit of "the show." With considerable ingenuity, Wallace weaves endless riffs on the possibilities and pathologies of competitive sport: the lonely kid from the Midwest who wins tennis tournaments by bringing along a rifle and threatening to shoot himself if he loses; the blind player who judges his shots by the sound of the ball alone; the German coach who elaborates a metaphysical system out of the borders of the court and the boundaries of the self.

But Wallace isn't only concerned with the grim comedy of enforced play. He also investigates the mundane troubles of being an adolescent in a confined environment. He wraps enormous amounts of technical information about tennis and drugs around an unhappy prep-school fable of school kid-taunting, furtive drug-taking and student-teacher seduction. As ever, he shuttles back and forth between the "infantile and goo-prone" and the baroquely, extravagantly cerebral. His writing has the information density of an encyclopedia at one moment, and the lurching awkwardness of a child's scribble at the next. And that's especially so when he's writing about Hal Incandenza, his shy and precocious teenager. For all his intelligence, Hal's desires are painfully straightforward: he wants to speak with his own voice, and to go to college. Neither of these ambitions is achieved.

Down the hill, Ennet House provides the setting for a different collage of affecting portraiture and jaded parody. Here Wallace invents an ingathering of addicts, who tell their various stories of desperation and recovery. The characters who migrate in and out of Ennet abuse a vast array of different substances: oral narcotics, heroin, marijuana, alcohol. In the novel's early pages, they drift toward the halfway house, living through their inexorable "decline and fall." Once there, they live under the benevolent eye of Don Gately, a 29-year-old ex-addict who is built like a bus, and presides over the desperations and the quarrels of the inmates with a quiet, collected dignity.

At the heart of *Infinite Jest* are the recovery meetings that the House residents attend. These scenes are small masterpieces of collective disclosure and digression. Wallace shows his addicts alternating between involvement and detachment, and the brilliance of his storytelling is that he makes both of these stances seem like equally valid options. Wallace wants to register everything phony and off-putting about a recovery meeting; and to suggest with earnest humility that perhaps "it just works, is all." He coils together the affecting and the absurd in ever more elaborate diagrams of confession and comedy.

Gately, a onetime thief as well as an abuser of oral narcotics, is the Everyman whom Wallace follows through the world of recovery. Gately is put off by the cliched slogans, the allusions to a "higher power," the numbing speeches that are "head-clutchingly prolix and involved." He recognizes that the recovery movement's logic implies that every kind of behavior can be understood as an addiction, including the habit of going to recovery meetings themselves. Still, he listens intently to the testimony that he hears in the "board cold salad bar'd" halls, and finds that when an addict talks about "this Substance you thought was your one true friend," or remembers drinking her way to the "old two-option welfare hotel window-ledge," the words are generally harrowing and sincere. An addict's story "has to be the truth to really go over, here," he notes. "It can't be a calculated crowd-pleaser, and it has to be the truth unslanted, unfortified. And maximally unironic. An ironist in a Boston A.A. meeting is a witch in church. Irony-free zone."

What's particularly Wallace-like about the recovery scenes, though, is that the addicts' stories often begin as candidly painful narratives, and then run off the rails into a kind of hideous slapstick violence. When a woman tries to throw herself off the John Hancock building, she is blown by a gust of hot air into an office on the thirty-first floor. When the son of a joke-shop proprietor gives his mother a birthday present, he actually kills her with a defective gag. At one meeting, Wallace relates the truly sickening and utterly sardonic story of a "totally paralyzed and retarded and catatonic" girl whose father puts a Raquel Welch mask on her face each night before raping her.

Eventually *Infinite Jest* comes to resemble a kind of manic Icelandic saga in which each character is introduced with a long testimonial to the bloody events of his or her youth. Only here the bloodshed doesn't involve the slaying of servants and priests: much of it sounds like something you'd hear about on an episode of Montel Williams sponsored by the OED. Wallace's America is a republic of the dysfunctional and the deformed. The novel's overture is the speech that a radio DJ named Madame Psychosis delivers over the MIT radio station wyyy: "Come on down," she intones, extending an invitation to the "phrenologically malformed. The suppuratively lesioned. The endoncrinologically malodorous of whatever ilk. . . . Run don't walk on down. The acervulus-nosed. The radically-ectomied. The morbidly diaphoretic with a hankie in every pocket. The chronically granulomatous . . . the hated and dateless and shunned, who keep to the shadows. Those who undress only in front of their pets . . ."

What, precisely, is Wallace trying to accomplish by all this? Isn't this winking catalog of cartoon violence and disease exactly what the literature of "reflexive irony" and "trendy sardonic exhaustion" is all about? At worst, Wallace uses the deformations of his characters as a kind of crutch; when in doubt about how to proceed with his novel, he resorts to inventing one more hideous tale that could have been lifted from the pages of an alternative comic book or Re/Search publications's Modern Primitives. His characters may be hideously disfigured, but, after several hundred pages, there doesn't seem to be anything improbable about their condition anymore. They are exactly alike in their crippled condition of defeat.

But Wallace gets more out of these stories than that. He wants to use the devices of fringe-culture sensationalism to get at a reservoir of real feeling that his characters share. The external disfigurations are a mark of some internal trauma, a terror of being seen in a culture obsessed with appearances and watching. This is the burden of self-consciousness that Wallace wants the reader to share, and that he writes about with directness and humor. It is a burden that weighs heavily on Hal, who imagines what it's like to be too emotionally tangled and physically grotesque to be viewed in public: ". . . to be really human (at least as he conceptualizes it) is probably to be unavoidably sentimental and naive and goo-prone and generally pathetic, is to be in some quite basic interior way forever infantile, some sort of not-quite-right looking infant dragging itself anaclitically around the map, with big wet eyes and froggy-soft skin, huge skull, gooey drool."

In his habit of zooming back and forth between the intimate and the grotesque, Wallace brings to mind a number of other contemporary novelists, such as William T. Vollman and A. M. Homes. Like Wallace, they pack their work with pathology, hoping to charge their art with the genuine shock of extreme experience and the lurid comedy of its overexposure. This approach has its dangers, ranging from the spurious impulse to identify nobility and suffering to the equally spurious impulse to present weird, tabloid-like scenarios with condescension and scorn. The fascination with "weirdness" can become an excuse to avoid the need to think critically, to analyze the oddity into its elements. Unlike so many of his peers, Wallace evades those traps, largely because he renders Hal and Gately as complex individuals, their "goo-prone" and adult selves somehow coexisting inside the same body.

But if Wallace grants Hal and Gately their humanity, he does not allow them to keep it for long. Finally both of his central characters slip away toward nothingness, toward the author's own private nightmare: the "death of lexical speech." Hal's father had once believed that his son could not speak, and now Hal finds that words really have failed him. Hal tries to give up smoking pot, but his efforts lead nowhere. After a hilarious visit to a men's movement meeting, he fades out of the narrative, succumbing to a growing sadness. Wallace treats this falling away with intimacy and care. As Hal's father foretold, he is "retreating to the periphery of life's frame."

A similar fate befalls Gately. After being beaten to a pulp by an angry mob outside Ennet House, Gately lies in a hospital bed, flickering in and out of consciousness. As Quebecois commandos bear down on the tennis academy, and Hal slips further into silence, he tumbles beneath the threshold of human communication. His hospital room becomes the scene of a tragicomic bedside vigil as a parade of visitors passes through: Ennet residents, who tell long stories about the minutiae of their tedious lives; the ravishing, veiled Joelle van Dyne, who comes to find Gately "romantic and heroic"; the hospital's terrifying doctor, who tempts him to ingest the very oral narcotic that he swore off in recovery; and—in a final flourish—the ghost of Hal's father, who flickers around the room, speaking obsessively, and sadly, of his failed relationship with his son. Gately is reduced to a state of complete passivity; he can only listen to the word-drunk, anguished souls that speak to him. He is a "huge, empty confessional booth" or a "statue of an ear."

Observing Gately's demise, Wallace orchestrates this subsiding of sentience very well. He has a gift for describing what it's like for a room to blur at the edges, or for words to lose their meaning and become part of an ambient surround:

He dreams he's riding due north on a bus the same color as its own exhaust, passing again and again the same gutted cottages and expanse of heaving sea, weeping . . . He dreams he looks in a mirror and sees nothing and keeps trying to clean the mirror with his sleeve. One dream consists only of the color blue, too vivid, like the blue of a pool. An unpleasant smell keeps coming up his throat. He's both in a bag and holding a bag.

Many readers have complained about *Infinite Jest*'s bitterly pessimistic ending. Hal's loss of speech, Gately's prospects of recovery, the resolution of the "continental emergency" that follows the circulation of the fatal "Entertainment": all of these plotlines are left hanging in the air, mysteries that refuse to be solved. (Some readers will probably spend decades combing the book for clues.) In many ways, however, the drive toward oblivion is the novel's proper end. Wallace can only hold together his commitments to genuine feelings, and to the ironic deflation of those feelings, by imagining a space where neither one is possible. When he gets there, the effect is oddly lulling, a song that's faded out. In an Enfield term paper, Hal had predicted that after the "bureaucratic hero" of postmodernism there would arise the "hero of nonaction," who is "one beyond calm, divorced from all stimulus." For all its hectic verve and incessant noise, *Infinite Jest* drives toward passivity and the cessation of action, toward a calm that lies somewhere between peacefulness and death. But not, of course, without protest: on the bus back from a tennis meet, the students read the immobile adventures of

Oblomov, and they appear, we are told, "very unhappy indeed."

> Whatever its other distinctions, Wallace's nonfiction is nearly as ambitious as his fiction. In *A Supposedly Fun Thing I'll Never Do Again,* he gathers essays and travelogues written over the course of the decade. They include lengthy excursions into the mind of David Lynch, the state of the novel in an age of television, and the uses of leisure time on a cruise ship holiday. Throughout the collection, Wallace paints a morose portrait of a TV-addled society obsessed with "watching and being watched." He also paints—it must be said—an equally morose portrait of himself.
>
> —*Alexander Star*

Whatever its other distinctions, Wallace's nonfiction is nearly as ambitious as his fiction. In *A Supposedly Fun Thing I'll Never Do Again,* he gathers essays and travelogues written over the course of the decade. They include lengthy excursions into the mind of David Lynch, the state of the novel in an age of television, and the uses of leisure time on a cruise ship holiday. Throughout the collection, Wallace paints a morose portrait of a TV-addled society obsessed with "watching and being watched." He also paints—it must be said—an equally morose portrait of himself. Wallace apologizes for losing track of his thesis; he convicts himself of being just as "aloof and sardonic and depressed" as the "hip young rebels" he complains about; and he confesses that he is just as concerned with how he appears to others as the cruise ship conformists he derides. The book might have been called Advertisements Against Myself.

As a reporter, Wallace practices a rather original brand of anti-journalism. He wants to watch, but he doesn't want to be seen. Like Hal, the frightened writer seems to retreat to the periphery of the room. In a profile of David Lynch, he explains that "[I] have no idea how to interview somebody." Visiting the Illinois State Fair, he avoids the rides, wanly pointing out that his chief goal in life is to "subject my nervous system to as little stress as possible." And his grand cruise ship adventure ends with a sullen retreat to his cabin. Hobbled by his hesitation, Wallace too often resorts to cheap caricature: the cruise ship passengers are a mass of "ectoplasm," the crowds at the state fair resemble a "Batan march of docile consumption." These are artfully turned banalities, mistakenly presented as if they were brilliantly derisive witticisms. It's hard to distinguish the scorn from the self-pity.

Still, Wallace's essays add up to a fine portrait of odd American detail. In the windswept plains of central Illinois, the inhabitants "[don't] comb their hair because why bother?" David Lynch's mailbox contains a "fresh shrink-wrapped copy of Jack Nicklaus's instructional video *Golf My Way.* Your guess is as good here as mine." Most memorable of all, perhaps, is Wallace's description of his cruise ship cabin's "fascinating and potentially malevolent" vacuum toilet: Its "concussive suction" is "so awesomely powerful that it's both scary and strangely comforting—your waste seems less removed than hurled from you, and hurled with a velocity that lets you feel as though the waste is going to end up someplace so far away from you that it will have become an abstraction."

It is when Wallace turns from the description of scenes and people to the analysis of ideas and artifacts that his weaknesses are most evident. Wallace's essays on contemporary fiction's flirtation with television and on David Lynch are full of arresting ideas, but they are frustrating performances, overcrowded with inflated arguments and randomly generated complications. Wallace makes being difficult all too easy on himself. These shortcomings are especially hard to miss in the essay on television and fiction, which was published in 1992. In much of the piece, he offers a sharp and persuasive attack on the literary culture of institutionalized irony. For writers like Pynchon and Gaddis, irony was a corrosive weapon against "the System," the status quo; but now irony's edge has been blunted by years of sitcom repetition, and so satirists of television such as Mark Leyner who "attempt to 'respond' to television via ironic genuflection" are "all too easily subsumed into the tired televisual ritual of mock-worship." The result, Wallace warns, is a writing that is "dead on the page," "some kind of line's end's end." Worst of all, the methods of this literature are "oppressive," because they prohibit the reader from asking the innocent question, "but what do you mean?" Wallace's conclusion about Leyner and associates is entirely on the mark: their work is "hilarious, upsetting, sophisticated, and extremely shallow."

This is a perfectly just assessment of much recent American writing, the smug, knowing style that strives to imitate the disingenuous self-mockery of a clever TV ad. But what is Wallace's corrective for this state of affairs? From which standpoint does he propose to offer serious resistance? The answer, we learn, is a new brand of literature that will "treat of plain old untrendy human troubles and emotions in U.S. life with reverence and conviction." Literature must not be afraid of its traditional mission, which is to provide "insights and guides to value." Indeed, virtually anything that promises to overcome the aesthetic of "trendy sardonic exhaustion" will do.

The problem is that Wallace's advocacy of earnestness turns out to be rather halfhearted. A reader quickly discovers that he can't use the words "reverence" and "conviction" without adding that he knows they are "untrendy"; he can't speak from the heart without adding a passing comment about how he knows he's not supposed to do that. The urge to escape irony and the urge to use it are all mixed up in his prose. As ever, Wallace's writing is full of side gestures and feints. But they are a greater liability in a work of criticism than in a work of fiction. Though his self-undermining asides are often quite funny, taken together they seem like a nervous act of self-defense. When he concludes by calling for a new breed of "anti-rebels" who will be "willing . . . to risk accusations of sentimentality, melodrama. Of overcredulity. Of softness," it is impossible to credit his profession that this is a role he would want for himself.

In the lengthy profile-essay on David Lynch, which was written on the set of Lost Highway, Wallace returns to many of the quandaries that inspire his own work, but from a different angle. Wallace admires Lynch, who charts a path between the "antiempathetic solipsism" of the avant-garde and the trite sentimentality of Hollywood. Lynch's films, in Wallace's estimation, are free of the self-protections of irony; instead, they are the work of an unaffected "genius" or "idiot" who seeks "psychic intimacy," who wants only to "get inside your head." Blue Velvet wasn't an exercise in satire or surrealism; it was an experimental film in which every detail—somehow, miraculously enough—"felt true."

As Wallace describes them, Lynch's methods come to sound an awful lot like Wallace's own. His films have rejected "conventional linear narrative" while "devot[ing] quite a lot of energy to character. I.e. they've had human beings in them." And they've also avoided the temptation to moralize, insisting that the capacity for evil may lie closer to home than we think. Lynch's films pass no moral judgments, but they are not a moral holiday: they require "empathetic confrontation with the exact same muddy bothness in ourselves and our intimates that makes the real world of moral selves so tense and uncomfortable." This is precisely the kind of complexity that Wallace wants to introduce into his own characters.

But do Lynch's films really succeed in exploring the "psychic spaces in which people are capable of evil"? A viewer of Lost Highway, certainly, will not think so. The film's concluding revelations about a character's sordid past hardly come across as a revelation of interior motives or feelings; they look, instead, like a ritualistic bow to a vaguely imagined "underworld" that is all too easily assumed to hold the sunlit world in its sway. In studying Lynch's influence, Wallace never contemplates the possibility that a belief in the omnipresence of evil can itself become a cliche, and no less reflexive than the tidy sorting of individuals into heroes and villains. If evil can show up everywhere, then all judgments are hypocritical. And if all judgments are hypocritical, then one might as well adopt a pose of blank, knowing indifference—the very stance of "trendy, sardonic exhaustion" that Wallace claims elsewhere to loathe.

While the admiration that Wallace expresses for Lynch's "artistic heroism" is genuine, his terms of admiration are not very persuasive. Wallace congratulates Lynch for avoiding the temptations of irony, but it is Lynch's gift for frustrating the audience's expectations that he wishes to emulate. He praises Lynch for refusing to judge his characters, but it is the capacity to make genuine and "unembarrassed" judgments that he believes contemporary artists must resurrect. He admires Lynch for his depth of characterization, but he has also mocked the very idea of providing characters with inner lives: "in our post-1950s inseparable-from-TV-association pool, brand loyalty is really synechdochic of character; this is simply a fact." Wallace delivers his critical judgments with great confidence, but they don't add up to a set of coherent propositions, much less a meaningful aesthetic.

Wallace's most artful essay, by contrast, is the title essay of his book, a novella-length account of a weeklong Caribbean cruise ship vacation. It begins tranquilly, rises to a considerable pitch of wicked laughter and mock horror, and then ends on a surprisingly gentle note. The furniture of the ship, its luxurious accommodations and its unsettling promise of "managed fun" are described with fanatical precision. Toward the end of the journey, the passengers gather for their most bizarre night of entertainment, a session with an English hypnotist, whose "boredom and hostility are not only undisguised, they are incorporated kind of ingeniously into the entertainment itself." The hypnotist robs selected audience members of their minds, creating "fantasies so vivid that the subjects do not even know they are fantasies." Watching grown adults act as if they were utterly lost, Wallace notes that it's "as if their heads were no longer their own."

This kind of willing self-surrender is Wallace's worst fear. It is the threat that drug addiction's slavery, and *Infinite Jest*'s "recursive loops," and the dreadful paranoia of the appearance-obsessed, all pose to the individual who would be "the rational and articulate protagonist of his own drama." But Wallace doesn't put the hypnosis scene to its expected use. It doesn't become one more allegory of Americans' loss of self-control or their slavery to artificial fantasies. Instead, he comes to see the experience of hypnosis as something neither "entertaining" nor "depressing" but merely, in his own fondly chosen word, "weird." The oddness of the occasion does not stimulate him to draw any lessons from it. Instead it frees him to do some fantasizing of his own.

And so, trying to avoid the mesmerist's influence, Wallace falls into his own "trance," where he comes to see the ship from the outside, through a drowning man's eyes. When he snaps out of it, he is back on shore. And now he believes that, having survived his adventure, he may be able to cope with "adult demands." It was "good to be on" and now it is "good to get off." The movement away from sentience is where *Infinite Jest* ends. But the essay reverses the novel's drift: it flirts with a reinvigorated sense of purpose and composure. Wallace is trying to live up to the straightforward, if not particularly demanding, ideal that he offered earlier in the essay: "Day to day I have to make all sorts of choices about what is good and important and fun, and then I have to live with the forfeiture of all the other options those choices foreclose."

What could these stumbling, ostentatiously sincere words mean? It is a little hard to accept Wallace's sudden humbleness. And his declarations of impending adulthood do not ring very true. "Good and demanding and fun": this is the very language of the awkward teenager that he aspires to leave behind. "Fun" is an ideal of quick, even instant gratification; it lowers the level of Wallace's ambition and takes back the seriousness that he just expressed. What if it turns out that the good and the demanding are not "fun"? It usually turns out that way. Still, Wallace's talk of "forfeitures" and foreclosures is encouraging. For once, his compulsion to make his own thoughts, though still present, is held in check. It's as if he's searching for a set of words that are simply too serious to play with, words that have the weight of deeds.

For all the brilliant expansiveness of his writing, Wallace's great subject is the anxiety of introspection. In his hands, self-awareness is a scary thing. What his fictional characters express with their vast piles of words is, essentially, terror; and with the same vast piles of words they try to hold off (and laugh at) that terror. The only options that are forbidden to them are self-confidence and self-forgetfulness. And so Wallace's universe is finally not as sprawling as his novel. His fiction would benefit greatly from the acknowledgment that strength and work and the transcendence of the self are also parts of the human comedy. With such a thought in mind, this remarkable writer might be able to create sober, autonomous human beings with as much intimacy, and as little caricature, as he brings to his descriptions of frightened teenagers and damaged adults.

FURTHER READING

Criticism

Bruni, Frank. "The Grunge American Novel." *New York Times*, (24 March 1996): 476-79.

Examines the release of *Infinite Jest*, Wallace's personality, and the publicity surrounding the novel.

Costello, Mark. "Fighting to Write: A Short Reminiscence of D. F. Wallace." *Review of Contemporary Fiction* 13, No. 2 (Summer 1993): 235-36.

    A brief remembrance by Mark Costello of the time he spent living with David Foster Wallace and collaborating on *Signifying Rappers.*

Rother, James. "Reading and Riding the Post-Scientific Wave: The Shorter Fiction of David Foster Wallace." *Review of Contemporary Fiction* 13, No. 2 (Summer 1993): 216-34.

    An in-depth examination of Wallace's *Girl with Curious Hair* and his story "Order and Flux in Northampton."

Additional coverage of Wallace's life and career is contained in the following sources published by Gale: *Contemporary Authors,* **Vol. 132; and** *Contemporary Authors New Revision Series,* **Vol. 59.**

□ Contemporary Literary Criticism

Indexes

Literary Criticism Series
Cumulative Author Index
Cumulative Topic Index
Cumulative Nationality Index
Title Index, Volume 114

How to Use This Index

The main references

Camus, Albert
1913-1960 ...... **CLC 1, 2, 4, 9, 11, 14,
32, 69; DA; DAB; DAC; DAM DRAM,
MST, NOV; DC2; SSC 9; WLC**

list all author entries in the following Gale Literary Criticism series:

BLC = *Black Literature Criticism*
BLCS = *Black Literature Criticism Supplement*
CLC = *Contemporary Literary Criticism*
CLR = *Children's Literature Review*
CMLC = *Classical and Medieval Literature Criticism*
DA = *DISCovering Authors*
DAB = *DISCovering Authors: British*
DAC = *DISCovering Authors: Canadian*
DAM = *DISCovering Authors Modules*
  DRAM = *dramatists;* *MST* = *most-studied
  authors;* *MULT* = *multicultural authors;* *NOV* =
  novelists; *POET* = *poets;* *POP* = *popular/genre
  writers;* *DC* = *Drama Criticism*
HLC = *Hispanic Literature Criticism*
LC = *Literature Criticism from 1400 to 1800*
NCLC = *Nineteenth-Century Literature Criticism*
PC = *Poetry Criticism*
SSC = *Short Story Criticism*
TCLC = *Twentieth-Century Literary Criticism*
WLC = *World Literature Criticism, 1500 to the Present*
WLCS = *World Literature Criticism Supplement*

The cross-references

See also CA 89-92; DLB 72; MTCW

list all author entries in the following Gale biographical and literary sources:

AAYA = *Authors & Artists for Young Adults*
AITN = *Authors in the News*
BEST = *Bestsellers*
BW = *Black Writers*
CA = *Contemporary Authors*
CAAS = *Contemporary Authors Autobiography
Series*
CABS = *Contemporary Authors Bibliographical
Series*
CANR = *Contemporary Authors New Revision Series*
CAP = *Contemporary Authors Permanent Series*
CDALB = *Concise Dictionary of American Literary
Biography*
CDBLB = *Concise Dictionary of British Literary
Biography*

DLB = *Dictionary of Literary Biography*
DLBD = *Dictionary of Literary Biography
Documentary Series*
DLBY = *Dictionary of Literary Biography Yearbook*
HW = *Hispanic Writers*
JRDA = *Junior DISCovering Authors*
MAICYA = *Major Authors and Illustrators for
Children and Young Adults*
MTCW = *Major 20th-Century Writers*
NNAL = *Native North American Literature*
SAAS = *Something about the Author Autobiography
Series*
SATA = *Something about the Author*
YABC = *Yesterday's Authors of Books for Children*

20/1631
See Upward, Allen
A/C Cross
See Lawrence, T(homas) E(dward)
Abasiyanik, Sait Faik 1906-1954
See Sait Faik
See also CA 123
Abbey, Edward 1927-1989 .... **CLC 36, 59**
See also CA 45-48; 128; CANR 2, 41
Abbott, Lee K(ittredge) 1947- .... **CLC 48**
See also CA 124; CANR 51; DLB 130
Abe, Kobo 1924-1993**CLC 8, 22, 53, 81; DAM NOV**
See also CA 65-68, 140; CANR 24, 60; DLB 182; MTCW 1
Abelard, Peter c. 1079-c. 1142 ...... **CMLC 11**
See also DLB 115
Abell, Kjeld 1901-1961 .... **CLC 15**
See also CA 111
Abish, Walter 1931- .... **CLC 22**
See also CA 101; CANR 37; DLB 130
Abrahams, Peter (Henry) 1919- ....**CLC 4**
See also BW 1; CA 57-60; CANR 26; DLB 117; MTCW 1
Abrams, M(eyer) H(oward) 1912- ... **CLC 24**
See also CA 57-60; CANR 13, 33; DLB 67
Abse, Dannie 1923-.. **CLC 7, 29; DAB; DAM POET**
See also CA 53-56; CAAS 1; CANR 4, 46; DLB 27
Achebe, (Albert) Chinua(lumogu) 1930-**C L C 1, 3, 5, 7, 11, 26, 51, 75; BLC 1; DA; DAB; DAC; DAM MST, MULT, NOV; WLC**
See also AAYA 15; BW 2; CA 1-4R; CANR 6, 26, 47; CLR 20; DLB 117; MAICYA; MTCW 1; SATA 40; SATA-Brief 38
Acker, Kathy 1948-1997 .... **CLC 45, 111**
See also CA 117; 122; 162; CANR 55
Ackroyd, Peter 1949- .... **CLC 34, 52**
See also CA 123; 127; CANR 51; DLB 155; INT 127
Acorn, Milton 1923- ....**CLC 15; DAC**
See also CA 103; DLB 53; INT 103
Adamov, Arthur 1908-1970**CLC 4, 25; DAM DRAM**
See also CA 17-18; 25-28R; CAP 2; MTCW 1
Adams, Alice (Boyd) 1926-**CLC 6, 13, 46; SSC 24**
See also CA 81-84; CANR 26, 53; DLBY 86; INT CANR-26; MTCW 1
Adams, Andy 1859-1935 .... **TCLC 56**
See also YABC 1
Adams, Brooks 1848-1927 .... **TCLC 80**
See also CA 123; DLB 47
Adams, Douglas (Noel) 1952- .... **CLC 27, 60; DAM POP**
See also AAYA 4; BEST 89:3; CA 106; CANR 34, 64; DLBY 83; JRDA

Adams, Francis 1862-1893 .... **NCLC 33**
Adams, Henry (Brooks) 1838-1918 **TCLC 4, 52; DA; DAB; DAC; DAM MST**
See also CA 104; 133; DLB 12, 47, 189
Adams, Richard (George) 1920-**CLC 4, 5, 18; DAM NOV**
See also AAYA 16; AITN 1, 2; CA 49-52; CANR 3, 35; CLR 20; JRDA; MAICYA; MTCW 1; SATA 7, 69
Adamson, Joy(-Friederike Victoria) 1910-1980 **CLC 17**
See also CA 69-72; 93-96; CANR 22; MTCW 1; SATA 11; SATA-Obit 22
Adcock, Fleur 1934- .... **CLC 41**
See also CA 25-28R; CAAS 23; CANR 11, 34, 69; DLB 40
Addams, Charles (Samuel) 1912-1988**CLC 30**
See also CA 61-64; 126; CANR 12
Addams, Jane 1860-1945 .... **TCLC 76**
Addison, Joseph 1672-1719 .... **LC 18**
See also CDBLB 1660-1789; DLB 101
Adler, Alfred (F.) 1870-1937 .... **TCLC 61**
See also CA 119; 159
Adler, C(arole) S(chwerdtfeger) 1932-..**C L C 35**
See also AAYA 4; CA 89-92; CANR 19, 40; JRDA; MAICYA; SAAS 15; SATA 26, 63, 102
Adler, Renata 1938- .... **CLC 8, 31**
See also CA 49-52; CANR 5, 22, 52; MTCW 1
Ady, Endre 1877-1919 .... **TCLC 11**
See also CA 107
A.E. 1867-1935 .... **TCLC 3, 10**
See also Russell, George William
Aeschylus 525B.C.-456B.C. ..**CMLC 11; DA; DAB; DAC; DAM DRAM, MST; DC 8; WLCS**
See also DLB 176
Aesop 620(?)B.C.-564(?)B.C. .... **CMLC 24**
See also CLR 14; MAICYA; SATA 64
Affable Hawk
See MacCarthy, Sir(Charles Otto) Desmond
Africa, Ben
See Bosman, Herman Charles
Afton, Effie
See Harper, Frances Ellen Watkins
Agapida, Fray Antonio
See Irving, Washington
Agee, James (Rufus) 1909-1955 **TCLC 1, 19; DAM NOV**
See also AITN 1; CA 108; 148; CDALB 1941-1968; DLB 2, 26, 152
Aghill, Gordon
See Silverberg, Robert
Agnon, S(hmuel) Y(osef Halevi) 1888-1970 **CLC 4, 8, 14; SSC 30**
See also CA 17-18; 25-28R; CANR 60; CAP 2; MTCW 1

Agrippa von Nettesheim, Henry Cornelius 1486-1535 .... **LC 27**
Aherne, Owen
See Cassill, R(onald) V(erlin)
Ai 1947- .... **CLC 4, 14, 69**
See also CA 85-88; CAAS 13; CANR 70; DLB 120
Aickman, Robert (Fordyce) 1914-1981**CLC 57**
See also CA 5-8R; CANR 3, 72
Aiken, Conrad (Potter) 1889-1973**CLC 1, 3, 5, 10, 52; DAM NOV, POET; SSC 9**
See also CA 5-8R; 45-48; CANR 4, 60; CDALB 1929-1941; DLB 9, 45, 102; MTCW 1; SATA 3, 30
Aiken, Joan (Delano) 1924- .... **CLC 35**
See also AAYA 1, 25; CA 9-12R; CANR 4, 23, 34, 64; CLR 1, 19; DLB 161; JRDA; MAICYA; MTCW 1; SAAS 1; SATA 2, 30, 73
Ainsworth, William Harrison 1805-1882 **NCLC 13**
See also DLB 21; SATA 24
Aitmatov, Chingiz (Torekulovich) 1928-**C L C 71**
See also CA 103; CANR 38; MTCW 1; SATA 56
Akers, Floyd
See Baum, L(yman) Frank
Akhmadulina, Bella Akhatovna 1937-**CLC 53; DAM POET**
See also CA 65-68
Akhmatova, Anna 1888-1966**CLC 11, 25, 64; DAM POET; PC 2**
See also CA 19-20; 25-28R; CANR 35; CAP 1; MTCW 1
Aksakov, Sergei Timofeyvich 1791-1859 **NCLC 2**
See also DLB 198
Aksenov, Vassily
See Aksyonov, Vassily (Pavlovich)
Akst, Daniel 1956- .... **CLC 109**
See also CA 161
Aksyonov, Vassily (Pavlovich) 1932-**CLC 22, 37, 101**
See also CA 53-56; CANR 12, 48
Akutagawa, Ryunosuke 1892-1927 **TCLC 16**
See also CA 117; 154
Alain 1868-1951 .... **TCLC 41**
See also CA 163
Alain-Fournier .... **TCLC 6**
See also Fournier, Henri Alban
See also DLB 65
Alarcon, Pedro Antonio de 1833-1891**NCLC 1**
Alas (y Urena), Leopoldo (Enrique Garcia) 1852-1901 .... **TCLC 29**
See also CA 113; 131; HW
Albee, Edward (Franklin III) 1928-**CLC 1, 2, 3, 5, 9, 11, 13, 25, 53, 86, 113; DA; DAB;**

TCLC 2
See also CA 104; 155; DLB 9, 78, 186
Atherton, Lucius
See Masters, Edgar Lee
Atkins, Jack
See Harris, Mark
Atkinson, Kate .... **CLC 99**
See also CA 166
Attaway, William (Alexander) 1911-1986
CLC 92; BLC 1; DAM MULT
See also BW 2; CA 143; DLB 76
Atticus
See Fleming, Ian (Lancaster); Wilson, (Thomas) Woodrow
Atwood, Margaret (Eleanor) 1939-CLC 2, 3, 4, 8, 13, 15, 25, 44, 84; DA; DAB; DAC; DAM MST, NOV, POET; PC 8; SSC 2; WLC
See also AAYA 12; BEST 89:2; CA 49-52; CANR 3, 24, 33, 59; DLB 53; INT CANR-24; MTCW 1; SATA 50
Aubigny, Pierre d'
See Mencken, H(enry) L(ouis)
Aubin, Penelope 1685-1731(?) .... **LC 9**
See also DLB 39
Auchincloss, Louis (Stanton) 1917-CLC 4, 6, 9, 18, 45; DAM NOV; SSC 22
See also CA 1-4R; CANR 6, 29, 55; DLB 2; DLBY 80; INT CANR-29; MTCW 1
Auden, W(ystan) H(ugh) 1907-1973CLC 1, 2, 3, 4, 6, 9, 11, 14, 43; DA; DAB; DAC; DAM DRAM, MST, POET; PC 1; WLC
See also AAYA 18; CA 9-12R; 45-48; CANR 5, 61; CDBLB 1914-1945; DLB 10, 20; MTCW 1
Audiberti, Jacques 1900-1965CLC 38; DAM DRAM
See also CA 25-28R
Audubon, John James 1785-1851 ..NCLC 47
Auel, Jean M(arie) 1936-CLC 31, 107; DAM POP
See also AAYA 7; BEST 90:4; CA 103; CANR 21, 64; INT CANR-21; SATA 91
Auerbach, Erich 1892-1957 .... **TCLC 43**
See also CA 118; 155
Augier, Emile 1820-1889 .... **NCLC 31**
See also DLB 192
August, John
See De Voto, Bernard (Augustine)
Augustine, St. 354-430 .... **CMLC 6; DAB**
Aurelius
See Bourne, Randolph S(illiman)
Aurobindo, Sri
See Ghose, Aurabinda
Austen, Jane 1775-1817 NCLC 1, 13, 19, 33, 51; DA; DAB; DAC; DAM MST, NOV; WLC
See also AAYA 19; CDBLB 1789-1832; DLB 116
Auster, Paul 1947- .... **CLC 47**
See also CA 69-72; CANR 23, 52
Austin, Frank
See Faust, Frederick (Schiller)
Austin, Mary (Hunter) 1868-1934 . TCLC 25
See also CA 109; DLB 9, 78
Autran Dourado, Waldomiro
See Dourado, (Waldomiro Freitas) Autran
Averroes 1126-1198 .... **CMLC 7**
See also DLB 115
Avicenna 980-1037 .... **CMLC 16**
See also DLB 115
Avison, Margaret 1918- CLC 2, 4, 97; DAC; DAM POET

See also CA 17-20R; DLB 53; MTCW 1
Axton, David
See Koontz, Dean R(ay)
Ayckbourn, Alan 1939- CLC 5, 8, 18, 33, 74; DAB; DAM DRAM
See also CA 21-24R; CANR 31, 59; DLB 13; MTCW 1
Aydy, Catherine
See Tennant, Emma (Christina)
Ayme, Marcel (Andre) 1902-1967 ..... CLC 11
See also CA 89-92; CANR 67; CLR 25; DLB 72; SATA 91
Ayrton, Michael 1921-1975 .... CLC 7
See also CA 5-8R; 61-64; CANR 9, 21
Azorin .... CLC 11
See also Martinez Ruiz, Jose
Azuela, Mariano 1873-1952 . TCLC 3; DAM MULT; HLC
See also CA 104; 131; HW; MTCW 1
Baastad, Babbis Friis
See Friis-Baastad, Babbis Ellinor
Bab
See Gilbert, W(illiam) S(chwenck)
Babbis, Eleanor
See Friis-Baastad, Babbis Ellinor
Babel, Isaac
See Babel, Isaak (Emmanuilovich)
Babel, Isaak (Emmanuilovich) 1894-1941(?) **TCLC 2, 13; SSC 16**
See also CA 104; 155
Babits, Mihaly 1883-1941 .... **TCLC 14**
See also CA 114
Babur 1483-1530 .... **LC 18**
Bacchelli, Riccardo 1891-1985 .... CLC 19
See also CA 29-32R; 117
Bach, Richard (David) 1936- CLC 14; DAM NOV, POP
See also AITN 1; BEST 89:2; CA 9-12R; CANR 18; MTCW 1; SATA 13
Bachman, Richard
See King, Stephen (Edwin)
Bachmann, Ingeborg 1926-1973 .... CLC 69
See also CA 93-96; 45-48; CANR 69; DLB 85
Bacon, Francis 1561-1626 .... LC 18, 32
See also CDBLB Before 1660; DLB 151
Bacon, Roger 1214(?)-1292 .... **CMLC 14**
See also DLB 115
Bacovia, George .... **TCLC 24**
See also Vasiliu, Gheorghe
Badanes, Jerome 1937- .... CLC 59
Bagehot, Walter 1826-1877 .... NCLC 10
See also DLB 55
Bagnold, Enid 1889-1981 ...... CLC 25; DAM DRAM
See also CA 5-8R; 103; CANR 5, 40; DLB 13, 160, 191; MAICYA; SATA 1, 25
Bagritsky, Eduard 1895-1934 .... TCLC 60
Bagrjana, Elisaveta
See Belcheva, Elisaveta
Bagryana, Elisaveta ....CLC 10
See also Belcheva, Elisaveta
See also DLB 147
Bailey, Paul 1937- .... CLC 45
See also CA 21-24R; CANR 16, 62; DLB 14
Baillie, Joanna 1762-1851 .... NCLC 71
See also DLB 93
Bainbridge, Beryl (Margaret) 1933-CLC 4, 5, 8, 10, 14, 18, 22, 62; DAM NOV
See also CA 21-24R; CANR 24, 55; DLB 14; MTCW 1
Baker, Elliott 1922- .... CLC 8
See also CA 45-48; CANR 2, 63
Baker, Jean H. .... TCLC 3, 10

See also Russell, George William
Baker, Nicholson 1957- . CLC 61; DAM POP
See also CA 135; CANR 63
Baker, Ray Stannard 1870-1946 .... TCLC 47
See also CA 118
Baker, Russell (Wayne) 1925- .... CLC 31
See also BEST 89:4; CA 57-60; CANR 11, 41, 59; MTCW 1
Bakhtin, M.
See Bakhtin, Mikhail Mikhailovich
Bakhtin, M. M.
See Bakhtin, Mikhail Mikhailovich
Bakhtin, Mikhail
See Bakhtin, Mikhail Mikhailovich
Bakhtin, Mikhail Mikhailovich 1895-1975 **CLC 83**
See also CA 128; 113
Bakshi, Ralph 1938(?)- .... CLC 26
See also CA 112; 138
Bakunin, Mikhail (Alexandrovich) 1814-1876 **NCLC 25, 58**
Baldwin, James (Arthur) 1924-1987CLC 1, 2, 3, 4, 5, 8, 13, 15, 17, 42, 50, 67, 90; BLC 1; DA; DAB; DAC; DAM MST, MULT, NOV, POP; DC 1; SSC 10; WLC
See also AAYA 4; BW 1; CA 1-4R; 124; CABS 1; CANR 3, 24; CDALB 1941-1968; DLB 2, 7, 33; DLBY 87; MTCW 1; SATA 9; SATA-Obit 54
Ballard, J(ames) G(raham) 1930-CLC 3, 6, 14, 36; DAM NOV, POP; SSC 1
See also AAYA 3; CA 5-8R; CANR 15, 39, 65; DLB 14; MTCW 1; SATA 93
Balmont, Konstantin (Dmitriyevich) 1867-1943 **TCLC 11**
See also CA 109; 155
Balzac, Honore de 1799-1850NCLC 5, 35, 53; DA; DAB; DAC; DAM MST, NOV; SSC 5; WLC
See also DLB 119
Bambara, Toni Cade 1939-1995 CLC 19, 88; BLC 1; DA; DAC; DAM MST, MULT; WLCS
See also AAYA 5; BW 2; CA 29-32R; 150; CANR 24, 49; DLB 38; MTCW 1
Bamdad, A.
See Shamlu, Ahmad
Banat, D. R.
See Bradbury, Ray (Douglas)
Bancroft, Laura
See Baum, L(yman) Frank
Banim, John 1798-1842 .... NCLC 13
See also DLB 116, 158, 159
Banim, Michael 1796-1874 .... NCLC 13
See also DLB 158, 159
Banjo, The
See Paterson, A(ndrew) B(arton)
Banks, Iain
See Banks, Iain M(enzies)
Banks, Iain M(enzies) 1954- .... CLC 34
See also CA 123; 128; CANR 61; DLB 194; INT 128
Banks, Lynne Reid .... CLC 23
See also Reid Banks, Lynne
See also AAYA 6
Banks, Russell 1940- .... CLC 37, 72
See also CA 65-68; CAAS 15; CANR 19, 52; DLB 130
Banville, John 1945- .... CLC 46
See also CA 117; 128; DLB 14; INT 128
Banville, Theodore (Faullain) de 1832-1891 **NCLC 9**
Baraka, Amiri 1934-CLC 1, 2, 3, 5, 10, 14, 33;

BLC 1; DA; DAC; DAM MST, MULT, POET, POP; DC 6; PC 4; WLCS
See also Jones, LeRoi
See also BW 2; CA 21-24R; CABS 3; CANR 27, 38, 61; CDALB 1941-1968; DLB 5, 7, 16, 38; DLBD 8; MTCW 1

Barbauld, Anna Laetitia 1743-1825NCLC 50
See also DLB 107, 109, 142, 158

Barbellion, W. N. P. .... TCLC 24
See also Cummings, Bruce F(rederick)

Barbera, Jack (Vincent) 1945- ....: CLC 44
See also CA 110; CANR 45

Barbey d'Aurevilly, Jules Amedee 1808-1889
NCLC 1; SSC 17
See also DLB 119

Barbusse, Henri 1873-1935 .... TCLC 5
See also CA 105; 154; DLB 65

Barclay, Bill
See Moorcock, Michael (John)

Barclay, William Ewert
See Moorcock, Michael (John)

Barea, Arturo 1897-1957 .... TCLC 14
See also CA 111

Barfoot, Joan 1946- .... CLC 18
See also CA 105

Baring, Maurice 1874-1945 .... TCLC 8
See also CA 105; 168; DLB 34

Barker, Clive 1952- .... CLC 52; DAM POP
See also AAYA 10; BEST 90:3; CA 121; 129; CANR 71; INT 129; MTCW 1

Barker, George Granville 1913-1991 CLC 8, 48; DAM POET
See also CA 9-12R; 135; CANR 7, 38; DLB 20; MTCW 1

Barker, Harley Granville
See Granville-Barker, Harley
See also DLB 10

Barker, Howard 1946- .... CLC 37
See also CA 102; DLB 13

Barker, Pat(ricia) 1943- .... CLC 32, 94
See also CA 117; 122; CANR 50; INT 122

Barlach, Ernst 1870-1938 .... TCLC 84
See also DLB 56, 118

Barlow, Joel 1754-1812 .... NCLC 23
See also DLB 37

Barnard, Mary (Ethel) 1909- .... CLC 48
See also CA 21-22; CAP 2

Barnes, Djuna 1892-1982CLC 3, 4, 8, 11, 29; SSC 3
See also CA 9-12R; 107; CANR 16, 55; DLB 4, 9, 45; MTCW 1

Barnes, Julian (Patrick) 1946-CLC 42; DAB
See also CA 102; CANR 19, 54; DLB 194; DLBY 93

Barnes, Peter 1931- .... CLC 5, 56
See also CA 65-68; CAAS 12; CANR 33, 34, 64; DLB 13; MTCW 1

Baroja (y Nessi), Pio 1872-1956TCLC 8; HLC
See also CA 104

Baron, David
See Pinter, Harold

Baron Corvo
See Rolfe, Frederick (William Serafino Austin Lewis Mary)

Barondess, Sue K(aufman) 1926-1977 CLC 8
See also Kaufman, Sue
See also CA 1-4R; 69-72; CANR 1

Baron de Teive
See Pessoa, Fernando (Antonio Nogueira)

Baroness Von S.
See Zangwill, Israel

Barres, (Auguste-) Maurice 1862-1923T C L C 47

See also CA 164; DLB 123

Barreto, Afonso Henrique de Lima
See Lima Barreto, Afonso Henrique de

Barrett, (Roger) Syd 1946- .... CLC 35

Barrett, William (Christopher) 1913-1992 CLC 27
See also CA 13-16R; 139; CANR 11, 67; INT CANR-11

Barrie, J(ames) M(atthew) 1860-1937 T C L C 2; DAB; DAM DRAM
See also CA 104; 136; CDBLB 1890-1914; CLR 16; DLB 10, 141, 156; MAICYA; SATA 100; YABC 1

Barrington, Michael
See Moorcock, Michael (John)

Barrol, Grady
See Bograd, Larry

Barry, Mike
See Malzberg, Barry N(athaniel)

Barry, Philip 1896-1949 .... TCLC 11
See also CA 109; DLB 7

Bart, Andre Schwarz
See Schwarz-Bart, Andre

Barth, John (Simmons) 1930-CLC 1, 2, 3, 5, 7, 9, 10, 14, 27, 51, 89; DAM NOV; SSC 10
See also AITN 1, 2; CA 1-4R; CABS 1; CANR 5, 23, 49, 64; DLB 2; MTCW 1

Barthelme, Donald 1931 1989CLC 1, 2, 3, 5, 6, 8, 13, 23, 46, 59; DAM NOV; SSC 2
See also CA 21-24R; 129; CANR 20, 58; DLB 2; DLBY 80, 89; MTCW 1; SATA 7; SATA-Obit 62

Barthelme, Frederick 1943- .... CLC 36
See also CA 114; 122; DLBY 85; INT 122

Barthes, Roland (Gerard) 1915-1980CLC 24, 83
See also CA 130; 97-100; CANR 66; MTCW 1

Barzun, Jacques (Martin) 1907- ...., CLC 51
See also CA 61-64; CANR 22

Bashevis, Isaac
See Singer, Isaac Bashevis

Bashkirtseff, Marie 1859-1884 .... NCLC 27

Basho
See Matsuo Basho

Bass, Kingsley B., Jr.
See Bullins, Ed

Bass, Rick 1958- .... CLC 79
See also CA 126; CANR 53

Bassani, Giorgio 1916- .... CLC 9
See also CA 65-68; CANR 33; DLB 128, 177; MTCW 1

Bastos, Augusto (Antonio) Roa
See Roa Bastos, Augusto (Antonio)

Bataille, Georges 1897-1962 .... CLC 29
See also CA 101; 89-92

Bates, H(erbert) E(rnest) 1905-1974CLC 46; DAB; DAM POP; SSC 10
See also CA 93-96; 45-48; CANR 34; DLB 162, 191; MTCW 1

Bauchart
See Camus, Albert

Baudelaire, Charles 1821-1867 NCLC 6, 29, 55; DA; DAB; DAC; DAM MST, POET; PC 1; SSC 18; WLC

Baudrillard, Jean 1929- .... CLC 60

Baum, L(yman) Frank 1856-1919 ... TCLC 7
See also CA 108; 133; CLR 15; DLB 22; JRDA; MAICYA; MTCW 1; SATA 18, 100

Baum, Louis F.
See Baum, L(yman) Frank

Baumbach, Jonathan 1933- .... CLC 6, 23
See also CA 13-16R; CAAS 5; CANR 12, 66; DLBY 80; INT CANR-12; MTCW 1

Bausch, Richard (Carl) 1945- .... CLC 51
See also CA 101; CAAS 14; CANR 43, 61; DLB 130

Baxter, Charles (Morley) 1947- CLC 45, 78; DAM POP
See also CA 57-60; CANR 40, 64; DLB 130

Baxter, George Owen
See Faust, Frederick (Schiller)

Baxter, James K(eir) 1926-1972 .... CLC 14
See also CA 77-80

Baxter, John
See Hunt, E(verette) Howard, (Jr.)

Bayer, Sylvia
See Glassco, John

Baynton, Barbara 1857-1929 .... TCLC 57

Beagle, Peter S(oyer) 1939- .... CLC 7, 104
See also CA 9-12R; CANR 4, 51; DLBY 80; INT CANR-4; SATA 60

Bean, Normal
See Burroughs, Edgar Rice

Beard, Charles A(ustin) 1874-1948 TCLC 15
See also CA 115; DLB 17; SATA 18

Beardsley, Aubrey 1872-1898 .... NCLC 6

Beattie, Ann 1947-CLC 8, 13, 18, 40, 63; DAM NOV, POP; SSC 11
See also BEST 90:2; CA 81-84; CANR 53; DLBY 82; MTCW 1

Beattie, James 1735-1803 .... NCLC 25
See also DLB 109

Beauchamp, Kathleen Mansfield 1888-1923
See Mansfield, Katherine
See also CA 104; 134; DA; DAC; DAM MST

Beaumarchais, Pierre-Augustin Caron de 1732-1799 .... DC 4
See also DAM DRAM

Beaumont, Francis 1584(?)-1616LC 33; DC 6
See also CDBLB Before 1660; DLB 58, 121

Beauvoir, Simone (Lucie Ernestine Marie Bertrand) de 1908-1986 CLC 1, 2, 4, 8, 14, 31, 44, 50, 71; DA; DAB; DAC; DAM MST, NOV; WLC
See also CA 9-12R; 118; CANR 28, 61; DLB 72; DLBY 86; MTCW 1

Becker, Carl (Lotus) 1873-1945 ..... TCLC 63
See also CA 157; DLB 17

Becker, Jurek 1937-1997 .... CLC 7, 19
See also CA 85-88; 157; CANR 60; DLB 75

Becker, Walter 1950- .... CLC 26

Beckett, Samuel (Barclay) 1906-1989 CLC 1, 2, 3, 4, 6, 9, 10, 11, 14, 18, 29, 57, 59, 83; DA; DAB; DAC; DAM DRAM, MST, NOV; SSC 16; WLC
See also CA 5-8R; 130; CANR 33, 61; CDBLB 1945-1960; DLB 13, 15; DLBY 90; MTCW 1

Beckford, William 1760-1844 .... NCLC 16
See also DLB 39

Beckman, Gunnel 1910- .... CLC 26
See also CA 33-36R; CANR 15; CLR 25; MAICYA; SAAS 9; SATA 6

Becque, Henri 1837-1899 .... NCLC 3
See also DLB 192

Beddoes, Thomas Lovell 1803-1849 NCLC 3
See also DLB 96

Bede c. 673-735 .... CMLC 20
See also DLB 146

Bedford, Donald F.
See Fearing, Kenneth (Flexner)

Beecher, Catharine Esther 1800-1878 N C L C 30
See also DLB 1

Beecher, John 1904-1980 .... CLC 6
See also AITN 1; CA 5-8R; 105; CANR 8

Beer, Johann 1655-1700 .... LC 5
See also DLB 168
Beer, Patricia 1924- .... CLC 58
See also CA 61-64; CANR 13, 46; DLB 40
Beerbohm, Max
See Beerbohm, (Henry) Max(imilian)
Beerbohm, (Henry) Max(imilian) 1872-1956
TCLC 1, 24
See also CA 104; 154; DLB 34, 100
Beer-Hofmann, Richard 1866-1945TCLC 60
See also CA 160; DLB 81
Begiebing, Robert J(ohn) 1946- .... CLC 70
See also CA 122; CANR 40
Behan, Brendan 1923-1964 CLC 1, 8, 11, 15,
79; DAM DRAM
See also CA 73-76; CANR 33; CDBLB 1945-
1960; DLB 13; MTCW 1
Behn, Aphra 1640(?)-1689LC 1, 30; DA; DAB;
DAC; DAM DRAM, MST, NOV, POET;
DC 4; PC 13; WLC
See also DLB 39, 80, 131
Behrman, S(amuel) N(athaniel) 1893-1973
CLC 40
See also CA 13-16; 45-48; CAP 1; DLB 7, 44
Belasco, David 1853-1931 .... TCLC 3
See also CA 104; 168; DLB 7
Belcheva, Elisaveta 1893- .... CLC 10
See also Bagryana, Elisaveta
Beldone, Phil "Cheech"
See Ellison, Harlan (Jay)
Beleno
See Azuela, Mariano
Belinski, Vissarion Grigoryevich 1811-1848
NCLC 5
See also DLB 198
Belitt, Ben 1911- .... CLC 22
See also CA 13-16R; CAAS 4; CANR 7; DLB
5
Bell, Gertrude (Margaret Lowthian) 1868-1926
TCLC 67
See also CA 167; DLB 174
Bell, J. Freeman
See Zangwill, Israel
Bell, James Madison 1826-1902 ... TCLC 43;
BLC 1; DAM MULT
See also BW 1; CA 122; 124; DLB 50
Bell, Madison Smartt 1957- ...... CLC 41, 102
See also CA 111; CANR 28, 54
Bell, Marvin (Hartley) 1937-CLC 8, 31; DAM
POET
See also CA 21-24R; CAAS 14; CANR 59; DLB
5; MTCW 1
Bell, W. L. D.
See Mencken, H(enry) L(ouis)
Bellamy, Atwood C.
See Mencken, H(enry) L(ouis)
Bellamy, Edward 1850-1898 .... NCLC 4
See also DLB 12
Bellin, Edward J.
See Kuttner, Henry
**Belloc, (Joseph) Hilaire (Pierre Sebastien Rene
Swanton)** 1870-1953 TCLC 7, 18; DAM
POET; PC 24
See also CA 106; 152; DLB 19, 100, 141, 174;
YABC 1
Belloc, Joseph Peter Rene Hilaire
See Belloc, (Joseph) Hilaire (Pierre Sebastien
Rene Swanton)
Belloc, Joseph Pierre Hilaire
See Belloc, (Joseph) Hilaire (Pierre Sebastien
Rene Swanton)
Belloc, M. A.
See Lowndes, Marie Adelaide (Belloc)

Bellow, Saul 1915-CLC 1, 2, 3, 6, 8, 10, 13, 15,
25, 33, 34, 63, 79; DA; DAB; DAC; DAM
MST, NOV, POP; SSC 14; WLC
See also AITN 2; BEST 89:3; CA 5-8R; CABS
1; CANR 29, 53; CDALB 1941-1968; DLB
2, 28; DLBD 3; DLBY 82; MTCW 1
Belser, Reimond Karel Maria de 1929-
See Ruyslinck, Ward
See also CA 152
Bely, Andrey .... TCLC 7; PC 11
See also Bugayev, Boris Nikolayevich
Belyi, Andrei
See Bugayev, Boris Nikolayevich
Benary, Margot
See Benary-Isbert, Margot
Benary-Isbert, Margot 1889-1979 .... CLC 12
See also CA 5-8R; 89-92; CANR 4, 72; CLR
12; MAICYA; SATA 2; SATA-Obit 21
Benavente (y Martinez), Jacinto 1866-1954
TCLC 3; DAM DRAM, MULT
See also CA 106; 131; HW; MTCW 1
Benchley, Peter (Bradford) 1940-. CLC 4, 8;
DAM NOV, POP
See also AAYA 14; AITN 2; CA 17-20R; CANR
12, 35, 66; MTCW 1; SATA 3, 89
Benchley, Robert (Charles) 1889-1945T C L C
1, 55
See also CA 105; 153; DLB 11
Benda, Julien 1867-1956 .... TCLC 60
See also CA 120; 154
Benedict, Ruth (Fulton) 1887-1948 TCLC 60
See also CA 158
Benedict, Saint c. 480-c. 547 .... CMLC 29
Benedikt, Michael 1935- .... CLC 4, 14
See also CA 13-16R; CANR 7; DLB 5
Benet, Juan 1927- .... CLC 28
See also CA 143
Benet, Stephen Vincent 1898-1943 . TCLC 7;
DAM POET; SSC 10
See also CA 104; 152; DLB 4, 48, 102; DLBY
97; YABC 1
Benet, William Rose 1886-1950 ... TCLC 28;
DAM POET
See also CA 118; 152; DLB 45
Benford, Gregory (Albert) 1941-....... CLC 52
See also CA 69-72; CAAS 27; CANR 12, 24,
49; DLBY 82
Bengtsson, Frans (Gunnar) 1894-1954T C L C
48
Benjamin, David
See Slavitt, David R(ytman)
Benjamin, Lois
See Gould, Lois
Benjamin, Walter 1892-1940 .... TCLC 39
See also CA 164
Benn, Gottfried 1886-1956 .... TCLC 3
See also CA 106; 153; DLB 56
Bennett, Alan 1934-CLC 45, 77; DAB; DAM
MST
See also CA 103; CANR 35, 55; MTCW 1
Bennett, (Enoch) Arnold 1867-1931 TCLC 5,
20
See also CA 106; 155; CDBLB 1890-1914;
DLB 10, 34, 98, 135
Bennett, Elizabeth
See Mitchell, Margaret (Munnerlyn)
Bennett, George Harold 1930-
See Bennett, Hal
See also BW 1; CA 97-100
Bennett, Hal .... CLC 5
See also Bennett, George Harold
See also DLB 33
Bennett, Jay 1912- .... CLC 35

See also AAYA 10; CA 69-72; CANR 11, 42;
JRDA; SAAS 4; SATA 41, 87; SATA-Brief
27
Bennett, Louise (Simone) 1919-CLC 28; BLC
1; DAM MULT
See also BW 2; CA 151; DLB 117
Benson, E(dward) F(rederic) 1867-1940
TCLC 27
See also CA 114; 157; DLB 135, 153
Benson, Jackson J. 1930- .... CLC 34
See also CA 25-28R; DLB 111
Benson, Sally 1900-1972 .... CLC 17
See also CA 19-20; 37-40R; CAP 1; SATA 1,
35; SATA-Obit 27
Benson, Stella 1892-1933 .... TCLC 17
See also CA 117; 155; DLB 36, 162
Bentham, Jeremy 1748-1832 .... NCLC 38
See also DLB 107, 158
Bentley, E(dmund) C(lerihew) 1875-1956
TCLC 12
See also CA 108; DLB 70
Bentley, Eric (Russell) 1916- .... CLC 24
See also CA 5-8R; CANR 6, 67; INT CANR-6
Beranger, Pierre Jean de 1780-1857NCLC 34
Berdyaev, Nicolas
See Berdyaev, Nikolai (Aleksandrovich)
Berdyaev, Nikolai (Aleksandrovich) 1874-1948
TCLC 67
See also CA 120; 157
Berdyayev, Nikolai (Aleksandrovich)
See Berdyaev, Nikolai (Aleksandrovich)
Berendt, John (Lawrence) 1939- ..... CLC 86
See also CA 146
Beresford, J(ohn) D(avys) 1873-1947 . T C L C
81
See also CA 112; 155; DLB 162, 178, 197
Bergelson, David 1884-1952 .... TCLC 81
Berger, Colonel
See Malraux, (Georges-)Andre
Berger, John (Peter) 1926- .... CLC 2, 19
See also CA 81-84; CANR 51; DLB 14
Berger, Melvin H. 1927-................... CLC 12
See also CA 5-8R; CANR 4; CLR 32; SAAS 2;
SATA 5, 88
Berger, Thomas (Louis) 1924-CLC 3, 5, 8, 11,
18, 38; DAM NOV
See also CA 1-4R; CANR 5, 28, 51; DLB 2;
DLBY 80; INT CANR-28; MTCW 1
Bergman, (Ernst) Ingmar 1918- CLC 16, 72
See also CA 81-84; CANR 33, 70
Bergson, Henri(-Louis) 1859-1941 TCLC 32
See also CA 164
Bergstein, Eleanor 1938- ....CLC 4
See also CA 53-56; CANR 5
Berkoff, Steven 1937-........................ CLC 56
See also CA 104; CANR 72
Bermant, Chaim (Icyk) 1929- .... CLC 40
See also CA 57-60; CANR 6, 31, 57
Bern, Victoria
See Fisher, M(ary) F(rances) K(ennedy)
Bernanos, (Paul Louis) Georges 1888-1948
TCLC 3
See also CA 104; 130; DLB 72
Bernard, April 1956-........................ CLC 59
See also CA 131
Berne, Victoria
See Fisher, M(ary) F(rances) K(ennedy)
Bernhard, Thomas 1931-1989 CLC 3, 32, 61
See also CA 85-88; 127; CANR 32, 57; DLB
85, 124; MTCW 1
Bernhardt, Sarah (Henriette Rosine) 1844-1923
TCLC 75
See also CA 157

See also CDBLB 1832-1890; DLB 32, 163;
    YABC 1

Browning, Tod 1882-1962 .... **CLC 16**
    See also CA 141; 117

Brownson, Orestes Augustus 1803-1876
    NCLC 50
    See also DLB 1, 59, 73

Bruccoli, Matthew J(oseph) 1931-... **CLC 34**
    See also CA 9-12R; CANR 7; DLB 103

Bruce, Lenny .... **CLC 21**
    See also Schneider, Leonard Alfred

Bruin, John
    See Brutus, Dennis

Brulard, Henri
    See Stendhal

Brulls, Christian
    See Simenon, Georges (Jacques Christian)

Brunner, John (Kilian Houston) 1934-1995
    CLC 8, 10; DAM POP
    See also CA 1-4R; 149; CAAS 8; CANR 2, 37;
    MTCW 1

Bruno, Giordano 1548-1600 .... **LC 27**

Brutus, Dennis 1924- **CLC 43; BLC 1; DAM
    MULT, POET; PC 24**
    See also BW 2; CA 49-52; CAAS 14; CANR 2,
    27, 42; DLB 117

Bryan, C(ourtlandt) D(ixon) B(arnes) 1936-
    CLC 29
    See also CA 73-76; CANR 13, 68; DLB 185;
    INT CANR-13

Bryan, Michael
    See Moore, Brian

Bryant, William Cullen 1794-1878 . **NCLC 6,
    46; DA; DAB; DAC; DAM MST, POET;
    PC 20**
    See also CDALB 1640-1865; DLB 3, 43, 59,
    189

Bryusov, Valery Yakovlevich 1873-1924
    TCLC 10
    See also CA 107; 155

Buchan, John 1875-1940 .... **TCLC 41; DAB;
    DAM POP**
    See also CA 108; 145; DLB 34, 70, 156; YABC
    2

Buchanan, George 1506-1582 .... **LC 4**
    See also DLB 152

Buchheim, Lothar-Guenther 1918- .... **CLC 6**
    See also CA 85-88

Buchner, (Karl) Georg 1813-1837 . **NCLC 26**

Buchwald, Art(hur) 1925- .... **CLC 33**
    See also AITN 1; CA 5-8R; CANR 21, 67;
    MTCW 1; SATA 10

Buck, Pearl S(ydenstricker) 1892-1973 **CLC 7,
    11, 18; DA; DAB; DAC; DAM MST, NOV**
    See also AITN 1; CA 1-4R; 41-44R; CANR 1,
    34; DLB 9, 102; MTCW 1; SATA 1, 25

Buckler, Ernest 1908-1984 .... **CLC 13; DAC;
    DAM MST**
    See also CA 11-12; 114; CAP 1; DLB 68; SATA
    47

Buckley, Vincent (Thomas) 1925-1988 **CLC 57**
    See also CA 101

Buckley, William F(rank), Jr. 1925- **CLC 7, 18,
    37; DAM POP**
    See also AITN 1; CA 1-4R; CANR 1, 24, 53;
    DLB 137; DLBY 80; INT CANR-24; MTCW
    1

Buechner, (Carl) Frederick 1926- **CLC 2, 4, 6,
    9; DAM NOV**
    See also CA 13-16R; CANR 11, 39, 64; DLBY
    80; INT CANR-11; MTCW 1

Buell, John (Edward) 1927- .... **CLC 10**
    See also CA 1-4R; CANR 71; DLB 53

Buero Vallejo, Antonio 1916- ..... **CLC 15, 46**
    See also CA 106; CANR 24, 49; HW; MTCW
    1

Bufalino, Gesualdo 1920(?)- .... **CLC 74**
    See also DLB 196

Bugayev, Boris Nikolayevich 1880-1934
    TCLC 7; PC 11
    See also Bely, Andrey
    See also CA 104; 165

Bukowski, Charles 1920-1994 **CLC 2, 5, 9, 41,
    82, 108; DAM NOV, POET; PC 18**
    See also CA 17-20R; 144; CANR 40, 62; DLB
    5, 130, 169; MTCW 1

Bulgakov, Mikhail (Afanas'evich) 1891-1940
    TCLC 2, 16; DAM DRAM, NOV; SSC 18
    See also CA 105; 152

Bulgya, Alexander Alexandrovich 1901-1956
    TCLC 53
    See also Fadeyev, Alexander
    See also CA 117

Bullins, Ed 1935- **CLC 1, 5, 7; BLC 1; DAM
    DRAM, MULT; DC 6**
    See also BW 2; CA 49-52; CAAS 16; CANR
    24, 46; DLB 7, 38; MTCW 1

Bulwer-Lytton, Edward (George Earle Lytton)
    1803-1873 .... **NCLC 1, 45**
    See also DLB 21

Bunin, Ivan Alexeyevich 1870-1953 **TCLC 6;
    SSC 5**
    See also CA 104

Bunting, Basil 1900-1985 ..... **CLC 10, 39, 47;
    DAM POET**
    See also CA 53-56; 115; CANR 7; DLB 20

Bunuel, Luis 1900-1983 .. **CLC 16, 80; DAM
    MULT; HLC**
    See also CA 101; 110; CANR 32; HW

Bunyan, John 1628-1688 ... **LC 4; DA; DAB;
    DAC; DAM MST; WLC**
    See also CDBLB 1660-1789; DLB 39

Burckhardt, Jacob (Christoph) 1818-1897
    NCLC 49

Burford, Eleanor
    See Hibbert, Eleanor Alice Burford

**Burgess, Anthony CLC 1, 2, 4, 5, 8, 10, 13, 15,
    22, 40, 62, 81, 94; DAB**
    See also Wilson, John (Anthony) Burgess
    See also AAYA 25; AITN 1; CDBLB 1960 to
    Present; DLB 14, 194

Burke, Edmund 1729(?)-1797 **LC 7, 36; DA;
    DAB; DAC; DAM MST; WLC**
    See also DLB 104

Burke, Kenneth (Duva) 1897-1993 **CLC 2, 24**
    See also CA 5-8R; 143; CANR 39; DLB 45,
    63; MTCW 1

Burke, Leda
    See Garnett, David

Burke, Ralph
    See Silverberg, Robert

Burke, Thomas 1886-1945 .... **TCLC 63**
    See also CA 113; 155; DLB 197

Burney, Fanny 1752-1840 .... **NCLC 12, 54**
    See also DLB 39

Burns, Robert 1759-1796 .... **PC 6**
    See also CDBLB 1789-1832; DA; DAB; DAC;
    DAM MST, POET; DLB 109; WLC

Burns, Tex
    See L'Amour, Louis (Dearborn)

Burnshaw, Stanley 1906- .... **CLC 3, 13, 44**
    See also CA 9-12R; DLB 48; DLBY 97

Burr, Anne 1937- .... **CLC 6**
    See also CA 25-28R

Burroughs, Edgar Rice 1875-1950 . **TCLC 2,
    32; DAM NOV**

See also AAYA 11; CA 104; 132; DLB 8;
    MTCW 1; SATA 41

Burroughs, William S(eward) 1914-1997 **CLC
    1, 2, 5, 15, 22, 42, 75, 109; DA; DAB; DAC;
    DAM MST, NOV, POP; WLC**
    See also AITN 2; CA 9-12R; 160; CANR 20,
    52; DLB 2, 8, 16, 152; DLBY 81, 97; MTCW
    1

Burton, Richard F. 1821-1890 .... **NCLC 42**
    See also DLB 55, 184

Busch, Frederick 1941- ..... **CLC 7, 10, 18, 47**
    See also CA 33-36R; CAAS 1; CANR 45; DLB
    6

Bush, Ronald 1946- .... **CLC 34**
    See also CA 136

Bustos, F(rancisco)
    See Borges, Jorge Luis

Bustos Domecq, H(onorio)
    See Bioy Casares, Adolfo; Borges, Jorge Luis

Butler, Octavia E(stelle) 1947- **CLC 38; BLCS;
    DAM MULT, POP**
    See also AAYA 18; BW 2; CA 73-76; CANR
    12, 24, 38; DLB 33; MTCW 1; SATA 84

Butler, Robert Olen (Jr.) 1945- **CLC 81; DAM
    POP**
    See also CA 112; CANR 66; DLB 173; INT 112

Butler, Samuel 1612-1680 .... **LC 16, 43**
    See also DLB 101, 126

Butler, Samuel 1835-1902 . **TCLC 1, 33; DA;
    DAB; DAC; DAM MST, NOV; WLC**
    See also CA 143; CDBLB 1890-1914; DLB 18,
    57, 174

Butler, Walter C.
    See Faust, Frederick (Schiller)

Butor, Michel (Marie Francois) 1926- **CLC 1,
    3, 8, 11, 15**
    See also CA 9-12R; CANR 33, 66; DLB 83;
    MTCW 1

Butts, Mary 1892(?)-1937 .... **TCLC 77**
    See also CA 148

Buzo, Alexander (John) 1944- .... **CLC 61**
    See also CA 97-100; CANR 17, 39, 69

Buzzati, Dino 1906-1972 .... **CLC 36**
    See also CA 160; 33-36R; DLB 177

Byars, Betsy (Cromer) 1928- .... **CLC 35**
    See also AAYA 19; CA 33-36R; CANR 18, 36,
    57; CLR 1, 16; DLB 52; INT CANR-18;
    JRDA; MAICYA; MTCW 1; SAAS 1; SATA
    4, 46, 80

Byatt, A(ntonia) S(usan Drabble) 1936- **C L C
    19, 65; DAM NOV, POP**
    See also CA 13-16R; CANR 13, 33, 50; DLB
    14, 194; MTCW 1

Byrne, David 1952- .... **CLC 26**
    See also CA 127

Byrne, John Keyes 1926-
    See Leonard, Hugh
    See also CA 102; INT 102

Byron, George Gordon (Noel) 1788-1824
    **NCLC 2, 12; DA; DAB; DAC; DAM MST,
    POET; PC 16; WLC**
    See also CDBLB 1789-1832; DLB 96, 110

Byron, Robert 1905-1941 .... **TCLC 67**
    See also CA 160; DLB 195

C. 3. 3.
    See Wilde, Oscar (Fingal O'Flahertie Wills)

Caballero, Fernan 1796-1877 .... **NCLC 10**

Cabell, Branch
    See Cabell, James Branch

Cabell, James Branch 1879-1958 .... **TCLC 6**
    See also CA 105; 152; DLB 9, 78

Cable, George Washington 1844-1925 **T C L C
    4; SSC 4**

Author Index

See also CA 104; 155; DLB 12, 74; DLBD 13

Cabral de Melo Neto, Joao 1920- ... **CLC 76; DAM MULT**
   See also CA 151

Cabrera Infante, G(uillermo) 1929- .. **CLC 5, 25, 45; DAM MULT; HLC**
   See also CA 85-88; CANR 29, 65; DLB 113; HW; MTCW 1

Cade, Toni
   See Bambara, Toni Cade

Cadmus and Harmonia
   See Buchan, John

Caedmon fl. 658-680 .... **CMLC 7**
   See also DLB 146

Caeiro, Alberto
   See Pessoa, Fernando (Antonio Nogueira)

Cage, John (Milton, Jr.) 1912- .... **CLC 41**
   See also CA 13-16R; CANR 9; DLB 193; INT CANR-9

Cahan, Abraham 1860-1951 .... **TCLC 71**
   See also CA 108; 154; DLB 9, 25, 28

Cain, G.
   See Cabrera Infante, G(uillermo)

Cain, Guillermo
   See Cabrera Infante, G(uillermo)

Cain, James M(allahan) 1892-1977CLC 3, 11, 28
   See also AITN 1, CA 17-20R, 73-76, CANR 8, 34, 61; MTCW 1

Caine, Mark
   See Raphael, Frederic (Michael)

Calasso, Roberto 1941- .... **CLC 81**
   See also CA 143

Calderon de la Barca, Pedro 1600-1681 . **LC 23; DC 3**

Caldwell, Erskine (Preston) 1903-1987CLC 1, 8, 14, 50, 60; DAM NOV; SSC 19
   See also AITN 1; CA 1-4R; 121; CAAS 1; CANR 2, 33; DLB 9, 86; MTCW 1

Caldwell, (Janet Miriam) Taylor (Holland) 1900-1985CLC 2, 28, 39; DAM NOV, POP
   See also CA 5-8R; 116; CANR 5; DLBD 17

Calhoun, John Caldwell 1782-1850NCLC 15
   See also DLB 3

Calisher, Hortense 1911-CLC 2, 4, 8, 38; DAM NOV; SSC 15
   See also CA 1-4R; CANR 1, 22, 67; DLB 2; INT CANR-22; MTCW 1

Callaghan, Morley Edward 1903-1990CLC 3, 14, 41, 65; DAC; DAM MST
   See also CA 9-12R; 132; CANR 33; DLB 68; MTCW 1

Callimachus c. 305B.C.-c. 240B.C. **CMLC 18**
   See also DLB 176

Calvin, John 1509-1564 .... **LC 37**

Calvino, Italo 1923-1985CLC 5, 8, 11, 22, 33, 39, 73; DAM NOV; SSC 3
   See also CA 85-88; 116; CANR 23, 61; DLB 196; MTCW 1

Cameron, Carey 1952- .... **CLC 59**
   See also CA 135

Cameron, Peter 1959- .... **CLC 44**
   See also CA 125; CANR 50

Campana, Dino 1885-1932 .... **TCLC 20**
   See also CA 117; DLB 114

Campanella, Tommaso 1568-1639 ...... **LC 32**

Campbell, John W(ood, Jr.) 1910-1971 **C L C 32**
   See also CA 21-22; 29-32R; CANR 34; CAP 2; DLB 8; MTCW 1

Campbell, Joseph 1904-1987 .... **CLC 69**
   See also AAYA 3; BEST 89:2; CA 1-4R; 124; CANR 3, 28, 61; MTCW 1

Campbell, Maria 1940- .... **CLC 85; DAC**
   See also CA 102; CANR 54; NNAL

Campbell, (John) Ramsey 1946-CLC 42; SSC 19
   See also CA 57-60; CANR 7; INT CANR-7

Campbell, (Ignatius) Roy (Dunnachie) 1901-1957 .... **TCLC 5**
   See also CA 104; 155; DLB 20

Campbell, Thomas 1777-1844 .... **NCLC 19**
   See also DLB 93; 144

Campbell, Wilfred .... **TCLC 9**
   See also Campbell, William

Campbell, William 1858(?)-1918
   See Campbell, Wilfred
   See also CA 106; DLB 92

Campion, Jane .... **CLC 95**
   See also CA 138

Campos, Alvaro de
   See Pessoa, Fernando (Antonio Nogueira)

Camus, Albert 1913-1960CLC 1, 2, 4, 9, 11, 14, 32, 63, 69; DA; DAB; DAC; DAM DRAM, MST, NOV; DC 2; SSC 9; WLC
   See also CA 89-92; DLB 72; MTCW 1

Canby, Vincent 1924- .... **CLC 13**
   See also CA 81-84

Cancale
   See Desnos, Robert

Canetti, Elias 1905-1994CLC 3, 14, 25, 75, 86
   See also CA 21-24R; 146; CANR 23, 61; DLB 85, 124; MTCW 1

Canin, Ethan 1960- .... **CLC 55**
   See also CA 131; 135

Cannon, Curt
   See Hunter, Evan

Cao, Lan 1961- .... **CLC 109**
   See also CA 165

Cape, Judith
   See Page, P(atricia) K(athleen)

Capek, Karel 1890-1938 ... **TCLC 6, 37; DA; DAB; DAC; DAM DRAM, MST, NOV; DC 1; WLC**
   See also CA 104; 140

Capote, Truman 1924-1984CLC 1, 3, 8, 13, 19, 34, 38, 58; DA; DAB; DAC; DAM MST, NOV, POP; SSC 2; WLC
   See also CA 5-8R; 113; CANR 18, 62; CDALB 1941-1968; DLB 2, 185; DLBY 80, 84; MTCW 1; SATA 91

Capra, Frank 1897-1991 .... **CLC 16**
   See also CA 61-64; 135

Caputo, Philip 1941- .... **CLC 32**
   See also CA 73-76; CANR 40

Caragiale, Ion Luca 1852-1912 ...... **TCLC 76**
   See also CA 157

Card, Orson Scott 1951-CLC 44, 47, 50; DAM POP
   See also AAYA 11; CA 102; CANR 27, 47; INT CANR-27; MTCW 1; SATA 83

Cardenal, Ernesto 1925- .... **CLC 31; DAM MULT, POET; HLC; PC 22**
   See also CA 49-52; CANR 2, 32, 66; HW; MTCW 1

Cardozo, Benjamin N(athan) 1870-1938 **TCLC 65**
   See also CA 117; 164

Carducci, Giosue (Alessandro Giuseppe) 1835-1907 .... **TCLC 32**
   See also CA 163

Carew, Thomas 1595(?)-1640 .... **LC 13**
   See also DLB 126

Carey, Ernestine Gilbreth 1908- .... **CLC 17**
   See also CA 5-8R; CANR 71; SATA 2

Carey, Peter 1943- .... **CLC 40, 55, 96**

See also CA 123; 127; CANR 53; INT 127; MTCW 1; SATA 94

Carleton, William 1794-1869 .... **NCLC 3**
   See also DLB 159

Carlisle, Henry (Coffin) 1926- .... **CLC 33**
   See also CA 13-16R; CANR 15

Carlsen, Chris
   See Holdstock, Robert P.

Carlson, Ron(ald F.) 1947- .... **CLC 54**
   See also CA 105; CANR 27

Carlyle, Thomas 1795-1881 . **NCLC 70; DA; DAB; DAC; DAM MST**
   See also CDBLB 1789-1832; DLB 55; 144

Carman, (William) Bliss 1861-1929 **TCLC 7; DAC**
   See also CA 104; 152; DLB 92

Carnegie, Dale 1888-1955 .... **TCLC 53**

Carossa, Hans 1878-1956 .... **TCLC 48**
   See also DLB 66

Carpenter, Don(ald Richard) 1931-1995**C L C 41**
   See also CA 45-48; 149; CANR 1, 71

Carpentier (y Valmont), Alejo 1904-1980CLC 8, 11, 38, 110; DAM MULT; HLC
   See also CA 65-68; 97-100; CANR 11, 70; DLB 113; HW

Carr, Caleb 1955(?)- .... **CLC 86**
   See also CA 147

Carr, Emily 1871-1945 .... **TCLC 32**
   See also CA 159; DLB 68

Carr, John Dickson 1906-1977 .... **CLC 3**
   See also Fairbairn, Roger
   See also CA 49-52; 69-72; CANR 3, 33, 60; MTCW 1

Carr, Philippa
   See Hibbert, Eleanor Alice Burford

Carr, Virginia Spencer 1929- .... **CLC 34**
   See also CA 61-64; DLB 111

Carrere, Emmanuel 1957- .... **CLC 89**

Carrier, Roch 1937-CLC 13, 78; DAC; DAM MST
   See also CA 130; CANR 61; DLB 53

Carroll, James P. 1943(?)- .... **CLC 38**
   See also CA 81-84

Carroll, Jim 1951- .... **CLC 35**
   See also AAYA 17; CA 45-48; CANR 42

Carroll, Lewis .... **NCLC 2, 53; PC 18; WLC**
   See also Dodgson, Charles Lutwidge
   See also CDBLB 1832-1890; CLR 2, 18; DLB 18, 163, 178; JRDA

Carroll, Paul Vincent 1900-1968 ...... **CLC 10**
   See also CA 9-12R; 25-28R; DLB 10

Carruth, Hayden 1921- **CLC 4, 7, 10, 18, 84; PC 10**
   See also CA 9-12R; CANR 4, 38, 59; DLB 5, 165; INT CANR-4; MTCW 1; SATA 47

Carson, Rachel Louise 1907-1964 .. **CLC 71; DAM POP**
   See also CA 77-80; CANR 35; MTCW 1; SATA 23

Carter, Angela (Olive) 1940-1992 **CLC 5, 41, 76; SSC 13**
   See also CA 53-56; 136; CANR 12, 36, 61; DLB 14; MTCW 1; SATA 66; SATA-Obit 70

Carter, Nick
   See Smith, Martin Cruz

Carver, Raymond 1938-1988 **CLC 22, 36, 53, 55; DAM NOV; SSC 8**
   See also CA 33-36R; 126; CANR 17, 34, 61; DLB 130; DLBY 84, 88; MTCW 1

Cary, Elizabeth, Lady Falkland 1585-1639 **LC 30**

Cary, (Arthur) Joyce (Lunel) 1888-1957

TCLC 1, 29
See also CA 104; 164; CDBLB 1914-1945;
DLB 15, 100

Casanova de Seingalt, Giovanni Jacopo 1725-
1798 .... **LC 13**

Casares, Adolfo Bioy
See Bioy Casares, Adolfo

Casely-Hayford, J(oseph) E(phraim) 1866-1930
TCLC 24; BLC 1; DAM MULT
See also BW 2; CA 123; 152

Casey, John (Dudley) 1939- .... **CLC 59**
See also BEST 90:2; CA 69-72; CANR 23

Casey, Michael 1947- .... **CLC 2**
See also CA 65-68; DLB 5

Casey, Patrick
See Thurman, Wallace (Henry)

Casey, Warren (Peter) 1935-1988 .... **CLC 12**
See also CA 101; 127; INT 101

Casona, Alejandro .... **CLC 49**
See also Alvarez, Alejandro Rodriguez

Cassavetes, John 1929-1989 .... **CLC 20**
See also CA 85-88; 127

Cassian, Nina 1924- .... **PC 17**

Cassill, R(onald) V(erlin) 1919- ... **CLC 4, 23**
See also CA 9-12R; CAAS 1; CANR 7, 45; DLB
6

Cassirer, Ernst 1874-1945 .... **TCLC 61**
See also CA 157

Cassity, (Allen) Turner 1929- .... **CLC 6, 42**
See also CA 17-20R; CAAS 8; CANR 11; DLB
105

Castaneda, Carlos 1931(?)- .... **CLC 12**
See also CA 25-28R; CANR 32, 66; HW;
MTCW 1

Castedo, Elena 1937- .... **CLC 65**
See also CA 132

Castedo-Ellerman, Elena
See Castedo, Elena

Castellanos, Rosario 1925-1974 **CLC 66; DAM
MULT; HLC**
See also CA 131; 53-56; CANR 58; DLB 113;
HW

Castelvetro, Lodovico 1505-1571 .... **LC 12**

Castiglione, Baldassare 1478-1529 ..... **LC 12**

Castle, Robert
See Hamilton, Edmond

Castro, Guillen de 1569-1631 .... **LC 19**

Castro, Rosalia de 1837-1885 **NCLC 3; DAM
MULT**

Cather, Willa
See Cather, Willa Sibert

Cather, Willa Sibert 1873-1947. **TCLC 1, 11,
31; DA; DAB; DAC; DAM MST, NOV;
SSC 2; WLC**
See also AAYA 24; CA 104; 128; CDALB 1865-
1917; DLB 9, 54, 78; DLBD 1; MTCW 1;
SATA 30

Catherine, Saint 1347-1380 .... **CMLC 27**

Cato, Marcus Porcius 234B.C.-149B.C.
CMLC 21

Catton, (Charles) Bruce 1899-1978. **CLC 35**
See also AITN 1; CA 5-8R; 81-84; CANR 7;
DLB 17; SATA 2; SATA-Obit 24

Catullus c. 84B.C.-c. 54B.C. .... **CMLC 18**

Cauldwell, Frank
See King, Francis (Henry)

Caunitz, William J. 1933-1996 .... **CLC 34**
See also BEST 89:3; CA 125; 130; 152; INT
130

Causley, Charles (Stanley) 1917- .... **CLC 7**
See also CA 9-12R; CANR 5, 35; CLR 30; DLB
27; MTCW 1; SATA 3, 66

Caute, (John) David 1936- ..... **CLC 29; DAM**

NOV
See also CA 1-4R; CAAS 4; CANR 1, 33, 64;
DLB 14

Cavafy, C(onstantine) P(eter) 1863-1933
TCLC 2, 7; DAM POET
See also Kavafis, Konstantinos Petrou
See also CA 148

Cavallo, Evelyn
See Spark, Muriel (Sarah)

Cavanna, Betty .... **CLC 12**
See also Harrison, Elizabeth Cavanna
See also JRDA; MAICYA; SAAS 4; SATA 1,
30

Cavendish, Margaret Lucas 1623-1673 **LC 30**
See also DLB 131

Caxton, William 1421(?)-1491(?) .... **LC 17**
See also DLB 170

Cayer, D. M.
See Duffy, Maureen

Cayrol, Jean 1911- .... **CLC 11**
See also CA 89-92; DLB 83

Cela, Camilo Jose 1916- **CLC 4, 13, 59; DAM
MULT; HLC**
See also BEST 90:2; CA 21-24R; CAAS 10;
CANR 21, 32; DLBY 89; HW; MTCW 1

Celan, Paul .... **CLC 10, 19, 53, 82; PC 10**
See also Antschel, Paul
See also DLB 69

Celine, Louis-Ferdinand **CLC 1, 3, 4, 7, 9, 15,
47**
See also Destouches, Louis-Ferdinand
See also DLB 72

Cellini, Benvenuto 1500-1571 .... **LC 7**

Cendrars, Blaise 1887-1961 ..... **CLC 18, 106**
See also Sauser-Hall, Frederic

Cernuda (y Bidon), Luis 1902-1963 **CLC 54;
DAM POET**
See also CA 131; 89-92; DLB 134; HW

Cervantes (Saavedra), Miguel de 1547-1616
**LC 6, 23; DA; DAB; DAC; DAM MST,
NOV; SSC 12; WLC**

Cesaire, Aime (Fernand) 1913- . **CLC 19, 32,
112; BLC 1; DAM MULT, POET**
See also BW 2; CA 65-68; CANR 24, 43;
MTCW 1

Chabon, Michael 1963- .... **CLC 55**
See also CA 139; CANR 57

Chabrol, Claude 1930- .... **CLC 16**
See also CA 110

Challans, Mary 1905-1983
See Renault, Mary
See also CA 81-84; 111; SATA 23; SATA-Obit
36

Challis, George
See Faust, Frederick (Schiller)

Chambers, Aidan 1934- .... **CLC 35**
See also AAYA 27; CA 25-28R; CANR 12, 31,
58; JRDA; MAICYA; SAAS 12; SATA 1, 69

Chambers, James 1948-
See Cliff, Jimmy
See also CA 124

Chambers, Jessie
See Lawrence, D(avid) H(erbert Richards)

Chambers, Robert W(illiam) 1865-1933
TCLC 41
See also CA 165; DLB 202

Chandler, Raymond (Thornton) 1888-1959
TCLC 1, 7; SSC 23
See also AAYA 25; CA 104; 129; CANR 60;
CDALB 1929-1941; DLBD 6; MTCW 1

Chang, Eileen 1920-1995 .... **SSC 28**
See also CA 166

Chang, Jung 1952- .... **CLC 71**

See also CA 142

Chang Ai-Ling
See Chang, Eileen

Channing, William Ellery 1780-1842 . **NCLC
17**
See also DLB 1, 59

Chaplin, Charles Spencer 1889-1977 **CLC 16**
See also Chaplin, Charlie
See also CA 81-84; 73-76

Chaplin, Charlie
See Chaplin, Charles Spencer
See also DLB 44

Chapman, George 1559(?)-1634 **LC 22; DAM
DRAM**
See also DLB 62, 121

Chapman, Graham 1941-1989 .... **CLC 21**
See also Monty Python
See also CA 116; 129; CANR 35

Chapman, John Jay 1862-1933 .... **TCLC 7**
See also CA 104

Chapman, Lee
See Bradley, Marion Zimmer

Chapman, Walker
See Silverberg, Robert

Chappell, Fred (Davis) 1936- ..... **CLC 40, 78**
See also CA 5-8R; CAAS 4; CANR 8, 33, 67;
DLB 6, 105

Char, Rene(-Emile) 1907-1988 **CLC 9, 11, 14,
55; DAM POET**
See also CA 13-16R; 124; CANR 32; MTCW 1

Charby, Jay
See Ellison, Harlan (Jay)

Chardin, Pierre Teilhard de
See Teilhard de Chardin, (Marie Joseph) Pierre

Charles I 1600-1649 .... **LC 13**

Charriere, Isabelle de 1740-1805 ... **NCLC 66**

Charyn, Jerome 1937- .... **CLC 5, 8, 18**
See also CA 5-8R; CAAS 1; CANR 7, 61;
DLBY 83; MTCW 1

Chase, Mary (Coyle) 1907-1981 .... **DC 1**
See also CA 77-80; 105; SATA 17; SATA-Obit
29

Chase, Mary Ellen 1887-1973 .... **CLC 2**
See also CA 13-16; 41-44R; CAP 1; SATA 10

Chase, Nicholas
See Hyde, Anthony

Chateaubriand, Francois Rene de 1768-1848
NCLC 3
See also DLB 119

Chatterje, Sarat Chandra 1876-1936(?)
See Chatterji, Saratchandra
See also CA 109

Chatterji, Bankim Chandra 1838-1894 **NCLC
19**

Chatterji, Saratchandra .... **TCLC 13**
See also Chatterje, Sarat Chandra

Chatterton, Thomas 1752-1770 . **LC 3; DAM
POET**
See also DLB 109

Chatwin, (Charles) Bruce 1940-1989 **CLC 28,
57, 59; DAM POP**
See also AAYA 4; BEST 90:1; CA 85-88; 127;
DLB 194

Chaucer, Daniel
See Ford, Ford Madox

Chaucer, Geoffrey 1340(?)-1400 **LC 17; DA;
DAB; DAC; DAM MST, POET; PC 19;
WLCS**
See also CDBLB Before 1660; DLB 146

Chaviaras, Strates 1935-
See Haviaras, Stratis
See also CA 105

Chayefsky, Paddy .... **CLC 23**

DLBY 81; MTCW 1

Copeland, Stewart (Armstrong) 1952-**CLC 26**

Copernicus, Nicolaus 1473-1543 .... **LC 45**

Coppard, A(lfred) E(dgar) 1878-1957 **T C L C 5; SSC 21**
See also CA 114; 167; DLB 162; YABC 1

Coppee, Francois 1842-1908 .... **TCLC 25**

Coppola, Francis Ford 1939- .... **CLC 16**
See also CA 77-80; CANR 40; DLB 44

Corbiere, Tristan 1845-1875 .... **NCLC 43**

Corcoran, Barbara 1911- .... **CLC 17**
See also AAYA 14; CA 21-24R; CAAS 2;
CANR 11, 28, 48; CLR 50; DLB 52; JRDA;
SAAS 20; SATA 3, 77

Cordelier, Maurice
See Giraudoux, (Hippolyte) Jean

Corelli, Marie 1855-1924 .... **TCLC 51**
See also Mackay, Mary
See also DLB 34, 156

Corman, Cid 1924- .... **CLC 9**
See also Corman, Sidney
See also CAAS 2; DLB 5, 193

Corman, Sidney 1924-
See Corman, Cid
See also CA 85-88; CANR 44; DAM POET

Cormier, Robert (Edmund) 1925-**CLC 12, 30; DA; DAB; DAC; DAM MST, NOV**
See also AAYA 3, 19; CA 1-4R; CANR 5, 23;
CDALB 1968-1988; CLR 12; DLB 52; INT
CANR-23; JRDA; MAICYA; MTCW 1;
SATA 10, 45, 83

Corn, Alfred (DeWitt III) 1943- ...... **CLC 33**
See also CA 104; CAAS 25; CANR 44; DLB
120; DLBY 80

Corneille, Pierre 1606-1684 .... **LC 28; DAB; DAM MST**

Cornwell, David (John Moore) 1931- **CLC 9, 15; DAM POP**
See also le Carre, John
See also CA 5-8R; CANR 13, 33, 59; MTCW 1

Corso, (Nunzio) Gregory 1930- .... **CLC 1, 11**
See also CA 5-8R; CANR 41; DLB 5, 16;
MTCW 1

Cortazar, Julio 1914-1984**CLC 2, 3, 5, 10, 13, 15, 33, 34, 92; DAM MULT, NOV; HLC; SSC 7**
See also CA 21-24R; CANR 12, 32; DLB 113;
HW; MTCW 1

CORTES, HERNAN 1484-1547 .... **LC 31**

Corvinus, Jakob
See Raabe, Wilhelm (Karl)

Corwin, Cecil
See Kornbluth, C(yril) M.

Cosic, Dobrica 1921- .... **CLC 14**
See also CA 122; 138; DLB 181

Costain, Thomas B(ertram) 1885-1965 . **C L C 30**
See also CA 5-8R; 25-28R; DLB 9

Costantini, Humberto 1924(?)-1987 **CLC 49**
See also CA 131; 122; HW

Costello, Elvis 1955- .... **CLC 21**

Cotes, Cecil V.
See Duncan, Sara Jeannette

Cotter, Joseph Seamon Sr. 1861-1949 **T C L C 28; BLC 1; DAM MULT**
See also BW 1; CA 124; DLB 50

Couch, Arthur Thomas Quiller
See Quiller-Couch, SirArthur (Thomas)

Coulton, James
See Hansen, Joseph

Couperus, Louis (Marie Anne) 1863-1923 **TCLC 15**
See also CA 115

Coupland, Douglas 1961-**CLC 85; DAC; DAM POP**
See also CA 142; CANR 57

Court, Wesli
See Turco, Lewis (Putnam)

Courtenay, Bryce 1933- .... **CLC 59**
See also CA 138

Courtney, Robert
See Ellison, Harlan (Jay)

Cousteau, Jacques-Yves 1910-1997 ..**CLC 30**
See also CA 65-68; 159; CANR 15, 67; MTCW
1; SATA 38, 98

Cowan, Peter (Walkinshaw) 1914- ....**SSC 28**
See also CA 21-24R; CANR 9, 25, 50

Coward, Noel (Peirce) 1899-1973**CLC 1, 9, 29, 51; DAM DRAM**
See also AITN 1; CA 17-18; 41-44R; CANR
35; CAP 2; CDBLB 1914-1945; DLB 10;
MTCW 1

Cowley, Abraham 1618-1667 .... **LC 43**
See also DLB 131, 151

Cowley, Malcolm 1898-1989 .... **CLC 39**
See also CA 5-8R; 128; CANR 3, 55; DLB 4,
48; DLBY 81, 89; MTCW 1

Cowper, William 1731-1800 . **NCLC 8; DAM POET**
See also DLB 104, 109

Cox, William Trevor 1928- .... **CLC 9, 14, 71; DAM NOV**
See also Trevor, William
See also CA 9-12R; CANR 4, 37, 55; DLB 14;
INT CANR-37; MTCW 1

Coyne, P. J.
See Masters, Hilary

Cozzens, James Gould 1903-1978**CLC 1, 4, 11, 92**
See also CA 9-12R; 81-84; CANR 19; CDALB
1941-1968; DLB 9; DLBD 2; DLBY 84, 97;
MTCW 1

Crabbe, George 1754-1832 .... **NCLC 26**
See also DLB 93

Craddock, Charles Egbert
See Murfree, Mary Noailles

Craig, A. A.
See Anderson, Poul (William)

Craik, Dinah Maria (Mulock) 1826-1887
NCLC 38
See also DLB 35, 163; MAICYA; SATA 34

Cram, Ralph Adams 1863-1942 ..... **TCLC 45**
See also CA 160

Crane, (Harold) Hart 1899-1932 **TCLC 2, 5, 80; DA; DAB; DAC; DAM MST, POET; PC 3; WLC**
See also CA 104; 127; CDALB 1917-1929;
DLB 4, 48; MTCW 1

Crane, R(onald) S(almon) 1886-1967**CLC 27**
See also CA 85-88; DLB 63

Crane, Stephen (Townley) 1871-1900 **T C L C 11, 17, 32; DA; DAB; DAC; DAM MST, NOV, POET; SSC 7; WLC**
See also AAYA 21; CA 109; 140; CDALB 1865-
1917; DLB 12, 54, 78; YABC 2

Crase, Douglas 1944- .... **CLC 58**
See also CA 106

Crashaw, Richard 1612(?)-1649 .... **LC 24**
See also DLB 126

Craven, Margaret 1901-1980 . **CLC 17; DAC**
See also CA 103

Crawford, F(rancis) Marion 1854-1909**TCLC 10**
See also CA 107; 168; DLB 71

Crawford, Isabella Valancy 1850-1887**N C L C 12**

See also DLB 92

Crayon, Geoffrey
See Irving, Washington

Creasey, John 1908-1973 .... **CLC 11**
See also CA 5-8R; 41-44R; CANR 8, 59; DLB
77; MTCW 1

Crebillon, Claude Prosper Jolyot de (fils) 1707-
1777 .... **LC 28**

Credo
See Creasey, John

Credo, Alvaro J. de
See Prado (Calvo), Pedro

Creeley, Robert (White) 1926-**CLC 1, 2, 4, 8, 11, 15, 36, 78; DAM POET**
See also CA 1-4R; CAAS 10; CANR 23, 43;
DLB 5, 16, 169; DLBD 17; MTCW 1

Crews, Harry (Eugene) 1935- **CLC 6, 23, 49**
See also AITN 1; CA 25-28R; CANR 20, 57;
DLB 6, 143, 185; MTCW 1

Crichton, (John) Michael 1942-**CLC 2, 6, 54, 90; DAM NOV, POP**
See also AAYA 10; AITN 2; CA 25-28R; CANR
13, 40, 54; DLBY 81; INT CANR-13; JRDA;
MTCW 1; SATA 9, 88

Crispin, Edmund .... **CLC 22**
See also Montgomery, (Robert) Bruce
See also DLB 87

Cristofer, Michael 1945(?)- .... **CLC 28; DAM DRAM**
See also CA 110; 152; DLB 7

Croce, Benedetto 1866-1952 .... **TCLC 37**
See also CA 120; 155

Crockett, David 1786-1836 .... **NCLC 8**
See also DLB 3, 11

Crockett, Davy
See Crockett, David

Crofts, Freeman Wills 1879-1957 .. **TCLC 55**
See also CA 115; DLB 77

Croker, John Wilson 1780-1857 ..... **NCLC 10**
See also DLB 110

Crommelynck, Fernand 1885-1970 ..**CLC 75**
See also CA 89-92

Cromwell, Oliver 1599-1658 .... **LC 43**

Cronin, A(rchibald) J(oseph) 1896-1981**C L C 32**
See also CA 1-4R; 102; CANR 5; DLB 191;
SATA 47; SATA-Obit 25

Cross, Amanda
See Heilbrun, Carolyn G(old)

Crothers, Rachel 1878(?)-1958 .... **TCLC 19**
See also CA 113; DLB 7

Croves, Hal
See Traven, B.

Crow Dog, Mary (Ellen) (?)- .... **CLC 93**
See also Brave Bird, Mary
See also CA 154

Crowfield, Christopher
See Stowe, Harriet (Elizabeth) Beecher

Crowley, Aleister .... **TCLC 7**
See also Crowley, Edward Alexander

Crowley, Edward Alexander 1875-1947
See Crowley, Aleister
See also CA 104

Crowley, John 1942- .... **CLC 57**
See also CA 61-64; CANR 43; DLBY 82; SATA
65

Crud
See Crumb, R(obert)

Crumarums
See Crumb, R(obert)

Crumb, R(obert) 1943- .... **CLC 17**
See also CA 106

Crumbum

See Bosman, Herman Charles
de Brissac, Malcolm
   See Dickinson, Peter (Malcolm)
de Chardin, Pierre Teilhard
   See Teilhard de Chardin, (Marie Joseph) Pierre
Dee, John 1527-1608 .... **LC 20**
Deer, Sandra 1940- .... **CLC 45**
De Ferrari, Gabriella 1941- .... **CLC 65**
   See also CA 146
Defoe, Daniel 1660(?)-1731 **LC 1; DA; DAB;**
   DAC; DAM MST, NOV; WLC
   See also AAYA 27; CDBLB 1660-1789; DLB
   39, 95, 101; JRDA; MAICYA; SATA 22
de Gourmont, Remy(-Marie-Charles)
   See Gourmont, Remy (-Marie-Charles) de
de Hartog, Jan 1914- .... **CLC 19**
   See also CA 1-4R; CANR 1
de Hostos, E. M.
   See Hostos (y Bonilla), Eugenio Maria de
de Hostos, Eugenio M.
   See Hostos (y Bonilla), Eugenio Maria de
Deighton, Len .... **CLC 4, 7, 22, 46**
   See also Deighton, Leonard Cyril
   See also AAYA 6; BEST 89:2; CDBLB 1960 to
   Present; DLB 87
Deighton, Leonard Cyril 1929-
   See Deighton, Len
   See also CA 9-12R, CANR 19, 33, 68, DAM
   NOV, POP; MTCW 1
Dekker, Thomas 1572(?)-1632 .. **LC 22; DAM**
   DRAM
   See also CDBLB Before 1660; DLB 62, 172
Delafield, E. M. 1890-1943 .... **TCLC 61**
   See also Dashwood, Edmee Elizabeth Monica
   de la Pasture
   See also DLB 34
de la Mare, Walter (John) 1873-1956**TCLC 4,**
   53; DAB; DAC; DAM MST, POET; SSC
   14; WLC
   See also CA 163; CDBLB 1914-1945; CLR 23;
   DLB 162; SATA 16
Delaney, Franey
   See O'Hara, John (Henry)
Delaney, Shelagh 1939-**CLC 29; DAM DRAM**
   See also CA 17-20R; CANR 30, 67; CDBLB
   1960 to Present; DLB 13; MTCW 1
Delany, Mary (Granville Pendarves) 1700-1788
   LC 12
Delany, Samuel R(ay, Jr.) 1942-**CLC 8, 14, 38;**
   BLC 1; DAM MULT
   See also AAYA 24; BW 2; CA 81-84; CANR
   27, 43; DLB 8, 33; MTCW 1
De La Ramee, (Marie) Louise 1839-1908
   See Ouida
   See also SATA 20
de la Roche, Mazo 1879-1961 .... **CLC 14**
   See also CA 85-88; CANR 30; DLB 68; SATA
   64
De La Salle, Innocent
   See Hartmann, Sadakichi
Delbanco, Nicholas (Franklin) 1942- **CLC 6,**
   13
   See also CA 17-20R; CAAS 2; CANR 29, 55;
   DLB 6
del Castillo, Michel 1933- .... **CLC 38**
   See also CA 109
Deledda, Grazia (Cosima) 1875(?)-1936
   TCLC 23
   See also CA 123
Delibes, Miguel .... **CLC 8, 18**
   See also Delibes Setien, Miguel
Delibes Setien, Miguel 1920-
   See Delibes, Miguel

See also CA 45-48; CANR 1, 32; HW; MTCW
   1
DeLillo, Don 1936- **CLC 8, 10, 13, 27, 39, 54,**
   76; DAM NOV, POP
   See also BEST 89:1; CA 81-84; CANR 21; DLB
   6, 173; MTCW 1
de Lisser, H. G.
   See De Lisser, H(erbert) G(eorge)
   See also DLB 117
De Lisser, H(erbert) G(eorge) 1878-1944
   TCLC 12
   See also de Lisser, H. G.
   See also BW 2; CA 109; 152
Deloney, Thomas (?)-1600 .... **LC 41**
   See also DLB 167
Deloria, Vine (Victor), Jr. 1933- ..... **CLC 21;**
   DAM MULT
   See also CA 53-56; CANR 5, 20, 48; DLB 175;
   MTCW 1; NNAL; SATA 21
Del Vecchio, John M(ichael) 1947- ... **CLC 29**
   See also CA 110; DLBD 9
de Man, Paul (Adolph Michel) 1919-1983
   CLC 55
   See also CA 128; 111; CANR 61; DLB 67;
   MTCW 1
De Marinis, Rick 1934- .... **CLC 54**
   See also CA 57-60; CAAS 24; CANR 9, 25, 50
Dembry, R. Emmet
   See Murfree, Mary Noailles
Demby, William 1922-**CLC 53; BLC 1; DAM**
   MULT
   See also BW 1; CA 81-84; DLB 33
de Menton, Francisco
   See Chin, Frank (Chew, Jr.)
Demijohn, Thom
   See Disch, Thomas M(ichael)
de Montherlant, Henry (Milon)
   See Montherlant, Henry (Milon) de
Demosthenes 384B.C.-322B.C. ...... **CMLC 13**
   See also DLB 176
de Natale, Francine
   See Malzberg, Barry N(athaniel)
Denby, Edwin (Orr) 1903-1983 .... **CLC 48**
   See also CA 138; 110
Denis, Julio
   See Cortazar, Julio
Denmark, Harrison
   See Zelazny, Roger (Joseph)
Dennis, John 1658-1734 .... **LC 11**
   See also DLB 101
Dennis, Nigel (Forbes) 1912-1989 .... **CLC 8**
   See also CA 25-28R; 129; DLB 13, 15; MTCW
   1
Dent, Lester 1904(?)-1959 .... **TCLC 72**
   See also CA 112; 161
De Palma, Brian (Russell) 1940- .... **CLC 20**
   See also CA 109
De Quincey, Thomas 1785-1859 .... **NCLC 4**
   See also CDBLB 1789-1832; DLB 110; 144
Deren, Eleanora 1908(?)-1961
   See Deren, Maya
   See also CA 111
Deren, Maya 1917-1961 .... **CLC 16, 102**
   See also Deren, Eleanora
Derleth, August (William) 1909-1971**CLC 31**
   See also CA 1-4R; 29-32R; CANR 4; DLB 9;
   DLBD 17; SATA 5
Der Nister 1884-1950 .... **TCLC 56**
de Routisie, Albert
   See Aragon, Louis
Derrida, Jacques 1930- .... **CLC 24, 87**
   See also CA 124; 127
Derry Down Derry

See Lear, Edward
Dersonnes, Jacques
   See Simenon, Georges (Jacques Christian)
Desai, Anita 1937-**CLC 19, 37, 97; DAB; DAM**
   NOV
   See also CA 81-84; CANR 33, 53; MTCW 1;
   SATA 63
de Saint-Luc, Jean
   See Glassco, John
de Saint Roman, Arnaud
   See Aragon, Louis
Descartes, Rene 1596-1650 .... **LC 20, 35**
De Sica, Vittorio 1901(?)-1974 ....**CLC 20**
   See also CA 117
Desnos, Robert 1900-1945 .... **TCLC 22**
   See also CA 121; 151
Destouches, Louis-Ferdinand 1894-1961**C L C**
   9, 15
   See also Celine, Louis-Ferdinand
   See also CA 85-88; CANR 28; MTCW 1
de Tolignac, Gaston
   See Griffith, D(avid Lewelyn) W(ark)
Deutsch, Babette 1895-1982 ....**CLC 18**
   See also CA 1-4R; 108; CANR 4; DLB 45;
   SATA 1; SATA-Obit 33
Devenant, William 1606-1649 .... **LC 13**
Devkota, Laxmiprasad 1909-1959 . **TCLC 23**
   See also CA 123
De Voto, Bernard (Augustine) 1897-1955
   TCLC 29
   See also CA 113; 160; DLB 9
De Vries, Peter 1910-1993 **CLC 1, 2, 3, 7, 10,**
   28, 46; DAM NOV
   See also CA 17-20R; 142; CANR 41; DLB 6;
   DLBY 82; MTCW 1
Dexter, John
   See Bradley, Marion Zimmer
Dexter, Martin
   See Faust, Frederick (Schiller)
Dexter, Pete 1943- ... **CLC 34, 55; DAM POP**
   See also BEST 89:2; CA 127; 131; INT 131;
   MTCW 1
Diamano, Silmang
   See Senghor, Leopold Sedar
Diamond, Neil 1941-.........................**CLC 30**
   See also CA 108
Diaz del Castillo, Bernal 1496-1584 ... **LC 31**
di Bassetto, Corno
   See Shaw, George Bernard
Dick, Philip K(indred) 1928-1982**CLC 10, 30,**
   72; DAM NOV, POP
   See also AAYA 24; CA 49-52; 106; CANR 2,
   16; DLB 8; MTCW 1
Dickens, Charles (John Huffam) 1812-1870
   NCLC 3, 8, 18, 26, 37, 50; DA; DAB; DAC;
   DAM MST, NOV; SSC 17; WLC
   See also AAYA 23; CDBLB 1832-1890; DLB
   21, 55, 70, 159, 166; JRDA; MAICYA; SATA
   15
Dickey, James (Lafayette) 1923-1997 **CLC 1,**
   2, 4, 7, 10, 15, 47, 109; DAM NOV, POET,
   POP
   See also AITN 1, 2; CA 9-12R; 156; CABS 2;
   CANR 10, 48, 61; CDALB 1968-1988; DLB
   5, 193; DLBD 7; DLBY 82, 93, 96, 97; INT
   CANR-10; MTCW 1
Dickey, William 1928-1994 .... **CLC 3, 28**
   See also CA 9-12R; 145; CANR 24; DLB 5
Dickinson, Charles 1951- .... **CLC 49**
   See also CA 128
Dickinson, Emily (Elizabeth) 1830-1886
   NCLC 21; DA; DAB; DAC; DAM MST,
   POET; PC 1; WLC

See also CA 104; DLB 10
Gregory, J. Dennis
See Williams, John A(lfred)
Grendon, Stephen
See Derleth, August (William)
Grenville, Kate 1950- .... **CLC 61**
See also CA 118; CANR 53
Grenville, Pelham
See Wodehouse, P(elham) G(renville)
Greve, Felix Paul (Berthold Friedrich) 1879-
1948
See Grove, Frederick Philip
See also CA 104; 141; DAC; DAM MST
Grey, Zane 1872-1939 .. **TCLC 6; DAM POP**
See also CA 104; 132; DLB 9; MTCW 1
Grieg, (Johan) Nordahl (Brun) 1902-1943
TCLC 10
See also CA 107
Grieve, C(hristopher) M(urray) 1892-1978
CLC 11, 19; DAM POET
See MacDiarmid, Hugh; Pteleon
See also CA 5-8R; 85-88; CANR 33; MTCW 1
Griffin, Gerald 1803-1840 .... **NCLC 7**
See also DLB 159
Griffin, John Howard 1920-1980 .... **CLC 68**
See also AITN 1; CA 1-4R; 101; CANR 2
Griffin, Peter 1942- .... **CLC 39**
See also CA 136
Griffith, D(avid Lewelyn) W(ark) 1875(?)-1948
TCLC 68
See also CA 119; 150
Griffith, Lawrence
See Griffith, D(avid Lewelyn) W(ark)
Griffiths, Trevor 1935- .... **CLC 13, 52**
See also CA 97-100; CANR 45; DLB 13
Griggs, Sutton Elbert 1872-1930(?)**TCLC 77**
See also CA 123; DLB 50
Grigson, Geoffrey (Edward Harvey) 1905-1985
CLC 7, 39
See also CA 25-28R; 118; CANR 20, 33; DLB
27; MTCW 1
Grillparzer, Franz 1791-1872 .... **NCLC 1**
See also DLB 133
Grimble, Reverend Charles James
See Eliot, T(homas) S(tearns)
Grimke, Charlotte L(ottie) Forten 1837(?)-1914
See Forten, Charlotte L.
See also BW 1; CA 117; 124; DAM MULT,
POET
Grimm, Jacob Ludwig Karl 1785-1863**NCLC**
3
See also DLB 90; MAICYA; SATA 22
Grimm, Wilhelm Karl 1786-1859 .... **NCLC 3**
See also DLB 90; MAICYA; SATA 22
Grimmelshausen, Johann Jakob Christoffel von
1621-1676 .... **LC 6**
See also DLB 168
Grindel, Eugene 1895-1952
See Eluard, Paul
See also CA 104
Grisham, John 1955- ..... **CLC 84; DAM POP**
See also AAYA 14; CA 138; CANR 47, 69
Grossman, David 1954- .... **CLC 67**
See also CA 138
Grossman, Vasily (Semenovich) 1905-1964
CLC 41
See also CA 124; 130; MTCW 1
Grove, Frederick Philip .... **TCLC 4**
See also Greve, Felix Paul (Berthold Friedrich)
See also DLB 92
Grubb
See Crumb, R(obert)
Grumbach, Doris (Isaac) 1918-**CLC 13, 22, 64**

See also CA 5-8R; CAAS 2; CANR 9, 42, 70;
INT CANR-9
Grundtvig, Nicolai Frederik Severin 1783-1872
NCLC 1
Grunge
See Crumb, R(obert)
Grunwald, Lisa 1959- .... **CLC 44**
See also CA 120
Guare, John 1938- . **CLC 8, 14, 29, 67; DAM**
DRAM
See also CA 73-76; CANR 21, 69; DLB 7;
MTCW 1
Gudjonsson, Halldor Kiljan 1902-1998
See Laxness, Halldor
See also CA 103; 164
Guenter, Erich
See Eich, Guenter
Guest, Barbara 1920- .... **CLC 34**
See also CA 25-28R; CANR 11, 44; DLB 5,
193
Guest, Judith (Ann) 1936- . **CLC 8, 30; DAM**
NOV, POP
See also AAYA 7; CA 77-80; CANR 15; INT
CANR-15; MTCW 1
Guevara, Che .... **CLC 87; HLC**
See also Guevara (Serna), Ernesto
Guevara (Serna), Ernesto 1928-1967
See Guevara, Che
See also CA 127; 111; CANR 56; DAM MULT;
HW
Guild, Nicholas M. 1944- .... **CLC 33**
See also CA 93-96
Guillemin, Jacques
See Sartre, Jean-Paul
Guillen, Jorge 1893-1984 .... **CLC 11; DAM**
MULT, POET
See also CA 89-92; 112; DLB 108; HW
Guillen, Nicolas (Cristobal) 1902-1989 . **C L C**
48, 79; BLC 2; DAM MST, MULT, POET;
HLC; PC 23
See also BW 2; CA 116; 125; 129; HW
Guillevic, (Eugene) 1907- .... **CLC 33**
See also CA 93-96
Guillois
See Desnos, Robert
Guillois, Valentin
See Desnos, Robert
Guiney, Louise Imogen 1861-1920 **TCLC 41**
See also CA 160; DLB 54
Guiraldes, Ricardo (Guillermo) 1886-1927
TCLC 39
See also CA 131; HW; MTCW 1
Gumilev, Nikolai (Stepanovich) 1886-1921
TCLC 60
See also CA 165
Gunesekera, Romesh 1954- .... **CLC 91**
See also CA 159
Gunn, Bill .... **CLC 5**
See also Gunn, William Harrison
See also DLB 38
Gunn, Thom(son William) 1929-**CLC 3, 6, 18,**
32, 81; DAM POET
See also CA 17-20R; CANR 9, 33; CDBLB
1960 to Present; DLB 27; INT CANR-33;
MTCW 1
Gunn, William Harrison 1934(?)-1989
See Gunn, Bill
See also AITN 1; BW 1; CA 13-16R; 128;
CANR 12, 25
Gunnars, Kristjana 1948- .... **CLC 69**
See also CA 113; DLB 60
Gurdjieff, G(eorgei) I(vanovich) 1877(?)-1949
TCLC 71

See also CA 157
Gurganus, Allan 1947- .. **CLC 70; DAM POP**
See also BEST 90:1; CA 135
Gurney, A(lbert) R(amsdell), Jr. 1930- . **C L C**
32, 50, 54; DAM DRAM
See also CA 77-80; CANR 32, 64
Gurney, Ivor (Bertie) 1890-1937 ... **TCLC 33**
See also CA 167
Gurney, Peter
See Gurney, A(lbert) R(amsdell), Jr.
Guro, Elena 1877-1913 .... **TCLC 56**
Gustafson, James M(oody) 1925- .. **CLC 100**
See also CA 25-28R; CANR 37
Gustafson, Ralph (Barker) 1909- ..... **CLC 36**
See also CA 21-24R; CANR 8, 45; DLB 88
Gut, Gom
See Simenon, Georges (Jacques Christian)
Guterson, David 1956- .... **CLC 91**
See also CA 132
Guthrie, A(lfred) B(ertram), Jr. 1901-1991
CLC 23
See also CA 57-60; 134; CANR 24; DLB 6;
SATA 62; SATA-Obit 67
Guthrie, Isobel
See Grieve, C(hristopher) M(urray)
Guthrie, Woodrow Wilson 1912-1967
See Guthrie, Woody
See also CA 113; 93-96
Guthrie, Woody .... **CLC 35**
See also Guthrie, Woodrow Wilson
Guy, Rosa (Cuthbert) 1928- .... **CLC 26**
See also AAYA 4; BW 2; CA 17-20R; CANR
14, 34; CLR 13; DLB 33; JRDA; MAICYA;
SATA 14, 62
Gwendolyn
See Bennett, (Enoch) Arnold
H. D. .... **CLC 3, 8, 14, 31, 34, 73; PC 5**
See also Doolittle, Hilda
H. de V.
See Buchan, John
Haavikko, Paavo Juhani 1931- .. **CLC 18, 34**
See also CA 106
Habbema, Koos
See Heijermans, Herman
Habermas, Juergen 1929- .... **CLC 104**
See also CA 109
Habermas, Jurgen
See Habermas, Juergen
Hacker, Marilyn 1942- . **CLC 5, 9, 23, 72, 91;**
DAM POET
See also CA 77-80; CANR 68; DLB 120
Haeckel, Ernst Heinrich (Philipp August) 1834-
1919 .... **TCLC 83**
See also CA 157
Haggard, H(enry) Rider 1856-1925**TCLC 11**
See also CA 108; 148; DLB 70, 156, 174, 178;
SATA 16
Hagiosy, L.
See Larbaud, Valery (Nicolas)
Hagiwara Sakutaro 1886-1942**TCLC 60; PC**
18
Haig, Fenil
See Ford, Ford Madox
Haig-Brown, Roderick (Langmere) 1908-1976
CLC 21
See also CA 5-8R; 69-72; CANR 4, 38; CLR
31; DLB 88; MAICYA; SATA 12
Hailey, Arthur 1920-**CLC 5; DAM NOV, POP**
See also AITN 2; BEST 90:3; CA 1-4R; CANR
2, 36; DLB 88; DLBY 82; MTCW 1
Hailey, Elizabeth Forsythe 1938- ..... **CLC 40**
See also CA 93-96; CAAS 1; CANR 15, 48;
INT CANR-15

Haines, John (Meade) 1924- .... **CLC 58**
  See also CA 17-20R; CANR 13, 34; DLB 5
Hakluyt, Richard 1552-1616 .... **LC 31**
Haldeman, Joe (William) 1943- .... **CLC 61**
  See also CA 53-56; CAAS 25; CANR 6, 70,
  72; DLB 8; INT CANR-6
Haley, Alex(ander Murray Palmer) 1921-1992
  CLC 8, 12, 76; BLC 2; DA; DAB; DAC;
  DAM MST, MULT, POP
  See also AAYA 26; BW 2; CA 77-80; 136;
  CANR 61; DLB 38; MTCW 1
Haliburton, Thomas Chandler 1796-1865
  NCLC 15
  See also DLB 11, 99
Hall, Donald (Andrew, Jr.) 1928- **CLC 1, 13,**
  37, 59; DAM POET
  See also CA 5-8R; CAAS 7; CANR 2, 44, 64;
  DLB 5; SATA 23, 97
Hall, Frederic Sauser
  See Sauser-Hall, Frederic
Hall, James
  See Kuttner, Henry
Hall, James Norman 1887-1951 ..... **TCLC 23**
  See also CA 123; SATA 21
Hall, (Marguerite) Radclyffe 1886-1943
  TCLC 12
  See also CA 110; 150
Hall, Rodney 1935- .... **CLC 51**
  See also CA 109; CANR 69
Halleck, Fitz-Greene 1790-1867 .... **NCLC 47**
  See also DLB 3
Halliday, Michael
  See Creasey, John
Halpern, Daniel 1945- .... **CLC 14**
  See also CA 33-36R
Hamburger, Michael (Peter Leopold) 1924-
  CLC 5, 14
  See also CA 5-8R; CAAS 4; CANR 2, 47; DLB
  27
Hamill, Pete 1935- .... **CLC 10**
  See also CA 25-28R; CANR 18, 71
Hamilton, Alexander 1755(?)-1804 **NCLC 49**
  See also DLB 37
Hamilton, Clive
  See Lewis, C(live) S(taples)
Hamilton, Edmond 1904-1977 .... **CLC 1**
  See also CA 1-4R; CANR 3; DLB 8
Hamilton, Eugene (Jacob) Lee
  See Lee-Hamilton, Eugene (Jacob)
Hamilton, Franklin
  See Silverberg, Robert
Hamilton, Gail
  See Corcoran, Barbara
Hamilton, Mollie
  See Kaye, M(ary) M(argaret)
Hamilton, (Anthony Walter) Patrick 1904-1962
  CLC 51
  See also CA 113; DLB 10
Hamilton, Virginia 1936- .... **CLC 26; DAM**
  MULT
  See also AAYA 2, 21; BW 2; CA 25-28R;
  CANR 20, 37; CLR 1, 11, 40; DLB 33, 52;
  INT CANR-20; JRDA; MAICYA; MTCW 1;
  SATA 4, 56, 79
Hammett, (Samuel) Dashiell 1894-1961 **C L C**
  3, 5, 10, 19, 47; SSC 17
  See also AITN 1; CA 81-84; CANR 42; CDALB
  1929-1941; DLBD 6; DLBY 96; MTCW 1
Hammon, Jupiter 1711(?)-1800(?) . **NCLC 5;**
  BLC 2; DAM MULT, POET; PC 16
  See also DLB 31, 50
Hammond, Keith
  See Kuttner, Henry

Hamner, Earl (Henry), Jr. 1923- ...... **CLC 12**
  See also AITN 2; CA 73-76; DLB 6
Hampton, Christopher (James) 1946- **CLC 4**
  See also CA 25-28R; DLB 13; MTCW 1
Hamsun, Knut .... **TCLC 2, 14, 49**
  See also Pedersen, Knut
Handke, Peter 1942-**CLC 5, 8, 10, 15, 38; DAM**
  DRAM, NOV
  See also CA 77-80; CANR 33; DLB 85, 124;
  MTCW 1
Hanley, James 1901-1985 ..... **CLC 3, 5, 8, 13**
  See also CA 73-76; 117; CANR 36; DLB 191;
  MTCW 1
Hannah, Barry 1942- .... **CLC 23, 38, 90**
  See also CA 108; 110; CANR 43, 68; DLB 6;
  INT 110; MTCW 1
Hannon, Ezra
  See Hunter, Evan
Hansberry, Lorraine (Vivian) 1930-1965**CLC**
  17, 62; BLC 2; DA; DAB; DAC; DAM
  DRAM, MST, MULT; DC 2
  See also AAYA 25; BW 1; CA 109; 25-28R;
  CABS 3; CANR 58; CDALB 1941-1968;
  DLB 7, 38; MTCW 1
Hansen, Joseph 1923-.......................... **CLC 38**
  See also CA 29-32R; CAAS 17; CANR 16, 44,
  66; INT CANR-16
Hansen, Martin A(lfred) 1909-1955**TCLC 32**
  See also CA 167
Hanson, Kenneth O(stlin) 1922- .... **CLC 13**
  See also CA 53-56; CANR 7
Hardwick, Elizabeth (Bruce) 1916- **CLC 13;**
  DAM NOV
  See also CA 5-8R; CANR 3, 32, 70; DLB 6;
  MTCW 1
Hardy, Thomas 1840-1928**TCLC 4, 10, 18, 32,**
  48, 53, 72; DA; DAB; DAC; DAM MST,
  NOV, POET; PC 8; SSC 2; WLC
  See also CA 104; 123; CDBLB 1890-1914;
  DLB 18, 19, 135; MTCW 1
Hare, David 1947- .... **CLC 29, 58**
  See also CA 97-100; CANR 39; DLB 13;
  MTCW 1
Harewood, John
  See Van Druten, John (William)
Harford, Henry
  See Hudson, W(illiam) H(enry)
Hargrave, Leonie
  See Disch, Thomas M(ichael)
Harjo, Joy 1951- .... **CLC 83; DAM MULT**
  See also CA 114; CANR 35, 67; DLB 120, 175;
  NNAL
Harlan, Louis R(udolph) 1922-......... **CLC 34**
  See also CA 21-24R; CANR 25, 55
Harling, Robert 1951(?)- .... **CLC 53**
  See also CA 147
Harmon, William (Ruth) 1938-......... **CLC 38**
  See also CA 33-36R; CANR 14, 32, 35; SATA
  65
Harper, F. E. W.
  See Harper, Frances Ellen Watkins
Harper, Frances E. W.
  See Harper, Frances Ellen Watkins
Harper, Frances E. Watkins
  See Harper, Frances Ellen Watkins
Harper, Frances Ellen
  See Harper, Frances Ellen Watkins
Harper, Frances Ellen Watkins 1825-1911
  TCLC 14; BLC 2; DAM MULT, POET;
  PC 21
  See also BW 1; CA 111; 125; DLB 50
Harper, Michael S(teven) 1938- ... **CLC 7, 22**
  See also BW 1; CA 33-36R; CANR 24; DLB

41
Harper, Mrs. F. E. W.
  See Harper, Frances Ellen Watkins
Harris, Christie (Lucy) Irwin 1907- **CLC 12**
  See also CA 5-8R; CANR 6; CLR 47; DLB 88;
  JRDA; MAICYA; SAAS 10; SATA 6, 74
Harris, Frank 1856-1931 .... **TCLC 24**
  See also CA 109; 150; DLB 156, 197
Harris, George Washington 1814-1869**NCLC**
  23
  See also DLB 3, 11
Harris, Joel Chandler 1848-1908 ...**TCLC 2;**
  SSC 19
  See also CA 104; 137; CLR 49; DLB 11, 23,
  42, 78, 91; MAICYA; SATA 100; YABC 1
Harris, John (Wyndham Parkes Lucas) Beynon
  1903-1969
  See Wyndham, John
  See also CA 102; 89-92
Harris, MacDonald ....**CLC 9**
  See also Heiney, Donald (William)
Harris, Mark 1922- .... **CLC 19**
  See also CA 5-8R; CAAS 3; CANR 2, 55; DLB
  2; DLBY 80
Harris, (Theodore) Wilson 1921-..... **CLC 25**
  See also BW 2; CA 65-68; CAAS 16; CANR
  11, 27, 69; DLB 117; MTCW 1
Harrison, Elizabeth Cavanna 1909-
  See Cavanna, Betty
  See also CA 9-12R; CANR 6, 27
Harrison, Harry (Max) 1925- .... **CLC 42**
  See also CA 1-4R; CANR 5, 21; DLB 8; SATA
  4
Harrison, James (Thomas) 1937- **CLC 6, 14,**
  33, 66; SSC 19
  See also CA 13-16R; CANR 8, 51; DLBY 82;
  INT CANR-8
Harrison, Jim
  See Harrison, James (Thomas)
Harrison, Kathryn 1961- .... **CLC 70**
  See also CA 144; CANR 68
Harrison, Tony 1937- .... **CLC 43**
  See also CA 65-68; CANR 44; DLB 40; MTCW
  1
Harriss, Will(ard Irvin) 1922- .... **CLC 34**
  See also CA 111
Harson, Sley
  See Ellison, Harlan (Jay)
Hart, Ellis
  See Ellison, Harlan (Jay)
Hart, Josephine 1942(?)-**CLC 70; DAM POP**
  See also CA 138; CANR 70
Hart, Moss 1904-1961**CLC 66; DAM DRAM**
  See also CA 109; 89-92; DLB 7
Harte, (Francis) Bret(t) 1836(?)-1902**TCLC 1,**
  25; DA; DAC; DAM MST; SSC 8; WLC
  See also CA 104; 140; CDALB 1865-1917;
  DLB 12, 64, 74, 79, 186; SATA 26
Hartley, L(eslie) P(oles) 1895-1972**CLC 2, 22**
  See also CA 45-48; 37-40R; CANR 33; DLB
  15, 139; MTCW 1
Hartman, Geoffrey H. 1929- .... **CLC 27**
  See also CA 117; 125; DLB 67
Hartmann, Sadakichi 1867-1944 ... **TCLC 73**
  See also CA 157; DLB 54
Hartmann von Aue c. 1160-c. 1205**CMLC 15**
  See also DLB 138
Hartmann von Aue 1170-1210 ...... **CMLC 15**
Haruf, Kent 1943- .... **CLC 34**
  See also CA 149
Harwood, Ronald 1934-......... **CLC 32; DAM**
  DRAM, MST
  See also CA 1-4R; CANR 4, 55; DLB 13

See also CA 89-92; CANR 36; MTCW 1
Herbst, Josephine (Frey) 1897-1969 **CLC 34**
See also CA 5-8R; 25-28R; DLB 9
Hergesheimer, Joseph 1880-1954 ... **TCLC 11**
See also CA 109; DLB 102, 9
Herlihy, James Leo 1927-1993 .... **CLC 6**
See also CA 1-4R; 143; CANR 2
Hermogenes fl. c. 175- .... **CMLC 6**
Hernandez, Jose 1834-1886 .... **NCLC 17**
Herodotus c. 484B.C.-429B.C. .... **CMLC 17**
See also DLB 176
Herrick, Robert 1591-1674**LC 13; DA; DAB; DAC; DAM MST, POP; PC 9**
See also DLB 126
Herring, Guilles
See Somerville, Edith
Herriot, James 1916-1995**CLC 12; DAM POP**
See also Wight, James Alfred
See also AAYA 1; CA 148; CANR 40; SATA 86
Herrmann, Dorothy 1941- .... **CLC 44**
See also CA 107
Herrmann, Taffy
See Herrmann, Dorothy
Hersey, John (Richard) 1914-1993**CLC 1, 2, 7, 9, 40, 81, 97; DAM POP**
See also CA 17-20R; 140; CANR 33; DLB 6, 185; MTCW 1; SATA 25; SATA-Obit 76
Herzen, Aleksandr Ivanovich 1812-1870 **NCLC 10, 61**
Herzl, Theodor 1860-1904 .... **TCLC 36**
See also CA 168
Herzog, Werner 1942- .... **CLC 16**
See also CA 89-92
Hesiod c. 8th cent. B.C.- .... **CMLC 5**
See also DLB 176
Hesse, Hermann 1877-1962**CLC 1, 2, 3, 6, 11, 17, 25, 69; DA; DAB; DAC; DAM MST, NOV; SSC 9; WLC**
See also CA 17-18; CAP 2; DLB 66; MTCW 1; SATA 50
Hewes, Cady
See De Voto, Bernard (Augustine)
Heyen, William 1940- .... **CLC 13, 18**
See also CA 33-36R; CAAS 9; DLB 5
Heyerdahl, Thor 1914- .... **CLC 26**
See also CA 5-8R; CANR 5, 22, 66; MTCW 1; SATA 2, 52
Heym, Georg (Theodor Franz Arthur) 1887-1912 .... **TCLC 9**
See also CA 106
Heym, Stefan 1913- .... **CLC 41**
See also CA 9-12R; CANR 4; DLB 69
Heyse, Paul (Johann Ludwig von) 1830-1914 **TCLC 8**
See also CA 104; DLB 129
Heyward, (Edwin) DuBose 1885-1940 **TCLC 59**
See also CA 108; 157; DLB 7, 9, 45; SATA 21
Hibbert, Eleanor Alice Burford 1906-1993 **CLC 7; DAM POP**
See also BEST 90:4; CA 17-20R; 140; CANR 9, 28, 59; SATA 2; SATA-Obit 74
Hichens, Robert (Smythe) 1864-1950 . **TCLC 64**
See also CA 162; DLB 153
Higgins, George V(incent) 1939-**CLC 4, 7, 10, 18**
See also CA 77-80; CAAS 5; CANR 17, 51; DLB 2; DLBY 81; INT CANR-17; MTCW 1
Higginson, Thomas Wentworth 1823-1911 **TCLC 36**

See also CA 162; DLB 1, 64
Highet, Helen
See MacInnes, Helen (Clark)
Highsmith, (Mary) Patricia 1921-1995**CLC 2, 4, 14, 42, 102; DAM NOV, POP**
See also CA 1-4R; 147; CANR 1, 20, 48, 62; MTCW 1
Highwater, Jamake (Mamake) 1942(?)- **C L C 12**
See also AAYA 7; CA 65-68; CAAS 7; CANR 10, 34; CLR 17; DLB 52; DLBY 85; JRDA; MAICYA; SATA 32, 69; SATA-Brief 30
Highway, Tomson 1951-**CLC 92; DAC; DAM MULT**
See also CA 151; NNAL
Higuchi, Ichiyo 1872-1896 .... **NCLC 49**
Hijuelos, Oscar 1951- **CLC 65; DAM MULT, POP; HLC**
See also AAYA 25; BEST 90:1; CA 123; CANR 50; DLB 145; HW
Hikmet, Nazim 1902(?)-1963 .... **CLC 40**
See also CA 141; 93-96
Hildegard von Bingen 1098-1179 . **CMLC 20**
See also DLB 148
Hildesheimer, Wolfgang 1916-1991 ..**CLC 49**
See also CA 101; 135; DLB 69, 124
Hill, Geoffrey (William) 1932- **CLC 5, 8, 18, 45; DAM POET**
See also CA 81-84; CANR 21; CDBLB 1960 to Present; DLB 40; MTCW 1
Hill, George Roy 1921- .... **CLC 26**
See also CA 110; 122
Hill, John
See Koontz, Dean R(ay)
Hill, Susan (Elizabeth) 1942- .... **CLC 4, 113; DAB; DAM MST, NOV**
See also CA 33-36R; CANR 29, 69; DLB 14, 139; MTCW 1
Hillerman, Tony 1925- ..**CLC 62; DAM POP**
See also AAYA 6; BEST 89:1; CA 29-32R; CANR 21, 42, 65; SATA 6
Hillesum, Etty 1914-1943 .... **TCLC 49**
See also CA 137
Hilliard, Noel (Harvey) 1929- .... **CLC 15**
See also CA 9-12R; CANR 7, 69
Hillis, Rick 1956- .... **CLC 66**
See also CA 134
Hilton, James 1900-1954 .... **TCLC 21**
See also CA 108; DLB 34, 77; SATA 34
Himes, Chester (Bomar) 1909-1984**CLC 2, 4, 7, 18, 58, 108; BLC 2; DAM MULT**
See also BW 2; CA 25-28R; 114; CANR 22; DLB 2, 76, 143; MTCW 1
Hinde, Thomas .... **CLC 6, 11**
See also Chitty, Thomas Willes
Hindin, Nathan
See Bloch, Robert (Albert)
Hine, (William) Daryl 1936-.............. **CLC 15**
See also CA 1-4R; CAAS 15; CANR 1, 20; DLB 60
Hinkson, Katharine Tynan
See Tynan, Katharine
Hinton, S(usan) E(loise) 1950- **CLC 30, 111; DA; DAB; DAC; DAM MST, NOV**
See also AAYA 2; CA 81-84; CANR 32, 62; CLR 3, 23; JRDA; MAICYA; MTCW 1; SATA 19, 58
Hippius, Zinaida .... **TCLC 9**
See also Gippius, Zinaida (Nikolayevna)
Hiraoka, Kimitake 1925-1970
See Mishima, Yukio
See also CA 97-100; 29-32R; DAM DRAM; MTCW 1

Hirsch, E(ric) D(onald), Jr. 1928-.... **CLC 79**
See also CA 25-28R; CANR 27, 51; DLB 67; INT CANR-27; MTCW 1
Hirsch, Edward 1950- .... **CLC 31, 50**
See also CA 104; CANR 20, 42; DLB 120
Hitchcock, Alfred (Joseph) 1899-1980**CLC 16**
See also AAYA 22; CA 159; 97-100; SATA 27; SATA-Obit 24
Hitler, Adolf 1889-1945 .... **TCLC 53**
See also CA 117; 147
Hoagland, Edward 1932-................... **CLC 28**
See also CA 1-4R; CANR 2, 31, 57; DLB 6; SATA 51
Hoban, Russell (Conwell) 1925- . **CLC 7, 25; DAM NOV**
See also CA 5-8R; CANR 23, 37, 66; CLR 3; DLB 52; MAICYA; MTCW 1; SATA 1, 40, 78
Hobbes, Thomas 1588-1679 .... **LC 36**
See also DLB 151
Hobbs, Perry
See Blackmur, R(ichard) P(almer)
Hobson, Laura Z(ametkin) 1900-1986**CLC 7, 25**
See also CA 17-20R; 118; CANR 55; DLB 28; SATA 52
Hochhuth, Rolf 1931-...**CLC 4, 11, 18; DAM DRAM**
See also CA 5-8R; CANR 33; DLB 124; MTCW 1
Hochman, Sandra 1936- .... **CLC 3, 8**
See also CA 5-8R; DLB 5
Hochwaelder, Fritz 1911-1986**CLC 36; DAM DRAM**
See also CA 29-32R; 120; CANR 42; MTCW 1
Hochwalder, Fritz
See Hochwaelder, Fritz
Hocking, Mary (Eunice) 1921-......... **CLC 13**
See also CA 101; CANR 18, 40
Hodgins, Jack 1938- .... **CLC 23**
See also CA 93-96; DLB 60
Hodgson, William Hope 1877(?)-1918 **T C L C 13**
See also CA 111; 164; DLB 70, 153, 156, 178
Hoeg, Peter 1957- .... **CLC 95**
See also CA 151
Hoffman, Alice 1952- ... **CLC 51; DAM NOV**
See also CA 77-80; CANR 34, 66; MTCW 1
Hoffman, Daniel (Gerard) 1923-**CLC 6, 13, 23**
See also CA 1-4R; CANR 4; DLB 5
Hoffman, Stanley 1944- .... **CLC 5**
See also CA 77-80
Hoffman, William M(oses) 1939-..... **CLC 40**
See also CA 57-60; CANR 11, 71
Hoffmann, E(rnst) T(heodor) A(madeus) 1776-1822 .... **NCLC 2; SSC 13**
See also DLB 90; SATA 27
Hofmann, Gert 1931- .... **CLC 54**
See also CA 128
Hofmannsthal, Hugo von 1874-1929**TCLC 11; DAM DRAM; DC 4**
See also CA 106; 153; DLB 81, 118
Hogan, Linda 1947-... **CLC 73; DAM MULT**
See also CA 120; CANR 45; DLB 175; NNAL
Hogarth, Charles
See Creasey, John
Hogarth, Emmett
See Polonsky, Abraham (Lincoln)
Hogg, James 1770-1835 .... **NCLC 4**
See also DLB 93, 116, 159
Holbach, Paul Henri Thiry Baron 1723-1789 **LC 14**
Holberg, Ludvig 1684-1754 .... **LC 6**

Holden, Ursula 1921- .... **CLC 18**
  See also CA 101; CAAS 8; CANR 22
Holderlin, (Johann Christian) Friedrich 1770-
  1843 .... **NCLC 16; PC 4**
Holdstock, Robert
  See Holdstock, Robert P.
Holdstock, Robert P. 1948- .... **CLC 39**
  See also CA 131
Holland, Isabelle 1920- .... **CLC 21**
  See also AAYA 11; CA 21-24R; CANR 10, 25,
  47; JRDA; MAICYA; SATA 8, 70
Holland, Marcus
  See Caldwell, (Janet Miriam) Taylor (Holland)
Hollander, John 1929- .... **CLC 2, 5, 8, 14**
  See also CA 1-4R; CANR 1, 52; DLB 5; SATA
  13
Hollander, Paul
  See Silverberg, Robert
Holleran, Andrew 1943(?)- .... **CLC 38**
  See also CA 144
Hollinghurst, Alan 1954- .... **CLC 55, 91**
  See also CA 114
Hollis, Jim
  See Summers, Hollis (Spurgeon, Jr.)
Holly, Buddy 1936-1959 .... **TCLC 65**
Holmes, Gordon
  See Shiel, M(atthew) P(hipps)
Holmes, John
  See Souster, (Holmes) Raymond
Holmes, John Clellon 1926-1988 ..... **CLC 56**
  See also CA 9-12R; 125; CANR 4; DLB 16
Holmes, Oliver Wendell, Jr. 1841-1935**TCLC**
  77
  See also CA 114
Holmes, Oliver Wendell 1809-1894 **NCLC 14**
  See also CDALB 1640-1865; DLB 1, 189;
  SATA 34
Holmes, Raymond
  See Souster, (Holmes) Raymond
Holt, Victoria
  See Hibbert, Eleanor Alice Burford
Holub, Miroslav 1923- .... **CLC 4**
  See also CA 21-24R; CANR 10
Homer c. 8th cent. B.C.- ... **CMLC 1, 16; DA;**
  DAB; DAC; DAM MST, POET; PC 23;
  WLCS
  See also DLB 176
Hongo, Garrett Kaoru 1951- .... **PC 23**
  See also CA 133; CAAS 22; DLB 120
Honig, Edwin 1919- .... **CLC 33**
  See also CA 5-8R; CAAS 8; CANR 4, 45; DLB
  5
Hood, Hugh (John Blagdon) 1928-**CLC 15, 28**
  See also CA 49-52; CAAS 17; CANR 1, 33;
  DLB 53
Hood, Thomas 1799-1845 .... **NCLC 16**
  See also DLB 96
Hooker, (Peter) Jeremy 1941- .... **CLC 43**
  See also CA 77-80; CANR 22; DLB 40
hooks, bell .... **CLC 94; BLCS**
  See also Watkins, Gloria
Hope, A(lec) D(erwent) 1907- ...... **CLC 3, 51**
  See also CA 21-24R; CANR 33; MTCW 1
Hope, Anthony 1863-1933 .... **TCLC 83**
  See also CA 157; DLB 153, 156
Hope, Brian
  See Creasey, John
Hope, Christopher (David Tully) 1944- **C L C**
  52
  See also CA 106; CANR 47; SATA 62
Hopkins, Gerard Manley 1844-1889 ..**N C L**
  17; DA; DAB; DAC; DAM MST, POET;
  PC 15; WLC

See also CDBLB 1890-1914; DLB 35, 57
Hopkins, John (Richard) 1931-...........**CLC 4**
  See also CA 85-88
Hopkins, Pauline Elizabeth 1859-1930**T C L C**
  28; BLC 2; DAM MULT
  See also BW 2; CA 141; DLB 50
Hopkinson, Francis 1737-1791 .... **LC 25**
  See also DLB 31
Hopley-Woolrich, Cornell George 1903-1968
  See Woolrich, Cornell
  See also CA 13-14; CANR 58; CAP 1
Horatio
  See Proust, (Valentin-Louis-George-Eugene-)
  Marcel
Horgan, Paul (George Vincent O'Shaughnessy)
  1903-1995 .... **CLC 9, 53; DAM NOV**
  See also CA 13-16R; 147; CANR 9, 35; DLB
  102; DLBY 85; INT CANR-9; MTCW 1;
  SATA 13; SATA-Obit 84
Horn, Peter
  See Kuttner, Henry
Hornem, Horace Esq.
  See Byron, George Gordon (Noel)
Horney, Karen (Clementine Theodore
  Danielsen) 1885-1952 .... **TCLC 71**
  See also CA 114; 165
Hornung, E(rnest) W(illiam) 1866-1921
  TCLC 59
  See also CA 108; 160; DLB 70
Horovitz, Israel (Arthur) 1939-**CLC 56; DAM**
  DRAM
  See also CA 33-36R; CANR 46, 59; DLB 7
Horvath, Odon von
  See Horvath, Oedoen von
  See also DLB 85, 124
Horvath, Oedoen von 1901-1938 ... **TCLC 45**
  See also Horvath, Odon von
  See also CA 118
Horwitz, Julius 1920-1986 .... **CLC 14**
  See also CA 9-12R; 119; CANR 12
Hospital, Janette Turner 1942- .... **CLC 42**
  See also CA 108; CANR 48
Hostos, E. M. de
  See Hostos (y Bonilla), Eugenio Maria de
Hostos, Eugenio M. de
  See Hostos (y Bonilla), Eugenio Maria de
Hostos, Eugenio Maria
  See Hostos (y Bonilla), Eugenio Maria de
Hostos (y Bonilla), Eugenio Maria de 1839-1903
  TCLC 24
  See also CA 123; 131; HW
Houdini
  See Lovecraft, H(oward) P(hillips)
Hougan, Carolyn 1943-......................**CLC 34**
  See also CA 139
Household, Geoffrey (Edward West) 1900-1988
  CLC 11
  See also CA 77-80; 126; CANR 58; DLB 87;
  SATA 14; SATA-Obit 59
Housman, A(lfred) E(dward) 1859-1936
  TCLC 1, 10; DA; DAB; DAC; DAM MST,
  POET; PC 2; WLCS
  See also CA 104; 125; DLB 19; MTCW 1
Housman, Laurence 1865-1959 .... **TCLC 7**
  See also CA 106; 155; DLB 10; SATA 25
Howard, Elizabeth Jane 1923-..... **CLC 7, 29**
  See also CA 5-8R; CANR 8, 62
Howard, Maureen 1930-......... **CLC 5, 14, 46**
  See also CA 53-56; CANR 31; DLBY 83; INT
  CANR-31; MTCW 1
Howard, Richard 1929- .... **CLC 7, 10, 47**
  See also AITN 1; CA 85-88; CANR 25; DLB 5;
  INT CANR-25

Howard, Robert E(rvin) 1906-1936 **TCLC 8**
  See also CA 105; 157
Howard, Warren F.
  See Pohl, Frederik
Howe, Fanny (Quincy) 1940- ....**CLC 47**
  See also CA 117; CAAS 27; CANR 70; SATA-
  Brief 52
Howe, Irving 1920-1993 .... **CLC 85**
  See also CA 9-12R; 141; CANR 21, 50; DLB
  67; MTCW 1
Howe, Julia Ward 1819-1910 .... **TCLC 21**
  See also CA 117; DLB 1, 189
Howe, Susan 1937- ....**CLC 72**
  See also CA 160; DLB 120
Howe, Tina 1937- ....**CLC 48**
  See also CA 109
Howell, James 1594(?)-1666 .... **LC 13**
  See also DLB 151
Howells, W. D.
  See Howells, William Dean
Howells, William D.
  See Howells, William Dean
Howells, William Dean 1837-1920**TCLC 7, 17,**
  41
  See also CA 104; 134; CDALB 1865-1917;
  DLB 12, 64, 74, 79, 189
Howes, Barbara 1914-1996 .... **CLC 15**
  See also CA 9-12R; 151; CAAS 3; CANR 53;
  SATA 5
Hrabal, Bohumil 1914-1997 .... **CLC 13, 67**
  See also CA 106; 156; CAAS 12; CANR 57
Hroswitha of Gandersheim c. 935-c. 1002
  CMLC 29
  See also DLB 148
Hsun, Lu
  See Lu Hsun
Hubbard, L(afayette) Ron(ald) 1911-1986
  CLC 43; DAM POP
  See also CA 77-80; 118; CANR 52
Huch, Ricarda (Octavia) 1864-1947**TCLC 13**
  See also CA 111; DLB 66
Huddle, David 1942-..........................**CLC 49**
  See also CA 57-60; CAAS 20; DLB 130
Hudson, Jeffrey
  See Crichton, (John) Michael
Hudson, W(illiam) H(enry) 1841-1922**T C L C**
  29
  See also CA 115; DLB 98, 153, 174; SATA 35
Hueffer, Ford Madox
  See Ford, Ford Madox
Hughart, Barry 1934- ....**CLC 39**
  See also CA 137
Hughes, Colin
  See Creasey, John
Hughes, David (John) 1930- ....**CLC 48**
  See also CA 116; 129; DLB 14
Hughes, Edward James
  See Hughes, Ted
  See also DAM MST, POET
Hughes, (James) Langston 1902-1967**CLC 1,**
  5, 10, 15, 35, 44, 108; BLC 2; DA; DAB;
  DAC; DAM DRAM, MST, MULT, POET;
  DC 3; PC 1; SSC 6; WLC
  See also AAYA 12; BW 1; CA 1-4R; 25-28R;
  CANR 1, 34; CDALB 1929-1941; CLR 17;
  DLB 4, 7, 48, 51, 86; JRDA; MAICYA;
  MTCW 1; SATA 4, 33
Hughes, Richard (Arthur Warren) 1900-1976
  CLC 1, 11; DAM NOV
  See also CA 5-8R; 65-68; CANR 4; DLB 15,
  161; MTCW 1; SATA 8; SATA-Obit 25
Hughes, Ted 1930-**CLC 2, 4, 9, 14, 37; DAB;**
  DAC; PC 7

See also CDBLB 1789-1832; DLB 96, 110

Keene, Donald 1922- .... **CLC 34**
See also CA 1-4R; CANR 5

Keillor, Garrison .... **CLC 40**
See also Keillor, Gary (Edward)
See also AAYA 2; BEST 89:3; DLBY 87; SATA 58

Keillor, Gary (Edward) 1942-
See Keillor, Garrison
See also CA 111; 117; CANR 36, 59; DAM POP; MTCW 1

Keith, Michael
See Hubbard, L(afayette) Ron(ald)

Keller, Gottfried 1819-1890 **NCLC 2; SSC 26**
See also DLB 129

Keller, Nora Okja .... **CLC 109**

Kellerman, Jonathan 1949- ... **CLC 44; DAM POP**
See also BEST 90:1; CA 106; CANR 29, 51; INT CANR-29

Kelley, William Melvin 1937- .... **CLC 22**
See also BW 1; CA 77-80; CANR 27; DLB 33

Kellogg, Marjorie 1922- .... **CLC 2**
See also CA 81-84

Kellow, Kathleen
See Hibbert, Eleanor Alice Burford

Kelly, M(ilton) T(erry) 1947- .... **CLC 55**
See also CA 97-100; CAAS 22; CANR 19, 43

Kelman, James 1946- .... **CLC 58, 86**
See also CA 148; DLB 194

Kemal, Yashar 1923- .... **CLC 14, 29**
See also CA 89-92; CANR 44

Kemble, Fanny 1809-1893 .... **NCLC 18**
See also DLB 32

Kemelman, Harry 1908-1996 .... **CLC 2**
See also AITN 1; CA 9-12R; 155; CANR 6, 71; DLB 28

Kempe, Margery 1373(?)-1440(?) .... **LC 6**
See also DLB 146

Kempis, Thomas a 1380-1471 .... **LC 11**

Kendall, Henry 1839-1882 .... **NCLC 12**

Keneally, Thomas (Michael) 1935- **CLC 5, 8, 10, 14, 19, 27, 43; DAM NOV**
See also CA 85-88; CANR 10, 50; MTCW 1

Kennedy, Adrienne (Lita) 1931- **CLC 66; BLC 2; DAM MULT; DC 5**
See also BW 2; CA 103; CAAS 20; CABS 3; CANR 26, 53; DLB 38

Kennedy, John Pendleton 1795-1870 **NCLC 2**
See also DLB 3

Kennedy, Joseph Charles 1929-
See Kennedy, X. J.
See also CA 1-4R; CANR 4, 30, 40; SATA 14, 86

Kennedy, William 1928- .. **CLC 6, 28, 34, 53; DAM NOV**
See also AAYA 1; CA 85-88; CANR 14, 31; DLB 143; DLBY 85; INT CANR-31; MTCW 1; SATA 57

Kennedy, X. J. .... **CLC 8, 42**
See also Kennedy, Joseph Charles
See also CAAS 9; CLR 27; DLB 5; SAAS 22

Kenny, Maurice (Francis) 1929- ..... **CLC 87; DAM MULT**
See also CA 144; CAAS 22; DLB 175; NNAL

Kent, Kelvin
See Kuttner, Henry

Kenton, Maxwell
See Southern, Terry

Kenyon, Robert O.
See Kuttner, Henry

Kepler, Johannes 1571-1630 .... **LC 45**

Kerouac, Jack .... **CLC 1, 2, 3, 5, 14, 29, 61**

See also Kerouac, Jean-Louis Lebris de
See also AAYA 25; CDALB 1941-1968; DLB 2, 16; DLBD 3; DLBY 95

Kerouac, Jean-Louis Lebris de 1922-1969
See Kerouac, Jack
See also AITN 1; CA 5-8R; 25-28R; CANR 26, 54; DA; DAB; DAC; DAM MST, NOV, POET, POP; MTCW 1; WLC

Kerr, Jean 1923- .... **CLC 22**
See also CA 5-8R; CANR 7; INT CANR-7

Kerr, M. E. .... **CLC 12, 35**
See also Meaker, Marijane (Agnes)
See also AAYA 2, 23; CLR 29; SAAS 1

Kerr, Robert .... **CLC 55**

Kerrigan, (Thomas) Anthony 1918- **CLC 4, 6**
See also CA 49-52; CAAS 11; CANR 4

Kerry, Lois
See Duncan, Lois

Kesey, Ken (Elton) 1935- **CLC 1, 3, 6, 11, 46, 64; DA; DAB; DAC; DAM MST, NOV, POP; WLC**
See also AAYA 25; CA 1-4R; CANR 22, 38, 66; CDALB 1968-1988; DLB 2, 16; MTCW 1; SATA 66

Kesselring, Joseph (Otto) 1902-1967 **CLC 45; DAM DRAM, MST**
See also CA 150

Kessler, Jascha (Frederick) 1929- .... **CLC 4**
See also CA 17-20R; CANR 8, 48

Kettelkamp, Larry (Dale) 1933- .... **CLC 12**
See also CA 29-32R; CANR 16; SAAS 3; SATA 2

Key, Ellen 1849-1926 .... **TCLC 65**

Keyber, Conny
See Fielding, Henry

Keyes, Daniel 1927- **CLC 80; DA; DAC; DAM MST, NOV**
See also AAYA 23; CA 17-20R; CANR 10, 26, 54; SATA 37

Keynes, John Maynard 1883-1946 **TCLC 64**
See also CA 114; 162, 163; DLBD 10

Khanshendel, Chiron
See Rose, Wendy

Khayyam, Omar 1048-1131 **CMLC 11; DAM POET; PC 8**

Kherdian, David 1931- .... **CLC 6, 9**
See also CA 21-24R; CAAS 2; CANR 39; CLR 24; JRDA; MAICYA; SATA 16, 74

Khlebnikov, Velimir .... **TCLC 20**
See also Khlebnikov, Viktor Vladimirovich

Khlebnikov, Viktor Vladimirovich 1885-1922
See Khlebnikov, Velimir
See also CA 117

Khodasevich, Vladislav (Felitsianovich) 1886-1939 .... **TCLC 15**
See also CA 115

Kielland, Alexander Lange 1849-1906 **TCLC 5**
See also CA 104

Kiely, Benedict 1919- .... **CLC 23, 43**
See also CA 1-4R; CANR 2; DLB 15

Kienzle, William X(avier) 1928- ..... **CLC 25; DAM POP**
See also CA 93-96; CAAS 1; CANR 9, 31, 59; INT CANR-31; MTCW 1

Kierkegaard, Soren 1813-1855 ...... **NCLC 34**

Killens, John Oliver 1916-1987 .... **CLC 10**
See also BW 2; CA 77-80; 123; CAAS 2; CANR 26; DLB 33

Killigrew, Anne 1660-1685 .... **LC 4**
See also DLB 131

Kim
See Simenon, Georges (Jacques Christian)

Kincaid, Jamaica 1949- **CLC 43, 68; BLC 2; DAM MULT, NOV**
See also AAYA 13; BW 2; CA 125; CANR 47, 59; DLB 157

King, Francis (Henry) 1923- **CLC 8, 53; DAM NOV**
See also CA 1-4R; CANR 1, 33; DLB 15, 139; MTCW 1

King, Kennedy
See Brown, George Douglas

King, Martin Luther, Jr. 1929-1968 **CLC 83; BLC 2; DA; DAB; DAC; DAM MST, MULT; WLCS**
See also BW 2; CA 25-28; CANR 27, 44; CAP 2; MTCW 1; SATA 14

King, Stephen (Edwin) 1947- **CLC 12, 26, 37, 61, 113; DAM NOV, POP; SSC 17**
See also AAYA 1, 17; BEST 90:1; CA 61-64; CANR 1, 30, 52; DLB 143; DLBY 80; JRDA; MTCW 1; SATA 9, 55

King, Steve
See King, Stephen (Edwin)

King, Thomas 1943- .... **CLC 89; DAC; DAM MULT**
See also CA 144; DLB 175; NNAL; SATA 96

Kingman, Lee .... **CLC 17**
See also Natti, (Mary) Lee
See also SAAS 3; SATA 1, 67

Kingsley, Charles 1819-1875 .... **NCLC 35**
See also DLB 21, 32, 163, 190; YABC 2

Kingsley, Sidney 1906-1995 .... **CLC 44**
See also CA 85-88; 147; DLB 7

Kingsolver, Barbara 1955- **CLC 55, 81; DAM POP**
See also AAYA 15; CA 129; 134; CANR 60; INT 134

Kingston, Maxine (Ting Ting) Hong 1940- **CLC 12, 19, 58; DAM MULT, NOV; WLCS**
See also AAYA 8; CA 69-72; CANR 13, 38; DLB 173; DLBY 80; INT CANR-13; MTCW 1; SATA 53

Kinnell, Galway 1927- **CLC 1, 2, 3, 5, 13, 29**
See also CA 9-12R; CANR 10, 34, 66; DLB 5; DLBY 87; INT CANR-34; MTCW 1

Kinsella, Thomas 1928- .... **CLC 4, 19**
See also CA 17-20R; CANR 15; DLB 27; MTCW 1

Kinsella, W(illiam) P(atrick) 1935- **CLC 27, 43; DAC; DAM NOV, POP**
See also AAYA 7; CA 97-100; CAAS 7; CANR 21, 35, 66; INT CANR-21; MTCW 1

Kipling, (Joseph) Rudyard 1865-1936 **TCLC 8, 17; DA; DAB; DAC; DAM MST, POET; PC 3; SSC 5; WLC**
See also CA 105; 120; CANR 33; CDBLB 1890-1914; CLR 39; DLB 19, 34, 141, 156; MAICYA; MTCW 1; SATA 100; YABC 2

Kirkup, James 1918- .... **CLC 1**
See also CA 1-4R; CAAS 4; CANR 2; DLB 27; SATA 12

Kirkwood, James 1930(?)-1989 .... **CLC 9**
See also AITN 2; CA 1-4R; 128; CANR 6, 40

Kirshner, Sidney
See Kingsley, Sidney

Kis, Danilo 1935-1989 .... **CLC 57**
See also CA 109; 118; 129; CANR 61; DLB 181; MTCW 1

Kivi, Aleksis 1834-1872 .... **NCLC 30**

Kizer, Carolyn (Ashley) 1925- **CLC 15, 39, 80; DAM POET**
See also CA 65-68; CAAS 5; CANR 24, 70; DLB 5, 169

Klabund 1890-1928 .... TCLC 44
See also CA 162; DLB 66
Klappert, Peter 1942- .... CLC 57
See also CA 33-36R; DLB 5
Klein, A(braham) M(oses) 1909-1972CLC 19;
DAB; DAC; DAM MST
See also CA 101; 37-40R; DLB 68
Klein, Norma 1938-1989 .... CLC 30
See also AAYA 2; CA 41-44R; 128; CANR 15,
37; CLR 2, 19; INT CANR-15; JRDA;
MAICYA; SAAS 1; SATA 7, 57
Klein, T(heodore) E(ibon) D(onald) 1947-
CLC 34
See also CA 119; CANR 44
Kleist, Heinrich von 1777-1811 NCLC 2, 37;
DAM DRAM; SSC 22
See also DLB 90
Klima, Ivan 1931- .... CLC 56; DAM NOV
See also CA 25-28R; CANR 17, 50
Klimentov, Andrei Platonovich 1899-1951
See Platonov, Andrei
See also CA 108
Klinger, Friedrich Maximilian von 1752-1831
NCLC 1
See also DLB 94
Klingsor the Magician
See Hartmann, Sadakichi
Klopstock, Friedrich Gottlieb 1724-1803
NCLC 11
See also DLB 97
Knapp, Caroline 1959- .... CLC 99
See also CA 154
Knebel, Fletcher 1911-1993 .... CLC 14
See also AITN 1; CA 1-4R; 140; CAAS 3;
CANR 1, 36; SATA 36; SATA-Obit 75
Knickerbocker, Diedrich
See Irving, Washington
Knight, Etheridge 1931-1991CLC 40; BLC 2;
DAM POET; PC 14
See also BW 1; CA 21-24R; 133; CANR 23;
DLB 41
Knight, Sarah Kemble 1666-1727 .... LC 7
See also DLB 24, 200
Knister, Raymond 1899-1932 .... TCLC 56
See also DLB 68
Knowles, John 1926- ..CLC 1, 4, 10, 26; DA;
DAC; DAM MST, NOV
See also AAYA 10; CA 17-20R; CANR 40;
CDALB 1968-1988; DLB 6; MTCW 1;
SATA 8, 89
Knox, Calvin M.
See Silverberg, Robert
Knox, John c. 1505-1572 .... LC 37
See also DLB 132
Knye, Cassandra
See Disch, Thomas M(ichael)
Koch, C(hristopher) J(ohn) 1932- ... CLC 42
See also CA 127
Koch, Christopher
See Koch, C(hristopher) J(ohn)
Koch, Kenneth 1925- .... CLC 5, 8, 44; DAM
POET
See also CA 1-4R; CANR 6, 36, 57; DLB 5;
INT CANR-36; SATA 65
Kochanowski, Jan 1530-1584 .... LC 10
Kock, Charles Paul de 1794-1871 ..NCLC 16
Koda Shigeyuki 1867-1947
See Rohan, Koda
See also CA 121
Koestler, Arthur 1905-1983CLC 1, 3, 6, 8, 15,
33
See also CA 1-4R; 109; CANR 1, 33; CDBLB
1945-1960; DLBY 83; MTCW 1

Kogawa, Joy Nozomi 1935- .. CLC 78; DAC;
DAM MST, MULT
See also CA 101; CANR 19, 62; SATA 99
Kohout, Pavel 1928- .... CLC 13
See also CA 45-48; CANR 3
Koizumi, Yakumo
See Hearn, (Patricio) Lafcadio (Tessima Carlos)
Kolmar, Gertrud 1894-1943 .... TCLC 40
See also CA 167
Komunyakaa, Yusef 1947-CLC 86, 94; BLCS
See also CA 147; DLB 120
Konrad, George
See Konrad, Gyoergy
Konrad, Gyoergy 1933- .... CLC 4, 10, 73
See also CA 85-88
Konwicki, Tadeusz 1926- .... CLC 8, 28, 54
See also CA 101; CAAS 9; CANR 39, 59;
MTCW 1
Koontz, Dean R(ay) 1945- ..... CLC 78; DAM
NOV, POP
See also AAYA 9; BEST 89:3, 90:2; CA 108;
CANR 19, 36, 52; MTCW 1; SATA 92
Kopernik, Mikolaj
See Copernicus, Nicolaus
Kopit, Arthur (Lee) 1937-CLC 1, 18, 33; DAM
DRAM
See also AITN 1; CA 81-84; CABS 3; DLB 7;
MTCW 1
Kops, Bernard 1926- .... CLC 4
See also CA 5-8R; DLB 13
Kornbluth, C(yril) M. 1923-1958 .... TCLC 8
See also CA 105; 160; DLB 8
Korolenko, V. G.
See Korolenko, Vladimir Galaktionovich
Korolenko, Vladimir
See Korolenko, Vladimir Galaktionovich
Korolenko, Vladimir G.
See Korolenko, Vladimir Galaktionovich
Korolenko, Vladimir Galaktionovich 1853-
1921 .... TCLC 22
See also CA 121
Korzybski, Alfred (Habdank Skarbek) 1879-
1950 .... TCLC 61
See also CA 123; 160
Kosinski, Jerzy (Nikodem) 1933-1991CLC 1,
2, 3, 6, 10, 15, 53, 70; DAM NOV
See also CA 17-20R; 134; CANR 9, 46; DLB
2; DLBY 82; MTCW 1
Kostelanetz, Richard (Cory) 1940-... CLC 28
See also CA 13-16R; CAAS 8; CANR 38
Kostrowitzki, Wilhelm Apollinaris de 1880-
1918
See Apollinaire, Guillaume
See also CA 104
Kotlowitz, Robert 1924- .... CLC 4
See also CA 33-36R; CANR 36
Kotzebue, August (Friedrich Ferdinand) von
1761-1819 .... NCLC 25
See also DLB 94
Kotzwinkle, William 1938- ..... CLC 5, 14, 35
See also CA 45-48; CANR 3, 44; CLR 6; DLB
173; MAICYA; SATA 24, 70
Kowna, Stancy
See Szymborska, Wislawa
Kozol, Jonathan 1936- .... CLC 17
See also CA 61-64; CANR 16, 45
Kozoll, Michael 1940(?)- .... CLC 35
Kramer, Kathryn 19(?)- .... CLC 34
Kramer, Larry 1935-CLC 42; DAM POP; DC
8
See also CA 124; 126; CANR 60
Krasicki, Ignacy 1735-1801 .... NCLC 8
Krasinski, Zygmunt 1812-1859 .... NCLC 4

Kraus, Karl 1874-1936 .... TCLC 5
See also CA 104; DLB 118
Kreve (Mickevicius), Vincas 1882-1954TCLC
27
Kristeva, Julia 1941- .... CLC 77
See also CA 154
Kristofferson, Kris 1936- .... CLC 26
See also CA 104
Krizanc, John 1956- .... CLC 57
Krleza, Miroslav 1893-1981 .... CLC 8, 114
See also CA 97-100; 105; CANR 50; DLB 147
Kroetsch, Robert 1927-CLC 5, 23, 57; DAC;
DAM POET
See also CA 17-20R; CANR 8, 38; DLB 53;
MTCW 1
Kroetz, Franz
See Kroetz, Franz Xaver
Kroetz, Franz Xaver 1946- .... CLC 41
See also CA 130
Kroker, Arthur (W.) 1945- .... CLC 77
See also CA 161
Kropotkin, Peter (Aleksieevich) 1842-1921
TCLC 36
See also CA 119
Krotkov, Yuri 1917- .... CLC 19
See also CA 102
Krumb
See Crumb, R(obert)
Krumgold, Joseph (Quincy) 1908-1980 C L C
12
See also CA 9-12R; 101; CANR 7; MAICYA;
SATA 1, 48; SATA-Obit 23
Krumwitz
See Crumb, R(obert)
Krutch, Joseph Wood 1893-1970 ..... CLC 24
See also CA 1-4R; 25-28R; CANR 4; DLB 63
Krutzch, Gus
See Eliot, T(homas) S(tearns)
Krylov, Ivan Andreevich 1768(?)-1844N C L C
1
See also DLB 150
Kubin, Alfred (Leopold Isidor) 1877-1959
TCLC 23
See also CA 112; 149; DLB 81
Kubrick, Stanley 1928- .... CLC 16
See also CA 81-84; CANR 33; DLB 26
Kumin, Maxine (Winokur) 1925- CLC 5, 13,
28; DAM POET; PC 15
See also AITN 2; CA 1-4R; CAAS 8; CANR 1,
21, 69; DLB 5; MTCW 1; SATA 12
Kundera, Milan 1929-..CLC 4, 9, 19, 32, 68;
DAM NOV; SSC 24
See also AAYA 2; CA 85-88; CANR 19, 52;
MTCW 1
Kunene, Mazisi (Raymond) 1930- ... CLC 85
See also BW 1; CA 125; DLB 117
Kunitz, Stanley (Jasspon) 1905-CLC 6, 11, 14;
PC 19
See also CA 41-44R; CANR 26, 57; DLB 48;
INT CANR-26; MTCW 1
Kunze, Reiner 1933- .... CLC 10
See also CA 93-96; DLB 75
Kuprin, Aleksandr Ivanovich 1870-1938
TCLC 5
See also CA 104
Kureishi, Hanif 1954(?)- .... CLC 64
See also CA 139; DLB 194
Kurosawa, Akira 1910-CLC 16; DAM MULT
See also AAYA 11; CA 101; CANR 46
Kushner, Tony 1957(?)-CLC 81; DAM DRAM
See also CA 144
Kuttner, Henry 1915-1958 .... TCLC 10
See also Vance, Jack

See also CA 104; 128; DLB 66; MTCW 1
Mannheim, Karl 1893-1947 .... **TCLC 65**
Manning, David
  See Faust, Frederick (Schiller)
Manning, Frederic 1887(?)-1935 ... **TCLC 25**
  See also CA 124
Manning, Olivia 1915-1980 .... **CLC 5, 19**
  See also CA 5-8R; 101; CANR 29; MTCW 1
Mano, D. Keith 1942- .... **CLC 2, 10**
  See also CA 25-28R; CAAS 6; CANR 26, 57;
  DLB 6
Mansfield, Katherine **TCLC 2, 8, 39; DAB; SSC 9, 23; WLC**
  See also Beauchamp, Kathleen Mansfield
  See also DLB 162
Manso, Peter 1940- .... **CLC 39**
  See also CA 29-32R; CANR 44
Mantecon, Juan Jimenez
  See Jimenez (Mantecon), Juan Ramon
Manton, Peter
  See Creasey, John
Man Without a Spleen, A
  See Chekhov, Anton (Pavlovich)
Manzoni, Alessandro 1785-1873 .... **NCLC 29**
Mapu, Abraham (ben Jekutiel) 1808-1867 **NCLC 18**
Mara, Sally
  See Queneau, Raymond
Marat, Jean Paul 1743-1793 .... **LC 10**
Marcel, Gabriel Honore 1889-1973 . **CLC 15**
  See also CA 102; 45-48; MTCW 1
Marchbanks, Samuel
  See Davies, (William) Robertson
Marchi, Giacomo
  See Bassani, Giorgio
Margulies, Donald .... **CLC 76**
Marie de France c. 12th cent. - **CMLC 8; PC 22**
Marie de l'Incarnation 1599-1672 ...... **LC 10**
Marier, Captain Victor
  See Griffith, D(avid Lewelyn) W(ark)
Mariner, Scott
  See Pohl, Frederik
Marinetti, Filippo Tommaso 1876-1944 **TCLC 10**
  See also CA 107; DLB 114
Marivaux, Pierre Carlet de Chamblain de 1688-1763 .... **LC 4; DC 7**
Markandaya, Kamala .... **CLC 8, 38**
  See also Taylor, Kamala (Purnaiya)
Markfield, Wallace 1926- .... **CLC 8**
  See also CA 69-72; CAAS 3; DLB 2, 28
Markham, Edwin 1852-1940 .... **TCLC 47**
  See also CA 160; DLB 54, 186
Markham, Robert
  See Amis, Kingsley (William)
Marks, J
  See Highwater, Jamake (Mamake)
Marks-Highwater, J
  See Highwater, Jamake (Mamake)
Markson, David M(errill) 1927- ...... **CLC 67**
  See also CA 49-52; CANR 1
Marley, Bob .... **CLC 17**
  See also Marley, Robert Nesta
Marley, Robert Nesta 1945-1981
  See Marley, Bob
  See also CA 107; 103
Marlowe, Christopher 1564-1593 **LC 22; DA; DAB; DAC; DAM DRAM, MST; DC 1; WLC**
  See also CDBLB Before 1660; DLB 62
Marlowe, Stephen 1928-
  See Queen, Ellery

See also CA 13-16R; CANR 6, 55
Marmontel, Jean-Francois 1723-1799 . **LC 2**
Marquand, John P(hillips) 1893-1960 **CLC 2, 10**
  See also CA 85-88; DLB 9, 102
Marques, Rene 1919-1979 ..... **CLC 96; DAM MULT; HLC**
  See also CA 97-100; 85-88; DLB 113; HW
Marquez, Gabriel (Jose) Garcia
  See Garcia Marquez, Gabriel (Jose)
Marquis, Don(ald Robert Perry) 1878-1937 **TCLC 7**
  See also CA 104; 166; DLB 11, 25
Marric, J. J.
  See Creasey, John
Marryat, Frederick 1792-1848 .... **NCLC 3**
  See also DLB 21, 163
Marsden, James
  See Creasey, John
Marsh, (Edith) Ngaio 1899-1982 **CLC 7, 53; DAM POP**
  See also CA 9-12R; CANR 6, 58; DLB 77;
  MTCW 1
Marshall, Garry 1934- .... **CLC 17**
  See also AAYA 3; CA 111; SATA 60
Marshall, Paule 1929- .. **CLC 27, 72; BLC 3; DAM MULT; SSC 3**
  See also BW 2; CA 77-80; CANR 25; DLB 157;
  MTCW 1
Marshallik
  See Zangwill, Israel
Marsten, Richard
  See Hunter, Evan
Marston, John 1576-1634 **LC 33; DAM DRAM**
  See also DLB 58, 172
Martha, Henry
  See Harris, Mark
Marti, Jose 1853-1895 **NCLC 63; DAM MULT; HLC**
Martial c. 40-c. 104 .... **PC 10**
Martin, Ken
  See Hubbard, L(afayette) Ron(ald)
Martin, Richard
  See Creasey, John
Martin, Steve 1945- .... **CLC 30**
  See also CA 97-100; CANR 30; MTCW 1
Martin, Valerie 1948- .... **CLC 89**
  See also BEST 90:2; CA 85-88; CANR 49
Martin, Violet Florence 1862-1915 **TCLC 51**
Martin, Webber
  See Silverberg, Robert
Martindale, Patrick Victor
  See White, Patrick (Victor Martindale)
Martin du Gard, Roger 1881-1958 **TCLC 24**
  See also CA 118; DLB 65
Martineau, Harriet 1802-1876 .... **NCLC 26**
  See also DLB 21, 55, 159, 163, 166, 190; YABC 2
Martines, Julia
  See O'Faolain, Julia
Martinez, Enrique Gonzalez
  See Gonzalez Martinez, Enrique
Martinez, Jacinto Benavente y
  See Benavente (y Martinez), Jacinto
Martinez Ruiz, Jose 1873-1967
  See Azorin; Ruiz, Jose Martinez
  See also CA 93-96; HW
Martinez Sierra, Gregorio 1881-1947 **TCLC 6**
  See also CA 115
Martinez Sierra, Maria (de la O'LeJarraga) 1874-1974 .... **TCLC 6**
  See also CA 115
Martinsen, Martin

See Follett, Ken(neth Martin)
Martinson, Harry (Edmund) 1904-1978 **CLC 14**
  See also CA 77-80; CANR 34
Marut, Ret
  See Traven, B.
Marut, Robert
  See Traven, B.
Marvell, Andrew 1621-1678 ... **LC 4, 43; DA; DAB; DAC; DAM MST, POET; PC 10; WLC**
  See also CDBLB 1660-1789; DLB 131
Marx, Karl (Heinrich) 1818-1883 . **NCLC 17**
  See also DLB 129
Masaoka Shiki .... **TCLC 18**
  See also Masaoka Tsunenori
Masaoka Tsunenori 1867-1902
  See Masaoka Shiki
  See also CA 117
Masefield, John (Edward) 1878-1967 **CLC 11, 47; DAM POET**
  See also CA 19-20; 25-28R; CANR 33; CAP 2;
  CDBLB 1890-1914; DLB 10, 19, 153, 160;
  MTCW 1; SATA 19
Maso, Carole 19(?)- .... **CLC 44**
Mason, Bobbie Ann 1940- **CLC 28, 43, 82; SSC 4**
  See also AAYA 5; CA 53-56; CANR 11, 31,
  58; DLB 173; DLBY 87; INT CANR-31;
  MTCW 1
Mason, Ernst
  See Pohl, Frederik
Mason, Lee W.
  See Malzberg, Barry N(athaniel)
Mason, Nick 1945- .... **CLC 35**
Mason, Tally
  See Derleth, August (William)
Mass, William
  See Gibson, William
Masters, Edgar Lee 1868-1950 **TCLC 2, 25; DA; DAC; DAM MST, POET; PC 1; WLCS**
  See also CA 104; 133; CDALB 1865-1917;
  DLB 54; MTCW 1
Masters, Hilary 1928- .... **CLC 48**
  See also CA 25-28R; CANR 13, 47
Mastrosimone, William 19(?)- .... **CLC 36**
Mathe, Albert
  See Camus, Albert
Mather, Cotton 1663-1728 .... **LC 38**
  See also CDALB 1640-1865; DLB 24, 30, 140
Mather, Increase 1639-1723 .... **LC 38**
  See also DLB 24
Matheson, Richard Burton 1926- .... **CLC 37**
  See also CA 97-100; DLB 8, 44; INT 97-100
Mathews, Harry 1930- .... **CLC 6, 52**
  See also CA 21-24R; CAAS 6; CANR 18, 40
Mathews, John Joseph 1894-1979 .. **CLC 84; DAM MULT**
  See also CA 19-20; 142; CANR 45; CAP 2;
  DLB 175; NNAL
Mathias, Roland (Glyn) 1915- .... **CLC 45**
  See also CA 97-100; CANR 19, 41; DLB 27
Matsuo Basho 1644-1694 .... **PC 3**
  See also DAM POET
Mattheson, Rodney
  See Creasey, John
Matthews, Greg 1949- .... **CLC 45**
  See also CA 135
Matthews, William (Procter, III) 1942-1997 **CLC 40**
  See also CA 29-32R; 162; CAAS 18; CANR
  12, 57; DLB 5

Author Index

Matthias, John (Edward) 1941- .... **CLC 9**
  See also CA 33-36R; CANR 56
Matthiessen, Peter 1927-**CLC 5, 7, 11, 32, 64;**
  DAM NOV
  See also AAYA 6; BEST 90:4; CA 9-12R;
  CANR 21, 50; DLB 6, 173; MTCW 1; SATA
  27
Maturin, Charles Robert 1780(?)-1824**NCLC**
  6
  See also DLB 178
Matute (Ausejo), Ana Maria 1925- .. **CLC 11**
  See also CA 89-92; MTCW 1
Maugham, W. S.
  See Maugham, W(illiam) Somerset
Maugham, W(illiam) Somerset 1874-1965
  CLC 1, 11, 15, 67, 93; DA; DAB; DAC;
  DAM DRAM, MST, NOV; SSC 8; WLC
  See also CA 5-8R; 25-28R; CANR 40; CDBLB
  1914-1945; DLB 10, 36, 77, 100, 162, 195;
  MTCW 1; SATA 54
Maugham, William Somerset
  See Maugham, W(illiam) Somerset
Maupassant, (Henri Rene Albert) Guy de 1850-
  1893**NCLC 1, 42; DA; DAB; DAC; DAM**
  MST; SSC 1; WLC
  See also DLB 123
Maupin, Armistead 1944-**CLC 95; DAM POP**
  See also CA 125; 130; CANR 58; INT 130
Maurhut, Richard
  See Traven, B.
Mauriac, Claude 1914-1996 .... **CLC 9**
  See also CA 89-92; 152; DLB 83
Mauriac, Francois (Charles) 1885-1970**C L C**
  4, 9, 56; SSC 24
  See also CA 25-28; CAP 2; DLB 65; MTCW 1
Mavor, Osborne Henry 1888-1951
  See Bridie, James
  See also CA 104
Maxwell, William (Keepers, Jr.) 1908-**CLC 19**
  See also CA 93-96; CANR 54; DLBY 80; INT
  93-96
May, Elaine 1932- .... **CLC 16**
  See also CA 124; 142; DLB 44
Mayakovski, Vladimir (Vladimirovich) 1893-
  1930 .... **TCLC 4, 18**
  See also CA 104; 158
Mayhew, Henry 1812-1887 .... **NCLC 31**
  See also DLB 18, 55, 190
Mayle, Peter 1939(?)- .... **CLC 89**
  See also CA 139; CANR 64
Maynard, Joyce 1953- .... **CLC 23**
  See also CA 111; 129; CANR 64
Mayne, William (James Carter) 1928-**CLC 12**
  See also AAYA 20; CA 9-12R; CANR 37; CLR
  25; JRDA; MAICYA; SAAS 11; SATA 6, 68
Mayo, Jim
  See L'Amour, Louis (Dearborn)
Maysles, Albert 1926- .... **CLC 16**
  See also CA 29-32R
Maysles, David 1932- .... **CLC 16**
Mazer, Norma Fox 1931- .... **CLC 26**
  See also AAYA 5; CA 69-72; CANR 12, 32,
  66; CLR 23; JRDA; MAICYA; SAAS 1;
  SATA 24, 67
Mazzini, Guiseppe 1805-1872 .... **NCLC 34**
McAuley, James Phillip 1917-1976 . **CLC 45**
  See also CA 97-100
McBain, Ed
  See Hunter, Evan
McBrien, William Augustine 1930- . **CLC 44**
  See also CA 107
McCaffrey, Anne (Inez) 1926-**CLC 17; DAM**
  NOV, POP

See also AAYA 6; AITN 2; BEST 89:2; CA 25-
  28R; CANR 15, 35, 55; CLR 49; DLB 8;
  JRDA; MAICYA; MTCW 1; SAAS 11; SATA
  8, 70
McCall, Nathan 1955(?)- .... **CLC 86**
  See also CA 146
McCann, Arthur
  See Campbell, John W(ood, Jr.)
McCann, Edson
  See Pohl, Frederik
McCarthy, Charles, Jr. 1933-
  See McCarthy, Cormac
  See also CANR 42, 69; DAM POP
McCarthy, Cormac 1933- **CLC 4, 57, 59, 101**
  See also McCarthy, Charles, Jr.
  See also DLB 6, 143
McCarthy, Mary (Therese) 1912-1989**CLC 1,**
  3, 5, 14, 24, 39, 59; SSC 24
  See also CA 5-8R; 129; CANR 16, 50, 64; DLB
  2; DLBY 81; INT CANR-16; MTCW 1
McCartney, (James) Paul 1942-. **CLC 12, 35**
  See also CA 146
McCauley, Stephen (D.) 1955- .... **CLC 50**
  See also CA 141
McClure, Michael (Thomas) 1932-**CLC 6, 10**
  See also CA 21-24R; CANR 17, 46; DLB 16
McCorkle, Jill (Collins) 1958-........... **CLC 51**
  See also CA 121; DLBY 87
McCourt, Frank 1930- .... **CLC 109**
  See also CA 157
McCourt, James 1941- .... **CLC 5**
  See also CA 57-60
McCoy, Horace (Stanley) 1897-1955**TCLC 28**
  See also CA 108; 155; DLB 9
McCrae, John 1872-1918 .... **TCLC 12**
  See also CA 109; DLB 92
McCreigh, James
  See Pohl, Frederik
McCullers, (Lula) Carson (Smith) 1917-1967
  CLC 1, 4, 10, 12, 48, 100; DA; DAB; DAC;
  DAM MST, NOV; SSC 9, 24; WLC
  See also AAYA 21; CA 5-8R; 25-28R; CABS
  1, 3; CANR 18; CDALB 1941-1968; DLB
  2, 7, 173; MTCW 1; SATA 27
McCulloch, John Tyler
  See Burroughs, Edgar Rice
McCullough, Colleen 1938(?)- **CLC 27, 107;**
  DAM NOV, POP
  See also CA 81-84; CANR 17, 46, 67; MTCW
  1
McDermott, Alice 1953-...................... **CLC 90**
  See also CA 109; CANR 40
McElroy, Joseph 1930- .... **CLC 5, 47**
  See also CA 17-20R
McEwan, Ian (Russell) 1948- .... **CLC 13, 66;**
  DAM NOV
  See also BEST 90:4; CA 61-64; CANR 14, 41,
  69; DLB 14, 194; MTCW 1
McFadden, David 1940-..................... **CLC 48**
  See also CA 104; DLB 60; INT 104
McFarland, Dennis 1950- .... **CLC 65**
  See also CA 165
McGahern, John 1934-**CLC 5, 9, 48; SSC 17**
  See also CA 17-20R; CANR 29, 68; DLB 14;
  MTCW 1
McGinley, Patrick (Anthony) 1937- .**CLC 41**
  See also CA 120; 127; CANR 56; INT 127
McGinley, Phyllis 1905-1978 .... **CLC 14**
  See also CA 9-12R; 77-80; CANR 19; DLB 11,
  48; SATA 2, 44; SATA-Obit 24
McGinniss, Joe 1942- .... **CLC 32**
  See also AITN 2; BEST 89:2; CA 25-28R;
  CANR 26, 70; DLB 185; INT CANR-26

McGivern, Maureen Daly
  See Daly, Maureen
McGrath, Patrick 1950-..................... **CLC 55**
  See also CA 136; CANR 65
McGrath, Thomas (Matthew) 1916-1990**CLC**
  28, 59; DAM POET
  See also CA 9-12R; 132; CANR 6, 33; MTCW
  1; SATA 41; SATA-Obit 66
McGuane, Thomas (Francis III) 1939-**CLC 3,**
  7, 18, 45
  See also AITN 2; CA 49-52; CANR 5, 24, 49;
  DLB 2; DLBY 80; INT CANR-24; MTCW
  1
McGuckian, Medbh 1950- ..... **CLC 48; DAM**
  POET
  See also CA 143; DLB 40
McHale, Tom 1942(?)-1982 .... **CLC 3, 5**
  See also AITN 1; CA 77-80; 106
McIlvanney, William 1936- .... **CLC 42**
  See also CA 25-28R; CANR 61; DLB 14
McIlwraith, Maureen Mollie Hunter
  See Hunter, Mollie
  See also SATA 2
McInerney, Jay 1955-**CLC 34, 112; DAM POP**
  See also AAYA 18; CA 116; 123; CANR 45,
  68; INT 123
McIntyre, Vonda N(eel) 1948-........... **CLC 18**
  See also CA 81-84; CANR 17, 34, 69; MTCW
  1
McKay, ClaudeTCLC 7, 41; BLC 3; DAB; PC
  2
  See also McKay, Festus Claudius
  See also DLB 4, 45, 51, 117
McKay, Festus Claudius 1889-1948
  See McKay, Claude
  See also BW 1; CA 104; 124; DA; DAC; DAM
  MST, MULT, NOV, POET; MTCW 1; WLC
McKuen, Rod 1933- .... **CLC 1, 3**
  See also AITN 1; CA 41-44R; CANR 40
McLoughlin, R. B.
  See Mencken, H(enry) L(ouis)
McLuhan, (Herbert) Marshall 1911-1980
  CLC 37, 83
  See also CA 9-12R; 102; CANR 12, 34, 61;
  DLB 88; INT CANR-12; MTCW 1
McMillan, Terry (L.) 1951- **CLC 50, 61, 112;**
  BLCS; DAM MULT, NOV, POP
  See also AAYA 21; BW 2; CA 140; CANR 60
McMurtry, Larry (Jeff) 1936-**CLC 2, 3, 7, 11,**
  27, 44; DAM NOV, POP
  See also AAYA 15; AITN 2; BEST 89:2; CA 5-
  8R; CANR 19, 43, 64; CDALB 1968-1988;
  DLB 2, 143; DLBY 80, 87; MTCW 1
McNally, T. M. 1961-......................... **CLC 82**
McNally, Terrence 1939- ... **CLC 4, 7, 41, 91;**
  DAM DRAM
  See also CA 45-48; CANR 2, 56; DLB 7
McNamer, Deirdre 1950- .... **CLC 70**
McNeile, Herman Cyril 1888-1937
  See Sapper
  See also DLB 77
McNickle, (William) D'Arcy 1904-1977 **C L C**
  89; DAM MULT
  See also CA 9-12R; 85-88; CANR 5, 45; DLB
  175; NNAL; SATA-Obit 22
McPhee, John (Angus) 1931- .... **CLC 36**
  See also BEST 90:1; CA 65-68; CANR 20, 46,
  64, 69; DLB 185; MTCW 1
McPherson, James Alan 1943-.. **CLC 19, 77;**
  BLCS
  See also BW 1; CA 25-28R; CAAS 17; CANR
  24; DLB 38; MTCW 1
McPherson, William (Alexander) 1933- **C L C**

See also CA 111

Morris, William 1834-1896 .... NCLC 4
  See also CDBLB 1832-1890; DLB 18, 35, 57, 156, 178, 184

Morris, Wright 1910-1998CLC 1, 3, 7, 18, 37
  See also CA 9-12R; 167; CANR 21; DLB 2; DLBY 81; MTCW 1

Morrison, Arthur 1863-1945 .... TCLC 72
  See also CA 120; 157; DLB 70, 135, 197

Morrison, Chloe Anthony Wofford
  See Morrison, Toni

Morrison, James Douglas 1943-1971
  See Morrison, Jim
  See also CA 73-76; CANR 40

Morrison, Jim .... CLC 17
  See also Morrison, James Douglas

Morrison, Toni 1931-CLC 4, 10, 22, 55, 81, 87; **BLC 3; DA; DAB; DAC; DAM MST, MULT, NOV, POP**
  See also AAYA 1, 22; BW 2; CA 29-32R; CANR 27, 42, 67; CDALB 1968-1988; DLB 6, 33, 143; DLBY 81; MTCW 1; SATA 57

Morrison, Van 1945- .... CLC 21
  See also CA 116; 168

Morrissy, Mary 1958- .... CLC 99

Mortimer, John (Clifford) 1923-CLC 28, 43; **DAM DRAM, POP**
  See also CA 13-16R; CANR 21, 69; CDBLB 1960 to Present; DLB 13; INT CANR-21; MTCW 1

Mortimer, Penelope (Ruth) 1918- .... CLC 5
  See also CA 57-60; CANR 45

Morton, Anthony
  See Creasey, John

Mosca, Gaetano 1858-1941 .... TCLC 75

Mosher, Howard Frank 1943- .... CLC 62
  See also CA 139; CANR 65

Mosley, Nicholas 1923- .... CLC 43, 70
  See also CA 69-72; CANR 41, 60; DLB 14

Mosley, Walter 1952- CLC 97; BLCS; DAM MULT, POP
  See also AAYA 17; BW 2; CA 142; CANR 57

Moss, Howard 1922-1987 CLC 7, 14, 45, 50; **DAM POET**
  See also CA 1-4R; 123; CANR 1, 44; DLB 5

Mossgiel, Rab
  See Burns, Robert

Motion, Andrew (Peter) 1952- .... CLC 47
  See also CA 146; DLB 40

Motley, Willard (Francis) 1909-1965CLC 18
  See also BW 1; CA 117; 106; DLB 76, 143

Motoori, Norinaga 1730-1801 .... NCLC 45

Mott, Michael (Charles Alston) 1930-CLC 15, 34
  See also CA 5-8R; CAAS 7; CANR 7, 29

Mountain Wolf Woman 1884-1960 .. CLC 92
  See also CA 144; NNAL

Moure, Erin 1955- .... CLC 88
  See also CA 113; DLB 60

Mowat, Farley (McGill) 1921-CLC 26; DAC; **DAM MST**
  See also AAYA 1; CA 1-4R; CANR 4, 24, 42, 68; CLR 20; DLB 68; INT CANAR-24; JRDA; MAICYA; MTCW 1; SATA 3, 55

Moyers, Bill 1934- .... CLC 74
  See also AITN 2; CA 61-64; CANR 31, 52

Mphahlele, Es'kia
  See Mphahlele, Ezekiel
  See also DLB 125

Mphahlele, Ezekiel 1919-1983 CLC 25; **BLC 3; DAM MULT**
  See also Mphahlele, Es'kia
  See also BW 2; CA 81-84; CANR 26

Mqhayi, S(amuel) E(dward) K(rune Loliwe) 1875-1945TCLC 25; BLC 3; DAM MULT
  See also CA 153

Mrozek, Slawomir 1930- .... CLC 3, 13
  See also CA 13-16R; CAAS 10; CANR 29; MTCW 1

Mrs. Belloc-Lowndes
  See Lowndes, Marie Adelaide (Belloc)

Mtwa, Percy (?)- .... CLC 47

Mueller, Lisel 1924- .... CLC 13, 51
  See also CA 93-96; DLB 105

Muir, Edwin 1887-1959 .... TCLC 2
  See also CA 104; DLB 20, 100, 191

Muir, John 1838-1914 .... TCLC 28
  See also CA 165; DLB 186

Mujica Lainez, Manuel 1910-1984 ... CLC 31
  See also Lainez, Manuel Mujica
  See also CA 81-84; 112; CANR 32; HW

Mukherjee, Bharati 1940-CLC 53; DAM NOV
  See also BEST 89:2; CA 107; CANR 45, 72; DLB 60; MTCW 1

Muldoon, Paul 1951-CLC 32, 72; DAM POET
  See also CA 113; 129; CANR 52; DLB 40; INT 129

Mulisch, Harry 1927- .... CLC 42
  See also CA 9-12R; CANR 6, 26, 56

Mull, Martin 1943- .... CLC 17
  See also CA 105

Mulock, Dinah Maria
  See Craik, Dinah Maria (Mulock)

Munford, Robert 1737(?)-1783 .... LC 5
  See also DLB 31

Mungo, Raymond 1946- .... CLC 72
  See also CA 49-52; CANR 2

Munro, Alice 1931-.... CLC 6, 10, 19, 50, 95; **DAC; DAM MST, NOV; SSC 3; WLCS**
  See also AITN 2; CA 33-36R; CANR 33, 53; DLB 53; MTCW 1; SATA 29

Munro, H(ector) H(ugh) 1870-1916
  See Saki
  See also CA 104; 130; CDBLB 1890-1914; DA; DAB; DAC; DAM MST, NOV; DLB 34, 162; MTCW 1; WLC

Murasaki, Lady .... CMLC 1

Murdoch, (Jean) Iris 1919-CLC 1, 2, 3, 4, 6, 8, 11, 15, 22, 31, 51; DAB; DAC; DAM MST, NOV
  See also CA 13-16R; CANR 8, 43, 68; CDBLB 1960 to Present; DLB 14, 194; INT CANR-8; MTCW 1

Murfree, Mary Noailles 1850-1922 ... SSC 22
  See also CA 122; DLB 12, 74

Murnau, Friedrich Wilhelm
  See Plumpe, Friedrich Wilhelm

Murphy, Richard 1927- .... CLC 41
  See also CA 29-32R; DLB 40

Murphy, Sylvia 1937- .... CLC 34
  See also CA 121

Murphy, Thomas (Bernard) 1935- ... CLC 51
  See also CA 101

Murray, Albert L. 1916- .... CLC 73
  See also BW 2; CA 49-52; CANR 26, 52; DLB 38

Murray, Judith Sargent 1751-1820NCLC 63
  See also DLB 37, 200

Murray, Les(lie) A(llan) 1938-CLC 40; DAM POET
  See also CA 21-24R; CANR 11, 27, 56

Murry, J. Middleton
  See Murry, John Middleton

Murry, John Middleton 1889-1957 TCLC 16
  See also CA 118; DLB 149

Musgrave, Susan 1951- .... CLC 13, 54

See also CA 69-72; CANR 45

Musil, Robert (Edler von) 1880-1942 . T C L C 12, 68; SSC 18
  See also CA 109; CANR 55; DLB 81, 124

Muske, Carol 1945- .... CLC 90
  See also Muske-Dukes, Carol (Anne)

Muske-Dukes, Carol (Anne) 1945-
  See Muske, Carol
  See also CA 65-68; CANR 32, 70

Musset, (Louis Charles) Alfred de 1810-1857 NCLC 7
  See also DLB 192

My Brother's Brother
  See Chekhov, Anton (Pavlovich)

Myers, L(eopold) H(amilton) 1881-1944 TCLC 59
  See also CA 157; DLB 15

Myers, Walter Dean 1937-. CLC 35; BLC 3; **DAM MULT, NOV**
  See also AAYA 4, 23; BW 2; CA 33-36R; CANR 20, 42, 67; CLR 4, 16, 35; DLB 33; INT CANR-20; JRDA; MAICYA; SAAS 2; SATA 41, 71; SATA-Brief 27

Myers, Walter M.
  See Myers, Walter Dean

Myles, Symon
  See Follett, Ken(neth Martin)

Nabokov, Vladimir (Vladimirovich) 1899-1977 CLC 1, 2, 3, 6, 8, 11, 15, 23, 44, 46, 64; **DA; DAB; DAC; DAM MST, NOV; SSC 11; WLC**
  See also CA 5-8R; 69-72; CANR 20; CDALB 1941-1968; DLB 2; DLBD 3; DLBY 80, 91; MTCW 1

Nagai Kafu 1879-1959 .... TCLC 51
  See also Nagai Sokichi
  See also DLB 180

Nagai Sokichi 1879-1959
  See Nagai Kafu
  See also CA 117

Nagy, Laszlo 1925-1978 .... CLC 7
  See also CA 129; 112

Naidu, Sarojini 1879-1943 .... TCLC 80

Naipaul, Shiva(dhar Srinivasa) 1945-1985 CLC 32, 39; DAM NOV
  See also CA 110; 112; 116; CANR 33; DLB 157; DLBY 85; MTCW 1

Naipaul, V(idiadhar) S(urajprasad) 1932- CLC 4, 7, 9, 13, 18, 37, 105; DAB; DAC; **DAM MST, NOV**
  See also CA 1-4R; CANR 1, 33, 51; CDBLB 1960 to Present; DLB 125; DLBY 85; MTCW 1

Nakos, Lilika 1899(?)- .... CLC 29

Narayan, R(asipuram) K(rishnaswami) 1906- CLC 7, 28, 47; DAM NOV; SSC 25
  See also CA 81-84; CANR 33, 61; MTCW 1; SATA 62

Nash, (Frediric) Ogden 1902-1971 . CLC 23; **DAM POET; PC 21**
  See also CA 13-14; 29-32R; CANR 34, 61; CAP 1; DLB 11; MAICYA; MTCW 1; SATA 2, 46

Nashe, Thomas 1567-1601(?) .... LC 41
  See also DLB 167

Nashe, Thomas 1567-1601 .... LC 41

Nathan, Daniel
  See Dannay, Frederic

Nathan, George Jean 1882-1958 .... TCLC 18
  See also Hatteras, Owen
  See also CA 114; DLB 137

Natsume, Kinnosuke 1867-1916
  See Natsume, Soseki

2

Owen, Hugh
See Faust, Frederick (Schiller)

Owen, Wilfred (Edward Salter) 1893-1918
TCLC 5, 27; DA; DAB; DAC; DAM MST, POET; PC 19; WLC
See also CA 104; 141; CDBLB 1914-1945; DLB 20

Owens, Rochelle 1936- .... CLC 8
See also CA 17-20R; CAAS 2; CANR 39

Oz, Amos 1939-CLC 5, 8, 11, 27, 33, 54; DAM NOV
See also CA 53-56; CANR 27, 47, 65; MTCW 1

Ozick, Cynthia 1928-CLC 3, 7, 28, 62; DAM NOV, POP; SSC 15
See also BEST 90:1; CA 17-20R; CANR 23, 58; DLB 28, 152; DLBY 82; INT CANR-23; MTCW 1

Ozu, Yasujiro 1903-1963 .... CLC 16
See also CA 112

Pacheco, C.
See Pessoa, Fernando (Antonio Nogueira)

Pa Chin .... CLC 18
See also Li Fei-kan

Pack, Robert 1929- .... CLC 13
See also CA 1-4R; CANR 3, 44; DLB 5

Padgett, Lewis
See Kuttner, Henry

Padilla (Lorenzo), Heberto 1932- .... CLC 38
See also AITN 1; CA 123; 131; HW

Page, Jimmy 1944- .... CLC 12

Page, Louise 1955-........................... CLC 40
See also CA 140

Page, P(atricia) K(athleen) 1916- CLC 7, 18; DAC; DAM MST; PC 12
See also CA 53-56; CANR 4, 22, 65; DLB 68; MTCW 1

Page, Thomas Nelson 1853-1922 .... SSC 23
See also CA 118; DLB 12, 78; DLBD 13

Pagels, Elaine Hiesey 1943-............ CLC 104
See also CA 45-48; CANR 2, 24, 51

Paget, Violet 1856-1935
See Lee, Vernon
See also CA 104; 166

Paget-Lowe, Henry
See Lovecraft, H(oward) P(hillips)

Paglia, Camille (Anna) 1947- .... CLC 68
See also CA 140; CANR 72

Paige, Richard
See Koontz, Dean R(ay)

Paine, Thomas 1737-1809 .... NCLC 62
See also CDALB 1640-1865; DLB 31, 43, 73, 158

Pakenham, Antonia
See Fraser, (Lady) Antonia (Pakenham)

Palamas, Kostes 1859-1943 .... TCLC 5
See also CA 105

Palazzeschi, Aldo 1885-1974 .... CLC 11
See also CA 89-92; 53-56; DLB 114

Paley, Grace 1922-CLC 4, 6, 37; DAM POP; SSC 8
See also CA 25-28R; CANR 13, 46; DLB 28; INT CANR-13; MTCW 1

Palin, Michael (Edward) 1943- .... CLC 21
See also Monty Python
See also CA 107; CANR 35; SATA 67

Palliser, Charles 1947- .... CLC 65
See also CA 136

Palma, Ricardo 1833-1919 .... TCLC 29
See also CA 168

Pancake, Breece Dexter 1952-1979
See Pancake, Breece D'J

See also CA 123; 109

Pancake, Breece D'J .... CLC 29
See also Pancake, Breece Dexter
See also DLB 130

Panko, Rudy
See Gogol, Nikolai (Vasilyevich)

Papadiamantis, Alexandros 1851-1911 T C L C 29
See also CA 168

Papadiamantopoulos, Johannes 1856-1910
See Moreas, Jean
See also CA 117

Papini, Giovanni 1881-1956 .... TCLC 22
See also CA 121

Paracelsus 1493-1541 .... LC 14
See also DLB 179

Parasol, Peter
See Stevens, Wallace

Pardo Bazan, Emilia 1851-1921 .... SSC 30

Pareto, Vilfredo 1848-1923 .... TCLC 69

Parfenie, Maria
See Codrescu, Andrei

Parini, Jay (Lee) 1948- .... CLC 54
See also CA 97-100; CAAS 16; CANR 32

Park, Jordan
See Kornbluth, C(yril) M.; Pohl, Frederik

Park, Robert E(zra) 1864-1944 ...... TCLC 73
See also CA 122, 165

Parker, Bert
See Ellison, Harlan (Jay)

Parker, Dorothy (Rothschild) 1893-1967C L C 15, 68; DAM POET; SSC 2
See also CA 19-20; 25-28R; CAP 2; DLB 11, 45, 86; MTCW 1

Parker, Robert B(rown) 1932-CLC 27; DAM NOV, POP
See also BEST 89:4; CA 49-52; CANR 1, 26, 52; INT CANR-26; MTCW 1

Parkin, Frank 1940- .... CLC 43
See also CA 147

Parkman, Francis, Jr. 1823-1893 ... NCLC 12
See also DLB 1, 30, 186

Parks, Gordon (Alexander Buchanan) 1912-CLC 1, 16; BLC 3; DAM MULT
See also AITN 2; BW 2; CA 41-44R; CANR 26, 66; DLB 33; SATA 8

Parmenides c. 515B.C.-c. 450B.C. CMLC 22
See also DLB 176

Parnell, Thomas 1679-1718 .... LC 3
See also DLB 94

Parra, Nicanor 1914- .... CLC 2, 102; DAM MULT; HLC
See also CA 85-88; CANR 32; HW; MTCW 1

Parrish, Mary Frances
See Fisher, M(ary) F(rances) K(ennedy)

Parson
See Coleridge, Samuel Taylor

Parson Lot
See Kingsley, Charles

Partridge, Anthony
See Oppenheim, E(dward) Phillips

Pascal, Blaise 1623-1662 .... LC 35

Pascoli, Giovanni 1855-1912 .... TCLC 45

Pasolini, Pier Paolo 1922-1975 . CLC 20, 37, 106; PC 17
See also CA 93-96; 61-64; CANR 63; DLB 128, 177; MTCW 1

Pasquini
See Silone, Ignazio

Pastan, Linda (Olenik) 1932- CLC 27; DAM POET
See also CA 61-64; CANR 18, 40, 61; DLB 5

Pasternak, Boris (Leonidovich) 1890-1960

CLC 7, 10, 18, 63; DA; DAB; DAC; DAM MST, NOV, POET; PC 6; SSC 31; WLC
See also CA 127; 116; MTCW 1

Patchen, Kenneth 1911-1972 ... CLC 1, 2, 18; DAM POET
See also CA 1-4R; 33-36R; CANR 3, 35; DLB 16, 48; MTCW 1

Pater, Walter (Horatio) 1839-1894 .. NCLC 7
See also CDBLB 1832-1890; DLB 57, 156

Paterson, A(ndrew) B(arton) 1864-1941 TCLC 32
See also CA 155; SATA 97

Paterson, Katherine (Womeldorf) 1932-C L C 12, 30
See also AAYA 1; CA 21-24R; CANR 28, 59; CLR 7, 50; DLB 52; JRDA; MAICYA; MTCW 1; SATA 13, 53, 92

Patmore, Coventry Kersey Dighton 1823-1896 NCLC 9
See also DLB 35, 98

Paton, Alan (Stewart) 1903-1988 CLC 4, 10, 25, 55, 106; DA; DAB; DAC; DAM MST, NOV; WLC
See also AAYA 26; CA 13-16; 125; CANR 22; CAP 1; DLBD 17; MTCW 1; SATA 11; SATA-Obit 56

Paton Walsh, Gillian 1937-
See Walsh, Jill Paton
See also CANR 38; JRDA; MAICYA; SAAS 3; SATA 4, 72

Patton, George S. 1885-1945 .... TCLC 79

Paulding, James Kirke 1778-1860 ... NCLC 2
See also DLB 3, 59, 74

Paulin, Thomas Neilson 1949-
See Paulin, Tom
See also CA 123; 128

Paulin, Tom .... CLC 37
See also Paulin, Thomas Neilson
See also DLB 40

Paustovsky, Konstantin (Georgievich) 1892-1968 .... CLC 40
See also CA 93-96; 25-28R

Pavese, Cesare 1908-1950 ... TCLC 3; PC 13; SSC 19
See also CA 104; DLB 128, 177

Pavic, Milorad 1929- .... CLC 60
See also CA 136; DLB 181

Payne, Alan
See Jakes, John (William)

Paz, Gil
See Lugones, Leopoldo

Paz, Octavio 1914-1998CLC 3, 4, 6, 10, 19, 51, 65; DA; DAB; DAC; DAM MST, MULT, POET; HLC; PC 1; WLC
See also CA 73-76; 165; CANR 32, 65; DLBY 90; HW; MTCW 1

p'Bitek, Okot 1931-1982 .... CLC 96; BLC 3; DAM MULT
See also BW 2; CA 124; 107; DLB 125; MTCW 1

Peacock, Molly 1947- .... CLC 60
See also CA 103; CAAS 21; CANR 52; DLB 120

Peacock, Thomas Love 1785-1866 . NCLC 22
See also DLB 96, 116

Peake, Mervyn 1911-1968 .... CLC 7, 54
See also CA 5-8R; 25-28R; CANR 3; DLB 15, 160; MTCW 1; SATA 23

Pearce, Philippa .... CLC 21
See also Christie, (Ann) Philippa
See also CLR 9; DLB 161; MAICYA; SATA 1, 67

Pearl, Eric

See Elman, Richard (Martin)

Pearson, T(homas) R(eid) 1956- ...... **CLC 39**
See also CA 120; 130; INT 130

Peck, Dale 1967- .... **CLC 81**
See also CA 146; CANR 72

Peck, John 1941-................................**CLC 3**
See also CA 49-52; CANR 3

Peck, Richard (Wayne) 1934-........... **CLC 21**
See also AAYA 1, 24; CA 85-88; CANR 19,
38; CLR 15; INT CANR-19; JRDA;
MAICYA; SAAS 2; SATA 18, 55, 97

Peck, Robert Newton 1928- ..... **CLC 17; DA;**
DAC; DAM MST
See also AAYA 3; CA 81-84; CANR 31, 63;
CLR 45; JRDA; MAICYA; SAAS 1; SATA
21, 62

Peckinpah, (David) Sam(uel) 1925-1984 **C L C**
20
See also CA 109; 114

Pedersen, Knut 1859-1952
See Hamsun, Knut
See also CA 104; 119; CANR 63; MTCW 1

Peeslake, Gaffer
See Durrell, Lawrence (George)

Peguy, Charles Pierre 1873-1914 ... **TCLC 10**
See also CA 107

Peirce, Charles Sanders 1839-1914 **TCLC 81**

Pena, Ramon del Valle y
See Valle-Inclan, Ramon (Maria) del

Pendennis, Arthur Esquir
See Thackeray, William Makepeace

Penn, William 1644-1718 .... **LC 25**
See also DLB 24

PEPECE
See Prado (Calvo), Pedro

Pepys, Samuel 1633-1703 **LC 11; DA; DAB;**
DAC; DAM MST; WLC
See also CDBLB 1660-1789; DLB 101

Percy, Walker 1916-1990 **CLC 2, 3, 6, 8, 14, 18,**
47, 65; DAM NOV, POP
See also CA 1-4R; 131; CANR 1, 23, 64; DLB
2; DLBY 80, 90; MTCW 1

Percy, William Alexander 1885-1942 **TCLC 84**
See also CA 163

Perec, Georges 1936-1982 .... **CLC 56**
See also CA 141; DLB 83

Pereda (y Sanchez de Porrua), Jose Maria de
1833-1906................................. **TCLC 16**
See also CA 117

Pereda y Porrua, Jose Maria de
See Pereda (y Sanchez de Porrua), Jose Maria
de

Peregoy, George Weems
See Mencken, H(enry) L(ouis)

Perelman, S(idney) J(oseph) 1904-1979 **C L C**
3, 5, 9, 15, 23, 44, 49; DAM DRAM; SSC
32
See also AITN 1, 2; CA 73-76; 89-92; CANR
18; DLB 11, 44; MTCW 1

Peret, Benjamin 1899-1959 .... **TCLC 20**
See also CA 117

Peretz, Isaac Loeb 1851(?)-1915 .. **TCLC 16;**
SSC 26
See also CA 109

Peretz, Yitzkhok Leibush
See Peretz, Isaac Loeb

Perez Galdos, Benito 1843-1920 .... **TCLC 27**
See also CA 125; 153; HW

Perrault, Charles 1628-1703 .... **LC 2**
See also MAICYA; SATA 25

Perry, Brighton
See Sherwood, Robert E(mmet)

Perse, St.-John

See Leger, (Marie-Rene Auguste) Alexis Saint-
Leger

Perutz, Leo 1882-1957 .... **TCLC 60**
See also DLB 81

Peseenz, Tulio F.
See Lopez y Fuentes, Gregorio

Pesetsky, Bette 1932- .... **CLC 28**
See also CA 133; DLB 130

Peshkov, Alexei Maximovich 1868-1936
See Gorky, Maxim
See also CA 105; 141; DA; DAC; DAM DRAM,
MST, NOV

Pessoa, Fernando (Antonio Nogueira) 1898-
1935 .... **TCLC 27; HLC; PC 20**
See also CA 125

Peterkin, Julia Mood 1880-1961 .... **CLC 31**
See also CA 102; DLB 9

Peters, Joan K(aren) 1945-................ **CLC 39**
See also CA 158

Peters, Robert L(ouis) 1924- .... **CLC 7**
See also CA 13-16R; CAAS 8; DLB 105

Petofi, Sandor 1823-1849 .... **NCLC 21**

Petrakis, Harry Mark 1923-................ **CLC 3**
See also CA 9-12R; CANR 4, 30

Petrarch 1304-1374 **CMLC 20; DAM POET;**
PC 8

Petrov, Evgeny .... **TCLC 21**
See also Kataev, Evgeny Petrovich

Petry, Ann (Lane) 1908-1997 ... **CLC 1, 7, 18**
See also BW 1; CA 5-8R; 157; CAAS 6; CANR
4, 46; CLR 12; DLB 76; JRDA; MAICYA;
MTCW 1; SATA 5; SATA-Obit 94

Petursson, Halligrimur 1614-1674 .... **LC 8**

Peychinovich
See Vazov, Ivan (Minchov)

Phaedrus 18(?)B.C.-55(?) .... **CMLC 25**

Philips, Katherine 1632-1664 .... **LC 30**
See also DLB 131

Philipson, Morris H. 1926-................ **CLC 53**
See also CA 1-4R; CANR 4

Phillips, Caryl 1958- . **CLC 96; BLCS; DAM**
MULT
See also BW 2; CA 141; CANR 63; DLB 157

Phillips, David Graham 1867-1911 **TCLC 44**
See also CA 108; DLB 9, 12

Phillips, Jack
See Sandburg, Carl (August)

Phillips, Jayne Anne 1952- **CLC 15, 33; SSC 16**
See also CA 101; CANR 24, 50; DLBY 80; INT
CANR-24; MTCW 1

Phillips, Richard
See Dick, Philip K(indred)

Phillips, Robert (Schaeffer) 1938- .... **CLC 28**
See also CA 17-20R; CAAS 13; CANR 8; DLB
105

Phillips, Ward
See Lovecraft, H(oward) P(hillips)

Piccolo, Lucio 1901-1969 .... **CLC 13**
See also CA 97-100; DLB 114

Pickthall, Marjorie L(owry) C(hristie) 1883-
1922 .... **TCLC 21**
See also CA 107; DLB 92

Pico della Mirandola, Giovanni 1463-1494 **LC**
15

Piercy, Marge 1936- **CLC 3, 6, 14, 18, 27, 62**
See also CA 21-24R; CAAS 1; CANR 13, 43,
66; DLB 120; MTCW 1

Piers, Robert
See Anthony, Piers

Pieyre de Mandiargues, Andre 1909-1991
See Mandiargues, Andre Pieyre de
See also CA 103; 136; CANR 22

Pilnyak, Boris.................................. **TCLC 23**

See also Vogau, Boris Andreyevich

Pincherle, Alberto 1907-1990 .... **CLC 11, 18;**
DAM NOV
See also Moravia, Alberto
See also CA 25-28R; 132; CANR 33, 63;
MTCW 1

Pinckney, Darryl 1953- .... **CLC 76**
See also BW 2; CA 143

Pindar 518B.C.-446B.C...... **CMLC 12; PC 19**
See also DLB 176

Pineda, Cecile 1942- .... **CLC 39**
See also CA 118

Pinero, Arthur Wing 1855-1934 .. **TCLC 32;**
DAM DRAM
See also CA 110; 153; DLB 10

Pinero, Miguel (Antonio Gomez) 1946-1988
CLC 4, 55
See also CA 61-64; 125; CANR 29; HW

Pinget, Robert 1919-1997 .... **CLC 7, 13, 37**
See also CA 85-88; 160; DLB 83

Pink Floyd
See Barrett, (Roger) Syd; Gilmour, David; Mason, Nick; Waters, Roger; Wright, Rick

Pinkney, Edward 1802-1828 .... **NCLC 31**

Pinkwater, Daniel Manus 1941-....... **CLC 35**
See also Pinkwater, Manus
See also AAYA 1; CA 29-32R; CANR 12, 38;
CLR 4; JRDA; MAICYA; SAAS 3; SATA 46,
76

Pinkwater, Manus
See Pinkwater, Daniel Manus
See also SATA 8

Pinsky, Robert 1940-**CLC 9, 19, 38, 94; DAM**
POET
See also CA 29-32R; CAAS 4; CANR 58;
DLBY 82

Pinta, Harold
See Pinter, Harold

Pinter, Harold 1930-**CLC 1, 3, 6, 9, 11, 15, 27,**
58, 73; DA; DAB; DAC; DAM DRAM,
MST; WLC
See also CA 5-8R; CANR 33, 65; CDBLB 1960
to Present; DLB 13; MTCW 1

Piozzi, Hester Lynch (Thrale) 1741-1821
NCLC 57
See also DLB 104, 142

Pirandello, Luigi 1867-1936 **TCLC 4, 29; DA;**
DAB; DAC; DAM DRAM, MST; DC 5;
SSC 22; WLC
See also CA 104; 153

Pirsig, Robert M(aynard) 1928-**CLC 4, 6, 73;**
DAM POP
See also CA 53-56; CANR 42; MTCW 1; SATA
39

Pisarev, Dmitry Ivanovich 1840-1868 **N C L C**
25

Pix, Mary (Griffith) 1666-1709 .... **LC 8**
See also DLB 80

Pixerecourt, (Rene Charles) Guilbert de 1773-
1844 .... **NCLC 39**
See also DLB 192

Plaatje, Sol(omon) T(shekisho) 1876-1932
TCLC 73; BLCS
See also BW 2; CA 141

Plaidy, Jean
See Hibbert, Eleanor Alice Burford

Planche, James Robinson 1796-1880**NCLC 42**

Plant, Robert 1948- .... **CLC 12**

Plante, David (Robert) 1940- **CLC 7, 23, 38;**
DAM NOV
See also CA 37-40R; CANR 12, 36, 58; DLBY
83; INT CANR-12; MTCW 1

Plath, Sylvia 1932-1963 **CLC 1, 2, 3, 5, 9, 11,**

See also BEST 90:3; CA 1-4R; CANR 1, 22, 36, 55; CDALB 1968-1988; DLB 2, 28, 173; DLBY 82; MTCW 1

Rothenberg, Jerome 1931- .... **CLC 6, 57**
See also CA 45-48; CANR 1; DLB 5, 193

Roumain, Jacques (Jean Baptiste) 1907-1944 **TCLC 19; BLC 3; DAM MULT**
See also BW 1; CA 117; 125

Rourke, Constance (Mayfield) 1885-1941 **TCLC 12**
See also CA 107; YABC 1

Rousseau, Jean-Baptiste 1671-1741 ..... **LC 9**

Rousseau, Jean-Jacques 1712-1778**LC 14, 36; DA; DAB; DAC; DAM MST; WLC**

Roussel, Raymond 1877-1933 .... **TCLC 20**
See also CA 117

Rovit, Earl (Herbert) 1927- .... **CLC 7**
See also CA 5-8R; CANR 12

Rowe, Elizabeth Singer 1674-1737 ..... **LC 44**
See also DLB 39, 95

Rowe, Nicholas 1674-1718 .... **LC 8**
See also DLB 84

Rowley, Ames Dorrance
See Lovecraft, H(oward) P(hillips)

Rowson, Susanna Haswell 1762(?)-1824 **NCLC 5, 69**
See also DLB 37, 200

Roy, Arundhati 1960(?)- .... **CLC 109**
See also CA 163; DLBY 97

Roy, Gabrielle 1909-1983 **CLC 10, 14; DAB; DAC; DAM MST**
See also CA 53-56; 110; CANR 5, 61; DLB 68; MTCW 1

Royko, Mike 1932-1997 .... **CLC 109**
See also CA 89-92; 157; CANR 26

Rozewicz, Tadeusz 1921- ...**CLC 9, 23; DAM POET**
See also CA 108; CANR 36, 66; MTCW 1

Ruark, Gibbons 1941- .... **CLC 3**
See also CA 33-36R; CAAS 23; CANR 14, 31, 57; DLB 120

Rubens, Bernice (Ruth) 1923- .... **CLC 19, 31**
See also CA 25-28R; CANR 33, 65; DLB 14; MTCW 1

Rubin, Harold
See Robbins, Harold

Rudkin, (James) David 1936- .... **CLC 14**
See also CA 89-92; DLB 13

Rudnik, Raphael 1933- .... **CLC 7**
See also CA 29-32R

Ruffian, M.
See Hasek, Jaroslav (Matej Frantisek)

Ruiz, Jose Martinez .... **CLC 11**
See also Martinez Ruiz, Jose

Rukeyser, Muriel 1913-1980**CLC 6, 10, 15, 27; DAM POET; PC 12**
See also CA 5-8R; 93-96; CANR 26, 60; DLB 48; MTCW 1; SATA-Obit 22

Rule, Jane (Vance) 1931- .... **CLC 27**
See also CA 25-28R; CAAS 18; CANR 12; DLB 60

Rulfo, Juan 1918-1986 ....**CLC 8, 80; DAM MULT; HLC; SSC 25**
See also CA 85-88; 118; CANR 26; DLB 113; HW; MTCW 1

Rumi, Jalal al-Din 1297-1373 .... **CMLC 20**

Runeberg, Johan 1804-1877 .... **NCLC 41**

Runyon, (Alfred) Damon 1884(?)-1946**T C L C 10**
See also CA 107; 165; DLB 11, 86, 171

Rush, Norman 1933- .... **CLC 44**
See also CA 121; 126; INT 126

Rushdie, (Ahmed) Salman 1947-**CLC 23, 31,** 55, 100; **DAB; DAC; DAM MST, NOV, POP; WLCS**
See also BEST 89:3; CA 108; 111; CANR 33, 56; DLB 194; INT 111; MTCW 1

Rushforth, Peter (Scott) 1945- .... **CLC 19**
See also CA 101

Ruskin, John 1819-1900 .... **TCLC 63**
See also CA 114; 129; CDBLB 1832-1890; DLB 55, 163, 190; SATA 24

Russ, Joanna 1937-............................ **CLC 15**
See also CANR 11, 31, 65; DLB 8; MTCW 1

Russell, George William 1867-1935
See Baker, Jean H.
See also CA 104; 153; CDBLB 1890-1914; DAM POET

Russell, (Henry) Ken(neth Alfred) 1927-**C L C 16**
See also CA 105

Russell, William Martin 1947- .... **CLC 60**
See also CA 164

Rutherford, Mark .... **TCLC 25**
See also White, William Hale
See also DLB 18

Ruyslinck, Ward 1929- .... **CLC 14**
See also Belser, Reimond Karel Maria de

Ryan, Cornelius (John) 1920-1974 ..... **CLC 7**
See also CA 69-72; 53-56; CANR 38

Ryan, Michael 1946- .... **CLC 65**
See also CA 49-52; DLBY 82

Ryan, Tim
See Dent, Lester

Rybakov, Anatoli (Naumovich) 1911-**CLC 23, 53**
See also CA 126; 135; SATA 79

Ryder, Jonathan
See Ludlum, Robert

Ryga, George 1932-1987**CLC 14; DAC; DAM MST**
See also CA 101; 124; CANR 43; DLB 60

S. H.
See Hartmann, Sadakichi

S. S.
See Sassoon, Siegfried (Lorraine)

Saba, Umberto 1883-1957 .... **TCLC 33**
See also CA 144; DLB 114

Sabatini, Rafael 1875-1950 .... **TCLC 47**
See also CA 162

Sabato, Ernesto (R.) 1911-**CLC 10, 23; DAM MULT; HLC**
See also CA 97-100; CANR 32, 65; DLB 145; HW; MTCW 1

Sa-Carniero, Mario de 1890-1916 . **TCLC 83**

Sacastru, Martin
See Bioy Casares, Adolfo

Sacher-Masoch, Leopold von 1836(?)-1895 **NCLC 31**

Sachs, Marilyn (Stickle) 1927- .... **CLC 35**
See also AAYA 2; CA 17-20R; CANR 13, 47; CLR 2; JRDA; MAICYA; SAAS 2; SATA 3, 68

Sachs, Nelly 1891-1970 .... **CLC 14, 98**
See also CA 17-18; 25-28R; CAP 2

Sackler, Howard (Oliver) 1929-1982 **CLC 14**
See also CA 61-64; 108; CANR 30; DLB 7

Sacks, Oliver (Wolf) 1933-................. **CLC 67**
See also CA 53-56; CANR 28, 50; INT CANR-28; MTCW 1

Sadakichi
See Hartmann, Sadakichi

Sade, Donatien Alphonse Francois, Comte de 1740-1814 .... **NCLC 47**

Sadoff, Ira 1945- .... **CLC 9**
See also CA 53-56; CANR 5, 21; DLB 120

Saetone
See Camus, Albert

Safire, William 1929- ....**CLC 10**
See also CA 17-20R; CANR 31, 54

Sagan, Carl (Edward) 1934-1996**CLC 30, 112**
See also AAYA 2; CA 25-28R; 155; CANR 11, 36; MTCW 1; SATA 58; SATA-Obit 94

Sagan, Francoise .... **CLC 3, 6, 9, 17, 36**
See also Quoirez, Francoise
See also DLB 83

Sahgal, Nayantara (Pandit) 1927- ....**CLC 41**
See also CA 9-12R; CANR 11

Saint, H(arry) F. 1941- ....**CLC 50**
See also CA 127

St. Aubin de Teran, Lisa 1953-
See Teran, Lisa St. Aubin de
See also CA 118; 126; INT 126

Saint Birgitta of Sweden c. 1303-1373**C M L C 24**

Sainte-Beuve, Charles Augustin 1804-1869 **NCLC 5**

Saint-Exupery, Antoine (Jean Baptiste Marie Roger) de 1900-1944 ....
TCLC 2, 56; DAM NOV; WLC
See also CA 108; 132; CLR 10; DLB 72; MAICYA; MTCW 1; SATA 20

St. John, David
See Hunt, E(verette) Howard, (Jr.)

Saint-John Perse
See Leger, (Marie-Rene Auguste) Alexis Saint-Leger

Saintsbury, George (Edward Bateman) 1845-1933 .... **TCLC 31**
See also CA 160; DLB 57, 149

Sait Faik .... **TCLC 23**
See also Abasiyanik, Sait Faik

Saki .... **TCLC 3; SSC 12**
See also Munro, H(ector) H(ugh)

Sala, George Augustus .... **NCLC 46**

Salama, Hannu 1936- .... **CLC 18**

Salamanca, J(ack) R(ichard) 1922-**CLC 4, 15**
See also CA 25-28R

Sale, J. Kirkpatrick
See Sale, Kirkpatrick

Sale, Kirkpatrick 1937- .... **CLC 68**
See also CA 13-16R; CANR 10

Salinas, Luis Omar 1937- ...... **CLC 90; DAM MULT; HLC**
See also CA 131; DLB 82; HW

Salinas (y Serrano), Pedro 1891(?)-1951 **TCLC 17**
See also CA 117, DLB 134

Salinger, J(erome) D(avid) 1919-**CLC 1, 3, 8, 12, 55, 56; DA; DAB; DAC; DAM MST, NOV, POP; SSC 2, 28; WLC**
See also AAYA 2; CA 5-8R; CANR 39; CDALB 1941-1968; CLR 18; DLB 2, 102, 173; MAICYA; MTCW 1; SATA 67

Salisbury, John
See Caute, (John) David

Salter, James 1925- .... **CLC 7, 52, 59**
See also CA 73-76; DLB 130

Saltus, Edgar (Everton) 1855-1921 . **TCLC 8**
See also CA 105; DLB 202

Saltykov, Mikhail Evgrafovich 1826-1889 **NCLC 16**

Samarakis, Antonis 1919- .... **CLC 5**
See also CA 25-28R; CAAS 16; CANR 36

Sanchez, Florencio 1875-1910 .... **TCLC 37**
See also CA 153; HW

Sanchez, Luis Rafael 1936- .... **CLC 23**
See also CA 128; DLB 145; HW

Sanchez, Sonia 1934-... **CLC 5; BLC 3; DAM**

MTCW 1

Sheldon, Alice Hastings Bradley 1915(?)-1987
See Tiptree, James, Jr.
See also CA 108; 122; CANR 34; INT 108;
MTCW 1

Sheldon, John
See Bloch, Robert (Albert)

Shelley, Mary Wollstonecraft (Godwin) 1797-
1851NCLC **14, 59; DA; DAB; DAC; DAM
MST, NOV; WLC**
See also AAYA 20; CDBLB 1789-1832; DLB
110, 116, 159, 178; SATA 29

Shelley, Percy Bysshe 1792-1822 . NCLC **18;
DA; DAB; DAC; DAM MST, POET; PC
14; WLC**
See also CDBLB 1789-1832; DLB 96, 110, 158

Shepard, Jim 1956- .... CLC **36**
See also CA 137; CANR 59; SATA 90

Shepard, Lucius 1947- .... CLC **34**
See also CA 128; 141

Shepard, Sam 1943-CLC **4, 6, 17, 34, 41, 44;
DAM DRAM; DC 5**
See also AAYA 1; CA 69-72; CABS 3; CANR
22; DLB 7; MTCW 1

Shepherd, Michael
See Ludlum, Robert

Sherburne, Zoa (Morin) 1912- .... CLC **30**
See also AAYA 13; CA 1-4R; CANR 3, 37;
MAICYA; SAAS 18; SATA 3

Sheridan, Frances 1724-1766 .... LC **7**
See also DLB 39, 84

Sheridan, Richard Brinsley 1751-1816N C L C
**5; DA; DAB; DAC; DAM DRAM, MST;
DC 1; WLC**
See also CDBLB 1660-1789; DLB 89

Sherman, Jonathan Marc .... CLC **55**

Sherman, Martin 1941(?)- .... CLC **19**
See also CA 116; 123

Sherwin, Judith Johnson 1936- .... CLC **7, 15**
See also CA 25-28R; CANR 34

Sherwood, Frances 1940- .... CLC **81**
See also CA 146

Sherwood, Robert E(mmet) 1896-1955T C L C
3; DAM DRAM
See also CA 104; 153; DLB 7, 26

Shestov, Lev 1866-1938 .... TCLC **56**

Shevchenko, Taras 1814-1861 .... NCLC **54**

Shiel, M(atthew) P(hipps) 1865-1947TCLC **8**
See also Holmes, Gordon
See also CA 106; 160; DLB 153

Shields, Carol 1935- .... CLC **91, 113; DAC**
See also CA 81-84; CANR 51

Shields, David 1956- .... CLC **97**
See also CA 124; CANR 48

Shiga, Naoya 1883-1971 ..... CLC **33; SSC 23**
See also CA 101; 33-36R; DLB 180

Shilts, Randy 1951-1994 .... CLC **85**
See also AAYA 19; CA 115; 127; 144; CANR
45; INT 127

Shimazaki, Haruki 1872-1943
See Shimazaki Toson
See also CA 105; 134

Shimazaki Toson 1872-1943 .... TCLC **5**
See also Shimazaki, Haruki
See also DLB 180

Sholokhov, Mikhail (Aleksandrovich) 1905-
1984 .... CLC **7, 15**
See also CA 101; 112; MTCW 1; SATA-Obit
36

Shone, Patric
See Hanley, James

Shreve, Susan Richards 1939- .... CLC **23**
See also CA 49-52; CAAS 5; CANR 5, 38, 69;

MAICYA; SATA 46, 95; SATA-Brief 41

Shue, Larry 1946-1985CLC **52; DAM DRAM**
See also CA 145; 117

Shu-Jen, Chou 1881-1936
See Lu Hsun
See also CA 104

Shulman, Alix Kates 1932- .... CLC **2, 10**
See also CA 29-32R; CANR 43; SATA 7

Shuster, Joe 1914- .... CLC **21**

Shute, Nevil .... CLC **30**
See also Norway, Nevil Shute

Shuttle, Penelope (Diane) 1947- .... CLC **7**
See also CA 93-96; CANR 39; DLB 14, 40

Sidney, Mary 1561-1621 .... LC **19, 39**

Sidney, Sir Philip 1554-1586 LC **19, 39; DA;
DAB; DAC; DAM MST, POET**
See also CDBLB Before 1660; DLB 167

Siegel, Jerome 1914-1996 .... CLC **21**
See also CA 116; 151

Siegel, Jerry
See Siegel, Jerome

Sienkiewicz, Henryk (Adam Alexander Pius)
1846-1916 .... TCLC **3**
See also CA 104; 134

Sierra, Gregorio Martinez
See Martinez Sierra, Gregorio

Sierra, Maria (de la O'LeJarraga) Martinez
See Martinez Sierra, Maria (de la O'LeJarraga)

Sigal, Clancy 1926- .... CLC **7**
See also CA 1-4R

Sigourney, Lydia Howard (Huntley) 1791-1865
NCLC **21**
See also DLB 1, 42, 73

Siguenza y Gongora, Carlos de 1645-1700L C
8

Sigurjonsson, Johann 1880-1919 ... TCLC **27**

Sikelianos, Angelos 1884-1951 .... TCLC **39**

Silkin, Jon 1930- .... CLC **2, 6, 43**
See also CA 5-8R; CAAS 5; DLB 27

Silko, Leslie (Marmon) 1948-CLC **23, 74, 114;
DA; DAC; DAM MST, MULT, POP;
WLCS**
See also AAYA 14; CA 115; 122; CANR 45,
65; DLB 143, 175; NNAL

Sillanpaa, Frans Eemil 1888-1964 .... CLC **19**
See also CA 129; 93-96; MTCW 1

Sillitoe, Alan 1928- .... CLC **1, 3, 6, 10, 19, 57**
See also AITN 1; CA 9-12R; CAAS 2; CANR
8, 26, 55; CDBLB 1960 to Present; DLB 14,
139; MTCW 1; SATA 61

Silone, Ignazio 1900-1978 .... CLC **4**
See also CA 25-28; 81-84; CANR 34; CAP 2;
MTCW 1

Silver, Joan Micklin 1935- .... CLC **20**
See also CA 114; 121; INT 121

Silver, Nicholas
See Faust, Frederick (Schiller)

Silverberg, Robert 1935- CLC **7; DAM POP**
See also AAYA 24; CA 1-4R; CAAS 3; CANR
1, 20, 36; DLB 8; INT CANR-20; MAICYA;
MTCW 1; SATA 13, 91

Silverstein, Alvin 1933- .... CLC **17**
See also CA 49-52; CANR 2; CLR 25; JRDA;
MAICYA; SATA 8, 69

Silverstein, Virginia B(arbara Opshelor) 1937-
CLC **17**
See also CA 49-52; CANR 2; CLR 25; JRDA;
MAICYA; SATA 8, 69

Sim, Georges
See Simenon, Georges (Jacques Christian)

Simak, Clifford D(onald) 1904-1988CLC **1, 55**
See also CA 1-4R; 125; CANR 1, 35; DLB 8;
MTCW 1; SATA-Obit 56

Simenon, Georges (Jacques Christian) 1903-
1989 .. CLC **1, 2, 3, 8, 18, 47; DAM POP**
See also CA 85-88; 129; CANR 35; DLB 72;
DLBY 89; MTCW 1

Simic, Charles 1938- ....CLC **6, 9, 22, 49, 68;
DAM POET**
See also CA 29-32R; CAAS 4; CANR 12, 33,
52, 61; DLB 105

Simmel, Georg 1858-1918 .... TCLC **64**
See also CA 157

Simmons, Charles (Paul) 1924- .... CLC **57**
See also CA 89-92; INT 89-92

Simmons, Dan 1948- ...... CLC **44; DAM POP**
See also AAYA 16; CA 138; CANR 53

Simmons, James (Stewart Alexander) 1933-
CLC **43**
See also CA 105; CAAS 21; DLB 40

Simms, William Gilmore 1806-1870 NCLC **3**
See also DLB 3, 30, 59, 73

Simon, Carly 1945- .... CLC **26**
See also CA 105

Simon, Claude 1913-1984 .. CLC **4, 9, 15, 39;
DAM NOV**
See also CA 89-92; CANR 33; DLB 83; MTCW
1

Simon, (Marvin) Neil 1927-CLC **6, 11, 31, 39,
70; DAM DRAM**
See also AITN 1; CA 21-24R; CANR 26, 54;
DLB 7; MTCW 1

Simon, Paul (Frederick) 1941(?)- ..... CLC **17**
See also CA 116; 153

Simonon, Paul 1956(?)- .... CLC **30**

Simpson, Harriette
See Arnow, Harriette (Louisa) Simpson

Simpson, Louis (Aston Marantz) 1923-CLC **4,
7, 9, 32; DAM POET**
See also CA 1-4R; CAAS 4; CANR 1, 61; DLB
5; MTCW 1

Simpson, Mona (Elizabeth) 1957- ... CLC **44**
See also CA 122; 135; CANR 68

Simpson, N(orman) F(rederick) 1919-CLC **29**
See also CA 13-16R; DLB 13

Sinclair, Andrew (Annandale) 1935-.CLC **2,
14**
See also CA 9-12R; CAAS 5; CANR 14, 38;
DLB 14; MTCW 1

Sinclair, Emil
See Hesse, Hermann

Sinclair, Iain 1943- .... CLC **76**
See also CA 132

Sinclair, Iain MacGregor
See Sinclair, Iain

Sinclair, Irene
See Griffith, D(avid Lewelyn) W(ark)

Sinclair, Mary Amelia St. Clair 1865(?)-1946
See Sinclair, May
See also CA 104

Sinclair, May 1863-1946 .... TCLC **3, 11**
See also Sinclair, Mary Amelia St. Clair
See also CA 166; DLB 36, 135

Sinclair, Roy
See Griffith, D(avid Lewelyn) W(ark)

Sinclair, Upton (Beall) 1878-1968 CLC **1, 11,
15, 63; DA; DAB; DAC; DAM MST, NOV;
WLC**
See also CA 5-8R; 25-28R; CANR 7; CDALB
1929-1941; DLB 9; INT CANR-7; MTCW
1; SATA 9

Singer, Isaac
See Singer, Isaac Bashevis

Singer, Isaac Bashevis 1904-1991CLC **1, 3, 6,
9, 11, 15, 23, 38, 69, 111; DA; DAB; DAC;
DAM MST, NOV; SSC 3; WLC**

Swift, Jonathan 1667-1745 **LC 1; DA; DAB; DAC; DAM MST, NOV, POET; PC 9; WLC**
See also CDBLB 1660-1789; DLB 39, 95, 101; SATA 19
Swinburne, Algernon Charles 1837-1909 **TCLC 8, 36; DA; DAB; DAC; DAM MST, POET; PC 24; WLC**
See also CA 105; 140; CDBLB 1832-1890; DLB 35, 57
Swinfen, Ann .... **CLC 34**
Swinnerton, Frank Arthur 1884-1982**CLC 31**
See also CA 108; DLB 34
Swithen, John
See King, Stephen (Edwin)
Sylvia
See Ashton-Warner, Sylvia (Constance)
Symmes, Robert Edward
See Duncan, Robert (Edward)
Symonds, John Addington 1840-1893 **N C L C 34**
See also DLB 57, 144
Symons, Arthur 1865-1945 .... **TCLC 11**
See also CA 107; DLB 19, 57, 149
Symons, Julian (Gustave) 1912-1994 **CLC 2, 14, 32**
See also CA 49-52; 147; CAAS 3; CANR 3, 33, 59; DLB 87, 155; DLBY 92; MTCW 1
Synge, (Edmund) J(ohn) M(illington) 1871-1909 .. **TCLC 6, 37; DAM DRAM; DC 2**
See also CA 104; 141; CDBLB 1890-1914; DLB 10, 19
Syruc, J.
See Milosz, Czeslaw
Szirtes, George 1948- .... **CLC 46**
See also CA 109; CANR 27, 61
Szymborska, Wislawa 1923- .... **CLC 99**
See also CA 154; DLBY 96
T. O., Nik
See Annensky, Innokenty (Fyodorovich)
Tabori, George 1914- .... **CLC 19**
See also CA 49-52; CANR 4, 69
Tagore, Rabindranath 1861-1941**TCLC 3, 53; DAM DRAM, POET; PC 8**
See also CA 104; 120; MTCW 1
Taine, Hippolyte Adolphe 1828-1893 . **N C L C 15**
Talese, Gay 1932- .... **CLC 37**
See also AITN 1; CA 1-4R; CANR 9, 58; DLB 185; INT CANR-9; MTCW 1
Tallent, Elizabeth (Ann) 1954- .... **CLC 45**
See also CA 117; CANR 72; DLB 130
Tally, Ted 1952-............................... **CLC 42**
See also CA 120; 124; INT 124
Tamayo y Baus, Manuel 1829-1898 . **NCLC 1**
Tammsaare, A(nton) H(ansen) 1878-1940 **TCLC 27**
See also CA 164
Tam'si, Tchicaya U
See Tchicaya, Gerald Felix
Tan, Amy (Ruth) 1952-**CLC 59; DAM MULT, NOV, POP**
See also AAYA 9; BEST 89:3; CA 136; CANR 54; DLB 173; SATA 75
Tandem, Felix
See Spitteler, Carl (Friedrich Georg)
Tanizaki, Jun'ichiro 1886-1965**CLC 8, 14, 28; SSC 21**
See also CA 93-96; 25-28R; DLB 180
Tanner, William
See Amis, Kingsley (William)
Tao Lao
See Storni, Alfonsina

Tarassoff, Lev
See Troyat, Henri
Tarbell, Ida M(inerva) 1857-1944 . **TCLC 40**
See also CA 122; DLB 47
Tarkington, (Newton) Booth 1869-1946**TCLC 9**
See also CA 110; 143; DLB 9, 102; SATA 17
Tarkovsky, Andrei (Arsenyevich) 1932-1986 **CLC 75**
See also CA 127
Tartt, Donna 1964(?)- ....**CLC 76**
See also CA 142
Tasso, Torquato 1544-1595 .... **LC 5**
Tate, (John Orley) Allen 1899-1979**CLC 2, 4, 6, 9, 11, 14, 24**
See also CA 5-8R; 85-88; CANR 32; DLB 4, 45, 63; DLBD 17; MTCW 1
Tate, Ellalice
See Hibbert, Eleanor Alice Burford
Tate, James (Vincent) 1943- ..... **CLC 2, 6, 25**
See also CA 21-24R; CANR 29, 57; DLB 5, 169
Tavel, Ronald 1940- ....**CLC 6**
See also CA 21-24R; CANR 33
Taylor, C(ecil) P(hilip) 1929-1981 ..... **CLC 27**
See also CA 25-28R; 105; CANR 47
Taylor, Edward 1642(?)-1729 ..... **LC 11; DA; DAB; DAC; DAM MST, POET**
See also DLB 24
Taylor, Eleanor Ross 1920- .... **CLC 5**
See also CA 81-84; CANR 70
Taylor, Elizabeth 1912-1975 ..... **CLC 2, 4, 29**
See also CA 13-16R; CANR 9, 70; DLB 139; MTCW 1; SATA 13
Taylor, Frederick Winslow 1856-1915 **T C L C 76**
Taylor, Henry (Splawn) 1942- ....**CLC 44**
See also CA 33-36R; CAAS 7; CANR 31; DLB 5
Taylor, Kamala (Purnaiya) 1924-
See Markandaya, Kamala
See also CA 77-80
Taylor, Mildred D. ....**CLC 21**
See also AAYA 10; BW 1; CA 85-88; CANR 25; CLR 9; DLB 52; JRDA; MAICYA; SAAS 5; SATA 15, 70
Taylor, Peter (Hillsman) 1917-1994**CLC 1, 4, 18, 37, 44, 50, 71; SSC 10**
See also CA 13-16R; 147; CANR 9, 50; DLBY 81, 94; INT CANR-9; MTCW 1
Taylor, Robert Lewis 1912- ....**CLC 14**
See also CA 1-4R; CANR 3, 64; SATA 10
Tchekhov, Anton
See Chekhov, Anton (Pavlovich)
Tchicaya, Gerald Felix 1931-1988 . **CLC 101**
See also CA 129; 125
Tchicaya U Tam'si
See Tchicaya, Gerald Felix
Teasdale, Sara 1884-1933 .... **TCLC 4**
See also CA 104; 163; DLB 45; SATA 32
Tegner, Esaias 1782-1846 .... **NCLC 2**
Teilhard de Chardin, (Marie Joseph) Pierre 1881-1955 .... **TCLC 9**
See also CA 105
Temple, Ann
See Mortimer, Penelope (Ruth)
Tennant, Emma (Christina) 1937-**CLC 13, 52**
See also CA 65-68; CAAS 9; CANR 10, 38, 59; DLB 14
Tenneshaw, S. M.
See Silverberg, Robert
Tennyson, Alfred 1809-1892 ... **NCLC 30, 65; DA; DAB; DAC; DAM MST, POET; PC**

6; **WLC**
See also CDBLB 1832-1890; DLB 32
Teran, Lisa St. Aubin de .... **CLC 36**
See also St. Aubin de Teran, Lisa
Terence 195(?)B.C.-159B.C. **CMLC 14; DC 7**
Teresa de Jesus, St. 1515-1582 .... **LC 18**
Terkel, Louis 1912-
See Terkel, Studs
See also CA 57-60; CANR 18, 45, 67; MTCW 1
Terkel, Studs .... **CLC 38**
See also Terkel, Louis
See also AITN 1
Terry, C. V.
See Slaughter, Frank G(ill)
Terry, Megan 1932- .... **CLC 19**
See also CA 77-80; CABS 3; CANR 43; DLB 7
Tertullian c. 155-c. 245 .... **CMLC 29**
Tertz, Abram
See Sinyavsky, Andrei (Donatevich)
Tesich, Steve 1943(?)-1996 .... **CLC 40, 69**
See also CA 105; 152; DLBY 83
Teternikov, Fyodor Kuzmich 1863-1927
See Sologub, Fyodor
See also CA 104
Tevis, Walter 1928-1984 .... **CLC 42**
See also CA 113
Tey, Josephine .... **TCLC 14**
See also Mackintosh, Elizabeth
See also DLB 77
Thackeray, William Makepeace 1811-1863 **NCLC 5, 14, 22, 43; DA; DAB; DAC; DAM MST, NOV; WLC**
See also CDBLB 1832-1890; DLB 21, 55, 159, 163; SATA 23
Thakura, Ravindranatha
See Tagore, Rabindranath
Tharoor, Shashi 1956- .... **CLC 70**
See also CA 141
Thelwell, Michael Miles 1939- .... **CLC 22**
See also BW 2; CA 101
Theobald, Lewis, Jr.
See Lovecraft, H(oward) P(hillips)
Theodorescu, Ion N. 1880-1967
See Arghezi, Tudor
See also CA 116
Theriault, Yves 1915-1983 .... **CLC 79; DAC; DAM MST**
See also CA 102; DLB 88
Theroux, Alexander (Louis) 1939-**CLC 2, 25**
See also CA 85-88; CANR 20, 63
Theroux, Paul (Edward) 1941- **CLC 5, 8, 11, 15, 28, 46; DAM POP**
See also BEST 89:4; CA 33-36R; CANR 20, 45; DLB 2; MTCW 1; SATA 44
Thesen, Sharon 1946-....................... **CLC 56**
See also CA 163
Thevenin, Denis
See Duhamel, Georges
Thibault, Jacques Anatole Francois 1844-1924
See France, Anatole
See also CA 106; 127; DAM NOV; MTCW 1
Thiele, Colin (Milton) 1920-............. **CLC 17**
See also CA 29-32R; CANR 12, 28, 53; CLR 27; MAICYA; SAAS 2; SATA 14, 72
Thomas, Audrey (Callahan) 1935-**CLC 7, 13, 37, 107; SSC 20**
See also AITN 2; CA 21-24R; CAAS 19; CANR 36, 58; DLB 60; MTCW 1
Thomas, D(onald) M(ichael) 1935-. **CLC 13, 22, 31**
See also CA 61-64; CAAS 11; CANR 17, 45; CDBLB 1960 to Present; DLB 40; INT

DAM POET
See also CA 9-12R; CANR 7, 38, 60; DLB 5

Van Dyne, Edith
See Baum, L(yman) Frank

van Itallie, Jean-Claude 1936- ....CLC 3
See also CA 45-48; CAAS 2; CANR 1, 48; DLB 7

van Ostaijen, Paul 1896-1928 .... TCLC 33
See also CA 163

Van Peebles, Melvin 1932-.CLC 2, 20; DAM MULT
See also BW 2; CA 85-88; CANR 27, 67

Vansittart, Peter 1920-...................... CLC 42
See also CA 1-4R; CANR 3, 49

Van Vechten, Carl 1880-1964 .... CLC 33
See also CA 89-92; DLB 4, 9, 51

Van Vogt, A(lfred) E(lton) 1912-.........CLC 1
See also CA 21-24R; CANR 28; DLB 8; SATA 14

Varda, Agnes 1928- .... CLC 16
See also CA 116; 122

Vargas Llosa, (Jorge) Mario (Pedro) 1936-
CLC 3, 6, 9, 10, 15, 31, 42, 85; DA; DAB; DAC; DAM MST, MULT, NOV; HLC
See also CA 73-76; CANR 18, 32, 42, 67; DLB 145; HW; MTCW 1

Vasiliu, Gheorghe 1881-1957
See Bacovia, George
See also CA 123

Vassa, Gustavus
See Equiano, Olaudah

Vassilikos, Vassilis 1933- .... CLC 4, 8
See also CA 81-84

Vaughan, Henry 1621-1695 .... LC 27
See also DLB 131

Vaughn, Stephanie .... CLC 62

Vazov, Ivan (Minchov) 1850-1921 . TCLC 25
See also CA 121; 167; DLB 147

Veblen, Thorstein B(unde) 1857-1929 T C L C 31
See also CA 115; 165

Vega, Lope de 1562-1635 .... LC 23

Venison, Alfred
See Pound, Ezra (Weston Loomis)

Verdi, Marie de
See Mencken, H(enry) L(ouis)

Verdu, Matilde
See Cela, Camilo Jose

Verga, Giovanni (Carmelo) 1840-1922T C L C 3; SSC 21
See also CA 104; 123

Vergil 70B.C.-19B.C. .....CMLC 9; DA; DAB; DAC; DAM MST, POET; PC 12; WLCS

Verhaeren, Emile (Adolphe Gustave) 1855-1916 TCLC 12
See also CA 109

Verlaine, Paul (Marie) 1844-1896NCLC 2, 51; DAM POET; PC 2

Verne, Jules (Gabriel) 1828-1905TCLC 6, 52
See also AAYA 16; CA 110; 131; DLB 123; JRDA; MAICYA; SATA 21

Very, Jones 1813-1880 .... NCLC 9
See also DLB 1

Vesaas, Tarjei 1897-1970 .... CLC 48
See also CA 29-32R

Vialis, Gaston
See Simenon, Georges (Jacques Christian)

Vian, Boris 1920-1959 .... TCLC 9
See also CA 106; 164; DLB 72

Viaud, (Louis Marie) Julien 1850-1923
See Loti, Pierre
See also CA 107

Vicar, Henry

See Felsen, Henry Gregor

Vicker, Angus
See Felsen, Henry Gregor

Vidal, Gore 1925-CLC 2, 4, 6, 8, 10, 22, 33, 72; DAM NOV, POP
See also AITN 1; BEST 90:2; CA 5-8R; CANR 13, 45, 65; DLB 6, 152; INT CANR-13; MTCW 1

Viereck, Peter (Robert Edwin) 1916-.CLC 4
See also CA 1-4R; CANR 1, 47; DLB 5

Vigny, Alfred (Victor) de 1797-1863NCLC 7; DAM POET
See also DLB 119, 192

Vilakazi, Benedict Wallet 1906-1947TCLC 37
See also CA 168

Villa, Jose Garcia 1904-1997 .... PC 22
See also CA 25-28R; CANR 12

Villaurrutia, Xavier 1903-1950 ...... TCLC 80
See also HW

Villiers de l'Isle Adam, Jean Marie Mathias Philippe Auguste, Comte de 1838-1889 NCLC 3; SSC 14
See also DLB 123

Villon, Francois 1431-1463(?) .... PC 13

Vinci, Leonardo da 1452-1519 .... LC 12

Vine, Barbara ....CLC 50
See also Rendell, Ruth (Barbara)
See also BEST 90:4

Vinge, Joan (Carol) D(ennison) 1948-CLC 30; SSC 24
See also CA 93-96; CANR 72; SATA 36

Violis, G.
See Simenon, Georges (Jacques Christian)

Virgil
See Vergil

Visconti, Luchino 1906-1976 ....CLC 16
See also CA 81-84; 65-68; CANR 39

Vittorini, Elio 1908-1966 .... CLC 6, 9, 14
See also CA 133; 25-28R

Vizenor, Gerald Robert 1934-CLC 103; DAM MULT
See also CA 13-16R; CAAS 22; CANR 5, 21, 44, 67; DLB 175; NNAL

Vizinczey, Stephen 1933- ....CLC 40
See also CA 128; INT 128

Vliet, R(ussell) G(ordon) 1929-1984 .CLC 22
See also CA 37-40R; 112; CANR 18

Vogau, Boris Andreyevich 1894-1937(?)
See Pilnyak, Boris
See also CA 123

Vogel, Paula A(nne) 1951- ....CLC 76
See also CA 108

Voigt, Cynthia 1942- ....CLC 30
See also AAYA 3; CA 106; CANR 18, 37, 40; CLR 13,48; INT CANR-18; JRDA; MAICYA; SATA 48, 79; SATA-Brief 33

Voigt, Ellen Bryant 1943- ....CLC 54
See also CA 69-72; CANR 11, 29, 55; DLB 120

Voinovich, Vladimir (Nikolaevich) 1932-C L C 10, 49
See also CA 81-84; CAAS 12; CANR 33, 67; MTCW 1

Vollmann, William T. 1959-...CLC 89; DAM NOV, POP
See also CA 134; CANR 67

Voloshinov, V. N.
See Bakhtin, Mikhail Mikhailovich

Voltaire 1694-1778 LC 14; DA; DAB; DAC; DAM DRAM, MST; SSC 12; WLC

von Daeniken, Erich 1935-.................CLC 30
See also AITN 1; CA 37-40R; CANR 17, 44

von Daniken, Erich
See von Daeniken, Erich

von Heidenstam, (Carl Gustaf) Verner
See Heidenstam, (Carl Gustaf) Verner von

von Heyse, Paul (Johann Ludwig)
See Heyse, Paul (Johann Ludwig von)

von Hofmannsthal, Hugo
See Hofmannsthal, Hugo von

von Horvath, Odon
See Horvath, Oedoen von

von Horvath, Oedoen
See Horvath, Oedoen von

von Liliencron, (Friedrich Adolf Axel) Detlev
See Liliencron, (Friedrich Adolf Axel) Detlev von

Vonnegut, Kurt, Jr. 1922-CLC 1, 2, 3, 4, 5, 8, 12, 22, 40, 60, 111; DA; DAB; DAC; DAM MST, NOV, POP; SSC 8; WLC
See also AAYA 6; AITN 1; BEST 90:4; CA 1-4R; CANR 1, 25, 49; CDALB 1968-1988; DLB 2, 8, 152; DLBD 3; DLBY 80; MTCW 1

Von Rachen, Kurt
See Hubbard, L(afayette) Ron(ald)

von Rezzori (d'Arezzo), Gregor
See Rezzori (d'Arezzo), Gregor von

von Sternberg, Josef
See Sternberg, Josef von

Vorster, Gordon 1924- ....CLC 34
See also CA 133

Vosce, Trudie
See Ozick, Cynthia

Voznesensky, Andrei (Andreievich) 1933-
CLC 1, 15, 57; DAM POET
See also CA 89-92; CANR 37; MTCW 1

Waddington, Miriam 1917-...............CLC 28
See also CA 21-24R; CANR 12, 30; DLB 68

Wagman, Fredrica 1937- ....CLC 7
See also CA 97-100; INT 97-100

Wagner, Linda W.
See Wagner-Martin, Linda (C.)

Wagner, Linda Welshimer
See Wagner-Martin, Linda (C.)

Wagner, Richard 1813-1883 ....NCLC 9
See also DLB 129

Wagner-Martin, Linda (C.) 1936- ....CLC 50
See also CA 159

Wagoner, David (Russell) 1926- CLC 3, 5, 15
See also CA 1-4R; CAAS 3; CANR 2, 71; DLB 5; SATA 14

Wah, Fred(erick James) 1939- ....CLC 44
See also CA 107; 141; DLB 60

Wahloo, Per 1926-1975 ....CLC 7
See also CA 61-64

Wahloo, Peter
See Wahloo, Per

Wain, John (Barrington) 1925-1994 .CLC 2, 11, 15, 46
See also CA 5-8R; 145; CAAS 4; CANR 23, 54; CDBLB 1960 to Present; DLB 15, 27, 139, 155; MTCW 1

Wajda, Andrzej 1926- ....CLC 16
See also CA 102

Wakefield, Dan 1932- ....CLC 7
See also CA 21-24R; CAAS 7

Wakoski, Diane 1937-.CLC 2, 4, 7, 9, 11, 40; DAM POET; PC 15
See also CA 13-16R; CAAS 1; CANR 9, 60; DLB 5; INT CANR-9

Wakoski-Sherbell, Diane
See Wakoski, Diane

Walcott, Derek (Alton) 1930-CLC 2, 4, 9, 14, 25, 42, 67, 76; BLC 3; DAB; DAC; DAM MST, MULT, POET; DC 7
See also BW 2; CA 89-92; CANR 26, 47; DLB

See also CA 121; 148

Welch, James 1940- ..... CLC 6, 14, 52; **DAM MULT, POP**
See also CA 85-88; CANR 42, 66; DLB 175; NNAL

Weldon, Fay 1931-..CLC 6, 9, 11, 19, 36, 59; **DAM POP**
See also CA 21-24R; CANR 16, 46, 63; CDBLB 1960 to Present; DLB 14, 194; INT CANR-16; MTCW 1

Wellek, Rene 1903-1995 .... CLC 28
See also CA 5-8R; 150; CAAS 7; CANR 8; DLB 63; INT CANR-8

Weller, Michael 1942- .... CLC 10, 53
See also CA 85-88

Weller, Paul 1958- .... CLC 26

Wellershoff, Dieter 1925- .... CLC 46
See also CA 89-92; CANR 16, 37

Welles, (George) Orson 1915-1985CLC 20, 80
See also CA 93-96; 117

Wellman, John McDowell 1945-
See Wellman, Mac
See also CA 166

Wellman, Mac 1945- .... CLC 65
See also Wellman, John McDowell; Wellman, John McDowell

Wellman, Manly Wade 1903-1986 ... CLC 49
See also CA 1-4R; 118; CANR 6, 16, 44; SATA 6; SATA-Obit 47

Wells, Carolyn 1869(?)-1942 .... TCLC 35
See also CA 113; DLB 11

Wells, H(erbert) G(eorge) 1866-1946TCLC 6, 12, 19; DA; DAB; DAC; **DAM MST, NOV; SSC 6; WLC**
See also AAYA 18; CA 110; 121; CDBLB 1914-1945; DLB 34, 70, 156, 178; MTCW 1; SATA 20

Wells, Rosemary 1943-..................... CLC 12
See also AAYA 13; CA 85-88; CANR 48; CLR 16; MAICYA; SAAS 1; SATA 18, 69

Welty, Eudora 1909-.CLC 1, 2, 5, 14, 22, 33, 105; DA; DAB; DAC; **DAM MST, NOV; SSC 1, 27; WLC**
See also CA 9-12R; CABS 1; CANR 32, 65; CDALB 1941-1968; DLB 2, 102, 143; DLBD 12; DLBY 87; MTCW 1

Wen I-to 1899-1946 .... TCLC 28

Wentworth, Robert
See Hamilton, Edmond

Werfel, Franz (Viktor) 1890-1945 ... TCLC 8
See also CA 104; 161; DLB 81, 124

Wergeland, Henrik Arnold 1808-1845N C L C 5

Wersba, Barbara 1932-..................... CLC 30
See also AAYA 2; CA 29-32R; CANR 16, 38; CLR 3; DLB 52; JRDA; MAICYA; SAAS 2; SATA 1, 58

Wertmueller, Lina 1928- .... CLC 16
See also CA 97-100; CANR 39

Wescott, Glenway 1901-1987 .... CLC 13
See also CA 13-16R; 121; CANR 23, 70; DLB 4, 9, 102

Wesker, Arnold 1932-.... CLC 3, 5, 42; DAB; **DAM DRAM**
See also CA 1-4R; CAAS 7; CANR 1, 33; CDBLB 1960 to Present; DLB 13; MTCW 1

Wesley, Richard (Errol) 1945- .... CLC 7
See also BW 1; CA 57-60; CANR 27; DLB 38

Wessel, Johan Herman 1742-1785 .... LC 7

West, Anthony (Panther) 1914-1987 CLC 50
See also CA 45-48; 124; CANR 3, 19; DLB 15

West, C. P.
See Wodehouse, P(elham) G(renville)

West, (Mary) Jessamyn 1902-1984CLC 7, 17
See also CA 9-12R; 112; CANR 27; DLB 6; DLBY 84; MTCW 1; SATA-Obit 37

West, Morris L(anglo) 1916-........ CLC 6, 33
See also CA 5-8R; CANR 24, 49, 64; MTCW 1

West, Nathanael 1903-1940 TCLC 1, 14, 44; **SSC 16**
See also CA 104; 125; CDALB 1929-1941; DLB 4, 9, 28; MTCW 1

West, Owen
See Koontz, Dean R(ay)

West, Paul 1930- .... CLC 7, 14, 96
See also CA 13-16R; CAAS 7; CANR 22, 53; DLB 14; INT CANR-22

West, Rebecca 1892-1983 ... CLC 7, 9, 31, 50
See also CA 5-8R; 109; CANR 19; DLB 36; DLBY 83; MTCW 1

Westall, Robert (Atkinson) 1929-1993CLC 17
See also AAYA 12; CA 69-72; 141; CANR 18, 68; CLR 13; JRDA; MAICYA; SAAS 2; SATA 23, 69; SATA-Obit 75

Westlake, Donald E(dwin) 1933- CLC 7, 33; **DAM POP**
See also CA 17-20R; CAAS 13; CANR 16, 44, 65; INT CANR-16

Westmacott, Mary
See Christie, Agatha (Mary Clarissa)

Weston, Allen
See Norton, Andre

Wetcheek, J. L.
See Feuchtwanger, Lion

Wetering, Janwillem van de
See van de Wetering, Janwillem

Wetherald, Agnes Ethelwyn 1857-1940TCLC 81
See also DLB 99

Wetherell, Elizabeth
See Warner, Susan (Bogert)

Whale, James 1889-1957 .... TCLC 63

Whalen, Philip 1923- .... CLC 6, 29
See also CA 9-12R; CANR 5, 39; DLB 16

Wharton, Edith (Newbold Jones) 1862-1937 TCLC 3, 9, 27, 53; DA; DAB; DAC; **DAM MST, NOV; SSC 6; WLC**
See also AAYA 25; CA 104; 132; CDALB 1865-1917; DLB 4, 9, 12, 78, 189; DLBD 13; MTCW 1

Wharton, James
See Mencken, H(enry) L(ouis)

Wharton, William (a pseudonym) CLC 18, 37
See also CA 93-96; DLBY 80; INT 93-96

Wheatley (Peters), Phillis 1754(?)-1784LC 3; BLC 3; DA; DAC; **DAM MST, MULT, POET; PC 3; WLC**
See also CDALB 1640-1865; DLB 31, 50

Wheelock, John Hall 1886-1978 .... CLC 14
See also CA 13-16R; 77-80; CANR 14; DLB 45

White, E(lwyn) B(rooks) 1899-1985 CLC 10, 34, 39; **DAM POP**
See also AITN 2; CA 13-16R; 116; CANR 16, 37; CLR 1, 21; DLB 11, 22; MAICYA; MTCW 1; SATA 2, 29, 100; SATA-Obit 44

White, Edmund (Valentine III) 1940-CLC 27, 110; **DAM POP**
See also AAYA 7; CA 45-48; CANR 3, 19, 36, 62; MTCW 1

White, Patrick (Victor Martindale) 1912-1990 CLC 3, 4, 5, 7, 9, 18, 65, 69
See also CA 81-84; 132; CANR 43; MTCW 1

White, Phyllis Dorothy James 1920-
See James, P. D.
See also CA 21-24R; CANR 17, 43, 65; DAM

POP; MTCW 1

White, T(erence) H(anbury) 1906-1964 C L C 30
See also AAYA 22; CA 73-76; CANR 37; DLB 160; JRDA; MAICYA; SATA 12

White, Terence de Vere 1912-1994 ...CLC 49
See also CA 49-52; 145; CANR 3

White, Walter F(rancis) 1893-1955 TCLC 15
See also White, Walter
See also BW 1; CA 115; 124; DLB 51

White, William Hale 1831-1913
See Rutherford, Mark
See also CA 121

Whitehead, E(dward) A(nthony) 1933-CLC 5
See also CA 65-68; CANR 58

Whitemore, Hugh (John) 1936- ....CLC 37
See also CA 132; INT 132

Whitman, Sarah Helen (Power) 1803-1878 **NCLC 19**
See also DLB 1

Whitman, Walt(er) 1819-1892..NCLC 4, 31; DA; DAB; DAC; **DAM MST, POET; PC 3; WLC**
See also CDALB 1640-1865; DLB 3, 64; SATA 20

Whitney, Phyllis A(yame) 1903- ..... CLC 42; **DAM POP**
See also AITN 2; BEST 90:3; CA 1-4R; CANR 3, 25, 38, 60; JRDA; MAICYA; SATA 1, 30

Whittemore, (Edward) Reed (Jr.) 1919-CLC 4
See also CA 9-12R; CAAS 8; CANR 4; DLB 5

Whittier, John Greenleaf 1807-1892NCLC 8, 59
See also DLB 1

Whittlebot, Hernia
See Coward, Noel (Peirce)

Wicker, Thomas Grey 1926-
See Wicker, Tom
See also CA 65-68; CANR 21, 46

Wicker, Tom ....CLC 7
See also Wicker, Thomas Grey

Wideman, John Edgar 1941- CLC 5, 34, 36, 67; BLC 3; **DAM MULT**
See also BW 2; CA 85-88; CANR 14, 42, 67; DLB 33, 143

Wiebe, Rudy (Henry) 1934- .. CLC 6, 11, 14; DAC; **DAM MST**
See also CA 37-40R; CANR 42, 67; DLB 60

Wieland, Christoph Martin 1733-1813N C L C 17
See also DLB 97

Wiene, Robert 1881-1938 .... TCLC 56

Wieners, John 1934-............................CLC 7
See also CA 13-16R; DLB 16

Wiesel, Elie(zer) 1928- CLC 3, 5, 11, 37; DA; DAB; DAC; **DAM MST, NOV; WLCS 2**
See also AAYA 7; AITN 1; CA 5-8R; CAAS 4; CANR 8, 40, 65; DLB 83; DLBY 87; INT CANR-8; MTCW 1; SATA 56

Wiggins, Marianne 1947- ....CLC 57
See also BEST 89:3; CA 130; CANR 60

Wight, James Alfred 1916-1995
See Herriot, James
See also CA 77-80; SATA 55; SATA-Brief 44

Wilbur, Richard (Purdy) 1921-CLC 3, 6, 9, 14, 53, 110; DA; DAB; DAC; **DAM MST, POET**
See also CA 1-4R; CABS 2; CANR 2, 29; DLB 5, 169; INT CANR-29; MTCW 1; SATA 9

Wild, Peter 1940- ....CLC 14
See also CA 37-40R; DLB 5

Wilde, Oscar (Fingal O'Flahertie Wills) 1854(?)-1900TCLC 1, 8, 23, 41; DA; DAB;

Wolfe, Thomas Kennerly, Jr. 1930-
See Wolfe, Tom
See also CA 13-16R; CANR 9, 33, 70; DAM
POP; DLB 185; INT CANR-9; MTCW 1
Wolfe, Tom .... CLC 1, 2, 9, 15, 35, 51
See also Wolfe, Thomas Kennerly, Jr.
See also AAYA 8; AITN 2; BEST 89:1; DLB
152
Wolff, Geoffrey (Ansell) 1937- .... CLC 41
See also CA 29-32R; CANR 29, 43
Wolff, Sonia
See Levitin, Sonia (Wolff)
Wolff, Tobias (Jonathan Ansell) 1945-.. C L C
39, 64
See also AAYA 16; BEST 90:2; CA 114; 117;
CAAS 22; CANR 54; DLB 130; INT 117
Wolfram von Eschenbach c. 1170-c. 1220
CMLC 5
See also DLB 138
Wolitzer, Hilma 1930- .... CLC 17
See also CA 65-68; CANR 18, 40; INT CANR-
18; SATA 31
Wollstonecraft, Mary 1759-1797 .... LC 5
See also CDBLB 1789-1832; DLB 39, 104, 158
Wonder, Stevie .... CLC 12
See also Morris, Steveland Judkins
Wong, Jade Snow 1922- .... CLC 17
See also CA 109
Woodberry, George Edward 1855-1930
TCLC 73
See also CA 165; DLB 71, 103
Woodcott, Keith
See Brunner, John (Kilian Houston)
Woodruff, Robert W.
See Mencken, H(enry) L(ouis)
Woolf, (Adeline) Virginia 1882-1941TCLC 1,
5, 20, 43, 56; DA; DAB; DAC; DAM MST,
NOV; SSC 7; WLC
See also CA 104; 130; CANR 64; CDBLB
1914-1945; DLB 36, 100, 162; DLBD 10;
MTCW 1
Woolf, Virginia Adeline
See Woolf, (Adeline) Virginia
Woollcott, Alexander (Humphreys) 1887-1943
TCLC 5
See also CA 105; 161; DLB 29
Woolrich, Cornell 1903-1968 .... CLC 77
See also Hopley-Woolrich, Cornell George
Wordsworth, Dorothy 1771-1855 ..NCLC 25
See also DLB 107
Wordsworth, William 1770-1850 ..NCLC 12,
38; DA; DAB; DAC; DAM MST, POET;
PC 4; WLC
See also CDBLB 1789-1832; DLB 93, 107
Wouk, Herman 1915-CLC 1, 9, 38; DAM NOV,
POP
See also CA 5-8R; CANR 6, 33, 67; DLBY 82;
INT CANR-6; MTCW 1
Wright, Charles (Penzel, Jr.) 1935-CLC 6, 13,
28
See also CA 29-32R; CAAS 7; CANR 23, 36,
62; DLB 165; DLBY 82; MTCW 1
Wright, Charles Stevenson 1932- ... CLC 49;
BLC 3; DAM MULT, POET
See also BW 1; CA 9-12R; CANR 26; DLB 33
Wright, Jack R.
See Harris, Mark
Wright, James (Arlington) 1927-1980CLC 3,
5, 10, 28; DAM POET
See also AITN 2; CA 49-52; 97-100; CANR 4,
34, 64; DLB 5, 169; MTCW 1
Wright, Judith (Arandell) 1915- CLC 11, 53;
PC 14

See also CA 13-16R; CANR 31; MTCW 1;
SATA 14
Wright, L(aurali) R. 1939- .... CLC 44
See also CA 138
Wright, Richard (Nathaniel) 1908-1960 C L C
1, 3, 4, 9, 14, 21, 48, 74; BLC 3; DA; DAB;
DAC; DAM MST, MULT, NOV; SSC 2;
WLC
See also AAYA 5; BW 1; CA 108; CANR 64;
CDALB 1929-1941; DLB 76, 102; DLBD
2; MTCW 1
Wright, Richard B(ruce) 1937-........... CLC 6
See also CA 85-88; DLB 53
Wright, Rick 1945- .... CLC 35
Wright, Rowland
See Wells, Carolyn
Wright, Stephen 1946- .... CLC 33
Wright, Willard Huntington 1888-1939
See Van Dine, S. S.
See also CA 115; DLBD 16
Wright, William 1930- .... CLC 44
See also CA 53-56; CANR 7, 23
Wroth, LadyMary 1587-1653(?) .... LC 30
See also DLB 121
Wu Ch'eng-en 1500(?)-1582(?) .... LC 7
Wu Ching-tzu 1701-1754 .... LC 2
Wurlitzer, Rudolph 1938(?)- .... CLC 2, 4, 15
See also CA 85-88; DLB 173
Wycherley, William 1641-1715LC 8, 21; DAM
DRAM
See also CDBLB 1660-1789; DLB 80
Wylie, Elinor (Morton Hoyt) 1885-1928
TCLC 8; PC 23
See also CA 105; 162; DLB 9, 45
Wylie, Philip (Gordon) 1902-1971 ....CLC 43
See also CA 21-22; 33-36R; CAP 2; DLB 9
Wyndham, John .... CLC 19
See also Harris, John (Wyndham Parkes Lucas)
Beynon
Wyss, Johann David Von 1743-1818NCLC 10
See also JRDA; MAICYA; SATA 29; SATA-
Brief 27
Xenophon c. 430B.C.-c. 354B.C. ... CMLC 17
See also DLB 176
Yakumo Koizumi
See Hearn, (Patricio) Lafcadio (Tessima Carlos)
Yanez, Jose Donoso
See Donoso (Yanez), Jose
Yanovsky, Basile S.
See Yanovsky, V(assily) S(emenovich)
Yanovsky, V(assily) S(emenovich) 1906-1989
CLC 2, 18
See also CA 97-100; 129
Yates, Richard 1926-1992 .... CLC 7, 8, 23
See also CA 5-8R; 139; CANR 10, 43; DLB 2;
DLBY 81, 92; INT CANR-10
Yeats, W. B.
See Yeats, William Butler
Yeats, William Butler 1865-1939TCLC 1, 11,
18, 31; DA; DAB; DAC; DAM DRAM,
MST, POET; PC 20; WLC
See also CA 104; 127; CANR 45; CDBLB
1890-1914; DLB 10, 19, 98, 156; MTCW 1
Yehoshua, A(braham) B. 1936-.. CLC 13, 31
See also CA 33-36R; CANR 43
Yep, Laurence Michael 1948-............ CLC 35
See also AAYA 5; CA 49-52; CANR 1, 46; CLR
3, 17; DLB 52; JRDA; MAICYA; SATA 7,
69
Yerby, Frank G(arvin) 1916-1991 CLC 1, 7,
22; BLC 3; DAM MULT
See also BW 1; CA 9-12R; 136; CANR 16, 52;
DLB 76; INT CANR-16; MTCW 1

Yesenin, Sergei Alexandrovich
See Esenin, Sergei (Alexandrovich)
Yevtushenko, Yevgeny (Alexandrovich) 1933-
CLC 1, 3, 13, 26, 51; DAM POET
See also CA 81-84; CANR 33, 54; MTCW 1
Yezierska, Anzia 1885(?)-1970 ....CLC 46
See also CA 126; 89-92; DLB 28; MTCW 1
Yglesias, Helen 1915- .... CLC 7, 22
See also CA 37-40R; CAAS 20; CANR 15, 65;
INT CANR-15; MTCW 1
Yokomitsu Riichi 1898-1947 .... TCLC 47
Yonge, Charlotte (Mary) 1823-1901TCLC 48
See also CA 109; 163; DLB 18, 163; SATA 17
York, Jeremy
See Creasey, John
York, Simon
See Heinlein, Robert A(nson)
Yorke, Henry Vincent 1905-1974 ....CLC 13
See also Green, Henry
See also CA 85-88; 49-52
Yosano Akiko 1878-1942 .... TCLC 59; PC 11
See also CA 161
Yoshimoto, Banana ....CLC 84
See also Yoshimoto, Mahoko
Yoshimoto, Mahoko 1964-
See Yoshimoto, Banana
See also CA 144
Young, Al(bert James) 1939-CLC 19; BLC 3;
DAM MULT
See also BW 2; CA 29-32R; CANR 26, 65; DLB
33
Young, Andrew (John) 1885-1971 ......CLC 5
See also CA 5-8R; CANR 7, 29
Young, Collier
See Bloch, Robert (Albert)
Young, Edward 1683-1765 .... LC 3, 40
See also DLB 95
Young, Marguerite (Vivian) 1909-1995 C L C
82
See also CA 13-16; 150; CAP 1
Young, Neil 1945- .... CLC 17
See also CA 110
Young Bear, Ray A. 1950- ..... CLC 94; DAM
MULT
See also CA 146; DLB 175; NNAL
Yourcenar, Marguerite 1903-1987CLC 19, 38,
50, 87; DAM NOV
See also CA 69-72; CANR 23, 60; DLB 72;
DLBY 88; MTCW 1
Yurick, Sol 1925- .... CLC 6
See also CA 13-16R; CANR 25
Zabolotsky, Nikolai Alekseevich 1903-1958
TCLC 52
See also CA 116; 164
Zamiatin, Yevgenii
See Zamyatin, Evgeny Ivanovich
Zamora, Bernice (B. Ortiz) 1938-... CLC 89;
DAM MULT; HLC
See also CA 151; DLB 82; HW
Zamyatin, Evgeny Ivanovich 1884-1937
TCLC 8, 37
See also CA 105; 166
Zangwill, Israel 1864-1926 .... TCLC 16
See also CA 109; 167; DLB 10, 135, 197
Zappa, Francis Vincent, Jr. 1940-1993
See Zappa, Frank
See also CA 108; 143; CANR 57
Zappa, Frank ....CLC 17
See also Zappa, Francis Vincent, Jr.
Zaturenska, Marya 1902-1982 ...... CLC 6, 11
See also CA 13-16R; 105; CANR 22
Zeami 1363-1443 .... DC 7
Zelazny, Roger (Joseph) 1937-1995 .CLC 21

Literary Criticism Series
Cumulative Topic Index

This index lists all topic entries in Gale's *Classical and Medieval Literature Criticism, Contemporary Literary Criticism, Literature Criticism from 1400 to 1800, Nineteenth-Century Literature Criticism,* and *Twentieth-Century Literary Criticism.*

Topic Index

Topic Index

Contemporary Literary Criticism
Cumulative Nationality Index

Nationality Index

Nationality Index

Nationality Index

Nationality Index

Nationality Index

CLC-114 Title Index

ISBN 0-7876-2211-7

90000

9 780787 622114